THE LAW AND PRACTICE OF

MARINE INSURANCE AND AVERAGE

Associate Authors

BRIAN M. WALTHAM and JONATHAN LUX
Ince & Co., Solicitors
London, England

JOHN R. CUNNINGHAM
Campney & Murphy, Barristers & Solicitors
Vancouver, Canada

DEREK R. HENTZE
Senior Legal Officer, Caltex Australia Limited
Sydney, Australia

T. J. BROADMORE
Chapman Tripp Sheffield Young, Barristers & Solicitors
Wellington, New Zealand

CARTER QUINBY
Derby, Cook, Quinby & Tweedt, Attorneys at Law
San Francisco, California

MARTIN P. DETELS, JR.
Attorney at Law
Seattle, Washington

PAUL N. WONACOTT
Wood Tatum Mosser Brooke & Landis, Attorneys at Law
Portland, Oregon

THE LAW AND PRACTICE OF
MARINE INSURANCE
AND AVERAGE

VOLUME II

BY ALEX L. PARKS

Member of the Oregon State Bar
and the Bars of the United States District Court, District of Oregon;
Court of Appeals, Ninth Circuit; Court of Appeals, District of Columbia;
United States Supreme Court;
Member of the Maritime Law Association of the United States; Associate
Member of the Association of Average Adjusters of the United States;
Adjunct Professor (Admiralty and Insurance),
Willamette University College of Law

CORNELL MARITIME PRESS
Centreville, Maryland

Library of Congress Cataloging in Publication Data

Parks, Alex Leon, 1925–
The law and practice of marine insurance and average.

Includes index.
1. Insurance, Marine—United States. 2. Average
(Maritime law) 3. Insurance, Marine. I. Title.
KF1135.P35 1987   346'.086   87-13667
ISBN 0-87033-368-2   342.686

Manufactured in the United States of America
First edition

CONTENTS : VOLUME II

THE LAW AND PRACTICE OF

MARINE INSURANCE AND AVERAGE

CHAPTER XIX

RUNNING DOWN CLAUSE

Running Down or Collision Clause

Prior to the decision in *De Vaux v. Salvador (La Valeur)*,[1] there was no Running Down or Collision Clause in marine policies. In that case, two vessels collided, both sustained damage, and both were held at fault. On balance (see "Limitation of Liability, Cross Liabilities, and Single Liability," *infra*) one of the owners had to pay an amount to the other vessel, whereupon he sought to recover the amount paid as a particular average loss falling under the perils clause. It was held that the liability of the insured vessel was not caused by a peril insured against; rather, it grew out of an arbitrary provision in the law of nations from views of general expediency—not as dictated by natural justice, nor (possibly) quite consistent with it—and could no more be charged against underwriters than a penalty incurred by contravention of the revenue laws. The decision was followed shortly by *General Mutual Ins. Co. v. Sherwood*[2] in which the underwriter, although required to pay the owner for his hull damage, was held not liable for collision and cargo damages sustained by the other vessel.

The decision in *De Vaux v. Salvador* led to the introduction of the Running Down Clause whereby the underwriter agreed to insure the risk of liability of the owner of the insured vessel for damage done by the vessel owing to collision with another vessel. As first adopted (and as now still current in the Institute Time Hulls form of the Institute of London Underwriters), the clause only covered three-fourths of the owner's collision liability to the other vessel. Apparently, it was thought that by limiting the coverage to three-fourths, thereby compelling the owner to bear one-fourth of his loss, greater care would be exercised by the owner.

American forms (of which the American Institute Hulls form, June, 1977, is a typical example) invariably cover four-fourths of the owner's collision liability. The clause, as set forth in the AIH form, reads in its entirety as follows:

> And it is further agreed that:
> (a) If the Vessel shall come into collision with any other ship or vessel, and the Assured or the Surety in consequence of the Vessel being at fault shall become liable to pay and shall pay by way of damages to

---

1. (1836) 5 L.J.K.B. 134, 111 E.R. 845.
2. 55 U.S. 351 (1847).

any other person or persons any sum or sums in respect of such collision, the Underwriters will pay to the Assured or the Surety whichever
shall have paid, such proportion of such sum or sums so paid as their
respective subscriptions hereto bear to the Agreed Value, provided always that their liability in respect to any one such collision shall not
exceed their proportionate part of the Agreed Value.

(b) In cases where, with the consent in writing of a majority (in
amount) of Hull Underwriters, the liability of the Vessel has been contested, or proceedings have been taken to limit liability, the Underwriters will also pay a like proportion of the costs which the Assured
shall thereby incur or be compelled to pay.

When both vessels are to blame, then, unless the liability of the
owners or charterers of one or both such vessels becomes limited by
law, claims under the Collision Liability Clause shall be settled on the
principle of Cross-Liabilities as if the owners or charterers of each vessel had been compelled to pay to the owners or charterers of the other
of such vessels such one-half or other proportion of the latter's
damages as may have been properly allowed in ascertaining the balance or sum payable by or to the Assured in consequence of such
collision.

The principles involved in this clause shall apply to the case where
both vessels are the property, in part or in whole, of the same owners
or charterers, all questions of responsibility and amount of liability as
between the two vessels being left to the decision of a single Arbitrator,
if the parties can agree on a single arbitrator, or failing such agreement, to the decision of Arbitrators, one to be appointed by the assured and one to be appointed by the majority (in amount) of Hull
Underwriters interested; the two Arbitrators chosen to choose a third
Arbitrator before entering upon the reference, and the decision of
such single Arbitrator, or of any two of such three Arbitrators, appointed as above, to be final and binding.

Provided always that this Clause shall in no case extend to any sum
which the Assured or the Surety may become liable to pay or shall pay
in consequence of, or with respect to:

(a) removal or disposal of obstructions, wrecks or their cargoes under statutory powers or otherwise pursuant to law;

(b) injury to real or personal property of every description;

(c) the discharge, spillage, emission or leakage of oil, petroleum
products, chemicals or other substances of any kind or description
whatever;

(d) cargo or other property on or the engagements of the Vessel;

(e) loss of life, personal injury or illness;

Provided further that exclusions (b) and (c) above shall not apply to
injury to other vessels or property thereon except to the extent that

such injury arises out of any action taken to avoid, minimize or remove any discharge, spillage, emission or leakage described in (c) above.

Mutual Insurance (Protection and Indemnity—P & I)

It will be observed that, notwithstanding the apparent broadness of the Collision Clause, certain categories or risks are wholly excluded; i.e., removal or disposal of obstructions and wrecks, injury to real or personal property of every description, etc. The present forms of P & I insurance policies (and the club rules where no written policy is issued) pick up the risks which are currently excluded from the hull policy and, in fact, have been described as a "complement" to collision insurance.[3]

It has been said that the uninsured one-quarter of the collision liability under the standard English clause led shipowners to attempt to protect themselves by placing the one-quarter uninsured collision liability in the protection associations. The first "club" or society was formed to cover "extra risks not covered by ordinary marine policies on ships with a collision or running down clause therein"; that is, excess collision liability and liability for loss of life and personal injury.[4]

Today, the P & I clubs are now usually incorporated. The club itself is therefore the insurer and the assured's right of action lies against the club and not the other members, the consideration being the assured's ability to contribute to the losses of the other members and the expenses of the club.[5]

The rules vary from association to association in England and elsewhere and it is therefore difficult to lay down any hard and fast rule applicable to every situation; in the end, each case must be decided on its own facts. The most common American forms are discussed in some detail in Chapter XXI, *infra*.

---

3. *Trinidad Corp. v. American S.S. Owners Mutual P & I Ass'n*, 130 F.Supp. 46, 1955 AMC 1280, *aff'd* 229 F.2d 57 (2d Cir.), 1956 AMC 1464.

4. "The History and Development of P & I Insurance: The British Scene," William R.A. Birch Reynardson, Vol. 43, No. 3, *Tulane Law Review*, "A Symposium on the P & I Policy," 1969. Also, prior to *De Vaux v. Salvador, supra*, mutual associations called "hull clubs" competed with underwriters at Lloyd's, although the coverage supplied by them did not appear to be extensive. Some of the hull clubs did insure their members for third-party liabilities to crew members, passengers, and cargo. The transition from hull clubs to protection and indemnity clubs was therefore logical and natural.

5. *North-Eastern 100A S.S. Ins. Ass'n v. Red S. Steamship Co.*, (1906) 22 T.L.R. 692, 12 Com.Cas. 26, C.A.

Collision Clause is a Supplementary Contract

Reference to the standard clause in the AIH form, quoted above, will reveal that the opening phrase "And it is further agreed that:" provides supplementary coverage to the basic hull coverage. That is, a liability may accrue under the collision clause *in addition to* a claim for total loss or partial loss arising out of the same accident. Thus, a vessel may be sunk in a collision and totally lost, and, at the same time, the insured owner be found liable to the other vessel for damages done to it. In that instance, the hull underwriters would be liable to the insured owner for the total loss of his vessel and, in addition, for their proportionate amount of damages paid to the other vessel.[6]

Collision with Another "Vessel"

At the outset, it must be emphasized that the opening sentence of the clause requires that the collision be with another ship or vessel. The leading case in the United States is *Lehigh & Wilkes-Barre Coal Co. v. Globe & Rutgers Fire Ins. Co. (The Honeybrook)*.[7] That case involved barges which struck rock abutments and the bank of a canal while under tow. The court held that this was not a "collision" as comprehended by the clause. In that instance, the clause covered a "collision with any other vessel, craft or structure, floating or otherwise." See, also, *Bennett S.S. Co. v. Hull Mutual S.S. Protecting Society*,[8] where the insured vessel ran into nets attached to and extending from a fishing vessel about a mile distant, there being no contact between the hulls of the two vessels. The court held the insured vessel had not come into collision with any other "ship or vessel."

A number of cases involving this point have arisen with respect to tug and tow. The most controversial from the standpoint of the United States market is *M'Cowan v. Baine & Johnston (The Niobe)*.[9] There, the *Niobe* was in tow of the tug *Flying Serpent*. The tug collided with another vessel, the *Valetta*, sinking the latter. The owners of the *Valetta* brought suit against the tug and the *Niobe* and recovered damages against both the tug and the *Niobe*. After the owners of the *Niobe* had paid the owners of the *Valetta*, they brought an action against underwriters on the Running Down Clause. Recovery was allowed even though the *Niobe* never came in con-

---

6. See *New York Trap Rock Co.*, 1956 AMC 469 (Arb.); *Adelaide Steamship Co., Ltd. v. The Crown (The Warilda)*, (1926) A.C. 172.
7. 6 F.2d 736, 1925 AMC 717, 22 Ll.L.Rep. 82 (2d Cir.).
8. (1914) 3 K.B. 57, 12 Asp. M.L.C. 522, C.A.
9. (1891) A.C. 401, 7 Asp. M.L.C. 89, H.L.

tact with the *Valetta*. The judgment clearly followed the doctrine that a tug and tow are legally regarded as one vessel and, in this case, the control and command of the flotilla rested with the crew of the tow.[10]

The case has been severely criticized in the United States.[11] In *Western Transit v. Brown*[12] and in *The Richmond*,[13] the insured vessels by their suction caused another vessel to sheer and come into collision with a third vessel. Although the third vessel was held liable in damages, the courts in both instances held there was no recovery against the insured vessels as neither of them had come into contact with the injured vessel. See, in this respect, *William France, Fenwick & Co. Ltd. v. Merchants' Marine Ins. Co.*,[14] where the insured vessel collided with another vessel which, in turn, collided with a third vessel causing a large amount of damage. The insured vessel was held at fault for both collisions and paid the owners of both vessels. In a suit against its underwriters by the insured vessel's owners, it was held that the Running Down Clause covered. Compare, also, *The Schodack*,[15] where the tow, assisted by three tugs, caused one of the assisting tugs to come into contact with a moored vessel. The tow was held liable to the moored vessel and its owners then brought suit against their P & I underwriters. In holding that neither *Western Transit v. Brown* nor *The Niobe* governed, the court denied recovery, stating that the Running Down Clause in the hull policy insuring against the risk of collision plainly covered the loss. The distinction is clear: in *France Fenwick* and in *The Schodack,* there was a collision with another vessel which vessel, in an unbroken chain of causation, collided with and caused damage to a third vessel.

What Is a Ship or Vessel

The question of what is a ship or vessel is a vexing one. For example, in *Chandler v. Blogg*,[16] the insured vessel collided with a barge which had just been struck and sunk by a collision with another vessel. The barge was raised the next day, sailed to her home port, and repaired. The court,

---

10. *The Niobe* antedated the decision in *Devonshire v. Owners of the Barge Leslie*, (1912) P. 21, C.A., where Lord Atkinson set forth the proposition that "the question of the identity of the tow with the tug that tows her is one of fact, not law, to be determined upon the particular facts and circumstances of each case." This brought the English rule into conformity with the rule in the United States. See *Sturgis v. Boyer*, 65 U.S. 110 (1861).

11. See *Western Transit v. Brown*, 161 F. 869 (2d Cir., 1908); *Coastwise S.S. Co. v. Aetna Ins. Co. (The Richmond)*, 161 F. 871 (S.D.N.Y., 1908); *Trinidad Corp. v. American S.S. Owners Mut. Protection & Indemnity Ass'n*, 130 F.Supp. 46, 1955 AMC 1280, *aff'd* 229 F.2d 57, 1956 AMC 1464 (2d Cir.); *Lehigh & Wilkes-Barre Coal Co. v. Globe & Rutgers Fire Ins. Co., supra*, n. 7.

12. Id., n. 11.

13. Id., n. 11.

14. (1915) 3 K.B. 290, 13 Asp. M.L.C. 106, C.A.

15. 89 F.2d 8, 1937 AMC 548 (2d Cir.).

16. (1898) 1 Q.B. 32, 8 Asp. M.L.C. 349.

obviously impressed by the fact that the barge was so promptly raised, applied a "navigability" test and held that the sunken barge was a "vessel" and allowed recovery against the underwriters. By contrast, in *Pelton S.S. Co. Ltd. v. North of England Protecting and Indemnity Ass'n (The Zelo)*,[17] the insured vessel collided with the wreck of another vessel upon which salvage efforts were then being conducted rather unsuccessfully. The collision with the insured vessel caused additional damage which made any salvage operations hopeless. The owners of the insured vessel claimed against hull underwriters under the Running Down Clause; the latter refused to pay because the wreck was no longer a "vessel." The insured then brought suit against the P & I underwriters who paid one-quarter of the loss but refused to pay the remaining three-quarters on the ground that the wreck was a "vessel" at the time of the collision. The court, in concluding that the wreck was a "vessel," applied a test as to whether or not any reasonably minded owner would have continued salvage operations just prior to the collision in hope of completely recovering and repairing her. In doing so, the "navigability" test applied in *Chandler v. Blogg* was disapproved.[18]

An anchor is an integral part of a ship or vessel. Where the insured tug collided with the anchor of another vessel, it was held that a collision had occurred with a "vessel."[19] However, in *Trinidad Corp. v. American S.S. Owners Mut. P & I Ass'n*,[20] it was held that a dredge pipeline and pontoon, attached to the dredge, were not a part of a "vessel." In that case, the insured vessel ran into a dredge's pipeline and pontoons, forcing a pontoon into another vessel and causing damage to the pipeline, the pontoon, and the other vessel. After an exhaustive analysis of the English cases, the court held that the collision did not occur to the dredge itself—there was no collision with a "vessel"—and, consequently, the loss fell within the ambit of the P & I policy which, in that instance, covered liability for damage to "any fixed or moveable object or property whatsoever, except another vessel or craft."

A flying boat is not a ship or vessel within the intendment of the Running Down Clause.[21]

---

17. (1925) 22 Ll.L.Rep. 510, K.B.D.
18. See, in this connection, *Burnham v. China Mut. Ins. Co.*, 189 Mass. 100, 75 N.E. 74, 109 Am.St.Rep. 627 (1905), where the insured vessel struck a wrecked vessel which had been sunk several hours before and never raised. Although it was practicable to raise her, the cost would have exceeded her value when raised. The court held that the insured vessel did not come into collision with another "vessel" within the meaning of the Running Down Clause.
19. *Re Margetts and Ocean Accident and Guarantee Corp.*, (1901) 2 K.B. 792, 9 Asp. M.L.C. 217.
20. Id., n. 11.
21. *Polpen Shipping Co. Ltd. v. Commercial Union Assur. Co., Ltd.*, (1943) 1 All E.R. 162, (1943) K.B. 161, 74 Ll.L.Rep. 157, 1943 AMC 438.

In *Merchants' Marine Ins. Co., Ltd. v. North of England Protecting and Indemnity Ass'n*,[22] a pontoon barge, with a crane permanently mounted on it, with no motive power of its own, not capable of being steered and with no rudder, having been moved only five or six times in twelve years, was held not to be a vessel. By contrast, in *Coelleda-Swallow*,[23] it was held that the hull of a former naval sloop, stripped of her fittings and for many years used as a storage vessel for gunpowder, permanently anchored in a river and not attached to or moored to the shore, was a "ship or vessel" within the meaning of the Running Down Clause.[24]

22. (1926) 26 Ll.L.Rep. 201, C.A.
23. 1932 AMC 1044 (Arb.).
24. See, also, the following cases, all of which involved the definition of a vessel, although not necessarily in the context of construing the term in the Running Down Clause or a P & I policy: *The Craighall*, (1910) P. 207 (a landing stage not a vessel); *The Gas Float Whitton No. 2*, (1897) A.C. 337 (a gas float not a vessel); *Marine Craft v. Blomquist*, (1953) 1 Lloyd's Rep. 541 (a pontoon is a vessel); *The Hezekiah Baldwin*, (1878) 8 Benedict 556 (a floating elevator on a canal boat held to be a vessel); *Cope v. Vallette Dry Dock Co.*, 119 U.S. 625 (1887) (floating drydock not a vessel); *Connors Marine v. Northwestern Ins.*, 16 F.Supp. 626, 1936 AMC 1061 (S.D.N.Y.) and *U.S. v. Bethlehem Steel*, 1966 AMC 2748, *cert. den.* 1967 AMC 2530 (pontoons are not vessels); *Evansville v. Chero Cola Co.*, 271 U.S. 19, 1926 AMC 684 (houseboat used as a warehouse and office and not for the carriage of cargo not a vessel); *Halvorsen v. Aetna Ins. Co.*, 1954 AMC 1996 (St.,Wash.) (tow of logs not a vessel or craft); *Quarter Boat No. 1*, 19 F.Supp. 419, 1937 AMC 1042 (W.D., Mo.) (floating rooming house, maintained for employees and intended to be moved about from time to time, held to be a vessel); *Pirate Ship*, 21 F.2d 231, 1927 AMC 1378 (E.D.,La.) (vessel without propelling machinery moored to a wharf and used as a dancing platform held to be a vessel); *The Ark*, 1927 AMC 38 (S.D.,Fla.) (houseboat without machinery or sails moored to the shore and used as a floating supper club held to be sufficiently a "vessel" to be within admiralty jurisdiction).
With respect to "dead ships," in mothball fleets, withdrawn from navigation and/or indefinitely laid up, see *West v. U.S.*, 361 U.S. 118, 1960 AMC 15; *Roper v. U.S.*, 368 U.S. 20, 1961 AMC 2499; *Hillcone S.S. Co. v. Steffen*, 136 F.2d 965, 1943 AMC 1022 (9th Cir.); *Yost v. General Electric Co.*, 173 F.Supp. 630, 1960 AMC 635 (S.D.N.Y.); *Kissinger v. U.S.*, 176 F.Supp. 828, 1960 AMC 1468 (E.D.N.Y.); *White v. U.S.*, 400 F.2d 74, 1968 AMC 2036 (4th Cir.); *Lupo v. Consolidated Mariners, Inc.*, 261 F.Supp. 450, 1966 AMC 1833 (S.D.N.Y.); *McKinney v. U.S.*, 1966 AMC 600, *aff'd* 368 F.2d 542, 1967 AMC 2528 (9th Cir.); *Rogers v. Ralph Bollinger*, 279 F.Supp. 92, 1968 AMC 1766 (E.D.,La.); and *In the Matter of the Queen*, 361 F.Supp. 1009, 1973 AMC 2510 (E.D.,Pa.) (owner's intent to continue using the *Queen Elizabeth* in commerce or navigation of less importance than the extent of her permanent attachment to land; rejecting the Second Circuit's "dead ship" doctrine).
Generally speaking, the courts in the United States have tended to expand the definition of what is a "vessel," holding that such special purpose rigs as offshore drilling platforms, drill barges, ferries, small motorboats, LASH barges, floating cranes, derrick barges, etc., are "vessels." See *The Dixie III*, 1965 AMC 2629 (St.,La.) (submersible-type drilling barge held a vessel); *Offshore Co. v. Robison*, 266 F.2d 769, 1959 AMC 2049 (5th Cir.) (offshore mobile drilling platform held to be a vessel); *Senko v. LaCrosse Dredging Co.*, 352 U.S. 370, 1957 AMC 891 (inland, landlocked dredge held to be a vessel); *Sylvester v. Offshore Food*, 1968 AMC 1183 (St.La.) (quarter boat used for personnel working with offshore drilling platform held to be a vessel); *Miami River Boat Yard v. 60 ft. Houseboat*, 390 F.2d 596, 1968 AMC 336 (5th Cir.) (houseboat used for living quarters and from time to time towed from place to place held to be a vessel); *Loftis v. Southeastern Drilling*, 43 F.R.D. 32, 1969 AMC 729 (E.D.,La.) (submersible drilling barge located 50-75 miles offshore held to be a vessel); *Dardar v. Louisiana*, 322 F.Supp. 1115, 1971 AMC 1560 (E.D.La.) (ferry with crew of three, "walked" across a bayou by use of cables and winches held to be a vessel); *Spiller, Admx v. Lowe*, 328 F.Supp. 54, 1971 AMC 2661 (W.D.,Ark.) (16-foot aluminum motorboat used for

Regrettably, the courts seem to have proceeded on an *ad hoc* basis on the theory that one knows a ship when one sees one. Lord Justice Scrutton in *Merchants' Marine Ins. Co. v. North of England Protecting and Indemnity Ass'n, supra,* stated that approach very well when he said:

> I find myself in the not very courageous position of saying that all the contribution I can make is to say that I am not convinced that the Learned Judge below was wrong. One might possibly take the position of the gentleman who dealt with the elephant by saying he could not define an elephant but he knew what it was when he saw one; and it may be that this is the foundation of the Learned Judge's judgment, that he cannot define "ship or vessel" but he knows this thing is not a ship or vessel. I should have liked to have given a definition here because considering that these words are the words in every ordinary marine policy and in every Club policy, and that they are also, with some addition, the words in the Merchant Shipping Act, it is rather a pity that the Courts are not able to give a definition of the words, which are constantly turning up in a mercantile transaction.

Hybrid Clauses

Running Down Clauses are not necessarily limited in their scope to collisions with "vessels," but depend upon the wording of the particular clause in the hull policy. For example, see *John O. Carroll*,[25] (collision with a floating but non-navigable object); *Glover v. Phila. F. & M. Ins. Co.*,[26] (damage to the tow-rail of a yacht from striking timbers of a wharf); *Mancomunidad*

---

surveying navigable waters held to be a vessel); *Salgado v. Rudolph Co.*, 514 F.2d 750, 1975 AMC 888 (2d Cir.) (mobile floating crane without motive power held to be a vessel); *Wirth v. Acadia Forest*, 537 F.2d 1272, 1976 AMC 2178 (5th Cir.) (LASH barge, even though transported for part of the transportation movement aboard a "mother" ship held to be a vessel); *Moye v. Henderson*, 496 F.2d 973, 1974 AMC 2661 (8th Cir.), *cert. den.* 419 U.S. 884, 1974 AMC 2661 (18-foot motorboat held to be a vessel); *Montgomery v. Greenville Gravel*, 1974 AMC 2524 (N.D.,Miss.) (floating derrick barge held to be a vessel); *Foremost Ins. Co. v. Richardson*, 457 U.S. 668, 1982 AMC 2253 (two pleasure boats colliding on navigable waters held to be within admiralty jurisdiction and thus, inferentially, to be "vessels").

Compare, however, *Loffland Bros. Co. v. Roberts*, 386 F.2d 540, 1968 AMC 1463 (5th Cir.) (fixed offshore drilling platform held not to be a vessel); *Cookmeyer v. La. Dept. of Highways*, 309 F.Supp. 881, 1970 AMC 584 (E.D.,La.) (floating pontoon bridge, consisting of two steel barges permanently attached to piling while pivoting to permit water traffic to pass, held not to be a vessel); *Peytavin v. Gov't Emp. Ins.*, 1971 AMC 2311 (E.D.,La.) (ferry ramp supported by floating pontoon and attached permanently to shore by cables held not to be a vessel); *Dresser Industries v. Fidelity & Cas. Co.*, 580 F.2d 806, 1978 AMC 2588 (5th Cir.) (self-elevating drilling unit, capable of being navigated, but jacked up on its legs 40 feet above the ocean surface, held not to be a vessel).

25. 203 NYAD 430, 1923 AMC 77 (St., N.Y.).
26. 1956 AMC 1210 (St.,Md.).

del Vapor "Frumiz" v. Royal Exchange Assur.[27] ("collision with any object [ice included] other than water" held to cover a stranding and pumping on rocks); *Vestey Bros. v. Motor Union Ins. Co., Ltd.*[28] ("collision with ice or any other substance other than water" held to cover collision of vessel with the chain of a gate while navigating through a lock). And see *Harding v. Amer. Univ. Ins. Co.,*[29] where the propeller shaft of the insured vessel struck an unidentified submerged object while traveling through shoal waters. The court held that striking a submerged object is a "peril of the sea" and the fact that such a striking is not a collision and therefore not covered by the Running Down Clause does not mean that the loss was not covered by the perils clause, the two clauses being distinct rights of recovery unrelated to one another.

In *The Munroe,*[30] the clause covered collision with " . . . any . . . sunken . . . wreck." The vessel ran aground and on the tide falling was found to be resting amidship on the wreck of a vessel sunk more than a year before. The vessel subsequently shifted her position off the wreck and onto a bank of iron ore which, two or three years earlier, had formed part of the cargo of another vessel. It was held that the policy covered. In *Union Marine Ins. Co. v. Borwick,*[31] the policy covered collision with "piers, or stages, or similar structures." Two vessels covered by the policy went adrift in a storm and onto the toe of a breakwater whereupon they went to pieces. It was held to be a collision and not a mere stranding.

Towers' Liability Coverage

It will be recognized that certain aspects of towers' liability insurance are in reality insurance against collision liabilities. But first, it must be remembered that both hull and P & I policies contain rather standard towage exclusion clauses. The AIH (June, 1977) form provides, in part, that:

> . . . The Vessel may not be towed, except as is customary or when in need of assistance, nor shall the Vessel render assistance or undertake

---

27. (1927) 1 K.B. 567, 17 Asp. M.L.C. 205, 26 Ll.L.Rep. 191.

28. (1922) 10 Ll.L.Rep. 194, 270. See, also, *Newtown Creek Towing Co. v. Aetna Ins. Co.,* 163 N.Y. 114, 57 N.E. 302, where a boat lashed to the starboard side of a tug and projecting 45 to 50 feet beyond it was damaged by being forced through a heavy ice floe in the night when the master could not see whether the ice was so heavy or dangerous that he should stop. The contract of towers' liability insurance covered the tow for any damage caused by collision; the court held that the term "collision" covered damage sustained by striking the heavy ice floe.

29. 130 So.2d 86, 1962 AMC 2423 (St.,Fla.). Compare, however *Cline v. Western Assur. Co.,* 101 Va. 496, 44 S.E. 700 (1903).

30. (1893) P. 248, 7 Asp. M.L.C. 407.

31. (1895) 2 Q.B. 279, 8 Asp. M.L.C. 71.

towage or salvage services under contract previously arranged by the Assured, the Owners, the Managers or the Charterers of the Vessel . . .

Correspondingly, the towage exclusion clause in the American S.S. Mutual P & I form provides that where the policy insures tugs, the underwriter is not liable directly or indirectly for:

> Loss or damage to any vessel or vessels in tow and/or their cargoes, whether such loss or damage occurs before, during or after actual towage; provided, that this exception shall not apply to claims for loss of life, injury or illness.

It is apparent that the foregoing exclusions relate to *contract* towing; i.e., where the owner of the insured vessel is engaged in towing as a regular business or on a planned and deliberate basis even though possibly sporadic.[32]

Since an innocent tow is not liable *in rem* where it is brought into collision with another vessel by the negligence of its tug,[33] and since the Running Down Clause in the hull policy of the tug generally requires actual contact between the insured vessel and the other vessel, the tug is without protection under its hull policy as respects collision damage to its tow— unless, of course, special towers' liability endorsements are attached to the hull policy.[34] Moreover, the towage exclusion in the P & I policy eliminates coverage under that policy except for personal injuries, loss of life, or illness.[35]

The dilemma is well illustrated in *Emmco Ins. Co. v. Southern Terminal and Transp. Co.*,[36] and *Florida Waterways Properties, Inc. v. The Oceanus Mutual Underwriting Association (Bermuda) Ltd. et al.*[37] In *Emmco*, the P & I policy insured specified tugs and barges of Southern against liability to the full extent of their hull values. Following a collision in which Southern's insured tug was at fault while towing one of its uninsured barges, the underwriter denied coverage because the policy excluded liability for any loss, damage, expense, or claim arising out of or having relation to the

---

32. This is not to say that towers' liability coverage cannot be procured under a standard form of hull policy. To the contrary, as discussed *infra*, special endorsements to a standard form hull policy can be obtained which, in essence, extend the coverage of the Running Down Clause to collision damage to a tow.

33. *Sturgis v. Boyer*, 65 U.S. 110 (1860); *The Eugene F. Moran*, 212 U.S. 466 (1909).

34. *Coastwise S.S. Co. v. Aetna Ins. Co.*, 161 F. 871 (S.D.N.Y., 1908); cf., *The Schodack*, 89 F.2d 8, 1937 AMC 548 (2d Cir.).

35. See *Atlantic Lighterage Co. v. Continental Ins. Co.*, 75 F.2d 288, 1935 AMC 305 (2d Cir.) where the P & I policy expressly excluded liability arising out of towing except as to passengers and crew of the tug. The policy also contained a typewritten rider excluding "towers' liability." It was held that the rider was a further restriction of the risk.

36. 333 So.2d 80 (Fla.,D.C.A.).

37. 1977 AMC 70 (M.D.,Fla.).

towing of any other vessel or craft. At first instance, the assured prevailed on a motion for summary judgment on the ground that there was an irreconcilable conflict or ambiguity between the insuring clause and the exclusion, and the ambiguity should be resolved in favor of the assured as the underwriter well knew that the assured was engaged in the business of towing. On appeal, the court held that there was no conflict; that the risk of collision and damage therefrom was affected by the towing relationship because of the reduced maneuverability of the vessels and, that being so, the underwriter could contract to limit its liability to those collisions in which a premium had been paid for both tug and barge. Consequently, there was no coverage. In *Florida Properties*, the court held that the P & I underwriters were not required to indemnify the assured for amounts paid in settlement of collision claims where the policy contained a specific exception or exclusion with respect to risks which would have been covered under the "Tug Syndicate" form.

Towers' liability coverage for collision is generally provided by one of four different methods: (1) by special endorsements to a standard hull policy which, in essence, expand or extend the coverage of the Running Down Clause; (2) by special tug hull policies; (3) by specially constructed endorsements to a P & I policy; and (4) by utilizing a comprehensive general liability policy with the watercraft exclusion deleted. These four types or methods of coverage are discussed in depth in Chapter XXI, "Protection & Indemnity" under the heading of "Collision" and "Special Tug Provisions and Exclusions."

Complexities of Tug and Tow Collisions

When a multitude of interests are involved, such as a collision between a tow, which may be commonly owned with its tug, or separately owned by a third party, and other vessels, apportionment of the ultimate liability among underwriters—not to mention whether liability exists at all—can become incredibly complex. For example, compare *Augusta—Detroit*[38] and *Ariosa and D-22*,[39] discussed *infra*.

A further example is *New York Trap Rock Co.*[40] In that case, a barge in a large tow in the Hudson River listed, dumped its cargo, and then righted itself, sustaining damage. Part of its cargo struck an adjacent barge, damaging it so that it capsized, damaging other barges. In analyzing the hull cover, P & I cover, and the excess liability cover, it was held that (1) the hull cover was liable for the direct hull loss to the insured barge; (2) the

---

38. 290 F. 685, 1923 AMC 754; 1923 AMC 816; 1924 AMC 872, *aff'd* 5 F.2d 773, 1925 AMC 756 (4th Cir.).

39. 144 F.2d 262, 1944 AMC 1035 (2d Cir.), *cert. den.* 323 U.S. 797 (1944).

40. 1956 AMC 469 (Arb.).

hull cover and the P & I cover were liable for the loss to the adjacent barges, the Running Down Clause up to its limit (minus deductible), and the P & I cover for the balance (minus deductible); and (3) the excess cover was not liable for anything as the losses were within the limits of the hull and P & I cover.

Harbor Towing Co. v. Atlantic Mutual Ins. Co.[41] involved a negligent tug which caused its innocent barge to collide with another vessel. The tug and barge were owned by the same person. The Fourth Circuit held that the Running Down Clause covered only the insured vessel's liability and could not be stretched to protect the owner of the innocent barge not at fault even though the same owner owned both vessels. The same result was reached in *Norman Kelly*.[42]

Essentially the same facts were present in *The Fanny D (Eggers v. Southern S.S. Co)*,[43] but there the Fifth Circuit held that the fact that the barge was not liable *in rem* as the offending thing did not prevent a recovery, as coverage under the policy was not restricted to cases in which the insured vessel was at fault and was broad enough to cover the *in personam* liability of its owner. Since all three cases involved an earlier version of the clause, such a conflict should no longer arise in view of the later inclusion of the words "in consequence of the insured vessel being *at fault*." Compare *Driftwood Land and Timber Ltd. v. U.S. Fire Ins. Co.*,[44] where the insurance was "in respect of" a barge. The insured also owned a tug. While the tug was towing the barge, the tug crew was negligent such that the barge struck and damaged a dock. It was held that the damage was not covered as the intent of the policy was to cover the insured only in its capacity as owner of the barge and not against the liability arising out of the operation of the tug.

Counsel confronted with the problem of analyzing liability under applicable insurance policies for a collision involving a tug and its tow must take into consideration such myriad factors as the following:

(1) Does the hull policy on the tug, either directly or by special endorsement, provide running down coverage with respect to the tow and its cargo;

(2) Does the P & I policy provide coverage and, if so, to what extent;

(3) Is either the tug or the tow entitled to limit liability and, if so, what is the impact upon the extent of recoverable damages;

(4) What impact, if any, does the cross liabilities clause in the Running Down Clause have upon ultimate coverage and the consequent recovery of damages.

41. 189 F.2d 409, 1951 AMC 1070 (4th Cir.).

42. 1923 AMC 959 (St., Ohio).

43. 112 F.2d 347, 1940 AMC 1101 (5th Cir.), *cert. den.* 311 U.S. 680.

44. (1954) O.R. 733, *aff'd* (1954) O.W.N. 935, (1955) D.L.R. 176, (C.A., Can.), 1955 AMC 844.

These and allied problems are discussed in subsequent sections under the appropriate headings.

Attention is also directed to the potential impact of cross-insurance endorsements between the owner of the tug and the owner of the tow, a practice which is quite prevalent in the towing industry. Such endorsements are a relatively new development and only recently have received judicial approbation. Clearly, such endorsements came into being in an attempt to circumvent the decision of the Supreme Court in *Bisso v. Inland Waterways Corp.* and its progeny,[45] which in essence hold that a towing company cannot exculpate itself from the consequences of its own negligence as a matter of public policy.

There is, of course, a distinct difference between an outright exculpatory clause relieving the tug of all consequences of its own negligence, and a contractual provision between the owners of a tug and tow that each will procure appropriate insurance on the respective vessels and name the other as an additional assured with waiver of subrogation. The net effect of properly drafted cross-endorsements (which would include, of course, both hull and P & I insurance) whereby each party fully insures its own vessel, effects a waiver of subrogation, and names the other party as an additional assured, would be to compel each party to absorb hull damages arising out of a collision by virtue of their own insurance coverage and eliminate subrogation rights of the respective underwriters against the parties to the towing venture.[46] This obviously impacts upon the loss experience of hull underwriters forced to respond to claims under the Running Down Clauses in their policies.

Liability for Tort Only

A careful reading of the first paragraph of the Clause will reveal that it only comes into play where the insured vessel is *at fault* and the insured

---

45. 349 U.S. 85, 1955 AMC 899; *Boston Metals Co. v. The Winding Gulf,* 349 U.S. 122, 1955 AMC 927; *Dixilyn Drilling Corp. v. Crescent Towing & Salvage Co.,* 372 U.S. 697, 1963 AMC 829. Other examples are: *Kincaid v. Trans-Pacific,* 367 F.2d 857, 1966 AMC 2663 (9th Cir.); *Juno—Drill Barge 58,* 262 F.Supp. 282, 1966 AMC 2172, (S.D.,Tex.); *Seley Barges, Inc. v. Tug El Leon Grande,* 396 F.Supp. 1020 (E.D.,La., 1974), *aff'd* 513 F.2d 628 (5th Cir., 1974).

46. The leading case is *Twenty Grand Offshore v. West India Carriers,* 492 F.2d 679, 1974 AMC 2254 (5th Cir.). See, also, *Tenneco Oil Co. v. Tug Tony and Coastal Towing Corp.,* 324 F.Supp. 834, 1971 AMC 2335 (S.D.,Tex.); *Slade v. Samson Towing Co.,* 327 F.Supp. 555, 1971 AMC 2342 (E.D.,Tex.); *Hartford Fire Ins. Co. v. Port Everglades Towing Co.,* 454 F.2d 276, 1972 AMC 316 (5th Cir.); *BASF Wyandotte v. Leander,* 590 F.2d 96, 1979 AMC 1721 (5th Cir.); *Dillingham Tug & Barge v. Collier Carbon et al,* 707 F.2d 1086 (9th Cir., 1983) (agreeing with the Fifth Circuit, citing with approval *Twenty Grand Offshore v. West India Carriers,* and affirming the district court's finding that the towing company breached the implied warranty of workmanlike performance). Compare, however, *Dow Chemical Co. v. Ashland Oil, Inc.,* 579 F.2d 902 (5th Cir.); *Dow Chemical Co. v. M/V Charles F. Detmar, Jr.,* 545 F.2d 1091 (7th Cir., 1976); *PPG Industries, Inc. v. Ashland Oil Co. et al,* 592 F.2d 138, 1979 AMC 2056 (3d.Cir.).

actually pays damages. In short, the liabilities contemplated by the Clause refer to those arising from "tort" rather than contract. This was first established in *Furness, Withy & Co., Ltd. v. Duder,*[47] where the insured vessel was under tow. She collided with the towing tug due to the negligence of the tug. Under the U. K. Towing Conditions then in effect, she was contractually obligated to pay for the damages to the tug. The court held that this was a liability created by contract and not by tort and the clause therefore did not cover. A comparable situation occurred in *Hall Bros. Steamship Co., Ltd. v. Young*[48] where the assured was forced by French law to pay for damages sustained by a French pilot boat which collided with the assured's vessel through no fault on the part of the latter. The court held, in essence, that payment was made because of the provisions of French law and not by reason of collision liability *per se.*

In *Taylor v. Dewar,*[49] the vessel *Rouen* ran down another ship whereby some of her crew were drowned. By order of the court of admiralty, the owners of the *Rouen* were compelled to pay damages to the personal representatives of the deceaseds. It was held the clause did not apply.

The question seems to have first arisen in the United States in *Norman Kelly.*[50] In that case, the barge *Norman Kelly* was insured under a hull policy which contained a collision clause reading:

> And it is further agreed that if the ship hereby insured shall come into collision with any other ship or vessel, and the Assured shall in consequence thereof become liable to pay, and shall pay by way of damages to any other person or persons any sum or sums not exceeding _____ , we, the Assurers, will pay the Assured such proportion of such sum or sums so paid.

The barge, while in tow of a commonly owned tug, collided with a steamer, causing damage to both the steamer and the barge. In a suit by the steamer, the court found the collision to have been due to the sole negligence of the tug. The tug and barge owner then sought to recover what had been paid from the underwriters on the barge hull policy. The court said, in part:

> . . . The liability as a result of such collision must be such a liability as would permit the third person or persons to recover in a suit at law for the damage done. . . . Unless the collision occurred by the fault of the barge, and such fault was either a proximate or contributing cause of the collision, there could be no liability on the part of (the owner) in

47. [1936] 2 All E.R. 119, 55 Ll.L.Rep. 52.
48. [1939] 1 All E.R. 809, 63 Ll.L.Rep. 143, C.A.
49. [1864] 33 L.J.Q.B. 141, 122 E.R. 754.
50. 1923 AMC 959 (St., Ohio).

its capacity as *owner of the barge* to pay any third person for any damage resulting from said collision. [emphasis supplied]

Essentially the same facts were presented in *The Fanny D (Eggers v. Southern S.S. Co.)*[51] seventeen years later, but there the Fifth Circuit held that the fact that the barge was not liable *in rem* did not prevent a recovery, as coverage under the policy was not restricted to cases in which the insured vessel was a fault and was broad enough to cover the *in personam* liability of its owner.

The same question was later presented in *Harbor Towing Co. v. Atlantic Mutual Ins. Co.*[52] involving essentially the same facts. The Fourth Circuit, citing *Furness, Withy & Co., supra,* and *Norman Kelly, supra,* held squarely that the indemnity furnished by the underwriter under the Clause was confined to protection from the vessel's misdeeds; i.e., "fault." As the barge was not at "fault" there was no coverage.

Since all three cases involved an earlier version of the clause, and the current clause has been amended to include the phrase "in consequence of the Vessel being *at fault,*" the question in the United States has now been laid to rest.[53]

Indemnity Only

The clause provides, in part, that the underwriters will pay the assured when "in consequence of the Vessel being at fault" the assured "shall become liable to pay *and shall pay* by way of damages . . . any sum or sums in respect of such collision." In nearly all jurisdictions, this renders the policy one of indemnity and not liability.[54]

Narco—Lolita, supra, is instructive. In that case, the *Narco* collided with the *Lolita* which then filed an action against *Narco,* the *Narco*'s owner, and *Nardelli,* the charterer. Nardelli, in turn, impleaded the hull underwriter seeking recovery under the policy in the event the *Narco* should be held

---

51. 112 F.2d 347, 1940 AMC 1101, *cert. den.* 331 U.S. 680 (5th Cir.).

52. 189 F.2d 409, 1951 AMC 1070 (4th Cir.).

53. See, also, *Thompson v. Reynolds,* (1857) 119 E.R. 1211; *The London S.S. Owners' Ass'n v. The Gampian S.S. Co.,* (1890) 24 Q.B.D. 663, C.A.; *Field S.S. Co. v. Burr,* (1899) 1 Q.B. 579; *The Narco and The Lolita,* 258 F.2d 718, 1958 AMC 2404, modified 286 F.2d 600, 1961 AMC 1999 (5th Cir.); *Augusta-Detroit,* 290 F. 685, 1923 AMC 754, 816, 1924 AMC 872, *aff'd* 5 F.2d 773, 1925 AMC 756 (4th Cir.); *Ariosa and D-22,* 144 F.2d 262, 1944 AMC 1035, *cert. den.* 323 U.S. 797 (1944).

54. *Narco—Lolita (Stuyvesant Ins. Co. v. Nardelli),* 286 F.2d 600, 1961 AMC 1999 (5th Cir.); *Cucurillo v. American S.S. Owners' Mut. Prot. & Indemn. Ass'n, Inc.,* 1969 AMC 2334 (St., N.Y.); *Liman, Trustee v. American S.S. Owners' Mut. Prot. & Indemn. Ass'n, Inc.,* 299 F.Supp. 106, 1969 AMC 1669 (S.D.N.Y.), *aff'd* 417 F.2d 627 (2d Cir.), *cert. den.* 397 U.S. 936, 1971 AMC 814; *Ahmed v. American S.S. Owners' Mut. Prot. & Indemn. Ass'n, Inc.,* 640 F.2d 993, 1981 AMC 897, on remand 1982 AMC 1228 (N.D.,Cal.).

liable. After decisions in the lower court and on appeal, upon rehearing it was held that the Running Down Clause covered Nardelli, the charterer, up to the full amount of the policy.

The case was remanded. No further evidence was taken and the charterer was awarded the full amount of the policy plus his attorneys' fees expended in establishing liability under the policy. The case was again appealed. The Fifth Circuit, in an opinion somewhat difficult to follow, held that since Nardelli had paid nothing on the judgment in favor of the *Lolita*, the requirement that there be "payment" precluded him from recovery; i.e., the policy was one of indemnity and not liability and there could be no recovery in the absence of proof that actual payment had been made. Nardelli did, however, recover his attorneys' fees as these were actually incurred and paid.

State law may, however, have a dramatic effect upon the classification of a policy as being one of indemnity rather than liability. In *Liman, Trustee v. American S.S. Owners Mut. Prot. & Indemnity Ass'n, Inc.*,[55] the court held that under New York law, an insurer under an indemnity policy may not escape its obligation to indemnify by showing that the assured's payment of claims was advanced by a third party or financed in some other fashion. In *Orion Ins. Co. v. Firemen's Fund Ins. Co. (The Barcelona)*,[56] after judgment in a cargo action holding both the time charterer and the shipowner at fault but granting the former indemnity over against the shipowner because of the vessel's unseaworthiness, the time charterer's underwriter paid the judgment and sought recovery from the shipowner's P & I underwriters. They asserted that since their policy covered only "liabilities and expenses which [the assured] shall have become liable to pay and shall have in fact paid" they were not liable until the assured shipowner had paid the loss. As the shipowner was bankrupt and could never pay, the plaintiff underwriters could prevail only if they could convince the court that the P & I policy issued to the shipowner was one which indemnified for liability rather than indemnified for loss.

Holding the P & I policy ambiguous, in somewhat tortuous reasoning, the court held that as applied to "expenses" to be paid under the policy, the policy was one of indemnity, but as applied to "liabilities" it was one of liability.

Moreover, direct action statutes such as that of Louisiana and Puerto Rico may render nugatory the effect of the words "and shall pay." See "Limitation of Liability," *infra.*

---

55. 46 C.A.3d 374, 1975 AMC 1183 (St.,Cal.).

56. The court cited, among others, *Saunders v. Austin W. Fishing Corp.*, 353 Mass. 169, 224 N.E.2d 215, 1967 AMC 984 (St.,Mass.), which held that the policy in question (identical in its terms) was an indemnity policy but thereafter held that it violated a Massachusetts statute which prohibited the issuance of a policy which indemnified an insured only for actual loss and not liability.

Exceptions Proviso

Under the proviso, the clause in no case extends to any sum which the assured may become liable to pay and shall pay in consequence of, or with respect to:

(a) removal or disposal of obstructions, wrecks, or their cargoes under statutory powers or otherwise pursuant to law;

(b) injury to real or personal property of every description;

(c) the discharge, spillage, emission, or leakage of oil, petroleum products, chemicals, or other substances of any kind or description whatever;

(d) cargo or other property on or the engagements of the vessel;

(e) loss of life, personal injury or illness.

However, by the express language of the clause in the AIH (1977) form, exclusions (b) and (c) above do not apply to injury to other vessels or property thereon except to the extent that such injury arises out of any action taken to avoid, minimize or remove any discharge, spillage, emission, or leakage described in (c) above.

By contrast, the new London Institute Time Clauses (Hulls) (1/10/83) reads rather more simply but somewhat more broadly:

Provided always that this Clause 8 shall in no case extend to any sum which the Assured shall pay for or in respect of:

8.4.1 removal or disposal of obstructions, wrecks cargoes or any other thing whatsoever

8.4.2 any real or personal property or thing whatsoever except other vessels or property on other vessels

8.4.3 the cargo or other property on, or the engagements of, the insured Vessel

8.4.4 loss of life, personal injury or illness

8.4.5 pollution or contamination of any real or personal property or thing whatsoever (except other vessels with which the insured Vessel is in collision or property on such other vessels).

The liabilities enumerated in the respective provisos are, however, usually recoverable by the shipowner from his P & I underwriter, and are discussed more fully in Chapter XXI, "Protection and Indemnity," subheading "Collision."

Costs of Attack or Defense

The clause provides in subsection (b) of the AIH (1977) form " . . . In cases where, with the consent in writing of a majority (in amount) of Hull

Underwriters, the liability of the Vessel has been contested, or proceedings have been taken to limit liability, the Underwriters will also pay a like proportion of the costs which the Assured shall thereby incur or be compelled to pay."[57] The covenant to pay costs is supplementary to the earlier provision of the Clause and, therefore, costs are payable in addition to the maximum liability in respect of damages—which, in the case of the Running Down Clause in the AIH (1977) form, is the "Agreed Value."[58] In the new London form it is the "Insured Value."

The coverage with respect to costs was inserted in the clause as a consequence of *Xenos v. Fox*[59] in which it was held (under the wording of the clause as it then was) that the costs of defending a claim for collision damages, even though successful, could not be recovered under the clause nor as sue and labor inasmuch as such costs were not incurred to prevent loss or damage to the vessel itself.

It should be immediately apparent that the underwriters' willingness to bear costs is not altogether altruistic as the paramount objective is to minimize, insofar as possible, liability to third parties. As costs of defense they are borne by the hull underwriters under the clause.[60] Obviously, damage to the insured vessel is of no concern to the P & I underwriters nor are they interested in the costs applicable to obtaining a recovery from the colliding vessel.

Categories of Collision Cases

Logically, collision cases can be divided into three categories: (1) where neither vessel is to blame;[61] (2) where one vessel is entirely to blame; and

---

57. The new London Institute hull form (1/10/83) provides with respect to such costs:
8.3 The Underwriters will also pay three-fourths of the legal costs incurred by the Assured or which the Assured may be compelled to pay in contesting liability or taking proceedings to limit liability, with the prior written consent of the Underwriters.
58. A comparison of the last several lines of paragraph (a) of the clause in the AIH form (relating to liability for damages) with the last several lines of paragraph (b) (relating to costs) will reveal that the former contains a proviso that underwriters' liability in respect to any one collision shall not exceed *their proportionate part of the Agreed Value;* no such proviso appears with respect to liability for costs.
The language of the new London hull form is that the underwriters will *also* pay three-fourths of the legal costs—thus clearly indicating that coverage provided for legal costs is supplementary to the other coverages.
59. (1868) L.R. 4 C.P. 665. See, also, *Cunard S.S. Co. v. Marten,* [1902] 2 K.B. 624, 9 Asp. M.L.C. 343, C.A., [1903] 2 K.B. 511 9 Asp. M.L.C. 452.
60. This is true, of course, under American practice where the Collision Clause covers four-fourths of the shipowners' liability; under English practice where the clause only covers three-fourths of the shipowners' liability, the P & I underwriters are responsible for the remaining one-fourth and are, therefore, interested to that extent in the payment of costs.
61. By "inevitable accident" is meant a collision which occurs without legal fault (i.e., violation of rule or lack of due care) on the part of either vessel. See *Olympia,* 61 F. 120, (6th Cir., 1894); *The Lackawanna,* 210 F. 262 (2d Cir., 1913); *Anna C. Minch,* 271 F. 192 (2d Cir.,

(3) where both vessels are to blame.[62]

One would assume that if the insured vessel is found solely at fault all costs incurred, including those expended to limit liability, should be considered as costs of defense. However, this does not necessarily follow as a practical matter because at the time legal proceedings are in progress, counsel for the vessel are almost invariably defending the insured vessel and, at the same time, pressing claims against the colliding vessel, the actual outcome not being known until the trial has been concluded and the court has rendered its decision. As a matter of practice, the allocation of legal expenses and costs among the parties in interest is a function of the average adjusters rather than decisional law, and, in practice, such costs are commonly treated as general costs with the underwriters or other interests involved each paying their share.[63]

Costs fall rather neatly into three classes. These are: general, attack, and defense.

General Costs

These are costs incurred in determining liability. This category would include costs incurred in endeavoring to establish liability up to the time liability is definitively established, such as investigation of the facts of the collision, interviewing witnesses, attending hearings of regulatory agencies such as the Coast Guard, and depositions on the issue of liability. These embrace, of course, efforts to prove that the other vessel was liable and that the insured vessel was not. Also included are any other costs which cannot be specifically attributed to attack or defense; i.e., efforts which are expended which are common to both attack and defense and which must be apportioned rateably over the amounts involved.

1921). It does not mean one which "could not have been avoided by any degree of care or skill." *The Fontana*, 119 F. 853 (6th Cir., 1903); *The Jumna*, 149 F. 171 (2d Cir., 1906). Thus, since inevitable accident presupposes that there is no legal fault on either side, there is, of course, no liability; the loss remains where it falls. *Stainbeck v. Rae*, 55 U.S. 532 (1853); *The Continental*, 81 U.S. 345 (1872); *The Sunnyside*, 91 U.S. 208 (1875). A typical case may also be postulated where vessels operate in wartime without lights.

62. Prior to *U.S. v. Reliable Transfer Co., Inc.*, 421 U.S. 397, 1975 AMC 541, [1975] 2 Lloyd's Rep. 286, the rule in the United States, of course, was that of an equal division in the absence of facts calling for the application of the major-minor rule. This, too, was the rule in England until 1911, when the Maritime Conventions Act, 1911 was passed, following the Brussels Convention of 1910. In both jurisdictions, the rule of proportionate fault is now applied.

63. In a typical collision involving two vessels, each carrying cargo, there are three parties involved with respect to the insured vessel: the owner as to uninsured losses and deductibles; the hull underwriters as to liabilities and costs under the Running Down Clause; and P & I underwriters (in most instances) as to death and personal injury claims, claims of cargo on the insured vessel, as well as other allied claims of a P & I nature. The task of the adjuster is to apportion costs among them.

Attack Costs

These are costs which relate to prosecuting the claim against the other vessel. Examples are: preparation and filing of the complaint against the other vessel; arranging service of process; obtaining security from the other vessel; examining evidence in support of damages to the insured vessel, both property as well as detention; obtaining evidence as necessary, including fees paid to witnesses called solely for the purpose of proving the damages to the insured vessel as contrasted with those called in connection with establishing liability of the vessel. Costs incurred in attempting to defeat the other vessel's right to limit liability or relating to the size of her limitation fund would also fall within this category.

The average adjuster apportions the attack costs over the various items of the claim which is recovered, or, if recovery has been denied, over the various interests which have benefitted by a successful outcome. For example, costs referrable to efforts to recover for physical damage are charged to the hull underwriters; costs of the vessel's detention claim are charged to the owner.

Defense Costs

These are costs which specifically relate to defending the claims of the other vessel. Included are: preparing the answer to the complaint of the other vessel; making provision for posting security for the other vessel; investigating and ascertaining the other vessel's damages and expenses incurred in contesting the other vessel's damages. Also included would be the costs incurred in filing and prosecuting limitation proceedings on behalf of the insured vessel.

The average adjuster here apportions the defense costs to the interests benefitted or intended to be benefitted; i.e., to the hull underwriters with respect to those claims falling within the Running Down Clause (damage to the other vessel) and to P & I underwriters with respect to any claims falling within the scope of the club rules such as personal injury and death claims, claims of cargo on the insured vessel, and other allied claims of a P & I nature.

Costs in General

If both vessels are to blame, the rule has long been that each vessel should bear her own costs. In England, this rule prevailed for a time despite the Maritime Conventions Act, 1911, under which the degree of blame (as under *U.S. v. Reliable Transfer Co.*) can vary considerably. See, for example, *Berbera v. The Bravo*,[64] in which the court stated:

> I think on the whole the practice which has prevailed of each vessel paying her own costs when both vessels are to blame ought to be applied to new cases under the Maritime Conventions Act. The preparation of the case does not alter in character by reason of the degree of fault being great or small. . . . Apart from special circumstances, each delinquent vessel, if she come into court either to make an attack or to repel an attack, will have to bear her own costs.

The more modern rule, however, is that costs are awarded to follow the event and, in the absence of special circumstances, the order for costs made generally reflects any differing degrees of blame attaching to the vessels.[65] The rule in the United States, insofar as it can be deduced at this time, appears to be the same.

It should be observed that the clause with respect to costs provides that such costs must be incurred with the "consent in writing of a majority (in amount) of Hull Underwriters." This does not mean, however, that a vessel owner should not take the necessary steps to preserve and protect his interests, as well as those of his underwriters, irrespective of such written consent. For example, such immediate and obvious steps as conducting a survey of the other vessel and taking down statements of witnesses should be undertaken without delay and will invariably be treated by underwriters as costs of defense.

Association of Average Adjusters' Rules of Practice

As noted above, the allocation of legal expenses and costs among the various parties in interest is generally a matter for average adjusters rather than decisional law. In this connection, in the United States these are generally apportioned in accordance with Rule XX of the Association of Average Adjusters, reading as follows:[66]

---

64. [1912] 29 T.L.R. 122, 12 Asp. M.L.C. 311.
65. *The Osprey*, [1967] 1 Lloyd's Rep. 76.
66. The corresponding rule of the Association of Average Adjusters of Great Britain (Rule A8) provides:
That when a vessel sustains and does damage by collision, and litigation consequently results for the purpose of testing liability, the technicality of the vessel having been plaintiff or defendant in the litigation shall not necessarily govern the apportionment of the costs of such litigation, which shall be apportioned between claim and counter-claim in proportion to the amount, excluding interest, which has been or would have been allowed in respect of each in the event of the claim or counter-claim being established; provided that when a claim or counter-claim is made solely for the purpose of defence, and is not allowed, the costs apportioned thereto shall be treated as costs of defence.

In cases involving collisions, the legal costs and/or other expenses incurred to determine liability either by court action, arbitration or determination by consent of the parties shall be apportioned rateably over the full provable damages, excluding interest and costs, of the claim and counter-claim which have been or would have been allowed.

Nothing contained in this rule shall affect those legal costs and/or other expenses incurred specifically for the purpose of defense or recovery which shall be charged accordingly.

The corresponding rule of the Association of Average Adjusters of Canada (Rule 13) is rather more specific and detailed:

(1) Legal expense shall be divided into the following categories:

(a) Attack relating to the proceedings for the recovery of damages sustained by the insured ship in collision.
(b) Defense relating to proceedings against the insured ship for damage sustained by another ship in collision.

(2) Owner and underwriters shall contribute to the legal expense of attack in proportion that owner's claim for deductible average, demurrage or other expense, and underwriters' claim for the balance, bears to the entire provable damage of the insured ship.

(3) Where the insured ship becomes legally liable for the demurrage sustained by another ship, the legal expense of defense shall be charged to the underwriters, but where defense is successfully maintained legal expense shall be divided between owner and underwriters in the proportion which the owner's deductible average, the payment of which is avoided, bears to the estimated potential liability of the insured ship to the other ship.

This latter method of apportionment of legal expense shall also be applied to any case where the collision damages, as finally determined, are less than the owner's deductible average, provided the collision liability claim as originally asserted, based upon reasonable and proper estimates, exceeds the deductible average, the owner's participation in the claim and legal expense not to exceed the amount of his deductible average.

(4) In cross actions involving both attack and defense, legal expense shall be apportioned between owner and underwriters to the extent to which each is interested in accordance with the foregoing principles. That is to say:

(a) Attack expenses charged to owners and underwriters in proportion to the extent to which they are interested.
(b) Defense expenses charged to underwriters.

(5) The foregoing principles shall govern in respect to compromise settlements and arbitrations.

Example of Cost Computations

Take the case of a vessel, insured under the AIH (1977) form, which collides with another vessel on Long Island Sound. Following the collision, the insured vessel is surveyed by both underwriters' and owners' surveyors, the estimated cost of repairs being $100,000. The charges for owners' superintendance and survey fees amount to $500.[67]

The case proceeded to trial, but having gone badly was settled after two days with opposing counsel on the basis of the insured vessel bearing 75 percent of the other vessel's damages and the other vessel's costs for contesting liability, as well as withdrawing her counterclaim for damages. There still being a dispute as to damages, this was referred to an arbitrator who calculated the other vessel's damages at $200,000.

There being no dispute that the claim was covered by the Running Down Clause, the apportionment would be as follows:

Item	General	Defense	R.D.C.	Hull U/R's
Arbitrator's award of damages				
$200,000				
75% $150,000				
Interest 1,500				
$151,500			$151,500	
Vessel's own hull damage				$100,000
Survey of other vessel		$ 750		
Survey of own vessel				500
Witness fees for testing liability	$ 950			
Own attorneys' fees for testing liability	10,000			
Own attorneys' fees for challenging claim and				

---

67. Fees for underwriters' surveyors are normally of no concern to the other colliding vessel as that vessel is not interested in whether the other vessel was insured or not. See, however, *Gulf Oil v. Panama Canal*, 471 F.2d 561, 1973 AMC 1582 (5th Cir.) (shipowner not limited to recovering only one surveyor's fee; allowance of cost of second survey, performed at shipowner's request, in addition to the cost of an ABS classification survey); and *Reliable Transfer v. U.S.*, 53 F.R.D. 24, 1973 AMC 930 (E.D.N.Y.) (even though surveyors were engaged by vessel's underwriters to determine the extent of damage and to supervise repairs, their fees were recoverable as damages by the vessel owner to whom they also reported). See, also, *Kay—F.S. 219*, 202 F.Supp. 67, 1965 AMC 984 (E.D.,Va.), where notice of survey was given, there was no duplication of fees, and both parties were represented by the same surveyor; and *The Moliere*, [1925] P. 27, 20 Ll.L.Rep. 101, where the only survey carried out was by underwriters' surveyor.

arbitration of damages		7,500		
Other vessel's fees and costs—testing liability	15,000			
Other vessel's fees and costs—proving claim and arbitration of damages		6,500		
Assured's miscellaneous	165			
	$26,115			

Division of General Costs:

Own claim $100,000 =	$ 8,705			8,705
Opposition claim $200,000 =	$17,410		17,410	
	$300,000 = $26,115			
		$14,750	$14,750	
			$183,660	$109,205

As a practical matter, the claim of the owner of the insured vessel would be deferred until after actual repairs were completed or an agreed settlement being reached in the event the damage remained unrepaired.

Limitation of Liability, Cross Liabilities, and Single Liability

All maritime nations subscribe to the theory that a vessel owner should be entitled to limit his liability. But what that "liability" should be has been a stumbling block.

In brief summary, in the United States at the present time, the Limitation of Liability Act[68] permits a shipowner to limit his liability for the damage arising out of a collision (provided the collision occurred without his privity or knowledge) to the value of the vessel *after* the accident plus the freight actually earned on the voyage. If the vessel is lost as a consequence of a collision, or before the end of the intended voyage, the value of the owner's interest may well be nothing.[69] But, if the vessel is repaired and thereafter completes her voyage, her value for limitation purposes appears to be her "repaired value."[70] Clearly, however, if the vessel is lost any prepaid or guaranteed freight would constitute a part of the limitation fund as the freight is, in fact, deemed to have been "earned" on the voyage. Moreover, in the event of a collision, the owner's interest in his vessel also includes any claim against a tortfeasor for damaging it such as by a collision.[71]

68. 46 U.S.C. 181-186.
69. *The City of Norwich*, 118 U.S. 468 (1886); *The Scotland*, 118 U.S.507 (1886).
70. *The Lara*, 1947 AMC 27 (S.D.N.Y.).
71. *O'Brien v. Miller*, 168 U.S. 287 (1897); *Oliver J. Olson v. S.S. Marine Leopard*, 356 F.2d 728, 1966 AMC 1064 (9th Cir.).

If the limitation fund is insufficient to pay all claimants in full, and if the proportion of the fund available for claimants in respect of personal injury claims is less than $60 per ton of the vessel's gross tonnage, the limitation fund must be increased so that there is $60 per ton available for claims of that type.[72]

Under general maritime principles, it has long been settled that when both vessels are to blame in a collision, only one payment is to be made, the vessel with the greater liability on balance to the other having to pay accordingly. This principle is known as "single liability,"[73] and can be simply illustrated by the following example in which vessel A is found 70 percent at fault and vessel B is found 30 percent at fault:

	Vessel A		Vessel B
Damage	$100,000	Damage	$50,000
Demurrage	5,000	Demurrage	2,000
	$105,000		$52,000

A is liable for 70% of $52,000	= $36,400
B is liable for 30% of $105,000	= $31,500
A pays B on balance	$4,900

So far, so good, but the principle of single liability came a cropper when it came to applying it to policies of insurance. This became apparent in *London Steamship Owners' Mutual Ins. Ass'n v. The Grampian Steamship Co.*[74] where it was held that, having received a payment of the balance due from the other vessel, the insured vessel was unable to recover under its Running Down Clause any part of the amount deducted by the other vessel for damage done to it because the insured vessel had not made any payment as to that amount to the other vessel. This created an obvious inequity and led to language in the Running Down Clause providing that, *unless the liability of the owners or charterers of one or both of such vessels becomes limited by law,* claims under the clause are to be settled on the principle of cross-liabilities just as if the owners or charterers of each vessel had been compelled to pay the owners or charterers of the other such vessel such proportion of the latter's damaqes as may have been properly allowed in ascertaining the balance or sum payable by or to the assured in consequence of such collision.

72. The subject of limitation of liability is rather exhaustively discussed in the Admiralty Law Institute: "Symposium on Limitation of Liability," *Tulane Law Review,* Vol. 53, No. 4, June, 1979, to which the reader is commended. Other source references are: Gilmore & Black, *The Law of Admiralty* (2d ed.), The Foundation Press, Inc., 1975; A. Parks, *The Law of Tug, Tow & Pilotage* (2d ed.), Cornell Maritime Press, Inc., 1982. For the purposes of the present discussion, it is sufficient to refer only generally to the principles of limitation.
73. *The North Star,* 106 U.S. 17 (1882); *Stoomvaart Maatschappij Nederland v. P. & O. Steam Navigation Co. (The Khedive),* (1882) 5 App.Cas. 876, 7 App. Cas. 795.
74. [1890] 24 Q.B.D. 663, 59 L.J.Q.B. 549, 6 Asp. M.L.C. 506.

Fundamentally, however, the owner's right to limit is exercised in re-spect of the balance payable by him on a "single liability" basis. Thus, in the example given, vessel A would not normally pursue her right to limit liability unless the limited amount would be less than $4,900. If she could, however, limit her liability to, say, $4,000 that is the sum which vessel B would receive and this would then calculate out as follows:

Vessel B's damage	$50,000 but receives only	$3,840
Demurrage	2,000 but receives only	160
	$52,000	$4,000

The Running Down Clause thus specifically precludes claims being adjusted on a cross-liabilities basis when both vessels are to blame and either one or both of them are successful in limiting liability. When either vessel limits liability, it is impossible to reconcile the principle of cross-liabilities with the legal requirement of single liability and, as a conse-quence, equitable principles must be subordinated to expedience. The effect is that while vessel B pays nothing in satisfaction of the claim of vessel A, the underwriters of vessel B have paid $50,000 toward her hull damage but will receive only $3,840 in diminution of their liability. In short, it is indisputable that when a vessel's liability is limited to a certain figure, this amount remains the same whatever damage the vessel may receive and whatever may be her degree of fault.[75]

75. As the principle is rather difficult to grasp, another example may well be helpful. Mullins, *Marine Insurance Digest*, Cornell Maritime Press, Inc., 1959, contains this example with respect to two vessels found to be mutually at fault (i.e., 50 percent with respect to each):

. . . Suppose that vessel X and Y (both fully covered by full form insurance including the Four-Fourths Collision Clause) collide, are both damaged and are mutually at fault for the collision. Take X's physical damages as $20,000 and her demurrage claim as $10,000, making $30,000 in all, and Y's physical damage as $6,000 and her demurrage claim as $3,000, making $9,000 in all. The actual settlement between the vessels would be made on the principle of single liability as provided by law. Vessel Y having sustained the lesser damage would pay to Vessel X 50% of the difference between the damages or $10,500. The recovery thus made by vessel X would then be apportioned between her physical damages of $20,000 and her demurrage claim of $10,000. The recovery appli-cable to the demurrage claim would be $3,500, leaving the owner of X with a net de-murrage loss of $6,500. The owner of Y would have his demurrage loss of $3,000 un-diminished by any recovery.

Under a Cross Liability settlement the fiction would be that X paid Y $4,500 (being half her total damages) and that Y paid X $15,000 (being half her total damages). The suppositious recovery of $4,500 made by vessel Y would be apportioned over her total damages. The proportion applicable to the demurrage claim would be $1,500, leaving the owner of Y with a net demurrage loss of $1,500. Similarly the suppositious recovery of $15,000 made by vessel X would be apportioned over her total damages, $5,000 being applicable to the demurrage claim, leaving her owner with a net demurrage loss of $5,000. Both vessel owners would recover $1,500 more demurrage under the Cross Liability settlement. Their respective underwriters would be correspondingly worse off.

It is important to understand precisely what is meant by the phrase "limited by law." A leading adjuster has described the concept in language which cannot be improved:[76]

> . . . It frequently happens that in the case of a serious collision the *potential* liability of each vessel exceeds the amount to which the vessel owner may be entitled to limit his liability under the limitation statutes and, in such cases, *both* vessels often institute proceedings for limitation of liability. Nevertheless, after the case is concluded by litigation or settlement, it may well be that the total actual liabilities of each vessel fall below the amount to which each vessel's owner is entitled to limit its liability. Furthermore, it is the single liability balance payable by the debtor vessel which is the criterion which determines whether the debtor vessel's liability has been *limited by law* within the meaning of the collision clause. That a shipowner has been granted the right to limit does not in itself mean that his liability has been *limited by law*. Only if the final settlement on a single liability basis between the colliding vessels is reduced or cancelled by reason of the insufficient limitation fund can it be said that that vessel's liability has been *limited by law*. In short, if the debtor vessel has a limitation fund sufficient to discharge its single liability to the other vessel, i.e., the imbalance owing, there has been no *effective* limitation of liability and a cross-liabilities settlement under the collision clause would be permissible. Thus, the principle to be applied in adjusting the claims between the two vessels might, under their hull policies, differ radically from the single liability principle which would then be applied by the court in the collision case itself.

Under English law and the laws of all nations subscribing to the Brussels Collision Convention, where both vessels are held at fault, the cargo in either vessel can only recover from the colliding vessel the same percentage of its loss (including if applicable the cargo's contribution to general average)[77] as the percentage of blame attaching to that vessel.[78] For example, if two vessels, A and B, collide, and A is held 80 percent to blame and B 20 percent to blame, the cargo in B can only recover 80 percent of its damages from shipowner A. The cargo owners' right of recovery for the remaining 20 percent of their loss is only against the owner of

---

76. Buglass, *Marine Insurance and General Average in the United States* (2d ed.), Cornell Maritime Press, Inc., 1981.

77. *Greystoke Castle (Cargo Owners) v. Morrison Steamship Co., Ltd.*, [1947] A.C., [1946] 80 Ll.L.Rep. 55, affirming *The Cheldale*, [1945] P. 10, [1945] 78 Ll.L.Rep. 129. The American rule as to inclusion of cargo's contribution to general average is the same. See *Toluma— Sucarseco*, 294 U.S. 394, 1935 AMC 412, affirming 1934 AMC 1083 (2d Cir.), 50 Ll.L.Rep. 28. Note, also, *Hamilton—Mexico*, 72 F.2d 694, 1934 AMC 1090 (2d.Cir.).

78. *The Drumlanrig*, [1911] A.C. 16, 27 T.L.R. 146, confirming the rule enunciated in *The Milan*, (1861) 31 L.J. Adm., (1861) Lush. 388.

the carrying vessel which, however, is usually insulated from liability pursuant to the terms of the contract of affreightment which exempts the carrying vessel from liability where negligent navigation of the vessel by master or crew caused the collision.

The rule in the United States unfortunately differs, for in a both-to-blame collision the cargo owner can recover in full from the non-carrying vessel. This was decided in *The Chattahoochee*.[79] That case involved a collision between the *Chattahoochee* and the schooner *Golden Rule*. Both vessels were at fault. At that time (prior to *Reliable Transfer*) the American rule relating to division of damages in mutual fault collision cases was that each vessel was liable for one-half of the total damages; the result was (on a single liability principle) that the vessel suffering the smaller loss paid the other vessel one-half of the difference between its loss and that of the other vessel. In computing these amounts, the damages paid by the non-carrying vessel to the owners of the cargo on the carrying vessel were included as a part of the non-carrying vessel's damages. The net result, it will be seen, was that the carrying vessel remained indirectly liable for and paid one-half of the damages sustained by the cargo aboard it, even though under the Harter Act or Cogsa it would normally have been relieved of liability to cargo aboard it if the collision were due (as it usually is) to negligent navigation on the part of the carrying vessel. In *The Chattahoochee*, this anomaly was squarely presented and litigated, the carrying vessel claiming that the Harter Act should insulate it against such a result. The Supreme Court, however, held that the Act was not intended to affect the liabilities of the two vessels under the both-to-blame collision rule.

As a result of *The Chattahoochee,* carriers began inserting "both-to-blame" clauses in their bills of lading. These clauses, in substance, provide that where both vessels are at fault, the cargo owner must reimburse his carrier for any amount the carrier has had to pay to the non-carrying vessel, or has had set off against it by reason of the non-carrier having paid the cargo owner's loss. And so another rather awkward situation was created; i.e., if only one vessel is at fault, cargo can recover its full loss, but if both vessels are at fault, the cargo could recover only half its loss.

The interplay between these two conflicting interests came before the Supreme Court in *U.S. v. Atlantic Mutual Ins. Co.*,[80] whereupon the Supreme Court held the both-to-blame clause invalid, finding that there was no indication in the Harter Act to warrant changing the basic American rule of sharing losses when both vessels are to blame. The net result, of

---

79. 173 U.S. 540 (1899). See, also, *Toluma—Sucarseco* and *Hamilton—Mexico,* n. 77, *supra.* Where cargo is compelled, by virtue of a Jason Clause, to contribute in general average, such contribution is includible in the sum which cargo may assert against the non-carrying vessel.

80. 343 U.S. 236, 1952 AMC 659.

course, was to reinforce the rule in *The Chattahoochee* and invalidate contractual attempts *of common carriers* to offset it.[81]

Thus, not only were the carriers placed in an awkward position, so were the P & I underwriters, for if both vessels are guilty of negligent navigation, it is to the advantage of the P & I underwriters to establish that the other, or non-carrying, vessel is free from fault. That is, it is to their advantage (and the corresponding disadvantage of the hull underwriters on the same vessel) to seek to establish a sole fault situation even if this imposes liability on the vessel they have insured, whereas in a both-to-blame situation they would be compelled to pay half the damages of the carrying vessel's cargo.

Although it might well be argued that *Reliable Transfer* altered the American "cargo rule," this does not appear to have been the case. See, for example, *Vana Trading Co. v. S.S. Mette Skou;*[82] *Alamo Chemical Transp. Co. v. M/V Overseas Valdes;*[83] *Gulfcoast Transit Co. v. Anco Princess;*[84] *Re Malaysia Overseas Lines, Ltd.;*[85] *Matter of Flota Mercante Grancolumbiana, S.A.;*[86] *Allied Chemical v. Hess Tankship;*[87] and *Edmonds v. Compagnie Generale Transatlantique.*[88]

In *Alamo Chemical,* the Eastern District of Louisiana found a conflict between *Reliable Transfer* and the rule in *The Chattahoochee* and held that cargo could only recover proportionately to the fault of the other colliding vessel, i.e., 20 percent. In doing so, the district court expressly disapproved the holding in *Matter of Flota Mercante Grancolumbiana.* Subsequently, however, the Fifth Circuit in *Allied Chemical v. Hess Tankship* disagreed with the district court and held that the rule in *Flota Mercante Grancolumbiana* should be applied, citing *Edmonds* where the Supreme Court in a footnote had stated:

> *Reliable Transfer* merely changed the apportionment from equal division to division on the basis of relative fault. But we did not upset the

81. As the district court noted in *Alamo Chemical Transp. Co, v. M/V Overseas Valdes,* 469 F.Supp. 203, 1979 AMC 2033 (E.D.,La.), the context in which the both-to-blame clause was rejected in Atlantic Mutual *was confined to common carrier relationships.* See, also, *American Union Transport, Inc. v. U.S.,* 1976 AMC 1480 and *Commercial Molasses Corp. v. N.Y. Tank Barge Corp.,* 314 U.S. 104, 1941 AMC 1697 (holding that exculpatory clauses in *private* contracts of affreightment, as distinguished from *common* carriage, are not contrary to public policy). Presumably, therefore, both-to-blame clauses in *private* contracts of affreightment would be held to be valid.

82. 556 F.2d 100, 1977 AMC 702 (2d Cir.).

83. 469 F.Supp. 203, 1979 AMC 2033 (E.D.,La.).

84. 1978 AMC 2471 (E.D.,La.), [1978] 1 Lloyd's Rep. 293.

85. 1976 AMC 1287, 1306 (S.D.N.Y.).

86. 440 F.Supp. 704, 1979 AMC 156, *aff'd* without opinion, 573 F.2d 1290 (2d Cir.), *cert. den.* 436 U.S. 907 (1978).

87. 661 F.2d 1044, 1982 AMC 1271 (5th Cir.).

88. 443 U.S. 256, 1979 AMC 1167 (1979).

rule that the plaintiff may recover from *one* of the colliding vessels the damages concurrently caused by the negligence of both.

It should also be noted that in *Gulfcoast Transit v. Anco Princess, supra,* the district court, after finding that the innocent cargo aboard the towed barge could recover against the tug and its owner for 100 percent of its loss, also held that the tug and its owner could recover over against the owner of the tanker with which the collision took place, 85 percent of the amount paid to innocent cargo, i.e., that 85 percent which was the degree of fault assessed against the tanker and its owner. In *Allied Chemical v. Hess Tankship,* the Fifth Circuit, in a somewhat cryptic footnote, observed that *Allied Towing,* in proceedings fixing damages and striking a balance, could, of course, "urge all contractual exemptions and limitations from liability of cargo."

The anomaly which still exists unquestionably will lead to forum shopping since, under American law, cargo owners can recover in full from a negligent non-carrying vessel providing the vessel owner is solvent and cannot limit its liability. A classic illustration of forum shopping in this respect will be found in *The Giancinto Motta.*[89] In that case, the *World Mermaid* collided with the *Giancinto Motta* by reason of the negligent navigation of both vessels. The *Motta* was lost and her owners claimed damages of about £500,000; the cargo on the *Motta* was lost and its owners claimed £1,350,000; the *Mermaid* was damaged and her owners claimed £250,000. Two sets of proceedings were instituted. In the United States, the cargo owners' claim was settled by the payment of $2,485,880.37; in England, the owners of the *Motta* and the *Mermaid* were parties to a suit in which liability was established on the basis of equal fault. According to English law, the limitation fund of the *Mermaid* was £845,705; the owners of the *Motta* were not liable to the cargo owners for the loss of the cargo by virtue of the Hague Rules which applied to the contracts of carriage. The questions before the court were whether and to what extent the damages recoverable by the owners of the *Mermaid* from the owners of the *Motta* included the cargo claim; and whether, assuming the owners of the *Mermaid* had a right to limit liability, they were entitled to retain out of the limitation fund a sum in respect of the whole or any part of the cargo claim, or, alternatively, to have the whole or any part of the cargo claim taken into account in the distribution of the fund.

It was held (Queen's Bench Division, Admiralty Court) that there would be judgment for the owners of the *Motta.* While the owners of the *Mermaid* would be entitled to be credited in the distribution of their limitation fund in respect of the cargo claim, the amount of the credit could not exceed the amount of the dividend which would have been recoverable by the cargo owners from such fund if they had brought their claim

89. [1977] 2 Lloyd's Rep. 221.

against it instead of enforcing payment in respect of it in the United States. Consequently, the cargo owners were only entitled to bring a claim against the fund for 50 percent of their loss, and this was the extent to which the owners of the *Mermaid* were entitled to be credited.

It is clear that until the United States adopts *in toto* the proportionate fault rule of the Brussels Convention—or the U.S. Supreme Court addresses the problem directly and effects a change, so that there is no right of recovery by the non-carrying vessel against the carrying vessel with respect to payments to cargo—this anomaly will continue to plague P & I underwriters.

Examples of Dispositions on Single Liability versus Cross-Liability

By way of illustration of the differences between the single liability principle and settlement on the basis of cross-liabilities, take the following examples:

Vessels A and B are involved in a collision. Vessel A sustains $100,000 in hull damage and incurs a demurrage claim of $40,000; vessel B sustains $200,000 in hull damage and incurs a demurrage claim of $80,000. Vessel A is found to be 40 percent at fault; vessel B is found to be 60 percent at fault.

The *settlement at law* would involve one payment only; namely, the payment by A to B of $28,000, calculated as follows:

$$40\% \text{ of } \$280,000 = \$112,000 \text{ payable by A to B}$$
$$60\% \text{ of } \$140,000 = \underline{84,000} \text{ payable by B to A}$$
$$\$28,000 \text{ on balance paid by A to B}$$

On a single liability basis, the settlement under the respective policies (assuming each vessel to have been fully insured) would be as follows:

Hull underwriters of A—damage to vessel A	$100,000
plus	
Amount paid by A to B	28,000
A's total recovery under its policies	$128,000
Hull underwriters of B—damage to vessel B	$200,000
Less credit for the proportion of B's	
recovery from A; i.e., 200,00 of $28,000 =	20,000
280,000	
Net payable by B's underwriters	$180,000[90]

90. P & I underwriters of B make no payment.

As provided for in the Running Down Clause on the basis of cross-liabilities, the settlement under the policies would be as follows:

Damages	A	B
Ship	$100,000	$200,000
Demurrage	40,000	80,000
	$140,000	$280,000

Settlement between the parties:

Liability of A to B		
(40% of $280,000)	112,000	
Less liability of B to A		
(60% of 140,000)	84,000	
Single liability, A to B	$ 28,000	28,000
Total payments by A		28,000

Loss and damage to A:

Total payments	28,000
Own damages	140,000
	$168,000

Distribution of $168,000 if fully insured:

	P.A.	R.D.C.	Owners
Damage to ship	$100,000		
Demurrage			$40,000
Recovery from B	(60,000)		(24,000)
	$ 40,000		$16,000
Damages done:			
40% of $280,000		$112,000	
	$ 40,000	$112,000	$16,000

Underwriters would, therefore, pay the following to the owners of vessel A:

P.A.	$ 40,000
Collision claim	112,000
	$152,000[91]

Correspondingly:
Loss and damage to B:

Total payments	– – –
Own damages	$280,000

91. Deductibles in both policies are ignored for the purposes of illustration.

Distribution of $280,000 if fully insured:

	P.A.	R.D.C.	Owners
Damage to ship	$200,000		
Demurrage			$80,000
Recovery from A	(80,000)		(32,000)
	$120,000		$48,000
Damages done:			
60% of $140,000		$84,000	
	$120,000	$84,000	$48,000

Underwriters would therefore pay the following to the owners of vessel B:

P.A.	$120,000
Collision claim	84,000
	$204,000

From the foregoing, it will be seen that on a cross-liabilities basis each shipowner will recover his proportionate share of demurrage.

For example, it is obvious that shipowner A is out of pocket by the sum of the damage to his vessel, his demurrage loss and the amount he has had to pay shipowner B in the settlement between the two vessels. Shipowner B is correspondingly out of pocket $280,000 less the sum he receives from shipowner A. On a single liability basis, shipowner A would receive only $128,000 and would have to bear his demurrage loss of $40,000. On a cross-liabilities basis, he receives $152,000 which represents $24,000 more than would be received on the single liability basis or 60 percent of his demurrage loss. Correspondingly, shipowner B would recover on a single liability basis only $180,000 but on a cross-liabilities basis $204,000—which represents an additional 40 percent of his demurrage claim of $80,000; i.e., an additional $32,000.

As an example of the calculations of a settlement between two vessels where liability is limited, assume that in the foregoing examples, the value of vessel A plus prepaid freight after the collision with vessel B was only $20,000—or $8,000 less than the amount to be paid on balance by vessel A to vessel B. The collision, insofar as vessel A is concerned, was caused by negligent navigation and, as the owner was not in privity with respect thereto, vessel A would be entitled to limit its liability to the $20,000 figure. The settlements with underwriters on their respective policies would then be as follows:

Vessel A's Underwriters

A's hull damages	$100,000
A's statutory (or limited) liability to B	20,000
A's total recovery from underwriters	$120,000

Vessel B's Underwriters

B's hull damages	$200,000
Less credit for the proportion of B's recovery from A; i.e., $\frac{\$200,000}{280,000}$ of $20,000 =	(14,200)
Net amount payable by B's underwriters	$185,800
Shipowner B would, of course, retain the proportion of his recovery from A applying to his loss of demurrage; i.e. $\frac{80,000}{280,000}$ of $20,000 =	$ 5,800

If, in the foregoing case there had been, in addition, damage to vessel B's cargo, under American law 100 percent could be claimed by the cargo owners against vessel A and would be ranked, together with vessel B's claim for $28,000 for payment out of the limitation fund, i.e., only $20,000. The effect of the inclusion of such cargo claims necessarily reduces shipowner B's recovery and consequently reduces the recovery of his underwriters.

The complex situation in *Diesel Tanker A.C. Dodge v. Stewart*,[92] affords a good example of the difference to underwriters of a settlement on the basis of single liability versus cross-liability. In that case, the *Dodge* collided with the *Michael* (and thereafter a fire occurred) with resultant loss of life to persons aboard both vessels, personal injuries aboard both vessels, loss of cargo on the *Dodge*, damage to the *Michael* and total loss of the *Dodge*.

Following the collision, the *Dodge* filed a petition for limitation of liability. After trial and appeal, it was held that the collision occurred by reason of the joint fault of the *Dodge* and the *Michael*. It was also held that the *Dodge* was entitled to limit liability.

The *Dodge* was required to deposit in its limitation fund $60.00 per ton of the vessel's gross tonnage for the benefit of personal injury and death claims. Out of this fund, the owners of the *Dodge* paid $64,531.50 to the estate of the master who had died in the collision.

Before the litigation terminated, the owner of the *Michael* had settled the majority of the personal injury death claims and the claim of the owner of the cargo on the *Dodge*. The *Michael's* owner also paid to the estate of the *Dodge's* master a total of $59,000 for a covenant not to sue the *Michael*. The *Dodge* was insured under hull policies (which contained a standard Running Down Clause) in the sum of $400,000 and its hull underwriters paid the full sum to the *Dodge's* owners. The *Dodge* was also insured separately against fire in the sum of $150,000, in excess of the

92. 262 F.Supp. 6, 1966 AMC 1746 (S.D.N.Y.), *aff'd per curiam* 376 F.2d 850, 1967 AMC 1689 (2d Cir.).

hull policy. The underwriters on that policy paid the *Dodge's* owner $75,000 on account of the total loss of the *Dodge.*

There were four additional P & I policies in effect on the *Dodge,* the latter three policies being in excess of the first, for an aggregate total of $1,000,000.

It being well settled that in a "both to blame" collision, if one of the colliding vessels pays third-party claims, such claims become part of the collision damage of the vessel paying the claim,[93] the *Michael* was able to offset one-half of her payments on account of these claims against one-half of the damages allowed to the *Dodge* for loss of the *Dodge* and incidental expenses. The total claims paid by the *Michael* amounted to some $650,000 and her hull claim amounted to $462,000. On a single liability basis (including payment of the third-party claims) the *Michael* was a creditor, her total damages (sustained or paid) having been greater than those of the *Dodge.*

However, in an ingenious approach, the *Dodge* sued its P & I underwriters for one-half the difference between the hull claim of the *Michael* and her own hull claim, i.e., $170,515.94. (This figure was arrived at because it was one-half the difference between the hull claim of the *Michael* [$462,618.69] and the total loss value of the *Dodge,* plus stand-by wreck and salvage expenses of $403,650.57, totalling $803,650.57.) The owners of the *Dodge* claimed, in essence, that Clause 4(a) of the P & I policies provided that if a claim arose under Clause 4, it would be settled on the basis of cross-liabilities. Therefore, if the principle of cross-liabilities applied, then the owner of the *Dodge* would be deemed to have paid a portion of the damages even though, in fact, he had not actually expended any of his own money.

The court noted that although Clause 4(a) provided for the use of the principle of cross-liabilities, it was clear that it could be used only to the same extent as provided in the standard Running Down Clause in the hull policy. As the standard Running Down Clause applied the cross-liability principle *unless* the liability of the insured owner was limited by law, and the owner of the *Dodge* had, in fact, limited its liability, the principle of cross-liability was not applicable to either the Running Down Clause or the P & I policy, even if the owner of the *Dodge* had incurred a liability for loss under Clause 4. Therefore, the *Dodge* could only recover under the P & I policy on the principle of strict indemnity and, since it has already been reimbursed for what it had actually paid out, it was entitled to no further recovery under the P & I policy.

To summarize, limitation of liability under American law is applied only after a balance has been struck and the single liability has been deter-

93. *Albert Dumois,* 177 U.S. 240 (1900); *N.Y. & Cuba S.S. Co. v. American S.S. Owners Mut. Prot. & Indemn. Ass'n, Inc.,* 72 F.2d 694, 1934 AMC 1090 (2d Cir.), *cert. den.* 293 U.S. 622 (1934).

mined, and limitation is effective only when that balance exceeds the statutory limit.

It should be noted, however, that application of "direct action" statutes such as that of Louisiana and Puerto Rico may have a dramatic effect on the liability of underwriters. The right to limit under the U.S. Limitation of Liability Act having been held to be personal to the owner, underwriters cannot limit their liability (to that limited by their assured) if they are sued directly by third parties in jurisdictions having direct action statutes.[94]

Moreover, the Louisiana statute appears to apply to every insurance policy, including P & I policies, having effect in Louisiana.[95] Happily, liability underwriters can take some comfort from *Alcoa S.S. Co. v. Charles Ferran & Co.*,[96] where a ship repairer's liability underwriter was held entitled to take advantage of a "red letter" clause in a ship repair contract limiting the repairer's liability to $300,000; i.e., the defense was not "personal" to the assured. In the language of the court, although insurers are not entitled to benefit from a defense based upon the insured's publicly protected legal statute, they should benefit from the contractual defenses of their assureds. And, in those jurisdictions where direct action statutes are not applicable or have not been enacted, the old rule continues to

---

94. *Maryland Casualty Co. v. Cushing*, 347 U.S. 409 (1954), 1954 AMC 837; *Olympia Towing Corp. v. Nebel Towing Co., Inc. and U.S. Casualty Co.*, 419 F.2d 230, 1969 AMC 1571 (5th Cir.), [1970] 1 Lloyd's Rep. 430, *cert. den.* 397 U.S. 989 (1970). Thus, under the Louisiana direct action statute, limitation is a personal defense available only to the vessel owner and a bareboat charterer and is not available to their insurers. *In Re Independent Towing Co.*, 242 F.Supp. 950, 1965 AMC 818 (E.D.,La.). For other cases involving direct action statutes, see: *Coleman v. Jahncke Service*, 1965 AMC 535, 341 F.2d 956, 1966 AMC 1115 (5th Cir.); *Alcoa Corsair*, 383 F.2d 46, 1967 AMC 2578 (5th Cir.); *Itco III*, 242 F.Supp. 784, 1968 AMC 818 (E.D.,La.); *Leebe & Tow*, 275 F.Supp. 784, 1968 AMC 367 (D., P.R.); *American Sugar v. Vainqueur*, 1970 AMC 405 (E.D.,La.); *Sincere Navigation Co. Lim. Procs.*, 317 F.Supp. 1, 1971 AMC 991 (E.D.,La.); *Nations v. Morris*, 1973 AMC 818 (5th Cir.); *Verret v. Travelers Ins. Co.*, 1969 AMC 2337 (St., La.); *St. Julien v. Diamond M. Drilling*, 403 F.Supp. 1256, 1975 AMC 1806 (E.D.,La.); *International Sea Food v. Campeche*, 566 F.2d 482, 1978 AMC 890 (5th Cir.); *McKeithen v. Frosta*, 430 F. Supp. 899, 1978 AMC 31 (E.D.,La.); *Signal Oil v. Barge W-701*, 468 F.Supp. 802, 1980 AMC 1445 (E.D.,La.) (where shipowner is entitled to limit but claimants have a right of direct action against underwriters, underwriters pay the proceeds into the limitation fund up to the amount of the fund; after receiving their pro-rata share of the fund, the claimants may then proceed directly against the balance of the insurance proceeds to satisfy their remaining claims); *Weiland v. Pyramid Ventures*, 511 F.Supp. 1034, 1981 AMC 2846 (M.D.,La.); *Red Star Barge Line Lim. Procs.*, 683 F.2d 42, 1982 AMC 2588 (2d Cir.) (the century-old "obsolescent" doctrine that insurance proceeds paid to a shipowner entitled to limit liability are not available to the injured party must be followed until re-examined by the Supreme Court).

95. *Sassoni v. Savoie*, 327 F.Supp. 474, 1971 AMC 1910 (E.D.,La.) (seaman granted direct action for injury sustained on high seas merely because the shipowner's insurance policy was written in Louisiana).

96. 383 F.2d 46, 1967 AMC 2578, 443 F.2d 250, 1971 AMC 1116 (5th Cir.), [1971] 2 Lloyd's Rep. 426.

apply that insurance proceeds paid to a shipowner entitled to limit liability are not available to the injured party.[97]

Sister Ship Clause

When two vessels, both in common ownership or management, are involved in a collision, it is impossible to resolve the question of liability by legal proceedings. This is so because an owner cannot be legally liable to himself; i.e., a person cannot sue himself. This principle was confirmed in *Simpson v. Thompson*.[98] It was to avoid this inequity arising simply out of an accident of ownership that the Sister Ship Clause was devised.

The Sister Ship Clause in the AIH (1977) form will be found in two different locations. The portion relating to collision will be found under the Collision Clause and reads:

> The principles involved in this clause shall apply to the case where both vessels are the property, in part or in whole, of the same owners or charterers, all questions of responsibility and amount of liability as between the two vessels being left to the decision of a single Arbitrator, if the parties can agree upon a single Arbitrator, or failing such agreement, to the decision of Arbitrators, one to be appointed by the Assured and one to be appointed by the majority (in amount) of Hull Underwriters interested; the two Arbitrators chosen to choose a third Arbitrator before entering upon the reference, and the decision of such single Arbitrator, or of any two of such three Arbitrators, appointed as above, to be final and binding.

A like provision appears under the General Average and Salvage Clause of the AIH (1977) form and reads:

> In the event of salvage, towage or other assistance being rendered to the Vessel by any vessel belonging in part or in whole to the same Owners or Charterers, the value of such services (without regard to the common ownership or control of the vessels) shall be ascertained by arbitration in the manner provided for under the Collision Liability clause in this Policy, and the amount so awarded so far as appli-

97. *Red Star Barge Line Lim. Procs.*, 683 F.2d 42, 1982 AMC 2588 (2d Cir.), citing *The City of Norwich*, 118 U.S. 468 (1886); *Dyer v. National Steam Navigation Co. (The Scotland)*, 118 U.S. 507 (1886); and *The Great Western*, 118 U.S. 507 (1886).

98. (1877) 38 L.T. 1, 3 Asp. M.L.C. 567, 3 A.C. 279. See, also, *City of New Bern*, 16 F.Supp. 1389, 1926 AMC 1651 (E.D.N.Y.), where a steamer was demise-chartered to the owner of a barge and during a tow injured the barge; no recovery *in rem* as the charterer-owner was owner *pro hac vice* of the steamer under the demise charter and could not recover against himself.

cable to the interest hereby insured shall constitute a charge under this Policy.

In English policies, whether the old Institute form or the new London Institute Hull Clauses (1/10/83),the Sister Ship Clause follows the Running Down Clause and reads as follows:

> Should the Vessel hereby insured come into collision with or receive salvage services from another vessel belonging wholly or in part to the same Owners or under the same management, the Assured shall have the same rights under this Policy as they would have were the other vessel entirely the property of Owners not interested in the Vessel hereby insured; but in such cases the liability for the collision or the amount payable for the services rendered shall be referred to a sole arbitrator to be agreed upon between the Underwriters and the Assured.

It will be seen, therefore, that under the Sister Ship Clause the assured can recover his demurrage with respect to the innocent vessel or a proportion of his demurrage on both vessels on a cross-liabilities basis if both vessels are to blame. If the principle of cross-liabilities were not applied, underwriters would simply pay for the damage suffered by each vessel and the shipowner would not recover any part of his demurrage.

The same principle applies where salvage services (and in the AIH form where towage services) are rendered by one vessel to another vessel owned by the same entity.

It is customary in sister-ship collisions where one vessel is clearly responsible for the collision and the other is wholly innocent to request underwriters' approval to present the claim for damage to the innocent vessel on the policy covering that particular vessel, thus obviating the necessity for an arbitration. Moreover, if no demurrage claims are involved, the claims are often stated as particular average claims under the respective policies on the vessels and the liability question becomes moot. However, if there is any doubt as to the question of liability for the collision and demurrage claims involved, it is necessary to follow the arbitration provisions.

The leading American cases involving sister-ship liabilities under the Running Down Clause will suffice to explain the principles involved.

In *Augusta-Detroit,*[99] a steamer towing a barge, both being in common ownership, collided with a third vessel. The steamer was found solely at fault and her owner limited liability. She also collided with her barge and sank it with its cargo. The steamer and the barge were separately insured through different hull underwriters, with the respective policies contain-

---

99. 290 F. 685, 1923 AMC 754, 1923 AMC 816, 1924 AMC 872, *aff'd* 5 F.2d 773, 1925 AMC 756 (4th Cir.).

ing the Running Down Sister Ship Clause. The owner of the barge received from its hull underwriters the sum of $25,932 on account of the loss of the barge.

Disagreement having arisen between the parties in respect of the amounts payable under the policies, by consent an arbitrator was appointed. The arbitrator, in effect, ruled that the liability of the steamer's underwriters to the owners thereof under the Sister Ship Clause was not limited to the amount which its owners had surrendered in the proceedings to limit liability, but so long as the steamer's loss exceeded the amount of the policies issued and the claim came within the provisions of the policies and was not affected by any of the excepting clauses, the steamer's hull underwriters were liable for the full sum insured.

Secondly, in response to a claim by the underwriters of the cargo on the barge and the hull underwriters on the barge that they were entitled to recover from the steamer's underwriters what sums they had paid with respect to the barge and its cargo, the arbitrator ruled that the steamer's underwriters were not liable for any sum whatsoever for the barge or its cargo or to the insurers of such cargo. Being dissatisfied, the barge and cargo underwriters threatened suit whereupon a suit was instituted to enjoin such action. The trial court affirmed the arbitrator's decision and, on appeal, the appeals court did likewise, adopting wholly the arbitrator's reasoning. In part, the appeals court observed that under the sister-ship provisions of the policy neither the underwriters of the barge and its cargo nor the owner thereof as such could assert any claim against the steamer's underwriters as they did not occupy such a relation to the latter or its underwriters so as to enable them to do so.

By contrast, in *Industry-Commerce*,[100] the distinguished arbitrator reached a different conclusion. The facts in that case were remarkably similar to *Augusta-Detroit* except that in *Industry-Commerce* the hull underwriters of the innocent barge paid in full rather than approximately one-quarter by virtue of the limitation proceeding, and further, payment was made under a loan receipt rather than making an outright payment. The arbitrator distinguished *Augusta-Detroit* and held that the hull underwriters of the innocent barge were entitled to contribution from the hull underwriters of the steamer.

In the *Ariosa and D-22*,[101] the Second Circuit took a slightly different tack. In that case, *Ariosa*, towing the *D-22* (both being in common ownership), caused the *D-22* to collide with a steamer. Fault was divided half on the *Ariosa* and the steamer; *D-22* was found blameless. The *D-22* and the steamer suffered damage; the *Ariosa* was undamaged. The hull under-

---

100. 1939 AMC 717 (Arb.).
101. 144 F.2d 262, 1944 AMC 1035 (2d Cir.), *cert. den.* 323 U.S. 797 (1944).

writers on the *D-22* advanced the repair costs on a loan receipt. Other underwriters had insured the *Ariosa* with tower's risk, and a Running Down Clause containing a sister-ship provision. The damage to the *D-22* was less in amount than that sustained by the steamer and the half damages due the latter were paid by her owners by the payment of the excess of one-half its damages over one-half the damages of the *D-22*.

The underwriters on the *Ariosa* filed a declaratory judgment action to determine their liability, contending that because there happened to be hull insurance on a vessel not at fault which was injured through the fault of their assured, their liability should be reduced by the amount of that other insurance on the ground that they could compel its collection for their benefit. Apparently, the parties to the litigation agreed to abide the result of the court action in lieu of arbitration under the Sister Ship Clause.

The court, noting that the liability of the underwriters on the *Ariosa* having been established, held that they were bound to pay in accordance with the terms of their policy regardless of any insurance the owner of the *D-22* had on it. The court stated, in part:

> . . . Even though for present purposes, the owner of the *Ariosa* and the owner of the [*D-22*], though in fact the same, are to be treated as separate and distinct parties, it is obvious that payment by the underwriters of the legal liability of the *Ariosa* can give them no rights by way of subrogation, except to be put in the position in which a separate and distinct owner of the *Ariosa* would have been upon making such payment. The owner of the ship partially at fault certainly has no claim against the owner, treated as a third party, of the blameless scow and has no recognizable interest in any insurance which that owner may have had on the hull of that scow. We need not decide whether the insurer of the scow, if and when it paid, would be subrogated to the rights of the scow owner against the *Ariosa* and the [steamer]. That was unnecessary because the defendants (underwriters of the *D-22*) have in the loan receipt given effect to the equivalent of a right of subrogation and made double recovery by the scow owner an impossibility.

The underwriters on the *Ariosa* insisted that they were entitled to recover under the *Augusta-Detroit* decision, and that the Sister Ship Clause should be construed so as to relieve them from liability under their policy to the extent of the hull insurance. The court discussed the *Augusta-Detroit* decision and concluded that what was denied underwriters in that decision was, in effect what was being denied the underwriters in the instant case.

The ultimate outcome in the case was that:

(1) The hull underwriters on the *D-22* recovered in full for its damages, one-half from the steamer and one-half from the *Ariosa;*

(2) The steamer recovered one-half of her damages from the *Ariosa;*

(3) The hull underwriters of the *Ariosa* reimbursed the *Ariosa* for the one-half damages paid to the steamer;

(4) The hull underwriters of the *Ariosa* reimbursed the hull underwriters on the *D-22* for one-half of the damage to it;

(5) It was not necessary to decide the subrogation rights of the hull underwriters on the *D-22* because the loan receipt method of payment was effective as the equivalent of subrogation; and

(6) The tower's and running down risk underwriters on the *Ariosa* were not relieved of liability under the policy to the extent of the hull insurance on the *D-22.*

In *Bushey & Sons v. Tugboat Underwriting Syndicate,*[102] the assured sought an order compelling arbitration of a claim under a policy issued by defendant underwriters insuring the tug *Frances A. Small.* The claim arose out of a collision between the *Small* and the Barge *Hygrade 95.* The *Small* was, at the time of the collision, owned by Bulk Navigation & Towing, Inc., and was under bareboat charter to plaintiff Red Star. The barge *Hygrade 95* was owned by Barge Hygrade No. 95 Corp. In effect, the parent company, Ira S. Bushey & Sons, Inc., owned both vessels; i.e., its subsidiary Barge Hygrade No. 95 Corp. owned the barge *Hygrade 95* and its subsidiary Red Star was bareboat charterer of the towing tug *Frances A. Small.* The term "Assured" in the policy was defined to mean the parent as well as its subsidiaries.

The court noted that the assured corporations were separate entities and could, if need be, sue each other and recover a judgment. However, the court held on a construction of the Sister Ship Clause that it would be inherently wasteful and unreasonable for sister corporations to be required to pursue litigation against each other which, defendant underwriters conceded, but for the use of separate fictional identities, would have been obviated by the Sister Ship Clause. Finding an expressed intention and a valid written agreement to arbitrate the controversy, the court ordered it so.

In *Sucre—Tamare,*[103] the *Sucre* was time-chartered to the Creole Petroleum Corporation. It was struck while lying at its berth by the *Tamare,* which was bareboat chartered to a wholly owned subsidiary of the Creole Petroleum Corporation. (It was common ground that the wholly owned subsidiary was the equivalent of the Creole Petroleum Corporation.) The *Sucre* sustained substantial damage, the cost of repairs having been collected by its owner from the *Sucre's* underwriters. A claim was thereupon filed on behalf of the *Sucre* against the *Tamare* for the physical damages and time lost during repairs. The *Tamare* interests denied liability for the

102. 1975 AMC 392 (S.D.N.Y.).
103. 1950 AMC 493 (Arb.).

claim, basing such denial upon a provision in the policies of insurance that " . . . for the duration of period while vessels are under time charter the within insurance shall be extended to cover the interest of (Creole Petroleum Corporation) . . . " and a provision in the charter party that the owner would, during the period of the charter," . . . include as insured interest in the owner's policies of insurance (both hull and P & I) the charterer and/or associated and/or affiliated companies."

The arbitrator ruled that the underwriters could not collect the cost of repairs and the detention loss from the time charterer or his ship for the reason that they had effectively waived their subrogation rights in respect of any damage caused by the time charterer by extending their policies to cover the time charterer's interest.

Chapter XX

PARTICULAR AVERAGE

Definition

There can be no doubt that by far the most frequent claims under marine insurance policies are those for partial losses of the subject-matter insured.

What is "average"? *Webster's New World Dictionary* defines the term as "(a) a loss incurred by damage to a ship at sea or to its cargo, (b) an incurring of such loss, (c) the equitable division of such loss among the interested parties, (d) a charge arising from such loss, (e) any of various small charges paid by the master of a ship, as for pilotage or towage."

Gow[1] defines the term with precision: "Particular average is the liability attaching to a marine insurance policy in respect of damage or partial loss accidentally and immediately caused by some of the perils insured against, to some particular interest (as the ship alone or the cargo alone) which has arrived at the destination of the venture."

Phillips[2] states: "A particular average is a loss borne wholly by the party upon whose property it takes place, and is so called in distinction from a general average for which divers parties contribute."

The Marine Insurance Act, 1906, Section 56(1) provides that:

"A loss may be either total or partial. Any loss other than a total loss, as hereinafter defined, is a partial loss."

Examples of Particular Average

Ship: Where, for example, a vessel encounters heavy weather with violent seas sweeping her decks; strikes an obstruction; strands, incurring damage to her plates, propeller, or rudder; collides with another vessel; or catches on fire and deck houses, furniture, or fittings are damaged. Unless the damage is so serious as to qualify for a constructive total loss, the damage is particular average.

Cargo: Where, for example, the cargo is damaged by seawater during heavy weather; by fire; by cargo stowed breaking way during heavy

---

1. William Gow, *Marine Insurance, A Handbook,* Macmillan & Co., London, 4th ed., 1913.
2. Willard Phillips, *A Treatise on the Law of Insurance,* Hurd and Houghton, New York, 1867. See, also, *Padelford v. Boardman,* 4 Mass. 548 (1808).

weather; leakage for the same reason; the vessel striking an obstruction; or by sweat damage due to an inability to properly ventilate the hold as a consequence of prolonged heavy weather.

Freight: Where, for example, freight is payable on delivery of cargo at destination and a cargo of sugar is partially dissolved by seawater, thus occasioning a loss of part of the shipowner's freight.

Damage Must Be Accidental and Fortuitous

As noted in the above definitions, a particular average loss or damage concerns solely the person interested in the subject matter of the insurance and his underwriter. It must be accidental and it must be fortuitous. Consequently, it is clearly distinguishable from *general average* as where property is deliberately sacrificed for the general benefit of the common venture in time of peril—such as throwing cargo overboard in order to lighten a vessel so as to get off a strand and thereby save the vessel and other cargo on board. In such an instance, the loss of the jettisoned cargo would be a general average loss to which the owners of the other property would have to contribute.[3]

Section 64 of the Marine Insurance Act defines a particular average loss with total simplicity:

(1) A particular average loss is a partial loss of the subject-matter insured, caused by a peril insured against, and which is not a general average loss.

(2) Expenses incurred by or on behalf of the assured for the safety or preservation of the subject-matter insured, other than general average and salvage charges, are called particular charges. Particular charges are not included in particular average.[4]

It is necessary to distinguish a particular average loss from the total loss of a part. Suppose that an insured cargo consists of 100 bales of jute, the value of which is $10 per bale. A fire occurs in the cargo hold of the carrying vessel and 10 bales of jute are totally destroyed. This is nonetheless a particular average loss. Suppose, however, that the insured cargo consists of 100 bales of jute, 20 cartons of tobacco, and 15 boxes of apples. The jute, tobacco, and apples are insured on separate valuations and upon distinct and different premiums. A fire occurs in the cargo hold of the carrying vessel and all 20 cartons of tobacco are destroyed. This is not

---

3. The subject of general average is treated in depth in Chapter XVII, *supra.*

4. The leading case on particular charges is *Kidston v. Empire Marine Ins. Co.*, (1867) L.R. 2 C.P. 357, 36 L.J.C.P. 156, 16 L.T. 119, 15 W.R. 769, 2 Mar. L.C. 468, Ex. Ch., involving a loss of freight.

a particular average loss but instead a total loss of a distinct part of an entire shipment.[5]

Measure of Indemnity

One of the fundamental rules pervading all insurance is that a contract of insurance is a contract of indemnity and of indemnity only, and where an insured loss occurs, the assured is entitled to a full indemnity but no more. As Brett, L. J., said, in the old non-marine case of *Castellain v. Preston:*[6]

> The very foundation, in my opinion, of every rule which has been applied to insurance law is this, namely that the contract of insurance contained in a marine or fire policy is a contract of indemnity, and of indemnity only, and that this contract means that the assured, in case of a loss against which the policy has been made, shall be fully indemnified, but shall never be more than fully indemnified. That is the fundamental principle of insurance, and if ever a proposition is brought forward which is at variance with it—that is to say, which either will prevent the assured from obtaining a full indemnity, or which will give to the assured more than a full indemnity—that proposition must certainly be wrong.

It is clear, however, that a "valued" policy on a vessel may, and often does, violate this basic principle because the insured value agreed upon is binding between the assurer and assured regardless of whether or not it represents the actual value of the vessel. And particular average claims under the policy on a vessel are not affected because such claims are not based on the insured value stipulated in the policy but on the cost of repairs regardless of overinsurance or underinsurance.[7]

5. See *Duff v. Mackenzie*, (1857) 140 E.R. 643, and *La Fabrique de Produits Chimiques S.A. v. Large*, (1923) 13 Ll.L.Rep. 269.

6. *Castellain v. Preston*, (1883) 11 Q.B.D. 380, C.A. See, also, the recent non-marine case of *Leppard v. Excess Ins. Co.*, [1979] 1 W.L.R. 512. The principle was emphasized in a leading marine case, *Rickards v. Forestal Land, Timber and Railways Co., Ltd.*, [1941] 3 All E.R. 62, H.L. In *Goole and Hull Steam Towing Co., Ltd. v. Ocean Marine Ins. Co., Ltd.*, (1927) 20 Ll.L.Rep. 242, K.B.D., the court properly pointed out that it must always be remembered that a marine insurance policy is not a contract of indemnity ideally, but of an indemnity according to the conventional terms of the bargain; i.e. the real question in any case is: What is the measure of indemnity which by the convention of the parties has been promised to the assured? A striking illustration will be found in *Balmoral Steamship Co. v. Marten*, [1902] A.C. 511, where the vessel was valued in the policy at less than her value arrived at in the general average statement. It was held that the underwriter was only liable to pay to her owner an amount which bore the same ratio to the ship's contribution as the valuation in the policy bore to the valuation in the general average statement.

7. *Lohre v. Aitchison*, (1878) 3 Q.B.D. 558, on appeal, *sub nom Aitchison v. Lohre*, (1879) 4

734 MARINE INSURANCE AND AVERAGE

Section 67 of the Marine Insurance Act covers in general the extent of liability of an insurer for loss. It reads:

(1) The sum which the assured can recover in respect of a loss on a policy by which he is insured, in the case of an unvalued policy, to the full extent of the insurable value, or, in the case of a valued policy, to the full extent of the value fixed by the policy, is called the measure of indemnity.[8]

(2) Where there is a loss recoverable under the policy, the insurer, or each insurer if there be more than one, is liable for such proportion of the measure of indemnity as the amount of his subscription bears to the value fixed by the policy, in the case of a valued policy, or to the insurable value, in the case of an unvalued policy.[9]

Section 81 of the Act relates to the effect of underinsurance and reads:

Where the assured is insured for an amount less than the insurable value, or, in the case of a valued policy, for an amount less than the policy valuation, he is deemed to be his own insurer in respect of the uninsured balance.[10]

The key words here are "an amount less than the policy valuation." Thus, if the vessel's value is expressed in the policy as being a certain amount, and the insured value as being a different and *lesser* sum, then the assured is his own insurer in respect of the uninsured balance. On the other hand, if the vessel is valued in the policy at a certain amount, and that amount is expressed in the policy as being the insured value, then the assured is entitled to the full amount of the policy valuation in the event of a total or constructive total loss and up to the full amount of the policy valuation as respects repairs should the repairs amount to as much as the policy valuation and the assured elects to repair instead of claiming for a constructive total loss.

The following illustrations may be helpful:

(a) A ship whose intrinsic or "real" value is $100,000, but whose value is expressed in the policy as being $50,000, is insured for $50,000 by two underwriters, each of whom subscribes for $25,000. The ship grounds

---

App.Cas. 755, H.L.; *International Nav. Co. v. Atlantic Mutual Ins. Co.*, 100 F. 304 (1900), *aff'd* on rehearing 108 F. 987 (2d Cir.).

8. *Papadimitrio v. Henderson*, [1939] 3 All E.R. 908, K.B.

9. *Id.*, n. 7.

10. *The Commonwealth*, [1907] P. 216 (apportioning a sum received from a tortfeasor); *Duus, Brown & Co. v. Binning*, (1906) 11 Com.Cas. 190 (costs of unsuccessful litigation divided between assured and underwriters in proportion to their interests). Compare, however, *Mason v. Marine Ins. Co.*, 110 F. 452 (Mich., 1901) where it was held, contrary to the English rule, that the abandonment of an underinsured vessel to underwriters as a constructive total loss vested the entire ownership in the underwriters.

and the owners spend $10,000 in making repairs, and another $1,000 under the Sue and Labor Clause in getting her off her strand. Each hull underwriter must pay $5,000 under his policy and another $500 under the Sue and Labor Clause. The real or "intrinsic" value of the ship is wholly immaterial as it is a "valued" policy.

(b) A ship valued in the policy at $100,000 is insured for only $50,000 by two hull underwriters, each of whom subscribes for $25,000. The ship grounds and the owners spend $10,000 in making repairs, and another $1,000 under the Sue and Labor Clause in getting her off her strand. The vessel owner, being deemed to be his own insurer in respect of the uninsured balance, must bear $5,500 of the costs and the two underwriters will bear the remaining proportion, i.e., $2,750 each.

(c) A ship valued at $100,000 in the policy is insured for $100,000 by two hull underwriters, each of whom subscribes for $50,000 of the risk. The ship grounds and the owners reasonably spend $11,000 in attempting to get her off her strand. Notwithstanding their efforts, eventually the ship is totally lost. The hull underwriters must each pay $50,000 on their policies and another $5,500 under the sue and labor clauses.

(d) Cargo valued at $50,000 is insured for $10,000 by five underwriters, each of whom subscribes for $2,000. The cargo is damaged by a sea peril to the extent of $10,000. Each insurer is liable for $400 only.

(e) A freight policy is issued by one underwriter to the ocean carrier for $10,000. The total freight payable is $20,000 and is expressed as being not prepaid but being payable only upon delivery of the goods at destination. Enroute, due to sea perils, one tenth of the cargo is destroyed by seawater entering the holds. As the freight was underinsured by one-half, the underwriter is liable for only one-half of the freight loss, i.e., $500.

The foregoing points up the materially different rules with respect to the measure of indemnity for ship, freight, and cargo, and these different rules are examined in detail in the discussion which follows.

Particular Average on Ship

The Marine Insurance Act, Section 69, provides the measure of indemnity for particular average claims on ships or vessels, as follows:

Where a ship is damaged, but is not totally lost, the measure of indemnity, subject to any express provision in the policy, is as follows:

(1) Where the ship has been repaired, the assured is entitled to the reasonable cost of the repairs, less the customary deductions, but not exceeding the sum insured in respect of any one casualty;

(2) Where the ship has been only partially repaired, the assured is entitled to the reasonable cost of such repairs, computed as above, and also to be indemnified for the reasonable depreciation, if any, arising from the unrepaired damage, provided that the aggregate amount shall not exceed the cost of repairing the whole damage, computed as above;

(3) Where the ship has not been repaired, and has not been sold in her damaged state during the risk, the assured is entitled to be indemnified for the reasonable depreciation arising from the unrepaired damage, but not exceeding the reasonable cost of repairing such damages, computed as above.

Subsection (1) of Section 69 means precisely what it says—where the ship is repaired, the assured is entitled to the reasonable cost of repairs but not exceeding the sum insured in respect of any one casualty and less customary deductions. Thus, the fact that the insured value may be less than the real or intrinsic value of the vessel is immaterial if, in fact, the assured effects repairs, the costs of such repairs are reasonable, and the costs of the repairs do not exceed the sum for which the vessel was insured.[11]

The reasons for the difference in treatment of damage to ships, damage to cargo, and loss of freight are well set forth by Judge Brown in *International Nav. Co. v. Atlantic Mutual Ins. Co.* where he said:[12]

In cases of partial loss, the different rule applied to goods and freight from that applied to ships, has not arisen from any theoretical or even logical construction of the policy; but from practical considerations, having reference to the different purposes in insuring, the

---

11. *International Nav. Co. v. Atlantic Mutual Ins. Co.*, 100 F. 304 (1900), *aff'd* on rehearing, 108 F. 987 (2d Cir.), where Judge Brown said, in part:
. . . This rule, therefore, seems to me as firmly established as any point in the law of marine insurance—that insurers pay for a particular average loss to a ship *in the proportion that the loss bears to the policy value,* and not in proportion of the loss to the *actual value* [of the vessel] . . . [Emphasis supplied].
Judge Brown also quoted with approval from *Irving v. Manning,* (1847) 1 H.L. Cas. 287, as follows:
That for the purpose of ascertaining the amount of compensation to be paid to the assured, when the loss has happened, the value shall be taken to be the sum fixed, in order to avoid disputes as to the quantum of the assured's interest. . . . In a valued policy, the agreed total value is conclusive.
Again, from *Insurance Ass'n v. Armstrong,* L.R. 5 Q.B. 244, he quotes:
. . . The assured is not at liberty to say it is worth more. He is bound by that amount. It is for the purpose of avoiding all questions about the value that the parties agree to fix that amount, and for that purpose, therefore, of adjusting the right under that policy, both the parties are bound by that value.
See, also, *The Potomac,* 105 U.S. 630 (1881); *Providence & S.S.S. Co. v. Phoenix Ins. Co.,* 89 N.Y. 559 (1882); and *Disrude v. Commercial Fish., etc.,* 570 P.2d 963 (Or. 1978), 1978 AMC 261.
12. *Id.,* n. 11.

different circumstances of the subjects of insurance and the evident difference in the appropriate measure of indemnity.

The reason assigned by Lord Mansfield for the rule as respects goods, was in order that the proportion of the insurance chargeable to the insurers on a partial loss, might be the true proportion of the merchant's actual loss by the sea peril, and not fluctuate with the market price of profits, but be the same proportion, whether the goods came to a rising or falling market.

The reasons have little or no application to ships. Ships are not employed as merchandise, nor insured as such; but as carriers. If damaged, they are not expected to be sold, but to be repaired for continued use by the owner, or for the necessary completion of the voyage. Nor is there any such usual market for vessels as for goods, by which the loss or damage could be fairly ascertained by a sale; nor could sales of damaged vessels be ordinarily made or required, without great prejudice to all concerned—to the underwriters as well as to the assured [citing Brett, L. J., in *Pitman v. Insurance Co.*, 9 Q.B. Div. 207]. In fact, to require a sale of the ship on every marine accident, would be destructive of commerce. The absolute right of the owner, therefore, to repair the damage, is a commercial necessity; and it is perfectly established [Citing cases]. The policy by its terms requires the insurer "to bear all the loss and damage that may come to the ship by sea perils," within the limit of the value named in the policy; and hence the repairs necessary to make the ship as good as before are evidently the proper measure of indemnity.

New for Old

The reference to "customary deductions" in Section 69(1) is with respect to the old practice of deducting a certain sum (usually one-third) from the cost of furnishing new materials for old on the theory that supplying new materials resulted in a betterment of the vessel. The deduction would not be made with respect to straightening a bent plate or removing a dent in a plate as there would be no "new" material and no betterment, but is applied solely to new materials, such as removing a badly damaged plate and replacing it with a totally new one. In any event, insurance is seldom placed today on a vessel without a stipulation in the policy that there will be no deduction, new for old.

Reasonable Costs of Repairs

No subject is fraught with more difficulties than determining the reasonable cost of repairs to a vessel. About the best that can be said is that it is a

738 MARINE INSURANCE AND AVERAGE

question of fact to be determined in each particular case, giving consideration to all the circumstances.

Essentially, it is a matter of common sense; i.e., what a fair-minded shipowner of average prudence would do in effecting repairs in similar circumstances. A vessel is an income-producing instrumentality and, therefore, should be brought back into service as soon as reasonably practicable. That this is a primary consideration and one which was (or certainly should have been) within the contemplation of the underwriters at the time the policy was issued seems beyond doubt. The question is not whether the shipowner benefits from quicker repairs but whether the cost of repairs, in the manner actually consummated, is reasonable. And the question of reasonableness must be tested from the standpoint of both the underwriter and the shipowner. If the assured acts imprudently, then any extra costs incurred are for the assured's account.

The language of Maule, J., in this respect is instructive. He said:[13]

> Let us see upon what principle the expenses of repairing an insured ship can be recovered from the underwriters. I apprehend they can be recovered in two ways only. One is, where they are the expenses of repairs actually incurred, and properly incurred, to remedy a loss within the policy; they are then a fit measure of the damage which the assured has sustained—he is then so much the worse for a peril within the policy. It is not sufficient that they should be actually incurred in order to recover them; it is necessary also that they should be properly and prudently incurred, to make them a fit measure for the amount of the loss of the assured. Suppose they are actually incurred, but incurred with a view to a job, in order to put money into the pockets of carpenters and shipbuilders, friends of the owner or his agent, these would be expenses actually incurred but not properly incurred and, therefore, not chargeable to underwriters, as a proper measure of damages. Or suppose though actually incurred, they have been incurred foolishly and absurdly, under circumstances no prudent man would think of repairing the damage, but would leave his ship or other article unrepaired, and treat it as so much the worse for the injury. The assured may therefore recover the expenses of repairs, not *eo nomine* as expenses, but as a measure of his loss, where those ex-

---

13. *Stewart v. Steele*, (1842) 11 L.J.C.P. 155. See, also, *Pitman v. Universal Marine Ins.*, (1882) 9 Q.B.D. 192, 51 L.J.Q.B. 561 ("sums expended in repairing the ship in a reasonable and proper way"); *Aitchison v. Lohre*, n. 7, *supra* ("the actual outlay on the repairs, if bona fide, would be strong evidence what the reasonable cost was"); *McBride v. Marine Ins. Co.*, 7 Johns 431 (N.Y.,1810); *The Fortitude*, F.Cas. 4,953, (necessary repairs are those which are reasonably fit and proper in the circumstances and not merely those which are absolutely indispensable); *Lesicich v. North River Ins. Co.*, 191 Wash. 305, 71 P.2d 35 (St. Wash. 1937) (in the absence of evidence requiring an examination of the reasonable cost of repairs, the amounts actually paid for repairs are controlling and may be recovered without further proof as to the reasonable value).

penses have been bona fide and prudently incurred; and a jury might fairly be liberal in their allowance of expenses so incurred.

Phillips puts it that the underwriter is responsible for the repair or restoration of the damaged or destroyed part of the ship or article belonging to it with materials, workmanship, style, and finish corresponding to its original character.[14] Various expressions have been used in the cases construing what repairs are sufficient. For example, that the vessel should be so far repaired as to keep it a ship, though, perhaps, not so good a ship as before;[15] to put her in as good a state and condition as she was when the policy was made;[16] restoring the ship to its former state;[17] repairs fairly executed to replace damage occasioned by one of the underwritten perils;[18] and to get it afloat and cause it to be repaired and used again as a ship.[19]

Average Adjusters

By far the majority of general average claims are adjusted by average adjusters. This is not necessarily so with respect to particular average claims. In the United States, probably the majority of particular average claims are adjusted by brokers on an "in house" basis, although there is no impediment whatever to an assured-owner submitting his own proof of loss and supporting data to the underwriters where the claim may either be paid as presented, denied in its entirety, or paid in part and rejected in part. Frequently, an assured will present the facts to his broker, who, in turn, will assist in preparing the formal claim and submitting it to underwriters.

Although an average adjuster's statement has no legal force, *per se*, such statements in general average situations are rarely questioned by the courts.[20] And, in the case of general average, the parties frequently agree that they will be bound by the determinations of the average adjuster. What the effect of such agreements may be is not entirely clear. For example, in *Corrado Societa Anonima Di Navigazione v. L. Mundet Sons, Inc.*,[21] it was held that the agreement was not one to pay a general average contribution but an agreement upon the sum payable, if any. As the court found no general contribution was due, the average statement was held to have

14. Phillips, Sec. 1428, citing *Waller v. Louisiana Ins. Co.*, 9 Mart. N.S. La. 276.
15. *Rankin v. Potter*, (1873) L.R. 6 H.L.
16. *Giles v. Eagle Ins. Co.*, 43 Mass. 140 (1840).
17. *American Ins. Co. v. Center*, 4 Wend. 45 (N.Y., 1829).
18. *Aitchison v. Lohre*, n. 7, *supra*.
19. *Phoenix Ins. Co. v. McGhee*, 18 S.C. 70 (Can.)
20. The U. S. Supreme Court has stated, in fact, that an adjuster's statement is nothing more "than a provisional estimate and calculation which his principal, the owner, is free to adopt or to put aside."
21. 18 F.Supp. 37 (E.D. Pa.), 1936 AMC 1740.

no effect. The only question in the case was whether or not the statement was conclusive as to liability. In *Navigazione Generale Italiana v. Spencer Kellogg & Sons. Inc.*,[22] the parties agreed to be bound by the determinations of certain average adjusters. In that case, the court determined that a general average act had taken place and hence the cargo was liable to contribute its proportion of the expenditures incurred by the ship for the common benefit of ship and cargo. The court thereupon held that the agreement to pay whatever the adjuster found to be due to the shipowner was enforceable. But the court somewhat diluted the force of its holding in stating:

> Upon examination of the statement of the adjuster we find that the expenditures classed by them as general average expenses were proper ones. Nor do we find any attacks made upon the adjustment by the respondent other than certain claims that the case was not one for general average and that the vessel was unseaworthy.

Thus, it may be said that the case stands only for the proposition that such an agreement is enforceable after the court has found that a general average situation has occurred and that the contents of the adjuster's statement are correct.

In *Cia. Atlantica Pacifica v. Humble Oil & Refining Co. (M/V Clydewater)*,[23] however, the court made a very clear holding that a general average statement prepared pursuant to an agreement of the parties constitutes *prima facie* evidence of its details, computations and allocation of general average. Consequently, in the absence of any evidence tending to contradict it, in whole or in part, the [statement] would compel a direction by the court to the jury, assuming that it is a case of general average. Specifically, the court stated that the portions of a general average statement which should be taken as *prima facie* proof are: (1) the losses, damages, and expenses which as factual matters are the direct consequence of a general average act, (2) the values attaching to such losses, damages, and expenses, and (3) the computations proportioning these losses, damages, and expenses between the parties to the venture.

In *Gemini Navigation v. Philipp Bros.*,[24] the Second Circuit had occasion to comment on *Cia. Atlantica Pacifica*. In the *Gemini* case, the plaintiff-

---

22. 92 F.2d (2d Cir.), 1937 AMC 1506, *cert. den.* 302 U.S. 751 (1937).
23. 247 F.Supp. 884 (D. Md.), 1967 AMC 1474.
24. 499 F.2d 745 (2d Cir), 1974 AMC 1122. See, also, *Master Shipping Agency, Inc. v. M/S Farida et al*, 571 F.2d 131 (2d Cir.), 1978 AMC 1267 (where an ocean carrier had no basis for believing its claim against cargo for general average contributions would fail, it was justified in spending $100,000 in preparing a general average statement, and although the claim ultimately failed, third party stevedores found 50 percent at fault must indemnify the carrier for one-half the sums so expended); *Great Eastern Associates, Inc. and Farrell Lines v. Republic of India*, 1978 AMC 1288 (S.D.N.Y.) (in the absence of an agreement to the contrary, a

shipowner sought to impose general average contributions upon the cargo owners and their underwriters. At first instance, the district court found for the plaintiff-shipowner. On appeal, however, the appeals court reversed, holding that improper stowage was the proximate cause of the cargo shifting and the consequent restowing expenses. The plaintiff-shipowner urged, in reliance upon *Cia. Atlantica Pacifica,* that the general average statement was *prima facie* proof as to the loss, the values attributable thereto, and the computations proportioning the losses between ship and cargo. The court said, in part:

> That case involved a general average statement identical to the one signed by Phillip here. *Cia. Atlantica* makes clear, however, that, whatever evidentiary value may be assigned to the general average statement once the cargo owner's underlying liability for *some* general average has been independently established, the signing of that general average statement does not in any way preclude the cargo owner, as that owner does here, from denying *all* liability for general average on the grounds that the shipowner's fault produced the expense alleged to be subject to general average, and that, under Cogsa, that fault would make the shipowner liable for any damage to the cargo. . . . The general average agreement here thus has no bearing on our resolution of the seminal issue of *Gemini's* fault.

The profession of average adjusting is an old and honorable one and rules of practice in that profession are of inestimable assistance in ascertaining how particular average claims should be determined. The rules are designed as aids for general construction and not to be worn as a straitjacket. But within those parameters, resort to the rules as general principles is most helpful. For example, Rule A4 of the Rules of Practice of the Association of Average Adjusters of Great Britain provides:

> That in adjusting particular average on ship or general average which includes repairs, it is the duty of the adjuster to satisfy himself that such reasonable and usual precautions have been taken to keep down the cost of repairs as a prudent shipowner would have taken if uninsured.

As a statement of the principle by which the question of the reasonable cost of repairs should be approached, it can scarcely be improved upon.

It should also be noted that the question of "reasonableness" must be examined from the standpoint of both the vessel owner and the underwriter. For example, suppose that the part damaged is a ship's engines and machinery but the vessel is old and nearly obsolete. The cost of spe-

---

general average statement is without legal effect and is not conclusive on cargo's liability to contribute).

cially building a new engine and machinery would be exorbitant. In such instances, an adequate used or reconditioned part is all that underwriters should be expected to provide. Moreover, in such a situation, there should logically be no deduction for new for old. This question arose in *Ferrante v. Detroit Fire and Marine Insurance Company, et al,*[25] where, due to the negligence of an engineer in failing to lubricate, a crankshaft broke. After the casualty, the surveyor's report noted that a new crankshaft was not immediately available from the factory. A second-hand shaft of the same type and model as the original was located, accordingly checked between centers, and found to be true. It was thereupon installed in the vessel. The second-hand shaft and its testing and preparation for installation amounted to $2,578.40; the new crankshaft would have cost $3,887.00. Use of the second-hand crankshaft thus effected a saving of $1,309.00. The total cost of the repairs amounted to $11,682.05.

The court held that the assured was entitled to recover the cost of repairs, less the deductible, but denied the assured's claim for the difference between the cost of a new crankshaft and the cost of the used crankshaft, noting that the used crankshaft was an adequate replacement and was installed by the assured for his own convenience.

While the underwriter may be liable for the whole cost of repairs, he is likewise entitled to credit for any allowances in respect of the value of old material, scrap metal, cable, shafts, etc. This principle is formalized in Rule A5 of the British association reading:

> That in all claims for ship's machinery for repairs, no claim for a new propeller or new shaft shall be admitted into an adjustment unless the adjuster shall obtain and insert into his statement evidence showing what has become of the old propeller or shaft.

Wear and Tear

Nor is the underwriter liable for the cost of repairing what may be termed "wear and tear".[26] Moreover, the underwriter is not liable for the loss of any part of the ship's gear being stowed in improper locations.[27]

---

25. 125 F.Supp. 621 (S.D. Cal.), 1954 AMC 2026.
26. Sec. 55(2)(c), Marine Insurance Act. See, also, cases cited in Chapter XIV, "Inchmaree Clause," where the causes of loss were held, in many instances, to be due to wear and tear rather than the presence of a latent defect.
27. Rule A6 of the British association notes that water casks or tanks carried on a ship's deck are not paid for by underwriters as general or particular average; nor are warps or other articles when improperly carried on deck. See, also, Rule D3 (chafed rigging) and Rule D4 (sails split or blown away). In *Brooks v. Oriental Ins. Co.,* 38 Mass. 472 (1839), the court noted that underwriters are liable for the loss of a boat from the stern davits unless it be proved that the boat was improperly carried or slung in that location.

Incidental Expenses

Invariably, where a particular average claim arises, the costs incurred exceed the nominally bare costs of the repairer's invoices. As the question of what is the reasonable cost of repair is one of fact, resort must be had to the cases to determine in particular factual situations what has been regarded as an incidental expense which is recoverable. In this connection, a veritable smorgasbord of incidental expenses was involved in *Helmville, Ltd. v. Yorkshire Ins. Co., Ltd. (The Medina Princess).*[28] In that case, the vessel was engaged on a voyage from Bremen via Rotterdam to China with a cargo of flour in bags. Her owners had previously arranged that she should call at Djibouti to replenish her bunkers. She limped into that port with a four-degree list to port, having had a list for a considerable period of time. Her owners claimed that enroute from Europe to Djibouti her engines, boilers, and auxiliaries suffered severe damage by reason of the negligence of the engine room staff. After the vessel arrived at Djibouti, she grounded on two successive occasions, which, the owners claimed, occasioned bottom damage, damage to her tank tops, main deck, and port and starboard side plating. Sometime afterwards, the port authority at Djibouti ordered her to leave her berth and moor in an anchorage. Shortly thereafter, her owners gave notice of abandonment to underwriters as for a constructive total loss. Underwriters declined to accept notice but, as is customary in such cases, agreed to place the plaintiff vessel owners in the same position as if a writ had been issued as of the date of notice of abandonment.

At the time, the vessel was insured on a valued policy on hull and machinery in the sum of £350,000. It was common ground between the parties that pursuant to Clause 15 of the Institute Time Clauses (hulls), the plaintiffs could not succeed in a claim for a constructive total loss unless they showed that the cost of repairs exceeded £350,000. Her sound value prior to her successive casualties was in the order of £65,000, and her damaged value nil.

The court found, after an exhaustive analysis of the evidence and law, that the cost of repairs to the hull would have been £123,230; that the damage to machinery was £28,761; that incidental expenses totalled £722; and towage expenses were £14,560. The court then observed that even if these expenses were added together, plus £75,000 claimed for expenses in discharging the cargo, the total sum would not exceed £350,000 and, therefore, the plaintiffs had established only a partial loss.

As the vessel was not repaired nor sold during the risk, *prima facie* the measure of indemnity was the depreciation (not exceeding the reasonable

---

28. [1965] 1 Lloyd's Rep. 361, Q.B.D.

cost of repairs) arising from the unrepaired damage (Section 69(3) of the Act). However, as the damaged value of the vessel was practically nil, the indemnity would be limited to the reasonable cost of repairs.

Although plaintiffs claimed for a rather large amount of incidental expenses while the vessel was at Djibouti, in the final analysis the court allowed a portion, consisting of expenses of the consultant's assistant (air fare, hotel bill, etc.), communications expense, and attendance of the classification surveyor for one day only. The total of all "incidental" expenses was £722.

The case is exceedingly valuable for its discussion of what repair costs were recoverable and how much could be recovered as being reasonable.

Other major items of repair costs have to be considered in relation to reasonable cost of repairs. These are considered *seriatim:*

Temporary Repairs

The term "reasonable cost of repairs" is not limited merely to permanent repairs. Generally speaking, temporary repairs are allowed: where complete repairs cannot be made at the port where the vessel then lies; when made to effect a saving in the cost of permanent repairs; or when the material or parts necessary for permanent repairs are unobtainable at the port where the vessel then lies, except after unreasonable delay.[29] Generally speaking, expenses necessarily incurred to place the vessel in a position to be repaired are includible in a claim for repairs.[30]

Inherent in the question of temporary repairs is the question of incurring an extraordinary expense initially in order to save expenses which would otherwise be payable; e.g., airfreighting an essential part or piece of machinery at a greater cost where the part or piece could be shipped at a much lower cost but with a greater consequent delay in effecting temporary repairs. This question arose in a general average situation where the difference between airfreight and seafreight on a replacement tailshaft was allowed as a substitute expense by reason of saving on port of refuge expenses.[31]

It should be emphasized, however, that the *reason* for making temporary repairs is a governing factor. If, for example, permanent repairs could be made at the port of refuge but the shipowner elects to make temporary repairs for his own business reasons, such as, for instance, to

29. This states in substance Rule XI of the Association of Average Adjusters of the United States. See, also, Rule Dl of the British association, reproduced in the Appendix, relating to removal expenses, discussed *infra.*
30. *Bradlie v. Maryland Ins. Co.,* 37 U.S. 378 (1838); *Orient Marine Ins. Co. v. Adams,* 123 U.S. 67 (1887); *Sewall v. U.S. Inc. Co.,* 28 Mass. 90 (1831); *The Joseph Farwell,* 31 F. 844 ; *Potter v. Ocean Ins. Co.,* F.Cas. 11,335 (1837).
31. See *Western Canada S.S. Co., Ltd. v. Canadian Commercial Corp.,* [1960] 2 Ll.L.Rep.

meet a sailing schedule or to procure a lucrative contract of affreightment, then underwriters are not liable for the expense of the temporary
repairs.

Deferred Repairs

Generally speaking, underwriters are not liable for any resulting increase
in costs of repair arising out of a conscious decision on the part of the
vessel owner to defer making repairs for his own business convenience.[32]
But, as a practical matter, shipowners frequently defer making repairs
(where the seaworthiness of the vessel is not impaired) until their vessel's
next scheduled drydocking. And, occasionally, it is simply impossible to
effect repairs until a later date due to total unavailability of materials due,
for example, to war conditions.[33]

In any event, any prudent shipowner should seriously consider the ad-
visability of making repairs at the first drydocking after the casualty to
avoid being met with a contention on the part of underwriters that repairs
were deferred for the owner's business convenience.

Removal Expenses

Removal expenses, reasonably and prudently incurred by the assured,
are recoverable from underwriters as a part of the reasonable cost of repairs.[34] Rule D1 of the British association states the principles applicable:

> Where a vessel is in need of repair at any port, and is removed
> thence to some other port for the purpose of repairs, either because
> the repairs cannot be effected, or cannot be effected prudently:

---

313. See, also, Rule XXI, Association of Average Adjusters, United States, reading:
   The cost of air freight on repair parts shall be allowed as part of the reasonable cost of
   repairs when the shipment of such parts by water and/or land conveyance would result
   in unreasonable delay.
   Nevertheless, when shipment by air saves General Average expense the extra cost of
   shipment by air over the cost of water and/or land conveyance shall be allowed in General Average up to the expense saved.
   It should also be observed that in the *Medina Princess*, Justice Roskill apparently accepted without reservation the underwriters' surveyors' view that two damaged feed pumps
could have been disconnected and flown from Djibouti, where the vessel was then lying, to
Aden for reconditioning. Airfreighting in that instance appears to have been accepted as a
normal and prudent practice.
   32. See the remarks of Lord Blackburn in *Marine Insurance Co., Ltd. v. China Transpacific
S.S. Co., Ltd. (The Vancouver)*, (1886) 11 A.C. 573.
   33. This was the situation in *Irvin v. Hine*, (1949) 83 Ll.L.Rep. 162, where, due to wartime restrictions, the vessel could not be repaired until after the war. The court refused to
accept the underwriters' contention that the estimated increase in cost due to the lapse of
time should be disallowed.
   34. *Compania Maritima Astra v. Archdale (The Armar)*, 134 N.Y.S.2d 20 (St. N.Y.), 1954
AMC 1674, [1954] 2 Ll.L.Rep. 95; *Young v. Union Ins. Co.*, 24 F. 279 (N.D. Ill.); *North Atlantic
S.S. Co., Ltd. v. Burr*, (1904) 9 Com.Cas. 164; *Moran v. Taylor*, (1884) 24 N.B.R. 39 (Can.).

(a) The necessary expenses incurred in moving the vessel to the port of repair shall be allowed as part of the cost of repair, and where the vessel after repairing forthwith returns to the port from which she was removed, the necessary expenses incurred in so returning shall also be allowed.

(b) Where by moving the vessel to the port of repair any new freight is earned, or any expenses are saved in relation to the current voyage of the vessel, such net earnings or savings shall be deducted from the expenses of moving her, and where the vessel loads a new cargo at the port of repair no expenses subsequent to the completion of repair shall be allowed.

The expenses of removal include the cost of temporary repair, ballasting, wages and provisions of crew and/or runners, pilotage, towage, extra marine insurance, port charges, fuel and engineroom stores.

(c) This rule shall not admit any ordinary expenses incurred in fulfilment of a contract of affreightment, though such expenses are increased by the removal to a port of repair.

Rule D2, relating to fuel and stores used in repair of damages to a vessel, reads:

That the cost of replacing fuel and stores consumed either in the repair of damages to a vessel, in working the engines or winches to assist in the repairs of damage, or in moving her to a place of repair within the limits of the port where she is lying, shall be treated as part of the cost of repairs.

The Claims (General Provisions) Clause in the current AIH form (1977) relates to removal expenses when such expenses are incurred at the request of underwriters. The clause reads, in part:

In the event of any accident or occurrence which could give rise to a claim under this Policy, prompt notice thereof shall be given to the Underwriters, and:

(a) where practicable, the Underwriters shall be advised prior to survey, so that they may appoint their own surveyor, if they so desire;

(b) the Underwriters shall be entitled to decide where the Vessel shall proceed for docking and/or repair (allowance to be made to the Assured for the actual additional expense of the voyage arising from compliance with the Underwriters' requirement);

(c) the Underwriters shall have the right of veto in connection with any repair firm proposed;

(d) the Underwriters may take tenders, or may require in writing that tenders be taken for the repair of the Vessel, in which event, upon acceptance of a tender with the approval of Underwriters, an allowance shall be made at the rate of 30 per cent per annum on the amount insured, for each day or pro rata for part of a day, for time lost between the issuance of invitations to tender and the acceptance of a tender, to the extent that such time is lost solely as the result of tenders having been taken and provided the tender is accepted without delay after receipt of the Underwriters' approval.

Due credit shall be given against the allowances in (b) and (d) above for any amount recovered:

(1) In respect of fuel, stores, and wages and maintenance of the Master, Officers or Crew allowed in General or Particular Average;
(2) from third parties in respect of damages for detention and/or loss of profit and/or running expenses; for the period covered by the allowances or any part thereof.[35]

As Buglass[36] notes, where there are various classes of repairs which must be accomplished, there must be an allocation of expenses. For example, if the vessel is removed from a port where repairs cannot be effected, it is the usual practice to apportion removal costs pro rata to the individual cost of each class of repairs for which the removal was made. But, where the removal does not effect any savings with regard to a particular repair port, the cost of that part should not be reflected in the apportionment of the removal expenses.

Wages and Provisions

It is well settled that underwriters on a vessel are not liable for the cost of wages and provisions of the crew during repairs unless the members of the crew are paid extra sums to do work for which the underwriters would be liable and which would otherwise have required outside labor.[37]

35. While under the clause underwriters can exercise control over repairs to the vessel and selection of the port where repairs are to be effected, underwriters seldom avail themselves of this right. Where the underwriters do exercise their rights under the tender clause, the owners are not charged with any part of the removal expenses regardless of the nature of repairs effected for owners' account. To qualify for an allowance, it is necessary that tenders be taken at the express request of the underwriters in writing.

36. Buglass, *Marine Insurance and General Average in the United States*, (2d ed.), 1981.

37. *Helmville, Ltd. v. Yorkshire Insurance Co., Ltd. (The Medina Princess)*, n. 28, *supra; Robinson v. Ewer*, (1786) 1 T.R. 182, (1786) 99 E.R. 1111; *De Vaux v. Salvador*, (1836) 111 E.R. 845; *The Armar*, n. 34, *supra; Hobson v. Lord*, 92 U.S. 397 (1875); *Walsh v. Smith*, (1875) 6 Nfld. L.R. 35 (Can.).

Attention is directed, in this connection, to allowances for crew's wages under the 1977 AIH form of policy which reads: (Lines 107-110)

> No claim shall be allowed in Particular Average for wages and maintenance of the Master, Officers or Crew, except when incurred solely for the necessary removal of the Vessel from one port to another for average repairs or for trial trips to test average repairs, in which cases wages and maintenance will be allowed only while the Vessel is under way. This exclusion shall not apply to overtime or similar extraordinary payments to the Master, Officers or Crew incurred in shifting the Vessel for tank cleaninq or repairs or while specifically engaged in these activities, either in port or at sea.

Fuel and Stores

Fuel and stores necessarily consumed while the vessel is undergoing average repairs, and in assisting with the repair work, are recoverable as part of the costs of repair.[38]

Drydocking Expenses

Ordinarily, the cost of drydocking in order to effect repairs, and dock dues payable during the time the vessel is in drydock, are recoverable as part of the cost of repairs.[39]

Rule IX of the Association of Average Adjusters of the United States states:

> When a vessel is drydocked:
>
> (1) For owners' account and repairs are found necessary for which underwriters are liable and which can only be effected in drydock; or
> (2) For survey and/or repairs for which underwriters are liable and repairs for owners' accounts are made which are immediately necessary for her seaworthiness, or she is due for ordinary drydocking (in accordance with the owners' custom), the cost of removing the vessel to and from the drydock, of docking and undocking, and as much of the dock dues as is common to both classes of work, shall be divided equally between the owners and underwriters.

---

38. See Rule D2 of the British association, discussed *supra*.
39. *The Armar*, n. 34, *supra*; *Chicago S.S. Lines v. U.S. Lloyd*, 2 F.2d 767 (N.D. Ill.), 1924 AMC 1479; *Young v. Union Ins. Co.*, 24 F. 279 (N.D. Ill.).

When the vessel is drydocked for underwriters' account and the owners avail of her being in drydock to scrape and paint or to do other work for their own account which is not immediately necessary for seaworthiness, all the expenses incidental to the drydocking of the vessel shall be charged to the underwriters.

The Adjuster shall insert a note in the average statement in explanation of the allowances made.

The same subject is covered in Rule D5 of the British association and is not dissimilar.

The subject of drydocking expenses was involved in two leading English cases, *Marine Insurance Co. v. China Transpacific S.S. Co. (The Vancouver)*[40] and *Ruabon S.S. Co. v. London Assurance Corp.*[41] In *The Vancouver*, the vessel was put into drydock initially for the owners' account to clean, scrape, and paint the vessel's bottom. While in drydock it was discovered that her stern post had been fractured. Repairs were effected over a period of eight days, during the first three of which cleaning, scraping, and painting were concurrently performed. As a consequence of the simultaneous performance of both operations, three days' dock dues were saved. At issue was whether the underwriters were liable for any portion of the three days while the cleaning, scraping, and painting were going on. The House of Lords held that the three days' dock dues would be divided equally between the shipowner and the underwriters.

In *The Ruabon*, the vessel grounded and was drydocked for inspection. In eleven months it would have been necessary to drydock the vessel in any event for her classification survey in order to retain her class. As the rules of the classification society provided for an acceleration of drydocking at the owners' option, the owners took advantage of the earlier drydocking for repairs in order to have her surveyed for class. Underwriters contended that a portion of the docking expenses should be borne by the owner. However, the House of Lords held that the docking expenses, including the cost of putting in and taking out of drydock, as well as dues for the hire of the dock, were to be borne solely by the underwriters.

Generally speaking, *The Ruabon* has been followed while *The Vancouver* has not been.[42]

It has been held in the United States that where the underwriters repair the vessel and then tender it to the assured, the assured has a right to

---

40. Id., n. 32, *supra.*
41. (1900) A.C. 6, 9 Asp. M.L.C. 2.
42. See *The Acanthus*, [1902] P. 17; *Carslogie S.S. Co. v. Royal Norwegian Gov't*, [1952] 1 All E.R. 20; *The Haversham Grange*, [1905] P. 307; *Pyman S.S. Co. v. Admiralty Commissioners*, [1918] 1 K.B. 480; *Admiralty Commissioners v. S.S. Chekiang*, [1926] A.C. 637; *Morrison S.S. Co. v. Greystoke Castle S.S. (Cargo Owners)*, [1946] 2 All E.R. 696; *The Ferdinand Retzlaff*, (1972) 2 Lloyd's Rep. 120.

a reasonable test to determine whether or not the repairs were sufficient.[43]

Overtime

It is often necessary to incur overtime in order to expedite the repair of a vessel. The test again is whether the overtime was reasonably incurred in the circumstances then existing. If incurring overtime results in a saving of other expenses, such as drydocking dues, then logically the assured is entitled to an amount up to that saved.[44]

Surveyors' and Superintendents' Fees

It would be most unusual today for repairs to be effected to a vessel with the shipowner and underwriter not having a surveyor in attendance. Their functions are to inspect the damage, agree (if possible) on the extent of the repairs necessary, and agree (if possible) on the sums to be paid for the repairs. Moreover, frequently the shipowner hires the surveyor or someone else qualified to supervise the carrying out of the work of repair. In these circumstances, the underwriters are, of course, liable to pay the fees of their own surveyor. Underwriters must also reimburse the shipowner for surveyors' and supervisors' fees *reasonably incurred* in connection with the repairs. It should be noted that the cost of *surveying the damage* is not recoverable as this represents only the cost of ascertaining and proving the loss, but the cost of supervision or superintendence of the actual repairs is recoverable.[45]

43. *Kahmann v. Aetna Ins. Co.*, 242 F. 20 (5th Cir. 1917).
44. Rule X of the American association provides:
The bonus or extra cost of overtime work on repairs shall be allowed in general and/or particular average up to the amount of the saving of drydock dues or other charges, which otherwise would have been incurred and allowed in general and/or particular average; and where the overtime work effects a savings both of general average expense (excluding general average repairs) and in the cost of repairs the extra cost for overtime shall be apportioned over the general average expenses saved and the savings in the cost of repairs.
    The Adjuster shall insert a note in the average statement in explanation of the allowances made.
45. *Helmville, Ltd. v. Yorkshire Ins. Co., Ltd. (The Medina Princess)*, n. 28, *supra*. See, also, Rule XV of the American association reading:
Fees of Classification Societies for surveys of particular average damages shall be allowed (notwithstanding that a survey of such damages would have been required for classification purposes) in addition to a fee paid an independent surveyor.
See, also, Rule XVI of the American association, reading:
In cases where a superintendent, or other shore employee, in the permanent employ of the owner of a vessel, superintends the repair of average damage, compensation for such service and incidental expenses shall be allowed in average:
    First—When an independent surveyor, or outside man, has not been employed for this purpose, and the vessel is repaired at a port other than where the superintendent, or other employee, makes his headquarters; or

A perfect illustration of the requirement of reasonableness is provided by *Agenoria S.S. Co. v. Merchants' Marine Ins. Co.*[46] In that case, the assured's vessel sustained heavy weather damage and stranding damage. After being temporarily repaired in New Zealand the vessel proceeded to Melbourne for permanent repairs. The assured decided to send out a surveyor (who was regularly employed by it) from the United Kingdom to Melbourne to look out for its interests, and claimed against underwriters for his fees and expenses. Underwriters refused to pay and the court ruled that in the circumstances the assured's conduct was unreasonable. The court did allow, however, a much lesser sum which represented the probable cost of a competent local surveyor.

Cost of Providing Funds

In *Agenoria S.S. Co.*, above, the assured further claimed to recover their bankers' charges for an overdraft which they had to obtain to send money to Melbourne to pay the repair bill. The court held that it was proper to include, as a part of the cost of repairs, expenses properly and reasonably incurred in providing funds for payment at the repair port.

When and Where Repairs Are to Be Effected

Generally speaking, subject to any special provision in the applicable hull policy,[47] the shipowner is entitled to decide where and when the repairs to his ship are to be effected, but, again, subject to the requirement of reasonableness.

Costs of Discharging Cargo in Order to Effect Repairs

Clearly, the costs of removal of cargo in order to effect repairs at a port of refuge are recoverable if under general average. As such, these would be general average expenses.

But, where such costs are incurred as a part of a particular average loss, the question becomes more difficult. If the repairs cannot be effected without the removal of the cargo (as, for example, where a tanker is damaged and repairs cannot be effected without removing its hazardous cargo and, moreover, the vessel cannot be put on drydock

---

Second—When the owner has incurred extra expense by employing, temporarily, another man to do the work of the superintendent, or other shore employee, while either of the latter is engaged in superintending repair of average damage.
Rule 3 of the Rules of the Great Lakes Association is similar. Compare, however, *Bond v. Reliance Ins. Co.*, 173 F.Supp. 828 (D. Fla. 1961).
46. (1903) 19 T.L.R. 442, 8 Com.Cas. 212.
47. See discussion, *supra*, relating to the tender clause.

MARINE INSURANCE AND AVERAGE

without removing the cargo) then this expense would fall under Section 69(1) of the Marine Insurance Act where the measure of damage is the reasonable cost of repairs.[48]

Where, however, the cargo is damaged or destroyed, so as no longer to be, in specie, the cargo which was shipped, a different principle applies.

The question of the liability for such discharge expenses was the subject of an arbitration in *Barge J. Whitney (Asphalt Incident)*.[49] There, the owners of a barge contracted to transport a cargo of asphalt from California to Alaska. This necessitated heating the asphalt to a temperature sufficient to liquefy it, and keeping it at a certain temperature so that it could be unloaded upon reaching destination.

As the hot asphalt was being loaded into the barge, condensate still present in the heating tubes inside the barge flashed into steam and created internal pressures which ruptured the heating tubes inside the barge and rendered the heating system inoperable.

Upon arrival at Alaska, this unfortunate condition was discovered and, after several efforts to repair the heating system, the barge was returned to California with what amounted to a complete load of completely solidified asphalt.

The owners then commenced Herculean efforts to discharge the asphalt cargo, involving cutting accesses in the main deck and installing

48. See, for example, Rule D6 of the British association which provides, in part:
1. That, in practice, where repairs, for the cost of which the underwriters are liable, require the tanks to be rough cleaned and/or gas-freed as an immediate consequence of the casualty, or the vessel is taken out of service especially to effect such repairs, the cost of such rough cleaning and/or gas-freeing shall be chargeable in full to the underwriters notwithstanding that the shipowner may have taken advantage of the vessel being rough cleaned and/or gas-freed to carry out survey for classification purposes or to effect repairs on his account which are not immediately necessary to make the vessel seaworthy.
2(a). Where repairs on Owners' account which are immediately necessary to make the vessel seaworthy and which require the tanks being rough cleaned and/or gas-freed are executed concurrently with other repairs, for the cost of which underwriters are liable, and which also require the tanks being rough cleaned and/or gas-freed,
   (b). Where the repairs, for the cost of which underwriters are liable, are deferred until a routine drydocking or repair period, at which time repairs on Owners' account which also require the tanks being rough cleaned and/or gas-freed are effected, whether or not such Owners' repairs affect the seaworthiness of the vessel, the cost of such rough cleaning and/or gas-freeing as is common to both repairs shall be divided equally between the shipowners and the underwriters, irrespective of the fact that the repairs for which underwriters are liable may relate to more than one voyage or accident or may be payable by more than one set of underwriters.
   3. The cost of fine cleaning specifically for a particular repair or particular repairs shall be divided in accordance with the principles set forth above.. . . .
49. 1968 AMC 995. Compare *Antilles S.S. v. American Hull*, 539 F.Supp. 572, 1983 AMC 1100 (S.D.N.Y.), where the court, distinguishing *Field S.S.* and *Barge J. Whitney*, held that the hull policy covered the assured's expenses in removing a cargo of acrylic acid which exploded and solidified inside the cargo tanks, causing structural damage to the vessel. On appeal, however, the Second Circuit reversed, relying on *Field S.S.* 733 F.2d 195, 1984 AMC 2444 (2d Cir., 1984).

portable heating units. After this had been accomplished and the repair of the heating coil system had been effected, the total costs amounted to $229,860.22.

The barge owners claimed for recovery of all costs under the heading of general average or particular average. To the contrary, the underwriters contended that the unfortunate situation gave rise to no claim in general average and that the expenses, other than repairing the coils and *removing the asphalt adhering to the inside of the tanks,* were not recoverable under the hull policy.

The arbitrator ruled, in essence, that neither the *vessel* nor the *cargo* was in "apparently imminent peril" sufficient to call into play general average principles. That is, the loss of *economic value*—as respects the barge because it could carry no cargoes and earn no freight, and as respects the cargo because it could not be used to pave roads—was not the kind of peril envisioned in the doctrine of general average.

Moving to the claim for particular average, the arbitrator, relying upon *Field Steamship Co. v. Burr,*[50] ruled that the hull underwriters were liable only for the cost of repairing physical damage *done to the vessel* including the heating system, during loading, and cutting accesses in the main deck during discharge to install portable heating coils, the cost of repairing the permanent coils, and the cost of removing materials adhering to the tanks after all the sound cargo had been discharged (minus the deductible). These costs amounted to only $40,229.60 as contrasted with the actual expenditures incurred by the barge owners of in excess of $250,000.

The arbitrator quoted extensively from *Field Steamship Co. v. Burr.* In that case, the vessel was insured under a hull and machinery policy against the usual risks. Carrying a cargo of cottonseed and almost at destination, she was in collision with another vessel and seriously damaged below the waterline. She was run aground to avoid sinking and a part of her cargo removed in lighters. She was then towed to a drydock where temporary repairs were made. She was moved thence to a pier for discharge where it was discovered that the remaining cargo, as a result of the water and mud that had entered the hull, had become a putrid mass which the consignees and their underwriters refused to accept and therefore abandoned.

The vessel owner was obliged to find a site where the mass of material could be dumped and stevedores could be hired at extra rates to remove the material. He claimed for this cost (or, alternatively, for the excess over normal discharging costs), pointing out, quite logically, that permanent repairs could not be effected until the material had been removed.

---

50. (1899) 1 Q.B. 579 (C.A.).

In rejecting his claim against underwriters, the court noted that the shipowner must be deprived of his ship or the use of her and that the damage must be caused to *the ship*. On appeal, the lord justice gave as an example the case of a cargo of cement in bags solidified by a sea peril so as to become stone, and thus to cost more to discharge than would otherwise be the case. He noted that if, by the solidification, the cement got affixed to the hull or machinery, so that either the hull or machinery became damaged, the underwriters on the hull and machinery might have to pay, but for the mere extra cost of removal of the cargo at destination, with which removal the underwriters upon hull and machinery had nothing to do, the underwriters were not liable.

Collins, L.J., commented:

> How can the presence of a putrid cargo in the ship be said to be a damage to the hull? The fabric of the ship is not injured by it; so far as it affects the ship at all, it is by interfering with its use until it is removed. But this is not damage to the hull, which is insured, but damage to the shipowner . . . in his business as carrier.[51]

Successive Losses

While ordinarily the liability of a hull underwriter is limited to the amount of the policy insofar as any one accident is concerned, it may happen that the insured vessel is involved in more than one accident during the currency of the policy. If the assured makes repairs to the damage arising out of the multiple casualties during the currency of the policy, the liability of the underwriter may exceed the amount of the policy.[52]

Particular Average (Unrepaired) Followed by Total Loss

But where, under the same policy, a partial loss *is not repaired or made good*, and is followed by a total loss, the partial loss is merged in the total loss and the assured can recover only for the total loss.[53]

---

51. It should be observed that *Field Steamship* was decided before enactment of the Marine Insurance Act, 1906, and the court relied upon the principle that the measure of damage was the depreciation of the subject-matter insured. Under Sec. 69(1) of the Act, the rule is the reasonable cost of the repairs.

52. *Matheson v. Equitable Marine Ins. Co.*, 118 Mass. 209 (1875); *Le Cheminant v. Pearson*, (1812) 128 E.R. 372; *George W. Clyde*, 2 F.Supp. 767 (N.D. Ill.), 1924 AMC 1479; *Christie v. Buckeye Ins. Co.*, F.Cas. 2,700 (6th Cir. 1872). It should also be observed that sue and labor charges and claims under the Running Down Clause may be recoverable, in addition to the amount of the policy, as those insurances are supplementary to the regular hull coverage.

53. *Livie v. Janson*, (1810) 104 E.R. 253; *British & Foreign Ins. Co., Ltd. v. Wilson Shipping Co., Ltd.*, [1921] A.C. 188; compare, however, *Gulf Florida v. Interstate F.& C.*, 423 F.2d 269 (5th Cir.), 1970 AMC 28, where an underwriter which had paid a total loss under a later policy was held liable for unrepaired damage suffered under an earlier policy, now expired,

These rules are set forth in Section 77 of the Marine Insurance Act, which reads:

(1) Unless the policy otherwise provides, and subject to the provisions of this Act, the insurer is liable for successive losses, even though the total amount of such losses may exceed the sum insured.

(2) Where, under the same policy, a partial loss, which has not been repaired or otherwise made good, is followed by a total loss, the assured can only recover in respect of the total loss;

Provided that nothing in this section shall affect the liability of the insurer under the suing and labouring clause.

Policy conditions can, of course, vary the rule. However, the AIH (1977) form expressly follows Section 77 in providing:

In no case shall the Underwriters be liable for unrepaired damage in addition to a subsequent Total Loss sustained during the period covered by this Policy.

The derivation of Section 77 sheds light on why the principle was adopted. In *Livie v. Janson*,[54] a ship was insured under a hull policy which warranted the vessel "free from American condemnation." The vessel, in leaving an American port, stranded and was abandoned by her crew. She was thereafter seized by the American government, refloated, and later condemned. The risk of condemnation was not insured against. The assured claimed from underwriters in respect of the particular average damage sustained by the vessel as a consequence of the stranding but the court held that such damage was merged in the subsequent total loss by seizure and condemnation—which, being an uninsured risk, meant the assured recovered nothing.

Livie v. Janson was followed more than 100 years later by *Wilson Shipping Co., Ltd. v. British & Foreign Marine Ins. Co., Ltd.*[55] In that case, the vessel was insured against customary marine risks and while so insured was chartered to the British government which assumed liability for war risks. During the term of the policy, the vessel sustained three casualties due to marine risks, but before the damage could be repaired, she was torpedoed and totally lost. The British government paid the owners her sound value as a consequence of the total loss but deducted the estimated costs of repairing the particular average damages previously sustained. The vessel's owners thereupon claimed against the hull and machinery underwriters, contending that *Livie v. Janson* did not apply as they had

where the later policy excluded liability after total loss for prior unrepaired damage "under *this* policy," although the later policy was expressed to be a "revival" of the earlier policy.

54. *Id.*, n. 53.
55. (1919) 2 K.B. 653, (1921) 1 A.C. 188, 4 Ll.L.Rep. 371.

been prejudiced by reason of the existence of the unrepaired damage, i.e., because the government deducted the cost of such unrepaired damage from the sound value of the vessel. The House of Lords disagreed, holding that so long as the total loss occurred during the term of the policy, whether caused by an insured peril or not, there could be no claim for a particular average loss.

The decision, although consistent with the provisions of Section 77(2) of the Marine Insurance Act, must be considered as having applied Section 91(2) of the Act which reads:

> (2) The rules of the common law including the law merchant, save in so far as they are inconsistent with the express provisions of this Act, shall continue to apply to contracts of marine insurance.

In effect, the House of Lords reaffirmed *Livie v. Janson*, decided over a century before because, by its very terms, Section 77(2) only applies where the total loss is caused by a peril insured against in the policy.

Liability of Underwriters Where Assured Claims for a Total Loss But Proves Only a Partial Loss

It bears repeating that where the assured sues for a total loss but proves only a partial loss, he is entitled to recover the latter.[56] And the assured is not bound to claim for a constructive total loss (even though he could do so in the circumstances), but may, instead, refuse to abandon his vessel to underwriters and sue as for a particular average loss but not exceeding the cost of repairs.[57]

Liability of Underwriters for Unrepaired Damage

It will be remembered that both in *Livie v. Janson* and in *Wilson Shipping*, the previous particular average loss and the total loss occurred within the same policy period. What is the rule if a vessel is damaged but on expiration of the policy period (or any extensions thereof pursuant to policy provisions) the damage has not been repaired and the vessel is not a total loss? The assured presumptively has a right of recovery in respect of the unrepaired damage. There are, obviously, three possible situations:

(1) The vessel is only partially repaired;
(2) The vessel is not repaired at all; or

---

56. Sec. 56(4) of the Act. See, also, *Merchants Marine Ins. Co. v. Ross*, (1884) 10 Q.L.R. 236 (C.A. Can.); *The Tornado*, 1 F.Supp. 137 (W.D. Pa.), 1924 AMC 452; *George W. Clyde*, 2 F.Supp. 767 (N.D. Ill.), 1924 AMC 1479; *Harkley v. Prov. Ins. Co.*, (1868) 18 U.C.C.P. 335 (C.A. Can.); *Western Assur. Co. v. Scanlan*, (1886) 13 S.C.R. 207 (Can.); *Troop v. Union Ins. Co.*, (1893) 32 N.B.R. 135 (C.A. Can.). And, see Chapter XVI, "Actual and Constructive Total Loss."
57. *Disrude v. Commercial Fish, etc.*, 570 P.2d 963 (Or. 1978), 1978 AMC 261.

(3) The vessel is not repaired and the owner sells her during the policy period.

Section 69 directly applies to the first two possible situations (sub-sections [2] and [3]), but the Act is totally silent with respect to the third.[58]

It will be seen that both sub-sections (2) and (3) provide for the same indemnity whether repairs have been taken in hand only in part or have not been taken in hand at all, the measure of indemnity in each instance being fixed as the reasonable depreciation in the value of the vessel but not exceeding the cost of repairs.

The principle involved was derived from the case of *Lidgett v. Secretan.*[59] In that case, a vessel was insured under one policy for a voyage from London to Calcutta and for 30 days after arrival, and under another policy for the return voyage. On the voyage from London to Calcutta the vessel sustained damage and repairs were undertaken in Calcutta. Before the repairs could be completed, but after the 30-day period had expired, the vessel caught fire and was a total loss. By this time, the second policy had gone into effect. The underwriters on the first policy admitted liability for only the cost of repairs completed at the time of the fire and denied liability for the cost of the repairs not yet concluded; the underwriters on the second policy (by coincidence, the underwriters were the same) paid on the basis of a total loss.

The court found that upon the expiration of the first policy the underwriters on that policy were only liable to make good the diminution in value in the vessel by reason of the repairs not having been completed, i.e., reasonable depreciation.[60]

Although the question seems not to have arisen in the United States, there are cases which appear to follow the general principle involved. For example, in *Walker v. Liverpool & London & Globe Ins. Co.,*[61] the policy

---

58. For convenience, both sub-sections bear repeating:
(2) Where the ship has been only partially repaired, the assured is entitled to the reasonable cost of such repairs, computed as above, and also to be indemnified for the reasonable depreciation, if any, arising from the unrepaired damage, provided that the aggregate amount shall not exceed the cost of repairing the whole damage, computed as above;
    (3) Where the ship has not been repaired, and has not been sold in her damaged state during the risk, the assured is entitled to be indemnified for the reasonable depreciation arising from the unrepaired damage, but not exceeding the reasonable cost of repairing such damage, computed as above.
59. (1871) L.R. 6 C.P. 616, 1 Asp. M.L.C. 95.
60. The measure of indemnity is calculated as of the time the policy expires. *Helmville, Ltd. v. Yorkshire Ins. Co., Ltd. (The Medina Princess)*, [1965] 1 Lloyd's Rep. 361. This is so because it is only when the risk is ended that it can be predicted for certain that neither repair nor sale will take place during the risk. *Helmville, supra*, p. 516. Moreover, where the damaged value of the vessel is, for practical purposes, nothing, indemnity is limited to the reasonable cost of the repairs. *Helmville, supra*, p. 515.
61. 190 N.Y.S. 255, *aff'd Walker v. Western Assur. Co. of City of Toronto*, 193 N.Y.S. 957, 201 App.Div. 886 (St. N.Y. 1922).

provided, in essence, that no claim of loss should go beyond the cost of actual repairs. That provision, considered with a provision for estimating loss, was held merely to limit the claim for loss to the cost of repairs, if made, and if no repairs were made, the assured could recover the amount of damages found on the survey, i.e., estimated cost of repairs. In *O'Boyle v. American Equitable Assur. Co.*,[62] the insured barge was not repaired as the assured notified the underwriters that he was financially unable to do so until he was reimbursed by insurance proceeds. The policy provided that it was the underwriters' intent to "fully indemnify" the assured but also provided that the loss could not go "beyond the extent or cost of actual repairs." The underwriters contended that since no repairs were made, they were not liable. The court disagreed, holding that the underwriters' contention would render the policy one to indemnify, not against loss, but against only such loss as the assured might repair, and would leave out of consideration the words "the extent" in the phrase last quoted.

In *Norwich & N.Y. Transp. Co. v. Western Massachusetts Ins. Co.*,[63] a steamboat, insured against fire owing to a collision, caught fire after a collision in consequence of which it sank. The policy provided that the measure of computing any loss thereunder was the cash value of the vessel before the fire. The plaintiffs (assureds) offered to prove the cash value, deducting the amount the vessel was damaged by the collision, including all the necessary consequences, to which mode the underwriters objected. The court held that as the only mode of estimating the loss was to prove what it would have cost to repair the damages necessarily resulting from the fire, the assureds would be permitted to do so.

In *Giles v. Eagle Ins. Co.*,[64] the vessel received a strain which altered her shape so that she could not be repaired without rebuilding her. Her value was thereby diminished. The underwriters were held liable to the extent of such diminished value in addition to the expenses of the repairs even though the vessel was made seaworthy by the repairs and was afterwards insured at the same premium and at the same valuation as before the casualty. In this respect, the decision does not differ from *Agenoria S.S. Co. v. Merchants Marine Ins. Co., Ltd.*,[65] where the vessel sustained damage to her keel which was repaired by "shoeing." The repair was perfectly safe and adequate although somewhat disfiguring but would no doubt have affected the resale value of the vessel. The court held that in addition to the cost of repairs, the underwriters would have to pay for the diminution in the value of the vessel.

What is the measure of indemnity if the vessel is repaired and, after such repairs, further damage or defects are discovered? In *Reynolds v.*

62. 189 N.Y.S. 46, 116 Misc. Rep. 39 (St. N.Y. 1921).
63. F.Cas. 10,363, *aff'd* 79 U.S. 201, 20 L.ed. 380 (1870).
64. 43 Mass. 140 (St. Mass. 1840).
65. *Id.*, n. 46, *supra*.

Ocean Ins. Co.,[66] this question arose. In that case, the vessel was abandoned to underwriters who afterwards repaired her and tendered her back to the assured who accepted her. Later the assured found a marked deficiency in her repairs and successfully made claim against the underwriters.

A delay in ascertaining a loss should not be deemed to prejudice the assured. This was the holding in *Berry v. Columbian Ins. Co.*[67] There, the vessel stranded but it was not possible to give the ship a thorough examination at that time and the vessel proceeded on her voyage. Subsequently, she was found to be leaking badly, due mainly to the original stranding. The court held that the delay in discovering the loss did not prevent a recovery for the partial loss incurred.

It should also be noted that loss of use of a vessel is not generally covered under a hull and machinery policy. Such a loss may be specifically insured (as well as other incidental losses referrable to vessels such as profits, disbursements, freight, anticipated freight, charter hire, premiums, etc.) and, in fact, provision is made for such insurance in lines 210-255 of the AIH form (1977). But if such insurances are not taken out, the hull underwriters are not liable for loss of use, etc.[68]

Vessel Sold Unrepaired

As noted above, the Marine Insurance Act does not cover the situation where the vessel is sold in an unrepaired state during the currency of the policy. No guidance whatever is given in the Act as to the measure of an underwriter's liability in such circumstance.

However, in *Pitman v. Universal Marine Insurance Co.,*[69] the question was presented although not decided in a fashion which can be regarded as totally definitive. In that case, an insured ship was damaged during the continuance of the risk by perils insured against, and was sold by the owners without being repaired. The amount required to restore her to the same condition as she was in at the commencement of the risk would have exceeded her value when repaired so that no reasonable uninsured owner would have repaired her. The owners effected some slight repairs for the purposes of sale, sold her, and then claimed to recover from the underwriters the cost of repairs estimated as being necessary to put the

---

66. 39 Mass. 191 (St. Mass. 1839).

67. (1866) 12 Gr. 418 (Can.).

68. *Jarvis Towing & Transp. Corp. v. Aetna Ins. Co.,* 298 N.Y. 280, 82 N.E.2d 577 (St. N.Y.1948). See, also, *Brown v. Merchants' Marine Ins. Co.,* 152 F. 411 (9th Cir.,1917), where there was a separate policy on "disbursements and/or increased value." The ship was sunk in a collision and held at mutual fault although recovering a sum on balance less than the insured value. Both underwriters shared in the subrogation recovery.

69. (1882) 9 Q.B.D. 192, 4 Asp. M.L.C. 544, C.A.

ship in the same condition as she was prior to the damage, less one-third deduction, new for old. The court held that the assureds were not entitled to recover the amount claimed and that the underwriters were only liable to pay the amount of the difference between the value of the ship at the port of departure and the amount of the net proceeds of the sale after deducting the sum spent on repairs.

At first instance, Lindley, J. held that the value of the vessel at the port of destination was £4,000 (the vessel was valued in a time policy at £3,700 at the time of leaving the port of origin—Singapore). He further held that the assured could recover the difference between the proceeds of the sale, less the cost of repairs actually effected, and the sound value of the vessel, that proportion being applied to the value in the policy in determining the amount payable by the underwriter.

His decision was affirmed by a majority of the court of appeal but the reasons given by the three justices are not entirely clear.

M. R. Jessel obviously thought the case was one of constructive total loss, and, although he did not approve of the reasons given by Lindley, J., thought that the assured should not recover more than as for a total loss which was basically the result reached by Lindley, J. Cotton, L. J., although he agreed with Lindley, J., expressed his views differently, saying:

> Probably, the most accurate way of stating the measure of what, under such circumstances the assured is to recover, is that it will be the estimated cost of repairs less the actual deduction, not exceeding the depreciation in value of the vessel as ascertained by the sale.

In the last analysis, the views of Lindley, J., Cotton, L. J., and Jessel, M. R., limited the assured to the cost of repair or the depreciation, whichever was less.

Brett, L. J., was of the opinion that the estimated cost of repairs was the absolute measure of the loss and the fact that the assured was able to sell the vessel at a good price was merely a fortuituous circumstance which should not be given consideration. He also noted that the fact that the assured was able to achieve more than a mere indemnity was not grounds for reaching a different result.

If *Pitman* expresses the correct result, the difference in wording between sub-sections (2) and (3) of Section 69 would appear to be of no consequence.

How is the "reasonable depreciation" to be ascertained? The Marine Insurance Act provides no guidance and the point does not appear to have been decided by the English courts. The question was approached in *Irvin v. Hine*[70] but was not decided, as the methods of calculation ad-

---

70. [1949] 2 All E.R. 1089, [1950] 1 K.B. 555, 65 T.L.R. 768, 83 Ll.L.Rep. 162.

vanced by the parties would have resulted in figures in excess of the estimated costs of repairs.

In that case, the insured vessel stranded in January 1942. The assured claimed as for a constructive total loss because it was unlikely that he would be able to repair her within a reasonable time due to wartime conditions and the licensing program then in force. On this point, it was held that, whether or not the loss would have been a constructive total loss at common law, it was not such a constructive total loss as defined by Section 60 of the Act.

Alternatively, the assured claimed for a partial loss; i.e., as the vessel had not been repaired he was entitled under Section 69(3) of the Act "to be indemnified for the reasonable depreciation arising from the unrepaired damage, but not exceeding the reasonable cost of repairing such damage." That cost would have been £4,620. The value of the vessel was agreed in the policy to be £9,000. Her actual value before the stranding was £3,000 and £685 after the stranding. Section 27(3) of the Act provides, of course, that "subject to the provisions of the Act," the value fixed by the policy is conclusive, whether the loss be total or partial. It was held that by reason of Section 27(3), in computing her depreciation it was not correct to subtract her true value after the stranding from her true value before the stranding (£3,000 - £685); that either (1) the true damaged value must be subtracted from the conventional value (£9,000 - £685), or (2) the proportion of her actual depreciation must be applied to her conventional value (£9,000); but that, as, in either case, the result exceeded £4,620, the cost of repairs, the assured was only entitled to recover that sum.[71]

Whatever may be the rule in England, the principle of applying the percentage of actual depreciation to the agreed insured value has been adopted in the United States, in *Compania Maritima Astra, S.A. v. Archdale (The Armar),*[72] followed by *Delta Supply Co. v. Liberty Mutual Ins. Co.*[73]

In *Armar,* the vessel grounded. Efforts to relieve her of her strand having proved unavailing, a salvage tug was procured to assist her. She was then towed to a shipyard where her cargo was discharged and she was drydocked for the purpose of ascertaining the extent of her damages. A few days prior to her ill-fated voyage, her owners had insured her against, among other losses, total or constructive total loss in the sum of $1.2 million.

71. Interestingly, shortly before *Irvin v. Hine* was decided, in *Elcock v. Thompson,* (1949) 82 Ll.L.Rep. 892, a non-marine case involving a fire policy on a mansion, the court, after reviewing the marine cases and the analogous provisions of the Marine Insurance Act, adopted as the correct method the proportion of the actual depreciation as applied to conventional or agreed insured value.

72. 134 N.Y.S.2d 20 (St. N.Y.), 1954 AMC 1674, [1954] 2 Lloyd's Rep. 95.

73. 211 F.Supp. 429 (S.D. Tex.), 1963 AMC 1540.

The assureds contended that they were entitled to recover as for a constructive total loss because, based on their calculations, the cost of repair would exceed her insured value. The evidence was clear that her sound, replacement value was about $675,000. The underwriters contended that the repair costs would not exceed the insured value, i.e., $1.2 million.

In ruling on the measure of indemnity, the court also held, *inter alia* (principal citations as shown in footnotes):

(1) The disproportion between insured value and replacement value of the vessel did not raise questions of wagering and gambling contracts as the validity of valued policies in hull insurance was long ago established,[74] and the purpose and function of a valued policy was to eliminate uncertainty in the valuation of a total loss;[75]

(2) Although at common law the American rule was that repair and recovery costs in excess of 50% of stated value constituted a constructive total loss,[76] the policy (apparently in consonance with the Marine Insurance Act of 1906) required proof of costs in excess of 100% of insured value;[77]

(3) In calculating repair and recovery costs, it is proper to include expenditures necessary to deliver the ship from its peril to a port of safety and thereafter to make it a seaworthy vessel;[78]

(4) Accordingly, in addition to repair costs, the expenses of salvage;[79] drydock and surveys;[80] pilotage and towage;[81] and superintendence[82] were allowable. Not to be included, however, was any allowance provided for by the Tender Clause of the policy whereby the assured was to be awarded 30% per annum of the assured value from the time of completion of the survey to the acceptance of the tender for repairs "in cases where a tender is accepted with the approval of Underwriters" for in the instant case there had been no acceptance by the underwriters;

74. *Klein v. Globe & Rutgers Fire Ins. Co. of New York*, 2 F.2d 137 (3rd Cir.), 1924 AMC 452; *Murray v. Great Western Ins. Co.*, 25 N.Y. Supp. 414; *Irving v. Manning*, 1 H.L.C. 287.

75. *Calmar S.S. Corp. v. Scott (The Portmar)*, 209 F.2d 852, 853-4 (4th Cir.), 1954 AMC 558; see, also, *Rhinelander v. The Insurance Co. of Pennsylvania*, 8 U.S. 29.

76. *Bradlie et al v. The Maryland Insurance Co.*, 37 U.S. 378; *Fireman's Fund Ins. Co. v. Globe Navigation Co.*, 236 F. 618 (9th Cir.).

77. Sec. 60(2)(ii).

78. *Young v. Union Ins. Co.*, 24 F. 279, 283 (N.E. Ill.); *North Atlantic S.S. Co., Ltd. v. Burr*, 8 Com.Cas. 164.

79. *Hall v. Hayman*, 17 Com.Cas. 81; *Bradlie et al v. The Maryland Insurance Co.*, supra, n. 76.

80. *Chicago S.S. Lines v. U.S. Lloyd*, 2 F.2d 767 (N.D. Ill.), 1924 AMC 1479, 12 F.2d 733 (7th Cir.), *aff'd* 1926 AMC 807; *Young v. Union Ins. Co.*, supra, n. 78.

81. Arnould, *Marine Insurance*, (13th ed.) 1031; Hurd, *Marine Insurance*, 55; Templeman, *Marine Insurance*, 171.

82. *Agenoria S.S. Co., Ltd. v. Merchants' Marine Ins. Co.*, 8 Com.Cas. 212.

(5) The burden of proving costs in excess of insured value lies upon the assured[83] and he must show the actual and other necessary costs to be in fact, not just "probably," above the insured value;[84]

(6) In ascertaining whether the plaintiff met his burden of proving a constructive total loss, the bids reported by the plaintiff must, in the facts involved in the case, be put to one side for, while a reasonable, acceptable, bona fide bid is of probative value,[85] bids solicited with no intent of letting the work are of no probative value[86] as where there is a patent discrepancy between the repairs requested and replacement value and the bidders must have known that insurance recovery, and not repair, was the true objective of the solicitation; and

(7) No bid or tender is of value unless the specifications upon which they are based fairly represent the extent of damage sustained and fairly state the work required to be done to restore the vessel to its former condition. An estimate based upon an exaggerated statement of damage and on an extravagant listing of the repair work to be done is not a proper guide in determining the cost of repair.

After determining that there was no constructive total loss, the court turned to the question of determining the proper measure of recovery for a partial loss. Citing numerous cases, the court concluded that federal law, and not state law, should be applied.[87] And, based thereon, the court further held that federal law would look to the laws of England for guidance with respect to matters involving insurance.[88]

---

83. *Fireman's Fund Ins. Co. v. Globe Navigation Co., supra,* n. 76.

84. *Jeffcott v. Aetna Insurance Co.—Yacht Dauntless,* 40 F.Supp. 404, 410-11 (S.D.N.Y.), 1941 AMC 1317, 129 F.2d 582 (2d Cir.), *aff'd* 1942 AMC 1021; *Wallace v. Thames & Mersey Ins. Co.,* 22 F. 66 (C.C.E.D. Mich.); *Fireman's Fund Ins. Co. v. Globe Navigation Co., supra,* n. 76; *Bradlie et al. v. The Maryland Insurance Co., supra,* n. 76; *Fontaine v. Phoenix Ins. Co.,* 11 Johns (N.Y.) 293; *Orient Ins. Co. v. Adams,* 123 U.S. 67; 2 Phillips, *Insurance* (3d ed.), 258.

85. *Jeffcott v. Aetna Insurance Co., supra,* n. 84.

86. *Streckfus Steamboat Line v. U.S.,* 27 F.2d 251, 252 (5th Cir.), 1928 AMC 1325.

87. *Southern Pacific Co. v. Jensen,* 244 U.S. 205; *Peters v. Veasey,* 251 U.S. 121; *Maryland Casualty Co. v. Cushing,* 347 U.S. 409, 1954 AMC 837; *Aetna Ins. Co. v. Houston Oil & Transport Co.,* 49 F.2d 121 (5th Cir.), 1931 AMC 995, *cert. den.,* 284 U.S. 628; *Lanasa Fruit S.S. & Importing Co. v. Universal Ins. Co.,* 89 F.2d 545 (4th Cir.), 1937 AMC 651; *Wilburn Boat Co. v. Firemen's Fund Ins. Co.,* 201 F.2d 833 (5th Cir.), 1953 AMC 284. [Author's note: *The Armar* was decided shortly before *Wilburn Boat Co. v. Firemen's Fund Ins. Co.* was appealed to the U.S. Supreme Court and before that court refused to formulate a warranties rule, thus applying state law. See discussion, *supra,* Chapter I, subheading "What Law Applies," where *Wilburn Boat* is discussed in detail, and the refusal or reluctance commented upon of lower courts to apply *Wilburn* except where a state statute clearly applies].

88. *Aetna Ins. Co. v. Houston Oil & Transport Co., supra,* n. 87; *Queen Ins. Co. of America v. Globe & Rutgers Fire Ins. Co. (The Napoli),* 263 U.S. 487, 1924 AMC 107; *New York & Oriental S.S. Co. v. Automobile Ins. Co.,* 37 F.2d 461, 463 (2d Cir.), 1930 AMC 328; *Lanasa Fruit S.S. & Importing Co. v. Universal Ins. Co., supra,* n. 87, and 88 F.2d 549 (2d Cir.), 1937 AMC 651; see, also, *The Eliza Lines,* 199 U.S. 119, 128; *Calmar S.S. Corp. v. Scott (The Portmar), supra,* 209 F.2d 855, 1954 AMC 558.

Applying English law, the court held that Section 69(3) of the Marine Insurance Act, 1906, applied, by which the assured was entitled to be indemnified for the reasonable depreciation arising from the unrepaired damage, but not exceeding the reasonable cost of repairing such damage, citing *Elcock v. Thompson, Pitman v. Universal Marine Ins. Co.*, and noting the application of one suggested method in *Irvin v. Hine*. The court concluded by stating:

> . . . In my view the formula [following Section 69(3)] most nearly comports with the purpose of sec. 69(3) in the case of valued hull insurance; is not inconsistent with rule or decision of our Federal courts; and will here be employed.

> Applying the formula to the instant case, the evidence shows the value of the vessel in her present condition is $218,000. Her sound value undamaged was $675,000. The depreciation was therefore 67.7%. An equal percentage of the insured value would be $812,400 which would be the maximum plaintiff could recover for repairs. Since I have found the cost of repairs to be $736,315 it is within the bounds of the limitation imposed by the formula and thus recoverable. In so far as the measure of damages is concerned, there is accordingly no conflict with plaintiff's theory.

> To this figure must be added the cost of recovery amounting to $77,384.10 as heretofore found, plus an additional amount of $2,600 [owners' superintendent's fee and expenses for preliminary survey] which, while not considered with respect to constructive total loss, is allowable in arriving at partial total loss.

> Judgment is therefore granted to plaintiff on the first cause of action for a partial loss, in the sum of $816,299.10.

In light of the facts of the case, the court refused to allow pre-judgment interest.[89]

In *Delta Supply Co. v. Liberty Mutual Ins. Co.*,[90] the assured was the owner of a yacht which sank while berthed in its regular place. Prior to the sinking, the assured had procured a policy of hull insurance in which the vessel was insured for $15,000. The yacht was raised and thereafter the assured sold it, receiving therefor as salvage the sum of $4,500.

The assured alleged that the sinking was caused by the negligence of the berth owner and that the sinking occurred under such conditions that the loss was covered by the hull policy.

---

89. The author pleads forgiveness for belaboring *The Armar* in such detail, but the decision is so well reasoned and the citations of authority so numerous that full treatment is warranted. Moreover, the case report throws valuable light upon what items of repair costs are allowable in particular average and the reasoning of the court in allowing or disallowing claimed items of costs.

90. *Id.*, n. 73, *supra*.

The jury, in answering special issues, exonerated the berth owner but held that the hull policy covered. The jury also found that the reasonable cash market value of the yacht immediately prior to her sinking was $18,000 even though the yacht was valued in the insurance policy for only $15,000. The jury further found that the reasonable cash market value of the yacht in its damaged condition immediately after it had been raised was $4,500 and that the cost of repairs reasonably necessary to restore the yacht to her condition immediately prior to the sinking was $12,700.

The defendant underwriter contended that the yacht should be treated as a constructive total loss with the result that the defendant would be credited with the $4,500 realized by the assured as a result of the sale, thus reducing the company's liability from $15,000 (the maximum) to $10,500.

The policy provided, in part:

> No recovery for a "constructive total loss" shall be had hereunder unless the expense of recovering and repairing the vessel shall exceed the insured value of the vessel.

The court found that since the cost of repairs did not exceed the insured value of the vessel, there was no constructive total loss under the policy.

The plaintiff assured contended that it was entitled to recover the estimated cost of repairs just as if the repairs had been actually made. The court, noting that if the assured had *actually* made the repairs, the actual cost of those repairs would have been the measure of the loss, emphasized that, in fact, the yacht was sold unrepaired. The court then declared that *Pitman v. Universal Marine Ins. Co.* was the controlling case and, based thereon, followed that decision in ascertaining the measure of indemnity. Interestingly, although the court cited *Armar* with respect to whether interest was or was not recoverable, it did not appear to focus on the fact that *Armar* involved precisely the same question. In fact, the judge stated that he had been unable to find any United States authority on the exact question involved in the present case. However, the court did note that several cases in *dicta* had assumed that the rule in *Pitman* was the correct one to apply in determining damages in a situation where the vessel is sold unrepaired.[91]

The law would seem to be well settled in the United States that the rule in *Armar* should be followed in all cases involving the measure of indemnity in particular average claims on a ship where the assured sells the vessel without making repairs.

---

91. Citing *Aetna Ins. Co. v. United Fruit Co.*, 92 F.2d 576 (2d Cir.), 1938 AMC 22; *Gulf Refining Co. v. Atlantic Mutual Ins. Co.*, 279 U.S. 708, 1929 AMC 825, and *International Navigation Co. v. Atlantic Mutual Ins. Co.*, 100 F. 304 (S.D.N.Y. 1900).

Miscellaneous Cases Involving Particular Average Claims on Vessels

In *Providence Washington Ins. Co. v. Paducah Towing Co.*,[92] the policy provided that a deduction of one-third would be made from a partial loss claim for repairs to the vessel after the first two years from the date of her original customhouse survey. The underwriters claimed that the policy language entitled them to deduct one-third, in addition to the one-third which they were otherwise entitled to deduct by virtue of the one-third, new for old deduction. The court held for underwriters.

In *Aetna Cas. & Surety Co. v. Bell*,[93] the court held that while the insurer was liable only for the fair value of repairs made necessary by injury to the vessel, the insurer had the burden of establishing that the charges incurred for repair were excessive.

Marine policies normally do not contain a condition precedent with respect to filing proofs of loss with underwriters as one commonly finds in fire insurance policies. This fundamental distinction was commented on by Ritchie, J., in *Robertson v. Pugh*,[94] where he noted the American cases on the subject and pointed out that such a clause in a marine policy only required that reasonable information be given to the underwriters of the circumstances attending the loss so that they might be able to judge of their rights and liabilities before being called upon to pay, and was not to be understood as requiring proof in a legal or technical sense.

In *Milledge v. Stymest*,[95] the plaintiff claimed for a constructive total loss but the evidence showed a partial loss only. No evidence was given as to the amount of repairs and the trial court nonsuited the plaintiff. On appeal, the court held that the plaintiff was at the least and in all events entitled to nominal damages.

The policy valuation set forth in the policy is absolutely binding in the absence of fraud. This was demonstrated in *Barker v. Janson*.[96] In that case, the vessel was insured by a valued time policy and its value stated in the policy as being £8,000. At the time the policy was made, but unknown to the parties, the vessel had been damaged in a storm so that the expense of repairs would have exceeded its value when repaired. During the currency of the risk, the vessel was totally lost. In an action against the underwriters, the court held that the policy attached, notwithstanding the previous damage to the ship, and there being no fraud, the value of the vessel as stated in the policy was conclusive as between the parties.

92. 28 Ky. 622, 89 S.W. 722 (St. Ky. 1905).
93. 390 F.2d 612 (lst Cir. 1968).
94. (1887) 20 N.S.R. 15, *aff'd* 15 S.C.R. 706 (Can.).
95. (1866) N.B. Dig. 737 (Can.).
96. (1868) L.R. 3 C.P. 303, 17 L.T. 473, 3 Mar. L.C. 28.

Attention is directed to *American S.S. Co. v. Indemnity Mut. Marine Assur. Co.*,[97] in which the policy contained two separate valuations. One included the hull, tackle, etc., and the other the engines, propeller, boilers, and machinery. The policy also contained clauses providing that in the event of particular average, the underwriters would be liable only for the excess of one-half percent upon the entire value and that average was payable on each valuation as if separately insured, or on the whole. It was held that the effect of the latter cause was to entitle the assured to treat the policy as a single policy on the whole, or as two separate policies, for the purpose of computing the deductible average in case of a partial loss, and that in case of a loss which did not affect any of the items included in the second class, the half percent deductible under the franchise clause should be computed only on the amount of the first valuation.[98]

A clause in a hull policy stating that the policy is "free of particular average, unless the vessel be sunk, burned, stranded, or in collision" ceases to operate as soon as a collision has occurred, and underwriters are liable for a subsequent loss whether resulting from the collision or not; i.e., the collision "opens the franchise."[99]

The term "on fire" in a free from particular average clause is not synonymous with the word "burnt," but is merely indicative of a happening whereby the vessel is endangered by actual fire burning part of it, thus necessitating extraordinary efforts to prevent serious damage.[100]

Particular Average on Freight

As has already been noted, references in the Marine Insurance Act, 1906, to freight are relatively sparse.[101] This is so probably because the subject relates to an intangible, is very difficult to understand, and can be extraordinarily complex.[102] Other references to the subject will be found in this text in Chapter VII, "Insurable Interest," Chapter XV, "Proximate Cause," Chapter XVI, "Actual and Constructive Total Loss," Chapter XVII, "General Average," and Chapter XVIII, "Sue and Labor Clause."

---

97. 118 F. 1014 (lst Cir. 1902).

98. As noted heretofore, modern-day hull policies seldom contain a franchise clause and the question presented in *American S.S. Co.* is not likely to arise again.

99. *London Assurance v. Companhia De Moagens Do Barreiro*, 68 F. 247 (3rd Cir. 1895), *aff'd* 167 U.S. 149.

100. *Pacific Creosoting Co. v. Thames & Mersey Marine Ins. Co.*, 184 F. 947 (1914). Cf. *Service v. Mercantile Mar. Ins. Co. of South Australia*, (1878) 4 V.L.R. 436.

101. The original bill before Parliament (which ultimately became the Act), contained a sub-section in Sec. 60 relating to freight. The sub-section was deleted prior to final passage of the Act. Constructive total loss of freight is consequently governed by the general provisions contained in sub-section (1) of Sec. 60.

102. Goddard, L.J., in *Papadimitrious v. Henderson*, (1939) 64 Ll.L.R. 345, stated: "All cases of freight insurance, I think, as a rule raise questions of difficulty."

Section 90 of the Marine Insurance Act and Rule for Construction No. 16 define "freight" in identical terms:

> "Freight" includes the profit derivable by a shipowner from the employment of his ship to carry his own goods or moveables, as well as freight payable by a third party, but does not include passage money.

Section 70 of the Act states the rule with respect to the measure of indemnity of partial losses of freight:

> Subject to any express provision in the policy, where there is a partial loss of freight, the measure of indemnity is such proportion of the sum fixed by the policy in the case of a valued policy, or of the insurable value in the case of an unvalued policy, as the proportion of freight lost by the assured bears to the whole freight at the risk of the assured under the policy.

Section 16(2) of the Act states the measure of insurable value as follows:

> (2) In insurance on freight, whether paid in advance or otherwise, the insurable value is the gross amount of the freight at the risk of the assured, plus the charges of insurance.[103]

Being an intangible, freight in and of itself is not capable of sustaining "physical" depreciation by perils insured against as would a vessel or cargo. Therefore, to constitute a particular average loss on freight there must be a partial loss in respect of it.[103a]

Phillips defined particular average on freight as follows (Sec. 1438):

> A particular average or partial loss on freight is occasioned by the loss of the ship after a part of the voyage is performed, which makes it necessary to hire another ship to carry on the cargo to the port of destination in order to earn the freight.

Again, in Section 1439, he states:

> A loss of part of the cargo, whereby the ship is prevented from earning a part of its freight, is a particular average on freight; and it does not appear to make any difference in this respect that the loss is on an article of a perishable nature and of more than ordinary liability to damage; as in case of tobacco being damaged by sea-water.

---

103. This embodies the general custom upheld in *Palmer v. Blackburn*, (1822) 130 E.R. 25. For the purpose of the rule, see *Thames and Mersey Marine Ins. Co., Ltd. v. Gunford Ship Co., Ltd.*, [1911] A.C. 529. See, also, *U.S. Shipping Co. v. Empress Assurance Corp.*, [1907] 1 K.B. 259, *aff'd* [1908] 1 K.B. 115, C.A.; *The Bedouin*, [1894] P. 1, C.A.; *The Alps*, [1893] P. 109.
103a. See *Troop v. Merchants Mar. Ins. Co.*, (1886) 13 S.C.R. 506 (Can.).

As a practical matter, the measure of indemnity for loss of freight is governed by specific policy provisions. For example, the Institute Freight Clauses, whether for Time or Voyage, in reality serve a dual purpose since a loss of freight can occur either from a casualty to the vessel, or consequent on a loss of part of the cargo, or both. In this sense, they represent an amalgamation of hull and cargo clauses.

Clause 7 of the Institute Freight Clauses constitutes a significant departure from the basic principles of indemnity. It reads, in relevant part:

> . . . the amount recoverable hereunder for any claim for loss of freight shall not exceed gross freight actually lost. Where insurances on freight other than that effected by this policy are current at the time of the loss, all such insurances shall be taken into consideration in calculating the liability under this Policy and the amount recoverable hereunder shall not exceed the rateable proportion of the gross freight lost, notwithstanding any valuation in this or any other policy.

As a consequence of the above language, an aggregation must be made of all the insurance effected. The measure of indemnity for claims falling under the policy will be ascertained by applying to each insurance its proportion computed by a comparison of the sums insured with the total amount insured on freight. In no case can the claim exceed the gross freight lost even though there may be an overinsurance. The effect is that where the freight is over-insured the indemnity is not proportionately increased[104] but is proportionately reduced in the event of under-insurance. In light of this limitation of the assured's right to recover, there is little point in insuring freight under valued policies and they are rarely used.

It is now an almost universal custom for shipowners to demand payment of freight in advance, using such language as "ship and/or cargo lost or not lost." It will be seen that when freight is paid in advance, the shipowner has no insurable interest in it for he cannot be required to repay it whether the voyage is completed or not and thus runs no risk of losing it. Consequently, it is at the risk of the person paying it, usually the merchant shipping the cargo, who stands to lose if the vessel or cargo were lost. The insurable interest consequently vests in the owner of the cargo and customarily he insures it either as "advance freight" or includes it in the value of the cargo.

The principles involving advance freight are embodied in the Act in Section 12, reading:

> In the case of advance freight, the person advancing the freight has

---

104. As will be seen, this differs from a valued policy on cargo.

an insurable interest, in so far as such freight is not payable in advance.[105]

Whether the amount of the advance freight is set forth in the policy or not, the courts have held that the policy is to be construed as a policy on valued cargo and not as a separate insurance on advance freight; i.e., the advance freight is considered as being merged in the value of the cargo.[106]

Categories of Freight

Bill of Lading Freight. In the normal course of events, a shipowner will issue a bill of lading with respect to cargo put aboard his ship. The bill of lading serves as a receipt for the cargo and, if negotiable, is generally transferred by the shipper to his consignee upon payment by the consignee of the purchase price of the goods, plus freight charges and insurance. The bill of lading is, of course, the contract of affreightment. The amount earned from carriage under the bill of lading is generally termed "bill of lading freight," and the insurable interest in the freight is considered bound up with and a part of the cargo. Bill of lading freight almost invariably is paid in advance, "lost or not lost," so that no refund can be claimed from the shipowner if the cargo is not delivered. Not being repayable in the event of loss, the insurable interest is vested in the cargo owner who should include such payment in the value of the cargo. Thus, when cargo is lost, the assured cargo owner will seek reimbursement of the freight as a part of the valuation of the cargo paid by cargo underwriters in settlement of the claim. The cargo underwriter, in turn, will seek to recover the appropriate amount of freight from the carrier (shipowner) in connection with a claim for loss or damage to the cargo. Whether the underwriter will succeed in recouping from the carrier depends upon the cause of the loss and the terms and exceptions of the bill of lading. For example, under the Hague Rules (the applicable Carriage of Goods By Sea Acts), a shipowner is relieved of liability to the cargo if

---

105. See *Allison v. Bristol Marine Ins. Co.,* (1876) 1 App.Cas. 209, H.L., reviewing the cases. The case involved a policy by the shipowner on freight. By the terms of the charter party, half of the freight was to be paid in advance and half was to be paid on delivery of the cargo. The ship was lost but half of the cargo was saved and delivered to destination. It was held that no further freight was payable with respect to the half delivered because it was covered by the advance payment of half of the freight. Thus, there was a total loss of half of the freight, the advance freight having been at the charterer's risk and not the risk of the shipowner. See, also, *Manfield v. Maitland,* (1821) 4 B. & Ald. 582 (distinction between advance freight and a loan by charterer to shipowner) and *Hicks v. Shield,* (1857) 26 L.J.Q.B. 205 (distinction between advance freight and loan). See, also, *Solomon v. Miller,* (1865) 2 W.W. & A'.B. (E) 135 (Vic.Sup.Ct. Aus.).

106. *Thames & Mersey Marine Ins. Co., Ltd. v. Pitts, Son & King,* (1893) 1 Q.B. 476.

the loss was due to "error in navigation or management of the vessel," whereas he is not so relieved if the loss was due to negligence in the "care, custody and control" of the cargo.

If, on the other hand, the goods are shipped "freight collect," the shipowner has an insurable interest in the freight and if a part of the goods is lost and that part is not delivered, the shipowner has suffered a loss of freight. By the same token, the ship itself may be lost, but it may be possible for the shipowner to deliver the cargo to destination in another vessel. Where such action is taken to avoid a loss under the policy through perils insured against, expenses in forwarding the cargo give rise to a claim under the Sue and Labor Clause.[107] Should it become necessary to abandon the voyage due to perils for which the shipowner is not legally liable, there is no obligation on his part to provide alternative methods of forwarding the cargo unless the proximity of the port of destination is reasonably close and it would be reasonable for the shipowner to do so in light of his obligations to cargo.

Under English law, partial performance of a voyage does not give rise to a partial payment of freight; i.e. a proportionate payment of freight based upon the distance traveled, or freight *pro rata itineris peracti*. The laws of most foreign countries (and the United States) recognize the payment of distance freight.[108]

The basic problem, it will be seen, is to determine whether the freight is at the risk of the shipowner, or the cargo owner, or a charterer, if any. And the terms of the contract of affreightment clearly govern. For example, in *Renton & Co., Ltd. v. Palmyra Trading Corp. of Panama (The Caspiana)*,[109] freight was payable in advance. The express provisions of the so-called "liberties" clause of the bill of lading permitted the shipowner to abandon the voyage in specified circumstances. Notwithstanding abandonment of the voyage, the shipowner was entitled to retain the advance freight paid.

---

107. *Kidston v. Empire Marine Ins. Co.*, (1867) L.R. 1 C.P. 535, 36 L.J.C.P. 156; *Firemen's Fund v. Trojan Powder Co.*, 253 F. 305 (9th Cir. 1918); cf. *Lockwood v. Atlantic Mutual Ins. Co.*, 47 Mo. 50 (1870) (estimated expense of forwarding should not be deducted from claim).

108. If, under the contract of affreightment, the master is entitled to insist on a right to forward the cargo and he chooses to do so, or the owner of the cargo voluntarily and unconditionally accepts the cargo at an intermediate port, the law creates a promise to pay freight *pro rata itineris peracti*. See *Hurtin v. Phoenix Ins. Co.*, F.Cas. 6,942 (1806); *The Mohawk*, 8 Wall 153, 75 U.S. 153, 19 L.ed. 466 (1868); *The Velona*, F.Cas. 16,912; *Caze v. Baltimore Ins. Co.*, 7 Cranch 358, 11 U.S. 358, 3 L.ed. 370 (1813); *The Nathaniel Hooper*, F.Cas. 10,032; *Hugg v. Augusta I. & Bkg. Co.*, 48 U.S. 594, 12 L.ed. 834 (1849); *Weston v. Minot*, F.Cas. 17,453; *Williams v. Smith*, 2 Caines (N.Y.) 13 (1804); *McKibbin v. Peck*, 39 N.Y. 262 (1868); *M'Gaw v. Ocean Ins. Co.*, 40 Mass. 405 (1839); *Armroyd v. Union Ins. Co.*, 3 Binn (Pa.) 437 (1810); *Vlierboom v. Chapman*, 153 E.R. 96.

109. [1956] 2 Lloyd's Rep. 379, H.L.

Chartered Freight. Chartered freight is the sum payable to a shipowner for the use of his vessel, or cargo spaces therein, either for a specified period of time (time charter) or for a particular voyage (voyage charter).

The sum payable may be either a lump sum, or a certain sum per pay for the time the vessel is "on hire," or at a rate calculated according to the cargo to be carried. In any event, once the parties have reached an accord as to their business arrangement, the agreement is embodied in a "charter party."

If the charterer assumes complete control of the vessel with the consequent responsibility for employing the officers and crew, paying the operating costs, and assuming all liabilities in connection with its operation, the charter is a "demise" or "bareboat" charter. Of course, if he issues bills of lading to third-party cargo owners, he collects "bill of lading" freight. If, on the other hand, he utilizes the vessel to carry his own cargo, he is both shipper and carrier and the measure of indemnity for his "freight" is the difference in the value of the cargo at point of origin as contrasted with its value at destination. If he insures his freight, underwriters have literally no right of recovery against him in the event of damage or loss to the cargo as the carrier and shipper are one and the same and as a matter of law one cannot sue oneself. Thus, underwriters lose their subrogation rights.

If the vessel is chartered for a period of time, with the vessel owner providing the officers and crew and paying the vessel's operating costs, and the charterer paying the costs of loading and discharging the cargo, port charges, dues, etc., the agreement is a time charter. Charter hire is usually expressed in terms of a certain sum per day. The charterer may utilize the vessel to transport his own cargo, or he may let out space to other cargo owners, in which event he makes his profit by charging bill of lading freight. Such charters usually provide that the master will sign bills of lading as presented to him (usually based upon mate's receipts) or will permit the charterer to sign bills of lading as his agent. The bills of lading customarily provide that they are subject to the terms of the charter party. It will be seen that the contract between the owner and the charterer is the charter party while the bills of lading are the contracts between the charterer and the various shippers.

The time charterer frequently will enter into a sub-charter with one or more shippers and this sub-charter is more properly termed a "voyage charter." Generally speaking, freight is payable on the basis of a rate applied to each type of cargo. For example, in the instance of bulk cargoes, the rate will be specified as a certain sum per ton. It is customary in such voyage charters for the time charterer to require the voyage charterer to pay for all charges of loading and unloading and other charges incidental to the cargo. The difference between the bill of lading freight paid by the voyage charterer to the time charterer, on the one hand, and the time charter hire paid by the time charterer to the vessel owner, on the other, is the time charterer's "profit."

From the foregoing, it is apparent that more than one of the parties to a marine adventure involving transportation of goods under a charter party may have an insurable interest in the freight. When the parties seek to insure this interest in freight, it is clearly incumbent upon them to describe it accurately, if problems with the underwriters are to be avoided after a loss. This is well illustrated in *The Bedouin*.[110] In that case, the vessel was chartered for a voyage to South America and thence back to Europe. The freight was insured: "freight chartered and/or as if chartered on board or not on board," for three months, "one-third diminishing each month." In fact, the freight was payable monthly in advance. The issue was whether the underwriter should have perceived that he was insuring freight which was payable under a charter party and that the charter party was of the type which ordinarily contained a "cesser" clause by which hire ceases if the vessel is unable to proceed on its voyage (due to breakdowns, etc.) for a stipulated period of time.

While enroute on its voyage, a thrust shaft parted due to bad weather and as a consequence the vessel had to be towed into St. Vincent. Twenty-eight days of charter hire was lost as a result. Claim was made by the owner for the lost hire as "freight."

The court construed the effect of the insuring clause in the following words:

> What is the freight in this case which is said to be the subject matter of this insurance? It is not denied that it was chartered freight; and what was the charter? It was a charter of a ship on a voyage from Liverpool to the West Coast of South America, and back to Europe. That is a long voyage, but the freight was payable monthly in advance; that is, the freight by this charterparty was payable before it would otherwise be payable. If goods are shipped on board a vessel without any such terms no freight whatever is due until the arrival of the ship at the port of discharge, and till the goods are delivered. Therefore freight in advance can only be by means of contract, which is by the charterparty. It is advance freight and it is payable monthly. If that remains so and the ship comes into a port of distress by reason of the perils of the sea, the shipowner is not liable for injury done to the charterer by perils of the sea, and therefore the charterer would be bound, if the ship was kept for a month in the port of distress, to pay for that month; but the charterer, who takes a ship on these terms, wishes to throw off that liability, which is to pay a very large sum indeed for the ship at a time when, by perils of the seas, he cannot have the use of the ship, and the ship is in the hands of the shipowner, for

110. [1894] P. 1.

the shipowner is bound to repair the ship. Therefore he desires to get rid of that, and he does so by what is called the twenty-four hours' clause.

In such circumstances, it will be clearly apparent that the insurable interest in the "freight" is shifted from the charterer to the shipowner as respects loss of charter hire coming within the parameters of the cesser clause.

The court then discussed what the insuring clause must have told the underwriter, noting that he was asked to insure "freight chartered, and/ or as if chartered, on board or not on board." Thus, the court said, the insuring clause could not have meant freight on board or not on board because freight is never "on board," being the charge made for carrying the goods, and, therefore, the words "on board or not on board" was a shorthand way of saying that the underwriter was being asked to insure chartered freight, or, as if chartered, on goods on board or not on board. The court also noted that the words "on board or not on board" conclusively demonstrated that it must be chartered freight because if there is no charter or no contract equivalent to a charter, there cannot be freight payable on goods not on board. Consequently, the court held, the underwriter was deemed to be informed that the interest insured was charter hire and that the vessel owner could recover for the 28 days of hire which was lost.

In *Scottish Shire Line, Ltd. v. London and Provincial Marine and General Ins. Co., Ltd.*,[111] the court reviewed a number of cases in attempting to apply the term "freight chartered or as if chartered." The following conclusions are illuminating:

> There is no difficulty in understanding what is meant by chartered freight. It is contrasted with Bill of Lading freight. Chartered freight is remuneration paid to the shipowner by another who hires his ship or part of it, generally with an added contract that the shipowner's captain shall sign Bills of Lading for the charterer's benefit. On the other hand, Bill of Lading freight is *prima facie* the shipowner's own contracted remuneration for the carriage of goods in his own ship by his own servants. No doubt the word freight extends to other engagements which are binding although they do not take the form of either a charter or a Bill of Lading, such as berth notes. Vessels are often loaded on the berth, a middleman undertaking with the shipowner either to ship cargo or to procure cargo to be shipped. In those cases the shipowner has the right to receive cargo and to earn freight for its carriage; and as soon as in pursuance of such a contract his ship starts on the contracted voyage he has commenced to earn that remuneration, whether it be called freight, or chartered freight, or freight as if

111. [1912] 3 K.B. 51, 81 L.J.K.B. 1066.

chartered. It has often been said that freight involves the possession of goods implying a contract to carry or a legal right to have goods for carriage with a view to earning freight. But I cannot find that the words freight, or chartered freight, or freight as if chartered have ever been applied to the expectation, however well founded, that a ship's agents will procure a cargo for her where there is no actual binding engagement to that effect.

In the *Roanoke*,[112] two marine policies were issued on freight, one on "freight on board or not on board" the vessel at and from A to B, "while there and until loaded," and the other on "collect freight shipped or to be shipped" on board her at and from B to A. She sailed from A for several way ports with cargo on which the freight had been prepaid and earned, "vessel or goods lost or not lost," but foundered before reaching B. The court observed that in light of the circumstances, it was clear that the phrase "freight on board or not on board" referred to chartered freight and that the intention was to insure only the freight to be earned on the return voyage from B to A as the vessel owner had no other freight at risk since the bill of lading freight on the first leg of the voyage was prepaid and non-returnable.[113] The court also noted that it was by no means uncommon to insure during a previous voyage the freight to be earned on a subsequent voyage.

In *Williams & Co. v. Canton Ins. Office Ltd.*,[114] the court had occasion to construe the term "freight chartered or as if chartered" in these words:

> The term "chartered freight" is free from ambiguity, and means the freight, if any, made payable by the terms of the charterparty, i.e., in this case the lump sum of £3,000. The phrase, "chartered or as if chartered" is alternative in form; if there is a chartered freight for certain goods or for a certain space in the ship, that is the freight insured, and no other freight for the same goods or space can be added to it or substituted for it if the Underwriters' risk is altered. The alternative "or as if chartered" applies to freight, or what in business is treated as freight, although not made payable by the express terms of any charterparty—e.g. if the shipowner carries other people's goods without a charterparty, or perhaps if he carries his own goods. The phrase "as if chartered" would also cover freight payable under a charterparty entered into after the date of the policy, if the policy without those words would not extend to such freight.

112. 298 F. 1 (9th Cir.), 1924 AMC 790. See, also, *The Sephie*, 9 F.2d 304 (2d Cir.), 1926 AMC 447, and *Robinson v. Manufacturers' Ins. Co.*, 42 Mass. 143 (1840).

113. Citing *The Bedouin, supra*, and *Williams & Co. v. Canton Ins. Office Ltd.*, [1901] A.C. 462. See, also, *Santa Christina*, 26 F.2d 967 (2d Cir.), 1928 AMC 1074.

114. *Supra*, n. 113.

Insurable Interest

Although discussed in greater detail in Chapter VII, "Insurable Interest," it is timely to note that there must be a binding engagement with respect to cargo before there is an insurable interest in freight. Consequently, if only part of the cargo to which insurance on freight is to apply has been loaded on board the vessel or has actually been contracted for at the time the loss occurs, then the underwriter is liable only for such proportion of the amount insured as the part of the cargo actually aboard bears to the whole of the cargo which is to be shipped. This was the holding in *Forbes v. Aspinall*,[115] where part of the cargo had been loaded when the vessel was lost. As there was no contract for the cargo which had not been loaded, even though it was a moral certainty it would have been loaded but for the loss of the vessel, there was no loss of freight as to the portion not loaded. Moreover, a mere expectation of earning freight is not the same as there being freight at risk.[116] Unless the shipowner has a contract with another person under which he is to earn freight, and unless steps have been taken or expenses incurred toward earning it, then his interest is merely a contingent one. If, however, there is a contract, and steps have been taken to carry out the voyage, the interest ceases to be contingent and becomes inchoate.[116a] If that interest is subsequently destroyed by one of the perils insured against then freight has been lost and, if insured, underwriters are liable.

The rules relating to the attachment of freight risks is set forth in Rule for Construction No. 3(c) and (d) reading:

> (c) Where chartered freight is insured "at and from" a particular place, and the ship is at that place in good safety when the contract is concluded the risk attaches immediately. If she be not there when the contract is concluded, the risk attaches as soon as she arrives there in good safety.[117]

> (d) Where freight, other than chartered freight, is payable without special conditions and is insured "at and from" a particular place, the risk attaches pro rata as the goods or merchandise are shipped; provided that if there be cargo in readiness which belongs to the

---

115. (1811) 104 E.R. 394. See, also, *The Main*, (1894) P. 320. Compare, *Stillwell v. Home Ins. Co.*, F.Cas. 13,450 (Mo. 1874).

116. *Barber v. Fleming*, (1869) 39 L.J.Q.B. 25. See, also, *Manning v. National Fire & Marine Ins. Co. of New Zealand*, (1878) 1 S.C.R. (N.S.) (N.S.W.) 81 (insurance of "profits" without specifying what profits); *Robey v. Adelaide Ins. Co.*, (1878) 1 S.C.R. (N.S.) (N.S.W.) 236 ("profits" mean profits on goods as to which the risk does not run until laden on board).

116a. See *Jordan v. Great Western Ins. Co.*, (1885) 24 N.B.R. 421, *rev'd* on other grounds, 14 S.C.R. 734, relating to chartered freight where the voyage had commenced.

117. *Foley v. United Mar. Ins. Co.*, (1866) L.R. 1 Ex. 206.

shipowner, or which some other person has contracted with him to ship, the risk attaches as soon as the ship is ready to receive such cargo.[118]

Measure of Indemnity for Partial Loss of Freight

As noted heretofore, the measure of indemnity for a partial loss of freight is set forth in Section 70 of the Act. To illustrate, assume that the freight to be earned on a cargo of logs from the Pacific Northwest to Japan is $80,000. The freight is, however, insured for $100,000 "in and/or over."[119] During the voyage, the lashings break and a number of logs, on which the freight is $20,000, are washed overboard in heavy weather. Using the proportionate formula of Section 70, it will be observed that the actual freight was overinsured by 25 percent; applying the 25 percent to the $20,000 loss of deck cargo freight results in a loss payable by underwriters of $25,000.[120]

This seems relatively simple. But the calculation becomes more complex if, as to that portion paid in advance, the shipowner has no insurable interest. This was the situation in *The Main,*[121] where the valuation in the policy was based upon the current freight rates at the time and totalled £5,500. By the time the risk commenced, freight rates had declined to the point where the actual freight at risk was only £3,250, of which £952 had been paid in advance. While it was held that the valuation in the policy was binding, in view of the assured's lack of insurable interest in that portion paid in advance, the court held that the valuation had to be reduced proportionately. This was accomplished by deducting the advance freight paid from the total freight at risk, leaving the actual freight at risk only £2,298. Applying the proportionate formula resulted in a calculation that the £2,298 actually at risk should be insured for £3,889. The vessel was lost by fire on its voyage. The assured was held entitled to recover the sum of £3,889 as well as a small proportionate return of premium for the short interest. The underwriters attempted to argue that *Forbes v. Aspinwall* governed but the court distinguished that case by pointing out that it was not authority for the contention that if the value of what is about to be

118. As to special conditions, see *The Copernicus,* [1896] P. 237, C.A. ("engagement of goods"). Cf. *Jones v. Neptune Ins. Co.,* (1872) L.R. 7 Q.B. 702. As to "good safety," see *Lidgett v. Secretan,* (1870) L.R. 5 C.P. 190.

119. Meaning cargo which could be stowed either below decks or on deck. Generally speaking, a freight policy only covers freight to be carried under deck. *Adams v. Warren Ins. Co.,* 39 Mass. 163 (1839).

120. Subject, of course, to any express provision in the policy. As pointed out heretofore, Clause 7 of the Institute Freight Clauses limits a claim for loss of freight not to exceed the gross freight. Thus, had the shipment in the example been insured under the Institute Freight Clauses, maximum recovery would have been $20,000.

121. [1894] P. 320.

shipped, or the value of the freight on what is about to be shipped, is estimated too highly originally, and the assured is mistaken in his valuation, the valuation ought to be reduced.

Where there is a lump sum valuation covering a varied assortment of goods, it is very difficult to arrive at a correct valuation of a full interest on a constituent part of the goods when only a part is lost. It then becomes necessary for the court to examine all the constituents of the freight valuation in order to arrive at the correct determination of liability. This is termed "opening the valuation."[122]

Impact of Disbursements Warranty on Freight

The Disbursements Warranty (Clause 20 of the Institute Time Hulls form and Lines 210-238 of the American Institute Hulls (1977) form) has already been discussed elsewhere in relation to total losses. Essentially, it permits additional insurances such as disbursements, commissions, profits, freight, increased value, and the like. Freight insurances are permitted up to 25 percent of the hull value, less any sum insured on disbursements, etc., which are restricted to 10 percent of the hull value. Usually, the shipowner insures disbursements for 10 percent of hull value and freight for 15 percent of that value.

The task facing the shipowner is to calculate the freight which could be earned on any one voyage. If the anticipated freight to be earned exceeds the permitted limits, and he insures for the full anticipated freight, he could thereby breach the warranty and the underwriters would have the right to decline liability for claims on the ship as from the date of the breach. Under the provisions of the Disbursements Warranty, however, certain excess insurances are permitted under sub-sections (c), (d), and (e), after taking into account any sums insured under sub-section (b). It is quite possible that some of these excesses could be insured under a time policy and others under a voyage policy. In the event of a loss by an insured peril, resulting in a loss of freight, it is quite possible that the loss of freight would have to be apportioned between the respective underwriters on the time and voyage policies as the amount payable cannot exceed the gross freight at risk.

---

122. See *Asfar v. Blundell*, (1895) 2 Q.B. 196, (1896) 1 Q.B. 123, 65 L.J.Q.B. 138 (involving charterer's profit freight where the charterer recovered only the difference between chartered hire and bills of lading freight after taking into account advances and another insurance policy), and *Denoon v. Home and Colonial Assurance Co.*, (1872) L.R. 7 C.P. 341, 26 L.T. 628, 1 Asp. M.L.C. 309 (freight insurance on a cargo of rice where shipowner also carried coolies and obtained passage money). See, also, *McGaw v. Ocean Ins. Co.*, 23 Mass. 405 (1839), where the cargo was cotton and tobacco, the freight being valued at an entire sum. Thus, the valuation was applied proportionately.

Cesser Clause

The common "cesser clause" has been discussed in connection with *The Bedouin, supra*. The clause customarily comes into play where the vessel is under charter and is prevented from working for a period of more than 24 hours and continues until she is once more in an efficient state to resume the voyage. As noted, the loss of hire to the shipowner would be at his risk under the charter party and under the common form of freight policy would be insurable. Underwriters tend to regard this type of loss as being similar to delay as to which no underwriter wishes to insure. As a consequence, underwriters inserted the Time Penalty Clause in the standard Institute Freight Clauses, reading:

> Warranted free from any claim consequent on loss of time whether arising from a peril of the sea or otherwise.[123]

The efficacy of the Time Penalty Clause was tested in *Naviera de Canarias, S.A. v. Nacional Hispanica Aseguradora, S.A. (The Playa de las Nieves)*.[124] There, the vessel was chartered under the New York Produce Exchange time charter form. It stranded due to a latent defect causing a machinery breakdown but not from a want of due diligence by the shipowner. The vessel was eventually salved and taken to a port where repairs were effected, thereby enabling the vessel to resume her voyage. The shipowner plaintiff contended that the proximate cause of the loss was perils of the seas, or, alternatively, latent defects in the machinery, and that once these perils became operative and the vessel was damaged, hire was lost day by day. Thus, a claim could be submitted without relying upon loss of time. The plaintiff further argued that if the Time Penalty Clause applied, this would mean that recovery would be limited to a situation in which the vessel was an actual or constructive total loss, and the freight clauses would simply be a "trap for the unwary."

The trial judge was not impressed with the "trap" argument. He said, in part:

> First, marine insurance is a technical matter and marine policies on large commercial vessels are not intended for do-it-yourself enthusi-

123. This does not mean, of course, that loss of hire cannot be insured at all. To the contrary, Loss of Hire insurance is available and can be procured—for a premium.
124. [1976] 3 W.L.R. 45, [1976] 3 All E.R. 167, [1976] 2 Lloyd's Rep. 80, [1975] 1 Lloyd's Rep. 259, [1977] 1 Lloyd's Rep. 457, [1978] A.C. 853. See, also, *Bensaude v. Thames and Mersey Marine Ins. Co., Ltd.*, [1897] A.C. 809; *Atlantic Maritime Co., Inc. v. Gibbon*, [1954] 1 Q.B. 88; *Turnbull v. Hull Underwriters' Association*, [1900] 2 Q.B. 402; and *Russian Bank for Foreign Trade v. Excess Insurance Co.*, [1918] 2 K.B. 123, *aff'd* on other grounds [1919] 1 K.B. 39; *Wilson Bros. Bobbin Co. v. Green*, [1917] 22 Com.Cas. 185, 31 T.L.R. 605. Contrast, however, *Robertson v. Nomikos*, [1939] A.C. 371; *Roura & Forgas v. Townsend*, [1919] 1 K.B. 189; and *Carras v. London and Scottish Assurance Co.*, [1936] 1 K.B. 291.

asts. . . . Second, if the policy has the limited application suggested, this fact will no doubt be reflected in the premium.

The trial court also held that a loss of time remained an essential element. In order to prove a loss the shipowner had to resort to the appropriate clause in the time charter which necessarily involved him in showing some loss of time because of the wording of the clause. Although the court of appeal reversed, the House of Lords unanimously reinstated the trial court's decision on the ground that no other result was compatible with the plain meaning of the words of the Time Penalty Clause.[125]

Memorandum Clause in Freight Policies

The Institute Time Clauses (freight) contain a "memorandum clause" (Clause 4) reading:

> Warranted free from particular average under 3 per cent, unless the Vessel be stranded, sunk, or on fire, the Underwriters notwithstanding this warranty to pay for any loss caused by fire or collision with another vessel. Each craft and/or lighter to be deemed a separate insurance if desired by the Assured.

Thus, it will be seen that if the loss of freight is caused by fire or collision with another vessel, it is payable without regard to the franchise, while with respect to the vessel being stranded, sunk, or on fire, the warranty is nullified whether the loss of freight occurs before or after such occurrence.[125a] In the case of time policies, the 3 percent franchise is applied to the freight at risk at the time of loss, whereas in voyage policies it is applied to the freight at risk at the inception of the voyage.

Particular Average on Cargo

The rules with respect to partial loss of goods and merchandise differ significantly from partial loss of a ship or vessel. Section 71, Marine Insurance Act, 1906, states the rules with respect to particular average on cargo, as follows:

> Where there is a partial loss of goods, merchandise, or other moveables, the measure of indemnity, subject to any express provision of the policy, is as follows:

125. For illustrations of how freight claims for particular average losses are to be calculated, see the excellent discussion on this subject in *Marine Insurance Claims*, (2d ed.), by J. Kenneth Goodacre, p. 367-381, Witherby & Co. Ltd., London (1981).

125a. If the loss is not caused by one of the specified perils, the memorandum is not "opened" and underwriters are liable only for a total loss. *Hugg v. Augusta Ins. & Banking Co. of City of Augusta*, 48 U.S. 595 (1849).

(1) Where part of the goods, merchandise or other moveables insured by a valued policy is totally lost, the measure of indemnity is such proportion of the sum fixed by the policy as the insurable value of the part lost bears to the insurable value of the whole, ascertained as in the case of an unvalued policy;

(2) Where part of the goods, merchandise, or other moveables insured by an unvalued policy is totally lost, the measure of indemnity is the insurable value of the part lost, ascertained as in case of total loss;

As will be seen, sub-section (1) deals with a *total* loss of a part of the insured goods under *valued* policies. Sub-section (2) deals with a *total* loss of a part of the insured goods under *unvalued* policies.

In the case of sub-section (1) the liability for a total loss of a part of the cargo insured is the insured value of the part which is lost ascertained by a simple calculation; i.e., the proportion the insurable value bears to the insurable value of the whole cargo insured, which proportion is applied to the insured value. When the policy is an unvalued one, the liability is, of course, for the insurable value of the part lost.

The following examples will be helpful. Assume that 100 bales of cotton are insured under a policy for $100,000, valued at $1,000 per bale. One bale is totally lost by an insured peril. The liability under the policy is $1,000. However, let us suppose that the policy describes the interest insured as 100 bales of cotton valued at $100,000 but the insured interest consists of 10 lots, each consisting of 10 bales of a different grade of cotton and of a different value. In order to determine the amount recoverable, reference must be made to sub-section (1) of Section 71 to arrive at the insured value of the bale which is lost. The insurable value will fall to be determined in accordance with Section 16(3) of the Act; i.e., the prime cost of the bale insured, plus the expenses of, and incidental to, the shipping and charges of insurance upon the whole.

Where, however, different kinds of property are insured under one valuation, sub-sections (1) and (2) of Section 72 apply. For example, let us suppose that the policy describes the interest insured as "100 bales of cotton and 10 bales of rubber, valued at $110,000." Sub-sections (1) and (2) read:

(1) Where different species of property are insured under a single valuation, the valuation must be apportioned over the different species in proportion to their respective insured values, as in the case of an unvalued policy. The insured value of any part of a species is such proportion of the total insured value of the same as the insurable value of the part bears to the insurable value of the whole, ascertained in both cases as provided by this Act.

(2) Where a valuation has to be apportioned, and particulars of the prime cost of each separate species, quality, or description of goods cannot be ascertained, the division of the valuation may be made over the net arrived sound values of the different species, qualities, or descriptions of goods.

As a matter of practice, the apportionment of the valuation over the various interests insured is frequently based upon the invoice values of the goods insured. Although this method does not comport precisely with the provisions of the Act, it is certainly more convenient. In fact, this method has been approved by the average adjusters and has been incorporated in the British Average Adjusters Association Rules of Practice as Rule E(3). No such rule appears in the American Association of Average Adjusters' Rules but the same principle is applied.

It will be observed that sub-section (2) of Section 72 provides for situations in which there are no means of arriving at the insurable value of the goods lost. In such cases, the net arrived values of the different species are utilized. This problem frequently arises when the goods are sold on consignment. There, the goods are to be sold in the country of destination by agents for the best price obtainable. The insured values of the shipments are customarily based upon the shipper's best estimate of what the goods will bring on sale. If it becomes necessary to apportion a loss, the calculation is made in accordance with the provisions of sub-section (2). As a practical matter, the values ascertained by a sale usually take the place of invoice values. For example, one bale of cotton is offloaded in a damaged condition out of a consignment of four bales which have an insured value of $5,000. The calculation works out as follows:

	Sales Price
Bales 1 and 2 (sound) at $1,000 per bale	$2,000
Bale No. 3 (sound) at $1,100 per bale	1,100
Bale No. 4 (damaged) at $900 per bale	
Sound portion (50%)	450
Damaged portion (50%)	225
	$3,775

Insured Value Apportioned		
	Sound Value	*Insured Value*
Bales 1 and 2	$2,000	$2,500
Bale No. 3	1,100	1,375
Bale No. 4		
Damaged portion should realize	450	562.50
Sound portion brings	450	562.50
	$4,000	$5,000.00

Thus, instead of realizing $450, the damaged portion of the bale only brought in $225, demonstrating a loss of $225 on sale. Consequently, as $4,000 is insured for $5,000, $225 is insured for $281.

Apportionable Part

It is necessary, however, to draw a distinction between straight apportionments under Section 72 and what has been termed "apportionment of the contract." This can be quite important in F.P.A. policies. For example, Section 76(1) of the Act provides:

> Where the subject-matter insured is warranted free from particular average, the assured cannot recover for a loss of part, other than a loss incurred by a general average sacrifice, unless the contract contained in the policy be apportionable; but, if the contract be apportionable, the assured may recover for a total loss of any apportionable part.

Under F.P.A. policies, particular average claims are not generally recoverable but claims for total loss under the policy are recoverable. Consequently, *if the contract is apportionable,* the underwriters are liable for a total loss of an apportionable part.

This aspect of the damage calculus can be demonstrated by several cases. For example, in *Hills v. London Assurance Corp.,*[126] insurance was placed on wheat shipped in bulk and valued at £1,600, warranted free from average except general, or the ship be stranded. On the voyage the ship met with heavy weather and made considerable water. In pumping the water out, wheat to the value of about £75 was pumped out with the water and lost. It was held that the plaintiff insured could not recover as for a total loss of the part so lost.

Merely because the shipment is made in separate packages does not make the contract apportionable where the goods are all of one species and are insured in bulk. This was decided in *Ralli v. Janson*[127] where 2,688 bags of linseed were insured on the vessel *Waban* for £1,600. During the voyage, 1,023 bags were damaged by sea perils to the extent that a large portion of the linseed in them was thrown into the sea as being worthless and the rest was sold. The remaining bags were uninjured and were delivered to the assured. The goods were warranted "free from average, unless general, or the ship be stranded." As the ship was not stranded and there was no general average, it was held that the assured could not recover. In the absence of any separate valuation, or any other stipulation in the policy showing that it was intended to distinguish one portion of the seed from another, and to make a separate insurance upon each portion,

---

126. (1839) 9 L.J. Ex. 25, 151 E.R. 241.
127. (1856) 119 E.R. 922, *sub nom Janson v. Ralli,* 25 L.J.Q.B. 300.

as well as a joint one upon all, the policy was upon the whole of the seed. The loss was a partial loss only of the subject-matter insured and the underwriters were therefore protected by the memorandum clause.

Where, however, a single valuation is applied to cover goods of varying species, the valuation may be divided over the different species. As a result, even though the policy be on F.P.A. terms, underwriters respond to particular average claims. This first arose in *Duff v. McKenzie*,[128] where the master insured his personal effects "free from all average" and claimed successfully for the loss of a gold watch. The court held that the word "effects" was obviously employed to save the task of enumerating the nautical instruments, the chronometer, the clothes, the books, etc., of which they happened to consist, and, even though they were insured free of average and the insurer would not have been liable for any amount of sea damage to them short of a total loss, it did not do violence to the language to hold that underwriters would not be exempted from a total loss of any of the articles of which the "effects" consisted.

Where cargo is shipped in separate packages, each of which is separately insured, if there is a total loss of any package even under F.P.A. conditions, then the assured recovers for the total loss of each package. Consequently, if each barrel of a shipment is separately valued, the loss of one barrel would be paid as a total loss of a part of the shipment.[129]

Perhaps the best explanation of the principle of apportionable parts will be found in *La Fabrique de Produits Chimiques Societe Anonyme v. Large*.[130] In that case, three distinct parcels of perishable goods, namely,

---

128. (1857) 140 E.R. 643. See, also, *Wilkinson v. Hyde*, (1858) 140 E.R. 649, where the plaintiff insured £240 on any kind of goods aboard a ship against total loss, and afterwards put on board an emigrant's equipment, consisting of a variety of tools, materials, etc., in several separate packages, and all were lost except three small packages of small value. It was held he could recover for the total loss of the packages which were totally lost. See, also, *Canton Ins. Office v. Woodside*, 90 F. 301 (D. Cal. 1897), where there was a total loss of some personal effects under a policy warranted free from all average. The court held that the language, being ambiguous, would be construed as a severable contract and the assured was entitled to recover for each article totally lost.

129. See *Entwhistle v. Ellis*, (1857) 157 E.R. 226, where the insurance was on bags of rice, all valued at the same amount. Being the same species under one valuation, the assured was held not entitled to recovery for the loss of separate, individual bags. Cf. *Hills v. London Assur. Corp., supra*, n. 126. Frequently, however, underwriters will agree to amend the policies to state "each package is to be deemed a separate valuation."

130. [1923] 1 K.B. 203, [1922] All E.R. Rep. 372, 13 Ll.L.Rep. 269. See, also, *California Canneries Co. v. Canton Ins. Office*, 143 P. 549, 25 Cal.App. 303 (St. Cal. 1914); *Canton Ins. Office v. Woodside, supra*, n. 128; *Chicago Ins. Co. v. Graham & Morton Transp. Co.*, 108 F. 271 (7th Cir. 1901); *Singer Mfg. Co. v. Western Assur. Co.*, (1896) 10 Que. S.C. 379 (C.A. Can.) (policy on 116 sewing machines each valued at $30; assured held entitled to claim for a total loss on some only of the machines); *Mowat v. Boston Marine Ins. Co.*, (1896) 26 S.C.R. 47 (Can.) (policy language modified memorandum clause so as to cover total loss of a part); *Moore v. Provincial Ins. Co.*, (1873) 23 U.C.C.P. 383 (C.A. Can.) (where goods of the same species, shipped in packages, are insured free from average unless general, and it is not distinctly expressed that the packages are separately insured, the ordinary memorandum exempts underwriters from liability for a total loss of a part only, even though one or more

two parcels of vanillin and one parcel of caffeine, all separately valued, were insured against certain perils in a lump sum made up of the separate values of the parcels, the policy containing a clause by which it was warranted free from particular average. The two parcels of vanillin were lost by one of the perils insured against, i.e., thieves. The court held that the contract of insurance was apportionable as between the several parcels of goods, the loss being a total loss of a severable part of the goods insured and not a particular average loss of the whole. In doing so, the court said:

> Where perishable goods are insured for a lump sum and in bulk, and the bulk is of the same description, then the total loss of part of the bulk gives no claim under a policy which is F.P.A. It is a particular average loss . . . . Very often there are express words in a policy which makes each package a separate insurance. In that case the loss of one package is a total loss of that particular package, and the Underwriters are liable, although the policy is F.P.A. . . . Sometimes there is an insurance in one sum on goods actually distinct and of very different kinds. An instance was given of the master of a ship who insured all his effects, which were of such different kinds as a feather bed and a chronometer. They were insured by one sum, but it was held in that case that the effects were so distinguishable that the loss of one particular thing was a total loss of that particular article, and not a particular average loss of the whole. Another instance was the case of an immigrant going to a hotel who had all sorts of equipment, and although there was one general insurance of the whole, it was held that the packages were of such distinct character that the loss of one package was a total loss of that package, and not a particular average loss of the whole. It has been held that even though the species are the same, yet if contained in cases or packages which are themselves separately valued, that the loss of one of these packages is a total loss of that package, and not a particular average loss of the whole. In this case not only are the goods of different species—the two cases lost being vanillin and the one left being caffeine—but, as a matter of fact, each case has a separate value attributed to it.

In *Jones v. Niagara*,[131] the policy of cargo insurance covered a shipment of glazed ceramic tile from California to the Canal Zone. Upon arrival, it was found that about 10 percent of the shipment was broken. The policy contained a memorandum clause. The court held that partial loss

packages are totally lost by the specific perils named in the policy); *Sillars v. Royal Ins. Co.*, (1882) 6 Nfld. L.R. 410 (Can.); *Lempriere v. Miller*, (1871) 2 F.R. 26, 2 A.J.R. 18 (Aus.) (loss of 26 horses out of 66 insured; held, not a total loss of a part).

131. 170 F.2d 667 (4th Cir.), 1951 AMC 1401. The case has been criticized as not being in accord with the intent of the policy nor in accord with practice.

by breakage or negligence of stevedores is not a total loss of a part of the shipment even though the part totally lost consisted of one or more entire packages.

In *Larsen v. Ins. Co. of N.A.*,[132] 21 tierces of salmon were shipped from Alaska to Seattle, Washington. Upon arrival, it was found that 11 of the 21 tierces were spoiled. The policy contained a refrigeration insurance rider which read, in relevant part:

> Warranted free from Particular Average unless directly caused by the vessel being stranded, sunk, burnt or in collision with another ship or vessel or with ice or with any substance other than water . . . .

Plaintiff argued an entire loss of part of the goods of the same species, shipped and insured in bulk, was intended to be treated as a total loss. The court, however, held against this contention, noting that it seemed "clear that the 21 tierces of salmon were included as a single, unapportionable shipping packages and that the 11 tierces do not constitute an apportionable part of this package within the authorities." The court further held that although there had been a fire aboard the vessel and although the vessel had stranded for a short time, neither incident was "directly caused" as required by the clause. The court also held that the error of the ship's engineer in permitting the refrigeration equipment to be shut down for a short time was an error in the care, custody, and control of the vessel and not related to the navigation and management of the vessel.

By contrast, in *Panama City*,[133] there was a breakdown in one of the vessel's two boilers, necessitating the shutting off of steam to the refrigeration plant for more than 24 hours in order to maintain maneuverability at sea and reach port, resulting in an overripening of a cargo of bananas; the court held that the loss fell within the terms of the particular average clause covering damage or deterioration "caused by breakdown and/or latent defect of refrigerator machinery and/or plant."

Thus, what constitutes an "apportionable part" is clearly established by the decisions. Application of the principle actually results in an extension of underwriters' liability, and permits an assured to recover for the loss of an individual package which normally would not be recoverable as particular average unless the memorandum warranty is "opened" or the loss occurred during loading, transshipment, or discharge as is frequently provided in cargo coverage.

It should also be noted that the "Craft Clause" in standard cargo policies may be applicable as each "craft" is deemed to be a separate insurance. The standard form of policy covers craft risk at destination, but

---

132. 252 F.Supp. 458, 1965 AMC 2576 (W.D. Wash.).
133. 93 F.Supp. 431, 1950 AMC 1992 (S.D. Ala.).

does not cover this risk at the port of shipment. The Craft Clause (Clause 3 of Institute Cargo Clauses [F.P.A.]) overcomes this deficiency.[134]

Partial Damage to Cargo

Sub-sections (3) and (4) of Section 71 of the Act set forth the rules to be applied where cargo has been partially damaged by an insured peril. They read as follows:

> (3) Where the whole or any part of the goods or merchandise insured has been delivered damaged at its destination, the measure of indemnity is such proportion of the sum fixed by the policy in the case of a valued policy, or of the insurable value in the case of an unvalued policy, as the difference between the gross sound and damaged values at the place of arrival bears to the gross sound value.

> (4) "Gross value" means the wholesale price or, if there be no such price, the estimated value, with, in either case, freight, landing charges, and duty paid beforehand; provided that, in the case of goods or merchandise customarily sold in bond, the bonded price is deemed to be the gross value. "Gross proceeds" means the actual price obtainable at a sale where all charges on sale are paid by the sellers.

Shippers, in the event of damage to their goods, erroneously assume that the underwriters should pay them the difference between the insured value of the goods and the net amount derived from sale. This would, of course, result in the underwriters paying a different amount depending upon whether there was a rise or fall in the market—a subject which does not in the least interest underwriters. Payment on this basis is correctly termed a "salvage loss" and can only occur where there is a special wording in the policy,[135] or the cargo is necessarily sold short of its destination.[136] The following will illustrate the basic principle involved:

---

134. See, in this connection, *South British Fire & Marine Ins. Co. v. Da Costa*, [1906] 1 K.B. 456, and *General Ins. Co. of Trieste v. Royal Exchange Assurance*, [1897] 2 Com.Cas. 144.

135. See *Berns & Koppstein, Inc. v. Orion Ins. Co. Ltd.*, 273 F.2d 415, 1960 AMC 1379, [1960] 1 Lloyd's Rep. 276 (2d Cir.), affirming *per curiam* the District Court, 170 F.Supp. 707, 1959 AMC 2455 (S.D.N.Y.). There, the consignee of insect-infested peanuts, detained by U. S. customs authorities, notified its underwriters' New York agents who reconditioned the cargo to pass customs inspection and reduce the damages on resale to the insured's customers. The standard form of Lloyd's policy contained a special rider for "rejection" insurance covering loss from detention and/or rejection in customs "for any reasons whatsoever." It was held that under the rejection clause, the assured could recover its damages in full, reconditioning being solely at the expense and for the benefit of the insurer. Under the rejection clause, the peril insured against was the act of the government customs authorities, not the putrid condition of the goods. Compare *Snyder, Int. v. Dae Han Fire & Mar. Ins. Co.*, 1981 AMC 2685 (D. Mass.), where coverage was denied because the assured failed to comply with government regulations.

136. This can occur when the underwriter pays the difference between the total insured value and the net proceeds of sale at a place short of the destination of the goods,

	Rising market	Falling market
Arrived sound value (gross)	$1,500	$1,200
Arrived damaged value (gross)	1,000	800
	$ 500	$ 400
or	33 ⅓%	33⅓%

The percentage thus arrived at is then applied to the insured or insurable value depending upon whether the policy is valued or unvalued.

This principle was first laid down in *Lewis v. Rucker*,[137] where a cargo of sugar arrived damaged by seawater, the damaged hogsheads realizing £20 0s 8d each instead of £23 7s 8d per hogshead if sound, the difference being £3 7s 0d. The insured value of each hogshead was £30. The insured contended that he should recover £9 19s 4d per hogshead, the difference between £30 and £20 0s 8d. Lord Mansfield held, however, that the underwriter could not be concerned with fluctuations in market prices and pointed out the consequences if the assured's contention were to prevail; i.e., that the underwriter would pay a different sum on a falling market versus a rising market.

This point was again considered in *Johnson v. Sheddon*.[138] In that case, it was held that a settlement based on net values would result in fluctuation of claims by reason of the same charges being levied against damaged goods as against sound goods such as, for example, duty, freight, sales charges, etc.

Three examples will demonstrate the correct calculation:

Stable Market

	Sound value	Damaged value	Loss
Gross	$1,000	$500	$500 (50% of $1,000)
Freight, duties, etc.	200	200	
Net	800	300	$500 (62.5% of $800)

Rising Market

	Sound value	Damaged value	Loss
Gross	$1,200	$600	$600 (50% of $1,200)
Freight, duties, etc.	200	200	
Net	$1,000	$400	$600 (60% of $1,000)

---

because the goods can be sold to better advantage than if they were reconditioned and forwarded on to destination. The option to do so rests with the underwriter.

137. (1761) 97 E.R. 769. See, also, *Berns & Koppstein v. Orion Ins. Co.*, 170 F.Supp. 707, 1959 AMC 2455, 272 F.2d 415, 1960 AMC 1379 (S.D.N.Y.).

138. (1802) 102 E.R. 492.

Falling Market

	Sound value	Damaged value	Loss
Gross	$800	$400	$400 (50% of $800)
Freight, duties, etc.	200	200	
Net	$600	$200	$400 (66⅔% of $600)

In the three examples given, the percentage of depreciation on gross values remains constant at 50 percent but on net values the percentage rises as the market goes down.

Francis v. Boulton[139] involved another allied point; i.e., when damaged goods are sold and sound and damaged values are compared to determine the percentage depreciation, both values must be ascertained as of the date of sale; otherwise, market fluctuations would again distort the calculations. In that case, a lighter was sunk while carrying rice and subsequently raised, the rice being reconditioned and sold. It was held that there had not been a total loss of the rice as it was, in fact, sold as rice and that the proper method was by comparing sound and damaged values as of the date of sale. The underwriter was also held liable for the reconditioning costs under the Sue and Labor Clause.

In practice, the depreciation in value of damaged cargo is more often determined by agreement between the assured and the underwriter than by sale and the percentage depreciation is then applied to the insured value in order to fix the amount recoverable under the policy.

Goods Sold in Bond

Sub-section (4) of Section 71 contains an exception with respect to goods sold in bond, and provides that the bonded price is to be deemed the gross value. This is so because when goods are "in bond" they are stored under customs control in warehouses duty-free and the duty need only be paid when the goods are withdrawn. The "bonded price" is, therefore, the value before duty is paid. When the new owner (purchaser) withdraws damaged goods from bond, he must pay the duty. Consequently, "like must be compared with like" and the same basis is applied; i.e., when the damaged value is the bonded price, then the sound value must also be the bonded price.

Moveables Other Than Goods or Merchandise

Where goods or merchandise in general demand arrive at the port of destination, it is relatively simple to apply the proportionate calculation

---

139. (1895) 65 L.J.Q.B. 153, 8 Asp. M.L.C. 79. See, also, *Zack Metal v. Federal Ins. Co.*, 1960 AMC 1384 (N.Y.A.D.).

called for in sub-sections (3) and (4), because there are regular markets and auctions at which the values can be determined. This may not be the case where moveables of a specialized nature are involved as there may be no market demand whatever. Reference to Section 71 will show that while the first part of the section and sub-sections (1) and (2) use the terms "goods, merchandise, or other moveables," sub-sections (3) and (4) refer only to "goods or merchandise" and no rule is prescribed with respect to indemnity for "other moveables" which are delivered in a damaged condition. Reference must, therefore, be made to Section 75(1) of the Act which reads:

> (1) Where there has been a loss in respect of any subject-matter not expressly provided for in the foregoing provisions of this Act, the measure of indemnity shall be ascertained, as nearly as may be, in accordance with those provisions, in so far as applicable to the particular case.[140]

In practice, the extent of recovery is often resolved by the claim being settled on the basis of the cost of reconditioning or repair and the cost may be recoverable under the Sue and Labor Clause. See *Francis v. Boulton, supra.*

Replacement Clause

It is not at all unusual for shipments involving machinery to include the Institute Replacement Clause reading:

> In the event of loss of or damage to any part or parts of an insured machine caused by a peril covered by the Policy the sum recoverable shall not exceed the cost of replacement or repair of such part or parts, plus charges for forwarding and refitting, if incurred, but excluding duty unless the full duty is included in the amount insured, in which case loss, if any, sustained by payment of additional duty shall also be recoverable.
>
> Provided always that in no case shall the liability of underwriters exceed the insured value of the complete machine.

The limitation to the cost of repair or replacement, together with associated charges, enables the underwriter to avoid a forced sale and a consequent disproportionate loss. Moreover, the clause precludes the assured from claiming a total loss on the ground of a loss of "species."

---

140. For example, the loss of part of a machine rendering the whole machine valueless. See *British Columbia Sawmill Co. v. Nettleship*, (1868) L.R. 3 C.P. 499.

Unidentifiable Cargo

Occasionally, cargo will arrive at destination in specie but with all marks obliterated and, as a consequence, the owners cannot be identified. Section 56(5) of the Act provides that any loss of this type shall be treated as a partial loss:

> (5) Where goods reach their destination in specie, but by reason of obliteration of marks, or otherwise, they are incapable of indentification, the loss, if any, is partial, and not total.

It should be obvious that the absence or obliteration of marks on the cargo may be due to the fault of the shipper in which case there has been no insured peril. On the other hand, if the marks are missing or obliterated by reason of an insured peril, some method must be used to distribute the cargo to the consignees. In practice, the consignees are treated as tenants in common and the goods distributed as equitably as possible. Where, upon arrival, goods are so damaged and unidentifiable that there is no practical way to deliver them to the consignees, they are frequently sold and the proceeds of the sale distributed. This rather unusual situation occurred in *Spence v. Union Marine Ins. Co.*[141] There, the vessel was wrecked and only 617 bales of cotton arrived at destination with intact marks although some of the bales were damaged. These bales were sold in due course. Of the remaining 1,876 bales, 231 were totally lost and 1,645 were so damaged as to be incapable of identification. The solution of the court was to allocate to each consignee that proportion of the damaged and lost bales as he had failed to receive in accordance with the rule in cases of general average where it is not known whose goods have been sacrificed.

Increase in Weight by Reason of Water

Some articles, such as wool, hides, tobacco, etc., are hygroscopic; i.e., they gain in weight during transit due to their absorbent characteristics. It would be unfair to the underwriter to require him to pay for an increase in weight due to absorption of moisture. Consequently, to arrive at the sound value of the damaged goods, any increase in weight must be ascertained and deducted from the damaged weight. This poses no problem where some of the same cargo arrives in good condition, in which case a comparison is made with the weights of the sound portion of the cargo, and the percentage thus ascertained is then applied to the insured value.

---

141. (1868) L.R. 3 C.P. 427, 18 L.T. 632. See, also, *Gill Duffus (Liverpool) Ltd. v. Scruttons Ltd.*, [1953] 2 All E.R. 977.

But, where the actual increase in weight cannot be calculated (as where the entire shipment is damaged), an arbitrary allowance is taken which, in the case of wool, is 3 percent. Rule E6 of the Rules of Practice of the Association of Average Adjusters provides in this respect:

E6. Allowance for Water in Wool
Damaged wool from Australia, New Zealand, and the Cape is subject to a deduction of 3 per cent for wet, if the actual increase cannot be ascertained.

Pickings and Skimmings Claims

With respect to some articles such as cotton, it makes sense to pick off the damaged portion, leaving the bale picked for sale in "sound condition," the claim on underwriters being for the quantity picked off. This practice is confirmed in Rule E4 of the association, reading:

E4. Allowance for Water and/or Impurities in Picked Cotton
When bales of cotton are picked, and the pickings are sold wet, the allowance for water in the pickings (where there are no means of ascertaining it) is by custom fixed at one-third.
There is a similar custom to deduct one-sixth from the gross weight of pickings or country damaged cotton[142] to take account of dirt, moisture and other impurities.

The same custom prevails with respect to coffee and the damaged bag is "skimmed" by removing the damaged beans. By common usage, the losses are paid irrespective of percentage even though the claim may be less than the percentage set forth in the memorandum.

Garbling

Where the damaged portion of tobacco is cut off, the process is called "garbling" and, again, the loss on the garbled portion is paid irrespective of percentage. However, where there is an increase in weight by reason of water in the tobacco and the increase cannot be determined, by custom this is taken to be one-fourth of the weight of the garbled portion. This latter practice is embodied in Rule E5 of the rules of the association, which reads simply:

E5. Allowance for Water in Cut Tobacco
When damaged tobacco is cut off, the allowance for water in the cuttings is one-fourth if the actual increase cannot be ascertained.

---

142. "Country damaged" simply means damaged in the country of origin by reason of dirt, rain, mud, etc. Presumably, any water absorbed at that time would have had an opportunity to dry out. Consequently, the custom is to deduct one-sixth from the cotton picked off at destination to reflect dirt, moisture, and other impurities.

The underwriters also pay for the picking, skimming, or garbling charges in addition to the loss paid.

Natural or Normal Losses

Various kinds of commodities are subject to variations in weight. Some gain in weight through absorption of moisture; others dry out over the passage of time. Certain liquids tend to seep through their containers, small fungible type goods go through interstices in bagging. Such normal losses are not recoverable from underwriters even though underwritten on an all risks basis as all risks coverage covers risks but not certainties. Section 55(2)(c) makes it very clear that the underwriter is not liable for normal losses which would inevitably happen over a period of time. It reads:

> Unless the policy otherwise provides, the insurer is not liable for ordinary wear and tear, ordinary leakage and breakage, inherent vice or nature of the subject matter insured, or for any loss proximately caused by rats or vermin, or for any injury to machinery not proximately caused by maritime perils.

Policies very seldom "otherwise provide," although occasionally this may happen. For example, in *Overseas Commodities, Ltd. v. Style*,[143] the policy was on canned pork against all risks, including blowing of tins, inherent vice, and hidden defect, but "warranted all tins marked by manufacturers with a code for verification of date of manufacture." Although some of the tins were properly marked, others were not. A number of the tins were condemned while the balance sold below the market price. The court held that, considering the peculiar nature of the product, i.e., a pasteurized and not wholly sterilized pig product, it was inconceivable that the underwriters would, with their eyes open, have accepted liability for loss by inherent vice developing any time in the future since such a product must inevitably, if not timely consumed, suffer loss from inherent vice. Being perishable, the product necessarily contained the seeds of its own ultimate destruction. As the policy could not be severed into as many contracts as there were tins and because there was a substantial number of tins not marked, the court held that the warranty was breached and there was no recovery.[144]

143. [1958] 1 Lloyd's Rep. 339, Q.B.
144. See, also, *F.W. Berk & Co., Ltd. v. Style*, [1955] 2 Lloyd's Rep. 382 (rebaggage charges not recoverable as the original tearing due to the inadequacy of the bags); *Liberian Insurance Agency, Inc. v. Mosse*, [1977] 1 Lloyd's Rep. 560 (goods misdescribed); *Greene v. Cheetham*, 293 F.2d 933, 1961 AMC 2549 (2d Cir.) (inherent vice in cargo of fish; i.e., it was unfit before inception of the policy); *Berns & Koppstein, Inc. v. Orion Ins. Co.*, 170 F.Supp. 707, 1959 AMC

However, in *Soya G.M.B.H. Kommanditgesellschaft v. White (The Corfu Island),*[145] the policy insured, *inter alia,* against heat, sweat, and spontaneous combustion known collectively as the "HSSC clauses" for damage to a cargo of soya beans. The cargo arrived in damaged condition. The underwriters defended on the grounds that the cargo had been shipped in such a condition that it was unable to withstand the ordinary incidents of the voyage from Indonesia to Europe; i.e., the cargo was inherently vicious and therefore not covered by virtue of Section 55(2)(c) of the Act. The defense failed on the facts, the judge considering that underwriters had not established inherent vice and the damage was, therefore, not inevitable. However, interestingly, it appeared the judge was prepared to hold that as long as it was established that the damage was not inevitable, the HSSC clauses would cover the loss even if the damage to the cargo had been proximately caused by inherent vice. That is, the express coverage

---

2455, 272 F.2d 415, 1960 AMC 1379 (policy contained a special rider for rejection insurance covering loss from detention and/or rejection in customs "for any reason whatsoever"; insect-infested peanuts were reconditioned to pass customs inspection; insured entitled to recover reconditioning costs and diminished price); *Gillespie & Co. v. Continental Ins. Co.,* 1958 AMC 2437 (N.Y.M.) (shipment of walnuts found damaged by insects on arrival; insurer failed to prove that the insect eggs were present prior to shipment); *Nakasheff v. Continental Ins. Co.,* 1954 AMC 986 (S.D.N.Y.) (no recovery as the fluid shipped had the inherent vice of expanding with heat, causing it to force its way through and leak out of the tins in which it was shipped); *Coussa v. Westchester Fire Ins. Co.,* 1962 AMC 1805 (S.D.N.Y.) (loss due to gradual deterioration and inherent vice was excluded from the policy coverage); *Red Top Brewing Co. v. Mazzotti,* 202 F.2d 481, 1953 AMC 309 (2d Cir.) (policy on a shipment of cassava meal as to which the heart of the risk is insect infestation, requiring inspection and a particular certificate of condition; held, not satisfied by such inspection and certificate as was shown); *Monarch Industrial v. American Motorists,* 276 F.Supp. 972, 1967 AMC 2488 (S.D.N.Y.) (packaged steel sheets stored in open storage for four months prior to shipment and on arrival found to be badly rusted; although policy was on all risks of physical loss from exterior causes, the cargo owner's suit against underwriters was dismissed); *Teneria "El Popo" v. Home Ins. Co.,* 1955 AMC 328 (N.Y.M.) (cargo underwriter found liable for portion of larvae-infested skins and ocean carrier for the balance); *De Monchy v. Phoenix Ins. Co. of Hartford,* (1929) 34 Ll.L.Rep. 201 (leakage of turpentine); *U.S. v. Westchester F.I. Co.,* 154 F.Supp. 827, 1957 AMC 1014 (S.D.N.Y.) (shipment of refined sugar in bags, insured against "loss or damage due to contact with fresh water, other cargo, oil and/or coal, fuel oil, sweat and/or steam of hold"; bags were damaged by dampness at night during loading; held, damage was something which, in the circumstances, was inevitable and did not come within the perils named); *Roberts v. Calmar,* 59 F.Supp. 203, 1945 AMC 375 (E.D. Pa.) (canned goods, packed in gum veneer packing cases, found damaged by excessive moisture in the wood of the packing cases; the canned goods were insured under language very similar to that in *U.S. v. Westchester F.I. Co., supra;* held, policy did not cover any possible source of moisture during the voyage and since the insured had failed to sustain the burden of proof in establishing the cause of the moisture, the insurer was not liable); *Blackshaws (Pty) Ltd. v. Constantia Insurance Co. Ltd.,* [1983] (1) SA 120 (So.Af.) (defective packing of a container such that the contents were damaged constitutes per se inherent vice within terms of all risk policy).

145. [1980] 1 Lloyd's Rep. 491, *aff'd* [1982] 1 Lloyd's Rep. 136 (C.A.), *aff'd* [1983] 1 Lloyd's Rep. 122, H.L. See, also, *Guardian Industries Pty. Ltd. v. Transport & General Ins. Co. Ltd.,* [1965] N.S.W.R. 1430 (Aus.) (policy covered "bursting and blowing of tins and inherent vice"); *Victoria Overseas Trading Co. v. Southern Pac. Ins. Co.,* [1964-5] N.S.W.R. 824 (Aus.) (policy covered all risks, "including breakage"; shipment of ashtrays arrived damaged; held, policy covered breakage caused by ordinary handling as well as extraordinary).

provided for heat, sweat, and spontaneous combustion was a sufficient expression of intent to overrule the contrary provisions of the inherent vice exclusion in Section 55(2)(c).

Leakage of cargo such as turpentine in wooden barrels caused by heavy weather or some other peril insured by the policy is covered as particular average, but where such a claim arises, the liability (in the absence of special language in the policy) is only for the *extra leakage* due to the insured peril and not for customary or "trade" leakage or evaporation.[146]

However, if the terms of coverage are such that the leakage is recoverable, then if the remaining contents deteriorated as a result of the leakage, i.e., wine going bad when exposed to air in partially empty barrels, then the underwriter is liable for the additional deterioration.[147]

It cannot be overemphasized that the policy will cover normal losses only when the express words of the policy provide. Even the broadest possible language may not suffice.[148] But where the terms are unquestionably explicit, the courts will enforce them as written. This is demonstrated in *De Monchy v. Phoenix Ins. Co. of Hartford*[149] where turpentine in barrels was insured under a policy in which the relevant wording was: "To pay leakage from any cause, in excess of one per cent . . . " and the policy then continued to set forth how the leakage was to be ascertained, i.e., by a comparison of the gross shipped and delivered weights, but a formula was also set forth to convert from volume in American gallons and weight in kilograms. It was patent to the court that the agreed method of ascertaining leakage was incorrect as it made no allowance for variations in temperature or atmospheric pressure. The underwriters contended that there had been no showing of leakage as the barrels showed no signs of leakage. There was evidence, however, that aside from temperature and atmospheric differences, turpentine has a propensity to vaporize and its vapor is so penetrating that it will escape its container without leaving a sign. The court held that under the wording used, "leakage" would embrace a gradual escape of the turpentine through the joints in the barrels or even through the pores of the material of which the barrels were constructed. Compare, however, *Traders & General Ins. Ass'n v. Bankers & Gen-*

146. See *Traders & General Ins. Ass'n., Ltd. v. Bankers & General Insurance Co., Ltd.*, (1921) 9 Ll.L.Rep. 223, and *Dodwell & Co., Ltd. v. British Dominions & General Ins. Co., Ltd.* (otherwise unreported but extract from judgment reported [1955] 2 Lloyd's Rep. 391).

147. *Maignen & Co. v. National Benefit Assurance Co.*, (1922) 10 Ll.L.Rep. 30.

148. See *Maignen & Co. v. National Benefit Assurance Co.*, (1922) 10 Ll.L.Rep. 30, and *Wilson, Holgate & Co., Ltd. v. Lancashire & Cheshire Ins. Corp., Ltd.*, (1922) 13 Ll.L.Rep. 486. And, see *Dodwell & Co., Ltd. v. British Dominions & General Ins. Co., Ltd.*, n. 146, *supra*, where there were two policies, one of which simply said "including the risk of leakage" and the other which read "including the risk of leakage from whatever cause arising." It was held that the first policy covered extra leakage after deducting normal leakage, whereas the second policy covered all of the leakage proved.

149. (1929) 34 Ll.L.Rep. 201, H.L. See, also, *American Molasses Co. v. Robertson*, 95 N.Y.S.2d 866, *rev'd* 99 N.Y.S.2d 933.

eral Ins. Co.,[150] where the language used was: "Including leakage in excess of 2 percent each barrel *over trade ullage.*"

Bulk Oil Clauses

While the bulk oil clauses differ from region to region and country to country, the pattern is consistent with respect to calculation of losses. For example, in the United States, bulk oil carriers generally perform their services under tariffs or rate contracts or schedules which allow them a certain stipulated loss without penalty, and the method of calculating that loss is specified. By way of illustration, one such tariff allows a handling and/or evaporation loss allowance of three-quarters of one percent on the more volatile fuels (such as aviation gasoline) and an allowance of one-quarter of one per cent on the less volatile fuels such as diesel oil, distallate fuel oils, furnace oils, stove oil, etc. The carrier is charged with the quantity of petroleum product delivered to it by the shipper at the loading point, as determined by gauge of the conveyance (frequently by use of the Saybolt calibration) or by meter maintained in connection with the shipper's loading facility or by shore tank gauges. All quantity determinations are adjusted for temperature variations to (usually) 60 degrees Fahrenheit in accordance with standard volume correction tables for petroleum oils as approved by the industry institutes. The rates prescribed frequently do not include marine cargo insurance. However, if the shipper desires, the carriers usually will provide the insurance pursuant to relatively standard "bulk oil clauses," with the cost of such insurance being charged back against the consignor or consignee.

The bulk oil clauses in frequent use in the United States follow a fairly consistent pattern. The assureds are not prejudiced by the presence of a negligence clause and/or latent defect clause in the bills of lading. The seaworthiness of the vessel and/or craft as between the assured and assurers is admitted. It is generally agreed that in the event that unseaworthiness or a wrongful act or misconduct of the vessel owner, his agents, or servants, shall directly or indirectly cause loss or damage to the cargo by sinking, stranding, fire, explosions, contact with water, or by any other risk named in the policy, the underwriters (subject to the terms of average and other conditions of the policy) will pay to an innocent assured all of the resulting loss. Leave is given to sail with or without pilots and to tow and assist vessels in all situations.

There is usually a form of "transit clause" whereby the cargo is held covered in the event of transshipment, discharge short of destination, or overcarriage, and in the event of transshipment, each craft, lighter, or conveyance is considered as if separately insured. General average, sal-

---

150. (1921) 9 Ll.L.Rep. 223.

vage, and special charges are payable and a modified Jason Clause is almost invariably included.

The principal insuring clauses read:

> Against all risks whatsoever (excepting as hereinafter provided) from time of leaving tanks at port of shipment and while in transit and/or awaiting transit and until safely delivered in tanks at destination, but notwithstanding anything herein to the contrary, the assurers are not liable for shortage and/or leakage and/or contamination (except as elsewhere in this policy provided) unless caused by or arising out of the vessel or craft being stranded, sunk, burnt, in collision or in contact with any substance or thing (ice included) other than water, fire, explosion (however and wheresoever occurring) or there be a forced discharge of cargo; provided, however, that these assurers are liable for contamination resulting from stress of weather.

> It is agreed that notwithstanding anything herein to the contrary, this insurance is to pay the insured value of any oil lost from connecting pipe lines, flexible or otherwise, in loading, transhipment or discharge.

> Claims are to be paid irrespective of percentage, but subject to deduction for normal shortage hereunder, including shortage and/or leakage and/or contamination, through the bursting of boilers, breakage of shafts or through any latent defect in the machinery, hull or appliances, or from faults or errors in the navigation or management of the vessel by the master, mariners, mates, engineers or pilots; provided, however, that this clause shall not be construed as covering loss arising out of delay, deterioration or loss of market, unless otherwise provided elsewhere in this policy.

Such policies also generally contain a "held covered" clause extending coverage should the vessel at the expiration of the policy be at sea, or in distress, or at a port of refuge or of call, provided notice is given to the underwriters and an extra premium is paid. Also, coverage is generally provided for "both to blame" collision liability should the both-to-blame clause be included in the bill of lading. When the underwriter has been found liable on a cargo policy, and the percentage of depreciation has been applied to the insured value, any extra charges accruing, such as those incurred to determine the extent of the depreciation, including survey fees, are added to the claim insofar as they were incurred in connection with cargo damaged as would give rise to a claim against the policy. The underwriter is not liable for any such charges as may arise in connection with cargo found to be in sound condition[151] or for damage which

---

151. *Lysaght v. Coleman*, (1894) 64 L.J.Q.B. 175.

does not give rise to a claim under the policy. Nor is the underwriter liable for charges which would have been incurred in any event should the cargo arrived undamaged, such as sales charges on cargo shipped to selling agents on consignment.[152]

New London Cargo Clauses

For the dramatic impact that the new London cargo clauses promulgated in 1982 will have upon the foregoing discussion of particular average losses, see the discussion in Chapter III, "The Policy."

The Memorandum Clause

The memorandum clause has appeared in the standard Lloyd's form since 1749. It reads:

> N.B. Corn, fish, salt, fruit, flour, and seed are warranted free from average, unless general, or the ship be stranded—sugar, tobacco, hemp, flax, hides and skins are warranted free from average, under five pounds per cent., and all other goods, also the ship and freight, are warranted free from average, under three pounds per cent unless general, or the ship be stranded.[153]

Not uncommonly, the memorandum clause has been extended by the addition of words which extend the liability of underwriters to cases in which the vessel has been sunk, or burnt, or damage has been caused by collision.

Apparently, the original intention of the memorandum was to deny coverage for certain articles particularly susceptible to waste, leakage, or damage on a voyage whereby the underwriter would run a greater risk than he had calculated. It will be noted that the memorandum states nothing with respect to articles subject to leakage or breakage. This has been said to be due to a custom of Lloyd's whereby such articles are free from average unless it can be shown that the vessel struck ground with such force as to make it probable that the blow deranged her stowage.[154]

---

152. See Rule E7 of the Rules of Practice, Association of Average Adjusters, United Kingdom, reading:
> Extra charges payable by underwriters, when incurred at the port of destination, are recovered in full; but when charges of the same nature are incurred at an intermediate port they are subjected to the same treatment, in respect of insured and contributory values, as general average charges.

153. It has been held in the United States that potatoes are "perishable articles" within the memorandum clause. *Robinson v. Commonwealth Ins. Co.*, F.Cas. 11,949 (C.C. Mass. 1938).

154. See, generally, the following cases in the United States: *Biays v. Chesapeake Ins. Co.*, 11 U.S. 415 (1813); *Monderer v. Universal Ins. Co.*, 66 F.Supp. 477 (D.N.J. 1946) (certificate provided that insurance was "subject to particular average if amounting to three percent,

The memorandum has, in great measure, been superseded by various specialized clauses on different classes of goods.[155] Moreover, it will not be found in the new cargo clauses promulgated in 1982, which are discussed in considerable detail in Chapter III. However, as no text on marine insurance would be complete without a discussion of the memorandum, its essential features and the decisions flowing from it will be briefly analyzed.

It will be noted that the memorandum is, in reality, made up of three distinct sections. The first frees the underwriter from partial loss or damage of an accidental nature (excepting when the vessel has been

---

each bag insured separately." Total insurance was $18,000 and the insured shipped 520 bags; held, each bag insured for its proportion of the $18,000 providing the bag was damaged or there was loss to the extent of more than 3%); *Kuh v. British American Assur. Co.*, 114 N.Y.S. 268, *aff'd* 195 N.Y. 571 (1909) (essentially same holding as in *Monderer, supra*); *Chicago Ins. Co. v. Graham & Morton Transp. Co.*, 108 F. 271, reh. den. 109 F. 352 (7th Cir. 1901) (5% franchise applicable to each kind of cargo and each bill of lading interest separately); *Morean v. U.S. Ins. Co.*, 14 U.S. 219 (1816) (underwriter not liable under memorandum where part of memorandum cargo arrived safely); *Washburn & Moen Mfg. Co. v. Reliance Marine Ins. Co.*, 179 U.S. 1 (1906) (rider stating: "Free of particular average, but liable for absolute total loss of a part if amounting to 5 per cent," is *in pari materia* with memorandum by which goods were "warranted by the assured free from average unless general" and qualifies the memorandum so that, instead of limiting liability to an actual total loss, it permits recovery for an actual total loss of a part); *Potter v. Suffolk Ins. Co.*, F.Cas. 11,339 (1835) (effect of memorandum clause is not to enlarge the perils insured against but to exempt the underwriter from certain losses within those perils); *Pacific Creosoting Co. v. Thames & Mersey Mar. Ins. Co.*, 184 F. 947 (1911) (under memorandum, underwriter does not assume liability for a partial loss); *Humphrey v. Union Ins. Co.*, F.Cas. 6,871 (1824) (insurance on cargo of lemons and oranges; the whole of the oranges were lost but the lemons arrived safely; held, underwriter not liable under memorandum for loss of the oranges where the memorandum warranted the underwriter free from particular average on "fruit"); *Bull v. Insurance Co. of N.A.*, 218 F. 616 (1914) (liability of underwriter for partial loss considered under policy limiting liability to a loss amounting to 3% of insured value); *Louisville Mar. & F. Ins. Co. v. Bland*, 39 Ky. 143 (1839) (percentage to be ascertained with respect to value of one of several articles specified in the clause to which the damage has occurred); *Rosen-Reichardt Brokerage Co. v. London Assur. Corp.*, 214 Mo.App. 672, 264 S.W. 443 (1924) ("deterioration" distinguished from "soiling damage" under specifically drafted memorandum clause); *Borgemeister v. Union Ins. Soc. of Canton*, 214 N.Y.S. 548 (1926), 1926 AMC 277 (words "to pay average irrespective of percentage" stamped on policy held applicable only to memorandum clause and not repugnant to warranty against particular average unless vessel was stranded, sunk, or burnt); *Devitt v. Providence Washington Ins. Co.*, 65 N.E. 777, 173 N.Y. 17 (1902) ("free of particular average" means the underwriter is liable only for a total loss); *Jones v. Niagara*, 170 F.2d 667, 1951 AMC 1401 (4th Cir.) (warranty exempts underwriter from a claim for total loss of a part only, even if the part totally lost consists of one or more entire packages; under memorandum clause, partial breakage loss due to rough handling in loading and unloading not covered); *Hood Rubber Co. v. Atlantic Mut. Ins. Co.*, 170 F. 939 (2d Cir. 1909), cert den. 215 U.S. 601; *Pierce v. Columbian Ins. Co.*, 96 Mass. 320 (1867) (vessel condemned; goods thereon, insured against total loss only, were transshipped into two other vessels, one of which was totally lost with its cargo and the other of which arrived safely; held, underwriters liable on the policy for the goods which were lost); *Dominican Import v. Lloyd's*, 1981 AMC 2981 (E.D. Va.) (losses arising from inherent vice and delay are not perils insured against, and the memorandum does not operate to enlarge those perils but only to exempt underwriters from certain losses within those perils).

155. See discussion, *infra*, under heading "Clauses for Special Trades."

stranded) on corn, fish, salt, fruit, flour, and seed—all of which are peculiarly susceptible to seawater damage. The second frees the underwriter on sugar, tobacco, hemp, flax, hides, and skins, all of which are subject to deterioration in transit, unless the loss reaches 5 percent of the insured value of the goods. And, finally, to eliminate small losses, all other goods, including ship and freight if those are the subject matters of the insurance, must sustain accidental damage or loss amounting to 3 percent of the insured value before there is a claim under the policy—unless, of course, the ship be stranded.

The most important point to remember is that once the percentage of loss has been reached or exceeded, the claim is payable in full.[156] This type of exception is commonly termed a "franchise," as distinguished from a deductible. Where the underwriter is to be held liable only for the excess over a certain amount, the term "deductible" is more appropriate and in the United States the term "deductible average" or "deductible franchise" will occasionally be encountered.

The following simple example will explain the point. Suppose a shipment of goods is insured for $1,000 subject to the 3 percent franchise which, of course, equals $30.

> (1) Goods are damaged by an insured peril—loss $20 (2%)
> No Claim
> (2) Goods are damaged by an insured peril—loss $30 (3%)
> Claim for $30
> (3) Goods are damaged by an insured peril—loss $40 (4%)
> Claim for $40

It must also be observed that the franchise does not apply to general average losses but only to particular average, i.e., fortuitous partial losses. Thus, Rule for Construction No. 13 states:

> The term "average unless general" means a partial loss of the subject-matter insured other than a general average loss, and does not include "particular charges."[157]

Section 76(4) of the Act also bears on the point. It reads:

> (4) For the purpose of ascertaining whether the specified percentage has been reached, regard shall be had only to the actual loss suffered by the subject-matter insured. Particular charges and the ex-

156. See cases cited *supra*, n. 154.
157. *Kidston v. Empire Ins. Co.*, (1866) L.R. 1 C.P. 535; *Lohre v. Aitchison*, (1878) 3 Q.B.D. 558, C.A.; *Price v. Al Small Damages Ass'n*, (1889) 22 Q.B.D. 580, C.A., 5 T.L.R. 356, 6 Asp. M.L.C. 435, C.A.; *Buzby v. Phoenix Ins. Co.*, 31 F. 422 (1887). And see *Donnell v. Columbian Ins. Co.*, F.Cas. 3,987 (1836).

penses of and incidental to ascertaining and proving the loss must be excluded.[158]

Moreover, general average and particular average losses cannot be added together to reach or attain the franchise amount. This was the ruling in *Price & Co. v. The Al Ships' Small Damage Ins. Ass'n*,[159] where the vessel sustained damage amounting to less than the 3 percent franchise, through heavy weather. On the same voyage, there was a general average sacrifice of part of the rigging. The two losses, added together, would have exceeded the 3 percent franchise. The court held that this was improper and the ruling is now embodied in Section 76(3) reading:

(3) Unless the policy otherwise provides, where the subject-matter insured is warranted free from particular average under a specified percentage, a general average loss cannot be added to a particular average loss to make up the specified percentage.

Also, the memorandum does not apply at all if the "ship be stranded." Thus, if the ship is stranded, the provisions of the memorandum never come into play. Consequently, all particular average losses are recoverable regardless of the percentage of loss. This principle is contained in Rule for Construction No. 14, reading:

Where the ship has stranded, the insurer is liable for the excepted losses, although the loss is not attributable to the stranding, provided that when the stranding takes place the risk has attached and, if the policy be on goods, that the damaged goods are on board.[160]

It will be observed from the foregoing that the risk must have attached at the time of the stranding and the cargo must be on board. This is demonstrated in two leading cases. In *Thames & Mersey Mar. Ins. Co. v. Pitts, Son & King*,[161] a cargo of maize was insured from San Nicholas and Buenos Aires to a port in Europe: 26,910 bags were insured from San Nicholas; 8,299 from Buenos Aires. The policy covered all risks in craft and contained a warranty against particular average unless the ship or craft be stranded. After loading the 29,910 bags at San Nicholas and while enroute to Buenos Aires, the vessel stranded; at that time the 8,299 bags were in lighters at Buenos Aires awaiting her arrival. The ship was gotten off her strand and found to be seaworthy. The cargo from San Nicholas, which had been taken out of the ship, was re-shipped, the 8,299

---

158. See, also, *Donnell v. Columbian Ins. Co.*, F.Cas. 3,987 (1836).
159. *Supra*, n. 157.
160. *Burnett v. Kensington*, (1797) 7 T.R. 210, 101 E.R. 937; *Barrow v. Bell*, (1825) 4 B. & C. 736; *Washington Iron Works v. St. Paul Fire & Marine Ins. Co.*, 128 Wash. 349, 222 P. 487 (1924); *De Farconnet v. Western Assur. Co.*, 110 F. 405, *aff'd* 122 F. 448, *cert. den.* 190 U.S. 558 (1901).
161. [1893] 1 Q.B. 476, 7 Asp. M.L.C. 302.

bags waiting in the lighters were put aboard, and the ship proceeded on her voyage to Europe, in the course of which a large part of the cargo was damaged by water owing to perils of the seas. It was admitted that a claim for particular average arose in respect of the 26,910 bags loaded at San Nicholas, but the assured also contended that a particular average claim existed with respect to the 8,299 bags loaded at Buenos Aires as the vessel had stranded. The court held that the claim for particular average only applied with respect to the cargo aboard the ship, i.e., the 29,910 bags loaded at San Nichols, and not to the 8,299 bags in lighters in Buenos Aires at the time of stranding, as the latter were not at risk at the time of the stranding.

In the *Alsace-Lorraine,*[162] the policy covered a cargo of rice on a voyage from Calcutta to Barbados. The policy contained the common memorandum by which rice is warranted free from average unless general or the ship be stranded and a special memorandum by which the rice was "warranted free from particular average unless the ship be stranded . . . ." The vessel encountered heavy weather and some of the rice was jettisoned. The ship subsequently put into Mauritius where, in order to effect repairs, the cargo was discharged. A part of it, including some of the rice in question, being damaged, was condemned as unfit to be forwarded and was sold. While the vessel was being repaired and while the whole of the cargo was ashore, a cyclone struck during which the vessel stranded and was found to be so damaged that she was condemned and abandoned. The remainder of her cargo was shipped on another vessel and after a portion of it, including some of the rice in question, had been, in the course of the voyage, damaged by sea perils, was finally delivered to Barbados. The assured claimed on the policy for the particular average damage to the rice on the ground that the original vessel on which the rice had been loaded had been stranded. The court held that the underwriters were not liable as the stranding took place at a time when the insured goods were not on board the vessel and, therefore, the warranty against particular average remained in force.

Warehouse to Warehouse

Originally, it was held that the memorandum applied only to shipped goods, and goods damaged during transit from a warehouse to a ship were not subject to the free from particular average warranty.[163]

---

162. [1893] P. 209, 7 Asp. M.L.C. 362.
163. *William H. Muller & Co. v. L'Unione Maritime of Paris, et al,* (1924) Ll.L.Rep. 90, H.L.; see, also, *Renton & Co. Ltd. v. Cornhill Ins. Co., Ltd.,* (1933) Ll.L.Rep. 14, where under the Timber Trade Federation Clauses the phrase "deckload warranted free from particular average" was held to apply only while the timber was actually loaded on deck. The point was raised in *Shaver v. Travelers Ind. Co.,* 481 F.Supp. 892, 1980 AMC 393 (D. Ore.), but, as the

However, cargo policies in use today almost invariably contain a provision to the effect that the warranty applies and operates during the warehouse-to-warehouse risk.

What Is a "Stranding"

A vessel is "stranded" within the meaning of the memorandum only when, as a consequence of an accidental or unusual occurrence, she comes in contact with the ground or some other object and remains hard and fast upon it for some appreciable time.[164] A vessel is not stranded if she sinks in deep water.[165]

Meaning of the Word "Sunk"

A ship is not sunk within the meaning of the memorandum unless she physically sinks. This is clearly demonstrated in *Bryant & May Ltd. v. London Assur. Corp.*,[166] where the vessel was loaded with match splits. On arrival in port she had water over her deck as far aft as the mainmast. The match splits obviously kept her from sinking further although had the cargo absorbed more water she probably would have sunk further. It was

---

court found the loss (by contamination) was not covered by an insured peril, was not decided.

164. *Bowring v. Emslie*, (1790) 101 E.R. 939 (there must be a bona fide stranding); *Bishop v. Pentland*, (1827) 108 E.R. 705 (stranding must be accidental and out of the ordinary course of the voyage); *Harman v. Vaux*, (1813) 3 Camp. 429, N.P. (not necessary that the vessel upon stranding has received any material damage); *M'Dougle v. Royal Exchange Assur. Co.*, (1816) 105 E.R. 921 (striking a rock and remaining stationary for a minute and a half is not a stranding even though the striking caused a total loss of the vessel); *Baker v. Towry*, (1816) 1 Stark 436, N.P. (striking a rock and remaining fixed there for fifteen or twenty minutes in consequence of which the vessel sustained a material injury is a stranding); *Hearne v. Edmunds*, (1819) 129 E.R. 772 (vessel took ground in the ordinary course of navigation and afterwards, being moored at a quay, took ground and fell over on an ebbing of the tide; held, not a stranding); *De Farconnet v. Western Ins. Co.*, 110 F. 405, aff'd 122 F. 448, *cert. den.* 190 U.S. 558 (vessel being disabled was towed into port; while being towed she ran upon a coral reef and pounded for half an hour; held, a stranding); *Washington Iron Works v. St. Paul Fire & Mar. Ins. Co.*, 128 Wash. 349, 222 P. 387 (1924) (master erroneously thought he could enter port without touching bottom but did so; held, a stranding); *Carruthers v. Sydebotham*, (1815) 105 E.R 764 (vessel tied up improperly through negligence of a pilot fell over on the tide and bilged; held, a stranding); *Barrow v. Bell*, (1825) 107 E.R. 1234 (vessel forced to take shelter in a harbor struck an anchor while entering and was found to be leaking; she was hauled up with warps higher in the harbor where she took ground for half an hour; held, a stranding); *Raynor v. Godmond*, (1821) 106 E.R. 1175 (vessel in a canal when the waters in the canal were drained off to effect repairs to the canal; vessel went fast upon some pilings which were not known to be there; held, a stranding); *Letchford v. Oldham*, (1880) 5 Q.B.D. 538 (vessel grounded upon approaching a quay. She was left there to await the next high tide so she could come alongside the quay; as the tide receded, she settled down but pitched by the head into a hole which was not known to be there and was damaged. Held: a stranding).

165. *Baker Whitely Coal Co. v. Marten*, (1910) 26 T.L.R. 314.

166. (1886) 2 T.L.R. 591.

held that this was not a sinking within the meaning of the term "sunk." Likewise, a mere capsizing of the vessel does not mean she is sunk. For example, in *Snare & Triest Co. v. Fireman's Fund Ins. Co.*,[167] a barge upon which a concrete mixer was secured capsized at sea and the concrete mixer broke free and was lost. The barge was towed upside down 30 miles to port. This was held not to be a "sinking."

Meaning of the Word "Burnt"

A vessel is not burnt within the meaning of the memorandum unless the injury by fire is such as to constitute a substantial burning of the ship as a whole,[168] but it has been held in the United States that a vessel is deemed to be "on fire" if a structural part is on fire regardless of the extent.[169] Because of the restrictive nature of the term "burnt," it is not uncommon to find policies in which the words "or on fire" have been added.

Meaning of the Term "Collision"

When the memorandum contains the additional words "or in collision," this generally refers only to a collision with another ship or vessel, and not with other objects such as wharves, piers, and the like.[170] Chapter XIX, "The Running Down Clause," contains a discussion in depth of what constitutes a "collision" with another "ship or vessel."

Particular Cargo Clauses

For many years, so far as cargo insurance was concerned, there were three sets of standard cargo clauses in use in England and the American market generally followed the English *modus operandi*. These classes were:

(1) Institute Cargo Clauses (W.A.) 1.1.63
(2) Institute Cargo Clauses (F.P.A.) 1.1.63
(3) Institute Cargo Clauses (All Risks) 1.1.63

As discussed in Chapter III, "The Policy," these forms have now been supplanted by the new London Cargo Clauses which became effective on January 1, 1982. However, a transition period was necessary and the old

---

167. 261 F. 777 (2d Cir. 1919).
168. *The Glenlivet*, (1894) P. 48, 7 Asp. M.L.C. 395. See, also, *Service v. Mercantile Mar. Ins. Co. of S. Australia*, (1878) 4 V.L.R. 436 (Aus.).
169. *Thames & Mersey Marine Ins. Co. v. Pacific Creosoting Co.*, 223 F. 561 (9th Cir. 1915).
170. *Richardson v. Burrows*, (1880), note to [1904] P. 198. And see *London Assur. v. Companhia de Moagens Do Barreiro*, 68 F. 247 (3rd Cir. 1895), *aff'd* 167 U.S. 149, where the Supreme Court also discussed the meaning of the words "burned" and "stranded" although the principal issue in the case was the meaning of the word "collision."

policy form and clauses could be used insofar as the London market was concerned until March 31, 1983.

Because the American market is continuing to use forms which are substantially identical to the old Institute clauses, it is necessary that the form of those clauses and the judicial decisions construing them be considered. It is common practice in the American market to utilize what is commonly known as a "manuscript" form, frequently printed but occasionally specially typed. These manuscript forms generally are 15 to 20 or more printed pages in length and are so constructed that they are, in effect, "open policies" with the assured being given the right to issue "certificates" under the open policy to cover specific shipments. The shipments are then "declared" to the underwriter and a premium paid accordingly.

For example, in one common American marine open cargo policy, one specific paragraph, denominated "Average Terms and Conditions," contains sufficient blank space to insert phrasing which refers to an attached endorsement. The endorsement, in turn, specifically states what the average terms are with respect to the particular types of cargo transported, or likely to be transported. Thus, for example, if lumber is to be insured, the Timber Trade Federation Clauses will most likely be the subject of the endorsement and the "Risks Covered" paragraph of those particular clauses reads in part as follows:

6. (a) Subject to 6(b) below this insurance is against all risks of loss of or damage to the subject-matter insured but shall in no case be deemed to extend to cover loss damage or expense proximately caused by delay or inherent vice or nature of the subject-matter insured.

(b) Deckload warranted free from Particular Average unless the vessel or craft be stranded, sunk, burnt, on fire, or in collision, but notwithstanding this warranty the Underwriters are to pay the insured value of any portion of the cargo which may be totally lost by jettison or washing overboard or in loading transhipment or discharge, also for any loss of or damage to the interest insured which may reasonably be attributed to fire, explosion, collision, or contact of the vessel and/or craft and/or conveyance with any external substance (ice included) other than water, or to discharge of cargo at port of distress, also to pay special charges for landing warehousing and forwarding if incurred at a port of loading call or refuge, for which Underwriters would be liable under the Standard Form of English Marine Policy with the Institute Cargo Clauses (W.A.) attached. Cargo stowed in poop, forecastle, deck house, shelter deck, or other enclosed space, shall be deemed to be cargo under deck.

The Institute Particular Average Warranties

Section 76 of the Marine Insurance Act deals with particular average warranties and reads as follows:

(1) Where the subject-matter insured is warranted free from particular average, the assured cannot recover for a loss of part, other than a loss incurred by a general average sacrifice, unless the contract contained in the policy by apportionable; but if the contract be apportionable, the assured may recover for a total loss of any apportionable part.

(2) Where the subject-matter insured is warranted free from particular average, either wholly or under a certain percentage, the insurer is nevertheless liable for salvage charges, and for particular charges and other expenses properly incurred pursuant to the provisions of the suing and laboring clause in order to avert a loss insured against.

(3) Unless the policy otherwise provides, where the subject-matter insured is warranted free from particular average under a specified percentage, a general average loss cannot be added to a particular average loss to make up the specified percentage.

(4) For the purpose of ascertaining whether the specified percentage has been reached, regard shall be had only to the actual loss suffered by the subject-matter insured. Particular charges and the expenses of and incidental to ascertaining and proving the loss must be excluded.

Institute Cargo Clauses (F.P.A.)

It will be observed that sub-section (1) of Section 76 covers situations where the subject-matter insured is warranted free from particular average. The standard form of "free from particular average" warranty will be found in the Institute Cargo Clauses (F.P.A.) which reads as follows:[171]

Warranted free from Particular Average unless the vessel or craft be stranded, sunk, or burnt, but notwithstanding this warranty the Underwriters are to pay the insured value of any package or packages which may be totally lost in loading, transhipment or discharge, also for any loss of or damage to the interest insured which may reasonably be attributed to fire, explosion, collision or contact of the vessel and/or craft and/or conveyance with any external substance (ice included)

171. The Institute Cargo Clauses will be found reproduced in the Appendix.

other than water, or to discharge of cargo at a port of distress, also to pay special charges for landing, warehousing and forwarding if incurred at an intermediate port of call or refuge, for which Underwriters would be liable under the standard form of English Marine Policy with the Institute Cargo Clauses (W.A.) attached.

This Clause shall operate during the whole period covered by the policy.[172]

From a close reading of the warranty, it will be seen that a total loss of a part of the subject-matter insured will not be recoverable at all unless the warranty is "broken" by one of the contingencies occurring; i.e., the carrying vessel is sunk, stranded or burnt, or the loss or damage may be attributed to fire, explosion, collision, etc. It will also be observed that heavy weather damage is not included among the contingencies specified nor is damage to the subject matter by reason of seawater.[173]

Moreover, it will be observed that the warranty does provide for payment of "special charges" which fall within the description of sue and labor. As sue and labor charges are recoverable if incurred to minimize or prevent a claim under the policy, and it is often difficult to determine whether or not a total loss has been averted, underwriters agree to pay special charges as though the cargo was insured on "with average" conditions. In this respect, therefore, the coverage afforded by the with average clause and the F.P.A. clause are identical.

Apportionable Part

It will also be observed that even under the F.P.A. Clause, sub-section (1) of Section 76 makes it clear that if the subject-matter insured is comprised of a number of *apportionable parts,* a total loss of any one part is recoverable whether or not one of the contingencies may happen to open the warranty. This subject is discussed in detail in this chapter under the heading "Particular Average on Cargo."

---

172. The last sentence was added to make it clear that the memorandum provisions are applicable to the whole period covered by the policy, including, of course, land transit, and follows the decision in *William H. Muller & Co. v. L'Unione Maritime of Paris, et al, supra,* n. 163.

173. For example, in *Shaver v. Travelers Ind. Co.,* 481 F.Supp. 892, 1980 AMC 393 (D. Ore.), a cargo of caustic soda being carried under F.P.A. conditions in a barge was found to be contaminated by reason of animal fats and tallow being left in the barge's input and discharge lines. No insured peril having occurred and none of the contingencies having occurred, there was no coverage. See, also, *Boon & Cheah Steel Pipes v. Asia Insurance Co. Ltd.,* [1975] 1 Lloyd's Rep. 452 (Malaysia), where 656 pipes out of 668 were lost overboard by perils of the sea. The court held that the 12 pipes remaining were too high a proportion to be treated as *de minimis* and recovery was not allowed. See, also, *Jones v. Niagara, supra,* n. 131; *Larsen v. Ins. Co. of N.A., supra,* n. 132; *Ralli v. Janson, supra,* n. 127.

Craft, Etc., Clause

The Institute Cargo Clauses (F.P.A.) contain a special clause relating to total loss of the insured subject matter when it is in separate craft such as lighters. The clause reads:

> 3. Including transit by craft, raft or lighter to or from the vessel. Each craft, raft or lighter to be deemed a separate insurance. The Assured are not to be prejudiced by any agreement exempting lightermen from liability.

Consequently, a total loss by an insured peril of the insured cargo carried in any one craft, raft, etc., will be recoverable. Correspondingly, if the policy contains (as some policies do) the statement that "each package is to be deemed a separate insurance," then a total loss of one package by reason of an insured peril would be recoverable even though the policy is warranted free of particular average.[174]

Sub-section (2) of Section 76 makes it quite clear that salvage charges and sue and labor charges are recoverable under F.P.A. cargo policies. However, sue and labor charges incurred to prevent a *partial* loss of cargo are not recoverable under a policy warranting the goods free from particular average. That is, only sue and labor charges incurred to prevent a loss insured against are recoverable and, as F.P.A. policies insure only against total losses, only sue and labor charges incurred to prevent a total loss would be recoverable.[175]

---

174. The sentence relating to agreements exempting lightermen from liability is an illustration of underwriters being willing to extend coverage to avoid the effect of cases such as *Tate v. Hyslop*, (1885) 15 Q.B.D. 368, 5 Asp. M.L.C. 487, C.A., where the assured failed to communicate to the underwriters that the goods would be lightered on the basis of the lighterman being exempted from his common carrier liability and thus liable only for negligence. As it is common practice today that lightermen will only carry goods on the basis of an almost complete immunity from liability, the underwriters have, in effect, conceded that they waive any obligation on the part of the assured to communicate this fact to them in advance.

175. See *Meyer v. Ralli*, (1876) 45 L.J.Q.B. 741, 3 Asp. M.L.C. 324; *Wilson Bros. Bobbin Co. v. Green*, (1917) 1 K.B. 860, 14 Asp. M.L.C. 119; *Booth v. Gair*, (1863) 33 L.J.C.P. 99, 143 E.R. 796; *Great Indian Peninsular Railway v. Saunders*, (1862) 31 L.J.Q.B. 206, 121 E.R. 1072, Ex.Ch.; *Kidston v. Empire Marine Ins. Co.*, (1866) L.R. 2 C.P., 2 Mar. L.C. 468, Ex.Ch. The decisions in *Great Indian* and *Booth v. Gair*, involving charges for forwarding cargo from a port of refuge to port of destination, are likely mooted by the clause in the Institute Cargo Clauses (F.P.A.) in which underwriters agree to pay "special charges for landing, warehousing and forwarding if incurred at an intermediate port of call or refuge for which Underwriters would be liable under the standard form of English Marine Policy with the Institute Cargo Clauses (W.A.) attached."

Institute Cargo Clauses (W.A.)

The abbreviation "W.A." means "with average." As the word "average" means partial loss, either particular or general, and the Average Clause by its wording expressly does not apply to general average, the clause relates to particular average losses. Occasionally, the term "W.P.A." is encountered, meaning "with particular average." There is no difference between the two terms.

The Institute Cargo Clauses (W.A.) read:

5. Warranted free from average under the percentage specified in the policy, unless general, or the vessel or craft be stranded, sunk or burnt, but notwithstanding this warranty the Underwriters are to pay the insured value of any package which may be totally lost in loading, transhipment or discharge, also for any loss of or damage to the interest insured which may reasonably be attributed to fire, explosion, collision or contact of the vessel and/or craft and/or conveyance with any external substance (ice included) other than water, or to discharge of cargo at a port of distress.

This Clause shall operate during the whole period covered by the policy.

A comparison of the above-quoted clause with the Institute Cargo Clauses (F.P.A.) will demonstrate that all the risks covered by the F.P.A. Clause are covered, and also all other particular average losses arising from insured perils, provided that the loss attains the minimum percentage or franchise specified in the policy. Substituting this clause for the F.P.A. Clause has the effect, in practice, of adding coverage for partial losses (subject to the franchise) which arise from heavy weather. This usually involves seawater damage to the cargo and/or leakage or breakage of the goods as a result of heavy weather.

In summary, the W.A. Clause does not cover handling damage, freshwater damage, leakage, breakage, or damage caused by contact with other cargo, unless caused by heavy weather or some other insured peril.

An analysis of the F.P.A. and W.A. clauses will disclose that the risks insured against in those clauses are those primarily resulting from maritime perils. There are, of course, many other types of what may be termed "extraneous risks" for a lack of a better term. These include, but are not limited to, such risks as theft, pilferage, short delivery, non-delivery, freshwater damage, oil damage, stevedoring damage, sweating, damage by other cargo, ordinary leakage and breakage, discoloration, heat, sweat, spontaneous combustion, chipping, scratching, and denting, rust, inherent vice such as the "blowing of tins," etc. As will be demonstrated in the discussion of all risks coverage which follows, even an all risk policy does not necessarily cover all the above enumerated extraneous risks, and a sophisticated assured would be well advised to weigh the risks to which his goods may be subjected against the cost of higher premiums for coverage against such extraneous risks.

All Risks Clauses

The Institute Cargo Clauses (All Risks) reads simply:

> This insurance is against all risks of loss of or damage to the subject-matter insured but shall in no case be deemed to extend to cover loss damage or expense proximately caused by delay or inherent vice or nature of the subject-matter insured. Claims recoverable hereunder shall be payable irrespective of percentage.

These clauses were first introduced in 1951, although there are reported decisions on the meaning of "all risks" which antedate the adoption of the Institute All Risks Clauses.[176]

It will be remembered that delay and inherent vice are specifically excluded by Section 55 of the Marine Insurance Act *unless the policy otherwise provides*.[177] It would appear that by expressly excepting delay or inherent vice in the insuring clause quoted above, underwriters intended to put the assured on notice that claims, even under all risks conditions, would not be paid if the proximate cause of loss or damage was delay or inherent vice. Correspondingly, the last sentence specifying that claims are recoverable and payable irrespective of percentage could only have the purpose of clarifying that the memorandum is rendered ineffective.

Notwithstanding the apparent broadness of the term "all risks," it is clear that an all risks policy does not, in fact, cover all risks—only those that are fortuitous. As Lord Birkenhead, L.C., said in *British and Foreign Marine Ins. Co. Ltd. v. Gaunt:*[178]

> . . . These words cannot, of course, be held to cover all damage however caused, for such damage as is inevitable from ordinary wear

---

176. Notable among these are: *British and Foreign Marine Insurance Co. Ltd. v. Gaunt,* [1921] 2 A.C. 41, H.L.; *Theodorou v. Chester,* [1951] 1 Lloyd's Rep. 204 (policy covered "all risks of loss and/or damage however arising, irrespective of percentage"); *Schloss Bros. v. Stevens,* [1906] 2 K.B. 665 (policy covered "all risks by land and by water by any conveyance"; held, damage by abnormal delay exposing goods to dampness and damage by wetting and injury by worms covered under the policy); *London & Provincial Leather Processes Ltd. v. Hudson,* [1939] 3 All E.R. 857, 64 Ll.L.Rep. 352 (fortuitous event under all risk policy held to include assured being deprived of his goods through conversion). See, also, *Goix v. Knox,* 1 Johns 337 (N.Y., 1800); *Parkhurst v. Gloucester M.F. Ins. Co.,* 100 Mass. 301 (1868).
177. See discussion, supra, "Particular Average on Cargo," p. 793 to p. 796, where policies did so "otherwise provide."
178. *Supra,* n. 176.

and tear and inevitable depreciation is not within the policies. . . .
Damage, in other words, if it is to be covered by policies such as these,
must be due to some fortuitous circumstance or casualty . . . .

In *Schloss Bros. v. Stevens*,[179] the words used were "accidental cause of
any kind" and in *Theodorou v. Chester*,[180] the phrase employed was "extraneous and accidental cause."[181]

"All Loss or Damage"

It would appear that the omission of the word "risks" from the insuring
words should mean something more than "all risks." Assuming that the
assured has an insurable interest and has sustained a financial loss, any
loss or damage, even natural losses sustained in transit, such as evaporation, should be covered, except, perhaps, losses arising from wilful misconduct of the assured,[182] or shipment of cargo in an improper condition
with the knowledge of the assured, thus constituting non-disclosure of a
material fact.[183]

General Average May Not Be Added to Particular Average

Sub-section (3) of Section 76 of the Marine Insurance Act provides quite
clearly that general average losses may not be added to particular average
losses to make up the percentage of loss specified in a particular average

---

179. *Supra*, n. 176.
180. *Supra*, n. 176.
181. The American cases do not differ. See *Goodman v. Fireman's Fund*, 600 F.2d 1040,
1979 AMC 2534 (4th Cir.); *Heindl-Evans v. Reliance Ins.*, 1980 AMC 2823 (E.D. Va.); *Morrison
Grain v. Utica Mut.*, 632 F.2d 424, 1982 AMC 658 (5th Cir.); *Contractors Realty Company, Inc. v.
Insurance Co. of N.A.*, 469 F.Supp. 1287, 1979 AMC 1864 (S.D.N.Y.); *Anders v. Poland*, 181
So.2d 879, 1966 AMC 1867 (St. La.); *Mathis v. Hanover Ins. Co.*, 127 Ga.App. 89, 192 S.E.2d
510 (St. Ga.,1972); *Liberty Mut. Ins. Co. v. Flitman*, 234 So.2d 390 (St. Fla., 1970); *Brandt v.
Premier Ins. Co.*, 260 Or. 392, 490 P.2d 984 (St. Ore., 1971); *Egan v. Washington Gen. Ins. Corp.*,
240 So.2d 875 (St. Fla., 1970). See, also, *Northwestern v. Chandler*, 1982 AMC 1631 (N.D. Cal.)
(loss of insured containers by "mysterious disappearance" covered under all risks policy);
Consolidated Int. v. Falcon, 1983 AMC 270 (S.D.N.Y.) (all risks policy covering "new machinery" also includes unused machinery stored in original crates); *Welded Tube v. Hartford Fire*,
1973 AMC 555 (E.D. Pa.) (proof by assured under all risks policy of shipment in good condition and subsequent damage in transit; underwriters held to have burden of establishing
that loss was caused by one of the enumerated exceptions). *Quattrochiocchi v. Albany Ins.*, 1983
AMC 1152 (N.D. Cal.).
182. In *Sassoon v. Yorkshire Ins. Co.*, (1923) 14 Ll.L.Rep. 167, *aff'd* 16 Ll.L.Rep. 129, C.A.,
damage by mould and mildew was specifically included. See, also, *Soya G.M.B.H. v. White*,
[1980] 1 Lloyd's Rep. 491 (heat, sweat, and spontaneous combustion specifically covered);
Traders and Gen. Ins. Ass'n Ltd. v. Bankers and Gen. Ins. Co., Ltd., (1921) 9 Ll.L.Rep. 223 (peril
insured was "leakage," not the "risk of leakage"; held, leakage was intended to cover leakage
of any kind and from whatever cause). Compare, however, *Gee and Garnham Ltd. v. Whittal*,
[1955] 2 Lloyd's Rep. 562, where there was no evidence that the loss occurred during transit.
183. *Greenhill v. Federal Ins. Co. Ltd.*, (1926) 95 L.J.K.B. 717.

warranty.[184] Although such a general average loss may be recovered in full, no matter how small, the particular average loss, alone, must amount to the requisite percentage.

Survey Fees, Etc.

Sub-section (4) of Section 76 provides that for the purpose of ascertaining whether the specified percentage has been reached, only the actual loss suffered by the subject matter may be considered. Particular charges and the expenses of and incidental to ascertaining and proving the loss must be excluded. However, such extra charges are payable by underwriters when the requisite percentage has been reached and if the claim is in other respects recoverable under the policy.

These are commonly referred to as "franchise charges" and are the subject of Rule of Practice No. A9 of the British Association, reading:

> The expenses of protest, survey, and other proofs of loss, including the commission or other expenses of a sale by auction, are not admitted to make up the percentage of a claim; and are only paid by the underwriters in case the loss amounts to a claim without them.

It should be here observed that particular charges are more comprehensive than sue and labor charges, although the latter are included in and are a form of particular charges. While coverage for sue and labor charges is supplementary to the basic coverage, even up to 100 percent of the sum insured in addition to a total loss, the Marine Insurance Act has no provisions with respect to the measure of indemnity for particular charges. Consequently, recovery for particular charges (other than sue and labor) will be limited to the sum insured in the absence of any special provisions in the policy.

Moreover, as particular charges cannot be added to particular average damage in order to overcome the franchise, reconditioning charges at destination are charges which are payable only if the loss itself is recoverable, and are not includable as sue and labor inasmuch as the subject-matter insured has attained a state of safety by virtue of reaching destination.

Thus, for example, where the franchise is 3 percent of the insured value, and the particular average damage claim is only 2 percent of that value, and even though reconditioning (or extraordinary) charges would bring the total up to, say, 5 percent, underwriters are not liable for either the particular average claim or the extraordinary charges incurred.[185]

---

184. *Price & Co. v. The Al Ships' Small Damage Ins. Ass'n,* (1889) 22 Q.B.D. 580, 6 Asp. M.L.C. 435.

185. A detailed discussion of the intricacies involved in determining whether extraordinary expenses are recoverable and to what extent is beyond the scope of this text. Refer-

What Is Includable to Reach the Franchise Cargo Claims

What may be included to reach the franchise differs, of course, as to ship, cargo, and freight. In the case of cargo, as has already been noted, only the actual loss sustained by the goods may be taken into account in ascertaining whether or not the requisite percentage has been reached. Once the franchise amount has been reached, or exceeded, the actual loss sustained as well as extraordinary charges (such as survey fees, sales charges incurred solely in determining the damaged value, and reconditioning charges, if any, etc.) are recoverable.

Freight Claims

As with cargo, only the actual loss sustained with respect to freight is recoverable. The Institute Time Clauses (freight) provide that, except with respect to total loss (actual or constructive) the amount recoverable shall not exceed the gross freight actually lost. And the clauses also provide, with respect to the average warranty, as follows:

> Warranted free from particular average under 3 per cent. unless the Vessel be stranded, sunk or on fire, the Underwriters notwithstanding this warranty to pay for any loss caused by fire or collision with another vessel. Each craft and/or lighter to be deemed a separate insurance if desired by the Assured.

Hull Claims

As a matter of logic, it is apparent that the cost of repairs to the insured vessel is the measure of underwriters' liability where there is a partial loss. Consequently, as a general rule, those items which go to make up the cost of repairs may also be included in order to reach the franchise. These would include not only the actual cost of the repair work but ancillary expenses such as drydocking, dock dues, fuel, and engine room stores allowable, etc.[186]

It is common practice today that commercial vessels are insured, not on the basis of a franchise, but with a deductible. Occasionally, however, vessels will be insured on restricted conditions such as "F.P.A. Absolutely,"

---

ence should be made to such excellent texts as *Marine Insurance Claims,* J. Kenneth Goodacre, Witherby & Co. Ltd., London, where the practical problems involved in arriving at a proper ascertainment are discussed in a clear and concise manner.

186. See discussion, *supra,* this chapter, "Particular Average on Ship," as to what is includable in cost of repair.

"Free of Damage Absolutely," or "Total Loss Only."[187]

To the contrary, yachts are frequently insured on an all risks basis,[188] or irrespective of percentage,[189] thus obviating the application of the memorandum. It is not uncommon for such yacht policies to contain a deductible.

Only Losses by Insured Perils May Be Considered

It cannot be overemphasized that only losses proximately caused by insured perils can be considered in determining whether the franchise has been reached under a policy warranted free from particular average under a specific percent or whether there has been a total loss under a policy warranted free from particular average. For example, in *Dominican Import v. Lloyd's*,[190] the freezing and "cooking" damage to a banana shipment insured under the Institute Cargo Clauses (F.P.A.) was found to have been caused by delay in unloading due to the assured's failure to provide a properly functioning conveyor system. Thus, losses arising from inherent vice and delay are not perils insured against. In *Jones v. Niagara*,[191] a partial loss by breakage of a shipment of glazed ceramic tile due to the inherent nature of the goods or negligence of a stevedore was held not to be a loss arising from perils of the seas, nor covered as perils underdeck 3 percent on on-deck, nor as landing expenses, nor as total loss of a part of a shipment. And in *Continental Grain Co., Inc. v. Twitchell*,[192] involving a time-charterer's freight policy, the vessel was stranded. The policy insured only against total and/or constructive total loss of the vessel. The repairs took a considerable period of time and cost so much that the ship was for practical purposes a constructive total loss although its owners did not treat it as such. Later, after the ship was put back into service, the charter was cancelled by the time-charterers by making a payment to the shipowner as by that time a fall in freight rates rendered further subchartering unprofitable. As a consequence, only a partial loss of earnings was caused by the stranding, the remainder being due to a fall in the market. There being no total loss of earnings, the proximate cause of which was the constructive total loss of the ship by reason of an insured peril, there was no recovery.

---

187. An example of coverage on the basis of total loss only will be found in the recent decision in *Edinburgh Assur. v. R.L. Burns*, 479 F.Supp. 138, 1980 AMC 1261, *aff'd* 669 F.2d 1269, 1982 AMC 2532 (9th Cir.), where an offshore drilling platform, already damaged and declared to be a constructive total loss, was insured on those terms by purchasers who desired to salve it.

188. See, for example, *Goodman v. Fireman's Fund*, 600 F.2d 1040, 1979 AMC 2534 (4th Cir.).

189. As in the Institute Yacht Clauses.

190. 1981 AMC 2981 (E.D. Va.).

191. 170 F.2d 667, 1951 AMC 1401 (4th Cir.).

192. (1945) 78 Ll.L.Rep. 251, C.A.

"Series"

As vessels became larger and larger, the size and values of individual shipments likewise became larger, thus making the franchise progressively greater. As a concession, shippers have been permitted to subdivide shipments for franchise purposes into smaller lots or divisions, each being known as a "series." If the damage amounts to the requisite percentage on a series, the loss would be recoverable as to that series. For example, partial losses would be paid with respect to cotton, 3 percent each bale; sugar, 5 percent each 30 bags; wool on each bale; cocoa on 20 bags, etc.

Obviously, if the particular average reaches the required percentage on the whole of the interest insured there will be no necessity of considering each series separately.

Occasionally, a number of odd packages, bales, or bags may remain after dividing the shipment into series, the packages, bales or bags remaining being referred to as a "tail series." As to these tail series, the claim is payable if the franchise percentage is reached even though the number involved is smaller. For example, in the example given above with respect to sugar, assume that there were 305 bags altogether shipped. If the damage amounts to 5 percent on the value of the last five bags, the loss would be recoverable even though the depreciation in value did not reach the stipulated 5 percent on a series of 30 bags.

"Irrespective of Percentage"

As has already been noted, it is not uncommon for cargo to be insured, average being payable "irrespective of percentage." This totally eliminates the application of the percentages set forth in the memorandum.[193] As already observed, the Institute Cargo Clauses (All Risks) contains such a provision.

Bulk liquid cargos are frequently insured on the basis of a franchise such as, say, 1 percent. This was the case in *American Molasses Co. v. Robertson*,[194] where the policy included coverage for leakage, shortage,

---

193. See, in this connection, *The Kazembe*, 1926 AMC 277 (N.Y.M.). There, the policy contained a common form memorandum clause. Stamped on the face of the policy was the legend "To pay average irrespective of percentage." The cargo of rubber insured sustained water damage while enroute. The assured contended the legend superseded the provision whereby the defendant underwriter was liable for partial loss only if the vessel stranded, sunk, or burnt, whereas the defendant contended that the legend was merely a modification of the memorandum clause which made payment of average on certain classes of goods depend on the percentage of damage. The court sustained the defendant's contention, holding that there was nothing in the stamped legend which was repugnant to the warranty requiring the vessel to be stranded, sunk, or burnt, and as the vessel had not been stranded, sunk, or burnt, the assured could not recover.

194. 95 N.Y.S.2d 866, 197 Misc. 919, *rev'd* 99 N.Y.S.2d 933, 277 App.Div. 967 (St. N.Y., 1950).

and contamination, each in excess of 1 percent of each tank of syrup shipped, or on the whole, and also provided all claims payable irrespective of percentage. The court held that this constituted a clear agreement to pay all loss if it exceeded 1 percent and the underwriter was held liable in full for leaking and contamination loss of syrup which exceeded 1 percent.

Successive Losses

With respect to hull coverages, it frequently happens that successive losses may occur at different times during a voyage, each one of which may be under the requisite percentage. The question arises: May the successive losses be added together for the purpose of reaching the necessary percentage?

Insofar as voyage policies are concerned, whether hull, cargo, or freight, it would appear that this is entirely proper as the time for ascertaining the damage is at the end of the voyage.[195] Where, however, the insurance is hull coverage under a time policy, the rule appears to be that, in order to determine whether the required "franchise" amount has been reached, the assured may add together the losses occurring on one round voyage only and not losses occurring during the whole currency of the policy.[196] No definition of a "voyage" was given and the market proceeded to do so, resulting in the so-called "voyage clause." The clause was rather tortuous and complex and, as will be explained below, is no longer used. In any event, in *Portvale Steamship Company Ltd. v. Royal Exchange Assur.*,[197] it was concluded that a period of four and a half months in port came within the scope of the then-extant clause. In succession, underwriters introduced a multiple values clause (which incorporated separate values for hull and machinery) and, later, a ship's gear clause by which hull and machinery parts were segregated and identified.

In 1969, the Institute Time Clauses were amended to replace the franchise with a sum to be deducted from the aggregate of all claims (excepting claims for total and constructive total loss) arising out of each separate accident or occurrence. The same holds true with respect to American Institute Hull Clauses (June 2, 1977). Consequently, it is most unlikely

---

195. *Blackett v. Royal Exchange Assur.*, (1832) 1 L.J. Ex. 101, 149 E.R 106.
196. *Stewart v. Merchants' Marine Ins. Co.*, (1885) 55 L.J.Q.B. 81, 5 Asp. M.L.C. 506, C.A.
197. (1932) 43 Ll.L.Rep. 161. See, also, *American Pacific S.S. Co. v. Hull Underwriters*, 1952 AMC 1016 (Arb.), and *American President Lines, Ltd. v. Hull Underwriters*, 1952 AMC 1021, where the distinguished arbitrators, Russell T. Mount and Joseph J. Geary, respectively, were confronted with the task of arbitrating claims under "voyage clause" in the AITH hull forms as they were constituted at that time.

that anyone in the industry will be any longer confronted with the old voyage clause and its successors.

The deductible franchise in the American Institute Hull Clauses (June 2, 1977) reads as follows:

Notwithstanding anything in this Policy to the contrary, there shall be deducted from the aggregate of all claims (including claims under the Sue and Labor clause and claims under the Collision Liability Clause) arising out of each separate accident, the sum of $ _____ unless the accident results in a Total Loss of the Vessel in which case this clause shall not apply. A recovery from other interests, however, shall not operate to exclude claims under this Policy provided the aggregate of such claims arising out of one separate accident if unreduced by such recovery exceeds that sum. For the purpose of this clause each accident shall be treated separately, but it is agreed that (a) a sequence of damages arising from the same accident shall be treated as due to that accident and (b) all heavy weather damage, or damage caused by contact with floating ice, which occurs during a single sea passage between two successive ports shall be treated as though due to one accident.

The comparable deductible franchise appearing in the Institute Time Clauses (hulls) is rather more complicated but the essential purpose is the same.

F.P.A. Absolutely

It is possible to secure a more restricted form of hull insurance by the Institute Voyage Clauses (hulls)—F.P.A. Absolutely.[198] The average warranty in that form reads:

Warranted free from particular average absolutely and from claims for general average damage to hull but, notwithstanding anything herein to the contrary, Vessel's proportion of general average shall be payable when it arises in respect of loss of or damage to equipment, hawsepipes, machinery, boilers, donkey boilers, winches, cranes, windlasses, steering gear (rudder excepted), electric light installation, refrigerating machinery, insulation, masts, spars, anchors, chains, ropes, sails, boats and the connections of any of the foregoing, also in

---

198. A most useful text containing all the Institute Clauses as well as the principal American clauses is *The Reference Book of Marine Insurance Clauses*, published by Witherby & Co., Ltd., London, now in its 54th edition, 1982. The new 54th edition also includes the new London clauses, i.e., cargo clauses, malicious damage, cargo (air), standard conditions for cargo contracts, strikes (both cargo and air cargo), war, and war strikes.

respect of any damage to the Vessel or her equipment caused in extinguishing fire, or by contact with other vessels in salvage operations.

Free of Damage Absolutely

More restricted cover is afforded by the Institute Time Clauses (hulls)—Free of Damage Absolutely, in which the following warranty appears:

Warranted free from any claim in respect of partial loss of and/or damage to the property hereby insured, whether included as general average or otherwise.

Deductible Franchise (Restricted Conditions)

Both the F.P.A. Absolutely and the Free of Damage Absolutely forms contain a deductible franchise clause, reading as follows:

No claim arising from a peril insured against shall be payable under this insurance unless the aggregate of all such claims arising out of each separate accident or occurrence (including claims under the Running Down and Suing and Labouring Clauses) exceeds _____ in which case this sum shall be deducted. This paragraph shall not apply to a claim for total or constructive total loss of the Vessel.

Excluding any interest comprised therein, recoveries against any claim which is subject to the above deductible shall be credited to the Underwriters in full to the extent of the sum by which the aggregate of the claim unreduced by any recoveries exceeds the above deductible.

Interest comprised in recoveries shall be apportioned between the Assured and the Underwriters, taking into account the sums paid by Underwriters and the dates when such payments were made, notwithstanding that by the addition of interest the Underwriters may receive a larger sum than they have paid.

Total Loss Only

It is also possible to insure vessels on a "Total Loss Only" basis. The American Institute form is known as "Total Loss Endorsement, 6Z-3" (Nov. 1, 1975); the Institute form is denominated the Institute Standard T.L.O. Clauses (hulls).

Clauses for Special Trades

A number of trade associations, in conjunction with underwriters, have adopted special clauses for particular types of cargo. The Institute

Clauses previously discussed, as well as their American counterparts, were drafted to meet the needs of shippers of general merchandise. As already noted, some brokers and underwriters have prepared their own special manuscript forms which they guard rather jealously.

However, there are a considerable number of so-called "trade clauses" which are basic in those trades and will be found reproduced in *Witherby's Reference Book of Marine Insurance Clauses.* An examination of these trade clauses will reveal a great many similarities with the standard and basic clauses. The modifications and amendments found in the trade clauses will, for the most part, be found to involve variations on coverage during transit and the perils insured against.

It is beyond the scope of this text to consider all the minute differences between the trade clauses and their standard counterparts, but the major differences warrant discussion. It is to be anticipated that many of the trade clauses will be substantially amended, in due course, to conform to the new London cargo clauses which became effective on January 1, 1982. However, it would be too much to expect that the use of the present standard clauses would cease so abruptly that underwriters, brokers, adjusters, surveyors—and their attorneys—would not continue to be confronted with questions involving the old clauses for many years to come.

Timber Trade Federation Clauses (1/1/62)

The precise phraseology of the insuring clause (Clause 6) in the Timber Trade Federation Clauses is set forth, *supra,* at page 805. It will be seen that as to underdeck stowage of logs or timber, the insurance is on an all risks basis. However, it is customary in the timber trade industry to transport considerable quantities of logs and/or timber on deck. As to the on-deck carriage, Clause 6(b) establishes a "modified" F.P.A. basis. An examination of Clause 6(b) will disclose that

(1) deckload is warranted free from particular average unless the vessel or craft is stranded, sunk, burnt, on fire, or in collision. However, notwithstanding the warranty, underwriters agree to pay the insured value of any portion of the cargo which may be totally lost:

(a) by jettison or washing overboard;
(b) in loading, transshipment or discharge;

Also, for any loss or damage to the interest insured which may be *reasonably attributed to:*

(c) fire, explosion, collision, or contact of the vessel and/or craft and/or conveyance with any external substance (ice included) other than water;
(d) discharge of cargo at port of distress;

Also, to pay special charges for landing, warehousing, and forwarding if incurred at a port of loading, call, or refuge, for which underwriters would be liable under the standard form of English policy with the Institute Cargo Clauses (W.A.) attached.

The Transit Clause contained in the Timber Trade Clauses is very, very wide. It reads:

Notwithstanding that the description of the voyage contained in the body of the policy may state only the ports and places of shipment and discharge, this insurance shall attach subject to the Assured then having an insurable interest at any time on or after the loading of the goods insured hereunder on land and/or water conveyances or their floating at the mill, warehouse, factory, yard or premises wheresoever, from which the despatch to the overseas vessel is made, and shall continue while the goods remain in transit until delivery by land or water into the mill, warehouse, factory, yard or premises at their final destination, whether at the port of discharge of the overseas vessel or (further sea voyage excepted) elsewhere and are there made available to the Assured or Receivers.

Provided always that where the insured goods are to be stored at the place at which they are finally landed from vessel or craft, the Underwriters' liability for loss or damage by fire shall not extend beyond 15 days from midnight of the day of the completion of such final landing notwithstanding that the goods have not then been made available to the Assured or Receivers.

Subject to the qualification that the assured has an insurable interest, (and in most instances this will be found to be at the mill, factory, warehouse, yard, or other premises in the interior), the insurance cover then extends onward and continues to the final destination until such time as the subject-matter insured is *made available to the Assured or Receivers*. The words emphasized were added to the Timber Trade Clauses as a consequence of *Renton and Co. Ltd. v. Black Sea and Baltic General Ins. Co. Ltd.*,[199] where the final destination of the cargo was the shed or space to which the cargo was delivered dockside at the Port of London.

There, in accordance with a long-standing custom, the timber was unloaded on the dock alongside the vessel in a stack without any separation of any kind as respects marks, size, or description. Ostensibly, at that point the obligation of the vessel was ended. Thereafter, the timber was carried into a shed and there stacked. Until this was done, it was impossible to allot the timber to any particular receiver. When this process was completed, it was found that 12 standards were missing.

199. (1940) 68 Ll.L.Rep. 71, 110 L.J.K.B. 329.

The question presented was whether the risk had ended at dockside (there being evidence that the entire shipment had been discharged), or whether it continued until the stacking had been completed, or until the receivers could physically take possession and remove it.

The court held that the timber had reached its final destination when removed from the vessel by the Port of London Authority, even though the task of sorting and piling the goods had to be completed before the receivers could take it away. The suit to recover the missing standards was, therefore, dismissed, leading, however, to the amendment to the clause making it clear that coverage extended until the goods were "made available to the assured or receivers."

It should be noted, however, that whether or not the goods have been so made available, coverage expires as to the fire risk 15 days from midnight on the day final landing is completed.

It not infrequently happens that when the vessel is initially unloaded, pieces are found to be missing although the loading tally shows that they should have been aboard. In the absence of any evidence as to the operation of an insured peril, such as heavy weather which might account for pieces washing overboard, coupled with, for example, loose slings, such losses would not ordinarily be recoverable. However, underwriters will frequently (for a premium) extend coverage to include all shortages of deck cargo.

Sub-section (c) of Clause 6 (the insuring clause) also provides that each raft, or craft, or deckload, or bill of lading, or deckload of each bill of lading is to be deemed a separate insurance if required by the assured. This language was involved in *Renton and Company Ltd. v. Cornhill Ins. Co.*,[200] where cargo intended to be shipped on deck was damaged while in lighters due to perils of the sea. The court held that the intention was that the underwriters should be free from liability for damage while the goods were actually deckload, but that they were liable for damage incurred while they were not actually deckload even though they might afterwards become deckload. Thus, the assured prevailed.

It will be observed that if timber loaded into craft or lighters is thus not considered to be deckload, it may well be possible for a lighter to be so constructed that it could carry a deckload. Sub-section (a) of Clause 6 makes it very clear that all timber not stowed on deck is insured under all risks terms. Consequently, (unless the lighter is specially constructed as noted above), timber loaded in craft or other conveyances and timber loaded under deck are being carried under all risks terms.

The final sentence of Clause 6 provides that claims falling under the clause are payable if amounting to 1/2 percent of the insured value or £10, whichever is lesser. If the loss claimed is more than £10 there is no prob-

---

200. (1933) 46 Ll.L.Rep. 14, [1933] All E.R. Rep. 577.

lem, but if not, then calculations must be made to see if 1/2 percent of the insured value is less than £10. If so, then sub-section (c) must then be applied whereby different lots can be treated as separate insurances and the 1/2 percent franchise applied to them.

Timber in the North American trade is generally insured on the basis of board feet measure and the invoice value calculated on the basis of 1,000 board feet. Plywood, on the other hand, is usually shipped in bundles or packages of predetermined size and claims are therefore dealt with on the basis of cubic capacity.

The Timber Trade Clauses, in common with other trade clauses, contain an "Increased Value" clause. This clause was devised so as to permit the increased value underwriters to participate with the primary underwriters in subrogation claims and was triggered by the decision in *Boag v. Standard Marine Insurance Co.*[201] There, goods were jettisoned. In the subrogation suit which followed, the primary underwriters were held entitled to the full general average contribution up to 100 percent of their payment and that the increased value underwriters would only be entitled to any excess of this amount.

The Increased Value Clause reads:

14. In the event of any additional insurance being placed by the Assured for the time being on the cargo herein insured, the value stated in this policy shall, in the event of loss or claim, be deemed to be increased to the total amount insured at the time of loss or accident.

Where the insurance is on "increased value" the following Clause shall apply:

£ _____ being increased value of cargo to be deemed to be part of the total amount insured on the cargo valued at such total amount. Where the original policies effected on the cargo cover

201. (1937) 57 Ll.L.Rep. 83. See, also, *Standard Marine Ins. Co. Ltd. v. Scottish Metropolitan Assurance Co. Ltd. (The Glenorchy)*, 283 U.S. 284, 1931 AMC 839, in which a cargo of wheat was insured under the seller's open policy for its c.i.f. value plus 3½ cents charge. The same cargo of wheat was insured under the buyer's open policy for the "increased value" of market over c.i.f. price. The carrying steamer was sunk in a collision with another vessel and the cargo was lost. Cargo, in the limitation proceedings which followed, recovered for the market value of the wheat at the time and place of shipment. Underwriters on the seller's open policy had paid the assured the c.i.f. value while underwriters on the buyer's open policy had also paid the assured the difference between the c.i.f. value and the highest market value. Both underwriters sued to establish subrogation rights against the sums recovered by the cargo owner in the limitation proceedings. The Supreme Court denied subrogation rights to the underwriter of increased value and awarded the underwriter of c.i.f. value full reimbursement, noting that, in essence, there was not a case of double insurance, as the seller's policy insured loss of the cargo whereas the buyer's policy, being insurance on increased value above market value at port of shipment, was of the same nature as insurance of profits.

also Advanced Freight then the word "cargo" in this policy shall be deemed also to include "Advanced Freight."

In the event of any additional insurance being placed by the Assured for the time being on the cargo herein insured, the value of the cargo shall, in the event of loss or claim, be deemed to be increased to the total amount insured at the time of loss or accident.

The necessity for increased value insurance is not at all academic. In the timber trade, as in many others, ownership of the cargo may change hands several times as well as increase considerably in value during the course of a voyage. The new owner, faced with knowledge of such increases, will doubtless wish to protect himself by obtaining additional insurance.

If this could be done easily and conveniently by approaching the original underwriters and requesting that the sum insured and the insured value be increased, the solution would be simple. But this is frequently not the case as the new owner may do business in one country and the underwriters be domiciled in another. As a practical matter, the new owner will place the increased value insurance through his own broker. If the increased value underwriters are to be protected in their subrogation rights, they must be able to rely on the Increased Value Clause.

The Timber Trade Federation Clauses also contain the Extended Cover Clause and the Termination of Adventure Clause which are customarily found in other trade clauses. Under the Extended Cover Clause, the insurance cover remains in force during any deviation, delay beyond the control of the assured, forced discharge, reshipment, transshipment, and any other variation of the adventure permitted to the carrier under the contract of affreightment. Under the Termination of Adventure Clause, if through no fault of the assured either the contract of affreightment is terminated or the adventure is otherwise terminated before delivery at destination, then provided notice is given immediately after receipt of advice of termination and subject to an additional premium if required, the insurance remains in force until the goods are sold and delivered at such port or place, or, if forwarded to destination, until the goods have arrived at the destination covered by the Transit Clause.

Corn Trade F.P.A. Clauses

A comparison of the Corn Trade Clauses with the standard Institute Cargo Clauses (F.P.A.) will disclose several significant differences. First, the Transit Clause in the Corn Trade Clauses differs in that the coverage attaches when the cargo leaves the warehouse at the place named in the policy for the commencement of the transit and continues until the goods are delivered to the consignees' or other final warehouse at the destination named in the policy. Moreover, the Corn Trade Clauses do not impose a time limit after discharge, but instead provide that coverage continues while in craft to or from the vessel, during any deviation, delay beyond the control of the assured, forced discharge, reshipment, transshipment, change of voyage, or any variation of the adventure by reason of any liberty granted to the carrier under the contract of affreightment.

The F.P.A. warranty is substantially the same as the Institute Cargo Clauses (F.P.A.) but contains minor variations. The Corn Trade F.P.A. warranty reads:

6. Warranted free from particular average unless the vessel and/or craft be stranded, sunk, burnt, or in collision with another ship or vessel but notwithstanding this warranty the Underwriters are to pay for loss of or damage to the interest hereby insured which may reasonably be attributed to fire, explosion or contact (other than collision with another ship or vessel) of the vessel and/or craft and/or conveyance with any substance, ice included, other than water, or owing to discharge of cargo at a port of distress. To pay partial loss occuring during transshipment and to pay the insured value of any bag which may be totally lost in loading or discharge, and the insured value of any portion of the cargo condemned at a port of distress owing to perils insured against. Also to pay special charges for landing warehousing and forwarding if incurred at an intermediate port of call or refuge, for which Underwriters would be liable under the Standard Form of English Marine Policy with the Institute Cargo Clauses (W.A.) attached.

This Clause shall operate during the whole period covered by the policy.

The variations between the standard F.P.A. Clause and the Corn Trade Clause can be summarized as follows:

(1) Under the Corn Trade Clause, the warranty is broken not only if the vessel is stranded, sunk, or burnt, but also if there is a collision with another ship or vessel. The standard F.P.A. Clause omits any reference to collision with another ship or vessel in respect of breaking the warranty.

(2) While the standard F.P.A. Clause pays for losses *reasonably attributable* to fire, explosion, collision, or contact with any external substance, the Corn Trade Clause does not mention collision with another ship or vessel in its "reasonably attributable" section of the wording. The practical effect would appear to be that claims from collision are limited to those *proximately* caused by that peril, rather than those *reasonably attributable* to such a peril.

(3) While bags totally lost in loading and discharge are recoverable, a partial loss is paid only if the loss occurs during transshipment.

It should be noted, however, that the Corn Trade Clause expands coverage with respect to any portion of the cargo which may be condemned at a port of distress due to perils insured against.

Corn Trade F.P.A. Clause (North Atlantic Shipments)

The North Atlantic Shipments form is identical to the standard Corn Trade Clause except that no coverage is provided with respect to inland transit prior to shipment or while awaiting shipment, the risk attaching only when the cargo is loaded on board the craft, lighter, or vessel at the place named in the policy for the commencement of the transit.

Coal Clauses (Coastwise Voyages)

The conditions of the Coal Clauses are essentially W.P.A. but as the memorandum franchise has been deleted, claims are payable irrespective of percentage.

Coverage attaches "at the time the subject-matter insured is at the risk of the assured within the limits of the port or place where the loading on board the coastwise vessel takes place" but only if the subject-matter is in conveyances in transit or awaiting transit (any prior attachment—such as when piled awaiting shipment—may be covered at a premium to be arranged). The risk continues during the ordinary course of transit, including transit by craft to the vessel, until the cargo is discharged from the coastwise vessel at port or place of destination, and, thereafter, during the course of transit ashore or afloat in any conveyance until delivered to stores, dumps, craft, or other vessels or storage hulks where it is intended that the cargo shall be finally deposited or delivered (in Great Britain) irrespective of the number or destinations of the craft or shore conveyances employed. If intended for coastwise or export vessels as bunkers or cargo, coverage is extended until delivered to vessels or craft afloat (other than storage hulks).

Interestingly, a time limit of 30 days is applied prior to shipment, but the risk can be extended at a premium to be arranged. Correspondingly, a 30-day time limit is also imposed between completion of discharge from the coastwise vessel at destination and final delivery. This may be contrasted with the 60-day time limit specified in the standard cargo clauses. However, extension of the latter 30-day time limit may also be had at a premium to be arranged.

Coverage is rather broad as it extends to include loss, damage, or depreciation, caused by "explosion, fire and heating of cargo even when caused by spontaneous combustion or inherent vice" and loss, damage, or depreciation which is attributable to discharge of cargo at a port of distress. Also covered are special charges for storage at, and re-shipping and forwarding from, a port of distress. Excluded, however is loss, damage, or expense proximately caused by delay.

Clause 10 provides special coverage where any portion of the cargo is discharged into craft to lighten the vessel (other than a general average act) where the water is not deep enough for the coastwise vessel to enter and discharge directly, but such coverage is on the basis of a premium to be arranged.

A special clause (Clause 11) provides that in the event of a claim for loss, damage, or contribution to general average or salvage charges, arising after discharge from the coastwise vessel and during the continuance of the insurance, there shall be added to the insured value of the cargo affected, for the adjustment of the claim, the proportionate part of the balance of freight due at the port of discharge from the coastwise vessel, and additional transport and delivery charges incurred on the cargo, but the total of all claims arising after discharge from the coastwise vessel shall not exceed the sum originally insured on the whole shipment. This reflects that in the bulk trades, freight is usually payable on the basis of outturn weights or volumes rather than being prepaid as is the usual case with respect to conventional packaged cargo. Thus, freight from the discharge of the vessel to final destination would not otherwise be covered unless the merchant arranged special freight contingency insurance.

These clauses also have the usual Increased Value Clause discussed, *supra*, with respect to the Timber Trade Federation Clauses.[202]

Flour "All Risks" Clauses

These clauses closely parallel the Institute Cargo Clauses "all risks" coverage but with a notable expansion; i.e., coverage embraces "all claims whatsoever irrespective of percentage for damage to the flour hereby insured arising from all the dangers and hazards of transportation including loss from short weight through bags being broken or torn in transit." However, excluded from coverage is any claim under £2 sterling on any one brand arriving on any one vessel, and coverage is warranted free from claims for loss, damage or expense proximately caused by weevils, insects, worms, grubs, delay or inherent vice or nature of the subject-matter insured.

It should be noted that although the title of the clauses refers to all risks, there is no mention of all risks. Rather, the term used is "any claims whatsoever." Interestingly, shortage claims for whole bags would not appear to be covered as the insuring clause refers only to "*damage* to the flour," etc.

---

202. Coal Clauses No. 116 are in common use for other regions but these forms are not reproduced in Witherby's *Reference Book of Clauses*.

Coverage attaches from the time the flour leaves the mill, or the shipper's warehouse at the place named in the policy for the commencement of the transit (unless otherwise stated), and continues until the flour is delivered to the consignee's or other final warehouse at the destination named in the policy or *until the expiration of 30 days from midnight of the day on which the vessel reports at the customs at the port of discharge, whichever may first occur.*[203]

The Termination of Adventure Clause follows standard wording except that the Flour Clauses have a 15-day limit instead of 60 days as in the standard cargo clauses.

Refrigerated Cargo Clauses

There are a number of such clauses and they appear to be continually evolving. For example, among the London Institute Clauses will be found the Frozen Food Clauses (All Risks—24 Hours Breakdown), Frozen Food Clauses (F.P.A. and Breakdown), Frozen Food Clauses (Full Conditions), Frozen Meat Clauses (Full Conditions), Frozen Meat Clauses (F.P.A. and 24 Hours Breakdown), and Frozen Meat Clauses (All Risks—24 Hours Breakdown). Similar clauses will be found in the American market and, of course, there are many special manuscript forms devised by various brokerage houses utilizing in major part the standard language and wording found in the comparable London Institute Clauses.

With respect to the Institute Clauses, the minimum cover is, of course, provided by the set entitled "F.P.A.—24 Hours Breakdown." The insuring clause reads:

7. This insurance is warranted free from Particular Average but nevertheless is extended to cover deterioration of or loss of the interest insured which is attributable to:

(a) breakdown of refrigerating machinery resulting in its stoppage for a period of not less than 24 consecutive hours;
(b) stranding, sinking, burning or collision of the vessel, craft or conveyance;
(c) contact of the vessel, craft or conveyance with any external substance (ice included) other than water;
(d) fire or explosion.

Excluded from coverage are claims arising from deterioration, loss, or damage on shore caused directly or indirectly by earthquake, volcanic eruption, and/or fire resulting therefrom.

---

203. It will be observed that this differs from the standard Institute Cargo Clauses, which specify a 60-day period which begins to run from midnight on the day discharge is completed.

More extensive coverage is provided by the "All Risks—24 Hours Breakdown" clauses. There, the insuring clause reads:

> This insurance is against all risks of loss of or damage to the interest insured other than loss or damage resulting from any variation in temperature howsoever caused, but this insurance shall not be deemed to extend to cover loss, damage or expense proximately caused by delay or inherent vice or nature of the subject-matter insured.

However, notwithstanding the foregoing, coverage is provided for loss of, or deterioration of or damage to the interest insured resulting from any variation in temperature which is attributable to (a) through (d) quoted above with respect to the F.P.A. form.

The "Full Conditions" form provides more extensive coverage and here the insuring clause covers deterioration of or loss of the interest insured from any cause (except bone taint or improper preparation, dressing, cooling, freezing, wrapping, and/or packing).

The assured is given the option, in all three sets of clauses, to have the risk commence:

(1) from the time the interest passes into the cooling and/or freezing chamber of the works, or

(2) from the time the interest is loaded into the conveyance at the freezing or cold store for transit to the oversea vessel; or

(3) on the loading of the interest on board the oversea vessel.

The Transit Clause is rather interesting and provides coverage during the ordinary course of transit until the vessel arrives at the final port of discharge, and thereafter continues while the cargo is on board the vessel at the discharge port for a period not exceeding 30 days, but this period may be extended upon payment of a premium to be arranged. Thereafter, coverage continues while the cargo is in transit to and while in cold store at the port of discharge and/or at the final destination. Oddly enough, the time periods vary depending upon the destination. For example, on shipments consigned to the United Kingdom or continent of Europe, the total period, on board the vessel, in transit to and while in cold store shall not exceed 60 days; on shipments to the United States and Canada the total period covered in transit to and while in cold store shall not exceed 30 days after discharge from the vessel; on shipments to other ports and places, the total period covered in transit to and while in cold store shall not exceed 5 days after final discharge from the vessel.

As in the standard Institute Cargo Clauses, and subject to prompt notice to underwriters and payment of a premium to be arranged, coverage continues during any deviation, forced discharge, reshipment, and transshipment, as well as during any variation of the adventure arising from the exercise of a liberty granted to carriers under the contract of affreightment, or during delay beyond the assured's control. The Termination of Adventure Clause has a limit of 30 days as compared to the 60 days usually granted in the standard cargo clauses.

Frozen Food Clauses

These clauses are used for all frozen foods but not frozen meat. At the risk of oversimplification, they partake of much of the frozen meat clauses and those of the standard cargo clauses, so much so that they can be considered to be an "amalgamation" of the two sets of clauses.

A variant of the Institute Frozen Food Clauses was litigated in *Panama City (sub nom, Fruit Distributing Co. v. Boag et al)*,[204] where the insuring clause read:

> Warranted Free from Particular Average and Loss unless caused by the vessel, craft or conveyances being stranded, sunk, burnt, on fire, or in collision or contact with any external substance (ice included) other than water, including breakdown of Refrigerator Machinery, but to pay all claims for all damage and/or deterioration to the Interest insured caused by breakdown and/or latent defect of Refrigerator Machinery and/or Plant and/or Insulation, but no claim shall be recoverable unless breakdown be for a period of not less than twenty-four hours.

The vessel, after being loaded with bananas, and while en route to its port of destination suffered a breakdown of its starboard boiler. The ship's boilers were the only source of steam for powering the vessel, its auxiliary equipment, and the refrigeration plant. The weather was inclement and the vessel could not maintain proper steerageway on one boiler if steam from that boiler had to be used also to power the refrigeration plant. Consequently, the steam to the refrigeration plant was shut off and the vessel proceeded to port. By the time it arrived, the refrigeration plant and machinery had been shut off more than 24 hours. By this time, the bananas were from 90 percent to 95 percent ripe, by reason of which they were materially impaired in value. There was no question but that the bananas were in proper condition for transporting without material injury had the refrigeration thereof continued during the voyage.

The issue before the court was whether the vessel's starboard boiler was an integral and indispensable part of the "Refrigerator Machinery and/or Plant" so that its malfunction would qualify under the insuring clause. The court, noting that the words "and/or Plant" had been added

204. 93 F.Supp. 431, 1950 AMC 1992 (S.D. Ala.).

to the word "Machinery" concluded that it was clear that the starboard boiler was within the contemplation of the insuring clause in the policy.

A broker's manuscript policy, covering *inter alia* refrigerated salmon, was involved in *Larsen v. Insurance Co. of N.A.*[205] There, the assured strove mightily to bring himself within the scope of the insuring clause, which read:

> Warranted free from Particular Average unless directly caused by the vessel being stranded, sunk, burnt or in collision with another ship or vessel or with ice or with any substance other than water. Notwithstanding this warranty, the Assurers are to pay the insured value of any package or packages which may be totally lost in loading, transshipment or discharge; also to pay landing, warehousing and special charges if incurred for which Underwriters would be liable under a policy covering Particular Average.
>
> Whilst stowed in Refrigeration Chambers of vessel named herein this insurance is extended to cover all loss or damage due to or caused by derangement or breakdown of the refrigerating machinery and/or refrigerating plant and/or insulation . . . .
>
> This insurance attaches from the time the goods leave the Warehouse and/or Store at the place named in the policy for the commencement of the transit and continues during the ordinary course of transit, including customary transhipment if any, until the goods are discharged overside from the overseas vessel at the final port.

The assured's contentions were many and varied, and included:

> (1) negligence of the crew in failing to maintain proper temperatures in the cargo holds below 40° Fahrenheit which, it was urged, constituted "faults or errors in the navigation and/or management of the vessel" within the meaning of the Inchmaree Clause in the policy;
>
> (2) the tierces of salmon that were lost were "separate and apportionable" packages within the exception to the F.P.A. warranty;
>
> (3) that the vessel stranded which opened the warranty;
>
> (4) that the loss of 11 tierces of salmon occurred during "transshipment" as was excepted from the warranty;
>
> (5) that there was a derangement in the refrigeration equipment;

---

205. 252 F.Supp. 458, 1965 AMC 2576 (W.D. Wash.). The contrast between such refrigeration policies written on an F.P.A. basis and those written on an all risks basis is amply demonstrated by comparing *Quattrochiocchi v. Albany Ins.*, 1983 AMC 1152 (N.D. Cal.). In the latter, the insurance was an all risk cargo policy on refrigerated dairy products, excluding "deterioration, decay or spoilage unless caused by derangement or breakdown of the refrigeration machinery, plant or insulation." The assured established that the cargo was in good order upon shipment and in bad condition on delivery. The court imposed upon the underwriters the burden of establishing that the assured's loss constituted "deterioration, decay or spoilage" and thereafter, that the damage was not caused by a "derangement or breakdown."

(6) that the flooding of the hold of the vessel as a result of the failure of a pipe was a peril of the sea; and

(7) that two special "free from particular average clauses" stamped in red ink on the policy applied.

The court held against the assured on all contentions. Specifically, as to No. (1), the negligence, if any, of the crew was held to be negligence in the care, custody, and control of the cargo. As to No. (2), the 11 damaged tierces were held not to be separate and apportionable packages. As to No. (3), although the vessel stranded, its stranding did not proximately and *directly* cause the loss. As to No. (4), the loss was more probably than not caused during the transit from inland origin to the vessel and the term "transshipment" was not applicable. As to No. (5), it was held that the failure of the crew to operate the machinery properly was not a "derangement." As to No. (6), the failure of the pipe, thus admitting water to the hold, was due to electrolysis or corrosion and not a "latent defect." As to No. (7), the special clauses stamped in red ink applied only with respect to other vessels in the fleet and not to the vessel on which the shipment was made.

CHAPTER XXI

PROTECTION AND INDEMNITY

Introduction and History

It has been said that protection and indemnity insurance arose out of the case of *De Vaux v. Salvador*,[1] which held, in essence, that hull underwriters were not liable for payment of the liabilities of the insured owner or his vessel arising out of negligence. There, two vessels collided and the court found mutual fault. On balance, one had to pay to the other and sought to recover the amount paid as a particular average loss arising from perils of the sea. Recovery was denied on the ground that the liability of the insured vessel was not caused by a peril insured against; rather, it grew out of an arbitrary provision in the law of nations from views of general expediency . . . not as dictated by natural justice, nor (possibly) quite consistent with it . . . and could no more be charged against underwriters than a penalty incurred by the contravention of revenue laws.[2]

As a consequence, the Running Down Clause evolved. But, reflecting the belief that a full loss should not be paid which might encourage negligence and carelessness on the part of the master and crew, the clause provided that only three-fourths of the liability would be paid. This led shipowners to attempt to protect themselves from the excess collision liability by placing the remaining one-fourth risk in protection associations.[3]

The first club or society was formed to cover "extra risks not covered by ordinary marine policies on ships with a collision or running down clause therein"; that is, excess collision liability and liability for loss of life and personal injury.[4]

---

1. (1836) 111 E.R. 845.

2. The decision in *De Vaux v. Salvador* was followed shortly in the United States by *General Mutual Ins. Co. v. Sherwood*, 55 U.S. 351 (1847), in which the underwriter, although required to pay the owner for his hull damage, was held not liable for collision and cargo damages sustained by the other vessel.

3. Prior to *De Vaux v. Salvador, supra,* mutual associations called "hull clubs" competed with underwriters at Lloyd's, although the coverage provided by them did not appear to be as extensive. Some of the hull clubs did insure their members for third-party liabilities to crew members, passengers, and cargo. The transition from hull clubs to protection & indemnity clubs was therefore logical and natural.

4. "The History and Development of P & I Insurance: The British Scene," William R. A. Birch Reynardson, 43 *Tulane Law Review* no. 3, "A Symposium on the P & I Policy" (April, 1969). See, also, "Report of Advanced Study Group No. 109 of the Insurance Institute of London," presented at a special meeting of the members on January 8, 1957, and reprinted by permission of the institute.

Shortly thereafter, the *Westenhope* was lost off South Africa, after having deviated from the port of original destination. The owners were forced to pay for the loss of cargo aboard, whereupon the protection association refused to reimburse the shipowners. As a consequence, and in due course, P & I policies were amended to provide coverage for cargo claims in certain instances.

By virtue of the Companies Act, 1862, in Great Britain mutual protection associations are invariably registered under the Act, either as a company limited by shares or by guarantee.[5] The association itself is the insurer, and the assured's right of action lies against the association and not against the individual members, the consideration being the assured's liability to contribute to the losses of the other members and the expenses of the association.[6]

Mutual insurances are expressly made subject to the articles of association and to the rules and regulations thereof, which are by express reference incorporated in the club rules or form of policy as the case may be. A knowledge of the rules by which a member has agreed to be bound will be imputed to him.[7]

Although the rules vary from association to association,[8] there are a number of rules which appear to be common to nearly all. For example, the non-assignability of claims without the express consent of the association; an option on the part of the association to cancel if the vessel is sold or requisitioned, or if the entire management, control and possession of the entered vessel is transferred by demise charter or by a change in corporate ownership or control; a requirement that prompt notice of claims be made; and time limits with respect to filing suit.[9] For example, see *Lemar Towing v. Fireman's Fund,*[10] where no breach of the management warranty was found.

Because the rules do vary from association to association, it is difficult to lay down any hard and fast rule applicable to every situation; in the end, each case must be decided upon its own facts and the club rules applicable thereto. For example, the question has been raised as to whether or not there can be claims for loss or contributions by or against part

5. See *Lion Insurance Ass'n v. Tucker,* (1883) 12 Q.B.D. 176, C.A.
6. See *North-Eastern 100A S.S. Insurance Ass'n v. Red S. Steamship Co.,* (1906) 22 T.L.R. 692, 12 Com.Cas. 26, C.A. Policies of P and I insurance are invariably issued in the United States, and the assured's right of action lies against the association and not the individual members.
7. *Turnbull v. Wolfe,* (1862) 7 L.T. 483.
8. See vol. 7A, *Benedict on Admiralty* (2d ed.) for the text of the principal P and I club rules.
9. English policies almost invariably require a reference to arbitration as a condition precedent to the right of a member to bring an action against the association. See, for example, *Wells Fargo v. London S.S. Owners,* 408 F.Supp. 626, 1976 AMC 592 (S.D.N.Y.), [1977] 1 Lloyd's Rep. 213.
10. 471 F.2d 609, 1973 AMC 1843 (5th Cir.).

owners of vessels insured other than members. In *United Kingdom Mutual S.S. Ass'n v. Nevill,*[11] it was held that a part owner could not be sued for contributions as an undisclosed principal of the manager and as a part owner who was entered as the member. However, in other decisions, it has been held that part owners were liable for contributions.[12]

By the same token, whether a rule is a warranty, the non-compliance with which discharges the insurer, or is only an exception from the risks insured against, is a question of construction depending upon the language of the rule and the nature of the risk to which it relates. For example, in *Harrison v. Douglas,*[13] the policy contained a condition that all chain cables were to be properly tested. This was not done. The court held that it was a jury question and the payment of money into court by the insurer waived any objection as to the non-performance. To the contrary, in *Stewart v. Wilson,*[14] and *Colledge v. Harty,*[15] the rules were construed as warranties, the breach of which relieved the underwriters of liability.

Estoppel by conduct may also come into play in construing the rules.[16]

The method of making calls on assessments has also been litigated. In *Turner v. American Steamship Owners P & I Ass'n,*[17] the court held that a plan of assessing vessels entered in the association on the basis of "contributing tonnage" was fair if the discretion of the directors was exercised in good faith and not arbitrarily. In *Columbia S.S. v. American S.S. Owners P & I Ass'n,*[18] the P & I association simultaneously declared a dividend based on the results of certain insurance years which lowered the association's surplus below the amount required by the New York law and levied an assessment against current policyholders, including the plaintiff, to restore the surplus to the minimum level. The court held that the simultaneous dividend-assessment scheme was proper and lawful. In *Volkswagenwerk A. G. and Wolfsburger Transport G.m.b.H. v. International Mutual Strike Assur. Co. (Bermuda) Ltd.,*[19] the association directors had to decide on

11. (1887) 19 Q.B.D. 110, C.A.

12. *Ocean Iron S.S. Ins. Ass'n v. Leslie,* (1887) 22 Q.B.D. 722; *Great Britain 100 A1 Steamship Ins. Ass'n v. Wyllie,* (1899) 22 Q.B.D. 710, C.A.; and *British Marine Mut. Ins. Co. v. Jenkins,* (1900) 111 E.R. 299.

13. (1835) 111 E.R. 463.

14. (1843) 153 E.R. 1089 (failure to comply with an order of the managing underwriters after an inspection).

15. (1851) 155 E.R. 515 (violation of a rule not to sail to a particular area during specified dates).

16. See *Teignmouth & Ge. Shipping Ass'n, Martin's Claim,* (1872) L.R. 14 Eq. 148 (policy not stamped but there was a sufficient admission of liability in the books of the association); *Barrow Mutual Ship Ins. Co. Ltd. v. Ashburner,* (1885) 54 L.J.Q.B. 377, C.A. (policy not stamped but member held liable for calls for losses after having previously paid calls and acted otherwise as if he were a member); *Jones v. Bangor Mut. Shipping Ins. Soc. Ltd.,* (1889) 61 L.T. 727, 6 Asp. M.L.C. 450, D.C. (violation of rule against overinsurance with knowledge of the association; association held estopped to rely on the rule).

17. 16 F.2d 707, 1927 AMC 337 (5th Cir.).

18. 1974 AMC 982 (D.,Ore.).

19. [1977] 2 Lloyd's Rep. 503.

the amount of "advance calls" and "supplementary calls." Although the respondents' membership had ceased, they still remained liable for supplementary calls made thereafter with respect to the last policy year. They were insured in respect of strikes of persons working on shore only and not for crew strike risks. Some members were insured against both risks. The respondents refused to pay the calls. After an arbitration took place and questions were certified to the court of appeal, the court held that the association was not bound to administer as a separate fund the calls and claims of members insuring against shore risks only to the exclusion of members insured against other risks, and that in levying, the association was bound to levy on all members at the same percentage or rate per unit of currency of the contributing value of their respective entered vessels.

In *First Nat'l Bank of Chicago v. West of England, etc. (The Evelpidis Era)*,[20] the assured assigned rights under the policy to the mortgagee bank. The club was given notice of the assignment. It was held that the club had no right to offset delinquent calls on other vessels of the assured against sums due for repatriation expenses payable under the policy. In *West of Scotland Ship Owners Mut. P & I Ass'n v. Aifanourios Shipping (The Aifanourios)*,[21] the club insured the defendant's vessel for P & I risks and claimed unpaid release calls amounting to some $26,000, for which the vessel was arrested. It was held that as a contract of insurance did not fall within the scope of the statute as an agreement "relating to the use or hire of any ship or to the carriage of goods," the arrest was vacated and the security theretofore posted was voided. In *West of England v. Patriarch*,[22] it was held that unpaid insurance premiums do not give rise to a maritime lien. Consequently, the bank's mortgage lien was held to have priority over the claims for unpaid insurance premiums. In *Weiland v. Pyramid Ventures*,[23] it was held that the club was not entitled to cancellation of coverage or set-off for "release calls" against a personal injury judgment because of the assured's failure to pay calls where the assured's delinquency (including ultimate insolvency) occurred after the date of the accident giving rise to the judgment.

P & I Policy Is a "Time Policy"

Section 85, Marine Insurance Act, 1906, refers tangentially to protection and indemnity insurance in its provisions with respect to "mutual insurance." Section 85 provides:

---

20. [1981] 1 Lloyd's Rep. 54.
21. [1980] 2 Lloyd's Rep. 403.
22. 491 F.Supp. 539, 1981 AMC 423 (D.,Mass.).
23. 511 F.Supp. 1034, 1981 AMC 2846 (M.D.,La.).

(1) Where two or more persons mutually agree to insure each other against marine losses there is said to be a mutual insurance.

(2) The provisions of this Act relating to the premium do not apply to mutual insurance, but a guarantee, or such other arrangement as may be agreed upon, may be substituted for the premium.

(3) The provisions of this Act in so far as they may be modified by the agreement of the parties, may in the case of mutual insurance be modified by the terms of the policies issued by the association, or by the rules and regulations of the association.

(4) Subject to the exceptions mentioned in this section, the provisions of this Act apply to a mutual insurance.[24]

More specifically, as to the application of the Act with respect to protection and indemnity policies, see *Compania Maritima San Basilio S.A. v. Oceanus Mutual Underwriting Ass'n (Bermuda) Ltd. (The Eurysthenes).*[25] In that case, the plaintiffs' vessel stranded while carrying cargo and the cargo interests made claim against the plaintiffs. The defendant club suggested that, as the vessel did not have her full complement of deck officers, proper charts, a serviceable echo sounder, or an operative boiler, she was unseaworthy when she embarked on the voyage. Three questions were certified which the court was requested to answer:

1. Whether it constituted a defense to prove that the ship was sent to sea in an unseaworthy state with the privity of the plaintiffs within Section 39(5) of the Act;

2. If so, whether in order to prove "privity" within that section it was necessary for the defendants to prove (a) negligence . . . and/or . . . (b) knowledge . . . of the fact constituting unseaworthiness and/or (c) some deliberate or reckless conduct . . . in sending the ship to sea in an unseaworthy state; and

3. Whether the defendants' discretion to reject or reduce a claim may be exercised where the only evidence relevant to the exercise of such discretion concerned the conduct of the member before any claim against him had arisen in sending the ship to sea in an unseaworthy state.

The court of appeal answered the first question "yes," as the contract of insurance constituted a time policy and, accordingly, Section 39(5) formed part of the cover. As to the second question, it was held that the word "privity" in Section 39(5) meant "with knowledge and consent" and it was therefore necessary to prove knowledge and concurrence on the part of the shipowner personally to the ship being sent to sea in an un-

24. See, generally, *British Marine Mutual Ins. Co. v. Jenkins,* [1900] 1 Q.B. 299; *Ocean Iron S.S. Ass'n Ltd. v. Leslie,* (1887) 22 Q.B.D. 722.
25. [1976] 2 Lloyd's Rep. 171, C.A.

seaworthy state, though such privity did not necessarily amount to "wilful misconduct." The third question was answered "no," for the plaintiffs were not required to take steps to protect their interests before the casualty occurred.

Essentially, the same result obtained in the United States until 1941, notwithstanding that the general rule is that there is not an implied warranty of seaworthiness in a P & I policy under United States law. This conclusion, however, involves a comparison of and harmonization with a number of decisions which bear on the question.

In 1926, the Ninth Circuit in *The C.S. Holmes*,[26] held that there was no implied warranty of seaworthiness in a P & I policy, and that the policy covered liability of the assured for damage to cargo founded upon the vessel's unseaworthiness where the assured was without privity or knowledge.

In *The T.W. Lake (Hanover Fire Ins. v. Merchants Transp. Co.)*,[27] the court held that there was no implied warranty of seaworthiness in the P & I policy; that while limitation was denied in a proceeding for limitation of liability, this did not constitute a defense on behalf of the P & I underwriter; that the failure of the assured to give the insurer information concerning the unseaworthiness of the vessel was, in the absence of fraud and on account of a failure on the part of the underwriter to seek information, no defense to liability, nor did it avoid the policy; and that the policy covered damage arising from the negligence of the ship unless such negligence was so gross as to amount to wilful, deliberate, and intentional wrong.

Concurrently, the Fourth Circuit in *Sorenson & Neilson v. Boston Ins. Co.*,[28] held that a P & I policy is not voided by privity and knowledge of the assured as to the unseaworthiness of the vessel unless there is either fraud or wilful exposure to a known danger.

However, in *Edgar F. Coney and Tow*,[29] the Fifth Circuit held that a shipowner who paid liability claims and whose petition to limit liability for such claims was denied on the grounds of "privity and knowledge" could not recover under his P & I policy covering losses sustained "with-

---

26. 9 F.2d 296, 1926 AMC 126.
27. 15 F.2d 949, 1927 AMC 1 (9th Cir.).
28. 20 F.2d 640, 1927 AMC 1288 (4th Cir.). This decision was cited with approval in *T.N. No. 73*, 1939 AMC 673, *aff'd* 1940 AMC 1361 (2d Cir.), 1941 AMC 1697 (U.S. Sup.Ct., 1941). See, also, *Rose Murphy*, 1933 AMC 444 (St.,Ala.), where the owner of a vessel lost at sea sued his protection and indemnity underwriter to recover sums paid to the owner of the lost cargo. The underwriter entered a plea that the assured had wilfully cast away the ship and cargo. The owner demurred to the plea. The court held that the plea was good and sufficiently alleged that the cargo was wilfully destroyed, noting that there can be no insurance coverage which will indemnify the assured against a loss which he may purposely and wilfully create or which may arise from his immoral, fraudulent, or felonious conduct.
29. 117 F.2d 694, 1941 AMC 262 (5th Cir.).

out fault or privity on the part of the assured." The court further held
that the terms "fault or privity" as used in the policy had substantially the
same meaning as those terms had in the English and American limitation
of liability statutes—they did not mean negligence so gross as to amount
to a wilful, deliberate, and intentional wrong.

In 1941, the Second Circuit in *The Morro Castle (P & I Insurance)*,[30]
held that the words "owner or owners" in the limitation of liability statute
and the word "assured" in the policy should be interpreted to include all
members of the staff of the corporation to whom duties of a managerial
nature were assigned, and were not to be limited to the executive officers
of the corporate owner. Consequently, the corporate owner was bound by
the acts and omissions of its "managing officer," the shore superintendent
to whom had been delegated the supervision of the vessel; thus, the
failure to take efficient measures to assure that all laws and regulations
were properly observed was an omission sufficient to charge the owners
with "privity or knowledge" such as to avoid the P & I underwriters' liability to reimburse for resulting losses.

This strict construction by the court in *Morro Castle* of the term "privity" led to a deletion of the "fault or privity" clause from American P & I
policies. In fact, in 1941, the U.S. Maritime Commission required, by
order, the deletion of all "privity" clauses in respect of vessels in which it
had an interest.[31]

As a consequence of the deletion of the "privity" clause, P & I underwriters are liable for claims arising from any improper condition of the
vessel even though management might be aware of it or the condition
may have resulted from the design or neglect of management.[32]

The question which arose in *The Eurysthenes*—that is, the applicability
of Section 39(5) of the Act—does not appear to have been decided in the
United States. While, as noted heretofore, the Act does not apply of its
own force in the United States, Section 39(5) is merely declarative of the
common law.[33] However, as also noted, the American rule is expressed in
the negative that a vessel owner, from bad faith or neglect, will not knowingly permit his vessel to break ground in an unseaworthy condition, the
consequence of which is a denial of liability if the loss or damage was
caused proximately by such unseaworthiness.

It is to be hoped that this discordance between American law and English law in this respect will eventually be resolved. If, in America, under a
time hull policy, there is no liability if the owner, from bad faith or neglect, knowingly permits his vessel to break ground in an unseaworthy

30. 117 F.2d 404, 1941 AMC 243 (2d Cir.).
31. See 1941 AMC 429 for the text of the order.
32. See, for example, *Martin & Robinson v. Orion Ins. Co.*, 1971 AMC 515 (St.,Cal.).
33. See discussion on the subject of warranties of seaworthiness and implied warranties
of seaworthiness in time policies, Chapter XI, "Warranties."

condition which proximately causes loss, then the same result should follow under a P & I policy which, after all, is but a species of "time" policy—and this is true notwithstanding the physical deletion of "privity" clauses from American P & I policies.

Construction in General

There are, of course, many different types of protection and indemnity policies other than the classic form originally intended to cover collision liabilities which were not then provided by the hull policies.[34] There are freight, demurrage, and defense associations, and associations covering shipbuilders' liabilities, ship repairers' liabilities, and the like. More importantly, there are employers' liability-type policies which carry special endorsements such as the marina operators' liability policy construed in *Pillgrem v. Cliff Richardson Boats Ltd. and Richardson: Switzerland Gen. Ins. Co., Third Party*,[35] and comprehensive personal liability insurance (with special endorsements) such as was construed in *Security Nat. Ins. Co. v. Sequoyah Marina.*[36]

In general, such policies are construed like any other insurance policy and the same rules apply. And as in every insurance policy, such liability policies must be construed in light of the *purpose* of such insurance. See, for example, *Cunard S.S. Co. v. Marten*,[37] where, even though the policy contained a suing and laboring clause, it was held to be inappropriate and inapplicable in a protection and indemnity policy.

Further examples will serve to illustrate this proposition. In *Seaboard Shipping v. Jocharanne Tugboat*,[38] the court noted that P and I policies are intended to apply chiefly to situations not covered by other insurance and thereupon upheld a "no contribution" clause where the assured had expended sums for sue and labor expenses and its hull underwriters sought to recoup a portion of them from the P & I underwriters. The court reached this conclusion even though the efforts and sums expended might well have avoided possible explosion, abandonment, wreck removal and other expenses and liabilities which otherwise would have fallen upon the P & I underwriters.

In *Caballery v. Sea-Land Services, etc.*,[39] the policies were endorsed to provide that if the assured's vessel was chartered to any affiliated or re-

---

34. As a result of legislation over the years and the imposition of new liabilities on shipowners, underwriters had continually been required to add new risks to the coverages originally provided.
35. [1977] 1 Lloyd's Rep. 297 (Can.).
36. 246 F.2d 830, 1958 AMC 143 (10th Cir.).
37. [1903] 2 K.B. 511, C.A.
38. 461 F.2d 500, 1972 AMC 2151 (2d Cir.).
39. 1973 AMC 479 (D.,R.I.).

lated companies, coverage would be extended to protect the charterers "in any capacity." One of the assured's related companies was engaged in stevedoring operations, during the course of which liability was imposed on the vessel. After payment, underwriters brought a subrogation action against the related company but failed in the action.

In *Lanasse v. Travelers Ins. Co.*,[40] there was a charter provision requiring the owner to indemnify the time charterer against all claims "directly or indirectly connected with the possession, navigation, management and operation of the vessel." Where the vessel was merely the "inert locale" of the seaman's injury, which in turn resulted solely from the negligence of the charterer's crane operator during loading operations, the court denied indemnity from the underwriter, as the operation of the crane was not even remotely connected or related to the vessel's "operation and management."

See, also, *Bee Line Transp. Co. v. Connecticut Fire Ins. Co. of Hartford*,[41] construing a specially constructed tower's liability endorsement attached to a general liability policy; *American Ins. Co. v. Keane*,[42] involving the construction of a combination hull and P & I policy covering a racing boat; *Hinkle & Finlayson v. Globe & Rutgers*,[43] defining the term "vehicle" under Section 109 of the New York Insurance Code as including a water vehicle, a vessel, or tugboat); *Security Nat. Ins. Co. v. Sequoyah Marina*,[44] construing a comprehensive personal liability policy defining the insured as "any person legally responsible therefor"; *Miller v. American S.S. Mut. P & I Ass'n*,[45] where the court held that a P & I policy is an indemnity policy, not a liability policy, and the underwriter was liable only for payments actually made by the assured; *Ahmed v. American S.S. Owners Mut. P & I Ass'n*,[46] holding that to receive reimbursement from a P & I underwriter, the assured shipowner must first actually pay the loss; *Offshore Logistics v. Mutual Marine*,[47] holding that a bareboat charterer is an owner *pro hac vice* and, as such, is covered by a P & I policy insuring its liability as "owner"; *Progress Marine v. Foremost*,[48] holding that removal of a wreck is "com-

---

40. 450 F.2d 580, 1972 AMC 818 (5th Cir.).
41. 76 F.2d 759, 1935 AMC 670 (2d Cir.).
42. 233 F.2d 354, 1956 AMC 488 (D.C. Cir.).
43. 1936 AMC 1289 (St.,N.Y.).
44. 246 F.2d 830, 1958 AMC 143 (10th Cir.).
45. 509 F.Supp. 1047, 1981 AMC 903 (S.D.N.Y.).
46. 444 F.Supp. 569, 1978 AMC 586 (N.D.,Cal.), *aff'd* 640 F.2d 993, 1981 AMC 897 (9th Cir.), subsequent proceedings, 1982 AMC 1228 (N.D.,Cal.), *aff'd* 701 F.2d 824, 1983 AMC 2712 (9th Cir.), *cert. den.* 1984 AMC 2401. The subsequent proceedings involved the question of whether the New York statute, denying a right of direct action against a liability underwriter, was constitutional. The court held that it was.
47. 462 F.Supp. 486, 1981 AMC 1154 (E.D.,La.).
48. 642 F.2d 816, 1981 AMC 2315 (5th Cir.). Compare this case with *Seaboard Shipping v. Jocharanne Tugboat, supra.*

pulsory by law" under a P & I policy if the assured incurs the cost in a subjective belief that removal is reasonably necessary to avoid potential legal liability justifying the expense; *St. Paul Fire v. Vest*,[49] where the P & I underwriter on a barge was held not liable for wreck removal expenses when the barge sank solely because of the negligence of the towing tug; *La Cross v. Craighead*,[50] where a supply boat owner's P & I underwriter was found to owe no duty to defend or indemnify a time charterer for liability to an injured seaman arising out of the time charterer's status as the owner of a drilling rig rather than as the "owner and charterer" of the supply boat; *Parfait v. Central Towing*,[51] holding that the sale of all the stock in a closely held tug-owning corporation and election of new directors and officers voided the policy under the "change of management" clause; *Rini v. Transocean*,[52] where the assured held two policies covering the same risk, each containing an "escape" clause, and liability was prorated on the basis of the monetary limits of the respective policies; *Healy Tibbetts v. Foremost*,[53] holding that an oil spill is not part of the "wreck" of a sunken oil barge within the meaning of the wreck removal clause and was excluded from liability by a "pollution exclusion clause"; *Michaels v. Mutual Marine*,[54] where it was held that a policy containing a $10,000 deductible for "any one loss, accident or disaster" covered damage to a ship's deck caused by repeated contacts of grab buckets during the discharge of scrap, as the repeated contacts constituted a single event or occurrence; *Farmers Home v. I.N.A.*,[55] where the court held that a policy insuring a yacht owner against liability for bodily injury arising by reason of his "interest" was ambiguous and was therefore construed to cover injury to a guest who fell through an opening in a pier while assisting another passenger to disembark; *Continental v. Bonanza*,[56] holding that since a vessel's time charterer, named as a co-assured in a shipowner's P & I policy, had no "ownership" interest in the vessel, the charterer had no duty as "owner" to remove the vessel's wreck and the P & I club was not liable to reimburse the charterer for its costs of removing the wreck from its leased underwater property; and *M.J. Rudolf v. Lumber Mut. Fire; Luria International et al, Third Parties (The Cape Borer)*,[57] where the court construed the P & I policy as covering the expense of wreck removal when such removal was ordered by a department of the city in whose waters the vessel sank.

49. 500 F.Supp. 1365, 1982 AMC 450 (N.D.,Miss.).
50. 466 F.Supp. 880, 1982 AMC 2692 (E.D.,La.).
51. 660 F.2d 608, 1982 AMC 698 (5th Cir.).
52. 1981 AMC 1128 (W.D.,La.).
53. 1980 AMC 1600 (N.D.,Cal.).
54. 472 F.Supp. 26, 1979 AMC 1673 (S.D.N.Y.).
55. 1979 AMC 2549 (St.,Wash.).
56. 706 F.2d 1365, 1983 AMC 2059 (5th Cir.).
57. 371 F.Supp. 1325, 1974 AMC 1990 (E.D.N.Y.), [1975] 2 Lloyd's Rep. 108.

Eagle Leasing Corp. v. Hartford Fire[58] involved an interesting point of construction. Generally speaking, an insurance policy is construed most strongly against the underwriter, as it normally represents the underwriter's handiwork and draftsmanship.[59] However, in *Eagle Leasing*, the vessel owner was a corporation managed by sophisticated and knowledgeable personnel. It placed its coverage with the P & I underwriter through knowledgeable and sophisticated insurance brokers who were in part, at least, responsible for the ultimate provisions of the policy. When the loss occurred, the policy term had expired. The assured contended that the act of neglect leading to the loss and consequent expenditures occurred during the policy period although the actual event occurred afterwards, and therefore the underwriters should be required to indemnify. At first instance, the assured succeeded. On appeal, although conceding that the coverage provision was ambiguous, the appellate court refused to apply the general rule but instead denied recovery, giving effect to the most probable intentions of the parties and one considered most reasonable from a business point of view.

A modern P & I policy covers many diverse risks.[60] These include: loss of life, personal injury, and illness of *any person* except employees covered by a Workmen's Compensation Act (the term "any person" as used here includes the crew, passengers or other persons lawfully on board the vessel, stevedores, and any person injured on shore by the vessel); repatriation expenses; excess collision risks; damage caused otherwise than by collision; damage to docks, buoys, structures, etc.; wreck removal; cargo losses; fines and penalties; mutiny and misconduct; quarantine expenses; putting-in expenses (incurred with respect to landing injured or sick seamen and passengers); cargo's proportion of general average[61]; pollution liabilities; expenses of investigation and defense; and expenses incurred with the express authorization of the association in the interest of the association.[62]

---

58. 540 F.2d 1257, 1978 AMC 604 (5th Cir.).

59. See discussion, *supra*, Chapter IV, "Principles of Construction," where the maxim *verba chartarum fortius accipiuntur contra proferentem* is considered.

60. For the discussion which follows, the American Steamship Owners Mutual Protection and Indemnity Association, Inc., form of policy, revised February 20, 1972, is taken as the model, referred to herein for convenience as the "ASM" form. Also discussed and compared, as appropriate, will be the SP-23 (revised 1/56) form and the SP-38 form, the former being in fairly common usage in the United States. Where appropriate, the comparable rule from one of the major P and I clubs in Great Britain will be set forth and comparisons drawn.

61. This has validity with respect only to contributions assessed against cargo which cannot be collected from the cargo because of a breach of the contract of affreightment on the part of the vessel owner.

62. Coverage provided with the "express authorization of the Association in the interest of the Association" is generally referred to in the so-called "Omnibus Rule" of the principal P & I clubs. For example, Rule 20(25) of the Britannia Steam Ship Insurance Associated Limited provides coverage for:

Introduction and General Observations concerning Shipowners' and Charterers' Liabilities for Loss of Life and Personal Injury[63]

It is helpful to keep in mind the historical division between "protection" risks and "indemnity" risks. Protection risks are, generally speaking, those which concern liability for loss of life and personal injury, collision liabilities, damage to piers, removal of wreck, wash damage and the like. Indemnity risks involve primarily damage to or loss of cargo and fines and penalties. At first, the two classes of risks were insured in separate mutual associations, but today the two classes have been merged into the same form of policy or club rules.

Unquestionably, one of the principal reasons for the formation and rapid growth of the protection associations was the ever increasing liabilities imposed upon shipowners for loss of life and personal injuries to crew and passengers. Although as of 1846 when Parliament enacted the Fatal Accidents Act (commonly known as Lord Campbell's Act), liability of shipowners for loss of life and personal injury was governed by the common law and was virtually unlimited, dependents of persons killed had no right to sue for damages. This was corrected by Lord Campbell's Act, which imposed still further liability upon shipowners, among others.[64]

For many years, the laws in the United States relating to shipowners' liability for loss of life and personal injury generally paralleled those of Great Britain. For example, under the common law, a shipowner was obliged to respond in damages for negligent injury to persons but not for loss of life.[65]

Liabilities, costs and expenses incidental to the business of owning, operating or managing ships which, in the discretion of the Committee, come within the scope of the cover afforded by the Association. Claims under this paragraph shall be recoverable to such extent only as the Committee may determine.

63. The entire section of this chapter with respect to shipowners' and charterers' liabilities for loss of life and personal injury was prepared by Paul N. Wonacott, a partner in the firm of Wood Tatum Mosser Brooke & Landis, Portland, Oregon, for which the author expresses his deepest appreciation. Mr. Wonacott is a noted expert in this area, and his firm for many years has represented with great distinction all, or nearly all, the P & I clubs in their matters arising on the Pacific Coast of the United States.

64. For the history and development of P & I insurance in Great Britain, the reader is highly recommended to the excellent article in 43 *Tulane Law Review* no. 3 (1969) by William R. A. Birch Reynardson. As an illustration of how cheaply life was valued prior to the turn of the century, Mr. Reynardson gives the example of a claim filed with the United Kingdom Association in 1876 involving the vessel *Talisman*, which collided with and sank a French lugger loaded with potatoes and also drowned the captain's wife. The claim was honored, valuing the potatoes at £71 and the captain's wife at £5. One need only examine the judgments obtained against shipowners for loss of life in the last several decades to appreciate the wide disparity between the size of claims one hundred years ago and those being advanced today, with a concomitant increase in exposure of the P & I underwriters.

65. See the excellent article, "The History and Development of P & I Insurance: The American Scene," by John P. Kipp, 43 *Tulane Law Review* no. 3 (1969), for a discussion of how P & I insurance evolved in the United States.

The United States, of all the major maritime nations in the world, stands alone in its refusal to adopt a "workmen's compensation" approach to seamen's claims for injuries and death. Instead, commencing with *The Osceola*,[66] amplified by the passage of the so-called "Jones Act,"[67] and expanded astronomically by the courts on a case-by-case basis, the system in the United States has been to relegate the problem to the courts. As a consequence, there has been a steady expansion of liabilities imposed upon shipowners and charterers, with concomitant restrictions on their defenses.

The evolution of personal injury law in maritime law has been steady and dramatic. The tendency of the courts, in adopting a most liberal approach to interpreting the statutes and case law involving maritime workers, has produced a host of new "plaintiffs," and the ingenious application of old and new theories by the very competent maritime plaintiffs' bar has produced new areas of recovery which were never dreamed of fifty years ago.[68]

Under the principle of pendent jurisdiction, seamen/claimants today file suit in the state courts, pray for maintenance and cure (an admiralty concept), allege their injuries were caused by unseaworthiness of their vessels (another admiralty concept), seek money damages for their injuries under the Jones Act—and still have their claims adjudicated by a jury. Although P & I insurance covers a whole spectrum of liabilities, it is little wonder that the liabilities of P & I underwriters in the field of maritime personal injury have reached literally incredible proportions as compared with claims falling under the remaining rules and policy provisions.

Consequently, unless the extent and nature of these liabilities are fully understood, it is difficult if not impossible to understand and predict with any degree of accuracy how the American courts will construe the policy provisions or club rules applicable to claims for loss of life or personal injury. Consequently, in the discussion that follows, the case law and stat-

66. 189 U.S. 158, 23 S.Ct. 483, 47 L.Ed. 760 (1903).
67. 46 U.S.C. 688, Sec. 33 of the Merchant Marine Act of 1920. Technically, the term "Jones Act" can be confusing. The term is also used with respect to the cabotage laws of the United States, i.e., the body of laws restricting the carriage of merchandise in the "coastwise trade" to vessels built in and owned by citizens of the United States. See, for example, 46 U.S.C. 883. Thus, one hears of a "Jones Act seaman"—used in the sense of one who is entitled to the benefits of 46 U.S.C. 688—and the prohibitions of the "Jones Act," meaning the impediments to the use of foreign-built or owned vessels in the American coastwise trade. The two are, of course, totally dissimilar.
68. For example, collisions between strictly pleasure boats are now within the purview of admiralty, not to mention injuries to water skiers. A "seaman" today can include a bartender and hairdresser aboard a cruise ship who are thus members of the "crew." Moreover, such "seamen" can include workers who live ashore and do handy jobs aboard such craft as landlocked dredges. Because of the prevalence of jury trials in the American system, it will be found that the cases support the proposition that a "seaman is a seaman if the jury says he is."

utes relating to maritime personal injury and loss of life in the United States will be discussed in considerable detail.[69]

Organization of Discussion to Follow

The easiest and most convenient way to organize this topic is to examine separately the various liabilities of a vessel owner and arrange them by categories. Thus, the owner's liabilities are segregated as follows: (1) liability to seamen under general maritime law for maintenance and cure and for damages under both the Jones Act and general maritime law; (2) liability to third party shoreworkers for negligence under 33 U.S.C. 905—one of the sections of the Longshoremen's and Harbor Workers' Compensation Act; (3) liabilities to passengers, guests, and shipboard visitors; and (4) other miscellaneous liabilities and related subjects such as maritime rights to indemnity or contribution.

The discussion of the charterer's liabilities relates only to the contractual shift of responsibility from the vessel owner to the time or voyage charterer for injury or death of a third party shoreworker. Liabilities of a bareboat charterer require no separate inquiry since they are derivatively those of the vessel owner.

The text on damage issues for maritime personal injury or death is bifurcated. The first logical placement for personal injury damages was at the conclusion of the section on the Jones Act. Death actions, however, invoke a variety of distinct rules and refinements and thus appear in a separate section.

Finally, any discussion of a vessel owner's liabilities would be incomplete without some mention of the owner's rights to indemnity and contribution, which comprise the last part of the discussion.

Maintenance and Cure

As long as the vessel owner has employed seamen, he has had the obligation to provide maintenance and cure.[70] It is an incident of the employ-

69. There are several excellent texts covering the general topic of the maritime law of personal injury and loss of life in the United States to which reference should be made by the serious student. Among these are: M. Norris, *The Law of Maritime Personal Injuries* (3rd ed., 1975); M. Norris, *The Law of Seamen* (4th ed., 1985); G. Gilmore and C. Black, *The Law of Admiralty* (2d ed., 1975); Admiralty Law Institute: Symposium on Maritime Personal Injury and Death under American Law, 55 *Tulane Law Review* no. 4 (June, 1981). The symposium, consisting of papers by outstanding admiralty lawyers and scholars on the various topics in the field, is especially commended and brings the status of the law up to date through 1981.

70. The term "seaman" is used because Justice Story used it in *Harden v. Gordon*, 11 F.Cas. 480, No. 6,047 (C.C.,Me., 1823), the seminal case on the maintenance and cure obligation, when he examined the laws of the "principal maritime nations" and found the remedy universal. Some opinions still use "crew member" and "seaman" synonymously. The definitions of "seaman" will depend upon context and may vary according to the remedy

ment status and applies equally to owners of cargo vessels, yachts, tugboats, and fishing vessels. The seaman's right grows out of the employment relationship. Created in the sea codes of the Middle Ages and surviving through the whole of American jurisprudence, the nature of the obligation has not changed, but the application has expanded.[71] Thus, if the seaman becomes injured or ill "in the service of the ship," the shipowner's obligation arises. It is an obligation that the seaman can enforce against his employer *in personam* or against the vessel *in rem*.[72]

Usually, the employer is the shipowner (or disponent owner) but this is not necessarily so; the maintenance and cure obligation attaches to the seaman's employer and not to the shipowner. Thus, a ship's concessionaire may employ the seaman, whose remedies are only against the concessionaire.[73] The *in rem* nature of the seaman's claim has particular significance in determining priorities to a fund created by sale of the vessel where there are competing claims of creditors. The maritime lien for maintenance and cure enjoys a high ranking.[74]

The remedy for maintenance and cure is to be distinguished from damage remedies, such as those predicated upon Jones Act negligence or breach of the shipowner's warranty of seaworthiness. The right to maintenance and cure exists irrespective of shipowner fault or vessel unseaworthiness. It is a form of judge-created worker's compensation.

Components of the Remedy

Maintenance is *per diem* subsistence; cure is medical care, covering a broad spectrum of hospital and related medical costs. The seaman also has the

---

invoked. For example, a statutory definition may be relevant to a Jones Act claim (see 46 U.S.C. 10101(3)), but of little help in a maintenance and cure claim. 46 U.S.C. 10303, 10304.

There is therefore validity in one writer's cautionary remark that use of the term "seaman" can be an inexact label and a substitute for reason. T. Byrne, "Liability for Personal Injury and Death, Including Third Party Liability and the *Ryan* Doctrine," 43 *Tulane Law Review* 509, 510, n. 5 (1969). In the end, the terms "seaman" or "vessel" or "member of the crew" range too widely in meaning to be decided by a court as a matter of law. Definition almost always presents a question of fact. *Braniff v. Jackson Avenue-Gretna Ferry, Inc.*, 280 F.2d 523, 1961 AMC 1739 (5th Cir., 1960). See, also, discussion on "Establishing Status as a Jones Act Seaman," *infra*.

71. See, generally, T. Byrne, n. 70; J. Shields, "Seamen's Rights to Recover Maintenance and Cure Benefits," 55 *Tulane Law Review* 1046 (1981).

72. *Padre Island (Stranding)*, 447 F.2d 438, 1971 AMC 2192 (5th Cir.); *The Osceola*, 189 U.S. 158 (1903). Even if the shipowner is not the employer, it may well be that the vessel is nonetheless liable *in rem*. *Solet v. M/V Capt. H.V. Dufresne*, 303 F.Supp. 980, 1970 AMC 571 (E.D.,La., 1969).

73. *Mahramas v. American Export Isbrandtsen Lines, Inc.*, 475 F.2d 165, 1973 AMC 587 (2d Cir., 1973).

74. See, generally, *Padre Island (Stranding)*, 447 F.2d 438, 1971 AMC 2192 (5th Cir.) (seaman's lien for maintenance and cure, including unearned wages to the end of the voyage, is in the highest category of priority, ranking right after, if not alongside, earned wages, and above salvage).

right to unearned wages in certain instances, and this right was considered part of the maintenance and cure remedy.[75] Originally, the right to unearned wages continued for the duration of the voyage for which the seaman had signed articles, which also defined the duration of the right to maintenance and cure. Today, however, unearned wages are recoverable for the contract period, whether a definite term or a voyage. The right to full wages for the period of employment is normally pleaded as part of a damage action under the Jones Act for negligence and under the general maritime law for unseaworthiness.[76] The right to maintenance and cure now extends for a reasonable time after the voyage. See discussion, *infra,* on this proposition.

Eligibility

Eligibility requires satisfying dual criteria of (1) "seaman status" and (2) that the illness or injury manifested itself as a consequence of the seaman being "in the service of the ship." These criteria have undergone considerable stretching, as the history and rationale behind the remedy help to explain.

1. Historical Rationale: The Wardship Doctrine. An excellent historical review of maintenance and cure will be found in *Hudspeth v. Atlantic & Gulf Stevedores, Inc.,*[77] which begins by quoting Justice Story's classic justification for protecting seamen:

> They are generally poor and friendless, and acquire habits of gross indulgence, carelessness and improvidence; . . . are unprotected and need counsel; . . . are thoughtless and require indulgence; . . . are credulous and complying; . . . and are easily overreached.[78]

Judicial solicitude early on made seamen wards of the admiralty, and the "wardship" doctrine continues in decisions today:

> The "ancient solicitude of courts of admiralty for those who labor at sea" continues unchanged despite the progress from canvass sails to diesel engines.[79]

Whether protective wardship should legitimately continue is open to question.[80] To his advantage, the seaman's workplace today is totally dif-

---

75. *The Osceola,* 189 U.S. 158 (1903).
76. See *Dardar v. State of Louisiana,* 322 F.Supp. 1115, 1971 AMC 1560 (E.D.,La.).
77. 266 F.Supp. 937, 1967 AMC 2108 (E.D.,La.).
78. *Harden v. Gordon,* 11 F.Cas. 480 (C.C., Me., 1823).
79. *Hudspeth v. Atlantic & Gulf Stevedores, Inc., supra* n. 77, quoting from *Weiss v. Central Railroad of New Jersey,* 235 F.2d 309, 1956 AMC 1473 (2d Cir.).
80. See Lovitt, "Things Are Seldom What They Seem: The Jolly Little Wards of the Admiralty," 46 A.B.A.J. 171 (1960), in which the author characterizes Justice Story's wardship doctrine as "solemn nonsense":

ferent. Stringent and pervasive regulatory standards and technological advances in navigation, to say nothing of the force of union protectionism, have vastly improved working conditions aboard ship. Nevertheless, the wardship doctrine remains alive although modern day decisions invoking the doctrine are not so critical of the seaman's shipboard environment. Today, when the rationale of a decision is explained in terms of the wardship doctrine, the facts will frequently involve a seaman's release coupled with questionable claims practices by shipowners.[81] One illustration of a court's concern for a seaman's business acumen will be found in *United States v. Johnson*,[82] where the court, in striking down a release, noted:

> It is true that appellee [a seaman with one year of college courses in business administration] is undoubtedly more intelligent than an average seaman, but it does not appear that he was versed in medical and legal matters.

2. Seaman's Status Today[83]. The claim for maintenance and cure and the claim under the Jones Act for negligence depend on the same relationship between the parties. In each instance it is a plaintiff seaman claiming against his employer.[84] The notion of a seaman is no longer restricted to the watch-standing sailor who has satisfied U.S. Coast Guard requirements. Today, the role of the seaman is broadly defined.[85]

Story, of course was thinking of a "seaman" as one who could reef a sail aloft or steer a course, but the courts have extended the term to include practically the vessel's entire personnel—thus the engineer who holds degrees from M.I.T., the head chef and entertainers on a luxury liner are all "insane" when they step into a court of admiralty.

81. For a collection of such cases, see E. Wood, "Old Father Antic the Law: The Favorites of the Courts of Admiralty," 41 *A.B.A.J.* 924, 927 (1955).

82. 160 F.2d 789, 1947 AMC 765 (9th Cir.).

83. "Seaman's status" is also discussed *infra* in connection with the Jones Act negligence remedy.

84. *Fink v. Shepherd Steamship Co.*, 337 U.S. 810, 69 S.Ct. 1330, 93 L.Ed. 1709 (1949), 1949 AMC 1045.

85. See M. Norris, *The Law of Seamen*, sec. 2:3 (4th ed., 1985), cataloging the diverse roles of the members of ships' companies who would be entitled to maintenance and cure, as follows:

Early in our maritime history, cooks and stewards were held to be mariners, and in *The James H. Shrigley*, a woman cook was considered to be a "seaman." The list can be extended to include a clerk, engineers and firemen, a barber employed on the vessel and on articles, a bartender, and a muleteer, i.e., one in charge of a shipment of mules aboard ship.

To this list can be added, a coal passer, a dipper tender on a dredge, a fisherman, ferry hand, deck hand on a dredge, a civil service ferryboat engineer, a diver, a foreman on a dredge, fireman on a floating derrick, horseman, sealer, steward, pursers, pilot, watchman on a vessel during a voyage, porter, longshoreman, wrecker, and laundress. [footnotes omitted]

A vessel's master is also entitled to maintenance and cure,[86] as are fishermen on lay shares.[87]

3. Service of the Ship. Once the status requirement has been satisfied, the seaman must next show that the injury or illness manifested itself while "in the service of the ship." Courts examine the structure of the "ship" and the nature of the "service." Service on a "vessel," no matter what kind, is a basis for admiralty jurisdiction.[88] "In the service of the ship" means "subject to the call of duty and earning wages as such."[89] A contract of employment must be shown to exist to establish the "service of the ship" requirement.[90] Longshoremen, even though doing traditional work of seamen, are not eligible since they are employed by the contracting stevedore and not by the shipowner.[91] Neither are other shore-based non-employees, such as a shore watchman, "in the service of the ship."[92]

How courts define a "vessel" is discussed at length, *infra*, under "Jones Act Negligence." The proper definition is almost always a question of fact,[93] and insofar as the plaintiff must show he is a seaman on a vessel, Jones Act and maintenance and cure cases may be read interchangeably.[94]

While the employment nexus must be to a vessel, the injury or illness need not happen there. A seaman injured on shore leave is still subject to the call of duty, and the personal nature of the seaman's activity is of no consequence in assessing the claim for recovery.[95] Since shore leave is considered an integral and necessary part of the seaman's duties, injury ashore gives rise to maintenance and cure. Manifestation of the injury or

---

86. *Murphy v. Light*, 224 F.2d 944, 1955 AMC 1986 (5th Cir.), *cert. den.* 350 U.S. 960 (1956).

87. *Luksich v. Misetich*, 140 F.2d 812, 1944 AMC 206 (9th Cir., 1944), *cert.den.* 322 U.S. 761 (1944).

88. See *Offshore Co. v. Robison*, 266 F.2d 769, 1959 AMC 2049 (5th Cir.).

89. *Aguilar v. Standard Oil Co.*, 318 U. S. 724, 1942 AMC 1045.

90. *Baker v. Raymond International*, 656 F.2d 173, 1982 AMC 2752 (5th Cir., 1981).

91. *Yaconi v. Grady & Gioe, Inc.*, 246 N.Y. 300, 158 N.E. 876, 1928 AMC 204 (1927), *cert.den.* 276 U.S. 636 (1927).

92. *Bagnoll v. Silver Line, Ltd.*, 1931 AMC 1608 (E.D.N.Y., 1931).

93. *Braniff v. Jackson Avenue-Gretna Ferry, Inc.*, 280 F.2d 523, 1961 AMC 1739 (5th Cir., 1960).

94. *Mahamras v. American Export Isbrandtsen Lines, Inc.*, 475 F.2d 165, 1973 AMC 587 (2d Cir.).

95. See *Koistinen v. American Export Lines, Inc.*, 83 N.Y.S. 2d 297, 1952 AMC 2066 (St.,N.Y.), where a seaman was injured when he was enticed into a woman's room for illicit purposes and, finding himself the potential victim of a robbery scam, jumped out the nearest exit, which happened to be a window. He later sued for maintenance and cure as a result of his injuries in doing so. The court granted recovery, noting that the courts have been liberal in their attitude toward seamen who receive injuries on shore leave through their notorious penchants not stemming from intoxication or deliberate acts of indiscretion. See, also, *Warren v. United States*, 340 U.S. 523, 1951 AMC 416.

illness during the shipboard employment is all that is required. Original causation during that period is not required. A member of the ship's company who is primarily based on shore but suffers injury aboard ship may be eligible for maintenance and cure.[96]

The Remedy of Cure

Cure is simply medical care. The seaman is entitled to cure from the time he pays for, or incurs liability for, medicines and related treatment.[97]

Formerly, medical care for seamen was provided free at United States government hospitals. 42 U.S.C. 249. But, in 1981, the statute was amended, and U.S. Public Health Service hospitals are no longer in existence and available for seamen.[98] Formerly, because of the free governmental treatment program, there was seldom a cost of cure; consequently, the seaman could not allege costs as special damages. However, when the free public health service care was for some reason unavailable, the shipowner was nevertheless obliged to provide it, and so the situation stands today.

Of course, there can be no recovery for cure when it consists of simply convalescing at a place for which no expense or obligation to pay has been incurred or imposed.[99] However, a claimant may show special circumstances which, though falling short of a contractual obligation to pay for lodging, will nevertheless support an award for cure during convalescence.[100]

The Remedy of Maintenance

Maintenance is the obligation of a shipowner to provide the seaman with compensation sufficient to supply him with food and lodging during his

96. See *Weiss v. Central Railroad Co. of New Jersey*, 235 F.2d 309, 1956 AMC 1473 (2d Cir., 1956), involving an extra hand on a railroad whose work was to substitute for regular men working (1) around the ferryhouse and (2) on the ferryboats. Plaintiff contracted tuberculosis shortly after being hired. On the basis of the fact that on a few occasions he had held the wheel of several different ferryboats on Hudson River crossings, the court held this justified classifying him as a seaman. But, see *Brown v. ITT Rayonier, Inc.*, 497 F.2d 234, 1975 AMC 634 (5th Cir.), in which a college student, working during Christmas vacations as an inside pulp tester, was held not entitled to Jones Act seaman's status during a motorboat trip to collect water samples in connection with his employer's effluent control program).
97. *Kelmore Steamship Corp. v. Taylor*, 303 U.S. 525, 1938 AMC 341 (1938).
98. Public Law 97-35, August 13, 1981.
99. *Marine Drilling, Inc. v. Landry*, 302 F.2d 127, 1962 AMC 1957 (5th Cir.).
100. *McCormick Shipping Corp. v. Duvalier*, 311 F.2d 933, 1963 AMC 1967 (5th Cir.) (no intention that seaman's convalescence at a cousin's home was to be the subject of charity).

medical care.[101] In theory, the amount is equal to compensate for the quality the seaman would have received aboard his ship.[102] And if, while on the vessel, the seaman always paid for his own meals, the owner cannot use non-payment to excuse his obligation to pay maintenance.[103]

Until fairly recently, the maintenance rate was more or less liquidated at $8 per day pursuant to collective bargaining agreements with the unions. Admiralty courts had consistently used that rate, at least for union vessels, and the sum had become entrenched over the years as the "standard figure."[104]

On non-union ships, it has always been a question for the trier-of-fact: On the basis of all evidence before the court, what is the compensable *per diem* rate? Evidence would include actual costs incurred by the seaman for food and lodging in the area, rates provided in union contracts, and previous court awards. Actual cost is the preferred basis.[105] The seaman's testimony concerning his own expenses is probative on the amount of maintenance owing,[106] and the burden of production is "feather light."[107] Expert testimony may also be used.[108]

Increasingly, in cases involving non-union seamen, some courts have found the $8 per day award constitutes a "starvation payment."[109]

Similarly, in *Rutherford v. Sealand Service, Inc.*,[110] a seaman was not bound by the collective bargaining rate of $8 per day, which was found to be inadequate as a matter of law, so that evidence of actual costs of maintenance was allowed to establish the rate as a factual matter on a case-by-case basis. The authority of *Rutherford* has, however, been severely eroded. At this writing the Ninth Circuit has just enforced the $8 per diem rate for union seamen in recognition of "the broad policies which undergird the labor laws, as well as the nature of the collective bargaining process."[110a]

101. *Vaughn v. Atkinson*, 369 U.S. 527, 1962 AMC 1131 (1962).
102. *Calmar S.S. Corp. v. Taylor*, 303 U.S. 525, 1938 AMC 341 (1938).
103. *The City of Avalon*, 156 F.2d 500, 1946 AMC 1606 (9th Cir.).
104. *Harper v. Zapata Off-Shore Co.*, 741 F.2d 87, 1985 AMC 979 (5th Cir., 1984).
105. *Morer v. Sabine Towing & Transportation Co., Inc.*, 669 F.2d 345 (5th Cir., 1982) (awarding $20 per day).
106. *Caulfield v. A.C. & D. Marine*, 633 F.2d 1129, 1982 AMC 1033 (5th Cir., 1981).
107. *Yelverton v. Mobile Laboratories, Inc.*, 782 F.2d 555 (5th Cir., 1986)
108. *Robinson v. Plimsoll Marine*, 460 F.Supp. 949, 1979 AMC 1973 (E.D.,La., 1978).
109. *Harper v. Zapata Off-Shore Co.*, 563 F.Supp. 576, 1985 AMC 979 (E.D.,La., 1983), awarding $40 per day in light of the high quality of food aboard the drilling barge although the amount was remitted on appeal to $20 per day. 741 F.2d 87, 1985 AMC 979 (5th Cir., 1984). See, also, *Incandela*, 659 F.2d 11, 1981 AMC 2401 (2d Cir.), awarding $26.80 per day based upon pro-rated actual costs.
110. 575 F.Supp. 1365, 1984 AMC 1496 (N.D.,Cal.).
110a. *Gardiner v. Sea-Land Service, Inc.*, 786 F.2d 943, 1986 AMC 1521 (9th Cir., 1986), possibly signalling judicial reconsideration of the wardship doctrine.

Duration of the Obligation

1. Palliative vs. Curative. The vessel owner's oligation extends so long as medical treatment will improve the seaman's condition and so long as the seaman himself does nothing to cause the right to terminate.

The extent of the obligation is commonly phrased in terms of "maximum medical cure." Thus, in *Farrell v. U.S.,*[111] a seaman, blinded in accident, was held entitled to payment of therapeutic hospital expenses until the point of "maximum cure," but there was no entitlement for life. So when the condition is diagnosed as incurable or when future treatment is merely palliative, if treatment will not improve the condition itself (i.e., if it is non-curative), the shipowner has no obligation to continue with it.[112] If the treating physician testifies that a seaman would benefit from further treatment, the seaman has *prima facie* established that maximum cure has not been attained.

2. Voluntary Rejection. Even if medical improvement is still possible, a seaman's voluntary refusal to receive medical care at a hospital may abbreviate the shipowner's obligation.[113] Conversely, the act of returning to work does not necessarily terminate the right to maintenance and cure.[114] Nor is there a right to set off the seaman's shoreside earnings against maintenance liability.[115]

Of course, if the seaman shows that services at one medical facility are inadequate and that is why the services were discontinued, the shipowner's obligation to provide maintenance and cure continues.[116]

Defenses to Obligation to Pay

Aside from the foregoing defenses, which merely abbreviate the period for which maintenance is owing, the vessel owner has little else, since obligation does not depend on fault.

As a general rule, it is better to err on the side of payment because of the "traditional liberality displayed towards seamen"[117] and the fact that

---

111. 336 U.S. 511, 1949 AMC 613 (1949).

112. *Pelotto v. L & N Towing Company,* 604 F.2d 396, 1981 AMC 1047 (5th Cir., 1979).

113. *United States v. Johnson,* 160 F.2d 789, 1947 AMC 765 (9th Cir.), *modified,* 333 U.S. 46, 92 L.Ed. 468 (1948).

114. *Permanente Steamship Corp. v. Martinez,* 369 F.2d 297, 1967 AMC 192 (9th Cir., 1966).

115. *Vaughn v. Atkinson,* 369 U.S. 527, 1962 AMC 997 (1962).

116. *Kratzer v. Capital Marine Supply, Inc.,* 645 F.2d 477, 1982 AMC 2691 (5th Cir., 1981).

117. *Aguilar v. Standard Oil Co. of New Jersey,* 318 U.S. 724, 1943 AMC 451 (1943). But the tradition may have ended. See *Gardiner v. Sea-Land Service, Inc.,* 786 F.2d 943, 1986 AMC 1521 (9th Cir. 1986).

in certain instances, non-payment may create liabilities for attorneys' fees, punitive damages, and even a new cause of action. Especially in the area of punitive damages, courts have closely scrutinized the employer's behavior. Non-payment due to faulty investigation can be costly and provide a basis for damages.[118]

While the seaman's right is absolute and independent of proof of vessel fault, there are certain limited circumstances where recovery will be denied. Thus, if the seaman incurred the illness or injury while *not* in the service of the ship, or if, at the inception of employment, he intentionally concealed the illness or injury, or the cause was the seaman's own wilful misbehavior, deliberate act, or indiscretion, recovery will be denied.[119]

1. Seaman's Fraud. The most obvious defense to payment is the seaman's fraud. If investigation discloses no factual basis for the claim, it should be denied. For example, if the shipowner's investigation discloses that the injury or the aggravating incident occurred outside the term of the employment relationship, there should be no oligation to provide maintenance and cure.

Similarly, when a seaman fraudulently conceals a known illness or disability, maintenance and cure will be denied.[120] Courts distinguish, however, between concealment and non-disclosure. If the shipowner does not require a pre-employment medical examination, and the seaman does not disclose material medical facts, the question then is whether reasonable grounds existed for the seaman's good faith belief he was fit for duty.[121] Of course, in case of either concealment or non-disclosure there must be a causal link between the pre-existing disability and what is claimed was incurred in the service of the ship.[122]

A pre-existing condition may support an award of maintenance and cure for an aggravation, as, for example, where a seaman with a known tubercular condition was washed against a ship's rail during heavy seas; an award for maintenance due to the aggravation of the illness was affirmed.[123]

---

118. See *Tullos v. Resource Drilling, Inc.,* 750 F.2d 380 (5th Cir. 1985) and discussion *infra.*
119. *McCorpen v. Central Gulf Steamship Corp.,* 396 F.2d 547, 1970 AMC 257 (5th Cir., 1968); *Warren v. U.S.,* 340 U.S. 523, 1951 AMC 416 (1951).
120. *McCorpen v. Central Gulf Steamship Corp.,* 396 F.2d 547, 1970 AMC 257 (5th Cir., 1968) (concealment of known diabetes during a pre-employment medical examination); *Siders v. Ohio River Co.,* 351 F.Supp. 987 (W.D.,Pa., 1971), *aff'd* 469 F.2d 1093, 1974 AMC 531 (3rd Cir., 1972) (seaman's specific denial of previous back injury which was aggravated aboard ship).
121. *Couts v. Erickson,* 241 F.2d 499, 1957 AMC 515 (9th Cir.).
122. *Hazelton v. Luckenbach Steamship Co.,* 134 F.Supp. 525, 1955 AMC 2096 (D.,Mass., 1955).
123. *Sentilles v. Intercaribbean Shipping Corp.,* 361 U.S. 107, 1960 AMC 10 (1960).

Generally speaking, an honest failure to disclose a prior condition will not defeat a claim for maintenance and cure.[124] If the disabling potential of the illness is not known by the seaman, he will not be precluded from recovery.[125]

2. Wilful Misconduct. Direct disobedience of orders may afford a defense based upon wilful misbehavior. For example, in *Equilease Corp. v. Millston Tankers, Inc.,*[126] because the seaman returned to a bar after being specifically ordered not to do so, it was held there was no obligation to pay maintenance and cure.

Sometimes intoxication, if extreme, may be held to relieve the shipowner of the obligation of paying maintenance and cure, but the defense has been weakened.[127] There may be no maintenance and cure obligation in cases of venereal disease as courts have held that contracting the disease is wilful.[128]

3. Laches. If the elements of laches are established, i.e., inexcusable delay in asserting the claim and resultant prejudice to the shipowner, the shipowner is absolved of the duty to pay maintenance and cure. There is no particular limitation period involved, only the traditional laches considerations based upon particular facts.[129]

4. Seaman's Own Negligence Is No Bar. The seaman's own negligence is no bar to his protection. It does not matter if his contributory negligence brought on the injury. There is no fellow servant rule or doctrine of assumption of risk. The quality of conduct sufficient to constitute a defense is articulated in *Aguilar v. Standard Oil Co. of New Jersey*:[130] "Only some wilful misbehavior or deliberate act of indiscretion suffices to deprive the seaman of his protection." The shipowner has the burden of proof to show wilful misbehavior, the typical situation of alleged wilful misbehavior being the seaman engaging in a fight.[131]

124. *Sammon v. Central Gulf Steamship Corp.,* 442 F.2d 1028, 1971 AMC 1113 (2d Cir.).
125. *Blouin v. American Export Isbrandtsen Lines, Inc.,* 319 F. Supp. 1150, 1970 AMC 712 (S.D.N.Y.).
126. 1980 AMC 1390 (D.,Alaska, 1978).
127. *Daily v. Alcoa S.S. Co.,* 337 F.2d 611, 1966 AMC 1281 (5th Cir., 1964), but, see *Ellis v. American Steamship Co.,* 165 F.2d 999, 1948 AMC 707 (9th Cir.).
128. *Ressler v. States Marine Lines, Inc.,* 517 F.2d 579, 1975 AMC 819 (2d Cir.), *cert.den.* 423 U.S. 894, 1975 AMC 2159 (1975).
129. See *West v. Marine Resources Commission,* 330 F.Supp. 966, 1971 AMC 418 (E.D.,Va., 1966), where the court analogized the Jones Act 3-year period, rather than a limitation period of 10 years for contracts. A claim for maintenance and cure would seem to be outside the Uniform Statute of Limitations for Maritime Torts, 46 U.S.C. 763a.
130. 318 U.S. 724, 1943 AMC 451 (1943).
131. See *Gulledge v. U.S.,* 337 F.Supp. 1108, 1972 AMC 1187, *aff'd* 474 F.2d 1344 (3d Cir., 1972). (recurring fight between seamen not sufficient); *Mears v. American Export Lines, Inc.,* 457 F.Supp. 846, 1979 AMC 395 (S.D.N.Y., 1978).

Collateral Source Rule

The question frequently arises as to what extent a shipowner may offset compensation the seaman receives from collateral sources such as state unemployment disability benefits and health insurance proceeds. The collateral source rule precludes a credit for amounts received through health insurance furnished by the shipowner. In *Owens v. Conticarriers and Terminals, Inc.,*[132] the shipowner paid for the policy but it was held nevertheless to be a fringe benefit to the seaman/employee. Similarly, in *Gypsum Carrier, Inc. v. Handelsman,*[133] benefits from the California Disability Fund could not be used to diminish the amount of maintenance and cure the shipowner owed to the seaman. Even though the payments constituted a double recovery, the shipowner was not subjected to a double burden. In *Gauthier v. Crosby Marine Service, Inc.,*[134] it was shown as a factual matter that the plaintiff had paid the premiums for the medical insurance policy and thus had actually incurred expense. The collateral source rule barred a set-off.

A contrary result was reached in *Shaw v. Ohio River Co.,*[135] where Blue Cross/Blue Shield payments were allowed to substitute for maintenance and cure payments, the court ruling that the collateral source was inapplicable in a "no fault" situation such as one giving rise to maintenance and cure. Since no out-of-pocket expenses had been incurred, there was nothing to reimburse, and so the maintenance and cure obligation was negated.

Attorneys' Fees

The seaman's maintenance and cure recovery may include "necessary expenses" where the shipowner is callous in his actions, makes no investigation of the seaman's claim, and his default is wilful and persistent, thus requiring the seaman to hire an attorney. In such a case, the seaman may recover an award for attorneys' fees.[136] The *Vaughn* test is to evaluate the shipowner's conduct to determine whether the refusal to pay was arbitrary, recalcitrant, or unreasonable. The conduct must be wrongful to provide a basis for attorneys' fees. If the owner's tardiness in payment cannot fairly be characterized as callous under the *Vaughn* test, attorneys' fees are not recoverable.[137] In *Hollingsworth v. Maritime Overseas Corp.,*[138]

132. 591 F.Supp. 777 (W.D.,Tenn., 1984).
133. 307 F.2d 525, 1963 AMC 175 (9th Cir., 1962).
134. 752 F.2d 1085, 1985 AMC 2477 (5th Cir., 1985).
135. 526 F.2d 193, 1976 AMC 1164 (3d Cir., 1975).
136. *Vaughn v. Atkinson*, 369 U.S. 527, 1962 AMC 1131 (1962).
137. *Ober v. Penrod Drilling Co.*, 726 F.2d 1035 (5th Cir., 1984).
138. 363 F.Supp. 1393, 1973 AMC 2328 (E.D.,Pa.).

attorneys' fees were denied where the shipowner had an honest belief that
the seaman was guilty of gross misconduct, even though the later findings
at trial were to the contrary. It follows, therefore, that there is no absolute
right to attorneys' fees as a matter of law, even though maintenance is
awarded.[139]

The attorneys' fees issue is one for the trier of fact. If maintenance and
cure is a single claim under general maritime law, it lies in admiralty and
the court will make the determination. Frequently, however, such claims
are combined with Jones Act causes of action, and both are tried to a jury.
It has been held that the attorneys' fees issue is a non-severable part of the
cause of action, and so the jury may determine both entitlement and
amount unless the parties expressly waive the jury determination.[140]
Other courts allow the jury to decide entitlement but the court must determine what is a reasonable amount.[141]

Punitive Damages

Some courts recognize that liability for the seaman's attorneys' fees is itself
punitive in nature and accordingly restrict damage awards to reasonable
attorneys' fees; in other words, the punitive award is payment of the
plaintiff's attorneys' fees.[142]

There appears to be a trend toward granting damages without limiting them to attorneys' fees.[143] A failure to pay *adequate maintenance* is not a
basis for punitive damages where the shipowner decided to rely upon the
legal minimum of $8 per day, there being no element of bad faith.[144]
There must be evidence of malice or a deliberate purpose on the part of
the shipowner to frustrate the seaman's admitted rights. A failure to re-

---

139. *Kopczynski v. The Jacqueline*, 742 F.2d 555, 1985 AMC 769 (9th Cir., 1984), *cert. den.*
105 S.Ct. 2677.

140. *Holmes v. J. Ray McDermott & Co.*, 734 F.2d 1110, 1985 AMC 2024 (5th Cir., 1984).

141. *Incandela v. American Dredging Co.*, 659 F.2d 11, 1981 AMC 2401 (2d Cir., 1981).

142. *Kraljic v. Berman Enterprises, Inc.*, 575 F.2d 412, 1978 AMC 1297 (2d Cir.).

143. See, for example, *Robinson v. Pocahontas, Inc.*, 477 F.2d 1048, 1973 AMC 2268 (1st
Cir.) and *Harper v. Zapata Off-Shore Co.*, 741 F.2d 87, 1985 AMC 979 (5th Cir., 1984). In
Harper, the court gave examples of employer behavior that could merit punitive damages,
including (1) laxness in investigating a claim; (2) termination of benefits in response to the
seaman's retention of counsel or refusal of a settlement offer; or (3) failure to reinstate benefits after diagnosis of an ailment previously not medically determined. An element of bad
faith is needed, and if there is evidence of arbitrary and capricious conduct, it will be for the
jury to determine. See, also, *Tullos v. Resource Drilling, Inc.*, 750 F.2d 380 (5th Cir., 1985),
where the case was remanded for determination whether the employer's reliance on a medical report it had requested in order to terminate benefits justified the refusal, or whether it
was an act of bad faith, making the owner liable for punitive damages.

144. *Tullos v. Resource Drilling, Inc., supra*, n. 143.

spond to a single demand letter cannot support an award of punitive damages.[145]

Duty to Investigate

A shipowner has the duty to commence with reasonable diligence an investigation into the need for maintenance and cure.[146] Breach of the duty may result in a finding under *Vaughn* of a callous disregard and arbitrary refusal. The fact that the investigation was merely slow is no defense.[147]

Additional Cause of Action

A new tort arises if a wrongful refusal to provide maintenance and cure aggravates the condition. To the extent the new injury is caused by the aggravation, the seaman has an additional cause of action for compensatory damages.[148]

Prejudgment Interest

A court in admiralty has discretion to award prejudgment interest on an award for maintenance and cure when the court is the trier of fact. Where the jury makes the fact determination, the court abuses its discretion if it adds on an award for prejudgment interest.[149]

Vessel Owner's Warranty of Seaworthiness

Dictum in *The Osceola*[150] is the origin for the proposition that both owner and vessel are "liable for an indemnity for injuries received by seamen in consequence of the unseaworthiness of the ship, or a failure to supply and keep in order the proper appliances appurtenant to the ship." Today, this liability is phrased in terms of an owner's implied warranty owing to Jones Act seamen. The warranty of seaworthiness describes a duty that is absolute, continuing and non-delegable.[151] The duty is absolute since it does

---

145. *Farnham v. Baker*, No. 82-3006 (9th Cir., Jan. 31, 1984) not otherwise reported.
146. *Wilson v. Twin Rivers Towing Co.*, 413 F.Supp. 154 (W.D.,Pa., 1976).
147. *Stewart v. S.S. Richmond*, 214 F.Supp. 135, 1963 AMC 922 (E.D.,La.), *appeal dismissed* 326 F.2d 208 (5th Cir., 1964).
148. *Central Gulf Steamship Corp. v. Sambula*, 405 F.2d 291, 1968 AMC 2521 (5th Cir.); *Downie v. United States Lines Co.*, 359 F.2d 344, 1964 AMC 2289, 2297 (3d Cir., 1966), *cert.den.* 385 U.S. 897.
149. *Robinson v. Pocahontas, Inc.*, 477 F.2d 1048, 1973 AMC 2268 (1st Cir.).
150. 189 U.S. 158 (1903).
151. *Mahnich v. Southern Steamship Co.*, 321 U.S. 96, 1944 AMC 1 (1944).

not require proof of fault; it continues though the condition arose after the voyage began, and it is a duty irrevocably placed on the owner, meaning it cannot be delegated.

To claim protection of the warranty, a plaintiff must prove seaman status (see discussion under Jones Act, *infra*) in order to qualify as "a ward of the admiralty and to place large responsibility for his safety on the owner." The warranty extends not only to appurtenances but to defective gear, equipment, and crew.[152] Thus, a seaman may have a savage disposition disproportionate to that of other seamen. If that seaman attacks another and causes injury, the vessel and owner will be liable for unseaworthiness.[152a] Similarly, if there is an insufficient complement of crew necessary for the tasks assigned, liability may be imposed.[153]

Liability for unseaworthiness depends on neither negligence nor notice, which are predicates for Jones Act recovery. The Supreme Court has termed the warranty of seaworthiness "essentially a species of liability without fault . . . neither limited by concepts of negligence nor contractual in character . . . ." An unseaworthy condition may exist only momentarily, undetected by the shipowner.[154]

During the period between 1946 (when *Seas Shipping Co. v. Sieracki, supra,* was decided) and 1972, when the amendments to the Longshoremen's and Harbor Workers' Compensation Act[155] abolished the warranty for maritime employees (as opposed to seamen), the class of *Sieracki* seamen grew to encompass almost any maritime business invitee doing work traditionally done by seamen. With the expanded class of seamen came extensive judicial refinements of the warranty of seaworthiness. Thus, the warranty came to embrace containers and packaging of cargo, cargo littering the deck, broken metal bands on bales of cargo, and even methods of loading cargo.[156] As the doctrine expanded to protect the *Sieracki* seamen, it drew criticism for making the vessel owner liable for almost any kind of shipboard accident.[157]

152. *Seas Shipping Co. v. Sieracki*, 328 U.S. 85, 1946 AMC 698 (1946) (defective gear); *Michalic v. Cleveland Tankers, Inc.*, 364 U.S. 325, 1960 AMC 2251 (1960) (defective equipment); *Boudoin v. Lykes Bros. S.S. Co.*, 348 U.S. 336, 1955 AMC 488 (1955) (unfit crew).

152a. *Boudoin v. Lykes Bros. S.S. Co.*, 348 U.S. 336, 1955 AMC 488 (1955).

153. *Waldron v. Moore-McCormack Lines, Inc.*, 386 U.S. 724, 1967 AMC 579 (1967).

154. *Mitchell v. Trawler Racer, Inc.*, 362 U.S. 539, 1960 AMC 1503 (1960).

155. Codified (as amended from time to time) at 33 U.S.C. 901-950.

156. *Gutierrez v. Waterman S.S. Corp.*, 373 U.S. 206, 1963 AMC 1649 (1963) (beans spilled onto deck); *Atlantic & Gulf Stevedores, Inc. v. Ellerman Lines, Ltd.*, 369 U.S. 355, 1962 AMC 565 (1962) (broken metal bands on cargo bales); *Morales v. City of Galveston*, 370 U.S. 165, 1962 AMC 1450 (1962) (improper method of loading cargo).

157. "Notwithstanding the rhetoric of many decisions, the shipowner has become virtually an insurer of the injured seaman." L. Guzmano, "Seamen's Rights to Recover for Injury against Either Shipowner or Charterer," 55 *Tulane Law Review* 1029, 1031 (1981). See,

There appear to be few survivors of the *Sieracki* seamen. The 1972 amendments to the LHWCA decimated the class by broadly defining maritime employees who were covered by the LHWCA and thus relegated solely to a negligence remedy in a third party action against the shipowner. One *Sieracki* survivor may be the river pilot, an independent contractor, who is not subject to the LHWCA and thus is still entitled to assert a claim for unseaworthiness.[157a]

In legal theory, however, some limitations on the warranty do exist. Perfection is not required, only reasonable fitness for the purpose intended.[158] Further, if negligent operation of seaworthy equipment consists of an "isolated, personal negligent act," the vessel is not unseaworthy.[159]

The warranty applies the standard for causation under general maritime law. Liability for unseaworthiness requires the "substantial factor" causal connection between the shipboard condition and the plaintiff's injury. The causation requirement is to be distinguished from the Jones Act standard, where the inquiry is whether the owner's negligence played "any part, no matter how small," in the plaintiff's injury.

The plaintiff's own negligence in a suit for unseaworthiness under general maritime law is merely a defense in mitigation. As in Jones Act actions, it serves only to reduce recovery.[160] However, the sole negligence of the plaintiff will preclude recovery under either theory.[161]

A general maritime law claim based upon unseaworthiness is no longer governed by the doctrine of laches; rather, the three-year limitation period of the Uniform Statute of Limitations for Maritime Torts, 46 U.S.C. 763(a) imposes a three year period, the same as prescribed by the Jones Act.[162]

---

also, dissent by Justice Powell in *Webb v. Dresser Industries*, 536 F.2d 603, 1976 AMC 2671 (5th Cir., 1976), *cert. den.* 429 U.S. 1121, 1976 AMC 2684 (1976). The dissent is to the denial of certiorari and is also quoted in *Gusmano, supra*, at 1033:

> The doctrine of "seaworthiness," on which this recovery is predicated, has been extended beyond all reason. In that case, the vessel was unseaworthy because the master was required to go ashore in Alaska without adequate boots.

157a. *Clark v. Solomon Nav. Ltd*, 631 F.Supp. 1275, 1986 AMC 2141 (S.D.N.Y., 1986).

158. *Little v. Green*, 428 F.2d 1061 (5th Cir., 1970), *cert.den.* 400 U.S. 964, 1971 AMC 818 (1971), "There is no requirement, however, that the newest or best equipment be provided, only that it be suitable for its intended use." The duty, however, is not discharged merely by meeting the custom and practice of the trade. *June T. Inc. v. King*, 290 F.2d 404, 1961 AMC 1431 (5th Cir., 1961); *Schlicter v. Port Arthur Towing Co.*, 288 F.2d 801, 1961 AMC 1164 (5th Cir., 1961).

159. *Usner v. Luckenbach Overseas Corp.*, 400 U.S. 494, 1971 AMC 810 (1971).

160. *Comeaux v. T.L. James & Co., Inc.*, 666 F.2d 294 (5th Cir., 1982).

161. *Robinson v. Zapata Corp.*, 664 F.2d 45 (5th Cir., 1981).

162. See *Nasser v. Hudson Waterways Corp.*, 563 F.Supp. 88, 1984 AMC 180 (W.D., Wash., 1983), where the court acknowledged that the uniform statute would bar an unseaworthiness claim but refused retroactive application of the statute.

Liability under the Jones Act

General Observations

An injured American seaman (and sometimes an injured alien sea-man)[163] has a remedy under the Jones Act (46 U.S.C. 688) if the injury was caused by the negligence of the employer, who is usually the shipowner.[164] Before enactment of the relevant legislation, the plaintiff seaman's action could be defeated by such defenses as assumption of risk and the fellow servant doctrine; namely, that the negligence of another crew member was not actionable. That was one of the propositions of *The Osceola.*[165]

There is no doubt that the clear purpose of the Jones Act was to extend to *seamen* a cause of action against their employers measured by the provisions of the Federal Employers Liability Act applicable to railroad workers. What were thought of as "seamen" at that time were clearly so-called blue water seamen employed on ships which plied the high seas. In any event, the legislative notion in 1920 may seem anachronistic today, given the expansive definition of "seamen" as meaning almost anyone.[166]

With the proliferation of special purpose vessels, diverse occupations now employed aboard many vessels, and the segmentation of vessel ownership and operation, the terms "Jones Act seaman" and "Jones Act employer" have acquired meanings which the Congress, in 1920, could never have foreseen.

If plaintiff qualifies as a Jones Act seaman and the defendant has obligations as a Jones Act employer, a simply proved and liberal negligence remedy immediately becomes available. First, however, the statutory status on both sides of the employment relationship must be established.

---

163. If the vessel flies the U.S. flag, the seamen on board (whether of American citizenship or not) are covered by the Jones Act. Jones Act benefits have been steadily extended to alien seamen on foreign flag vessels if certain criteria are met. See, in the evolution of Jones Act benefits to seamen, *Lauritzen v. Larsen,* 345 U.S. 571, 1953 AMC 1210 (1953); *Romero v. International Terminal Operating Co,* 358 U.S. 354, 1959 AMC 1603 (1959); and *Hellenic Lines v. Rhoditis,* 398 U.S. 306, 1970 AMC 994 (1970). In *Hellenic Lines,* the Supreme Court held that a resident alien shipowner, engaged in an extensive business operation in the United States, was a Jones Act "employer." See, also, *Kyriakos v. Goulandris,* 151 F.2d 132, 1945 AMC 1041 (2d Cir.), and *Bartholomew v. Universe Tankships,* 279 F.2d 911, 1960 AMC 1816 (2d Cir., 1960).
164. See discussion *infra* on "Employer as Non-Vessel Owner."
165. 189 U.S. 158 (1903).
166. *Carumbo v. Cape Cod S.S. Co.,* 123 F.2d 991, 1942 AMC 215 (1st Cir., 1941) (one who does any sort of work aboard a ship in navigation is a "seaman" within the meaning of the Jones Act; this includes, for example, even a ship's beautician). *Mahramas v. American Export Lines,* 475 F.2d 165, 1973 AMC 587 (2d Cir.).

These questions of maritime status, which are initial fact determinations, will yield significant consequences in measuring the nature and extent of liabilities for tortiously caused injury or death.

The status determination may dictate whether the plaintiff is entitled to a remedy for damages. To illustrate, if the maritime employee is not a Jones Act seaman, he is probably subject to the Longshoremen's and Harbor Workers' Compensation Act, codified (as amended from time to time) at 33 U.S.C. 901-50. If so, his exclusive remedy is the right to compensation under the L.H.W.C.A., which provides a compensation remedy for any maritime worker who is *not* a "master or member of the crew of any vessel." 33 U.S.C. 902(3), 903(a) (1). This L.H.W.C.A. exclusion has helped to define eligibility for Jones Act remedies; i.e., those available to a crew member. It will be readily seen that judicial expansion of the Jones Act status test correspondingly restricts coverage under the L.H.W.C.A. Normally, such L.H.W.C.A. coverage is excluded from a P & I policy, so liberalization of Jones Act liability directly affects the P & I underwriter.

The recurrent exercise is to draw a line between the Jones Act seaman (variously termed a member of the ship's crew, or a "member of the ship's company") and the maritime employee covered by the L.H.W.C.A. Naturally, it depends upon the circumstances of the litigation whether the plaintiff will seek to qualify as a Jones Act seaman. He may want to do so when the circumstances suggest fault of the shipowner contributing to his injury. Recovery under the Jones Act, with its very slight burden of proof, is clear inducement for the maritime employee to strive to escape the L.H.W.C.A.'s exclusive remedy provisions, generous as the benefits granted under those provisions may be.

Line drawing is not limited to a separation of the Jones Act seaman from the maritime employee under the L.H.W.C.A. A shipowner, and by extension the P & I underwriter, may draw the same kinds of lines, using different tests, between the Jones Act seaman and a passenger on a commercial vessel; between a Jones Act seaman and guests on a pleasure vessel; or between a Jones Act seaman and employees of subcontractors working aboard the vessel. In each instance, significant procedural and substantive results follow.

Establishing Status as a Jones Act Seaman

To qualify as a Jones Act seaman, a plaintiff must show:

   (a) employment as a member of the crew
   (b) of a vessel
   (c) which is in navigation
   (d) on navigable waters

(e) and that the employment demonstrates a more or less permanent connection with the vessel and that the plaintiff's reason for
being on board was primarily to aid in navigation.[167]

Each element, discussed separately below, must exist as a matter of
fact, and each is defined by an increasingly intricate body of law.

Employment as a Member of the Crew. The classic test required seamen to
have been possessed of some skill in navigation. They had to be able to
"hand, reef and steer," which was the ordinary test of seamanship.[168]
Nautical skill is no longer the criterion. The concept that all co-laborers
on a vessel should have the status of seamen had its origin in an opinion of
Justice Story in an early decision in which he equated the word "crew"
with "ship's company." This opened the floodgates to permit all sorts of
workers aboard ship, such as bartenders, cooks, and beauticians, to attain
seaman status.[169]

Whereas the concept of co-laborer may be all-embracing, the requirement of an employment contract is not. It is the contract of employment
that distinguishes a plaintiff seaman from a business invitee.[170] The Jones
Act expressly requires an employee/employer relationship as a prerequisite to recovery.[171] For example, the classification of a "pilot" as a Jones
Act seaman turns upon the particular facts. He may have an employment
contract with a vessel owner in which case he is a seaman if he is permanently assigned to act as a pilot on one or another of the vessel owner's
tugs.[172] Early authority indicated that a river or bar pilot whose services
were provided through pilots' associations to seagoing vessels on a per
trip basis was a seaman.[173] Later cases, however, recognize that a compulsory pilot is not a seaman in the classical sense of someone being under
contract with the vessel owner to serve as a crewman or officer.[174] The
pilot may be entitled to assert a warranty of seaworthiness, however, as a

---

167. Any discussion of the status test requires a caveat up front. The test is so often
refined and coated with "extensive judicial gloss" that periodic re-evaluation is essential. See,
for example, *Barrett v. Chevron U.S.A., Inc.,* 781 F.2d 1067, 1986 AMC 2455 (5th Cir., 1986) in
which the court *en banc* found it time to re-evaluate its own leading case of *Offshore Company
v. Robison,* 266 F.2d 769, 1959 AMC 2049 (5th Cir., 1959).

168. *The Canton,* 5 F.Cas. 29 (D.,Mass, 1858).

169. See footnote 85, *supra.*

170. *Miller v. Browning S.S. Co.,* 165 F.2d 209, 1947 AMC 1043 (2d Cir.).

171. *Spinks v. Chevron Oil Co.,* 507 F.2d 216 (5th Cir., 1975), *reh. den.,* opinion clarified
546 F.2d 675, 1979 AMC 1165.

172. *Magnolia Towing Company v. Pace,* 378 F.2d 12, 1967 AMC 2079 (5th Cir., 1967).

173. See *The Mary Elizabeth,* 24 F. 397 (C.C. Ala., 1885), in which a pilot on a steamboat
had a lien for seaman's wages, having been hired by the master on authority of the owner
and in compliance with compulsory pilotage laws.

174. One such case is *Walsh v. Zuisei Kaiun K.K.,* 606 F.2d 259, 1980 AMC 2788 (9th Cir.,
1979), where the court affirmed the owner's duty to rescue the decedent pilot, having "no
hesitation in holding that the pilot in this case, even a compulsory pilot, was entitled to the
same duty of rescue as a seaman . . . ."

survivor of the *Sieracki* seamen after the 1972 amendments to the LHWCA.

For Jones Act liability to attach, the employer need not be the owner or the operator of the vessel.[175] Although it is clear that a stowaway is not a Jones Act seaman,[176] a "workaway" may be.[177] A master may also recover under the Jones Act.[178]

Questions of status also arise in actions brought by passengers. Since they have no employment relationship, there is no Jones Act protection.[179] Guests on pleasure boats are not generally considered Jones Act seamen.[180] See the discussion *infra* concerning the vesselowner's obligations to passengers and guests.

Once the employment relationship and the nature of activities establish status as a Jones Act seaman, there is no requirement of a causal connection between the injury and the type of work the seaman was doing when injured. For example, an employee who was assigned "light duty" was injured ashore while cleaning out a duck blind. Seaman's status was upheld.[181]

It is equally clear that a "volunteer" aboard a vessel is not a seaman, there being no employment relationship.[182]

There is also a class of crew members which is statutorily excluded from Jones Act protection. These are scientific personnel serving aboard oceanographic research vessels. The Oceanographic Research Vessels Act precludes Jones Act recovery.[183]

Employment on a Vessel. Plaintiff's employment must call for performance of service on a "vessel." Like the term "crew member," the word "vessel"

175. *Barrios v. Louisiana Construction Materials Co.*, 465 F.2d 1157, 1972 AMC 2659 (5th Cir., 1972); *Spinks v. Chevron Oil Co., supra*, n. 171.

176. *The Laura Madsen*, 112 F. 72 (D.,Wash., 1901).

177. *The Tashmoo*, 48 F.2d 366, 1931 AMC 48 (D., N.Y., 1930) (by signing articles and assuming duties of a crew member, the plaintiff became a crew member and thus was precluded from recovering a salvage award as a "passenger").

178. *Warner v. Goltra*, 293 U.S. 55, 1934 AMC 1436 (1934).

179. *Beard v. Shell Oil Co.*, 606 F.2d 515, 1980 AMC 1880 (5th Cir.).

180. *Shaver v. Erikson*, 1979 AMC 2308 (N.D.,Ill.), which follows the general rule of *Kermarec v. Compagnie Generale Transatlantique*, 358 U.S. 625, 1959 AMC 597 (1959), holding that the shipowner owes a duty of reasonable care to all those aboard his vessel for purposes not inimical to his interests.

181. *Savoie v. Otto Candies, Inc.*, 692 F.2d 363 (5th Cir., 1982). It is very clear that the situs of the injury is not limited to occurrences aboard a vessel. The employer's "negligence" can extend ashore, as happened in *Hopson v. Texaco, Inc.*, 383 U.S. 262, 1966 AMC 281 (1966), where a cab driver was held to be the servant of the shipowner in transporting an injured seaman when an automobile accident ensued.

182. *G.I. Ferry Co. v. Williams*, 25 F.2d 612, 1928 AMC 1223 (2d Cir.), where the plaintiff was aboard a ferry to assist for one day.

183. 46 U.S.C. 441-445. Scientific personnel may, however, recover for unseaworthiness under general maritime law. *Sennett v. Shell Oil Co.*, 325 F.Supp. 1, 1072 AMC 1346 (E.D.,La.). But see *Presley v. M/V Caribbean Seal*, 537 F.Supp. 956, 1983 AMC 75 (S.D.,Tex.), *rev'd* 709 F.2d 406, 1984 AMC 2307 (5th Cir., 1983), *cert.den.* 1984 AMC 2404.

carries an expansive meaning, but in this instance it is statutory. A vessel includes "every description of water craft or other artificial contrivance used, or capable of being used, as a means of transportation on water."[184] There are, however, a great many "special purpose vessels," the definition of which sets the outer limits of what is a "vessel."

Unique factual problems arise under the Outer Continental Shelf Lands Act.[185] That act specifically applies the provisions of the L.H.W.C.A. to disability or death in connection with operations on the continental shelf. If a structure is affixed to the continental shelf, it is not a vessel in navigation for purposes of the Jones Act.[186] Furthermore, summary judgment is proper to deny Jones Act status when the injury is sustained on a fixed oil rig.[187]

The expanded practical application of a vessel in navigation was formulated in the leading case of *Offshore Co. v. Robison*,[188] which held that a worker on an off-shore drilling platform was a seaman. The opinion expands the traditional concept of vessel "consistent with the liberal construction of the [Jones] Act that has characterized it from the beginning and is consistent with its purposes." After *Robison*, vessels could be special purpose vessels, not usually employed as a means of transportation by water, but designed to float on water.

The vessel need not be in navigation, but need only possess a potential for water movement.[189] Naturally, barges without power but capable of being towed are vessels.[190] An amphibious marsh buggy, being operated in 12 inches of water, was held not to be a vessel, although the court said it could be a vessel if at the time of the accident it had been operated in a navigable waterway.[191]

Employment on drydocks or on work boats raises the "vessel" issue in determinations of Jones Act status. Like larger drydocks, a floating drydock permanently attached to shore is not a vessel,[192] nor is a floating construction platform permanently affixed to shore.[193]

184. 1 U.S.C. 3.

185. 43 U.S.C. 1331 *et seq.*

186. *Rodrigue v. Aetna Cas. & Sur. Co.*, 395 U.S. 352, 1969 AMC 1082 (1969).

187. *Stansbury v. Sikorski Aircraft*, 681 F.2d 948, 1984 AMC 2482 (5th Cir., 1982).

188. 266 F.2d 769, 1959 AMC 2049 (5th Cir.), which was recently re-evaluated in *Barrett v. Chevron U.S.A., Inc.*, n. 167.

189. *The Ark*, 17 F.2d 446, 1927 AMC 38 (S.D., Fla.) (a powerless houseboat held to be a vessel); *The Showboat*, 47 F.2d 286, 1931 AMC 19 (D.,Mass., 1930) (schooner tied to a wharf and used as a restaurant held to be a vessel); *Pirate Ship*, 21 F.2d 231, 1927 AMC 1378 (E.D.,La.) (vessel without propelling machinery moored to a wharf and used as a dancing platform held to be a vessel).

190. *Los Angeles v. United Dredging Co.*, 14 F.2d 364. 1927 AMC 188 (9th Cir.).

191. *Percle v. Western Geophysical Co.*, 528 F.Supp. 227 (E.D.,La., 1981). See, however, *Senko v. LaCrosse Dredging Co.*, 352 U.S. 370, 1957 AMC 891 (1957), where the plaintiff was employed as a handyman aboard a land-locked dredge, anchored to the shore.

192. *Atkins v. Greenville Shipbuilding*, 411 F.2d 279, 1969 AMC 1728 (5th Cir.).

193. *Cook v. Belden Concrete Products*, 472 F.2d 999, 1973 AMC 285 (5th Cir.).

A recent case dealing exhaustively with the subject is *Bernard v. Binnings Constr. Co., Inc.*,[194] holding that a small "work punt," though capable of being moved, was stationary at the time and the situation was analogized to that of a drydock. The work punt was not a vessel. The *Bernard* court said: " . . . mere capacity to float or move across navigable waters does not necessarily make a structure a vessel for Jones Act purposes."

Vessel in Navigation. Even though the plaintiff can establish he was assigned to work on a "vessel," that vessel must be "in navigation." The factual determinations, of course, are intertwined, but the navigational aspect seems to raise three principal questions: (1) For vessels under construction, what was the stage of completion at the time of the accident? (2) Although the structure may once have been a vessel, what is her purpose and employment following conversion to a more terrestrial use? (3) Although unquestionably a vessel, is she nevertheless a "dead ship"?

The broad test for establishing that a vessel is in navigation is that the vessel must be an "instrumentality of commerce." For example, in *Williams v. Avondale Shipyards, Inc.*,[195] an incomplete vessel was undergoing sea trials to determine what additional work was required. It was held that the craft was not yet an instrumentality of commerce and hence not a vessel in navigation.

A subsidiary question is whether a vessel undergoing repairs remains "in navigation" or whether she is "dead." A leading case which refines the criteria for that determination is *Martinez v. Dixie Carriers, Inc.*;[196] i.e., was the contracted work minor or major, who had custody of the vessel while work was being done, and was the work traditionally and ordinarily done by seamen, etc.?

The duration of the repair work may be determinative. Thus, in *Wixom v. Bolen Marine & Mfg. Co., Inc.*,[197] seaman's status was denied to an employee working on a ship which had remained in the repair yard for three years. Vessel status may also depend upon whether the repair work was preparatory to lay-up of the vessel or preparatory to the season. For example, in *Warner v. Fish Meal Co.*,[198] a vessel undergoing year-end main-

194. 741 F.2d 824, 1985 AMC 784 (5th Cir.,1985). Special purpose vessels such as submersible oil facilities are, however, Jones Act vessels. *Hicks v. Ocean Drilling and Exploration Co.*, 512 F.2d 817, 1975 AMC 1378 (5th Cir.); *Producers Drilling Co. v. Gray*, 361 F.2d 432, 1966 AMC 1260 (5th Cir.). It is apparently immaterial whether such a submersible rig is moored to the bottom at the time of the injury. *McCarty v. Service Contracting, Inc.*, 317 F.Supp. 629, 1971 AMC 90 (E.D.,La.).

195. 452 F.2d 955, 1971 AMC 2124 (5th Cir.).

196. 529 F.2d 457 (5th Cir., 1976).

197. 614 F.2d 956, 1980 AMC 2992 (5th Cir.).

198. 548 F.2d 1193 (5th Cir., 1977). See, also, *Wixom v. Bolen Marine Mfg. Co.*, *supra*, n. 197.

tenance was held to be in navigation, giving rise to the owner's warranty of seaworthiness, which is also authority for vessel status under the Jones Act. On the other hand, in *Desper v. Starved Rock Ferry Co.,*[199] a plaintiff preparing a laid-up vessel for the upcoming season was held not to be a Jones Act seaman.

Where the vessel has no crew, an expired Coast Guard certificate, and has been inoperable for over a year, a directed verdict denying seaman's status was affirmed. The vessel had been permanently withdrawn from navigation and was a "dead ship."[199] Similarly, a deactivated vessel is no longer in maritime commerce.[200]

Where a vessel is used in connection with land-based activities, the courts make an additional inquiry. Thus, in *Garcia v. Universal Seafoods Ltd.,*[201] an old navy ship was converted into a floating seafood processor. It had not been moved, and the owners had no intention of moving it. Held: Not a vessel in navigation, citing *Hicks v. Ocean Drilling & Exploration Co.,*[202] which established the test that the purpose for which a facility was constructed and the business in which it is engaged are controlling considerations in determining whether a facility is a "vessel." In that case, an oil storage facility was held to be a vessel.

A vessel may be in navigation but not on "navigable waters." The issue seldom arises because the three elements of navigability are usually present: (1) waters which are navigable in fact; (2) waters which are public; and (3) waters which connect in their own ordinary condition, or with other waters, to navigable waters. Thus, mill ponds, borrow pits, or artificially created bodies of water may not be navigable since they may not connect with other navigable bodies of water nor are they capable of being used as an artery of commerce.[203]

Connection between Employment and the Vessel. The leading case establishing the substantive test for seaman's status, as heretofore noted, is *Offshore Co. v. Robison,* discussed *supra.* Robison was a roughneck assigned to a drilling rig mounted on a barge in the Gulf of Mexico. He contended he was a member of the crew of the barge. His jury verdict was affirmed. The case typifies how the proliferation of special purpose vessels and the hybrid nature of amphibious assignments has spawned so much litigation.

---

199. 342 U.S. 187, 1952 AMC 12 (1952). But see *Butler v. Whiteman,* 356 U.S. 271, 1959 AMC 2566 (1959).

200. *West v. United States,* 361 U.S. 118, 1960 AMC 15 (1959). Nor is a vessel used to store grain, towed to and from the grain silos, a vessel in navigation. *Roper v. United States,* 368 U.S. 20, 1961 AMC 2499 (1961).

201. 459 F.Supp. 463, 1980 AMC 2654 (W.D.,Wash, 1978).

202. 512 F.2d 817, 1975 AMC 1378 (5th Cir.), *cert.den.* 423 U.S. 1050 (1976).

203. See *Adams v. Montana Power Co.,* 528 F.2d 437, 1973 AMC 1189 (9th Cir., 1975).

A recent articulation of the nexus element (relationship of employment to vessel navigation) is found in *Barrett v. Chevron U.S.A., Inc.*,[204] where the court reviewed the leading cases and reaffirmed the principle of "permanency" between the work and the vessel. While each determination rests on particular facts, it appears that the claimant must show some regularity and continuity for a significant part of his work on a vessel or on an identifiable fleet, meaning a group of vessels acting together or under common control. The Fifth Circuit test appears to be the majority view, but not without criticism even from members of that court.[205]

If the worker's primary duties are on land or fixed platforms, and if the work is only fortuitously maritime (i.e., where the only maritime connection is the location of the accident), seaman's status will be denied.[206] If the plaintiff's activity is traditionally maritime, Jones Act status may be established even though the connection with the vessel or vessels is only temporary.[207] If it is merely a transitory relationship between the land-based worker (i.e., not traditional maritime employment) and several vessels not in a fleet, there is no Jones Act status.[208]

Employer as Non-Vessel Owner. A plaintiff's seaman status may not be defeated simply by showing that his employer was not the owner or operator of the vessel. The employment on a particular vessel, though not owned by the employer, may be sufficiently "permanent" to satisfy the status test. The permanency requirement has been expanded beyond a single vessel. Thus, one can be a member of the crew of numerous vessels which have common ownership or control.[209] Moreover, when the plaintiff's assignment is to several vessels under common ownership, the fact that the employer is not the owner of the vessels will not defeat Jones Act status.[210]

It is readily apparent that exposure to Jones Act liabilities has transcended traditional thinking. Independent contractors may be liable un-

---

204. 781 F.2d 1067, 1986 AMC 2455 (5th Cir., 1986).

205. See dissent in *Barrett, supra,* giving approval to the more conservative test of *Johnson v. John F. Beasley Construction Co.,* 742 F.2d 1054, 1985 AMC 369 (7th Cir., 1984) which focuses more sharply on the requirement that the claimant must perform significant navigational functions before his status as a Jones Act seaman is met. Such a focus helps to define a bright-line rule: " . . . A bright line rule is called for, one that nudges coverages back toward the blue-water sailors for whom the Jones Act was meant." The dissent reasoned that passage of the Outer Continental Shelf Lands Act, 43 U.S.C. 1333(b), and the 1972 amendments to the L.H.W.C.A., both examples of beneficence, removed much of the rationale for the liberal Jones Act tests.

206. *Guidrey v. Continental Oil Co.,* 640 F.2d 523, 1982 AMC 2845 (5th Cir., 1981).

207. *Wallace v. Oceaneering International,* 727 F.2d 427 (5th Cir., 1984).

208. *Jones v. Mississippi River Grain Elevator Co.,* 703 F.2d 108, 1983 AMC 2403 (5th Cir., 1983).

209. *Braniff v. Jackson Avenue-Gretna Ferry, Inc.,* 280 F.2d 523, 1961 AMC 1739 (5th Cir.).

210. *Bertran v. International Mooring Marine, Inc.,* 700 F.2d 240, 1984 AMC 1740 (5th Cir., 1983).

der the Jones Act.[211] Furthermore, one may become the employer by assuming sufficient control over a worker, even though not the contractual employer. Thus, the borrowed servant doctrine, using control as the critical inquiry, can produce one more entity that may be found liable under the Jones Act.[212]

Primarily to Aid in Navigation. Closely aligned to the permanency requirement is the criterion that the plaintiff seeking Jones Act status must have been aboard the vessel primarily to aid in its navigation.[213]

This criterion takes on greatest importance outside the employment context. Thus, passengers on commercial vessels and guests on pleasure vessels must first establish a purpose to aid in navigation. The plaintiff is not a seaman as a matter of law if, when the "nature and location of his occupation is taken as a whole," there is no permanent assignment to a vessel or any identifiable fleet of vessels.[214] It has been said that the test of "contributing to the vessel's function or mission" has been liberalized to the point that it excludes only passengers who happen to perform some seamen's duties.[215] A cook on board is a member of the crew in aid of navigation,[216] as is a fireman on a derrick stationed in a river.[217] Though some of the foregoing cases do not directly involve "aid to navigation" in the strict sense, they do illustrate the liberalization of the test. On the other hand, a laborer assigned to clean a barge is not a Jones Act seaman without a showing that he was aboard primarily to aid in navigation.[218]

Standards of Proof under the Jones Act

Once seaman's status is shown, the plaintiff will encounter an "extremely low evidentiary standard," which applies to questions of liability and

---

211. *Guidry v. South Louisiana Contractors, Inc.*, 614 F.2d 447, 1983 AMC 455 (5th Cir., 1980); *Mahramas v. American Export Isbrandtsen Lines, Inc.*, 475 F.2d 165, 1973 AMC 587 (2d Cir., 1973).

212. *Ruiz v. Shell Oil Co.*, 413 F.2d 310 (5th Cir., 1969). See, also, *Spinks v. Chevron Oil Co.*, 507 F.2d 216, opinion clarified, 546 F.2d 675, 1979 AMC 1165 (5th Cir., 1960).

213. *Braniff v. Jackson Avenue-Gretna Ferry, Inc.*, 280 F.2d 523, 1961 AMC 1739 (5th Cir.); *Abshire v. Sea Coast Products*, 668 F.2d 832 (5th Cir., 1982).

214. *White v. Valley Line Company*, 736 F.2d 304, 1985 AMC 1172 (5th Cir., 1984).

215. See *Dove v. Belcher Oil Co.*, 686 F.2d 329 (5th Cir., 1982), in which a captain was a passenger on a different vessel and did not contribute to its function or mission.

216. *A.L. Mechling Barge Line v. Bassett*, 119 F.2d 995 (7th Cir., 1941).

217. *Summerlin v. Massman Constr. Co.*, 199 F.2d 715, 1952 AMC 1965 (4th Cir., 1952).

218. *Simko v. C. & C. Marine Maintenance Co.*, 594 F.2d 960, 1980 AMC 1995 (3d Cir., 1979), *cert.den.* 1980 AMC 2102, on remand, 484 F.Supp. 401 (W.D.,Pa., 1980). Also representing the stricter view is *Wolbert v. City of New York*, 314 F.Supp. 528, 1971 AMC 102 (S.D.N.Y.), where a deckhand whose duties were to secure lines was held not to be a Jones Act seaman because he was predominantly shorebound.

damages. However, the low standard does not apply to the threshold issue of seaman status.[219]

Proof of liability is facilitated because of the language of the Act. The Act (46 U.S.C. 688) expressly incorporates the Federal Employer's Liability Act (45 U.S.C. 51 *et seq*), which gives a remedy for injury or death when it results "in whole or in part from the negligence of the officers, agents or employees." It was the interpretation by the U.S. Supreme Court in *Rogers v. Missouri R.R. Co.*,[220] which translated "in whole or in part" to mean "any part, however small." Today, the usual jury charge allows a finding of liability if the employer's negligence contributed "even in the slightest degree." There is thus no requirement of proximate cause. It is fair to say that almost every Jones Act claim is submitted to the jury on issues of negligence and causation. The standard of proof for causation, which is almost non-existent, has tended to relax the burden of proving negligence as well. Trial judges are reluctant to draw the lines between scanty causation and scanty negligence.

Comparative Fault

The seaman's own negligence may be considered only in mitigation of damages. Thus, to the extent to which the seaman's negligence has contributed to cause injury, his recovery is proportionately reduced. This is true even if the plaintiff's negligence was greater than that of the employer.[221] In the same vein, however, if the seaman's negligence is 100 percent, he is barred from recovery. This not because of his own negligence, but rather because the chain of causation was never established.[222] Comparative negligence, then, is merely a defense in mitigation. Defenses to a seaman's negligence remedy prior to enactment of the Jones Act have been abolished. These include the fellow servant doctrine and assumption of risk. Exculpatory contracts or similar devices also are prohibited.[223] Some courts have strictly construed the seaman's duty of care for his own safety under certain circumstances. Thus, it has been held that a seaman owes only a slight duty of care.[224] Similarly, under the "rescue doctrine," evidence of a seaman's lack of judgment or ordinary negligence will not support a jury charge for comparative negligence. There must be a showing of reckless or wanton conduct on his part.[225] Where the

219. *Wallace v. Oceaneering International*, 727 F.2d 427 (5th Cir., 1984).

220. 353 U.S. 500, 1957 AMC 652 (1957).

221. *Asaro v. Parisi*, 297 F.2d 859, 1962 AMC 1155 (1st Cir.), *cert.den.* 370 U.S. 904, where plaintiff was guilty of 75% causal negligence.

222. *Chesapeake & Ohio R.R. Co. v. Newman*, 243 F.2d 804, 1957 AMC 2369 (6th Cir.).

223. *Boyd v. Grand Trunk Western R.R. Co.*, 338 U.S. 263. 1950 AMC 26 (1949).

224. *Brooks v. Great Lakes Dredge & Drydock Co.*, 754 F.2d 536 (5th Cir., 1984).

225. *Furka v. Great Lakes Dredge & Dock Co.*, 755 F.2d 1085, 1985 AMC 2914 (4th Cir., 1985). This case also discusses the other "prong of the rescue doctrine, viz., that violation of

vessel owner violates a statute enacted for the safety of crew, a finding of comparative fault under the Jones Act is prohibited.[226]

By extension, the factual bases of jury awards for the Jones Act seaman demonstrate the liberal reception of evidence by the courts.

Limitation Period

The Jones Act incorporates the three-year statute of limitation found in the Federal Employers' Liability Act. 45 U.S.C. 56. The limitation period is therefore a part of the cause of action and for that reason is strictly construed.[227] That is not to say, however, that the limitation period cannot be tolled by misrepresentation or other inducement to the seaman to delay filing.[228]

The limitation period begins to run when the cause of action accrues. The "discovery rule" would seem to apply in Jones Act actions. For example, in *Dubose v. Kansas City Southern Railway*,[229] a FELA case, it was held that the limitation period was tolled because the plaintiff was not aware of, and had no reasonable opportunity to discover, the critical facts of his injury and its cause. However, where the seaman has knowledge of the injuries at the time he is injured and soon learns that they are substantial, his lack of knowledge of all claimed consequences of the injury cannot justify tolling the limitation period.[230]

Jones Act Damages

Additional Liabilities to Seamen. Recently, resourceful plaintiffs' counsel have fused maintenance and cure theories into Jones Act damage claims. The cause of action seeks to recover damages for aggravation of a physical condition caused by a delay in paying, or a refusal to pay, maintenance and cure.[231]

There is also authority that retaliatory discharge of a seaman who has filed a Jones Act claim against his employer gives rise to a new maritime tort under general maritime law, even though the employment is terminable at will by either party.[231a] The claim may be joined with a Jones Act

---

a duty owed to one who is imperiled is also a violation of duty to rescuer," following *Grigsby v. Coastal Marine Service of Texas, Inc.*, 412 F.2d 1011 (5th Cir., 1969).

226. *Brunner v. Maritime Overseas Corp.*, 779 F.2d 296, 1986 AMC 2630 (5th Cir., 1986).

227. *Holifield v. Cities Service Tanker Corp.*, 552 F.2d 367 (5th Cir., 1977).

228. *Glus v. Brooklyn Eastern District Terminal*, 359 U.S. 231, 1959 AMC 2092 (1959).

229. 729 F.2d 1026 (5th Cir., 1985).

230. *Albertson v. T.J. Stevenson & Co., Inc.*, 749 F.2d 223 (5th Cir., 1984).

231. See discussion, *supra*, under "Maintenance and Cure."

231a. There is no right to a federal jury trial in an action for retaliatory discharge since the action is founded on maritime law and there is no underlying state cause of action and thus no basis for diversity jurisdiction. *Schultheiss v. Mobil Oil*, 757 F.2d 282, 1986 AMC 1028 (5th Cir., 1985).

claim.[232] Moreover, although the seaman's Jones Act complaint alleges significant disability, which would make the vessel owner potentially liable for continuing employment, such potential liability is still no defense to a complaint for retaliatory discharge.[233] The shipowner may, however, defeat a claim of retaliatory discharge by demonstrating that the personal injury action was not a substantial motivating factor for the discharge.[234]

Compensatory Damages for Maritime Personal Injury. Broadly speaking, the rules governing the measure of general damages for personal injury in Jones Act cases are those followed in other maritime personal injury actions and also in non-maritime cases.

The award for compensatory damages may include compensation for the actual physical injury, past and future pain and suffering, past and future mental anguish, and impaired enjoyment of life.[235]

Maritime personal injury actions tend to result in abnormally large jury awards, a fact for which any foreign or domestic P & I underwriter will sadly vouch. The reasons and their validity may be debated. It is difficult to say whether the cause lies in a certain mystique of the maritime calling or in consideration of evidence of comparatively high wage loss figures, or in the disparate sympathies evoked, for example, by the corporate vessel owner and the injured maritime worker. Certainly, there are the obvious factors affecting the awards, such as the nature and extent of the injury, how demonstrable it is, demographics of the forum, and the ability of the plaintiff and support witnesses to "market" the plaintiff's case. So-called special damages include the following: reimbursement for maintenance and cure (see discussion, *supra*); medical expenses (past and future); lost earnings (past and future); impaired earning capacity; and past and future economic loss, if any, other than earnings.[236]

---

232. *Smith v. Atlas Off-Shore Boat Services,* 653 F.2d 1057 (5th Cir., 1981).

233. *Roberson v. Rebstock Drilling Co., Inc.,* 749 F.2d 1182 (5th Cir., 1985). This cause of action must be distinguished from the statutory claim of wrongful discharge under 46 U.S.C. 594. That statute provides the seaman a summary method of establishing damages for breach of an employment agreement which specifies a definite term or voyage. See *Annot.,* Liability to Improperly Discharged Seaman under 46 U.S.C. 594, 41 A.L.R. Fed. 811 (1979). To be further distinguished is the statutory claim for penalty wages. 46 U.S.C. 596. Under that statute, the court has no discretion and must award double wages for each day the shipowner/employer withholds wages without sufficient cause. See *Griffin v. Oceanic Contractors, Inc.,* 458 U.S. 564, 1982 AMC 2377 (1982), where a seaman was held entitled to recover more than $300,000 in penalties because his employer withheld $412.40 in wages due him.

234. *Smith v. Atlas Off-Shore Boat Services,* n. 232, *supra.*

235. See Fallon, "Personal Injury Damages Obtainable in Jones Act and/or General Maritime Law Claims," *Damages Recoverable in Maritime Matters,* American Bar Association, 1984.

236. *Downie v. United States Lines Co.,* 359 F.2d 344, 1964 AMC 2289, 2297 (3d Cir., 1960), *cert.den.* 385 U.S. 897 (1967).

Medical Expenses. Usually, the seaman's medical expenses have been paid by the shipowner as part of the maintenance and cure obligation. In such instances, of course, the expenses may not be alleged and proved at trial; otherwise, they are properly recoverable.

Lost Earnings. Normally, the plaintiff will offer proof by wage vouchers of actual earnings over the last several years prior to his injury, plus fringe benefits. A seaman's employment is often sporadic or, if not sporadic, less than 12 months on an annual basis. It then becomes necessary to determine an average over the last several years.

Courts have taken different approaches with respect to fringe benefits. One approach simply computes those fringe benefits existing at the time of injury; another approach averages the fringe benefits with the wages.[237] The proper measure of fringe benefits is their value to the plaintiff, although proof of value may come in through the cost to defendant of providing the benefits.[238]

Unearned wages are those wages recoverable as part of maintenance and cure. See discussion *supra.* The vessel owner (and P & I underwriters) are liable for such payment independently of any damage claim. If already paid, they may not be alleged and proved in the Jones Act action. However, unearned wages do not cover lost overtime, which may be alleged and proved.

Juries should be instructed that the measure for future wage loss is net wages *after* deduction for applicable taxes.[239]

Loss of Earning Capacity. The measure for impaired earning capacity is normally the diminution in wages after the accident when compared to pre-accident earnings. However, the plaintiff may prove that equal or higher post-accident wages are not indicative and that his earning capacity has, in fact, been impaired.[240]

Future Wage Loss. An award for future wage loss should be discounted to present value. The discount rate is what could be earned on "the best and safest investments."[241] The court should properly take into account the effects of inflation in setting an award for future wage loss. However, how the trial court should properly instruct on the interaction of inflation and

---

237. Compare *United States Steel Corp. v. Lamp,* 436 F.2d 1256, 1971 AMC 2666 (6th Cir., 1970) with *Davis v. Hill Engineering,* 549 F.2d 314, 1977 AMC 1090 (5th Cir.).

238. *Williams v. Reading & Bates Drilling Co.,* 750 F.2d 487 (5th Cir., 1985).

239. *Norfolk & Western Railway v. Liepelt,* 444 U.S. 490, 1980 AMC 1811 (1980), reh.den. 445 U.S. 972 (1980).

240. *Wiles v. New York, Chicago & St. Louis R.R. Co.,* 283 F.2d 328 (3d Cir., 1960).

241. *Jones & Laughlin Steel Corp. v. Pfeifer,* 76 L.Ed.2d 768, 1983 AMC 1881 (1983).

discounting to present value apparently is unsettled.[242] Prejudgment interest may not be calculated on an award of future damages.[243]

Remittitur and Additur. Occasionally, the verdict may be so high that the court will conclude it is grossly excessive, in which case the remedy of remittitur may be available.[244] In some states, remittitur is precluded no matter how much the trial judge may be tempted to apply the principle. In many federal decisions, under maritime law, it has been held that the trial judge has discretion to order a new trial for an excessive verdict unless the plaintiff is willing to accept a remitted amount.

Duty to Effect Cure. It is a question of fact whether the seaman's decision to decline surgery is reasonable. If it is not, he is precluded from damages for the consequences which surgery would have corrected.[245]

Collateral Source Rule. A shipowner cannot normally claim benefit of amounts the seaman received, such as money in a pension fund, as mitigation of damages. The collateral source rule precludes such application.[246] It does not matter whether the amounts were funded by the shipowner,[247] or whether the benefits came from a third party without participation from a source to which neither the plaintiff nor the shipowner contributed. But where the seaman recovers on a negligence claim under the Jones Act, he may not recover medical expenses for maintenance and cure where such expenses were paid by a union plan. He must offer proof of expenditures made or liability incurred.[248]

Prejudgment Interest. An admiralty judge has discretion to award prejudgment interest and may do so if the court is the trier of fact in a Jones Act case. However, a jury award in favor of a Jones Act seaman may not bear prejudgment interest.[249] Where the Jones Act claim is tried jointly with a general maritime law claim, an award of prejudgment interest is within the judge's discretion.[250] Conversely, when the Jones Act and general maritime law actions are combined in a jury trial, a court may exercise discretion to award prejudgment interest on the purely admiralty item of

242. *Jones & Laughlin Steel Corp. v. Pfeifer, supra,* n. 241.
243. *Williams v. Reading & Bates Drilling Co.,* 750 F.2d 487 (5th Cir., 1985).
244. *Schottka v. American Export Isbrandtsen Lines, Inc.,* 311 F.Supp. 77, 1970 AMC 2160 (S.D.N.Y., 1969).
245. *Young v. American Export Isbrandtsen Lines, Inc.,* 291 F.Supp. 447, 1969 AMC 63 (S.D.N.Y., 1968).
246. *Russo v. Matson Navigation Co.,* 486 F.2d 1018, 1973 AMC 2334 (9th Cir.).
247. *Bourque v. Diamond M. Drilling Co.,* 623 F.2d 351, 1982 AMC 1810 (5th Cir., 1980).
248. *Gosnell v. Sea-Land Service, Inc.,* 782 F.2d 464 (4th Cir., 1986).
249. *Theriot v. J. Ray McDermott & Co.,* 742 F.2d 877 (5th Cir., 1984).
250. *Ceja v. Mike Hooks, Inc.,* 690 F.2d 1191 (5th Cir., 1982).

damages, such as those caused by unseaworthiness, provided they are sufficiently identified in the jury verdict.[251]

If the admiralty court, in its discretion, awards prejudgment interest, the rate will be the market rate as established by the prevailing party. There is authority in the Ninth Circuit,[252] that the rate of prejudgment interest is the federal post-judgment rate.[253] However, since the award is discretionary, substantial evidence may establish that the equities require a different rate.[254] The date prejudgment interest begins to accrue is normally from the date of the injury. In maritime tort claims against the United States, pursuant to the Suits in Admiralty Act,[255] prejudgment interest runs from the date suit was commenced. In that instance, the statute itself sets the annual rate at 4 percent.[256]

Punitive Damages. The courts appear to be split on whether punitive damages may be recovered under the Jones Act. The Ninth Circuit denies them.[257] The Fifth Circuit expressly left the issue undecided in *In re Merry Shipping, Inc.*,[258] but the court did express doubt that Congress intended to provide such a remedy when it incorporated the Federal Employers' Liability Act. Apparently, the Sixth Circuit concludes otherwise; i.e., punitive damage may be recoverable if the shipowner either engaged in or ratified malicious conduct.[259]

Liabilities for Section 905(b) Negligence

For the P & I underwriter, Section 905(b) of the Longshoremen's and Harbor Workers' Compensation Act of the United States represents a significant exposure which has undergone dramatic expansion since the section was added to the L.H.W.C.A. in 1972. The 1972 amendments attempted to accomplish several basic objectives:

(1) Abolish the warranty of seaworthiness which had been enjoyed by longshoremen and harbor workers by virtue of their court-created status as "Sieracki seamen."[260]

---

251. *Domanque v. Penrod Drilling Co.,* 748 F.2d 999 (5th Cir., 1984).
252. *Western Pacific Fisheries, Inc. v. S.S. President Grant,* 730 F.2d 1280 (9th Cir., 1984). At this writing there are no known personal injury cases applying the statutory rate of prejudgment interest.
253. 28 U.S.C. 1961(a).
254. *Western Pacific Fisheries, Inc. v. S.S. President Grant,* n. 252 *supra.*
255. 46 U.S.C. 745.
256. 46 U.S.C. 743.
257. *Kopczynski v. The Jacqueline,* 742 F.2d 555, 1985 AMC 769 (9th Cir., 1984).
258. 650 F.2d 622, 1981 AMC 2839 (6th Cir., 1981).
259. See *Kozar v. Chesapeake and Ohio R.R. Co.,* 449 F.2d 1238 (6th Cir., 1971).
260. See discussion, *infra,* concerning *Seas Shipping Co. v. Sieracki,* 328 U.S. 85, 1946 AMC 698 (1946).

(2) Abolish the shipowners' *Ryan* indemnity rights against the employer of the longshoremen and/or harbor workers.[261]

(3) Increase the workers' benefits under the L.H.W.C.A. for which the employer was liable without fault.

In short, the worker was to be appeased by receipt of very generous compensation benefits for work-related injury, illness, or death, which benefits were presumably large enough to induce him to accept a sole negligence remedy against the shipowner. Before 1972, he had had two available theories: a tort remedy for negligence and the seaworthiness warranty. The stevedore employer accepted these enlarged compensation obligations in exchange for the abolition of the *Ryan* warranty and what some would say had amounted to "pass-through" liabilities of the vessel. The inducement for the shipowners' interests, of course, was the end of the era of *Sieracki* seamen.

Before addressing what kind of recovery the shore worker gained from Section 905(b) negligence protection, it is useful to understand the evolution of the shore worker's third-party rights against the shipowner.

The shore worker had a negligence remedy against the shipowner, even before his brother seamen. It was not until the Jones Act was enacted in 1920 that a seaman was able to sue his shipowner-employer for negligence. That is, before the Jones Act, the fourth proposition of *The Osceola*[262] held that the seaman was not allowed to recover from the employer for negligence of the master or any member of the crew; rather, the seaman was relegated to his remedy for maintenance and cure.

Until 1946, the shore worker (who by then was protected by the L.H.W.C.A. of 1927) asserted negligence theories against the shipowner based upon general maritime law; namely, that the owner owed the business invitee a duty to exercise reasonable care for his safety while aboard the vessel.

Following enactment of the Jones Act, the shore worker sought standing as a Jones Act seaman, but this was unavailing since he had no employment relationship with the shipowner.

In 1946, the U.S. Supreme Court decided *Seas Shipping Co. v. Sieracki.*[263] That case held that the warranty of seaworthiness, traditionally owed by a shipowner to a seaman, extended to a longshoreman injured while working aboard a ship. Longshoremen and other harbor workers thus became "Sieracki seamen" because they performed work traditionally done by members of the crew. With their newfound warranty remedy, *Sieracki* seamen had little use for negligence theories. Conse-

---

261. See discussion, *infra.*

262. 189 U.S. 158 (1903).

263. *Supra*, n. 260. Following *Sieracki*, in *Pope & Talbot v. Hawn*, 346 U.S. 406, 1954 AMC 1 (1953), the Supreme Court extended the same right to shore-based employees such as shipfitters and carpenters. The shipowner's right of indemnity over against the stevedore

quently, case law defining a maritime business invitee's negligence remedy from 1946 to 1972 was very sparse indeed. In turn, the paucity of legal precedent, following the 1972 amendments and enactment of Section 905(b), led the courts to develop a new body of federal maritime law pertaining to the shore worker's negligence remedy.

Today, by virtue of Section 905(b) of the L.H.W.C.A., a shore worker coming under the Act may recover against the shipowner for injuries "caused by the negligence of a vessel." The discussion below centers upon the degree of requisite causation, the contours of the 905(b) negligence standard, and the statutory definition of the third-party defendant in terms of a "vessel." First, however, some broad understanding of the Act itself is helpful.

Longshoremen's and Harbor Workers' Compensation Act

It must be recognized at the outset that liability for coverage under the L.H.W.C.A. is usually excluded under a P & I policy or club cover, although it is not unusual to provide for "L & H cover" by endorsement to the P & I policy.

The Act itself draws the line between maritime shore workers and the vessel's complement, the latter being excluded from the L.H.W.C.A. benefits which are not considered P & I risks.

A thorough understanding of the statutory benefits, administrative proceedings, and jurisdictional nuances is beyond the scope of this text and, therefore, must yield to a rather simplistic summary.[264]

---

was fully perfected in *Pan-Atlantic S.S. v. Ryan Stevedoring Co.*, 350 U.S. 124, 1956 AMC 9 (1956), where the Supreme Court held that the "exclusive" features of the L.H.W.C.A. did not, after all, apply to the stevedoring company in the shipowner's action for indemnity. Even if the ship is unseaworthy, if the act or omission of the stevedore "brings into play" the unseaworthy condition so that injuries result, the shipowner prevails on an indemnity theory. The expansion, however, is not over. In *Reed v. The Yaka*, 373 U.S. 410, 1963 AMC 1373 (1963), an *in rem* action was filed by a longshoreman against the *S.S. Yaka*. The shipowner impleaded the direct stevedoring employer of the injured worker. The stevedoring company also happened to be the bareboat or demise charterer of the vessel. Although the Act then provided that the worker's remedy against his employer was under the Act and was "exclusive," the Supreme Court nonetheless held that the worker could recover on the warranty of seaworthiness and his employer was thereupon held liable as the "owner" *pro hac vice*. After *Reed*, it was but a short step to permitting direct *in personam* recovery by a longshoreman against his employer where the employer was carrying on stevedoring activities and also owned and operated the vessel. *Jackson v. Lykes Bros. S.S. Co.*, 386 U.S. 731, 1967 AMC 584 (1967). As might be expected, it did not take very long for shore-based mechanics, sent aboard vessels to perform work, to perceive that they, too, could sue their employer directly. See *Course v. Pacific Inland Navigation Co.*, 368 F.2d 540, 1967 AMC 333 (9th Cir.); *Chamberlain v. Shaver Transportation Co.*, 399 F.2d 893, 1968 AMC 2031 (9th Cir.). Thus, the stage was set for the 1972 amendments to the Act which were supposed to correct all the inequities.

264. Three sources should be consulted for what has here been merely summarized. See G. Gilmore & C. Black, *The Law of Admiralty*, 408-55 (2d ed., 1975); 1 M. Norris, *The Law*

As with other workers' compensation acts, liability under the L.H.W.C.A. is absolute. Unlike the shore worker's third-party claim against the vessel, recovery does not depend upon proof of fault.

Frequently, however, the incident giving rise to the compensation remedy may also provide a basis for alleging injury "caused by the negligence of a vessel." In that instance, certain procedures must be observed in order to preserve a third-party election. If the shore worker ultimately recovers from the third-party vessel, further issues arise which involve competing interests of the worker, his attorney, his employer, and the compensation carrier—some or all of whom may have pecuniary interests in the fund created by the third-party settlement or judgment.

While the substance and mechanics of the L.H.W.C.A. compensation remedy are of only tangential interest here, the issue of the shore worker's eligibility has a direct bearing. The Act defines who qualifies as a maritime "employee" and who must answer as a "vessel."[265] As the jurisdictional net of the L.H.W.C.A. is spread landward by the 1972 amendments, coverage under the Act increases, both for those eligible for compensation benefits and those potentially holding a Section 905(b) negligence remedy against a vessel. However, the statutory definition of maritime "employee" under the Act does not automatically endow a class of third-party plaintiffs, since the negligence theory under Section 905(b) still needed vessel causation. It is now helpful to examine the principal issues arising under the 905(b) negligence cases.

905(b) Causation—Only Partial under Edmonds. The usual scenario for a shore worker's Section 905(b) negligence case involves multiple parties with intertwining responsibilities for shipboard conditions. Typically, a stevedore company's procedures, the shore worker's inattentiveness, and the vessel's equipment may all share the involvement. As between the vessel and the shore worker, the latter's negligence serves only as a defense in mitigation; that is, the usual maritime rule of comparative negligence reduces recovery in proportion to the plaintiff worker's comparative fault. The situation is not so equitable where the stevedore company (the

---

of Maritime Personal Injuries, sec. 55-113 (3d ed., 1975), with annual supplements; C. Tucker, "Coverage and Procedure under the Longshoremen's and Harbor Workers' Compensation Act Subsequent to the 1972 Amendments," 55 *Tulane Law Review* 1056 (1981).

265. The definitional section of the Act, 902(3), defines an "employee" to mean "any person engaged in maritime employment, including any longshoreman or other person engaged in longshoring operations, and any harbor worker including a ship repairman, ship builder, and ship breaker, but such term does not include a master or member of a crew of any vessel, or any person engaged by the master to load or unload or repair any small vessel under 18 tons net." Sec. 33 U.S.C. 902(21) defines the term "vessel" to mean "any vessel upon which or in connection with any person entitled to benefits under this chapter suffers injury or death arising out of or in the course of his employment, and said vessel's owner, owner *pro hac vice,* agent, operator, charterer or bareboat charterer, master, officer, or crewmember."

worker's employer) has itself been concurrently negligent, and such negligence is the cause of the injury. In that situation, the vessel bears the "burden of the inequity" and must respond in damages to the shore worker for the combined negligence of the vessel and the stevedore.[266]

It is clear from the definitional section of the Act that the term "vessel" means "any vessel" and also a broad spectrum of vessel interests. Assuming the requisite substantive basis can be shown, the shore worker may proceed in a 905(b) negligence case either *in personam* against the owner, bareboat charterer, agent, operator, time charterer, master, officer, or crew member, or *in rem* against the vessel. For present purposes, the term "vessel" includes both the *res* and the *in personam* interests.[267]

905(b) Negligence and the Shipowner's Standard of Care. In 1981, the Supreme Court attempted to define the kinds of duties the shipowner owed to a 905(b) shore worker.[268] Prior to that time, the lower courts had formulated various standards of care, primarily for those cases which involved negligence arising after the stevedore had come aboard to commence cargo operations.[269] For negligence relating to conditions arising *prior* to cargo operations, the traditional duties enunciated in *Marine Terminals v. Burnside Shipping* were affirmed.[270]

Stated with shameful simplicity, the duties articulated in *Santos* may be broken down into three categories: (1) The "turn-over" duty of *Marine*

---

266. *Edmonds v. Compagnie Generale Transatlantique*, 443 U.S. 256, 1979 AMC 1167 (1979). The precise holding in *Edmonds* was that a longshoreman injured by the concurrent negligence of his stevedoring employer and a shipowner may recover *all* his proven damages from the shipowner, reduced only by the percentage of his own contributory fault.

267. Liability of a time charterer for a 905(b) injury is discussed *infra*.

268. *Scindia Steam Nav. Co., Ltd. v. De los Santos*, 451 U.S. 156, 68 L.Ed.2d 1, 1981 AMC 601 (1981), hereinafter referred to as "Santos."

269. On facts arising within the confines of cargo operations, the courts of appeal applied at least four standards to measure the requisite duty of care binding upon the shipowner. After the stevedore assumed control of the cargo operations, the inquiry is made, when and to what extent does the shipowner have continuing duties? Some courts strictly apply a "control test," so that once the shipowner relinquishes control of a reasonably safe vessel to the stevedore, liability of the shipowner ceases. *Cox v. Flota Mercante Grancolombiana*, 577 F.2d 798, 1979 AMC 2018 (2d Cir.); *Anuszewski v. Dynamic Mariners Corp.*, 391 F.Supp. 1143, 1975 AMC 899, *aff'd* 540 F.2d 757, 1976 AMC 2048 (4th Cir.), *cert.den.* 429 U.S. 1098 (1977). Other courts applied an "open and obvious" standard so that if the injury-causing condition was open and obvious to the stevedore, there was no shipowner liability. See, for example, *Gay v. Ocean Transport & Trading, Ltd.*, 546 F.2d 1233, 1977 AMC 996 (5th Cir.). The Second Circuit, most notably in *Evans v. Transportacion Maritime Mexicana*, 639 F.2d 848, 1981 AMC 622 (2d Cir.), used the Restatement of Torts, Sec. 343,343A "reasonable anticipation" test, which the Supreme Court in *Santos* arguably endorsed. Finally, the First and Ninth Circuits used a test of reasonable care in the circumstances. See, for example, *Johnson v. A/S Ivarans Rederi*, 613 F.2d 334, 1980 AMC 2738 (1st Cir.) and the Ninth Circuit opinion in *Santos*. That test fashioned a "continuing duty" for the shipowner even with respect to dangerous conditions arising during the course of cargo handling.

270. 394 U.S. 404, 1970 AMC 251 (1969).

Terminals; (2) the traditional duties if the vessel is actively engaged in cargo operations; and (3) the duty to intervene.

In *Santos* the independent contractor aboard the vessel was a stevedore company. The principles discussed, however, should apply equally to other independent contractors aboard ship where their maritime employees are subject to the L.H.W.C.A. Certainly, the *Santos* duties apply to independent ship repair contractors.[271]

The "Turn-Over" Duty. The turn-over duty of *Marine Terminals v. Burnside Shipping* obligates the vessel, as part of its duty to exercise reasonable care, "to have the ship and its equipment in such condition that an expert and experienced stevedore will be able by the exercise of reasonable care to carry on its cargo operations with reasonable safety to persons and property."[272] The turn-over duty also includes the duty to warn of hazards of which the shipowner knows or should have known, which the stevedore will likely encounter, but which are not known to the stevedore, nor would they be obvious or anticipated by him in the reasonable performance of his work.[273]

Recurrent issues arising under the turn-over duty are whether the shipowner had actual knowledge of a latent condition in the vessel;[274] whether a duty exists to warn of expectedly dangerous conditions which the contractor was hired to correct;[275] to what extent the shipowner is entitled to rely upon the expertise and safety procedures of the contractor, thus alleviating any protection duties allegedly owed to the contractor's employees;[276] whether there is a duty to warn of conditions which may be "non-obvious";[277] whether the turnover duty may be enlarged by OSHA regulations where the crew did work normally done by longshoremen;[278] the extent of the owner's inspection obligation prior to turning over the vessel;[279] whether the shipowner has the duty to warn of hazards in cargo created by foreign loading stevedores which cause injury to American longshoremen.[280]

271. *Cook v. Exxon Shipping Company,* 762 F.2d 750, 1986 AMC 2354 (9th Cir., 1985).
272. *Santos, supra,* n. 268, 451 U.S. at 167.
273. *Santos, supra,* n. 268. 451 U.S. at 167.
274. *Stass v. American Commercial Lines, Inc.,* 720 F.2d 879, 1984 AMC 2808 (5th Cir., 1983).
275. *Stass, supra,* n. 274.
276. *Duplantis v. Zigler Shipyards, Inc.,* 692 F.2d 372, 1983 AMC 2319 (5th Cir., 1982).
277. *Subingsubing v. Reardon Smith Line, Ltd.,* 682 F.2d 779, 1984 AMC 1069 (9th Cir., 1982).
278. *Ollestad v. Greenville Steamship Corp.,* 738 F.2d 1049. 1985 AMC 2257 (9th Cir., 1984).
279. *Hedrick v. Pine Oak Shipping,* 715 F.2d 1355, 1984 AMC 2701 (9th Cir., 1983).
280. *Turner v. Japan Lines, Ltd.,* 651 F.2d 1300, 1981 AMC 2223 (9th Cir., 1981).

The "Traditional" Duties. The traditional duties imposed upon a shipowner are fairly obvious. They derive from the standard that the vessel may not actively involve itself in the cargo operations and negligently injure a longshoreman.[281] The vessel will be liable to the longshoreman for negligently caused injury resulting from hazards under the active control of the vessel.

When the vessel has been charged with active negligence, the issues are basically to what extent the vessel retained control, or whether the vessel's method would foreseeably subject the shore worker to risk of injury;[282] or whether the vessel could reasonably anticipate that the maritime worker would go into a dangerous non-work area on the ship.[283] There are also the usual fact questions of who, as between the vessel and the contractor, created the condition causing the injury.

The Duty to Intervene. It is generally accepted that the vessel no longer has a continuing duty to discover and remedy a dangerous situation which develops after the stevedore has commenced cargo work. Before the 1972 amendments to the Act, such a duty did exist as part of the vessel's broad, non-delegable duty to provide a safe place to work. But the Supreme Court in *Santos* eliminated any continuing duty to inspect, subject, however, to the proviso that there are no contract provisions, positive law, or customs which otherwise create such a duty. In the absence of contract, positive law, or custom, there is no continuing duty to inspect, but there still remains the "pure *Santos*" duty to intervene in certain situations.

The more difficult duties, and those spawning the litigation which seemingly modifies and refines the rules on an almost daily basis, are those components of the so-called duty to intervene. This duty may arise in certain defined situations. The analytical framework of this duty requires three "conditions":

> (a) an independent stevedore contractor is aboard in charge of cargo operations;
> (b) a "dangerous condition" develops; and
> (c) the "dangerous condition" develops within the confines of the cargo operations.

The duty to intervene arises if (1) the condition is unreasonably hazardous to experienced workers; (2) the condition has developed in the workplace assigned to the stevedore; and (3) the vessel was aware of sufficient facts to activate the duty. Put another way, the new *Santos* duty requires evaluating the condition, where it arose, and whether there was

---

281. *Santos, supra*, n. 268. 451 U.S. at 167.
282. *Doucet v. Diamond M. Drilling Co.*, 683 F.2d 886, 1983 AMC 2999 (5th Cir., 1982).
283. *U.S. Fidelity & Guar. Co. v. Plovidba*, 683 F.2d 1022, 1983 AMC 2473 (7th Cir., 1982).
284. *Santos, supra*, n. 268. 451 U.S. at 170.

knowledge chargeable to the vessel and, if so, whether inaction was justified by reliance upon the stevedore.

Unreasonably Dangerous Condition. The starting point for analysis is the Supreme Court's recognition that the stevedore is the expert: "As a general matter, the shipowner may rely on the stevedore to avoid exposing the longshoremen to unreasonable hazards."[284]

In isolation, a condition may present an element of danger, but when evaluated with reference to an experienced stevedore, the danger may be completely manageable. Cases involving transitory conditions are particularly illustrative. The combination of grain dust and morning dew, for example, may pose "only a limited and accepted hazard."[285] If so, the vessel is entitled to rely on the stevedore to do the necessary to provide a safe workplace for its own employees. Similarly, elimination of the condition, in accordance with obligations imposed on the employer by OSHA, may be so easy that the vessel, as a matter of law, may reasonably anticipate that the stevedore will correct it, and a vessel duty to intervene does not arise.[286] The contrary may be true if there is independent evidence that the vessel knew the stevedore was ignoring the regulatory requirements.[287] Generally, sole responsibility for compliance with OSHA rests with the stevedore.[288] The stevedore has the statutory duty to provide a reasonably safe workplace.[289] Regulations embodied in OSHA, however, do not necessarily bind the stevedore to the exclusion of the vessel.[290]

The dangerous condition must exist in the stevedore's assigned work area. If it does not develop within the physical workspace for stevedore's cargo operations, the vessel may have no duty to intervene.[291] Areas constituting vessel ingress and egress are subject to vessel supervision and outside the "confines" rule.[292]

The vessel has no duty to intervene unless there is (1) actual knowledge of the dangerous condition, *and* (2) actual knowledge that the stevedore-employer will not respond appropriately to protect the employees.[293]

285. *Thompson v. Cargill, Inc.,* 585 F.Supp. 1332, (E.D.,La., 1984).

286. *Albergo v. Hellenic Lines, Inc.,* 658 F.2d 66, 1981 AMC 2417 (2d Cir., 1981). There, an untidy condition on deck consisted of skinny rope cuttings which could be, and had been, swept aside by the longshoremen.

287. *Landsem v. Isuzu Motors, Ltd.,* 534 F.Supp. 448 (D.,Ore., 1982), 1985 AMC 1518, *aff'd* 711 F.2d 1064 (9th Cir., 1983).

288. *Bachtel v. Mammoth Bulk Carriers,* 605 F.2d 438, 1980 AMC 172 (9th Cir., 1979), *cert. granted* and judgment vacated, 451 U.S. 978 (1981), 1981 AMC 2097.

289. 33 U.S.C. 941.

290. *Subingsubing v. Reardon Smith Line, Ltd.,* 682 F.2d 779, 1984 AMC 1069 (9th Cir., 1982).

291. *Turner v. Costa Line,* 744 F.2d 505, (5th Cir., 1984).

292. *Sarauw v. Oceanic Navigation Corp.,* 655 F.2d 526, 1981 AMC 2989 (3d Cir., 1981).

293. *Helaire v. Mobil Oil Co.,* 709 F.2d 1031, 1984 AMC 820 (5th Cir., 1983).

Distinguished from transitory conditions, such as hazardous substances on deck surfaces, are conditions of the ship's gear or in the cargo
itself. So, when a winch slips and causes suspended cargo to injure a
worker, the vessel will be liable for 905(b) negligence upon proof of earlier episodes and attempted, but unsuccessful, repairs.[294] Liability will not
be imposed on the vessel when there is no *actual* knowledge that the repair contractor was using a device in a fashion that made it unsafe. A
guardrail when used as a ladder was held to be defective and unreasonably dangerous. Even though it provided the sole access to a deck, there
being no proof that the vessel actually knew of the contractor's use, there
is no showing that the vessel was aware of the contractor's improvi-
dence.[295] The result would be different if the device had been furnished
for use as a ladder.[296]

Dangerous conditions in the cargo will not impose vessel liability
where the stevedore uses an inappropriate method for dealing with the
cargo.[297] On the other hand, placement of the cargo in the stow, coupled
with a known and inherently dangerous stevedore method, may require
vessel intervention.[298]

A vessel may be liable for negligently stowed cargo of which the vessel
has actual knowledge.[299] There is no liability for dangerous conditions in
the stow that develop after control of the vessel has been turned over to
the stevedore, or for conditions created during loading, of which the vessel reasonably has no knowledge.[300]

It is no defense simply to show that the pre-existing condition in the
stow was open and obvious. It depends on the vessel's knowledge as to
how the stevedore is responding. If the longshoremen's only alternatives
to working with obviously dangerous cargo are leaving the job or facing
trouble for a work delay, the vessel may be liable.[301]

Notwithstanding the foregoing commentary concerning the duty to
intervene, in certain limited circumstances the vessel may have a continuing duty of inspection or supervision even after the vessel has been
turned over to the stevedore. This general duty, however, requires proof
of contract provision, positive law, or custom creating the duty:

294. *Webster v. M/V Moolchand, Sethia Lines, Ltd.*, 730 F.2d 1035, 1986 AMC 2854 (5th Cir., 1984).
295. *Wild v. Lykes Bros. Steamship Co.*, 734 F.2d 1124 (5th Cir., 1984).
296. *Pluyer v. Mitsui O.S.K. Lines, Ltd.*, 664 F.2d 1243, 1984 AMC 534 (5th Cir., 1982). See, also, *sub nom., Pluyer v. Amer. Mut. Liab. Ins. Co.*
297. *Taylor v. Federal Commerce & Nav. Co.*, 738 F.2d 442 (7th Cir., 1984) (where the stevedore "breaks out" a cargo of steel products with improper tools there is no duty to supervise the manner of discharging).
298. *Gill v. Hango-Ship Owners A/B*, 682 F.2d 1070, 1982 AMC 2955 (4th Cir., 1982).
299. *Lemon v. Bank Lines, Ltd.*, 656 F.2d 110 (5th Cir., 1981).
300. *Moser v. Texas Trailer Corp.*, 694 F.2d 96, 1984 AMC 725 (5th Cir., 1982). But, compare *Turner v. Japan Lines, Ltd.*, 702 F.2d 752, 1984 AMC 2703 (9th Cir., 1983).
301. *Stass v. American Commercial Lines, Inc.*, 720 F.2d 879, 1984 AMC 2808 (5th Cir., 1982).

We are of the view that absent contract provision, positive law, or custom to the contrary . . . the shipowner has no general duty by way of supervision or inspection to exercise reasonable care to discover dangerous conditions that develop within the confines of the cargo operations that are assigned to the stevedore.[302]

One example of positive law is the OSHA regulations discussed heretofore. See, for example, *Ollstead v. Greenville Steamship Corp.*,[303] where, because the crew did the normal work of longshoremen, the jury was allowed to consider OSHA regulations on the issue of the vessel's standard of care.

A ship repair contract which reserved to the shipowner the right to inspect the contractor's work did not create an affirmative contractual duty to discover and remedy a dangerous condition. So, there was no vessel liability for failure to discover and clean up a grease spot.[304] Likewise, a provision in a charter agreement that cargo work was to be "under the supervision of the captain" was not a special contractual promise creating new vessel duties.[305]

Expert testimony of custom established a master's inspection duty in overseeing the cargo stow in Japan in *Turner v. Japan Lines, Ltd.*,[306] and vessel liability followed for the defective stow. Custom was also considered material in the concurring opinion in *Sarauw v. Oceanic Navigation Corp.*,[307] which traced the vessel's duties as to the gangway to the custom of good seamanship. However, the customary power of the mate to countermand stevedore procedures is not a duty imposed by custom to assure the safety of longshoremen.[308]

To summarize, the new *Santos* duty requires the vessel to intervene in cargo operations only in fact situations which are undergoing refinement every day and then, only if there is no continuing duty established elsewhere as, for example, in a contract, a regulation, or by custom. Absent these, the vessel's duty to intervene is the product of the nature of the allegedly dangerous condition, its location, the stevedore response, and the shipowner's knowledge of all of these.

Admittedly, the synopsis above conveys only a general sense of the subject. The decisions interpreting the 905(b) negligence standard and applying *Santos* are being rendered too rapidly, are far too numerous, and establish too many refinements to fit comfortably within the scope of a chapter on P & I insurance.

302. *Santos, supra*, n. 268. 451 U.S. at 172.
303. 738 F.2d 1049, 1985 AMC 2257 (9th Cir., 1984).
304. *Westerman v. United States*, 568 F.Supp. 485 (E.D.N.Y., 1983).
305. *Spence v. Mariehamns R/S*, 766 F.2d 1504, 1986 AMC 685 (11th Cir., 1985).
306. 651 F.2d 1300, 1984 AMC 2703 (9th Cir., 1981).
307. 655 F.2d 526, 1981 AMC 2989 (3d Cir., 1981).
308. *Spence v. Mariehamns R/S*, 766 F.2d 1504 (11th Cir.), 1986 AMC 685 (1985).

Dual Capacity of the Shipowner. As discussed heretofore, before enactment of the 1972 amendments to the Act, it was established that a longshoreman was not precluded by the exclusive remedy provision of the Act from bringing an action against his employer if that employer wore two hats. Put another way, if the longshoreman were employed by a stevedore company which doubled as an owner of a vessel, the longshoreman could still maintain an action against his employer for injuries incurred while performing work as a longshoreman aboard the vessel.[309]

The 1972 amendments did not preclude piercing the employer's dual status. Thus, in *Smith v. M/V Captain Fred,*[310] a maritime employee was held entitled to maintain a negligence tort action against his employer who was also the shipowner; the owner received no insulation from third-party liability by arguing that he was a "covered" employer and thus shielded by the exclusive remedy prescribed in the L.H.W.C.A.

Application of the *Captain Fred* has now been restricted by the 1984 amendment to Section 905. That amendment restricts an employee engaged in "shipbuilding, repairing, or breaking services" from maintaining a 905(b) action against his "employer," even if that employer is also the owner, operator or charterer of the vessel. 33 U.S.C. 905(c). Third-party *Yaka* actions by shipyard employees against shipbuilders who happen to own the vessel are consequently now barred. Compensation is the exclusive remedy. It appears clear, however, that the amendments do not change the remedies of the employee who provides longshoring or stevedoring services to the vessel. That employee would still be entitled, under *Captain Fred,* to maintain a negligence action against the employer/shipowner.

Reed v. S.S. Yaka exposure is largely unaffected. It remains true that in dual capacity situations, the P & I exposure may be far greater than initially contemplated by owners or underwriters when analyzing the protection seemingly offered by the exclusive remedy provisions of the L.H.W.C.A.

Time Charterers' Liability for 905(b) Negligence

The time charterer may also experience disillusionment (or, if he were astute, his P & I underwriter would feel it) when faced with a 905(b) negligence liability. Several cases hold that the time charterer is a viable 905(b) defendant within the meaning of the term "vessel," which the L.H.W.C.A. defines to include "charterer or bareboat charterer." The fact situation giving rise to a time charterer's potential liability involves

309. See discussion, *supra,* citing *Reed v. S.S. Yaka* and *Jackson v. Lykes Bros. S.S. Co.*
310. 546 F.2d 119, 1977 AMC 353 (5th Cir., 1977).

cargo handling; that is, liability for a condition arising either during stowage of cargo or cargo discharge.

Broadly speaking, the litigated cases involve three basic fact situations: (1) active participation by the charterer in the cargo handling process; (2) fault of the stevedore for whom the charterer is responsible by contract; or (3) loss occurring through conduct of the ship's personnel while acting for cargo (and thus charterer's) interests. This body of law is just now developing; it is confusing, and it is inconclusive. While many of the cases cited below are cargo cases, the principles have been expanded to the personal injury area.

It is now generally accepted that a time charterer may be held liable to a 905(b) plaintiff, as the following cases demonstrate. Principles of charterer liability derive from cases involving cargo loss or damage and, in the usual instance, depend upon the particular wording of the charter party between the owner and the time charterer.

Charterer's Active Participation

Where charterer's representatives are visible in the cargo handling process, with some degree of active participation, the charterer is frequently held liable for the loss. This is especially true where the charterer acts as its own stevedore.[311] For example, where the charterer actually erects the cribbing for deck cargo, which subsequently fails, the charterer is liable for the cargo loss.[312]

Where the charterer is responsible for the safe performance of stevedoring services, the charterer is answerable to the plaintiff.[313] The New York Produce Exchange form (1946) (herein the NYPE form) contains, in Clause 8, the frequently litigated provision:

> The Captain (although appointed by the Owners), shall be under the orders and directions of the charterers as regards employment and agency; and charterers are to load, stow, and trim the cargo at their expense under the supervision of the captain.

Clause 8 is often modified by marginal clauses and endorsements. However, the basic issue is the same. That is, does the master, officer, or crew, when acting in the cargo process, act on behalf of the charterer or the owner? Analysis of the issue divides into two competing inquiries. Is the master, officer, or crew member subject to control or right of control

---

311. *Hopson v. M/V Karl Grammerstorf*, 330 F.Supp. 1260, 1972 AMC 1815 (E.D.,La., 1971).

312. *Oxford Paper Co. v. Nidarholm*, 282 U.S. 681, 1931 AMC 522 (1931).

313. *Revel v. American Export Lines, Inc.*, 162 F.Supp. 279, 1959 AMC 360 (E.D.,Va., 1958), *aff'd* 266 F.2d 82, 1959 AMC 1073 (4th Cir., 1959).

in the time charterer? If not, the owner and not the charterer is responsible for conditions in the stow causing loss or injury.[314]

The other inquiry focuses on purpose, and the classic language is that of Judge Friendly in *Nichimen Co. v. M/V Farland*.[315] If the purpose behind the conduct of owner's personnel is to protect the vessel's safety, consequences flowing from such conduct are the responsibility of the owner; on the other hand, where the intervention of the owner's personnel in the stowage process is to protect cargo, responsibility for the conduct of the crew in that instance is on the charterer.[316]

Thus, in *Turner v. Japan Lines, Ltd.*,[317] the Ninth Circuit held that improper loading itself (through negligent supervision by master or mates) created primary liability on the part of the charterer. As an aside, the *Turner* decision also warped the *Santos* duty to intervene. The vessel was held to a duty to inspect activities of the independent contractor/loading stevedore since that entity was foreign.

While it is difficult to articulate a single rule or rules from the charterer liability cases, the trend is easily discernible. Chartering activities, in the commercial context anyway, have introduced new P & I risks.

Generally on Recovery in Death Actions

Maritime death actions involve recurrent tensions among federal statutory remedies, state wrongful death acts, and general maritime law. This subject is fraught with inconsistencies and contradiction in policy.[318]

The survivor's recovery of damages necessarily requires inquiry into the status of the decedent; i.e., whether a Jones Act seaman or non-seaman, the class of beneficiary to which the survivor belongs, in what waters the cause of action arose, and what items of damage are compensable. Death recoveries may involve different measures of damages and different substantive theories, depending upon whether the cause of action arose within or beyond one marine league (the so-called three-mile

314. *Ove Skou v. Hebert*, 365 F.2d 341, 1966 AMC 447 (5th Cir., 1966). Using that inquiry, the court found Clause 8 imposed merely a financial burden to pay for costs of loading, stowing, and trimming the cargo, but did not confer actual operational control over the activities. Thus, there was no liability on the charterer for his misperformance.

315. 462 F.2d 319, 1972 AMC 1573 (2d Cir., 1971).

316. *Nichimen* was relied upon in *Fernandez v. Chios Shipping Co., Ltd.*, 542 F.2d 145, 1976 AMC 1780 (2d Cir., 1976). While the dual agency concept was extended to personal injury cases in *Fernandez*, it may have yielded to an even broader test, and that is simply whether an activity is "cargo-related." If it is, considerations of purpose or whether that activity affected cargo or vessel may be moot.

317. 651 F.2d 1300, 1981 AMC 2223 (9th Cir., 1981).

318. See the comprehensive discussion by Chief Judge John Brown, *Bodden v. American Offshore, Inc.*, 681 F.2d 319, 1982 AMC 2409 (5th Cir., 1982). For a more complete treatment of these damage issues and the related (but far more complex) issues of conflicts of law, see the thorough discussion by Edelman, "Recovery for Wrongful Death Under General Maritime Law," 55 *Tulane Law Review* 1123 (1981).

limit).[319] The three-mile limit is the line between the state's territorial waters and the high seas. As discussed below, the three-mile limit materially affects the applicable remedy.

After the three-mile line has been drawn, to determine applicable law the next consideration is the status of the decedent; i.e., whether or not a "seaman" within the Jones Act. Status may dictate whether certain items of damage are compensable.

Death damages must be distinguished from survival damages. Death damages are those of the beneficiary bringing the action for the decedent's wrongful death. Survival damages are those compensable damages suffered by the decedent while alive. They would have been recoverable had plaintiff's decedent survived. While *Moragne*[320] created a uniform federal wrongful death action, it did not create a bar to survival actions in territorial waters.[321] Nor are survival actions barred by the Death on the High Seas Act[322] (herein DOHSA) for deaths occurring beyond one marine league. Survival actions merely supplement DOHSA.[323] The decedent's conscious pain and suffering is therefore compensable irrespective of where the death occurred, and such damages are recoverable under both federal maritime law and the Jones Act. Recoveries under general maritime law and federal statutory laws are next examined.

Recovery under General Maritime Law

Federal maritime law includes both the general maritime law developed by the admiralty courts and also federal maritime statutory law. In the context of maritime death remedies, these statutes most notably include the Death on the High Seas Act, 46 U.S.C. 761 *et seq.* (DOHSA), the Jones Act, 46 U.S.C. 688, incorporating the Federal Employees' Liability Act (FELA), 45 U.S.C. 51-60 (1976) (which allows recovery for death resulting "in whole or in part" from negligence of the employer), and the Longshoreman's and Harbor Workers' Compensation Act (LHWCA), 33 U.S.C. 901 *et seq.*, providing statutory death benefits according to formula.[324]

319. More frequently than not, death and the causative event occur in the same waters. But this is not always the case. See *Chute v. United States*, 466 F.Supp. 61, 1980 AMC 954 (D.,Mass., 1978). Nonetheless, these distinctions will not be pursued, and future references to where the death occurred assume identity of place of wrong and place of death and mean simply where the "cause of action" arose.

320. *Moragne v. States Marine Lines*, 398 U.S. 375, 1970 AMC 967 (1970).

321. *Sea-Land Services v. Gaudet*, 414 U.S. 573, 1973 AMC 2572 (1973).

322. 46 U.S.C. 761 *et seq.*

323. *Azzopardi v. Ocean Drilling & Exploration Co.*, 742 F.2d 890, 1986 AMC 434 (5th Cir., 1985) *Evich v. Connelly*, 759 F.2d 1432, 1986 AMC 356 (9th Cir., 1985).

324. 33 U.S.C. 909 (1976). See, also, Outer Continental Shelf Lands Act, 43 U.S.C. 1333(b), which ties into the benefits schedule of the L.H.W.C.A., 33 U.S.C. 909—both containing worker's compensation schemes operating independently of the damage remedies under discussion.

Before the U. S. Supreme Court decision in *Moragne v. States Marine Lines, Inc.*, deaths occurring within the territorial waters of the states were governed by the coastal state's wrongful death statute. *Moragne* made wrongful death actionable under general maritime law. State wrongful death statutes no longer govern recovery for deaths occurring in state territorial water although they may supplement the general maritime law. Past the three-mile limit it is not clear to what extent state statutory schemes are preempted by DOHSA.[325]

In *Moragne*, a longshoreman was killed allegedly as a result of the unseaworthiness of the vessel on which he was then working. It was held that the state's wrongful death statute was preempted even though the vessel was afloat on navigable waters within state territorial limits. *Moragne* thus provides for recovery under general maritime law for death caused by vessel unseaworthiness as well as owner's negligence. If relying upon unseaworthiness, of course, plaintiff's decedent must come within the class of persons entitled to the warranty.

The general maritime law of admiralty also recognizes death claims based upon intentional torts and the doctrine of strict liability in tort, under Restatement (second) of Torts, Section 402(A).[326]

As noted heretofore, survivors of scientific personnel on oceanographic research vessels are precluded from bringing suit based on negligence under the Jones Act or "wrongful act, neglect or default" under DOHSA.[327] While survivors of such personnel have a remedy under general maritime law, they are not entitled to the benefit of a warranty of seaworthiness since they are not "seamen."[328]

Compensable Items of Damage under General Maritime Law

Under general maritime law, items of recoverable damages for a wrongful death action within a state's territorial waters (again distinguishing from the high seas) consist of the following: (1) loss of pecuniary support; (2) loss of services of the decedent; (3) loss of society; and (4) funeral expenses.[329] Each item is discussed below.

Of the four basic items of damages, the most controversial is "loss of society." Recovery of damages for loss of society depends entirely upon

---

325. *Tallentire v. Offshore Logistics, Inc.*, 91 L.Ed.2d 174, 1986 AMC 2113 (1986) holding that DOHSA, to the exclusion of state statutes, provides the remedy and measure of recovery but (in dictum) that state courts retain jurisdiction to enforce a claim under DOHSA. The dictum will likely create new confusion over when and where the right to jury trial exists in a DOHSA case.

326. *Lindsay v. McDonnell Douglas Aircraft Corp.*, 460 F.2d 631, 1974 AMC 1341 (8th Cir., 1972).

327. See Oceanographic Research Vessels Act, 46 U.S.C. 444.

328. *Craig v. M/V Peacock*, 760 F.2d 953, 1986 AMC 2565 (9th Cir., 1985). The decision is questionable. See dissent by Judge Wisdom, Circuit Judge of the Fifth Circuit, sitting by designation.

whether the death occurred within or beyond the three-mile limit. The *Moragne/Gaudet* damage measure compensates for loss of society where the death occurred within the state's territorial waters. Beyond that limit, however, general maritime law does not allow recovery for loss of society. There, recovery is controlled by DOHSA and thus limited to "just compensation for the pecuniary loss sustained by the persons for whose benefit the suit is brought."[330]

Loss of society represents deprivation of "love, affection, care, attention, companionship, comfort and protection."[331] Mental anguish or grief, on the other hand, is distinguishable from loss of society. Mental anguish represents the survivor's emotional response to the wrongful act.[332] Loss of society is a deprivation of positive benefits. A survivor's mental anguish and grief are not compensable.

In summary, if death occurs beyond one marine league, there is no recovery for loss of society under the general maritime law of *Higginbotham*. Recovery is prescribed by DOHSA and limited to pecuniary loss. But if the death occurs within one marine league, i.e., within state territorial waters as defined by the three-mile limit, then the *Moragne/Gaudet* measure allows wrongful death recovery for non-pecuniary loss (of society). This is the same rule applicable in the loss of consortium cases, which is simply loss of society of the spouse who suffers a *non-fatal* injury.[333] It has recently been held that a minor child has no such right to recover for loss of companionship.[334]

In addition to allowing compensation for loss of society, the *Moragne/Gaudet* death damage measure may also (and primarily) compensate for pecuniary loss, being loss of support, loss of services, funeral expenses, and loss of prospective inheritance. Pecuniary losses are thus recoverable on either side of the three-mile limit.

Loss of pecuniary support is a straightforward element and often rests on proof of all financial contributions of decedent, had he lived, which may include a showing of decedent's wage-earning capacity over the expected work life, proof of dependency, and dependents' ages and relationships. Decedent's personal expenses are deducted.[335]

Loss of services also has a monetary value. Thus, when a parent is killed, it is proper to prove values for loss of training, education, guid-

329. *Sea-Land Services, Inc. v. Gaudet,* 414 U.S. 573, 1973 AMC 2572 (1974).
330. 46 U.S.C. 762. In *Mobil Oil Corp. v. Higginbotham,* 436 U.S. 618, 1978 AMC 1059 (1978), "pecuniary loss" was held to be exclusive of "loss of society."
331. *Sea-Land Services, Inc. v. Gaudet, supra,* n. 329.
332. *Gaudet,* at 585, n. 18.
333. *American Export Lines v. Alvez,* 446 U.S. 274, 1980 AMC 618 (1980).
334. *DeLoach v. Companhia de Navegacao Lloyd Brasileiro,* 782 F.2d 438, 986 AMC 1217 (3rd Cir., 1986).
335. See, for example, *In re U.S. Steel Corp.,* 436 F.2d 1256, 1971 AMC 914 (6th Cir., 1970), *cert.den.* 402 U.S. 987 (1971).

ance, and nurture.[336] If a child is killed, proof of actual monetary value of services may be more difficult.[337]

Funeral expenses are probably recoverable where they are actually a cost or liability of the survivor.[338] However, they have been disallowed.[339]

Loss of prospective inheritance has been allowed[340] but if the potential legacy becomes too remote under state intestacy laws, recovery will be denied.[341]

The class of beneficiaries entitled to bring an action for decedent's wrongful death under general maritime law of *Moragne* has not yet been precisely defined. The Supreme Court has suggested that federal courts look both to DOHSA and to state wrongful death statutes.[342]

Punitive damages may be recovered in a wrongful death action brought under federal maritime law, since exemplary damages are part of the survival rights inherent in the action.[343]

Recovery for Death under DOHSA

Recovery under DOHSA derives from "the death of a *person*," meaning seaman and non-seaman alike.[344]

The statute provides a remedy for death "caused by wrongful act, neglect, or default occurring beyond a league from the shore of any state."[345] The phrase "wrongful act, neglect or default" embraces a variety of substantive theories of recovery. DOHSA beneficiaries have a claim for negligence proximately causing decedent's death. Concepts of negligence and proximate cause are those developed under the general maritime law.[346] More liberal concepts of fault and causation exist under the Jones Act. See discussion *supra*. In addition to negligence theories, DOHSA allows recovery for the death of non-seamen based upon the

336. *Michigan Central R.R. v. Vreeland,* 227 U.S. 59 (1939).
337. *Ivy v. Security Barge Lines, Inc.,* 585 F.2d 732, 1979 AMC 2154 (5th Cir., 1978), *reh'g en banc* 606 F.2d 524, 1980 AMC 356 (5th Cir., 1979), *cert.den.* 446 U.S. 956, 1980 AMC 2101, involving a son who did occasional yardwork and babysitting but lived at home.
338. *Sea-Land Services v. Gaudet, supra,* n. 329.
339. See *Barbe v. Drummond,* 507 F.2d 794, 1975 AMC 204 (1st Cir., 1974), where the costs were an expense of the decedent's estate and not a loss suffered by beneficiaries.
340. *National Airlines, Inc. v. Stiles,* 268 F.2d 400, 1958 AMC 1158 (5th Cir., 1958), *cert.den.* 361 U.S. 885 (1959).
341. See, for example, *Complaint of Cambria S.S. Co.,* 505 F.2d 517, 1974 AMC 2411 (6th Cir., 1974), *cert.den.* 420 U.S. 975, 1975 AMC 2157 (1975).
342. *Moragne v. States Marine Lines, Inc.,* 398 U.S. 375, 1970 AMC 967 (1970). See, also, discussion concerning DOHSA, *infra,* and *Evich v. Connelly,* 759 F.2d 1432, 1986 AMC 356 (9th Cir., 1985).
343. *Renner v. Rockwell International Corp.,* 403 F.Supp. 849 (C.D.,Cal., 1975), vacated and remanded on other grounds, 587 F.2d 1030 (9th Cir., 1978).
344. 46 U.S.C. 761.
345. Id.
346. *Krause v. Sud-Aviation, Societe Nationale de Constructions Aeronautiques,* 413 F.2d 428 (2d Cir., 1969).

products-liability theory of strict liability in tort[347] under Restatement (Second) of Torts Section 402A. DOHSA also provides a remedy for unseaworthiness where decedent was a seaman.[348]

The classes of beneficiaries under DOHSA are broader than the classes under the Jones Act. DOHSA actions may be brought only for the benefit of the decedent's "wife, husband, parent, child, or dependent relative."[349] Thus, both remote and close relatives may recover and one class does not exclude a more remote class.[350] Siblings must prove dependency; otherwise there is no recovery.[351] A dependent divorced wife may not maintain an action.[352]

As in actions arising under general maritime law and actions under the Jones Act, a DOHSA decedent's conscious pain and suffering prior to death is compensable.[353]

Loss of society is not a compensable element of damages under DOHSA[354] nor is loss of consortium.[355] Recovery is limited to pecuniary loss. With that exclusion, however, the other elements of recovery in a *Moragne/Gaudet* death action are recoverable.

Punitive damages are probably not recoverable in actions under DOHSA, which allows recovery only for pecuniary loss.[356]

Recovery for Death under the Jones Act

Decedent's status as a Jones Act seaman brings into play a statutorily defined class of beneficiaries, a statutory remedy for negligence, and a measure of recovery specifically limited to pecuniary loss. The seaman's remedy will vary, depending upon where the death occurs. If the decedent died within one marine league from the shore of any state, the beneficiary is limited to a statutory negligence remedy, although the decedent's own personal injury suit for unseaworthiness may survive.[357] If the Jones Act seaman's death occurred beyond one marine league, the beneficiary has

347. *Lindsay v. McDonnell Douglas Aircraft Corp.*, 460 F.2d 631, 1974 AMC 1341 (8th Cir., 1972).

348. *Doyle v. Albatross Tanker Corp.*, 367 F.2d 465, 1967 AMC 201 (2d Cir., 1966), where a seaman's death was held compensable under both the Jones Act for negligence and DOHSA for unseaworthiness.

349. 46 U.S.C. 761.

350. *Safir v. Compagnie Generale Transatlantique*, 241 F.Supp. 501, 1965 AMC 2087 (S.D.N.Y., 1965), involving the death of a passenger.

351. *Evich v. Connelly*, 759 F.2d 1432, 1986 AMC 356 (9th Cir., 1985).

352. *In re Petition of ABC Charters, Inc.*, 558 F.Supp. 364, 1983 AMC 2025 (W.D.,Wash., 1983).

353. *Mobil Oil Corp. v. Higginbotham*, 436 U.S. 618, 1978 AMC 1059 (1978).

354. Id.

355. *Igneri v. Cie de Transport Oceaniques*, 323 F.2d 257, 1963 AMC 2318 (2d Cir., 1963).

356. *Renner v. Rockwell International Corp.*, 403 F.Supp. 849, (C.D. Cal., 1975), *vacated and remanded on other grounds*, 587 F.2d 1030 (9th Cir., 1978).

357. *Gillespie v. U.S. Steel Corp.*, 379 U.S. 148, 1965 AMC 1 (1964).

both Jones Act negligence and an unseaworthiness remedy under DOHSA.[358]

The Jones Act stratifies classes of beneficiaries entitled to recover. Superior classes of beneficiaries recover to the exclusion of classes below. In the first class are the spouse and children, next are parents, and next are dependent relatives.

Since Jones Act recovery is limited to pecuniary loss, there is no recovery for loss of society.[359] However, if a Jones Act claim is joined with an unseaworthiness claim, loss of society damages may be recoverable for death occurring in territorial waters.[360]

Conscious pain and suffering, an element of survival damages, is compensable in a Jones Act death case if accompanied by injury of a physical nature.[361] Punitive damages are probably not recoverable under the Jones Act, although there may be authority for a contrary argument.[362]

Shipowner's Exposure for Strict Liability in Tort

Admiralty recognizes recovery based upon strict liability in tort.[363] The law developed under Restatement (second) of Torts 402A is the federal maritime law of strict tort liability. A 402A claim is available both to the personal injury plaintiff and to the beneficiary plaintiff under DOHSA.[364]

The Restatement (second) of Torts 402A sets out the rules governing recovery:

402A Special Liability of Seller of Product for Physical Harm to User or Consumer.

a. One who sells any product in a defective condition unreasonably dangerous to the user or consumer or to his property is subject to liability for physical harm thereby caused to the ultimate user or consumer, or to his property, if (1) the seller is engaged in the business of selling such product, and (2) it is expected to and does reach the user

---

358. *Doyle v. Albatross Tanker Corp.*, 260 F.Supp. 303 (S.D.N.Y., 1965), *aff'd* 367 F.2d 465, 1967 AMC 201 (2d Cir., 1966).

359. *Ivy v. Security Barge Lines, Inc., supra*, n. 337; *Nygaard v. Peter Pan Seafoods, Inc,* 701 F.2d 77, 1985 AMC 2085 (9th Cir., 1983).

360. *Hlodan v. Ohio Barge Line, Inc.,* 611 F.2d 71, 1980 AMC 2644 (5th Cir., 1980).

361. *Cook v. Ross Island Sand & Gravel Co.,* 626 F.2d 746 (9th Cir., 1980), where an award of $100,000 for 2½ minutes of consciousness prior to drowning by asphyxiation was remitted to $35,000.

362. *Kopczynski v. The Jacqueline,* 742 F.2d 555, 1985 AMC 769 (9th Cir., 1984).

363. *East River Steamship Corp. v. Transamerica Delaval,* 106 S.Ct. 2295, 90 L.Ed. 2d 865, 1986 AMC 2027 (1986).

364. *Lindsay v. McDonnell Douglas Aircraft Corp.,* 460 F.2d 631, 1974 AMC 1341 (8th Cir., 1972).

or consumer without substantial change in the condition in which it is sold.

b. The rule stated in Subsection (1) applies although (1) the seller has exercised all possible care in the preparation and sale of his product, and (2) the user or consumer has not bought the product from or entered into any contractual relationship with the seller.

Thus, a claim for damages under Section 402A requires proof:

(1) That a defendant shipowner sold or manufactured the injury-causing product;

(2) That the condition of the product was "defective" at the time it left defendant's control; and

(3) That the defective condition proximately caused injury to plaintiff.

A shipowner cannot be a 402A defendant unless qualifying as a manufacturer or seller in the chain of production. Further, to be "defective" the product must be "unreasonably dangerous to the user." What is "unreasonably dangerous" will turn upon application of one or more tests:

(1) Whether the product was dangerous to an extent beyond that contemplated by the ordinary consumer who purchases it;[364a] or

(2) The utility of the product does not outweigh the magnitude of the danger.[364b]

A defective product may be demonstrated by a manufacturing defect (deficiency in production or distribution process)[364c] or the defect may consist of unsafe design or inadequate warning for a product inherently dangerous.

Usually, the shipowner is not a manufacturer or seller of a product. More commonly the shipowner is itself a consumer of an allegedly defective product, in which case there is no 402A liability.[365] Assuming the shipowner does qualify as a 402A defendant manufacturer or seller, the next question is, who is a proper plaintiff to invoke the 402A remedy under federal maritime law?

Case law upholding the right of a plaintiff to assert a 402A claim against a shipowner has thus far been quite limited.[365a] Passengers and

---

364a. See, e.g., *Pacific Power & Light Co. v. Diehl*, 1986 AMC 525 (D. Md. 1986).

364b. *Borel v. Fibreboard Paper Products Corp.*, 493 F.2d 1076, 1087 (5th Cir. 1973).

365. *Boncich v. M.P. Howlett, Inc.*, 421 F.Supp. 1300, 1978 AMC 2089 (E.D.N.Y., 1978).

365a. It is commonly appreciated, however, that a shipowner's potential exposure in products-liability for personal injury and death is vast. The trend in shoreside law is toward steady expansion of the class of protected plaintiffs. Common law trends in product liability law are harbingers of maritime decisions. *Lindsay v. McDonnell Douglas Aircraft Corp.*, 460 F.2d 631, 636-37, 1974 AMC 1341 (8th Cir. 1972). Nonusers and nonconsumers injured by a defective product have found increasing protection. See, for example, *Annot.* 33 ALR 3d 415. "Products Liability: Extension of Strict Liability in Tort to Permit Recovery by a Third Person Who was Neither a Purchaser nor User of Product." See, also, Judge John Brown's

their survivors may recover.[366] Shipboard guests and business invitees should likewise be entitled to recover for personal injury or death suffered as a result of a defective product.

On the other hand, longshoremen have no right of recovery under 402A, because their negligence remedy under the Longshoremen's and Harbor Workers' Compensation Act, 33 U.S.C. 905(b), is the exclusive remedy and precludes recovery on a theory of strict liability in tort.[367] The preclusion extends to the expansive class of American shoreworkers in maritime employment. They are covered by the LHWCA, as heretofore discussed.

While a seaman is a foreseeable plaintiff, in practical effect, his remedy is probably unaffected by the availability of a 402A action. His claim lies under the Jones Act based on liberal concepts of negligence, and he may claim under general maritime law for breach of the shipowner's warranty of seaworthiness which would certainly engulf any 402A claim. Of course, if the vessel's liability could be limited,[367a] the Jones Act seaman would seek redress directly against the manufacturer or seller. In this respect, a shipowner's unseaworthiness liability may be derivative of 402A liability of another party. Thus, where a defective shipboard product has been manufactured or sold by someone other than the shipowner, if the defect causes injury to a crewmember, for example, liability in the first instance will be based upon the warranty of seaworthiness, but the shipowner would have a right to indemnity or contribution from the 402A manufacturer or seller.

A claim for strict liability in tort is subject to the partial defense of comparative negligence. All of plaintiff's conduct is compared to that of

---

dissent in *China Union Lines, Ltd. v. A.O. Anderson & Co.*, 364 F.2d 769, 1966 AMC 1653 (5th Cir. 1966) forecasting "far reaching awesome liabilities" seemingly owed to the world:

> It [defendant shipper] owed a duty literally to the world—at least a world within the reach and protection of American jurisprudence, land-based, salt water and amphibious. It had to have in mind port workers at the place of loading, crew members on the carrying vessel, crew members of vessels with which the carrying vessel might come in contact by collision or otherwise, port officials, customs inspectors, immigration officers, maritime service personnel, and members of the public. The duties owed to this limitless group of protectees require as a minimum that it not knowingly participate in a method of handling or transport which would imprudently imperil the lives of these people. I do not suggest here that Cyanamid, the manufacturer-supplier-shipper, has the liability of an insurer, but it certainly has the far-reaching awesome liabilities now associated with products liability.

366. *Stoddard v. Ling-Temco-Vought, Inc.*, 513 F.2d 314, (9th Cir., 1980); *Chute v. United States*, 466 F.Supp. 61, 1980 AMC 954 (D.,Mass., 1978), *rev'd* 610 F.2d 7, 1980 AMC 941 (1st Cir., 1979).

367. *Wilhelm v. Associated Container Transportation (Australia) Ltd.*, 648 F.2d 1197, 1981 AMC 2233 (9th Cir., 1981).

367a. Limitation of Liability Act, 46 U.S.C. 181-189. But see *Streatch v. Associated Container Transport, Inc.*, 388 F.Supp. 939 (C.D.,Cal., 1975), where the shipowner provided the longshoremen with special loading vehicles carried on board. If the shipowner also qualifies as a commercial lessor, liability under 402A may follow.

the defendant.[368] To illustrate, the plaintiff may have been negligent in failing to discover the defect or negligent in the way plaintiff used the product. Misuse of the product under maritime law merely serves to mitigate the plaintiff's damages and is not a complete defense.[368a] Further, the plaintiff's voluntary assumption of the risk of a defective product is now subsumed within the maritime doctrine of comparative negligence.[368b]

While there are no reported cases yet on the point, it would appear that a personal injury or death action predicated on 402A would be subject to the Uniform Statute of Limitations for Maritime Torts, 46 U.S.C. 763(a), which prescribes a three-year limitation period running from the date the cause of action accrues.

Negligence: Liability to Shipboard Visitors

A shipowner's liability to a shipboard visitor is defined by reference to the visitor's purpose in being aboard. The purpose may be social as, for example, friends or relatives of the owner, crew, or passengers, assuming they are aboard with the express or implied permission of the owner; or the visitor may be a member of the public aboard as a social guest. Such were formerly classified as maritime licensees. The classification must now be considered obsolete by virtue of *Kermarec v. Compagnie Generale Transatlantique.*[369]

Distinguished from the social visitors are those aboard in connection with maritime business for the vessel, cargo, personnel, or the like. These were the maritime business invitees. In *Kermarec,* the Supreme Court abolished the distinctions in the common law standard of care owed to licensees and invitees. Now, the same duty of care is owed by a shipowner in navigable waters to all who are aboard for purposes not inimical to his legitimate interests. It is the duty to exercise reasonable care under the circumstances.

By definition, the *Kermarec* class excludes the trespasser, to whom the shipowner owes only the duty to avoid deliberate injury.

Today, consideration of the owner's liability to visitors normally precludes consideration of the business invitee, who is usually an employee of an independent contractor in maritime employment. Such persons are covered by the LHWCA. To them, the shipowner owes the duty of reasonable care but not as defined under general maritime law in accordance with *Kermarec* principles. For such injured maritime employees asserting

---

368. *Pan Alaska Fisheries, Inc. v. Marine Construction & Design Co.,* 565 F.2d 1129, 1978 AMC 2315 (9th Cir., 1977).

368a. *Lewis v. Timco,* 716 F.2d 1425, 1984 AMC 191 (5th Cir. 1983).

368b. *National Marine Service, Inc. v. Petroleum Service Corp.,* 736 F.2d 272 (5th Cir. 1984).

369. 358 U.S. 625, 1959 AMC 597 (1959).

vessel negligence, the standards are defined by the case law developing under Section 905(b) of the LHWCA. In fact, it is difficult to conceive of a *Kermarec* business invitee who is not a maritime employee subject to the LHWCA.

To be distinguished from the *Kermarec* social visitor is a member of the crew or a passenger. The crew member may, of course, sue on a Jones Act negligence theory or for breach of the warranty of seaworthiness, whereas the passenger may assert against the shipowner a common carrier's standard of highest care. A passenger is owed a high degree of care but is not entitled to the benefit of a warranty of seaworthiness. See discussion, *infra*, on "Liability to Passengers."

Apparently, there has been little litigation on the standard of care owed to a fare-paying passenger on a chartered fishing vessel; i.e., whether the owner owes the common carrier duty or the *Kermarec* duty, or whether assumption of risk may be asserted as a defense. The same kind of issue arises in defining the status of those aboard pleasure vessels, i.e., whether a member of the crew or a *Kermarec* visitor.[370]

Liability to Passengers

Passenger Status. Passenger status depends upon an underlying contract of carriage, either express or implied, generally requiring payment of fare or the equivalent. A passenger's injury gives rise to causes of action based both on breach of contract and on a tort theory of negligence.

Passengers must be distinguished from seamen who pay no fare but rather are paid a wage and who otherwise satisfy criteria of seaman's status. Thus, in *Buckley v. Oceanic S.S. Co.*,[371] the question whether a workaway was a passenger or a seaman was resolved in favor of the Jones Act remedy, since the plaintiff had become a member of the ship's company and was doing work of a maritime nature. A stowaway, by contrast, is neither a seaman nor a passenger.[372]

The passenger must also be distinguished from the *Kermarec* invitee, licensee, or trespasser. The distinction makes a difference in the standard of care to which the shipowner is held, and the defenses may vary.

Where plaintiff's relationship with the shipowner is that of a passenger, the owner has duties of a common carrier and must exercise "ex-

370. See, generally, P. Daigle, "Other Non-Seamen Claims Against Shipowners and Charterers," 55 *Tulane Law Review* 1104 (1981).
371. 5 F.2d 545, 1925 AMC 918 (9th Cir., 1925).
372. *The Laura Madsen*, 112 F. 72 (D.C.,Wash., 1901).

traordinary vigilance and the highest skill" for the passenger's safety.[373] However, the shipowner is not an *insurer* of safety.[374]

The common carrier's duty appears to rise to a standard of strict liability in the assault cases. There, the duty to protect a passenger from harm is contractual and absolute.[375] Similarly, civil liability of the shipowner follows as a result of a criminal assault on a passenger by a crew member.[376]

P & I coverage is unaffected by the theory of liability asserted; in other words, it makes no difference that plaintiff alleges a contractual basis, an intentional tort, or negligence. The language of the usual club rule, as well as the policy provisions of the American forms, is sufficiently broad to embrace all such theories, and there are no applicable exclusionary clauses.

Obviously, the carriage of passengers may be by cargo vessel, cruise ship, ferry boat, or the like. Issues of passenger "status" do not frequently arise in cruise ship litigation.

The shipowner's high degree of care embraces the duty to warn of dangers reasonably anticipated by the shipowner and not appreciated by the passenger, but the shipowner must, however, be on notice of the danger.[377]

Liability to Passengers for Conduct of Independent Contractors. Two recurrent fact situations arise: negligence of providers of shoreside transportation and negligence of physicians, either ashore or on board. Generally speaking, the shipowner will not be liable for the negligence of a provider of shoreside transportation simply on a theory of *respondeat superior.*[378] However, the nature of the contractual undertaking of a cruise shipowner/operator determines whether liability attaches. If the carrier contracts for stopovers at foreign ports, the duty to provide safe transportation will include the duty of safe embarkation and disembarkation at

373. *Allen v. Matson Navigation Co.*, 255 F.2d 273, 1958 AMC 1343 (9th Cir., 1958).
374. *Marshall v. Westfall-Larsen & Co.*, 259 F.2d 575, 1958 AMC 1665 (9th Cir., 1958).
375. *Pacific S.S. Co. v. Sutton*, 7 F.2d 579, 1925 AMC 64 1335 (9th Cir., 1925).
376. *Panama Mail S.S. Co. v. Vargas*, 33 F.2d 894, 1929 AMC 1345 (9th Cir., 1929), involving a rape by the ship's steward. See, also, 18 U.S.C. 2198, making seduction of a female passenger a crime. The assault cases make it clear that any defense that the seaman acted outside the scope of his employment is invalidated.
377. *Metzger v. Italian Line*, 1976 AMC 453 (S.D.N.Y.), *aff'd* 535 F.2d 1242 (2d Cir., 1975), where the plaintiffs went ashore in Jamaica and were injured in a car accident while passengers in a taxi they had hired. The taxis were unlicensed. It was held there could be no notice of different safety standards between commercially licensed and unlicensed vehicles, and Jamaica had both.
378. *Id.*

the intermediate ports.[379] There is always a duty to provide safe ingress and egress at the beginning and end of the voyage.[380]

In fulfilling its obligations, an American shipowner frequently has contractual relationships with physicians in foreign ports. When negligence is established on the part of the shoreside physician, the dual issue arises: (1) is the shipowner liable on grounds of *respondeat superior* for the negligence of the physician? (2) is the shipowner liable for its own negligence in failing to exercise the highest degree of care in selecting the shoreside physician? The general rule appears to be that a physician or surgeon taken on board the vessel pursuant to a statutory command is not a servant or agent of the shipowner, and the latter is not liable on a theory of *respondeat superior*, provided the duty of selecting a physician who was competent and duly qualified has been fulfilled, but there are cases to the contrary.[381] It would appear logical that the doctrine of *respondeat superior* would be even less frequently applied in the case of a shoreside physician in a foreign port.

It should also be observed that the shipowner has a duty to provide passengers with reasonable medical care which may require the services of the ship's doctor where the carriage is of more than 50 passengers. 46 U.S.C. 155.

Defenses to Passenger Liability

Passenger's Own Negligence. If admiralty jurisdiction exists, the court is governed by federal maritime law, which must be applied over any state law that would defeat or narrow maritime rights of recovery. A conflict may exist between the federal maritime rule of comparative negligence and state law defenses based upon common law contributory negligence, or a state's boat guest passenger statute. At common law, of course, contributory negligence would be a complete bar to recovery. And, for example, the typical boat guest passenger statute precludes recovery in favor of a non-paying passenger absent wilful or wanton operation of the boat. Thus, recovery may well depend entirely on the existence or absence of admiralty jurisdiction.

Admiralty jurisdiction exists when the tort occurred upon navigable waters and there is a "relationship of the wrong to traditional maritime

379. *Lawlor v. Incres Nassau S.S. Line*, 161 F.Supp. 764, 1958 AMC 1701 (D.,Mass., 1958).
380. *Marshall v. Westfall-Larsen & Co.*, 259 F.2d 575, 1958 AMC 1665 (9th Cir., 1958).
381. See *De Zon v. American President Lines, Ltd.*, 318 U.S.660. 1943 AMC 483 (1943); *Amdur v. Zim Israel Nav. Co.*, 310 F.Supp. 1033, 1969 AMC 2418 (S.D.N.Y., 1969). Compare, however, *Nietes v. American President Lines, Ltd.*, 188 F.Supp. 219, 1960 AMC 1603 (N.D.,Cal., 1959), where the court opined that if a ship's physician is in the regular employment of a vessel, as a salaried member of the crew, and subject to ship's discipline, he was a servant or employee of the shipowner.

activity."[382] Today, admiralty jurisdiction extends to almost all passenger cases occurring on navigable waters. There are no longer any useful distinctions based upon the type of vessel involved; i.e., whether commercial or pleasure.[383]

Ticket Defenses. Because of specific legislation on the subject, printed defenses on the passenger's ticket have limited efficacy. 46 U.S.C. 183. The shipowner may not exculpate itself for its own negligence, 46 U.S.C. 183(c), although exculpatory language on a boarding pass may be valid.[384] A ticket defense limiting the period of time within which to present notice of claim and/or bring suit may be valid if legible, if legally enforceable under 46 U.S.C. 183c, and if the limitation periods do not contravene 46 U.S.C. 183b(a), prohibiting a limitation period of less than a year. The recurrent issue in ticket defense litigation is whether the passenger had notice of the limitations.[385]

Miscellaneous Liabilities of Shipowners

Sometimes a party other than the injured plaintiff has brought an action against the shipowner to recover amounts paid to the injured person as a result of vessel negligence. The leading case creating the cause of action arose before the 1972 amendments to the LHWCA.[386] In *Burnside*, it was held that a plaintiff standing in the position of the injured shoreworker had a right of recovery from the shipowner for the amount of compensation payments occasioned by the shipowner's negligence; i.e., a right of subrogation against the third-party wrongdoer.

Following enactment of the 1972 amendments, and in particular 33 U.S.C. 905(b), some doubt existed whether a *Burnside* type of action survived the amendments. Thus, dictum in *Landon v. Lief Hoegh & Co.,*[387] suggests that the *Burnside* action was abrogated by 905(b), which states that "the remedy provided in this subsection shall be exclusive of all other remedies against the vessel except remedies available under this chapter."

---

382. *Executive Jet Aviation, Inc. v. City of Cleveland,* 409 U.S. 249, 1973 AMC 1 (1972).

383. *Foremost Insurance Co. v. Richardson,* 457 U.S. 668, 1982 AMC 2253 (1982). Of course, if the negligence of the passenger is so egregious that it constitutes the sole cause, the claim is barred under maritime law. *Collins v. Indiana & Michigan Electric Co.,* 516 F.Supp. 304, 1983 AMC 1814 (S.D.,Ind., 1981).

384. *Economy v. Peninsular & Orient Steam Nav. Co.,* 1977 AMC 2154 (St.,Cal., 1977).

385. The statute allows the passenger a period of not less than six months for filing a claim and not less than one year for bringing an action.

386. *Federal Marine Terminals, Inc. v. Burnside Shipping Co.,* 394 U.S. 404, 1970 AMC 251 (1969).

387. 521 F.2d 756, 1975 AMC 1106 (2d Cir., 1975), *cert.den.* 423 U.S. 1053, 1976 AMC 1500 (1976).

Contrasted to the dictum in *Landon* is a square holding in *Crescent Wharf and Warehouse Co. v. Barracuda Tankers Corp.*[388] That case held that the employer's remedy under the LHWCA was not the exclusive remedy and that the *Burnside* cause of action survived; i.e., the statutory subrogation provided by the LHWCA does not preclude a negligence action against third-party wrongdoers.

The measure of damages is based upon past compensation paid. The *Burnside* cause of action allowed the stevedore company to recover to the extent even of future compensation which was proven to be owing to the injured shoreworker. The holding in *Hinson v. S.S. Paros*[389] was that 905(b) modified *Burnside*, and the shipowner is now liable only for the past compensation paid. There is no recovery for compensation benefits probably payable in the future, absent a formal compensation award.

While the employer and its compensation carrier have the cause of action for indemnity, a person asserting subrogation rights against the shipowner on behalf of the special fund does not.[390]

Contractual Liability to Indemnify

Generally speaking, a personal injury liability imposed upon a shipowner by virtue of the shipowner's contractual undertakings will be excluded from P & I coverage under American practice. For example, Clause 29(e) of the ASM form excludes any liability:

> For any claim for loss of life, personal injury or illness in relation to the handling of cargo where such claim arises under a contract of indemnity between the Assured and his sub-contractor.

Such liabilities may be covered, however, under club rules and practice, and to this end the clubs commonly impose a requirement of pre-approval of any contractual indemnities the shipowner considers undertaking.

A common type of contractual indemnity is a shipyard's "red letter clause" whereby the shipowner is required to indemnify the shipyard for any liability for personal injury or death in excess of a certain amount. The issues in the red letter clause cases are usually whether the clause is valid and whether the contractual indemnity in favor of the shipyard is available to the shipyard's subrogated underwriters. Both issues were answered in the affirmative in *Alcoa S.S. Co. v. Charles Ferran & Co.*[391]

388. 696 F.2d 703 (9th Cir., 1983).
389. 461 F.Supp. 1219, 1980 AMC 1611 (S.D.,Tex., 1978).
390. *Crescent Wharf and Warehouse Co. v. Barracuda Tankers Corp., supra,* n.388.
391. 443 F.2d 250, 1971 AMC 1116 (5th Cir., 1971), [1971] 2 Lloyd's Rep. 426. See, also, *Hudson Waterways Corp. v. Coastal Marine Services, Inc.,* 436 F.Supp. 597, 1978 AMC 341 (E.D.,Tex.) Compare, however, *Todd Shipyards v. Turbine Service,* 467 F.Supp. 1257 (E.D.,La.,

A shipowner, faced with commercial and financial pressures which arise during vessel operations, will on some occasions logically see fit contractually to indemnify an independent contractor for injuries to the contractor or its employees arising out of vessel employment. Examples of such undertakings include the red letter clauses used by shipyards discussed *supra;* contracts for the employment of tugs where the shipowner is required by the terms of the tug employment contract to indemnify the owner of the tug; and contracts by which the shipowner agrees to indemnify a pilot (or the pilot's employer) for any damages which the pilot (or his employer) may be required to pay by virtue of the pilot's negligence while piloting the vessel.[392] It must again be emphasized, however, that whether the P & I underwriter will respond to such a contractual undertaking depends wholly upon the wording of the applicable club rules or policy form.

Liability for Intentional Torts

As discussed heretofore, a shipowner has an absolute and non-delegable duty to provide a crew composed of seamen of an equal temperament, disposition, and seamanship to ordinary men in the calling. Liability may flow from a seaman's assault. It does not matter that the assault came on suddenly, unexpectedly, and without notice or warning.[393]

Vicarious Tort Liability—Ship's Officers

The vessel owner may have vicarious tort liability when its officers intentionally inflict injury within the scope of their employment. In this regard, certain criminal liabilities are relevant. It is a crime for an officer or master intentionally to inflict corporal punishment without justifiable cause. 18 U.S.C. 2191. A beating may leave the officer both criminally and civilly liable, and it appears that the injured person may get attorneys' fees as an element of damages.[394] The master, the vessel, or its owner may have

---

1978), where a red letter clause was held invalid as being against public policy where the shipyard's conduct was "greatly below the standard established by law for the protection of others against unreasonable risk of harm," citing *Bisso v. Inland Waterways Corp.,* 349 U.S. 85, 1955 AMC 899 (1955).

392. See, for example, *Sun Oil Co. v. Dalzell,* 287 U.S. 291, 1933 AMC 35 (1932) and *U.S. v. Neilson,* 349 U.S. 129, 1955 AMC 2231 (1955), upholding the validity of "pilotage clauses." See, also, ORS Chapter 776, (Oregon, 1983), compelling indemnity by shipowners of pilots employed on Oregon waters. See, generally, A. Parks, *Law of Tug, Tow & Pilotage* (2d ed.), (Centreville, Md.: Cornell Maritime Press, 1982) and supplements.

393. *Deakle v. John E. Graham & Sons,* 756 F.2d 821, 1985 AMC 2979 (11th Cir., 1985); *Boudoin v. Lykes Bros. S.S. Co.,* 348 U.S. 336, 1955 AMC 488 (1955).

394. *Riley v. Allen,* 23 F. 46 (E.D.,Tenn., 1885); *Hanson v. Fowle,* F.Cas. No. 6,042 (D. Or., 1871).

criminal liability arising out of an assault if the master had actual knowledge of the assault and did not use due diligence to surrender the officer
of the vessel (U.S. flag vessels only) who inflicted the corporal punishment
and who escaped because of the master's non-compliance. 46 U.S.C. 712.

Liability in Rescue Situations

An owner of a rescuing vessel is held to a standard of care making it liable
only for (a) negligent conduct that worsens the position of the victim, or
(b) reckless or wanton conduct in performing the rescue.[395] That standard of care, however, is owed to strangers. The standard of care is different, of course, with respect to passengers to whom the highest degree
of care is owed, and crew members, who are entitled to the warranty of
seaworthiness.[396]

Liability for Injuries Arising out of Collision

Persons aboard a vessel have a negligence remedy against the owner of
another vessel for personal injury or death resulting from collision where
the other vessel is found to have any degree of negligence. The standard
of care is negligence under general maritime law. Such liabilities are discussed, *infra*, under the heading of "Collision." Normally, a P & I policy
covers collision liabilities for personal injury and death.

Shipowners' Rights to Indemnity and Contribution

In the course of risk evaluation by shipowners and P & I underwriters,
thought must be given to recouping the loss directly, or indirectly by subrogation, either in the existing action or through a separate action. These
potential recoveries and rights of indemnity or contribution are integral
to an evaluation of the P & I risk.[397]

Courts today are loath to award indemnity to a shipowner except in
two situations and then, of course, only if there is no statutory prohibition. The first situation requires a written contract clearly and expressly
creating the indemnity obligation. The usual question is whether the ex-

---

395. *Berg v. Chevron U.S.A., Inc.*, 759 F.2d 1425, 1986 AMC 360 (9th Cir., 1985); *Caminiti
v. Tomlinson Fleet*, 1981 AMC 201 (N.D.,Ohio); *Shaver v. Erickson*, 1979 AMC 2308 (N.D.,Ill.).

396. See discussion, *supra*, as respects passengers; as to crew members, see *Reyes v. Van-
tage S.S.*, 609 F.2d 104, 1981 AMC 1255 (5th Cir., 1980), *sub.proc.* 672 F.2d 556, 1982 AMC
1814 (5th Cir., 1982).

397. An exceptionally clear and comprehensive analysis of these rights is F. Gorman,
"Indemnity and Contribution under Maritime Law," 55 *Tulane Law Review* 1165 (1981) to
which the reader is commended for historical background and conceptual analysis of maritime indemnity and contribution rights.

press language contains an indemnification for the indemnitee's own negligence.[398] An indemnity provision in a maritime contract is interpreted
according to federal maritime law, not state law.[399] If the provision is unambiguous, the court makes the determination; otherwise it is a question
of fact and determination of the parties' intent is central. For example,
did the parties mean for "A" to indemnify "B" for damages caused by
"A's" negligence alone? Or, was the intent that "A" indemnify "B" for
damages caused in any part by "B"? Or, did the parties intend an indemnity based upon respective fault; that is, must "B" indemnify "A" only for
the proportion of "B's" fault causal to the accident?[400]

Even if the contract does create an indemnity obligation, it may be unlawful in some instances; e.g., where the indemnitor is a maritime employer under the LHWCA. Thus, a claim based upon a contractual right
to indemnity, as with claims based on either a *Ryan* warranty or tort theory (discussed *infra*), may be expressly prohibited by the 1972 amendments to the LHWCA. 33 U.S.C. 905(b).

Section 905(b) is clear in its prohibition:

> In the event of injury to a person covered by this chapter caused by
> the negligence of a vessel, then such person, or anyone otherwise en-
> titled to recover damage by reason thereof, may bring an action
> against such vessel as a third party in accordance with the provisions
> of Sec. 933 of this title, and *the employer shall not be liable to the vessel for
> such damages directly or indirectly and any agreements or warranties to the
> contrary shall be void.* [Emphasis supplied]

It appears, however, that 905(b), of its own force, does not prohibit
indemnity actions by "non-vessels."[401] Furthermore, even though the LH-
WCA prohibits indemnity agreements between the covered employer
and the vessel, it does not void an agreement by a stevedore to name a
shipowner as an additional assured on the stevedore's liability insurance
policy.[402] Just as the Act does not preclude indemnity actions by non-vessel owners, neither does it prohibit an indemnity action by the vessel
against an employer not subject to the Act, as, for example, a manufacturer of ship's equipment.[403] The Act would not appear to preclude indemnity against another shipowner whose employee caused injury,[404] nor

398. See *Seal Offshore, Inc. v. American Standard, Inc.*, 736 F.2d 1078 (5th Cir., 1984).
399. *Lirette v. Popich Bros. Water Transport, Inc.*, 699 F.2d 725 (5th Cir., 1983).
400. See, generally, *American Stevedores, Inc. v. Porello*, 330 U.S. 446, 1947 AMC 349
(1947).
401. *Aparicio v. Swan Lake*, 643 F.2d 1109, 1981 AMC 1887 (5th Cir., 1981).
402. *Boisin v. O.D.E.C.O. Drilling Co.*, 744 F.2d 1174 (5th Cir., 1984).
403. *Williams v. Brasea, Inc.*, 497 F.2d 67, 1976 AMC 708 (5th Cir., 1974).
404. *Norris v. Great Lakes Towing*, 1979 AMC 1080 (W.D.N.Y.).
405. *Doca v. Marina Mercante Nicaraguense*, 634 F.2d 30, 1980 AMC 2401 (2d Cir., 1980),
recognizing that the stevedore who is not the injured party's employer may, upon proper

does it include a stevedore who was not the employer of the covered workman.[405]

Ryan *Warranty*

The U.S. Supreme Court created the *Ryan* doctrine of indemnity to ameliorate the effect of two other cases creating inequities for the shipowner.[406] One was *Seas Shipping Co. v. Sieracki*,[407] extending the warranty of seaworthiness traditionally owed to seamen to shore-based workers who do the work traditionally done by seamen. These greatly expanded warranty liabilities made little sense in the recurring factual situation where the employer of the "Sieracki" seaman was also at fault. However, in *Halcyon Lines v. Haenn Ship Ceiling & Refitting Corp.*,[408] the Supreme Court had held that there was no right to maritime contribution in a non-collision case, thus precluding the shipowner from recovering anything from the concurrently negligent stevedore-employer.

In *Ryan,* indemnity was awarded on the basis that the contractual relationship existing between the stevedore and the shipowner carried an implied warranty of workmanlike performance. Thus, the effect of the shipowner's far-reaching liability for breach of the warranty of seaworthiness was counteracted by a corresponding right to recover indemnity from the employing stevedore for breach of the warranty of workmanlike performance.

That counteraction is important, because following the 1972 amendments to the LHWCA, courts have been reluctant to imply a *Ryan* warranty in favor of a shipowner unless the contractor's breach of the warranty of workmanlike performance "renders the vessel unseaworthy and imposes liability on the owner for the consequences of that unseaworthiness."[409]

The *Ryan* warranty is a powerful tool, but even when available it is not without limitations. The warranty is for workmanlike performance and is supposedly independent of considerations of fault. Yet, where the contractor and the shipowner share control over the injury-producing instrumentality, courts seem to require evidence approximating proof of

---

proof, be liable for indemnity. See, also, *Rindome v. Arya National Shipping Co.*, 1980 AMC 196 (S.D.N.Y, 1979). Sec. 905(c) of the 1984 amendments also removed a bar for a vessel seeking indemnity in the limited circumstance where the vessel is liable under the LHWCA pursuant to the Outer Continental Shelf Lands Act, 43 U.S.C. 1333 and there exists a "reciprocal indemnity" between the vessel and the employer-indemnitee.

406. *Ryan Stevedoring Co. v. Pan-Atlantic Steamship Corp.*, 350 U.S. 124, 1956 AMC 9 (1956).

407. 328 U.S. 85, 1946 AMC 698 (1946).

408. 342 U.S. 282, 1952 AMC 1 (1952).

409. *Sandoval v. Mitsui Sampaku*, 460 F.2d 1163, 1973 AMC 135 (5th Cir., 1972); *Davis v. Charles Kurz & Co.*, 483 F.2d 184, 1974 AMC 1862 (9th Cir., 1973).

fault before allowing a *Ryan* recovery.[410] If the shipowner has equal ability to minimize the risk, the rationale of *Italia Societa v. Oregon Stevedoring Co.*[411] may be missing, and a *Ryan* warranty will be denied.

However, once the breach of the warranty is established, though only a partial cause of the injury, indemnity may follow.[412] A lawsuit by an injured seaman would be one of the foreseeable harms resulting from the breach; so proximate causation exists.[413]

Where the shipowner and the contractor are concurrently at fault, a further evaluation of the shipowner's conduct is critical. If the owner's conduct prevents the contractor from performing in a workmanlike manner, *Ryan* indemnity is precluded.[414]

In some circuits, simple causal negligence of the shipowner will preclude *Ryan* indemnity. The Ninth Circuit is far more liberal toward the shipowner and requires "egregious conduct" "which effectively prevents the stevedore from satisfying its implied warranty."[415] Even then, conduct which does handicap the contractor will not necessarily preclude indemnification.[416]

Assuming the corresponding seaworthiness obligation does exist, and further assuming no prohibition by virtue of 905(b), there is authority that a *Ryan* right of recovery is still alive.[417] There is also contrary authority—that *Ryan* is a "withered doctrine."[418]

Right to Indemnity Based upon Tort

It appears that the bases of common law indemnity, i.e., active/passive negligence or primary/secondary fault, are no longer applicable in maritime indemnity actions. Comparative fault principles, applicable in maritime cases involving both negligence and strict liability, have made the common law distinctions "at best a redundancy."[419] Thus, in *Loose v. Off-*

---

410. See *Coffman v. Hawkins & Hawkins Drilling Co., Inc.*, 594 F.2d 152, 1981 AMC 893 (5th Cir., 1979).

411. 376 U.S. 315, 1964 AMC 1927 (1964).

412. *Simko v. C & C Marine Maintenance Co.*, 594 F.2d 960, 1980 AMC 1995 (3rd Cir., 1979).

413. *Arista Cia De Vapores, S.A. v. Howard Terminal*, 372 F.2d 152, 1967 AMC 312 (9th Cir., 1967).

414. *Weyerhaeuser S.S. Co. v. Nacirema Operating Co.*, 355 U.S. 563, 1958 AMC 501 (1958).

415. *Hanseatische Reederei Emil Offen v. Marine Terminals*, 590 F.2d 778, 1979 AMC 303 (9th Cir., 1979).

416. Id.; *Victory Carriers, Inc. v. Stockton Stevedoring Co.*, 399 F.2d 955, 1968 AMC 344 (9th Cir., 1968).

417. *Zapico v. Bucyrus-Erie Co.*, 579 F.2d 714, 1978 AMC 1629 (2d Cir., 1978).

418. *Gator Marine Service v. J. Ray McDermott & Co.*, 651 F.2d 1096, 1984 AMC 1927 (5th Cir., 1981), particularly in light of a preference for comparative negligence principles. *Bass v. Phoenix Seadrill 78, Ltd.*, 749 F.2d 1154 (5th Cir., 1985).

419. *Seal Offshore, Inc. v. American Standard, Inc.*, 736 F.2d 1078 (5th Cir., 1984).

shore Navigation, Inc.,[420] the Fifth Circuit buried the traditional distinctions as it relied upon two U.S. Supreme Court cases, *Cooper Stevedoring Co. v. Fritz Kopke, Inc.*[421] and *United States v. Reliable Transfer Co.*[422] *Cooper Stevedore* said there is a maritime right to contribution between joint tortfeasors in non-collision cases unless one of the joint tortfeasors enjoys statutory immunity as, for example, by 905(b).[422a] *Reliable Transfer* held that contribution may be based on proportion of fault and not on a pro rata basis. The emerging view is that these two cases replace maritime tort indemnity with maritime contribution according to causal fault.

In summary, any rights of indemnity otherwise held by a shipowner may be prohibited by 905(b) of the LHWCA. There is no such prohibition if the party claiming indemnity is not the "vessel" within the meaning of the statute, nor does the prohibition extend to a vessel's claim for indemnity against a non-employer; i.e., an employer not subject to the LHWCA or an employer who, although within the coverage of the LHWCA, is not the employer of the injured person. Assuming no 905(b) prohibition, the shipowner's rights of recoupment may be based upon an express contract of indemnity, possibly a *Ryan* warranty, and, with frequency safe to forecast, upon a contribution theory based on proportionate fault.

Annotations for a P & I Policy or Club Rules

Loss of Life, Injury or Illness

The relevant portion of the insuring clause of the ASM form of policy (after reciting the name of the insured vessel, the assured, the sum insured, the policy period, and provisions as to assessability of the assured) reads as follows:

> The Association agrees to indemnify the Assured against any loss, damage or expense which the Assured shall become liable to pay and shall pay by reason of the fact that the Assured is the owner (or operator, manager, charterer, mortgagee, trustee, receiver or agent, as the case may be) of the insured vessel and which shall result from the following liabilities, risks, events, occurrences and expenditures:
>
> *Loss of Life, Injury and Illness*
>
> (1) Liability for life salvage, loss of life of, or personal injury to, or illness of any person, not including, however, unless otherwise agreed by endorsement hereon, liability to an employee (other than hereafter excepted) of the assured, or in case of his death to his beneficiaries,

---

420. 670 F.2d 493, 1984 AMC 1216 (5th Cir., 1982).
421. 417 U.S. 106, 1974 AMC 537 (1974).
422. 421 U.S. 397, 1975 AMC 541 (1975).
422a. See *Edmonds v. Compagnie Generale Transatlantique, supra,* n. 266.

under any compensation act. Liability hereunder with respect to a member of the crew shall include liability arising ashore or afloat. Liability hereunder shall also include burial expenses not exceeding $500.00, where reasonably incurred by the assured for the burial of any seaman.

(a) Liability hereunder shall include the liability of the Assured for claims under any Compensation Act (other than hereafter excepted), in respect of an employee (i) who is a member of the crew of the insured vessel, or (ii) who is on board the insured vessel with the intention of becoming a member of her crew, or (iii) who, in the event of the vessel being laid up and out of commission, is engaged in the upkeep, maintenance or watching of the insured vessel, or (iv) who is engaged by the insured vessel or its Master to perform stevedoring work in connection with the vessel's cargo at ports in Alaska and ports outside the Continental United States where contract stevedores are not readily available. This insurance, however, shall not be considered as a qualification under any Compensation Act, but, without diminishing in any way the liability of the Association under this policy, the Assured may have in effect policies covering such liabilities. All claims under such Compensation Act for which the Association is liable under the terms of this policy are to be paid without regard to such other policies.

(b) Liability hereunder shall not cover any liability under the provisions of the Act of Congress approved September 7, 1916 and as amended, Public Act No. 267, Sixty-Fourth Congress, known as the U.S. Employees Compensation Act.

(c) Liability hereunder in connection with the handling of cargo for the insured vessel shall commence from the time of receipt by the Assured of the cargo on dock or wharf, or on craft alongside for loading, and shall continue until due delivery thereof from dock or wharf of discharge or until discharge from the insured vessel on to a craft alongside.

(d) Liability hereunder may, by endorsement hereon, be made payable to an employee of the Assured or in the event of his death to his beneficiaries or estate.

(e) Claims hereunder, other than for burial expenses, are subject to a deduction of $ _____ with respect to each accident or occurrence.

By contrast, the recent Protection and Indemnity (P and I) Clauses (June 2, 1983) issued by the American Institute of Marine Underwriters, as respects loss of life, injury, or illness, read rather more simply:

(1) Loss of life and bodily injury or illness; but excluding amounts paid under any compensation act.

(2) Hospital, medical or other expenses necessarily and reasonably

incurred with respect to loss of life, bodily injury to, or illness of, any person.

(3) Crew member burial expense not to exceed $1,000 per person.

The SP-23 (revised) form of P & I policy, very common in the United States, like the AIMU (June 2, 1983) form, precedes the actual coverage provisions with an "insuring clause," which, in the case of SP-23, reads as follows:

> The Assurer hereby undertakes to make good to the Assured or the Assured's executors, administrators and/or successors, all such loss and/or damage and/or expense as the Assured shall *as owners of the vessel named herein* have become liable to pay and shall pay on account of the liabilities, risks, events and/or happenings herein set forth. [Emphasis supplied][423]

Thereafter, the coverage with respect to loss of life, injury and illness reads:

> (1) Liability for loss of life of, or personal injury to, or illness of, any person, *excluding, however, unless otherwise agreed by endorsement hereon,* liability under any Compensation Act to any employee of the Assured (other than a seaman) or in case of death to his beneficiaries or others.

> [Here follows language substantially identical to Clause (1)(c) of the ASM form relating to liability in connection with the handling of cargo.]

> (2) Liability for hospital, medical, or other expenses necessarily and reasonably incurred in respect of loss of life of, personal injury to, or illness of any member of the crew of the vessel named herein or any other person. Liability hereunder shall also include burial expenses not exceeding Two Hundred ($200) Dollars, when necessarily and reasonably incurred by the Assured for the burial of any seaman of said vessel.

The language of SP-38 (P & I, 1955) in respect of the same liability is even more simple. It reads:

> Loss of life of, or injury to, or illness of, any person;
> Hospital, medical, or other expenses necessarily and reasonably incurred in respect of loss of life of, injury to or illness of any member of the crew of the vessel named herein.[424]

---

423. The importance of the italicized phrase will be apparent in the discussion of the decisions which follows.

424. It should be noted, however, that under the "exclusions" portion of the SP-38 form (lines 44-45), liability is excluded with respect to "any claim arising directly or indi-

By comparison, the comparable rule [rule 20(1)] of the Britannia Steam Ship Insurance Association, Limited, reads:

20(1) Damages, compensation, wages, maintenance and hospital, medical and funeral expenses for which a Member may be liable (including liabilities under collective or special agreements approved by the Managers) arising out of loss of life, personal injury or illness of:

(a) the master or a member of the crew;
(b) any other person on board or near an entered ship;
(c) any person on board any other ship.[425]

It is somewhat difficult to compare the SP-23 form with the ASM form because the latter is generally in use with so-called blue water ships while SP-23 is most commonly used with respect to inland and coastal vessels. By the same token, the language of SP-38 is somewhat broader than that in SP-23, but the former does not cover claims for loss of, damage to, or expense in respect to cargo aboard the insured vessel.

It will be observed from a comparison of the language in the ASM form with that of SP-23 and SP-38 that the ASM form purports to indemnify the assured against loss, damage, or expense which he becomes liable to pay, not only as "owner" of the entered vessel but also as "operator, manager, charterer, mortgagee, trustee, receiver or agent, as the case may be," whereas both SP-23 and SP-38 provide coverage only to the assured as the "owner" of the entered vessel. The inclusion of the words "trustee, receiver or agent," however, must be read *in pari materia* with Clause 28(a) of the ASM form which permits the underwriter to cancel the policy if the management, control, or possession of the entered vessel is transferred whether by demise charter, change in corporate ownership, or transfer of control.

Cases Interpreting the Scope of P & I Coverage for Loss of Life and Personal Injury

Coverage in General. The cases illustrating and interpreting the scope of coverage for loss of life, personal injury, or illness under P & I policies and comparable employers' liability and comprehensive liability policies in the United States are rather numerous. For example, in *Upper Columbia*

---

rectly under the Longshoremen's and Harbor Workers' Compensation Act or any workmen's compensation act of any state or nation." This is consistent, of course, with the approach taken by SP-23.

425. A proviso then excludes recovery arising out of a member's liability under a contract of indemnity between the member and a third party, and as to supernumeraries and passengers except as set forth in other subsections of the rule.

River Towing Co. v. Glens Falls Ins. Co.,[426] the assured towboat company utilized crew members of its towing tugs to unload and load barges being towed. It was shown that the P & I underwriter was aware of this. A crew member from the towing tug was injured aboard a barge and brought suit, which the towboat company settled. The towboat company then brought suit against the P & I underwriter that had previously refused to defend the Jones Act claim. The court held that although the injury had been sustained on board the barge and not on board the insured tug, the Jones Act action was within the scope of the cover of the P & I policy.

In *Tidewater Oil Co. v. Amer. S.S. Owners M.P. & I. Ass'n,*[427] a seaman who was connecting a steam hose from a pier to a tanker to supply her with steam during a period when fires were to be extinguished was held not to be engaging in stevedoring work within an exception in the policy.

In *Brinkman v. Oil Transfer Co.,*[428] maintenance and cure obligations were paid by the injured seaman's parents. The maintenance underwriter defended on ground that the seaman owed no duty to reimburse his parents. It was held that the shipowner was not excused from liability for sums actually expended in an emergency by relatives or other interested parties.

In *Harbor Tug v. Zurich,*[429] the plaintiff insured

> . . . against loss from the liability imposed by law . . . for damages on account of bodily injury or death accidentally suffered . . . by any person or persons not employed by the assured . . . by reason of the ownership, maintenance or use of vessels covered by the policy or by reason of collision or other perils of navigation while said vessels are being used in the waters described in the policy.

The insured vessel was negligently operated so as to precipitate a cargo of pipe into the water, and the pipe was neither removed nor marked by the assured. Another vessel collided with the sunken pipe and was sunk, thereby drowning one of its crewmen, whose estate recovered against the plaintiff-assured. It was held that the insurer was liable only for losses proximately caused by perils insured against and not for losses for which an insured peril was a remote cause; the proximate cause was the assured's failure to mark or remove the pipe and the remote cause the negligence in precipitating the pipe into the water; consequently there was no recovery.

Dryden v. Ocean Acc. & Guar. Co.[430] involved a suit for maintenance and cure, in which the insurer resisted liability on ground that the policy cov-

426. 179 F.Supp. 705, 1960 AMC 389 (D.,Ore., 1960)
427. 1935 AMC 936 (St.,N.Y.).
428. 1950 AMC 341 (St.,N.Y.).
429. 25 F.Supp. 847, 1938 AMC 1197 (N.D.,Cal.).
430. 138 F.2d 291, 1944 AMC 680 (7th Cir.).

ered only "liability imposed by law" and that maintenance and cure arose from an employer-employee contract relation. It was held, inter alia, that maintenance and cure was a right whose source arose in law, although applicable only to persons standing in the contractual relationship of employer and employee, and, therefore, coverage was provided.

Liman, Trustees v. American S.S. Owners,[431] involved a situation in which P & I underwriters refused to defend personal injury claims against a bankrupt shipowner. The bankruptcy trustee paid such claims on a basis whereby the claimants waived the $1,000 deductible. It was held that the underwriter could not avoid payment by showing that the assured's payment of claims was advanced by a third person or financed in some other fashion. Otherwise, the underwriters would reap a benefit at the expense of the intended beneficiaries.

In *Citizens Casualty v. Seafood Packers,*[432] a wholesale purchaser of fish, as a gratuitous service, permitted the masters of vessels delivering fish to his wharf to select and use fishboxes from his wharf. A fishing boat owner was injured by reason of a defect in one of the boxes. It was held that the wholesale purchaser did not warrant the condition of his fish boxes and was not therefore liable to indemnify the fish boat owner for injuries suffered by reason thereof. Moreover, the court held that there was no right of subrogation on the part of the fishing boat owner's underwriters.

In *Lanasse v. Travelers Ins.,*[433] the shipowner's P & I policy named the time charterer as an additional assured with waiver of subrogation. A seaman was injured by reason of the sole negligence of the time charterer's crane operator, and the P & I underwriter paid a sum in settlement of the seaman's claim. The P & I underwriter then brought a subrogation action against the time charterer to recoup the amount paid in the settle-

---

431. 299 F.Supp. 106, 1969 AMC 1669 (S.D.N.Y.), *aff'd* 417 F.2d 627 (2d Cir., 1969).
432. 1972 AMC 770 (D.,Mass.).
433. 450 F.2d 580, 1972 AMC 818 (5th Cir., 1971), *cert. den.* 406 U.S. 921. See, also, *LaCross v. Craighead,* 466 F.Supp. 880, 1982 AMC 2692 (E.D.,La., 1979), where, on the authority of *Lanasse* that "there must be causal operational relation between the vessel and resulting injury," an oil exploration rig owner who had been named as an additional assured under a tug owner's P & I policy as the charterer of the tug was denied recovery because the injury-producing event arose out of the oil rig operator's negligence *qua* rig or platform operator and not as a charterer of the tug. See, also, *Dow Chemical Co. v. Tug Thomas Allen et al,* 349 F.Supp. 1354, 1974 AMC 781 (E.D.,La.), where a tug owner by contract was obligated to and did name the owner of the tow as an assured under the tug owner's P & I policy. An employee of the tow owner was injured by reason of the tow owner's negligence. It was held that there was no coverage under the P & I policy as liability did not stem from fault on the part of the tug or its crew. *Wedcock v. Gulf Mississippi Marine Corp.,* 554 F.2d 240 (5th Cir., 1977) extended the principle one step further. There, a charterer was named as an additional assured with respect to a tug owner's tug. A tug employee was injured aboard the charterer's barge. Although the injury occurred as a result of concurrent negligence of the employees of both the tug owner and the barge charterer, the tug's P & I policy was held not to cover because the charterer was an additional assured only as to the tug and not as to the barge.

ment and was awarded judgment. The court reasoned that the policy by its language only covered liabilities of the assured as "owner" of the insured vessel, and neither the shipowner's crew nor his vessel was at fault. In short, although the time charterer was a named assured in the policy with a waiver of subrogation, this did not prevent recovery against him where the proximate cause of the injury was negligence of his employee in a sense wholly disassociated from the insured vessel, and the policy only covered the assured(s) in his or their capacity as "owners" of the vessel.

Essentially the same principle was applied in *American Motorists v. American Employers Ins.*,[434] where it was held that there was no coverage under the P & I policy for injury sustained by the plaintiff as a result of being struck by a bullet fired by an employee of the assured in the absence of any connection between ownership of the insured vessel and the employee's negligent act.

A like decision is *Employers Mut. Ins. Co. v. Aetna Ins. Co.*[435] There, a tug owner's P & I policy was held not to cover an injury to an employee by a dynamite explosion which occurred during a dredging operation. The employee was on a charterer's barge attached to the tug. It was held that the policy did not cover because the employee was engaged in operations wholly disassociated from the operation of the insured tug.

In *Offshore Logistics v. Mutual Marine*,[436] the bareboat charterer of a crewboat contracted with the crewboat's legal owner for the latter to "man, victual, maintain, navigate and supply" the crewboat. The charterer negligently ordered the crewboat out to sea in rough weather and third persons were injured thereby. The contract with the legal owner to man and operate the crewboat was held not to vitiate the charterer's status as an "owner *pro hac vice*," and the excess P & I policy was held to cover the charterer's liability as "owner."

In *Gryar v. Odeco*,[437] an oil rig worker was injured attempting to jump from a crewboat to a workboat and thence to his employer's submersible drilling rig. The crewboat owner's P & I policy did not specifically name the drilling owner as an additional assured but had been amended to provide for granting permission to charter the insured vessel and the nomination of anyone as an additional assured for whom the vessel was working. The crewboat owner's P & I policy covered all liability that the assured, *as owner of the vessel*, should incur. The drilling rig owner's negligence consisted of a failure to provide reasonably safe access to the drilling rig. It was held that the negligence of the drilling rig owner arose out

434. 447 F.Supp. 1314, 1978 AMC 1467 (W.D.,La., 1978).
435. 254 F.Supp. 263 (E.D., Mich., 1966).
436. 462 F.Supp. 485, 1981 AMC 1154 (E.D.,La., 1978).
437. 1982 AMC 143 (E.D.,La., 1981).

of his status as owner of the drilling rig and not as operator of the crewboat, and, therefore, the P & I policy afforded no coverage.

The foregoing cases demonstrate graphically that the *status* of the named insured in a P & I policy is governing. If the policy provides coverage to the named insured only as "owner" of the vessel, then a named additional assured can bring himself under the coverage of the policy only if his status at the time of the claim arising was that of an "owner." This is pointed up by the decision in *Helaire v. Mobil Oil Corp.*,[438] where the phrase "as owners of the vessel named herein" was physically deleted from the policy. The insured vessel was chartered to an oil company. While it was under charter, a longshoreman was injured while off-loading casings from the chartered vessel to the oil company's drilling platform. It was held that the P & I policy covered the liability of the oil company as charterer.

The principles involved in the construction of P & I policies have already been discussed, *supra*. It is well, however, to emphasize that both the insuring language and exclusionary language should be carefully drafted because of the tendency of the courts to construe insurance policies most strongly against the party which drafted them, and to hold that coverage exists when the policy contains an ambiguity. For example, in *Guarantee Mutual Assur. Co. v. Middlesex Mut. Ins. Co.*,[439] the assured's homeowner policy excluded coverage of boating accidents if the boat had (1) an inboard motor exceeding 50 horsepower, or (2) an outboard motor exceeding 24 horsepower. At the time of an accident involving the insured vessel, it was powered by a 120 horsepower inboard-outboard motor. As this third type of motor was not referred to in the exclusionary clause, it was held that the underwriter had to defend the insured. Another example will be found in *Kelloch v. S. & H. Sub Water Salvage*,[440] where a liability policy was endorsed to limit maritime coverage on employees to an injury which "occurs whilst diving." It was construed as applying to the entire

---

438. 497 F.Supp. 633 (E.D.,La., 1980).

439. 339 A.2d 6 (St.,N.H., 1975), 1975 AMC 2327. See, also, *Continental Automobile v. Hansen*, 334 So.2d 437 (App., La., 1976), involving a similar policy and similar exclusionary language where the court held that the exclusionary language did not apply to the vessel, powered by an outboard motor acquired *after* the inception of the policy; and *Farmers Home v. I.N.A.*, 1979 AMC 2549 (St.,Wash.) where the policy insured a yacht owner against liability for bodily injury arising by reason of his "interest" in the yacht. The term "interest" was held to be ambiguous and was construed to cover injury to a guest who fell through an opening in a pier while attempting to assist another passenger to disembark from the yacht. Admittedly, such policies involved pleasure craft where the courts' tendency to find ambiguities and award coverage based on the assured's "reasonable expectations" seems to run rampant. In this connection, see the discussion, *supra*, in Chapter XIV, "The Inchmaree Clause," and specifically *Lewis v. Aetna Ins. Co.*, 264 Or. 314, 505 P.2d 914 (St.,Ore., 1973) where the concurring justices expressly predicated their concurrence on the "reasonable expectations" of the assured as respects an interpretation of the Inchmaree Clause in the policy.

440. 1974 AMC 2516 (E.D.,La., 1972).

diving operation and, therefore, did not exclude coverage for injury to an assistant of a diver *prior* to the latter entering into the water.[441]

"Other Insurance" Clauses. "Other insurance" clauses in liability policies can be quite troublesome, particularly where two or more policies exist and each other insurance clause purports to exclude or limit liability if other insurance exists. Such clauses take different forms in different policies. One type purports to exclude all liability whatever if other insurance exists; another type provides that it will be in excess of any other existing insurance. The following decisions will demonstrate how the courts have treated such clauses in the context of a P & I policy or like liability policies.

For example, in *Voison v. Ocean Protein,*[442] an employer-shipowner's liability was covered under both his workmen's compensation policy and a P & I policy, each policy containing an exclusion with respect to other insurance. It was held that the liability would be apportioned between the two policies. To the same effect is *Keys Engineering Co. v. Boston Ins. Co.,*[443] where coverage was afforded under two policies. One policy contained a valid other insurance proration provision; the other policy only prohibited double insurance. In this instance, the proration formula was applied by the court.

By contrast, in *Viger v. Geophysical Services, Inc.,*[444] a time charterer's liability policy contained an other insurance clause providing for pro rata payment by insurers if other insurance existed. The time charterer was also an additional assured under the vessel owner's P & I policy, which contained an escape clause disclaiming any participation if other insurance existed. The court held that all clauses in insurance policies must be given effect if possible and, therefore, the escape clause in the P & I policy meant that the time charterer's liability insurer was responsible for the entire loss. In *Morslich's Case,*[445] the shipowner was covered against a personal injury claim of its longshoreman-employee by both a P & I policy and an employer's liability policy, each containing differently worded other insurance clauses. It was held that the employer's liability policy provided "existing coverage," which, under the other insurance language of the P & I policy, rendered the latter inapplicable.

In *Rini v. Transocean Contractors,*[446] the shipowner had two primary insurance policies, both of which were claused to cover the shipowner's lia-

---

441. See, also, *Geehan v. Trawler Arlington Inc.,* 547 F.2d 132, 1976 AMC 2510 (1st Cir., 1976) where the court held that any ambiguity in the P & I policy would not be construed to benefit an excess insurer at the expense of the vessel owner, who was insured under both the P & I and excess policies.
442. 321 F.Supp. 173, 1971 AMC 464 (E.D.,La.)
443. 192 F.Supp. 574 (S.D.,Fla., 1961).
444. 338 F.Supp. 808, 1972 AMC 2113 (W.D.,La., 1972).
445. 1972 AMC 2655 (S.D.N.Y.).

bility for injuries to employees aboard his vessel. One policy was a typed employer's liability policy with an endorsement covering maritime exposures. The other was a P & I policy issued by a separate underwriter. Both policies contained a provision negating coverage if the same risk were insured elsewhere. As the two provisions were mutually repugnant, the shipowner's recovery against underwriters was pro-rated on the basis of the monetary limits of the respective policies.

A like result was reached in *Port of Portland v. Water Quality Ins. Syndicate,*[447] where the assured port had two policies presumptively applicable to the same vessel, an inland dredge. One policy was a comprehensive general liability covering the port, with the watercraft exclusion deleted; the other policy was one issued by the Water Quality Insurance Syndicate specifically insuring the port, as owner of the insured dredge, against pollution cleanup expenses and costs. The dredge sank at its mooring, releasing rather considerable quantities of fuel oil into the waters of the harbor. The court held that under the comprehensive general liability policy, the term "sudden and accidental" pollution of navigable waters constituted "property damage" under that portion of the policy covering "physical injury to or destruction of tangible property." That policy had limits of $1,000,000; the WQIS policy had a limit of $350,000. The court pro-rated the assured's recovery against both underwriters on the basis of the monetary limits of the respective policies.

In *Lodrique v. Montegut,*[448] one policy provided that "there shall be no contribution by the company on the basis of double insurance or otherwise." The other policy (a comprehensive general liability policy) provided that it would be "excess above insured's other available collectible insurance." The "escape clause" in the first policy negated any other "available and collectible" insurance and, therefore, it was held that the general liability underwriter was liable to pay any loss the barge owner sustained to the plaintiff employee.

In *Berkeley v. Firemen's Fund,*[449] the owner, a demise charterer, and a sub-bareboat charterer of a fishing vessel were named insureds in a "layered employer's liability policy." The demise charterer also had a separate employer's liability policy and a separate "umbrella" policy. After a casualty at sea, causing deaths and injuries to the crew, all three parties petitioned to limit liability. The loss was found due to the negligence of the sub-bareboat charterer, who was found to be the employer of the crew. The underwriter on the "layered" policy sought to enforce contribution against the other two insurers. It was held that the coverage pri-

---

446. 1981 AMC 1128 (W.D., La., 1981).
447. 1984 AMC 2019 (D.,Ore., 1984). The trial court's decision has been appealed to the Ninth Circuit Court of Appeals and was recently affirmed.
448. 1978 AMC 2272 (E.D., La., 1977).
449. 1976 AMC 856 (W.D., Wash.).

orities should be determined in light of the total policy insuring intent; and that the insurer on the "layered" policy properly should bear the entire loss, as the actual employer of the crew was a named assured but was not a named assured on the other policies; and that the umbrella policy was clearly intended to be excess. In ruling, the court stated in part:

> It is a disfavored approach to resolve disputes among insurance carriers on the basis of dogmatic reliance upon the "other insurance" clauses of respective policies without regard to the intent of the parties as manifested in the overall pattern of insurance coverage.

Interrelationship between Primary and Excess Coverages. It is clear that a primary P & I underwriter owes a good faith duty to take the excess insurer's interests into account along with those of the assured in reaching settlement decisions and to balance those interests just as if the primary insurer were liable for any excess judgment.[450]

In *Nilsen v. Mutual Marine Office, Inc.,*[451] the excess marine P & I policy contained no notice of claims clause. The primary P & I policy did, however, contain a requirement of notice by the assured. The assured gave such notice, and the excess carrier knew that suit had been filed against the primary assured before default judgment was taken. The excess carrier also knew that the primary insurer was bankrupt. The prevailing rule in the insurance industry that the assured or its broker should notify the excess carrier when there is a likelihood that the claim or loss would invade the excess coverage, would not be deemed to vary the terms of the excess carrier's policy, and, therefore, could not justify the excess carrier's disclaimer of liability because of absence of notice.

Occupational Disease. Occupational diseases such as silicosis, developed over an extended period of time, are compensable under P & I policies. Thus, in *Froust v. Coating Specialists,*[452] and *McMillan v. Coating Specialists,*[453] it was held that liability for prolonged exposure to silicon during sandblasting operations falls upon the underwriter covering the risk on the last day of exposure.

Longshoring Exception. Notwithstanding the rather clear exclusions of P & I policies with respect to coverage for payments made, or liability in-

---

450. *Bohemia v. Home Ins. Co.,* 1983 AMC 2770 (D.,Ore.), *aff'd* 725 F.2d 506 (9th Cir., 1984). In the instant case, however, on the facts it was held that the primary insurer did not breach its obligations to the excess insurer. There, no firm settlement demand was made by the wrongful death claimant at or prior to trial.

451. 428 F.Supp. 1375, 1977 AMC 1239 (D.,Mass., 1977).

452. 364 F.Supp. 1154, 1974 AMC 204 (E.D.,La.).

453. 427 F.Supp. 54, 1978 AMC 690 (E.D.,La.).

curred under workmens' compensation laws, the courts almost consistently have sought to interpret such policies so as to provide coverage for such claims under other provisions of the policies. For example, in *Voisin v. Ocean Protein, Inc.*,[454] there were two policies in existence, both of which the court found applied. Of primary interest in this discussion, the court held that the shipowner's P & I policy, which excluded liability to any employee under any compensation act, nonetheless covered a claim based on general maritime law by an employee net mender who worked primarily ashore but was injured on board his employer's vessel while repairing a net. As the court noted, the claim of the plaintiff employee did not arise under any compensation act, but under the general maritime law pertaining to unseaworthiness, a decisional body of law which cannot be interpreted as a compensation act within the meaning of the exclusionary clause of the policy.[455]

Legal Fees and Expenses of Litigation. It is not entirely clear whether legal fees and expenses incurred in defending a claim which presumptively falls within the scope of a P & I are includible as part of the overall limits provided by the policy. To state it in another fashion, if the limit of

454. 321 F.Supp. 173, 1971 AMC 564 (E.D.,La., 1970).
455. In the event, the court held that *both* the P & I policy and an applicable employers' liability policy covered, and recovery by the plaintiff was apportioned between the two insurers. See, also, *Harris v. Olympus Terminals & Transport Co.*, 516 F.2d 922 (5th Cir., 1975) (exclusionary language barring coverage for bodily injury where the insured might be held liable for workmens' compensation claims not applicable where a shore-based employee fell into the hold of a barge and sued his employee/barge owner for breach of warranty of seaworthiness); *Tidewater Oil Co. v. American Steamship Owners Mut. Protection & Indemnity Ass'n*, 1935 AMC 936 (St.,N.Y., 1935) (crewmember assisting in loading of oil on a vessel was injured while working on an adjacent dock. The work being done was not stevedoring work and the stevedoring exception in the P & I policy did not apply); *Brickley v. Offshore Shipyard, Inc.*, 270 F.Supp. 985, 1967 AMC 1886 (E.D.,La., 1967) (essentially the same holding as in *Voisin, supra*); *Parfait v. Jahncke Service, Inc.*, 484 F.2d 296 (5th Cir., 1973) (liability for indemnity under the *Ryan* doctrine covered under an employer's liability policy affording coverage for damages for personal injuries to employees and specifically covering liability resulting from suits brought against others; the exclusion as to master and crew or to employees subject to the LHWCA was narrower in scope than the broad insuring clause of the policy, and thus the indemnity claim was not excluded). Compare, however, *Rodrigues v. Litton Industries Corp.*, 428 F.Supp. 1232, 1977 AMC 1353 (D.,P.R., 1977), where the P & I insurer insured both the longshoremen's employer (a demise charterer) and the registered owner of the vessels on which the longshoremen were injured. Suit was brought by the injured longshoremen under the Puerto Rico direct action statute. The court held that there was no cause of action against the "owners" of the vessels, which had been demise chartered to the longshoremen's employer, and absent any showing of unseaworthiness preceding the demise charters. Thus, there was no "loss covered by the policy" as required under the direct action statute and therefore no recovery. See, also, *Lytle v. Freedom International Carrier, S.A. et al*, 519 F.2d 129, 1975 AMC 2670 (6th Cir.), where a stevedore's excess liability policy contained no specific coverage but was designed to fit on to the insured's primary policy, which covered the stevedore's liability vis-a-vis the shipowner under the *Ryan* doctrine. An endorsement on the excess policy excluding claims arising under "general maritime law" and "admiralty law" was held not sufficient to excuse the insurer from protecting its assured from claims by the shipowner in a longshoreman's suit.

coverage is $100,000 and, say, $20,000 are expended by the P & I underwriter in legal costs and expenses, must the underwriter pay the full
$100,000 limit plus legal fees and costs, or is it permissible to deduct the
$20,000 in fees and costs and pay over only the residue, i.e., $80,000?

The solution appears to be what the policy language states. For example, *Geehan v. Trawler Arlington, Inc.*,[456] involved a seaman's action against
a P & I underwriter and against the excess carrier seeking to satisfy a
judgment in a personal injury action. The excess carrier argued that the
primary P & I underwriter was not entitled to deduct the legal expenses
of the attorney appointed by it to defend the assured-shipowner. The
court held that the language of the policy issued by the primary P & I
underwriter was not ambiguous; that it clearly authorized the primary
underwriter to retain counsel and deduct the counsel fees; and that even
if the policy were ambiguous in this respect, it would not be construed to
benefit the excess underwriter at the expense of the shipowner, an assured under both the primary P & I policy and the excess policy.

By contrast, in *Verrett v. Ordoyne Towing Co., Inc.*,[457] the primary P & I
policy provided that the P & I underwriter was obligated to pay any judgment against its assured as well as defense costs incurred by the insured.
The injured plaintiff sued for personal injuries, settled with the vessel
owner directly, and then sought recovery against both the primary and
excess P & I underwriters. The primary underwriter attempted to deduct the attorneys' fees incurred by itself when sued under a direct action
statute. The court refused to permit this to be done.

In *Bohemia v. Home Ins. Co.*,[458] the policy limit of the primary policy
was $100,000. Legal fees expended in defending a death claim were in

456. 547 F.2d 132, 1976 AMC 2510 (1st Cir., 1976).
457. 1977 AMC 795 (E.D.,La., 1977).
458. 1983 AMC 2770 (D.,Ore.), aff'd 725 F.2d 506 (9th Cir., 1984). See, also, *McKeithen
v. The S.S. Frosta*, 430 F.Supp. 899, 1978 AMC 31 (E.D.,La., 1977), where, in an action involving a collision between a tanker and a ferry, the underwriter insuring the ferry sought a
declaration and interpleader determining that its liability under the policy could not exceed
$300,000 in respect to all claims arising out of the collision. While the court held that the
$300,000 limit was applicable to the claims, it did not include expenses of the underwriter in
filing the interpleader action. The policy expressly provided coverage to the *assured* with
respect to costs and expenses but was silent with respect to fees and expenses incurred by the
underwriter in filing an interpleader action. In *Faris, Ellis et al v. Jacob Towing, Inc.*, 324
So.2d 1284 (La. App. Cir 1977), a law firm retained by the underwriter to defend a maritime
claim against the assured brought an action against the assured for attorney's fees within the
deductible. At first instance, the law firm prevailed. On appeal, the court reversed, holding
that the deductible clause did not include a claim for attorney's fees in representing the
assured where the claim was brought against the assured but the attorneys were employed
by the underwriter. In essence, the court of appeal felt the deductible clause was ambiguous
and could have been phrased more precisely to cover "fees of attorneys selected by the insurer to represent the insured." And see, generally, *Wills v. Aetna Ins. Co.*, 1960 AMC 394
(St.,N.Y., 1959), where the policy language clearly limited the underwriter's obligation to the
policy limit, less the deductible.

excess of $8,000. The judgment was in excess of $177,000. The primary underwriter paid $100,000 less the legal fees; the excess underwriter paid the balance. Apparently, no contention was made by the excess underwriter that the policy limit of the primary policy of $100,000 did not include the legal fees and costs.

Warranties. As noted heretofore (see "Introduction and History," *supra*), there is no implied warranty of seaworthiness in a P & I policy. But the policy (or club rules) may well include or be subject to other warranties, either express or implied, which may affect coverage. This subject is discussed, *infra.*

Insolvency of Assured. It is a fundamental principle of a protection and indemnity policy that it constitutes an *indemnity* policy and not a liability policy. This principle is highlighted in the insuring clause of the ASM form, which commences, "The Association agrees to *indemnify* the Assured against any loss, damage or expense which the Assured shall become liable to pay *and shall pay* . . . " [Emphasis supplied] The interpretation of the various Club rules does not differ.

This principle was directly applied in *Ahmed v. American S.S. Owners Mutual,*[459] where, at first instance, the U.S. District Court for the Northern District of California held that in order to receive reimbursement from a P & I insurer, the assured shipowner must first have actually paid the loss. Construing New York law, the court held that the P & I insurer was not directly liable to seamen judgment creditors of the assured shipowner who had become insolvent, such coverage being indemnity and not liability insurance.

On appeal, the Ninth Circuit affirmed, noting that New York insurance law did not permit a direct action by an injured party against a marine indemnity underwriter. However, the court remanded to the trial court to rule on a contention by the plaintiffs that the provision of New York law violated the Equal Protection clause of the Constitution.

On remand, the trial court held that the New York provision exempting maritime insurance from the general application of the direct action statute did not constitute unlawful discrimination against the plaintiffs as merchant seamen. In doing so, the court relied heavily on *Miller v. American S.S. Owners Mutual,*[460] where the Southern District of New York had ruled on the same issue and concluded that the New York legislature, in excepting marine insurance from the direct action provision for other kinds of insurance, was expressly and primarily concerned with main-

---

459. 444 F.Supp. 569, 1978 AMC 586 (N.D.,Cal.), *aff'd* in part and modified in part, 640 F.2d 993, 1981 AMC 897 (9th Cir., 1981), on remand 1982 AMC 1228 (N.D.,Cal., 1982).
460. 509 F.Supp. 1047, 1981 AMC 903 (S.D.N.Y., 1981).

taining New York regulated maritime insurers on an equal, competitive basis with other insurers who write maritime insurance but which are not jurisdictionally subject to New York's requirement for placement of a direct action clause in their policies.

However, a contrary result was reached in *Weiland v. Pyramid Ventures Group*,[461] construing the Louisiana direct action statute, which expressly forbade any liability insurance "unless it contains provisions to the effect that the insolvency or bankruptcy of the insured shall not release the insurer from the payment of damages for the injuries sustained or loss occasioned during the existence of the policy." In *Weiland*, the P & I underwriters sought cancellation of coverage or a set-off against a personal injury plaintiff's judgment because of the assured shipowner's failure to pay prior "release calls" on account of an insolvency which occurred after the accident. The court held to the contrary, noting that to allow otherwise would enable the insurer to benefit from the assured's insolvency, which would have been in direct contravention to the "liability insurance" statutory provision.[462]

It must be emphasized, however, that a number of states in addition to Louisiana have passed statutes that compel insurers to include policy provisions to the effect that insolvency or bankruptcy of the assured does not relieve the insurers from the payment of damages for injuries or loss sustained during the currency of the policies. If the courts in those states feel constrained to follow *Wilburn Boat Co. v. Fireman's Fund Ins. Co.*,[463] then state law will govern and such statutes will prevail over the general rule and the decisions following it such as *Miller, supra*.

The question seems to be unsettled in Great Britain. The eminent authors of *Arnould* (16th ed.) have this to say:[464]

---

461. 511 F.Supp. 1034. 1981 AMC 2846 (M.D.,La., 1981).

462. See, also, construing Louisiana law, *Olympic Towing Corp. v. Nebel Towing Co.*, 419 F.2d 230, 1969 AMC 1571 (5th Cir.), *cert. den.* 397 U.S. 989 (1970), (1970) 1 Lloyd's Rep. 430, and *Maryland Casualty Co. v. Cushing*, 347 U.S. 409, 1954 AMC 837. See, also, discussion in Chapter XXIV, "Direct Action Statutes," *infra*. Compare, however, *Crown Zellerbach v. Ingram*, 745 F.2d 715, 1985 AMC 305 (5th Cir., 1984), *rev'd en banc*, 783 F.2d 1296, 1986 AMC 1471 (5th Cir., 1986), where *Nebel Towing* was overruled in part, the court *en banc* holding that the P & I club was not liable for sums in excess of the tug's liability limit.

463. 348 U.S. 310, 1955 AMC 467 (1955).

464. *Arnould, The Law of Marine Insurance and Average*, ed. M. Mustill and J. C. B. Gilman, 16th ed. (London: Stevens & Sons, 1981), Sec. 134, citing *Farrell v. Federated Employers' Ins. Ltd.*, (1970) 1 W.L.R. 1400; *Hassett v. Legal & General Assur. Soc. Ltd.*, 63 Ll.L.Rep. 278; *Barrett Bros. (Taxis) Ltd. v. Davies; United Dominions Trust Ltd. v. Eagle Aircraft Ltd.*, (1968) 1 W.L.R. 74; *Murray v. Legal and General Assur. Soc. Ltd.*, (1970) 2 Q.B. 495; *In Re Allobrogia S.S. Corp.*, (1979) 1 Lloyd's Rep. 190. In *In Re Allobrogia*, Slade J. expressed the view that there were substantial grounds for saying that a provision in club rules which purported to make payment by the member a condition precedent to recovery was invalidated by s. 1(3) of the Act of 1930. Whatever may be the rule in Great Britain, in those states in the United States which have direct action statutes such as Louisiana, forbidding policy provisions to the effect that insolvency or bankruptcy of the assured shall not release the underwriter from liability,

Conditions precedent in club policies can be relied upon as a defence in proceeding brought under the Third Parties (Rights Against Insurers) Act 1930, unless waived, except where the rule in question purports directly or indirectly to avoid the contract or to alter the rights of the parties in the event of bankruptcy or winding up of the member. The rules almost always make payment by the member of the claim against him and payment of calls conditions precedent to liability of the association. It has never been decided whether such rules are invalid in the context of proceedings under the Act of 1930, and professional opinion on this question is divided. It is the view of the present editors that there is no logical reason why such rules should not be valid against third party claimants, but it must be recognized that such a conclusion would deprive the Third Parties (Rights Against Insurers) Act 1930 of its efficacy, in the context of a club policy.

Notwithstanding countervailing statutes in some states and inconsistent provisions of direct action statutes, where those do not apply the general principle will be observed.[465]

Indemnity under the Ryan *Doctrine.* As noted heretofore,[466] assuming a seaworthiness obligation on the part of an assured shipowner does exist, and further assuming (where longshoremen may be involved) that Section 905(b) of the LHWCA does not prohibit recovery by way of indemnity, there is authority for the proposition that a *Ryan* right of recovery in indemnity is alive and well, although at least one court has called it a "withered doctrine." But whether or not *Ryan* indemnity is available to a shipowner (and more importantly to his P & I underwriter by way of subrogation), the shipowner and his P & I underwriter are nonetheless exposed to liability for personal injuries and death to persons injured

---

it is clear that P & I club rules which purport to require payment by the assured/member will not be enforced. See *Weiland, supra,* which involved the rules of the West of England Shipowners Mutual Indemnity Corporation.

465. For example, see *Willer v. Twin City Barge,* 1978 AMC 2008 (St.,N.Y.) (P & I underwriter's obligation to indemnify its assured arises, not on the happening of an accident, but only when the assured "shall have paid" the amount of its liability; until such payment is made, there is no "debt" or obligation on the part of the underwriter which can be attached to give a New York court jurisdiction over a non-resident defendant assured); *Diesel Tanker A.C. Dodge, Inc. v. Stewart,* 262 F.Supp. 6, 1966 AMC 1746 (S.D.N.Y.), *aff'd* 376 F.2d 850 (2d Cir.), *cert. den.* 389 U.S. 913 (insured must pay before insurer indemnifies, and where the insured is adjudicated a bankrupt, insurer is held to have a right to refuse to defend personal injury action); *Cucurillo v. American S.S. Owners' Mut.,* 1969 AMC 2334 (St.,N.Y., 1969); *Haun v. Guaranty Security Ins. Co.,* 1969 AMC 2068 (St.,Tenn., 1969). Compare, however, *Stuyvesant Ins. Co. of New York v. Nardelli,* 286 F.2d 600, 1961 AMC 1999 (5th Cir., 1961) (insurer liable for costs of defending even though the costs had not been paid); and *Liman v. American S.S. Owners' Mut.,* 299 F.Supp. 106, 1969 AMC 1669 (S.D.N.Y.), *aff'd* 417 F.2d 627 (2d Cir., 1969), discussed *supra.*

466. See discussion *supra,* "Ryan Warranty."

aboard or in connection with the covered vessel. This was the situation in *Parfait v. Jahncke Service, Inc.*,[467] where the plaintiff was an employee of a maritime contractor who was aboard a dredge to repair a broken cylinder block. Implicitly, the dredge owner recognized its liability and therefore settled. The contest was reduced, therefore, to a claim for indemnity by the dredge owner against the marine contractor and its liability underwriters. The marine contractor had two policies, a general liability policy covering bodily injury claims arising under its workmanlike performance warranty (but excluding bodily injury to any "employee") and an employer's liability policy containing an endorsement excluding "maritime liability," by which apparently was meant injuries sustained by a master or member of the crew of any vessel or by an person in the course of employment subject to the LHWCA. The underwriter on the latter policy contended that the "maritime liability" exclusion excluded both direct liability to employees covered by the LHWCA and *Ryan* warranty liability originating in injuries to such employees. The court held that the "maritime liability" endorsement did not exclude *Ryan* warranty indemnity.

In *Lytle v. Freedom International Carrier, S.A. et al*,[468] a stevedore's excess liability policy contained no specific coverage but was intended to fit on to the insured's primary policy, which covered the stevedore's liability vis-a-vis the shipowner under the *Ryan* doctrine. An endorsement on the excess policy excluding claims arising under "general maritime law" and "admiralty" law was held not sufficient to excuse the insurer from protecting its assured from claims by the shipowner in a longshoreman's suit.

In *Brown v. Ivarans Rederi*,[469] it was held that a longshoreman (or his estate) could not retain both a jury verdict against the ship and the compensation payable under the Longshoremen's Act, although the so-called equitable credit has been rejected by the courts which have considered it.

The problem of overlapping coverage or, worse yet, the possibility of no coverage at all, for *Yaka*-type claims, is amply demonstrated in *Pacific Inland Navigation Co. v. Fireman's Fund Ins. Co.*[470] That case involved a payment by the assured towboat company of $35,000 in settlement to a longshoreman injured aboard one of the assured's barges, who later sued in reliance upon *Reed v. S.S. Yaka.*[471] Thereafter, the assured brought suit against the insurer under the workmen's compensation-type policy it had issued to the assured in which LHWCA coverage had been provided. The court held that the language of the policy did not cover the liability of the assured to an employee injured by reason of the *Yaka*-type action, and that

467. 484 F.2d 296, 1973 AMC 2447 (5th Cir., 1973).
468. 519 F.2d 129, 1975 AMC 2670 (6th Cir.).
469. 545 F.2d 854, 1976 AMC 2212 (3rd Cir.).
470. 406 F.2d 1179, 1969 AMC 17 (9th Cir.).
471. 1963 AMC 1373 (1963).

the policy exclusions limited the coverage to workmens' compensation claims.

Life Salvage

Life salvage is covered under paragraph 1 of the ASM form, but the coverage may be more apparent than real, for, under general admiralty law, the saving of property is a condition precedent to an award for life salvage. Stating it another way, we may say that if a salvor while saving property also saves human life, the salvage award is almost invariably enhanced, and the underwriters on vessel and cargo (assuming the policies cover salvage) will respond.

For a time, the principles of life salvage in the United States and in Great Britain followed a parallel course. Compare, for example, the language of M. R. Brett in *The Renpor*[472] with Judge McCaleb's language in *Sturtevant et al v. The George Nicholaus*,[473] where the principle is enunciated with great clarity that a salvage award for the saving of life alone without the saving of ship, freight, or cargo, is not recoverable in the admiralty courts.

Great Britain first diverged by statutory enactment, the latest expression being Section 544 of the Merchant Shipping Act, 1894. The United States, in the Salvage Act, 1912 (46 U.S.C.A. 727-31), followed suit; but the United States statute is not so liberal as the statute in Great Britain. Essentially, the differences are: in Great Britain, no provision is made for life salvage per se but discretionary *ex gratia* awards may be made by the secretary of state for trade in circumstances where there is total property loss or where the recovered property is insufficient. In the United States, life salvage is not recognized per se, and there is no provision for discretionary ex gratia awards. In Great Britain and the United States, property recovery or assistance is a condition precedent to life salvage, but in the latter both life and property salvage must be performed either actually or substantially on the same occasion, whereas in the former the time element is not considered important. Compare, for example, *The Pacific*[474] with *Re Yamashita-Shinnihan Kisen*[475] and *St. Paul Marine Transp. Corp. v. Cerro Sales Corp. et al.*[476]

In Great Britain, the interests benefited must reward the life salvor; in the United States, the property salvor is obliged to reward the life salvor by sharing the award.

472. (1883) 8 P.D. 115, 5 Asp. M.L.C. 98, C.A.
473. F.Cas. No. 13,578 (E.D.,La., 1853).
474. (1898) P. 170, 8 Asp. M.L.C. 422.
475. 305 F.Supp. 796, 1969 AMC 2102 (W.D.,Wash.).
476. 313 F.Supp. 377, 1970 AMC 1742 (D.,Haw.), 505 F.2d 1115, 1975 AMC 503 (9th Cir.).

However, the Second Circuit, in *Peninsula & Oriental Steam Nav. Co. v. Overseas Oil Carriers, Inc.*,[477] may well be pointing the way to judicial recognition of life salvage where there has been no saving of property. There, a passenger vessel deviated to take on board an ill seaman from a tanker having no medical personnel. Overruling the district court, the Second Circuit held that the passenger vessel's owners were entitled to the reasonable value of the services rendered on the grounds that where admiralty jurisdiction is invoked, quasi-contractual claims may be considered.[478]

Repatriation Expenses

Paragraph 2 of the ASM form provides coverage for:

> Liability for expenses reasonably incurred in necessarily repatriating any member of the crew or any other person employed on board the insured vessel; provided, however, that the assured shall not be entitled to recover any such expenses incurred by reason of the expiration of the shipping agreement, other than by sea perils, or by the voluntary termination of the agreement. Wages shall be recoverable hereunder only when payable under statutory obligation during unemployment due to the wreck or loss of the insured vessel.

There do not appear to have been any reported decisions involving this paragraph.

Collision

Paragraph 3 of the ASM form provides coverage for:[479]

> Liability for loss or damage arising from collision of the insured vessel with another ship or vessel where the liability is of a type, character, or kind which would not be covered in any respect by the following portions of the Four-Fourths Collision Clause in the American Institute Hull Clauses (January 18, 1970) form including the June 4, 1970, Collision Clause Amendment A:[480]

477. 553 F.2d 830, 1977 AMC 283 (2d Cir.).
478. The subject is covered exhaustively and definitively in "Life Salvage in Anglo-American Law," D. Rhidian Thomas, 10, no. 1 *Journal of Maritime Law & Commerce* (Oct., 1978). See, also, Sir Barry Sheen, "Conventions on Salvage," and A. Parks, "The 1910 Brussels Convention, The United States Salvage Act of 1912, and Arbitration of Salvage Cases in the United States," 57 *Tulane Law Review* (June, 1983).
479. English Running Down Clauses, as a general rule, still cover only three-fourths of the collision liability. However, in the American market, four-fourths clauses are customary. This is also true with respect to the English Institute Yacht Clauses (1/8/77) because yachts are not entered in the P & I clubs. For this reason, the yacht clauses include a Protection and Indemnity Clause.
480. It is specifically emphasized that if the vessel covered is a tug, then the collision clause in the hull policy referred to in paragraph 3 of the ASM form is rendered inoperative

And it is further agreed that:

> (a) if the Vessel shall come into collision with any other ship or vessel, and the Assured or the Surety in consequence of the Vessel being at fault shall become liable to pay and shall pay by way of damages to any other person or persons any sum or sums in respect of such collision, the Underwriters will pay the Assured or the Surety, whichever shall have paid, such proportion of such sum or sums so paid as their respective subscriptions hereto bear to the Agreed Value, provided always that their liability in respect to any one such collision shall not exceed their proportionate part of the Agreed Value;
> (b) in cases where, with the consent in writing of a majority (in amount) of Hull Underwriters, the liability of the Vessel has been contested, or proceedings have been taken to limit liability, the Underwriters will also pay a like proportion of the costs which the Assured shall thereby incur or be compelled to pay.

When both vessels are to blame, then, unless the liability of the owners or charterers of one or both such vessels becomes limited by law, claims under the Collision Liability clause shall be settled on the principles of Cross-Liabilities as if the owners or charterers of each vessel had been compelled to pay to the owners or charterers of the other such vessels such one-half or other proportion of the latter's damages as may have been properly allowed in ascertaining the balance or sum payable by or to the Assured in consequence of such collision.

The principles involved in this clause shall apply to the case where both vessels are the property, in part or in whole, of the same owners or charterers, all questions of responsibility and amount of liability as between the two vessels being left to the decision of a single Arbitrator, if the parties can agree upon a single Arbitrator, or failing such agreement, to the decision of Arbitrators, one to be appointed by the Assured and one to be appointed by the majority (in amount) of Hull Underwriters interested; two Arbitrators chosen to choose a third Arbitrator before entering upon the reference, and the decision of such single Arbitrator, or of any two of such three Arbitrators, appointed as above, to be final and binding.

Providing that this clause shall in no case extend to any sum which the Assured or the Surety may become liable to pay in consequence of, or with respect to:

---

by Clause 30 of the ASM form, and instead, the collision clause in the American Institute Tug Form, January, 1984 (rev. Nov. 30, 1959), is deemed incorporated in lieu thereof. The special rules applicable to collisions by tugs and their tows with other vessels are discussed in detail *infra*.

(a) removal or disposal of obstructions, wrecks or their cargoes under statutory powers or otherwise pursuant to law;
(b) injury to real or personal property of every description;
(c) the discharge, spillage, emission or leakage of oil, petroleum products, chemicals or other substances of any kind or description whatsoever;
(d) cargo or other property on or the engagements of the Vessel;
(e) loss of life, personal injury or illness.

Provided further that exclusions (b) and (c) above shall not apply to injury to other vessels or property thereon except to the extent that such injury arises out of any action taken to avoid, minimize or remove any discharge, spillage, emission or leakage described in (c).

Provided, however, that insurance hereunder shall not extend to any liability, whether direct or indirect, in respect of engagements of or the detention or loss of time of the insured Vessel.

(a) Claims hereunder shall be settled on the principles of Cross-Liabilities to the same extent only as provided in the four-fourths Collision Clause above mentioned.
(b) Where both vessels are the property, in part or in whole, of the same Owners or Charterers, claims hereunder shall be settled on the basis of the principles set forth in the four-fourths Collision Clause above mentioned.
(c) Claims hereunder shall be separated among and take the identity of the several classes of liability for loss, damage, and expense enumerated in this policy and each class shall be subject to the deductions, inclusions, exclusions and special conditions applicable in respect to such class.
(d) Notwithstanding the foregoing, the Association shall not be liable for any claims hereunder where the various liabilities resulting from such collision, or any of them, have been compromised, settled or adjusted without the written consent of the Association.

By contrast, Rule 15(D) of the Rules of the West of England Ship Owners Mutual Protection and Indemnity Association (Luxembourg) provides collision coverage rather more simply as follows:

(1) For the one fourth proportion (without regard to any limit as to the amount referred to therein) of the collision liability not covered under the Running Down Clause referred to in Rule 21 and set out in the First Schedule.[481]

481. Rule 21, in relevant part, provides that unless otherwise agreed in writing the Association is not liable to indemnify an insured owner against any liabilities, costs, or ex-

(2) For the excess collision liability not recoverable under the Hull and Excess Liability Policies (referred to in Rule 21) solely by reason of such liability exceeding the maximum amount recoverable under said policies. PROVIDED THAT:

> (a) Should an insured vessel come into collision with another vessel belonging wholly or in part to the same Owner, the Owner of the insured vessel (being the insured Owner) shall have the same rights of recovery from the Association as he would have were the other vessel entirely the property of Owners not interested in the insured vessel.
>
> (b) When both vessels are to blame for the Collision then unless the liability of the Owners of one or both of such vessels becomes limited by law, claims under this Sub-Rule shall be settled on the principle of cross liabilities, as if the Owner of each vessel had been compelled to pay to the Owner of the other of such vessels one-half or such other proportion of the latter's damages, as may have been properly allowed in ascertaining the balance or sum payable by or to the former in consequence of the Collision.

Special attention is drawn to Rule 21.

The interrelationship between the underwriters' exposure under the Running Down Clause and the P & I policy is clearly demonstrated in *Trinidad Corp. v. American S.S. Owners Mut. P & I Ass'n*.[482] In that case, the insured vessel ran into a dredge's pipeline and pontoons, forcing the pontoons into another vessel and causing damage to the pipeline, the pontoons, and the other vessel. After fully discussing the English decisions, the court held that the collision did not occur to the dredge itself and, consequently, fell within the ambit of the P & I policy which, in that instance, covered liability for damage to "any fixed or moveable object or property whatsoever, except another vessel or craft."

What is a "Collision". What is a "collision" can be troublesome. For example, in *Lehigh & Wilkes-Barre Coal Co. v. Globe & Rutgers Fire Ins. Co. (The Honeybrook)*,[483] barges in tow struck rock abutments and the bank of a canal. The court held this was not a collision as comprehended by the Running Down Clause, and reviewed most extensively the authorities.

---

penses to the extent that the same would be recoverable if the insured vessel were at all times fully insured under hull and excess liability policies on terms not less wide than those of the standard Lloyd's policy with Institute Time Clauses (hulls) (including the Running Down Clause) attached. The first schedule referred to sets forth verbatim the Running Down Clause in the Institute Time Clauses (hulls).

482. 229 F.2d 57, 1956 AMC 1464 (2d Cir.).

483. 6 F.2d 736, 1925 AMC 717 (2d Cir.), 26 Ll.L.Rep. 82.

See, however, *Mancommunidad del Vapor "Frumiz" v. Royal Exchange Assurance*,[484] where the policy was on F.P.A. conditions except damage received by "collision with any object (ice included) other than water." The vessel came in contact with rocky ground and stranded. The court held that a collision with an "object" had taken place.

In *France (William) Fenwick & Co., Ltd. v. Merchants' Marine Ins. Co., Ltd.*,[485] the insured vessel negligently came in contact with a vessel she was overtaking. The other vessel, as a direct result, came into contact with a third vessel to which a great amount of damage was done. The insured vessel was held liable and paid sums in respect of the damage to both vessels and brought suit against underwriters to recover the sums paid. It was held that underwriters were liable under the collision clause for the damages to both vessels.

The American cases on what is a collision are rather numerous. For example, in *London Assurance v. Companhia de Moagens do Barreiro*,[486] the Supreme Court observed that a vessel may be in collision with another vessel where only one is in motion and the other tied to a wharf. Moreover, an impairment of the seaworthiness of a vessel by contact with another vessel is not necessary to constitute a collision where, as a result of the impact, cracks from $\frac{1}{2}$ to $1\frac{1}{2}$ inches wide for a distance of 11 feet in the hull plating were made.

Generally speaking, contact with a sunken or floating obstruction of undetermined nature is not considered a collision within the meaning of the term as used in insurance policies, and this is unquestionably so where the Running Down Clause is specifically limited to another "vessel." However, the American cases are far from being consistent. For example, in *Baum v.. Girard Fire & Marine Insurance Co.*[487] and *Cline v. Western Assurance Co.*,[488] striking a submerged or sunken object was held not to be a collision, but in *Carroll Towing Co. v. Aetna Ins. Co.*,[489] it was held that a collision included an accidental contact between a vessel and a floating but non-navigable object, and in *Burnham v. China Mutual Ins. Co.*,[490] coverage for collision was found where the vessel came in contact with a wreck, sunk several hours before, the cost of whose raising would have exceeded her value when raised.[491] By contrast, in *Harding v. American Universal Ins. Co.*,[492] the court held that striking a submerged object was a peril of the

484. (1926) 26 Ll.L.Rep. 191, 17 Asp. M.L.C. 205.
485. (1915) 3 K.B. 290, 13 Asp. M.L.C. 106, C.A.
486. 167 U.S. 149 (1896).
487. 228 N.C. 525, 46 S.E. 2d 324 (1948).
488. 101 Va. 496, 44 S.E. 700 (1903).
489. 196 N.Y.S. 198, 203 App.Div. 430 (1922).
490. 189 Mass. 100, 75 N.E. 74 (1905).
491. Compare, in this respect, *Chandler v. Blogg*, (1898) 1 Q.B. 32, 8 Asp. M.L.C. 349, where the object collided with was a sunken barge which, however, was raised the next day and sailed into port. The court held the collision had been with a "vessel."
492. 130 So.2d 86 (St.,Fla., 1961), 1962 AMC 2423.

sea as that term is used in a policy and did not fall within the collision coverage of the policy. And in *Hanover Ins. Co. v. Sonfield*,[493] the court concluded that the term "collision" generally had reference to contact between two vessels or between a vessel while navigating and some other floating object and, also, according to some authorities, contact between a vessel and various fixed objects such as piers, docks, pilings, and wharves.

It has been held that a deliberate running into a perfectly apparent obstruction, with the hope or expectation that the vessel will survive the collision, is not a collision within the meaning of an insurance policy.[494] However, the pounding together of vessels in a common tow has been deemed to be a collision within the terms of the policy.[495]

The English cases are interesting and instructive on what is a collision. For example, in *Reischer v. Borwick*,[496] the vessel was insured for collision damage but not as to "perils of the sea." The vessel ran against a snag in the river that caused a leak, which was temporarily plugged. Later, the vessel was being towed to safety when the plug fell out because of the motion of the vessel through the water. It was held that the proximate cause of the damage to the vessel was the initial collision with the snag.

In *Union Marine Ins. Co. v. Borwick*,[497] the insured vessel was driven by high winds and seas upon an artificial bank of boulders outside a breakwater of a harbor. The loss was held to have been caused by a collision.

France (William) Fenwick & Co. Ltd. v. Merchants' Marine Ins. Co., Ltd.[498] involved the Running Down Clause in a hull policy, and where insured vessel came into slight contact with another vessel which, in consequence thereof and while navigating, collided with another vessel and damaged it, the underwriters on the hull policy were held liable for damages to the third vessel. By contrast, *The Schodack*[499] involved the coverage of the P & I policy to a similar set of facts. As the Running Down Clause in the hull policy plainly covered the damage to the third vessel, and as the P & I policy (as is customary) expressly excluded losses covered by the ordinary form of hull policy, there was no coverage under the P & I policy. The rationale is, of course, that the collision blow, in such a three-vessel incident, is merely transmitted through the hull of the vessel interposed between the vessel insured and the vessel damaged and there is nonetheless a collision between the insured vessel and the third vessel.

---

493. 386 S.W.2d 160 (St.,Tex., 1965)
494. *Newton Creek Towing Co. v. Aetna Ins. Co.*, 48 N.Y.S. 927, 23 App.Div. 152 (1897), *rev'd* 163 N.Y. 114, 57 N.E. 302 (1900).
495. *Tice Towing Line v. Western Assur. Co.*, 214 N.Y.S. 637, 216 App.Div. 202.
496. [1894] 2 Q.B. 548.
497. [1895] 2 Q.B. 279.
498. [1915] 3 K.B. 290.
499. 89 F.2d 8, 1937 AMC 548 (2d Cir.).

What Is a "Ship or Vessel". As noted heretofore in Chapter XIX, "Running Down Clause," *supra,* what is or is not a "ship or vessel" can be most troublesome. For example, in *Chandler v. Blogg,*[500] the object collided with was a sunken barge which was raised the next day and sailed into her home port. The court held that there was a collision between two "vessels." In *Pelton S.S. Co., Ltd. v. North of England Protecting & Indemnity Ass'n: The Zelo)*[501] the insured vessel collided with the wreck of a sunken vessel. Shortly after the latter vessel had sunk, salvage efforts had begun, but these efforts were unsuccessful. The collision with the insured vessel so damaged her that further salvage efforts would have been fruitless. The assured brought suit against the hull underwriters under the Running Down Clause, but they declined to pay, whereupon the assured claimed against the P & I underwriters. There being a three-fourths Running Down Clause, the P & I underwriters paid one-fourth of the loss but contended that since the wreck was a "vessel" at the time of the collision, they were not liable for the remaining three-quarters. The court upheld the contention on the ground that at the time of the collision the owners of the wreck had a "reasonable expectation" of completely recovering her.

In *Bennett S.S. Co. v. Hull Mutual S.S. Protecting Society,*[502] the insured vessel ran into fishing nets attached to and extending from a fishing vessel which was about a mile distant from the insured vessel; there was no contact between the hulls of the two vessels. It was held that there was no collision with any other ship or vessel within the meaning of the usual Running Down Clause.

In *Polpen Shipping Co., Ltd. v. Commercial Union Assur. Co., Ltd.,*[503] the insured vessel collided with a flying boat. It was held that the flying boat was not a "ship or vessel" under the Running Down Clause.

In *Merchants' Marine Insurance Co., Ltd. v. North of Eng-land Protecting & Indemnity Ass'n,*[504] the insured vessel collided with a pontoon crane. Under the rules of the association, the assured was protected against one-fourth of any damages arising out of a collision with a "ship or vessel" and under another rule, against the whole of any damage to "any harbour, dock . . . or any fixed or moveable things, other than ships or vessel." The court held the assured was entitled to collect as to the whole of the damage, as the pontoon crane was not a ship or vessel within the rules.

In *Halvorsen v. Aetna Ins. Co.,*[505] the P & I policy insured a tug against liability for damage to any buoy, beacon, etc., but with an exclusionary clause against liability for damage arising out of or having relation to the

500. [1889] 1 Q.B. 32, 8 Asp. M.L.C. 349.
501. (1925) 22 Ll.L.Rep. 510, K.B.D.
502. [1914] 3 K.B. 57, 12 Asp. M.L.C. 522, C.A.
503. [1943] 1 All E.R. 162, K.B.D., 74 Ll.L.Rep. 157, C.A., 1943 AMC 438.
504. (1926) 26 Ll.L.Rep. 201, C.A.
505. 1954 AMC 1996 (St.,Wash.).

towage of any other vessel or craft. During a tow of a raft of logs, the tug's towline fouled in a government beacon. The court held that the tow of logs did not constitute a "vessel or craft," and consequently the exclusionary clause was inapplicable.

In *Wheeler v. South British Fire & Marine Ins. Co.*,[506] the assured had leave to tow vessels. In attempting to tow a derelict wreck upside down, the assured lost his ship. The court held that the derelict was not a "vessel."

In *Dresser v. Fidelity & Guaranty*,[507] the insured vessel collided with a jackup drilling rig while the rig was jacked up out of the water in preparation for drilling. The court held that it was not a collision with a "vessel" for policy coverage purposes.

By contrast, in *Re Margetts & Ocean Accident & Guarantee Corp.*,[508] the assured's tug was damaged by striking upon a vessel's anchor, to which the vessel was riding attached by a chain. The court held that a collision with a "vessel" had occurred and, therefore, the underwriters on the Running Down Clause were liable.

And in *Coelleda-Swallow*,[509] the object collided with was a former naval sloop, stripped of her fittings and for many years used as a storage vessel for gunpowder. The sloop had been left permanently at anchor and was not attached or moored to the shore. The arbitrator held that the sloop was a "ship or vessel" under the Running Down Clause of the hull policy.

The American cases involving the definition of a "vessel" are exceedingly numerous, although not necessarily in the context of construing the term in the Running Down Clause or a P & I policy. These cases involved, for the most part, questions of admiralty jurisdiction for the purpose of determining whether a maritime lien for necessaries would be imposed, or whether a floating object was a vessel for the purpose of determining seaman status under the Jones Act. They will be found cited in Chapter XIX, "The Running Down Clause."

Cross-Liability versus Single Liability. It will be remembered that paragraph 3 of the ASM form expressly contains cross-liabilities and Sister Ship clauses essentially similar to those found in the hull collision clause.

In *New York & Cuba Mail S.S. Co. v. American S.S. Owners' Mutual Protection & Indemnity Ass'n (Hamilton-Mexico)*,[510] the vessel owner was insured under a four-fourths Running Down Clause, with settlement on the basis of cross-liabilities. The vessel was also entered in a P & I club. In a mutual

506. (1899) 6 W.N. (N.S.W.) 39 (Aus.).
507. 580 F.2d 806 (5th Cir., 1978).
508. [1901] 2 K.B. 792, 9 Asp. M.L.C. 217, D.C.
509. 1932 AMC 1044 (Arb., N.Y., 1932).
510. 72 F.2d 694, 1934 AMC 1090, *cert.den.* 293 U.S. 622, 1934 AMC 1594.

fault collision, the court held that the vessel owner could recover from the club only the balance of cargo liability on the principle of single liability. Moreover, the vessel was held liable for only the amount of direct damage to the other vessel's cargo, and not for the amount of its contributions in general average.

The result under admiralty law where two vessels collide and both are at fault is that the owner of the less damaged vessel pays to the owner of the other vessel the difference between one-half of the damages sustained by one and one-half of the damages sustained by the other. This creates only a single liability against the less damaged vessel. See *Stoomvaart Maatschappiy Nederland v. Peninsular and Oriental Steam Navigation Co.*[511] The clause relating to settlement on the basis of cross-liabilities was added to the Running Down Clause as a consequence of that case, and of *London S.S. Owners' Ins. Co v. Grampian S.S. Co.*[512] However, as the clause notes, this does not apply where the liability of one or both vessels is limited by law.

In *Diesel Tanker A.C. Dodge v. Stewart,*[513] the vessel *Michael* made a recovery under the principle of single liability against the vessel *Dodge* by reason of having made some $610,360 in payments to settle third-party claims, but, since the *Dodge* limited its liability, was unable to recover. The court had held that the *Michael,* in making such voluntary and reasonable settlements with cargo, death, and injury claimants, did not become the assignee of such claimants, and therefore the vessels involved were required to present their claims to each other as single sums of loss suffered by each. The *Dodge,* after having been paid in full by its hull underwriters, including $75,000 in excess insurance coverage against fire perils, then filed suit against its P & I underwriters, contending that were it not for the *Michael* having paid the third-party claims, the *Dodge* would have recovered, on balance, the sum of $170,515.94, being one-half the difference between the hull claim of the *Michael* and the total loss value of the *Dodge,* plus standby wreck and salvage expenses. Although the court found that the P & I policy provided for the use of the principle of cross-liabilities, such principle could be used only to the same extent as that provided in the hull policy Running Down Clause. The court said, in part:

> . . . Since the liability of the owner of the *Dodge* has been limited, it follows that the cross-liabilities theory principle mentioned in . . . the P & I policy could not be used even if the libelant had incurred a liability for loss under Clause 4. Therefore, the libelant could only recover under the P & I policies on the principle of strict indemnity and

511. (1882) 7 App.Cas. 795, [1881-85] All E.R. Rep. 342, 4 Asp. M.L.C. 567, H.L.
512. (1890) 24 Q.B.D. 663, 6 Asp. M.L.C. 506, C.A.
513. 262 F.Supp. 6, 1966 AMC 1746 (S.D.N.Y.).

since libelant has already been reimbursed for what it has actually paid, it is entitled to no further recovery under the P & I policies.

For applications of the Sister-Ship Clause, see the discussion in Chapter XIX, "The Running Down Clause," *supra,* involving *Augusta—Detroit,*[514] and *Ariosa and D-22.*[515]

In a nightmarish chain of proximate causation, both hull and P & I underwriters paid losses in *New York Trap Rock Co.*[516] In that case a barge in a large tow in the Hudson River listed, dumped its cargo, and then righted itself, sustaining damage. Part of its cargo struck an adjacent barge, damaging it so that it capsized, damaging other barges. In analyzing the hull cover, P & I cover, and the excess liability cover, it was held that (1) the hull cover was liable for the direct hull loss to the insured barge; (2) the hull cover and the P & I cover were liable for the loss to adjacent barges, the Running Down Clause up to its limit (minus deductible) and the P & I cover for the balance (minus its deductible); and (3) the excess cover was not liable for anything as the losses were within the limits of the primary coverage.

In the *Massmar,*[517] the vessel in tow sustained damage by stranding, owing partly to negligence of the leading tug and partly to negligence of the tug captain acting as pilot on board the vessel in tow. It was held that loss should fall equally upon the hull and P & I underwriters where both the joint tortfeasors were proceeded against by the party suffering the damages.

In certain circumstances, as where the vessel carries insufficient hull insurance to pay off collision losses in full, an "excess" collision liability may result. This was the situation in *Landry v. Steamship Mut. Underwriting Association,*[518] There, the owner had insured his vessel for $20,000 and obtained a P & I policy for $50,000. The vessel collided with another, whose damages amounted to $24,000 plus. The vessel owner paid off the $24,000 liability, was reimbursed $20,000 by his hull underwriters, and thereafter brought suit against the P & I underwriters for the difference of $4,000. Much to the surprise of the underwriters, the court held that the vessel owner could recover for the excess liability from the P & I underwriters. As a consequence, some P & I clubs and underwriters amended their rules or policies to exclude this excess liability of which paragraph 29(c) of the ASM form is an example. It provides that there shall be no liability by reason of:

---

514. 290 F. 685, 1923 AMC 754, 1923 AMC 816, 1924 AMC 872, *aff'd* 5 F.2d 773, 1925 AMC 756 (4th Cir.).

515. 144 F.2d 262, 1944 AMC 1035 (2d Cir.), *cert.den.* 323 U.S. 797 (1944).

516. 1956 AMC 469 (Arb.).

517. 1942 AMC 227 (Arb.).

518. 177 F.Supp. 142, 1960 AMC 54 (D.,Mass.), 281 F.2d 482, 1960 AMC 1650 (lst Cir.).

Any loss, damage, sacrifice or expense of a type, character or kind which would be payable under the terms of a policy written on the American Institute Hull Clauses (January 18, 1970) Form including the June 4, 1970 Collission Clause Amendment A, and a policy written on the American Institute Increased Value and Excess Liabilities Clauses (January 18, 1970) Form *whether or not the insured vessel is fully covered under those policies by insurance and excess insurance sufficient in amount to pay in full, and without limit all such loss, damage, sacrifice or expense.* [Emphasis added]

As noted, *supra,* if the insured vessel is a tug, the reference in paragraph 29(c) to the AIH (January 18, 1970) form should read "American Institute Tug Form, January, 1954 (revised November 30, 1959)."

See, however, *Stuyvesant Insurance v. Leloup Shrimp,*[519] where the P & I policy excluded liability "in connection with any accident covered under the Four-Fourths Running Down Clause." The court held that the P & I underwriter was not required to pay a $21,500 difference between a $34,000 judgment against the insured in collision litigation and the $12,500 for which the insurer was liable under the Running Down Clause.

It should be noted that it is immaterial whether or not the assured under a P & I policy actually procures the hull insurance (with Running Down Clause) required by the terms of the P & I policy. This was the holding in *DeBardeleben Coal Corp. v. P & I Underwriting Syndicate,*[520] where the P & I cover excluded any loss, damage, or expense that would be payable under the terms of the American Tug Syndicate form of policy on hull and machinery, etc., whether or not the vessel were fully covered by such insurance sufficient in amount to pay such loss, damage, or expense. The court held that the exclusionary provision was unambiguous and it was immaterial whether or not the assured actually procured and maintained the required insurance.

It is emphasized that the cross-liabilities provision applies only to the Running Down Clause. If there is reinsurance on terms different from the primary hull cover (which contains the Running Down Clause), then the reinsuring underwriter may not recover against the primary underwriter for any difference in the sums paid by them between single liability and the principles of cross-liabilities. This was made clear in *Young v. Merchants' Marine Insurance Co.*[521] There, the primary underwriters issued a policy on a vessel for total loss, and also for three-fourths of the collision liability on the principle of cross-liabilities. However, they reinsured only

519. 333 F.Supp. 233, 1962 AMC 1286 (S.D.,Tex.).
520. 34 So.2d 62 (St.,La., 1948).
521. [1932] 2 K.B. 705.

for total loss. The insured vessel collided with another, both vessels were held to blame, and the insured vessel's one-half of the damages was exceeded by the damages to the other vessel, as a consequence of which the insured vessel had to pay, under the admiralty rule of single liability, one-half of the difference. The primary underwriters' payments to the vessel owners for total loss and under the Running Down Clause were calculated on the principle of cross-liabilities. The reinsurer sought a credit in respect of the other vessel's liability on the principle of cross-liability, but the court held that since the reinsurer was only a reinsurer for total loss and not with respect to the Running Down Clause coverage, the reinsurer was not entitled to such credit.

It will be seen that paragraph 3 of the ASM form covers the liability for loss of or damage to any other vessel or craft or the freight thereof, or property on such other vessel or craft, caused by collision with the insured vessel, subject, always to the qualification that such liability would not be covered by full insurance under a four-fourths Running Down Clause.

What happens, then, when the insured vessel collides with another vessel, each vessel is at fault, both vessels are damaged, and the cargo on each is damaged or lost? The American rule, exemplified by *The Chattahoochee*,[522] and further expanded by *U.S. v. Atlantic Mutual Ins. Co.*,[523] creates a Pandora's box of troubles.

In this connection, it must be remembered that the liability of a shipowner in this country to the cargo carried aboard his vessel is governed by either the Harter Act or the Carriage of Goods by Sea Act, unless, of course, the carriage is on the basis of a private contract of affreightment. Under either the United States system or the continental system, each vessel pays its proper share of hull damages to the other vessel, and under the Harter Act, the Carriage of Goods by Sea Act, or the Hague Rules in force in Europe, a shipowner is not liable to the cargo for cargo damage caused by the negligent navigation of the vessel by its master or crew. But under the collision law of the United States, in a both-to-blame situation, a cargo owner can recover in full from the non-carrying vessel, whereas in Europe under the Brussels Convention cargo recovers from the non-carrying vessel its damages in the same proportion as the vessel's fault.

To understand how this anomalous situation was created, it is necessary to understand the earlier cases which arose under the Harter Act. In *The Irrawaddy*,[524] the vessel stranded. Cargo was jettisoned and expenses incurred in getting the vessel off. The vessel owner then claimed contribution in general average from the remaining cargo. There was no clause

522. 173 U.S. 540, 19 S.Ct. 491, 43 L.ed. 801 (1899).
523. 343 U.S. 236, 1952 AMC 659 (1952).
524. 171 U.S. 187, 43 L.ed. 130 (1898).

in the bill of lading providing for such contributions. The Supreme Court held that the Harter Act operated to relieve the vessel owner of negligence under certain circumstances but did not, of its own force and effect, create a right of general average contribution where the loss was caused by negligent navigation.

A few years later, the court had before it *The Jason*.[525] The facts were almost identical except that in *The Jason* the bill of lading contained the general average contribution clause which today bears the name of the "Jason Clause." Essentially, the clause merely provides that where the carrier has exercised due diligence to make his vessel seaworthy and properly manned, equipped, and supplied, both cargo and the shipowner shall contribute in general average just as if the loss had not occurred from negligent navigation. The Supreme Court held the clause valid.

Meanwhile, a few years before, the Supreme Court had decided *The Chattahoochee*.[526] That case involved a collision between the *Chattahoochee* and the schooner *Golden Rule*. Both vessels were at fault. Keeping in mind that under the American rule relating to division of damages in mutual fault collision cases each vessel is liable for one-half of the total damages, the result is that the vessel suffering the smaller loss pays the other vessel one-half of the difference between its loss and that of the first vessel. In computing these amounts, the damages paid by the non-carrying vessel to the owners of the cargo on the carrying vessel are included as a part of the non-carrying vessel's damages. The net result is that the carrying vessel is indirectly liable for and pays one-half of the damages sustained by the cargo aboard it, even though under the Harter Act or the Carriage of Goods by Sea Act, it would normally be relieved of liability to the cargo aboard it as a result of negligent navigation.

In *The Chattahoochee*, this anomaly was squarely presented and litigated, the carrying vessel claiming that the Harter Act should insulate it against such a result. The Supreme Court held that the Act was not intended to affect the liabilities of the two vessels under the both-to-blame collision rule.

As a result of *Chattahoochee*, carriers began inserting both-to-blame clauses in their bills of ladings. The clause, in substance, provides that where both vessels are at fault the cargo owner reimburses his carrier for any amount the carrier has had to pay to the non-carrying vessel, or has had set off against it by reason of the non-carrier having paid the cargo owner's loss. And so another rather awkward situation was created; i.e., if only one vessel is at fault, cargo on the other vessel can recover its full loss, but if both vessels are at fault, the cargo could recover only half its loss.

525. 225 U.S. 32, 56 L.ed. 969 (1912).
526. 173 U.S. 540, 43 L.ed. 901 (1899).

The interplay between these two conflicting interests came before the Supreme Court in *U.S. v. Atlantic Mutual Ins. Co.*[527] whereupon the Supreme Court held the both-to-blame clause invalid, finding that there was no indication in the Harter Act to change the basic American rule of sharing losses equally when both vessels are to blame. The net result, of course, was to reinforce the *Chattahoochee* rule and invalidate contractual attempts of the carriers to offset it.[528]

Thus, not only were the carriers placed in an awkward position—so were the P & I underwriters; for if both vessels are guilty of negligent navigation, it is to the advantage of the P & I underwriters to establish that the other, or non-carrying vessel, was free from fault. That is, it is to their advantage to seek to establish a sole fault situation even if this imposes liability on the vessel they have insured, whereas in a both-to-blame situation they will pay half the damages of the carrying vessel's cargo.

Apparently, the new proportionate fault rule established in *U.S. v. Reliable Transfer Co.*,[529] has not altered the situation, although arguably it could be said that *Reliable Transfer* did change the rule. See, for example, *Vana Trading Co. v. S.S. Mette Skou*,[530] and *Gulfcoast Transit Co. v. Anco Princess*.[531] In *Gulfcoast*, a collision occurred between a tug and its tow and a tanker. A large quantity of cargo on board the tanker was lost, for which its owners claimed damages. At trial, blame was apportioned by the court at 85 percent to the tanker and 15 percent to the tug. The court held that the cargo owners were barred from recovering from the carrying tanker because of the statutory exoneration from navigational errors in the Carriage of Goods by Sea Act, but that they could recover in full from the tug because some blame had been attached to her. The tug owner could then, in its own right, recover 85 percent of its liability to the cargo owners from the tanker owner.[532]

527. 343 U.S. 236, 1952 AMC 659 (1952).

528. *Atlantic Mutual* involved, however, a common carrier and the interplay of the clause with the Harter Act and Cogsa. The Supreme Court expressly laid its decision on public policy with respect to *common carriers*. Thus, such a clause in a private contract of affreightment, or, for example, under a charter party where the charterer's goods utilize the full carrying capacity of the vessel and no bills of lading are issued, would be valid. See *American Union Transport, Inc. v. U.S.*, 1976 AMC 1480 (N.D.,Cal.).

529. 421 U.S. 397, 1975 AMC 541 (1975).

530. 556 F.2d 100, 1977 AMC 702 (2d Cir.).

531. 1978 AMC 2471 (E.D.,La.), [1978] 1 Lloyd's Rep. 293. See, also, *Alamo Chemical Transp. Co. v. M/V Overseas Valdes*, 469 F.Supp. 203, 1979 AMC 2033 (E.D.,La.).

532. See, however, *Re Malaysia Overseas Lines, Ltd.*, 1976 AMC 1287 (S.D.N.Y.); *Matter of Flota Mercante Grancolumbiana, S.A.*, 440 F.Supp. 704, 1979 AMC 156, *aff'd* without opinion 573 F.2d 1290 (2d Cir., 1978), *cert.den.* 436 U.S. 907 (1978); and *Edmonds v. Compagnie Generale Transatlantique*, 443 U.S. 256, 1979 AMC 1167 (1979) where the Supreme Court said in a footnote:

. . . *Reliable Transfer* merely changed the apportionment from equal division to division on the basis of relative fault. But we did not upset the rule that the plaintiff may recover from one of the colliding vessels the damage concurrently caused by the negligence of both.

The anomaly still existing will unquestionably lead to forum shopping, since under American law cargo owners can recover in full from a negligent non-carrying vessel, provided the vessel is solvent and cannot limit its liability. This is so because under American law those in control of negligent vessels are jointly and severally liable to cargo, and the cargo owner may elect to sue either vessel for the entire amount of his damages.[533] Obviously, in most instances the cargo owner would sue the non-carrying vessel, as the carrying vessel could well be insulated from liability by the Harter Act or Cogsa. Having recovered from the non-carrying vessel, the latter, in turn, could claim contribution from the carrying vessel by reason of the computation of damages on principles of single liability.[534]

A classic illustration of the evils of forum shopping will be found in *The Giancinto Motta*.[535] In that case the *World Mermaid* collided with the *Giancinto Motta* by reason of the negligent navigation of both vessels. The *Motta* was lost, and her owners claimed damages of about £500,000; the cargo on the *Motta* was lost, and its owners claimed £1,350,000; the *Mermaid* was damaged, and her owners claimed £250,000. Two sets of proceedings were instituted. In the United States, the cargo owners' claim was settled by the payment of $2,485,880.37; in England, the owners of the *Motta* and the *Mermaid* were parties in a suit in which liability was established on the basis of equal blame. According to English law, the limitation fund of the *Mermaid* was £845,705; the owners of the *Motta* were not liable to the cargo owners for the loss of the cargo by virtue of the Hague Rules, which applied to the contracts of carriage. The questions before the court were whether and to what extent the damages recoverable by the owners of the *Mermaid* from the owners of the *Motta* included the cargo claim; and whether, assuming the owners of the *Mermaid* had a right to limit liability, they were entitled to retain out of the limitation fund a sum in respect of the whole or any part of the cargo claim or, alternatively, to have the whole or any part of the cargo claim taken into account in the distribution of the fund.

It was held by the Queen's Bench division (Admiralty Court) that there would be judgment for the owners of the *Motta*. While the owners of the *Mermaid* were entitled to be credited in the distribution of their limitation fund in respect of the cargo claim, the amount of the credit could not exceed the amount of the dividend which would have been receivable by the cargo owners from such fund if they had brought their claim against it instead of enforcing payment in respect of it in the United States. Con-

---

533. *The Alabama and the Gamecock*, 92 U.S. 695 (1875); *The Atlas*, 93 U.S. 302 (1876).
534. See *The Chattahoochee, supra; The Juniata*, 93 U.S. 337; and *The Sapphire*, 85 U.S. 51 (1873).
535. [1977] 2 Lloyd's Rep. 221.

sequently, the cargo owners were only entitled to bring a claim against the fund for 50 percent of their loss.

It is clear that until the United States adopts *in toto* the proportionate fault rule of the Brussels Convention, or the U. S. Supreme Court addresses the problem directly and effects a change, so that the right of cargo to proceed against the non-carrying vessel is limited to the proportionate fault of the latter, this anomaly will continue to plague assureds and the P & I underwriters.

Consequential Damages Arising from Collisions. Generally speaking, running down clauses have provided cover only for physical damage to the other vessel collided with, and no coverage is provided with respect to damages by way of detention of the vessel for repairs, or losses sustained by the other vessel because she cannot carry out her engagements.[536]

Nearly all running down clauses in current use expressly exclude, of course, *inter alia*, "engagements of the vessel" and "loss of life, personal injury or illness." If these are to be covered at all, it can only be by virtue of the P & I policies or rules.[537]

Fault. The concept of "fault" in collision law is the basic premise upon which liability insurance is predicated. If the insured vessel is not "at fault," i.e., liable in tort, then the underwriters generally do not have to respond. One of the best examples is *Furness Withy & Co. v. Duder.*[538] In that case, the insured vessel collided with a government tug, but damages could not be recovered because the owner of the insured vessel had agreed by contract to indemnify the government for all liability and claims. The underwriters were relieved of liability because the policy (hull with Running Down Clause) was held not to cover liability incurred by way of contract but only by way of tort.

---

536. See *Shelbourne & Co. v. Law Investment & Insurance Co.*,[1898] 2 Q.B. 626; *Chapman v. Fisher*, [1904] 20 T.L.R. 319. In *Shelbourne*, the court held that a loss by detention was not a loss proximately caused by the collision, in that it was a consequence of the repair and therefore not covered by the three-fourths Running Down Clause. In *Chapman*, it was held that the Running Down Clause did not cover the costs to the salvage company for the increased costs of raising the sunken vessel with which the insured vessel collided.

537. See, for example, *Taylor v. Dewar*, [1864] 5 B. & S. 58, 122 E.R. 754, where the court observed that loss of life is not covered under the Running Down Clause as it is limited to damage to the other vessel. See, however, *Coey v. Smith*, 22 D. 955 (Ct. of Sess.) (Scot.) where the converse was held. The date of the decision reflects, no doubt, an earlier version of the Running Down Clause.

538. [1936] 2 K.B. 461, 2 All E.R. Rep. 119. To the same effect, see *Hall Brothers Steamship Co. v. Young*, [1939] 1 K.B. 748, where the insured vessel collided with a French pilot boat. Under French law, the pilot was entitled to recover from the insured vessel even though the insured vessel was not at fault; but the insurance was held not to cover, because the liability arose by virtue of foreign law and not because of a breach of duty owed by the insured vessel.

For additional cases involving tug and tow collisions, see the discussion which follows. These fall into a completely separate category because here one is dealing with more than one vessel, which vastly complicates the coverage solution.

Towers' Liability and the Placement Thereof

If the interrelationship of the Running Down Clause with a standard P & I policy is difficult to comprehend, even more difficulties are encountered when dealing with hull and P & I coverages on tugs and barges. The primary reasons are that tug hull policies frequently have towers' liability clauses attached by special endorsements or, in the case of specially written tug hull forms, such clauses are incorporated in the body of the hull policy. Some towers' liability clauses provide cover for the object being towed; others do not. Some provide cover for not only the object being towed, but any cargo aboard the tow. It happens all too frequently that the tug has a hull policy (which may or may not incorporate towers' liability clauses) as well as a P & I policy. But the P & I policy does not cover the tow unless specially so endorsed, for the simple reason that P & I policies cover only the *named* vessel or, in the case of the British clubs, only the *entered* vessel.

First, it must be remembered that both hull and P & I policies contain rather standard towage exclusion clauses. For example, the standard AIH (June 2, 1977) policy provides, in part, under the "Adventures" clause, that:

> . . . The Vessel may not be towed, except as is customary or when in need of assistance, nor shall the Vessel render assistance or undertake towage or salvage services under contract previously arranged by the Assured, the Owners, the Managers or the Charterers of the Vessel.

By contrast, the towage exclusion clause in the ASM form provides that where the policy insures tugs, the underwriter is not liable directly or indirectly for:

> Loss of or damage to any vessel or vessels in tow and/or their cargoes, whether such loss or damage occurs before, during or after actual towage; provided, that this exception shall not apply to claims for loss of life, injury or illness.

Rule 20(15) of the Rules of the Britannia Steam Ship Insurance Association Limited reads rather differently. It provides coverage for:

> Liability which a Member may incur under the terms of a contract for:
> (a) the customary towage *of* an entered ship. *Provided always* that the Committee may reject or reduce a claim arising out of such a contract

if it decides that it was unreasonable having regard to all the circumstances to have arranged for the towage to be performed or to have agreed to the terms of the contract;

(b) any other towage *of* an entered ship. *Provided always* that there shall be no recovery unless the Member has paid or agreed to pay such additional call or premium as may be required by the Association and unless the towage contract has been approved by the Managers. [Emphasis supplied]

Rule 20(16) provides cover with respect to liability which a member may incur where the towage is performed *by* the entered vessel. It reads:

Liability which a Member may incur under the terms of a contract for the towage *by* an entered ship of any other ship or object shall be recoverable only if the Committee in its discretion regards the terms of the contract as reasonable and the liability as coming within the scope of the cover afforded by the Association. *Provided always* that an entered ship specially designed or converted for the purpose of towage shall be declared as such to the Managers at the time of entry or at the time of conversion for the purpose of towage.

It is apparent that the primary thrust of the towage exclusion (certainly this is true with respect to the ASM form) relates to *contract* towage; i.e., where the owner is engaged in towage as a regular business or on a planned and deliberate basis, even though sporadic.

The concern of hull underwriters under the Running Down Clause and the equal concern of P & I underwriters with respect to a tower's liability are highlighted by reference to the language of the ASM form in Clause 30 which reads:

In every case where this policy insures tugs, Clause (b) of Paragraph (6) and Clause (c) of Paragraph (29) shall be deemed to refer to the American Institute Tug Form, August 1, 1976 instead of the American Institute Hull Clauses (June 2, 1977) Form and Paragraph (3) shall be deemed to incorporate the Collision Clause contained in said policy (American Institute Tug Form, August 1, 1976) instead of the Collision Clause quoted in said Paragraph (3) and the following clause shall be substituted for and supersede Clause (d) of Paragraph (29) namely

Loss of or damage to any vessel or vessels in tow and/or their cargoes, whether such loss or damage occurs before, during or after actual towage; provided, that this exception shall not apply to claims under Paragraph (1) of this policy.

Since an innocent tow is not liable in rem where it is brought into collision with another vessel by the negligence of its towing tug,[539] and since the Running Down Clause in a hull Policy requires actual contact between the insured tug and the other vessel collided with, the tug is without protection under its hull policy as respects damage to its tow unless:[540] (a) Its hull policy specifically contains coverage with respect to the tow—and desirably, to the cargo aboard the tow; or (b) The owner of the tow is specifically named in the tug's hull policy as an additional assured and the intent of the policy is clear that coverage is extended to the owner of the tow under the tug's Running Down Clause.

Moreover, the towage exclusion in a P & I policy eliminates coverage under that policy, except for personal injuries and death of the crew and passengers of the named tug.[541]

One would think that where a tug owner contracts with underwriters for standard hull and P & I coverages and the underwriters issue such policies, knowing that the vessel(s) covered is a tug and that it will engage in towing as a customary business, the exclusionary clauses should not apply. Unfortunately, this is not so. In *Emmco Ins. Co. v. Southern Terminal and Transp. Co.*,[542] the P & I policy insured specified tugs and barges of Southern against liability to the full extent of their hull value. Following a collision in which Southern's insured tug was at fault while towing one of its uninsured barges, the underwriters denied coverage because of a clause in the policy excluding liability for any loss, damage, expense, or claim arising out of or having relation to the towage of any other vessel or craft. The assured prevailed in the trial court on motion for summary judgment on the grounds there was an irreconcilable conflict or ambigu-

---

539. *Sturgis v. Boyer*, 65 U.S. 110 (1860); *The Eugene F. Moran*, 212 U.S. 466 (1909).

540. *Coastwise S.S. Co. v. Aetna Ins. Co.*, 161 F. 871 (S.D.N.Y.,1908). See, also, *Western Transit Co. v. Brown*, 161 F. 869 (2d Cir., 1908), *cert.den.* 210 U.S. 434 (1908), where a tug and tow going downriver met two upbound steamers. One of the steamers collided with the tow. In the litigation resulting, it was held that the other upbound steamer had come too close to the colliding steamer, causing it to sheer into the tow. As the offending steamer did not itself come into contact with the injured tow, the court held that its Running Down Clause did not cover. Compare *The Niobe*, discussed in Chapter XIX, "Running Down Clause," where a contrary result was reached. The decision has been criticized in the United States and has not been followed. By contrast, in *The Schodack*, 89 F.2d 8, 1937 AMC 548 (2d Cir.), the tow, assisted by three tugs, caused one of the assisting tugs to come into contact with a moored vessel. The tow was held liable to the moored vessel, and its owners brought suit against the P & I underwriters. In holding that neither *Western Transit* nor *The Niobe* governed, the court denied recovery, stating that the Running Down Clause in the hull plainly covered the damage. The rationale was that the collision blow was merely transmitted through the hull of a vessel interposed between the insured vessel and the damaged vessel.

541. See *Atlantic Lighterage Co. v. Continental Ins. Co.*, 75 F.2d 288, 1935 AMC 305 (2d Cir.), where a printed clause in the P & I policy expressly excluded liability arising out of towing except as to passengers and crew of the tug. The policy also contained a typewritten rider excluding "tower's liability." The court held the rider to be a further restriction of the risk.

542. 333 So.2d 80 (Fla., D.C.A.).

ity between the insuring clause and the exclusion, and the ambiguity should be resolved in favor of the assured. On appeal, it was held that there was no conflict; that the risk of collision and damage therefrom is affected by the towing relationship because of the reduced maneuverability of the vessels and, that being so, the underwriter could contract to limit its liability to those collisions in which a premium had been paid for both tug and barges. Consequently, there was no coverage. In *Florida Waterway Properties v. Oceanus Mutual Underwriting Association (Bermuda) Ltd. et al*,[543] the court held that the P & I underwriters were not required to indemnify the assured for amounts paid in settlement of collision claims where the policy contained a specific exception as to risks covered under the "Tug Syndicate" form.

Clearly, also, where the tug owner deliberately conceals from underwriters that the vessel will be used for towing on a regular basis, the policy can be avoided by underwriters.[544]

The problems arising out of providing tower's liability coverages are myriad, and they are well illustrated in the following cases.

In *Halvorsen v. Aetna Ins. Co.*,[545] the P & I policy insured the tug against liability for damage to any buoy, beacon, etc., but with an exclusionary clause against liability for damage "arising out of or having relation to the towage of any other vessel or craft." During a tow of a raft of logs, the tug's towline fouled in a government beacon. The court held the tow of logs did not constitute a "vessel or craft" and, consequently, the exclusion in the policy was inapplicable.

In *Connors Marine v. Northwestern Fire Ins. Co.*,[546] the court held that pontoons cannot properly be included in the category of either hulls, barges, or cargoes, and their loss while being towed under a towage contract was held not covered by a policy covering carrier's liabilities as "owners, operators, carriers, forwarders, or freighters." The court also commented unfavorably upon the use of riders to supersede all the printed terms of the policy, stating:

> This litigation illustrates once more the likelihood of controversy when underwriters pursue their inveterate and abominable practice of using an inappropriate printed form and attaching thereto a type-written rider which describes elliptically the real terms of the insurance contract and contradicts nearly everything in the printed form . . . .

543. 1977 AMC 70 (M.D.,Fla.).
544. See, in connection with concealment or non-disclosure, such decisions as *The Papoose*, 409 F.2d 974, 1969 AMC 781; *Hauser v. Amer. Central Ins. Co.*, 216 F.Supp. 318, 1964 AMC 526; *The Pacific Queen*, 1962 AMC 574, aff'd 307 F.2d 700, 1962 AMC 1845 (9th Cir.), and other cases on the same point in Chap. X, "Disclosures and Representations," and Chap. XI, "Warranties."
545. 1954 AMC 1996 (St.,Wash.).
546. 88 F.2d 637, 1937 AMC 344 (2d Cir.).

In *Soil Mechanics v. Empire Mut. Ins. Co.*,[547] a raft or float used to mount soil-bearing equipment was held not to be a "water craft" and therefore was not excluded from the policy.

In *Driftwood L. & T. v. U.S. Fire Ins. Co.*,[548] a towed barge struck a dock solely because of the negligence of the tug. Both tug and barge were owned by the same person. The tug owner paid the damages to the dock and sought to recoup his damages from the P & I underwriters. The court held that under the language of the policy the plaintiff tugowner was intended to be protected only in his capacity as owner of the barge and not in his capacity as master of those negligently operating the tug, and denied coverage.

In *New York Trap Rock*,[549] a barge in a large tow in the Hudson River listed, dumped its cargo, and then righted itself, sustaining damage. Part of its cargo struck an adjacent barge, damaging it so that it, in turn, capsized and caused damage to other adjacent barges. In analyzing the hull cover, P & I cover, and excess cover, the arbitrator held that the hull cover was liable for the direct hull loss to the first barge; the hull cover and P & I cover were liable for the loss to the adjacent barges, the hull Running Down Clause up to its limit (minus deductible) and the P & I cover for the remainder, minus its deductible; and the excess cover was not involved as the losses were within the limits of the primary coverages.

In *Massey, Trustee v. Globe & Rutgers*,[550] the Hedger Company, as carrier, agreed to carry cargo in its barge at a rate which included "complete coverage of insurance." Hedger took out two policies, one for cargo and the other for towage risks of its tug including "loss of goods on any other ship caused proximately by the tug insofar as not covered by the Running Down Clause." The cargo was lost by reason of negligence of Hedger's tug. The cargo then sued on the cargo policy but failed to recover because of breach of an inspection warranty. Cargo then sued Hedger for breach of contract and recovered. Hedger's trustee then filed suit on the towage policy and proved that the loss was proximately caused by the negligence of the tug and that Hedger had paid the loss on a judgment for breach of contract. The court held:

1. That failure to maintain insurance for the cargo's benefit effected a change in the nature of Hedger's liability from that of a carrier to that of an insurer;

2. Under the broad wording of the policy, the defendant insurance company had agreed to indemnify Hedger in every case in which it was required to pay a loss due to the operation of the insured tug;

---

547. 1968 AMC 491 (St.,N.Y.).
548. [1954] O.R. 733, *aff'd* [1954] 1 D.L.R. 176 (C.A.,Can.), 1955 AMC 884.
549. 1956 AMC 469 (Arb.).
550. 1936 AMC 656 (St.,N.Y.).

3. Nothing in the policy required that payment be made only after liability had been adjudicated. If Hedger was, in fact, liable, it did not have to await a judgment; and

4. Hedger's trustee was entitled to collect under the broad provisions of the towage liability policy.

At trial, it appeared that the cargo had pressed its suit on a theory of breach of contract at the instance of the insurance company, thereby deliberately not raising the issue of the tug's negligence. The court, in this connection, said:

> The good faith of the defendant (insurance company) in thus obtaining a result favorable to itself in litigation to which it was not a party is open to question. The net result of this was that the defendant became its assured's adversary. The court will not lend its aid to lock the door which defendant no doubt hoped it had effectively closed on the issue of the Hedger Company's negligence.

In *N.Y. & L.B.R.R. v. U.S.*,[551] the tug owner was specifically included as a named assured in the towed barge's P & I policy. The tug negligently brought the barge into collision with a bridge without any fault on the part of the barge. Although the court held that the tug owner (who might be found negligent in towing the barge) had sufficient "insurable interest" to warrant its being included as a named assured in the barge's P & I policy, it was also held that the policy did not cover the towing tug's liability for negligence where there was no fault on the part of the insured vessel, the barge.

In *Brittingham v. Tugboat Underwriting*,[552] the tug owner chartered a barge under a demise charter. The tug owner's tower's liability policy excluded coverage for any vessel "owned by" the insured tug owner. After a casualty to the barge, it was held that the policy did not cover, as the bareboat charterer of a vessel is an owner *pro hac vice;* i.e., an "owner" for the time being.

"Other insurance" can also have a marked bearing on the P & I underwriters' liability. In *Sample No. 1*,[553] an unmanned barge, under complete control of its tug, sustained damage, losing oil cargo overboard which damaged shore properties. The barge was covered by a P & I policy and the tug by the Tug Syndicate form. The court held that the loss of the cargo and shoreside damage were within the tug's syndicate hull form policy and not within the barge's P & I policy, in view of the latter's express provision against liability where the assured had "other insurance."

---

551. 1976 AMC 2253 (S.D.N.Y.) (otherwise unreported). See, also, *U.S. Fire Ins. Co. v. Gulf States Marine & Min. Co.*, 262 F.2d 565, 1959 AMC 397.
552. 1971 AMC 1639 (St.,Md.).
553. 262 F.2d 565, 1959 AMC 397 (5th Cir.).

In *Marine Transit Corporation v. Northwestern Fire & Marine Ins. Co.*,[554] the carrier had both a tower's liability clause in its hull policy as well as a separate policy covering its legal liability to cargo on the tow. The latter policy provided that if the interest insured were covered by other insurance, the loss would be collected from the several policies in the order of the date of their attachment. It also provided that if other insurance were procured, the legal liability policy would be void except as such other insurance might be deficient toward fully covering the loss. The court held that the towers' liability policy must respond up to the limits of its policy and the legal liability policy thereafter for any liability beyond that limit.

Reference is made to the fundamental nature of the Running Down Clause. It comes into play only where the insured vessel is *at fault* and the insured *actually pays damages*.[555] *Norman Kelly*[556] presents the question neatly. There, a barge was insured under a hull policy containing the usual collision clause. The barge, while in tow of a commonly owned tug, collided with a steamer, causing damage to both the steamer and the barge. In a suit by the steamer, the court found the collision to have been due to the sole negligence of the tug. The owner of the tug and the barge then sought to recover what had been paid from the underwriters on the barge hull policy. The court said, in part:

> . . . The liability as a result of such collision must be such a liability as would permit the third person or persons to recover in a suit at law for the damage done . . . . Unless the collision occurred by the fault of the barge, and such fault was either a proximate or contributing cause of the collision, there could be no liability on the part of [the owner] in its capacity as *owner of the barge* to pay any third person for any damage resulting from said collision. [Emphasis supplied]

Towage does not necessarily end when the tug casts loose its its lines from the tow.[557] For example, in *Bronx Towing*,[557a] the tug left its barge in an unsafe berth. Loss did not occur to the barge until eight hours after the tug had departed. The tug's P & I policy excluded damage to another vessel caused by collision or by contact, or any loss covered by a standard tug syndicate policy. The court held it was absurd to say that the tug syndicate policy had spent its force the minute the tow was moored and held

---

554. 67 F.2d 544, 1933 AMC 1631 (2d Cir.).
555. See Chap. XIX, "The Running Down Clause," "Liability for Tort Only," citing, *inter alia, Furness Withy & Co. Ltd. v. Duder*, [1936] 2 All E.R. 119, 55 Ll.L.Rep. 52; *Hall Bros. Steamship Co. Ltd. v. Young*, [1939] 1 All E.R. 809, 63 Ll.L.Rep. 143, C.A.; *Taylor v. Rouen*, [1864] 33 L.J.Q.B. 14, 122 E.R. 754; *Norman Kelly*, 1923 AMC 959 (St.,Ohio); *Harbor Towing Co. v. Atlantic Mutual Ins. Co.*, 189 F.2d 409, 1951 AMC 1070 (4th Cir.).
556. 1923 AMC 959 (Ohio App.).
557. *Crain Bros.,Inc. v. Hartford Fire Ins. Co.*, 149 F.Supp. 663 (E.D.,Pa., 1957); *Bronx Towing Line v. Continental Ins. Co.*, 204 F.2d 512, 1953 AMC 1039 (2d Cir.).

that the tug's P & I policy did not cover a loss caused by leaving the tow in an unsafe berth.

Nor does a tower's liability policy cover intentional acts by the assured or its agents; only negligence is covered. This is illustrated in *Louis O'Donnell—Scipio*,[558] where the tug stranded its tow without damage on a well-known shoal which blocked a canal, and then proceeded to drag the tow across the shoal by main force. The court held that, assuming the tug was at fault, there could be no recovery under the tower's liability policy because the damage was intentional and not fortuitous.[559]

The pounding, chafing, riding, or bumping together of barges in a common tow has been held to be a "collision" within the scope of a tower's liability policy.[560]

As an illustration of the construction given to the words in marine policies, see *Ohio Valley Eng. v. Ove 102*,[561] involving the simultaneous stranding of two barges while in tow. The court held that the tower's liability insurer was entitled to only one $2,000 deductible; i.e., the deductible clause referred to claims "resulting from any one accident." In *Lehigh & Wilkes Barre Coal Co. v. Globe & Rutgers Fire Ins.Co.*,[562] the tug caused its tow to be dragged against the sides of a canal. The court held that the extended Running Down Clause used in the tower's liability policy did not cover damage to the tow, as the language covered "collision and/or stranding . . . of any vessel . . . while in tow," and the impact of the tow with the wall of the canal was neither a stranding nor a collision.

However, in *Marine Transit Corp. v. Northwestern Fire & Marine Ins. Co. (The Edward Ryan)*,[563] the tow was brought into collision with the wall of a government lock, and its cargo of wheat became a total loss. The language of the tower's liability clause expressly covered a collision of the tow "with any other vessel, craft or structure, floating or otherwise." The court held that the striking of the lock by the tow was a collision with a "structure" and, consequently, *Lehigh, supra,* was not applicable.

That the liability of a tug, and correspondingly, the liability of its tower's liability underwriters, is predicated upon actionable negligence of the tug is aptly demonstrated in *Rosabelle—Montezuma No. 2*,[564] where the tug owner was found not liable for the grounding of a barge whose draft

558. 1933 AMC 316 (Arb.).
559. See, also, *Newton Creek Towing Co. v. Aetna Ins. Co.*, 48 N.Y.S. 927, 23 App.Div. 152 (St.,N.Y.), *rev'd* 163 N.Y. 114, 57 N.E. 302 (1900).
560. *Tice Towing Line v. Western Assur. Co. (John Rugge-Numatic)*, 214 N.Y.S. 637, 216 App.Div. 202, 1926 AMC 904 (St.,N.Y.). See, also, *The Wyoming*, 76 F.2d 759, 1935 AMC 670 (2d Cir.).
561. 214 F.Supp. 784, 1963 AMC 728 (E.D.,La.).
562. 6 F.2d 735, 1925 AMC 717 (2d Cir.).
563. 67 F.2d 544, 1933 AMC 1631 (2d Cir.), modifying 1933 AMC 350.
564. 1927 AMC 557 (E.D.N.Y.).

had been misrepresented by its owner's agent. And in the *Jason*,[565] a large vessel under repair and without steam was being shifted from one berth to another by a harbor pilot (who was on the payroll of the towing company) and four tugs belonging to the towing company. A strong wind blew her against a pier, which was damaged. The towing company was insured under two policies, the first being a Tug Form 1930 and the second a legal liability policy. The latter excluded any liability which would be covered under the terms of the Tug Form 1930. The Running Down Clause in the Tug Form 1930 was in customary form; i.e., insuring the tug and its tow for collision with vessels and other objects where the assured, *as owner of the vessel,* should become liable to pay and shall pay. The arbitrator found that the sole cause of the collision with the pier was the negligence of the harbor pilot and that none of the assisting tugs was negligent. Consequently, as the towing company was not liable, *as owner of the tugs,* the Tug Form 1930 afforded no cover and the legal liability underwriters had to respond.[566]

Agreement to Obtain Coverage for Another. In the absence of contractual provisions therefor, the owner of the tow is under no obligation to obtain insurance for the tug insuring against unforeseen accidents.[567] But where such contractual provisions exist, they will be enforced. See, for example, *Slade v. Samson Towing,*[568] where a provision in a charter provided that the owner of the tow would provide liability insurance against negligence of the towing tug. The court held that in the absence of any "monopolistic compulsion"—a concept utilized in *Bisso v. Inland Waterways Corp,*[569]—breach of such a provision disentitled the tow owner from recovering for

---

565. 1942 AMC 1358 (Arb.).

566. Much of the litigation involving towing companies and harbor pilots has arisen from collision damage occasioned while vessels are under command of local, non-compulsory harbor pilots. In many American ports, the local pilots are customarily masters of one of the assisting tugs, who go aboard the vessel to be piloted and act as the pilot during the maneuver. In due time, the towing companies developed the so-called "pilotage clause," the validity of which was upheld by the Supreme Court in *Sun Oil Co. v. Dalzell,* 287 U.S. 291, 1933 AMC 35 (1932), reaffirmed in *U.S. v. Neilson,* 349 U.S. 129, 1954 AMC 2231 (1955). The clause, essentially, establishes that when such harbor pilots are engaging in pilotage duties, they are acting on their own, beyond the scope of their duties to their regular tug company employers, and that they are, in fact, analogous to the well-known "loaned employee" situation. A full treatment of the "pilotage clause" and the corresponding liabilities of the parties to it is beyond the scope of this text, but the subject is treated in great depth in A. Parks, *Law of Tug, Tow & Pilotage,* 2d ed. (Centreville, Md.: Cornell Maritime Press, 1982), with biennial supplements, pp. 1048-70.

567. *National Metal v. Mariner,* 1971 AMC 1913 (N.D.,Cal.).

568. 327 F.Supp. 555, 1971 AMC 2342 (E.D.,Tex.).

569. 349 U.S. 85, 1955 AMC 899 (1955), holding that it is against public policy in the United States for a tug owner to exculpate himself from his own negligence.

losses which would have been covered by such insurance had it been procured.[570]

It appears now to be well established that the *Bisso* doctrine does not apply to a contract whereby a tow owner is required to procure insurance to protect the towing company. That is, although while a tug owner cannot contract away his own negligence, he can, by insisting that the owner of the tow provide insurance coverage, accomplish essentially the same goal.[571]

Simply naming a party to the towing venture as an additional assured may not, however, always be a satisfactory answer. For example, in *Dow Chemical v. Thomas Allen*,[572] the barge owner was named as an additional assured on the tug's P & I policy for liability "in respect of" the tug. It was held that the policy afforded no coverage to a barge owner whose liability arose from its negligence in ordering dangerous navigation by the tug in order to perform services for its customers without delay.[573]

Providing Towers' Liability Coverage. Towers' liability coverage is generally provided by one of three different methods: (1) by special endorsements to the hull policy which, in essence, extend the coverage of the running down clause; (2) by special tug hull policies; and (3) by specially constructed and drafted endorsements to a P & I policy, or a general liability policy.

Taking these *seriatim*, the first method involves substituting printed endorsements (A, B, C, or D) for the usual Running Down Clause in the hull policy. The insuring clause in Endorsement A reads, in relevant part:

> . . . If the Vessel hereby insured and/or her tow shall come into collision with any other ship or vessel, etc., etc.

The insuring clause in Endorsement B expands this language as follows (italicized portion new):

---

570. See, also, *Calcasieu Chemical Corp. v. Canal Barge Company, et al*, 404 F.2d 1227, 1969 AMC 114 (7th Cir.), *aff'ming* 1969 AMC 1618, involving the failure of a charterer to procure, as promised, insurance covering not only its cargo but also any liability of the tug owner, and *Dillingham Tug & Barge Corp. v. Collier Carbon & Chemical Corp.*, 707 F.2d 1086, 1984 AMC 1990 (9th Cir.), *cert.den.* 1984 AMC 2402 (1984) where the contract required the barge owner to insure its barge to its full value, naming the towing company as an additional assured. It failed to do so, insuring instead with a $1 million deductible. The court held the insurance provision valid and denied the barge owner its $1 million shortfall.

571. See *Twenty Grand Offshore v. West India Carriers*, 492 F.2d 679, 1974 AMC 2254 (5th Cir.) and recent decisions following it. The subject is discussed in Chap. XIX, "The Running Down Clause," and the cases cited.

572. 349 F.Supp. 1354, 1974 AMC 781 (E.D.,La.).

573. See, also, *Dow Chemical Co. v. Ashland Oil Co.*, 579 F.2d 902 (5th Cir.); *Dow Chemical Co. v. M/V Charles F. Detmar, Jr.*, 545 F.2d 1091 (7th Cir.); and *PPG Industries, Inc. v. Ashland Oil Co. et al*, 592 F.2d 138, 1979 AMC 2056 (3rd Cir.).

. . . If the Vessel hereby insured and/or her tow shall come into collision with any other Ship, Vessel, *Craft or Structure, floating or otherwise,
or shall strand or ground such other Vessel or Craft,* etc., etc. . . .

The insuring clause in Endorsement C further expands the language
as follows (italicized portion new):

. . . If the Vessel hereby insured and/or her tow shall come into collision with any other Ship, Vessel, Craft, Structure *or object, other than
water,* floating or otherwise; or shall strand, ground or sink such other
Vessel, Craft *or object,* etc. etc . . . . *And it is further agreed that this policy
shall also extend to and cover the legal liability of the Vessel hereby insured
arising from any collision, grounding, stranding or sinking which may occur
to any Vessel(s) or Craft(s) while in tow of said Vessel.*

The insuring clause in Endorsement D expands the latter portion of
the new language in Endorsement C as follows (italicized portion new):

. . . And it is further agreed that this policy shall also extend to and
cover the legal liability of the Vessel hereby insured arising from any
collision, grounding, stranding or sinking which may occur to any
Vessel(s) or Craft(s) *or their cargo and/or freight* while in tow of the said
Vessel . . . .

All four endorsements contain substantially the same exclusions, except that the exclusions in Form A are more extensive. Moreover, all four
endorsements cover the liability of a collision of the tow after breaking
away if the breaking away is the consequence of a collision as defined in
the clause. The relevant language reads as follows (that portion of Form A
which is omitted in Forms B, C, and D is indicated in brackets):

Provided always that this clause shall in no case extend to any sum
which the Assured or Charterers may become liable to pay or shall pay
for removal of obstructions under statutory powers [for injury to harbors, wharves, piers, stages and similar structures], consequent on
such collision, or in respect of the cargo or engagements of [either] the
vessel hereby insured [or her tow], or a collision of the tow after breaking away, unless such break be the consequence of a collision as specified herein; or for loss of life, or personal injury . . . .

It appears likely that all four endorsements will eventually be
amended, in light of *Wyandotte Transp. Co. v. U.S.,*[574] to add, in addition to
the clause excluding liability for removal of obstructions "under statutory
powers," the phrase "or otherwise pursuant to law."[575]

---

574. 389 U.S. 191, 1967 AMC 2553 (1967).
575. See discussion, *supra,* Chap. XVI, "Actual and Constructive Total Loss," relating
to the ramifications of *Wyandotte.*

Special Tug Hull Policies. The J & H Tug Hull Form (September 1959) and the McLelland Tug Hull Form, No. 1706, are illustrative of the Towers' Liability Clauses used in special tug hull policies. The language in each is identical, reading in relevant part:

And it is further agreed that if any Vessel hereby insured and/or her tow shall come into collision with any other Ship or Vessel, and the Assured and/or Charterers and/or Operators and/or Lessees in consequence thereof or the Surety for any or all of them in consequence of their undertaking shall become liable to pay and shall pay by way of damages to any other person or persons any sum or sums in respect to such collision . . . .

And it is further agreed that this Policy shall also extend to and cover the liability of the vessel hereby insured from any collision and/or grounding and/or stranding and/or loss or damage which may occur to any vessel or vessels or craft or their cargo and/or freight while in tow of said vessel, subject to all the terms and conditions of the above clause.

And it is further agreed that if the Vessel hereby insured and/or her tow shall come into collision or contact with any structure floating or otherwise or with any substance or thing other than water or shall cause any other ship, vessel or craft to strand, ground, or collide or come into contact with any substance or thing other than water . . . .

In no case shall the above clauses extend to claims for removal of obstructions under statutory powers, or in respect of the cargo or engagements of the insured Vessel, or for loss of life or personal injury.

There is, also, the relatively new Pacific Coast Tug/Barge Form (1979), which constitutes a major step in the evolution of insurance forms for the tug and barge industry.

The major features of the form are:

1. An implied suggestion that tugs and tows should be insured on the same conditions and with the same underwriters. As has been noted, the impossibility of arranging insurance on that basis was a principal reason for the demise of the Tugboat Underwriter Syndicate;[576]

2. A "standard" perils clause;

3. An Inchmaree Clause which is a model of brevity and inclusiveness. The new language not only expands coverage; it also shifts the burden of proof of loss by a peril insured against from the tug owner to the insurer and thereby imposes upon the latter the burden of proving that loss or damage to the vessel is excluded from coverage; and

576. See "Insurance of Tugboats and Liabilities of Tugboat Operators," by Martin P. Detels, Jr., of Seattle, Washington, delivered at the International Maritime Law Seminar, *The Law of Tug and Tow*, Vancouver, B.C., 1979.

4. The Collision and Towers' Liability Clause provides the same broad coverage as provided by Form D discussed above, except that unlike the latter it does not exclude liability flowing from "a collision of the tow after breaking away." However, it does exclude coverage for loss or damage to the tow if the tow is owned or operated by the assured or an affiliate, or to cargo aboard the tow if owned by the assured; i.e., the tugboat owner must look to other insurance for "first party losses" to his own vessel or cargo—ordinarily to the barge hull and marine cargo policies.

Specially Constructed Endorsements. It is not uncommon in the American market to find specially constructed endorsements tacked on to other existing forms used as P & I policies and general liability policies. Generally speaking, the towage exclusion in the P & I policy is deleted and a new endorsement added that essentially provides the same coverage as that of Forms A, B, C, or D, or that found in special tug hull policies; or, in the case of a comprehensive general liability policy, the "watercraft exclusion" is deleted and a towers' liability endorsement added.

Unfortunately, the highest degree of specificity in language in a towers' liability endorsement may prove dangerous. In *Bee Line Transportation Co. v. Connecticut Fire Ins. Co. of Hartford (The Wyoming)*,[577] the language used was quite similar to that of one of the insuring clauses in the Form C endorsement. Compare, for example, the language in *Bee Line, supra,* reading:

> . . . And it is further agreed that this policy shall also extend to and cover the said vessel's legal liability for any collision and/or grounding and/or stranding and/or loss or damage which may occur to any vessel or vessels or craft while in tow of said vessel, subject to all the terms and conditions of this clause . . . .

with the latter portion of the insuring clause in the Form C endorsement reading:

> . . . And it is further agreed that this policy shall also extend to and cover the legal liability of the Vessel hereby insured arising from any collision, grounding, stranding or sinking which may occur to any Vessel(s) or Craft(s) while in tow of said vessel.

In *Bee Line,* the phrasing "said vessel's legal liability for any collision and/or grounding and/or stranding and/or loss or damage . . . " was held to be sufficiently broad to cover the tug's legal liability to the *owner of the*

---

577. 76 F.2d 759, 1935 AMC 670 (2d Cir.). See, also, *Port of Portland v. WQIS*, 549 F.Supp. 233, 1984 AMC 2019 (D., Ore.), where a dredge was held to be insured as to oil pollution claims by use of a comprehensive general liability policy with the "watercraft exclusion" deleted.

cargo on the tow, citing *Marine Transit Corp. v. Northwestern Fire & Marine Ins. Co.*[578]

The danger involved in incorporating other policies by reference is graphically demonstrated in *Bluewaters, Inc. v. Boag.*[579] In that case, a policy was issued incorporating the AIH form by reference, insofar as applicable. Since the basic policy was limited to total and/or constructive total loss only, the Running Down Clause in the AIH form was not considered "applicable." The incorporating language was typewritten and was held to prevail over the printed provisions.

When a multitude of interests are involved, such as a collision between a tow (commonly owned with its tug) and other vessels, apportionment of the ultimate liability among the respective underwriters can be both confusing and complicated.[580]

In view of the potential difficulties between tug and tow (and cargo on board the tow), it is not surprising that the methods developed to achieve protection have ranged from naming the tug and its owners as additional assureds on the tow's policy, to naming the tow on the tug's policies as an additional assured, to insisting on waivers of subrogation, etc. Nearly all towage contracts in use in the United States contain cross-insurance provisions similar to those mentioned above.[581]

It must be emphasized that the line of demarcation between a towage contract on the one hand, and a contract of affreightment utilizing a tug and barges on the other, may sometimes be difficult to determine. Consequently, in those instances in which the tug owner supplies both the tug and a barge with the customer's cargo on board under bills of lading, the contract usually is a contract of affreightment. However, if the tug owner demise charters his barge to the cargo owner, who loads the cargo aboard

---

578. 67 F.2d 544, 1933 AMC 1631 (2d Cir.).
579. 320 F.2d 833, 1964 AMC 71 (lst Cir.).
580. Compare *Augusta—Detroit,* 290 F. 685, 1923 AMC 754, 1923 AMC 816, 1924 AMC 872, *aff'd* 5 F.2d 773, 1925 AMC 756 (4th Cir.) and *Ariosa and D-22,* 144 F.2d 262, 1944 AMC 1035 (2d Cir.), *cert.den.* 323 U.S. 797 (1944).
581. For example, the towage contract in *Twenty Grand Offshore v. West India Carriers, supra,* reads as follows:

(3) Owner [the tug owner] agrees to procure, pay for and maintain in full force and effect throughout the term of this agreement, hull and machinery insurances in an amount at least equal to the value of the vessel and full form protection and indemnity insurance with a limit in the amount of at least one million dollars ($1,000,000). Principal shall be named as an additional assured in all of said policies and such policies shall contain a waiver of subrogation in favor of principal.

Principal [the barge owner] agrees to procure, pay for and maintain in full force and effect through the term of this agreement, hull and machinery insurance in an amount at least equal to the value of the barge and full form protection and indemnity insurance with a limit of at least one million dollars ($1,000,000). Owner, the vessel, its master and crew shall be named as additional assureds in all of said policies in favor of the owner, the vessel, its master and crew. Proper evidence of such insurance shall be furnished owner.

it, and the tug owner agrees to tow the barge to its destination, the agreement is probably one of towage. In the former, the tug owner may, by appropriate provisions, claim the benefit of the exemptions of the Harter Act or the Carriage of Goods by Sea Act.[582] In the latter, the tug owner must recognize that any exculpatory clauses (other than cross insurance endorsements) may be invalid as being against public policy in the United States.[583] Certainly, it behooves tug owner assureds and their underwriters to be aware of the various devices which may be utilized to limit or restrict liability, including, where possible, restructuring the agreement to avoid the imposition of greater liability under a towage contract than under a contract of affreightment.

Damage Caused Otherwise Than by Collision

Because only actual contact between the insured vessel and another ship or vessel (and other structures, objects, etc., under the broader forms of clauses) is covered under the Running Down Clause, damage claims arising where there is no collision contact are obviously left uninsured. Under this heading would come such items as swell damage, forcing another vessel aground, or causing it to collide with a third vessel or object.

Paragraph 4 of the ASM form covers this liability and reads:

> Liability for loss of or damage to any other vessel or craft, or to property on board such other vessel or craft, caused otherwise than by collision of the insured vessel with another vessel or craft.
>
> (a) Where such other vessel or craft or property on board such other vessel or craft belongs to the Assured, claims hereunder shall be

---

582. Compare, for example, *Mississippi Valley Barge Lines v. T.L. James & Co.*, 244 F.2d 263, 1957 AMC 1647 (5th Cir.) (towage contract) with *Texas Co. v. Lea River Lines*, 206 F.2d 55, 1953 AMC 1894 (3d Cir.) and *Allied Chem. Corp. v. Gulf Atlantic Towing Corp.*, 244 F.Supp. 2, 1965 AMC 776 (E.D.,Va.) (contracts of affreightment). See, also, *Agrico Chemical Co. v. M/V Ben W. Martin*, 664 F.2d 85 (5th Cir.), and *Hercules v. Stevens Shipping*, 698 F.2d 726, 1983 AMC 1786 (5th Cir., 1983). Note, also, that when only one shipper is involved in a contract of affreightment, as is often the case in barge movements, the rule in *The G.R. Crowe*, 294 F. 506, 1924 AMC 5 (2d Cir) would apply to make the contract one of private carriage in which case the parties are free to allocate the risks as they choose.
583. See *Bisso v. Inland Waterways Corp.*, 349 U.S. 85, 1955 AMC 899 (1955); *Boston Metals Co. v. The Winding Gulf*, 349 U.S. 122, 1955 AMC 927 (1955); and *Dixilyn Drilling Corp. v. Crescent Towage & Salvage Co.*, 372 U.S. 697, 1963 AMC 829 (1963). To the contrary, contractual stipulations in towage contracts exempting tug owners from liability for the negligence of their crews and servants and, in some instances, forcing the owner of the tow to indemnify the tugowner with respect to damages sustained even when occasioned by negligence of the tug's crew, have been consistently upheld in Great Britain and the Commonwealth nations, where the "United Kingdom Standard Towing Conditions" form is in common use. See *Walumba (Owners) v. Australian Coastal Shipping Commission*, [1964] 2 Lloyd's Rep. 387 (Aus., Vic. Sup. Ct.), on appeal *sub nom.*, *Australian Coastal Shipping Commission v. P.V. Wyuna*, [1964] 38 A.L.J.R. 321, [1965] 1 Lloyd's Rep. 121 (H.C., Aus.), and *Australian Coastal Shipping Commission v. Green*, [1971] 1 Q.B. 456, [1971] 1 All E.R. Rep. 353.

adjusted as if it belonged to a third person; provided, however, that if such vessel, craft or property be insured, the Association shall be liable hereunder only in so far as the loss or damage, but for the insurance herein provided, is not or would not be recoverable by the Assured under such other insurance.

(b) Claims hereunder are subject to a deduction of $ _____ with respect to each accident or occurrence.

See, in this connection, *Tucker v. Palmer et al, Trustees,*[584] where the vessel was testing its engines and sent a "quickwater" stream across a narrow channel, causing a passing tow to get out of shape and strike a bridge abutment, and *Baltimore—John Arbuckle,*[585] where the tug crowded an approaching tow into piers. Swell damage caused by the insured vessel is also covered by this clause.[586]

In *Bee Line Transportation Co. v. Connecticut Fire Ins. Co.,*[587] the policy was held to cover the tug's liability to the cargo owner for proceeding through heavy seas, causing the towed barge, owned by the insured, to pound, leak, and sink. Underwriters contended that the insured's tower's liability insurance included only damages paid to the owner of the towed vessel and not the cargo. The correctness of the decision, as respects liability to cargo, is doubted.

P & I club rules do not generally differ significantly. For example, Rule 20(13) of the rules of the Britannia Club provides coverage for:

> Damages for which a Member may be liable with costs and expenses incidental thereto for loss of or damage to any other ship or cargo or other property therein caused otherwise than by collision with an entered ship.
>
> *Provided always* that if the loss or damage relates to any ship or cargo or other property therein belonging to the Member, such Member shall be entitled to recover from the Association, and the Association shall have the same rights, as if such ship or cargo or other property belonged to a third party, but to the extent only that such loss or damage is not recoverable under any other insurance upon the said ship, cargo or other property.

Damage to Docks, Buoys, etc.

Paragraph 5 of the ASM form provides coverage for:

---

584. 45 F.Supp. 12, 1942 AMC 726 (S.D.N.Y.).
585. 1931 AMC 710 (E.D.N.Y.).
586. See the *Priscilla,* 15 F.2d 455, 1926 AMC 927 (S.D.N.Y.); the *Cameronia,* 41 F.2d 291, 1930 AMC 224 (E.D.N.Y.); and the *Arminda,* 1927 AMC 1523 (S.D.N.Y.).
587. 76 F.2d 759, 1935 AMC 670 (2d. Cir.).

Liability for damage to any dock, pier, jetty, bridge, harbor, break-water, structure, beacon, buoy, lighthouse, cable, or to any fixed or movable object or property whatsoever, except another vessel or craft or property on another vessel or craft, or to property on the insured vessel unless property on the insured vessel is elsewhere covered herein.

(a) Where any such object or property belongs to the Assured, claims hereunder shall be adjusted as if it belonged to a third person; provided, however, that if such object or property be insured, the Association shall be liable hereunder only in so far as the damage, but for the insurance herein provided, is not or would not be recoverable by the Assured under such other insurance.

(b) Claims hereunder are subject to a deduction of $ _____ with respect to each accident or occurrence.

The Britannia Club's comparable rule, Rule 20(12), does not differ significantly in its coverage. It reads, in relevant part, that coverage is provided for:

(a) Liability incurred by a Member for loss of or damage to, or for interference with rights in relation to any harbour, dock, pier, jetty or anything whatsoever moveable or immoveable, not being another ship or cargo or other property therein or cargo or other property carried in an entered ship.

(b) Liability incurred by a Member as a party to any agreement which relates to oil pollution for loss, damage or expense including expenditure reasonably incurred in accordance with the Member's obligations under such agreement.

A proviso clause, however, excludes recovery under sub-paragraph (a) above arising out of a contract of indemnity between a member and a third party (but such liability is covered under Rule 20[17] relating to, among others, contracts of indemnity between the member and the owners or operators of harbours, docks, drydocks, or canals, which rule also contains requirements for advance approval by the managers). Under sub-paragraph (b), such agreement must have been approved in advance by the managers, and any additional call or premium paid; and with respect to damage to such property owned by a member, the member is entitled to recover from the club but only to the extent "other insurance" is not available.

Some of the cases relating to this topic have already been discussed in connection with other paragraphs of the ASM form, but in the interest of an exhaustive compilation are mentioned again briefly here. For example, in *Halvorsen v. Aetna Ins. Co.*,[588] damage to a government beacon oc-

----

588. 1954 AMC 1996 (St.,Wash.).

curred when the insured tug was towing a raft of logs. As the raft was not considered a "ship or vessel" within the scope of a clause excluding liabilities arising out of towage of a ship or vessel, this portion of the policy was relied upon to grant recovery to the assured. In *Trinidad Corp. v. American Steamship Owners Mutual Protection & Indemnity Ass'n*,[589] the insured vessel struck a pipeline and associated pontoons belong to a dredge. It was held that the liability fell within the scope of the P & I policy and not under the Running Down Clause of the hull policy because the objects struck were not "ships or vessels."[590] In *Driftwood L. & T. v. U.S. Fire Ins. Co.*,[591] a towed barge was insured under a P & I policy; the barge struck a dock because of the negligence of a commonly owned tug. In this instance, the court held that the tug owner was insured only in his capacity as owner of the barge and the policy did not cover him in his capacity as employer of those employees negligently operating the tug, and coverage under the policy was denied. In *New York & L.B.R.R. v. U.S.*,[592] although the tug owner was specifically included as a named assured in the towed barge's P & I policy, coverage was not afforded under that policy where the tug's negligence permitted the barge to collide with a bridge and the barge was innocent of any fault.

In *Dresser v. Fidelity & Guaranty*,[593] a collision by the insured vessel with a jackup drilling rig while jacked up out of the water and in position to drill was held to be a collision with a fixed object and not a collision with a vessel for policy coverage purposes.

In *U.S. v. National Automobile & Cas. Ins. Co.*,[594] the common ownership clause was invoked to provide coverage to the owner of a tug insured under a P & I policy where the tug collided with and destroyed a gantry crane also belonging to the assured.

Gulf States Marine & Mining Co. v. Norwich Union Fire Ins. Soc.,[595] presented an interesting interplay between P & I coverage on a tug versus the same coverage on a chartered barge. In that case, liability was incurred by a barge charterer because of crude oil lost, which damaged shoreside properties. The loss was occasioned by negligence of the barge charterer's tankerman. It was held that coverage was not provided under

---

589. 130 F.Supp. 46, 1955 AMC 1280 (S.D.N.Y.), *aff'd* 229 F.2d 57, 1956 AMC 1464 (2d Cir.).

590. To the same effect, and applying the same principles, see *Bennett Steamship Co. v. Hull Mutual Steamship Protecting Society*, [1913] 3 K.B. 372, *aff'd* [1914] 3 K.B. 57, where the insured vessel became entangled with fishing nets of a fishing vessel located over a mile away.

591. n. 482, *supra*.

592. n. 551, *supra*.

593. 580 F.2d 806, 1978 AMC 2588 (5th Cir., 1978).

594. 1962 AMC 971 (N.D.,Cal., 1961). See, also, *Crown Zellerbach v. Ingram*, 745 F.2d 715, 1985 AMC 305 (5th Cir., 1985) (tug struck a bridge).

595. 168 F.Supp. 863 (S.D.,Tex., 1957).

the P & I policy that the charterer carried on its tug, nor under the hull policy on the tug, notwithstanding a tower's liability clause therein, because the liability had been incurred not by reason of the ownership of the tug but by reason of its employment of the tankerman. Moreover, there was no coverage under the barge owner's hull policy on which the charterer had been endorsed as an additional assured. However, the liability was found to be within the coverage of the P & I policy on the barge, which policy had also been endorsed to show the charterer as an additional assured. On appeal, *sub nom. U.S. Fire Ins. Co. v. Gulf States Marine & Mining Co. (Barge Sample No. 1)*,[596] the Fifth Circuit reversed, holding that where a tug is towing an unmanned barge without motive power, the tug, being the active instrument in charge of the undertaking, is responsible for and liable to respond to third persons damaged by the tow, the unmanned barge and its owner being merely passive participants. In short, as is common in the towing industry in the United States, the tankerman was actually a member of the crew of the tug who also held a tankerman's certificate. His negligence, therefore, was as a member of the insured tug. Consequently, the appeals court held that the Tug Syndicate Form hull insurance underwriters must respond, and there was no liability on the underwriters on the P & I policy.

Wreck Removal

The ASM form of policy provides coverage for wreck removal in the following terms:

> Liability for costs or expenses of or incidental to the removal of the wreck of the insured vessel; provided, however, that:
>
> (a) From such costs and expenses shall be deducted the value of any salvage from or which might have been recovered from the wreck inuring, or which might have inured, to the benefit of the Assured;
>
> (b) The Association shall not be liable for any costs or expenses of a type, character or kind which would be payable under the terms of a policy written on the American Institute Hull Clauses (June 2, 1977) Form and a policy written on the American Institute Increased Value and Excess Liabilities Clauses (November 3, 1977) Form;
>
> (c) In the event that the wreck of the insured vessel is upon property owned, leased, rented or otherwise occupied by the Assured, the Association shall be liable for any liability for removal of the wreck which would be imposed upon the Assured by law in the absence of contract if the wreck had been upon the property belonging to another, but only for the excess over any amount recoverable under any other insurance applicable thereto;

596. 262 F.2d 565, 1959 AMC 397 (5th Cir.).

(d) Each claim hereunder is subject to a deduction $ _____

The landmark decision in *Wyandotte Transportation Co. v. U.S.*,[597] has already been discussed in connection with the necessity for notice of abandonment.[598] It bears repetition in summary form. There, a barge loaded with liquid chlorine sank in the Mississippi River. Some months later, it was located, and, it having been abandoned by its owner, the United States undertook to raise it and dispose of the dangerous chlorine cargo, thereafter seeking reimbursement from its owner for the costs incurred. The Supreme Court held that the removal costs could be recovered against the owner, stating, in part:

> . . . There is no indication anywhere else—in the legislative history of the Act, in the predecessor statutes, or in nonstatutory law—that Congress might have intended that a party who negligently sinks a vessel should be shielded from personal responsibility . . . we conclude that other remedies, including those sought here, are available to the Government.

Promptly after the *Wyandotte* decision, the American Hull Insurance Syndicate amended its collision clause to exclude liability for removal or disposal of obstructions, wrecks, or their cargoes under statutory powers *or otherwise pursuant to law.* Since a P & I policy is designed to cover those liabilities not recoverable under the hull policy, it then follows (unless the P & I policy is so phrased that it either affords no coverage or excludes such coverage) that expenses of, or incidental to, removal of the wreck of the insured vessel are recoverable where removal is mandatory under statutory powers or otherwise pursuant to law.

Wyandotte seems to speak in terms of liability being imposed upon the owner who negligently sinks his vessel. It is also clear that such an owner is responsible for marking and lighting the wreck immediately and until it is legally abandoned or removed.[599] It would also appear that liability to mark and remove the wreck continues indefinitely.[600]

Two post-*Wyandotte* cases have held that any negligence by an owner will render him liable for removal costs.[601] And unless the vessel is unequivocably in control of another, the owner's negligence may be inferred from an unexplained sinking.[602] Such negligence may also be sometimes proved under the doctrine of *res ipsa loquitur.*[603]

597. 389 U.S. 191, 1967 AMC 2553 (1967).
598. See discussion, Chap. XVI, "Actual and Constructive Total Loss."
599. The Wreck Act, 33 U.S.C. 409, *et seq.*
600. *Humble v. Tug Crochet,* 422 F.2d 602, 1972 AMC 1843 (5th Cir.).
601. *In Re Marine Leasing Services, Inc.,* 471 F.2d 255, 1974 AMC 534 (5th Cir.); *Humble v. Tug Crochet, supra,* n. 600.
602. *U.S. v. Osage Co., Inc.,* 414 F.Supp. 1097 (D.,Pa., 1976).
603. *U.S. v. Chesapeake & Delaware Shipyard, Inc.,* 369 F.Supp. 714, 1974 AMC 511 (D.,Md.).

One of the leading cases dealing with the interplay of the P & I policy and the hull Running Down Clause is *M.J. Rudolph v. Lumber Mutual Fire; Luria International et al, Third Parties (The Cape Borer),*[604] In that case, the plaintiff owners of a barge insured her with defendant P & I underwriters under the usual form of policy in which the underwriters agreed to cover, *inter alia,* for wreck removal expenses except as to costs or expenses which would have been covered by full insurance under the AIH hull clauses (1/10/70). The barge was not covered by any hull policy. Later, while being towed, she capsized. She was then towed to a pier in New York City, where she sank. A department of the city ordered her removal, as she was a menace to navigation and was obstructing the pier. The plaintiffs had her removed and claimed against the P & I underwriters. The underwriters denied liability, contending that if the barge had been covered under the AIH hull policy, the hull underwriters would have been liable to plaintiffs under the Sue and Labor Clause. The court held that the barge had been completely sunk, rendered unnavigable, and therefore a wreck which the plaintiffs were under compulsion of law to remove, and that even if the plaintiffs had insured her under an AIH policy, the Sue and Labor Clause would not have applied because such clauses do not provide an indemnity with respect to the cost of wreck removal.

Compare, however, *Seaboard Shipping Corp. v. Jocharanne Tugboat Corp. et al,*[605] where a gasoline barge stranded and was damaged. The owner of the barge was insured under a hull policy, an open cargo legal liability policy, and a P & I policy. The usable gasoline was offloaded from the barge and salvage expenses were incurred in getting her off her strand. Later, the barge was towed to New York City, where it was declared to be a constructive total loss. The trial court held that the leaking and damaged condition of the barge threatened the distinct and separate interests of each underwriter and that the barge owner, in incurring towing and removal costs, was seeking to protect the hull, save the cargo, and prevent explosion and resultant disaster. On that premise, the trial court divided the costs and expenses three ways. The P & I underwriter appealed. The hull underwriters contended pressure from authorities made the removal of the barge from her strand "compulsory in law." The P & I underwriter contended its policy did not apply at all. The appeals court agreed, noting that there had been no compulsory removal of the barge. To the contrary, the owner and the hull underwriters, far from abandoning their interest in the vessel, had it towed to another location in a vain hope of salvaging the hull. As such, the "removal," salvage and towing

---

604. 371 F.Supp. 1325, 1974 AMC 1990 (E.D.N.Y.), [1975] 2 Lloyd's Rep. 108.
605. 461 F.2d 500, 1972 AMC 2151 (2d Cir.).

expenses were sue and labor claims and fell upon the hull underwriters and the open cargo legal liability underwriters.[606]

The question of what is removal that is "compulsory by law" was touched upon in *M.J. Rudolph, supra,* where the court said that apparently a sunken vessel damaged to the extent of being rendered unnavigable is a wreck and that where the authorities legitimately and lawfully order it removed, even though those authorities are city officials and not the Corps of Engineers, the owner is under "compulsion of law" to remove it.

The point surfaced again in *Progress Marine v. Foremost,*[607] where the owner voluntarily raised its vessel which had been sunk by the owner's negligence. The policy form was SP-38, which covered the cost of removal when such removal is "compulsory by law." The court disapproved the holding in *Jocharanne, supra,* and held that no express order from a governmental agency was required in order for the removal to be "compulsory by law." Instead, a three-pronged test was enunciated; i.e., (a) if removal was reasonably required by law, or (b) if failure to remove would expose the insured to liability of such magnitude as to justify removal, and (c) if the insured believed that removal was necessary to avoid legal consequences of the type covered by the policy. However, the *Progress Marine* test was later modified slightly by the Fifth Circuit sitting *en banc* in *Continental Oil Co. v. Bonanza Corp.,*[608] where the court held that the "subjective" portion of the *Progress Marine* test was not necessary.

Although the Supreme Court's decision in *Wyandotte* left unresolved the question of whether an *in personam* action could lie against a non-negligent owner of a sunken vessel, subsequent decisions have made it clear that, although a non-negligent owner has a statutory duty to remove the sunken vessel or abandon it, such an owner cannot be held personally liable for the government's cost of removing the sunken vessel.[609] Thus, the innocent owner has an option: he may either raise the vessel himself and seek recovery of the expenses from the party responsible for wrecking it, or, he may abandon the vessel and allow the United States to bear

---

606. From the decision, it is not at all clear whether the barge was "removed" because it was a wreck or "removed" because of the owner's hope of salvaging the hull. The appeals court held it was the latter. The seminal question of whether or not the barge, while stranded, was a "wreck" as that term was used in the policies, or was merely a stranded barge which could be got off her strand without too much difficulty, was not addressed. One usually assumes that a "wreck" is just that; a vessel which is either sunk or partially so and which is so irreparably damaged as not to be the "thing insured," thus entitling the assured to abandon as for actual or constructive total loss. In *Jocharanne,* it was certainly questionable that the barge was a "wreck" at all.

607. 642 F.2d 816, 1981 AMC 2315 (5th Cir.).

608. 706 F.2d 1365, 1983 AMC 1059 (5th Cir.). This decision is discussed, *infra,* in connection with the question of liability of a charterer for wreck removal.

609. *Tennessee Valley Sand & Gravel Co. v. M/V Delta,* 598 F.2d 930 (5th Cir., 1979); *U.S. v. Raven,* 500 F.2d 728, 1975 AMC 603 (5th Cir., 1974), *cert.den.* 419 U.S. 1164 (1975); see, also, *University of Texas Medical Branch v. U.S.,* 557 F.2d 438, 1977 AMC 2607 (5th Cir., 1977).

the burden of removal and recovery of expenses from the negligent party.[610] If the non-negligent owner exercises his right to abandon, he is liable neither for the cost of removal nor for damages suffered by third parties as a result of the wreck.[611]

In *St. Paul Fire & Marine v. Vest*,[612] the innocent owner of a sunken barge was denied coverage under his P & I policy, where, by a consent decree, judgment was entered against him by the United States for nearly $400,000 expended by the government in raising the wreck of the barge. The fact situation was somewhat unusual. Legal title to the barge was apparently in Vest, but it was being used by Victory (a sister corporation having the same stockholders, directors, and officers), which was towing it, laden with oil, by its tug the *Johnny Dam*. There was no written agreement between Vest and Victory, but the circumstances led the court to infer that the arrangement constituted a bareboat or demise charter from Vest to Victory. The hull policy covered the tug, the barge, and some sister barges on which Vest was named as the primary assured and Victory was named as an additional assured. The primary P & I policy covered both the tug and the sunken barge, and the primary assured in this policy was Victory. The first excess P & I on the tug and barge named Vest as the assured, while Victory was not named at all. The second excess P & I policy covered both the tug and the barge and named both Vest and Victory as the assureds.

Each P & I policy incorporated into its provisions the special risk form SP-23 which, in essence, provided that the underwriter undertook to make good to the assured . . . all such loss and/or damage and/or expense as the assured as *"owners of the vessel named herein"* should become liable to pay and shall have paid with respect to, *inter alia,* "removal of the wreck of the *vessel named herein* when such removal is compulsory by law." The barge was brought into collision with a bridge pier through the negligence of the tug *Johnny Dam,* and the barge was innocent of any fault. It sank, and the United States raised it and removed it from the navigable channel.

The court noted that Vest was not legally liable for the removal expenses, as it was an innocent owner of the barge. The court also observed that Victory, as negligent owner of the tug, was personally liable for removal expenses. It then held that none of the P & I policies covered, because they provided coverage only if the *owner* was liable *as owner* of the wrecked barge. As the court put it, under the P & I policies the barge was

610. *In re Chinese Maritime Trust, Ltd.,* 478 F.2d 1357, 1973 AMC 1110 (2d Cir.); *United States v. Cargill, Inc.,* 367 F.2d 971, 1966 AMC 1974 (5th Cir.); *Western Transportation Co. v. Pac-Mar Services, Inc.,* 547 F.2d 97 (9th Cir., 1976).
611. *Lane v. U.S.,* 529 F.2d 175, 1976 AMC 66 (4th Cir.); *In re Marine Leasing Services, Inc.,* 471 F.2d 255, 1974 AMC 534 (5th Cir., 1973), and cases cited, *supra,* n. 609.
612. 500 F.Supp. 1365, 1982 AMC 450 (N.D.,Miss.).

covered if its owner was liable (and it was not), and although there was liability on the part of the tug, there was no coverage because it was not the wrecked vessel.[613]

It must be emphasized that expense of "removal" may not be confined merely to actual expenses of raising a sunken vessel and removing it from the water. For example, in *U.S. v. Ohio Barge Lines*,[614] the government recovered its costs in hiring a helper boat to escort other vessels safely past the wreck while the government was removing it. The defendant vessel owner's negligence was presumed.

Continental Oil Co. v. Bonanza Corp.[615] is probably a high-water mark in decisions relating to liability for wreck removal. There, a vessel under time charter to Conoco sank near an offshore platform which sat upon submerged lands leased to Conoco. Conoco paid to have it removed. Conoco was an additional assured on the P & I policy covering the vessel which incorporated the SP-38 clauses. Conoco sued the vessel owner/operator and the P & I underwriter for the costs of removal. The court held, *inter alia*, that since Conoco was not exposed to any liability as "owner" of the vessel, it could not recover from the P & I underwriter under wreck removal coverage; i.e., a time charterer has no obligation to remove the wreck of a vessel under time charter to it. The court also noted that even an owner has no obligation to remove a wreck if the sinking was not due to his negligence. Moreover, Conoco was denied recovery under the policy provision covering "expense in connection with any fixed or movable object," as its expense was incurred as a lease operator and not "as owner" of the vessel.

Right of a Negligent Owner to Limit Liability. The law seems well settled that neither negligent owners nor negligent third parties can limit liability for removal expenses. Thus, in *Re Pacific Far East Line, Inc.*[616] the court held that the statutory duty of diligence in removing a wreck was a mandatory obligation personal to the owner; that failure to remove was within the privity and knowledge of the owner; and therefore the limitation peti-

---

613. The case does not mention, nor does it appear from the court's opinion, that if, in fact (as the court found), Victory were a bareboat or demise charterer, it would in legal intendment be an "owner *pro hac vice*" of the barge and, as such, should qualify as an "owner" of that vessel under the P & I policies . . . or at least the primary and second layer excess policies. Compare *Brittingham v. Tugboat Underwriting*, 1971 AMC 1639 (St.,Md.), where the tug owner chartered a barge under a demise charter. The tower's liability policy there excluded coverage for any vessel "owned by" the insured tug owner. After a casualty to the barge, it was held that the policy did not cover, as the bareboat charterer of a vessel is the owner *pro hac vice*; i.e., an "owner" for the time being.

614. 432 F.Supp. 1023, 1977 AMC 1200 (W.D.,Pa.).

615. 706 F.2d 1365, 1983 AMC 2059 (5th Cir.) *en banc.*

616. 314 F.Supp. 1339, 1970 AMC 1592 (N.D.,Cal.), *aff'd per curiam* 472 F.2d 1382 (9th Cir., 1973).

tioner was not entitled to limit. And in *Re Chinese Maritime Trust, Ltd.*[617] the owner of a vessel sunk in the Panama Canal was denied limitation because the regulations of the Panama Canal Zone created an obligation "personal" to the owner and the costs incurred were within the owner's privity and knowledge once it became aware of the sinking.

In *University of Texas Medical Branch v. U.S.*,[618] a negligent third party was held liable for the sinking of a government dredge. The government immediately removed the wreck and sought recovery of its costs. The court assumed that the limitation plaintiff's vessel had been negligent and that her owner lacked privity or knowledge with respect to causal negligence. Nonetheless, the court held the Limitation Act inapplicable.

In a decision refreshing to underwriters who have become accustomed to their policies being construed most strongly against them, the Fifth Circuit in *Eagle Leasing Corp. et al v. Hartford Fire*[619] declined to apply the almost universal rule of construction in marine policies. In that case, the vessel owner had procured P & I insurance on a fleet of barges. One of the barges sank during the policy period. The assured initiated search and salvage efforts, which, however, were discontinued when it was deemed economically inadvisable, and the sunken wreck was abandoned and sold. Afterwards, a tanker struck the sunken barge and was damaged. Suit was brought against the plaintiff owner who defended when the underwriter refused to do so. The suit was dismissed, and the plaintiff owner brought an action against the P & I underwriter, alleging, in effect, that the suit it had defended was predicated upon neglect during the policy period even though the actual striking took place after expiration of the policy. In the lower court, judgment was given for the plaintiff insured for the full amount of costs, expenses, and attorneys' fees incurred in defense of the suit by the tanker owner. On appeal, the Fifth Circuit reversed. Although conceding that the coverage provision was ambiguous, in this instance the court refused to apply the general rule that a policy is construed most strongly against the underwriters on the ground that the plaintiff-assured was a large corporation, managed by sophisticated businessmen. Instead, the court denied recovery, giving effect to the most probable intentions of the parties, intentions considered commercially reasonable from a business point of view.

It is worthwhile to note that the new AIMU form of policy (June 2, 1983) provides with respect to wreck removal for indemnification for attempted or actual removal or disposal of obstructions, wrecks, or cargoes "under statutory power or otherwise pursuant to law." This qualification is lacking in the ASM form.

---

617. 478 F.2d 1357, 1973 AMC 1110 (2d Cir.), *cert.den.* 414 U.S. 1143 (1974).
618. 557 F.2d 438, 1977 AMC 2607 (5th Cir.).
619. 540 F.2d 1257, 1978 AMC 604 (5th Cir.).

Great Britain and the Commonwealth Nations. In Canada, the owner of a wreck is himself liable, without limitation, for the expense of wreck removal, and he can secure an indemnity from the owner of another vessel at fault only to the extent that that owner cannot limit his liability.[620]

In Great Britain, under Sections 530-34, Merchant Shipping Act, 1894, where a wreck constitutes a danger or obstruction, the authority may remove it, sell the wreck, and sell any cargo in order to recoup its expenses. The Act gives no personal remedy against the shipowner, nor does the authority have a common law remedy unless the obstruction was caused by negligent or improper acts for which the owner may be held liable. Personal remedies may, however, be given by special acts; e.g., the Port of London Act, 1968.[621]

Cargo

The ASM form provides coverage for:

Liability for loss of or damage to or in connection with cargo or other property (except mail or parcels post), including baggage and personal effects of passengers, to be carried, carried or which has been carried on board the insured vessel.[622]

As noted at the commencement of this chapter, there is no implied warranty of seaworthiness in a P & I policy. The reason is simple and was well expressed in *The C.S. Holmes*[623] in the following language;

If a warranty of seaworthiness was implied in a P & I policy, it would mean that in practically every instance the insurance company had assumed no risk [as to cargo loss], because, generally speaking, a ship is not liable to cargo unless it is unseaworthy.[624]

---

620. See *Maxwell Equipment Ltd et al v. Vancouver Tugboat Co. et al*, [1961] S.C.R. 43, and *Margrande Compania Naviera S.A. et al v. The Leecliffe Hull's Owners et al*, [1970] Ex. C.R. 870.
621. In Australia, see *Smith (William Howard) & Sons Ltd. v. Wilson*, [1896] A.C. 579, P.C. (Aus.); *Musgrove v. Mitchell*, [1891] 17 V.L.R. 346, 13 A.L.T. 62; *Ramsden v. Payne*, [1875] 1 V.L.R. (L.) 250; *Payne v. Fishley*, [1870] 1 A.J.R. 122; and *Melbourne Harbour Trust Comm'rs v. Victorian Lighterage Pty. Ltd.*, [1930] V.L.R. 357, 36 A.L.R. 293. And in New Zealand, see *Griffin v. Whitney*, [1914] 33 N.Z.L.R. 1028.
      In Great Britain, see *The Stonedale No. 1 v. Manchester Ship Canal Co.*, [1955] 2 Lloyd's Rep. 9, H.L.; *The Berwyn*, [1977] 2 Lloyd's Rep. 99, C.A.; *The Tremontana*, [1969] 2 Lloyd's Rep. 94 (on duty of harbor authorities to mark the position of a wreck by an appropriate buoy); *The Douglas*, [1882] 7 P.D. 151, C.A. and *The Utopia*, [1893] A.C. 492, P.C. (duty of reasonable care and skill imposed on harbor authorities to buoy wrecks).
622. By contrast, the SP-23 form also provides cargo coverage, but neither SP-38 nor the new AIMU forms provide such coverage, although there is an AIMU endorsement form for cargo liability to be attached if cargo liability is desired.
623. 9 F.2d 296, 1926 AMC 126 (9th Cir.).
624. See, also, *Puritan Insurance Co. v. The 13th Regional Corp.*, 1983 AMC 298 (W.D, Wash., 1983), a personal injury case, where the court said that to read into the policy an implied warranty of seaworthiness would definitely defeat the entire object of the policy.

There are numerous exclusions under the cargo liability clause, which will be discussed *seriatim* after the general coverage of the clause is explained.

General Coverage of the Cargo Liability Clause. Surprisingly, there are relatively few cases bearing on this portion of a P & I policy. One of the earliest was *Good v. London S.S. Owners' Mutual Prot. Ass'n.*[625] The policy in that case covered, *inter alia,* damage to goods on board the covered vessel caused by "improper navigation." Sea cocks were negligently left open, and, as a consequence, water entered the ship's holds, damaging the cargo. The court held this to be "improper navigation" within the meaning of the policy. In *Carmichael v. Liverpool Sailing Ship Owners' Mut. Ind. Ass'n,*[626] an opening or port in the side of the vessel was negligently left open during the loading of the cargo. During the voyage, water leaked in and damaged the cargo of wheat. The leak did not hinder or impede the navigation of the vessel in the course of her voyage. It was held that the damage arose from "improper navigation," for which the P & I club was liable under its policy. However, in *Canada Shipping Co. v. British Shipowners' Mut. Prot. Ass'n,*[627] a cargo of wheat suffered taint damage by reason of insufficiently cleaned holds. This was held not to be due to "improper navigation," and recovery against the club was denied.

In *The Exmoor,*[628] tobacco was damaged by its proximity to valonia. Part of the damage occurred when one P & I policy was in effect; the remainder when the second P & I policy was in effect. The damage was apportioned between the two policies on the basis of the damage occurring during the currency of each respective policy.

In *Barcelona, Orion Ins. Co. Ltd. v. Firemen's Fund,*[629] judgment was obtained against a time charterer and the shipowner in respect of cargo damage. The time charterer was granted indemnity from the shipowner because the vessel was unseaworthy. The time charterer's underwriters paid the judgment and sought to recover indemnity from the shipowner's P & I insurer, who refused, contending that its policy covered only liabilities and expenses which the assured shall have become liable to pay and shall have in fact paid. The insured shipowner had not paid and was not expected to pay anything on the judgment. The court held that the policy was ambiguous, that it would therefore be construed as one of liability insurance with respect to all but the relatively small expenses of a kind the shipowner assured would pay in the normal course of business

---

625. (1871) L.R. 6 C.P. 523, 20 W.R. 33.
626. (1887) 19 Q.B.D. 242, C.A.
627. (1889) 23 Q.B.D. 342, C.A.
628. 106 F.2d 9, 1939 AMC 1095 (2d Cir.).
629. 1975 AMC 1183 (St. Cal.).

and, therefore, the P & I underwriter's duty to pay arose as of the date of the judgment.[630]

In *Kuehne & Nagel, Inc. v. F.W. Baiden*,[631] the plaintiff held a charterer's liability policy issued by the defendant. Some jeeps, stowed on deck, were swept overboard by heavy seas. The consignee, on arrival, claimed that the plaintiff should have given adequate notice of on-deck storage, so that the consignee could have arranged insurance. The claim with the consignee was settled for an agreed sum, the consignee claiming no further compensation and the plaintiff waiving any freight charged. The plaintiff then sued on the charterer's liability policy for the unpaid freight. The New York Court of Appeal held that the plaintiff could settle claims and recover under the policy so long as the settlement was reasonable and the cause of the liability was an insured risk. Since the defendant was unable to submit evidentiary facts or materials to show the existence of a triable issue, and the risk was one insured against, the plaintiff was held entitled to summary judgment.

In *Steamship Mutual Underwriting Ass'n Ltd. v. Bureau Veritas*,[632] the P & I club advanced an interesting and novel concept. There, the subrogated P & I club brought a negligence action against a classification society to recover cargo losses and other expenses arising out of the sinking of the insured cargo vessel. The court held that, although the classification society was negligent in failing to comply with its own rules in inspecting and testing the vessel's shell plating and double bottom tanks, plaintiff's evidence failed to establish that this negligence was the proximate cause of the vessel's sinking; i.e., the presumption of unseaworthiness arising from a vessel's sinking cannot be used against a classification society which merely classed but did not control the vessel.

As will become very clear from the discussion which follows, the P & I underwriter is prepared to indemnify the shipowner for *negligence* that causes damage to cargo carried aboard, but not for damage resulting from intentional or wilful acts of the shipowner, nor for damage resulting from a failure of the shipowner to avail himself of all the limitations of liability which the law permits him by ensuring that the bills of lading or contracts of affreightment are properly claused, nor for a variety of other potential liabilities which the P & I underwriters do not consider "commercially reasonable" to bear and which a careful and prudent shipowner presumably should be prepared to guard against. Thus, a policy covering liability for loss of cargo "from any cause whatsoever" does not provide

---

630. The decision demonstrates the proclivity of the courts to construe a policy in favor of an assured where the slightest ambiguity can be found in the policy.

631. 354 N.Y.S.2d 648, 1974 AMC 1373 (St. N.Y.), *rev'd* [1977] 1 Lloyd's Rep. 90 (N.Y.C.A.).

632. 1973 AMC 2184 (E.D. La.).

indemnity for losses arising from the vessel owner's intentional act such as loss by willful scuttling of the vessel.[633]

It is helpful, also, to note that the insuring clause as to cargo refers to "liability for loss of or damage to *or in connection with* cargo, or *other property.*" Consequently, the proper interpretation of the insuring clause would seem to dictate that, for example, delay in delivery of the cargo such that it was rendered totally worthless would be covered as being "in connection with" cargo loss and damage,[634] and the term "other property" should certainly embrace property on board other than, strictly speaking, cargo.[635]

Policy Exclusions and Protective Clauses. The ASM form provides under Clause 7 relating to cargo as follows:

> *Provided, However, that no liability shall exist hereunder, for:*
> (a) Loss, damage or expense incurred in connection with the custody, carriage or delivery of specie, bullion, precious metals, precious stones, jewelry, silks, furs, currency, bonds or other negotiable documents, or similar valuable property, unless specially agreed to and accepted for transportation under a form of contract approved, in writing, by the Association.

The intent here is quite clear: the P & I underwriter expects the shipowner to take advantage of limitations of liability to which he is entitled by law.[636] By requiring advance approval of special contracts, the underwriter is in a position to condition approval upon the taking of special precautions such as extra guards, burglar-proof compartments, and the like.

633. *Fidelity-Phoenix Fire Ins. Co. v. Murphy,* 146 So. 387, 1933 AMC 444 (St. Ala.). Reference should in all events be made to the excellent article by J. Moore, "Liability for Damage to Property Carried, to be Carried, or Which Has been Carried; Both-to-Blame Cases and Liability for Recovery Over by Non-Carrier; Liability for Cargo's Proportion of General Average Not Otherwise Collectible, Policy Exclusions and Protective Clauses," 43 *Tulane Law Review* 581 (1969).

634. Mr. Moore (see n. 633) gives as an example a situation where the assured had not validly contracted for exemption from liability for delay, and a shipment of 1969 calendars having gone astray and not delivered until 1970, were rendered worthless. Here, in the absence of other policy exclusions, the P & I underwriter should respond. As noted heretofore, marine policies do not ordinarily provide coverage for "delay." See *Amoroso v. Sea Insurance Co.,* 157 N.E. 156, 1927 AMC 1196 (St. N.Y.). The decision in *Lanasa Fruit Steamship & Importing Co. v. Universal Ins. Co.,* 302 U.S. 556, 1938 AMC 1 (1938) is clearly an anomaly. There, the policy was held to cover a loss of bananas due to delay and the inherent nature of the bananas to rot, occasioned by a delay due to a stranding. The decision triggered policy amendments making it clear that damage due to delay is not a covered peril even though the delay was occasioned by a peril insured against.

635. Mr. Moore (see footnote 617) gives as an example, personal effects of the crew, pilots and longshoremen, unaccompanied baggage, salvaged property, and property which is carried as a courtesy.

636. See 46 U.S.C. 1306 and 46 U.S.C. 181.

(b) Loss, damage or expense arising out of or in connection with the care, custody, carriage or delivery of cargo requiring refrigeration, unless the spaces, apparatus and means used for the care, custody and carriage thereof have been surveyed by a classification or other competent disinterested surveyor under working conditions before commencement of each round voyage and found in all respects fit, and unless the Association has approved in writing the form of the contract under which such cargo is accepted for transportation.

Even minor malfunctions in refrigeration equipment can cause major cargo losses, nearly all of which are expensive. It is therefore logical that the P & I underwriter wishes assurance that all reasonable steps have been taken to guard against losses due to malfunctioning of refrigeration equipment. For example, see the cargo policy cases of *Larson v. Ins. Co. of N.A.*,[637] and *Quattrochiocchi v. Albany Ins. Co.*,[638] both of which involved refrigerated cargo and claims involving alleged derangement of refrigerating equipment. In those cases, although P & I insurance was not involved (or at least not referred to), cargo underwriters were confronted with claims of cargo loss involving possible derangement of refrigerating equipment. It would be interesting to speculate whether such claims were ultimately presented to P & I underwriters, either by cargo owners who failed to recover on their cargo policies, or by cargo underwriters who were compelled to pay and subrogated against the P & I carrier on the vessel.

(c) Loss or damage to any passenger's baggage or personal effects, unless the form of the ticket issued to the passenger shall have been approved, in writing, by the Association.

This exclusion falls into the same category as the exclusion with respect to specie, bullion, jewelry, etc. The P & I underwriter wishes to limit its liability to the maximum permitted by law and, therefore, desires to exercise some degree of control over what liabilities its assured/shipowner may have in the carriage of passengers. Such limitations generally take the form, for example, of clauses exculpating the carrier from liability for failing to adhere to its published itinerary,[639] limiting the time in which a passenger can file suit for damage or loss to baggage,[640] and limiting the vessel's liability for injuries sustained by passengers while on land excursions.[641]

---

637. 252 F.Supp. 458, 1965 AMC 2576 (W.D. Wash.).
638. 1983 AMC 1152 (N.D. Cal.).
639. See *Desmond v. Holland American Lines*, 1981 AMC 211 (S.D.N.Y.).
640. See *Morak v. Costa Arm.*, 1982 AMC 1859 (E.D.N.Y.).
641. See *Lohman v. Royal Viking*, 1981 AMC 1104 (D. Col.).

(d) Loss, damage or expense arising from any deviation in breach of the Assured's obligation to cargo, known to the Assured in time to enable him specifically to insure his liability therefor, unless notice thereof has been given the Association, and the Association has agreed, in writing, that such insurance was unnecessary.

It will be noted that this exclusion does not come into play unless it is *known to the Assured* in time for him to insure his liability or unless the association agrees in writing that the insurance was unnecessary. Thus, coverage is still provided under the P & I policy if the assured/shipowner is unaware of the deviation or if it occurs contrary to the assured's instructions.[642]

(e) Loss, damage or expense arising from stowage of underdeck cargo on deck, or stowage of cargo in spaces not suitable for its carriage, unless the Assured shall show that every reasonable precaution has been taken by him to prevent such improper stowage.

It is fundamental in water carriage that a clean bill of lading, both before the Hague Rules and since, has always meant that the cargo is to be carried under deck.[643] Deck cargo is not subject to the Hague Rules,[644] and the carrier is free to insert exculpatory clauses in the bill of lading. However, Cogsa would apply where the cargo is carried on deck, and is stated as being carried on deck and the bill of lading, by special wording, applies Cogsa to deck cargo.[645] In this instance, however, the carrier would have to comply with all the other provisions of Cogsa.[646]

It is not surprising, therefore, that P & I underwriters are understandably reluctant to undertake liability in such circumstances and expressly exclude liability therefor.[647]

(f) Loss, damage or expense arising from issuance of clean bills of lading for goods known to be missing, unsound or damaged.

---

642. Compare, for example, *Maryland Ins. Co. v. LeRoy, Bayard and M'Evers*, 11 U.S. 26 (1812), where additional cargo was taken on not approved under the insurance contract and the underwriter was discharged from liability.

643. *Roberts & Co. v. Calmar S.S. Corp.*, 1945 AMC 375.

644. Read here, of course, the various carriage of goods by sea acts which follow the Hague Rules, such as the United States Carriage of Goods by Sea Act, 1936, 46 U.S.C. 1300-15.

645. See *Diethelm & Co. v. S.S. Flying Trader*, 1956 AMC 1550 (S.D.N.Y.); *General Motors Corp. v. S.S. Mormacoak*, 327 F.Supp. 666, 1971 AMC 1647 (S.D.N.Y.).

646. See, generally, *Marine Cargo Claims* (2d), W. Tetley, Chap. 29, Butterworths, 1978.

647. Representative cases are: *Transatlantic Shipping Co. v. St. Paul Fire & Marine Ins. Co.*, 298 F. 551, 1924 AMC 628 (S.D.N.Y.), *aff'd* 9 F.2d 720, 1926 AMC 83 (2d Cir.); *Allegre's Admr. v. Maryland Ins. Co.*, 2 Gill and J. 139 (St. Md. 1830); *Tauton Copper Co. v. Merchants Ins. Co.*, 40 Mass. 108 (St. Mass. 1839); *Kuehne & Nagel v. Baiden*, 1974 AMC 1373 (St. N.Y.).

The key word in this exclusionary clause is "known"; i.e., "known" to the carrier to be missing, unsound, or damaged. Thus, it would appear that coverage would be voided under this clause only in instances in which the carrier incurs liability to a bona fide third party purchaser based upon issuance of a bill of lading.[648]

This is a recurring problem in the shipping industry because many shipments are made on letters of credit specifying that the bills of lading must describe the goods as being in apparent good order and condition, or shipped on or before a certain date. Thus, carriers are frequently brought under pressure by shippers to issue bills of lading describing the goods as being in apparent good order and condition whereas in fact that may not be the case at all. As Moore points out,[649] letters of indemnity are often offered by shippers as an inducement to the carrier to issue clean bills of lading for goods in bad condition or shipped late. In any event, issuance of such bills is clearly a fraud and the only protection the carrier has is the solvency and moral responsibility of the shipper. In any event, the reluctance of P & I underwriters to accept liability in such circumstances is readily understandable.

(g) Loss, damage or expense arising from the intentional issuance of bills of lading prior to receipt of the goods described therein, or covering goods not received at all.[650]

(h) Loss, damage or expense arising from delivery of cargo without surrender of the bills of lading.

Bills of lading are, generally speaking, documents of title and the holder of the bill is considered the owner of the goods described therein. In the commercial world of reality, delivery of goods without surrender of bills of lading covering them is sometimes made when the bills have been lost or mislaid and the parties are reluctant to delay delivery. Such delivery is, however, an open invitation to fraud on the part of the consignee who dishonestly claims that the bill has gone astray where, in fact, he simply lacks funds to pay for the goods. Taking a letter of indemnity from such a consignee involves a conscious decision on the part of the carrier to rely on the credit of the consignee—a chancy decision at best.

It is interesting to note that the preceding exclusions require knowledge or intention on the part of the assured, whereas sub-clause (h) by its language excludes liability in absolute terms and seemingly would therefore exclude liability under the P & I policy where the assured's servants *negligently* permit delivery of the cargo without surrender of the bills of lading.

---

648. See, in the United States, Sec. 22 of the Pomerene Act, 49 U.S.C. 102.
649. See n. 633.
650. See discussion *supra*, with respect to the preceding exclusionary clause (f).

(i) Freight on cargo short-delivered, whether or not prepaid, or whether or not included in the claim and paid by the Assured.

The clear purpose of this clause is to enable the underwriter to avoid payment to the assured of freight on cargo which may never have existed. Presumably, the assured/carrier has been paid the freight for carrying non-existent cargo and, therefore, should not profit at the expense of the P & I underwriter. This is true because even where the cargo is not delivered because of theft or loss overboard, the freight includes an element of shipowner's profit.

(j) Liability hereunder shall in no event exceed that which would be imposed by law in the absence of contract.

This clause again emphasizes language in the ASM form of policy which restricts losses to those due to the assured's *negligence*. And Clause 29 reiterates this premise by specifying that in no event shall the policy cover such matters as: cancellment or breach of any charter or contract, detention of the vessel, bad debts, insolvency, fraud of agents, loss of freight, passage money, hire, demurrage, or any other loss of revenue. Clearly, none of these latter items could be construed as liabilities for which an assured could reasonably expect that his P & I underwriters would indemnify him.

(k) Liability hereunder shall be limited to such as would exist if the charter party, bill of lading or contract of affreightment contained (A) a negligence general average clause in the form hereinafter specified under Paragraph (12); (B) a clause providing that any provision of the charter party, bill of lading or contract of affreightment to the contrary notwithstanding, the Assured and the insured vessel shall have the benefit of all limitations of and exemptions from liability accorded to the owner or chartered owner of the vessels by any statute or rule of law for the time being in force; (C) such clauses, if any, as are required by law to be stated therein; (D) and such other protective clauses as are commonly in use in the particular trade.

Clause 12 of the ASM form, is discussed *infra,* and relates to the P & I underwriters' liability for cargo's proportion of general average. Subparagraph B requires the assured to keep his liability within the bounds of the Harter Act if coastwise trade in the United States, or within the bounds of the Carriage of Goods by Sea Act (Cogsa) if in foreign trade or if the vessel owner opts to avail himself of the so-called "coastwise option" by incorporating the provisions of Cogsa even though the contract of carriage may be in the coastwise trade. Moreover, the vessel owner is expected to avail himself, by contractual stipulation, of the benefits of the U.S. Limitation of Liability Act (46 U.S.C. 181-89).

Sub-paragraphs C and D are catch-all requirements to ensure that the assured takes full advantage of any and all clauses of which he can avail himself. Sub-paragraph C, in particular, contains clauses which are required by law to be stated in the bill of lading. The fifth paragraph of Section 13 of Cogsa expressly requires that in every bill of lading which is evidence of a contract of carriage by sea from ports of the United States in foreign trade, there must be a statement that the contract shall have effect subject to the provisions of Cogsa.

An exhaustive discussion of the complexities involved in the efforts of shipowners to restrict their liabilities with respect to cargo is beyond the scope of this text.[651] It will be observed that the exclusionary clause above refers not just to bills of lading but also to charter parties and contracts of affreightment. The following general observations on the principles of law governing carriage of goods by sea, with examples, should prove helpful.

At common law, a common carrier of goods was an insurer and the mere fact that cargo was lost or damaged during a voyage by a cause beyond the carrier's control did not protect him from liability for the loss or damage. There were three exceptions to the common law rule: inherent vice of the cargo, act of God, and act of the "Queen's enemies." The former two exceptions are literally self-explanatory; the last is of limited value and only refers to enemies of the sovereign of the shipowner's country and then only to states at war with that sovereign. It most probably does not cover pirates, vandals, rebellious subjects of the sovereign, and acts of terrorists.

In England, contracts of exoneration in ocean shipping were held valid, whereas in the United States (with a few minor exceptions) this was not the case. As a consequence, the English carriers developed bills of lading which were unsurpassed in length and prolixity, and which required the application of English law. Shipping in American bottoms fell to a low ebb, and English vessels enjoyed an almost complete monopoly. It was readily apparent that some method would have to be devised to encourage shipowning in the United States and to afford some equitable measure of protection—and competitive position—to American shipowners. The Harter Act was the result.

The first and second sections banned clauses of exoneration; the third allowed exemptions from liability if the shipowner used "due diligence"

---

651. The following texts will be found to be helpful; *Marine Cargo Claims* (2d ed.), W. Tetley (Butterworths, 1978); *Time Charters* (2d ed.), M. Wilford, T. Coghlin, N. Healy, Jr., J. Kimball (Lloyd's of London Press, Ltd., 1984); and the British Shipping Laws series including *Carriage by Sea*, Carver; *C.I.F. and F.O.B. Contracts*, Sassoon; *Law of General Average and York-Antwerp Rules*, Lowndes & Rudolf; *Merchant Shipping Acts*, Temperley; and *Ship Owners*, Singh and Colinvaux. In the field of tug and tow, see *Law of Tug, Tow & Pilotage* (2d ed.), A. Parks (Cornell Maritime Press, 1982).

to make his vessel seaworthy prior to commencing the voyage; the fourth required the issuance of bills of lading showing numbers and marks; the fifth authorized customs officers to deny clearance to vessels whose bills of lading were not in compliance with the Act; the sixth preserved the Fire Statute and Limitation of Liability Statute; and the seventh made the Act inapplicable to the transportation of live animals.

The Harter Act worked well in the United States and, subsequently, it was copied by Australia, New Zealand and Canada. The genius of the Harter Act lay in what that eminent authority Mr. Arnold Knauth called the "fortunate formula"; i.e., that, if a shipowner exercised due diligence to make his vessel seaworthy prior to the commencement of the voyage, he was entitled to exemption from liability for faults or errors in the navigation or management of his vessel, but held liable for negligence, fault or failure in the proper loading, stowage, custody, care, or proper delivery of cargo entrusted to his charge.

Following enactment of the Harter Act, there were many international efforts toward achieving uniformity in bills of lading, culminating in a conference at The Hague in 1921. After intensive study, the draft of an acceptable ocean bill of lading was agreed upon. The result was known as "The Hague Rules," the intention being that the rules would be voluntarily incorporated in bills of lading much as were the well-known York-Antwerp Rules relating to general average. Minor amendments were made at later conferences in 1922 and 1923. In 1924 the convention was signed by most of the eventual signatory nations, including the United States. However, it was not until 1936 that the Congress finally adopted the Hague Rules, with minor amendments, as the law of the United States (46 U.S.C. 1300-15), referred to as the Carriage of Goods by Sea Act, 1936, more familiarly known as "Cogsa."

By its terms, the Harter Act covered shipments between ports of the United States and its possessions as well as shipments with foreign countries. Cogsa, on the other hand, applies to contracts for the carriage of goods by sea *to and from ports of the United States in foreign trade.* But Cogsa also provides that, by express agreement, it may be made applicable to shipments between any port of the United States or its possessions and any other port of the United States or its possessions; i.e., the so-called "coastwise option."

A close reading of Cogsa, as compared with the Harter Act, will reveal that the former applies to the parties to a shipping contract only while the cargo is being moved by water. Consequently, since Cogsa expressly preserved the Harter Act insofar as the provisions of that Act related to the duties, responsibilities, and liabilities of the ship or carrier prior to the time when the goods are loaded on and after the time they are discharged from the ship, the Harter Act to this extent still applies.

Knauth, in his excellent little text *Ocean Bills of Lading,* American Maritime Cases, Inc., has so graphically described the "essential theoretical" difference between the two Acts that his comment has been extensively quoted and deserves repetition here:

> The essential theoretical difference between the Harter Act and the Hague Rules or Carriage of Goods by Sea Acts is that the negligence or exception clause of the Harter Act . . . Section 3 . . . is conditional; it never operates to exonerate the carrier unless due diligence has been used to make the vessel seaworthy *in all respects,* regardless of causal connections; whereas the exemption clause of the Hague Rules . . . Article 4 . . . is positive; it always operates to exonerate the carrier unless due diligence has not been used in some respect proximately causing or contributing to the loss. While both the Harter Act and the Act of 1936 are statutory negligence clauses to which the shipper and carrier must conform, the Harter Act is expressed in a conditional way, whereas the Act of 1936 is expressed to declare the law.[652]

It is clear that Cogsa does not condition exemptions from liability on due diligence to make the vessel seaworthy. It is only liability for loss due to unseaworthiness that is conditioned. That is, the unseaworthiness must be the proximate cause of the cargo loss or damage. This is clear from a reading of Section 4(1) which states flatly that:

> Neither the carrier nor the ship shall be liable for the loss or damage arising or resulting from unseaworthiness *unless caused* by want of due diligence on the part of the carrier to make the ship seaworthy . . . .

The due diligence required by the Harter Act and Cogsa is *non-delegable.* The failure of independent contractors hired by the shipowner, even though of the highest repute, to use due diligence saddles the shipowner with liability just as certainly as if the negligence were that of the general manager of the shipowner or its executive vice president.[653]

---

652. The more onerous burden of the Harter Act was not, however, judicially established until 1933 in *The Isis,* 290 U.S. 333, 1933 AMC 1565, 48 Ll.L.Rep. 35. There, the Supreme Court held that the shipowner was not entitled to exemption under the Harter Act because he had failed to exercise due diligence to make the vessel seaworthy although there was no causal connection between the unseaworthy condition and the negligent stranding of the vessel. Moreover, in the *Carib Prince,* 170 U.S. 655 (1898), the Supreme Court had already held that where the shipowner had inserted a provision in the bill of lading exempting him from liability due to latent defects in the hull, this was insufficient to protect him from liability from latent defects in the hull existing *at the commencement of the voyage.* A close reading of the case will reveal that had the shipowner stated specifically that the exemption was to apply to latent defects existing both *at* and *after* the commencement of the voyage, he would have been insulated from liability.

653. See *International Navigation Co. v. Farr & Bailey Mfg. Co.,* 181 U.S. 218 (1901), and the *Muncaster Castle,* decided by the House of Lords in 1961 and reported at [1961] A.C. 807, 1961 AMC 1357, [1961] 1 Lloyd's Rep. 57.

It is important, however, to recognize that the Harter Act and Cogsa are applicable only when bills of lading are issued with respect to *common carriage,* unless the parties to the contract of affreightment expressly incorporate either of those acts in the contract of affreightment even though it may involve private carriage. For example, Section 1(a) of Cogsa defines the term "carrier" as including the owner or charterer who enters into a contract of carriage with a shipper, and sub-section b provides that the term "contract of carriage" applies only to contracts of carriage covered by a bill of lading or any similar document of title, insofar as such document relates to the carriage of goods by sea, including any bill of lading or any similar document issued under or pursuant to a charter party from the moment at which such bill of lading or similar document of title regulates the relations between a carrier and a holder of the same. Subsequently, the second paragraph of Section 5 provides that the provisions of the Act shall not apply to charter parties, but if bills of lading are issued in the case of a ship under a charter party, they shall comply with the provisions of the Act.

It is quite clear that the purpose is to preserve the sanctity of negotiable bills of lading in ocean shipping. Such bills are relied upon in international trade and commercial practices, being, as they are, *documents of title.* This is demonstrated by the line of cases holding that where the contract is one of private carriage, where (for example) the entire reach of the vessel is utilized for the shipment of one cargo belonging to one shipper, any bills of lading are treated as receipts only and the parties are free to contract as they choose concerning their respective duties, each to the other.[654] Certainly, a private carrier is not an "insurer," as was a common carrier prior to the Harter Act and Cogsa. For example, in a contract of private carriage, the burden is upon the shipper to establish that the cargo damage resulted from a cause for which the carrier was liable.[655]

The question of private carriage by tug and tow as distinguished from common carriage or a contract of towage has been before the court on numerous occasions.[656]

654. Courts in the United States early decided that the carriage of an entire vessel-load for a single shipper is "private carriage" and not common carriage, and thus not governed by the Harter Act. *G.R. Crowe,* 294 F. 506, 1924 AMC 5 (2d Cir.); *The Munamar,* 23 F.2d 194, 1927 AMC 1437, *aff'd* 32 F.2d 1021 (2d Cir.). The rule in other jurisdictions appears to be the same. Compare *Liver Alkali Co. v. Johnson,* (1874) L.R. 7 Ex. 267 with *Consolidated Tea Co. v. Oliver's Wharf,* [1910] 2 K.B. 395, although the issuance of a bill of lading or other "shipping document" may well bring into play the Harter Act, or Cogsa, or the Hague Rules. See *Consolidated Mining and Smelting Co. v. Straits Towing Ltd.,* [1972] F.C. 804 (Can.). Unfortunately, not all the courts have applied this principle uniformly, particularly in the area of contracts of affreightment to be performed by tug and tow.

655. See *Commercial Molasses Corp. v. New York Tank Barge Co.,* 314 U.S. 104, 1941 AMC 1697 (1941); *G.R. Crowe, supra,* n. 658; *The Fernandina,* 1926 AMC 1663 (S.D.N.Y.).

656. A good example is *Allied Chemical Corp. v. Gulf Atlantic Towing Corp.,* 244 F.Supp. 2, 1965 AMC 776 (E.D. Va.). See, also, *Texas Co. v. Lea River Lines,* 206 F.2d 55, 1953 AMC 1894

There appears to be no question of the right of a private carrier to stipulate for the benefits and exemptions of the Harter Act or Cogsa if the carrier so chooses.[657]

Difficulties may arise for the shipowner, however, when the shipowner charters his vessel to another. For example, it is not uncommon for a shipowner to bareboat (demise) charter his vessel to a vessel-operating shipping company, say, the ABC Co. The ABC Co. crews the vessel and time charters it to the DEF Co. That company, in turn, voyage charters it to the XYZ Co., which books cargo for a number of individual shippers. The XYZ Co., as voyage charterer, causes bills of lading to be issued to the various shippers.

The demise charter from the owner to the ABC Co. contains an express disclaimer, in unequivocal terms, of any warranty of seaworthiness. Moreover, the demise charter requires that the charterer, its successors and assigns, covenant and agree that any cargo transported on the vessel be so transported on bills of lading, contracts of affreightment, etc. standard and customary, and include the Jason Clause, the both-to-blame clause, general average clause, liberties clause, etc. This is coupled with an express indemnity from the charterer to the owner to hold the owner harmless from any liens, claims, or demands incurred by reason of the charterer failing to observe such covenant.

In the event, it so happens that the XYZ Co., the voyage charterer, issues bills of lading signed by it, "for the master," even though neither the demise charterer, the owner, nor the master actually authorized such signature by the charterer.

As it happened, the vessel was actually unseaworthy by reason of a defect (defective ballasting system) of which the owner was unaware, and such unseaworthiness existed at the inception of the charter to the ABC Co. and prior to delivery to that company. Because of the defect, water entered the cargo holds and damaged the cargo. Cargo owners instituted suit for their damages. The court was thereupon confronted with a multitude of questions, not the least of which is whether the vessel owner was liable to the cargo interests.

At the outset, bills of lading signed by the master on behalf of the *vessel owner* would, of course, evidence a contract between the owner and the holders of the bills of lading.[658] But, in the example given, the master did

(3rd Cir.); *Commercial Transport Corp. v. Martin Oil Service*, 374 F.2d 813, 1967 AMC 2185; *Kerr-McGee Corp. v. Law*, 479 F.2d 61, 1973 AMC 1667 (4th Cir.). The foregoing is but a mere sampling.

657. See *U.S. v. South Star*, 210 F.2d 44, 1954 AMC 418 (2d Cir.); *Raleigh—Cynthia II*, 1943 AMC 1016 (D. Md.); *Bathgate*, 1928 AMC 233 (3rd Cir.); *U. S. v. Wessel, Duval & Co.*, 115 F.Supp. 678, 1953 AMC 2056 (S.D.N.Y.); *PPG Industries, Inc. v. Ashland Oil Co.*, 527 F.2d 502 (3rd Cir. 1975); *American Union Transport, Inc. v. U.S.*, 1976 AMC 1480 (N.D. Cal.); *Kerr-McGee Corp. v. Law*, 479 F.2d 61, 1973 AMC 1667 (4th Cir.).

658. *Gans S.S. Lines v. Wilhelmsen*, 275 F. 254 (2d Cir. 1921), *cert. den.* 257 U.S. 655 (1921); *Aljassim v. S.S. South Star*, 323 F.Supp. 918, 1971 AMC 1703 (S.D.N.Y.). In this instance, however, the master did not sign the bills of lading, nor was he the "owner's man."

not sign the bills of lading and, moreover, he was not the "owner's man" but instead the employee of the demise charterer, the ABC company.

It is clear under American law that the vessel owner is not personally liable on bills of lading issued by a charterer and not signed by the master where the owner's name does not appear on the bill of lading.[659] And, unless the master or owner actually authorizes signature by the charterer, a bill of lading signed by the charterer "for the master" is the charterer's bill of lading for which the owner is not personally liable.[660]

This does not mean, however, that the shipowner's vessel may not be liable *in rem* for the cargo damage. Quite to the contrary, under American law once the cargo is loaded aboard with the knowledge of the master, the unity of ship and cargo comes into existence,[661] although the shipowner is entitled to full indemnity from the charterer.[662]

Charters frequently stipulate that bills of lading are to be signed "without prejudice to the charter party." The decisions reflect that this is a term of contract between shipowners and charterers that, notwithstanding any engagements made by the bills of lading, this contract shall remain unaltered, and when the master signs the bills, it does not affect the contract in the charter party.[663]

In one significant area, American and English law differ, and that is with respect to the so-called demise clause. Under such a clause, charterers attempt to make the bill of lading a contract exclusively between cargo and the shipowner. That is, the clause spells out in unequivocal terms that the bill of lading is intended to be a shipowners' bill of lading, the theory being that since the charter party entitles the charterer to present to the master for signature by him, on the owner's behalf, all bills of lading, the shipowner should be liable to the exclusion of the charterer.

---

659. *Tube Products of India v. S.S. Rio Grande,* 334 F.Supp. 1039, 1971 AMC 1629 (S.D.N.Y.); *United Nations Children's Fund v. The Nordstern,* 251 F.Supp. 833 (S.D.N.Y. 1965).

660. *Demsey & Associates v. S.S. Sea Star,* 461 F.2d 1009 (2d Cir. 1972). Compare, under English law, *Wilston v. Andrew Weir,* (1925) 22 Ll.L.Rep. 521; *Elder Dempster v. Paterson, Zochonis,* [1924] A.C. 522; *The Berkshire,* [1974] 1 Lloyd's Rep. 185; *Tillmans & Co. v. S.S. Knutsford,* [1908] 2 K.B. 385, [1908] A.C. 406; *Kruger & Co. Ltd. v. Moel Tryvan Ship Co. Ltd.,* [1907] A.C. 272; *Samuel v. West Hartlepool Steam Navigation,* (1906) 11 Com.Cas. 115. The English decisions seemingly impose a greater degree of liability upon shipowners in such circumstances than does American law, although a right of indemnity over by the shipowners against the offending charterer seems equally clear. See *Milburn v. Jamaica Fruit,* [1900] 2 Q.B. 540; *Kruger v. Moel Tryvan, supra; Strathlone Steamship v. Andrew Weir,* (1934) 50 Ll.L.Rep. 185; *Dawson Line v. Adler,* (1932) 41 Ll.L.Rep. 75.

661. *The G.A. Tomlinson,* 293 F. 51 (W.D.N.Y. 1923). This is true even though the master did not know of the terms of the charterer's bill of lading as he is presumed to have knowledge of its terms. See, also, *British West Indies Produce, Inc. v. S.S. Atlantic Clipper,* 353 F.Supp. 548, 1973 AMC 163 (S.D.N.Y.).

662. *British West Indies Produce, Inc. v. S. S. Atlantic Clipper, supra,* n. 661.

663. *Hansen v. Harrold,* [1894] 1 Q.B. 612; *Gledstanes v. Allen,* (1852) 12 C.B. 202; *Shand v. Sanderson,* (1859) 28 L.J.Ex. 278; *Turner v. Haji Goolam,* [1904] A.C. 826.

Under English law, such clauses are honored;[664] under American law they are void.[665]

It is also clear that under American law a charterer who books cargo and who issues his own bills of lading will also be held liable as a "carrier" under Cogsa.[666] The situation differs where there is an intermediate time charterer who does not book cargo nor issue its own bill of lading. This question was presented in *Thyssen Steel Corp. v. The Adonis,*[667] where the vessel was time chartered by Adonis to Teseo. Teseo, in turn, entered into a sub-voyage charter with Atlantic. Thyssen's cargo was loaded aboard the vessel under bills of lading issued by Atlantic. The cargo suffered damage and Thyssen brought an action against Teseo for the damage. It was held that since Teseo had not issued the bills of lading it was not liable for the loss; i.e., since the contract of carriage was between Thyssen and Atlantic, and there was no contract of carriage between Teseo and Thyssen, Teseo was not a "carrier" under Cogsa.[668]

Additionally, there is a line of cases in the United States which imposes liability upon the shipowner on a theory of tort. Thus, even in a situation where there is no contractual liability—no privity of contract—between a shipowner and a subsequent charterer or the owner of cargo on board the vessel, liability may be imposed upon the shipowner if he is negligent and the vessel he provides to the demise charterer is unseaworthy by reason of such negligence.[669]

Applying the above principles in the illustration given, it is quite apparent that, *absent contractual stipulations between the respective parties, or cross-insurance endorsements between them,* a vessel may be held liable *in rem* and its owner *in personam* where the vessel was unseaworthy on delivery even though such unseaworthiness was without the shipowner's knowledge and privity.[670]

---

664. *The Berkshire,* [1974] 1 Lloyd's Rep. 185.

665. *Epstein v. U.S.,* 86 F.Supp. 740 (S.D.N.Y. 1949).

666. *The Quarrington Court,* 36 F.Supp. 278 (S.D.N.Y. 1940), *aff'd* 122 F.2d 266 (2d Cir. 1941), 1940 AMC 1546, 1941 AMC 1234.

667. 1974 AMC 389 (S.D.N.Y. 1973).

668. From the record it appeared that the master did not sign the bills of lading, and no evidence was presented to show that he authorized Atlantic or its agents to sign on his behalf. Also rejected was the contention by Thyssen that it was a third-party beneficiary of the charter between Adonis and Teseo which provided that Teseo was responsible for the loading and stowage of the cargo. See, also, *The Muskegon,* 10 F.2d 817 (S.D.N.Y. 1924); *The Poznan,* 276 F. 418 (S.D.N.Y. 1921); *The Blandon,* 287 F. 722 (S.D.N.Y. 1922); *United Nations Children's Fund v. The Nordstern,* 251 F.Supp. 833 (S.D.N.Y. 1965).

669. See *The Poznan,* 276 F. 418 (S.D.N.Y. 1921); *Sunil Industries v. The Ogden Fraser,* 1981 AMC 2670 (S.D.N.Y. 1981). It should be noted, also, that when the vessel owner is not a party to the contract of carriage, he will not be entitled to the exceptions from and limitations of liability which may be contained in the contract of carriage. *Toho Bussan Kaisha Ltd. v. American President Lines,* 265 F.2d 418, 1959 AMC 1114 (2d Cir. 1959); *Sunil Industries v. The Ogden Fraser, supra.*

670. See, generally, "Charter Parties in Relation to Cargo," A. Zock, Admiralty Law Institute: Symposium on Carriage of Goods by Water, 45 *Tulane Law Review* 733 (1971); "De-

It is, therefore, not surprising that P & I underwriters are understandably insistent that their assured shipowner avail himself of each and every limitation of liability provision which either the custom of the trade or organic law permits.

Exclusionary Clause 1 reads:

> When cargo carried by the insured vessel is under a bill of lading or similar document of title subject or made subject to the Carriage of Goods by Sea Act of the United States or a law of any other country of similar import, liability hereunder shall be limited to such as imposed by said Act or law, and if the Assured or the insured vessel assumes any greater liability or obligation, either in respect of the valuation of the cargo or in any other respect, than the minimum liabilities and obligations imposed by said Act or law, such greater liability or obligation shall not be covered hereunder.

There do not appear to have been any cases involving the interpretation of the above clause, although its meaning is certainly clear. P & I underwriters simply do not intend to provide coverage under their policies or rules if the shipowner/assured does not avail himself of the protections afforded by the statutes implementing the Hague Rules in the respective countries which may be involved, nor do they intend to provide coverage where the shipowner/assured assumes greater liabilities or obligations than the minimum liabilities and obligations imposed by the applicable statutes following the Hague Rules.

> (m) When cargo carried by the insured vessel is under a charter party, bill of lading or contract of affreightment not subject or made subject to the Carriage of Goods by Sea Act of the United States or a law of any other country of similar import, liability hereunder shall be limited to such as would exist if said charter party, bill of lading or contract of affreightment contained a clause exempting the Assured and the insured vessel from liability for loss arising from unseaworthiness provided that due diligence shall have been exercised to make said vessel seaworthy and properly manned, equipped and supplied, and a clause effectively limiting the Assured's liability for total loss or damage to goods shipped to $500 per package, or in case of goods not shipped in packages, per customary freight unit, and providing for pro rata adjustment on such basis for partial loss or damage.

---

mise Charters: Responsibilities of Owner or Charterer for Loss or Damage," E. Harper, Admiralty Law Institute: Symposium on Charter Parties, 49 *Tuland Law Review* 785 (1975); "Responsibilities of Owner and Charterer to Third Parties: Consequences under Time and Voyage Charters," R. G. Bauer, Admiralty Law Institute: Symposium on Charter Parties, 49 *Tulane Law Review* 995 (1975).

Although there do not appear to be any cases interpreting the above clause, it appears quite clearly that P & I underwriters anticipate that where, for example, cargo is carried on the entered vessel on the basis of a contract of *private* carriage, the shipowner/assured will, at the very least, take advantage of the minimum liabilities and obligations which Cogsa permits him to enjoy. It would have been possible, of course, for the underwriters to have made the clause even more restrictive on the shipowner/assured by requiring, for example, that in a contract of private carriage the shipowner must stipulate for even more rigorous limitation of liability provisions, as he is permitted to do under such private contracts. This, however, would have posed an almost insuperable drafting problem, as the provisions which *could* be inserted in a private contract of affreightment to protect the shipowner are so multitudinous and varied that no suitable requirement could be drafted which could envision all the scenarios which could be utilized. Apparently, P & I underwriters were content to insist upon the minima permitted by Cogsa.

(n) In the event cargo is carried under an arrangement not reduced to writing, the Association's liability hereunder shall be no greater than if such cargo has been carried under a charter party, bill of lading or contract of affreightment containing the clauses referred to herein.

While there have been no cases involving P & I policies and rules which refer to the above clause, its meaning is perfectly clear.

(o) Where cargo on board the insured vessel is the property of the Assured, such cargo shall be deemed to be carried under a contract containing the protective clauses described in clauses (k), (l) and (m) herein; and such cargo shall be deemed to be fully insured under the usual form of cargo policy, and in case of loss of or damage to such cargo the Assured shall be insured hereunder in respect of such loss or damage only to the extent that he would have been if the cargo belonged to another, but only in the event and to the extent that the loss or damage would not have been recoverable from marine insurers under a cargo policy as above specified.

The above somewhat tortuous language has never been construed by the courts. In any event, it is difficult to see how P & I underwriters could ever be held liable for loss of or damage to the assured's own cargo on board the insured vessel. One obvious question does exist, however, and that is the meaning of the words "fully insured" under the usual form of cargo policy. Does this mean "fully insured" as in an "all risks" policy, or would a cargo policy written under "with average" conditions suffice? It would seem, logically, that a cargo policy written on F.P.A. conditions would not qualify as being "fully insured."

(p) No liability shall exist hereunder for any loss, damage or expense in respect of cargo, or baggage or personal effects of passengers before loading on land or while on another vessel or craft unless such loss, damage or expense is caused directly by the insured vessel, her master, officers and crew.

There do not appear to be any cases construing the above language.

(q) No liability shall exist hereunder for any loss, damage or expense in respect of cargo, or baggage or personal effects of passengers before loading on or after discharge from the insured vessel caused by floods, tide, windstorm, earthquake, fire, explosion, heat, cold, deterioration, collapse of wharf, leaky shed, theft or pilferage unless such loss, damage or expense is caused directly by the insured vessel, her master, officers or crew.

There do not appear to have been any cases construing the above language. The meaning, however appears to be clear.

(r) A deduction of $ _____ shall be made from any claim or claims with respect to each cargo carried, including passengers' baggage and personal effects.

This clause is self-explanatory. There are no decisions construing it.

The comparable exclusionary provisions of the respective English clubs do not appear to differ significantly.

Fines and Penalties

Clause 8 of the ASM form provides coverage for fines and penalties for the violation of any laws of the United States, or of any state thereof, or of any foreign country. However, underwriters exclude liability for any such fines or penalties resulting directly or indirectly from the failure, fault, or neglect of the assured or its managing officers to exercise the highest degree of diligence to prevent a violation of any such laws.[671]

Mutiny, Misconduct

Clause 9 of the ASM form provides coverage for liability for expenses incurred in resisting any unfounded claim by a seaman or other person employed on board the insured vessel, or in prosecuting such person or persons in case of mutiny or other misconduct; not including, however,

---

671. No cases can be found construing this clause, or similar clauses in the English club rules.

costs of successfully defending claims elsewhere protected in the ASM form of policy.[672]

Quarantine Expenses

Clause 10 of the ASM form covers quarantine expenses and reads:

(10) Liability for extraordinary expenses incurred in consequence of the outbreak of plague or other disease on the insured vessel, for disinfection of the vessel or of persons on board, or for quarantine expenses, not being the ordinary expenses of loading or discharging, nor the ordinary wages or provisions of the crew or passengers; provided, however, that no liability shall exist hereunder if the vessel be ordered to proceed to a port where it is known that she will be subjected to quarantine.[673]

Putting in Expenses

Clause 11 of the ASM form covers liability for putting in expenses in the following language:

(11) Liability for port charges incurred solely for the purpose of putting in to land an injured or sick seaman or passenger, and the net loss to the assured in respect of bunkers, insurance, stores, and provisions as the result of the decision.

A deviation in maritime law is a departure from the stated route not contemplated by the parties to the contract, and not rendered necessary to save life or property at sea. Cogsa recognizes the principle of "necessity" in Section 4(4), which reads:

Any deviation in saving or attempting to save life or property at sea, or any reasonable deviation shall not be deemed to be an infringement or breach of this Act or the contract of carriage, and the carrier shall not be liable for any loss or damage resulting therefrom: Provided, however, That if the deviation is for the purpose of loading or unloading cargo or passengers it shall, *prima facie* be regarded as unreasonable.

It has long been held that a departure from the route for the purpose of saving human life is not a deviation, nor is a policy avoided when the

672. No cases can be found construing this clause or similar clauses in the English club rules.
673. No cases can be found construing this clause, or similar clauses in the English club rules.

ship goes out of her course to obtain necessary medical assistance for those lawfully on board.[674] Such decisions frequently result in disputes between a shipowner and a time charterer as to whether the shipowner or the charterer has to pay for the lost time and expenses,[675] but the obligation to depart from the course in such circumstances is quite clear for humanitarian reasons. P & I underwriters are prepared to bear the expenses of doing so within the scope of the language used in Clause 11. In this connection, it will be observed that the clause really covers only the *out-of-pocket* expenses of the shipowner directly consequent on the departure from route. Nothing is said about any possible loss of charter hire or loss of profits which may occur by reason of the departure. The general rule as respects charter hire is that the vessel is off-hire from the time she departs from her regular course until she reaches a point the same mileage distance from the ultimate destination.[676]

In this connection, attention is directed to the rather unusual decision in *Peninsula & Oriental Steamship Co. v. Overseas Oil Carriers, Inc.*[677] In that case, a passenger vessel, responding to a radio request, deviated to take on board an ailing seaman from a tanker having no medical staff. There was no agreement that the owner of the tanker would reimburse the owner of the passenger vessel. The master of the passenger vessel did advise the master of the tanker that reimbursement might be sought for diversion costs, medical and out-of-pocket expenses but did not demand payment. The tanker owner paid the charges of the passenger vessel's surgeon but refused to pay for the crewman's accommodation and nursing and rejected a claim for the additional fuel consumed because of the deviation and the excess speed to get the crewman to adequate medical attention as soon as possible. The trial granted recovery of $500 for nursing services but denied the additional fuel expenses. On appeal, the Second Circuit, reasoning that since the tanker was obligated to make reasonable efforts to provide the stricken seaman with swift medical care and had requested the passenger vessel to perform that obligation in her stead, held that the tanker owner was liable for the reasonable value of the services rendered. The court referred to the "questionable doctrine" that pure life salvage merits no compensation as being irrelevant and held that the passenger vessel owner's claim fell within an exception to the rule denying recovery in quasi-contract to mere volunteers. As the bunkers consumed by the passenger vessel in rushing the stricken seaman to medical attention were not, of course, bunkers consumed by the tanker, any claim presented by the tanker owner to his P & I underwriters would not have fallen within

674. *Bond v. Brig Cora,* 2 Wash. C.C. 80; *Perkins v. Augusta Ins. Co.,* 76 Mass. 312; *The Ada,* 1926 AMC 1 (St. N.Y., 1925).
675. See, for example, *The Myriam,* 1952 AMC 1625 (Arb., 1952).
676. See *The Myriam, supra,* n. 675.
677. 553 F.2d 830, 1977 AMC 283 (2d Cir.).

the precise scope of the above clause, but the principle should, by analogy, be the same.

Cargo's Proportion of General Average

Clause 12 of the ASM form provides coverage for liability of the shipowner for the cargo owner's proportion of general average in the following terms:

> Liability for cargo's proportion of general average, including special charges, so far as the assured is not entitled to recover the same from any other source: provided, however, that if the charter party, bill of lading or contract of affreightment does not contain the negligence general average clause quoted below, the Association's liability hereunder shall be limited to such as would exist if such clause were contained therein: viz.

> > In the event of accident, danger, damage or disaster, before or after commencement of the voyage resulting from any cause whatsoever, whether due to negligence or not, for which, or for the consequence of which, the Carrier is not responsible, by statute, contract, or otherwise, the goods, the shipper and the consignee shall contribute with the Carrier in general average to the payment of any sacrifices, losses or expenses of a general average nature that may be made or incurred, and shall pay salvage and special charges incurred in respect of the goods. If a salving ship is owned or operated by the Carrier, salvage shall be paid for as fully and in the same manner as if such salving ship or ships belonged to strangers.

The principal purpose of the above clause is to provide coverage to the assured/shipowner for loss of cargo's proportion of general average due to circumstances for which the assured is directly or vicariously liable. That is, where cargo cannot be made to contribute to general average because the shipowner failed to exercise due diligence to make the vessel seaworthy, either directly by a failure on the part of the shipowner, or, by failure on the part of those to whom he may have delegated responsibility for the exercise of that duty. Reference here should be made to the relevant words in the Jason Clause quoted above, which requires the cargo owner to contribute in general average where but only where the obligation to contribute arises from a cause, *whether due to negligence or not,* for which or for the consequence of which "the carrier is not responsible, by statute, contract, or otherwise . . . ." If, therefore, the carrier *is* liable to cargo by reason of statute, contract or otherwise, then cargo is under no obligation to contribute in general average, and the P & I underwriters must indemnify the assured/shipowner for cargo's proportion of general average which was not recoverable.

It will be observed that the clause is not restricted to situations where the assured cannot recover such proportion from the cargo owner solely by reason of the assured's breach of the contract of affreightment, but provides coverage where the inability of the assured is due to insolvency of the cargo interests, the running of the statutes of limitation, or even failure to recover in full because of fluctuations in exchange rates. It will also be noted that the clause covers general average *expenditures,* not sacrifices. It also would appear that coverage is provided for the excess of the ship's portion of general average over the amount covered in the hull policy when, because of an increase in the value of the ship, the contributory value of the ship in the general average adjustment is greater than the insured value of the hull.

Where, for example, the ship strands because of the negligence of the master and crew, and the shipowner has availed himself of the limitations of the Hague Rules or their statutory counterpart, general average expenditures may well be incurred. Since, in this illustration, the cause was one for which the shipowner (as carrier) was not responsible, cargo under the Jason Clause would be required to contribute in general average, and no coverage would be provided under Clause 12 of the ASM form.

The foregoing is relatively simple and understandable. A serious difficulty arises, however, under American law when the insured vessel collides with another and both vessels are at fault because of the rule in the United States that cargo can recover in full from either tortfeasor. Therefore, even though cargo may not be able to recover against its carrying vessel by virtue of the limitations of liability afforded to the carrier under Cogsa, it can recover against the other and non-carrying vessel. That vessel, in turn, can include the sums it has to pay to cargo on the carrying vessel in its damage calculations in the collision liability litigation. The net result, of course, is that the carrying vessel—although it has no direct liability to its cargo—can be compelled to absorb a proportion of the non-carrying vessel's damages when a balance is struck between the two vessels on the maritime principle of single liability. It was to avoid this problem that the both-to-blame clause was devised but, as noted heretofore, that clause has been held invalid in contracts of *common carriage.*

The difficulties adverted to above are very well illustrated in two companion cases, both of which were decided on appeal by the Second Circuit on the same day. The first, *Aktieselskabet Cuzco v. S.S. Sucarseco (Toluma—Sucarseco),*[678] involved a suit by owners of the cargo on the *Toluma* against the *Sucarseco* to recover their damages, including their contributions as

---

678. 72 F.2d 690, 1934 AMC 1083 (2d Cir.).

cargo in general average to the owners of the *Toluma*. At trial, cargo recovered only for physical damage sustained; recovery for general average contributions was denied on the ground that the rights of an owner of cargo against a vessel at fault for a collision with the carrying vessel are derivative only, and on the additional ground that an obligation to contribute in general average under the Jason Clause rests wholly on a special contract to which the non-carrying vessel is not a party and that such damage is too remote to be recoverable. The Second Circuit reversed. Citing the *Energia*,[679] the court held that in a suit by cargo for collision damages no distinction purely as an element of damage is to be made broadly between physical cargo damage and damages sustained by cargo by reason of general average contribution, noting that the two stand, generally speaking, on the same footing, and citing additional American cases and the leading case in England.[680] The practical result of the decision was that the cargo owners on the *Toluma* recovered from the *Sucarseco* the amount of their general average contributions made to the *Toluma;* the *Sucarseco* then, in turn, included this sum in its damage calculation against the *Toluma;* and the *Toluma* had to bear a proportionate part of that sum in the collision litigation, which applied the maritime principle of single liability.

The second decision, *New York & Cuba Mail S.S. Co. v. American Steamship Owners Mutual Protection and Indemnity Association, Inc.*,[681] involved a similar factual situation but slightly different issues. There, the parties were in equal fault. In the computation between ships, the contributions in general average made by the cargo on the *Mexico* were treated as a liability of the other vessel, the *Hamilton,* and accordingly as part of its collision damages. When the balance was struck, the *Hamilton,* having sustained less damage than the *Mexico,* paid the difference to the owners of the *Mexico.* Those owners, in turn, paid to the cargo on the *Mexico* the amount recovered from the *Hamilton* to reimburse them for the general average contributions they had paid to the *Mexico.*

The *Mexico* carried hull insurance with collision clauses that provided for settlement of losses on the basis of cross liabilities. Its owners attempted to collect thereunder one-half of the amount which had been treated as the *Hamilton's* collision damages in the settlement between the two vessels. Hull underwriters paid one-half of the amount of the direct damage sustained by the *Hamilton* but refused to pay what the owners of the *Mexico* had actually lost by the reduction of its recovery from the

679. 66 F. 604.
680. *Ralli et al v. Societa Anonima Di Navigazione etc.*, 222 F. 994; *Erie & Western Trans. Co. v. Chicago*, 178 F. 42; *Gray's Harbor Tugboat Co. v. Petersen*, 250 F. 956; *The Minnetonka*, [1905] P.D. 206.
681. 72 F.2d 694, 1934 AMC 1090 (2d Cir.).

Hamilton due to the offset for the general average contributions which the *Hamilton* had included in its damage calculation. The refusal was based on a provision in the collision clauses in the policies that such clauses "in no case shall extend to any sum the assured may become liable to pay . . . in respect to cargo . . . of the insured vessel."

The *Mexico* was insured with the defendant P & I underwriters on the then current ASM form, which provided, of course, that the association would indemnify the *Mexico* for its liability for loss or damage arising from collision with another vessel or craft to the extent that such liability was not covered by the hull insurance described, *inter alia*, as being subject to settlement on the principle of cross-liabilities.

The issue was simply whether claims wholly outside the collision clauses must by implication be settled on the same basis that governed the settlement of claims within them. The court held that the owners of the *Mexico* had sustained a loss in respect of its cargo by reason of the application of the admiralty rule of dividing damages on the basis of single liability and not because of any liability of the *Mexico* to its own cargo or to the *Hamilton*.[682] What resulted was a single liability of the *Hamilton* for the balance struck on the division of damages between the two ships and, because in that division the *Hamilton* had to pay the *Mexico*, the latter had no liability upon which payment could be predicated.

Until the anomaly created by the adherence of the United States to its rule that cargo can recover in full from the non-carrying vessel, rather than proportionately as under the Brussel's Convention, is rectified, this problem will continue to plague American shipowners.

Cleanup Expense

Clause 13 of the ASM form provides coverage for liability of its entered vessels for cleanup expenses arising out of pollution incidents. It reads:

> (13) Liability for expenses arising out of action taken in compliance with the laws of the United States or any state or subdivision thereof or of any country to avoid damage from, or to minimize or remove, any discharge, spillage, emission or leakage of oil, petroleum products, chemicals or other substances.

> (a) Claims hereunder are subject to a deduction of $ _____ with respect to each accident or occurrence.

There do not appear to be any decisions construing this clause and relating to coverage questions. However, comparable provisions of other

---

682. Citing, *inter alia*, *Erie R. Co. v. Erie & W. Transp. Co.*, 204 U.S. 220; *The Khedive*, 7 A.C. 795; and *London Steamship Owners Ins. Co. v. Grampian Steamship Co.*, 24 Q.B.D. 663.

forms of policies have produced decisions, and these are discussed hereinafter.

The language of the clause must be read carefully. It only covers liability for expenses:

(a) Arising out of action taken in compliance with the laws of the United States or any state or subdivision thereof or of any country—

    (1) to avoid damage from; or
    (2) to minimize; or
    (3) to remove

(b) Any discharge, spillage, emission, or leakage of:

    (1) oil
    (2) petroleum products
    (3) chemicals
    (4) other substances.

Unless the expenses incurred by the assured fall within one or more of the above categories, the policy does not cover.

It is very difficult in a text of this nature to cover adequately the proliferating statutes and regulations in the United States, Great Britain, and the Commonwealth nations relating to pollution by oil and other substances. Moreover, the subject is in such a state of flux, and questions about the impact of limitation of liability statutes on it have generated so much uncertainty (particularly in the United States) that the wisdom of Solomon, coupled with the judicial acumen of Justice Holmes, would prove inadequate to the task. All that can be done is to summarize briefly the developing status of the law and call to the attention of the practitioner the few cases which now exist that bear upon the problem.[683]

In the United States, the leading case with respect to the dichotomy between the federal government and state governments is *Askew v. American Waterways Operators, Inc.*,[684] in which, *inter alia*, the U.S. Supreme

---

683. The following articles on the subject will be found to be of material assistance: Davis, "The Ports and Waterways Safety Act of 1972: An Expansion of the Federal Approach to Oil Pollution," 10 *Journal of Marine Law and Commerce* 249 (1978); Sisson, "Oil Pollution and the Limitation of Liability Act: A Murky Sea for Claimants against Vessels," 9 *Journal of Marine Law and Commerce* 285 (1978); Cusine, "The International Oil Pollution Fund as Implemented in the Kingdom," 9 *Journal of Marine Law and Commerce* 495 (1978); Wood, "An Integrated International and Domestic Approach to Civil Liability for Vessel-Source Oil Pollution," 7 *Journal of Marine Law and Commerce* 1 (1975); Dubais, "The Liability of a Salvor Responsible for Oil Pollution Damage," 8 *Journal of Marine Law and Commerce* 375 (1977); Cusine, "Liability for Oil Pollution under the Merchant Shipping (Oil Pollution) Act, 1971," 10 *Journal of Marine Law and Commerce* 105 (1978); Jacobsen and Yellen, "Oil Pollution: The 1984 London Protocols and the AMOCO CADIZ," 15 *Journal of Marine Law and Commerce* 467 (1984); Clark, "The Future of Tovalop," [1978] 4 LMCLQ 572.

684. 411 U.S. 325, 1973 AMC 811 (1973).

Court held that the states could impose liability on vessel owners for pollution cleanup expenses; i.e., the federal preemption doctrine does not forbid states from imposing liability upon vessel owners for oil pollution, even though the federal government has a corresponding statute. Unfortunately, in *Askew* the Court declined to decide whether liabilities imposed by a state statute would be subject to the limited liability provided by the Federal Pollution Act (then termed the Water Quality Improvement Act), subsequently amended by the Federal Water Pollution Control Act (FWPCA), 33 U.S.C. 1251 *et seq.*, or the Limitation of Liability Act, 46 U.S.C. 183 *et seq.*

However, recent decisions have cast some light on the question and have clarified some of the questions left unsettled by *Askew. In re Oswego Barge Corp.*[685] stands for the proposition that the Limitation of Liability Act is applicable to claims under a state statute imposing strict liability for cleanup expenses, and *In re Steuart Transportation Co.*[686] holds that the amount a state may recover for such expenses under a state statute is not limited by the FWPCA.

The latest expression of the courts with respect to oil pollution liability is *U.S. v. Big Sam,*[687] where the Fifth Circuit held, *inter alia,* that the words "owner or operator" were included in the FWPCA so as to preclude an owner from being insulated from liability for cleanup costs (which Congress intended to be joint and several) by bareboat chartering its vessel to another; that notwithstanding the FWPCA, the government may assert a traditional maritime tort lien for cleanup costs against a negligent non-discharging vessel responsible for oil pollution without the per-ton limitation available to the discharging vessel under sub-section g of the FWPCA; that the liability of the owner or bareboat charterer of a non-discharging vessel responsible for oil pollution is subject to the Limitation of Liability Act; and that the government may not assert a cause of action under the Refuse Act, 33 U.S.C. 407, to recover its cleanup costs from a third-party, non-discharging vessel which caused or contributed to an oil spill.[688]

In *Oswego Barge Line,* a barge grounded and oil spilled into the St. Lawrence Seaway. The state of New York asserted claims, three of which were based on the New York Environmental Conservation Law, which provided for strict liability for oil spill cleanup costs. The court held that Congress, in enacting the Limitation of Liability Act, never intended that

---

685. 439 F.Supp. 312, 1979 AMC 333 (N.D.N.Y.).
686. 435 F.Supp. 798, 1978 AMC 1906, *aff'd* 596 F.2d 609, 1979 AMC 1187 (4th Cir.).
687. 681 F.2d 432, 1983 AMC 2730 (5th Cir.).
688. Compare, however, *U.S. v. Dixie Carriers,* 627 F.2d 736, 1982 AMC 409 (5th Cir.), which, seemingly, is wholly inconsistent.

claims brought under statutes of strict liability be exempted from limitation of liability and allowed limitation.[689]

In *Steuart,* a barge sank in the Chesapeake Bay while fully loaded with
oil, and its owners filed a petition for exoneration or limitation under the
Limitation of Liability Act. Claims were filed by the state of Virginia and
by the federal government. Limitation was denied because the sinking
was the result of a cause within the privity and knowledge of the barge
owner. However, liability was limited to $100 per ton of the barge's gross
tonnage pursuant to the FWPCA and this provided the upper limit of
recovery for the cleanup expenses of the federal government. As the
combined state and federal costs exceeded the amount recoverable under
the FWPCA, the state contended its recovery was not limited by the per-
ton limitation of the FWPCA. The court agreed, holding that the FWPCA
limits recovery only as to the federal cleanup expenses, placing heavy reliance upon *Portland Pipe Line v. Environment Improvement Commission.*[690]

In *Complaint of Harbor Towing Corp.,*[691] the claims for damage under
Maryland's strict liability statute exceeded $500,000, while the value of
the vessel totaled a little over $33,000. No federal cleanup expenses were
involved. Although the Water Quality Improvement Act was in force, the
court did not consider its possible effect in removing existing limitations
on state cleanup and other expenses. Limitation was granted. The court
also reaffirmed the holdings in *In Re Pacific Island Navigation Co.*[692] and
Pettus v. Jones & Laughlin Steel Corp.,[693] to the effect that the owner's hull
and machinery and P & I insurances are not to be included in the limitation fund and, notwithstanding that Maryland had a direct action statute,
refused to permit a suit against the owner's P & I carrier because it would
contravene *The City of Norwich.*[694]

In *U.S. v. Boyd,*[695] the court upheld the coast guard's "sheen" test, incorporated in its regulations, stating that the test complied with the con-
gressional mandate to determine what was a harmful quantity. The case
involved a spill of only 30 gallons of oil. In *U.S. v. LeBoeuf Bros. Towing
Co.,*[696] the court held that the civil penalty under the WQIA was not a
criminal sanction within the scope of the Act's immunity provision.

---

689. A collateral issue was also involved; i.e., whether the state could collect for removal
expenses incurred by the U.S. Coast Guard under the section of the New York law allowing
for recovery of removal costs "incurred by or on behalf of the people of the State." The court
denied this claim, holding that in that respect the state legislation conflicted with the
FWPCA.
690. 307 A.2d 1, 1973 AMC 1341 (Me., 1973), appeal dismissed 414 U.S. 1035 (1973).
691. 335 F.Supp. 1150, 1972 AMC 597 (D.,Md.).
692. 263 F.Supp. 915 (D.,Haw., 1967).
693. 322 F.Supp. 1078, 1972 AMC 170 (W.D.,Pa., 1971).
694. 118 U.S. 468 (1886).
695. 491 F.2d 1163, 1973 AMC 1498 (9th Cir.).
696. 537 F.2d 149, 1976 AMC 1416 (5th Cir.), *cert.den.* 430 U.S. 987.

In *Tug Ocean Prince v. U.S.*,[697] the court held that, although the FWPCA is not a "model of clarity," the government's claim for cleanup costs is subject to the Limitation of Liability Act except where the discharge is caused by the shipowner's "wilful misconduct"—a term which, under the Warsaw Convention, has been construed to mean a reckless disregard of the probability of harm. Applying that standard to a stranding of the tug's oil barge, the court held the tug company liable without limitation where it failed to designate a tug captain and to eliminate the known practice of sending deckhand lookouts below to fetch coffee.

A third-party defense under the FWPCA was originally sustained by the trial court in *U.S. v. Leboeuf Bros. Towing Co.*[698] where 60 gallons of oil were discharged from the defendant's barge by a negligent crewman of the towing tug. The tug belonged to a third party. The coast guard assessed a fine and sought to recover its cleanup expenses. The trial court held that the negligence of the tug's crewman could not be ascribed to the defendant merely because it owned the barge from which the oil escaped, dismissed the claim for cleanup expenses, and remanded the penalty to the coast guard for reconsideration. The Fifth Circuit reversed,[699] holding that the term "third party" must be narrowly construed in order to encourage barge owners to select tugs carefully and to insure against potential losses.

Port of Portland v. Water Quality Ins. Synd. et al[700] involved several questions of coverage of policies which presumably covered oil pollution cleanup expenses. In that case, a dredge owned by the Port of Portland sank at her moorings, creating a rather large oil spill. The port contracted with third parties for the cleanup. The port had two policies that presumptively provided coverage: i.e., a policy of the Water Quality Insurance Syndicate under which the dredge was named as an insured vessel,[701] and a comprehensive general liability policy underwritten by St. Paul Fire & Marine Insurance Co. The watercraft exclusion normally contained in such policies was stricken in the St. Paul policy. Although WQIS had received prompt notice of the sinking of the dredge, the as-

697. 584 F.2d 1151, 1978 AMC 1786 (2d Cir.).
698. 1978 AMC 2195 (E.D.,La.).
699. 621 F.2d 787, 1981 AMC 1947 (5th Cir.), *cert.den.* 452 U.S. 906, 1981 AMC 2104. See, also, *Hollywood Marine, Inc. et al v. U.S.*, 625 F.2d 524 (1981), *cert.den.* 68 L.ed.2d 955 (1981).
700. 549 F.Supp. 233, 1984 AMC 2019, 1984 AMC 2012 (D.,Ore., 1984).
701. The Water Quality Insurance Syndicate was (and is) a syndicate composed of 29 major domestic marine insurance companies who banded together to provide a "pool" of coverage for pollution incidents on the inland waters of the United States. The WQIS policy was expressly keyed to the provisions of the FWPCA, the intent being that the syndicate would be liable only for costs and cleanup expenses mandated by the FWPCA. As the FWPCA exempts from its scope vessels owned by "public bodies," and the Port of Portland was a "public body," one of the questions presented vis-a-vis the WQIS policy was whether or not it provided coverage.

sured's agent represented to it that the oil spill was *de minimis* and should be fully cleaned up by the following day. Consequently, the WQIS took no action to determine the extent of the spill by, for example, sending a marine surveyor to examine the scene. Months later, WQIS was presented with a bill for approximately $480,000 in cleanup expenses—a sum which exceeded the amount of its policy coverage by more than $130,000.

The comprehensive liability policy issued by St. Paul provided coverage for "property damage," defined as "physical injury to or destruction of tangible property." The policy also had an exclusionary clause as to bodily injury and property damage arising out of the discharge, release, escape, etc., of smoke vapors, soot, fumes, toxic chemicals, liquids, gases, etc., or "other irritants, contaminants, or pollutants into or upon land, the atmosphere, or any water course or body of water." However, the exclusion did not apply if such discharge, dispersal, release, or escape was "sudden and accidental."

WQIS defended the suit on the grounds:

1. Its policy did not cover because the dredge was a "public vessel" at the time of the sinking;

2. The port failed to give it timely notice of the incident [in the sense that the "notice" given was inadequate and misleading]; and

3. The port failed to secure its consent to incurring the cleanup expenses [a condition of the policy].

St. Paul defended on the ground that the damage to the waterway was not "injury to or destruction of tangible property." St. Paul also contended that it should be able to introduce parol evidence to prove that it did not intend to cover such pollution losses and that the port did not intend to secure such coverage from the company.

The court held:

1. That the sinking of the dredge was "sudden and accidental";

2. That the state's interest in its water resources was sufficient to support an action for damages caused by pollution;

3. Relying upon *Lansco, Inc. v. Environmental Protection*,[702] that the sudden and accidental pollution was property damage;

4. That the dredge was not a "public vessel" as that term was used in the FWPCA;

5. That the silence of WQIS on the subject of the port undertaking removal operations constituted an acquiescence from which the port reasonably inferred that consent had been given;

6. That the WQIS policy therefore covered, as well as the St. Paul comprehensive liability policy; and

702. 138 N.J. Super. 275, 350 A.2d 520 (St.,N.J., 1975), *aff'd per curiam* 145 N.J. Super. 333, 368 A.2d 363 (App.Div., 1976).

7. That the port's claim would be paid by the respective insurers on a pro rata basis.[703]

The policy limit of the St. Paul policy was $1 million; that of the WQIS was $350,000. Both policies contained "other insurance" clauses by which neither policy was to respond where the assured had "other insurance." In the event, the two insurance companies paid on a proportionate basis reflecting the policy limits of each as applied to the total sums recovered by the port.[704]

Healy Tibbetts v. Foremost Ins. Co.[705] involved an ingenious argument by the assured. In that case, the plaintiff's barge was insured by the defendant P & I underwriter. The policy covered, *inter alia*, "liability for damage to any . . . property, whatsoever, except another vessel or craft . . . ." It also contained what was termed a pollution exclusion clause which, in essence, excluded any liability for any loss, damage, cost, expense, etc., of any kind or nature imposed upon the assured, arising directly or indirectly in consequence of the actual or potential discharge, spillage or leakage of oil, fuel, cargo, petroleum products, chemicals, or other substances of any kind or description.

While chartered to a third party, the barge sank. As it sank, oil escaped into the water through an open vent in the fuel tank which supplied a boiler for the barge's steam crane. The U. S. Navy undertook oil cleanup measures as the barge had sunk near one of its facilities. The barge was refloated and removed. Subsequently, the United States brought an action against the assured, the barge, and the charterer, seeking recovery of oil cleanup expenses exceeding $55,000.

The assured contended that, notwithstanding the pollution exclusion clause, the underwriter was liable because (1) an insured is entitled to coverage if a peril which was insured against causes the action of an excepted peril, which in turn causes the loss; (2) where two perils cause a loss, one being insured against and the other excepted, the insured is entitled to coverage; and (3) the insured was entitled to coverage under a separate section of the policy covering liability for cost or expenses of, or incidental to, the removal of the wreck of the insured vessel.

The court held that the policy did not insure against the peril of sinking but merely against *liability* for loss based on damage to certain property which may result from perils such as sinking. There was no insured peril acting concurrently with or causing the excepted peril of oil pollution. As the court observed, if the assured's argument were accepted—given the fact that oil can never escape from a barge without the interven-

---

703. *Lamb-Weston v. Or. Auto Ins. Co.*, 219 Or. 110, 341 P.2d 110 (1959).
704. The problems involving double insurance, "other insurance" clauses, etc., are discussed, *infra*, Chap. XXIII.
705. 1980 AMC 1600 (N.D.,Cal.).

tion of some other factor—the assured could claim that the policy made the underwriter liable whenever there was an oil spill. In such circumstances, the assured could always contend that the intervening factor was a "covered" peril which "caused" the excepted peril of oil pollution and would be tantamount to reading the pollution exclusion clause out of the policy altogether.

As to the assured's third contention that the expenses related to or were incidental to, the removal of the wreck, on the premise that the oil was part of the "wreck," the court held that the pollution exclusion clause would still apply.[706]

It has been held that a comprehensive general liability policy covering property damage and contractual liabilities does not cover liability for pollution penalties and fines.[707]

Oil Pollution Legislation

United States. In the United States, common law remedies have always been available against those causing damage through negligent or intentional discharges, under theories of negligence, nuisance or trespass. However, problems of proof of causation have always been troublesome.

The first act, ostensibly to avert navigational hazards, was the Refuse Act of 1899 (33 U.S.C. 407), which prohibited the discharge of refuse into navigable waters. It could be, and was, interpreted to apply to oil spillages.[708]

Next followed the Oil Pollution Act of 1924 (43 Stat. 604), but since proof of gross negligence was required for recovery, the burden of proof problems made the act unworkable as a practical matter.

The 1966 Clean Water Restoration Act (80 Stat. 1253) was equally ineffective, as it required claimants to prove wilful misconduct or gross negligence on the part of the shipowner, thus perpetuating the burden of proof problems found in the 1924 Act.

The first truly effective legislation was the 1970 Water Quality Improvement Act (84 Stat. 91-107) or, as it was familiarly known, the

---

706. The case also involved two other issues, the first being that the assured had been dilatory in giving notice of the pollution incident to the underwriter, and the second being that the underwriter owed a duty of defending the assured. As to the first issue, the court held that the underwriter had suffered no prejudice as a result of the delay in notification; as to the second issue, it was held that the pollution exclusion clause extended to the costs of defense and to the duty to defend, if any.

707. *West Waterway Lumber Co. v. Aetna Ins. Co.*, 14 Wash. App. 833, 545 P.2d 564 (1976). There, during dismantling, a ship caught fire, sank, and became an obstruction to navigation. The shipbreaker incurred wreck removal expenses and fines for oil pollution. The court held that the policy covered none of the expenses, including fines.

708. *La Merced*, 84 F.2d 444, 1936 AMC 1103 (9th Cir.); *U.S. v. Esso Standard Oil Co.*, 375 F.2d 621 (3d Cir., 1976). Compare *U.S. v. Big Sam*, 681 F.2d 432, 1983 AMC 2730 (5th Cir.).

"WQIA." In summary, it provided for fines for oil pollution from vessel owners and operators, and from operators of onshore and offshore facilities. Unless the owner or operator could prove that the pollution was caused solely by act of God, act of war, negligence on the part of the United States, or act or omission of a third party, the owner/operator could be held liable for the actual costs incurred for the removal of the oil, (a) in the case of a vessel, not to exceed $100 per gross ton of the vessel, or $14,000,000, whichever was lesser, and (b) in the case of onshore and offshore facilities, not to exceed $8,000,000. The full text of the Act will be found in 1970 AMC 741.

In 1972, Congress passed the Federal Water Pollution Control Act (FWPCA), 33 U.S.C. 1251-1376. The basic 1970 provisions were incorporated and, in addition, the act extended cleanup liability to dischargers of other "hazardous materials." It also imposed severe penalties for the discharge of soluble substances which cannot be removed, by authorizing the Environmental Protection Agency (EPA) to impose such penalties for the discharge of "hazardous substances" which it determines to be "not removable." At the same time, the Port and Waterways Safety Act (PWSA) authorized the coast guard to adopt regulations designed to reduce the likelihood of accidental spills through improved navigational aids.

In 1977, the FWPCA was amended by the Clean Water Act (91 Stat. 1566), amending 33 U.S.C. 1251-1376. The 1977 act removed the $14 million ceiling on liability as to vessels; increased the limits of liability for removal costs for inland oil barges to $125 per gross ton, or $125,000, whichever is greater; increased tanker limits to $150 per gross ton, or $250,000, whichever is greater; and increased the limits for other vessels to $150 per ton, with no floor. Since its passage, expenses incurred to prevent a threatened discharge, the costs of restoration or replacement of natural resources, and expenses incurred under the Intervention on the High Seas Act (33 U.S.C. 1471-87) are recoverable by the government as "removal costs." Liability for removal costs is extended to discharges beyond the contiguous zone when natural resources subject to the control of the United States may be affected. However, the notification and penalty provisions apply only to parties "otherwise subject to the jurisdiction of the United States."

Of interest are two decisions reached in 1977 and 1978, respectively, construing the 1972 FWPCA and the PWSA. In *U.S. v. Ohio Barge Lines*,[709] the defendant promptly notified the government of an alcohol spillage. However, at the time the EPA had not designated alcohol as a "hazardous substance." Although the statute, in requiring notice of discharge of a "hazardous substance," provides that information so obtained may not be

709. 410 F.Supp. 625, 1977 AMC 497 (W.D.,La.), *aff'd* by memorandum 531 F.2d 574, 1977 AMC 497 (5th Cir.).

used in any criminal case against the person making the disclosure, the defendant was found guilty on the basis of the reports made by it as the statute was not applicable in the absence of regulations defining "hazardous substances."

The Supreme Court in 1978 decided *Ray v. Atlantic Richfield Co.*,[710] upholding a three-judge district court which invalidated portions of the state of Washington tanker law on the grounds of preemption by the Ports and Waterways Safety Act. Among the provisions invalidated were those excluding any tanker exceeding 125,000 deadweight tons from Puget Sound, requiring enrolled tankers to be piloted by state-licensed pilots, and specifying certain design requirements.

Oil Pollution in Canada[711]. There are principally two acts in Canada that relate to oil pollution: Arctic Waters Pollution Prevention Act (R.S.C. 1970, 1st Supp. C1 [1970]), and Part 20 of the Canada Shipping Act (R.S.C. 1970, 2nd Supp. C27 [1971]). The first pertains to waters lying north of the 60th parallel of north latitude. The second contains a broad spectrum of delegated legislation to prevent the discharge of pollutants: defining substances classed as pollutants and prohibiting their discharge; setting standards as to hull, machinery, equipment, and crew with respect to vessels carrying pollutants; appointing inspectors with broad powers to prevent pollution incidents and to conduct investigations; and compelling ships' masters to report pollutant spillages or the danger of such occurring. The maximum penalty to be imposed against any ship or person violating the regulations is $100,000.

Part 20 and its implementing regulations (SOR/71-495) provide that both ship and cargo owner will be jointly and severally liable for damage resulting from a pollution incident and both will be liable for all actual loss or damage suffered by any person from the discharge of a pollutant. Both are liable for costs and expenses incidental to any action taken or authorized by the federal government to clean up a pollutant spillage or to reduce or mitigate any resulting damage to life and property.

Subject to four limited exceptions, the liability prescribed by Part 20 is absolute, being currently limited, however, to $150.52 for each ton of the ship's tonnage and $15,804,600, providing the pollution incident occurs without actual fault or privity on the part of the ship or the cargo owner.

Part 20 contains a provision for requiring owners of trading vessels in Canadian waters to post a bond or other security that will permit a victim of pollution to effect recovery for his loss without having to pursue either

710. 435 U.S. 151, 1978 AMC 527 (1978).
711. The author acknowledges his indebtedness to P. D. Lowry, Vancouver, B.C., for this summary of oil pollution legislation in Canada. The material is a condensation of a paper delivered by Mr. Lowry at the 1978 Pacific Northwest Admiralty Law Institute, Seattle, Washington.

the offending vessel, which may be lost, or her owner (who may be bankrupt or resident in a foreign jurisdiction). Part 20 also provides a fund derived from taxes on each ton of oil exported from or imported to Canada, which fund is available to victims of pollution damage who have a valid claim against a shipowner under Part 20 but who are unable to effect a partial or complete recovery.

While the preventive measures derived from Part 20 have proved effective in diminishing pollution incidents, the provisions for compensation have been proven all but wholly ineffective because the operable sections of the Act, though enacted, are not yet in force and in any event will be of advantage only to victims of incidents caused by vessels carrying pollutants as cargo. Both the federal government and private claimants are and will continue to be limited to common law remedies to recover losses sustained as a result of the spillage of pollutants which are not carried as cargoes.

Significantly, the provisions of Part 20 are limited to instances where pollutants are spilled or discharged in Canadian waters; no relief is available where the initial spill occurs outside Canadian waters and the pollutant is carried to Canadian shores.

Oil Pollution in the United Kingdom[712]. There are three acts which, together with subordinate legislation issued thereunder, regulate oil pollution in the United Kingdom. These are:

(a) The Merchant Shipping (Oil Pollution) Act, 1971;

(b) The Merchant Shipping Act, 1974, and

(c) The Prevention of Oil Pollution Act, 1971.   The Merchant Shipping (Oil Pollution) Act, 1971, is the act to give effect in the United Kingdom to the International Convention on Civil Liability for Oil Pollution Damages, 1969, which came into force on June 19, 1975. The act imposes strict liability on the owner of a ship carrying a cargo of persistent oil in bulk for any damage caused "in the area of the United Kingdom by contamination" and for the cost of any measures taken to prevent or reduce such damage.

The only exceptions from liability are where the escape of oil resulted from war; hostilities, etc.; exceptional, inevitable, and irresistible natural phenomena; sabotage by any person who is neither a servant or agent of the owner; or wrongful acts of governments, etc., in exercising their functions of maintaining lights or other navigational aids.

Section 3 contains an important provision to the effect that an owner shall not be liable for oil pollution damage otherwise than in accordance

---

712. The author expresses his sincere appreciation to John Lux, of Ince & Co., London, England, for this portion of the text relating to pollution laws in the United Kingdom.

with the act, and that no recourse for such loss damage is to be had against any servant or agent of the owner.

Sections 4 and 5 govern the amount to which an owner may limit his liability. As most recently revised, the limit of liability is £86.83 per limitation ton, or £9,117,024 (whichever is lesser) in respect of claims arising under the act. The act also provides that where owners or insurers settle claims themselves or pay for cleanup costs, they may claim reimbursement against the limitation fund.

By Section 9 of the Merchant Shipping Act, 1974, an extra section has been added to the act, viz., Section 8A, the effect of which is that Sections 4-8 of the act do *not* apply to a ship which at the time of the oil escape was registered in a country which is (a) a non-convention (1969) country (i.e., a country in which the convention is not in force), and (b) a country where the 1957 limitation convention *is* in force. In other words, if (a) and (b) are satisfied, the owner's limit of liability is that calculated in accordance with the 1957 convention (i.e., in the United Kingdom in accordance with Section 503 of the Merchant Shipping Act as amended by the Merchant Shipping [Liability of Shipowners and Others] Act, 1958). It would appear that if a ship is registered in a non-convention (1969) country as defined above but in one where the 1957 convention is *not* in force, Sections 4-8 of the 1971 act *do* apply. In either case, the owner is not entitled to limit if the discharge or escape of oil occurred with his "actual fault or privity."

Actions to enforce a claim in respect of liability under the Act become time barred unless the action is commenced within three years after the claim arose and in no event later than six years after the occurrence resulting in the discharge or escape of oil.

Sections 10 and 11 provide that ships, other than government ships, carrying more than 2,000 tons of persistent oil in bulk are not to enter or leave United Kingdom ports or terminals without having in their possession a certificate evidencing compliance with the compulsory insurance requirements against liability for pollution.

Section 12 enables claims to be made directly against the insurers who are, however, entitled to avail themselves of the defenses which would have been open to the shipowner. The insurers are entitled to limit their liability regardless of actual fault or privity on the part of the owner. The insurers are absolved from liability if the spill was due to the wilful misconduct of the owner.

The act specifically extends the *in rem* jurisdiction of the courts of the United Kingdom to claims in respect of liability arising under the act.

The Merchant Shipping Act, 1974, gives effect to the 1971 fund convention, which is designed to complement the sums payable under the 1969 convention. The convention came into force internationally on October 16, 1978, and by Statutory Instrument No. 1466, Sections 1-9 came into force on the same date. Sections 2 and 3 regulate who shall contribute to the fund (in summary, importers of oil into the United Kingdom), assessment of contributions (by the assembly of the fund), security for payments, and the powers of the secretary of state to obtain information from importers of oil as to quantity and other relevant matters.

The fund sections were due to come into effect on February 16, 1979. At present, CRISTAL, a fund set up by the world's major oil companies, fulfills the function of the fund and is administered in London. Although CRISTAL operates only where the cargo involved is owned by a member company, member companies account for some 92 percent of the world's crude and fuel oil transported by sea.

Section 4 of the fund convention regulates when the fund will be liable to pay. In general terms, this occurs where a claimant has been unable to obtain full recompense under the Merchant Shipping (Oil Pollution) Act, 1971. Thus, the section provides coverage where the owner is exempted from liability under the 1971 act or where the owner (or his insurer) cannot pay or where the damage exceeds the liability as limited under the 1971 act. The claimant must first take all reasonable steps to recover his damages under the 1971 act. Owners/insurers who have paid for damages/cleanup costs may also claim recompense from the fund. Section 4 also lists certain limited circumstances in which the fund will be exempted from liability.

Section 5 provides indemnification for the owner of a ship registered in a fund convention country for that portion of damages he has had to pay in excess of £65.12 per limitation ton, or £5,426,800 (whichever is less), up to a maximum of £86.63 per limitation ton, or £9,117,024 (whichever is the less). In other words, the fund will reimburse owners/insurers for the top slice of the limitation fund under the 1971 act.

Sub-section 3 provides that the fund shall not be liable where the damage resulted from the owner's wilful misconduct. Likewise, sub-section 4 gives the fund a defense where it establishes that, as a result of the actual fault or privity of the owner, the ship did not comply with any requirements of the secretary of state as to marine safety which he had made when putting into effect marine safety conventions.

Section 6 provides for the jurisdiction of the admiralty courts in the United Kingdom and also for the enforcement of foreign judgments.

Section 7 in effect contains the same time limits for the commencement of the actions as the 1971 act, and Section 8 gives the fund, by subrogation, the right of claimants against the owners or insurers.

Part II (Section 10) of the act and subsequent sections provide that the secretary of state may make rules as to the construction of oil tankers, impose restrictions on tankers not complying with the rules, make orders imposing a variety of restrictions upon foreign seaborne trade by way of retaliation for measures taken by foreign governments against the interests of the United Kingdom (including Commonwealth governments),

and make safety regulations regarding submersible and supporting apparatus.

The Prevention of Oil Pollution Act, 1971, gives effect to the International Convention for the Prevention of Pollution of the Sea by Oil, 1954, the International Convention Relating to the Intervention on the High Seas in Cases of Oil Pollution Accidents and Collisions, 1969, and part of the Convention on the High Seas, 1958.

The act makes it a criminal offense on the part of the owner/master if (a) a United Kingdom-registered ship spills oil into any part of the sea outside United Kingdom territorial waters; or (b) *any* ship spills oil within United Kingdom waters. The secretary of state is empowered to make regulations requiring vessels registered in the United Kingdom to be fitted with equipment to prevent oil pollution. Failure to implement these regulations again amounts to an offense.

The owner or master charged with an offense under the act has a defense if the discharge of oil was (a) to secure the safety of the vessel or (b) to prevent damage to the vessel or her cargo, or to save life. Likewise, there is a defense if the escape of oil is attributable to (a) damage to the vessel (if all reasonable steps have been taken to prevent/reduce the escape) or (b) leakage from the vessel (if the leakage was not due to want of reasonable care and if, on discovery of the leakage, all appropriate steps were taken).

The act provides, *inter alia,* that harbor authorities exercising statutory powers regarding removal of wrecks and the prevention of obstruction/dangers to navigation shall not be guilty of an offense unless it be established that they failed to take reasonable steps.

The secretary of state may direct harbor authorities to make provision for oil reception facilities—that is, facilities for vessels using the harbor to discharge oil residues.

Sections 12-16 of the act govern the situation where a shipping casualty gives rise to the risk of oil pollution on a large scale in United Kingdom territorial waters. Section 12 empowers the secretary of state to give directions for the prevention/reduction of pollution to the owners or master of the ship, or salvors in possession of the ship at the time. The secretary of state has very wide powers under this section and, by sub-section 4, he may step in and take over control of operations *and the ship.*

Section 13 entitles any one suffering expense/damage as a result of the secretary of state acting unreasonably under Section 12 to recover recompense from the secretary of state.

Section 14 makes it an offense to fail to comply with orders under Section 12 or to obstruct their execution.

Section 16 sets out the circumstances in which Sections 12-15 may apply to ships (a) not registered in the United Kingdom and (b) outside United Kingdom territorial waters.

The act also provides for orders in council empowering inspection of foreign ships in United Kingdom waters both as to oil record books and compliance with United Kingdom equipment requirements. Sections 19 *et seq.* contain provisions regarding prosecutions, enforcement, and application of fines. Finally, there is an important provision at Section 23 which enables the secretary of state to exempt any vessel or class of vessels from all or any of the provisions of the act, either absolutely or on terms.

New Zealand Oil Pollution Legislation[713]. The New Zealand legislation relating to oil pollution is contained in the Marine Pollution Act, 1974. Part I of the statute gives effect to the provisions of the International Convention for the Prevention of Pollution of the Sea by Oil 1954, as amended in 1962 and 1968. An offense is committed under this part of the statute if any oil or pollutant is discharged or escapes into New Zealand waters from any place on land; from any ship, offshore installation, pipeline, or apparatus used for transferring oil from a ship; or as a result of explorations of the seabed. An owner or master also commits an offense if oil or a pollutant is discharged from a New Zealand ship or home-trade ship into any part of the sea outside New Zealand waters.

Part II of the statute concerns the dumping (as opposed to discharges and escapes) of wastes into the sea. An offense is committed if any waste (defined to include oil and any substance which has not been declared to be a pollutant for the purposes of the rest of the act) is dumped into New Zealand waters without a permit, from a ship, aircraft, offshore installation, or fixed or floating platform which is situated in the sea, or on the seabed under New Zealand jurisdiction. Provided the criteria specified in the act are satisfied, a special permit to dump may be issued by the Ocean Dumping Permit Authority.

The maximum penalty which can be imposed for an offense against Parts I and II of the act is a fine of $50,000, in addition to which the defendant may be ordered to pay the cost of removing or cleaning up or dispersing any oil or pollutant.

Part III of the statute gives effect to the provisions of the International Convention Relating to Intervention on the High Seas in Cases of Oil Pollution Casualties, 1969; it concerns any serious threat of pollution damage from oil or any pollutant to New Zealand or its territorial waters or "related interests" (as defined). If, as a result of a shipping casualty or an incident to an offshore installation or pipeline, a serious threat occurs, then the minister of transport is empowered to take measures to prevent, reduce, or eliminate the pollution, or risk of pollution. His powers in-

713. The author wishes to express his appreciation to Thomas J. Broadmore, of Chapman Tripp & Co., Wellington, New Zealand, for this portion of the text dealing with New Zealand legislation on oil pollution.

clude the removal of the ship or its cargo or both to another place; the salvage of the ship or its cargo; the sinking or destruction of the ship or its cargo; or the taking of control over the ship. If the minister exercises his powers in an unreasonable manner, the statute confers a right to compensation from the Crown.

Part IV of the statute implements the provisions of the International Convention on Civil Liability for Oil Pollution Damage, 1969. The act provides that where oil or pollutant is discharged or escapes into New Zealand waters, or the waters over the continental shelf from any installation, pipeline, or apparatus used to explore or exploit the seabed, the cost incurred by the Crown or a harbor board in removing the oil or pollutant will be recoverable from the owner of the offending device. In the case of pollution damage resulting from the discharge or escape of oil from ships, liability is limited to cases where the ship in question is carrying a cargo of persistent oil in bulk.

Part V of the statute implements the provisions of the International Convention on the Establishment of an International Fund for Compensation of Oil Pollution Damage, 1971, and provides compensation for persons suffering oil pollution damage beyond the damages covered under other parts of the act.

Expenses of Investigation and Defense

Clause 14 of the ASM form provides coverage for:

Liability for costs, charges and expenses reasonably incurred and paid by the assured in connection with any liability insured under this policy, subject, however, to the same deduction that would be applicable under the policy to the liability defended; provided that if any liability is incurred and paid by the assured as aforesaid, the deduction shall be applied to the aggregate of the claim and expenses; and provided further that the assured shall not be entitled to indemnity for expenses unless they were incurred with the approval in writing of the association, or the association shall be satisfied that such approval could not have been obtained under the circumstances without unreasonable delay, or that the expenses were reasonably and properly incurred; and provided further that any suggestion or approval of counsel, or incurring of expenses in connection with liabilities not insured under this policy, shall not be deemed an admission of the association's liability.

(a) It is understood and agreed that the association may undertake the investigation of any occurrence which develops into a claim against the assured, and may undertake the investigation and defense of any claim made against the assured with respect to which the assured shall be or may claim to be insured by the association, and that during such investigation and/or defense the association may incur expenses, which expenses shall be for the account of the assured, and such investigation and/or defense shall not be considered an admission of the association's liability for claim or expenses, and the liability of the association to the assured for any loss, damage or expense shall not be affected by any acts of the association prior to formal presentation to the association of the assured's claim for reimbursement or indemnity.

It cannot be overemphasized that a P & I policy is, strictly speaking, an *indemnity* policy and not a liability policy, although the indemnity is basically against liabilities. For example, the policy expressly excludes liabilities assumed by contract, and losses are payable to the assured only after liability has been established and when the assured has sustained a loss and paid it.

For example, in *Haun v. Guaranty Security Ins.*,[714] the court termed a river P & I policy as one of "indemnity" rather than of "liability"; i.e., the insurer had no obligation to provide a defense, merely to reimburse the assured when liability became fixed, and, consequently, the assured had to bear his own attorney's fees when he conducted his own defense.[715]

In *Cucurillo v. American S.S. Owner Mut.*,[716] the court held that under New York law the underwriters were not directly liable to judgment creditors of a bankrupt assured.[717]

In *Wm. Luckenbach—Powerful*,[718] a lighterage policy was held to cover only in the event of legal liability; hence it did not cover expenses incurred in the successful defense of an asserted liability claim.

In *Ahmed v. American S.S. Owners Mutual*,[719] the court held that in order for the assured to recover reimbursement from the P & I underwriter, he must first actually pay the loss, and under New York law (which

714. 1969 AMC 2068 (St.,Tex.).
715. In *Verrett v. Ordoyne Towing Co.*, 1977 AMC 795 (E.D.La.), the primary insurer settled the case after having been sued directly under the Louisiana Direct Action statute but in doing so expended $14,000 in legal fees. The policy provided that the underwriter was obligated to pay any judgment against its insured as well as any defense costs incurred by the *assured*. The court held that the primary insurer could not deduct the $14,000 in fees from the settlement amount, as it had no obligation to defend but only to indemnify the assured for legal costs it (the assured) had incurred.
716. 1969 AMC 2334 (St., N.Y.).
717. Compare, however, *Hinkle & Finlayson v. Globe & Rutgers*, 1936 AMC 37 (St.,N.Y.). In England, refer to the Third Parties (Rights against Insurers) Act, 1930. See, also, *Post Office v. Norwich Union F.I.S. Ltd.*, [1967] 1 Lloyd's Rep. 216, C.A.; *The Allobrogia*, [1979] 1 Lloyd's Rep. 190; *The Vainquer Jose*, [1979] 1 Lloyd's Rep. 557.
718. 1936 AMC 1796 (Arb.).
719. 444 F.Supp. 569, 1978 AMC 586 (N.D.,Cal.). See, also, *Miller v. American S.S. Owners Mutual*, 509 F.Supp. 1047, 1981 AMC 903 (S.D.N.Y.).

governed in the case) the P & I insurer is not directly liable to seamen judgment creditors of the insolvent shipowner.[720]

Under the ASM form there is no coverage for expenses of defense over and above the policy limits. In *Wills Lines, Inc. v. Aetna Ins. Co.,*[721] a shipowner with the knowledge and consent of the P & I underwriter settled a claim of $25,000—the policy limit. He then sued the underwriter for expenses in defending the claim. The court held that there was no liability on the part of the underwriter, as the full amount of the policy had already been paid. Where, however, claims in excess of the policy limits are successfully defended, the entire defense costs are recoverable if they do not exceed the policy limits.[722]

However, an underwriter's obligation to defend is broader than its obligation to indemnify. Thus, in *Monari v. Surfside Boat Club,*[723] it was held that the insurer had to pay legal costs incurred by the assured in defending against a claim which might reasonably have fallen within the scope of the policy even though the court ultimately held that no coverage existed. However, even though a P & I underwriter may acquiesce in the employment of certain counsel to defend a claim, a timely repudiation of liability under the policy—after issue is joined but before trial or settlement—relieves the underwriter of any obligation to reimburse for the counsel fee incurred.[724]

In keeping with the principle that a claim for indemnity requires that an actual liability be sustained by the indemnitee, a settlement by the indemnitee without a determination of the rights in question casts upon him the burden of proving an actual liability in the action over for indemnity.[725]

In the absence of fraud or negligence or bad faith, a P & I underwriter undertaking to defend an action against an assured is not liable to the assured for any excess amount of a verdict or judgment over the amount of the policy, although urged by the assured to settle for the amount of the policy at a stage of the case when the plaintiff was willing to accept that sum.[726]

Agents and brokers placing P & I insurance should assure themselves that the underwriters with whom coverage is placed are qualified to do business in the jurisdiction in which the assured resides and does busi-

---

720. But, see *Barcelona, Orion Ins. Co. Ltd. v. Firemen's Fund,* 1975 AMC 1183 (St.,Cal.).
721. 1960 AMC 394 (St.,N.Y., 1959). See, also, *Geehan, Admx v. Trawler Arlington,* 547 F.2d 132, 1976 AMC 2510 (1st Cir.)
722. *The Miramar,* 1931 AMC 984 (Arb.).
723. 469 F.2d 9, 1973 AMC 56 (2d Cir.). It is clear that the duty to defend and the duty to pay are independent. *American Casualty Co. v. Ins. Co. of North America,* 230 F.Supp. 617 (N.D. Ohio, 1964).
724. *Atlantic Lighterage Co. v. Continental Ins. Co.,* 75 F.2d 288, 1935 AMC 305 (2d Cir.).
725. *Toledo,* 122 F.2d 255, 1941 AMC 1219 (2d Cir.).
726. *Garcia & Diaz v. Liberty Mutual,* 1955 AMC 2336 (St.,N.Y.).

ness. Otherwise, the agent or broker may be held personally liable for a failure to defend on the part of the underwriter.[727]

Generally speaking, the intent of the parties to a contract of insurance to benefit a third party is shown by naming the third party as an additional assured. But that intent must be clearly shown.[728]

It must again be emphasized that under a P & I policy, the liability must relate to the assured's operations as the *owner* of the entered vessel. Thus, in *Barge BW 1933 Fire*,[729] the assured, although the owner of the entered barge, was held not covered for the negligence of its personnel while performing services for the owner in its capacity as a terminal operator.

It should be observed that a liability underwriter may, under the Federal Declaratory Judgments Act, seek and obtain a declaration of non-liability as to any obligation to protect or indemnify an assured against a specified action pending in court, although the granting of such relief is always discretionary with the court.[730]

The provisions of a policy with respect to deductibles must be clear and non-ambiguous. This was the teaching of *Faris, Ellis, Cutrone, Gilmore & Lautenschlaeger v. Jacob Towing, Inc.*[731] There, the policy provided for a deduction of $5,000 from the total amount of "any and all claims" under the policy. The underwriter provided legal representation for the assured. When it came time to settle up, the assured objected to application of the deductible as to legal fees. The court held that the phrase "any and all claims" was ambiguous insofar as legal fees were concerned. The court noted that the law firm was employed by the underwriter to defend the assured. Thus, the underwriter was the law firm's client, with no privity of contract between the insured and the law firm, and the legal fees were no part of the deductible charged against the assured.

---

727. *Cateora v. British Atlantic*, 282 F.Supp. 167, 1968 AMC 2160 (S.D.,Tex.); *Kelloch v. S. & H.*, 473 F.2d 767, 1973 AMC 948 (5th Cir.). See *Magnus Maritec v. St. Panteleimon*, 444 F.Supp. 567, 1978 AMC 687 (S.D.,Tex.), where a Luxembourg P & I club had no office in Texas but was nonetheless held subject to *in personam* jurisdiction in Texas as to its assured's vessels in Texas.

728. See *St. Julien v. Diamond M. Drilling*, 403 F.Supp. 1256, 1975 AMC 2625 (E.D.,La.). Compare, however, *Calcasieu Chemical Corp. v. Canal Barge Company, et al*, 404 F.2d 1227, 1969 AMC 114 (7th Cir.).

729. 1968 AMC 2738 (Arb.).

730. See, for example, *Association Indemnity Co. v. Garrow Co.*, 1942 AMC 390 (2d Cir.). However, the costs and expenses incurred by the underwriter in seeking declaratory relief and in prosecuting an interpleader action will not count toward the policy limits. *McKeithen v. The S.S. Frosta et al*, 430 F.Supp. 899, 1978 AMC 31 (E.D.,La.). For related proceedings in this protracted and complicated case, see 426 F.Supp. 307, 1978 AMC 12; 1978 AMC 24; 435 F.Supp. 584, 1978 AMC 43; 435 F.Supp. 572, 1978 AMC 51; 1978 AMC 2653; 1982 AMC 685.

731. 342 So.2d 1284 (St.,La., 1977).

Compare, however, *Board of Commissioners v. Rachel Guidry*,[732] where the policy clearly limited liability of the underwriter to a stated sum, *including* costs, fees, and expenses. Although the underwriter selected the counsel, the underwriter was permitted to apply the sum paid as counsel fees toward the policy limit.

An interesting question is presented under American law where the plaintiff's "injuries" consist of disease contracted by exposure to noxious substances over an extended period of time, such as exposure to silicon dust or asbestos. This question was presented in two related cases, *Froust v. Coating Specialists*,[733] and *McMillan v. Coating Specialists*.[734] Both cases involved employees who had contracted silicosis over an extended period of time. The question was, which of the various P & I underwriters on the risk during that protracted period was liable? In each instance, it was held that it was the underwriter who covered the risk on the last day of the plaintiff's exposure.

Prompt Notice of Loss, and Time Limits for Proof of Loss and Suit

Clause 16 of the ASM form requires prompt notice of loss to the underwriter when a claim arises. It reads:

> In the event of any happening which may result in loss, damage or expense for which the Association may become liable, prompt notice thereof, on being known to the Assured, shall be given by the Assured to the Association.

Clauses 17 and 18 of the ASM form are allied and read as follows:

> (17) The Association shall not be liable for any claim not presented to the Association with proper proofs of loss within one year after payment by the Assured.

> (18) In no event shall suit on any claim be maintainable against the Association unless commenced within two years after the loss, damage or expense resulting from liabilities, risks, events, occurrences and expenditures specified under this policy shall have been paid by the Assured.

Prompt Notice of Loss. Prompt notice is helpful to the P & I underwriter in minimizing (and perhaps avoiding) loss, by early appointment of counsel, initiation of the investigative process, and establishment of appropriate reserves well in advance of having to pay an anticipated loss.

732. 435 F.Supp. 661, 1977 AMC 791 (E.D.,La.).
733. 364 F.Supp. 1154, 1974 AMC 204 (E.D.,La.).
734. 427 F.Supp. 54, 1978 AMC 690 (E.D.,La.).

Generally speaking, compliance with prompt notice of loss is a condition precedent to recovery under a liability policy. For example, in *Neptune Lines v. Hudson Valley*,[735] the assured's action against his P & I underwriters was dismissed where no notice was given until 143 days after the accident and more than a month after the hull underwriters had disclaimed liability. And in *Navigazione Alta Italia v. Columbia Casualty Co.*,[736] a stevedoring company took out insurance to cover liability imposed upon shipowners for whom it performed stevedoring services. A longshoreman was injured; three years after the accident and one and one-half years after the judgment against the vessel was paid, the shipowner sued the insurer, contending that it did not know of the existence of the insurance and therefore had not complied with the clause requiring notice "as soon as practicable." The court held that notice to the stevedore of the existence of the policy was notice to the shipowner and that, therefore, the claim was barred for failure to comply with the requirements of notice.

Rather surprisingly, there are not too many decisions dealing with this point in P & I policies, although there are great numbers of cases concerning other types of policies such as hull, fire, general liability, and cargo. These are discussed in considerable detail in Chapter XXVI, "Practice and Procedures." There is no valid reason why cases involving cargo, hull, and other types of liability policies should not be equally persuasive in cases involving P & I policies.

The general rule is that the underwriter must be prejudiced by the delay in giving notice, although the minority view prescribes that the underwriter need show no prejudice. For example, in *American Stevedores, Inc. v. Sun Insurance Office, Ltd.*,[737] there was a six-month delay in giving the insurer notice of loss of a cargo of coffee. The court held this was an inexcusable delay voiding the policy. By contrast, in *Redna Marine v. Poland*,[738] the assured had no actual notice of the insurance policy requirement that immediate notice of damage be given to the Lloyd's agent at the

---

735. 1973 AMC 125 (S.D.N.Y.). It has been held that a requirement of prompt notice is a warranty to be governed by state law under the principle enunciated in *Wilburn Boat Co. v. Fireman's Fund Ins. Co.*, 348 U.S. 310, 1955 AMC 467 (1955). See *Granite State Minerals v. American Insurance Co.*, 435 F.Supp. 159 (D., Mass., 1977).

736. 256 F.2d 26, 1958 AMC 1099 (5th Cir.). See, also, *Watson v. Summers*, (1843) 4 N.B.R. 101 (Can.) (need to furnish proof of loss within a 60-day period held to be a condition precedent to recovery); *Baltic Shipping v. Maher*, 1980 AMC 410 (S.D.N.Y., 1979) (16-month delay in notification of claim precluded recovery); *Big Lift v. Bellefonte Ins.*, 594 F.Supp. 701, 1985 AMC 1201 (S.D.N.Y.) (interpretation of "notice of loss" provision governed by state law; 31-month delay in giving notice to the liability underwriter was unreasonable under controlling state law, and the charterer's negligence in notifying the wrong insurer provided no basis for equitable mitigation in view of the prejudice resulting from the delay).

737. 1964 AMC 1549 (St.,N.Y., 1964).

738. 1969 AMC 1809 (S.D.N.Y.).

port of discharge; the underwriters' defense on this ground was stricken on motion for summary judgment. In *Rock Transport v. Hartford Fire Ins. Co.*,[739] underwriters were held estopped to deny the assured's compliance with notice provisions where, after conducting surveys of every scow which was reported damaged, they raised no question as to the timeliness of the assured's notices of loss. Moreover, the assured gave notice prior to any surveys of the scows—the very purpose of the notice provision. In *Lemar Towing v. Fireman's Fund*,[740] it was held that not every seemingly trivial accident need be reported, especially where the anticipated repair cost did not exceed the deductible; i.e., the assured did not breach the warranty of prompt notice in not notifying the underwriter that the tug had been holed and was taking on water because the captain and the assured's president both believed pumps could control the water while the tug made a return voyage.[741] In *Healy Tibbetts v. Foremost Ins.*,[742] the court held that notice to the surplus lines broker six days after the casualty was proper; in addition, the underwriter failed to prove any prejudice by reason of the delay. In *Offshore Logistics v. Mutual Marine*,[743] a 16-month delay in notifying the excess P & I underwriter of an injury claim was held to be excusable where the assured reasonably assumed its liability would not exceed the $100,000 coverage of its primary policy, and the excess underwriter was given notice four weeks after the claimant had commenced suit. In *Port of Portland v. WQIS et al*,[744] the court held that the water pollution policy failed to specify what the assured was required to do to obtain underwriters' consent to cleanup costs. Consequently, the underwriters were precluded from defending on the ground that the assured failed to give prompt notice of the spill and of its intent to proceed with cleanup efforts.

Time Limit for Proof of Loss and Time for Suit. There do not appear to be any cases decided on the provisions of the ASM policy relating to a time limit for filing proofs of loss or filing suit. However, there are numerous cases involving similar provisions in the hull policies, cargo policies, fire pol-

739. 433 F.2d 152, 1970 AMC 2185 (2d Cir.).
740. 471 F.2d 609, 1973 AMC 1843 (5th Cir.).
741. To the same effect was *Utah Home Fire Ins. Co. v. Mechanical Equipment Co.*, 242 F.2d 513, 1957 AMC 805 (5th Cir.).
742. 1980 AMC 1600 (N.D.,Cal.).
743. 462 F.Supp. 485, 1981 AMC 1154 (E.D.,La.). See, however, *Arkwright-Boston v. Bauer*, 1978 AMC 1570 (S.D.,Tex.). There, the excess insurer was relieved of all liability to the insureds, who failed to give notice of a personal injury claim until 6 months after the insureds were aware that the case could involve coverage questions and 4 months after completion of the trial. The knowledge of the primary assurer's attorney and employees of the primary insurer that recovery might exceed the limits of the primary policy was imputed to the insureds. The knowledge of the insured's broker was not, however, imputed to the excess insurer.
744. 1984 AMC 2012 (D.,Ore.).

icies, and general liability policies. Nearly all the decisions uphold the validity of such contractual provisions unless there are extenuating circumstances.[745]

The validity of such time limit provisions extends even to those cases in which the assured was issued only a certificate or "binder" referring to the policy and was not aware of the time-for-suit clause contained in the policy itself.[746] The general rule is that the cause of action arises when the assured knew or should have known of the loss.[747]

It must be observed that in the United States a number of states have statutes specifically applicable to insurance policies forbidding contractual limitations of less than a specified time for bringing suit.[748] Many such statutes however, have been found not to be applicable to marine insurance.

Assured's Failure to Settle Claims

Clause 19 of the ASM form is very straightforward. It reads:

If the Assured shall fail or refuse to settle any claim as authorized or directed by the Association, the liability of the Association to the As-

---

745. See, discussion on the same topic in Chap. XXVI, "Practice and Procedures." In *Hesperos*, 15 F.2d 553, 1926 AMC 1614 (4th Cir.), the policy contained a clause providing that suit had to be brought against the vessel within 6 months. The charterer referred the claims to its P & I club, and the claimant engaged in rather lengthy correspondence with the club. The court held that the reference to the club and the correspondence which ensued did not constitute a waiver of the 6 months' requirement. In *Transpacific S.S. v. Marine Office*, 1957 AMC 1070 (St.,N.Y.), a cargo loss occurred in 1945. The P & I underwriter settled the claim in 1946. The carrier had paid a cargo surveyor and claimed in 1950 that the P & I underwriter should reimburse it on the same basis as the 1946 settlement. In 1955, a general average statement was issued, and in 1957 the carrier sought to amend its 1950 complaint so as to assert its claim in general average. The court held that the time bar began to run when the loss occurred (in 1945) and that the amendment was time-barred. In *McMillan v. Coating Specialists*, 427 F.Supp. 54, 1978 AMC 690 (E.D.,La.), there was a policy provision requiring written notice or suit within 36 months of the end of the policy period. The court held that the limitation provision was valid and barred a direct action by the claimant against the underwriter.
746. *Corsicana*, 1930 AMC 7 (St.,N.Y.); *Hart v. Automobile Ins. Co.*, 1931 AMC 24 (St.,N.Y.); *Suraga*, 37 F.2d 461, 1930 AMC 328 (2d Cir.). Compare, however, *Phoenix Ins. Co. of Hartford v. DeMonchy*, (1929) 141 L.T. 439, [1929] All E.R. Rep. 531, 34 Ll.L.Rep. 201, H.L., where a 1-year time for suit clause appeared in two policies of cargo insurance but were not mentioned in a certificate of insurance given to the plaintiff. The plaintiff, holder of the certificate, brought suit after the 1-year time for suit had expired. The court held that the time limitation clause did not bind the certificate holder. Note: The court in *Suraga* was aware of the decision in *DeMonchy* but refused to follow it.
747. See *Browning v. Providence Ins. Co.*, (1873) L.R. 5 P.C. 263, P.C.; *Gazija v. Jerns Co.*, 1975 AMC 975 (St.,Wash.).
748. Representative cases are: *Port Arthur Towing Co. v. Mission Ins. Co.*, 623 F.2d 367, 1982 AMC 606 (5th Cir., 1908) (policy had a 1-year time limitation for suit, but the state statute provided for 2 years. Suit was filed more than 2 years after the loss. The statutory limitation was upheld); *S.E.A. Towing Company v. Great Atlantic Ins. Co.*, 688 F.2d 1000, 1983 AMC 1520 (5th Cir., 1982), *cert. den.* 103 S.Ct. 1429 (hull policy prescribed 1 year for filing

sured shall be limited to the amount for which settlement could have been made, or, if the amount is unknown, to the amount which the Association authorized.

The provision is clearly intended to cover a situation where the underwriters believe that they could make a favorable settlement with the claimant but for whatever reason, the assured refuses to settle. This generally involves the reluctance of the assured to advance his deductible toward the settlement, but occasionally a stubborn assured may decline to settle simply as a matter of principle.[749]

There do not appear to be any decisions construing this particular clause in the ASM form, but the clear intent of the clause, by expressly limiting the insurer's liability, is to the effect that if the claim is within the scope of the policy and the insurer defends, full control of the litigation is vested in the insurer and settlement should be possible with or without the assured's agreement.[750]

Defense of Claims

Clause 20 of the ASM form reads:

> Whenever required by the Association, the Assured shall aid in securing information and evidence and in obtaining witnesses and shall cooperate with the Association in the defense of any claim or suit or in the appeal from any judgment, in respect of any occurrence as hereinbefore provided.[751]

As a general rule, the violation of the "cooperation" clause must be wilful, intentional, and prejudicial to the underwriter. Such non-cooperation must also be material.[752]

The duty of the insured under a cooperation clause is to make a fair, frank, and truthful disclosure of information reasonably demanded by the insurer to enable it to determine whether or not there is a genuine

---

suit; the state statute imposed a like limitation; the policy provision was held valid as to a suit filed more than 1 year after the loss); *R. Waverly,* 281 U.S. 338, 1930 AMC 981 (1930) (policy's 1-year-for-suit clause upheld although the state statute provided for 2 years).

749. See, for example, *Pratt v. U.S.,* 340 F.2d 174 (1st Cir., 1964).

750. See *Eureka Inv. Corp. v. Chicago Title Ins. Co.,* 530 F.Supp. 1110 (D.D.C., 1982).

751. There do not appear to be any maritime cases construing this clause or other similar clauses in marine policies. The cases which follow are selected from non-marine decisions where other types of cooperation clauses were involved, and are representative. See, also, *Annot.* 34 A.L.R.2d 264 (1954), 66 A.L.R.2d 1268 (1959), and 79 A.L.R.2d 1040 (1961).

752. See *Hart v. State Farm Mutual Automobile Ins. Co.,* 313 F.Supp. 289 (D.,Mass., 1970); *Peterson v. All City Ins. Co.,* 472 F.2d 71 (2d Cir., 1972); *State Farm Mutual Automobile Ins. Co. v. Palmer,* 237 F.2d 887 (9th Cir., 1956); *Metropolitan Casualty Ins. Co. of New York v. Johnston,* 146 F.Supp. 5 (D.,Kan., 1956); *Standard Accident Ins. Co. of Detroit v. Winget,* 197 F.2d 97 (9th Cir., 1952).

753. *Tillman v. Great American Indemnity Co. of New York,* 207 F.2d 588 (7th Cir., 1953).

defense.[753] The insured must reveal to the insurer all the true facts involving the incident leading to alleged liability, and he must adhere to that version of the facts throughout all proceedings. He cannot prejudice the underwriter in its defense by switching from one version of the facts to another,[754] although the fact that an insured testifies at trial in a manner inconsistent with prior statements he made to the underwriter does not, standing alone, demonstrate that the insured breached his duty of cooperation.[755]

Conduct on the part of the assured resulting in a breach of the cooperation clause has been found by the courts in such circumstances as: failing to respond to notice to admit inquiries from counsel, failure to attend depositions, and giving conflicting statements to the underwriters' investigators;[756] knowingly and intentionally making false statements to the insurer relating to the facts of the accident where such statements continued for a considerable period of time, were a material deception, and where the insurer relied upon the statements in preparing a defense;[757] collusively and voluntarily submitting to service in an out-of-state court and giving the insurer's investigators false and misleading information;[758] deliberately omitting and concealing facts within his knowledge bearing on the accident;[759] the insured voluntarily and inexcusably absenting himself from trial;[760] wilful and avowed obstruction on the part of the assured in the conduct of the preparation of the case for trial and in the trial itself;[761] and assisting the claimant in maintaining his suit rather than aiding the insurer in the conduct of the defense.[762]

The underwriter, however, owes some duties himself. For example, where the underwriter wrongfully refuses to defend, the insured has no duty of cooperation.[763] The underwriter must show good faith on his part to secure the cooperation of the assured, and the underwriter's conduct can be weighed in determining whether the assured was guilty of a breach of the cooperation clause.[764] Even if the assured breaches his duty to cooperate, the breach is deemed to be waived if the underwriter goes forward and defends the claim, but such a waiver can be avoided if the

754. *Home Indemnity Co. of New York v. Standard Accident Ins. Co. of Detroit,* 167 F.2d 919 (9th Cir., 1948).

755. *Century Indemnity Co. v. Serafine,* 311 F.2d 676 (7th Cir., 1963).

756. *Hart v. State Farm Mutual Automobile Ins. Co.,* 313 F.Supp. 289 (D.,Mass., 1970).

757. *Lumbermen's Mutual Cas. Co. v. Harleysville Mut. Cas. Co.,* 406 F.2d 836 (4th Cir., 1969).

758. *Metropolitan Cas. Ins. Co. of New York v. Johnston,* 146 F.Supp. 5 (D., Kan., 1956).

759. *Patterson v. American Mut. Liab. Ins. Co.,* 304 F.Supp. 1088 (D.,Conn., 1969).

760. *Potomac Ins. Co. v. Stanley,* 281 F.2d 775 (7th Cir., 1960).

761. *Peterson v. All City Ins. Co.,* 472 F.2d 71 (2d Cir., 1972).

762. *Elliott v. Metropolitan Cas. Ins. Co. of New York,* 250 F.2d 680 (10th Cir., 1957).

763. *Carter v. Aetna Cas. & Sur. Co.,* 437 F.2d 1071 (8th Cir., 1973).

764. *Iowa Home Mut. Cas. Co. v. Fulkerson,* 255 F.2d 242 (10th Cir., 1958).

underwriter discontinues the defense or secures an agreement that his continuation of the defense will not be deemed to operate as a waiver.[765] If, however, the underwriter defends because ordered to do so by the court, there is no waiver of the defense of non-cooperation, because the assumption of the defense was compulsory; but if the insurer appeals a judgment against the assured without reserving its rights to assert the defense of non-cooperation, there is a waiver.[766]

It is apparent that the courts do not lightly honor the defense of non-cooperation. For example, in *Martin v. Traveler's Indemnity Co.*,[767] the alleged misstatements by the assured related to coverage under the policy and not to liability for negligence, and it was held that no prejudice to the insurer had been shown. In *State Farm Mut. Automobile Ins. Co. v. Palmer*,[768] the court noted that the insured's cooperation with his insurer in the defense of an action implies, not abstract conformity to ideal conduct, but a pragmatic question to be determined in light of the particular facts and circumstances. In keeping with the general rule that the insured's conduct must be wilful, intentional, and wrongful, in *Standard Accident Ins. Co. of Detroit v. Winget*,[769] it was held that false facts which were withdrawn or corrected by the insured before any prejudice to the insurer had occurred did not constitute violation of the cooperation clause. In *U.S. v. Fidelity & Guarantee Co. v. Pierson*,[770] the insured refused to sign an affidavit for a change of venue. The affidavit stated that a fair and impartial trial could not be had in the court in which the case was then pending. The assured honestly and conscientiously believed that the affidavit was false. The court held this was not a failure to cooperate. And in *Ohio Cas. Ins. Co. v. Beckwith*,[771] the assured waived personal service of process and voluntarily appeared in the district where her personal residence was located. The court held that this did not violate the cooperation clause where she had fully notified the insurer, who then undertook the defense of the case.

It is clear that the defense of non-cooperation is an affirmative defense to be interposed by the insurer and must therefore be pleaded. Moreover, the insurer has the burden of proving the insured's non-cooperation and, in the majority of the states, to prove prejudice to the insurer resulting therefrom.[772]

---

765. *Fellows v. Mauser*, 302 F.Supp. 929 (D.,Va.,1969).
766. *Nationwide Mut. Ins. Co. v. Thomas*, 306 F.2d 767 (D.C.,Cir., 1962).
767. 450 F.2d 542 (5th Cir., 1971).
768. 237 F.2d 887 (9th Cir., 1956).
769. 197 F.2d 97 (9th Cir., 1952).
770. 89 F.2d 602 (8th Cir., 1937).
771. 74 F.2d 75 (5th Cir., 1935).
772. *Tennessee Farmers' Mut. Ins. Co. v. Wood*, 277 F.2d 21 (6th Cir., 1960).

Assumed Contractual Liability

Clause 21 of the ASM form provides:

> Unless otherwise agreed by endorsement hereon, the Association's liability shall in no event exceed that which would be imposed on the Assured by law in the absence of contract; provided, however, that the Assured's right of indemnity from the Association shall include any loss, damage or expense covered under the provisions of this policy arising as a result of any contract for the employment of tugs where such contract is one which is substantially similar to those customarily in use or in force during the currency of this policy. The Assured's right of indemnity hereunder shall not include any liability for loss, damage or expense arising from collision between the insured vessel and another vessel or craft, other than liability consequent on such collision, (a) for removal of obstructions under statutory powers, (b) for damage to any dock, pier, jetty, bridge, harbor, breakwater, structure, beacon, buoy, lighthouse, cable or similar structures, (c) in respect of the cargo of the insured vessel and (d) for loss of life, personal injury and illness.

There do not appear to be any decisions construing this particular clause. However, it must be presumed that the clause was designed to permit the assured to contract with harbor tug companies for the use of their tug captains as "loaned servants" to go aboard the insured vessel to pilot it in harbors, i.e., the so-called pilotage clause which is in such common use in harbors on the east coast of the United States. This practice arose because tug captains began to board oceangoing vessels in harbors to act as docking and undocking pilots at the invitation of the shipowners. A small gratuity was usually given them in recognition of the fact that they were acting on their own, beyond the scope of their duties to their regular tug company employers, and that they were, in fact, analogous to the well-known "loaned employee" situation.

Since this was a verbal understanding, some courts became confused over the relationship of such harbor pilots and, in some instances, their regular tug company employers were saddled with liability by reason of the negligence of their loaned harbor pilots. As a consequence, the pilotage clause came into being. Its validity was subsequently upheld in *Sun Oil Co. v. Dalzell*,[773] and the decision has never been overruled or distinguished.

___

773. 287 U.S. 291, 1933 AMC 35 (1932). See, also, *U.S. v. Neilson*, 349 U.S. 129, 1955 AMC 935 (1955).

The pilotage clause, *if properly drafted,* provides an indemnity to the tug company for damages sustained by its assisting tugs.[774] It does not, however, protect the tug company from liability to third parties if its assisting tugs are negligent.

Thus, Clause 21 in effect permits the assured to contract with tug companies on the basis of the usual and customary pilotage clause, but the right of indemnity, as clearly set forth, does not include any liabiity for loss or damage arising out of collision of the covered vessel with any other vessel except liability consequent on such a collision for wreck removal, damage to docks, wharves, etc., damage to cargo on the insured vessel, and loss of life, personal injury, or illness.

Assignment

Clause 22 of the ASM form relates to assignment of the policy and reads:

> No claim or demand against the Association shall be assigned or transferred without the written consent of the Association, and unless otherwise specifically agreed by endorsement hereon no person other than the Assured or Loss Payee named herein, or a receiver of the property or estate thereof, shall acquire any right against the Association hereunder.

The general rule and understanding has always been that marine liability policies are "personal" in nature, and this is generally true as respects other types of liability policies. Consequently, in the absence of waiver or estoppel, if the policy requires the written consent of the insurer to validate a transfer of the insured property, the policy is voidable where the insured property is conveyed without the requisite consent.[775] Such a requirement correctly reflects the liability underwriter's recognition of the "moral hazard" involved in insuring property—and the liability attendant thereto—owned by some third party of whom he has no knowledge. In a sense, it is akin to the "change of management" clause found in nearly all hull policies.

As noted, however, the liability underwriter may waive the requirement of notice, either expressly or by conduct. For example, in *Hilton v. Federal Ins. Co.,*[776] the insured owner sold his vessel to another and assigned to him the policy of insurance, although such an assignment was prohibited by the policy terms unless the consent of the insurer was ob-

---

774. *Penna. R.R. Co. v. Beatrice,* 161 F.Supp. 156, 1958 AMC 1612 (S.D.N.Y.); *Dalzell v. New York,* 77 F.Supp. 793, 1948 AMC 1230 (E.D.N.Y.); *American Oil Co. v. Lacon,* 337 F.Supp. 1123, 1973 AMC 1900 (S.D.,Ga.); *Nippon Yusen v. Zepher Shipping,* 1971 AMC 949 (D.,Mass.).

775. *Meridian Trading Corp. v. National Automobile & Cas. Ins. Co.,* 258 N.Y.S.2d 16, 1966 AMC 391 (St.,N.Y., 1964).

776. 1932 AMC 193 (St.,Cal., 1931).

tained, which was not done. The vessel stranded, and the insurer retained marine engineers to proceed to the scene and take the necessary
steps. The plaintiff/assignee on the following day discussed the matter
with the insurer and revealed his purchase of the vessel. The insurer did
not decline to pay until almost six weeks later. It was held that the delay in
refusing payment while the insurer's salvors worked on the wreck constituted a waiver of the prohibition of assignment clause.

In *Howell v. Globe & Rutgers Fire Ins. Co.*,[777] the policy contained a prohibition of assignment without consent of the insurer, but the policy also
had a rider attached to it which named an insured "for account of whom it
may concern." It was held that the rider superseded the printed terms of
the policy, and a sale of the vessel without the consent of the underwriter
did not invalidate the policy.[778]

Subrogation

Clause 23 of the ASM form relates to subrogation rights of the insurer
and reads:

> The Association shall be subrogated to all the rights which the As-
> sured may have against any other person or entity, in respect of any
> payment made under the policy, to the extent of such payment, and
> the Assured shall, upon the request of the Association, execute all doc-
> uments necessary to secure to the Association such rights.

Subrogation, of course, simply is the right of an underwriter who has
paid a loss to "take over" the rights which the assured had against third
parties and assert such rights against the offending third party. That is,
the underwriter becomes the beneficial owner of his assured's rights and
is entitled to sue the third party (either in the name of the assured or in
his own name) to recoup or recover the amount paid. Even in the absence
of a contractual stipulation in the policy relating to rights of surogation, a
right of subrogation arises by operation of law and no assignment or
transfer of the right of subrogation need be made.[779]

Section 79 of the Marine Insurance Act, 1906 restates the common law
as it existed prior to the Act, and reads:

> (1) Where the insurer pays for a total loss, either of the whole, or in
> the case of goods of any appreciable part, of the subject-matter in-

777. 1928 AMC 1806 (St.,N.Y.).
778. See, also, Chap. XI, "Warranties," and in particular the discussion with respect to
the change of management warranty.
779. *Phoenix Ins. Co. v. Erie & Western Transportation Co.*, 117 U.S. 312 (1886); *The Sydney*,
23 F. 88 (S.D.N.Y.. 1885); *Globe & Rutgers Fire Ins. Co. v. Hines*, 273 F. 774 (2d Cir., 1921);
Federal Insurance Co. v. Detroit F. & M. Ins. Co., 202 F. 648 (7th Cir., 1913).

sured, he thereupon becomes entitled to take over the interest of the assured in whatever may remain of the subject-matter so paid for, and he is thereby subrogated to all the rights and remedies of the assured in and in respect of the subject-matter as from the time of the casualty causing the loss.

(2) Subject to the foregoing provisions, where the insurer pays for a partial loss, he acquires no title to the subject-matter insured, or such part of it as may remain, but he is thereupon subrogated to all rights and remedies of the assured in and in respect of the subject-matter insured as from the time of the casualty causing the loss, insofar as the assured has been indemnified, according to this Act, by such payment for the loss.

The principle of subrogation obviously has a great impact in the field of marine insurance for, as a practical matter, underwriters frequently pay losses without delay, and the subsequent litigation which follows, against offending third parties, even though often prosecuted in the name of the assured as plaintiff, is actually carried forward by the underwriters and their counsel.

Surprisingly, there are relatively few cases discussing subrogation rights under P & I policies, although the literature abounds with cases involving rights of subrogation under hull and cargo policies. The subject in general under marine policies is discussed in detail in Chapter XXIII, "Subrogation, Waiver of Subrogation, Loan Receipts, and Double Insurance." The discussion here is limited to the few decisions involving P & I policies, or comparable liability policies insuring risks similar to those found in a standard P & I policy.

Rights of subrogation are not barred against one named as an additional assured under a P & I policy if the loss is caused by an activity of the additional assured which falls without the scope of the policy. Thus, in *Lanasse v. Travelers Ins.*,[780] the fact that the shipowner's P & I policy named the time charterer as an additional assured with waiver of subrogation was held not to prevent the P & I underwriter from recovering from the time charterer sums paid in settlement of a seaman's claim for personal injuries resulting solely from negligence of the time charterer's crane operator. The policy covered only liabilities of the assured "as owner" of the vessel, and neither the crew nor the vessel itself was at fault.

---

780. 450 F.2d 580, 1972 AMC 818 (5th Cir., 1971). To the same effect, essentially, see *Gryar v. Odeco*, 1982 AMC 143 (E.D., La., 1981), where an oil drilling company was named as an additional assured under a crewboat owner's P & I policy. An employee was injured as a result of the oil drilling company's independent negligence in failing to provide a safe means of access to its drilling rig. The court held that the policy covered only as to claims arising out of the operation of the crewboat.

A different result, however, was reached in *Caballery v. Sea-Land*,[781] where the P & I policy was endorsed to provide that if the assured's vessel were chartered to any affiliated or related companies, coverage would be extended to protect the charterers "in any capacity." The activities of the assured's related company in the *stevedoring* business occasioned the loss. It was held that the underwriter could not bring a subrogation action against the related company.

In *Callahan v. Cheramie Boats and Shell Oil Co.*,[782] it was held that an indemnitee is not barred from suing an indemnitor simply because both are named insureds under a liability policy obtained by the indemnitee pursuant to its charter agreement with the indemnitor. The case was decided upon the basis of preliminary motions in a suit involving a claim for personal injuries sustained by an employee of an independent contractor when he was disembarking from a fixed platform owned by the indemnitor. Although it is probable that the defense of the primary action was being conducted by the liability underwriter, and any judgment obtained against its assureds would be paid by it, this issue did not surface during the hearings on the preliminary motions.

In *American Auto Ins. v. Twenty Grand*,[783] a workmen's compensation insurer was held entitled to bring a subrogation action against the owner of a crewboat whose negligence allegedly injured the insured charterer's employee. The crewboat owner contended that the insurer could not, because of a lack of privity, avail itself of a hold harmless indemnity agreement in the charter. The court rejected this contention, holding that where the insurance contract expressly provided for subrogation upon payment by the insurer of the insured's claim, the contention was without merit; that subrogation includes both contractual and tortious rights; and that in Louisiana, a cause of action may be enforced by both subrogor and subrogee when subrogation is partial, but if the entire right has been subrogated, it may be enforced by the subrogee alone.

In *U.S. v. Alaska S.S. Co.*,[784] the insurer issued a policy insuring the defendant steamship company as a general agent under a service agreement with the United States, and also insuring the United States as the owner of the vessel. The service agreement precluded any right of subrogation by the United States or its insurer against the steamship company general agent. After settling a personal injury suit of a longshoreman employed by the steamship company's terminal and stevedoring division, the insurer in the name of the United States sought *Ryan* indemnity from the steamship company. The court held that the indemnity ac-

781. 1973 AMC 479 (D.P.R.).
782. 383 F.Supp. 1217, 1975 AMC 408 (E.D.,La., 1974).
783. 225 So.2d 114, 1969 AMC 2360 (St.,La.).
784. 491 F.2d 1147, 1974 AMC 630 (9th Cir.).

tion was not an improper subrogation action because the policy insured against general agent's liability whereas the indemnity claim was based on *stevedore* liability.

In *Prudential Lines v. General Tire*,[785] the issue was whether the P & I underwriter, a partial subrogee only, was a necessary or indispensable party under the Federal Rules of Civil Procedure. The case involved a suit by an ocean carrier against a party who had packed and secured the cargo, to recover a settlement paid by the P & I underwriter, to the consignee. The court held that the club need not be added as a party plaintiff since it would be estopped by *res adjudicata* principles from bringing a subsequent suit against the defendant.

In *Citizens Cas. Co. v. Seafood Packers*,[786] a wholesale purchaser of the catch of fishing vessels, as a gratuitous service to these vessels, allowed their masters to select and use fish-boxes from his wharf. A crewmember on a fishing boat was injured due to an allegedly deficient fish-box. The fishing vessel owner settled with the injured crewmember and its P & I insurer sought to recoup the sum paid against the wholesale purchaser. The court held that the wharf owner made no warranty of the condition of the boxes and was not liable to indemnify the fishing boat owner. Hence, the P & I insurer had no right of subrogation against the wharf owner.

In *Jones Tug & Barge Co. v. S.S. Liberty Manufacturer*,[787] the insured vessel stranded. The P & I underwriter was the Britannia Steamship Ins. Ass'n, Ltd. While stranded, the vessel began to leak oil. Britannia arranged with various parties to perform services on behalf of the vessel, including removal of the fuel oil from the vessel, salving the vessel and getting it off its strand, pumping services, oil control pollution services, ship husbanding and stevedore services, crane services, and tug assistance services. In many instances, Britannia paid those performing the requested services by way of loan receipts. The vessel was sold at a marshal's sale for only $136,000—a sum considerably less than the sales proceeds deposited in the registry of the court.

Britannia sought to acquire, by subrogation, rights against the vessel fund for the sums it had paid under loan receipts to those performing services. The court held that it was immaterial that the club's claims were asserted against the sale proceeds rather than the insured shipowner itself, and that payments made under the loan receipts had none of the indicia of true "loans." Consequently, the club was not entitled to claim subrogation, essentially against its own assured.

785. 74 FRD 474, 1978 AMC 93, related proceedings, 440 F.Supp. 556, 1978 AMC 2337, 448 F.Supp. 202, 1978 AMC 2344 (S.D.N.Y.).
786. 1972 AMC 770 (D.,Mass., 1971).
787. 1978 AMC 1183 (C.D.,Cal.).

In a rather unusual situation, the Ninth Circuit in *The Watsonville*,[788] denied subrogation rights on behalf of an insurance company which had paid for damage done by the insured vessel to dolphins and a light belonging to the United States. The trial court found that the damage was occasioned by the negligence of the pilot on board the insured vessel. Neither the pleadings nor the evidence at trial showed that the insurance company had issued a marine *liability* policy to the vessel owner, only a property damage policy insuring damage to property owned by the assured. As the assured had no property interest whatever in the dolphins and the light, and as the policy did not cover liabilities of the vessel owner to third parties, there was no right of subrogation in the insurance company; i.e., it had paid for the damage to the dolphins and the light as a volunteer.

In *Continental Casualty v. Canadian Universal Ins.*,[789] two insurance companies insured the same assured, the first company having issued a contractual indemnity policy and the second company having issued a liability policy covering Jones Act liabilities. The Jones Act insurer paid a substantial sum in settlement of a personal injury claim of an employee of the assured. The contractual liability policy provided coverage for unseaworthiness of a vessel on which the employee was injured, and the injuries occurred by reason of unseaworthiness. The court held that the Jones Act insurer was entitled to subrogate and obtain reimbursement from the contractual liability underwriter of a share of the sums paid to the injured claimant.

American Motorists v. American Employers[790] involved an action by the P & I underwriters against a comprehensive general liability underwriter for amounts contributed to settle a personal injury action arising when one of the assured's employees discharged a firearm ashore and injured a third party. The court held that the employee was not acting within the scope of his employment when he discharged the firearm and, consequently, neither policy covered the employer/assured. Hence, both insurance companies had to bear the losses resulting from their respective contributions and neither was entitled to contribution from the other.

Other Insurance

Clause 24 of the ASM form relieves the P & I underwriter from liability which would be covered by other insurance. It reads:

> The Association shall not be liable for any loss, damage or expense against which, but for the insurance herein provided, the assured is or would be insured under existing insurance.

788. 79 F.2d 716, 1935 AMC 1501 (9th Cir.).
789. 605 F.2d 1340, 1980 AMC 1907 (5th Cir., 1979).
790. 447 F.Supp. 1314, 1978 AMC 1467 (W.D.,La.).

In the United States, there is a split among the jurisdictions with respect to the effect to be given to "other insurance" clauses. The court, in *Lodrigue v. Montegut Auto Marine Service*,[791] gave a comprehensive review of the approaches taken by federal courts on the issue.

Generally speaking, such clauses take two forms. One type is known as an "excess" clause; the other an "escape" clause. Both types are commonly classified as "other insurance" clauses. The effect of the two clauses is, however, markedly different. Under an excess clause, the underwriter seeks to limit its liability to an amount in excess of any coverage provided by some other policy. Under an escape clause, the underwriter seeks complete relief from any coverage at all if the assured has other available insurance. The difficulty arises when, read together, only one of the two clauses can be given its intended effect.

The courts have adopted three different approaches to reconcile such differences. Some courts give effect to the escape clause, thereby relieving the insurer of any coverage at all.[792] Other courts have required the insurer whose policy contains an escape clause to provide primary coverage, while the excess clause insurer remains liable only for amounts in excess of the first company's policy limits.[793] A third line of cases disregards both clauses as mutually repugnant and apportions the liability on the basis of the primary limits of each insurance company's policy.[794]

In *Davis Yarn Co. v. Brooklyn Yarn Dye Co.*,[795] both policies had, in effect, excess clauses. Both underwriters defended on the ground of other insurance. The court held that one policy was more specific in its coverage than the other and therefore was primarily liable, to which the second policy was supplementary and secondary.

Essentially the same result was reached in *Marine Transit Corp. v. Northwestern Fire and Marine Ins. Co.*,[796] There, the carrier had both a tower's liability clause in its hull policy as well as a separate policy covering its legal liability to cargo on its tows. The clause in the latter policy provided that if other insurance were available, the policy would be void except as such other insurance might be deficient toward fully covering the loss. It was held that the tower's liability policy was primary up to its limit and the legal liability thereafter for any liability beyond that limit.

---

791. 1978 AMC 2272 (E.D.,La., 1977).

792. *Indiana Lumbermens Mut. Ins. Co. v. Mitchell*, 409 F.2d 392 (7th Cir., 1969); *Viger v. Geophysical Services, Inc.*, 338 F.Supp. 808, 1972 AMC 2113 (W.D.,La.), *aff'd* 476 F.2d 1288, 1973 AMC 1109 (5th Cir.), *reh. den. en banc*, 478 F.2d 1403 (5th Cir., 1973).

793. *Employers Liab. Assur. Corp., Ltd. v. Fireman's Fund*, 262 F.2d 239 (D.C.,Cir., 1958).

794. *Graves v. Traders & General Ins. Co.*, 252 La. 709, 214 So.2d 116 (1968); *Lamb-Weston, Inc. v. Oregon Auto Ins. Co.*, 219 Or. 110, 341 P.2d 110 (1959); *Werley v. United Services Auto. Ass'n*, 498 P.2d 112 (Alaska, 1972).

795. 1943 AMC 116 (St.,N.Y.).

796. 67 F.2d 544, 1933 AMC 1631 (2d Cir.).

In *Berkeley v. Fireman's Fund*,[797] the owner of a vessel, the demise charterer, and a sub-bareboat charterer were all named assureds in a "layered employer's liability policy." The demise charterer also had a separate employer's liability policy and a separate umbrella policy. The vessel broke apart at sea, causing multiple deaths and injuries to the crew. The loss was caused by the negligence of the sub-bareboat charterer, who was found to be the employer of the crew. The insurer on the layered employer's liability policy settled the crew claims and sought contribution from the other two insurers. The court held that the coverage priorities should be determined in light of the total policy insuring intent, and the insurer on the layered employer's liability policy was properly liable for the entire loss because (1) the actual employer (sub-bareboat charterer) was a named assured, (2) the actual employer was not a named assured in the other two policies, and (3) the umbrella policy was clearly intended to be excess. The court stated, in part, that it was a disfavored approach to resolve disputes among insurance carriers on the basis of a dogmatic reliance on other insurance clauses of respective policies without regard to the intent of the parties as manifested in the overall pattern of insurance coverage.[798]

No decision can be found construing the other insurance clause in the ASM form, but its wording is such that the only logical interpretation is that it is intended as an "escape" type of clause.

797. 1976 AMC 856 (W.D.,Wash.).
798. See, generally, *Irving—Seatrain Navana*, 103 F.2d 772, 1939 AMC 1043 (2d Cir.); *Zidell v. Travelers Indemnity*, 264 F.Supp. 496, 1967 AMC 1139 (D.,Ore.) (Lloyd's excess stevedore liability policy not required to contribute pro rata with the primary insurer); *Voison v. Ocean Protein*, 321 F.Supp. 173, 1971 AMC 464 (E.D.,La.) (workmen's compensation underwriter and P & I underwriter held to be co-insurers; disregarding the other insurance clauses in both policies, the court apportioned the liability equally between them); *Morslich's Case*, 1972 AMC 2655 (S.D.N.Y.) (employer's liability policy held to prevail over the P & I policy and liable to respond for the entire loss); *Barge BW 1933 Fire*, 1968 AMC 2738 (Arb.) (excess type clause given preference over escape clause, especially where this seemed to be in accord with the assured's intentions); *Lytle v. Freedom Int'l Carrier*, 519 F.2d 129, 1975 AMC 2670 (6th Cir.) (stevedore's excess liability policy dovetailed with the primary policy; exclusion in the excess policy was not sufficiently explicit to excuse the excess underwriter from responding to a claim against its assured); *Keys Eng. Co. v. Boston Ins. Co.*, 192 F.Supp. 574 (S.D.,Fla., 1961) (one policy contained an other insurance clause, the other only prohibited double insurance; the liability was pro-rated between the policies); *Offshore Logistics v. Mutual Marine*, 462 F.Supp. 485, 1981 AMC 1154 (E.D.,La.) (an excess P & I underwriter's policy contained two inconsistent clauses relating to other insurance, an excess clause and an escape clause; another liability policy—with an earlier date of attachment—also contained an excess clause; the court held that, construing the first policy most favorably to the assured, the excess clause would be given effect, and as between that policy and the other policy, the one attaching first would be deemed primary and the later attaching policy excess); *Rini v. Transocean*, 1981 AMC 1128 (W.D.,La.) (two P & I policies, both containing an escape clause with respect to other insurance; since they were mutually repugnant, liability was pro-rated between them); *Port of Portland v. WQIS*, 1984 AMC 2019 (D. Ore.) (a specific oil pollution policy and a comprehensive general liability policy, each containing an escape clause, held to cover the same liability arising out of an oil spill; liability pro-rated in proportion to the policy limits).

Rather surprisingly, there are relatively few cases in England and the Commonwealth construing such clauses, none of which involves P & I insurance. Section 80 of the Marine Insurance Act, 1906, relating to double insurance, merely expresses the law as it existed before the enactment of the 1906 Act. It reads:

> (1) Where the assured is over-insured by double insurance, each insurer is bound, as between himself and the other insurers, to contribute rateably to the loss in proportion to the amount for which he is liable under his contract.
> (2) If any insurer pays more than his proportion of loss, he is entitled to maintain an action for contribution against the other insurers, and is entitled to the like remedies as a surety who has paid more than his proportion of the debt.

Reference should be made to Chapter XXIII, "Subrogation, Waiver of Subrogation, Loan Receipts, and Double Insurance," for cases generally dealing with double insurance.[799]

A continuation of the practice among various maritime interests in the United States of insisting on being named as additional assureds on hull and P & I policies is certain to produce more cases in which the courts must decide which policies are primary and which are secondary. Many such situations never reach the courts but are amicably adjusted among the affected underwriters.

Limitation of Liability

Clause 25 of the ASM form limits the liability of the underwriter to a sum no greater than that to which the assured would be liable if entitled to rights of limitation. It reads:

> If and when the Assured under this policy has any interest other than as an owner or bareboat charterer of the insured vessel, in no event shall the Association be liable hereunder to any greater extent than if such Assured were the owner or bareboat charterer and were entitled to all the rights of limitation to which a shipowner is entitled.

Only one case can be found construing similar language, and that is *Crown Zellerbach Corp. v. Ingram and London Steamship Owners' Mutual In-*

---

799. Templeman, *Marine Insurance* (5th ed.), (McDonald & Evans, Ltd., 1981), p. 404, n. 41, notes that if both policies contain clauses excluding indemnity provided elsewhere, then it would be an unreasonable construction for the loss to be covered nowhere—consequently double insurance would exist, citing a motor insurance case, *Weddell and Another v. Road Transport and General Ins. Co.*, (1932) 41 Ll.L.Rep. 69, applied in *National Employers Mutual Gen. Ins. Ass'n Ltd. v. Hayden*, [1979] 2 Lloyd's Rep. 235, a professional indemnity case.

surance Ass'n, Ltd.[800] In that case, the assured's tug flotilla collided with the plaintiff's water intake structure on the Mississippi River, causing damage in excess of $3,900,000. The assured was found entitled to limitation and limited its liability to $2,134,918.88. The assured's primary P & I policy had a limit of $1,000,000; there was excess P & I coverage placed with the defendant London Steamship Owners' Mutual club. Following judgment, the assured and its two P & I underwriters made payments up to the limits of the assured's limited liability; i.e., $2,134,918.88. The excess P & I underwriter appealed. At first instance, the Fifth Circuit affirmed, holding, *inter alia,* that the excess underwriter had to respond for any excess over the limited amount, basing its decision on *Olympic Towing Corp. v. Nebel Towing Co., Inc.*[801] However, on rehearing *en banc,* the full court reversed itself and held that the excess P & I club was not liable for sums in excess of the tug's liability limit. The court pointed out that *Nebel Towing* had dealt solely with the contention that the P & I underwriters were entitled to the shipowner's *statutory* right to limit liability. In the present case, the claim was quite different and was premised on the terms of the club's rules, which expressly limited the maximum dollar amount to the dollar amount for which the shipowner/assured would be liable upon successfully maintaining the right to limit its liability. Although Louisiana had a direct action statute, that statute provided that any action brought under it would be subject to " . . . the defenses which could be urged by the insurer to a direct action brought by the insured." While the text of the London Steamship Mutual's rule differed in context from that set forth in the ASM policy, the net effect is the same. To the foregoing extent, *Nebel Towing* must be deemed overruled.

However, it must be emphasized that under American law—as it currently exists—only an owner or bareboat charterer of a vessel is entitled to limit liability under the U.S. Limitation of Liability Act, whereas under English law other types of legal entities are entitled to limit. The obvious intent of the ASM clause is to limit the underwriter's liability to an amount no greater than that to which the assured would be entitled to limit liability if that assured were the owner or bareboat charterer.

Lay-up Returns

Clause 26 of the ASM form, unlike many comparable P & I club forms, provides for lay-up returns. It reads:

---

800. 745 F.2d 715, 1985 AMC 305 (5th Cir., 1984), modified *en banc,* 783 F.2d 1296, 1986 AMC 1471 (5th Cir.).

801. 419 F.2d 230, 1969 AMC 1571 (5th Cir., 1969), *cert. den.* 397 U.S. 989, 1971 AMC 815 (1970).

If an insured vessel shall be and remain in any safe port for a period of thirty (30) or more consecutive days after finally mooring there (such period being computed from the day of arrival to the day of departure, one only being included) the Association is to return . . . percent of the initial annual premium, prorated daily, for the period the insured vessel shall be laid up without cargo and without crew (other than a skeleton crew) and to return . . . percent of the initial annual premium, prorated daily, for the period the insured vessel shall be laid up with cargo or crew on board, provided the Assured give written notice to the Association as soon as practicable after the commencement and termination of such lay up period. The Association shall have absolute discretion to determine whether a port is safe and how many crew members constitute a skeleton crew within the meaning of this paragraph.

No cases can be found construing this lay-up provision. However, the language is not too dissimilar to that found in standard forms of hulls clauses, and it must be assumed that decisions involving such hull lay-up clauses would be highly persuasive.

Limit of Amount Insured

Clause 27 of the ASM form limits the liability of the underwriter to the amount insured under the policy. It reads:

Liability hereunder in respect of any one accident or occurrence is limited to the amount hereby insured.

The approach taken under the ASM form thus differs from the customary British club rules, under which the liability of the club is not limited by any stated amount.

It is apparent that use of the phrase, "any one accident or occurrence" can lead to problems of construction. It is always difficult to determine whether or not a continuing series of disasters involving a covered vessel is one accident or occurrence or many such "occurrences."

For example, in *McKeithen v. Frosta*,[802] a tanker collided with a ferry, resulting in multiple deaths and injuries. The underwriter insuring the ferry sought a declaratory judgment action determining that its liability under the policy could not exceed $300,000 in respect of all claims arising out of the collision, that sum being the limit specified in the policy, with a clause limiting coverage to that sum for "claims arising out of or in consequence of any one occurrence." The court held that the insurer's liability was limited to $300,000 for all claims and not $300,000 for each victim.

---

802. 430 F.Supp. 899, 1978 AMC 51 (E.D.,La., 1977).

Cancellation

Clause 28 of the ASM form allows the underwriter to cancel the policy in certain circumstances. It reads:

(a) If the insured vessel should be sold or requisitioned, the Association shall have the option to cancel insurance hereunder with respect to the insured vessel, the Association to return . . . percent of the gross annual premium for each thirty (30) consecutive days of the unexpired term of the insurance with respect to the vessel. If the entire management, control and possession of the insured vessel be transferred whether by demise charter or by change in corporate ownership or control of the insured owner, the Association shall have the option to cancel insurance hereunder with respect to the insured vessel, the Association to return three (3) percent of the gross annual premium for each thirty (30) consecutive days of the unexpired term of the insurance with respect to said vessel. Cancellation shall not relieve the Assured from liability for premiums under this policy and for assessments levied and to be levied for deficiencies and impairments in respect to the insurance year for which the policy was originally written.

(b) In the event of non-payment of the full premium within sixty (60) days after attachment, or, if installment payment of the premium has been arranged, in the event of non-payment of any installment thereof within twenty (20) days after it is due, this policy may be cancelled by the Association upon five (5) days' written notice being given the Assured. Should this policy be cancelled under the provisions of this clause or otherwise or should the Assured fail to pay assessment within ten (10) days after it is due or should the Assured or any of them become insolvent or bankrupt or assign its property for the benefit of creditors or suffer the appointment of a receiver for its property or any part thereof or the institution of dissolution proceedings by or against it, the Association shall not be liable for any claims whatsoever under this policy unless within sixty (60) days from the date of such cancellation or the occurrence of such insolvency, bankruptcy assignment, receivership or dissolution proceedings, there are paid to the Association by or on behalf of the Assured all premiums due, and the payment of any premiums to become due as well as all possible assessments is unconditionally guaranteed by a responsible surety.

(c) In the event that Sections 182 to 189, both inclusive, of U.S. Code, Title 46, or any other existing law or laws determining or limiting liability of shipowners and carriers, or any of them, shall, while this policy is in force, be modified, amended or repealed, or the liabilities of shipowners or carriers be increased in any respect by legislative enactment, the Association shall have the right to cancel said insurance upon giving thirty (30) days' written notice of their intention so to do, and in the event of such cancellation, make return of premium upon a pro rata daily basis.

The reference to Sections 182 to 189 of Title 46 is, of course, to the U.S. Limitation of Liability Act.

The courts rather strictly construe such cancellation clauses, and if the underwriter does not strictly comply with the terms of the clause, or the clause does not provide for a return of premium in the event of cancellation, the courts are prone to hold the purported cancellation invalid.[803]

There are relatively few cases involving cancellation clauses in P & I policies and liability policies in general. The bulk of such cases have occurred in connection with hull policies.[804]

Where, however, the clause is clear and explicit, it will be honored. For example, in *Liman, Trustee v. United Kingdom Mut. Steamship Assur. Association,*[805] it was held that a trustee in bankruptcy could not seek the benefit of the bankrupt owner's P & I policy without assuming the obligations under the policy. Consequently, the P & I underwriters were held entitled to set off against the trustee's claim, their claims for unpaid calls and premiums which exceeded the trustee's claim.

Risks Excluded

Clause 29 of the ASM form expressly excludes certain types of claims. It reads:

---

803. See *Lemar Towing Co. v. Fireman's Fund Ins. Co.,* 471 F.2d 609, 1973 AMC 1843, *reh. den.* 478 F.2d 1402 (5th Cir.) (although the cancellation clause provided for return of premium, the insurer failed to do so); *Mustang Beach Development Corp. v. Fidelity and Cas. Co. of New York,* 348 F.Supp. 1270 (S.D.,Tex., 1972), *aff'd per curiam,* 463 F.2d 1136 (5th Cir., 1972) (the cancellation clause contained no provision for the return of premium; the policy remained in force); *Ruby Steamship Corp. v. American Merchant Marine Ins. Co. & Globe & Rutgers Fire Ins. Co.,* 1929 AMC 258 (St., N.Y., 1928) (threat by the underwriter prior to date cancellation could be made, followed by notice of cancellation after the prescribed period had run; the policy remained in force); *Saskatchewan Gov't Ins. Office v. Padgett,* 245 F.2d 48, 1958 AMC 1638 (5th Cir., 1957) (notice of cancellation sent for non-payment of a premium installation; no return of unearned premium was made; a loss occurring after notice of cancellation was held to be covered); *Weiland v. Pyramid Ventures Group,* 511 F.Supp. 1034, 1981 AMC 2846 (M.D., La.) (club not entitled to cancellation of coverage or set-off for "release calls" against a personal injury judgment because of the insured's failure to pay the calls when the insured's delinquency [including insolvency] occurred after the date of accident).

804. See, in this connection, Chap. XIII, under the subheading "Automatic Termination and Cancellation," where numerous cases involving cancellation under hull policies are collected.

805. 1971 AMC 727 (S.D.N.Y.).

Notwithstanding anything to the contrary contained in this policy, the Association shall not be liable for any loss, damage or expense sustained, directly or indirectly, by reason of:

(a) Loss, damage or expense to hull, machinery, equipment or fittings of the insured vessel, including refrigeration apparatus and wireless equipment, whether or not owned by the Assured;
(b) Cancelment or breach of any charter or contract, detention of the vessel, bad debts, insolvency, fraud of agents, loss of freight, passage money, hire, demurrage or any other loss of revenue;[806]
(c) Any loss, damage, sacrifice or expense of a type, character or kind which would be payable under the terms of a policy written on the American Institute Hull Clauses (June 2, 1977) Form and a policy written on the American Institute Increased Value and Excess Liabilities Clauses (November 3, 1977) Form whether or not the insured vessel is fully covered under those policies by insurance and excess insurance sufficient in amount to pay in full and without limit all such loss, damage, sacrifice or expense;
(d) The insured vessel towing any other vessel or craft, unless such towage was to assist such other vessel or craft in distress to a port or place of safety; provided, however, that this exception shall not apply to claims covered under Paragraph (1) of this policy;
(e) For any claim for loss of life, personal injury or illness in relation to the handling of cargo where such claim arises under a contract of indemnity between the Assured and his subcontractor.

Clause 30 of the ASM form relates to tugs specifically and must be read *in pari materia* with Clause 29. Clause 30 reads:

In every case where this policy insures tugs, Clause (b) of Paragraph (6) and Clause (c) of Paragraph 29 shall be deemed to refer to the American Institute Tug Form, August 1, 1976 instead of the American Institute Hull Clause (June 2, 1977) Form and Paragraph (3) shall be deemed to incorporate the Collision Clause contained in said policy (American Institute Tug Form, August 1, 1976) instead of the Collision Clause quoted in said Paragraph (3) and the following clause shall be substituted for and supersede Clause (d) of Paragraph (29) namely

806. See *Jamieson v. Newcastle Steamship Freight Ins. Ass'n*, (1895) 2 Q.B. 90, 7 Asp. M.L.C. 593, C.A., involving a similar clause, where the parties did not mutually consent to a cancellation of a charter although performance was rendered impossible on account of damages sustained by the vessel; i.e., cancellation of a charter was held to require mutual consent of both parties.

"Loss of damage to any vessel or vessels in tow and/or their cargoes, whether such loss or damage occurs before, during or after actual towage; provided, that this exception shall not apply to claims under Paragraph (1) of this policy."

Under a similar clause, which did not, however, include the phrase "whether or not the insured vessel is fully covered, etc.," the underwriters were held liable for the amount of a judgment in excess of the amount payable under the hull policy. The decision obviously triggered an amendment to the ASM form.[807]

In *DeBardeleben Coal Corp. v. Protection and Indemnity Underwriting Syndicate*,[808] a comparable clause was held to impose liability on the P & I underwriter for the share of the judgment above the insured's deductible of $350 to the limit of the lowest deductible available under the American Tug Syndicate standard form of hull and machinery policy.

In *The Schodack*,[809] the tow, assisted by three tugs, caused one of the assisting tugs to come into contact with a moored vessel. The tow was held liable to the moored vessel, and its owners brought suit against their P & I underwriters. The court held that the Running Down Clause in the hull policy plainly covered the loss. The rationale was that the collision blow was merely transmitted through the hull of a vessel interposed between the insured vessel and the vessel damaged.

Cases arising out of towage have occasioned a number of decisions involving the interrelationship of hull policies and P & I policies. These are discussed in depth in this chapter under the subheadings, *supra*, "Collision" and "Tower's Liability and the Placement Thereof."

One would think that where a tugowner contracts for standard hull and P & I coverages and the underwriters issue policies, knowing that the vessel covered is a tug and that it will be engaging in towage as a customary business, the exclusionary clauses should not apply. Unfortunately, this is not so.

For example, in *Emmco Ins. Co. v. Southern Terminal and Transp. Co.*,[810] the P & I policy insured specified tugs and barges of Southern against liability to the full extent of their hull value. Following a collision in which Southern's insured tug was at fault while towing one of its uninsured barges, the underwriter denied coverage because of a clause in the policy excluding liability for any loss, damage, expense, or claim arising out of or having relation to the towage of any other vessel or craft—language which is basically comparable to that contained in the ASM form. At the trial court level, the assured prevailed on a motion for summary judg-

807. 281 F.2d 482, 1960 AMC 1650 (1st Cir.).
808. 34 So.2d 63 (La.App., 1948).
809. 89 F.2d 8, 1937 AMC 548 (2d Cir.).
810. 333 So.2d 80 (St.,Fla.).

ment on the grounds that there was an irreconcilable conflict or ambiguity between the insuring clause and the exclusion, and the ambiguity should be resolved in favor of the assured. On appeal, it was held that there was no conflict; that the risk of collision and damage therefrom was affected by the towing relationship because of the reduced maneuverability of the vessels, and, that being so, the underwriter could contract to limit its liabilities to those collisions in which a premium had been paid for both tug and barge. Consequently, there was no coverage.

In *Florida Waterway Properties, Inc. v. The Oceanus Mutual Underwriting Association (Bermuda) Ltd.*,[811] the court held that the P & I underwriters were not required to indemnify the assured for amounts paid in settlement of collision claims where the policy contained a specific exclusion for risks covered under the "tug syndicate" form.

The task of coordinating various types of marine coverages such as hull and P & I is not an easy one. It is quite apparent that a careful analysis must be made of the coverages afforded by each type of policy, as well as of the exclusions which appear in each. Not only must the coverages afforded by each adequately accord with the assured's desires and needs, but also the exclusions must be scrutinized and, if necessary, deleted or modified so that there are no lacunae in the overall coverages afforded. In this area, there is no substitute for a competent and sophisticated broker.

War Risks

Clause 31 of the ASM form relates to war risks and reads as follows:

> Notwithstanding anything to the contrary contained in this policy, the Association shall not be liable for or in respect of any loss, damage or expense sustained by reasons of capture, seizure, arrest, restraint or detainment, or the consequences thereof or of any attempt thereat; or sustained in consequence of military, naval or air action by force of arms, including mines and torpedoes or other missiles or engines of war, whether of enemy or friendly origin; or sustained in consequence of placing the vessel in jeopardy as an act or measure of war taken in the actual process of a military engagement, including embarking or disembarking troops or material of war in the immediate zone of such engagement; and any such loss, damage or expense shall be excluded from this policy without regard to whether the Assured's liability therefor is based on negligence or otherwise, and whether before or after a declaration of war.

In a comparative sense, Rule 18 of the rules of Britannia Steam Ship Insurance Association, Limited, is quite similar although its semantical

811. 1977 AMC 70 (M.D.,Fla.).

construction is somewhat different. It provides that the association does not insure any member against any liabilities, costs, or expenses arising out of or in consequence of any of the perils, risks, or occurrences enumerated in the Lloyd's Free of Capture and Seizure Clause.

Rule 23 of the rules of the West of England Ship Owners Mutual Protection and Indemnity Association (Luxembourg) is quite similar, except that slightly broader cover is afforded with respect to fines and oil pollution containment or prevention measures of governments even though due to a war peril.

Surprisingly, no decisions appear to exist with respect to the war risk exclusionary clauses in P & I policies, although there are many such decisions with respect to hull policies, and the principles enunciated therein are, or should be, highly persuasive in the field of P & I insurance.[812]

Obligation to Insure

A number of interesting cases have arisen in the United States involving the right of a P & I underwriter to deny coverage.

In *Pino v. Trans-Atlantic Marine*,[813] the underwriter and its agent refused to provide P & I coverage to a Gloucester fisherman merely because he had previously brought an action to recover for injuries sustained aboard another fishing vessel. The court held this to be malicious and awarded damages and a permanent injunction.[814] Compare, however, *Goulart v. Trans-Atlantic Marine*,[815] where the court held that in the absence of statutory or other regulation, a marine underwriter had the right to cancel the shipowner's P & I coverage in respect of a particular crew member. In *Carroll v. Protection Marine Ins.*,[816] the First Circuit recognized that a cause of action for tortious inference—an alleged blacklisting of seamen by the P & I underwriters—was cognizable in admiralty because it was interwoven with seagoing employment and affected the operation of vessels at sea.

Omnibus Clause

Paragraph 15 of the ASM form provides coverage for:

Expenses which the assured may incur under authorization of the Association in the interest of the Association.

812. See, with respect to decisions involving the war risk exclusion under hull policies, Chap. XIII, "Frequent Coverages and Exclusions . . . " under the subheading "War Risks."
813. 1969 AMC 1369 (St.,Mass.), *aff'd* 1971 AMC 1721 (St.,Mass.).
814. To the same effect, see *Foley v. Trans-Atlantic Marine*, 1971 AMC 1085 (St.,Mass.).
815. 1970 AMC 1179 (St.,Mass.), [1970] 2 Lloyd's Rep. 389.
816. 512 F.2d 4, 1975 AMC 1633 (1st Cir.).

Not surprisingly, no cases appear to have arisen under this clause. The clause differs, of course, from that found in the United Kingdom club form, which reads:

> Liabilities, costs and expenses incidental to the business of owning, operating or managing ships which the Directors may decide to be within the scope of the Association. Claims under this paragraph shall be recoverable to such extent only as the Directors may determine.

Comparison of the Principal American P & I Policy Forms[817]

There are presently four principal forms of P & I policies in use in the United States. The form probably most widely used is the SP-23 (revised 1/56). There exists a form termed the SP-38, based essentially on SP-23, but which provides lesser coverage; i.e., notably with respect to claims for loss of or damage to or expense in connection with cargo on board the named vessel.[818] The third form to be compared is the ASM form, which has provided the basis for discussion throughout this chapter. The fourth form is comparatively new and was promulgated by the American Institute of Marine Underwriters in June, 1983.[819]

Generally speaking, the ASM form is primarily for so-called blue water vessels and, on account of the absence of a substantial blue water mar-

---

817. The Admiralty & Maritime Law Committee, Section of Tort and Insurance Practice, American Bar Association, in cooperation with the Committee on Marine Insurance, General Average and Salvage of the United States Maritime Law Association, has prepared *Annotations of the American Steamship Owners Mutual Protection and Indemnity Association Form Policy,* published by the American Bar Association Press, 1982, and supplemented by a First Addenda in 1985. The original edition contains a comparison between the ASM form and the American SP-23 (revised 1/56) form of policy, written by Sheldon Vogel, New York City. The First Addenda contains a comparison between the ASM and SP-23 forms on the one hand and the AIMU Protection and Indemnity (P & I) Clause of June 2, 1983, on the other, written by Nicholas J. Healy, Jr., New York City. The text which follows is a condensation and amalgamation of the material mentioned above, together with the author's own comments and observations. The author wishes to express his appreciation to Messrs. Vogel and Healy for their pioneering work in these comparative studies.

818. The coverage in SP-38 is expressed in broader language than SP-23 and will be discussed *infra.*

819. Technically, there is a fifth form, the 1962 Protection and Indemnity Clauses (Great Lakes), which, however, does not seem to be widely in use. It is the author's understanding that most of the vessels plying the Great Lakes are insured either in the English clubs or under the ASM form. Occasionally, however, risks are written under the form. Essentially, its cover parallels that of the ASM and SP-23 forms, with variations tailored to the needs of Great Lakes operations. Specifically, provisions are included for navigation limits, post and pre-season navigation, carriage of grain and/or seed cargo, and storage of grain in the vessel when she is not navigating. Interestingly, under the Great Lakes form, underwriters cover payments under the Longshoremens and Harbor Workers' Act and the Canadian Compensation Act if the assured has complied with the provisions of said acts. This provision is not limited to seamen. Moreover, there is a nuclear incident exclusion unlike the ASM and SP-23 forms.

ket in the United States, most inland, coastwise, and intercoastal risks are written on the SP-23 form. It is assumed that the AIMU form will probably be used primarily in the same markets as the SP-23 form. There is an AIMU form, Cargo Liability Endorsement, prepared for issuance with the basic AIMU form should cargo legal liability coverage be desired.

It is interesting to note that the coverage under the SP-38 form is expressed in more expansive language than is used in the SP-23 form, and no attempt has been made in the SP-38 form to avoid the impact of the decision in *Landry v. Steamship Mut. Underwriting Ass'n,*[820] which found liability on the part of the P & I underwriter for excess collision liability, i.e., where the collision liability coverage under the Running Down Clause of the hull policy was less in amount than the liability incurred in a collision with another vessel. More importantly, under SP-38 the navigation limits in the hull and machinery policy are deemed incorporated in the P & I policy. This can cause a serious problem where the hull policy is cancelled but the P & I policy remains in force and the vessel is lost outside the prescribed navigational limits.

The salient differences and similarities of the respective policies can be summarized as follows:

1. The coverage as respects the term "assured" in the ASM form is broader than that found in SP-23, SP-38, and the AIMU form. The ASM policy could conceivably inure to the benefit of a receiver or trustee of the assured, but it should be noted that the insurer can cancel the policy in the event of a change of management, control, etc. The AIMU form does contain a waiver of subrogation against affiliated or subsidiary companies of the assured but only to the extent that they are uninsured.

2. The coverage under the ASM form for loss of life, personal injury, etc., is broader in the sense that it expands the concept of a member of the crew to include stevedores engaged by the vessel in ports outside the continental United States and in Alaska. Also, coverage is provided with respect to claims under any compensation act for which the policy must respond.

3. Coverage for repatriation of crew members under the ASM form is broader than that of the other forms. The ASM form contains no requirement that the repatriation expenses must be incurred pursuant to statutory obligations, whereas the SP-23 form does. SP-38 does not mention repatriation coverage. The AIMU form provides such coverage except for that which arises from the termination of any agreement in accordance with its terms, or the sale of the vessel or other voluntary act of the assured.

---

820. 177 F.Supp. 143, 1960 AMC 54 (D.,Mass.), 281 F.2d 484 (1st Cir.). The *Landry* decision is discussed in detail in Chap. XIX, "The Running Down Clause."

3. The ASM policy has attempted to counter the effect of the *Landry* decision by excluding excess collision liabilities where the assured is underinsured under the hull policy. The SP-23 form has not been amended in this respect. SP-38 is worded more broadly. It reads simply that coverage is provided for loss of, or damage to, or expenses in connection with, *any fixed or movable object or property of whatever nature.* The AIMU form in this respect limits collision coverage in the following language:

> Damage to any fixed or movable object or property, howsoever caused, *excluding however, damage to another vessel or property aboard it caused by collision with the Vessel.*[821]

4. Under the ASM policy, wreck removal expenses need not be "compulsory by law," whereas under SP-23, SP-38, and the AIMU forms this is necessary, although the courts (particularly in the Fifth Circuit) have so liberally interpreted what is "compulsory by law" that the question may almost be rhetorical.

5. The ASM form and SP-23 provide coverage with respect to cargo but with specific limitations and exclusions; SP-38 flatly rejects any coverage with respect to cargo carried on board the insured vessel; the AIMU form excludes coverage with respect to cargo on board the insured vessel except liability imposed under the doctrine of cross liabilities for cargo on board for which there is no coverage under any other policy held by the assured.[822]

6. Fines and penalties coverages appear to be the same in all the forms.

7. Coverage for quarantine expenses appears to be broader in the AIMU form than in the ASM and SP-23 forms, because under the AIMU form coverage is provided where charterers order the vessel to a port known or supposed to be suffering from an outbreak of contagious disease, provided the charterers were not acting "on behalf of the assured."

8. Specific clauses in the ASM form provide for specific deductibles as to each clause. The AIMU form contains separate deductible clauses with respect to (a) loss of life, bodily injury or illness, and (b) all other claims. SP-23 does not contain a deductible clause, but one is frequently added by endorsement as a matter of underwriting practice. The SP-38 form contains a deductible clause (lines 31-35).

9. The ASM form provides pollution coverage; the other forms do not.[823]

---

821. Note that in the AIMU form the term used is "damage," as contrasted to the usual and customary phrase "loss of, or damage to, or expenses in connection with." The more restrictive term would appear to eliminate claims not directly attributable to physical damage, such as obstructing a pier.

822. Whether this would provide coverage for the deductible on the insured's hull policy is not clear.

823. The AIMU form expressly excludes pollution liabilities; SP-23 and 38 do not, the thought apparently being that since no cover has been provided, there is no necessity for an

10. The ASM form covers liabilities arising under a standard form of towage or pilotage contract. SP-38 does not, but neither is liability under such a contract expressly excluded. SP-38 excludes claims arising out of towage except as to salvage services rendered in an emergency and except as to claims for loss of life, injury, or illness of any person. The AIMU form excludes claims arising out of towage except emergency towage of a vessel in distress at sea to a port or place of safety, and except as to claims for loss of life, injury, or illness to any person. Emergency towage is defined to be towage undertaken as a salvage service while the vessel is on a voyage wholly unrelated to performance of such service.

11. The exclusions in all four forms follow the usual pattern, except as already noted above. In addition, the AIMU form expressly excludes punitive or exemplary damages, however described; an exclusion with respect to damage to the assured's own property; an exclusion with respect to engagement in unlawful trade or performance of an unlawful act "with knowledge of the assured;" an exclusion with respect to nuclear incidents; and an exclusion with respect to war risks, which includes piracy and also acts carried out for "political, ideological or terrorist purposes."

12. The new AIMU form also requires the assured not to make any admission of liability and to take such steps as a "prudent uninsured person" would take to minimize and avoid liability. The underwriters have an option to nominate attorneys to represent the assured and, in any event, the underwriters may direct the progress of such litigation.

13. The AIMU form contains a detailed subrogation clause and an extremely broad other insurance clause which eliminates participation on the basis of contribution or otherwise. While a receiver may acquire rights under the policy, this is limited to a period of ten days, whereupon the policy ceases to be in effect.

14. The time for notice and time for suit clauses in the four forms differ in some significant respects. These may be outlined as follows:

Form	Time for Notice	Time for Suit
ASM	Prompt	Two years
SP-23	Prompt	6 Months (for presentation of claims)

---

exclusion with respect to such pollution liabilities. However, the broad coverage under SP-38 with respect to loss of, or damage to, or expenses in connection with any *movable object or property* of whatever nature would seem to embrace damage to or expenses in connection with navigable *waters* to the extent to which such waters are considered to be a "property interest" as some of the court decisions seem to imply. Such waters would certainly seem to qualify as a "movable object or property." See *Port of Portland v. WQIS,* 549 F.Supp. 233, 1984 AMC 2019, 2021 (D.,Ore.), citing *Askew v. American Waterways Operators,* 411 U.S. 325, 1973 AMC 811 (1973), and noting that: "Oregon law establishes that the state's interest in its water resources is sufficient to support an action for damages caused by pollution."

| SP-38 | Prompt | One year |
| AIMU | Prompt | One year (or the shortest limit permitted by the applicable state laws) |

The foregoing summary is not intended to be exhaustive, and reference must necessarily be made to the precise terms of the four policy forms. The intent is to present the highlights of the respective forms.

Coverage with Respect to Punitive Damages[824]

Introduction. The concept of punitive or exemplary damages in admiralty arose quite early in English and American jurisprudence. The Supreme Court in *The Amiable Nancy*,[825] first recognized that punitive damages were recoverable in admiralty, although in *dictum* and in a case where the misconduct was on the part of the officers and crew of an American privateer. The innocent owner of the privateer was not assessed with punitive damages.[826]

The Northern District of California in *Gallagher v. The Yankee*,[827] first awarded punitive damages in an admiralty case against a ship's master who illegally transported the plaintiff against his will to Hawaii pursuant to a San Francisco vigilante committee's edict of banishment.

In 1893, in *Lake Shore, etc. Railway Co. v. Prentice*,[828] the Supreme Court clearly relied upon the law of England as it existed before the American Revolution, in declaring that under the English cases the recovery of damages beyond compensation for the injury received by way of punishing the guilty, and as an example to deter others from offending in a like manner, is clearly recognized.[829]

---

824. The author wishes to express his indebtedness to Theodore G. Dimitry and Francis I. Spagnoletti, Houston, Texas, who prepared the comparable section for the First Addenda to the *Annotations of the American Steamship Owners Mutual Protection and Indemnity Association Form Policy*, published by the American Bar Association Press and referred to in footnote 817, *supra*. Moreover, the author had the benefit of reading in manuscript the paper delivered in London in 1985 before the American Bar Association by George L. Waddell, San Francisco, California, entitled "Punitive Damages in Admiralty."

825. 16 U.S. 546 (1818).

826. Dicta in other early federal cases also recognized that such damages were recoverable. See *Emerson v. Howland*, F.Cas. No. 4,441 (D.,Mass., 1816); *Boston Manufacturing Co. v. Fiske*, F.Cas. No. 1,681 (D.,Mass., 1820); *Ralston et al v. The States Rights*, F.Cas. No. 11,540 (E.D.,Pa., 1836); *McGuire et al v. The Golden Gate*, F.Cas. No. 8,815 (N.D.,Cal., 1856).

827. F.Cas. No. 5,196 (N.D.,Cal., 1959), *aff'd* F.Cas. No. 18,124.

828. 147 U.S. 101 (1893).

829. The English authorities relied on were: *Wilkes v. Wood*, 98 E.R. 489 and *Huckle v. Money*, 95 E.R. 768.

Section 908 of the *Restatement (Second) of Torts* defines punitive damages as follows:

> Punitive damages are damages, other than compensatory or nominal damages, awarded against a person for his outrageous conduct and to deter him and others like him from similar conduct in the future . . . . Punitive damages may be awarded for conduct that is outrageous, because of the defendant's evil motive or his reckless indifference to the rights of others . . . .

Perhaps the principal controversy today with respect to punitive damages is whether an employer may be held liable vicariously . . . when he neither authorized nor ratified the act complained of. Section 909 of the *Restatement (Second) of Torts* sets forth the rule as follows:

> Punitive damages can be properly awarded against a master or other principal because of an act by an agent if, but only if,
> (a) the principal or a managerial agent authorized the doing and the manner of the act, or
> (b) the agent was unfit and the principal or a managerial agent was reckless in employing or retaining him, or
> (c) the agent was employed in a managerial capacity and was acting in the scope of employment, or
> (d) the principal or a managerial agent of the principal ratified or approved the act.

Punitive Damages in Personal Injury and Death Claims. There are relatively few cases in this area. Where the subject has been touched upon, the statements of the courts are to the effect that such damages are recoverable under the general maritime law upon a showing of wilful and wanton misconduct by the shipowner.[830]

As noted heretofore, death actions may be brought under the Jones Act, general maritime law, and the Death on the High Seas Act. As the Supreme Court in *Mobil Oil Corp. v. Higginbotham,*[831] held that under

---

830. *Complaint of Merry Shipping, Inc.*, 650 F.2d 622, 1981 AMC 2839 (5th Cir.); *Kopczynski v. The Jacqueline*, 742 F.2d 555, 1985 AMC 769 (9th Cir., 1984), cert.den. 1985 AMC 2397; *Baptiste v. Superior Court*, 164 Cal.Rptr. 789, 1980 AMC 1523 (St.Cal.); *Renner v. Rockwell International Corp.*, 403 F.Supp. 849 (C.D.,Cal., 1975), vacated and remanded on other grounds, 587 F.2d 1030 (9th Cir., 1978). Note that while such damages were recoverable under general maritime law, the question of recovery under the Jones Act was expressly left undecided. See, also, *In re Marine Sulphur Queen*, 460 F.2d 89, 1972 AMC 1122 (2d Cir., 1972) (punitive damages denied); *United States Steel Corp. v. Fuhrman*, 407 F.2d 1143, 1969 AMC 252, 1971 AMC 813 (6th Cir., 1969) (punitive damages denied); *Kozar v. Chesapeake and Ohio Railway Company*, 449 F.2d 1238 (6th Cir., 1971) (punitive damages not recoverable under the Federal Employers' Liability Act).

831. 436 U.S. 618, 1978 AMC 1059 (1978).

DOHSA damages are limited to compensation for the pecuniary loss sustained by the persons for whose benefit the suit was brought, pecuniary damages under that act would appear to be foreclosed.

Whether state wrongful death statutes may be applicable is very uncertain.[832] It may well be that where a state statute expressly authorizes punitive damages, they may be recovered.[833]

Maintenance and Cure Cases. Disagreement in the various circuits over the recoverability of punitive damages in maintenance and cure cases stems directly from the Supreme Court's decision in *Vaughn v. Atkinson*,[834] where the court treated the recoverability of attorneys' fees incurred in obtaining a recovery of maintenance and cure as a matter of damages. Thereafter, the circuits divided, the First and Fifth Circuits holding that an arbitrary and capricious failure to pay maintainance and cure warranted punitive damages not limited to attorneys' fees.[835] The Second Circuit has limited such recovery to attorneys' fees as has the Western District of Tennessee.[836] It would appear that the amount of attorneys' fees should be determined by the court rather than a jury.[837]

Punitive damages have been considered, whether ultimately granted or not, in cargo cases,[838] vessel damage cases,[839] products liability cases,[840]

---

832. Compare *Nygaard v. Peter Pan Seafoods, Inc.*, 701 F.2d 77 (9th Cir., 1983) (state wrongful death statutes do not apply) with *Tallentire v. Offshore Logistics, Inc.*, 754 F.2d 1274, 1986 AMC 23 (5th Cir., 1985) (state wrongful death statutes may apply on the high seas).

833. *McDonald v. The 204*, 194 F.Supp. 383, 1962 AMC 1540 (S.D.,Ala., 1961).

834. 369 U.S 527, 1962 AMC 1131 (1962).

835. *Robinson v. Pocahontas, Inc.*, 477 F.2d 1048, 1973 AMC 2268 (1st Cir., 1973); *Harper v. Zapata Offshore Co.*, 741 F.2d 87 (5th Cir., 1984); *Holmes v. J. Ray McDermott & Co.*, 734 F.2d 1110 (5th Cir.); *Hodges v. Keystone Shipping Co.*, 578 F.Supp. 620 (S.D.,Tex., 1983).

836. *Kraljic v. Berman Enterprises, Inc.*, 575 F.2d 412, 1978 AMC 1297 (2d Cir., 1978); *Owens v. Continental Carriers & Terminals, Inc.*, 591 F.Supp. 777 (W.D., Tenn., 1984).

837. *Incandela v. American Dredging Co.*, 659 F.2d 11, 1981 AMC 2401 (2d Cir.).

838. *Cosmos U.S.A. v. U.S. Lines*, 1983 AMC 1172 (N.D.,Cal., 1980) (claim denied on basis of Sec. 4(5) of Cogsa); *Seguros Banvenez, S.A. v. S.S. Oliver Drescher*, 587 F.Supp. 172 (S.D.N.Y., 1984) (claim denied); *Thyssen, Inc. v. S.S. Fortune Star*, 596 F.Supp. 865 (S.D.N.Y., 1984) (claim granted; underdeck cargo restowed on deck by order of a ship's officer and damaged by exposure to sea water); *B.F. McKernin & Co., Inc. v. U.S. Lines, Inc.*, 416 F.Supp. 1068, 1976 AMC 1527 (S.D.N.Y., 1976).

839. *Protectus Alpha Nav. v. North Pacific Grain Growers*, 585 F.Supp. 1062 (D.,Ore., 1984) (vessel caught fire at a grain dock; the grain dock foreman ordered it cast loose with crew and firemen aboard, one of whom was killed and another injured; award of $500,000 punitive damages). See, also, *Dredge General*, 1944 AMC 948 (S.D.,Fla., 1944) (punitive damages awarded against a dredger who damaged a submarine cable; owner complicity not mentioned); *The William H. Bailey*, 103 F.2d 799 (D.,Conn., 1900) (punitive damages denied; case was filed *in rem*); *The Seven Brothers*, 170 F. 126 (D.,R.I., 1909) (punitive damages disallowed because lack of owner complicity in case of alleged intentional damage to fish traps).

840. See *Gillham v. Admiral Corp.*, 523 F.2d 102 (6th Cir., 1975) (generally speaking, punitive damages are recoverable under state products liability law). Since products liability concepts have been now been incorporated into maritime law, it can only be a matter of time before recoveries are made of punitive damages in maritime products liability cases.

seamens' wrongful discharge,[841] wrongful imprisonment of seamen,[842] tortious interference with employment contracts,[843] fraud and deceit,[844] contract cases,[845] and bad faith insurance cases.[846]

Coverage for Liability for Punitive Damages. The seminal question is what law is to be applied. Is the governing law that of the Federal system or state law? The answer to the question was seriously compounded by the Supreme Court's decision in *Wilburn Boat Co. v. Fireman's Fund Ins. Co.,*[847] heretofore discussed at length in Chapter XI, "Warranties." Simply stated, *Wilburn* stands for the proposition that where there is no estab-

---

841. *Smith v. Atlas Off-Shore Boat Service, Inc.,* 653 F.2d 1057 (5th Cir., 1981) (damages not recoverable for a "retaliatory discharge"); *Schultheiss v. Mobil Oil Exploration & Producing,* 592 F.Supp. 628 (W.D.,La., 1981); *Nugent v. Sea-Land Services,* 1973 AMC 977 (N.D.,Cal., 1972) (malice present). Attention is directed, however, to the cases involving the statutory double-wage penalty under 46 U.S.C. 596. In a sense, awarding double wages is a species of punitive damages.

842. Seaman may not recover for wrongful imprisonment on a vessel by the master which was not authorized or ratified by the owner. *Pacific Packing & Navigation Co. v. Fielding,* 136 F. 577 (9th Cir., 1905); *The Ludlow,* 280 F. 162 (N.D., Fla., 1922).

843. See discussion, *supra,* under subheading "Obligation to Insure." On remand, in *Pino v. Protection Maritime Ins. Co., Ltd.,* 599 F.2d 10 (1st Cir., 1979), the district court awarded punitive damages to each plaintiff employee (490 F.Supp. at 281).

844. *The Normannia,* 62 F. 469 (S.D.N.Y., 1894) (punitive damages disallowed on grounds of lack of owner complicity).

845. The question is complicated because of the differing concepts as between contract and tort. However, if an act was characterized as a "tortious breach of contract", damages have been awarded. See *Fletcher v. Western National Life Ins. Co.,* 89 Cal.Rptr. 78 (St.,Cal., 1970). Compare, however, the earlier cases of *The Mascotte,* 72 F. 684 (D.,N.J., 1895), and *Crowley v. S. S. Arcadia,* 244 F.Supp. 597 (S.D.,Cal., 1964), denying recovery of punitive damages. In the first case, the owners acted on legal advice; in the second, no malice or wrongful intent was proved.

846. Bad faith cases are proliferating at an alarming rate. Whether such a concept exists in admiralty or may be applicable to marine policies remains to be seen. However, in light of the *Wilburn Boat* decision (which may result in the application of state law) and simple logic, there appears to be no reason why the doctrine will not be applied in all its vigor to marine policies. The author is currently involved in four marine insurance cases in which bad faith has been alleged on the part of underwriters. All four cases are currently pending and have not yet been decided. In a recent case, as yet unreported, *Poysky v. Pacific Marine Insurance Co. et al,* Civil No. 82-0731 (D.,Haw., 1985), the court found that there was no bad faith involved in the underwriter's refusal to pay benefits under the policy and that the plaintiff/insured had breached the warranty of seaworthiness. The case is now on appeal. Certain it is that consequential damages are increasingly being awarded for simple breach of contract, and where the assured is able to make out a case of bad faith, the traditional damage concept of *Hadley v. Baxendale,* 9 Exch. 341 (1854), may well not be applicable, but, instead, the assured may recover all damages naturally resulting from the insurer's breach, whether or not the insurer could have reasonably foreseen the particular type of injury. See "Reasonable and Foreseeable Damages for Breach of an Insurance Contract," 21 *Tort & Insurance Law Journal* 108 (1985), by Bob G. Freeman, Jr. See, also, *Bohemia, Inc. v. Home Ins. Co.,* 725 F.2d 506 (9th Cir., 1984), where excess underwriters claimed that the primary underwriter handled a claim in an improper and prejudicial manner, but the court disagreed.

847. 348 U.S. 310, 1955 AMC 367 (1955).

lished federal law on the point, state law will be applied. *Wilburn* involved the consequence of a breach of an express warranty and as has already been pointed out, it would appear that the tendency of the courts is to restrict that case to cases involving policy warranties—and even here, the courts are far from consistent. For example, in *Healy Tibbetts v. Foremost Ins. Co.*,[848] the court held that unless federal law has fashioned a rule of interpretation, a marine insurance policy will be construed under state law. By contrast, in *Bohemia, Inc. v. Home Ins. Co.*,[849] the court relied on federal case law which, as the court phrased it, "sufficiently established a federal admiralty rule governing the policy provisions." The court also stated that:

> State law will control the interpretation of a marine insurance policy only in the absence of a federal statute, a judicially fashioned admiralty rule, or a need for uniformity in admiralty practice.

To this litany of exceptions should probably be added one more category, i.e., where there is a countervailing state statute which conflicts with the admiralty rule (one could read here English law as to express warranties.)[850]

One distinguished commentator has suggested that *Wilburn* has been considered by a number of courts as not dealing with *interpretation* of policy language but as dealing with rules of marine insurance law independent of policy language, such as the legal effect of a breach of warranty. Thus, he states, a federal court faced with the question may have to decide whether coverage of punitive damages involves the application of a rule of law subject to *Wilburn* or whether it will be treated as a mere question of interpretation and, therefore, arguably not subject to *Wilburn*. If the former, the court will have to examine the law of the state (presumably the state having the most significant contacts with the facts) to decide if that state has a public policy against such coverage. If it finds none, the court may then consider the question to be one of mere interpretation as to which a federal court fashions its own rules.[851] The suggestion has much to commend it.

The basic insuring agreement in a P & I policy provides that the assured will be indemnified "against any loss, damage or expense which the assured shall become liable to pay and shall have paid" by reason of any

---

848. 1980 AMC 1600 (N.D.,Cal., 1979).

849. 725 F.2d 506 (9th Cir., 1984). See, also, *St. Paul Fire and Marine Ins. Co. v. Vest*, 500 F.Supp. 1365, 1982 AMC 450 (N.D.,Miss.), *aff'd per curiam* 666 F.2d 932 (5th Cir., 1982), where the court said that the interpretation of a policy of marine insurance is, of course, entirely a matter of federal, and not state, law.

850. *Wilburn* itself is a classic example. See, also, such decisions as *Continental Sea Foods, Inc. v. New Hampshire Fire Ins. Co.*, 1964 AMC 196 (S.D.N.Y.) where New York law required a strict literal compliance. Other decisions are cited in Chapter I, "Introduction."

851. George L. Waddell, San Francisco, California; see n. 824, *supra*.

occurrence covered by the policy. Absent an express exclusion, it would appear that this language is certainly broad enough to include punitive damages in respect of claims otherwise covered. It is noteworthy in this respect that the new AIMU form under "Exclusions" provides in (B) that the underwriter will not indemnify the assured in respect of "liability imposed on the Assured as punitive or exemplary damages, however described."

Only one case involving coverage for punitive damages under a P & I policy appears to have been decided and there the disposition by the court of a factual issue made it unnecessary to construe the insuring language in the policy. In *Ezell v. United States Fidelity & Guaranty*,[852] the court held that a conflict of interest between the P & I underwriter and its assured concerning the choice of available defenses in a Jones Act case made it reasonable for the insurer to refuse to assume the defense. As a consequence, the jury's award of $2 million in punitive damages against the insurer was reversed. The decision does not, of course, touch on the liability of the *underwriter* for wrongful conduct of its *assured* vis-a-vis the claimant.

Interpretation of Policy Language. The courts are divided on the question of whether the policy language in a standard form of liability policy is broad enough to cover punitive damages. Generally speaking, when coverage has been granted, the insuring language has been with respect to "all sums" or "any losses."[853]

Some courts, however, look to the *scope* of the insuring language. Thus, operative language preceded by the terms such as "caused by" or "arising out of" has been construed to limit policy coverage to compensatory damages only; i.e. such damages are the result of the insured's conduct, not the damages sustained by the insured person.[854] The rationale of this view is premised on the theory that punitive awards are not granted to compensate the plaintiff but rather to punish the defendant. In this light, it will be seen that philosophically such damages are not really damages for bodily injury or property damage sustained by the claimant, but instead are punishment to the defendant insured.

This distinction surfaces dramatically in such cases as *Southern Farm Bureau Cas. Ins. Co. v. Daniel*.[855] There, the claimant secured a judgment for compensatory damages against the assured as well as an award of

---

852. 1985 AMC 3000 [DRO] (5th Cir., 1985).

853. Representative cases are: *Harrel v. Travelers Indem. Co.*, 567 P.2d 1013 (Or. 1977); *Skyline Harvestore Systems v. Centennial Ins. Co.*, 331 N.W.2d 106 (Iowa 1983); *Ridgway v. Gulf Life Ins. Co.*, 578 F.2d 1026 (5th Cir., 1978) (applying Texas law).

854. Representative cases are: *Casperson v. Webber*, 213 N.W.2d 327 (Minn. 1973); *Schnuck Markets, Inc. v. Transamerica Ins. Co.*, 652 S.W.2d 206 (Mo. 1983); *Gleason v. Fryer*, 491 P.2d 85 (Colo. 1971).

855. 440 S.W.2d 582 (Ark. 1969).

$5,000 punitive damages under a comprehensive automobile policy. The assured then sued his underwriter to recover for the punitive damages award entered against him. Noting that the courts were divided on the question, the majority held that the policy covered punitive damages because those damages constituted a sum which the assured became legally obligated to pay as damages for bodily injuries sustained. The court observed that there was nothing in the state's public policy that prevented an insurer from indemnifying its assured against punitive damages arising out of an *accident,* as distinguished from an intentional tort, and noted that in a prior case, *Miller v. Blanton,* 210 S.W.2d 293 (Ark. 1948), it had held that recovery could be permitted against an employer for acts or admissions of an employee even though such acts were done without the employer's knowledge or authorization and were not subsequently ratified by him. There was a vigorous dissent in which it was emphasized that the term "compensatory damages" only included such items as pain and suffering, loss of time, medical attendance and support during a period of disablement, and for permanent injury and continuing disability. In the view of the dissent, the majority rule in the United States was that punitive damages were intended to punish the wrongdoer and not granted to compensate a claimant. The case is commended to the reader for its citation of the authorities on both sides of the issue.

Some courts rely on the doctrine of "reasonable expectations" in order to deny or grant coverage. Frequently, such cases involve ambiguities as to the scope of coverage, thus giving the courts free rein to speculate as to what the reasonable expectations of the assured may have been.[856]

As noted in Chapter IV, "Principles of Construction," under the doctrine of *contra proferentem* policy ambiguities are construed in favor of the assured and against the scrivener of the policy—most frequently the insurance company—but when commercial policies are involved, some courts have applied a construction which is "most reasonable from a business point of view."[857]

As a general rule, whether an injury is "accidental" as distinguished from "intentional" is determined under the majority of the liability cases in the United States from the standpoint of the *person injured.*[858] While

856. *Lazenby v. Universal Underwriters Ins. Co.,* 383 S.W.2d 1 (Tenn. 1964); *Harrel v. Travelers Indem. Co., supra,* n. 853; *Cieslewicz v. Mutual Serv. Cas. Ins. Co.,* 267 N.W.2d 595 (Wis. 1978).

857. *Eagle Leasing Corp. v. Hartford Fire Ins. Co.,* 540 F.2d 1257, 1978 AMC 604 (5th Cir., 1976). See, also, *Baltimore Bank & Trust Co. v. U.S.F. & G.,* 436 F.2d 743 (8th Cir., 1971).

858. *Fox Wisconsin v. Century Indemn.,* 263 N.W. 567 (Wis. 1935); *Hartford Accident v. Wolbarst,* 57 A.2d 151 (N.H. 1948); *New Amsterdam Cas. v. Jones,* 135 F.2d 191 (6th Cir., 1943); *City of Kimball v. St. Paul Fire & Marine,* 206 N.W.2d 632 (Neb. 1973). But where the insured deliberately intends the injury and the act was wilful and deliberate, this is no "accident." *Sontag v. Galer,* 181 N.E. 182 (Mass. 1932).

generally any injury which is unintended, unexpected and unusual from the standpoint of the injured claimant is deemed an "accident," even though resulting from acts which were intentionally done, some courts have held that where the acts were voluntary and intentional, the cause was not an accident.[859] The cases are very difficult to harmonize.

Public Policy. Even assuming coverage exists, courts have frequently denied coverage of punitive damages on the grounds of contravention of public policy.[860]

Other courts deny coverage on grounds of public policy except for vicarious liability of the assured. Here, the courts recognize that the assured in not personally at fault but rather that he has been held vicariously liable for another's wrongful conduct.[861]

More and more courts appear to be rejecting the policy arguments set forth in *McNulty* and have allowed recovery for punitive damages.[862] But, even in these jurisdictions, some courts have rejected recovery of punitive damages where the misconduct was intentional.[863]

In light of the conflicting theories and decisions, it seems a fair assumption that whether or not punitive damages are going to be allowed under P & I policies will be determined by the application of the public policy of the states in which the question arises. Certainly, the safest course of action for underwriters to pursue is to exclude such coverage by an express clause in the policy, as AIMU has done in its new policy.

859. *Argonaut Southwest v. Maupin,* 500 S.W.2d 633 (Tex. 1973).

860. The leading case is *Northwestern Nat. Cas. Co. v. McNulty,* 307 F.2d 432 (5th Cir., 1962). See, also, *Hartford Accident & Indemn. Co. v. Hempstead,* 397 N.E.2d 737 (N.Y. 1979); *Padavan v. Clemente,* 350 N.Y.S. 2d 694 (N.Y. 1973). The rationale is that to allow punitive damages would frustrate the public's interest in punishing or deterring extreme misconduct.

861. *U.S. Concrete Pipe Co. v. Bould,* 437 So.2d 1061 (Fla. 1983); *Dayton Hudson Corp. v. American Mut. Ins. Co.,* 621 P.2d 1155 (Okla. 1980); *Colson v. Lloyd's of London,* 435 S.W.2d 42 (Mo. 1968).

862. *Lazenby v. Universal Underwriters Ins. Co.,* 383 S.W.2d 1 (Tenn. 1964); *Universal Ins. Co. v. Tenery,* 39 P.2d 776 (Colo. 1934); *Southern Farm Bureau Cas. Ins. v. Daniel,* 440 S.W.2d 582 (Ark 1969); *Harrel v. Travelers Indemn. Co.,* 567 P.2d 1013 (Or. 1977). The cases cited here are not, of course, all-inclusive. There are many others. Only the leading cases have been cited.

863. *Lasenby v. Universal Underwriters Ins. Co., supra,* n. 862; *Harrel v. Travelers Indemn. Co., supra,* n. 862; *Southern Farm Bureau Cas. Ins. Co. v. Daniels, supra,* n. 862; *Hensley v. Erie Ins. Co.,* 283 S.E.2d 227 (W.Va. 1981); *Continental Ins. Co. v. Hancock,* 507 S.W.2d 146 1 (Ky. 1973).

CHAPTER XXII

SHIPBUILDERS', REPAIRERS', AND MARINA OPERATORS' LIABILITY; PRODUCTS LIABILITY

Introduction

Policies for shipbuilders, ship repairers, and marina operators are, in general, special forms and clauses which have been developed over the years for insurance of some of the liabilities and risks which those traditional members of the maritime fraternity face in the conduct of their businesses. It will be observed that the language used above refers to *some* of the liabilities and risks to which those types of businesses are exposed; most assuredly, the typical forms and clauses in general use today fall far short of providing the optimum coverages which are necessary in today's modern business world.

Generally speaking, the forms and clauses in use provide property damage coverage to ships and vessels while in the custody of the builder, repairer, or marina operator. Other coverages are also provided, in a limited sense, for collision and circumscribed P & I risks. The policy exclusions are numerous and almost all-encompassing. As compared to the rather broad and extensive types of risks which are covered in a comprehensive general liability clause (with the watercraft exclusion deleted), the coverages under such policies are, to put it bluntly, distressingly minimal.

Shipbuilders' Liability Policies

Among the coverages historically provided by the marine insurance industry, as opposed to casualty insurance, are those encompassed in the Builders' Risks forms.

Two forms are in rather common use; i.e., the American Institute Builders' Risks Clauses (Feb. 8, 1979) (Form 13-L), and the London Institute Clauses for Builders' Risks (1/12/72) (Form CL.13).[1] As will be seen, the coverages afforded by both forms are similar, and are primarily intended as first party property damage coverage to protect the builder and the buyer. In scope they correspond generally to a "course of construction" policy used in the general building industry.

---

1. These forms will be found reproduced in the Appendix, Vol. 2.

The American Institute Form of Policy

The American Institute form provides in pertinent part as follows:

> The Subject Matter of this insurance (herein referred as the Vessel) is the hull, launches, lifeboats, rafts, furniture, bunkers, stores, tackle, fittings, equipment, apparatus, machinery, boilers, refrigeration machinery, insulation, motor generators and other electrical machinery, ordnance, munitions, and appurtenances, including materials, plans, patterns and moulds, staging, scaffolding and similar temporary construction to the extent only that the cost of any of the foregoing is included in the Agreed Value incorporated in or allocated to Hull No. _____ Type _____ building at the yard of the Builder at _____ . The policy insures only . . . while the Vessel (ashore or afloat) is at the building location named above; while in transit within the port of construction to and from such location; and while on trial trips (including proceeding to and returning from the trial course), as often as required, within a distance by water of 250 nautical miles of the port of construction, or held covered at an additional premium to be named by the Underwriters in the event of deviation of voyage, provided prompt notice thereof is given to Underwriters.

By its terms, the policy expires in any event on delivery of the vessel to the buyer. The London Institute form has a comparable geographic and time limitation.

In terms of first party property damage, the policy insures against all risks of physical loss of or damage to the vessel occurring during the currency of the policy, except as otherwise provided. In case of failure to launch, the underwriters bear all necessary expenses incurred in completing the launch. Deliberate damage (pollution hazard), general average and salvage, total loss, and sue and labor coverages are also provided.

Under the liability section of the policy, collision liability (limited to colliding with another ship or vessel) is provided in the usual form and the Protection and Indemnity section enumerates some, but not all, of the coverages provided by a P & I policy in standard form. However, the policy form concludes by providing coverage for liabilities " . . . from causes not hereinbefore specified, but which are recoverable under the Protection and Indemnity policy form known as Lazard No. SP 23."[2]

Of paramount importance, however, is the fact that the form expressly excludes loss of life of, or bodily injury to, or illness of " . . . an employee of *an Assured* under this Policy." The lack of coverage in this area is often

---

2. See Chapter XXI, "Protection & Indemnity," "Comparison of the Principal American P & I Forms" for a discussion on the risks covered under the SP 23 form.

overlooked but can be disastrous from the standpoint of the builder as well as the vessel owner.[3]

While worded in a slightly different fashion, Clauses 17 and 19 of the London Institute form achieve the same result.

The underwriters have also been careful to exclude the cost of repairing, modifying, replacing, or renewing any part or parts when arising from faulty design. Although the underwriters will pay for *consequential damage* to the subject matter insured arising from faulty design, sums expended for betterment or alteration of design are not paid. But, if during the term of the insurance any part is condemned solely by reason of discovery of a latent defect, the policy will pay the cost of repairing, replacing, or renewing the defective part. The foregoing is a summary of the provisions in the London Institute form. The comparable American form (13-L), as supplemented and amended by Addendum No. 2, is rather more specific. Addendum No. 2 deletes lines 61-62 of the basic form and substitutes the following:

> Subject to the provisions of exclusion (b) of the following paragraph, in the event that faulty design of any part or parts should cause physical loss of or damage to the Vessel, this insurance shall not cover the cost or expense of repairing, replacing or renewing such part or parts, nor any expenditures incurred by reason of a betterment or alteration in the design. Fault design shall include, but not be limited to, errors, omissions or deficiencies in plans, drawings, specifications or calculations.
>
> Further, Underwriters shall not pay for any loss, damage or expense caused by or arising in consequence of:
>
> > (a) faulty workmanship, or the installation or use of improper or defective materials, unless resulting in destruction, deformation, breaking, tearing, bursting, holing or cracking of the Vessel, or any other like condition, and which loss, damage or expense is not otherwise excluded under the terms and conditions of the War, Strikes and Other Exclusions Clause of the attached Policy; provided that Underwriters in no event shall respond for the cost or expense of repairing, replacing or renewing any improper or defective materials.
> > (b) faulty production or assembly procedures even if constituting faulty design.

3. The policy is designed such that the builder *and* the vessel owner are usually the named assureds. This simply recognizes that the vessel owner, in the usual situation, acquires an interest in the uncompleted vessel commensurate with the amount of progress payments made by him to the builder, as well as in materials, equipment, plans, etc., acquired by the builder for the vessel but not incorporated therein at the time of a particular loss.

It should also be observed that the American form contains an exclusion with respect to delay or disruption, i.e., "consequential damages." Lines 225-26 exclude in this respect:

> Delay or disruption of any type whatsoever, including but not limited to, loss of earnings or use of the Vessel, howsoever caused, except to the extent, if any, covered by the Collision Liability or the Protection and Indemnity Clauses of this Policy.[4]

Neither of the forms contemplate insuring liabilities of the builder to the buyer for post-delivery failures, i.e., failures occurring after the vessel has had its trial trips and has been finally delivered to, and accepted by, the buyer. The "delay or disruption" or "consequential damage" exclusion in the American form would seem to restate and reinforce this conclusion. However, this did not insulate the underwriters against liability for lost profits and post-delivery repairs in *Stanley v. Onetta Boat Works*.[5]

In that case, a new fishing vessel just completed fell off the launching ways during the process of lauching and was damaged. The impact also caused built-in stresses in the hull and machinery which did not manifest themselves until later when the vessel was in service in the Gulf of Alaska at which time cracks were discovered in the fuel and water tanks. Although the shipbuilder's policy excluded "consequential damages" or any loss through delay, the underwriters were held liable for all damages, including lost profits, sustained by the vessel owner as a result of the vessel's unseaworthiness at time of delivery. Underwriters were also held liable on the theory that they negligently performed a voluntarily assumed obligation to repair the vessel after the launching accident.[6]

By contrast, however, in *Rydman et al v. Martinolich Shipbuilding Corp. et al*,[7] the underwriters were held not liable for the sinking of a vessel after her delivery when the policy period had expired and the loss occurred more than 100 miles from the construction site, although the vessel owner alleged and urged that the cause of the sinking was defective construction during the policy period.[8] The court found the same language construed (or ignored) in *Stanley, supra,* to be unambiguous and that it limited the

---

4. Comparable language is not found in the London Institute form, but Sec. 55(2)(b) of the Marine Insurance Act would appear to exclude any loss proximately caused by delay although the delay is caused by a peril insured against, unless the policy otherwise provides —and the London Institute form does not.

5. 431 F.2d 241, 1971 AMC 74 (9th Cir.).

6. Underwriters' surveyor examined the vessel after the launching accident and more or less took over the direction of the repairs. It is difficult, however, to explain the case in light of the express exclusion in the policy and the absence of any disclosure of the terms of the policy as to expiration or geographic limitation. It does not appear to have been followed by any American court.

7. 1975 AMC 1005 (St.,Wash.).

8. Ironically, in both *Stanley* and *Rydman* the author represented the vessel owners.

coverage of the policy to damage occurring prior to delivery and within the geographic limits of the policy.

Other decisions involving the construction and interpretation of shipbuilders' policies are helpful in understanding the extent of coverage. For example, in *Bushey v. Home Ins. Co.*,[9] a builders' risk policy, extending to "all risks of launching and breakage of ways" was held to include the cost of repairing building ways which broke during the launching, and not merely to damage sustained by the vessel when the building ways broke. By contrast, in *Charleston v. Atlantic*,[10] the policy covered common marine risks as applied to a marine railway. During efforts to launch a repaired vessel, the cradle stuck and repairs to the cradle in excess of $8,000 were paid under the policy. The assured also claimed for the cost of completing the launch, amounting to a sum in excess of $7,000. The arbitrator held that the policy did not cover the expense of removing the vessel from the cradle as the policy covered the marine railway but did not extend to builders' risks.

In *Wheeler v. Aetna Ins. Co.*,[11] a builders' risks policy covered "trial trips." The vessel was completed and while enroute to the assured's showroom (where it was to be exhibited) stranded, causing damage to one of the engines. The engine was removed, overhauled, and replaced at another shipyard belonging to the assured and it was recommended that the vessel be run and tried out for 30 or 40 hours at slow speed. The vessel went along in company with another vessel owned by the assured, proceeding at slow speed. Enroute, the captain stopped off and took on board his wife and two friends. After arrival at destination, the vessel was sent into an inlet to load gasoline. After the gasoline was loaded, the captain attempted to start the engine whereupon the vessel exploded. The court held that the vessel was on a "trial trip" at the time it exploded and, as the explosion was within the geographical limits of the policy, the policy covered—a very expansive and liberal interpretation of what is a trial trip.

In *Hanney v. Franklin F. I. Co.*,[12] a builders' risks policy was issued to the owner and the builder of a halibut boat then under construction in Tacoma, Washington. Fire destroyed certain materials while stored in Seattle, Washington, but destined for use in the boat. The court held that the coverage granted was in terms so broad as to indemnify against loss of any material belonging to and destined for the boat whether for building or outfitting.

9. 1926 AMC 1111 (St.,N.Y.).
10. 1946 AMC 1611 (Arb.).
11. 68 F.2d 30, 1934 AMC 436 (2d Cir.).
12. 142 F.2d 864, 1944 AMC 868, 1945 AMC 712 (9th Cir.).

In *North British & Mercantile v. Ullman*,[13] reinsurance companies accepted the risk of reinsuring the primary underwriters under a builders' risks policy covering 24 hulls. The policy warranted that the keels would be laid before May 22, 1943. The court held, based on its interpretation of rather ambiguous extension agreements in the treaty of reinsurance, that the reinsurers contined to be bound upon a loss occurring on keels laid after May 22, 1943.

In *Atlantic Basin Iron Works v. American Ins. Co.*,[14] an ordinary hull policy was purportedly adapted to cover builders' and repairmen's liability risks by means of written and printed riders. The court held that the riders overrode such portions of the printed hull policy as were not reconcilable and, as so interpreted, the policy did not cover legal liability to third parties for damage negligently done but, to the contrary, was specifically limited to liability for loss or damage to vessels which might be in the hands of the assured or on which it might be engaged in work.

In *U. S. v. Mary Ann*,[15] the United States, as mortgagee of a fishing vessel purchased under a Fish and Wildlife Act loan, was named as the sole loss payee in a builders' risks insurance endorsement providing that the mortgagee would not be prejudiced by any act or neglect of the mortgagor. The mortgagor paid $77,000 for repairs to the vessel and insisted that the mortgagee bring an action against the builders' risks underwriters. The mortgagee refused. It was held that the mortgagor acquired no rights as a third-party beneficiary under the endorsement or otherwise to compel the mortgagee to sue the underwriters to recover the repair costs.[16]

A builders' risks policy is a marine policy and subject to all the defenses which underwriters can raise under marine policies. Thus, in *James Yachts Ltd. v. Thames & Mersey Marine Insurance Co. Ltd. et al*,[17] involving a builder's risk policy, the assured failed to inform the insurer that a

---

13. 1946 AMC 1622 (Arb.).

14. 1927 AMC 319 (St.,N.Y.), *sub nom Monterey - Dixie*, 1929 AMC 336 (St., N.Y.).

15. 466 F.2d 63, 1972 AMC 2652 (5th Cir.).

16. At the time the mortgagor made the demand on the mortgagee, the mortgagor was not then in default under the mortgage. Subsequently, the mortgagor defaulted and the mortgagee forclosed its preferred ship's mortgage. One of the defenses of the mortgagor was that the mortgagee had wrongfully refused to bring a suit on the insurance policy containing the loss payable mortgage clause. The court correctly noted that the mortgagee clause creates an independent agreement between the insurer and the mortgagee for the latter's benefit and the mortgagor had no rights under it. The mortgagee owed no duty to the mortgagee to bring an action against the insurer and its refusal to do so did not change or modify the obligation of the mortgagor to the mortgagee under the note and mortgage. The result would no doubt have been different if the mortgagor had been named as an additional assured under the mortgagee clause and named as a loss payee under the loss payable clause. Interestingly, when the mortgagor brought suit directly against the underwriter, the defense was that the damage did not occur while the vessel was in the shipyard or during a trial run.

17. [1976] 1 Lloyd's Rep. 206 (B.C., Canada).

permit to carry on business at its premises had been refused by the local authorities, and the assured's impecuniosity was not disclosed. It was held, in a suit by the assured against the underwriter, that there had been a non-disclosure of material facts and the assured's behavior in carrying on a boat building business was in breach of the implied warranty of legality contained in British Columbia's version of the Marine Insurance Act, 1906.

It is important to remember that, under United States law, a contract for vessel construction is not a maritime contract and, therefore, an admiralty court has no jurisdiction of an action based on a breach of a vessel construction contract.[18] To the contrary, an admiralty court under United States law does have jurisdiction of an action based on breach of a vessel *repair* contract.[19] But, disputes involving marine insurance contracts do fall within admiralty and maritime jurisdiction.[20] Thus, the anomaly is presented that a vessel owner cannot sue the shipbuilder directly in admiralty for damages arising out of defective design or construction, but if the shipbuilder also engages in ship repair work (as most of them do), and the cause of action arises out of alleged defective repairs, then he can sue the ship repairer directly in admiralty. If, on the other hand, the vessel owner sues the underwriter on a builders' risks policy, jurisdiction can be laid in admiralty because the policy is a marine insurance policy.

This subject and the right of vessel owners to bring suit against shipbuilders and ship repairers in products liability actions is discussed, *infra.*

It must also be remembered that ship construction contracts take several varied forms. In one instance, the shipbuilder may contract with the putative shipowner to supply an entire vessel, fully completed, consisting of hull, machinery, electronics, etc., sometimes referred to in the vernacular as a "turn-key" project. The shipbuilder may, and probably will, subcontract with independent suppliers for the supply of certain component parts. Here, the contract is between the shipbuilder and the shipowner, and there is no privity of contract between the shipowner and the independent suppliers or subcontractors. In such circumstances, the shipbuilder may arrange insurance cover only after the subcontractor has made delivery, and, correspondingly, the subcontractor should arrange cover while the component parts are being fabricated by him and prior to delivery to the principal shipbuilder.

18. See *inter alia, North Pacific Steamship Co. v. Hall Bros. Marine Railway and Shipbuilding Co.,* 249 U.S. 119 (1919); *Kelly, Inc. v. Bruno & Stillman,* 1981 AMC 104 (D, N.H.).
19. *North Pacific Steamship Co., supra; Houston-New Orleans, Inc. v. Page Engineering,* 353 F.Supp. 890 (E.D.,La., 1972).
20. *Delovio v. Boit,* 7 F.Cas. 418 (C.C.,Mass., 1815); *Insurance Co. v. Dunham,* 78 U.S. 1 (1870); *Queen Ins. Co. v. Globe & Rutgers Fire Ins. Co.,* 263 U.S. 487, 1924 AMC 107 (1924).

In another scenario, the principal contract is between the shipbuilder and vessel owner and calls for the construction of hull and/or machinery, with the shipowner contracting with third parties for certain component parts or machinery independently of the main contract. Here, there is no privity of contract between the shipbuilder and the independent contractors. Clearly, each contractor ought to insure his own property but liabilities can easily arise between the shipbuilder and the independent contractors such as, for example, where negligence of the independent contractor damages work which the shipbuilder has constructed.

It is important in this context that the ship construction contract clearly delineate the respective rights and liabilities of the respective contractors. Assuming this is done, the policies of the respective contractors can be tailored to the liabilities to which they may be exposed, each to the other, and to their right to claim reimbursement for damage to property in their care, custody, control, or ownership. As a practical matter, it would be wise to furnish the broker obtaining the coverage with a copy of all relevant construction and purchase contracts in order that he may ascertain what liabilities should be covered. Not only the contracts of construction and supply but also the policies should clearly enunciate the intention of the parties with respect to liability and the concomitant responsibilities of each, such as, for example, liability for consequential damages such as delay and loss of profits.[21]

Ship Repairers' Liability[22]

Two forms are in common usage in the United States, the American Institute Ship Repairers' Liability Clauses (November 3, 1977) and Ship Re-

21. See, for example, *Saint Line v. Richardsons Westgarth & Co.*, [1940] 2 K.B. 99 (engines, after installation, found to be inefficient; owners rejected the engines, purchased others elsewhere at a cost in excess of the contract price, and brought suit for the extra cost, incidental expenses, and loss of profits; held, engine suppliers liable for all damages claimed); *Wilson v. General Screw Colliery Co.*, (1877) 47 L.J.Q.B. 239 (propeller shaft and other fittings for a steamer found to be defective; shipowner recovered damages for the cost of replacement and the delay while rectifying the problem); *Alison & Co. v. Wallsend Slipway Co.*, 26 Ll.L.Rep. 159 (cylinders supplied were defective; replacements had to be procured involving delay to the vessel; cylinder suppliers held liable for damages for delay to the vessel). It will be observed that in all the above examples, the standard London form would not have provided coverage for damages for delay. Attention is also called to the provisions of the Uniform Commercial Code, now in effect in nearly all the states in the United States and the Sale of Goods Act in the United Kingdom. Under those acts, there may well be warranties such as the warranty of reasonable fitness for the purpose intended which, if not complied with, could impose liability on the part of the supplier. See *Cammell Laird & Co. v. Manganese Bronze & Brass Co.*, [1934] A.C. 402, where propellers supplied proved to be unsuitable; the subcontractors were held liable to the shipbuilder for the loss sustained by them, including the expense of running a succession of trials to determine and correct the problem. See, also, *Todd Shipyards v. Turbine Service*, 674 F.2d 401, 1982 AMC 1976 (5th Cir.).

22. The author wishes to express his appreciation for the aid available to him through reference to the excellent paper on the same subject by Martin P. Detels, Jr., entitled "The

pairers' Liability (Form SP 9B) (McLelland 1504). The forms are substantially similar.

It is not uncommon for the underwriter to endorse the policy to restrict coverage to liabilities arising out of the performance of services under a form of contract approved by the underwriter in advance, the object being to require the repairer to utilize some form of "red letter" clause acceptable to the underwriter.

The primary cover under such forms is, unfortunately, exceedingly narrow and restricted. The coverage extends to watercraft and their equipment, etc., *occurring only while such watercraft are in the care, custody or control of the Insured for the purpose of repair or alteration,* and only as to liabilities imposed upon the repairer *because of property damage caused by . . . such watercraft while in the repairer's care, custody and control and being operated away from the repairer's premises but within permitted waters.* Legal expenses are covered in defending the repairer against claims based upon liability or alleged liability if the amount claimed exceeds the deductible. Such legal expenses are not recoverable under the policy unless incurred with the written consent of the underwriter. The underwriter reserves the right to conduct such defense at its own expense. If the repairer has a claim, by subrogation or otherwise, the cost and expense of pursuing the claim is proportioned between the underwriter and the repairer.

By contrast, the exclusions are exceedingly numerous. No coverage is provided for liability for loss of life or personal injury, consequential damage, contractually-assumed liabilities, or for any damage occurring after completion of repairs or relinquishment of care, custody, and control, or for vessels in the repairer's custody or at his premises only for storage. Also excluded is the cost of redoing defective work or repairing or replacing any defective part. Loss or damage not discovered within 60 days of delivery of the vessel to its owner, or completion of the work, whichever first occurs, is also excluded.

Clearly, underwriters insuring under these forms intend that the major liabilities incident to the business of ship repairing be insured elsewhere or not at all. As has been noted,[23] the surgical skills required to modify the forms to afford adequate protection to a ship repairer would be better utilized by the preparation of a manuscript form, or modification of the standard form of comprehensive general liability policy.

The American Institute Excess Marine Liabilities Clause (November 3, 1977) (Form 8-A) makes provision for the insuring of excess ship repairers' liabilities but the coverage, of course, extends only to liabilities

---

Insurance of the Liability of Shipbuilders, Repairers and Suppliers," presented at the Second International Maritime Law Seminar, Pacific Northwest Admiralty Law Institute, Vancouver, B.C., June, 1981.

23. Detels, *supra*, n. 22.

insured under the primary policy, but in excess of its limits. Thus, whatever primary form coverage is utilized, it must be scheduled in the excess liabilities policy.

The cases construing ship repairers' liabilities policies are rather numerous in the United States. In *America*,[24] the repair contract provided that the shipowner would continue its "present insurance" up to $2 million; that the repair yard would provide adequate builders' risks, casualty, and other insurance; and that the repair yard would not be released from any liability, however arising. Due to the negligence of the repair yard, a fire broke out on the insured vessel. The court held that in view of ambiguities in the contract, and in view of the transactions leading up to the contract, that the contract operated to give the repair yard the benefit of the owner's fire insurance up to the sum named. (The shipowner had in effect a type of self-insurance by means of an insurance fund and bookkeeping methods.) The court further held that the shipowner's program did not differ from insurance through outside companies insofar as the rights of the repair yard were concerned.

In *Faith*,[25] the ship repairer was insured against liability for losses to vessels "while in the assured's charge being altered and/or repaired." A vessel was lost while tied up at the repairer's wharf at a fixed rental for dockage space. The court held that the loss was not covered as the vessel was not in charge of the ship repairer/assured and was not being altered or repaired.

In *Wyoming*,[26] a ship repairer in whose yard a vessel suffered fire damage and who repaired such damage was held not entitled to recover the cost thereof from his underwriters without showing that he was liable to the owner of the vessel by reason of a judgment, or that the underwriter had waived proof of liability by authorizing the repair.

In *Monterey—Dixie*,[27] an ordinary printed form of hull policy was adapted to cover builders' and repairers' liabilities by means of written and printed riders and purportedly included "legal liability." The court held that the parts of the contract must be examined to determine what kind of legal liability was meant, and, as examined, the cover did not extend to the legal liability of the repairer for its workmen carelessly setting fire to a nearby vessel although the cause of the fire was work being done on the insured vessel.

In *Boyce-Harvey v. Standard Fire Ins. Co.*,[28] a vessel was damaged while being hauled out for repairs when the marine railway collapsed. The

24. 34 F.2d 100, 1929 AMC 1219 (2d Cir.).
25. 1931 AMC 1250 (St.,N.Y.).
26. 1932 AMC 561 (St., N.Y.).
27. 1929 AMC 336 (St.,N.Y.).
28. 1955 AMC 563 (E.D.,La.).

court allowed recovery under the policy for the cost of repair and restoration in the amount of the low bid, plus fees and expenses paid to the naval architect and marine surveyor, plus interest from the date of judicial demand, but disallowed penalties and attorneys' fees under Louisiana law on the ground that a dispute existed as to the origin, cause, and extent of damage and the insurer's refusal to pay was not arbitrary and without probable cause.

American Ship Building Co. v. Orion Insurance Co., Ltd.,[29] illustrates the rather narrow coverage afforded under the standard forms of policies. In that case, the issue before the court was whether damage to the assured's dry dock was covered under policies which incorporated the Institute Clauses for Builders' Risks. The court held that the clauses expressly covered only the assured's *liability to others* and not for damage sustained by the assured's own property.

In *Heipershausen Bros. v. Continental Ins. Co.,*[30] the court held that an underwriter who was sued for a fire loss which occurred just before the policy expired could not implead another underwriter whose policy attached at the moment when the previous policy expired. The liability under either policy could not be affected by the provisions of the other.

In *Cardinal v. U.S. Casualty Co.,*[31] a miscellaneous liability (payroll) type ship repairers' policy was held to cover the liability of a ship repairer who was impleaded into a suit by the owner of a vessel where repairmen aboard had been injured and had sued the vessel owner. The vessel owner settled the claim to which the ship repairer contributed.

In *Monarch Ins. Co. of Ohio v. Cook,*[32] the ship repairers' policy was in the usual form and covered the legal liability of the ship repairer for loss or damage to vessels in its care, custody, or control for the purpose of alteration or repair at locations within the United States or while such vessels or craft were being shifted and/or moved not in excess of 15 miles. The court held that the policy covered two types of risks in the disjunctive and thus where the vessel sank while in the assured's possession for extensive repairs and while repairs were being actually performed at a location within the United States, coverage was provided although the vessel had previously been moved in excess of 15 miles.

Todd Shipyard Corp v. Turbine Service, Inc.,[33] amounts to an instructive treatise on nearly all aspects of repairer's liability vis-a-vis its customers, as well as an equally valuable and instructive treatise on the coverage

---

29. [1969] 2 Lloyd's Rep. 251 (S.D.N.Y., 1969), apparently not otherwise reported.
30. 25 F.Supp. 1010, 1938 AMC 277, 1938 AMC 1591 (S.D.N.Y.).
31. 1949 AMC 2025 (St.,N.Y.).
32. 336 So.2d 738 (St.,Miss.,1976).
33. 674 F.2d 401, 1982 AMC 1976 (5th Cir.).

provided to a repairer by an appropriately worded comprehensive general liability policy. In that incredibly complicated and lengthy case,[34] the owners of the vessel *Katrin* contracted with Todd Shipyards for the performance of various repairs, including repairs to the turbines. The low pressure (LP) turbine was found to be badly damaged. The repairs consisted, in part, of removing four rows of the LP turbine for complete renewal. Necessary blading was to be manufactured. The remaining blading was to be faired, dressed, and renewed. Other bladings in the stator of the turbine were to be removed, faired, and reinstalled in good order. Because Todd's labor force was fully occupied, it hired Turbine Service to perform these repairs. Todd's contract with owners contained a red letter clause limiting its liability to $300,000.

The blades obtained by Turbine Service for making the repairs were incompatible and had to be modified for insertion in the turbine by milling off the blade roots and welding the old roots to the new turbines—found to be a totally unacceptable and negligent method of accomplishing the work. Turbine Service hired Gonzales, a welding company, to do this work without the knowledge of Todd or the owners under a subcontract from Turbine Service in violation of the terms of Todd's purchase order to Turbine Service.

The work was improper and the welds defective through the joint and concurring negligence of both Turbine and Gonzales. After installation and during a river test, it was found that there was a failure of welds in two rotor blades and the broken blades caused considerable damage. Owners elected to ship the entire turbine to Germany to its original manufacturer for rebuilding. Months later, it was returned and installed in the vessel. On examination of the high pressure (HP) turbine, it was found that it had excessive gaps between the tips of the rotor blades and the outer casing of the turbine. Owners decided to have the vessel sail from New Orleans notwithstanding.

Four months later while off the Irish coast near Cork, the turbines suddenly seized up and stopped. The damage to the HP and LP turbines was found to be so extensive that the vessel was sold for scrap. This litigation then followed. The claims, counterclaims, and crossclaims at trial were as follows:

1. Owners sought to recover from all other parties approximately $3.5 million for costs of repairs, loss of the vessel's value, loss of use, and related expenses;

---

34. The court of appeal noted that the action began in November, 1977, and ended in May, 1978. There were 67 days of trial, 28 witnesses, over 7,000 pages of depositions, and more than 600 exhibits offered. The record on appeal comprised 83 volumes.

2. Todd sought to recover from owners its unpaid repair invoices, and sought indemnity from Turbine Service/Travelers Insurance and Gonzales/Sentry Insurance in the event Todd was found liable to owners;

3. Turbine Service/Travelers sought indemnity from Gonzales/Sentry for negligent workmanship by Gonzales and sought to recover from Todd and owners unpaid repair invoices;

4. Gonzales/Sentry sought to recover unpaid repair invoices from all other parties, and sought indemnity from Turbine Service in the event that Gonzales/Sentry were found liable to owners or Todd.

The district court made findings of fact and conclusions of law in which it found, *inter alia,* that the failure of one or more of the LP blades caused the river casualty; that all the repairers had been negligent and had breached implied warranties of workmanlike service, and were consequently liable for damages arising from the river casualty; that no repairer was responsible for the excessive tip clearances that caused the casualty off Cork; that Todd was entitled to indemnity from Turbine and Gonzales; that no exclusion of the insurance policies of Travelers and Sentry relieved them from liability for the damages caused by their insureds; that Todd's red letter clause was valid but was ineffective in this instance because Todd was grossly negligent. Todd was ordered to pay owners $967,633.20 plus costs, attorneys' fees, and post-judgment interest (subject to Todd's right of indemnity, except attorneys' fees, against Turbine/Travelers and Gonzales/Sentry). All parties appealed.

On appeal, the appeals court affirmed the judgment holding Todd, Turbine Service, and Gonzales liable to owners in damages for the improper repair of the LP turbine rotor; affirmed the judgment requiring indemnification of Todd by Turbine Service and Gonzales and denial of indemnification of Turbine by Gonzales; reversed the finding that Todd was guilty of gross negligence; modified the district court's calculation of loss of use damages; affirmed the award of attorneys' fees to owners; directed the district court to enter pre-judgment interest; affirmed the judgment exonerating the defendants from liability suffered by the vessel in the Cork casualty; and reversed the judgment holding that exclusion (o) of the two policies was not applicable.

The discussion by the appeals court, of the various exclusions which the comprehensive general liability insurers urged should apply, is very instructive. All the exclusions were held inapplicable except exclusion (o) which excluded coverage for "property damage to work performed by or on behalf of the named insured arising out of the work or any portion thereof, or out of the materials, parts or equipment furnished in connection therewith . . . "; i.e., the "work product" exclusion. This holding by the court necessitated determining what was the assureds' work product. The insurers contended it was the entire LP turbine; the assureds contended it was merely the specific component parts they attempted to repair and at the most the exclusion eliminated coverage for the cost of repairing or replacing those components. The court upheld the assureds' contention. In the final analysis, the exclusion was held to eliminate coverage for the cost of repairing or replacing any components of the assureds' work product that required such repair or replacement as a result of the assureds' negligence, whether or not such components were themselves defective, and further, that the exclusion did not exclude the other economic losses caused by the assureds' faulty workmanship, i.e., damages for loss of use—by far the largest element of damages in the case.

In the event, Todd as the prime contractor/ship repairer was able to limit its liability to $300,000 under its red letter clause and was found entitled to indemnity for at least a portion of the $300,000 from Turbine Service and Gonzales. The case illustrates graphically the complex questions of liability of ship repairers and their subcontractors, and the equally complex and difficult task of providing insurance coverage for those liabilities. It also demonstrates the inadequacy of the coverage provided under the standard American forms of ship repairers' liabilities insurance. Most of the damage items involved in *Todd Shipyards* would not have been covered under either of the two common American forms. It is fortunate that at least the brokers for Turbine Service and Gonzales recognized this and sought to protect their clients by utilizing comprehensive general liability policies.

Hercules Co. v. Royal Indemnity Co.[35] involved another comprehensive general liability policy used to cover the liabilities of a contractor. In that case, a ship cleaners' policy was held to cover the subsequent loss of cargo caused by careless work as against a contention that the policy did not cover accidents arising out of "completed work." The cause of the loss was cleaning rags negligently left aboard which obstructed a valve. The court held the work was not "completed" until the rags were removed.

"Red Letter" Clauses

Nearly all ship repairers include in their repair contracts a so-called red letter clause limiting the repairers' liabilities to a stipulated amount. A typical example will be found in *Hudson Waterways v. Coastal Marine Service*,[36] the validity of which was sustained as against a contention that the

35. 171 F.Supp. 746, 1960 AMC 157 (S.D.N.Y.).
36. 436 F.Supp. 597, 1978 AMC 341 (E.D.,Tex.).

Bisso[37] decision rendered it void as against public policy. A further and more recent example will be found in *Northwest Marine Iron Works v. Exxon Shipping Co. et al.*[37a] In that case, a ship repairer sued in declaratory judgment against the shipowner and three insurance companies. The suit was based on diversity. The ship repairer contended its liability under the repair contract was limited to $300,000 by virtue of a red letter clause. The shipowner claimed an offset of $975,000 for delay damages by virtue of a liquidated damages provision calling for $39,000 per calendar day for each day's delay in completing the work. The ship repairer's insurers claimed their policies did not cover the ship repairer's liability for liquidated damages as that provision was a contracted-for liability excluded from coverage under the policies.

The clause limiting liability read:

> In further consideration of the making of this Agreement, it is hereby stipulated and agreed that the undertaking of the Contractor to perform work on and dry dock the vessel and provide berth, wharfage, towage and other services and facilities is made only upon the condition that it shall not be liable in respect to any one vessel, directly or indirectly, in contract, tort or otherwise, to its owners, demised charterers, or underwriters for any injury to such vessel, its equipment or movable stores, to cargo owned by the shipowner or demised charterer, or for any consequences thereof, in an amount in excess of $300,000.

The court upheld the validity of the limiting clause, and construed the liquidated damages provision in light of that clause, thus holding, in essence, that the liquidated damages provision simply provided a method of computing damages for delay within the limit established by the limiting clause. This rendered moot the insurers' contention that their policies did not cover because of the liquidated damages provision being a contracted-for liability excluded from their policies.

In *Alcoa Steamship Co. v. Charles Ferran & Co., Inc.*,[38] it was held that a ship repairers' legal liabilities underwriter, sued under a direct action statute, could avail himself of the red letter clause in the ship repair contract. The court distinguished *Olympic Towing Co. v. Nebel Towing Co.*,[39]

37. 349 U.S. 85, 1955 AMC 899 (1955). The same contention was made in *Morton v. Zidell*, 695 F.2d 347, 1983 AMC 2929 (9th Cir.), with the same result.

37a. U.S.D.C., Dist. of Oregon, Civil No. 83-909-RE, February 14, 1984, not yet reported.

38. See *Alcoa Corsair*, 383 F.2d 46, 1967 AMC 2578 (5th Cir.), and subsequent proceedings, sub nom *Alcoa Steamship Co. v. Charles Ferran & Co.*, 443 F.2d 250, 1971 AMC 1116, [1971] 2 Lloyd's Rep. 426 (5th Cir.,1971).

39. 419 F.2d 230, 1969 AMC 1571 (5th Cir.).

where the Limitation of Liability Act was held inapplicable as being a "personal defense" not available to underwriters, and held that the defense of the red letter clause resulted from the nature of the obligation and was not a personal defense.[40]

A cautionary note is in order. Generally speaking, under American law, exculpatory clauses which result in "overreaching" by one party by reason of disparate bargaining power will not be enforced. This was the thrust of the *Bisso* decision. Thus, in towing contracts, such exculpatory clauses are not generally enforced whereas in ship repair contracts, the red letter clause is generally upheld.

Marina Operators' Liability

Marina operators face considerable liabilities in their operations, whether they be operators of pleasure boat marinas or, as is rather common in the United States, operators of "barge fleeting" moorages. A marina operator's liability does not differ significantly from the liability imposed upon a wharfinger as respects vessels coming to his wharf. For example, in *Trade Banner Line, Inc. v. Caribbean Steamship Co., S.A.*,[41] the court noted that while a wharfinger is not a guarantor of the safety of a ship coming to his wharf, he is under a duty to exercise reasonable diligence to furnish a safe berth, which includes the duty of ascertaining the condition of the berth, to make it safe, or to warn the vessel of any hidden hazard or deficiency known to him which, in the exercise of reasonable care and inspection, should be known to him and not reasonably known to the shipowner. This includes underwater obstructions.[42]

To render a berth "safe" means suitable fastenings and lines.[43] While

---

40. It should also be noted that 15 years later the Fifth Circuit in *Crown Zellerbach Corp. v. Ingram Industries, Inc.*, 783 F.2d 1296, 1986 AMC 1471 (5th Cir., 1986), expressly overruled *Olympic Towing* and sustained the validity of a P & I policy provision restricting the underwriters' maximum liability to the amount of the shipowner/assured's judicially declared liability under the Limitation of Liability Act.

41. 521 F.2d 229, 1975 AMC 2515 (5th Cir., 1975).

42. See *The Dave and Mose*, 61 F. 336 (2d Cir., 1893); *Smith v. Burnett*, 173 U.S. 430 (1899); *Bilkay Holding Corp. v. Cons. Iron & Metal Co.*, 330 F.Supp. 1313, 1972 AMC 440 (S.D.N.Y., 1971); *Bouchard Transport Co. v. Tug Gillen Bros.*, 389 F.Supp. 77, 1975 AMC 2030 (S.D.N.Y., 1975).

43. See *Petition of Kingsman Transit Co.*, 338 F.2d 708, 1964 AMC 2503 (2d Cir., 1964); *City Compress & Warehouse Co. v. U.S.*, 190 F.2d 699, 1951 AMC 1511 (4th Cir., 1951); *Porto Ronco v. American Oriole*, 1977 AMC 467 (E.D.,La.); *Medomsley Steam Shipping Co. v. Elizabeth River Terminals*, 354 F.2d 476, 1966 AMC 903 (4th Cir., 1966); *Federal Barge Lines v. Star Towing Co.*, 263 F.Supp. 981 (E.D.,La., 1967); *Wisconsin Barge Line, Inc. v. Barge Chem 301*, 390 F.Supp. 1388, 1976 AMC 2305 (M.D., La.); *Ohio River Co. v. Continental Grain Co.*, 352 F.Supp. 505 (N.D., Ill., 1972). But, bad weather alone, not coupled with negligence on the part of the marina operator, does not impose liability on the marina operator. *Federal Ins. Co. v. Herreshoff Mfg. Co.*, 6 F.Supp. 827 (D.,R.I., 1934); *Buntin v. Fletchas*, 257 F.2d 512 (5th Cir., 1958); *Stegemann v. Miami Boat Slips, Inc.*, 213 F.2d 561 (5th Cir., 1954).

normally there is no duty to provide a watchman, a marina operator may be held liable where he voluntarily undertakes to provide one and a loss occurs because of the watchman's negligence.[44] There is also a duty to provide for safe ingress and egress.[45]

Marina operators frequently find that independent contractors appear upon their premises to do work on vessels moored at the marina. This can lead to difficulties for the marine operator where damage occurs and a question arises as to who was responsible, the marina operator or the independent contractor. This was the situation in *Ertel v. General Motors Corp.*, where a vessel sank through the sole negligence of an independent contractor.[46]

Typical of the liabilities insured are those involved in *Pillgrem v. Cliff Richardson Boats, Ltd. and Richardson: Switzerland General Ins. Co., Third Party*.[47] In that case, the marina operator had effected a marina operators' legal liabilities policy which insured, *inter alia*, the legal liability of the marina operator for loss or damage to vessels which were in the care, custody, and control of the operator, as well as operations involving the alteration, repair, maintenance, or storage of such vessels. In addition, a P & I endorsement extended coverage for liability of the marina operator for loss of, or damage to, or expense in connection with, "any fixed or movable object or property of whatsoever nature." Excluded, however, under the P & I endorsement, was any liability which was recoverable, in whole or in part, under the basic policy as described above.

The assured agreed to build a hull, install a motor, and do such other work as the plaintiff vessel owner was unable to do himself. The vessel owner applied fiberglass to the hull, while the marina operator/assured installed the motor and fuel tanks. One day after delivery, the owner saw moisture on a weld of the starboard tank and reported it to the marina operator who removed the tank. While doing so, fuel oil was spilled on the deck of the boat. While the operator was attempting to pump the

---

44. Compare *Sisung v. Tiger Pass Shipyard Co.*, 303 F.2d 318 (5th Cir., 1962), with *Noonan Constr. Co. v. Federal Barge Lines*, 453 F.2d 637, 1972 AMC 1195 (5th Cir., 1972). Where a marina is merely renting mooring space without more, there does not appear to be a bailment relationship and the marina operator would not normally be considered to have "charge" of the boat. See *Niagara Fire Ins. Co. v. Dog River Boat Service, Inc.*, 187 F.Supp. 528 (S.E.,Ala., 1960); *Security National Ins. Co. v. Sequoyah Marina, Inc.*, 246 F.2d 830 (10th Cir., 1957); *Richardson v. Port Vincent Boat Works, Inc.*, 284 F.Supp. 353 (E.D.,La.). Compare, also, *Stegemann v. Miami Boat Slips, Inc.*, 213 F.2d 561 (5th Cir., 1954) (bailment found), and *Erlbacher v. Republic Homes Corp.*, 263 F.2d 217 (8th Cir., 1959) (bailment found), with *Isbell Enterprises v. Citizens Casualty of New York*, 431 F.2d 409 (5th Cir., 1970) (bailment not found), and *The Dupont*, 14 F.Supp. 193 (D.,Md., 1936) (bailment not found).
45. See *Bailey v. Texas Co.*, 47 F.2d 153, 1931 AMC 771 (2d Cir., 1931); *Harris v. Bremerton*, 85 Wash. 64, 147 P. 638 (St., Wash., 1915); *Enerson v. Anderson*, 55 Wn.2d 486, 348 P.2d 401 (St.,Wash., 1960); *Shannon v. City of Anchorage*, 429 P.2d 17 (St., Alaska, 1967).
46. 41 Fla.App. 166 (Fla., 4th Cir.).
47. [1977] 1 Lloyd's Rep. 297 (Ont. S.C., Can.).

tank, a spark ignited the fuel, causing a fire which destroyed the boat. The plaintiff owner claimed against the marina operator who, in turn, claimed indemnity from his underwriters.

The court held that the marina operator had been negligent and found for the plaintiff. As to the operator's claim against the underwriter, the court held that the rewelding of the tanks would fall within the meaning of the words "alteration, repair or maintenance." The court also held that even if the boat were in the yard for storage only, the operator would be liable for spilling the oil in the manner he adopted and such negligence would fall within the meaning of the term "storage." The insurer was also held liable under the P & I endorsement for the method attempted in removing the oil.

There appears little doubt that a marina operator's policy under English and Commonwealth law is a form of "marine policy."[48] The same is no doubt true under American law.

There is a surprising dearth of decisions involving marina operators' liabilities policies, and, on a national level, there do not appear to be any "standard" forms such as one finds with respect to ship repairers' liabilities, i.e., American Institute Ship Repairer's Liability Clauses (November 3, 1977) and the SP 9B form (McClelland 1504).[49] However, decisions involving ship repairer's liability policies are probably analogous.

It is not uncommon for marinas to provide "dry storage" of boats on land, either in the open or inside buildings. Such dry storage may well result in the liability of the marina being tested on the basis of "land law" rather than admiralty law, and may bring into play state statutes such as the Uniform Commercial Code.[50] In any event, any marina operator's policy should take this into consideration and should be so constructed that coverage extends to liabilities incurred during dry storage.

Products Liability in Maritime Law

Liability for defective or dangerous products in the maritime field is of comparatively recent origin but the incidence of cases in which this principle has been applied is rapidly increasing.

---

48. See *James Yachts Ltd. v. Thames & Mersey Marine Ins. Co. Ltd. et al*, [1977] 1 Lloyd's Rep. 206 (B.C., Can.), discussed *supra* under the heading, "Shipbuilder's Liabilities."

49. A form of marina operator's liability policy is reproduced in the *Journal of Maritime Law & Commerce*, Vol. 6, No. 4 (July 1975), which is apparently in use in Florida. See "Marina Liability and Insurance," by James F. Moseley. While the form of policy there reproduced is broader in some respects than the standard form of ship repairer's liability, the exclusions are equally broad and all-inclusive and marina operators and their advisors would do well to consider procuring something in the nature of a comprehensive general liability policy with the watercraft exclusion deleted.

50. See, for example, *Fireman's Fund American Ins. Co. v. Boston Harbor Marina*, 406 F.2d 917 (1st Cir., 1969).

Historically, manufacturers of defective products were insulated from
liability to those injured by such products by reason of the "privity of contract" rule if the injured party did not purchase the product himself.[51]
Over the years, a number of exceptions developed, the most notable of
which was to impose liability where a product was inherently dangerous
to the user such as tainted foods, explosives, poisons, etc.

In recent years, liability has been predicated upon one or more of
three theories: i.e., negligence, breach of warranty, and strict liability.[52]

Negligence

MacPherson v. Buick Motor Co.,[53] was the first case to eliminate the privity
rule in negligence cases where the product was dangerous if defectively
made. Although not generally enunciating the principle under the rubric
of "products liability," in *Sieracki v. Seas Shipping Co.*,[54] a shipbuilder was
held liable for negligence in making a shackle which broke under strain
on the ground that the duty of reasonable care required more searching
tests than the one actually carried out.

Breach of Warranty

Long before the Uniform Commercial Code (UCC) was drafted, in *Jones
v. Bright*,[55] a supplier of copper sheathing for a vessel was held liable for
its deterioration on the ground of a breach of an express warranty. In
doing so, the court also enunciated implied warranty principles by noting
that when a man sells an article he warrants that it is merchantable—that
is, fit for some purpose—and if he sells it for a particular purpose, he
warrants it for that purpose.

In 1960, in *Henningson v. Bloomfield Motors, Inc.*,[56] the purchaser of an
automobile was injured and she sued both the retailer and the manufacturer, claiming a breach of the implied warranty of merchantability and
thus sought to impose liability without proof of negligence as well as without privity of contract. The court upheld her claim, stating in part:

51. See *Winterbottom v. Wright*, (1842) 152 E.R. 402.
52. See *Hill v. James Crowe (Cases) Ltd.*, [1977] 2 Lloyd's Rep. 450, indicating a trend in
Great Britain to broaden the duty of care. In that case, the manufacturers of a wooden
packing case were held liable to a third party lorry driver who was injured when the packing
case caved in as the driver was standing on it during the course of loading the lorry. The fact
of the accident was held to prove negligent manufacture and the injury to the plaintiff was
held to be a reasonably foreseeable consequence of the negligent manufacture. The facts
were remarkably similar to *Parks v. Simpson Timber Co.*, 388 U.S. 459, 1967 AMC 1696 (1967),
and the same result was reached.
53. 111 N.E. 1050 (N.Y.C.A., 1916).
54. 328 U.S. 85, 90 L.Ed. 1099, 1946 AMC 698 (1946).
55. (1929) 130 E.R. 1167.
56. 32 N.J. 358, 161 A.2d 69 (St.,N.J., 1960).

. . . Where the commodities sold are such that if defectively manufactured they will be *dangerous to life and limb,* then society's interests
can only be protected by eliminating the requirement of privity between the maker and his dealers and the reasonably expected ultimate
consumer. In that way the burden of losses consequent upon the use of
defective articles is borne by those who are in a position to either control the danger or make an equitable distribution of the losses when
they do occur.

Henningson has been called the "fall of the citadel of privity of
contract."[57]

The UCC, which is based upon common law principles, specifically
sets forth three kinds of warranties. These are: express warranty (Section
2-313), implied warranty of merchantability (Section 2-314), and implied
warranty of fitness (Section 2-315).

There have been, as might be expected, a number of maritime cases
where manufacturers have been held liable on warranty principles.[58]

It should be emphasized that under the UCC, a manufacturer or supplier may disclaim warranties. However, such a disclaimer must be in
writing, be conspicuous, and be reasonable before it will be given effect.[59]

Strict Liability

It is generally agreed that the strict liability doctrine had its genesis in
Greenman v. Yuba Power Products, Inc.,[60] where the court embraced the doctrine of "strict liability in tort" and expressly rejected the contention that
recovery depended upon a finding of breach of any statutorily implied
warranty. And in *Vandermark v. Ford Motor Co.,*[61] the California supreme

57. Prosser, "The Fall of the Citadel (Strict Liability to the Consumer)," 69 *Yale L.J.* 1099
(1960).
58. See, for example, *Gambino v. United Fruit,* 1969 AMC 704 (S.D.N.Y.) (bottle of ket-
chup exploded and injured a seaman; damages of the seaman held recoverable by the
shipowner from the manufacturer); *Pabellon v. Grace Line, Inc.,* 191 F.2d 169, 1951 AMC 1751
(2d Cir., 1951) (injuries to seaman from the explosion of three commercial cleansers mixed
together; recovery over by the shipowner against the manufacturer); *Condensor Service &
Engineering Co. v. Compania Maritima, S.A.,* 1954 AMC 1243 (E.D.,Va.) (express warranty that
an evaporator would make 12 tons of fresh water per day; instead, it only produced 5 tons
per day; held, the breach of warranty by the manufacturer precluded its claim for the unpaid purchase price); *Jig the Third Corp. v. Puritan Maritime Insurance Underwriting Syndicate,*
519 F.2d 171, 1976 AMC 118 (5th Cir., 1975) (negligent design and construction of a propeller shaft assembly on a shrimp boat). The foregoing are not intended to be, and are not,
all-inclusive, but are representative of the cases.
59. Sec. 2-316, UCC. See, in this connection, *Jig the Third Corp., supra,* n. 58, where a
disclaimer was disallowed when it made no specific mention of negligence or of tort liability.
Moreover, under UCC Sec. 2-715, consequential damages may be recovered in appropriate
circumstances.
60. 59 Cal.2d 67, 377 P.2d 897 (St.,Cal., 1963).
61. 61 Cal.2d 256, 391 P.2d 168 (St.,Cal., 1964).

court took the next step in imposing strict liability in tort on the retailer, thereby declining to enforce contractual limitations on warranties and other disclaimers.

Strict liability in tort under U.S. law is most definitively expressed in the Restatement (Second) of Torts, Section 402-A (1965) which reads:

> (1) One who sells any product in a defective condition unreasonably dangerous to the user or consumer or to his property is subject to liability for physical harm thereby caused to the ultimate user or consumer, or to his property, if

> (a) the seller is engaged in the business of selling such product, and
> (b) it is expected to and does reach the user or consumer without substantial change in the condition in which it is sold.

> (2) The rule stated in Subsection (1) applies although

> (a) the seller has exercised all possible care in the preparation and sale of his product, and
> (b) the user or consumer has not bought the product from or entered into any contractual relation with the seller.

Although maritime law in the United States has long embraced the concept of strict liability as applied to shipowners, notably with respect to unseaworthiness,[62] the battle has been hard fought when the liability of manufacturers, suppliers, or other non-shipowners has been involved.

It appears that the first maritime case to follow *MacPherson* as to the liability of the remote shipbuilder was *Sieracki v. Seas Shipping Co.*[63] *Parks v. Simpson Timber Co.*,[64] foreshadowed the application of strict liability without fault to cargo shippers, when a longshoreman was injured when he fell through a deceptively packaged bundle of lumber.[65]

---

62. See, for example, *Mahnich v. Southern S. S. Co.*, 321 U.S. 96, 1944 AMC 1 (1944); *Seas Shipping v. Sieracki*, 328 U.S. 85, 1946 AMC 698 (1946); *Italia Societa Per Azioni di Navigazioni v. Oregon Stevedoring Co.*, 376 U.S. 315, 1964 AMC 1075 (1964).

63. 149 F.2d 98, 1945 AMC 407 (3rd Cir., 1945). That case ultimately reached the Supreme Court and is best known under its case title for the proposition of liability of the shipowner but, additionally, in the Third Circuit the shipbuilder was held liable for actionable negligence in failing to test the defective shackle that caused injury to the longshoreman.

64. 390 F.2d 353, 1968 AMC 566 (9th Cir., 1968), *cert. denied*, 373 U.S. 858 (1968).

65. *Cunningham v. Bethlehem Steel Co.*, 231 F.Supp. 934, 1965 AMC 340 (S.D.N.Y., 1964), and *China Union Lines v. A.O. Anderson & Co.*, 364 F.2d 769, 1966 AMC 1653 (5th Cir., 1966), both rejected application of the doctrine of strict liability in tort, but *Harrison v. Flota Mercante Grancolumbiana*, 577 F.2d 968, 1979 AMC 824 (5th Cir., 1978), emphatically embraced the doctrine and specifically declared that the Restatement (Second) of Torts, Sec. 402-A governed the liability of a shipper of toxic chemicals.

In *McKee v. Brunswick Corp.*,[66] a pleasure yacht exploded. The cause was attributed to an ignition coil, negligently manufactured and negligently installed. The yacht was damaged and the owner and his passengers injured. The owner and his passengers sued the negligent manufacturer of the ignition coil, the negligent manufacturer/assembler of the yacht, and the seller. All recovered against all defendants on all theories. It was held that the seller's warranties ran to both his immediate customer and the passengers; that both the component manufacturer and the manufacturer/assembler were liable for negligence; that privity of contract was not required; that the property damage to the vessel itself was recoverable; and that the federal court had admiralty jurisdiction of the case although the manufacture and sale of the yacht were non-maritime contracts.[67]

In *Pan-Alaska Fisheries, Inc. v. Marine Construction & Design Co., etc.*,[68] a long-term charterer of a crab boat contracted with the Marine Construction & Design Co. (Marco) for a major reconstruction job on the fishing boat. In April, 1969, Caterpillar had sold a new marine diesel engine to Northern Commercial Marine, a local dealer in marine engines. In turn, in October, 1969, Northern Commercial sold the engine to Marco which installed it in the fishing vessel. In December, 1969, a fuel filter cracked, spraying fuel over the engine room. The vessel caught fire, sank, and was a total loss. Pan-Alaska sued Marco, Northern Commercial Marine and Caterpillar. The trial court found Northern Commercial Marine, the dealer, negligent and responsible for one-third the loss. Pan-Alaska was held negligent and two-thirds responsible for the loss. Caterpillar and Northern Commercial Marine were exonerated from liability. The evidence showed that approximately nine days before the sale of the engine by Northern Commercial to Marco, Caterpillar had advised its dealers, including Northern Commercial, that filters installed on that particular model of engine at the factory should be replaced. The letter instructed dealers to furnish new and different filters to owners of that type engine. Caterpillar had no communication with either Pan-Alaska or Marco about the filters. At the time of receipt of the warning, Northern

---

66. 354 F.2d 577, 1966 AMC 344 (7th Cir., 1965).

67. *Schaeffer v. Michigan-Ohio Navigation Co.*, 416 F.2d 217 (6th Cir., 1969), appears to be the first case in which an admiralty court squarely considered the question whether a products liability suit is cognizable in admiralty. In that case, a seaman was injured by a dumbwaiter. The vessel owner paid the claim and sought indemnity against the contractor who had agreed to install and maintain the dumbwaiter, and from two subcontractors. The court allowed recovery, finding a breach of the implied warranty of workmanlike service. In the same year, an admiralty court expressly applied 402-A of the Restatement (Second) of Torts in a case involving the Death on the High Seas Act. *Soileau v. Nicklos Drilling Co.*, 302 F.Supp. 119 (W.D.,La., 1969).

68. 565 F.2d 1129, 1978 AMC 2315 (9th Cir., 1977).

Commercial had not resold the engine to Marco. Northern Commercial did not change the filters or advise or warn Marco or Pan-Alaska.

The court of appeals reversed, holding that strict liability in tort applied to suits in admiralty; that Section 402-A of the Restatement of Torts was to be accepted as the law of products liability in the Ninth Circuit; that under that law Marco, the repairer, and Caterpillar, the manufacturer, were liable, relying upon *Vandermark* and *Greenman, supra;* that a repairer is a "seller" under Section 402-A as to goods which it installs; that the manufacturer could not escape liability by its warning to Northern Commercial—which was held to be "irrelevant"; and that the doctrine of comparative fault applied as a partial defense to a strict liability claim in tort under maritime law.[69]

The courts and Congress[70] have been wrestling with the question whether "economic loss" standing alone should be recoverable under a products liability theory; that is, whether a claim for injury to a product itself may be brought in tort. At one end of the spectrum, the case that created the majority land-based approach, *Seely v. White Motor Co.,*[71] held that preserving a proper role for the law of warranty precludes imposing tort liability if a defective product causes purely monetary harm.

At the other end of the spectrum was the minority land-based approach whose progenitor, *Santor v. A and M Karagheusian, Inc.,*[72] held that a manufacturer's duty to make nondefective products encompassed injury to the product itself, whether or not the defect created an unreasonable risk of harm.[73]

Between the two poles fall a number of cases which would permit a product liability action under certain circumstances when a product injures only itself. These cases attempt to differentiate between "the disappointed users . . . and the endangered ones and permit only the latter to sue in tort." The determination has been said to turn on the nature of the defect, the type of risk, and the manner in which the injury arose.[74]

69. This is far from being universal. For example, under Washington law, contributory/comparative negligence is neither a total nor a partial defense to a 402-A claim. *Seay v. Chrysler Corp.,* 93 Wash.2d 319, 609 P.2d 1382 (1980).

70. See, for example, S. 1999. 131 Cong. Rec. 18321, H.R. 2568, 99th Cong., 1st Sess. (1985), and H.R. 4425, 99th Cong., 2d Sess. (1986)—bills which were introduced to formulate national products liability legislation.

71. 63 Cal.2d 9, 403 P.2d 145 (1965) (defective truck). See, also, *Jones & Laughlin Steel Corp. v. Johns-Manville Sales Corp.,* 626 F.2d 280 (3rd Cir., 1980).

72. 44 N.J. 52, 207 A.2d 305 (marred carpeting).

73. See, also, *LaCrosse v. Schubert,* 72 Wis.2d 38, 240 N.W.2d 124 (1976); *Emerson G.M. Diesel, Inc. v. Alaskan Enterprise,* 732 F.2d 1468, 1985 AMC 2069 (9th Cir., 1984). Most of the admiralty cases have arisen in federal courts and have concerned fishing vessels. It must be conceded that the courts and Congress have shown special solicitude for fishermen and this may explain more fully the result in *Emerson.*

74. See *Russell v. Ford Motor Co.,* 281 Or. 587, 575 P.2d 1383 (1978); *Pennsylvania Glass Sand Corp. v. Caterpillar Tractor Co.,* 652 F.2d 1165 (3rd Cir., 1981); *Northern Power & Engineering Corp. v. Caterpillar Tractor Co.,* 623 P.2d 329 (1981) (allowing a tort action if the defective

In any event, the Supreme Court finally set the question to rest in *East River Steamship Corp. v. Transamerica Delaval Inc.*[75] In that case, Seatrain Shipbuilding Corp. announced it was building four supertankers. Each tanker was constructed under a contract in which a separate wholly owned subsidiary of Seatrain Lines, Inc., engaged Shipbuilding. Shipbuilding in turn contracted with the respondent, now known as Transamerica Delaval, Inc. (Delaval), to design, manufacture, and supervise the installation of turbines, costing $1.4 million each, that would be the main propulsion units for the supertankers. When each ship was completed, its title was transferred from the contracting subsidiary to a trust company (as trustee for the owner), which in turn chartered the ship to one of the petitioners, also subsidiaries of Seatrain Lines, Inc. Each petitioner operated under a bareboat charter by which it took control of the vessel for a number of years as though it owned it, with the obligation afterwards to return the ship to the real owner. Each charterer assumed responsibility for the cost of any repairs to the ships.

Defects in high pressure turbines of three of the vessels forced the charterers to take those vessels out of service in order to repair the defective turbines. Negligent installation of a valve in the fourth vessel forced the charterer to take that vessel out of service in order to repair the low pressure turbine.

The charterers brought suit against the manufacturer (Delaval) in tort to recover the repair costs and lost profits under product liability theories of negligence and strict liability.

First, the court held that the charterers' claims fell within admiralty jurisdiction, citing *The Plymouth*,[76] *Executive Jet Aviation, Inc. v. City of Cleveland*,[77] and *Foremost Ins. Co. v. Richardson*.[78] The "locality" test of *The Plymouth* was met because the damage to each vessel occurred at sea and was discovered either at sea or in port. The vessels' involvement in maritime commerce satisifed the nexus requirement established for inland waters by *Executive Jet*. However, the court refrained from deciding whether that requirement applies to torts on the high seas. The court noted that the traditional exclusion of ship construction contracts from admiralty jurisdiction mandated exclusion of the warranty action for repair costs and lost profits.

The court then squarely held that products liability including strict liability is part of the general maritime law.[79] Since general maritime law

---

product creates a situation potentially dangerous to persons or other property, and loss occurs as a proximate result of that danger and under dangerous circumstances).

75. 106 S.Ct. 2295 (June 16, 1986), 1986 AMC 2027 (1986).
76. 70 U.S. 20 (1866).
77. 409 U.S. 249, 1973 AMC 1.
78. 457 U.S. 668, 1982 AMC 2253 (1982).
79. As noted heretofore, the incorporation of product liability into admiralty law had previously been recognized by numerous courts of appeal. See *inter alia, Ocean Barge Trans-*

governs actions in admiralty, the incorporation of products liability into admiralty enabled the court to ground its decision on products liability considerations of general commercial application. Those considerations were primarily that (1) products liability and warranty theories of liability should be kept separate; (2) that the customer needs less protection from the courts when the only damage is to the defective product itself, and (3) manufacturers should not be exposed to the vast liabilities which would result if recovery were permitted in tort for all foreseeable economic losses.

Prior to *East River,* at least three courts of appeal had allowed recovery in products liability for economic loss unaccompanied by physical injury to persons or property in certain circumstances. The Supreme Court's decision in *East River* reversed the rule in the Eighth Circuit and narrowed the rule in the Third Circuit. It is inconsistent with language adopted in the Ninth and Eleventh Circuits. However, the Supreme Court observed that commercial fishermen had received special protection from the courts but were not involved in the case before it, thus leaving open the possibility that *East River* will not be applied to commercial fishermen. The Court also reserved the question of whether a tort cause of action can ever be stated in admiralty when the only damages sought are economic.[80]

The Supreme Court also observed that damage to a product itself is most naturally understood as a warranty claim and that such damage means simply that the product has not met the customer's expectations. The maintenance of product value and quality is precisely the purpose of express and implied warranties. If the charterers' claims had been brought as breach of warranty actions, they would not have been within the admiralty jurisdiction since contracts relating to the construction of or supply of materials to a ship are not within the admiralty jurisdiction and neither are warranty actions grounded in such contracts.[81]

The opinion leaves open the possibility that recovery may be available in tort for damage to other components of a vessel where a defective component fails, but squarely forecloses recovery in tort where the damage occurs solely to the defective part.

---

port v. Hess Oil Virgin Islands, 726 F.2d 121 (3rd Cir., 1984); Lewis v. Timco, Inc., 697 F.2d 1252 (5th Cir., 1983); Schaeffer v. Michigan-Ohio Navigation Co., 416 F.2d 217 (6th Cir., 1969); Lindsay v. McDonnell Douglas Aircraft Corp., 460 F.2d 631 (8th Cir., 1972); Pan-Alaska Fisheries, Inc. v. Marine Construction & Design Co., 565 F.2d 1129, 1978 AMC 2315 (9th Cir., 1977). Prior to East River, the Supreme Court had not opined on the subject.

    80. Citing Robins Dry Dock & Repair Co. v. Flint, 275 U.S. 303, 1928 AMC 61 (1927).

    81. See Thames Towboat Co. v. The Schooner Francis McDonald, 254 U.S. 242 (1920). As the court observed, state law would govern such actions and, in particular, the Uniform Commercial Code which has been adopted by 49 states would apply.

Conclusion

It is now settled that admiralty law has successfully absorbed the principles of products liability law ashore. A suit predicated upon a contract also governed by the Uniform Commercial Code, such as may be found in a contract to repair a vessel as contrasted with a contract to build one, may be brought in admiralty and UCC defenses may be allowed. Moreover, a non-maritime claim based on the UCC, although not cognizable in admiralty, may nonetheless be sued on in federal court if there is diversity jurisdiction.

Use of Comprehensive General Liability Policies for Shipbuilders, Repairers, and Marina Operators

Unquestionably, a properly claused comprehensive general liability policy provides more comprehensive coverage to a shipbuilder, ship repairer, or marina operator than the standard forms of shipbuilders' and ship repairers' policies. However, even the broadest comprehensive general liability policy is far from being an "all risks" policy and contains certain limitations, restrictions, and exclusions with which assureds and assurers should be familiar.

Policies of general liability insurance have traditionally provided coverage for legal liability imposed upon an insured as a result of *unintentional* and *unexpected* personal injury or property damage. Prior to 1966, the American form of policy expressed this concept in terms of coverage for personal injury or property damage "caused by accident." Revisions in 1966 changed the terminology to coverage for an "occurrence." In 1973, further revisions were made to amend the definition of an occurrence. The new definition defines an occurrence as:

> an accident, including continuous or repeated exposure to conditions, which result in bodily injury or property damage neither expected nor intended from the standpoint of the insured.

Before 1966, the word "accident" was generally undefined in the policies. This led to a number of judicial definitions of the term. One common definition of an accident was "any happening resulting in injury . . . which is undesigned and unintended and not foreseeable as the natural and probable consequence of the initiating act."[82]

It is obvious that when an insured has some prior knowledge, actual or constructive, of possible damage from his activities the question of foreseeability can arise. This was apparent in *Town of Tieton v. General Ins. Co.*

---

82. See *Western Casualty & Surety Co. v. City of Frankfort,* 516 S.W.2d 859 (St., Ky., 1974). Another comparable definition will be found in *Moffat v. Metropolitan Cas. Ins. Co.,* 238 F.Supp. 165 (M.D.,Pa., 1964).

of America.[83] There, the insured city constructed a sewage lagoon which allegedly contaminated the claimant's well. The question arose prior to construction whether or not the lagoon might contaminate adjoining property owners' wells but the city engineers disagreed, claiming that the possibility was "slight." In reversing the trial court's determination in favor of the insured, the Supreme Court held that the damage was foreseeable and therefore not an accident. It will be seen that there was certainly no intent on the part of the insured city to contaminate anyone's well but the result was equally not "unforeseen." Since the city was aware of the possible result, there was a "calculated business risk" in building the lagoon at that particular location. Thus, when damage actually occurred, it could not be said to be "unusual, unexpected and unintended."[84]

Those courts not subscribing to the "foreseeability" test concluded that it was the result or consequence of an act rather than the act itself which mattered. Nearly all conduct leading to damage is in some way intentional, although the consequence may not be foreseen or intended. Therefore, it was not an intentional act which barred coverage so much as the nature of the consequence of that act.

Some courts held that some form of intent to do harm was necessary before coverage could be denied. Thus, the unintended consequence of an intentional act was covered.[85] Other courts emphasized the word "expected." Consequently, although foreseeability may be rejected as an element of an accident, there is no coverage if the accident was expected or could have been expected.[86]

Unfortunately, after the 1966 amendments, the definition of the term "accident" continued to cause problems. This is apparent from a comparison of *Millard Warehouse, Inc. v. Hartford Ins. Co.*[87] and *Geurin Contractors, Inc. v. Bituminous Cas. Corp.*[88] Neither of the above cases attempted to distinguish "expected" from "foreseeable." However, in *City of Carter Lake v. Aetna Cas. & Surety Co.*,[89] the court placed emphasis on the expected nature of the damage. In that case, a sewage backup occurred due to an overload to the city's sewage pump. The city did not correct the underly-

---

83. 61 Wn.2d 716, 380 P.2d 127 (St.,Wash., 1963).
84. Other cases reaching the same result are *Hutchison Water Co. v. U. S. Fidelity and Guaranty Co.*, 250 F.2d 892 (10th Cir., 1957); *Kuckenberg v. Hartford Accident Indemnity Co.*, 226 F.2d 225 (9th Cir., 1955) (not necessary to foresee the precise damage which occurred in order to bar coverage). Other courts rejected the "foreseeability" or "natural and probable consequences" as an element of an accident. See *Iowa Mut. v. Simmons*, 262 N.C. 691, 138 S.E.2d 512 (1964)(foreseeability rejected as a test as it would preclude coverage for negligence and render the policy meaningless).
85. See *Moffat v. Metropolitan Cas. Ins. Co. of New York*, 238 F.Supp. 165 (M.D.,Pa., 1964); *Cross v. Zurich Gen. Accident and Liability Ins. Co.*, 184 F.2d 609 (7th Cir., 1950).
86. *Bennett v. Fidelity & Cas. Co. of New York*, 132 So.2d 788 (Fla. App. 1961); Annot., 7 A.L.R. 3d 1262 (1966); Annot., 20 A.L.R. 3d 520 (1968).
87. 204 Neb. 518, 283 N.W.2d 56 (1979).
88. 5 Ark.App. 229, 636 S.W.2d 638 (1982).
89. 604 F.2d 1052 (8th Cir., 1979).

ing problem and there were subsequent backups. Instead of using the foreseeability test, the court focused on the issue in terms of probability; i.e., should the city know or should it have known that there was a "substantial probability" that injury or damage would result from its acts. In the event, the court held that the first backup was covered but the subsequent ones were not, the city having taken a "calculated risk."[90]

From Whose Viewpoint Must Coverage Be Viewed

Prior to 1966, a split of authority existed with respect to whether the happening of an event should be determined from the standpoint of the insured or from the standpoint of the victim. If the latter, then nearly all instances of personal injury or property damage would appear to be "accidents." Clearly, the victim of a personal injury or property damage does not intend or expect it to happen.

The 1966 amendments clearly and unequivocally require that the matter be viewed from the standpoint of the insured.[91] The effect of this change is graphically demonstrated in *Ashland Oil Co., Inc. v. Miller Oil Purchasing Co.*,[92] where the assured had a primary policy and an umbrella policy. Under the primary policy, the amended "occurrence" definition appeared; under the umbrella policy, that definition was absent. The assured deliberately injected a corrosive liquid resembling crude oil into an oil company's pipeline in order to dispose of it surreptitiously. The court held that under the primary policy, the damage ensuing was both intended and expected from the assured's standpoint; under the umbrella policy coverage was upheld as the matter had to be viewed from the standpoint of the injured party.[93]

Vicarious Liability

Where vicarious liability is involved, the courts view it from the standpoint of the insured to determine whether he expected or intended the injury. Thus, in *McBride v. Lyles*,[94] a father was held covered for the intentional assault by one of his sons.

90. Compare *City of Carter Lake* with *Auto Owners Ins. Co. v. Jensen*, 667 F.2d 714 (8th Cir., 1981).
91. *Continental Cas. Co. v. Parker*, 288 S.E.2d 776 (Ga.App., 1982).
92. 678 F.2d 1293 (5th Cir., 1982).
93. See, also, *Merchants Mut. Ins. Co. v. City of Concord*, 117 N.H. 482, 374 A.2d 945 (1977)(suicide by an inmate in the city jail; held that from the standpoint of the insured city, the matter must be viewed from the standpoint of the assured, the city, and was an accident); *Lansco, Inc. v. Dept. of Environmental Protection*, 145 N.J. Super. 433, 368 A.2d 363 (1976), *cert.den.*, 73 N.J. 57, 372 A.2d 322 (St.,N.J., 1976) (release of oil by unknown persons contaminating a reservoir held to be neither expected nor intended by the assured).
94. 303 So.2d 795 (La.App., 1974). See, also, *Edwards v. Akion*, 52 N.C. App. 688, 279 S.E.2d 894, *aff'd* 304 N.C. 585, 284 S.E.2d 518 (1981) (city held covered for an assault by one

Where corporations are involved, the courts view it from the standpoint of whether the wrongdoer was sufficiently high up in the hierarachy of the corporation to impute his act to the corporation.[95]

Coverage Involving Defective Products

From the standpoint of shipbuilders and ship repairers, coverage for products liability is a very important consideration. A threshold question is always involved: whether an accident occurred under the "occurrence" definition. Although the act of manufacturing or fabricating is, of course, a deliberate and intentional act, from the standpoint of the insured a failure of the product is generally unexpected and unintended and coverage is therefore afforded.[96]

Coverage Involving Defective Workmanship

As might be expected, several cases have addressed the question whether defective workmanship falls under the "occurrence" definition. For example, in *Johnson v. Aid Ins. Co. of Des Moines, Iowa*,[97] there were flagrant violations and deficiencies in a construction contract. Holding that obvious violations of contract standards are not "unexpected and unintended" from the standpoint of the insured, the court denied coverage. While carelessness is covered, an insured cannot be allowed to control the risk under the policy through his own intentional or reckless conduct. A similar result was reached in *Bacon v. Diamond Motors, Inc.*[98]

By contrast, in *Barber v. Harleysville Mut. Ins. Co.*,[99] and in *Travelers Ins. Co. v. Volentine*,[100] coverage was upheld. The distinction seems to be that in the latter two cases, the failure to perform and of improper performance could easily have been both accidental and neither intended nor expected by the insured.

---

of its sanitation workers); *Armstrong v. Security Ins. Co.*, 292 Ala. 27, 288 So.2d 134 (1974) (wife who was additional assured held covered for liability for an intentional shooting of a customer by her husband); *Baltizar v. Williams*, 254 So.2d 470 (La.App., 1971) (city held covered for assault by a deputy town marshal).

95. *St. Paul Ins. Co. v. Talledega Nursing Home*, 606 F.2d 631 (5th Cir., 1979) (intentional tort committed by directors of a company; no coverage); *Aetna Cas. & Sur. Co. v. Shuler*, 100 Misc.2d 33, 421 N.Y.S.2d 285 (1979) (intentional tort committed by officer, director, and shareholder of corporation; no coverage).

96. See *Aetna Cas. & Sur. Co. v. General Time Corp.*, 704 F.2d 80 (2d Cir., 1983) (defective electric motors of the insured used by the claimant in fabricating radiators; coverage upheld); *Yakima Cement Products Co. v. Great American Ins.*, 93 Wash.2d 210, 608 P.2d 254 (1980) (defective concrete wall panels supplied by the insured; coverage upheld).

97. 287 N.W.2d 663 (Minn., 1980).

98. 424 So.2d 1155 (La.App., 1982).

99. 450 A.2d 718 (Pa. Super.Ct., 1982)

100. 578 S.W.2d 501 (Tex.Civ.App.. 1979).

Mistakes of law and fact can cause problems for the insured. The mistake may entail damage to property of others in which case the question arises whether the damage was intentional on the part of the assured.[101]

Continuing Damage

The courts have also addressed the problem arising where the insured fails to correct a condition or problem which continues to cause damage. The first occurrence could easily be an "accident"; it is difficult, however, to view continuing damage as an "accident" or "occurrence" when the insured has been alerted that damage is being caused and fails to correct it.[102]

"Bodily Injury"

The coverages clause of the comprehensive general liability policy in use today reads:

The company will pay on behalf of the *insured* all sums which the *insured* shall become legally obligated to pay as damages because of

Coverage A. *bodily injury* or
Coverage B. *property damage*

to which this insurance applies, caused by an *occurrence,*and the company shall have the right and duty to defend any suit against the *insured* seeking damages on account of such *bodily injury* or *property damage,* even if any of the allegations of the suit are groundless, false or fraudulent, and may make such investigation and settlement of any claim or suit as it deems expedient, but the company shall not be obligated to pay any claim or judgment or to defend any suit after the applicable limit of the company's liability has been exhausted by payment of judgments or settlements. [Emphasis original]

A comprehensive discussion of what constitutes "bodily injury," when a bodily injury "triggers" coverage under the policy, and, once triggered,

---

101. Compare *Argonaut v. Maupin,* 500 S.W.2d 633 (Tex., 1973), and *Foxley & Co. v. United States Fidelity & Guaranty Co.,* 203 Neb. 165, 277 N.W.2d 686 (1979), with *State v. Glens Falls Ins. Co.,* 137 Vt. 313, 404 Å.2d 101 (1979). In the first two cases, there was a mistake as to legal ownership of property as a consequence of which the insured damaged property of others; in the last case, a sheriff seized property of a third party, honestly but mistakenly believing that it was owned by another. Coverage was denied in the first two cases but upheld in the last.

102. See *United States Fidelity & Guaranty Co. v. Bonitz Insulation Co. of Alabama,* 424 So.2d 569 (Ala., 1982); *City of Carter Lake v. Aetna Cas. & Sur. Co.,* 604 F.2d 1052 (8th Cir., 1979); *Grand River Lime Co. v. Ohio Cas. Co.,* 32 Ohio App.2d 178, 289 N.E.2d 360 (Ohio App., 1972).

the scope of the coverage afforded is beyond the scope of this chapter.[103] The discussion which follows is a drastically abbreviated outline of the subject.

Prior to the 1966 and 1973 revisions to the standard form of policy, much confusion existed over whether an accident was confined to a single, sudden event, or whether it included bodily injuries resulting from gradual or repeated exposures to dangerous conditions. The 1973 revisions defined an "occurrence" as meaning an accident, including continuous or repeated exposure to conditions which results in bodily injury or property damage neither expected nor intended from the standpoint of the insured. "Bodily injury" was defined as bodily injury, sickness, or disease sustained by any person which occurs during the policy period, including death at any time resulting therefrom.

It is undisputed that the revisions were intended to make it clear that coverage under the policy was triggered by a bodily injury *resulting during the policy period.* Thus, the insurable event is the bodily injury, and not the accident or negligent act. Moreover, a sudden identifiable accident is not necessary to trigger coverage and coverage is thus provided for injury which is the result of gradual or repeated injurious exposures to conditions over a period of time. Consequently, progressive injury resulting from cumulative exposures over a long period of time would be covered by *all policies which provided coverage during the period of injury.* The significance of this change in cases of asbestosis is readily apparent.

The proper inquiry is not when a particular disease results from exposure but rather when bodily injury results. Thus, the current CGL policy provides coverage for injury which occurs during the policy period, *regardless of when the exposure to harmful conditions takes place, or when injury becomes known or manifest.* If an injury results from cumulative exposures over a period of time, it will be covered by all policies providing coverage during the period of exposure.[104]

Keeping in mind that it is the injury, not the exposure, which triggers coverage and as long as the injury continues to happen the policies in effect during those times are activated, most courts which have considered the question have concluded that interpretation of the term "bodily injury" did not require the taking of medical evidence. Thus, the question whether there is "injury" within the meaning of the policy is a legal

---

103. The subject is treated in depth in the excellent article by Marcy Louise Kahn, in *The Forum*, Vol. XIX, No. 4, Summer 1984, published under the auspices of the Tort and Insurance Practice Section, American Bar Association, to which readers are commended.

104. See *Keene Corp. v. I.N.A.*, 667 F.2d 1034 (D.C., Cir., 1981); *ACandS, Inc. v. Aetna Cas. & Sur. Co.*, 567 F.Supp. 936 (E.D., Pa., 1983); *Sandoz, Inc. v. Employers' Liability Assur. Corp.*, 554 F.Supp. 257 (D.N.J., 1983); *American Home Products Corp. v. Liberty Mut. Ins. Co.*, 565 F.Supp. 1485 (S.D.N.Y., 1983).

one, not a medical one,[105] and hinges on the reasonable expectations which the policyholder would have as to the extent of its insurance coverage for liability for any particular bodily injury claim.

It is notable that with several minor exceptions, the courts which have considered the above questions have concluded that the standard policy provisions which trigger coverage are ambiguous. It is to hoped that the industry can, in subsequent revisions, make the language more clear and precise.

Completed Operations Hazard vs. Products Hazard

Since the 1966 amendments to the standard form of CGL policy, the "Completed Operations Hazard" and the "Products Hazard" have been separated. The Completed Operations Hazard reads (italicized phrases in the original are omitted):

> "Completed operations hazard" includes bodily injury and property damage arising out of operations or reliance upon a representation or warranty made at any time with respect thereto, but only if the bodily injury or property damage occurs after such operations have been completed or abandoned and occurs away from the premises owned by or rented to the named assured. "Operations" includes materials, parts or equipment furnished in connection therewith. Operations shall be deemed completed at the earliest of the following times:
>
> (1) when all operations to be performed by or on behalf of the named insured under the contract have been completed,
> (2) when all operations to be performed by or on behalf of the named insured at the site of the operations have been completed, or
> (3) when the portion of the work out of which the injury or damage arises has been put to its intended use by any person or organization other than another contractor or subcontractor engaged in performing operations for a principal as a part of the same project.
>
> Operations which may require further services or maintenance work, or correction, repair or replacement because of any defect or deficiency, but which are otherwise complete, shall be deemed complete.

---

105. *Commercial Union Ins. Co. v. Pittsburgh Corning Corp.*, 553 F.Supp. 425 (E.D.,Pa., 1981).

The completed operations hazard does not include bodily injury or property damage arising out of

> (a) operations in connection with the transportation of property unless the bodily injury or property damage arises out of a condition in or on a vehicle created by the loading or unloading thereof,
> (b) the existence of tools, uninstalled equipment or abandoned or unused materials, or
> (c) operations for which the classification stated in the policy or in the company's manual specifies "including completed operations."

By comparison, the Products Hazard reads:

> "Products hazard" includes bodily injury and property damage arising out of the named insured's products or reliance upon a representation or warranty made at any time with respect thereto but only if the bodily injury or property damage occurs away from premises owned by or rented to the named insured and after physical possession of such products has been relinquished to others.

The courts have taken a rather practical, commonsense approach toward the distinction between an "operation" and a "product." A product is a tangible piece of goods; an operation is work performed by the assured and includes not only a "pure service" but also acts taken with respect to products, such as their installation, delivery, repair, sale, or even manufacture. In short, the court decisions make it clear that the completed operations hazard does not cover *only* pure services. In resolving the question, the courts try to identify the *cause* of the accident or occurrence. If the cause of the accident or occurrence was a defect in the product itself, then the products hazard applies; if the cause was a defect in the manner in which the product was installed or repaired or otherwise treated, the completed operations hazard determines coverage.

The leading case to date on this dichotomy is *Friestad v. Travelers Indemnity Co.*[106] There, the insured was sued for the faulty installation of a furnace which had been built by another company. The policy clearly excluded coverage for the products hazard but it was not clear whether or not the completed operations hazard had been excluded. The insurer contended that the definition in the products hazard, which included the term "handled," made the furnace one of the insured's products so that coverage was excluded. The court disagreed, holding that the exclusion should be applied only when a product, rather than a service, is the *cause in fact* of damages or injury to a third person. In fact, the cause in fact was

---

106. 260 Pa. 178, 393 A.2d 1212 (1979).

the faulty installation of the furnace—a service—not a defect in the product itself.

On the other hand, products liability also includes such product-related activities as sales, warranties, manufacture, and the publication of warnings. Consequently, the reasonable expectations of an assured would be that such activities are included within the products hazard.

The only logical way to harmonize the two hazards with the reasonable expectations of an assured is to accept that the two definitions are not mutually exclusive.[107] As a practical matter, products hazard coverage and completed operations coverage should be purchased together. If the coverages differ, or one is excluded and the other not excluded, problems will arise in distinguishing between the two and this only leads to further litigation.

When is an Operation "Completed"

Reference to the new policy language will demonstrate that three independent conditions can suffice for completion, the earliest of which "completes" the operation. The first, completion of the contract, is a legal question.[108] The second and third present factual issues.[109] Despite the clarifying language in the 1966 amendments, it is clear that factual questions will continue to arise to plague insurers and insureds alike.

What is "Property Damage"

The new standard CGL policy defines property damage as follows:

> "Property Damage" means (1) the physical injury to or destruction of tangible property which occurs during the policy period including the loss of use thereof at any time resulting therefrom, or (2) loss of use of tangible property which has not been physically injured or destroyed provided such loss of use is caused by an occurrence during the policy period. [Italicized portions in original are not indicated.]

An example of the first type is a demolition contractor who causes damage to an adjoining building. Following the damage, it is discovered

---

107. See *Indiana Ins. Co. v. DeZuti*, 408 N.E.2d 12 (Ind., 1980), where liability for a breach of implied warranty in the construction of concrete footings of a building was treated as falling within either the products hazard or the completed operations hazard.

108. See *Casey v. Employees National Ins. Co.*, 538 S.W.2d 181 (Tex.Civ.App. 1976); *Bell Telephone Co. v. Travelers Indemnity Co.*, 252 Ark. 400, 479 S.W.2d 232 (1972).

109. See *Martinez v. Hawkeye Security Ins. Co.*, 195 Colo. 184, 576 P.2d 1017 (Colo. 1978); *Woodward v. North Carolina Farm Bureau Mut. Ins. Co.*, 44 N.C. App. 282, 261 S.E.2d 43 (1979); *Nogales Avenue Baptist Church v. Peyton*, 576 P.2d 1164 (Okla. 1978); *Abco Tank & Mfg. Co. v. Federal Ins. Co.*, 550 S.W.2d 193 (Mo. 1977); *Hanover Ins. Co. v. Hawkins*, 493 F.2d 377 (7th Cir., 1974).

that the adjoining building was also rendered structurally unsound and will have to be repaired over a period of time. Any loss of use resulting therefrom, such as interruption of business sustained by occupants of that building, is considered to be a property damage loss. An example of the second type would be the case where a contractor's crane topples onto a main roadway. Although the accident does not physically damage any property, access to several business establishments is inhibited until the crane can be removed. This would be considered a loss of use of tangible property (the businesses) that has not been physically damaged or destroyed. However, the covered loss must be "sudden and accidental" and must occur during the policy period.

The definition seems clear; the difficulties arise when the various policy exclusions are examined. The exclusions are rather numerous.

Exclusions

The following exclusions appear in the new standard form of policy and read as follows:

Contractual Liability. This insurance does not apply:

> to liability assumed by the assured under any contract or agreement except an incidental contract; but this exclusion does not apply to a warranty of fitness or quality of the named insured's products or a warranty that work performed by or on behalf of the named insured will be done in a workmanlike manner.

The purpose of the exception as to warranties in the overall exclusion is to make warranties of the insured's products the subject of products liability insurance, rather than contractual liability insurance. Generally speaking, protection for liability contractually assumed by a business must be separately covered for an additional premium. However, certain of the contractual liability exposures—the so-called "incidental contracts"—are automatically covered under most CGL policies. The term "incidental contract" is defined to mean any *written* (1) lease agreement; (2) easement agreement; (3) agreements required by municipalities; (4) railroad sidetrack agreements; or (5) elevator maintenance agreements.

Performance. This insurance does not apply:

> to loss of use of tangible property which has not been physically injured or destroyed resulting from
>
>> (1) a delay in or lack of performance by or on behalf of the named insured or any contract or agreement, or
>> (2) the failure of the named insured's products or work per-

formed by or on behalf of the named insured to meet the level of performance, quality, fitness or durability warranted or represented by the named insured;

but this exclusion does not apply to loss of use of other tangible property resulting from the sudden and accidental physical injury to or destruction of the named insured's products or work performed by or on behalf of the named insured after such products or work have been put to use by any person or organization other than insured.

For example, a manufacturer makes and sells a steam turbine with a guaranty that the unit will produce a specified level of power within a certain period. The turbine fails to produce power to expected levels thereby causing its owner to lose the use of certain machinery dependent upon the power, as well as causing corresponding losses of production and revenue. These resulting damages constitute loss of use of *undamaged* tangible property, as well as loss of intangibles; they are excluded under the standard CGL policy. If, however, the steam turbine suddenly and accidentally explodes, the manufacturer would have coverage against the owner's loss of use of tangible property, *other than the turbine itself*.[110] And bodily injuries to others resulting from the turbine explosion would also be covered.

The basic requirement—and a very important one—is that someone else other than the named insured must be using the product at the time of loss. The net result of the exclusion is to insulate insurers from losses normally considered to be a part of the cost of producing products. The rationale is that when a product does not perform properly, the burden of any loss of use stemming from that product should fall upon its maker or assembler who should be the best judge of the product and its capabilities and who has the responsibility for making it work as warranted or represented.

Business Risk. This insurance does not apply:

to bodily injury or property damage resulting from the failure of the named insured's products or work completed by or for the named insured to perform the function or serve the purpose intended by the named insured, if such failure is due to a mistake or deficiency in any design, formula, plan, specifications, advertising material or printed instructions prepared or developed by any insured; but this exclusion does not apply to bodily injury or property damage resulting from the active malfunctioning of such products or work.

---

110. Coverage applies because the failure to perform exclusion makes exception to loss of use of other tangible property resulting from sudden and accidental damage or destruction of the named insured's products.

This exclusion seems self-explanatory.

Damage to the Product. This insurance does not apply:

to property damage to the named insured's products arising out of such products or any part of such products . . . .

Damage to the Work Performed. This insurance does not apply:

to property damage to work performed by or on behalf of the named insured arising out of the work or any portion thereof, or out of materials, parts or equipment furnished in connection therewith . . . .

As noted heretofore, there is no coverage under a CGL policy for damage simply to the named insured's product. It is immaterial whether the product is physically damaged or merely rendered useless because it fails to work. The rationale is simple: the underwriter is to be insulated from liability for having to pay for the repair or replacement of a product incorrectly designed or defectively produced.

There are two important aspects to remember. First, when damage arises out of a portion of a product and the damage makes the remaining part of the product useless, the exclusion applies to the whole product, not just the part from which the damage arose. Second, damage to a product arising from any portion of the product is excluded, whether the underlying cause of the damage was attributable to the work of a manufacturer, an assembler, or a supplier of a component.

The following example may be helpful:

The ABC company manufactures electric generators which the XYZ Shipbuilding Company uses in constructing its vessels. One of the generators is defective and burns out and causes damage (physical injury or loss of use) to the main propulsion engine while the vessel owner is operating the vessel. The XYZ company would be without products liability coverage under its products liability coverage for damages to the electric generator and main engine because both are considered to be its products.[111] The ABC company has a legal responsibility for the costs of repairing or replacing its defective generator, probably without benefit of insurance, because that component is considered to be its product. The products liability insurer of the ABC company should respond for the payment of damage to the damaged main engine since that engine was

---

111. While the shipbuilder may be responsible for repairing or replacing the electric generator, it has a right of recourse against the ABC company whose defective component was the proximate cause of the loss.

not the ABC company's product; i.e., the engine was not manufactured, sold, handled, or distributed by the ABC company.

If the damage to the generator and main engine were sudden and accidental, however, the XYZ company would have coverage under its products liability policy for loss of use of other undamaged tangible property sustained by the vessel owner under the exception of the failure to perform exclusion.

Sister Ship Liability Exclusion. The so-called "Sister Ship" exclusion is an important exclusion that affects products liability coverage. It is directed at costs incurred by a business entity for the withdrawal, inspection, repair, or replacement of its products, including their loss of use, when its products must be withdrawn from the market or from use because they are either known to be or suspected to be defective. Such product recalls are common in the automotive and drug industry. Insurance for this risk, commonly referred to as products recapture or recall insurance, is available for a premium but the risk is definitely not covered under a standard CGL policy.

It reads:

This insurance does not apply:

> to damages claimed for the withdrawal, inspection, repair, replacement, or loss of use of the named insured's products or work completed by or for the named insured or of any property of which such products or work form a part, if such products, work or property are withdrawn from the market or from use because of any known or suspected defect or deficiency therein.

Care, Custody, or Control Exclusion. In keeping with the basic philosophy of a CGL policy which is to cover *liabilities to others,* this exclusion removes coverage for property damage (1) to property owned or occupied by or rented to the insured; (2) to property used by the insured; or (3) property in the care, custody, or control of the insured or as to which the insured is for any purpose exercising physical control. Excepted from the exclusion, however, are liabilities under a written sidetrack agreement, and liability for property damage (other than to elevators) arising out of the use of an elevator at premises owned by, rented to, or controlled by the named insured.[112]

---

112. The term "elevator" is defined in the policy as meaning any hoisting or lowering device to connect floors or landings, including its appliances, such as any car, platform, stairway, power equipment, or machinery. The term does not include, however, such items as an automobile servicing hoist, a hoist without mechanical power and without a platform which is used outside a building, an inclined conveyor used exclusively for conveying property, etc. Whether a marine elevator used in pulling ships out of the water in order to perform repairs or maintenance work is an "elevator" seems to be an open question; no decisions can be found in which this issue was presented.

The "Watercraft" Exclusion. This exclusion can be of critical importance to a ship repairer who wishes to procure more expansive liability coverage by using a CGL policy rather than one of the standard ship repairers' forms, discussed *supra*. It reads:

This insurance does not apply:

to bodily injury or property damage arising out of the ownership, maintenance, operation, use, loading or unloading of

(1) any watercraft owned or operated by or rented or loaned to any insured, or
(2) any other watercraft operated by any person in the course of his employment by any insured;

but this exclusion does not apply to watercraft while ashore on premises owned by, rented to or controlled by the named insured.

A careful reading of the entire exclusion leads to several interesting observations. It clearly would not cover, for example, a vessel under *construction* by a shipbuilder as the vessel would be a watercraft owned by the named insured so long as title to the uncompleted vessel is still in the name of the shipbuilder. It would appear to cover bodily injury or property damage arising out of the presence of a watercraft at the ship repairer's dock or wharf unless that watercraft was being "operated" by a person employed by the named insured at the time the damage was sustained. This exclusion by itself, without reference to the exclusion of property in the care, custody, or control of the assured, would not appear to apply to a vessel pulled up on shore on a ship repairer's marine railway because of the exception contained therein. However, the exclusion (and its exception) cannot be read as if it stands alone but must be construed *in para materia* with the other covering clauses as well as the other exclusionary clauses. And in this respect, it would appear that the care, custody, and control exclusion would exclude liability for property damage to the vessel under repair. Liability for property damage or bodily injury to third parties arising out of an explosion, for example, on board a vessel on shore, would appear to be covered.

The precise meaning of the exclusion does not appear to have been adjudicated. It is submitted that if a putative assured, such as a shipbuilder, ship repairer, or marina operator, wishes to utilize a CGL policy in conjunction with a first party property damage policy such as the American Institute Builders' Risk Clauses (Feb. 8, 1979) or the American Institute Ship Repairer's Liability Clauses, he should arrange to have the watercraft exclusion clause in the CGL policy deleted.

In this area, there is simply no substitute for a well-informed and sophisticated broker who can procure coverage using the standard forms discussed herein, including a CGL policy, as modified by endorsements, to effect the coverages which his clients desire and must have to protect themselves. Another alternative would be the production of a manuscript policy incorporating the best features of all the relevant standard forms.

CHAPTER XXIII

SUBROGATION, WAIVER OF SUBROGATION, LOAN RECEIPTS, AND DOUBLE INSURANCE

It is difficult to conceive of a more important subject in marine insurance than the doctrine of subrogation. This doctrine, it also must be remembered, led directly to the "benefit of insurance" clauses which, in turn, precipitated the countervailing use of "loan receipts."

Although subrogation, the use of loan receipts, waiver of subrogation, and double insurance can be treated as separate sub-topics, the interrelations are such that some degree of overlapping necessarily occurs.

Subrogation

Subrogation, simply, is the right of an underwriter who has paid a loss to his assured to "take over" the rights which the assured had against a third party and assert such rights against the third party. That is, the underwriter becomes the beneficial owner of his assured's rights and is entitled to sue the third party (either in the name of the assured or in his own name) to recoup or recover the amount paid.

The doctrine obviously has a great impact in the maritime field for, as a practical matter, underwriters frequently pay losses without delay to their assureds and the subsequent litigation against negligent third parties, even though often prosecuted in the name of the assured as plaintiff, is actually carried forward by the underwriters and their counsel.

For example, the underwriters will pay promptly the collision damage to a tug even though the tug owner has a meritorious claim against the colliding vessel. The underwriters then (frequently in the name of the tug owner) will prosecute the claim for collision damage against the other colliding vessel in an effort to recoup that which has been paid to their assured.

The Marine Insurance Act, 1906, in Section 79 describes the rights of an underwriter after payment of a loss as follows:

> (1) Where the insurer pays for a total loss, either of the whole, or in the case of goods of any appreciable part, of the subject-matter insured, he thereupon becomes entitled to take over the interest of the assured in whatever may remain of the subject-matter so paid for, and he is thereby subrogated to all the rights and remedies of the assured

in and in respect of that subject-matter as from the time of the casualty causing the loss.

(2) Subject to the foregoing provisions, where the insurer pays for a partial loss, he acquires no title to the subject-matter insured, or such part of it as may remain, but he is thereupon subrogated to all rights and remedies of the assured in and in respect of the subject-matter insured as from the time of the casualty causing the loss, insofar as the assured has been indemnified, according to this Act, by such payment for the loss.

It will be observed that, after payment of a total loss, the underwriters have two correlative rights instead of merely one; i.e., they have a right to exercise ownership of the subject-matter insured and also to acquire rights of action against offending third parties who caused the loss.[1] However, if rights of ownership are exercised, they may prove to be expensive.[2] In *Wong v. Utah Home Fire Ins. Co, supra,* the subject vessel was deposited by a tidal wave in a commercial fishpond. After the insurance company had paid the vessel owner's loss, the fishpond owner sued the insurance company for damages and trespass for failure to remove the wreck. Recovery was granted. In *Cleary Bros. v. Boston Ins. Co.,*[3] a subrogated cargo insurer attempted to avoid liability for general average and salvage expenses by saying it was not a party to the contract of carriage. The defense was not allowed. In the *Tashmoo,*[4] the underwriters avoided this complication by declining abandonment and, after paying a total loss, disclaiming any interest in the wreck. In so doing, they also lost the benefit of an offset (moneys received from salvage) to which they otherwise would have been entitled. This is also in accord with English law.[5]

Abandonment of a wrecked vessel to the United States may create problems. In *U.S. v. Cargo Salvage,*[6] the United States under 33 U.S.C.A. 419 notified the owner that his sunken ship constituted an obstruction to navigation but failed to notify the underwriters on the cargo being carried in the vessel. The cargo underwriters were held entitled to the salvage.

Subrogation is an equitable remedy based on general principles of contract and does not spring from contract, although it may be confirmed or modified by contract. The rights of underwriters after payment of a

1. *Wong v. Utah Home Fire Ins. Co,* 167 F.Supp. 230, 1960 AMC 649 (D.,Haw.).
2. The cases appear to reflect that an abandonment takes place in every total loss, either by express notice in case of constructive total loss, or by implication in case of an actual total loss; i.e., an underwriter who pays a total loss without qualification could legally become the owner of the wreck, although he may avoid that result by appropriate disclaimer.
3. 177 F.Supp. 807, 1960 AMC 397 (E.D.N.Y.).
4. 48 F.Supp. 808, 1943 AMC 399 (E.D.,Mich.).
5. See *Brooks v. McDonnell,* (1835) 4 L.J. Ex. Cheq. 60, 160 E.R. 204.
6. 228 F.Supp. 145, 1966 AMC 158 (S.D.N.Y.).

loss are purely derivative; they may assert all that, but no more than, that the assured might have claimed.[7]

In *Bleakley No. 76*,[8] a barge owner whose barge was damaged by its negligent tug sought limitation. The underwriters on the barge paid the loss and intervened in the limitation proceeding. The court held the underwriters' rights were subordinated to the rights of other claimants against the fund because the underwriters were entitled to no greater rights than the vessel itself was entitled to, and its rights, including damage claims, were subject to the claims of the other vessels and the cargo owner. (It should be observed that since the vessel owner, in a limitation proceeding in the United States, is not required to surrender the proceeds of any hull insurance recovery, it necessarily follows that his underwriters should not be put in a preferred position vis-a-vis other claimants against the fund.)[9]

In *Yorkshire Ins. Co., Ltd. v. Nisbet Shipping Co., Ltd,*[10] the insured vessel came into collision with a Canadian government vessel, and the underwriters paid £72,000. The assured claimed damages against the Canadian government and succeeded. Meanwhile, the pound had been devalued, and when the loss was converted into English currency it totaled nearly £127,000. The assured repaid the £72,000 to the underwriters and retained the balance of £55,000. The underwriters brought an action to recover. The court held that the suit failed, as the underwriters were entitled to recover no more than they had paid.

Stating it in a slightly different context, we may say that the right of subrogation does not carry with it a right to recoup any more than that which was paid out.[11] In *Almirante, supra,* the Supreme Court held that a valued hull policy is a contract of indemnity and that the insurer could not make a profit out of his subrogation rights. In that case, the owner of a vessel totally lost in a collision recovered from the owner of the other vessel at fault a sum in excess of the agreed value of his vessel under his hull insurance policies. Although the owner was required to reimburse his hull underwriters for the sums they paid him, after deducting pro rata the legal expenses of the collision litigation, the underwriters were held not to be entitled to any overage. In *Eunice and Lillian, supra,* a vessel

---

7. *Eunice and Lillian,* 232 F.Supp. 472, 1964 AMC 1894 (D.,Mass.); *City of Bangor,* 60 F.2d 124, 1932 AMC 1049 (6th Cir.); *Sea Insurance Co. v. Hadden,* (1884) 13 Q.B.D. 706, C.A.; *Glen Line Ltd. v. A.G.,* (1930) 37 Ll.L.Rep. 55, H.L.; *Burnand v. Rodocanachi,* 7 App.Cas. 333, 4 Asp. M.L.C. 576, H.L.

8. 56 F.2d 1037, 1932 AMC 307 (S.D.N.Y.).

9. Subrogees are, however, entitled to intervene in limitation actions. *The Gloria,* 1931 AMC 1048 (5th Cir.).

10. [1961] All E.R. 487, 2 Q.B. 330.

11. *Almirante,* 304 U.S. 430, 1938 AMC 707 (1938); *Rose and Lucy—Saint Anna Maria,* 284 F.Supp. 141, 1968 AMC 1612 (D.,Mass.); *Eunice and Lillian,* 232 F.Supp. 472, 1964 AMC 1894 (D.,Mass.).

worth $60,000 but insured for $30,000 was totally lost in a collision in which both vessels were to blame. The court held that the owner was a 50 percent co-insurer with his insurance company and entitled as subrogee to one-half of the damages collected by his insurance company from the other vessel, less attorneys' fees and expenses.

The facts in *Rose and Lucy—Saint Anna Maria, supra,* were even more unusual. There, the same insurance company insured both the colliding vessels. The innocent vessel was paid the full amount of its hull policy ($30,000) although less than its value ($40,000). Thereafter, the owner of the innocent vessel sued the offending vessel for the full amount of $40,000. The court held that an assignment to the underwriter of the subrogation rights of the innocent vessel upon payment of the $30,000 was valid and that the offending vessel was entitled to a credit of $30,000 on the judgment in favor of the innocent vessel. The underwriter was refused its litigation expenses since it was the insurer of both vessels and therefore received no benefit from the defense.

A subrogee cannot improve his position or augment his right of recovery beyond that of the party he succeeds merely because he sues in his own name without bringing in the latter as a party. The right he asserts is subject to the same infirmities and set-offs as though its original owner were asserting it.[12]

Where the owner of a vessel has no rights against another vessel at fault, by reason of common ownership of the two vessels, then the underwriters who paid the loss on one vessel may not claim subrogated rights against the other vessel.[13]

Just as an assured cannot sue himself, neither can the underwriters sue the assured or one standing in the same relationship.[14]

Generally speaking, the right to subrogate does not arise until a loss has been paid.[15] However, in *Welded Tube v. Hartford,*[16] it was held that a

12. *Coal Operators' Casualty Co. v. U.S.,* 76 F.Supp. 681, 1948 AMC 127 (E.D.,Pa.). See, also, *Yates v. Whyte,* (1838) 132 E.R. 793 and *Boag v. Standard Marine Ins. Co., Ltd,* (1937) 1 All E.R. 714, [1937] 2 K.B. 113, 19 Asp. M.L.C. 107.

13. *Augusta-Detroit,* 5 F.2d 773, 1925 AMC 756 (4th Cir.); *Simpson v. Thomson,* (1877) 3 App.Cas. 279 , H.L.

14. *Caballery v. Sea-Land,* 1973 AMC 479 (D.,P.R.) (P & I policy endorsed to cover any affiliated or related companies if vessel chartered to them, and charterers would be protected in "any capacity"; assured's related company's activities as a stevedore imposed liability on the assured's vessel); *Atlas Assurance v. Harper, Robinson Shipping,* 508 F.2d 1381, 1975 AMC 2358 (9th Cir.) (when cargo was damaged during loading and unloading operations, cargo underwriters would not, after payment of consignee's claim, be allowed equitable subrogation against an ocean carrier where such litigation, in effect, would be a suit against their own insured); *Canadian Co-op v. John Russell,* 68 F.2d 901, 1934 AMC 7 (2d Cir.) (cargo underwriter insured cargo "for account of whom it may concern"; the shipowner paid the premium in accordance with the charter party; the underwriter paid the loss to cargo owners under loan receipts and sued the shipowner in subrogation; held, no recovery).

15. *West Aleta,* 12 F.2d 855, 1926 AMC 855 (9th Cir.); *Frank J. Fobert,* 129 F.2d 319, 1942 AMC 1052 (2d Cir.).

16. 1973 AMC 555 (E.D.,Pa.).

cargo underwriter could implead an ocean carrier in an action brought by its assured even though it had not technically acquired any subrogation rights by making payment to the assured, and in *Callahan v. Cheramie Boats,*[17] it was held that an indemnitee was not barred from suing the indemnitor merely because both were named insureds under a liability policy obtained by the indemnitee pursuant to its charter agreement with the indemnitor.

In *Marine Sulphur Queen,*[18] it was contended the underwriters had waived their rights of subrogation under a clause by which the underwriters had waived subrogation against the vessel and affiliated and associated companies in the event the vessel was chartered by such affiliated and/or associated companies. Finding that the owner and charterer both knew of the unseaworthy condition of the vessel, the court held that the underwriter was entitled to recovery through subrogation against the shipowner and charterer in the absence of clear proof of identity or control by the cargo owner, and that the term "chartered" in the clause meant "demise chartered."

The subrogation rights of the underwriter may be easily prejudiced and, if not pursued within the time limit imposed upon the assured himself by applicable law, may be totally lost. In *Meredith v. Ionian Trader,*[19] and *Government of Pakistan v. Ionian Trader,*[20] the cargo underwriter did not settle and pay off the loss prior to the one-year time limit imposed by Cogsa. A libel was brought, however, in the name of the assured before the expiration of the one-year period. The court held that the timely filing of the libel was a nullity as it was done without authority. To the contrary, the underwriter may pay the loss, subrogate, and if it files suit within the one-year period recoup its payment, or, if sued within the one-year period by the cargo owner, it may implead the carrier to enforce its potential subrogation claims before the insurance payment is actually made on the insured's claim.[21] However, as the court pointed out in *New Hampshire F.I. Co. v. Perla,*[22] a delay in adjudication of the claim against the vessel will not be tolerated while the cargo owners and the underwriters settle their liabilities.[23]

Parties to a marine venture may, by contract, waive their rights against other parties in the same venture and when they do so, they effectively

17. 383 F.Supp. 1217, 1975 AMC 408 (E.D.,La.).
18. 312 F.Supp. 1081, 1970 AMC 1004, [1970] 2 Lloyd's Rep. 285.
19. 279 F.2d 471, 1962 AMC 2660 (2d Cir.).
20. 173 F.Supp. 29, 1961 AMC 206 (S.D.N.Y.).
21. *St. Paul Fire & Marine Ins. Co. v. U.S. Lines,* 258 F.2d 374, 1958 AMC 2358 (2d Cir.); *Boston Ins. Co. v. Alferra Schiffahrtsges,* 1963 AMC 312 (Can.).
22. 84 F.Supp. 715, 1949 AMC 1324 (D.,Md.).
23. In *Monarch Industrial v. American Motorists,* 276 F.Supp. 972, 1967 AMC 2488 (S.D.N.Y.), the cargo underwriter protected its position by obtaining letters of extension from the carrier, continued to deny liability to its assured, and yet filed suit to litigate its claim against the carrier. The court held this could be done under Federal Rules of Civil Procedure, Rule 14.

cut off the subrogation rights of their underwriters.[24] In *Narco, supra*, the negligent charterers were included among the named insureds; in *Duchess, supra*, and *Northwestern, supra*, the owners agreed to insure and to relieve the charterers of any liability; in *Allied Chemical, supra*, the cargo underwriters waived subrogation against the carrier in a private contract of affreightment and included the interest of the carrier in the policy of cargo insurance.

In a number of recent cases, waivers of subrogation have proved effective and have been found not to be against public policy. In *Tenneco Oil Co. v. Tony*,[25] the court squarely held that a clause in a contract to carry cargo in towed vessels, whereby the cargo owner agreed to obtain insurance upon the cargo and waive subrogation rights against the carrier, was not invalid as against public policy. In *Hartford Fire v. Port Everglades*,[26] the general conditions in a marine hull policy on a barge contained a conditional waiver of subrogation against any tug towing the insured barge. In an action against the tug by the barge hull underwriters, the tug owner was held entitled to summary judgment under the waiver of subrogation as a matter of law. In *Fluor Western v. G. H. Offshore*,[27] the court held that a cargo owner's agreement in a towing contract to obtain a waiver of subrogation against the towing company was not the same as an exemption from liability for negligent towage and was not void as against public policy. In *Twenty Grand Offshore v. West India Carriers*[28] and *Slade v. Samson Towing*,[29] it was held that the *Bisso*[30] decision did not invalidate compulsory insurance clauses in which the barge owner was required to provide and pay for insurance to protect the tower, as an assured, with waiver of subrogation. In *Dillingham Tug & Barge Corp. v. Collier Carbon & Chemical*,[31] the Ninth Circuit followed *Twenty Grand Offshore* with approval.

The following are of collateral interest.

In *Travelers Ins. Co. v. Graye*,[32] it was held that an underwriter's attempted salvage of the sunken vessel after payment of a total loss collision claim did not estop it from claiming subrogation against the party re-

---

24. *Narco—Lolita*, 258 F.2d 718, 1958 AMC 2404 (5th Cir.); *Duchess*, 15 F.2d 198, 1926 AMC 1389 (E.D.N.Y.); *Northwestern F. & M. Co. v. Ley & Co.*, 1933 AMC 559 (St.,N.Y.); *Allied Chemical v. Gulf Atlantic*, 244 F.Supp. 2, 1965 AMC 776 (E.D.,Va.).
25. 324 F.Supp. 834, 1971 AMC 2336 (S.D.,Tex.).
26. 454 F.2d 276, 1972 AMC 316 (5th Cir.).
27. 447 F.2d 35, 1972 AMC 406 (5th Cir.).
28. 492 F.2d 679, 1974 AMC 2254 (5th Cir.).
29. 327 F.Supp. 555, 1971 AMC 2342 (E.D.,Tex.).
30. 349 U.S. 85, 1955 AMC 899 (1955). In *Bisso*, the Supreme Court invalidated attempts by towers to exculpate themselves from liability to their tows by straight contractual terms, holding such attempts invalid as being against public policy.
31. 707 F.2d 1086, 1984 AMC 1990 (9th Cir.), cert. den. 467 U.S. 520, 1984 AMC 2402 (1984).
32. 1971 AMC 409 (St.,Mass.).

sponsible for the collision, even in the absence of an express subrogation clause in the policy.

In *Lanasse v. Travelers Ins.*,[33] the shipowner's P & I policy named the time charterer as an additional assured with waiver of subrogation. A crane operator employed by the charterer was negligent and injured a seaman on board the insured vessel, whose claim was paid by the P & I underwriters. Underwriters then brought an action against the time charterer. It was held that the underwriters could recover, as the policy covered only liabilities of the assured "as owner" of the vessel, and neither the vessel nor the crew was at fault.

In *Cosid v. Rolwi*,[34] the plaintiff consignee sued the vessel and stevedore for cargo damage after having been partially reimbursed by its numerous cargo insurance underwriters. It was held that the insurance companies could be required to join as parties plaintiff, as they were the real parties in interest. To the same effect, see *Jefferson Chemical v. Grena*.[35] However, in *Prudential Lines v. General Tires*,[36] the court, stating that whether or not a partial subrogee is a necessary or indispensable party must be decided on a case-by-case basis, held that the P & I club which paid a cargo loss to the consignee need not be added as a party plaintiff since it would be estopped by *res judicata* principles from bringing a subsequent suit against the defendants who caused the loss.

In *Jones Tug & Barge v. Liberty Mutual*,[37] the court held that a P & I club which had paid claims against the insured vessel under "loan receipts" could not acquire subrogation rights against the proceeds of the vessel's sale. The mere tender of the vessel to underwriters did not, absent acceptance, constitute an abandonment which would sever the insurance relationship, and it was immaterial whether the club's claims were asserted against the sale proceeds rather than the vessel itself. On the facts, the court held that the payments made had none of the indicia of true loans.

In *Allied Chemical—Piermay*,[38] it was held that the subrogated cargo underwriter was entitled to the benefit of charter party arbitration provisions entered into by its assured.

In *Willamette-Western v. Columbia-Pacific*,[39] a provision in a barge owner's hull policy, waiving subrogation against "charterers," made the barge's demise charterer a donee beneficiary whose rights could not be taken away retroactively without its consent even if it was unaware of the policy provision. Consequently, in the barge owner's action against the de-

---

33. 450 F.2d 580, 1972 AMC 818 (5th Cir.).
34. 1972 AMC 2157 (7th Cir.).
35. 292 F.Supp. 500, 1968 AMC 1202 (S.D.,Tex.).
36. 78 F.R.D. 474, 1978 AMC 93 (S.D.N.Y.).
37. 1978 AMC 1183 (C.D.,Cal.).
38. 1978 AMC 773 (Arb.).
39. 466 F.2d 1390, 1972 AMC 2128 (9th Cir.).

mise charterer for damage to the vessel, it was held that the plaintiff barge owner was not entitled to recover in respect of moneys already paid to it by hull underwriters under loan receipts, since this would constitute "indirect subrogation" and permit underwriters to escape the effect of the waiver provision.

In *African Neptune (Claim of Denny)*,[40] a cargo underwriter had paid a claim for goods lost when the truck carrying the goods sank to the bottom of a river following a ship-bridge collision. The court allowed the underwriter to recover against the vessel even though the claim was nominally filed by the truck driver who had no real interest under the policy.

In *American Auto Ins. Co. v. Twenty Grand*,[41] it was held that subrogation includes both contractual as well as tortious rights, and a workmen's compensation underwriter was held entitled to bring a subrogation action against the owner of a crewboat whose negligence injured the insured charterer's employee. The crewboat owner's claim that the underwriter could not, because of lack of privity, avail itself of a hold harmless indemnity agreement in the charter was rejected where the insurance policy expressly provided for subrogation upon payment by the underwriter of the insured's claim.

In *Gibbs v. Dona Paz*,[42] it was held in a cargo damage action brought by a subrogated insurer that the defendant ocean carriers could bring a third-party action against the plaintiff's assured on the ground that it had acted negligently in its capacity as stevedore in discharging its own cargo. Considerations of judicial economy justified such a third-party action; otherwise, a successful defendant would have to bring a separate suit to recover its expenses incurred in defending the principal action.

In *Blasser v. Northern Pan-Am*,[43] it was held that although a cargo insurer generally has no right to sue the ocean carrier until it has become subrogated by payment of its assured's loss, such subrogation can occur where the assured has sued both the insurer and the carrier in the same action and both are found liable. The insurer was permitted to recover on its cross-claim against the carrier for cargo damage found to have been covered by its policy.

In *Mr. Galvanized v. Shin Ming*,[44] a cargo owner who had been reimbursed in full by his underwriter for cargo damage was held not to be the real party in interest in an action against the ocean carrier and a terminal operator. By contrast, in *Seguros v. Oliver Drescher*,[45] an assured cargo owner was held to be a proper party entitled to sue the carrier, even

40. 1976 AMC 1674 (S.D.,Ga.).
41. 1969 AMC 2360 (St.,La.).
42. 96 F.R.D. 597, 1984 AMC 516.
43. 628 F.2d 376, 1982 AMC 84 (5th Cir.).
44. 1982 AMC 1949 (S.D.N.Y.).
45. 761 F.2d 855, 1985 AMC 2168 (2d Cir.).

though the cargo underwriter's own recovery on a subrogated claim could not exceed the amount paid under its policy. This was so because if the insurer has paid only part of its assured's loss, the assured is entitled to recover the residue and, hence, is a proper plaintiff.[46]

It should also be noted that the settlement of an insured loss is a matter between the underwriter and the assured. A third party sued by the underwriter is therefore not entitled to assert as a defense that, as between the assured and the insurer, there was not a good claim for a total loss. Subrogation is essentially equivalent to the assignment of a cause of action.[47]

Right to Sue as Assignee

In *Mandu—Denderah*,[48] the court of appeals held that an American underwriter, having taken absolute assignments of paid cargo claims from foreign cargo underwriters, had standing to sue even though it was clear that the suit was filed to collect moneys due the assignors. This is in accord with the liberal practice in admiralty of permitting *bona fide* representatives to maintain suits for loss or damage on condition that the true party in interest appears before the conclusion of the matter. *Mandu* also stands for the further proposition that an assignee of a cause of action must state the names of his assignors but need not reveal what he paid for the assignments.

However, an assignment of insurance moneys by a mortgagor is ineffective as to the mortgagee unless the latter consents.[49] In *Meridian Trading v. National Automobile & Casualty*,[50] after the mortgagor's default the mortgagee voluntarily settled a claim against the mortgaged vessel when the P & I underwriters refused to take over the defense. Holding that the underwriters had never consented to the mortgagee's becoming a party to the insurance contract, that the action was not commenced within the period prescribed in the policy, and that the mortgagee had no rights to settle the claim without the underwriters' consent, the court dismissed the mortgagee's suit against the P & I underwriters.

In *Liman, Trustee v. United Kingdom*,[51] it was held that a trustee in bankruptcy could not seek the benefit of the bankrupt shipowner's P & I policy without assuming the obligations under the policy. Consequently, the P &

46. See, in this connection, *Mitsui & Co. v. American Export Lines*, 636 F.2d 708, 1981 AMC 331 (2d Cir.), and *Rohner, Gehrig & Co. v. Capital City Bank*, 655 F.2d 571 (5th Cir., 1981).
47. *King v. Victoria Ins. Co., Ltd*, (1896) A.C. 250, 12 T.L.R. 285, P.C.
48. 102 F.2d 459, 1939 AMC 287 (2d Cir.).
49. *National Motorship v. Home Indemnity*, 1938 AMC 737 (2d Cir.).
50. 1966 AMC 391 (St.N.Y.).
51. 1971 AMC 727 (S.D.N.Y.).

I underwriters were held entitled to set off against the trustee's claim, their claims for unpaid calls and premiums.

Under English law, Section 50, Marine Insurance Act, governs. It provides:

(1) A marine policy is assignable unless it contains terms expressly prohibiting assignment. It may be assigned either before or after loss.

(2) Where a marine policy has been assigned so as to pass the beneficial interest in such policy, the assignee of the policy is entitled to sue thereon in his own name; and the defendant is entitled to make any defense arising out of the contract which he would have been entitled to make if the action has been brought in the name of the person by or on behalf of whom the policy was effected.

(3) A marine policy may be assigned by endorsement thereon or in other customary manner.

Clause 14 of the Institute Time Clauses (freight) and Clause 5 of the new London Institute Time Clauses (hulls) contain identical restrictions with respect to assignment.

Under sub-section 2, if the defense of the underwriter would not have been good against the assignor, it will be of no avail against the assignee.[52] In *William v. Atlantic Assur. Co., Ltd.*,[53] it was held that as a partial assignment of the policy did not convey the full beneficial interest under the policy, the assignee could not sue on the policy without joining his assignors. Moreover, the policy was an unvalued one and the plaintiff did not prove the value of the goods which had been lost.[54]

An assured who no longer has an interest cannot assign the policy. In this connection, see Section 51, Marine Insurance Act, reading:

Where the assured has parted with or lost his interest in the subject matter insured, and has not, before or at the time of so doing, expressly or impliedly agreed to assign the policy, any subsequent assignment of the policy is inoperative:

Provided that nothing in this section affects the assignment of a policy after loss.

---

52. *Baker v. Adam*, (1910) 102 L.T. 248, [1908-10] All E.R. 632; *Pellas v. Neptune Marine Ins. Co*, (1879) 49 L.J.Q.B. 153, C.A.

53. [1932] All E.R. Rep. 32, 43 Ll.L.Rep. 177, C.A.

54. For further examples of instances in which the underwriters' defense prevailed, see *Bank of New South Wales v. South British Ins. Co., Ltd.*, (1920) 4 Ll.L.Rep. 266, 384, C.A. (assignee took from enemy aliens and policy was null and void by reason thereof); *Pickersgill & Sons v. London and Marine Prov. Ins. Co., Ltd.*, (1912) 3 K.B. 614, [1911-13] All E.R. Rep. 861 (non-disclosure of a material fact); *Graham Joint Stock Shipping Co., Ltd. v. Merchants' Marine Ins. Co., Ltd.*, [1924] A.C. 294, 17 Ll.L.Rep. 44, H.L. (mortgagees' interest under an equitable assignment derivative from the assured and the fraud of the assured precluded recovery).

See, in connection with the proviso, *Lloyd v. Fleming*,[55] where it was held that the loss having already occurred, there was no impediment to the assignment as it was liquidated.

As to the method of assignment, see *Baker v. Adam, supra*, holding that mere delivery of the policy is insufficient and *J. Aron & Co. v. Miall*,[56] (endorsement in blank held sufficient).

Loan Receipts in General

The loan receipt is a credit to the ingenuity of underwriters. It originally arose as a device to offset the "benefit of insurance" clause which the Supreme Court held valid in *Phoenix Ins. Co. v. Erie & Western Transp. Co.*[57] In turn, the "benefit of insurance" clause came into being to counteract the doctrine of subrogation, which permitted the cargo underwriter to sue the carrier, in the name of the shipper, to recoup its insurance payment on the cargo. To defeat the cargo underwriters' subrogation rights, the carriers inserted in their bills of lading a clause allowing the carrier to have the "benefit of the shipper's insurance."

Not to be outdone, the underwriters began paying their assureds' cargo losses by merely "lending" them the amount of the loss, with the "loan" to be repaid only if the assured was able to collect from the carrier. Though admittedly a subterfuge, it clearly was no more so than the "benefit of insurance" clause and, as might be expected, the Supreme Court upheld the validity of such receipts in *Luckenbach v. W. J. McCahan Sugar Co.*[58] Although the payment in a loan receipt is termed a loan, other provisions in the receipt require the assured to prosecute, in his own name but at the expense of the underwriter, a suit against any third party causing the loss. The proceeds of the recovery belong to the underwriter by virtue of the repayment.[59]

Although the doctrine of subrogation requires that the subrogee pay his principal's loss, and although a loan receipt by its terms refers to the

55. (1872) L.R. 7 Q.B. 299.
56. (1928) L.J.K.B. 204, 31 Ll.L.Rep. 242, C.A.
57. 117 U.S. 312.
58. 248 U.S. 139 (1918). The U.S. Carriage of Goods by Sea Act now expressly forbids "benefit of insurance" clauses.
59. See, in this connection, *City General v. St. Paul F. & M. Ins. Co.*, 1963 AMC 2362 (S.D.N.Y.) For other cases involving loan receipts, see *Turret Crown*, 297 F.2d. 766, 1924 AMC 253 (2d Cir.); *Merrimack v. Lowell*, 1944 AMC 511 (St., N.Y.); *Morton Coal Co. v. Garcia*, 1945 AMC 594 (St.,N.Y.); *Sosnow v. Storatti Co.*, 1945 AMC 645 (St., N.Y.); *Textron v. Lowell Trucking Co.*, 1947 AMC 1276 (S.D.N.Y.); *Hercules*, 322 F.2d 846, 1964 AMC 2037 (3rd Cir.); *Bonitas*, 197 F.Supp. 699, 1962 AMC 977 (E.D.,Va.); *Mitchell v. Luckenbach S.S. Co.*, 1929 AMC 39 (St., N.Y.).

payment as a loan, the courts commendably have treated loan receipt payments as the equivalent of subrogation.[60]

However, loan receipts may not always accomplish that which the underwriters hope to accomplish.[61] But, where effective, the underwriter may succeed in recouping his payment. Thus, in *Federation Ins. v. Coret Accessories*,[62] the underwriter had paid a claim under a loan receipt for goods allegedly lost during transit but which were subsequently found and delivered by the ocean carrier. It was held that the underwriter could recover the payment from the assured.

Effecting a Waiver of Subrogation by Naming a Party as an "Additional Assured"

It is a very common practice for parties to a marine venture to seek to have themselves named as additional assureds in order to insulate themselves against liability, the theory being that if they are named as additional assureds on the applicable policies of insurance, the underwriters on those policies cannot file suit against their own assureds.

Being named as an additional assured may not, in all instances, achieve the desired result of waiving subrogation. This is illustrated in *Sample No. 1*.[63] There, tug and barge owners each had their hull policies endorsed so that the other was named as an additional assured, but the tug owner was not named as an additional assured on the cargo policy. The tug negligently stranded the barge, resulting in damage to the cargo. Cargo underwriters sued. Since the negligence was that of the tug, the tug's underwriters were compelled to respond in damages. Obviously, had the tug owner secured a waiver of subrogation from the cargo underwriters, or had been named as an additional assured on the cargo policy, he would have been protected.

Sucre—Tamare[64] illustrates success in cutting off subrogation rights by being named as an additional assured. In that case, the *Sucre* was time chartered and the vessel's hull and P & I policies endorsed to include the

---

60. *Ariosa and D-22*, 144 F.2d 262, 1944 AMC 1035 (2d Cir.); *Auto Ins. Co. v. Hamburg-Amerika*, 1937 AMC 1057 (St.,N.Y.); *Irving-Seatrain Havana*, 103 F.2d 722, 1939 AMC 1043 (2d Cir.); *City General v. St. Paul*, 1963 AMC 2362 (S.D.N.Y.); *Manila Motors Co. v. Ivaran*, 46 F.Supp. 394, 1942 AMC 947 (S.D.N.Y.).

61. See, for example, *Willamette-Western v. Columbia-Pacific, supra*, and *Jones Tug & Barge v. Liberty Mutual, supra*. See, also, *American Dredging v. Federal Insurance*, 309 F.Supp. 425, 1970 AMC 1163 (S.D.N.Y), where two sets of marine underwriters insured the same risk under separate policies. Although recognizing that the set which paid the assured's claim had a right of contribution from the other, the court held that the real party in interest rule prevented the paying set from suing in the name of the assured.

62. 1968 AMC 1796 (Can.).

63. 262 F.2d 565, 1959 AMC 397 (5th Cir.).

64. 1960 AMC 493 (Arb.).

time charterer's interests. The vessel was damaged in a collision with the *Tamare*, the latter being solely at fault. The *Sucre's* underwriters having paid the repairs, claims were made for the repairs and detention loss against the *Tamare* which, it so happened, was bareboat chartered to the same company which had time chartered the *Sucre*. There being an identity of interest, the arbitrator held that the underwriters on the *Sucre* had waived their subrogation rights by extending their policies to cover the interests of the time charterer. See, also, *Allied Chemical & Dye Corp. v. Tug Christine Moran*,[65] where the court held that while ordinarily a time charterer of a barge is secondarily liable to the barge owner for damage caused by the negligence of a tug engaged by the time charterer, where the barge owner agreed to include the time charterer as an additional assured under its hull policies, the time charterer was relieved of this liability to the extent that the hull underwriters reimbursed the owner of the barge.[66]

Clearly, it is much the better practice in adding parties as additional assureds for the purpose of waiving subrogation to request expressly that the underwriters waive subrogation *per se*. Even the addition of an involved party as an additional assured with express waiver of subrogation can leave a tower in an awkward situation with respect to the actual policy terms and conditions; i.e., large deductibles, exclusionary clauses of which the tower is unaware, and simple failure of the policies to cover all the expectable liabilities which the venture might encounter.[67]

Double Insurance[68]

There appears to be no legal impediment to an assured procuring two policies on the same risk. However, as a practical matter, it does little good as the assured can only make one recovery. Section 80, Marine Insurance Act, 1906, spells this out with particular clarity, and the court decisions are to the same effect. Section 80 reads:

---

65. 303 F.2d 197, 1962 AMC 1198 (2d Cir.).

66. For a more definitive discussion of the problems which can develop and the gaps in coverage which may occur by reliance upon being named as an "additional assured" with the expectation that in so doing, the underwriters will have waived subrogation, see the subheading "Towers' Liability," *supra*, Chapter XXI. See, also, subheading entitled "Disclosures and Representations," Chapter X, with respect to the duty to disclose to underwriters *every material circumstance which is known to the assured with respect to the risk undertaken*. In the author's opinion, if adding an additional assured is intended for the purpose of waiving subrogation and the underwriter is unaware that this is the real purpose, the underwriter may elect to declare the policy void.

67. See, for example, *Driftwood Land and Timber Ltd. v. U. S. Fire Ins. Co.*, 1955 AMC 884 (Can.), and *Sample No. 1, supra*.

68. Included in this subheading will also be found cases relating to "other insurance"; e.g., where liability, in whole or in part, is imposed upon two sets of underwriters under different policies for the same loss.

(1) Where the assured is over-insured by double insurance, each insurer is bound, as between himself and the other insurers, to contribute rateably to the loss in proportion to the amount for which he is liable under his contract.

(2) If any insurer pays more than his proportion of the loss, he is entitled to maintain an action for contribution against the other insurers, and is entitled to the like remedies as a surety who has paid more than his proportion of debt.

Double insurance is defined in the Act in Section 32, which also specifies the duties and obligations of the assured in such instances. It reads:

(1) Where two or more policies are effected by or on behalf of the assured on the same adventure and interest or any part thereof, and the sums insured exceed the indemnity allowed by this Act, the assured is said to be over-insured by double insurance.

(2) Where the assured is over-insured by double insurance:

(a) The assured, unless the policy otherwise provides, may claim payment from the insurers in such order as he may think fit, provided that he is not entitled to receive any sum in excess of the indemnity allowed by this Act;

(b) Where the policy under which the assured claims is a valued policy, the assured must give credit as against the valuation, for any sum received by him under any other policy without regard to the actual value of the subject-matter insured;

(c) Where the policy under which the assured claims is an unvalued policy he must give credit, as against the full insurable value, for any sum received by him under any other policy;

(d) Where the assured receives any sum in excess of the indemnity allowed by this Act, he is deemed to hold such sum in trust for the insurers, according to their right of contribution among themselves.

Sections 32 and 80 should also be read *in pari materia* with Section 84, the relevant portion of which reads:

(1) Where the consideration for the payment of the premium totally fails, and there has been no fraud or illegality on the part of the assured or his agents, the premium is thereupon returnable to the assured.

. . . . . .

(3) (e) Where the assured has over-insured under an unvalued policy, a proportionate part of the premium is returnable;

(f) Subject to the foregoing provisions, where the assured has over-insured by double insurance, a proportionate part of the several premiums is returnable;

Provided, that, if the policies are effected at different times, and any earlier policy has at any time borne the entire risk, or if a claim has been paid on the policy in respect of the full sum insured thereby, no premium is returnable in respect of that policy, and when the double insurance is effected knowingly by the assured no premium is returnable.

The question of "double insurance" arises most frequently where the assured is a party to a multi-vessel venture and is named as an additional assured on one or more policies. This situation has been more properly termed "other insurance." The question invariably arises: Which underwriter pays first and in what amounts?

A typical situation was presented in *Davis Yarn Co. v. Brooklyn Yarn Dye Co.*[69] Davis shipped yarn to Brooklyn for processing. Brooklyn insured with Commercial against risk of damage to yarn entrusted to it for processing with a clause that the insurance would be considered excess whenever Brooklyn's customers had other insurance covering the yarn. Davis also had a floater policy with Sentinel covering the yarn while in transit and at processing plants; the floater policy also had a similar "other insurance" provision. A loss occurred and both underwriters defended upon the ground that there was "other insurance." The court rejected the contention that the assureds could not recover at all because there was "other insurance" and held that Commercial's policy was more specific in coverage and therefore had a primary liability to which the floater policy was supplementary and secondary.

In *Zidell v. Travelers Indemnity*,[70] a Lloyd's excess stevedore liability policy provided that it should not apply if there was "other valid and collectible insurance." The court held that Lloyd's underwriters need not contribute *pro rata* with the primary insurer.

In *Glenorchy*,[71] a cargo of wheat was insured under the seller's open policy for its c.i.f. value plus $3\frac{1}{2}$ cents charge. The same cargo of wheat was insured under the buyer's open policy for the "increased value" of market over c.i.f. price. The carrying steamer was sunk in a collision with another vessel and the cargo lost. Cargo, in the limitation proceedings which followed, recovered for the market value of the wheat at the time and place of shipment. Underwriters on the seller's open policy had paid the assured the c.i.f. value while underwriters on the buyer's open policy had also paid the assured the difference between the c.i.f. value and the

69. 1943 AMC 116 (St.,N.Y.).
70. 264 F.Supp. 496, 1967 AMC 1139 (D.,Ore.).
71. 283 U.S. 284, 1931 AMC 839 (1931).

highest market value. Both underwriters sued to establish subrogation rights against the sums recovered by the cargo owner in the limitation proceedings. The Supreme Court denied subrogation rights to the underwriter of "increased value" and awarded the underwriter of c.i.f. value full reimbursement.

Irving—Seatrain Havana[72] presented a veritable nightmare of unravelling, overlapping coverages. In that case the Molasses Company owned cargo, insured by Atlantic, transported under a Seatrain bill of lading; Manhattan contracted to lighter the cargo for Seatrain and insured its liability with Aetna. Manhattan hired the lighter *Irving* from Connors; the lighter capsized and the cargo was lost. The cargo was actually worth $29,000 but under the bill of lading only $17,000 could be recovered. Atlantic paid Molasses Company $17,000. Aetna then paid Molasses Company the balance of the loss and took a loan receipt from Molasses Company under which repayment was to be made only out of any net recovery by Molasses from Connors and/or the *Irving* or anyone else, as directed by Manhattan. Molasses thereupon sued Seatrain, which impleaded Manhattan, who in turn impleaded Connors and the *Irving*. Connors and the *Irving* were held primarily liable, with secondary liability upon Manhattan and then upon Seatrain. The court further held that nothing in Aetna's policy covering Manhattan, nor the facts as to payments, loan receipts, and subrogation, was material with respect to the liability of Connors and the *Irving*, and that the Aetna policy did not cover the liability of the owner of a vessel chartered to Manhattan; i.e., the *Irving*.

In *Sample No. 1*,[73] an unmanned oil barge, without motive power, was damaged while in the complete control of its tug and quantities of its oil cargo lost. The question before the appeals court was whether the tug's Tug Syndicate Form Hull policy paid or the barge's P & I policy, which latter policy expressly provided against liability where the assured had other coverage. The court held that the hull policy was primary and had to respond for the loss. (The trial court was obviously confused by *in personam* considerations since the barge was chartered by the owner of the tug and the owner-charterer was named as an additional assured on the barge's hull and P & I policies.)

In *New York Trap Rock Co.*,[74] a barge in a large tow listed, dumped its cargo, and then righted itself, suffering damage. Part of its cargo struck an adjacent barge, damaging it so that it capsized, which then caused damage to other adjacent barges. In analyzing the hull cover, P & I cover,

72. 103 F.2d 772, 1939 AMC 1043 (2d Cir.).
73. 262 F.2d 565, 1959 AMC 397 (5th Cir.).
74. 1956 AMC 469 (Arb.).

and excess cover, the arbitrator held that the hull cover was liable for the direct hull loss to the first barge; the hull cover and P & I cover were liable for the loss to the adjacent barges, the hull Running Down Clause up to its limit (minus deductible) and the P & I cover for the balance (minus its deductible); and the excess cover was not required to respond as the losses were within the limits of the primary coverages.

True "double insurance" was involved in *Marine Transit Corporation v. Northwestern Fire and Marine Ins. Co.*[75] There, the carrier had both a towers' liability clause in its hull policy as well as a separate policy covering its legal liability to cargo on the tow. The latter policy provided that if the interest insured were covered by other insurance, the loss would be collected from the several policies in the order of the date of their attachment. It also provided that if other insurance were procured, the legal liability policy would be void except as such other insurance might be deficient toward fully covering the loss. The court held that the towers' liability policy must respond up to its limit, and the legal liability policy thereafter for any liability beyond that limit.[76]

---

75. 67 F.2d 544, 1933 AMC 1631 (2d Cir.).

76. Other American cases are: *Fuller v. Detroit Fire & Marine Ins. Co,* 36 F. 469 (7th Cir., 1888) (where there is a claim against several underwriters for the same loss, equity may apportion the loss among them and require a proportionate payment from each); *Howard Fire Ins. Co. v. Norwich & N.Y. Transp. Co,* 79 U.S. 194 (1870) (where two causes of loss concur, one at risk of the assured, and the other at risk of the insurer, or one insured against by one insurer and the other by another, if the damage by the perils respectively can be discriminated, each party must bear his proportion); *Leary v. Murray,* 178 F. 209 (3d Cir., 1910); *Hagan v. Delaware Ins. Co,* F. Cas. No. 6,582 (3d Cir., 1806); *Voison v. Ocean Protein,* 321 F.Supp. 173, 1971 AMC 464 (E.D., La.) (workmens' compensation underwriter and P & I underwriter held to be co-insurers, and disregarding "other insurance" clauses in both policies, the court apportioned the assured's liability equally between the insurers); *Viger v. Geophysical Services,* 338 F.Supp. 808, 1972 AMC 2113 (W.D.,La.) (time charterer's liability policy contained an "other insurance" clause providing for pro rata payment by insurers if other insurance existed; time charterer was also an additional assured under the vessel owner's P & I policy, which contained an escape clause disclaiming any participation if other insurance existed; held, clauses in policies must be given effect if possible, and the escape clause in the P & I policy meant that the time charterer's liability insurer was responsible for entire loss); *Morslich's Case,* 1972 AMC 2655 (S.D.N.Y.) (employer's liability policy held to prevail over P & I policy and to respond for entire loss); *BW 1933 Fire,* 1968 AMC 2738 (Arb.) (where two policies existed, each containing an "other insurance" clause, the "excess type" of clause will be given effect in preference to the "no liability" type, especially where this appears to be in accord with the assured's intentions); *Lytle v. Freedom Int'l Carrier,* 519 F.2d 129, 1975 AMC 2670 (6th Cir.) (stevedore's excess employer's liability policy contained no specific coverage but rather was dovetailed into primary policy which covered stevedore's liability to indemnify shipowner under the *Ryan* doctrine; an endorsement in the excess policy excluding liability arising under "general maritime law" and "admiralty law" was not sufficiently explicit to excuse excess insurer from protecting its assured from claim over by shipowner in a longshoreman's case); *Lodrigue v. Montegut,* 1978 AMC 2272 (E.D., La.) (escape clause in P & I policy, negating contribution "on the basis of double insurance or otherwise," is valid; hence, full liability must be borne by assured's comprehensive general liability underwriter, whose policy merely provided that it would be "excess above insured's other available and collectible insurance").

In *Berkeley v. Fireman's Fund*,[77] the owner, demise charterer, and sub-bareboat charterer were named assureds in a "layered employer's liability policy." The demise charterer also had a separate employer's liability policy and a separate umbrella policy. The vessel broke apart at sea, causing deaths and injuries to the crew, and all parties filed limitation of liability actions. The loss was caused by the negligence of the sub-bareboat charterer, who was found to be the employer of the crew. The insured on the layered employer's liability policy settled the crew claims and sought contribution against the other two insurers. Held: The coverage priorities should be determined in light of the total policy insuring intent, and the insurer on the layered employer's liability policy was properly liable for the entire loss because (1) the actual employer (sub-bareboat charterer) was a named assured; (2) the actual employer was not a named assured in the other policies; and (3) the umbrella policy was clearly intended to be excess. The court stated in part that it was a disfavored approach to resolve disputes among insurance carriers on the basis of dogmatic reliance on "other insurance" clauses of respective policies without regard to the intent of the parties as manifested in the overall pattern of insurance coverage.[78]

In *Gen. Ins. Co. v. Rocky Mt. F. & C. Co.*,[79] there were two policies covering the same risk. Both policies contained "other insurance" clauses, one being an "escape-excess" clause and the other a "pro rata" clause. The court held the clauses were not in conflict and that the "escape-excess" policy was not liable to pay a pro rata share of the loss.

In *Offshore Logistics v. Mutual Marine*,[80] the P & I policy contained two inconsistent clauses relating to "other insurance": an "excess clause" providing that the insurer should be liable only for an additional amount, and an "escape clause" negating any contribution from the insurer. Held: Construing the policy most favorably to the assured, only the "excess clause" would be given effect.

In *Ferromontan v. Georgetown Steel*,[81] the primary liability underwriter was not required to undertake the assured barge carrier's defense of a cargo action since the policy's valid "escape clause" was triggered by the existence of other insurance in the assured's favor.

77. 1976 AMC 856 (W.D., Wash.).
78. See, generally, *Murray v. Ins. Co. of Pa.*, F.Cas. No. 9,961 (3d Cir., 1808); *Potter v. Marine Ins. Co.*, F.Cas. No. 11,332 (1st Cir., 1822); *McAllister v. Hoadley*, 76 F. 1000 (S.D.N.Y., 1896); *International Nav. Co. v. British & Foreign Marine Ins. Co.*, 108 F. 987 (2d Cir., 1900); *Southern Cotton Oil Co. v. Merchants' & Miners' Transp. Co.*, 179 F. 133 (S.D.N.Y., 1910); *Export S.S. Corp. v. American Ins. Co.*, 108 F.2d 1013 (2d Cir., 1939); *Gulf Oil v. Margaret*, 441 F.Supp. 1, 1978 AMC 868 (E.D., La.), *aff'd per curiam*, 565 F.2d 958 (5th Cir.).
79. 1967 AMC 1148 (St.,Wash.).
80. 462 F.Supp. 485, 1981 AMC 1154 (E.D., La.), *aff'd* without opinion, 640 F.2d 382, 1982 AMC 1512 (5th Cir.).
81. 535 F.Supp. 1198, 1983 AMC 1849 (D.,S.C.).

In *Port of Portland v. Water Quality Ins. Synd., et al,*[82] the plaintiff port
had two policies, each of which presumptively covered the port's removal
costs for oil pollution. One policy was specifically directed to oil pollution
liabilities; the other policy was a comprehensive general liability policy
with the "watercraft exclusion" deleted. Both underwriters were held liable in proportion to the monetary limits of the respective policies.

The modern tendency in the United States clearly tends toward pro-
rating double coverage on the basis of the monetary limits of the respective policies.

Surprisingly, there are not many English and Commonwealth cases on
the topic. Section 80(2) merely expresses the law as it existed before the
enactment of the Marine Insurance Act, 1906, and where one insurer has
paid more than his proportion of a loss, he is entitled to maintain an action for contribution against the other insurers.[83]

See *Bank of British North America v. Western Assur. Co.,*[84] where the same
goods were insured under two different policies, the first policy being
taken out by the consignor and the second by the consignees. The extent
of coverage differed slightly in each policy. The court held that there was
a double insurance, the variations in the policies as to the extent of
coverage not varying the risk. In *Parsons v. Marine Ins. Co.,*[85] there was an
action on a policy for £500 on goods valued at £2,000. Upon a partial loss,
the defense was set up that under a policy of prior insurance for £1,500,
the whole loss was covered. Held: The company was liable on the second
policy for any deficiency not covered by the prior insurance.

A continuation of the practice in the maritime industry of insisting on
being named as additional assureds on the hull and liability policies of
vessels is certain to produce more cases in which the courts must decide
which policies are primary and which are secondary. Many of these situations never reach court but are amicably adjusted among the affected
underwriters.

82. 549 F.Supp. 233, 1984 AMC 2012, 2019 (D., Ore.).
83. See *Newby v. Reed,* (1763) 96 E.R. 237; *Irving v. Richardson,* (1831) 109 E.R. 1115;
Morgan v. Price, (1849) 4 Exch. 615; *Bousfield v. Barnes,* (1815) 4 Camp. 228, N.P.; *North British
& Mercantile Ins. Co. v. London, Liverpool & Globe Ins. Co.,* (1877) 5 Ch.D. 569, C.A. (the condition as to double insurance applies only to cases where the same property is the subject
matter of the insurance and where the interests are the same, and no right of contribution
exists between underwriters where different persons insure in respect of different rights);
Union Marine Ins. Co., Ltd. v. Martin, (1866) 35 L.J.C.P. 181; *Bruce v. Jones,* (1863) 158 E.R.
1094 (ship insured under several valued policies in some of which the vessel was valued at a
higher amount than in the policy in question; assured can recover, under the policy in question, only the difference between the sum already recovered and the amount at which the
vessel was valued in the present policy).
84. (1884) 7 O.R. 166 (Can.).
85. (1879) 6 Nfld. L.R. 193 (Can.).

CHAPTER XXIV

DIRECT ACTION STATUTES

Introduction

Because direct action statutes are becoming more common, and in at least one state (Florida), the courts have judicially created rights by third party claimants against underwriters, it is important to give those statutes and rights special mention.

Historically, the relationship between the assured and assurer under a liability policy has always been one of indemnification. Usually, the insurance contract requires the insurer to reimburse the insured after, but only after, the insured has paid the successful claimant.[1] If, for any reason, the claimant could not recover against the insured, he had no better rights against the insurer; e.g., if the insured became insolvent, the claimant could not avail himself of the insured's policy proceeds.

The general rule under the common law was that in the absence of a contractual provision authorizing a direct action by a claimant against a liability insurer, the claimant had no right of action against the insurer.[2] This rule was based on lack of privity between the claimant and the underwriter of the defendant assured. As a consequence, even though the injured party secured a judgment against an assured, if the assured were insolvent or unable to pay the judgment, the claimant could not maintain an action directly against the assured's underwriter.[3]

The inherent injustice is manifest because the fund created by the payment of insurance premiums was not available even though the precise situation it was designed to avoid had occurred—the victim of the negligence of the assured went uncompensated.

One means of avoiding the insurer's insulation from liability unless the insured had paid the claim was to declare such clauses invalid. This was the approach taken in Massachusetts in *Saunders v. Austin W. Fishing Corp.*[4] Another was to forbid the issuance of a policy within the state with-

---

1. The customary provision in a standard P & I policy reads with respect to the underwriters' commitment to reimburse: " . . . all such loss and/or damage and/or expense as the Assured shall as owners of the vessel . . . have become liable to pay and *shall pay* on account of the liabilities, risks, etc.. . . . "
2. See, for example, *Olokele Sugar Co. v. McCabe, Hamilton & Renny Co.*, 53 Haw. 69, 487 P.2d 769 (St.,Haw., 1971); *Severson v. Estate of Severson*, 627 P.2d 649 (St.,Alaska, 1981).
3. See, for example, *Cucurillo v. American S.S. Mutual P & I Ass'n*, 1969 AMC 2334 (St., N.Y., 1969); 25 Halsbury's Laws of England Sec. 704 (4th ed., 1978).
4. 224 N.E.2d 215, 1967 AMC 984 (St.,Mass.).

out an express provision therein to the effect that a claimant would have a right of action against the insurer in the event of the insured's insolvency. These approaches, however, still leave the claimant, faced with two lawsuits in many instances, the first against the assured to determine fault, and the second against the insurer.

Logically, one lawsuit could be eliminated by permitting a direct action against the insurer. A few states have passed such direct action legislation, albeit with some qualifications.[5] The Louisiana direct action statute is unquestionably the broadest, followed by its imitator, Puerto Rico.

Direct Action in Louisiana

The Louisiana statute reads in relevant part:[6]

> The injured person or his or her survivors or heirs . . . shall have a right of direct action against the insurer within the terms and limits of the policy . . . and such action may be brought against the insurer alone or against both the insured and insurer jointly and in solido. . . . This right of direct action shall exist whether the policy of insurance sued upon was written or delivered in the state of Louisiana or not and whether or not such policy contains a provision forbidding such direct action, provided the accident or injury occurred within the state of Louisiana. . . . It is the intent of this Section that any action brought hereunder shall be subject to all of the lawful conditions of the policy or contract and the defenses which could be urged by the insurer to a direct action brought by the insured, provided the terms and conditions of such policy or contracts are not in violation of the laws of this state.
>
> It is also the intent of this Section that all liability policies within their terms and limits are executed for benefit of all injured . . . to whom the insured is liable; and that it is the purpose of all liability policies to give protection and coverage to all insureds, whether they are named insureds or additional insureds under the omnibus clause, for any legal liability said insured may have as or for a tort-feasor within the terms and limits of said policy.

The Louisiana statute has received an exceedingly liberal and expansive interpretation. Under the statute, as will be noted, the policy need

---

5. See, for example, Rhode Island Gen. Laws 27-7-2 (on locally written policies if process is returned *non est inventus*); Arkansas Gen. Stat. Ann. 66-3240 (direct action permitted against insurers of immune governmental agencies and charitable organizations); Wisconsin Stat. Ann. 260.11 (direct action permitted with respect to automobile accident reparations). Florida occupied, until recently, a unique position in allowing such suits under a judicial interpretation of a procedural rule (30 Fla. R. Civ. Proc. 1.210). See discussion, *infra.*

6. La. R.S. 22.655 (1967).

not be written or delivered in the state. Thus, foreign insurance companies may be subjected to suit in Louisiana even though not qualified to do business in Louisiana and having no officers or agents within the state, provided that the accident happens in the state of Louisiana or that the policy is written or delivered in that state.[7]

It is not too surprising that little time elapsed before the Louisiana direct action statute ran headlong into the Federal Limitation of Liability Act.[8] This resulted in *Maryland Casualty Co. v. Cushing*,[9] which appears to be the only case in the history of the United States Supreme Court which was decided by the opinion of one justice.

In that case, a towboat under charter collided with a bridge pier and capsized. As a result, five seamen drowned. The charterer and owner filed consolidated petitions for limitation, in the course of which the district court issued an injunction prohibiting suits against the parties seeking limitation other than in the limitation proceeding itself. Subsequently, under the Louisiana direct action statute, personal representatives of the deceased seamen brought a direct suit against the liability underwriters in the same district court, based upon diversity and the Jones Act. One policy was a P & I policy in the amount of $170,000; the other was an employer's liability policy issued to the charterer in the sum of $10,000. The damages sought totaled $600,000.[10]

On reaching the Supreme Court, four justices felt that the direct action should be permitted; the other four felt otherwise. The latter supported their positions by pointing out that if the direct action were permitted to proceed, the $180,000 could be wholly exhausted, leaving the limitation petitioners subject to direct liability stripped of their insurance protection.[11]

---

7. *Dorr v. Marine Office of America*, 1977 AMC 653 (E.D.,La.); *Kirchman v. Mikula*, 443 F.2d 816 (5th Cir., 1971); *Webb v. Zurich Ins. Co.*, 251 La. 558, 205 So.2d 398 (1967); *Sacher v. Columbia Steamship Co.*, 493 F.2d 1109, 1974 AMC 2157 (5th Cir.). Stated in the obverse, the direct action statute does not apply with reference to an accident which does not take place in the state *and* where the policy was neither written nor delivered in the state. See, also, *McKeithen v. Frosta*, 435 F.Supp. 572, 1978 AMC 51 (E.D.,La.), where a Norwegian P & I club was held to be subject to personal jurisdiction in Louisiana because it insured 44 vessels entering state waters within a year, even though it maintained no offices, solicited no business, and delivered no policies in Louisiana. Thus, process in a Louisiana direct action suit could be validly served on the Louisiana secretary of state in a federal diversity action arising out of a collision on state waters. *McKeithen* involves the harmonious construction of LSA-R.S. 22:1249, 22:1253, and 22.655. Had not the court held that Sec. 22:1249 and 22:1253 applied (relating to transacting of business in the state by foreign or alien insurers), then Sec. 22:655 (the direct action statute) could not have been applied.
8. See the discussion, *supra*, Chapter XXI, on the Limitation of Liability Act.
9. 347 U.S. 409, 1954 AMC 837 (1954).
10. A stipulation for value filed in the limitation proceeding set the value of the tug at $25,000.
11. Hull insurance, of course, cannot be reached by claimants in a limitation proceeding under U. S. law. *City of Norwich*, 118 U.S. 468 (1886).

Justice Clark took a totally different view. He could see no logic in invalidating Louisiana's direct action statute by dismissing the actions. He felt that the district court could first conclude the limitation proceeding. If in that proceeding the limitation petitioners were held entitled to limit, their maximum liability would not exceed the value of the tug. At that point, the liability underwriters could discharge their obligations to their insureds by paying that amount into the limitation fund. Thereafter, the direct actions could continue against the insurance companies.

The result was both practical and in accordance with equitable principles as it protected both limitation petitioners and the damage claimants, while at the same time maintaining the integrity of the Limitation of Liability Act and the Louisiana direct action statute.

Maryland Casualty left unanswered a number of questions, but over the years, these have generally been resolved. Thus, in *In Re Independence Towing*,[12] the insurer intervened to enjoin civil actions brought against it. The court refused to issue an injunction on procedural grounds and held that an insurer is not entitled to claim the benefit of the limitation act because (1) limitation is an *in personam* proceeding based on defenses personal in nature and (2) the intent of the limitation statute was to reduce liabilities peculiar to vessel owners, not insurers.

In *Olympia Towing v. Nebel Towing*,[13] the court held *inter alia*, that the Louisiana direct action statute becomes part of every insurance policy, including P & I policies, having effect in Louisiana; that limitation of liability under the federal statutes is a personal defense available only to the shipowner and not to an insurer under the Louisiana direct action statute; that the direct action statute voided any policy clause requiring the injured person to obtain a judgment against the insured as a prerequisite to enforcing the contractual obligation of the insurer; and that the petitioners could proceed directly against the P & I insurer to satisfy that portion of their court award not satisfied due to the shipowner's limitation of liability defenses.

However, in *Crown Zellerbach Corp. v. Ingram and London Steamship Owners' Mutual Insurance Ass'n, Ltd.*,[14] the Fifth Circuit overruled *Olympic*

---

12. 242 F.Supp. 950 (E.D.,La., 1965). See, also, *Torres VDA v. Interstate Fire & Casualty Co.*, 275 F.Supp. 784 (DPR, 1967).

13. 419 F.2d 230, 1969 AMC 1571 (5th Cir.), [1970] 1 Lloyd's Rep. 430. To the same effect that a marine P & I policy is within the scope of the Louisiana direct action statute, see *American Sugar v. Vainqueur*, 1970 AMC 405 (E.D.,La.). With respect to underwriters being unable to assert defenses personal to the shipowner such as a statute of limitation or sovereign or interspousal immunity, see *Vasquez v. Litton Industries*, 1975 AMC 856 (DPR). With respect to abrogation of the defense that a P & I policy is an indemnity policy and the insurer need only pay if the assured has paid, see *Gonzalez v. Caribbean Carriers, Ltd.*, 379 F.Supp. 634 (DPR, 1974).

14. 745 F.2d 715, 1985 AMC 305 (5th Cir., 1984), modified *en banc*, 783 F.2d 1296, 1986 AMC 1471 (5th Cir., 1986).

Towing in part. In *Crown Zellerbach,* the assured's tug flotilla collided with the plaintiff's water intake structure on the Mississippi River causing damage in excess of $3.9 million. The assured was found entitled to limit its liability to $2,134,918.88. The assured's primary P & I policy had a limit of $1 million; there was excess P & I coverage placed with the defendant London Steamship Owners' Mutual club. Following judgment, the assured and its two P & I underwriters made payments up to the limits of the assured's limited liability, i.e., $2,134,918.88. The excess P & I underwriter appealed. At first instance, the Fifth Circuit affirmed, holding, *inter alia,* that the excess underwriter had to respond for any excess over the limited amount, basing its decision on *Olympia Towing.* However, on rehearing *en banc,* the full court reversed and held that the excess P & I club was not liable for sums in excess of the tug's liability limit. The court pointed out that *Olympic Towing* had dealt solely with the contention that the P & I underwriters were entitled to the shipowner's *statutory* right to limit liability. In the present case, the claim was quite different and was premised on the terms of the club's rules which expressly limited the maximum dollar amount to the dollar amount for which the shipowner/assured would be liable upon successfully maintaining the right to limit its liability. The Louisiana direct action statute provided that any action brought under it would be subject . . . "to the defenses which could be urged by the insurer in a direct action brought by the insured." The excess P & I club's rule provided in essence that in no event would the club be liable to any greater extent than if the assured were the owner or bareboat charterer of the entered vessel and were entitled to all the rights of limitation to which a shipowner is entitled.

Direct Actions in Puerto Rico

At this time, apparently Puerto Rico is the only other jurisdiction in the United States which has adopted a direct action statute comparable to that of Louisiana. The statute provides in essence that an insurer insuring against loss through liability for the bodily injury or death of a third person becomes absolutely liable whenever a loss covered by the policy occurs. Prior payment by the assured is not a prerequisite.[15] Thus, the indemnity aspect of a P & I policy is abrogated.

The Puerto Rico statute also provides that any individual sustaining losses has, at his option, a direct action against the insurer under the terms of the policy.[16] The statute was amended in 1958 to bring it into

15. P.R. Laws Ann., Tit. 26, Sec. 2001 (1977).
16. P.R. Laws Ann., Tit. 26, Sec. 2003(1) (1977).

conformity with that of Louisiana. Thus, under both statutes, the defense of limitation of liability is deemed personal and is unavailable to the insurer.

Other State Statutes

A number of states provide for direct action against an insurance company where the insured becomes insolvent. The terms of the relevant statutes must be scrutinized carefully however. Some of them by their terms apply only to *liability* policies—and as has been noted, a P & I policy is, strictly speaking, a policy of *indemnity* rather than liability. Some state insurance codes are expressly made inapplicable to marine insurance, or policies of "wet" marine insurance. Although those codes may contain a specific section authorizing direct action against the insurer when the insured is bankrupt, the exclusion of marine insurance or wet marine insurance renders a specific direct action section inapplicable.

A California statute, for example, provides that insolvency or bankruptcy of the assured will not release the insurer from liability for payment of damages. Upon a judgment being secured against the insured, an action may then be brought by the judgment creditor against the insurer to recover.[17] The effect is to create a contractual relationship which inures to the benefit of any person who is negligently injured by an insured tortfeasor.[18]

A Washington court has construed the California statute as allowing recovery for an injured seaman where the seaman's employer was insured under a marine policy issued in California. In *Williams v. Steamship Owners Mutual Underwriting Association*,[19] a seaman was injured when he fell into a manhole in a vessel's passageway. The seaman secured a judgment against the shipowner/employer, and subsequently brought an action against the insurer based on the California statute. The insurer raised the "indemnity" defense; i.e., it was liable only to the vessel owner and then only in the event and to the extent that the vessel owner paid the claim. The Washington court held that the California statute applied and granted recovery.

The insurer further contended that the policy was a maritime contract. As such, application of the California statute was unconstitutional because Article III, Section 2 of the U. S. Constitution mandated that it

17. Cal. Ins. Code Sec. 11580 (W.Supp. 1984).
18. *Zahn v. Canadian Indemnity Co.*, 57 Cal.App. 3d 509, 129 Cal.Rptr. 286 (1976); *Johnson v. Holmes Tuttle Lincoln Mercury*, 160 Cal.App.2d 290, 325 P.2d 193 (1958).
19. 45 Wash.2d 209, 273 P.2d 803 (1954).

be construed and interpreted according to general admiralty law. Citing *Maryland Casualty,* the court disagreed.

Joinder in Florida

The basis in Florida for permitting joinder of the insurer in an action against the insured is Florida Rule of Civil Procedure 1.210(c) which states that "any person may be made defendant who has or claims an interest adverse to the plaintiff." In the leading case of *Shingleton v. Bussey,*[20] the Florida supreme court held that the plaintiff, as a third party beneficiary of an automobile liability policy, had a direct cause of action against the insurer and could join the insurer as a party defendant under its rule of civil procedure. The court premised its holding upon the ground that public policy mandated that liability insurance policies could be construed as "quasi-third party beneficiary" contracts which give to the injured party an unquestionable right to bring a direct action against the insurer.

The following year, the Florida court expanded the rule in *Shingleton* to embrace forms of liability insurance other than insurance policies.[21]

However, in *Brent Towing Co., Inc. v. M/V Ruth Brent,*[22] the federal district court, Northern District of Florida, declined to allow joinder of the insurer with respect to maritime personal injury and death claims in a limitation of liability proceeding. The court said there was no authority for such procedure, relying on what it called the "general rule" that in admiralty proceedings an insurer may not be joined as a party defendant. Further, the court stated that to maintain uniformity in admiralty practice, the general rule of non-joinder should be followed unless clear grounds for exception exist—and it found none.

The federal courts in Florida have also refused to allow joinder with respect to suits on claims arising out of torts on the high seas.[23] However, a federal court in the Middle District of Florida recently allowed joinder of a liability insurer on a cargo claim, assuming that the tortious acts leading to the cargo loss occurred *on Florida waters.*[24] In rendering its decision, the court concentrated primarily on whether Florida's right of direct action conflicted with general maritime law, and concluded that the "constitutional imperative for the uniformity of admiralty" would not be offended

20. 223 So.2d 713 (St.,Fla., 1969).
21. *Beta Eta House Corp., Inc. v. Gregory,* 237 So.2d 163 (1970) (joinder allowed as to liability insurance carrier for a fraternity).
22. 414 F.Supp. 131 (N.D., Fla., 1975).
23. *Bangladesh Agricultural Development Corp. v. Millbank Shipping,* 1983 AMC 2631 (M.D.,Fla., 1983), and cases cited therein.
24. *Bangladesh Agricultural Development Corp. v. Millbank Shipping,* n. 23, *supra.*

by application of a judicially recognized right of direct action in maritime claims arising on inland waters of Florida.

In *Quinones v. Coral Rock, Inc.*,[25] a state trial court had held that a P & I underwriter could not be joined in an action against vessel owners for personal injuries, basing its decision on an interpretation of the policy as being one of pure indemnity. The appellate court reversed, construing the policy to be one of indemnity for liability only, rather than indemnity against loss paid. It is clear the court was influenced by a desire to maintain consistency in the decisional law and to implement the policies advocated in *Shingleton*.

However, in 1985, a Florida state court seemingly resolved the question adversely to the claimants in a direct action against a P & I underwriter. In *Macdonald v. Lexington Insurance Co., et al*,[26] the court referred to the holding in *Brent Towing* that there is a general maritime rule precluding joinder of insurers, and that the U. S. Supreme Court has held that the general maritime law applies to the resolution of lawsuits based on maritime accidents.[27] Continuing, the court noted that on three occasions, the Florida legislature had attempted to overturn the ruling in *Shingleton*, finally succeeding on the third attempt.[28] The court drew a clear distinction between a true liability policy and a true indemnity policy, noting that the defendant's policy was true indemnity, limiting its duty to pay a loss only after its assured had paid a loss for which he was legally liable to pay.

It thus appears that the efforts of the Florida courts to establish a right of direct action against insurers by reliance upon procedural rules have finally been thwarted by legislative action. It is probable, however, that the efforts of the Florida courts will not go unnoticed by other jurisdictions.

The New York "Anti-Direct Action" Statute[29]

Section 167(1) of the New York Insurance Code authorizes an injured party to sue an insurer directly if the insured is insolvent. Unfortunately,

25. 258 So.2d 485 (Fla.App. 1972).
26. 1985 AMC 2225 (St.,Fla., 1985).
27. Citing *inter alia, Pope & Talbot v. Hawn*, 346 U.S. 406, 1954 AMC 1 (1958); *Moragne v. States Marine Lines*, 398 U.S. 375, 1970 AMC 967 (1970); *Robertson v. Douglas Steamship Co.*, 510 F.2d 829, 1975 AMC 2338 (5th Cir.). *Wilburn Boat Co. v. Fireman's Fund Ins. Co.*, 348 U.S. 310, 1955 AMC 467 (1955), holding that no general maritime rule had been fashioned by the federal courts with respect to marine insurance policies, was neither cited nor mentioned.
28. Sec. 627.7262, Florida Statutes (Supp. 1982), held constitutional in *VanBibber v. Hartford Accident & Indemnity Insurance Co.*, 439 So.2d 888 (Sup.Ct., Fla., 1983).
29. The New York statute has such a limited application that one commentator has referred to it as an "anti-direct action" statute. Houdlett, "Direct Action Statutes and Marine P & I Insurance," *3 J. Mar. L. & Com.* 559, 560 (1972).

however, Section 167(4) specifically excludes from the direct action provision "insurance against the perils of navigation" and "marine protection and indemnity insurance."

In the personal injury field, attempts by injured seamen to recover directly against an insurer despite Section 167(4) have consistently met with failure in both state and federal courts.

This is immediately apparent by examining the state court decisions. For example, in *Cucurillo v. American Steamship Owners Mutual Protection and Indemnity Ass'n,*[30] the court held that under the New York law, P & I underwriters are not directly liable to judgment creditors of a bankrupt assured. More recently, in *Cowan v. Continental Insurance Co.,*[31] the survivors of a crew member of a tug lost off the coast of New Jersey brought a declaratory judgment action in New York seeking a declaration that there was coverage under a P & I policy on the tug issued to the decedent's employers. The court held that the survivors were clearly prohibited by Section 167(4) from obtaining relief.[32]

The federal courts have not been more sympathetic in this area. In *Ahmed v. American Steamship Owners Mutual P & I Ass'n,*[33] plaintiff seamen who had suffered personal injuries in the course of employment aboard the defendant assured's vessel brought suit. Default judgments were entered against the defendant assured but were unsatisfied because of the latter's insolvency. The court held (1) that the policies involved were ones of indemnity, (2) that New York law was applicable, and (3) that it was bound by the decision of the New York court in *Cucurillo.* It was apparent that the court felt the result was inequitable. The decision was appealed to the Ninth Circuit and affirmed in part. However the Ninth Circuit remanded, in part, to allow the plaintiffs to pursue their contention that Section 167(4) violated the equal protection clause of the Fourteenth Amendment to the U. S. Constitution. On remand, the court found no denial of equal protection.[34]

In *Miller v. American Steamship Owners Mutual P & I Ass'n,*[35] the district court of the Southern District of New York reinforced the conclusion that Section 167(4) barred a direct action against a P & I underwriter. There,

---

30. 1969 AMC 2334 (St., N.Y.).
31. 86 A.D.2d 646, 446 N.Y.S.2d 412 (St., N.Y., 1982).
32. The court further found that Connecticut had the most significant contacts with the litigation and that, therefore, the Connecticut statute should apply. That statute provided for direct action against an insurer by a judgment creditor of the insured defendant. However, in this instance, the plaintiff had not yet secured a judgment against the assured and the Connecticut statute therefore did not apply.
33. 444 F.Supp. 569, 1978 AMC 586 (N.D.,Cal.), *aff'd* in part 640 F.2d 993 (9th Cir., 1981), appeal after remand 701 F.2d 824 (9th Cir., 1983), *cert.den.* 104 S.Ct. 98.
34. 1982 AMC 1228, *aff'd* 701 F.2d 824, 1983 AMC 2712 (9th Cir., 1983).
35. 509 F.Supp. 1047, 1981 AMC 903 (S.D.N.Y.).

a seaman obtained a judgment against the owner of the vessel on which he was injured. The owner was insolvent and nothing was paid on the judgment. The plaintiff seaman then brought suit against the assured's underwriter. Although recognizing that the assured could never pay the judgment, and in reliance upon Section 167(4), the court granted the insurer's motion for summary judgment.

In *Wabco Trade Co. v. S.S. Iner Skou*,[36] cargo interests brought a direct action against underwriters to recover on a judgment obtained against the ocean carrier. The suit was based upon Section 3201(a) of the New York Procedural Code which provided that a money judgment could be enforced against any debt unless the debt were exempt from application to the satisfaction of a judgment, a debt being defined as consisting of a cause of action which could be assigned or transferred. Reversing the district court, the Second Circuit held that Section 167(4), being more specific, superseded the more general provisions of the rules of civil procedure. Consequently, a direct action was precluded against the insurer.

Other Decisions

Pennsylvania also has not viewed such direct actions with favor. In *Pettus v. Jones & Laughlin Steel Corp.*,[37] a plaintiff seaman brought suit against his employer for personal injuries sustained while engaged in making up a fleet of barges. In *dicta,* the court observed that under Pennsylvania law a claimant has no right of direct action unless the applicable insurance policy or a statute creates such a right. The statute provided for a direct action only upon the bankruptcy or insolvency of the assured, and the defendant employer was neither bankrupt nor insolvent. The insurance policy was not before the court and the court declined to rule on that phase of the question. In so ruling, the Pennsylvania court relied on a Hawaiian decision expressing a similar viewpoint.[38]

In the Hawaii case, the claimants attempted to rely on cases decided under Louisiana's direct action statute to compel the defendant to add its insurance coverage to the limitation fund. The court declined to permit this, observing that Hawaii's direct action statute was not even remotely comparable to the Louisiana statute. The court felt that if any change in

---

36. 663 F.2d 369, 1982 AMC 727 (2d Cir.).

37. 322 F.Supp. 1078, 1972 AMC 170 (W.D., Pa., 1971). See, also, *Robinson v. Shearer & Sons,* 429 F.2d 83, 1970 AMC 2360 (3rd Cir.) where the court held that the insurer's obligation to indemnify and duty to defend were aleatory; that it could never be absolute, and was not a "debt" subject to attachment under the federal rules or under Pennsylvania law before the defendant's liability had been established and determined to be within the policy coverage, nor was it attachable under a *quasi in rem* theory of jurisdiction.

38. *In Re Pacific Inland Navigation Co.,* 263 F.Supp. 915 (D., Haw., 1967).

this area were to be effected, it should come through legislation on a nationwide basis.[39]

Essentially the same result has been reached under Texas law. In *Continental Oil Co. v. Bonanza Corp.*, at first instance the district court for the Southern District of Texas held that the plaintiffs could proceed directly against the insurer based on privity of contract between the plaintiffs and the insurance company since the plaintiffs were named in the policy as additional assureds. Additionally, the court found that the plaintiffs could proceed against the insurers as third party beneficiaries of the contract. However, on appeal, this portion of the decision was reversed.[40] The appeals court noted that federal admiralty law provided no general right to sue an insurance company directly and, looking landwards, Texas law refused to permit a direct action against an insurance company.[41]

There are a few decisions in jurisdictions other than Louisiana and Puerto Rico where direct actions have been allowed but these seem to be the exception rather than the rule.[42]

Collateral Decisions of Interest

Notwithstanding a right of direct action, the rights of recovery of a claimant who proceeds against an underwriter are circumscribed by the liability which the underwriter owes to his primary assured. Thus, in *Ruiz Rod. v. Litton*,[43] since injured longshoremen are barred from suing a vessel's demise charterer, classified as an "employer" under the Puerto Rico

39. Subsequently, the Supreme Court of Hawaii in *Olokele Sugar Co. v. McCabe, Hamilton & Renny Co.*, 487 P.2d 769 (1971) arrived at the same conclusion.

40. 677 F.2d 455, 1983 AMC 387 (5th Cir., 1982). It should be observed that the Fifth Circuit, sitting *en banc*, reversed the prior panel on other grounds. 706 F.2d 1365, 1983 AMC 2059 (5th Cir., 1983).

41. Tex.R.Civ.P. 51(b); *Russell v. Hartford Casualty Ins. Co.*, 548 S.W.2d 737 (St.,Tex., 1977).

42. See, for example, *Finkelberg v. Continental Casualty Co.*, 125 Wash. 543, 219 P.2d 12 (1923), where a direct action was permitted against an indemnity insurer of an insolvent assured based on terms of the policy; *New Jersey Fidelity & Plate Glass Ins. Co. v. Clark*, 33 F.2d 235 (9th Cir., 1929), where a direct action was allowed based on provisions of the indemnity policy and a statute authorizing direct action in the event of bankruptcy; *Martin & Robertson v. Orion Ins. Co.*, 1971 AMC 515 (St., Cal.), where a ship was held to be a "vehicle" under the California Insurance Code and thus underwriters were subject to a direct action; *Hinkle & Finlayson v. Globe & Rutgers*, 1936 AMC 37, *aff'd* 1936 AMC 1289 (St.,N.Y.), where the word "vehicle" as used in Sec. 109 of the New York Insurance Code was held to include a water vehicle, a vessel, or tugboat, and a wharf owner whose property was damaged by a vessel owned by a bankrupt could proceed directly against the underwriter insuring the liability; see *St. Paul F. & M. Ins. Co. v. Mannie*, 91 F.R.D. 219 (D., N. Dakota, 1981), where the court adopted the majority rule prohibiting joinder of claims against insurers in declaratory judgment suits where the forum state does not allow direct actions against insurers. See, also, *Magras v. Puerto Rican American Ins. Co.*, 581 F.Supp. 427 (D., Virgin Is., 1982).

43. 574 F.2d 44, 1978 AMC 1004 (1st Cir.).

Workmen's Compensation Act, they likewise have no cause of action against the demise charterer's liability underwriter.

The Louisiana direct action statute does not govern over the Foreign Sovereign Immunities Act. It was the intent of Congress by that act to assure uniform treatment of foreign sovereigns. This requires denial of a right to jury trial in suits against a foreign sovereign's liability underwriters even in states such as Louisiana where direct action statute permits juries in actions against non-foreign sovereigns. Consequently, in *Goar v. Compania Peruana*,[44] it was held that the federal court did not have diversity jurisdiction over a Louisiana plaintiff's personal injury action against a Bermuda P & I club in which a foreign government shipowner was also named as a co-defendant.

In *Weiland v. Pyramid Ventures*,[45] P & I underwriters, sued under the Louisiana direct action statute, sought to cancel their coverage or to set off against a personal injury plaintiff's judgment unpaid "release calls" which their assured had failed to pay. The assured's delinquency (including insolvency) occurred after the date of the accident in which the plaintiff was injured. The court held to the contrary, noting that otherwise the insurer could benefit from the insured's insolvency in violation of the statute.

In *Shell Oil v. Orient Coral*,[46] it was held that under Louisiana law an underwriter's letter of undertaking issued to release a vessel from seizure was not a suretyship agreement since the underlying obligation arose *ex delicto* and the underwriter did not expressly agree in its letter to become a surety. Thus, the underwriter was not directly liable to the plaintiff in an action for collision which occurred outside Louisiana territorial waters.

In *International Sea Food v. Compeche*,[47] the appeals court held that the district court had erred in finding that it lacked subject matter jurisdiction in admiralty to enforce, by garnishment against insurance proceeds within the district, the maritime decree of the Supreme Court of Judicature, High Court (in admiralty) of the Isle of Barbados, awarding money damages to the plaintiff in a collision case. A court of admiralty in one nation can carry into effect the decree of the court of admiralty of another regardless of the maritime flavor of the underlying claim. Moreover, in the instant case, as the enforcement of the decree would require the interpretation of a marine insurance policy, a separate basis for jurisdiction existed.

---

44. 1981 AMC 1412 (E.D.,La.).
45. 688 F.2d 417, 1983 AMC 2178 (5th Cir.).
46. 548 F.Supp. 1385, 1983 AMC 1735 (E.D.,La.).
47. 506 F.2d 482, 1978 AMC 890 (5th Cir.).

A rather unusual situation was presented in *New York Marine Managers v. Helena Marine Service et al.*[48] There, a number of barges owned or operated by the assured were washed away from their moorings during a storm. They were swept downriver and allegedly damaged other vessels and property. Damages were alleged to amount to approximately $12 million. The assured had a primary policy of $1 million and an excess liability policy for $5 million. Petitions to limit were filed and *ad interim* stipulations for value purporting to assign the proceeds of the excess policy as Supplemental Rule F security. The claimants filed motions to dismiss the limitation proceedings based upon the inadequacy of the stipulations as Rule F security. The issues before the court were: (1) whether the excess underwriter was required to post security in the limitation actions; (2) if they were not, whether they were required to deposit the policy proceeds in the registry of the court; and (3) whether the limitation petitions were required to post security. The court held that absent an express policy provision or recognized custom in the marine insurance industry, excess hull underwriters could not be required to post security since this could expose them to potential risk exceeding the policy limits and create a priority in favor of parties whose claims were subject to limitation as opposed to other claimants. However, the court also held that the lower court did not abuse its discretion in requiring the excess underwriters to deposit the policy proceeds, less disbursements, in the registry of the court. (It will be seen that had the excess underwriters been forced to post security, that security presumably would have been co-equal to the total amount of the claims, i.e., $12 million—an amount $7 million in excess of the policy limits. If the petitioners failed to limit their liability, the total exposure could have been the $12 million). Finally, the court held that the limitation petitioners were required either to deposit cash in a sum equal to their interests in the vessel plus pending freight, or a corporate surety bond in the same amount, or to surrender the vessels.

It would appear that the exclusive liability provisions of the Longshoremen's Act, Section 905(a) and 933(i), bar a direct action against the employer's insurer as well as a suit against the employer.[49]

In *Deutsche-Schiff v. Bilbrough*,[50] the court held that the Louisiana direct action statute applied only to claims sounding in tort, not to claims based on contract or for quasi-contractual indemnity. Consequently, the action was dismissed against the vessel's P & I underwriters for breach of their contractual obligation to pay cargo damage claims arising out of the assured shipowner's tortious conduct vis-a-vis others.

---

48. 758 F.2d 313, 1986 AMC 662 (8th Cir., 1985).
49. *St Julien v. Diamond M. Drilling,* 403 F.Supp. 1256, 1975 AMC 1806 (E.D.,La.); *Johnson v. American Mutual,* 559 F.2d 382, 1979 AMC 1449.
50. 563 F.Supp. 1307, 1984 AMC 27 (E.D.,La.).

In *Oceanus Mutual v. Fuentes,*[51] although the registered owner had an insurable interest in its Panamanian flag vessel, the evidence established that the P & I coverage had been taken out by a charterer which was neither the agent nor the alter ego of the registered owner. Thus, the P & I underwriter was not liable to death claimants on a judgment previously obtained against the registered owner which was not a member of the P & I club.

In *Steelmet v. Caribe Towing,*[52] the court held that because Florida law recognized a cargo owner as a third party beneficiary of an ocean carrier's P & I policy, the cargo owner was entitled to bring a direct action against the P & I underwriter.

In *Fruehauf v. Royal Exchange,*[53] the Ninth Circuit held that even though the steamship company, as buyer under a conditional sales contract, was obligated to take insurance on tractors subject to a chattel mortgage, its policy did not name the seller-mortgagee as an assured. Consequently, the mortgagee's security interest in the tractors did not make it a party to the insurance contract and it could not prosecute a suit against the underwriters on the policy on the tractors.

In *Alcoa S.S. Co. v. Charles Ferran & Co.,*[54] it was held that a red letter clause in a ship repair contract, limiting damages recoverable to $300,000, was a defense based on a *contractual* limitation contained in an agreement which was the principal (if not the whole) source of rights and obligations and was not a defense which was "personal" to the assured. Consequently, the limitation was available to the ship repairman's liability underwriters when sued under the Louisiana direct action statute.

In *Signal Oil v. Barge W-701,*[55] the Fifth Circuit held that a barge owner, who was obliged by its contracts to procure "effectual insurance" covering its barge's operations, did not breach that contractual obligation by obtaining an excess policy which happened to have been delivered outside the state of Louisiana and thus not subject to that state's direct action statute. Also, the court held that the barge owner's warranty to the contractor that it had excess liability insurance did not constitute a personal contract which would preclude the barge owner from invoking the Limitation of Liability Act. In the event, a non-negligent party was held liable for a portion of the substantial loss, not from any contractual breach, but solely because of execution of an indemnity agreement and the application of the Limitation of Liability Act.

---

51. 1985 AMC 546 (St.,Fla.).
52. 747 F.2d 689, 1985 AMC 956 (11th Cir., 1984).
53. 704 F.2d 1168, 1984 AMC 1194 (9th Cir., 1983).
54. 1971 AMC 1116 (5th Cir.).
55. 654 F.2d 1164, 1982 AMC 2603 (5th Cir., 1981).

The Third Parties (Rights against Insurers) Act of 1930

As Arnould notes,[56] under English law, where the insured is insolvent, there are three avenues by which a claimant may proceed. The first is to treat the liability under the liability policy as an asset within the jurisdiction of the English courts, sufficient to found an application to wind up the assured in England.[57] The second is to proceed directly against the insurer under the Third Parties (Rights against Insurers) Act, 1930. The third is to obtain an injunction to restrain the assured from removing the proceeds of the policy beyond the jurisdiction of the court.[58]

The first method is relatively simple where the liability of the underwriter is not disputed and the claimant is a principal creditor of the assured. A claim under a club policy, payable in England, is an asset of the assured sufficient to warrant a winding up by the English courts.[59] Here, there are two methods of winding up the company: a creditors' voluntary winding up and a court ordered winding up. The first requires a resolution passed by a three-quarters majority of club members providing for the winding up and the appointment of a liquidator. The second requires a petition by a creditor to the court requesting that the company be wound up. Only if the members of the club approve by a special resolution can the company itself bring the petition. From that point on, the procedure follows its normal course: i.e., appointment of a liquidator, meeting of the creditors, possible appointment of an inspection committee, bringing proceedings, or compromising claims, etc. Proceeding by way of winding up is not, however, foolproof; the granting of an order to wind up is discretionary with the court and usually is not granted unless the claim against underwriters is likely to succeed,[60] and if there are other major creditors, the distributive share of the claimant may be de minimis.

Rather surprisingly, a company not incorporated in England may be wound up by the English courts if (a) the company is dissolved or has ceased to carry on a business or is carrying on a business for the purpose

56. *Law of Marine Insurance and Average* (16th ed.), Sec. 1356.
57. This procedure is not limited to liability policies. It could also be of value where, for example, the claimant has a cargo claim against a shipowner whose principal asset is a claim under the hull and machinery policies.
58. Such procedure is commonly known as a "Mareva injunction." See *Bakarim v. Victoria P. Shipping Co. (The Tatiangela)*, [1980] 2 Lloyd's Rep. 193; *Iraqui Ministry of Defence v. Arcepey Shipping Co., S.A. (The Angel Bell)*, [1980] 1 All E.R. 480; *Third Chandris Shipping Corp. v. Unimarine S.A.*, [1979] Q.B. 645 (discussing the general principles relating to the discretion of a court to issue the injunction).
59. See *Siderurgica del Orinoco S.A. v. London Steamship Owners' Mutual Insurance Ass'n (The Vainqueur Jose)*, [1979] 1 Lloyd's Rep. 557.
60. *In re Allobrogia S.S. Corp.*, [1978] 3 All E.R. 423.

of winding up its affairs, (b) if the company is unable to pay its debts, and (c) if the court concludes that it is just and equitable that the company be wound up.[61]

Most P & I clubs in England are either companies limited by guarantee or unlimited companies, formed under the Companies Acts.[62] It will also be remembered that it is customary in the British clubs that a member contributes calls only to the particular class for which he is entered, i.e., protection or indemnity, strikes, war risks, etc. Apparently, the clubs are under no obligation to segregate assets attributable to one class of business from other assets of the club. Where club articles permit the directors to borrow and pledge assets of the club as security, and if such borrowings are not made on a class-by-class basis, it will be seen that one class which has a surplus could see that surplus disappear into the hands of the secured creditor or liquidator.[63]

The second avenue available to creditors, of course, is to proceed under the Third Parties (Rights against Insurers) Act, 1930. The effect of the act, upon the bankruptcy or winding up of the assured, is to vest in the claimant the right of the assured to indemnity from the insurer. That the act applies to maritime liability policies is well established.[64]

The solution here, too, is not without its pitfalls. For example, many forms of club rules preclude a right of indemnity in the assured until his liability to the claimant has been quantified by a judgment or award. This necessitates, of course, the claimant prosecuting his claim against the assured to a successful conclusion before he can proceed directly against the underwriter.[65] Moreover, as the claimant stands in the shoes of the assured, he is subject to all the defenses, no matter how technical, which the club could have asserted against its assured.[66] The third hurdle the

61. Companies Act, 1948, 11 & 12 Geo. 6, ch. 38, amended by Companies Act, 1981, 29 and 30 Eliz. 2, ch. 62. See, also, *In re Compania Merabello San Nicholas, S.A.,* [1973] 1 Ch. 75. (*Merabello* involved the right to claim on an insurance contract which, if the order were made, would by virtue of the Third Parties Act 1930 become vested in the petitioner. The court also held that the burden is on those opposing the petition to prove that there is no possibility of any benefit accruing to the creditors.) A mere cause of action is an asset sufficient to give the court jurisdiction without proof that the action is certain to succeed. *In re Allobrogia S.S. Corp.,* n. 60, *supra.*

62. Companies Act, 1948, 11 & 12 Geo. 6, ch. 38; Insurance Companies Act, 1982, 30 & 31 Eliz. 2, ch. 50.

63. Where there is no separate trust fund for each class, the winding up rules under English corporate law cannot be circumvented. *British Eagle International Airlines v. Compagnie Nationale Air France,* [1975] 1 W.L.R. 758.

64. See *Merabello, supra,* n. 61; *Allobrogia, supra,* n. 60; and *Vainqueur Jose, supra,* n. 59.

65. *Post Office v. Norwich Union Fire Ins. Co.,* [1976] 2 Q.B. 363. See, also, *Vainqueur Jose, supra,* n. 59.

66. *Farrell v. Federated Employers Ins. Ass'n,* [1970] 1 W.L.R. 1400; *Post Office v. Norwich Union Fire Ins. Soc., supra,* n. 65; *Murray v. Legal & General Assur. Soc.,* [1970] 2 Q.B. 495 (if the policy makes payment of unpaid premiums a condition precedent to liability, the insurer may assert a right of set-off for the unpaid premiums; otherwise not). However, the act itself

claimant must overcome is where the club rules make coverage discretionary as under the "omnibus clause." While the claimant may demand that the club directors or committee exercise their discretionary powers just as they would do had the assured made the claim, the claim may be one for which the assured has no right of indemnity unless the directors or committee should determine, *in their discretion,* that it should be paid.[67]

It is very important to keep in mind that before the 1930 act may be resorted to, the right to sue the underwriters must exist. Most club rules require that if any difference or dispute between the member and the club arises, it must be arbitrated. Some club rules also provide that such a dispute must first be referred to the club's directors or committee for resolution or decision. Thus, not only may the claimant be required to submit the claim to the club's directors or committee, he may also be required to go to arbitration. Such rules have been upheld.[68]

---

voids any clauses which purport to relieve the underwriter from liability upon the insolvency of the assured. Such defenses may include such matters as a breach by the assured of the notice or cooperation requirements, cesser or cancellation, including retrospective cancellation, and failure of the shipowner to raise a good faith defense or to implead a necessary party.

67. See *Vainqueur Jose, supra.* The court held, *inter alia,* that such a claim, insofar as it relates to such a discretionary power, is not one of insurance to which the 1930 act applies and, hence, the claimant has no right of action against the underwriters.

68. *Socony Mobil Oil Co. v. West of England Ship Owners Mutual Insurance Ass'n (London),* [1984] 2 Lloyd's Rep. 408, citing *Scott v. Avery,* 10 E.R. 1121 (H.L.). See, also, *Freshwater v. Western Australia Assur. Co.,* [1933] 1 K.B. 515 and *Smith v. Pearl Assur. Co.,* [1939] 1 All E.R. 95.

CHAPTER XXV

REINSURANCE

Introduction[1]

Reinsurance is one of the most complex and difficult areas of insurance, and reinsurance of marine risks may well be the most difficult and complex of all.

It is probable that more people are employed in the practice of reinsurance than in any other branch of the insurance markets throughout the world.

While not essential, it is indeed desirable that a reinsurance underwriter be familiar with direct underwriting principles. As a matter of practice, reinsurance underwriters are generally dependent upon the skill and expertise of the direct (original) insurer for their underwriting profits.

The field of reinsurance has its own terminology as will be seen in the discussion which follows.

Origins of Marine Reinsurance

It is certain that reinsurance is as old as marine insurance itself. It apparently originated in Italy where insurance was practiced long before the Lloyd's market was created in London. The pre-eminence of Lloyd's as a marine insurance market is due more to successful underwriting for over three hundred years than to antiquity.

The road for reinsurance has not always been too smooth. As a consequence of the South Sea Bubble affair, by reason of which nearly all business ventures became suspect, Parliament passed the Bubble Act in 1720. Although directed at businesses in general, the scope of the act was sufficiently broad to have an impact on the reinsurance business. For example, the act prohibited underwriting in partnerships which, had the act continued in force, would have prevented the syndicate system at Lloyd's and its phenomenal growth over the years.

---

1. The author wishes to express his appreciation for the assistance available to him in *Marine Reinsurance*, by Robert Brown and Peter Reed, Witherby & Co. Ltd., London (1981) and *Reinsurance*, by Kenneth R. Thompson, The Chilton Company, Philadelphia, Pa. (4th ed., 1966). A debt of gratitude is also owed to Brian Waltham and Jonathan Lux of Ince & Co., London, who read the chapter in manuscript and made invaluable suggestions.

The writing of policies where the assureds had no insurable interest led to the enactment of a gaming and wagering act in 1746 which, incidentally, made reinsurance contracts illegal with several minor exceptions. Although the 1746 act was repealed in 1864, it is clear that reinsurance contracts continued to be written during the interval before repeal in 1864. And reinsurance contracts continued to be written on the Continent.

Originally, the majority of reinsurances were effected on a "facultative" basis; i.e.,where the reinsurer is given an option to reinsure rather than being obliged to do so. Thus, the reinsurer may accept or reject a risk tendered to him, he may determine the amount of the risk that he will accept and negotiate the premium rate for each acceptance.

Facultative reinsurance is still being written and will be discussed hereafter.

Purpose of Reinsurance

In simple terms, the purpose of reinsurance is to "spread the risk." There are a variety of reasons for effecting insurance and these are discussed, *infra*. The classic case of spreading the risk occurs when an underwriter is offered a large risk to underwrite. Rather than take the entire risk (which could expose him to an unacceptably large loss), he accepts only a small line with the balance being spread out among several other underwriters. He can then further spread the risk by reinsuring part of his acceptance with a reinsurer.

As is known, there is a strong sense of nationalism in the so-called developing countries which, by legislation, can manifest itself by forbidding payments of premium to underwriters located outside the country. This requires importers and exporters to procure their insurance from domestic companies which triggers in many cases a dramatic increase in potential liabilities. As a consequence such domestic companies, even state-controlled companies, can find it necessary to effect reinsurance treaties with reinsurers outside the country in order to provide full security to their policyholders.

Some countries have legislation which requires that part of any reinsurance be effected through a state-operated pool. The pool in turn will frequently find it necessary to reinsure abroad. This is well illustrated in *Empresa Lineas Maritimas Argentias v. Oceanus Mutual Underwriting Association (Bermuda) Ltd.*[2] In that case, Argentina required that state-owned bodies such as the plaintiffs (Elma) place their insurance with a state insurance company, Caja. However, Caja could not provide P & I cover nor

---

2. [1984] 2 Lloyd's Rep. 517.

could the state reinsurance company (Inder) provide reinsurance for such risks. As a result, both the state-owned and private fleets sought and obtained P & I cover direct in the international market by membership in one or more of the well-known clubs. Elma became a member of the United Kingdom Club. About 1975, the authorities decided that to save foreign exchange and strengthen the insurance market, shipowners should no longer be allowed to seek cover direct from overseas P & I clubs. In the future, owners would have to place their P & I coverage with Caja which would then reinsure with Inder which would in turn approach the P & I clubs. Inder did so and approached the defendant club. From 1976, the defendant had acted as reinsurers of a substantial proportion of Inder's P & I liabilities to Caja which in turn acted as insurers providing primary cover to Elma.

The defendant claimed unpaid calls from both Inder and Elma. To collect, the defendant club arrested one of the Elma fleet, in Rotterdam. Plaintiff posted a bank guaranty in order to release the vessel and sought a declaration that they were not party to any agreement by which the defendant club insured any of the plaintiffs' vessels and for the guaranty to be released. The court held for the plaintiffs on the ground that the only agreement between Argentina and the defendant was that made between Inder and the defendant to which Elma was not a party. The original claim for unpaid calls having failed, the bank guaranty was released. The case illustrates the cardinal principle, discussed *infra*, that reinsurance is a contract between the direct insurer and the reinsurer to which the original assured is not a party and which neither obligates the reinsurer to the assured nor the assured to the reinsurer. Section 9(2) of the Marine Insurance Act, 1906, codified the law on this point.

A further instance of reinsurance being placed in a foreign market is where state law requires that reinsurance must first be offered to domestic companies admitted in that state. Only the balance, after the local market has absorbed its maximum capacity, can be placed in the foreign market. The latter is sometimes achieved by "Surplus Line Reinsurance."

The original or direct insurer, as he is frequently termed, may transfer or "cede" the whole or part of a risk to another underwriter. This original or direct insurer, or "cedant" or "reassured" enters into a contractual relationship with the second underwriter who is called the reinsurer.

The original insurer is obligated directly to his insured or policyholder. The reinsurer, in turn, is obligated to the cedant, sometimes called the primary carrier, although this terminology sometimes causes confusion. The original insurer has to account to his assured in case of loss under the original policy. The original insurer by his contract of reinsurance may call upon his reinsurer by reason of the loss suffered by the former under the original policy.

The risk assumed in a reinsurance contract must be determined by examining the contract of reinsurance. It should not be taken for granted that the risk covered by the reinsurance contract is always the same as that covered by the original policy written by the direct insurer. The importance of this is emphasized subsequently.

Occasionally, a direct insurer will reinsure his whole line at the original premium rate. This appears strange until it is recognized that the direct insurer is, at least if his reinsurers are financially sound, taking a small risk, and should make a profit on the reinsurance commission (or "overrider") which he receives. The danger involved in this practice for the reinsurer is that the direct insurer, having no ultimate risk, may not be as discriminating as he should be in accepting risks, or may even write risks merely for the overrider. Reinsurers are understandably wary about such situations and nowadays almost always require that the direct insurer retain part of the original risk for his own account in the absence of special circumstances such as the need for "fronting" (see *infra*).

The Reinsurance Industry[3]

Reinsurance is an industry in its own right. Most direct insurers operate a reinsurance account which, in itself, assists in the principle of spreading the risk. This permits a form of reciprocal exchange whereby a direct insurer may reinsure with another company a certain risk. The latter company may itself write a direct line on a different risk and either by coincidence or design reinsure with the first direct insurer mentioned. This practice is so commonplace that it can be quite difficult to ascertain where the reinsurance market begins and ends. The varying relationships which can develop are almost incestuous in nature.

Generally speaking, a professional insurer is a large company dealing with reinsurance solely and covering most areas of insurance instead of concentrating on one type.

Sometimes, a group of reinsurers will band together to form a "pool." Under this type of arrangement, the pool members will vest an underwriter with authority to underwrite risks on behalf of the pool.

A different type of pool arrangement may be made whereby a group of insurers agrees to accept certain classes of risk, on the basis that risks of that type will be automatically reinsured by the pool. A classic example appears in non-marine business in the United States where the auto-

---

3. For those interested in the innermost workings of Lloyd's and the relationships between brokers, managing agents, and underwriters, see *Lloyd's of London, A Reputation at Risk*, by Geoffrey Hodgson, published by Allan Lane in Great Britain and The Viking Press in the United States (1984).

mobile liability underwriters formed a pool to insure young male drivers under a certain age—a class of risk that all felt obliged to write but as to which none of them wished to undertake too many risks in the specified class.

The London P & I clubs also operate a pool to spread the risks involved in very large P & I liability claims.

Reasons for Effecting Reinsurance

The most common reasons for effecting reinsurance are as follows:

1. To permit the direct insurer to write more business by increasing his capacity.

2. To protect against a catastrophic risk.

3. To retain that part of the risk which is desirable and lay off on the reinsurer that part which is undesirable.

4. To enable the direct insurer to accept risks which would exceed his economic limit in any one risk.

5. To provide overall protection for an underwriting account,thus enhancing solvency.

6. To close out an underwriting account.

The amount of liability a direct insurer accepts in any one risk or insurance contract is his "line." In evaluating his line, the direct insurer must consider the desirability of the risk, the adequacy of the premium, and the reserves which he has available to him to meet possible claims. The last factor is the direct insurer's "capacity."

It would be absurd, of course, to maintain large reserves to meet potential future claims if the same result could be accomplished by reinsuring at an economic premium. To the extent to which reinsurance shields the direct insurer from potential losses, he is thereby permitted to increase his capacity and write even more business. It is a fact of insurance life that brokers offer the best risks to underwriters who are capable of writing large lines, and as a consequence, insurers are constantly under pressure to write larger and larger lines merely to stay in business.

It is not uncommon for very large risks to be underwritten in certain areas and trades. For example, oil drilling rigs in the Gulf of Mexico cost into the millions and are exposed to the ever-present threat of hurricanes. An underwriter insuring such rigs can limit his maximum liability by retaining the amount of risk he feels he can handle with reasonable safety and by effecting a reinsurance contract on an "excess of loss" basis for the amount by which he feels overexposed.

Retaining part of the risk is rather common in hull insurances. While the underwriter may be prepared to cover rather large sums for repairs, he is understandably reluctant to take on a catastrophic loss such as a total or constructive total loss. He will therefore write the line on regular hull conditions but reinsure the line on "total loss only" conditions.

Direct insurers of cargo frequently insure under an open cover. The cover will contain a limit on any one acceptance, and is based on the maximum probable limit that the insured may wish to declare. Occasionally, an insured will wish to insure a risk which exceeds the limit. While the underwriter is not obliged to accept the amount by which his line is exceeded, he may wish to please his customer by accepting nonetheless. If he does so, he may wish to reinsure the excess. This may be done on a facultative basis but also may take the form of a treaty basis.

To protect his solvency, the underwriter can utilize reinsurance to ensure that his maximum possible loss will not exceed the solvency "margins" which he has established for himself as underwriting policy. This may also take place to satisfy regulatory authorities who examine solvency margins to determine that they come within the minima laid down by law.

An underwriter who is going out of business may reinsure his liabilities for losses which may be presented after the policies have expired but which arose when the policies were in force. For example, when a Lloyd's underwriter ceases to trade, his business will often be reinsured so that any losses attached to his account after he ceases business will be covered by insurance. This is common where a "name" on a syndicate dies and the syndicate effects reinsurance to cover his proportion of any claims attaching to accounts to which he had subscribed.

In the past, liquidators of insolvent insurance companies have sought reinsurance of the company's outstanding liabilities in order to be able to finalize the company's affairs. However, such reinsurances are nowadays rare, so that the liquidators either have to find a purchaser for the company, or run off its liabilities.

Reinsurance is also frequently resorted to in order to permit an underwriting agency, managing a syndicate, to close the account for an underwriting year which has run for its specified period so that the underwriting profit, if any, can be paid to the members of the syndicate. Such reinsurance is known as "reinsurance to close" and is a type of Stop Loss reinsurance.

Fundamental Principles

Insurable Interest

The same principles applicable to direct marine insurance apply to reinsurance. That is, the direct insurer who reinsures must have an insurable interest, although such an interest exists only during the period covered by the original insurance and only as against the risks therein assumed. Similarly, in a reinsurance upon a reinsurance the same principles apply; i.e., the risk of the first reinsurer constitutes an insurable interest sufficient to support the second reinsurance.[4] An exception to this rule exists in the United States (but not in England) as regards policies written "Policy Proof of Interest" (or "PPI"). Under the United States law, if the policy is written on PPI terms, then the reinsured does not have to show an insurable interest. Under English law, such policies are void under the Marine Insurance Act, 1906, Section 4. The parties would be liable to prosecution.

Utmost Good Faith

This very important principle in direct marine insurance applies with all vigor to reinsurance. The direct insurer is seldom in a position to verify the material facts which affect the subject matter he is asked to cover. The reinsurer is in an even worse position, as he must accept what he is told by the reassured in good faith. It is clear that there is no difference in the application of the principle between a direct insurer and a reinsurer.[5]

One of the problems facing a broker who is negotiating a reinsurance contract is whether or not he should disclose the details of clauses appearing in the original contract. The answer depends upon the clauses used. If the reinsurance contract contains general language such as "subject to all clauses in the original policy," then it appears that the reinsurance is subject to the clauses without having to set them out in detail.[6] But if the clauses in the original contract are unusual and differ from normal practice, their content must be disclosed to the reinsurer.[7]

---

4. *Sun Ins. Office v. Merz*, 64 N.J.L. 301 (St., N.J. 1900); *Bradford v. Symondson*, 7 Q.B.D. 456. See, also, generally, *In re National Benefit Assur. Co. Ltd.*, 8 La. 1 (St. La., 1835); *Philadelphia Ins. Co. v. Washington Ins. Co.*, 23 Pa. 250 (St., Pa., 1854); *Hewitt v. London General Ins. Co. Ltd.* (1925) 23 Ll.L.Rep. 243; *In re Overseas Marine Ins. Co., Ltd.*, (1930) 36 Ll.L.Rep. 183, C.A.

5. *Sun Mutual Ins. Co. v. Ocean Ins. Co.*, 107 U.S. 485 (1882); *Lambert v. Co-operative Ins. Soc. Ltd.*, [1975] 2 Lloyd's Rep. 485; *A/S Ivarans v. P.R. Ports Auth.*, 617 F.2d 903, 1982 AMC 2493 (1st Cir.); *Amer. Eagle F. I. Co. v. Eagle Star Ins. Co.*, 216 F.2d 176, 1954 AMC 1263 (9th Cir.); *Keresan*, 219 A.D. 636, 1927 AMC 577 (St. N.Y.). However, in *New Zealand Ins. Co. v. South Australian Ins. Co.*, (1878) 1 S.C.R. (N.S.) (N.S.W.) 214 (Aus.), it was held that concealment by the original assured of a material fact is not a defense to the reinsurer against the direct insurer if the direct insurer was not aware of the concealment and paid the loss in good faith. See, also, *London General Ins. Co. v. General Marine Underwriters' Ass'n.*, [1921] 1 K.B. 104, and *Commonwealth Ins. Co. of Vancouver v. Groupe Sprinks, S.A. et al.*, [1983] 1 Lloyd's Rep. 67 (reinsurers alleged misrepresentation and non-disclosure but failed in the burden of proof; however, held entitled to recover against the broker for negligence).

6. *Joyce v. Realm Marine Ins. Co.*, (1872) 41 L.J.Q.B. 356.

7. *Property Ins. Co. Ltd. v. National Protector Ins. Co. Ltd.*, (1913) 108 L.T. 104, 12 Asp. M.L.C. 287.

As is well known, an insurer is deemed to know the contents of standard clauses in use in the trade and the normal conditions on which direct marine insurance is written. For example, in *Marten v. Nippon Sea & Land Ins. Co., Ltd.*,[8] it was held that the "warehouse-to-warehouse" clause was such a common clause that the reinsurers ought to have known that it was included in the original policy and thus was incorporated into the reinsurance contract.

Policy

Since the reinsurer is deemed to know the usual terms of the original insurance, it behooves the reinsurer and the reinsurance broker to be familiar with and understand the cover afforded by the standard marine insurance policies. For several hundred years the "standard" marine policy in England and the Commonwealth nations was the old Lloyd S.G. form, utilized, more recently, with various forms of the Institute Clauses. It must be assumed that most brokers and insurers were, indeed, familiar with the policy forms then in use. The advent of the new London hull and cargo clauses will obviously require some degree of re-education on the part of brokers, insurers, and reinsurers.[9]

Marine Perils

A policy of reinsurance on a direct pure marine insurance contract covers, of course, only "marine" perils. The perils enumerated in the new London hull and cargo forms are those which are most usually covered in the English market, though other conditions are often found, particularly in the American forms. The American (AIH) form still follows the ancient perils clause in terminology.

Proximate Cause

The subject of proximate cause is a difficult one for many students. For a loss to be recoverable, it must be proximately caused by an insured peril. In order for the reassured to recover against the reinsurers, it is necessary, in the absence of specific contractual terms to the contrary, for him to prove his loss in a similar manner as the original assured must have proved it against the reassured. That is to say, the reinsurer is only bound to indemnify the reassured in respect of the latter's *legal liability* to the original assured. If the reassured improperly pays the original assured

---

8. (1889) 3 Com.Cas. 164. See, also, *Charlesworth v. Faber,* (1900) 5 Com.Cas. 408.
9. The new clauses are discussed in considerable detail in Chapter III, "The Policy."

then the reinsurer is not required to indemnify the reassured.[10] The widespread use of "Follow" clauses (see *infra*) alters the position in practice.

Indemnity

All marine insurance contracts are contracts of indemnity and a marine reinsurance contract is no exception.[11] As has been observed, pure indemnity is seldom applied in marine practice.[12] The basis of indemnity is generally tied to the agreed insured value which may or may not be the true value of the subject-matter insured. And, of course, in a valued policy the value fixed by the policy is, as between the assured and the assurer, conclusive as to the insurable value in the absence of fraud.

If, in a contract of reinsurance, the value is not stated the reinsurer is entitled to treat the policy as an unvalued policy. In such a policy, the insurable value falls to be determined by the rules which define the measure of insurable value. Section 16, Marine Insurance Act, 1906, specifies the manner of determination and American law does not differ. As the insurable value may be considerably different from the value inserted in the original policy of insurance between the direct underwriter and the original assured, a provision is almost invariably inserted in a contract of reinsurance reading "valued as original policy or policies."

It has happened, however, that the liability of a reinsurer may, even as to amount, and even where the policies are on the same terms, be either lesser or greater than the liability of the reassured. This comes about because of the operation of the Sue and Labor Clause. This is demonstrated in *Uzielli v. Boston Marine Insurance Co.*[13] In that case, a vessel was insured for £1,500. The original underwriter reinsured with the plaintiffs who, in turn, reinsured with the defendants for the sum of £1,000. The vessel became a constructive total loss which the original underwriters compromised by the payment of 88 percent but they had, in fact, expended sums amounting to 24 percent in getting the vessel to a place of safety. These underwriters were therefore entitled to recover this sum from the first

---

10. *Chippendale v. Holt*, (1895) 65 L.J.Q.B. 104; *Merchants' Mar. Ins. Co. v. Liverpool Mar. and General Ins. Co.*, (1928) 33 Com.Cas. 294; *Gurney v. Grimmer*, (1932) 38 Com.Cas. 7; *Excess Ins. Co. v. Matthews*, (1925) 31 Com.Cas. 43; *Yukon*, 1939 AMC 111 (Arb.); *Firemen's Ins. Co. v. Western Australian Ins. Co.*, (1927) 33 Com.Cas. (reinsurers successfully set up a defense of unseaworthiness although that defense had not been asserted by the reassured); *Commercial Standard Ins. Co. v. Fidelity Union Ins. Co.*, 111 S.W.2d 1167 (St. Tex. 1937) (reinsured assumed losses of one of its insolvent members; no liability).

11. *British Dominions Ins. Co. Ltd. v. Duder*, (1915) 2 K.B. 394, 13 Asp. M.L.C. 84.

12. See Chapter VII, "Insurable Interest," and Chapter IX, "Measure of Insurable Value."

13. (1884) 15 Q.B.D. 11.

reinsurers. The plaintiffs then sought to recover the 112 percent they had paid to the original underwriters from the second reinsurers, i.e., the defendants. It was held the Sue and Labor Clause did not apply and that the defendants were liable only for the amount which they had insured, i.e., £1,000.[14]

Almost all reinsurance policies contain a clause, in one form or another, reading "Being a reinsurance, subject to the same clauses and conditions as the original policy, and to pay as may be paid thereon." In one instance, involving reinsurance against total loss only, the language covered "compromised or arranged total losses" and in another "compromised and/or arranged total losses."[15]

The basic clause "to pay as may be paid thereon" does not preclude the reinsurer from insisting upon proof that a loss occurred within the terms of the policy. Thus, where the original underwriters accepted a notice of abandonment and in good faith paid their assured for a constructive total loss, those facts standing alone did not entitle them to recover from the reinsurer without proof that a constructive total loss had actually taken place.[16] However, where the liability of the original underwriter is definitely established, he is not required to prove actual payment to the original assured,[17] unless the reinsurance is "to pay as may be paid thereon," in which case prior payment of the claim by the reassured is essential. It may be necessary, however, to prove the *amount* of that liability before the reinsurer is liable where the reinsurance contract provides that the reinsurer is to "follow the settlements" of the reassured.[18]

14. In order for the plaintiffs to recover under the Sue and Labor Clause, they were required to show that they had sued and labored for the safety of the vessel. That expense had been incurred by the original underwriters and not by the plaintiffs and they were, therefore, not entitled to recover.

15. The former, *Street v. Royal Exch. Assur.,* (1913) 18 Com.Cas. 284, aff'd 19 Com.Cas. 339 (C.A.), involved a claim for a constructive total loss or in the alternative for a partial loss and was compromised by the original underwriters. The reinsurers were held liable. In the latter, *Gurney v. Grimmer,* (1932) 38 Com.Cas. 7, the words "arranged and/or compromised" were held to mean more than merely compromised, and again the reinsurers were held liable. There must, however, be a total loss or a genuine claim for one. The parties cannot create a total loss by arrangement. *Oscar L. Aronsen, Inc. v. Compton (The Megara),* 495 F.2d 674, 1974 AMC 480 (2d Cir.), [1973] 2 Lloyd's Rep. 361, [1974] 1 Lloyd's Rep. 590; *Bergens Dampskibs Ass. Forening v. Sun Ins. Office,* (1930) 46 T.L.R. 543.

16. See *Chippendale v. Holt, supra* n. 10; *Firemen's Fund Ins. Co. v. Western Australian Ins. Co.,* (1928) 43 T.L.R. 680; *China Traders Ins. Co. v. Royal Exchange Assur. Co.,* (1898) 2. Q.B. 187; *Gurney v. Grimmer, supra* n. 10; *Martin v. Steamship Owners' Underwriting Ass'n,* (1902) 7 Com.Cas. 195; *Western Ass. Co. v. Poole,* [1903] 1 K.B. 376, 9 Asp. M.L.C. 390.

17. *Allemannia Ins. Co. v. Firemen's Ins. Co.,* 209 U.S. 326 (1907); *Herckenrath v. American Mut. Ins. Co.,* 3 N.Y. 63 (1848); *British Union and National Ins. Co. v. Rawson,* [1916] 2 Ch. 476; *In Re Law Guarantee, etc., Soc.,* (1914) 2 Ch. 617; *Hicks v. Poe,* 269 U.S. 118, 1926 AMC 168 (1926); *R. Waverly,* 1929 AMC 1192 (St. Tex.), *rev'd* on other grounds, 281 U.S. 397, 1930 AMC 981 (Sup.Ct.).

18. *Beauchamp v. Fraser,* (1893) 3 Com.Cas. 308; *Verischerungs und Transport A.G. Daugava v. Henderson,* (1934) 39 Com.Cas. 312.

"Follow Clauses"

As a result of the difficulties which a reassured may find in establishing his own liability to the satisfaction of his reinsurer, it has become very common practice for marine insurance contracts to contain a "follow" clause. Such a clause might well read:

> To pay as may be paid thereon, and to follow original underwriters in settlement of claims.

Where a reinsurance contract contains such a provision, the insurer has merely to prove that he has paid the claim under the original insurance, and the amount of his payment. The effect of the follow clause is to preclude reinsurers from arguing that the reassured was not liable under the original policy. Under English law, there is an exception to this principle if reinsurers can prove that in settling the claims under the original policy, the reassured did not act in an honest and business like manner.

Subrogation

A discussion of rights of subrogation is beyond the scope of this chapter. Suffice it to say that generally a reinsurer is entitled to any recovery made by the original insurer. The amount of the credit will depend on the type of reinsurance. In the case of proportional reinsurance, the credit will be shared pro rata; in the case of non-proportional reinsurance, the recovery may not be distributed uniformly.

Types of Marine Reinsurance Systems

Proportional and Non-Proportional

Reinsurance contracts fall into two broad categories:
(1) Proportional Reinsurance
(2) Non-Proportional Reinsurance
    In proportional reinsurance, the reinsurer agrees to accept a proportion or percentage of the premium received by the cedant (less commissions), and, in exchange, agrees to pay a like proportion of all claims.

Example. A cedant has accepted, as direct insurer, a line of $100,000, in exchange for a premium of $2,000. He wishes to reinsure $50,000 on a proportional basis.

Fifty percent of $100,000 is $50,000. Leaving aside complications caused by commissions and brokerage, premium will be 50 percent of $2,000, or $1,000. If the cedant is liable to pay a claim of $10,000, then his reinsurer would be liable for 50 percent of this, or $5,000.

In non-proportional reinsurance, the premium is not directly proportional to the amount of the reinsurer's financial exposure, and he is not responsible simply for *a proportion* of all claims. One of the simplest examples of non-proportional reinsurance is Excess of Loss reinsurance. Under such a contract, the reinsurer is only liable to pay claims under the contract if the cedant's liability exceeds a threshold, sometimes known as the "excess point."

Example. The cedant has accepted $100,000 of a particular risk, for a premium of $2,000. He wishes to reinsure $50,000 excess of $50,000, so that in the event of a claim in excess of $50,000, the reinsurer will be liable to pay the excess of the claim over $50,000, up to a maximum of $50,000.

Although the reinsurer could be liable for as much as $50,000, he will be under no liability unless the cedant's liability is for a sum greater than $50,000. Thus, in this example, the reinsurer would probably expect a premium of rather less than 50 percent of the cedant's premium. If the cedant is liable to pay a claim of $20,000, then the reinsurer has no liability to the cedant; on the other hand, if the cedant is liable for $90,000, then the reinsurer will be liable for $40,000 ($90,000 less $50,000).

Facultative and Treaty

A further division is between facultative reinsurance and treaty reinsurance.

In facultative reinsurance, the reinsurer is offered each risk individually by the intending cedant, and is then able to decide, case by case, whether to accept or reject the risk offered, and on what terms.

On the other hand, a reinsurance treaty is a contract under which there is a longer term obligation between cedant and reinsurer governing what risks may or must be ceded to the reinsurer, and what risks the reinsurer may or must accept if offered to him, and on what terms.

Reinsurance treaties are often placed to ease the administrative inconvenience of having to reinsure each risk accepted by the cedant as and when it is offered to the cedant. Suitable treaty reinsurance also ensures that the cedant constantly has available to him reinsurance facilities tailored to his particular requirements. He can thus accept a direct risk knowing that he may immediately, and without question, reinsure it on known conditions.

Reinsurance treaties come in numerous forms. In particular, the terms of the treaty may compel one or the other party to cede or accept particular classes of risk; or the terms of the treaty may allow the cedant to choose which risks he cedes.

Contracts analogous to treaties are sometimes granted to intermediaries. This type of contract includes line slips, open covers, and binding authorities.

Particular Types of Treaties

Fronting Agreement. Sometimes, a direct insurer or a combination of direct insurers may not be acceptable to the insured. This commonly occurs because the original assured does not wish to be insured by a large number of direct insurers, or because there are legal restrictions on the activities of particular insurers in the country where the insured carries on business. In such cases, the broker may seek a "fronting" underwriter. That underwriter will receive 100 percent of the premium from the direct insured, and be directly and solely responsible to the assured for 100 percent of the claims. However, the underwriters who would otherwise have been the direct insurers of the assured agree to reinsure the fronting underwriter to the full extent that they would have insured the original assured.

The fronting underwriter will usually take a commission for this service, known as an "overrider." Apart from this overrider, he will pass all premiums received on to his reinsurers, and will expect his reinsurers to pay all claims in full.

It formerly was thought that the fronting underwriter ran no risk—until a spate of bankruptcies, particularly in the 1970s, that often left fronting underwriters insuring substantial lines of business for which they had retained no premium.

Example. A broker has insurers A, B, . . . W,X,Y, all prepared to insure the assured. The companies are not acceptable to the assured.

The broker therefore procures company Z to "front" the risk. Company Z is acceptable to the assured. Company Z demands a 5 percent overrider for the fronting service.

Company Z will receive a 100 percent premium (less brokerage) from the assured.

Company Z will pass 100 percent, minus 5 percent (i.e., 95 percent) of the premium received by Z on to companies A, B, . . . W,X,Y in their respective proportions.

Quota Share Treaties. A Quota Share Treaty is a proportional reinsurance contract under which the cedant is contractually bound to cede a proportion of all risks accepted by him which fall within the scope of the quota

share treaty concerned. By the same token, the reinsurer is equally bound
to accept his proportion of all risks so ceded. The reinsurer receives the
proportion of premium (less commissions), and is responsible for the like
proportions of claims. A quota share treaty does not permit the cedant to
select how much of each risk he retains. He must cede the specified proportion of the risk in each case falling within the scope of the treaty.
Quota share treaties have often been used to give the cedant the protection he needs to develop more capacity.

Surplus Treaties. A surplus treaty is a proportional treaty which, while laying down the circumstances in which the cedant must cede risks to his
reinsurer, permits the cedant to retain smaller lines in their entirety, and
gives the cedant the opportunity to increase his capacity to accept large
lines on incoming business.

The key to surplus reinsurance is the amount of the cedant's retained
line—that is, the maximum net exposure to which the cedant is prepared
to be exposed. A surplus treaty will then accept up to a maximum number
of further "lines"—that is, multiples of the cedant's retention.

Example. Cedant has a four-line surplus treaty, with a maximum line of
$10,000. The cedant is offered the opportunity to insure $20,000 of risk.
He can cede this to his surplus treaty in a number of ways:

(1) He can retain $10,000 and cede $10,000 (one line) to the surplus
treaty;

(2) He may retain $4,000, and cede $16,000 (four lines) to the surplus
treaty; or

(3) He may retain any amount between $4,000 and $10,000.

Once the cedant has decided his retention, and thus the sum to be
reinsured, premium will be divided between cedant and reinsurers in the
proportion which the cedant's retained line bears to the sum insured under the surplus treaty. Thus, in example (1) above, the reinsurers will received 50 percent of the premium (less any deduction), whereas in example (2), the reinsurers will receive 80 percent of the premium. Similarly, in
example (1), reinsurers will have to pay the cedant 50 percent of any
claim, whereas in example (2), reinsurers will have to pay the cedant 80
percent of any claims.

Not all surplus treaties permit this degree of flexibility. Many fix the
size of the reassured's retention for each category of business covered by
the treaty.

Facultative/Obligatory Contracts

Under a quota share treaty, the cedant is bound to cede and the reinsurer
to reinsure all risks falling within the scope of the treaty. In contrast, a

facultative/obligatory reinsurance contract is a contract under which, while the reinsurer is bound to accept any cession made to him within the terms of the treaty, the cedant may choose which risks he will cede to the treaty.

Under such a contract, there is clearly a risk that the cedant will select risks against the reinsurer. This is one reason why facultative/obligatory treaties cost more than quota share treaties.

Open Cover Line Slips and Binding Authorities[19]

Brokers who have a substantial volume of a particular type of contract to place may negotiate with reinsurers for a broker's open cover or a line slip.

Under the former, the reinsurers agree to accept any declaration made to the cover by the broker. The open cover will contain a rating provision so that, if a declaration is made within the scope of the open cover, the reinsurer is obliged to accept it. Thus, the broker's open cover may be thought of as analogous to a facultative/obligatory contract. Clearly, it differs from such a contract in that a facultative/obligatory treaty is a contract between cedant and the reinsurer, whereas a broker's open cover is a contract between brokers and reinsurers effectively giving the brokers power to bind the reinsurers to the reinsurance contract.

A broker's line slip may be used in similar circumstances. The major difference between a broker's line slip and a broker's open cover is that, whereas under the latter, reinsurers have no choice as to whether or not to accept a particular risk falling within the terms of the cover, the position under a typical line slip is that two leading underwriters subscribing to the line slip will usually have the power to fix the premium, terms, and conditions for each cession. The decision of the leading underwriters will bind the following underwriters.

A binding authority is a contract between a reinsurer and a coverholder, giving the coverholder the power to bind the reinsurer to the risk. Such authorities were formerly given in terms of allowing the coverholder a wide degree of latitude as to rating, terms, and conditions. Nowadays, such authorities are less usual, and when they are given, the prudent reinsurer exerts a close degree of control over the coverholder's activities.

Excess of Loss

Excess of loss reinsurance is usually taken out to protect a particular area of an insurer's business against the possibility of a large claim.

19. For a more complete discussion of open covers, see Chapter III, "The Policy."

Under excess of loss reinsurance, the reinsurer is only liable to pay if the loss suffered by the reassured exceeds a certain level (known as the "excess point"). The reinsurer is then liable for the excess of the cedant's claim over the excess point, up to the specified limit.

Premium on an excess of loss treaty is frequently calculated by reference to the total premium received by the cedant for the class of risk covered.

Excess of loss contracts are usually treaties covering a whole area of the cedant's business; however, facultative excess of loss contracts are also made.

Stop Loss Reinsurance

The form of stop loss insurance most commonly used protects the cedant against the possibility that his loss ratio will exceed a specified figure. Once his loss ratio has exceeded that figure, the cedant receives reimbursement from the reinsurer. The sum received will reimburse the reassured for a substantial portion of the excess.

Usually, the reinsurer will not make good the whole of the excess, but only a proportion of it; and the contract will be subject to a maximum fixed sum to be paid by the reinsurer, and to limits of loss ratio.

Another form of stop loss reinsurance is the "reinsurance to close" system used to close insurance accounts, for example, at Lloyd's. Under this system, the business of underwriters on a given year of account is reinsured into the next year of account. This exercise is usually done after the former year has run three years. A premium is fixed, taking into account both known losses and losses incurred but not reported ("IBNR"). In exchange for the premium, the second year reinsures the first year in respect of all unpaid losses as at the date of the reinsurance contract.

Facultative Reinsurance

(1) Facultative Reinsurance Methods. There are four principal methods of reinsuring on a facultative basis. These are:
1. Flat line (or first line).
2. Each or line.
3. Part of.
4. Surplus.

Within the foregoing principal methods are certain specific types of reinsurance:
1. Original conditions.
2. Limited terms (e.g., F.P.A. and T.L.O.).

Under the flat line method, the reinsurer reimburses the reassured for all losses up to the flat line, the amount of which is agreed upon, with the reassured retaining all losses in excess of the flat line. It is usually expressed in terms of percentage, either of the reassured's line or of the insured value on which the line is based. Where "signing down" occurs, the flat line reinsurance is not reduced except where the original line is reduced to a percentage which is lower than the flat line reinsurance percentage.[20]

Under the "each or line," a method relating to the hull market and involving original insurances covering fleets of vessels, the direct insurer cedes a flat line reinsurance on each vessel in the fleet up to an agreed amount. If the line on the direct insurance as respects any vessel is less than the flat line, the amount reinsured is limited to the line attaching to that vessel. This enables the reassured to pass on to the reinsurer all of his liability with respect to the low value vessels in the fleet, which is to his advantage because low value vessels tend to have worse claims records than the higher value vessels. The reinsurer can, of course, by the terms of his acceptance, agree to accept only the top value vessels. It is customary in fleet insurances to provide automatic coverage for new vessels joining the fleet.

In reinsurance placed on a "part of" basis, the reinsurer covers part of every loss paid on the direct policy and receives a like proportion of the premium. The reinsurer "follows the fortunes" of the direct insurer in respect to all valid claims presented under the direct policy.

For example, let us assume that the direct insurer takes a 10 percent line on a vessel valued at $1 million. His 10 percent line represents $100,000 of the total agreed value. He reinsures 50 percent of his line on a "part of" basis, on original conditions and at the original rate of premium. It will be seen that the direct insurer has retained 50 percent of the potential liability with the reinsurer bearing the other 50 percent. If we assume a premium of, say, $2,000, the reinsurer would receive one-half of that or the sum of $1,000. If the direct policy is oversubscribed, the direct insurer's line is "signed down" proportionate to the oversubscription. Let us say his line is signed down to 6 percent. His maximum liability under the direct policy would then become $60,000 and that of the reinsurer $30,000. By the same token, the reassured's premium would be $1,200 and the reinsuer's share of the premium would be $600.

Surplus (excess of line) cover operates directly opposite to flat line cover. That is, the reinsurer covers loss only when it exceeds an agreed

<hr/>

20. Signing down is discussed, *infra*. Essentially, it comes about because of the requirement of the London market that signings total 100% of the amount placed by the broker. If the signings, by all underwriters, total more than 100%, the sums subscribed are reduced proportionately.

amount with the reassured retaining all loss that does not reach the retention agreed upon. In this instance, the retained line is not reduced by signing down but the surplus line is reduced. Thus, the reassured would still have to bear his percentage retention but the reinsurer's liability would be reduced proportionately to the amount of the reduction.

The problems involved in signing down are graphically demonstrated in *General Accident Fire and Life Assur. Corp. et al v. Tanter et al.*[21] In that case, a prospective owner desiring to buy a vessel asked his brokers to obtain a quote for suitable insurance. The insurance to be placed by the brokers was to cover all the normal marine perils (a basis misleadingly known as "all risks" insurance). Since some all risks underwriters might wish to reinsure the whole or part of the total loss risk, the brokers obtained a quote from the first defendants, a total loss leading underwriter. Having obtained the first defendant's signature to the slip at an acceptable total loss rate of premium, the broker was then in a position to obtain quotes from some all risks underwriters.

The purchase was made and the brokers confirmed that all coverage requested had been placed. Subsequently, the vessel became a total loss and the all risks underwriters paid promptly. Notification was made to the defendant reinsurers but they refused to pay, contending that since an apparent reinsurance contract had been made by the brokers with an underwriter *before* any original insurance had been placed and before the brokers could have any principal on whose behalf they could place any reinsurance, the lead reinsurer and the following total loss underwriters could not be bound by the lead reinsurer initialing the slip. Alternatively, the reinsurers claimed against the brokers in contract and tort in respect of alleged excessive liability under the reinsurance slip. They argued that the signing indication limited the authority of the brokers to offer reinsurance to one-third and that the signing indication had contractual force as between the all risks underwriters as reassureds and the reinsuring total loss underwriters. The brokers denied any wrongdoing and contended that the signing indication merely had moral significance and no legal significance.

The court held that the slip was the contract between the assured and the T.L.O. underwriters and neither party could contend that part of the contract was to found elsewhere. If something was agreed between the broker and the reinsurance underwriters as part of the contract between the underwriters and the assured it had to be written in the slip. The contract of reinsurance was contained in a slip in exactly the same way as was a contract of original insurance; each reassured was put in a contractual relationship with each reinsurer who agreed to be liable for his proportion of any loss. The slip, together with the brokers advising the primary assured that cover had been obtained, was a binding contract of rein-

21. [1982] 1 Lloyd's Rep. 87.

surance. The reinsurers were liable to the reassureds up to the full amount of their written lines on the total loss slip.

Nonetheless, the brokers (who were also co-defendants) were held liable to the reinsurers for the difference between the actual "signing down" and a one-third signing. As the court stated, the market recognized an obligation on the part of the brokers to use their best efforts to achieve the indicated signing down; there was no reason why a duty of care on the part of the brokers to take such reasonable care should not be recognized, applying *Hedley Byrne & Co. Ltd v. Heller & Partners.*[22]

Facultative Original and Reinsurance Conditions. Hull and cargo policies of all types and their relevant policy conditions are discussed in detail elsewhere in this text. How do these conditions relate to facultative hull and cargo reinsurances?

There are a number of cardinal principles. First, the insurable interest of the direct insurer is commensurate with his liability under the policy. This means that if he has insured on limited conditions he cannot reinsure on full conditions, nor can he reinsure for more than his signed line on the original policy. If the line on the original policy is reduced, so is the reinsurance line by the same proportion, except as noted above, where the reinsurance is placed on a "part of" basis.

Consequently, the direct assurer may reinsure the full original conditions or on limited conditions. It is not uncommon to reinsure the total loss element of the risk and retain partial losses for his own account. In hull insurances, this is termed T.L.O. reinsurance; in cargo insurances, it is termed F.P.A. reinsurance.[23]

Reinsurance as Original. When reinsurance is effected on original conditions, it is customary to begin the clause with something similar to the following:

> "Being a reinsurance of . . . . Subject to the same terms and conditions as the original policy or policies and to pay as may be paid thereon."

The language seems quite clear but nonetheless has caused some confusion. As has been noted, under "Indemnity," *supra,* the obligation to pay as may be paid thereon is subject to the qualification that the reassured was actually liable for the loss for which payment is claimed from the reinsurer.[24] The reinsurance is likely to include a follow clause, the effect of which has already been mentioned.

---

22. [1963] 1 Lloyd's Rep. 485.
23. Whether cargo reinsurances will continue to be termed F.P.A. reinsurance in light of the advent of the new cargo clauses, A, B, and C, remains to be seen.
24. See discussion, *supra,* under subheading "Indemnity" and cases cited n. 10-15.

Of course, the language may be specially constructed and it then becomes the task of the courts to construe it if the parties cannot agree as to its meaning. For example, in *Ins. Co. of N.A. v. Hibernia Ins. Co.*,[25] the open policy issued to the defendant was endorsed:

> "To apply to the excess which the said company may have in all their various policies over $50,000, and to apply prorata with all reinsurance policies on same, but not to exceed $10,000."

The court held that the defendant, who had reinsured with the plaintiff the excess of its risks over $50,000, had the privilege to reinsure the other $50,000 with other companies, and it was not under an obligation to carry $50,000.

In *Boston Ins. Co. v. Globe Fire Ins. Co.*,[26] a reinsurer entered into an agreement to indemnify a reassured to the extent of one-half the reassured's losses by fire on marine risks it then held or might thereafter take during the life of the insurance contract. It was held that such a contract was not a wager policy but was governed by the laws and usages of marine insurance and was in the nature of an open policy, which, by such laws and usage, was valid. The court held that the validity of the open policy was not affected by the fact that it contained no stipulation for notice by the reassured of the policies it subsequently issued under the arrangement.

Hull T.L.O. Reinsurance Conditions. In the London market, a specialized form of hull T.L.O. reinsurance has attained common usage. The form will give some idea of how the market operates. It reads:

> This insurance is against the risks of total &/or constructive total loss of vessel only—
> To follow original underwriters in the event of a compromised or arranged total loss being settled,
> No salvage charges. No sue and labour,
> Negligence, Valuation, Sale & F.C.& S. clause as original,
> Continuation clause, extensions and agreements as original but with or without notice.
> Returns pro-rata as original, but No Lay-up returns.
> Original warranties and one half or scale additional premiums or held covered.
> Reinsurance Waiver Clause.

From the first sentence, it is clear that what is being covered is total loss only.

25. 140 U.S. 565 (1891).
26. 174 Mass. 229, 54 N.E. 543 (St. Mass. 1899).

In the absence of the second sentence, T.L.O. reinsurers would only have to pay in the event of the reassured being liable to pay a constructive or actual total loss. The effect of the second sentence is to compel T.L.O. reinsurers to pay their reassured in the event of a contentious actual or constructive total loss, irrespective of whether the reassured pays a full total loss, or pays a lesser sum on the basis of a compromised or arranged total loss.

The next sentence regarding no salvage and no sue and labor is clear and to the point. While one would normally think that a reinsurer would be liable for salvage and sue and labor if such charges were incurred to prevent a total loss, this is not always the case as was decided in *Uzielli v. Boston Marine*, discussed *supra*, and the sentence is designed to clarify any doubt about the matter.

"Negligence, Valuation, Sale and F.C. & S. clause as original" tells the reinsurer that the reinsurance will follow the terms of the original insurance in the respects mentioned. For example, the original policy may contain the liner negligence clause which is broader in scope than the customary Inchmaree Clause. The Valuation Clause is standard in hull policies and is necessary in the accepted method of determining a constructive total loss. Naturally, the reinsurer wants this clause included in the contract of reinsurance. The "sale" clause is simply a shorthand method of incorporating the change of management warranty in the reinsurance contract. Consequently, if the original insurer can avoid liability if there is a change of management or ownership or flag, the reinsurer has the same rights of termination as the reassured had on the original. Upon a lapse of the original policy, there would be an obligation for return of premium. The "returns" provision allows the reassured to recover a pro rata return of premiums from his reinsurer. All hull policies in use contain an F.C. & S. Clause, excluding war risks, and this language merely incorporates similar provisions into the reinsurance.

The "continuation clause, extensions and agreements but with or without notice" is necessary because incorporation of original conditions into the reinsurance gives the reinsurer the right to receive notice if such clauses are operative under the original policy. In the absence of the phrase, "with or without notice," such notice to the reinsurer would be necessary. It will be recalled that in general the only form of automatic continuance in original hull policies is that where the vessel is in distress, or in a port of refuge on the expiration date of the policy. By notifying the original insurer, the vessel owner can secure an extension by paying an additional premium. In practice, it would appear unusual for the original insurer not to confer with the reinsurer with respect to any extensions or agreements which might affect coverage for the risks insured against.

"Returns pro rata as original, but no lay-up returns" makes the reinsurer liable to make a refund of part of the premium where, for example, the original policy is cancelled due to a change of management or by mutual consent of the original assured and the original assurer. The reference to "no lay-up returns" makes an exception for lay-up returns. Since in most hull policies, the purpose of lay-up is to reduce *partial* losses during the period of lay-up, and in the event of a total loss, earned lay-up returns are forfeited anyway, a return premium for lay-up is really being allowed for a reduction in the partial loss risk rather than the total loss risk.

"Original warranties and one half or scale additional premiums or held covered" is nothing more than a shorthand method of telling the reinsurer that he will be bound to follow with respect to liberties granted by such warranties in the original policy with respect to navigation, trade, cargo, or towage, where the vessel owner notifies the original insurer and an additional premium is arranged. As the reinsurer is on the risk for T.L.O. only, he not entitled to the full additional premium when the original insurance is on broader conditions.

The "Reinsurance Waiver Clause" refers to a scheme at Lloyd's to obviate the bookkeeping and accounting tasks involved in settling up with respect to small additional premiums or return premiums which fall under the minimum agreed upon in the policy.

Cargo F.P.A. Reinsurance. It would logically seem that if one could write T.L.O. reinsurance on hulls, one could do so with respect to cargo. However, this is not the case because there are fundamental differences between hull coverages and cargo coverages.

The standard clause published by the Institute of London Underwriters reads:

> Being a reinsurance of _____ and to pay as may be paid on the original policy or policies, but only such claims as would be recoverable under the standard English form of marine policy with Institute Cargo Clauses (F.P.A.) attached.[27]

From the clear language of the clause, it is patent that the form can be used to reinsure an original policy on broader terms (such as "all risk" and "with average"—or to use the newer terminology, forms "A" and "B") but the reinsurance cover cannot be greater than that provided by F.P.A. cargo insurance. Of course, the original policy can be in broader terms than customary or the conditions may vary from the standard conditions.

27. It is likely, of course, that the form of the clause will have to be amended in light of the new London cargo clauses where form "C" corresponds most closely with the former F.P.A. Institute Clauses.

Here, the appropriate language to use would be "subject to all terms and conditions as original."[28]

It should also be emphasized that the term "as original" means as originally written by the original insurer. Unless the reinsurer agrees, he is not bound by an alteration of conditions by the original assured and original reassured *after* the inception of the original policy.[29]

Open Cover Reinsurance. Open cover reinsurances are discussed, generally, *supra.* The discussion which follows takes up the subject in more detail.

There are three basic situations in which open reinsurance cover is desirable and fits a commercial need. These are:

1. Open cover reinsurance procured by a direct insurer, either directly or through a broker, to cover the whole or part of each declaration under an open cover granted by the direct insurer;

2. Open cover reinsurance contracts negotiated by a broker for himself to take care of risks of specified categories which would otherwise have to be placed facultatively; and

3. Open cover reinsurance between a reassured and a reinsurer to handle declared risks which do not fall within the parameters of existent treaties but for which reinsurance protection is considered necessary.

Direct Insurance Open Cover. As noted before, an open cover is advantageous to a shipper because he can better cost his goods as he knows, in advance, essentially what his premium costs will be. He also will know that his goods will not commence their transit without there being insurance coverage. Here, however, the principle of utmost good faith applies with all vigor, and the merchant or shipper must declare every shipment which comes within the scope of the cover. He cannot pick and choose; he cannot shop around and place a desirable risk with other underwriters at a lower rate or on better terms. The underwriter, by the same token, is obliged, in good faith, to accept every valid declaration even if a loss has occurred before the declaration is made.

---

28. Where the original terms and conditions are substantially similar to standard market terms and conditions with which the market is generally familiar, the clauses need not be set out in full. *Joyce v. Realm Ins. Co.,* (1872) 41 L.J.Q.B. 356. But where the original terms and conditions are substantially different from those normally to be expected, the difference may be material and should be disclosed when the contract is concluded. *Property Ins. Co. v. National Protector Ins. Co. Ltd.,* (1913) 108 T.L.R. 104, 12 Asp. M.L.C. 287.

29. *Norwich Union Fire Ins. Soc. Ltd. v. Colonial Mutual Fire Ins. Co.,* [1922] 2 K.B. 461, 91 L.J.K.B. 881; *Nicholas Ins. Co. v. The Merchants' Mutual Fire & M. Ins. Co.,* 83 N.Y. 604 (St. N.Y. 1880); *Maritime Ins. Co. v. Sterns,* (1901) 2 K.B. 912; *Fire Ins. Ass'n Ltd. v. Canada F. & M. Ins. Co.,* 2 Ont. 481 (Can.). It goes without saying, of course, that neither the reassured nor the reassurer can make a change in the contract of an original assured without such assured's consent. *Southern Surety Co. v. Equitable Surety Co.,* 84 Okla. 23, 202 P. 295 (St. Okla. 1921); *Pacific Mutual Life Ins. Co. of California v. Pacific Surety Co.,* 182 Cal. 555, 189 P. 273 (St. Cal. 1930).

It should be noted, however, that not all cessions under an open cover are on an obligatory basis. This depends upon the terms and conditions of the open cover contract of reinsurance. Those terms and conditions will dictate whether or not the reassured is required to cede an item and, if ceded, whether it must be of the whole amount. While the duty to cede and to accept is obligatory when the reinsurance contract is on a "flat line" basis or "part of" basis, the reinsurance contract may be effected on a "surplus" basis to which different rules apply, as will be seen.

Cancellation Clauses. In modern practice, open covers usually commence on a specific date and remain open indefinitely—until and unless cancelled.

Under a cancellation clause both the underwriter and the assured may cancel by giving prescribed notice, usually upon 30 days (less for war). The same rules apply with respect to cancellation between the reassured and the reassurer, but it is customary to make the notice period somewhat longer. This is primarily to permit the broker time to effect a replacement.

Where items are covered and in transit (at risk) at the time of notice of cancellation, the items continue to be covered notwithstanding the notice until termination of transit.

Many policies provide for automatic termination notice on the anniversary date of the policy. Many reinsurers will, in the case of a policy of indefinite duration, write the risk and, at the same time, give notice to cancel at the anniversary date ("NCAD"). This is not convenient from the standpoint of assured or broker as it requires a reminder system to ensure that either the notice is withdrawn or a new cover effected with different underwriters. The advantage to underwriters is that the notice to cancel gives them a right to choose whether or not to continue with the contract after it has run for a year.

Coverage Limits. Almost all contracts of insurance (London P & I cover being a notable exception) contain, in one form or another, some limitation of coverage. In open policies on cargo, this is usually a maximum limit insured while being carried in one vessel, termed a "limit per bottom." This may also be coupled with a limit on accumulation of shipments at any one port and here the underwriter will insert a "location clause." This supplements the limit per bottom and is usually a multiple thereof.

Conveyances. Neither the direct underwriter nor the reinsurer has any control over what conveyance the shipper/assured uses to transport the goods. Of course, the open cover may specifically exclude certain types of conveyances, for example, transport by open scows or barges in which case the shipper has no coverage at all should he elect to ship by a forbidden conveyance.

Ships and vessels come in all sizes, configurations, and states of condition. In practice, the cargo underwriter is vitally concerned with such matters as: age of the vessel; whether or not it is classed; under what flag it operates; who owns it; and who manages the vessel. Under a facultative arrangement, the underwriter may reject the proposal for insurance or opt to charge a higher premium. But under an open cover, the underwriter must accept all valid declarations and he is not in a position to consider each risk separately or to assess it on the basis of the vessel being used, etc. To meet this problem, it is common to use a "classification clause," the effect of which is to charge a higher premium to shipments being carried on vessels which do not meet the requirements of the classification clause.

It is impossible to set forth in any detail the myriad indicia which the classification clause may include. For example, it may require the payment of an additional premium where the vessel is not on a regular trading pattern (a "tramp") and is over 15 years of age. Or, the vessel may be on a regular trading pattern but be over 25 years of age. Or, it may be a chartered vessel over 15 years old.

In most instances, premiums under a classification clause are based on an agreed market scale which takes into account such matters as the flag of the vessel, the operator of the vessel, the type of vessel, etc. Moreover, the nature of the coverage has a bearing on the premium; i.e., coverage on a F.P.A. basis would naturally be less in premium than coverage on an all risks basis, as would the corresponding reinsurance premium.

Original Open Cover—Schedules

Under an open cargo cover, schedules are usually incorporated which set forth a schedule of premium rates applicable to the various types of commodities being shipped. The schedules may well include amounts of maximum cover for particular categories of goods. Where the merchant/ assured is a major shipper, the schedules can be extraordinarily complex and extensive.

Declarations, Policies and Certificates. In practice under an open cover, the merchant supplies a declaration to the original insurer for each shipment as it is booked. Pursuant to agreement, the merchant is empowered to issue "certificates" of insurance as to each shipment which, of course, eliminates the need for a formal policy in each instance. In any event, the reinsurer is not interested in the individual certificates and does not, in turn, issue certificates to the original insurer.

As has been noted heretofore, from time to time, the original assurer may be called upon to honor a declaration which exceeds the cover limit in his open cover issued to the merchant/assured. Normally, the reassured cannot cede this in full to his reinsurer. Although this would be patently true where there is a 100 percent reinsurance, it may be that the reinsurance was effected on part of the reassured's line rather than the whole.

Take this example:

1. Original open cover

   Limit per bottom   U.S. $1,000,000
   Reassured's line   10%

2. Reinsurer's open cover

   Terms and conditions as per original
   Reinsured line   5% part of 10%

3. Declaration under original open cover

   Original insurer accepts declaration of U.S. 1,200,000 which exceeds his limit by $200,000.

4. Cession under reinsurance contract

   5% (part of 10%) of original cover limit $50,000.

It will be seen that the original insurer has no coverage under his reinsurance for the $20,000 accepted above and beyond his cover limit. Either he must renegotiate with his reinsurer or place the excess facultatively.

Broker's Open Covers, Line Slips, and Binding Authorities. Just as brokers of original placement find a series of facultative coverages time consuming and burdensome, so does a reinsurance broker. Consequently, if possible, he will seek to arrange an open cover reinsurance contract with a reinsurer under which he will attempt to establish the maximum probable limits which he might require for any one risk and arrange an open cover on that basis.[30]

Alternatively, he may arrange a line slip. If the broker has binding authority, he may accept the risk under the authority. Interesting questions arise as to the nature and extent of the broker's duties in ceding risks under open cover and binding authorities as regards the duty to disclose material information to reinsurers, the conflicting duties the broker may owe to cedants and reinsurers, and the effects of non-disclosure.

---

30. For a detailed discussion of the mechanics of broker's open covers, see *Marine Reinsurance*, by Robert Brown and Peter Reed, Witherby & Co. Ltd., London (1981).

Treaty Reinsurance

A treaty reinsurance, as previously discussed, is merely a long term binding agreement between the original (or ceding) underwriter and a reinsurer under which the ceding underwriter agrees to reinsure, and the reinsurer agrees to accept, all business coming *within the scope of the wording of the treaty within prearranged limits.*

One court described them as follows:

> . . . A reinsurance treaty is merely an agreement between two insurance companies whereby one agrees to cede and the other to accept reinsurance business pursuant to the provisions specified in the treaty. Reinsurance treaties and reinsurance policies are not synonymous: reinsurance treaties are contracts *for* insurance, and reinsurance policies are contracts *of* insurance.[31]

One form of treaty reinsurance is quota share. Under this form, the ceding underwriter retains a percentage of the business of a particular class with the balance being reinsured with the treaty underwriters up to a specified limit. For example, an 80 percent cargo quota share treaty would be one in which the reinsurer would accept 80 percent of the cargo coverages written by the original underwriter. Should the original underwriter be entitled to reinsure, for example, a top limit of $50,000, the treaty underwriters would be obliged to take 80 percent of the original risk written up to $50,000, or the sum of $40,000 while the original underwriter retains $10,000. Obviously, the reinsurer participates in claims to the extent of 80 percent. If the original underwriter accepts more than the $50,000 limit, he will seek facultative cover (in most instances) for the excess.

Alternatively, the reinsurance treaty may be one carried out on a surplus, or "excess of line" basis. Here, the ceding underwriter retains entirely the risk being underwritten up to a further defined limit. This may take the form of separate layers or steps in which case each step or layer is numbered consecutively; i.e., the first step would be called the First Surplus, the second the Second Surplus, and so on. Once a risk has been ceded to a surplus treaty, claims are shared between reinsured and reinsurer in proportion to the size of their lines.

Originally, treaty reassureds were expected to submit, in their periodic accounts, details of every risk ceded under the treaty. A single page of such information was termed a "bordereau." Several such sheets

---

31. *Pioneer Life Ins. Co. v. Alliance Life Ins. Co.*, 374 Ill. 576, 30 N.E. 66 (St. Ill. 1940); see, also, *Maurer v. International Reinsurance Corp.*, 74 A.2d 822 (St. Del. 1950).

were of course "bordereaux." The examination and review of such sheets was time consuming and, in many instances, non-productive. Consequently, the practice of submitting bordereaux has largely ceased but the original underwriter must still keep the required records which are available for inspection by the reinsurer. While this has eliminated the necessity for much bookkeeping on the part of the reinsurer's claims staff, it will be seen that the utmost good faith is a prerequisite on the part of the ceding underwriters.

Although it is simpler to deal with most treaties on an accounting basis, from time to time the cedant will require most prompt payment of larger losses. These are termed "cash losses" and some provision has to made with respect to their payment.

A typical clause governing their payment would read substantially as follows:

> Whenever the amount of a loss falling to be borne by this Treaty amounts to $5,000 or more or the equivalent in other currencies the Reinsurer shall pay its proportion of the amount due within 14 days after receiving notification thereof from the Company and if requested by the Company to do so.

Disputes. Disputes can and do arise between ceding companies and their reinsurers. These are most frequently settled by way of arbitration which is probably one reason why there are relatively so few court cases involving reinsurance. An arbitration clause in a reinsurance treaty is very common and is frequently worded most broadly, with the arbitrators given the power to "receive and act upon such evidence whether oral or written strictly admissible or not as [they] in their discretion think fit." Another clause which attracted the attention of the courts was worded as follows:

> The Arbitrators and Umpire are relieved from all judicial formalities and may abstain from following the strict rules of the law. They shall settle any dispute under this Agreement according to an equitable rather than a strictly legal interpretation of its terms, and their decision shall be final and not subject to appeal.

Such a clause was construed in *Orion Compania Espanola de Seguros v. Belfort Maatschappij Voor Algemene Verzegringeen,*[32] where the court held that the parties could not make a question of law any less a question of law by agreeing that a decision should be rendered on the basis of some extra-legal criterion. However, in *Eagle Star Ins. Co. Ltd. v. Yuval Ins. Co. Ltd.,*[33] the court felt that such a provision was reasonable and had the effect of

32. [1962] 2 Lloyd's Rep. 257.
33. [1978] 1 Lloyd's Rep. 357.

not ousting the court of jurisdiction but only eliminating technicalities and strict legal constructions.

A typical arbitration clause in an American treaty of reinsurance is as follows:

> Should an irreconcilable difference of opinion arise as to the interpretation of this Contract, it is hereby mutually agreed that such difference shall be submitted to arbitration, one arbiter to be chosen by the COMPANY, one by the REINSURER, and an umpire to be chosen by the two arbiters before they enter upon arbitration. The decision of the arbiters shall be final and binding upon both parties, but failing to agree they shall call in the umpire and the decision of the majority shall be final and binding upon both parties. Each party shall bear the expense of its own arbiter, and shall jointly and equally bear with the other the expense of the umpire and of the arbitration. Any such arbitration shall take place in _____ unless some other location is mutually agreed upon by the two parties.

Under English law, such an arbitration clause could not survive the avoidance of the contract or its termination through its breach. It is a moot point whether it is possible to draft an arbitration clause which does survive such events.

Excess of Loss Reinsurance. Under this method of reinsurance, the reassured retains a predetermined amount of loss with respect to any one casualty or event, and the reinsurer pays all losses which exceed the stipulated figure but only up to an agreed limit. This is a simple but extremely effective method of reinsuring against losses of a catastrophic nature, such as hurricanes, earthquakes, fires, floods, or casualties involving vessels and cargoes of great value, though the method is also used in other circumstances.

A typical insuring clause of an excess of loss treaty would read:

> The Reinsurer shall pay to the Company the amount of its ultimate net loss as hereinafter defined in excess of $ _____ arising out of any one occurrence _____ provided always that the liability of the Reinsurer shall not exceed $ _____ with respect to any one occurrence.

It is apparent from the foregoing that it would be possible, by reason of his retention, for a reassured to incur very considerable liabilities. By the same token, depending upon the amount of the losses and the retention of the reassured, the reinsurer could equally be exposed to a great loss. The secret lies in maintaining a well-balanced portfolio where the exposure is not disproportionately great in relation to the premium income.

There is a great variety of marine insurance risks. These are categorized in logical subdivisions such as war, cargo, hull, total loss only, P & I, etc. These various risks compose the reassured's portfolio. The reassured may elect to procure excess of loss protection for any one of the categories, or, he may decide to lump them together under his "whole account."

In the event of a truly catastrophic event, such as Hurricane Agnes in 1972, a reassured could suffer losses in a number of specific accounts such that the aggregate loss exceeds the agreed priority. Where the cover is on the whole account, the number of claims arising from the same event could be devastating.

Referring to the terms of the excess of loss insuring clause, it will be seen that reference is necessarily made with respect to "any one occurrence." The phrase "any one event" is also frequently used. The term is very difficult to define in particular circumstances and has occasioned much difficulty. For example, suppose that a vessel suffers an explosion but, after heroic efforts, the situation is brought under control. However, two weeks later a second explosion occurs and the vessel is a total loss. Should the two explosions be treated as separate occurrences or one event? As will be seen, the problems can become acute. It is a tribute to the profession that most of these perplexing questions are settled amicably by arbitration.

Again referring to the insuring clause quoted above, it will be observed that the reinsurer obligates himself to pay to the reassured the amount of its "ultimate net loss." That term is always defined in a treaty. It is often defined as the sum actually paid by the reassured in settlement of losses, after deducting for all recoveries, salvage, and claims upon other reinsurances. It includes, as one might expect, all adjustment expenses arising from the settlement of claims other than fixed costs such as office expense and salaries of the staff.[33a] Credit is often given for salvage recoveries.

It is not uncommon, in excess of loss reinsurances, to find that coverage is divided into a number of consecutive "layers." For example, the first layer could be $1 million excess of $750,000. The second layer could be $2 million excess of $1,750,000, and so on.

The upper layers would not, of course, be called upon to pay if recoveries obtained by the reassured under the lower layers were to be treated as reinsurance recoveries in arriving at the ultimate net loss. This is usually solved by including a provision that the reassured is to have the benefit of any recoveries under any underlying excess of loss reinsurance protecting the same account and covered by the same contract wording.

33a. Defined in *Stickel v. Excess Ins. Co. of America*, 23 N.E. 2d 839 (St. Ohio 1939).

Logically, where a loss occurs and is paid, the amount paid should reduce the amount of the cover remaining. For example, if the policy runs
for one year and, six months into that year, a major loss is incurred and
paid, this event would substantially consume the total cover. This possibility is usually allowed for by an agreement for automatic reinstatement
of the cover, with or without the payment of more premium. A maximum
number of reinstatements is usually specified.

While excess cover may be used by a reassured, the reassured must
exercise good faith in dealing with the reinsurer and this involves infor-
ming the reinsurer of any action taken in this connection so that the reinsurers will have knowledge of the reassured's retention under a treaty.

For example, in *Northwestern Mut. Fire Ass'n v. Union Mutual Fire Ins.
Co. of Providence*,[34] the reinsurance contract obligated the ceding company to a retention of not less than the sum ceded to the reinsurer. The
ceding company ceded $50,000 of reinsurance on a bridge but actually
retained only $32,000 because of the existence of an excess of loss insur-
ance contract. The reinsurer was held entitled to an adjustment of liability for damage to the bridge, reducing its liability to $32,000. The
court observed that the ceding company that made the investigation and
possessed all the details relating to the risk was obliged to exercise the
utmost good faith in all its dealings with the reinsurer.

In the matter of cessions, the reassured must be fair. He must be prepared to share his good business with the reassurer and not saddle him
merely with bad business. The reassured should parcel out his business in
such a fashion that a fair profit results to the reinsurer and in a bad year
the reassured can then expect to be assisted by the reinsurer. Thus, a reinsurer should be informed by the reassured as to the amount of the insurance the reassured is retaining for his own account and if the reassured
ceases to hold that retention before the reinsurance is completed, the reinsurance contract may be voidable.[35]

Stop Loss Reinsurance. Although excess of loss reinsurance enables the ceding underwriter to restrict his net liability on individual events to a predetermined level, nonetheless an influx of claims could still result in a
high claims ratio in any particular underwriting year. Stop loss insurance
is one method for limiting the loss ratio to an *agreed percentage of the premium income.*

A typical stop loss provision could read as follows:

> This reinsurance is to pay the net excess liability arising on the 1987
> marine underwriting year of account excess of an underwriting settle-

---

34. 144 F.2d 274 (9th Cir. 1944).
35. See *Foster v. Mentor Life,* [1854] 3 E.&B. 48; *Traill v. Baring,* [1864] 33 L.J. Ch. 521.

ment of 92% and is to indemnify the reinsured up to 30% of the reinsured's net premium income, or $90,000, whichever is the greater.

The reinsurer shall only be liable if and when the ultimate net loss sustained by the reinsured in respect of the above mentioned year of account exceeds an aggregate amount equal to 92% of the net premium income received by them which shall be determined by a comparison of net premiums and net claims as defined.

The agreement will define the net premiums and net claims and generally provide that the premium for the stop loss reinsurance is not to be taken into account nor any recovery which is made under that contract.

Defenses Available to Reinsurer

Generally speaking, a reinsurer may, in the absence of a follow clause, avail himself of every defense which could have been asserted by the reassured. When a reassured makes a claim against a reinsurer for reimbursement, he may well be met with defenses which he should have asserted against the original assured. This is so because the reinsurer is liable only for the amount which the reassured was under a duty to pay.[36] The effect of follow clauses has been discussed *supra*.

For example, in *Commercial Standard Ins. Co. v. Fidelity Union Ins. Co.*,[37] the reinsurer contracted to insure a reassured against loss to the extent of one-fourth of the reassured's liability under a syndicate contract, the purpose of which was to provide reciprocal insurance among the members of the syndicate (which was insuring cotton). It was held that the reinsurer could be held liable for only the legal liability of the reassured and not for any losses assumed by the reassured and other members of the syndicate because of the insolvency of one of its members.

36. *Eagle Ins. Co. v. Lafayette Ins. Co.*, 9 Ind. 443 (St. Ind. 1857); *New York etc. Ins. Co. v. Protection Ins. Co.*, 18 F.Cas. 160 (C.C.D. Mass. 1841); *Delaware Ins. Co. v. Quaker City Ins. Co.*, 3 Grant Cas. (Pa.) 71 (1859); *Hastie v. De Peyster*, 3 Caines 190 (St. N.Y. 1805); *Merchants M. Ins. Co. v. New Orleans Ins. Co.*, 224 La.Ann. 305 (St. La. 1872) (reassured paid a total loss; reinsurer held to be liable for only a partial loss because the loss paid by the reassured was, in fact, only a partial loss); *Yukon*, 1939 AMC 111 (Arb.); *Gurney v. Grimmer*, (1932) 38 Com.Cas. 7; *Firemen's Fund Ins. Co. v. Western Australian Ins. Co.*, (1927) 33 Com.Cas. 36 (reinsurer successfully defended on grounds the vessel was unseaworthy although the reassured did not assert the defense); *Chippendale v. Holt*, (1895) 65 L.J.Q.B. 104; *Merchants' Mar. Ins. Co. v. Liverpool Mar. and General Ins. Co.*, (1928) 33 Com.Cas. 294; *Western Assur. Co. of Toronto v. Poole*, (1903) 1 K.B. 376, 9 Asp. M.L.C. 390; *Martin v. Steamship Owners' Underwriting Ass'n*, (1902) 7 Com.Cas. 195; *Commercial Standard Ins. Co. v. Fidelity Union Ins. Co.*, 111 S.W.2d 1167 (St. Tex. 1937) (reinsurer not liable for losses assumed by the reinsured syndicate because of the insolvency of one of its members); *American Eagle F.I. Co. v. Eagle Star Ins. Co.*, 216 F.2d 176, 1954 AMC 1263 (9th Cir.); *National Mar. Ins. Co. of Australia v. Halfrey*, (1879) 5 V.L.R. 226 (Aus.). Cf. *China Union v. Amer. Marine*, 1985 AMC 1643 (2d Cir.) (lack of insurable interest held no defense).
37. *Id.*, n. 36.

In *American Eagle F. I. Co. v. Eagle Star Ins. Co.*,[38] the reinsurance contract contained a warranty that a Columbia River pilot would be in charge of the tug and barges used to carry the lumber cargo which had been reinsured. The barges were wrecked while being towed across the Columbia River bar without the services of a Columbia River pilot. The original insurer incurred expenses in attempting to salve the cargo and in unsuccessfully prosecuting a claim against the towing tug. The reinsurers apparently reimbursed the original assured for the amount of the cargo loss notwithstanding the breach of warranty but were held not liable for the additional expenses. The payment of the cargo loss could not be construed as an admission of further liability for such additional expenses.

The classic example is *Firemen's Fund Ins. Co. v. Western Australian Ins. Co.*,[39] where the reinsurer successfully defended on grounds that the vessel was unseaworthy although the reassured had not asserted that defense against the original assured.

If an original insurance is illegal for want of an insurable interest, it follows that all reinsurances are tainted with that illegality and are illegal and void.[40]

Contracts of reinsurance may also be avoided on grounds of fraud or mistake, just as any other contract, but the privilege of rescinding may be lost by waiver.[41] Retention of premiums after learning of a mistaken cession of risks greater than those contemplated in a treaty may also constitute a waiver.[42]

Fraudulent misrepresentations or concealment by a reassured as to the nature of a risk will entitle the reinsurer to avoid the contract of reinsurance notwithstanding the fact that the reassured remains liable to the original assured. As noted heretofore, the reassured is under a duty to disclose all details concerning the risk to the reinsurer. Any fact that is material to an underwriter and likely to influence his judgment in accepting the risk or fixing the premium should be disclosed. The Supreme Court in *Sun Mutual Insurance Co. v. Ocean Ins. Co.*[43] stated the rule very succinctly, as follows:

> In respect to the duty of disclosing all material facts, the case of reinsurance does not differ from that of an original insurance. The obligation in both cases is uberrimae fidei. The duty of communication,

38. *Id.*, n. 36.

39. *Id.*, n. 36.

40. *Re London County Commercial Reinsurance Office, Ltd.*, [1922] 2 Ch. 67.

41. *Commonwealth Mutual Fire Ins. Co. v. Eagle Fire Ins. Co.*, 163 Pa.Sup. 163 (1948); *Munich Reinsurance Co. v. Surety Co.*, 113 Md. 200 (St. Md. 1910).

42. *Commonwealth Mutual Fire. Ins. Co. v. Eagle Fire Ins. Co.*, 163 Pa.Sup. 163 (1948).

43. 107 U.S. 485 (1882); see, also, *A/S Ivarans v. P.R. Ports Auth.*, 617 F.2d 903, 1982 AMC 2493 (1st Cir.); and *New Zealand Ins. Co. v. South Australian Ins. Co.*, (1878) 1 S.C.R. (N.S.) (N.S.W.) 214 (Aus.).

indeed, is independent of the intention, and is violated by the fact of concealment even where there is no design to deceive. The exaction of information in some instances may be greater in the case of reinsurance than as between the parties to an original insurance.

Cancellation and Rectification

Policies of reinsurance may, of course, be cancelled where both parties consent. A reinsurer may cancel his policy when the policy of original insurance has come to an end. It should be emphasized, however, that if the reinsurer desires to cancel, he must make an unconditional demand to that effect or take direct action leading to that result. A mere expression of a desire to cancel is not sufficient.[44]

If the instrument embodying the agreement does not contain the true contract between the parties, the policy may be modified or amended to conform to the true intent of the parties under the legal principle of rectification or reformation.[45]

Avoidance, Forfeiture, and Conditions

The most common ground of avoidance or forfeiture is, of course, a breach of warranty. The language of the policy will determine whether words used constitute a warranty or merely a condition. Fulfillment of the warranty is a condition precedent to the underwriter's liability and if the warranty is not fulfilled, the underwriter is not liable.[46]

Increase of Risk

Many contracts of reinsurance are so constructed that they are subject to all the terms and conditions of the original policy of insurance existing between the assured and the reassured. The terms may grant to the reassured the right to assent or agree to reasonable changes requested by the original assured which do not increase the risk to the reinsurer. The reinsurer is obliged to follow along with the changes the reassured may make. If, of course, the policy permits a change with the written permission or

44. *Petersburg Sav. & Ins. Co. v. Manhattan Fire Ins. Co.*, 66 Ga. 446 (St. Ga. 1881); *Delaware Underwriters of West Chester Fire Co. v. National Union F. Ins. Co.*, 60 Pa.Sup. 325 (St. Pa. 1915); *Northwestern Fire & Marine Ins. Co. v. Connecticut Fire Ins. Co. of Hartford*, 117 N.W. 825, 105 Minn. 483 (St. Minn. 1908); *Tokio Marine & F. Ins. Co. v. National Union F. Ins. Co.*, 91 F.2d 964 (2d Cir. 1937); *Diamond T. Utah, Inc. v. Canal Ins. Co.*, 361 P.2d 665 (St. Utah 1961).
45. *Gullett v. Evans et al*, (1929) 35 Ll.L.Rep. 239.
46. *Bancroft v. Heath*, 6 Com.Cas. 137, 17 T.L.R. 425; *Central State Life Ins. Co. v. Employers' Indemnity Corp.*, 67 S.W.2d 543 (St. Mo. 1934).

consent of the reassured and the reassured gives his consent, then the re-insurer is bound by it.[47]

The changes must not, however, increase the risk to the reinsurer. If the reinsurer's liability is increased or prejudiced by the reassured, then the reinsurer may defend on this ground.[48]

For example, in *North British & Mercantile Ins. Co. Ltd. v. Ullman*,[49] the reinsuring companies accepted a risk in reinsuring the primary under-writers under a builders' risks policy covering 24 hulls that were war-ranted to be laid prior to May 22, 1943. As of May 22, 1943, only seven hulls had been laid at which time the reinsurance underwriter was ap-proached for a new binder which stated it was cancelling and replacing a provisional application dated May 25, 1942, and the binder was granted. The new binder, dated May 22, 1943, was identical to that placed May 25, 1942, except that it excluded the seven vessels whose hulls had been laid prior to May 26, 1943, and provided "warranted keels of all vessels be laid prior to May 22, 1944."

The question before the arbitrators was as to commissions due, and whether these risks, even though the keels were laid after May 22, 1944, were "accepted" prior to July 1, 1943, within the meaning of the reinsur-ing agreement between the parties.

In ruling that the risks had been accepted, the arbitrators stated in part:

> . . . while it is quite customary to issue builders' risk binders with a limitation as to the time during which risk may attach, yet this is customarily enforced only where there is a material change in the risks and conditions. Such a limitation is customarily treated as a safety de-vice inserted by the underwriter and it is customary and usual to make reasonable extensions of time when required, particularly where it can be foreseen, as here, that such extensions of time will be required. . . . We feel, therefore, that under the accepted custom in our busi-ness, the word "accepted" is broad enough to cover these risks under this extension.

If the reassured is to avoid a denial of liability on the part of the rein-surer, he must always communicate fully to the reinsurer the details of all policy changes or variations made with respect to all matters that may al-ter or have a material bearing on the risk.[50]

47. *Faneuil Hall Ins. Co. v. Liverpool*, 153 Mass. 63 (St. Mass. 1891); *North British and Merc. v. Ullman*, 1946 AMC 1622 (Arb.).
48. *St. Nicholas Ins. Co. v. The Merchants' Mutual Fire & M. Ins. Co.*, 83 N.Y. 604 (St. N.Y. 1880).
49. 1946 AMC 1622 (Arb.).
50. *Lower Rhine etc. Ins. v. Sedgwick*, (1899) 1 Q.B. 179; *Maritime Ins. Co. v. Sterns*, (1901) 2 K.B. 912; *Norwich U.F. Ins. Co. v. Mutual Fire Ins. Co. Ltd.*, (1922) 2 K.B. 461; *Fire Ins. Ass'n Ltd. v. Canada F. & M. Ins. Co.*, 2 Ont. 481 (Can.).

Subrogation by Reinsurer

A reinsurer, settling a claim, is entitled to subrogation to any right which the original assured and the reassured may have had in respect of the loss.[51] It has been held in the United States that the reassured may bring suit in his own name for the full amount of the subrogated rights but the recovery will be for the interests of its reinsurers and for its own interests, respectively, as the same may appear.[52]

The reinsurer as a matter of course has an interest in any salvage realized by the reassured and the right to insist that it be carefully and prudently managed.[53]

For example, in *Universal Ins. Co. v. Old Time Molasses Co.*,[54] the reinsurer reinsured the reassured to the extent of one-half of its losses arising out of an insurance contract by which the latter company had insured a cargo of molasses of the Molasses Company. The reassured paid the loss of the Molasses Company and the reinsurer paid the reassured. The reinsurer contended that it became subrogated to the rights of the Molasses Company against any vessel or person whatsoever and to receive from such person or vessel damages up to one-half the amount thereof. Citing *Liverpool & Great Western Steam Co. v. Phoenix Ins. Co.*,[55] the court agreed and held that the reinsurer was entitled to be subrogated to the original assured's right of action against the vessel or its owner for the loss.

Taxation and Non-Admitted Reinsurance Companies

If the fundamental principle of spreading risks as widely as possible is to remain viable, that principle should transcend national and other govern-

---

51. *Universal Ins. Co. v. Old Time Molasses Co. et al*, 46 F.2d 925 (5th Cir. 1931); *National Surety Co. v. Mass. Bonding Co.*, 19 F.2d 488; *Assicurazioni Generali di Trieste v. Empress Assur. Corp.*, (1907) 2 K.B. 814.

52. *Maryland Casualty Co. v. City of Cincinnati et al*, 291 F. 895 (S.D. Ohio 1923).

53. *Delaware Ins. Co. v. The Quaker City Ins. Co.*, 3 Grant's (Pa.) Cases 71 (1859); *Iowa Bonding & Cas. Co. v. Wagner*, 210 N.W. 775, 203 Iowa 179 (St. Iowa 1926); *Globe National F. Ins. Co. v. American Bonding & Cas. Co.*, 195 N.W. 728 (St. Iowa 1923).

54. 46 F.2d 925 (5th Cir. 1931). Compare, however, *Young v. Merchants M. Ins. Co.*, (1932) 2 K.B. 705, 42 Ll.L.Rep. 277, where the original insurance covered both total loss and collision liability under a Running Down Clause on the basis of cross liabilities. However, the reinsurance covered only the total loss. It was held that the reinsurer, having paid a total loss, was not entitled to subrogation to the rights of the original insurer under the Running Down Clause. And in *Standard Marine v. Westchester Fire*, 93 F.2d 457, 1938 AMC 31 (2d Cir. 1938), a British reinsurer was held not entitled to a share of an award made to the reassured underwriter by the U.S.- Germany Mixed Claims Commission. While normally the reinsurer would have been entitled to share in any recovery from a tort feasor, in this instance the payment was made to the U. S. government which, in turn, passed it along to the American underwriter.

55. 129 U.S. 397 (1889).

mental boundaries. Unfortunately, this principle has not always been observed. Some jurisdictions, notably states in the United States, have allowed their parochialism to outweigh the desirability of having access to international markets for placement of reinsurance risks, and have imposed special taxes on reinsurers and special legislative requirements which render placing of risks in the international market more difficult.

A full discussion of the cases involving taxation and regulation of reinsurers is beyond the scope of this text. However, attention is called to the cases cited in the accompanying footnote with respect to taxation.[56]

Moreover, reinsurers from "foreign" jurisdictions (which term as used here includes not only reinsurers from, say, England or other foreign countries, but also reinsurers from another state in the United States) should be aware that insurance regulatory schemes in the United States may involve multi-jurisdictional connotations which could easily have an impact on the rights of such reinsurers to subrogation.

A good example is *Excess and Casualty Reinsurance Ass'n v. Insurance Commissioner of the State of California and Florida Ins. Guaranty Ass'n et al.*[57] The facts briefly were: Signal had an excess reinsurance agreement with ECRA to cover excess losses on a book of medical malpractice insurance. Signal defended an assured in Florida until it became insolvent. The Florida Insurance Guaranty Ass'n (FIGA) assumed Signal's obligations, completed the defense of the pending action, and ultimately paid the claim. It then notified ECRA that it expected payment of the reinsurance proceeds. Payment demands were also made upon ECRA by the California

---

56. *Connecticut Gen. Life Ins. Co. v. Johnson*, 303 U.S. 77 (1938); *Morris v. Skandinavia Ins.*, 279 U.S. 405 (1929); *Allegeyer v. Louisiana*, 165 U.S. 578 (1897); *St. Louis Cotton Compress Co. v. Arkansas*, 260 U.S. 346 (1922). And see *Citizens Cas. Co. of New York v. American Glass Co.*, 166 F.2d 91 (7th Cir. 1948), where an insurance company that received money from the reinsurer refused to perform on the excuse it was not authorized to do business in the state and because the contracts were not approved by the director of insurance of the state. The court properly held that even assuming the contracts were unauthorized, there was no public policy which would permit the insurer to defend upon those grounds. Attention is also directed to *Stewart v. Oriental Fire & Marine Ins. Co. Ltd*, [1984] 2 Lloyd's Rep. 109, where the reassured placed a portion of the risk with foreign reinsurers who had no authority from the Department of Trade of Great Britain to conduct in Great Britain any relevant class of insurance business. The reassured was unaware whether any authority had been given to the defendant reinsurers by the Department of Trade or, indeed, whether any of them needed such authority. The difficulty arose because of the decision in *Bedford Ins. Co. Ltd. v. Institutio de Ressaguros do Brasil*, (1984) 1 Lloyd's Rep. 210, where it was held that where an insurer conducts business in Great Britain without authorization, contracts of insurance made in the course of that business are illegal and void with the probable result that the offending insurer could keep premiums paid by an innocent assured and yet not be liable to pay claims. To the credit of the defendant reinsurers in the *Stewart* case, they conceded their liability and challenged the correctness of the *Bedford* case. The court, Leggatt, J., held that the *Bedford* decision was incorrectly decided and awarded recovery to the plaintiff.

57. 656 F.2d 491 (9th Cir. 1981). See, also, F. W. Nutter, *Reinsurance Issues in Liquidation of Insolvent Insurers*, Vol. XVIII, *The Forum*, No. 2 (Winter 1983), p. 290-310.

Insurance Commissioner as official liquidator and by the Florida Insurance Commissioner as ancillary receiver. ECRA took advantage of interpleader procedures and paid the money into court.

The Signal/ECRA reinsurance agreement contained a relatively standard insolvency clause which stated, in part, that in the event of insolvency, payments would be made "directly to the Company or its liquidator, receiver or statutory successor."

FIGA's argument was based, of course, on the principle of subrogation. However, the court held that on the principle that an insured has no interest in a contract of reinsurance, neither do those paying claims as to insured/claimants. Thus, no equitable basis existed for the application of the principles of subrogation. The sum paid into court was granted to the California Insurance Commissioner.[58]

It is clear from the foregoing that foreign reinsurers should be aware of the ramifications and protect themselves by properly clausing the reinsurance agreements.

Punitive Damages in Reinsurance

It is rather unlikely that a reinsurance contract would be construed as a "maritime" contract because reinsurance contracts cover contractual obligations only, not torts. The reinsured's contract (policy) with the original assured may well be—indeed frequently is—a marine contract where it involves marine coverages, but the contract of the reinsurer with the reinsured is only a contract between those two parties requiring the reinsurer to reimburse the reinsured for claims paid out on the policy.

But what of the situation where the reinsured is held liable to the original assured for punitive damages based upon bad faith on the part of the reinsured in handling a claim? As a matter of principle, it would appear that a reinsurer, following the fortunes of the reinsured, would cover the reinsured's liability to pay punitive damages to the original assured, but would not be liable to cover any liability of the reinsured arising out of the latter's manner of handling claims.[59] However, it also appears that the re-

---

58. See, also, *American Re-Insurance Company v. The Insurance Commissioner of the State of California et al*, 696 F.2d 1267 (1983), where the reinsurer also filed an action for declaratory relief in order to clarify its liability as the reinsurer of an insolvent reassured company. There, the original assured intervened and filed a cross claim seeking damages from the reinsurer for an alleged failure to attempt to settle the litigation in good faith, relying upon a California statute. The court held that the statute did not impose a duty upon a reinsurer to participate in settlements and, consequently, the original assured could not recover damages.

59. *Employers Reinsurance Corp. v. American Fid. & Cas. Co.*, 196 F.Supp. 553 (W.D. Mo. 1959); *Reliance Ins. Co. v. General Reinsurance Corp.*, 506 F.Supp. 1042 (E.D. Pa. 1980).

insurer might be liable if it participates in the reinsured's handling of claims.[60]

One factor, however, may well have been overlooked and that is the increased cost of punitive damage litigation and the intimidating character of punitive damage claims which naturally lead to higher settlements. This increased cost is comprised of two elements: (1) greater expense arising from the diversion of the reinsurer's personnel into non-productive litigation matters; and (2) increased cost of defense counsel's efforts resulting from expanded discovery required into areas not directly related to the conduct which gave rise to the injury. Where a bad faith claim for wrongful declination to pay is involved, discovery procedures frequently involve such matters as underwriting history, claims-handling procedures, industry customs, advertising, use of manuals and guides, elements of motive (intent of the insurer), and the injury sustained (mental anguish of the assured).[61]

Complexities Involved in Construing Reinsurance Contracts

The complex nuances involved in construing reinsurance treaty contracts are well illustrated in two rather recent decisions. In *General Reinsurance Corporation et al v. Forsakringsaktiebolaget Fennia Patria*,[62] a reinsurance company brought suit for a declaration that the defendants, an insurance company, were bound by a slip policy that was amended retrospectively. Essentially, the facts were that the defendant insurance company had entered into two reinsurance contracts. The first, whole account cover, was considered insufficient and so the second, for specific cover, was concluded on the non-marine market in London with 28 reinsurance companies under a slip policy. On January 1, 1977, the whole account cover was increased so that it overlapped with the specific cover. On February 14, 1977, the defendant's brokers presented an amendment slip to the reinsurer. The reinsurer initialled the slip. The second reinsurer also ini-

---

60. *Peerless Ins. Co. v. Inland Mutual Ins. Co.*, 251 F.2d 696 (4th Cir. 1958).

61. See the excellent article by J. W. Morrison, *Punitive Damages and Why the Reinsurer Cares*, Vol. XX, *The Forum*, No. 1 (Fall 1984), p. 73-83, and the following cases cited therein: *Colonial Life & Accident Ins. Co. v. Superior Court*, 31 Cal.3d 785, 647 P.2d 86 (1982) (discovery of other claimants' files handled by same adjuster allowed); *Savio v. Travelers Ins. Co.*, 678 P.2d 549 (Colo.App. 1983) (evidence of insurer's financial worth discoverable); *Safeco Ins. Co. v. Campbell*, 433 So.2d 25 (Fla. Dist.App. 1983) (discovery of premium and profit records not allowable if punitive damages claim improper); *Jarvis v. Prudential Ins. Co.*, 448 A.2d 407 (N.H. 1982) (advertising materials not discoverable). For recent decisions regarding discovery in bad faith suit in general see *Brown v. Superior Court*, 137 Ariz. 327, 670 P.2d 725 (1973) (portions of claims file discoverable); *Aetna Cas. and Surety Co. v. Superior Court*, 153 Cal.App.3d 467, 200 Cal.Rptr. 471 (1984) (depositions and production of documents of insurer's former counsel's claims investigation not allowed); *Houston General Ins. Co. v. Superior Court*, 108 Cal.App.3d 958, 166 Cal.Rptr. 904 (1980) (portions of claims file protected by attorney-client privilege; joint client exception not applicable).

62. [1982] 1 Lloyd's Rep. 87.

tialled. The effect of the slip was to place the specific cover unequivocally on top of the whole account cover retrospectively from January 1, 1977. As a result, in respect of the loss (of paper in a warehouse) of 27 million finmarks, the specific reinsurers would bear only 2 million of the loss. If the amendment slip had not been prepared, then the specific reinsurers would have borne 12 million. The slip was not presented to or initialled by the remaining reinsurers.

The following day the defendant's brokers sought to obtain the first and second reinsurers' consent to cancel the amendment. The second reinsurers eventually agreed on the ground that they had known of the loss when they initialled the amendment slip.

The first issue was whether the first reinsurers were entitled to rely on the amendment slip or whether the defendant was entitled as of right to cancel it. The second issue was whether the title in the paper that was lost had been passed to the customers so that it was no longer within the terms of the specific cover at the time of the loss.

The court decided the issues based upon custom and usage of the London market. That is, the act of initialling a slip was an acceptance which then and there created a contract binding on both parties. However, while an original slip was being carried around the market and was not yet subscribed for 100 percent, the underwriters who had subscribed the slip recognized that it might be withdrawn but that, if so, they could require time-on-risk premium if the cover had already commenced. The right to cancel and the right to time-on-risk premiums were binding on both parties by reason of the custom and practice of the market. Thus, where underwriters subsequent to the leading underwriter altered the terms of the slip, business efficacy required an implied term that the earlier underwriters should have the option of adopting the terms inserted by the later underwriters but that if they did not do so, the assured had the option to cancel the whole slip but with liability for time-on-risk premiums. Consequently, it was held that the defendants were entitled to cancel the amendment slip and to recover on the counterclaim for the first plaintiff's proportion of the cover.

Balfour v. Belmont[63] involved the proper construction of a reinsurance slip issued in 1971, a primary slip issued in 1972, and a primary slip issued in 1971. The defendants, three reinsurers, had each subscribed to an excess of loss reinsurance policy by which the plaintiff had reinsured against certain losses. The loss in question involved a crash of a Turkish Airlines DC-10 manufactured by the McDonnell Douglas Corporation. That company was insured under four policies covering its third party liabilities. The first layer covered up to $15 million; the second, $35 million excess of $15 million; the third, $50 million excess of $50 million; and

---

63. [1982] 2 Lloyd's Rep. 493.

the fourth, $50 million excess of $100 million. The plaintiff was a party to all of the policies in all of the relevant years. The crash occurred on March 3, 1974. The 1972 reinsurance slip policy provided, *inter alia:*

> Period From: To: Losses occurring during twelve months at 1st December 1972 and/or as original; Interest: To reimburse the Re-Insured for all sums payable in respect of liability under the London Market Aviation Products Line Slip which includes products policies placed on a vertical basis with American Domestic Insurers' (mainly USAIG and AIU) and similar product policies.

In the event, the court construed the language of the 1972 slip policy as if a "notional" parenthesis were inserted after the word "Slip" and before "which," and a further parenthesis placed at the end of the text. As so construed, in light of the prior policies and renewals thereof, the defendants were not held liable. The decision must be read in its entirety to follow the reasoning of the court.

CHAPTER XXVI

MISTAKE AND REFORMATION

Mistake Must Be Mutual and Not Unilateral

The usual contract rules apply to reformation of policies and rectification of mistakes; i.e., the mistake must be a mutual mistake and not a mistake of merely one party to the contract of insurance.[1] The rule has been expressed that where both parties have an *identical intention* as to the terms to be embodied in a proposed written contract and a writing executed by them is materially at variance with that intention, either party can get a decree that the writing shall be reformed so that it shall express the intention of the parties, if innocent third persons will not be unfairly affected thereby.[2]

Reformation Allowed

For example, in *Wilson, Holgate & Co. Ltd. v. Lancashire and Cheshire Ins. Corp., Ltd.,*[3] a slip was executed which properly described the cargo as "palm oil" whereas the policy as actually issued described the cargo as "palm kernel oil." The court granted rectification of the policy to conform to the slip, noting that the language in the policy appeared there through a mistake, and, in addition, that palm oil was a better risk from the underwriters' standpoint than palm kernel oil.

American Employers Ins. Co. v. St. Paul Fire & Marine Ins. Co. Ltd.,[4] involved placement of an umbrella liability policy on the assured's vessels, together with excess P & I to bridge a "gap" in the existing primary cover caused by separate insurances, the full cover only existing if all the vessels were involved in a single accident. No mention was made as to whether

1. *American Employers Insurance Co. v. St. Paul Fire & Marine Ins. Co.,* 594 F.2d 973, 1979 AMC 1478 (4th Cir.), previous proceedings reported at 436 F.Supp. 873, 1977 AMC 2127, [1978] 1 Lloyd's Rep. 417 (N.D.,W.Va., 1977). See, also, *Emanuel & Co. v. Andrew Weir & Co.,* (1914) 30 T.L.R. 518; *Wilson, Holgate & Co. Ltd. v. Lancashire and Cheshire Ins. Corp. Ltd.,* (1922) 13 Ll.L.Rep. 486, K.B.D.; *Eagle Star and British Dominion Ins. Co. Ltd. v. Reiner,* (1927) 27 Ll.L.Rep. 173, K.B.D.; *Scott v. Coulson,* (1903) 2 Ch. 249; *Spalding v. Crocker,* (1897) 2 Com.Cas. 189; *Frederick v. Electro-Coal,* 548 F.Supp. 83, 1983 AMC 2364 (E.D.,La.). Of course, mutual mistake is not the only ground of rectification. Fraud or accident also give good grounds for reformation or rectification.
2. Restatement of Contracts, sec. 504.
3. (1922) 13 Ll.L.Rep. 486, K.B.D.
4. N. 1, *supra.*

the cover was to apply "per occurrence" or "per vessel." None of the parties noticed that a typographical error in the policy had the effect of making the coverage apply "per vessel." However, the insured and the insurer both credibly testified that they intended to have insurance providing coverage different from that in the written policy; i.e., that of "per occurrence" coverage. Based thereon, the appeals court reversed the lower court and reformed the policy.

Eagle Star and British Dominion Ins. Co., Ltd. v. Reiner,[5] involved a reinsurance policy in which the risk was stated to attach from Spain whereas the slip stated "at and from and off Gibraltar." The court reformed the policy to reflect that both the reinsured and reinsurer intended that it attach at and from and off Gibraltar and not from Spain as stated in the reinsurance policy. Emanuel & Co. v. Andrew Weir & Co.,[6] involved a reinsurance on the Titanic based on two slips and a mutual mistake of both parties. The policy was rectified.

In Frederick v. Electro-Coal,[7] the policy involved was a comprehensive general liability policy which covered a stevedore's liability. Exclusion (e) of the policy was the so-called watercraft exclusion. Exclusion (d) related to bodily injuries arising out of the transportation of mobile equipment by the insured by means of an automobile. The claimant was injured on a barge. At trial, testimony of the insurance agent was introduced in which he testified that he unknowingly ordered the wrong exclusion deleted from the policy; i.e., he meant to order that exclusion (e) be deleted and instead exclusion (d) was ordered deleted. The court found that exclusion (d) had nothing to do with vessels and that it was clear that the agent intended to have exclusion (e), the watercraft exclusion, deleted. Moreover, as the policy was ambiguous, it was proper for parol evidence in the form of the agent's deposition be introduced into evidence. Based thereon, the court reformed the policy.

Contract must be Ambiguous to Justify Admission of Parol Evidence

It must also be emphasized that under American law, the issue of mistake is one for decision by the court and not a jury.[8] That is, the court and not the jury decides whether a contract is so ambiguous as to justify admission of parol evidence to explain its meaning.

---

5. (1927) 27 Ll.L.Rep. 173, K.B.D.
6. (1914) 30 T.L.R. 518.
7. 548 F.Supp. 83, 1983 AMC 2364 (E.D.,La.).
8. Alcoa S.S. Co. v. Ryan, 1954 AMC 1121 (2d Cir.); Peterson v. Lexington Ins. Co., 753 F.2d 1016, 1985 AMC 2215 (11th Cir.).

For example, in *Peterson v. Lexington Insurance Co.,*[9] the policy contained a warranty against change of interest. The owner of the vessel purportedly sold it to another, using a standard form of Coast Guard bill of sale. When a loss occurred, the owner and purchaser both testified, over objection of the insurer, that there was not a real sale but merely a grant of an option by the seller. The court held that there was no ambiguity in the bill of sale whatsoever and that the trial court had erred in permitting parol evidence. The court emphasized that it was the duty of the trial court to determine whether or not the document was ambiguous and only if it were ambiguous could parol evidence be introduced to vary its terms.

Reformation Denied

Efforts to achieve reformation or rectification have failed more often than they have succeeded.[10]

For example, in *Baja California,*[11] the plaintiff, through a broker, insured three lots of cargo under an open policy against war risks, the name of the vessel and the sailing dates being unknown because secret. After the insurances were effected, the plaintiff caused them to be cancelled and applied for similar insurance under the government's cargo war risk insurance scheme at a lower rate. Meanwhile, unknown to the parties the vessel had sailed and had been attacked and sunk. The managers of the government scheme declined payment because the vessel was not in good safety. Plaintiff thereupon sued on his original policies claiming mistake and seeking reformation. The court held that the policies had been cancelled, there was no mistake and no basis for reformation.

In *Gagniere & Co. Ltd. v. Eastern Co. of Warehouses Insurance and Transport of Goods, Ltd.,*[12] the court refused to reform a policy covering cases of woolen goods being sent from England to Russia on the grounds that the terms of the contract had not been sufficiently proved. As the court put it, in the absence of clear evidence as to what the contract really was, it is very difficult to persuade a court that the policy should be rectified.

---

9. 753 F.2d 1016, 1985 AMC 2215 (11th Cir.).

10. *Baja California*, 60 F.Supp. 995, 1945 AMC 461 (S.D.N.Y.); *Zacharias v. Rhode Island Ins. Co.*, 213 F.2d 840, 1954 AMC 1522 (5th Cir.); *Hampton Roads Carriers v. Boston Ins. Co.*, 150 F.Supp. 338, 1958 AMC 425 (D.,Md.); *Scottish Metropolitan Assur. Co. v. Stewart*, (1923) 14 Ll.L.Rep. 55, K.B.D.; *Lowlands S.S. Co. v. North of England P & I Ass'n*, (1921) 6 Ll.L.Rep. 230, K.B.D.; *Maigenen & Co. v. National Benefit Assur. Co.*, (1922) 10 Ll.L.Rep. 30, K.B.D.; *Gagniere & Co. Ltd. v. Eastern Co. of Warehouses Ins. and Transport, Inc.*, (1921) 8 Ll.L.Rep. 365, C.A.; *Brogden & Sons v. Miller*, (1875) 3 N.Z.C.A. 109, 1 N.Z. Jur. (n.s.) C.A. 1.

11. 60 F.Supp. 995, 1945 AMC 461 (S.D.N.Y.).

12. (1921) 8 Ll.L.Rep. 365, C.A.

In *Zacharias v. Rhode Island Insurance Co.*,[13] the assured intended that all risks coverage would be procured to cover a shipment of textile machinery. However, due to oversight, or unilateral mistake on the part of the assured's representatives, this was not communicated to the insurer. The loss occurred during land transportation of the machinery and did not fall within the language of the policy. The assured contended the policy should be reformed. However, the court held that the assured had failed to prove that the insurer was instructed to insure on an all risks basis and the claim for reformation failed.

In *Hampton Roads Carriers v. Boston Ins. Co.*,[14] Hampton Roads requested a broker to procure insurance coverage on a barge "for total loss only." Instead, the broker procured a policy covering only "absolute physical total loss," and which specifically excluded a constructive total loss. The barge was damaged to the extent that it was a constructive total loss. Hampton Roads sued the insurance company and the broker, seeking reformation of the policy as to the insurance company, and, in the alternative, recovery from the broker for his failure to procure the insurance requested. The court awarded judgment against the broker but denied reformation as to the policy on grounds, in essence, that the mistake was unilateral and that the insurance company had never intended to issue any other policy than the one which it did issue.

In *Scottish Metropolitan Assur. Co. v. Stewart*,[15] there was a discrepancy between the slip and the actual policy. The slip stated that the vessel was reinsured "from September 20, 1922 until noon on February 20, 1923." The reinsurance policy expressly included September 20. The vessel became a total loss on September 20, 1922, and the reinsurer contended that the risk did not attach until midnight on September 20. The reinsurer claimed rectification of the policy to agree with the slip, but the court refused rectification on the basis there were no grounds therefor.

In *Maignen & Co. v. National Benefit Assur. Co.*,[16] the policy was on a shipment of burgundy and included the words "including leakage or breakage, however caused, irrespective of percentage." On arrival of the goods at destination, it was found that a considerable quantity of the wine had been lost by leakage. The underwriters contended that the policy was not in accordance with the ship and that under the slip, leakage was not a peril insured against. The court held that the slip did, in fact, cover leakage and the question of rectification therefore did not arise.

In *Lowlands S.S. Co. v. North of England P & I Ass'n*[17] the insured vessel was taken over by the Admiralty and manned for the purpose (or so the

---

13. 213 F.2d 840, 1954 AMC 1522 (5th Cir.).
14. 150 F.Supp. 338, 1958 AMC 425 (D.,Md.).
15. (1923) 15 Ll.L.Rep. 55, K.B.D.
16. (1922) 10 Ll.L.Rep. 30, K.B.D.
17. (1921) 6 Ll.L.Rep. 230, K.B.D.

insured thought) of being used to blockage a port in enemy occupation. The insured owners thereupon notified the P & I club and it was agreed the policy should be cancelled as of the date of her sailing. In fact, it was never intended that the vessel be used for blockading purposes but she was, in fact, subsequently lost on a voyage under an ordinary Admiralty charter. The insured owners contended that the agreement with the club to cancel the coverage had been entered into under a mutual mistake. The arbitrator held, and the court confirmed, that there been no mutual mistake; i.e., it was a mistake by the insured or someone in his employ as to the destination of the vessel and there were no grounds for rectification or reformation.

See, however, *Brown v. B.A. Assur. Co.*,[18] where the underwriter pled that the parties cancelled the policy before the loss, whereas the evidence showed that the cancellation took place after the loss. The court held that knowledge on the part of the insurer and ignorance on the part of the assured of the loss having occurred at the time of cancellation would render the cancellation inoperative and even if the insurer were equally ignorant along with the insured, the cancellation would be void as having been made under a common mistake of fact.

Attention is directed to those cases prior to 1959 (when the Stamp Act was repealed) in which claims were made to rectify a policy to make it accord with the slip.[19] In those instances, it was held that as the slip could not be stamped as a policy it was not a valid contract of insurance and could not be enforced as a contract to issue a policy. This is no longer true after repeal of the Stamp Act, nor has it ever been true under United States law.[20]

Cancellation of Policies

Cases will be found where policies have been cancelled or purportedly cancelled and a loss occurs. In these instances, it is frequently a question of fact whether the cancellation was effective before or after the loss.[21]

---

18. (1875) 25 U.C.C.P. 514, C.A. (Can.).

19. *Home Marine Ins. Co. Ltd. v. Smith*, (1898) 2 Q.B. 351; *Brogden & Sons v. Miller*, (1875) 3 N.Z.C.A. 109.

20. See *Bhugwandass v. Netherlands India Sea & Fire Insurance Co. of Batavia*, (1888) 14 App.Cas. 83 (P.C.) where the Privy Council held that an open cover issued in Rangoon where there were then no revenue laws similar to the Stamp Act could be enforced as a contract to insure.

21. See *Saskatchewan v. Padgett*, 245 F.2d 48, 1957 AMC 1638 (5th Cir.) (notice of intent to cancel given but as of the time of loss, the policy had not been cancelled nor had any return premium been made; Held: policy covered); *Weiland v. Pyramid Ventures*, 511 F.Supp. 1034, 1981 AMC 2846 (M.D.,La.) (P & I underwriters, sued under a direct action statute, not entitled to cancel or set-off for non-payment by the assured of "release calls" when the assured's delinquency, including insolvency, occurred after the accident); *Cram v. Sun Ins.*

Payment by Underwriters Under Mistake of Fact

Money paid by an underwriter on a claim under a mistake of fact is recoverable.[22] Thus, in *Norwich Union Fire Ins. Soc. Ltd. v. Price, Ltd.*,[23] the underwriters, believing a cargo of lemons had been damaged by an insured peril, paid the loss to the assured. It was later found that the lemons had not been so damaged but had been sold because they were found to be ripening. Recovery back of the payment was allowed.

In *Federation Ins. v. Coret Accessories*,[24] the underwriter paid a claim under a loan receipt for goods allegedly lost during transit but which were subsequently found and delivered by the ocean carrier. The underwriter was held entitled to recover back the payment.

In *Scottish Metropolitan Assur Co. v. Stewart*,[25] the plaintiff underwriters paid the broker but later learned that some of the other underwriters had declined to pay. The broker refused to refund, claiming a lien for premiums owed by the assured. The court held that the payment was made under mistake of fact and was not therefore money of the assured. Accordingly, the brokers had no lien upon it and were liable to refund to the underwriters.

In *Tynedale S.S. Co. v. Newcastle-on-Tyne Home Trade Ins. Ass'n*,[26] the underwriters recovered back moneys paid by them to the assured in ignorance of the true facts, there having been a misrepresentation and concealment on the part of the assured.

In *Lloyd's v. Dominion Film Co. Ltd.*,[27] a case of cinema films was insured on a shipment from Liverpool to Wellington. During the voyage certain of the cargo was jettisoned and agents of the steamship company, believ-

---

Office, 254 F.Supp. 702, 1966 AMC 2201 (D.,S.C.) (policy provision voiding coverage in event of vessel's sale without insurer's prior written consent held valid. Title had vested in the buyer and the seller's insurer not liable when the vessel was destroyed by fire); *Fruehauf v. Royal Exchange*, 704 F.2d 1168, 1984 AMC 1194 (9th Cir.) (no conversion of mortgaged tractors took place until the transferee refused to surrender the tractors to the plaintiff mortgagee and this was some six months after the policy was cancelled).

22. *Federation Ins. v. Coret Accessories*, 1968 AMC 1796 (Can.); *Scottish Metropolitan Assur. Co. v. Stewart*, (1923) 14 Ll.L.Rep. 55, K.B.D.; *Buller v. Harrison*, (1777) 2 Cowp. 565; *Norwich Union Fire Ins. Soc., Ltd. v. Price, Ltd.*, [1934] A.C. 455, 49 Ll.L.Rep. 55, P.C.; *Tynedale S.S. Co. v. Newcastle-on-Tyne Home Trade Ins. Ass'n*, (1890) 17 T.L.R. 81, *on appeal*, (1891) 17 T.L.R. 544, C.A.; *Lloyd's v. Dominion Film Co. Ltd.*, [1922] N.Z.L.R. 600, [1922] G.L.R. 106 (N.Z.).

23. [1934] A.C. 455, 49 Ll.L.Rep. 55, P.C.

24. 1968 AMC 1796 (Can.).

25. (1923) 14 Ll.L.Rep. 55, K.B.D.

26. *Supra*, n. 22.

27. *Supra*, n. 22.

ing the film had been jettisoned, issued a short-landed certificate to the consignee. The consignee presented the certificate to underwriters and was paid. In fact, the film had not been jettisoned but had been delivered to the harbor board. Underwriters demanded repayment which was refused. In the action that followed, the assured was ordered to disgorge the wrongful payment made in error.

CHAPTER XXVII

PRACTICE AND PROCEDURE

Following an insured loss, the insured must generally comply with all the policy provisions in order to recover. These provisions usually include a requirement that the insured notify the insurer of the loss and submit proofs of the loss. In addition, the insured must take steps to mitigate the damages and to determine the amount of the damages. It is therefore imperative that the policy be thoroughly examined to determine if there are additional requirements.

These provisions are typically conditions precedent to the insurer's obligation to perform under the insurance contract. Accordingly, the insured's failure to comply with the policy provisions can relieve the insurer of its obligation to pay for the loss unless the insured can produce a valid reason why the provision should not be enforced.

In most instances, the insured's claim is presented to underwriters through the insured's broker, or, in some instances, an average adjuster. Before presentation of the claim, however, it is exceedingly important that the insured and his broker/adjuster appraise the circumstances of the loss in light of the policy provisions. This preliminary, but vital, step requires that the insured confer with the broker *as soon as possible* after the loss. At this point, depending upon the policy provisions, it may well be imperative to forward preliminary advice of the loss to the underwriters without delay, such preliminary advice to be supplemented as soon as all of the facts and circumstances are fully developed. The subject of prompt notice of loss is discussed fully, *infra*.

The review of the policy provisions, in light of the facts, must be complete and exhaustive. The extent of coverage is most important. Nearly all hull policies on commercial vessels, for example, are on a "named perils" basis whereas nearly all policies on pleasure yachts are on an "all risks" basis. With respect to cargo policies, the coverage may be on an F.P.A. basis (free of particular average), a "with average" basis, or even an all risks basis. Unless the facts of the loss demonstrate that the loss is covered under the policy, the insured has no claim against underwriters under the policy. The policy, whether hull or cargo, should be checked for coverage under the Inchmaree Clause, i.e., additional perils.

The policy period and date of loss must be fixed. Hull coverages are usually "time policies" for a stated period, e.g., for one year, as are P & I policies. To the contrary, many cargo policies are so-called open policies where the insured undertakes to declare to underwriters all shipments that have been made, the type of cargo involved, and the values involved. While, in certain instances, it is possible to make a declaration after a loss, such a late declaration obviously creates problems.

Most important, the policy exclusions should be carefully examined. The type of loss which occurred could, for example, be totally excluded from coverage by reason of a specific exclusion. Moreover, the insured must have an insurable interest at the time of the loss. Under a hull policy this is usually that of an owner, a charterer, or a mortgagee. Under a cargo policy, whether the insured has an insurable interest depends upon the terms of shipment and when the risk of loss arises. For example, if the consignor procures the insurance in his name only, and title to the goods passes to the consignee *before* the loss, the consignor no longer has an insurable interest in the goods and cannot recover under the policy. If the consignee has failed to procure insurance covering the goods from the time title passes to him, he has no insurance at all although he certainly has an insurable interest.

Keeping in mind that it is the duty of the insured to disclose to the underwriter, before the insurance contract is concluded, every material circumstance known to him regarding the risk, it is important to determine that this duty was fulfilled by the insured and his broker or agent. Equally important is a determination that, if the policy contains any warranties, either express or implied, the insured complied with them.

If the subject matter of the insurance, whether ship or goods, has not been totally lost, it is of great importance that the loss be quantified. This entails prompt notification to the underwriter in order that a surveyor or surveyors can be appointed to carry out a survey of the ship or goods, as the case may be, so that the nature of the cause of the loss and/or damage and the extent thereof can be ascertained.

If the subject matter involves goods, prompt notification to the carrier must be made to keep open any rights which the insured and his underwriters may have against the carrier for loss or damage occasioned by breach of the contract of carriage. Here, it may be advisable to arrange for a joint survey by the surveyor appointed by the carrier and the surveyor appointed by the insured or his underwriters. The fact that the goods may be insured does not absolve the consignee from the obligation to give prompt notice to the carrier and all other interested parties.

If the goods have been landed at an intermediate port, this may mean either that the carrier has abandoned the voyage, or that the carrier is treating the contract of carriage as having been frustrated, or that the damage sustained by the goods is such that it would not be worthwhile to continue their shipment. Nearly all cargo policies provide that if there is a termination of the contract, or of the transit of the goods at an intermediate port, even where the insured is blameless, then the insurance cover terminates unless prompt notice is given to underwriters and a continuation of cover requested. Obviously, in these circumstances, the party interested in the goods, whether it be the agent, shipper, consignee, or freight forwarder, should immediately notify underwriters of the termination of the transit and request them to continue the coverage in force and appoint a surveyor to examine the goods and make recommendations as to their condition, and whether they should be reconditioned and forwarded or should be disposed of.

If the carrying vessel has sustained an accident on the voyage, giving rise to a general average situation, the ship's agent will generally notify the consignee of the goods in advance. If not, the consignee first learns of this when he tenders the bill of lading or other document entitling him to delivery. Generally speaking, at this time the consignee will be asked to furnish general average security, and prompt notice to underwriters of such request is necessary.

It is of paramount urgency that, if at all possible, the insured seek to mitigate damages and thus comply with his duty under the Sue and Labor Clause. The duties of the insured under the Sue and Labor Clause are discussed fully in Chapter XVIII.

Notice of Loss

Receipt of notice of loss from the insured is of primary importance to the underwriters. The earlier the notice the more promptly the underwriters can move to protect their interests. This includes, of course, with respect to hull insurance, the desirability of appointing surveyors; of selecting the repair firm; and of taking tenders for repairs. With respect to liability insurances, prompt notice is helpful to the underwriters in minimizing (or perhaps avoiding) the loss by early appointment of counsel, initiation of the investigative process, and establishment of appropriate reserves well in advance of having to pay an anticipated loss.

Hull Policies

The most common hull form in the United States is the American Institute Hull Clauses (June 2, 1977), referred to herein as the AIH form (1977). Neither it nor the other customary hull forms in the United States specifies when suit must be brought against underwriters; in such instances, the usual statute of limitations will govern as, perhaps, modified by the maritime doctrine of laches, unless the form should be endorsed with a specific "time for suit" clause.

The paragraph in the AIH form which most closely approaches a notice requirement is entitled "Claims (General Provisions)" and provides in relevant part:

In the event of any accident or occurrence which could give rise to a claim under this Policy, prompt notice thereof shall be given to the Underwriters, and:

(a) where practicable, the Underwriters shall be advised prior to survey, so that they may appoint their own surveyor, if they so desire. . . . .

By contrast, the new London Institute Time Clauses (Hulls) (1/10/83) provides, in Clause 10, entitled "Notice of Claim and Tenders," in part:

10.1 In the event of an accident whereby loss or damage may result in a claim under this insurance, notice shall be given to the Underwriters prior to survey and also, if the Vessel is abroad, to the nearest Lloyd's Agent so that a surveyor may be appointed to represent the Underwriters should they so desire.

The Pacific Coast Tug/Barge Form (1979) tracks, word for word, with the Claims (General Provisions) Clause in the AIH (1977) form.[1]

By contrast, the American Institute Builders' Risks Clauses (1979) is somewhat more specific. While the same "prompt notice" is required so that underwriters can appoint their own surveyor if they so desire, in addition, a later portion of the Claims Clause requires, under the Part II, "Liability" section, as follows:

B. In the event of any occurrence which may result in a loss, damage or expense for which the Underwriters are or may become liable under PART II of this Policy, the Assured will give prompt notice thereof and forward to the Underwriters as soon as practicable after receipt thereof all communications, processes, pleadings and other legal papers or documents relating to such occurrences.

No action shall lie against Underwriters under PART II of this Policy for the recovery of any loss sustained by the Assured unless such action is brought against the Underwriters within one year after the final judgment or decree is entered in the litigation against the Assured, or in case the claim against the Underwriters accrues without the entry of such final judgment or decree, unless such action is

---

1. For a scholarly and penetrating analysis of the Pacific Coast Tug/Barge Form (1979) and its precursors (Tugboat Underwriting Syndicate Form, American Institute Tug Form (1976), Tug Form (McClelland 1706), Tug Hull Form (McClelland 2139), and Collisions Clauses (Forms A, B, C and D)), see "Insurance of Tugboats and Liabilities of Tugboat Operators," International Maritime Law Seminar, *The Law of Tug and Tow*, Vancouver, B.C., by Martin P. Detels, Jr., Seattle, Washington. An invaluable guide to pursuing a hull claim against underwriters will be found in the proceedings of the Third International Maritime Law Conference, "Pursuing a Hull Claim" by Paul N. Wonacott of Portland, Oregon, June 5-6, 1986, Vancouver, British Columbia, sponsored by the Pacific Northwest Admiralty Law Institute.

brought within one year from the date of the payment of such claim by the Assured.

Cargo Policies

The new London Institute Cargo Clauses (A), (B), and (C) all contain several references to duties imposed upon the assureds which, when analyzed, are broad enough to cover "notice" requirements as respects the underwriters. For example, Clause 16 (which in essence is a Sue and Labor Clause) provides in part that it is the duty of the assured (and their servants and agents) in respect of loss recoverable under the policy to "ensure that all rights against carriers, bailees or other third parties are properly preserved and exercised." This entails, of course, notice being given to the carriers, bailees, etc., in a timely fashion in accordance with the bill of lading and the applicable statutes, such as Cogsa in the United States.

In addition, Clause 18 provides that it is a condition of the insurance that the assured shall act *with reasonable despatch in all circumstances within their control.*

And, lastly, as if to make assurance doubly sure, the policy forms contain a note at the foot of the last page which is printed in italics for emphasis and reads:

> NOTE:—It is necessary for the Assured when they become aware of an event which is "held covered" under this insurance to give prompt notice to the Underwriters and the right to such cover is dependent upon compliance with this obligation.

Protection and Indemnity

Generally speaking, P & I policies require "prompt" notice of loss, presentation of proper proofs of loss within a specified time period, and require that suit be brought within a certain time period. The ASM form is a good example; the relevant clauses read:

> (16) In the event of any happening which may result in loss, damage or expense for which the Association may become liable, prompt notice thereof, on being known to the Assured, shall be given by the Assured to the Association.

> (17) The Association shall not be liable for any claim not presented to the Association with proper proofs of loss within one year after payment by the Assured.

> (18) In no event shall suit on any claim be maintainable against the Association unless commenced within two years after the loss, damage or expense resulting from liabilities, risks, events, occurrences and ex-

penditures specified under this policy shall have been paid by the Assured.

Time for Notice

Generally speaking, the courts have insisted upon strict compliance with the policy requirements of prompt notice of loss.[2]

However, in *Redna Marine v. Poland*,[3] the assured had no actual notice of an insurance policy requirement that immediate notice of damage be given to Lloyd's agent at port of discharge; the underwriters' defense on this ground was stricken on a motion for summary judgment. Compare, however, *Navigazione Alta Italia v. Columbia Casualty Co.*,[4] where a stevedore took out insurance to cover liability imposed upon shipowners for whom it performed stevedoring services. A longshoreman was injured and three years after the accident and one and one-half years after the judgment against the vessel was paid, the shipowner sued the insurance company contending it did not know of the existence of the insurance and therefore had not complied with the clause requiring notice of claim "as soon as practicable." The court held that notice to the stevedore of the existence of the policy was notice to the shipowner and that the claim was barred for failure to comply with the requirements of notice. See also, *United Commercial Bank v. Commercial Union Ins. Co.*,[5] where a failure to

2. *Shadyside*, 1927 AMC 1003 (St.,N.Y.) (delay of 5 1/2 weeks in notifying that a laid-up vessel sank at her berth); *American Stevedores v. Sun Ins. Office*, 1964 AMC 1549 (St.,N.Y.) (6-month delay in giving the insurer notice of loss of coffee cargo held an inexcusable delay voiding the policy); *Greene v. Cheetham*, 293 F.2d 933, 1961 AMC 2549, 316 F.2d 730, 1963 AMC 1728 (2d Cir.) (consignee aware of bad condition of frozen fish on arrival but no notice given to underwriters until some months later when the goods were condemned; complaint against underwriters dismissed); *Neptune Lines v. Hudson Valley*, 1973 AMC 125 (S.D.N.Y.) (in absence of waiver, estoppel, or extenuating circumstances, compliance with prompt notice requirement is a condition precedent to recovery; assured's action against P & I underwriters dismissed where no notice was given until 143 days after the accident and more than a month after hull underwriters had disclaimed liability); *Watson v. Summers*, (1843) 4 N.B.R. (2 Kerr) 101 (Can.)(failure to furnish proof of loss within 60-day required period held a condition precedent to recovery); *Arkwright v. Bauer*, 1978 AMC 1570 (S.D.,Tex.) (excess insurer relieved of all liability to assureds who failed to give notice of personal injury suit until 6 months after the assureds were aware that the case could involve coverage and 4 months after completion of trial); *Howard Fuel v. Lloyd's*, 588 F.Supp. 1103, 1985 AMC 182 (S.D.N.Y.) (by investigating a claim for 6 months before denying it, cargo insurer did not waive defense that it was not given timely notice); *Big Lift v. Bellefonte Ins.*, 594 F.Supp. 701, 1985 AMC 1201 (S.D.N.Y.) (time charterer's 31-month delay in giving notice of a claim to its liability underwriter held to be unreasonable and the assured's negligence in notifying the wrong insurer provided no basis for equitable mitigation in view of the prejudice resulting from that delay).

3. 1969 AMC 1809 (S.D.N.Y.).

4. 246 F.2d 26, 1958 AMC 1099 (5th Cir.).

5. 1962 AMC 2421 (St.,N.Y.).

discover a loss of cargo for 17 months was held not to constitute "notice." In *Rock Transport Corp. v. Hartford Fire Ins. Co.,*[6] underwriters were held estopped to deny the assured's compliance with notice provisions where, after conducting surveys of every scow reported damaged, they raised no question as to the timeliness of the assured's notices of loss. Moreover, the assured gave notice prior to any surveys of the scows—the very purpose of the notice provision. In *Lemar Towing v. Fireman's Fund,*[7] it was held that not every seemingly trivial accident need be reported, especially where the anticipated repair cost would not exceed the deductible; e.g., assured did not breach the warranty of prompt notice in not notifying the underwriter where the tug had been holed and was taking on water when the captain and the assured's president both believed pumps could control the water while the tug made a return voyage. To the same effect, see *M/V Tuna Fish,*[8] where the vessel struck a submerged object, the policy had a $250 deductible, and the estimate of repairs was $150. The vessel sank enroute to the repair yard; recovery was allowed.

In *Dimock v. New Brunswick Marine Assur. Co.,*[9] the underwriter was held to have waived the production of preliminary proof of interest in the assured by objecting to paying the loss on a different ground. In *Gerow v. Providence Washington Ins. Co.,*[10] preliminary proofs of loss were given the underwriter with the statement that if any further proof was required, it would be supplied. It was held that the underwriter waived all defects in the proof of loss where he failed to notify the assured within a reasonable time of any claimed defects.

Choice of law rules can impact upon the question of whether notice of loss was sufficiently prompt and whether the underwriter must demonstrate prejudice by reason of allegedly tardy notice. For example, in *Baltic Shipping v. Maher,*[10a] there was a 16 months' delay by the assured stevedore in notifying the underwriter of a loss. A question was presented as to whether New York or New Jersey law applied. Under New York law, no prejudice need be shown; the assured must give notice as soon as reasonably possible. Under New Jersey law, prejudice to the underwriter is also a requirement. In the event, since the policy was issued in New York by a New York insurance company, New York law was held to apply although the business activities of the assured for which the policy was issued were

---

6. 433 F.2d 152, 1970 AMC 2185 (2d Cir.).
7. 471 F.2d 609, 1973 AMC 1843 (5th Cir.).
8. 242 F.2d 513, 1957 AMC 805 (5th Cir.).
9. (1848) 5 N.B.R. (3 Kerr) 654, subsequent proceedings, 6 N.B.R. (1 All.) 398 (Can.).
10. (1889) 28 N.B.R. 435, *aff'd* 14 S.C.R. 731 (Can.).
10a. 1980 AMC 410 (S.D.N.Y.). See, also, *Howard Fuel v. Lloyd's,* 588 F.Supp. 1103, 1985 AMC 182 (S.D.N.Y.), and *Big Lift v. Bellefonte Ins.,* 594 F.Supp. 701, 1985 AMC 1201 (S.D.N.Y.).

in New Jersey and Maryland. The delay in notifying of the loss was held to preclude recovery under the policy.

By contrast, in *Healy Tibbetts v. Foremost Ins. Co.*,[10b] the court applied California law (in the absence of any well-established federal doctrine) under which the underwriter has the burden of proving substantial prejudice. It was therefore held that the assured's notice to the "surplus line broker" within six days of the casualty was proper and the underwriter did not establish prejudice flowing from later delays in giving notice of litigation against the assured.

In *Offshore Logistics v. Mutual Marine*,[10c] the assured's 16-month delay in notifying the excess P & I insurer of a personal injury claim was held to be excusable where the assured reasonably assumed that its liability would not exceed the $100,000 coverage of its primary policy and the excess insurer was given notice four weeks after the plaintiff filed suit against the assured.

In *Grand Reserve v. Hartford Fire*,[10d] notice of claim was held to have been given a reasonable time after discovery of oxidation damage to a cargo of wine due to failure to maintain the temperature prescribed in the bill of lading. The cargo underwriter failed to sustain its burden of proving that the damage, acknowledged by its surveyor, was excluded from coverage.

The importance to the underwriter of prompt and *complete* notice was dramatically emphasized in *Port of Portland v. Water Quality Ins. Syndicate et al.*[10e] In that case, a dredge owned by the plaintiff port unexpectedly sank, releasing a considerable quantity of fuel oil into the harbor. The broker for the plaintiff notified the defendant pollution underwriter, but three days later followed up with a letter advising that the pollution was small, was being cleaned up, and the removal of all the oil should be accomplished by the next day. As it turned out, the oil was not cleaned up until several months later and costs for the cleanup totaled in excess of $450,000—the pollution cleanup policy having a limit of only $350,000—measured by the gross tonnage of the dredge under the Federal Water Pollution Control Act (FWPCA).

10b. 1980 AMC 1600 (N.D.,Cal.).
10c. 462 F.Supp. 485, 1981 AMC 1154 (E.D.,La.), *aff'd* without opinion, 640 F.2d 382, 1982 AMC 1512 (5th Cir.).
10d. 1984 AMC 1408 (N.D.,Ill.).
10e. 1984 AMC 2012 (D.,Ore.). Related proceedings will be found at 549 F.Supp. 233, 1982 AMC 2019 (D.,Ore., 1982). The significance of the lack of proper notice lies in the fact that under the FWPCA, the underwriter could have been required to pay twice under the policy had the expenses in excess of $350,000 been paid by the federal government rather than the plaintiff port. See *U.S. v. Dixie Carriers and WQIS*, 736 F.2d 180, 1985 AMC 815 (5th Cir.) (neither the language nor history of the FWPCA entitles the owner or operator of a discharging vessel to claim a "credit" for the $108,000 voluntarily expended for oil spill cleanup expenses against its $121,600 statutory non-fault limited liability).

A paragraph of the policy under general conditions and limitations required that the assured forward to the underwriter immediately "all information [and] communications . . . relating to the occurrence." No information whatever was furnished to the underwriter until more than a year later as to the greatly increased amount of the potential claim. Notwithstanding the delay, the court held that the underwriters' lack of diligence in determining the facts for themselves after notice of the dredge's sinking precluded their claim that the assured had delayed in forwarding the requisite information.

Time for Suit

The courts have consistently held time for suit clauses valid unless there are extenuating circumstances.[11] This extends even to those cases in which the assured was issued only a certificate or "binder" referring to the policy and was not aware of the time for suit provision contained in the policy itself.[12] Compare, however, *Phoenix Ins. Co. of Hartford v. DeMonchy*,[13] where a one-year time for suit clause appeared in two policies of cargo insurance but were not mentioned in a certificate of insurance given to the plaintiff. The plaintiff, holder of the certificate, brought suit after the one-year time for suit had expired. The court held that the time limitation clause did not bind the certificate holder.

The cause of action would appear to accrue when the assured knew or should have known of the loss. For example, in *Browning v. Providence Ins. Co.*,[14] a ship with flour as part of her cargo was seen in the Gulf of St. Lawrence on November 22, 1867. She was not heard of again until May 1868 when she was found driven ashore, all hands having been lost. On November 29, 1867, a violent storm had occurred in the gulf and it was probable that the vessel had been driven ashore at that time. Part of the

11. *Heffner v. Great Amer. Ins. Co.*, 1924 AMC 249 (St.Wash.); *Hart v. Automobile Ins. Co.*, 1931 AMC 24 (St.,N.Y.); *Moran T. & T. Co. v. Puerto Rico*, 1958 AMC 130 (S.D.N.Y.); *Pacific Queen*, 307 F.2d 700, 1962 AMC 1845 (9th Cir.); *Meridian Trading v. National Automobile Cas. Co*, 1966 AMC 391 (St.N.Y.); *Port Arthur Towing v. Mission Ins.*, 623 F.2d 367, 1982 AMC 606 (5th Cir.); *S.E.A. v. Great Atlantic*, 688 F.2d 1000, 1983 AMC 1520 (5th Cir.).
12. *Corsicana*, 1930 AMC 7 (St.,N.Y.); *Hart v. Automobile Ins. Co., supra; Suruga*, 37 F.2d 461, 1930 AMC 328 (2d Cir.). Compare, however, *Keresapa*, 1924 AMC 836 (St.N.Y.). See, also, *Magna Mercantile v. Great American*, 1969 AMC 2063 (St.,N.Y.) (cargo underwriter flatly denied liability at least 1 week before expiration of the policy's 1-year time for suit provision; held, assured did not act with due diligence in bringing suit 9 weeks later and underwriter's conduct did not estop him from asserting the time bar); *McMillian v. Coating Specialists*, 427 F.Supp. 54, 1978 AMC 690 (E.D.,La.) (policy provision requiring written notice or suit within 36 months of the end of the policy period is valid and bars a direct action against the insurer); *Robertson v. Lovett*, (1874) 9 N.S.R. 424 (Can.) (failure to bring suit within the specified 1-year time period).
13. (1929) 141 L.T. 439, [1929] All E.R. Rep. 531, 34 Ll.L.Rep. 201, H.L.
14. (1873) L.R. 5 P.C. 263, P.C.

flour was subsequently saved and sold by an agent of the underwriters. The action to recover on the policy was not brought until March 1869. The underwriter defended on the grounds of failure to bring suit within one year as required by the policy. Held: the loss was not in its inception total, and only became so where it was found that it was impossible to carry the flour to its destination, and that it was necessary to sell it. Consequently, the assured was not precluded by the lapse of time in bringing his action. In *Gazija v. Jerns Co.*,[15] there was an applicable three-year state statute of limitation. The assured's broker mistakenly cancelled coverage on one vessel when he was supposed to have cancelled the coverage on another vessel. The assured did not discover the error until four years later when the first vessel sank. In a suit against the broker, it was held that the cause of action accrued when the assured knew, or should have known, of the broker's error.

In *R. Waverly*,[16] a policy was issued in Mexico to be performed in Mexico and required that suit be brought within one year; the assured brought suit in Texas which had a statute of limitation prohibiting parties from contracting for a shorter period of limitation than two years. The court held the one-year provision valid.[17] *Port Arthur Towing v. Mission Ins.*[17a] is to the same effect. There, the vessel owner brought an action against the underwriter for grounding damage but the suit was not commenced until two and one-half years after the damage had been sustained. The policy provided that suit should be commenced "within the shortest limit of time permitted by" state law. The Texas statute invalidated any contractual time for suit period of less than two years. The trial court upheld the assured's action against the underwriter; the appeals court reversed. The same result was reached in *S.E.A. v. Great Atlantic*,[17b] where a suit for insurance proceeds, instituted twenty months after the vessel sank, was held barred by the policy's "one year from date of physical loss" limitation provision which was valid under Louisiana law.

Conduct on the part of the underwriter may constitute a waiver of the time requirements. It depends, of course, upon the circumstances involved.[18] For example, in one unreported case, the underwriters rejected the claim several months before the expiration of the time limitation; alleged "negotiations" and tacit understandings were held not a waiver by underwriters to insistence upon the time limitations. To the same effect

---

15. 1975 AMC 975 (St.,Wash.).

16. 281 U.S. 397, 1930 AMC 981.

17. See, also, *Hesperos*, 15 F.2d 553, 1926 AMC 1614 (4th Cir.); and *Transpacific S.S. v. Marine Office*, 1957 AMC 1070 (St.,N.Y.) (time bar of general average claim under state statute).

17a. 623 F.2d 367, 1982 AMC 606 (5th Cir.).

17b. 688 F.2d 1000, 1983 AMC 1520 (5th Cir.), *cert.den.* 1983 AMC 2111.

18. *Ada*, 1925 AMC 393 (St.,N.Y.).

was *American Stevedores v. Sun Ins. Office*,[19] where a nine-month interval between the first notice of loss and firm disclaimer was held not to estop the underwriters from asserting the time bar.

Interrelation of Cogsa to Cargo Policies

Cogsa, by express statutory provisions, covers the question of notice of loss. Section 3(6) provides, in essence, that unless notice of loss or damage and the general nature of such loss or damage is given in writing before or at the time of the removal of the goods, the removal is *prima facie* evidence on the delivery of the goods. If the loss or damage is not apparent, notice must be given within three days of delivery. Time for suit is within one year after delivery of the goods or the date when the goods should have been delivered.[20]

Form of Notice

As a practical matter, what form must the notice of claim take? Generally speaking, the assured must give the underwriters notice, in general terms, of the nature of the loss; the date of the occurrence; what steps were taken by the assured, if any, to minimize the damages; and the best estimate of the amount of the probable claim. In case of hull damage, it must be remembered that the underwriters should be notified, where possible, prior to survey in order that they may have a surveyor present; and that the underwriters have reserved the right to decide where the vessel should be repaired, the right to veto the repair firm proposed, and the right to make or require tenders for repair to be taken.[21]

Proof of Loss

Assuming proper notice of loss has been given and that the usual intermediate steps have been taken by the assured and the underwriters to effect prompt repair of the damage or to commence processing the claim of loss, what should the assured supply to the underwriters to "prove" his loss?

Generally speaking, an adequate proof of loss includes:

---

19. 1964 AMC 1549 (St.,N.Y.).

20. The express provisions of Cogsa appear to have overruled *Anchor Line v. Jackson*, 9 F.2d 543, 1926 AMC 221 (2d Cir.), that notice endorsed on the delivery receipt is insufficient and does not comply with a bill of lading requirement that notice must be given. *Quaere:* What about the Harter Act? Cogsa, *per se*, of course, has nothing to do with time for suit clauses in cargo policies but the insured must remember to pursue his rights diligently under the bill of lading or else prejudice his rights and those of his cargo underwriter.

21. See, for example, Lines 152-162, Pacific Coast Tug/Barge Form (1979).

1. A narrative statement, usually in the form of an affidavit, describing what occurred to produce the claim (usually termed a "Note of Protest");

2. A description of the insurance which the assured believes, or has reason to believe, covers the loss; again, this document should be under oath;[22]

3. The policies of insurance;

4. A certified or other authenticated copy of the vessel's document.

In cases of cargo loss, the underwriters must be supplied with the invoices establishing the value of the cargo and a set of the original bills of lading, appropriately endorsed, together with a description of the circumstances of the loss and the insurance policy (or certificates under an open policy), in the case of a total or constructive total loss.

In making up a proof of loss, an assured is not penalized for an honest mistake where the insurer has taken no action to its detriment in reliance upon the mistake. A substantial compliance with the requirement of a proof of loss is sufficient.[23] No formal presentation of a proof of loss is necessary where upon informal or other notification of loss, the underwriters issue a positive declination to pay the claim; i.e., formal proofs of loss are thereby waived.[24]

Rejection of proofs and a disclaimer of liability for a single designated reason is a waiver of other defenses, such as the existence of "other insurance," the availability of which was disclosed by the proof of loss.[25] However, in *Atlantic Lighterage Co. v. Continental Ins. Co.*,[26] the court held that a P & I underwriter was not estopped from denying coverage even though he acquiesced in retaining counsel and did not, for some months, deny liability after receiving the proof of loss.[27]

Notice of Abandonment

Unless the policy shows a different intention, total loss includes both actual and constructive total loss insurance. However, special problems of notice arise with respect to claims for constructive total loss; i.e., the insured must tender to the underwriter a formal written notice of abandonment as a prerequisite to a claim for constructive total loss. The subject of

---

22. In light of the discussion involving "other insurance," it is obvious why the underwriters are interested in what insurances are available to cover the loss.

23. *Maybrook,* 49 F.2d 713, 1931 AMC 1384 (2d Cir.).

24. *Holly,* 1925 AMC 1569; *Schodack,* 16 F.Supp. 218, 1936 AMC 1054, 89 F.2d 8, 1937 AMC 548 (2d Cir.).

25. *Anthony D. Nichols,* 41 F.2d 927, 1931 AMC 562 (S.D.N.Y.).

26. 75 F.2d 288, 1935 AMC 305 (2d Cir.).

27. See, also, *Dimock v. New Brunswick Marine Assur. Co., supra,* and *Gerow v. Providence Washington Ins. Co., supra,* under subheading "Time for Notice."

such notices, and the requirements thereof, are discussed in detail in Chapter XVI, "Actual and Constructive Total Loss."

Actions on Policies; Burden of Proof

It is settled law that an insured suing on an insurance policy has the burden of proving that the loss sued for resulted from one or more of the perils insured against.[28] The insured makes out a case, however, if the jury or the court finds that the evidence preponderates in favor of any one of the causes insured against, even though it may be impossible to say which of the several causes alleged was the actual or "proximate" cause of the loss.[29] Where, however, the fact finder can only speculate as to whether the loss was caused by an insured peril or some other cause not covered by the policy, or the evidence is in equipoise, the insured has failed to sustain his burden of proof and recovery on the policy must be denied.[30]

In England, it would appear that the assured has the burden of proving that there was a loss by an insured peril, although the degree of proof required is only to show a balance of probabilities in favor of a loss by the covered peril.[31]

In measuring whether or not the burden of proof has been sustained in a suit on a policy, the assured does not have to do more than in an ordinary case of so-called circumstantial evidence where proof is permitted to rest upon persuasive inference. An inference of fact is sufficient proof in a legal sense when all other reasonable inferences but the fact to be proven are reasonably excluded. If the inference does so prevail, it constitutes proof in a legal sense.[32]

28. *Lakeland*, 20 F.2d 619, 1927 AMC 1361 (6th Cir.); *Arbib v. 2nd Russell Ins. Co.*, 287 F. 722, 1923 AMC 240, reversed on other grounds, 294 F. 811, 1924 AMC 16 (2d. Cir.); *Redman*, 1930 AMC 1896, 43 F.2d 361 (E.D.,La.); *Continental Ins. Co. v. Patton-Tully*, 212 F.2d 543, 1954 AMC 889 (5th Cir.); *Zacharias v. Rhode Island Ins. Co.*, 213 F.2d 840, 1954 AMC 1522 (5th Cir.); *Mettler v. Phoenix Assur. Co.*, 107 F.Supp. 194, 1952 AMC 1734 (E.D.N.Y.); *Roberts v. Calmar*, 59 F.Supp. 203, 1945 AMC 375 (E.D.,Pa.); *Crist, Adm. v. U.S.*, 163 F.2d 145, 1947 AMC 932 (3d. Cir.); *Pacific Dredging Co. v. Hurley*, 1965 AMC 836 (St.Wash.); *Coburn v. Utah Home Ins. Co.*, 1963 AMC 410 (St.Ore.); *Russell Mining v. Northwestern F. & M. Ins.*, 207 F.Supp 162, 1963 AMC 130 (E.D.,Tenn.); *Mayan*, 1967 AMC 765 (S.D.,Fla.); *Wood v. Great American*, 289 F.Supp. 1014, 1968 AMC 1815A (E.D.,Wis.); *Welded Tube v. Hartford Fire*, 1973 AMC 555 (E.D.,Pa.); *College Point D. & S. v. National Union Fire*, 392 F.Supp. 772, 1976 AMC 1873 (S.D.N.Y.); *Northwestern Mutual Life Ins. Co. v. Linard (The Vainqueur)*, 498 F.2d 556, 1974 AMC 877 (5th Cir.), [1974] Lloyd's Rep. 398.

29. *Lakeland, supra; Zillah*, 1929 AMC 166 (St.,Minn.).

30. *Coburn v. Utah Home Ins. Co., supra; Cox v. Queen Ins. Co.*, 1963 AMC 2437 (St.Tex.); *Mayan, supra; Wood v. Great American, supra; Northwestern Life Ins. Co. v. Linard (The Vainqueur), supra; Astrovlanis Compania Naviera S.A. v. Linard (The Gold Sky)*, [1972] 2 LLoyd's Rep. 187, Q.B.D.

31. *Compania Martiartu v. Royal Exchange Assur. Corp.*, [1923] K.B. 650; *Compania Naviera Santi S.A. v. Indemnity Marine Assur. Co., Ltd. (The Tropaioforos)*, [1960] 2 Lloyd's Rep. 469.

32. *Thibert v. Union Ins. Soc.*, 1951 AMC 1661 (Arb.).

On the other hand, the insurer has the burden of proving non-coverage under the exclusions in the policy; i.e., that an exclusionary clause excludes a particular risk.[33] The same rule would appear to apply as respects an affirmative defense raised by the underwriter. If the underwriters, for example, raise the defense of scuttling, then it has been held that since the allegation is one of a crime, underwriters must prove beyond a reasonable doubt that the owner was privy to the scuttling.[34] Clearly, the burden of proving a breach of the implied warranty of seaworthiness is on the underwriter where he alleges it.[35]

As discussed, *supra*, the greatest difficulty seems to be occasioned when a vessel sinks in calm waters without any apparent cause. A presumption generally arises when a vessel sinks without explanation in calm waters or ordinary seas that the vessel was unseaworthy, and the mere fact of sinking does not establish that it was caused by an insured peril. Such a presumption does not arise so much from an express or implied warranty in the policy as from common sense and a sense of probabilities which establishes that well-found vessels do not usually sink in the absence of some fortuitous external cause. In this view, underwriters are equally entitled to the presumption in a case involving a time policy incorporating English law, under which there is no warranty of seaworthiness at all.

The courts diverge, however, when the insured then goes forward with evidence showing that the vessel was seaworthy immediately before the loss, although the weight of authority favors recovery by the assured.[36]

The insured's duty to prove that the cause of the loss was an insured peril extends to proving that when the loss occurred the policy was in effect.[37] The language used in the policy defining the insured perils will be closely scrutinized. While the insurer must at its peril make its policy exclusions clear and unmistakable—otherwise coverage exists (*Mayronne M. & C. Co. v. T-W Drilling Co., supra*)—the words will be defined in their usually accepted meaning. For example, in *Epstein v. Great American*,[38] the policy insured the vessel against damage caused by "collapse of buildings

33. *Ruffalo's v. National Ben-Franklin*, 1957 AMC 1233 (2d. Cir.); *Mayronne M. & C. Co. v. T-W Drilling Co.*, 168 F.Supp. 800, 1959 AMC 403 (S.D.,La.).

34. *Issaias v. Marine Insurance Co. Ltd.*, (1923) 15 Ll.L.Rep. 186, C.A. See, also, *Anghelatos v. Northern Assur. Co., Ltd.*, (1924) 19 Ll.L.Rep. 255, H.L.; and *Compania Vascongada v. British & Foreign Marine Ins. Co.*, (1936) 54 Ll.L.Rep. 35.

35. *Pickup v. Thames and Mersey Marine Ins. Co.*, (1878) 3 Q.B.D. 594, C.A.; *Davidson v. Burnand*, (1868) L.R. 4 C.P. 117.

36. Compare *Bertie Kay*, 106 F.Supp. 244, 1952 AMC 1812, (E.D.,N.C.) with *Zillah*, 1929 AMC 166 (Minn.State). See, also, *Glens Falls Ins. Co. v. Long*, 1953 AMC 1841 (St.Va.).

37. See *Alice Cooke*, 68 F.2d 827, 1934 AMC 222, (9th Cir.) (fire erupting 2 days after a cargo policy expired); *Heipershausen v. Continental*, 25 F.Supp. 1010, 1938 AMC 1591 (S.D.N.Y.)(fire found on vessel 19 hours after policy of repairman's liability had expired).

38. 1965 AMC 854 (St.Tenn.).

or other structures while not afloat." The vessel was damaged while afloat when a boathouse collapsed on it. Held: not a risk insured against.

Prosecuting an Insurance Claim[39]

When to File

At some point in time, despite the best efforts of the assured and his broker, it becomes apparent that the underwriters are going to reject the claim. Sometimes, the underwriters will flatly reject the claim and it is obvious at this point that there can be no recovery without filing suit. On other occasions, underwriters will not flatly reject, but will simply raise one objection after another to payment until it becomes equally obvious that payment will not be made without filing suit.

Generally speaking, a cause of action under an insurance policy accrues when the claim has been "rejected." If the assured is confronted with a time limitation, such as a requirement that suit be instituted within a stipulated period of time, there may be a question whether the "rejection" by underwriters has been unequivocal enough to trigger the running of the limitation period.[40] If the analogous contract action limitation period, under applicable law, is about to run and underwriters still have not paid or signified their willingness to pay, the only practical course of action to follow is to file suit before the statutory period runs.

Absent an express policy provision, the state statute of limitations for actions on contract applies. If however, suit is filed in admiralty, the limitation period is governed by the admiralty doctrine of laches with the state statute being applied by analogy. Consequently, if the statutory time has run, the plaintiff insured has the burden of proving both an excuse for the delay in filing and the absence of any resulting prejudice to the underwriter.[41]

As a tactical matter, it may be wise for the insured, when he perceives that underwriters are not going to respond to the claim, to file suit before the underwriters do so themselves by filing a declaratory judgment action. This approach, however, raises an issue whether there exists an "ac-

---

39. The author wishes to express his appreciation for the assistance provided to him in this portion of the chapter by virtue of the excellent paper, "Pursuing a Hull Claim," presented by Paul N. Wonacott at the Third International Maritime Law Conference, Pacific Maritime Law Institute, Vancouver, British Columbia, June, 1986.

40. *Bethlehem Steel Corp. v. Levante Societa*, 1983 AMC 6 (S.D.N.Y., 1982). In that case, the analogous limitations period for computing laches was, under New York law, 6 years. Early on, the underwriters unambiguously and emphatically rejected the insured's claim but subsequently continued negotiations. The insured finally filed suit, but 4 weeks after the applicable 6-year period had run. The court held that the claim was barred.

41. *Larios v. Victory Carriers, Inc.*, 316 F.2d 63, 1963 AMC 1704 (2d Cir. 1963).

tual controversy" under the Declaratory Judgment Act.[42] By first raising the issue, the insured can sometimes force underwriters to articulate a position inconsistent with eventual rejection.[43] While it is immaterial to the merits of a case who wins the race to the courts, as a tactical matter the party first filing frequently gains a psychological advantage.[44]

Where to File

This decision involves both legal and tactical considerations.

Generally speaking, *in personam* jurisdiction over the defendant insurer poses no problem. This is so because the underwriter is either "doing business" in the state, or is subject to jurisdiction under the state's "long arm statute," or has consented to acceptance of service by a "service of suit" clause in the policy.[45] Frequently, underwriters will give express permission to local defense counsel to enter a voluntary appearance.

Selection of the Forum. In the United States, an insured litigant generally has three choices of forum. He may either file in state court or in federal court. If in federal court, he may file in admiralty or as a civil action. If the latter, the federal rules require diversity of citizenship and the requisite jurisdictional amount.[46] Since a marine insurance policy is a maritime contract, the federal courts have original admiralty jurisdiction under 28 U.S.C. 1333, with the state court remedies being preserved through the "savings to suitors" clause.

Selection of the forum obviously presents tactical considerations. For example, a jury is available if the action is properly filed in state court or as a federal action on the civil side. If the suit is filed on the admiralty side, a jury is not available. Where the underwriters first file, in admiralty, in federal court, (such as in a declaratory judgment action), this tactic may well preclude the insured from having a jury try his counterclaims for damages for breach of contract.[47]

It must be kept in mind that if the suit is filed in state court, the underwriters may, and are quite likely to, move to remand to federal court pur-

---

42. 28 U.S.C. 2201.

43. Once an insurer has stated its reasons for denial of coverage, it may not rely on different grounds when sued by the insured. See, for example, *Ward v. Queen City Ins. Co.*, 69 Or. 347, 138 P. 1067 (St.,Ore., 1914).

44. *Arkwright-Boston Mfr. Mutual Ins. Co. v. Bauer Dredging Co.*, 74 F.R.D. 461, 1978 AMC 208 (S.D.,Tex. 1977).

45. "Service of suit" clauses are very common in policies issued by Lloyd's or the London companies.

46. See 28 U.S.C. 1332.

47. See *Underwriters at Lloyd's et al v. May*, 1983 AMC 2447 (S.D.,Cal., 1983), where the underwriters filed in admiralty and the insured counterclaimed for damages for breach of contract and bad faith, asserted pursuant to diversity and pendent jurisdiction. The insured's demand for a jury trial was stricken.

suant to 28 U.S.C. 1441. If such a motion is likely to be granted, then obviously a state court forum is not too viable an alternative.[48] Except in unusual circumstances, the federal court will remand if the state court action was based on underwriters' consent through a service of suit clause which constitutes a waiver of the right to remove.[49]

Basic Considerations in Selecting a Forum

Here, the practical practice of law shines its brightest. Innumerable considerations are involved. Among these are:

1. Do the provable facts on behalf of the insured appear to be sufficient to present a jury question?

2. Does the insured's claim have "jury appeal"?

3. What is the anticipated credibility of the witnesses for the insured and, in particular, will the insured make a "good witness"?

4. What is the nature of the underwriters' anticipated defenses; i.e., are they technical (such as a non-causal breach of a warranty) or fundamental (such as an allegation of deliberate scuttling, non-disclosure of unseaworthiness, etc.)?

5. How much discovery will be necessary? (Generally speaking, the discovery procedures in federal courts are more liberal and expansive than in state courts).

6. Judicial philosophical differences between state and federal courts may have a bearing. For example, many prefer the federal judiciary if the proper interpretation of the policy requires an application of English law. If there are, however, significant legal questions to be determined under the *Wilburn Boat* decision on the basis of state law, the state courts may be a better forum. This is particularly true in those states which recognize and adhere to the doctrine of "reasonable expectations of the assured."

7. What are the mechanical questions which arise during discovery? For example, are the non-party witnesses scattered in various jurisdictions? Will marshalling the documentary evidence be onerous?

No hard and fast rules can be laid down. Much depends upon the ingenuity of counsel and his intuitive perception of the best route to follow.

---

48. If any one of the defendants underwriters is a resident of the forum state, removal is improper. 28 U.S.C. 1441(b).

49. *Seattle First National Bank v. Underwriters at Lloyd's,* 1983 AMC 1874 (S.D.,Ala., 1981), distinguishing *Puritan Ins. Co. v. 13th Regional Corp.,* 1983 AMC 298 (W.D.,Wash. 1981), where the Washington federal district court retained jurisdiction because related actions were pending there and the policy provision had never been presented to the removing court.

The Complaint[50]

Parties and Jurisdiction

It is assumed here that underwriters have not sought declaratory relief which would, of course, require an answer and possible counterclaims.

The proper defendants must first be determined. This requires identifying all the underwriters on the risk and determining the method of serving process. This is done pursuant to Rule 4(d) of the Federal Rules of Civil Procedure, or by the applicable state statute if the suit is filed in state court. Frequently, counsel for the lead underwriter has already surfaced and it may be possible to obtain a voluntary appearance. This is particularly useful where, for example, the defendants comprise two dozen or more sets of underwriters.

Contents of the Complaint

Formal Allegations. No special rules apply to the common formal allegations. Notice pleading under the federal rules is quite straightforward and under the usual state code pleading statutes, pleading has been substantially liberalized. In many instances, particularly where the facts are complicated, it is helpful to begin with a concise paragraph describing the nature of the action. It is customary to describe the parties as individuals (or such other relationship as may be appropriate), or corporations, and to identify the residence or state of incorporation of the corporate parties.

Real Party in Interest. Pleading rules invariably require that the suit be prosecuted in the name of the real party in interest. This may, or may not be, the named insured or the named beneficiary in the policy. The real party in interest must be one who has a sufficient beneficial interest in the result of the action such that the insurer is discharged upon performance. This may be, for example, the trustee of an express trust, a judgment creditor of the insured,[51] a successor unit to a former governmental unit,

---

50. In the United States, the first pleading of the plaintiff is invariably styled as a "complaint." In Great Britain, suit is brought in the Commercial Court and the document is entitled "Points of Claim." In the Commonwealth nations it is usually referred to as a "statement of claim." For practical purposes, the terms are synonymous and the contents are remarkably similar.

51. If the policy is one of *indemnity* rather than *liability*, a judgment creditor may not be entitled to sue the insured's underwriter except in those jurisdictions which have direct action statutes, such as Louisiana and Puerto Rico. See, in this connection, Chapter XXIV, "Direct Action Statutes."

the assignee of the policy or the claim thereunder, an underwriter who is subrogated to the rights of the insured, the insured himself, either in his own right or suing under a loan receipt, or a named loss payee under the policy.

Existence and Terms of a Valid Contract of Insurance. A suit on an insurance policy is a contract claim. As such, it is axiomatic that the plaintiff/insured must allege sufficient facts from which the court can determine that a valid and enforceable contract of insurance existed between the parties and its terms and conditions. The same rules of pleading with respect to any contract apply here and care should be taken to include all the necessary elements for the existence of a contract of insurance.

Description of the Policy. The terms of the policy, the date of its issuance and delivery, the duration of the risk, the property covered, the perils insured against, the amount of the insurance, and the fact that the policy was in force at the time of the loss or occurrence should be alleged with particularity. Of course, the plaintiff must plead facts sufficient to bring the loss within the pertinent provisions of the policy.

It is often a convenience to the court and the parties to attach a copy of the policy to the complaint. Doing so, however, will not be adequate to supply any essential element missing from the complaint itself and it would be useless and improper for the pleader to allege a construction of the policy which conflicts with the policy terms.

Alternatively, it may be preferable to plead verbatim the appropriate provisions of the policy to ensure that the pertinent terms and conditions sufficiently support the essential elements of the claim for relief.

Insurable Interest. An insurable interest on the part of the plaintiff is a prerequisite to recovery in a suit on a policy.[52] A complaint which does not allege such insurable interest is fatally defective. The allegation need not be direct but may be taken from the four corners of the document.

Compliance with Terms and Conditions of the Policy. The insured must plead compliance with all the conditions precedent required by the policy, unless there is an excuse for non-compliance (such as waiver or estoppel), in which case sufficient ultimate facts must be pleaded to identify and support the excuse relied upon.

In pleading the performance or occurrence of conditions precedent, it is generally sufficient to allege generally that all conditions precedent have been performed or have occurred. It may be a safer practice for the insured to plead specifically compliance with a condition precedent (such

---

52. See Chapter VII, "Insurable Interest," for a discussion of this subject.

as, for example, timely submission of proofs of loss), or, if applicable, an excuse for non-compliance. If the insurer specifically denies the insured's compliance with such a requirement, the insured must prove at the trial that there has been compliance or, alternatively, a valid excuse for not complying. If the excuse for non-compliance is one that must be specifically pleaded in order to be relied upon, and the insured has not done so, he may be barred from presenting evidence on the matter at trial.

Waiver or estoppel may be pleaded by alleging the facts constituting waiver or estoppel without specifically labelling those terms.

Payment of Premium. It is the better practice to plead specifically payment of premium, or, if reliance is placed on waiver or estoppel rather than actual payment, those facts should be specifically pleaded.

Prematurity and Arbitration. Some policies (particularly some P & I club rules) have clauses providing for arbitration as a condition precedent to filing suit.[53] Therefore, it is the better practice to plead such matters, and certainly it is imperative that facts supporting any excuse for non-compliance be pleaded.

Loss from a Peril Insured Against. The complaint must allege facts sufficient to show that the plaintiff sustained a loss or that payment is due by reason of a peril insured against. The failure to allege such facts will render the complaint subject to challenge for failure to state facts sufficient to constitute a cause of action. The insured, of course, has the burden of proving that the loss was caused by a peril insured against.[54]

Amount of the Loss. It is essential that proof of the amount of the loss be pleaded and proved. If there is no allegation of the amount of the loss, the insured may be precluded from tendering proof of the amount of the loss at trial.

Other Insurance. Occasions have arisen in which two or more policies may cover a loss. In circumstances in which the substantive law prescribes a proration of the payment of the loss by the insurers, the other insurance should be pleaded with sufficient particularity to permit proof of the other policy and the extent of its coverage.

53. See, for example, *Deutsche-Schiff. v. Bilbrough*, 563 F.Supp. 1307, 1984 AMC 27 (E.D., La.), where the club's rules required arbitration. A stay was granted pending London arbitration.

54. A good example of this is *Case Existological Laboratories, Ltd. v. Foremost Ins. Co.*, [1984] B.C.L.R. 273 (Sup.Ct., Canada), where at first instance the assured failed to satisfy the trial court that a specially fabricated vessel, designed to be held afloat by a cushion of compressed air underneath its tanks, sank as the result of a "peril of the sea." On appeal, the decision was reversed.

Non-payment by the Insurer. It is the better practice in all instances for the plaintiff to include, in the nature of damages, an allegation of non-payment following the allegation of the amount due under the policy or the amount of the loss insured against.

Attorneys Fees. In some jurisdictions, a successful plaintiff/insured may, by statute, recover the attorneys fees incurred in successfully prosecuting an action on the policy. Generally speaking, such statutes invariably require that the party seeking such fees must assert the right to recover by alleging the facts, statute, or rule which provides the basis for the award of fees. Again generally speaking, it is not necessary to allege a right to a specific amount of fees and an allegation of a right to "reasonable attorneys fees" will be sufficient.

Prejudgment Interest. Allowance of prejudgment interest for breach of a marine policy is governed by federal maritime law irrespective of where the action may be filed. Generally speaking, unless the equities otherwise require, prejudgment interest is normally included in compensatory damages in maritime cases.[55] The rule is that established by federal statute for post-judgment interest.[56]

Sample Forms of Complaint. Sample forms of complaints from various jurisdictions will be found reproduced in the Appendix.

The Answer[57]

In General

Defense counsel should, as a first step, examine the applicable policy with all its endorsements and attachments to determine whether the insured has complied with all the conditions set forth concerning actions against the insurer and to ascertain what defenses are available.

If there is a possibility that state law may be held to govern, the applicable state statutes regarding insurance should be reviewed. Many state insurance codes contain numerous general and specific requirements for policies and actions on policies.

---

55. See *Western Pacific Fisheries v. S.S. President Grant,* 730 F.2d 1280 (9th Cir. 1984).
56. 28 U.S.C. 1961.
57. This is the terminology customarily used in the United States. In Great Britain, its counterpart is termed "Points of Defence." In the Commonwealth nations, it is customarily termed "Statement of Defence."

Formal Allegations. As in the case of a complaint, no special rules apply to the common formal allegations. It must be kept in mind, however, that allegations in an answer may cure a defect in the complaint.

Denials. If the defendant intends in good faith to contravert all of the allegations of the complaint, then a general denial is proper. However, an answer should ordinarily specifically deny all allegations in the complaint which the pleader intends to controvert. It is generally acceptable to deny an allegation by alleging that the defendant is without knowledge or information sufficient to form a belief as to the truth of the allegation. The failure to deny an allegation may result in such failure being deemed an admission of the truth of the allegation.

Affirmative Defenses. It appears to be a universal rule in the United States that all affirmative defenses must be pleaded. It is customary to plead the terms of the policy which are applicable to the defense asserted, either by describing the substance of the provisions or by quoting the relevant portions of the policy verbatim. If the policy has not been attached to the complaint, it is often helpful and convenient if the policy is attached to the answer.

Among the affirmative defenses which may be raised (and which should be affirmatively pleaded) are:

General Statutes of Limitation. If no special period of limitation has been prescribed, either by the insurance contract itself, or by statute, policies are subject to the general state statutory limitation for bringing an action on a contract. In probably the majority of all states, this is six years.

If the action, however, is tortious in nature, such as allegations of bad faith or breach of fiduciary duty by the underwriters, the applicable statute of limitations probably is the one which is ordinarily applied to torts. In many states, this may be as short as two years.

Special Statutes of Limitation. Some states have special statutes of limitation applicable to actions on marine insurance policies. These are usually contained in the insurance code of the particular state. One should not assume that the ordinary contract statute of limitation applies and should refer to the insurance code of the particular state to determine whether or not a shorter period of limitation may be applicable.

Contractual Limitations. Policy provisions limiting the time in which suit may be brought are not uncommon, and are valid if reasonable and not in conflict with specific statutes.

If the time defect in bringing the action on the policy does not appear on the face of the complaint, it must be affirmatively pleaded in the answer. If, however, the defect does appear on the face of the complaint, the defense can be raised by a motion to dismiss. The defense may be waived if not raised in one of these two ways.

Lack of Jurisdiction. Lack of jurisdiction over the insurance company is a defense that may be held to be waived if not raised by motion or pleaded in the answer.

Real Party in Interest. Keeping in mind that every action must be prosecuted in the name of the real party in interest, the defense of lack of real party in interest must be asserted in a motion to dismiss or be raised by answer in order to avoid waiver of the defense.

Exclusions from Coverage. If the general provisions of a policy cover a particular risk or peril and the insured proves a loss falling within that risk or peril, the underwriter must affirmatively plead and prove an exclusion from coverage in order to prevail on that defense.[58]

Exclusions from coverage are strictly construed against the underwriter although a clear and specific exclusion will be enforced as a contract between the parties.

Intentional Act Causing Loss. A conspiracy or wilful destruction of the insured property by the insured or with his connivance or consent is an act of wilful misconduct on the part of the assured and an exclusion from coverage. As such, it must be pleaded and proved. Thus, if underwriters believe that the assured scuttled the insured vessel, either personally or through agents, they must plead and prove the scuttling. It is not perfectly clear under English law what the burden of proof is in scuttling cases. The prevailing view seems to be that scuttling is a crime and the court will not find that it has been committed unless it is proved with the same degree of certainty as is required for proof of a crime.[59] This does not, however, necessarily mean that it must be proved beyond a reasonable doubt. As Arnould puts it,[60] an issue involving fraud or criminal conduct arising in the context of a civil action has, like any factual issue in a

---

58. See Chapter XIII, "Frequent Coverages and Exclusions, etc.," and *Ruffalo's v. National Ben-Franklin*, 1957 AMC 1233 (2d Cir.); *Mayronne M. & C. Co. v. T-W Drilling Co.*, 168 F.Supp. 800, 1959 AMC 403 (E.D., La.).

59. Compare, for example, *Compania Martiartu v. Royal Exchange Assur. Corp.*, [1923] 1 K.B. 650, [1924] A.C. 850, 19 Ll.L.Rep. 95 (H.L.), with *Issaias v. Marine Insurance Co.*, [1923] 15 Ll.L.Rep. 186. See, also, *The Gloria*, [1936] 54 Ll.L.Rep. 50; *Palmisto General Enterprises S.A. v. Ocean Marine Ins. Co. Ltd.*, [1972] 2 Q.B. 625, and *Astrovlanis Cia. Nav. S.A. v. Linard (No. 2)*, [1972] 2 Lloyd's Rep. 187. In the United States, see *Padre Island (Stranding)*, 1970 AMC 600 (S.D.,Tex.), [1971] 2 Lloyd's Rep. 431.

60. Arnould, *Law of Marine Insurance and Average*, Sec. 1358, (16th ed., 1981, London, Stevens & Sons) (Sir Michael J. Mustill and Jonathan C.B. Gilman).

civil case, to be decided upon the balance of probabilities, but the more serious the allegation, the higher will be the standard of proof required before the court will find that the burden has been discharged. The allegation of wilful misconduct must, therefore, be proved on a clear balance of probability if the defense is to succeed.

Nonpayment of Premium. Nonpayment of premium should be raised affirmatively by the insurer as an affirmative defense.

Misrepresentations Affecting Coverage; False Swearing; Fraud. The substantive law covering breach of warranty, misrepresentations, and fraud is covered in Chapter X, "Disclosures and Representations," and Chapter XI, "Warranties." Suffice it to say for the purposes of this chapter that the burden of correctly pleading and adequately proving a defense of wilful misrepresentation or fraud or false swearing is upon the insurer.

Concealment. Concealment is the designed and intentional concealment of any fact material to the risk that the insured in good faith should have communicated to the insurer. As such, it is a defense that must be affirmatively pleaded and proved.

Failure of Insured to Cooperate; Collusion. Failure of the insured to cooperate with the underwriters in connection with the loss coverage can be a defense provided that the insurer affirmatively pleads and proves that the insured's failure to cooperate prejudiced the insurer and that the insurer exercised reasonable diligence and good faith in conducting its own investigation of the loss and in seeking the insured's cooperation. As a practical matter, for this to be a viable defense, the insured's failure must be deliberate and wilful.

Notice and Proof of Loss. If the insurer intends to rely upon a defense of lack of notice or proof of loss, or the untimeliness of either, it should affirmatively plead the necessary facts to support that defense. This puts that condition precedent to recovery at issue and therefore requires proof by the assured that notice was timely given or proof of loss timely filed, or that there was a waiver.

Other Breaches. Non-performance or non-occurrence of a condition subsequent is a matter of defense which must be alleged affirmatively by the defendant.

Defenses against Loss Payees, Assignees, etc.. A loss payee may be suing in his own right, as, for example, a mortgagee who insures for his own account without reference to the mortgagor/insured. On the other hand, the loss payee may be one who derives his right under the policy through the insured. In the latter case, if the named insured cannot recover on the policy neither can an appointee such as a loss payee. That is, the appointee stands in the shoes of the original assured and any defenses good as against the named assured will be good as against the appointee. It is, therefore, important to determine at the outset whether or not the loss payee plaintiff sues by way of an original right or only in a derivative sense through the original insured.

Cancellation. Cancellation is an affirmative defense to an action on an insurance policy. It should be noted that the methods of cancellation and the circumstances under which purported cancellation occurs can be vitally important.[61]

Payment. Payment is a matter of defense to be alleged and proved by the defendant.

Res Judicata. If the parties have validly submitted to an award by an arbitrator or arbitrators and the award is not subject to impeachment, the amount of the plaintiff's loss is fixed such that an action cannot be maintained on the policy.

If a judgment has been entered in a prior action between the insured and the insurer, the insurer may interpose the defense of *res judicata* in a second action by the same parties based on the same set of operative facts as the first cause of action if the second claim could have been litigated in the first action.

Collateral estoppel by prior judgment in another action in which the parties are not identical may also be an affirmative defense for which the insurer will have the burden of proving that a particular issue upon which the defense is based was necessarily determined by the prior action.

Moreover, one must carefully distinguish between the issue of *liability*, which may have been determined in a prior action and be binding on the insurer, versus the issue of *coverage* under the policy, which may be different and may not have been litigated in the prior action. In the latter case, the insurer is not estopped by a prior judgment against the insured from raising coverage questions.

Special Considerations

Mitigation of Damages. Matters reducing the recovery under a policy should be alleged as an affirmative defense along with the facts showing

---

61. See, for example, *Vinnie's Market v. Canadian Marine*, 441 F.Supp. 314, 1978 AMC 977 (D.,Mass.).

in what manner and in what amount the liability should be reduced.

Generally, the insured has a duty to exercise reasonable care to minimize the loss covered by an insurance policy. This is particularly true under marine policies containing a Sue and Labor Clause.[62]

Although a defense of failure to mitigate or failure to exercise reasonable care to avoid consequences that increase the loss may be raised by a general denial, it is infinitely better practice in an action on an insurance policy to plead such failure as an affirmative defense.

Insolvency of the Insured. While the insolvency of the insured is not an affirmative defense to an action on a *liability* policy, it most certainly is a defense to an action on an *indemnity* policy. The language of the policy will disclose whether or not the policy is one covering liability or one covering an indemnity to the assured. Nearly all P & I policies are policies of indemnity and it therefore behooves the counsel for defendant underwriters to raise the defense if the insured is insolvent and has not actually paid the loss.[63]

Prematurity of Action. As noted heretofore, contractual provisions in a policy requiring the parties to first resort to arbitration prior to litigation are favored by the courts and may be considered conditions precedent to maintaining an action on the policy. If, therefore, such a provision exists in the policy and no arbitration has been had, the defense of prematurity should be raised as an affirmative defense.

Counterclaims. If the defendant underwriter has a counterclaim against the insured, whether legal or equitable in nature, it should be asserted as an affirmative defense.

The Reply

The reply serves the same function in an action against an insurer, on a policy or otherwise, as it does in other actions. Many states provide in their code pleading statutes that a reply must be filed with respect to a counterclaim denominated as such and to assert any affirmative allegations in avoidance of defenses asserted in the answer. Where this practice prevails, the plaintiff should, of course, file a reply. Replies are not necessary under federal practice, as affirmative matters raised in an answer are deemed denied.

---

62. See Chapter XVIII, "Sue and Labor Clause."
63. See, for example, such decisions as *Miller v. American S.S. Mutual, etc.,* 509 F.Supp. 1047, 1981 AMC 903 (S.D.N.Y.) (P & I policy is an indemnity policy, not a liability policy; insurer is liable only for payments actually made by the assured).

Great Britain and the Commonwealth Nations

Great Britain

Claims against insurers are brought before the Commercial Court of the High Court of Justice. Although the title of the pleadings may differ from practice in the United States, the necessity for specific allegations sufficient to plead a cause of action exists in full measure. Resort should be had to the Rules of the Supreme Court 1965 for specific problems, and, in particular, to an Order for Ship's Papers where the insurer alleges wilful misconduct of the assured.[64]

The Supreme Court Act of 1981 amended the Administration of Justice Act, 1956, in a number of particulars. Reference to that act should be made in order to determine and construe the changes made with respect to subjects of admiralty jurisdiction.

Australia

Each state and territory of Australia has its own court system. Each has a Supreme Court which is a superior court of record and has unlimited jurisdiction both at trial (first instance) level and on appeal. Civil trials are heard before a judge sitting alone. It is only in exceptional circumstances and for only some types of actions that a jury may be empaneled. On appeal, the court is constituted by three judges. In New South Wales, there is a separate court of appeal division within the Supreme Court and appeals are heard by the judges of that division. In the other states, the appellate court is called a "Full Court" and is constituted by any three judges.

Should a party be dissatisfied with the decision of a state appellate tribunal, he may apply to the High Court of Australia for special leave to appeal to it, or he may appeal to the Judicial Committee of the Privy Council.

High Court of Australia. Created by the Australian Constitution, this is the ultimate appellate court in Australia. It consists of seven justices, some of whom are also members of the Judicial Committee of the Privy Council.

The High Court has jurisdiction to hear any matter on appeal from any Supreme Court but special leave of the High Court itself must be obtained before any appeal can be brought to it.

---

64. See, in this connection, *Probatina Shipping Co. Ltd. v. Sun Insurance Office Ltd.*, [1973] 2 Lloyd's Rep. 520; *Palmisto General Enterprises S.A. v. Ocean Marine Ins. Co. Ltd.*, [1972] 2 Q.B. 625; *Astrovlanis Compania Naviera S.A. v. Linard*, [1972] 2 Q.B. 611.

The Constitution permitted appeals from the High Court to the Judicial Committee of the Privy Council but Section 74 provided that on questions *inter se* of the constitutional powers of the Commonwealth and the states, or as to constitutional powers of two or more states, the High Court had to give a certificate that the question was one which should be determined by the Privy Council. Only once has the High Court granted a certificate (*Colonial Sugar Refining Co. Ltd. v. Commonwealth*, (1912) 15 C.L.R. 182). In *Kirmani v. Captain Cook Cruises Pty. Ltd. (No. 2)*,[65] the High Court described the power to give a certificate as "the vestigial remnant of the hierarchical connexion which formerly existed between the Australian Courts exercising federal jurisdiction and the Privy Council." The Court went on to say, "Although the jurisdiction to grant a certificate stands in the Constitution, such limited purpose as it had has long since been spent."

Except in the unlikely event of the High Court granting a certificate under Section 74, all appeals to the Privy Council from the High Court were abolished by the Privy Council (Appeals from the High Court) Act, 1975. However, there remain some rights of appeal to the Judicial Committee of the Privy Council from the Supreme Courts of the various states in addition to the rights of appeal in admiralty matters.

Jurisdiction in Admiralty. At present, admiralty jurisdiction may only be exercised by the Supreme Courts of the respective states and by the High Court. Each of these courts is a "Colonial Court of Admiralty" within the meaning of a British statute, the Colonial Courts of Admiralty Act, 1890 (Imp.).

Section 2(2) of this act gives to the Colonial Courts of Admiralty the admiralty jurisdiction of the High Court of Justice in England "whether existing by virtue of any statute or otherwise" which is to be exercised over "the like places, persons, matters and things and in like manner and to as full an extent" as the High Court of Justice.

In *The Yuri Maru, The Woron*,[66] the Privy Council held that the jurisdiction which could be exercised by the Colonial Courts of Admiralty was fixed as at the time of the passing of the act.[67] The decision applies, of

---

65. (1985) 50 A.L.J.R. 480.
66. (1927) A.C. 906. Subsequent decisions have reinforced this view: *McIlwaith McEachern Ltd. v. Shell Regis*, (1939) 61 C.L.R. 688; *McIlwaith McEachern Ltd. v. Shell Company of Australia Ltd.*, (1945) 70 C.L.R. 175; *China Ocean Shipping Co. v. State of South Australia*, (1980) 27 A.L.R. 1.
67. The Colonial Courts of Admiralty Act applied the provisions of the Admiralty Court Act, 1840 (Imp.), and the Admiralty Court Act, 1961 (Imp.), which conferred jurisdiction on the High Court of Justice in England to the Colonial Courts of Admiralty (including those in Australia). Although those acts have long since been repealed in England, they remain in force in Australia. There are some important restrictions as to the circumstances in which claims can be brought which are not here relevant.

course, to all the Commonwealth nations then in existence and, in particular, Canada and New Zealand. The climate for correction was set, however, by passage of the Statute of Westminster, 1931, which gave the power to the Commonwealth nations to establish their own admiralty courts and to fix and determine their jurisdiction and regulate practice and procedure.

Procedure. Actions *in personam* are commenced by a writ in some jurisdictions and by a statement of claim in others. The writ, of course, is a formal document commanding the defendant to enter an appearance within a fixed time. Once he has done so, the plaintiff (claimant) files a statement of claim to commence the proceedings.

The defendant must file a statement of defence within a given time in which he pleads to the statement of claim. The defendant may also file a cross claim against the plaintiff or join another person to the action (a third party) by issuing a third-party notice. The "sub-action" in which the defendant is the claimant against the third party proceeds in the same way as the main action by the plaintiff against the defendant.

If the defendant believes that the statement of claim does not disclose a cause of action, he has the right to apply to the court for the action to be struck out for this reason. The plaintiff, who is the cross defendant in a cross action by the defendant and a possible third party in a third-party action commenced by the defendant, has a similar right.

An action *in rem* is commenced by filing a writ to which particulars of the plaintiff's claim must be annexed. If the vessel is to be arrested, the arrest is made as a result of the issue of the writ. Usually the vessel is not arrested, as the shipowner will put up security for the plaintiff's claim.

In both actions *in personam* and actions *in rem*, each party has the right to apply for orders to be made for discovery and inspection of the other party's documents and for the right to administer interrogatories. Usually it is not necessary to apply for orders as the parties give discovery and inspection, and administer and reply to interrogatories voluntarily. If one party believes that the pleadings of the other party do not disclose sufficient particulars of the matters pleaded, that party may seek further particulars of the pleading. If a party is required to plead to a particular pleading before particulars have been furnished, that party may amend his pleading after the particulars have been furnished.

If a party is dilatory in providing discovery, replying to interrogatories, or furnishing particulars, the other party may apply to the court for appropriate orders.

In the commercial and admiralty jurisdictions of the Supreme Courts, the judges tend to lay down a timetable in each action for pleadings and interlocutory steps and the parties are required to comply with the timetable.[68]

New Zealand

By virtue of the Statute of Westminster, 1931, New Zealand was empowered to adopt such legislation involving admiralty jurisdiction as it saw fit. This it has done in its Admiralty Act, 1973, which substantially adopted the provisions of the British Administration of Justice Act, 1956.

Canada

Pursuant to the authority of the Statute of Westminster, 1931, Canada adopted the Canadian Admiralty Act, 1934, which implemented Canada's decision to establish its own admiralty courts, to fix and determine its jurisdiction, and regulate practice and procedure.

The Federal Court Act, 1971, established a two-tier level of courts similar to those in the United States. While concurrent jurisdiction in admiralty is granted to the provincial courts, some doubt has been expressed as to the latter's jurisdiction *in rem*. Nonetheless, it appears clear that the federal courts can and do exercise equitable jurisdiction as well as jurisdiction to determine cases in quasi contract and unjust enrichment. Most assuredly, jurisdiction exists in the federal courts to hear and determine cases involving marine insurance.[69]

Summary

It is impossible in a text of this scope to set forth all of the practices and procedures that are applicable to actions by or against underwriters. Fortunately, the *basic* fundamentals applicable to such suits and actions are essentially identical in the United States, Great Britain, and the Commonwealth nations. The foregoing discussion is intended primarily as a broad overview with the expectation that prudent practitioners will inform themselves properly with respect to the minutiae of such actions and suits and govern themselves accordingly.

---

68. Proceedings are currently underway by the Federal Law Reform Commission to study admiralty jurisdiction in Australia and make proposals to the federal parliament. The consensus is that the federal parliament has sufficient constitutional authority to enact an admiralty act and to repeal the Colonial Courts of Admiralty Act.

69. *Zavarovalna Skupnost Triglav v. Terrasses Jewellers, Inc.*, [1983] I.L.R. 1-1627 (Can.Sup.Ct.).

APPENDICES

APPENDICES

DOCUMENTS

MARINE INSURANCE POLICY FORMS

American Forms

SAMPLE FORMS OF
PLEADINGS IN MARINE INSURANCE CASES

The author expresses his deep appreciation to Witherby & Co. Ltd. for supplying copies of the English
marine insurance forms for inclusion in the Appendices. Copies of the forms are available from Witherby
& Co. Ltd., 32/36 Aylesbury Street, London EC1R 0ET. He also is extremely grateful to Schmitz Graphics,
Inc., for supplying nearly all the American marine insurance forms for inclusion in the Appendices.
Copies of the forms are available from Schmitz Graphics, Inc., 2600 Alida Street, Oakland, California
94602.

Appendix 1

Marine Insurance Act, 1906

ARRANGEMENT OF SECTIONS

MARINE INSURANCE ACT, 1906

An Act to codify the Law relating to Marine Insurance.

Be it enacted by the King's most Excellent Majesty, by and with the advice and consent of the Lords Spiritual and Temporal, and Commons, in his present Parliament assembled, and by the authority of the same, as follows—

MARINE INSURANCE.

1. MARINE INSURANCE DEFINED. A contract of marine insurance is a contract whereby the insurer undertakes to indemnify the assured, in manner and to the extent thereby agreed, against marine losses, that is to say, the losses incident to marine adventure.

2. MIXED SEA AND LAND RISKS.
   (1) A contract of marine insurance may, by its express terms, or by usage of trade, be extended so as to protect the assured against losses on inland waters or on any land risk which may be incidental to any sea voyage.
   (2) Where a ship in course of building, or the launch of a ship, or any adventure analogous to a marine adventure, is covered by a policy in the

form of a marine policy, the provisions of this Act, in so far as applicable, shall apply thereto; but, except as by this section provided, nothing in this Act shall alter or affect any rule of law applicable to any contract of insurance other than a contract of marine insurance as by this Act defined.

3. MARINE ADVENTURE AND MARITIME PERILS DEFINED

(1) Subject to the provisions of this Act, every lawful marine adventure may be the subject of a contract of marine insurance.

(2) In particular there is a marine adventure where—

(a) Any ship goods or other movables are exposed to maritime perils. Such property is in this Act referred to as "insurable property";

(b) The earning or acquisition of any freight, passage money, commission, profit, or other pecuniary benefit, or the security for any advances, loan, or disbursements, is endangered by the exposure of insurable property to maritime perils;

(c) Any liability to a third party may be incurred by the owner of, or other person interested in or responsible for, insurable property, by reason of maritime perils.

"Maritime perils" means the perils consequent on, or incidental to, the navigation of the seas, fire, war perils, pirates, rovers, thieves, captures, seizures, restraints, and detainments of princes and peoples, jettisons, barratry, and any other perils, either of the like kind or which may be designated by the policy.

INSURABLE INTEREST.

4. AVOIDANCE OF WAGERING OR GAMING CONTRACTS

(1) Every contract of marine insurance by way of gaming or wagering is void.

(2) A contract of marine insurance is deemed to be a gaming or wagering contract-

(a) Where the assured has not an insurable interest as defined by this Act, and the contract is entered into with no expectation of acquiring such an interest; or

(b) Where the policy is made "interest or no interest," or "without further proof of interest than the policy itself," or "without benefit of salvage to the insurer," or subject to any other like term:

Provided that, where there is no possibility of salvage, a policy may be effected without benefit of salvage to the insurer.

5. INSURABLE INTEREST DEFINED

(1) Subject to the provisions of this Act, every person has an insurable interest who is interested in a marine adventure.

(2) In particular a person is interested in a marine adventure where he stands in any legal or equitable relation to the adventure or to any insurable property at risk therein, in consequence of which he may benefit by the safety or due arrival of insurable property, or may be prejudiced by its loss, or by damage thereto, or by the detention thereof, or may incur liability in respect thereof.

6. WHEN INTEREST MUST ATTACH

(1) The assured must be interested in the subject-matter insured at the time of the loss though he need not be interested when the assurance is effected:

Provided that where the subject-matter is insured "lost or not lost," the assured may recover although he may not have acquired his interest until after the loss, unless at the time of effecting the contract of insurance the assured was aware of the loss, and the insurer was not.

(2) Where the assured has no interest at the time of the loss, he cannot acquire interest by any act or election after he is aware of the loss.

7. DEFEASIBLE OR CONTINGENT INTEREST

(1) A defeasible interest is insurable, as also is a contingent interest.

(2) In particular, where the buyer of goods has insured them, he has an insurable interest, notwithstanding that he might, at his election, have rejected the goods, or have treated them as at the seller's risk, by reason of the latter's delay in making delivery or otherwise.

8. PARTIAL INTEREST. A partial interest of any nature is insurable.

9. REINSURANCE

(1) The insurer under a contract of marine insurance has an insurable interest in his risk, and may re-insure in respect of it.

(2) Unless the policy otherwise provides, the original assured has no right or interest in respect of such re-insurance.

10. BOTTOMRY. The lender of money on bottomry or respondentia has an insurable interest, in respect of the loan.

11. MASTER'S AND SEAMEN'S WAGES. The master or any member of the crew of a ship has an insurable interest, in respect of his wages.

12. ADVANCE FREIGHT. In the case of advance freight, the person advancing the freight has an insurable interest, in so far as such freight is not repayable in case of loss.

13. CHARGES OF INSURANCE. The assured has an insurable interest in the charges of any insurance which may he may effect.

14. QUANTUM OF INTEREST

(1) Where the subject-matter insured is mortgaged, the mortgagor has an insurable interest in the full value thereof, and the mortgagee has an insurable interest in respect of any sum due or to become due under the mortgage.

(2) A mortgagee, consignee, or other person having an interest in the subject-matter insured may insure on behalf and for the benefit of other persons interested as well as for his own benefit.

(3) The owner of insurable property has an insurable interest in respect of the full value thereof, notwithstanding that some third person may have agreed, or be liable, to indemnify him in case of loss.

15. ASSIGNMENT OF INTEREST. Where the assured assigns or otherwise parts with his interest in the subject-matter insured, he does not thereby transfer to the assignee his rights under the contract of insurance, unless there be an express or implied agreement with the assignee to that effect.

But the provisions of this section do not affect a transmission of interest by operation of law.

INSURABLE VALUE.

16. MEASURE OF INSURABLE VALUE. Subject to any express provision or valuation in the policy, the insurable value of the subject-matter insured must be ascertained as follows—

(1) In insurance on ship, the insurable value is the value, at the commencement of the risk, of the ship, including her outfit, provisions and stores for the officers and crew, money advanced for seamen's wages, and other disbursements (if any) incurred to make the ship fit for the voyage or adventure contemplated by the policy, plus the charges of insurance upon the whole:

The insurable value, in the case of a steamship, includes also the machinery, boilers, and coals and engine stores if owned by the assured, and, in the case of a ship engaged in special trade, the ordinary fittings requisite for that trade:

(2) In insurance on freight, whether paid in advance or otherwise, the insurable value is the gross amount of the freight at the risk of the assured, plus the charges of insurance:

(3) In insurance on goods or merchandise, the insurable value is the prime cost of the property insured, plus the expenses of and incidental to shipping and the charges of insurance upon the whole:

(4) In insurance on any other subject-matter, the insurable value is the amount at the risk of the assured when the policy attaches, plus the charges of insurance.

DISCLOSURE AND REPRESENTATIONS.

17. INSURANCE IS UBERRIMAE FIDEI. A contract of marine insurance is a contract based upon the utmost good faith, and, if the utmost good faith be not observed by either party, the contract may be avoided by the other party.

18. DISCLOSURE BY ASSURED

(1) Subject to the provisions of this section, the assured must disclose to the insurer, before the contract is concluded, every material circumstance which is known to the assured, and the assured is deemed to know every circumstance which, in the ordinary course of business, ought to be known by him. If the assured fails to make such disclosure, the insurer may avoid the contract.

(2) Every circumstance is material which would influence the judgment of a prudent insurer in fixing the premium, or determining whether he will take the risk.

(3) In the absence of inquiry the following circumstances need not be disclosed, namely—

(a) Any circumstance which diminishes the risk;

(b) Any circumstance which is known or presumed to be known to the insurer. The insurer is presumed to know matters of common notoriety or knowledge, and matters which an insurer in the ordinary course of his business, as such, ought to know;

(c) Any circumstance as to which information is waived by the insurer;

(d) Any circumstance which it is superfluous to disclose by reason of any express or implied warranty.

(4) Whether any particular circumstance, which is not disclosed, be material or not is, in each case, a question of fact.

(5) The term "circumstance" includes any communication made to, or information received by, the assured.

19. DISCLOSURE BY AGENT EFFECTING INSURANCE. Subject to the provisions of the preceding section as to circumstances which need not be disclosed, where an insurance is effected for the assured by an agent, the agent must disclose to the insurer—

(a) Every material circumstance which is known to himself, and an agent to insure is deemed to know every circumstance which in the ordinary course of business ought to be known by, or to have been communicated to, him; and

(b) Every material circumstance which the assured is bound to disclose, unless it comes to his knowledge too late to communicate it to the agent.

20. REPRESENTATIONS PENDING NEGOTIATION OF CONTRACT

(1) Every material representation made by the assured or his agent to the insurer during the negotiations for the contract, and before the contract is concluded, must be true. If it be untrue the insurer may avoid the contract.

(2) A representation is material which would influence the judgment of a prudent insurer in fixing the premium, or determining whether he will take the risk.

(3) A representation may be either a representation as to a matter of fact, or as to a matter of expectation or belief.

(4) A representation as to a matter of fact is true, if it be substantially correct, that is to say, if the difference between what is represented and what is actually correct would not be considered material by a prudent insurer.

(5) A representation as to a matter of expectation or belief is true if it be made in good faith.

(6) A representation may be withdrawn or corrected before the contract is concluded.

(7) Whether a particular representation be material or not is, in each case, a question of fact.

21. WHEN CONTRACT IS DEEMED TO BE CONCLUDED. A contract of marine insurance is deemed to be concluded when the proposal of the assured is accepted by the insurer, whether the policy be then issued or not; and for the purpose of showing when the proposal was accepted, reference may be made to the slip or covering note or other customary memorandum of the contract, although it be unstamped.

THE POLICY.

22. CONTRACT MUST BE EMBODIED IN POLICY. Subject to the provisions of any statute, a contract of marine insurance is inadmissible in evidence unless it is embodied in a marine policy in accordance with this Act. The policy may be executed and issued either at the time when the contract is concluded, or afterwards.

23. WHAT POLICY MUST SPECIFY. A marine policy must specify—

(1) The name of the assured, or of some person who effects the insurance on his behalf:

(2) The subject-matter insured and the risk insured against:

(3) The voyage, or period of time, or both, as the case may be, covered by the insurance:

(4) The sum or sums insured:

(5) The name or names of the insurers.

24. SIGNATURE OF INSURER

(1) A marine policy must be signed by or on behalf of the insurer, provided that in the case of a corporation the corporate seal may be sufficient, but nothing in this section shall be construed as requiring the subscription of a corporation to be under seal.

(2) Where a policy is subscribed by or on behalf of two or more insurers, each subscription, unless the contrary be expressed, constitutes a distinct contract with the assured.

25. VOYAGE AND TIME POLICIES

(1) Where the contract is to insure the subject-matter at and from, or from one place to another or others, the policy is called a "voyage policy," and where the contract is to insure the subject-matter for a definite period of time the policy is called a "time policy." A contract for both voyage and time may be included in the same policy.

(2) Subject to the provisions of section eleven of the Finance Act, 1901, a time policy which is made for any time exceeding twelve months is invalid.

26. DESIGNATION OF SUBJECT-MATTER

(1) The subject-matter insured must be designated in a marine policy with reasonable certainty.

(2) The nature and extent of the interest of the assured in the subject-matter insured need not be specified in the policy.

(3) Where the policy designates the subject-matter insured in general terms, it shall be construed to apply to the interest intended by the assured to be covered.

(4) In the application of this section regard shall be had to any usage regulating the designation of the subject-matter insured.

27. VALUED POLICY

(1) A policy may be either valued or unvalued.

(2) A valued policy is a policy which specifies the agreed value of the subject-matter insured.

(3) Subject to the provisions of this Act, and in the absence of fraud, the value fixed by the policy is, as between the insurer and assured, conclusive of the insurable value of the subject intended to be insured whether the loss be total or partial.

(4) Unless the policy otherwise provides, the value fixed by the policy is not conclusive for the purpose of determining whether there has been a constructive total loss.

28. UNVALUED POLICY. An unvalued policy is a policy which does not specify the value of the subject-matter insured, but, subject to the limit of the sum insured, leaves the insurable value to be subsequently ascertained, in the manner herein-before specified.

29. FLOATING POLICY BY SHIP OR SHIPS

(1) A floating policy is a policy which describes the insurance in general terms, and leaves the name of the ship or ships and other particulars to be defined by subsequent declaration.

(2) The subsequent declaration or declarations may be made by indorsement on the policy, or in other customary manner.

(3) Unless the policy otherwise provides, the declarations must be made in the order of dispatch or shipment. They must, in the case of goods, comprise all consignments within the terms of the policy, and the value of the goods or other property must be honestly stated, but an omission or erroneous declaration may be rectified even after loss or arrival, provided the omission or declaration was made in good faith.

(4) Unless the policy otherwise provides, where a declaration of value is not made until after notice of loss or arrival, the policy must be treated as an unvalued policy as regards the subject-matter of that declaration.

30. CONSTRUCTION OF TERMS IN POLICY

(1) A policy may be in the form in the First Schedule to this Act.

(2) Subject to the provisions of this Act, and unless the context of the policy otherwise requires, the terms and expressions mentioned in the First Schedule to this Act shall be construed as having the scope and meaning in that schedule assigned to them.

31. PREMIUM TO BE ARRANGED

(1) Where an insurance is effected at a premium to be arranged, and no arrangement is made, a reasonable premium is payable.

(2) Where an insurance is effected on the terms that an additional premium is to be arranged in a given event, and that event happens but no arrangement is made, then a reasonable additional premium is payable.

DOUBLE INSURANCE.

32. DOUBLE INSURANCE

(1) Where two or more policies are effected by or on behalf of the assured on the same adventure and interest or any part thereof, and the sums insured exceed the indemnity allowed by this Act, the assured is said to be over-insured by double insurance.

(2) Where the assured is over-insured by double insurance—

(a) The assured, unless the policy otherwise provides, may claim payment from the insurers in such order as he may think fit, provided that he is not entitled to receive any sum in excess of the indemnity allowed by this Act;

(b) Where the policy under which the assured claims is a valued policy, the assured must give credit as against the valuation for any sum received by him under any other policy without regard to the actual value of the subject-matter insured;

(c) Where the policy under which the assured claims is an unvalued policy he must give credit, as against the full insurable value, for any sum received by him under any other policy;

(d) Where the assured receives any sum in excess of the indemnity allowed by this Act, he is deemed to hold such sum in trust for the insurers, according to their right of contribution among themselves.

WARRANTIES, ETC.

33. NATURE OF WARRANTY

(1) A warranty, in the following sections relating to warranties, means a promissory warranty, that is to say, a warranty by which the assured undertakes that some particular thing shall or shall not be done, or that some condition shall be fulfilled, or whereby he affirms or negatives the existence of a particular state of facts.

(2) A warranty may be express or implied.

(3) A warranty, as above defined, is a condition which must be exactly complied with, whether it be material to the risk or not. If it be not so complied with, then, subject to any express provision in the policy, the insurer is discharged from liability as from the date of the breach of warranty, but without prejudice to any liability incurred by him before that date.

34. WHEN BREACH OF WARRANTY EXCUSED

(1) Non-compliance with a warranty is excused when, by reason of a change of circumstances, the warranty ceases to be applicable to the circumstances of the contract, or when compliance with the warranty is rendered unlawful by any subsequent law.

(2) Where a warranty is broken, the assured cannot avail himself of the defence that the breach has been remedied, and the warranty complied with, before loss.

(3) A breach of warranty may be waived by the insurer.

35. EXPRESS WARRANTIES

(1) An express warranty may be in any form of words from which the intention to warrant is to be inferred.

(2) An express warranty must be included in, or written upon, the policy, or must be contained in some document incorporated by reference into the policy.

(3) An express warranty does not exclude an implied warranty, unless it be inconsistent therewith.

36. WARRANTY OF NEUTRALITY

(1) Where insurable property, whether ship or goods, is expressly warranted neutral, there is an implied condition that the property shall have a neutral character at the commencement of the risk, and that, so far as the assured can control the matter, its neutral character shall be preserved during the risk.

(2) Where a ship is expressly warranted "neutral" there is also an implied condition that, so far as the assured can control the matter, she shall be properly documented, that is to say, that she shall carry the necessary papers to establish her neutrality, and that she shall not falsify or suppress her papers, or use simulated papers. If any loss occurs through breach of this condition, the insurer may avoid the contract.

37. NO IMPLIED WARRANTY OF NATIONALITY. There is no implied warranty as to the nationality of a ship, or that her nationality shall not be changed during the risk.

38. WARRANTY OF GOOD SAFETY. Where the subject-matter insured is warranted "well" or "in good safety" on a particular day, it is sufficient if it be safe at any time during that day.

39. WARRANTY OF SEAWORTHINESS OF SHIP
   (1) In a voyage policy there is an implied warranty that at the commencement of the voyage the ship shall be seaworthy for the purpose of the particular adventure insured.
   (2) Where the policy attaches while the ship is in port, there is also an implied warranty that she shall, at the commencement of the risk, be reasonably fit to encounter the ordinary perils of the port.
   (3) Where the policy relates to a voyage which is performed in different stages, during which the ship requires different kinds of or further preparation or equipment, there is an implied warranty that at the commencement of each stage the ship is seaworthy in respect of such preparation or equipment for the purposes of that stage.
   (4) A ship is deemed to be seaworthy when she is reasonably fit in all respects to encounter the ordinary perils of the seas of the adventure insured.
   (5) In a time policy there is no implied warranty that the ship shall be seaworthy at any stage of the adventure, but where, with the privity of the assured, the ship is sent to sea in an unseaworthy state, the insurer is not liable for any loss attributable to unseaworthiness.

40. NO IMPLIED WARRANTY THAT GOODS ARE SEAWORTHY
   (1) In a policy on goods or other movables there is no implied warranty that the goods or movables are seaworthy.
   (2) In a voyage policy on goods or other movables there is an implied warranty that at the commencement of the voyage the ship is not only seaworthy as a ship, but also that she is reasonably fit to carry the goods or other movables to the destination contemplated by the policy.

41. WARRANTY OF LEGALITY. There is an implied warranty that the adventure insured is a lawful one, and that, so far as the assured can control the matter, the adventure shall be carried out in a lawful manner.

THE VOYAGE.

42. IMPLIED CONDITION AS TO COMMENCEMENT OF RISK
   (1) Where the subject-matter is insured by a voyage policy "at and from" or "from" a particular place, it is not necessary that the ship should be at that place when the contract is concluded, but there is an implied condition that the adventure shall be commenced within a reasonable time, and that if the adventure be not so commenced the insurer may avoid the contract.
   (2) The implied condition may be negatived by showing that the delay was caused by circumstances known to the insurer before the contract was concluded, or by showing that he waived the condition.

43. ALTERATION OF PORT OF DEPARTURE. Where the place of departure is specified by the policy, and the ship instead of sailing from that place sails from any other place, the risk does not attach.

44. SAILING FOR DIFFERENT DESTINATION. Where the destination is specified in the policy, and the ship, instead of sailing for that destination, sails for any other destination, the risk does not attach.

45. CHANGE OF VOYAGE

   (1) Where, after the commencement of the risk, the destination of the ship is voluntarily changed from the destination contemplated by the policy, there is said to be a change of voyage.

   (2) Unless the policy otherwise provides, where there is a change of voyage, the insurer is discharged from liability as from the time of change, that is to say, as from the time when the determination to change it is manifested; and it is immaterial that the ship may not in fact have left the course of voyage contemplated by the policy when the loss occurs.

46. DEVIATION

   (1) Where a ship, without lawful excuse, deviates from the voyage contemplated by the policy, the insurer is discharged from liability as from the time of deviation, and it is immaterial that the ship may have regained her route before any loss occurs.

   (2) There is a deviation from the voyage contemplated by the policy—

      (a) Where the course of the voyage is specifically designated by the policy, and that course is departed from; or

      (b) Where the course of the voyage is not specifically designated by the policy, but the usual and customary course is departed from.

   (3) The intention to deviate is immaterial; there must be a deviation in fact to discharge the insurer from his liability under the contract.

47. SEVERAL PORTS OF DISCHARGE

   (1) Where several ports of discharge are specified by the policy, the ship may proceed to all or any of them, but, in the absence of any usage or sufficient cause to the contrary, she must proceed to them, or such of them as she goes to, in the order designated by the policy. If she does not there is a deviation.

   (2) Where the policy is to "ports of discharge," within a given area, which are not named, the ship must, in the absence of any usage or sufficient cause to the contrary, proceed to them, or such of them as she goes to, in their geographical order. If she does not there is a deviation.

48. DELAY IN VOYAGE. In the case of a voyage policy, the adventure insured must be prosecuted throughout its course with reasonable dispatch, and, if without lawful excuse it is not so prosecuted, the insurer is discharged from liability as from the time when the delay became unreasonable.

49. EXCUSES FOR DEVIATION OR DELAY

   (1) Deviation or delay in prosecuting the voyage contemplated by the policy is excused—

      (a) Where authorised by any special term in the policy; or

      (b) Where caused by circumstances beyond the control of the master and his employer; or

(c) Where reasonably necessary in order to comply with an express or implied warranty; or

(d) Where reasonably necessary for the safety of the ship or subject-matter insured; or

(e) For the purpose of saving human life, or aiding a ship in distress where human life may be in danger; or

(f) Where reasonably necessary for the purpose of obtaining medical or surgical aid for any person on board the ship; or

(g) Where caused by the barratrous conduct of the master or crew, if barratry be one of the perils insured against.

(2) When the cause excusing the deviation or delay ceases to operate, the ship must resume her course, and prosecute her voyage, with reasonable despatch.

ASSIGNMENT OF POLICY.

50. WHEN AND HOW POLICY IS ASSIGNABLE

(1) A marine policy is assignable unless it contains terms expressly prohibiting assignment. It may be assigned either before or after loss.

(2) Where a marine policy has been assigned so as to pass the beneficial interest in such policy, the assignee of the policy is entitled to sue thereon in his own name; and the defendant is entitled to make any defence arising out of the contract which he would have been entitled to make if the action had been brought in the name of the person by or on behalf of whom the policy was effected.

(3) A marine policy may be assigned by indorsement thereon or in other customary manner.

51. ASSURED WHO HAS NO INTEREST CANNOT ASSIGN. Where the assured has parted with or lost his interest in the subject-matter insured, and has not, before or at the time of so doing, expressly or impliedly agreed to assign the policy, any subsequent assignment of the policy is inoperative:

Provided that nothing in this section affects the assignment of a policy after loss.

THE PREMIUM.

52. WHEN PREMIUM PAYABLE. Unless otherwise agreed, the duty of the assured or his agent to pay the premium, and the duty of the insurer to issue the policy to the assured or his agent, are concurrent conditions, and the insurer is not bound to issue the policy until payment or tender of the premium.

53. POLICY EFFECTED THROUGH BROKER

(1) Unless otherwise agreed, where a marine policy is effected on behalf of the assured by a broker, the broker is directly responsible to the insurer for the premium, and the insurer is directly responsible to the assured for the amount which may be payable in respect of losses, or in respect of returnable premium.

(2) Unless otherwise agreed, the broker has, as against the assured, a lien upon the policy for the amount of the premium and his charges in respect of effecting the policy; and, where he has dealt with the person

who employs him as a principal, he has also a lien on the policy in respect of any balance on any insurance account which may be due to him from such person, unless when the debt was incurred he had reason to believe that such person was only an agent.

54. EFFECT OF RECEIPT ON POLICY. Where a marine policy effected on behalf of the assured by a broker acknowledges the receipt of the premium, such acknowledgment is, in the absence of fraud, conclusive as between the insurer and the assured, but not as between the insurer and broker.

LOSS AND ABANDONMENT.

55. INCLUDED AND EXCLUDED LOSSES

(1) Subject to the provisions of this Act, and unless the policy otherwise provides, the insurer is liable for any loss proximately caused by a peril insured against, but, subject as aforesaid, he is not liable for any loss which is not proximately caused by a peril insured against.

(2) In particular—

(a) The insurer is not liable for any loss attributable to the wilful misconduct of the assured, but, unless the policy otherwise provides, he is liable for any loss proximately caused by a peril insured against, even though the loss would not have happened but for the misconduct or negligence of the master or crew;

(b) Unless the policy otherwise provides, the insurer on ship or goods is not liable for any loss proximately caused by delay, although the delay be caused by a peril insured against;

(c) Unless the policy otherwise provides, the insurer is not liable for ordinary wear and tear, ordinary leakage and breakage, inherent vice or nature of the subject-matter insured, or for any loss proximately caused by rats or vermin, or for any injury to machinery not proximately caused by maritime perils.

56. PARTIAL AND TOTAL LOSS

(1) A loss may be either total or partial. Any loss other than a total loss, as hereinafter defined, is a partial loss.

(2) A total loss may be either an actual total loss, or a constructive total loss.

(3) Unless a different intention appears from the terms of the policy, an insurance against total loss includes a constructive, as well as an actual, total loss.

(4) Where the assured brings an action for a total loss and the evidence proves only a partial loss, he may, unless the policy otherwise provides, recover for a partial loss.

(5) Where goods reach their destination in specie, but by reason of obliteration of marks, or otherwise, they are incapable of identification, the loss, if any, is partial, and not total.

57. ACTUAL TOTAL LOSS

(1) Where the subject-matter insured is destroyed, or so damaged as to cease to be a thing of the kind insured, or where the assured is irretrievably deprived thereof, there is an actual total loss.

(2) In the case of an actual total loss no notice of abandonment need be given.

58. MISSING SHIP. Where the ship concerned in the adventure is missing, and after the lapse of a reasonable time no news of her has been received, an actual total loss may be presumed.

59. EFFECT OF TRANSHIPMENT, ETC. Where, by a peril insured against, the voyage is interrupted at an intermediate port or place, under such circumstances as, apart from any special stipulation in the contract of affreightment, to justify the master in landing and re-shipping the goods or other movables, or in transhipping them, and sending them on to their destination, the liability of the insurer continues, notwithstanding the landing or transhipment.

60. CONSTRUCTIVE TOTAL LOSS DEFINED
   (1) Subject to any express provision in the policy, there is a constructive total loss where the subject-matter insured is reasonably abandoned on account of its actual total loss appearing to be unavoidable, or because it could not be preserved from actual total loss without an expenditure which would exceed its value when the expenditure had been incurred.
   (2) In particular, there is a constructive total loss—
      (i) Where the assured is deprived of the possession of his ship or goods by a peril insured against, and (a) it is unlikely that he can recover the ship or goods, as the case may be, or (b) the cost of recovering the ship or goods, as the case may be, would exceed their value when recovered; or
      (ii) In the case of damage to a ship, where she is so damaged by a peril insured against that the cost of repairing the damage would exceed the value of the ship when repaired.

In estimating the cost of repairs, no deduction is to be made in respect of general average contributions to those repairs payable by other interests, but account is to be taken of the expense of future salvage operations and of any future general average contributions to which the ship would be liable if repaired; or

      (iii) In the case of damage to goods, where the cost of repairing the damage and forwarding the goods to their destination would exceed their value on arrival.

61. EFFECT OF CONSTRUCTIVE TOTAL LOSS. Where there is a constructive total loss the assured may either treat the loss as a partial loss, or abandon the subject-matter insured to the insurer and treat the loss as if it were an actual total loss.

62. NOTICE OF ABANDONMENT
   (1) Subject to the provisions of this section, where the assured elects to abandon the subject-matter insured to the insurer, he must give notice of abandonment. If he fails to do so the loss can only be treated as a partial loss.
   (2) Notice of abandonment may be given in writing, or by word of mouth, or partly in writing and partly by word of mouth, and may be given in any terms which indicate the intention of the assured to abandon his insured interest in the subject-matter insured unconditionally to the insurer.

(3) Notice of abandonment must be given with reasonable diligence after the receipt of reliable information of the loss, but where the information is of a doubtful character the assured is entitled to a reasonable time to make inquiry.

(4) Where notice of abandonment is properly given, the rights of the assured are not prejudiced by the fact that the insurer refuses to accept the abandonment.

(5) The acceptance of an abandonment may be either express or implied from the conduct of the insurer. The mere silence of the insurer after notice is not an acceptance.

(6) Where notice of abandonment is accepted the abandonment is irrevocable. The acceptance of the notice conclusively admits liability for the loss and the sufficiency of the notice.

(7) Notice of abandonment is unnecessary where, at the time when the assured receives information of the loss, there would be no possibility of benefit to the insurer if notice were given to him.

(8) Notice of abandonment may be waived by the insurer.

(9) Where an insurer has re-insured his risk, no notice of abandonment need be given by him.

63. EFFECT OF ABANDONMENT

(1) Where there is a valid abandonment the insurer is entitled to take over the interest of the assured in whatever may remain of the subject-matter insured, and all proprietary rights incidental thereto.

(2) Upon the abandonment of a ship, the insurer thereof is entitled to any freight in course of being earned, and which is earned by her subsequent to the casualty causing the loss, less the expenses of earning it incurred after the casualty; and, where the ship is carrying the owner's goods, the insurer is entitled to a reasonable remuneration for the carriage of them subsequent to the casualty causing the loss.

PARTIAL LOSSES (INCLUDING SALVAGE AND GENERAL AVERAGE AND PARTICULAR CHARGES).

64. PARTICULAR AVERAGE LOSS

(1) A particular average loss is a partial loss of that subject-matter insured, caused by a peril insured against, and which is not a general average loss.

(2) Expenses incurred by or on behalf of the assured for the safety or preservation of the subject-matter insured, other than general average and salvage charges, are called particular charges. Particular charges are not included in particular average.

65. SALVAGE CHARGES

(1) Subject to any express provision in the policy, salvage charges incurred in preventing a loss by perils insured against may be recovered as a loss by those perils.

(2) "Salvage charges" means the charges recoverable under maritime law by a salvor independently of contract. They do not include the expenses of services in the nature of salvage rendered by the assured or his agents, or any person employed for hire by them, for the purpose of averting a peril insured against. Such expenses, where properly incurred, may be

recovered as particular charges or as a general average loss, according to the circumstances under which they were incurred.

66. GENERAL AVERAGE LOSS

(1) A general average loss is a loss caused by or directly consequential on a general average act. It includes a general average expenditure as well as a general average sacrifice.

(2) There is a general average act where any extraordinary sacrifice or expenditure is voluntarily and reasonably made or incurred in time of peril for the purpose of preserving the property imperilled in the common adventure.

(3) Where there is a general average loss, the party on whom it falls is entitled, subject to the conditions imposed by maritime law, to a rateable contribution from the other parties interested, and such contribution is called a general average contribution.

(4) Subject to any express provision in the policy, where the assured has incurred a general average expenditure, he may recover from the insurer in respect of the proportion of the loss which falls upon him; and, in the case of a general average sacrifice, he may recover from the insurer in respect of the whole loss without having enforced his right of contribution from the other parties liable to contribute.

(5) Subject to any express provision in the policy, where the assured has paid, or is liable to pay, a general average contribution in respect of the subject insured, he may recover therefor from the insurer.

(6) In the absence of express stipulation, the insurer is not liable for any general average loss or contribution where the loss was not incurred for the purpose of avoiding, or in connexion with the avoidance of, a peril insured against.

(7) Where ship, freight, and cargo, or any two of those interests, are owned by the same assured, the liability of the insurer in respect of general average losses or contributions is to be determined as if those subjects were owned by different persons.

MEASURE OF INDEMNITY.

67. EXTENT OF LIABILITY OF INSURER FOR LOSS

(1) The sum which the assured can recover in respect of a loss on a policy by which he is insured, in the case of an unvalued policy to the full extent of the insurable value, or, in the case of a valued policy to the full extent of the value fixed by the policy, is called the measure of indemnity.

(2) Where there is a loss recoverable under the policy, the insurer, or each insurer if there be more than one, is liable for such proportion of the measure of indemnity as the amount of his subscription bears to the value fixed by the policy in the case of a valued policy, or to the insurable value in the case of an unvalued policy.

68. TOTAL LOSS. Subject to the provisions of this Act and to any express provision in the policy, where there is a total loss of the subject-matter insured—

(1) If the policy be a valued policy, the measure of indemnity is the sum fixed by the policy:

(2) If the policy be an unvalued policy, the measure of indemnity is the insurable value of the subject-matter insured.

69. PARTIAL LOSS OF SHIP. Where a ship is damaged, but is not totally lost, the measure of indemnity, subject to any express provision in the policy, is as follows—

(1) Where the ship has been repaired, the assured is entitled to the reasonable cost of the repairs, less the customary deductions, but not exceeding the sum insured in respect of any one casualty:

(2) Where the ship has been only partially repaired, the assured is entitled to the reasonable cost of such repairs, computed as above, and also to be indemnified for the reasonable depreciation, if any, arising from the unrepaired damage, provided that the aggregate amount shall not exceed the cost of repairing the whole damage, computed as above:

(3) Where the ship has not been repaired, and has not been sold in her damaged state during the risk, the assured is entitled to be indemnified for the reasonable depreciation arising from the unrepaired damage, but not exceeding the reasonable cost of repairing such damage, computed as above.

70. PARTIAL LOSS OF FREIGHT. Subject to any express provision in the policy, where there is a partial loss of freight, the measure of indemnity is such proportion of the sum fixed by the policy in the case of a valued policy, or of the insurable value in the case of an unvalued policy, as the proportion of freight lost by the assured bears to the whole freight at the risk of the assured under the policy.

71. PARTIAL LOSS OF GOODS, MERCHANDISE, ETC. Where there is a partial loss of goods, merchandise, or other movables, the measure of indemnity, subject to any express provision in the policy, is as follows—

(1) Where part of the goods, merchandise or other movables insured by a valued policy is totally lost, the measure of indemnity is such proportion of the sum fixed by the policy as the insurable value of the part lost bears to the insurable value of the whole, ascertained as in the case of an unvalued policy:

(2) Where part of the goods, merchandise, or other movables insured by an unvalued policy is totally lost, the measure of indemnity is the insurable value of the part lost, ascertained as in case of total loss:

(3) Where the whole or any part of the goods or merchandise insured has been delivered damaged at its destination, the measure of indemnity is such proportion of the sum fixed by the policy in the case of a valued policy, or of the insurable value in the case of an unvalued policy, as the difference between the gross sound and damaged values at the place of arrival bears to the gross sound value:

(4) "Gross value" means the wholesale price or, if there be no such price, the estimated value, with, in either case, freight, landing charges, and duty paid beforehand; provided that, in the case of goods or merchandise customarily sold in bond, the bonded price is deemed to be the gross value. "Gross proceeds" means the actual price obtained at a sale where all charges on sale are paid by the sellers.

72. APPORTIONMENT OF VALUATION
   (1) Where different species of property are insured under a single valuation, the valuation must be apportioned over the different species in proportion to their respective insurable values, as in the case of an unvalued policy. The insured value of any part of a species is such proportion of the total insured value of the same as the insurable value of the part bears to the insurable value of the whole, ascertained in both cases as provided by this Act.
   (2) Where a valuation has to be apportioned, and particulars of the prime cost of each separate species, quality, or description of goods cannot be ascertained, the division of the valuation may be made over the net arrived sound values of the different species, qualities, or descriptions of goods.

73. GENERAL AVERAGE CONTRIBUTIONS AND SALVAGE CHARGES
   (1) Subject to any express provision in the policy, where the assured has paid, or is liable for, any general average contribution, the measure of indemnity is the full amount of such contribution, if the subject-matter liable to contribution is insured for its full contributory value; but, if such subject-matter be not insured for its full contributory value, or if only part of it be insured, the indemnity payable by the insurer must be reduced in proportion to the under-insurance, and where there has been a particular average loss which constitutes a deduction from the contributory value, and for which the insurer is liable, that amount must be deducted from the insured value in order to ascertain what the insurer is liable to contribute.
   (2) Where the insurer is liable for salvage charges the extent of his liability must be determined on the like principle.

74. LIABILITIES TO THIRD PARTIES. Where the assured has effected an insurance in express terms against any liability to a third party, the measure of indemnity, subject to any express provision in the policy, is the amount paid or payable by him to such third party in respect of such liability.

75. GENERAL PROVISIONS AS TO MEASURE OF INDEMNITY
   (1) Where there has been a loss in respect of any subject-matter not expressly provided for in the foregoing provisions of this Act, the measure of indemnity shall be ascertained, as nearly as may be, in accordance with those provisions, in so far as applicable to the particular case.
   (2) Nothing in the provisions of this Act relating to the measure of indemnity shall affect the rules relating to double insurance, or prohibit the insurer from disproving interest wholly or in part, or from showing that at the time of the loss the whole or any part of the subject-matter insured was not at risk under the policy.

76. PARTICULAR AVERAGE WARRANTIES
   (1) Where the subject-matter insured is warranted free from particular average, the assured cannot recover for a loss of part, other than a loss incurred by a general average sacrifice, unless the contract contained in the policy be apportionable; but, if the contract be apportionable, the assured may recover for a total loss of any apportionable part.

(2) Where the subject-matter insured is warranted free from particular average, either wholly or under a certain percentage, the insurer is nevertheless liable for salvage charges, and for particular charges and other expenses properly incurred pursuant to the provisions of the suing and labouring clause in order to avert a loss insured against.

(3) Unless the policy otherwise provides, where the subject-matter insured is warranted free from particular average under a specified percentage, a general average loss cannot be added to a particular average loss to make up the specified percentage.

(4) For the purpose of ascertaining whether the specified percentage has been reached, regard shall be had only to the actual loss suffered by the subject-matter insured. Particular charges and the expenses of and incidental to ascertaining and proving the loss must be excluded.

77. SUCCESSIVE LOSSES

(1) Unless the policy otherwise provides, and subject to the provisions of this Act, the insurer is liable for successive losses, even though the total amount of such losses may exceed the sum insured.

(2) Where, under the same policy, a partial loss which has not been repaired or otherwise made good, is followed by a total loss, the assured can only recover in respect of the total loss:

Provided that nothing in this section shall affect the liability of the insurer under the suing and labouring clause.

78. SUING AND LABOURING CLAUSE

(1) Where the policy contains a suing and labouring clause, the engagement thereby entered into is deemed to be supplementary to the contract of insurance, and the assured may recover from the insurer any expenses properly incurred pursuant to the clause, notwithstanding that the insurer may have paid for a total loss, or that the subject-matter may have been warranted free from particular average, either wholly or under a certain percentage.

(2) General average losses and contributions and salvage charges, as defined by this Act, are not recoverable under the suing and labouring clause.

(3) Expenses incurred for the purpose of averting or diminishing any loss not covered by the policy are not recoverable under the suing and labouring clause.

(4) It is the duty of the assured and his agents, in all cases, to take such measures as may be reasonable for the purpose of averting or minimising a loss.

RIGHTS OF INSURER ON PAYMENT.

79. RIGHT OF SUBROGATION

(1) Where the insurer pays for a total loss, either of the whole, or in the case of goods of any apportionable part, of the subject-matter insured, he thereupon becomes entitled to take over the interest of the assured in whatever may remain of the subject-matter so paid for, and he is thereby subrogated to all rights and remedies of the assured in and in respect of that subject-matter as from the time of the casualty causing the loss.

(2) Subject to the foregoing provisions, where the insurer pays for a partial loss, he acquires no title to the subject-matter insured, or such part of it as may remain, but he is thereupon subrogated to all rights and remedies of the assured in and in respect of the subject-matter insured as from the time of the casualty causing the loss, in so far as the assured has been indemnified, according to this Act, by such payment for the loss.

80. RIGHT OF CONTRIBUTION

(1) Where the assured is over-insured by double insurance, each insurer is bound, as between himself and the other insurers, to contribute ratably to the loss in proportion to the amount for which he is liable under his contract.

(2) If any insurer pays more than his proportion of the loss, he is entitled to maintain an action for contribution against the other insurers, and is entitled to the like remedies as a surety who has paid more than his proportion of the debt.

81. EFFECT OF UNDER-INSURANCE. Where the assured is insured for an amount less than the insurable value or, in the case of a valued policy for an amount less than the policy valuation, he is deemed to be his own insurer in respect of the uninsured balance.

RETURN OF PREMIUM.

82. ENFORCEMENT OF RETURN. Where the premium, or a proportionate part thereof is, by this Act, declared to be returnable—

(a) If already paid, it may be recovered by the assured from the insurer; and

(b) If unpaid, it may be retained by the assured or his agent.

83. RETURN BY AGREEMENT. Where the policy contains a stipulation for the return of the premium, or a proportionate part thereof, on the happening of a certain event, and that event happens, the premium, or, as the case may be, the proportionate part thereof, is thereupon returnable to the assured.

84. RETURN FOR FAILURE OF CONSIDERATION

(1) Where the consideration for the payment of the premium totally fails, and there has been no fraud or illegality on the part of the assured or his agents, the premium is thereupon returnable to the assured.

(2) Where the consideration for the payment of the premium is apportionable and there is a total failure of any apportionable part of the consideration, a proportionate part of the premium is, under the like conditions, thereupon returnable to the assured.

(3) In particular—

(a) Where the policy is void, or is avoided by the insurer as from the commencement of the risk, the premium is returnable, provided that there has been no fraud or illegality on the part of the assured; but if the risk is not apportionable, and has once attached, the premium is not returnable;

(b) Where the subject-matter insured, or part thereof, has never been imperilled, the premium, or, as the case may be, a proportionate part thereof, is returnable:

Provided that where the subject-matter has been insured "lost or not lost" and has arrived in safety at the time when the contract is concluded, the premium is not returnable unless, at such time, the insurer knew of the safe arrival;

(c) Where the assured has no insurable interest throughout the currency of the risk, the premium is returnable, provided that this rule does not apply to a policy effected by way of gaming or wagering;

(d) Where the assured has a defeasible interest which is terminated during the currency of the risk, the premium is not returnable;

(e) Where the assured has over-insured under an unvalued policy, a proportionate part of the premium is returnable;

(f) Subject to the foregoing provisions, where the assured has over-insured by double insurance, a proportionate part of the several premiums is returnable:

Provided that, if the policies are effected at different times, and any earlier policy has at any time borne the entire risk, or if a claim has been paid on the policy in respect of the full sum insured thereby, no premium is returnable in respect of that policy, and when the double insurance is effected knowingly by the assured no premium is returnable.

MUTUAL INSURANCE.

85. MODIFICATION OF ACT IN CASE OF MUTUAL INSURANCE

(1) Where two or more persons mutually agree to insure each other against marine losses there is said to be a mutual insurance.

(2) The provisions of this Act relating to the premium do not apply to mutual insurance, but a guarantee, or such other arrangement as may be agreed upon, may be substituted for the premium.

(3) The provisions of this Act, in so far as they may be modified by the agreement of the parties, may in the case of mutual insurance be modified by the terms of the policies issued by the association, or by the rules and regulations of the association.

(4) Subject to the exceptions mentioned in this section the provisions of this Act apply to a mutual insurance.

SUPPLEMENTAL

86. RATIFICATION BY ASSURED. Where a contract of marine insurance is in good faith effected by one person on behalf of another, the person on whose behalf it is effected may ratify the contract even after he is aware of a loss.

87. IMPLIED OBLIGATIONS VARIED BY AGREEMENT OR USAGE

(1) Where any right, duty, or liability would arise under a contract of marine insurance by implication of law, it may be negatived or varied by express agreement, or by usage, if the usage be such as to bind both parties to the contract.

(2) The provisions of this section extend to any right, duty, or liability declared by this Act which may be lawfully modified by agreement.

88. REASONABLE TIME, ETC., A QUESTION OF FACT. Where by this Act any reference is made to reasonable time, reasonable premium, or reasonable diligence, the question what is reasonable is a question of fact.

89. SLIP AS EVIDENCE. Where there is a duly stamped policy, reference may be made, as heretofore, to the slip or covering note, in any legal proceeding.

90. INTERPRETATION OF TERMS. In this Act, unless the context or subject-matter otherwise requires—

"Action" includes counter-claim and set off:

"Freight" includes the profit derivable by a shipowner from the employment of his ship to carry his own goods or movables, as well as freight payable by a third party, but does not include passage money:

"Movables" means any movable tangible property, other than the ship, and includes money, valuable securities, and other documents:

"Policy" means a marine policy.

91. SAVINGS
  (1) Nothing in this Act, or in any repeal effected thereby, shall affect—
     (a) The provisions of the Stamp Act, 1891, or any enactment for the time being in force relating to the revenue;
     (b) The provisions of the Companies Act, 1862, or any enactment amended or substituted for the same;
     (c) The provisions of any statute not expressly repealed by this Act.
  (2) The rules of the common law including the law merchant, save in so far as they are inconsistent with the express provisions of this Act, shall continue to apply to contracts of marine insurance.

92. REPEALS. The enactments mentioned in the Second Schedule to this Act are hereby repealed to the extent specified in that schedule.

93. COMMENCEMENT. This Act shall come into operation on the first day of January one thousand nine hundred and seven.

94. SHORT TITLE. This act may be cited as the Marine Insurance Act, 1906.

SCHEDULES

First Schedule: Section 30, Form of Policy [Lloyd's S. G. Policy]

Be it known that   as well in
own name as for and in the name and names of all and every other person or
persons to whom the same doth, may, or shall appertain, in part or in all doth
make assurance and cause
and them, and every of them, to be insured lost or not lost, at and from

Upon any kind of goods and merchandises, and also upon the body, tackle, apparel, ordnance, munition, artillery, boat, and other furniture, of and in the good ship or vessel called the
whereof is master under God, for this present voyage,

or whosoever shall go for master in the said ship, or by whatsoever other name or names the said ship, or the master thereof, is or shall be named or called;

beginning the adventure upon the said goods and merchandises from the loading thereof aboard the said ship,

and so shall continue and endure during her abode there.
upon the said ship, etc. And further, until the said ship, with all her ordnance, tackle, apparel, etc., and goods and merchandises whatsoever shall be arrived at

upon the said ship, etc., until she hath moored at anchor twenty-four hours in good safety; and upon the goods and merchandises, until the same be there discharged and safely landed. And it shall be lawful for the said ship, etc., in this voyage, to proceed and sail to and touch and stay at any ports or places whatsoever

without prejudice to this insurance. The said ship, etc., goods and merchandises, etc., for so much as concerns the assured by agreement between the assured and assurers in this policy, are and shall be valued at

Touching the adventures and perils which we the assurers are contented to bear and do take upon us in this voyage: they are of the seas, men-of-war, fire, enemies, pirates, rovers, thieves, jettisons, letters of mart and countermart, surprisals, takings at sea, arrests, restraints, and detainments of all kings, princes, and people, of what nation, condition, or quality soever, barratry of the master and mariners, and of all other perils, losses, and misfortunes, that have or shall come to the hurt, detriment, or damage of the said goods and merchandises, and ship, etc., or any part thereof.

SUE AND LABOUR CLAUSE. And in case of any loss or misfortune it shall be lawful to the assured, their factors, servants and assigns, to sue, labour, and travel for, in and about the defence, safeguards, and recovery of the said goods and merchandises, and ship, etc., or any part thereof, without prejudice to this insurance; to the charges whereof we, the assurers, will contribute each one according to the rate and quantity of his sum herein assured.

WAIVER CLAUSE. And it is especially declared and agreed that no acts of the insurer or insured in recovering, saving or preserving the property insured shall be considered as a waiver, or acceptance of abandonment. And it is agreed by us, the insurers, that this writing or policy of assurance shall be of as much force and effect as the surest writing or policy of assurance heretofore made in Lombard Street, or in the Royal Exchange, or elsewhere in London. And so we, the assurers, are contented, and do hereby promise and bind ourselves, each one for his own part, our heirs, executors, and goods to the assured, their executors, administrators, and assigns, for the true performance of the premises, confessing ourselves paid the consideration due unto us for this assurance by the assured, at and after the rate of

IN WITNESS whereof we, the assurers, have subscribed our names and sums assured in London.

MEMORANDUM

N.B.—Corn, fish, salt, fruit, flour, and seed are warranted free from average, less general, or the ship be stranded—sugar, tobacco, hemp, flax, hides and skins are warranted free from average, under five pounds per cent., and all other goods, also the ship and freight, are warranted free from average, under three pounds per cent. unless general, or the ship be stranded.

RULES FOR CONSTRUCTION OF POLICY.

The following are the rules referred to by this Act for the construction of a policy in the above or other life form, where the context does not otherwise require—

1. LOST OR NOT LOST. Where the subject-matter is insured "lost or not lost," and the loss has occurred before the contract is concluded, the risk attaches unless, at such time the assured was aware of the loss, and the insurer was not.

2. FROM. Where the subject-matter is insured "from" a particular place, the risk does not attach until the ship starts on the voyage insured.

3. AT AND FROM SHIP.
    (a) Where a ship is insured "at and from" a particular place, and she is at that place in good safety when the contract is concluded, the risk attaches immediately.
    (b) If she be not at that place when the contract is concluded the risk attaches as soon as she arrives there in good safety, and, unless the policy otherwise provides, it is immaterial that she is covered by another policy for a specified time after arrival.
    FREIGHT
    (c) Where chartered freight is insured "at and from" a particular place, and the ship is at that place in good safety when the contract is concluded the risk attaches immediately. If she be not there when the contract is concluded, the risk attaches as soon as she arrives there in good safety.
    (d) Where freight, other than chartered freight, is payable without special conditions and is insured "at and from" a particular place, the risk attaches *pro rata* as the goods or merchandise are shipped; provided that if there be cargo in readiness which belongs to the shipowner, or which some other person has contracted with him to ship, the risk attaches as soon as the ship is ready to receive such cargo.

4. FROM THE LOADING THEREOF. Where goods or other movables are insured "from the loading thereof," the risk does not attach until such goods or movables are actually on board, and the insurer is not liable for them while in transit from the shore to the ship.

5. SAFELY LANDED. Where the risk on goods or other movables continues until they are "safely landed," they must be landed in the customary manner and within a reasonable time after arrival at the port of discharge, and if they are not so landed the risk ceases.

6. TOUCH AND STAY. In the absence of any further licence or usage, the liberty to touch and stay "at any port or place whatsoever" does not authorise the ship to depart from the course of her voyage from the port of departure to the port of destination.

7. PERILS OF THE SEAS. The term "perils of the seas" refers only to fortuitous accidents or casualties of the seas. It does not include the ordinary action of the winds and waves.

8. PIRATES. The term "pirates" includes passengers who mutiny and rioters who attack the ship from the shore.

9. THIEVES. The term "thieves" does not cover clandestine theft or a theft committed by any one of the ship's company, whether crew or passengers.

10. RESTRAINT OF PRINCES. The term "arrests, etc., of kings, princes, and people" refers to political or executive acts, and does not include a loss caused by riot or by ordinary judicial process.

11. BARRATRY. The term "barratry" includes every wrongful act wilfully committed by the master or crew to the prejudice of the owner, or, as the case may be, the charterer.

12. **ALL OTHER PERILS.** The term "all other perils" includes only perils similar in kind to the perils specifically mentioned in the policy.

13. AVERAGE UNLESS GENERAL. The term "average unless general" means a partial loss of the subject-matter insured other than a general average loss, and does not include "particular charges."

14. STRANDED. Where the ship has stranded, the insurer is liable for the excepted losses, although the loss is not attributable to the stranding, provided that when the stranding takes place the risk has attached and, if the policy be on goods, that the damaged goods are on board.

15. SHIP. The term "ship" includes the hull, materials and outfit, stores and provisions for the officers and crew, and, in the case of vessels engaged in a special trade, the ordinary fittings requisite for the trade, and also, in the case of a steamship, the machinery, boilers, and coals and engine stores, if owned by the assured.

16. FREIGHT. The term "freight" includes the profit derivable by a shipowner from the employment of his ship to carry his own goods or movables, as well as freight payable by a third party, but does not include passage money.

17. GOODS. The term "goods" means goods in the nature of merchandise, and does not include personal effects or provisions and stores for use on board.

In the absence of any usage to the contrary, deck cargo and living animals must be insured specifically, and not under the general denomination of goods.

Appendix 2

Rules of Practice of Association of Average Adjusters of the United States

I. COMPENSATION AND EXPENSES OF MASTER
Adopted February 17, 1885

Where the voyage is broken up by reason of shipwreck or condemnation of the ship at a place short of the port of destination, the master shall be entitled to compensation from the general interests for the time necessarily occupied by him in transacting the business growing out of the disaster until his departure thence for the home port with the proceeds, general accounts and vouchers.

He shall also be entitled to a reasonable indemnification for his necessary expenses and services in returning to the home port when needed or required, by the peculiar circumstances of the case, to justify his acts at the place of disaster, or to give information, not otherwise afforded, to finally adjust and apportion the average charges to be paid by the general or special interests for whom such services are performed, to be determined by the nature of the case.

These rules shall apply whether the vessel be in ballast or with cargo.

II. INTEREST ON ALLOWANCES IN GENERAL AVERAGE
Adopted April 21, 1885

Where allowances, sacrifices or expenditures are charged or made good in general average, interest shall be allowed thereon at the legal rate prevailing at the place of adjustment.

III. DECK LOAD JETTISON
Adopted October 9, 1894

Where cargo consisting of one kind of goods is in accordance with a custom of trade, carried on and under deck, that portion of the cargo loaded on deck shall be subject to the same rules of adjustment in case of jettison and expenses incurred, as if the same were laden under deck.

IV. LOSS OF FREIGHT ON CARGO SACRIFICED
Adopted January 16, 1900

Rescinded October 9, 1913: rescission to take effect December 9, 1913.

V. CREDIT FOR EXPENSES SAVED BY SALVAGE SERVICES, ETC.
Adopted October 9, 1902

Where salvage services are rendered to a vessel, or she becomes disabled and is necessarily towed to her port of destination, and the expenses of such towage are allowable in general average, there shall be credited against the allowance such ordinary expenses as would have been incurred, but have been saved by the salvage or towage services.

VI. CREDITS FOR OLD MATERIAL
Adopted October 13, 1910

Where old material is replaced by new, credit shall be given in the average statement for the value of proceeds of the old material, or, if there is no credit, the Adjuster shall insert a note in explanation.

VII. APPROVAL OF REPAIR ACCOUNTS
Adopted October 13, 1910

All repair accounts shall be examined, when practicable, by the owners' surveyor and a surveyor for underwriters before the statement is issued.

The Adjuster shall insert a note in the average statement that this has been done and the result of same.

VIII. SCRAPING AND PAINTING BOTTOM OF VESSEL
Adopted October 13, 1910; Rescinded October 5, 1961.

IX. DRYDOCKING CHARGES AND EXPENSES INCIDENTAL TO DRYDOCKING—PARTICULAR AVERAGE
Adopted October 13, 1910

When a vessel is drydocked:

(1) For owners' account and repairs are found necessary for which underwriters are liable and which can only be effected in drydock; or

(2) For survey and/or repairs for which underwriters are liable and repairs for owners' accounts are made which are immediately necessary for her seaworthiness, or she is due for ordinary drydocking (in accordance with the owners' custom), the cost of removing the vessel to and from the drydock, of docking and undocking, and as much of the dock dues as is common to both classes of work, shall be divided equally between the owners and underwriters.

When the vessel is drydocked for underwriters' account and the owners avail of her being in drydock to scrape and paint or to do other work for their own account which is not immediately necessary for seaworthiness, all the expenses incidental to the drydocking of the vessel shall be charged to the underwriters.

The Adjuster shall insert a note in the average statement in explanation of the allowances made.

X. OVERTIME WORK—GENERAL AND PARTICULAR AVERAGE SAVINGS—APPORTIONMENT
Adopted October 13, 1910; Amended October 14, 1937

The bonus or extra cost of overtime work on repairs shall be allowed in general and/or particular average up to the amount of the saving of drydock dues or other charges, which otherwise would have been incurred and allowed in general and/or particular average; and where the overtime work effects a savings both of general average expense (excluding general average repairs) and in the cost of repairs the extra cost for overtime shall be apportioned over the general average expenses saved and the savings in the cost of repairs.

The Adjuster shall insert a note in the average statement in explanation of the allowances made.

XI. TEMPORARY REPAIRS—PARTICULAR AVERAGE
Adopted October 13, 1910

The cost of reasonable temporary repairs shall be allowed:
When made in order to effect a saving in the cost of permanent repairs;
When complete repairs cannot be made at the port where the vessel is;
When the material or parts necessary for permanent repairs are unobtainable
   at the port where the vessel is, except after unreasonable delay.

The Adjuster shall insert a note in the average statement in explanation of the allowances made.

XII. ALLOWANCE IN RESPECT OF PROVISIONS
Adopted October 13, 1910; Amended 1913, 1917, 1920, 1922, 1923, 1930, 1942, 1947, May 19, 1952, October 1, 1970, October 6, 1976 & October 1, 1980

When allowance is made in General Average for provisions of Masters, Officers, and crews, the allowance shall be $8.00 per person per day for voyages beginning on or after October 1, 1980. For voyages beginning prior to October 6, 1976, the allowance shall be based on previous Rule XII.

The Rule shall apply to United States flag vessels in all instances and to vessels of other flags, on voyages to and from United States ports, including Territories and Insular possessions, when the general average is stated in accordance with the laws and usages of the United States, even though such laws and usages may be modified by York/Antwerp Rules.

XIII. ALLOWANCES IN GENERAL AVERAGE FOR REPAIRS TO VESSELS
Adopted April 10, 1913; Amended October 5, 1961 & October 4, 1979

Repairs to be allowed in general average shall not be subject to deductions in respect of "new for old" where old materials or parts are replaced by new unless the ship is over fifteen years old in which case there shall be a deduction of one third. The deductions shall be regulated by the age of the ship from the 31st December of the year of completion of construction to the date of the general average act, except for insulation, life- and similar boats, communications and navigational apparatus and equipment, machinery and boilers for which the deductions shall be regulated by the age of the particular parts to which they apply.

The deductions shall be made only from the cost of the new material or parts when finished and ready to be installed in the ship.

No deduction shall be made in respect of provisions, stores, anchors and chain cables.

Drydock and slipway dues and costs of shifting the ship shall be allowed in full.

The costs of cleaning, painting or coating of bottom shall not be allowed in general average unless the bottom has been painted or coated within the twelve months preceding the date of the general average act in which case one half of such costs shall be allowed.

XIV. FREIGHT—CONTRIBUTORY VALUE AND AMOUNT MADE GOOD IN GENERAL AVERAGE
Adopted October 9, 1913; Amended October 11, 1939 & October 11, 1950

The contributory value of freight shall be the amount at risk of the Shipowners or Charterers and earned on cargo on board, to which shall be added the allowance in general average for net freight lost, and from the total shall be deducted the expenses (except those allowed in general average) incurred to earn it after the date of the general average act; and if there be any cargo on board on which the freight is not at risk of the Shipowners or Charterers the charges to be deducted from the freight at their risk shall be only those which would have been incurred if such cargo had not been aboard.

And when loss of freight at risk of the Shipowners or Charterers is allowed in general average the allowance shall be for the net freight lost, to be ascertained by deducting from the gross freight sacrificed the expenses that would have been incurred, subsequent to the sacrifice, to earn it, but which, because of the sacrifice, have not been incurred.

Where the general average is prepared in accordance with York/Antwerp Rules and there be any cargo on board on which the freight is not at risk of the Shipowners or Charterers, the deductions made from the freight at their risk to arrive at the contributory value of freight shall be determined in accordance with the principles set forth above.

XV. CLASSIFICATION SURVEYORS' FEES—
PARTICULAR AVERAGE
Adopted April 19, 1923; Amended October 14, 1937

Fees of Classification Societies for surveys of particular average damages shall be allowed (notwithstanding that a survey of such damages would have been required for classification purposes) in addition to a fee paid an independent surveyor.

XVI. COMPENSATION AND EXPENSES OF
OWNERS' SUPERINTENDENT
Adopted April 19, 1923

In cases where a superintendent, or other shore employee, in the permanent employ of the owner of a vessel, superintends the repair of average damage, compensation for such service and incidental expenses shall be allowed in average:

First—When an independent surveyor, or outside man, has not been employed for this purpose, and the vessel is repaired at a port other than where the superintendent, or other employee, makes his headquarters; or

Second—When the owner has incurred extra expense by employing, temporarily, another man to do the work of the superintendent, or other shore employee, while either of the latter is engaged in superintending repair of average damage.

XVII. ALLOWANCES FOR CARGO DAMAGED AND SOLD
AND CONTRIBUTORY VALUE OF SAME
Adopted June 2, 1927

Where cargo is damaged, as a consequence of a general average act, and sold, and the extent of the loss has not been otherwise determined, the amount, if any, to be made good for same shall be based on the market value at the date of arrival or at the termination of the adventure (dependent on the facts) and shall be determined on the "salvage loss" basis irrespective of the date of sale.

The contributory value of such cargo shall be based on the proceeds of sale to which shall be added any amount made good; deduction being made of charges incurred subsequent to the general average act, except such charges as are allowed in general average.

"The date of arrival" in the case of a vessel herself delivering all cargo saved shall be the last day of discharge; and in complex cases this principle shall be followed as far as possible.

XVIII. WAGES AND PROVISIONS—GENERAL AVERAGE
Adopted October 14, 1937

In making allowance for wages and provisions in General Average either under American law or York/Antwerp Rules a period of less than twelve hours, either alone or in excess of a number of complete days, shall be disregarded and a period of twelve hours or more, either alone or in excess of a number of complete days, shall be treated as a whole day.

XIX. FIRE EXTINGUISHERS
Adopted October 14, 1937

The cost of replacing gas or any commodity used in efforts to extinguish a fire on board a vessel shall be allowed in general average even though the gas or commodity was on board the vessel at the time the fire was discovered.

XX. APPORTIONMENT OF LEGAL COSTS AND/OR OTHER EXPENSES IN COLLISION CASES
Adopted April 13, 1961

In cases involving collisions, the legal costs and/or other expenses incurred to determine liability either by court action, arbitration or determination by consent of the parties shall be apportioned rateably over the full provable damages, excluding interest and costs, of the claim and counter-claim which have been or would have been allowed.

Nothing contained in this rule shall affect those legal costs and/or other expenses incurred specifically for the purpose of defense or recovery which shall be charged accordingly.

XXI. AIR FREIGHT
Adopted April 13, 1961

The cost of air freight on repair parts shall be allowed as part of the reasonable cost of repairs when the shipment of such parts by water and/or land conveyance would result in unreasonable delay.

Nevertheless when shipment by air saves General Average expense the extra cost of shipment by air over the cost of water and/or land conveyance shall be allowed in General Average up to the expense saved.

Appendix 3

RULES OF PRACTICE
OF THE ASSOCIATION OF
AVERAGE ADJUSTERS [1]

SECTION A—GENERAL RULES

A1   ADJUSTMENTS FOR THE CONSIDERATION OF UNDERWRITERS

That any claim prepared for the consideration of underwriters shall include a statement of the reasons of the average adjuster for stating such a claim, and when submitted in conjunction with a claim for which underwriters are liable, shall be shown in such a manner as clearly to distinguish the claim for consideration from other claims embodied in the same adjustment.

An earlier Rule of Practice dealing with this subject was accepted in 1875, confirmed in 1876, and rescinded in 1894/95. The text of the earlier Rule is printed in the report for 1876, p. 12.

A2   INTEREST AND COMMISSION FOR ADVANCING FUNDS

That, in practice, interest and commission for advancing funds are only allowable in average when, proper and necessary steps having been taken to make a collection on account, an out-of-pocket expense for interest and/or commission for advancing funds is reasonably incurred.

See note under Rule A3.

A3   AGENCY COMMISSION AND AGENCY

That, in practice, neither commission (excepting bank commission) nor any charge by way of agency or remuneration for trouble is allowed to the shipowner in average, except in respect of services rendered on behalf of cargo when such services are not involved in the contract of affreightment.

An earlier Rule of Practice dealing with the subject of Agency fees chargeable by shipowners was accepted in 1879, confirmed in 1880, and rescinded in 1906/7, following the report of a Special Committee. The text of the earlier Rule is incorporated in the Committee's report, printed at 1906, p. 21.

---

[1] Adopted 1981. These Rules of Practice are reproduced by kind permission of the Association of Average Adjusters.

A4   Duty of Adjusters in respect of Cost of Repairs

That in adjusting particular average on ship or general average which inludes repairs, it is the duty of the adjuster to satisfy himself that such reasonable and usual precautions have been taken to keep down the cost of repairs as a prudent shipowner would have taken if uninsured.

A5   Claims on Ships Machinery

That in all claims on ship's machinery for repairs, no claim for a new propeller or new shaft shall be admitted into an adjustment, unless the adjuster shall obtain and insert into his statement evidence showing what has become of the old propeller or shaft.

A6   Water Casks

Water casks or tanks carried on a ship's deck are not paid for by underwriters as general or particular average; nor are warps or other articles when improperly carried on deck.

A7 Adjustment; Policies of Insurance and Names of Underwriters

That no adjustment shall be drawn up showing the amount of payments by or to the underwriters, unless the policies or copies of the policies of insurance or certificates of insurance, for which the statement is required, be produced to the average adjusters. Such statement shall set out sufficient details of the underwriters interested and the amounts due on the respective policies produced.

An earlier Rule of Practice dealing with this subject was accepted in 1889, confirmed in 1890, and rescinded in 1968/69. The text of the earlier Rule is printed in the report for 1890, p. 33.

A8   Apportionment of Costs in Collision Cases

That when a vessel sustains and does damage by collision, and litigation consequently results for the purpose of testing liability, the technicality of the vessel having been plaintiff or defendant in the litigation shall not necessarily govern the apportionment of the costs of such litigation, which shall be apportioned between claim and counter-claim in proportion to the amount, excluding interest, which has been or would have been allowed in respect of each in the event of the claim or counter-claim being established; provided that when a claim or counter-claim is made solely for the purpose of defence, and is not allowed, the costs apportioned thereto shall be treated as costs of defence.

A9   Franchise Charges

The expenses of protest, survey, and other proofs of loss, including the commission or other expenses of a sale by auction, are not admitted to make up the percentage of a claim; and are only paid by the underwriters in case the loss amounts to a claim without them.

SECTION B—GENERAL AVERAGE

RULES OF GENERAL APPLICATION

Note: In this edition, the Rules relating to the adjustment of general average under English law and practice have been transferred to Section F.

B1   BASIS OF ADJUSTMENT

That in any adjustment of general average not made in accordance with British law it shall be prefaced on what principle or according to what law the adjustment has been made, and the reason for so adjusting the claim shall be set forth.

In all cases the adjuster shall give particulars in a prominent position in the average statement of the clause or clauses contained in the charter-party and/or bills of lading with reference to the adjustment of general average.

B2-B8 inclusive — *transferred to section F.*

B9   CLAIMS ARISING OUT OF DEFICIENCY OF FUEL

That in adjusting general average arising out of deficiency of fuel, the facts on which the general average is based shall be set forth in the adjustment, including the material dates and distances, and particulars of fuel supplies and consumption.

B10-B23 inclusive — *transferred to section F.*

B24   CONTRIBUTORY VALUE OF SHIP

That in any adjustment of general average there shall be set forth the certificate on which the contributory value of the ship is based or, if there be no such certificate, the information adopted in lieu thereof, and any amount made good shall be specified.

B25   CONTRIBUTORY VALUE OF FREIGHT

That in any adjustment of general average there shall be set forth the amount of the gross freight and the freight advanced, if any; also the charges and wages deducted and any amount made good.

The first paragraph of Rule B25, dealing with the basis of adjustment under English law and practice, has been transferred to Section F and re-numbered F22.

B26   VESSEL IN BALLAST AND UNDER CHARTER: CONTRIBUTING INTERESTS

For the purpose of ascertaining the liability of Underwriters on British policies of insurance, the following provisions shall apply:—

When a vessel is proceeding in ballast to load under a voyage charter entered into by the shipowner before the general average act, the interests contributing to the general average shall be the vessel, such items of stores and equipment as belong to parties other than the owners of the vessel (e.g. bunkers, wireless installation and navigational instruments) and the freight earned under the voyage charter computed in the usual way after deduction of contingent expenses subsequent to the general average act. Failing a prior termination of the adventure, the place where the adventure shall be deemed to end and at which the values for contribution to general average shall be calculated is the final port of discharge of the cargo carried under the charter but in the event of the prior loss of the vessel and freight, or either of them, the general average shall attach to any surviving interest or interests including freight advanced at the loading port deducting therefrom contingent expenses subsequent to the general average act.

When a vessel is proceeding in ballast under a time charter alone or a time charter and a voyage charter entered into by the time charterer, the general average shall attach to the vessel and such items of stores and equipment as are indicated above. Failing a prior termination of the adventure, the adventure shall be deemed to end and the values for contribution to general average calculated at the first loading port upon the commencement of loading cargo.

When the charter to which the shipowner is a party provides for York–Antwerp Rules, the general average shall be adjusted in accordance with those Rules and British law and practice and without regard to the law and practice of any foreign port at which the adventure may terminate; and in the interpretation of Rule XI it shall be immaterial whether the extra period of detention takes place at a port of loading, call or refuge, provided that the detention is in consequence of accident, sacrifice or other extraordinary circumstance occurring whilst the vessel is in ballast.

In practice neither time charter hire, as such, nor time charterer's voyage freight shall contribute to general average.

The earliest Rule of Practice dealing with this subject was accepted in 1896, confirmed in 1897 and rescinded in 1926, when after reference to a Special Committee it was replaced by a new Rule, which was in its turn referred to a Special Committee in 1944 and rescinded in 1945/46. The text of the original Rule is printed in the report for 1897, pp. 34/35 and the subsequent Rule in the report for November 1926, p. 9.

B27   ULTERIOR CHARTERED FREIGHT: CONTRIBUTION TO GENERAL AVERAGE

That when at the time of a general average act the vessel has on board cargo shipped under charter-party or bills of lading, and is also under a separate charter to load another cargo after the cargo then in course of carriage has been discharged, the ulterior chartered freight shall not contribute to the general average.

B28   DEDUCTIONS FROM FREIGHT AT CHARTERER'S RISK

That freight at the risk of the charterer shall be subject to no deduction for wages and charges, except in the case of charters in which the wages or charges are payable by the charterer, in which case such freight shall be governed by the same rule as freight at the risk of the shipowner.

B29   FORWARDING CHARGES ON ADVANCED FREIGHT

That in case of wreck, the cargo being forwarded to its destination, the charterer, who has paid a lump sum on account of freight, which is not to be returned in the event of the vessel being lost, shall not be liable for any portion of the forwarding freight and charges, when the same are less than the balance of freight payable to the shipowner at the port of destination under the original charter-party.

B30   SACRIFICE FOR THE COMMON SAFETY: DIRECT LIABILITY OF UNDERWRITERS

That in case of general average sacrifice there is, under ordinary policies of insurance, a direct liability of an underwriter on ship for loss of or damage to ship's materials, and of an underwriter on goods or freight, for loss of or damage to goods or loss of freight so sacrificed as a general average loss; that such loss not being particular average is not taken into account in computing the memorandum percentages, and that the direct liability of an underwriter for such loss is consequently unaffected by the memorandum or any other warranty respecting particular average.

An earlier Rule of Practice dealing with this subject was accepted in 1874, confirmed in 1875 and rescinded in 1889. The text of this earlier Rule is printed in the report for 1875, p. 18.

B31   SACRIFICE OF SHIP'S STORES: DIRECT LIABILITY OF UNDERWRITERS

That underwriters insuring ship's stores, bunker coal or fuel, destroyed or used as part of a general average operation, shall only be liable for those articles as a direct claim on the policy when they formed part of the property at risk at the time of the peril giving rise to the general average act.

B32   ENFORCEMENT OF GENERAL AVERAGE LIEN BY SHIPOWNERS

That in all cases where general average damage to ship is claimed direct from the underwriters on that interest, the average adjusters shall ascertain whether the shipowners have taken the necessary steps to enforce their lien for general average on the cargo, and shall insert in the average statement a note giving the result of their enquiries.

B33   UNDERWRITER'S LIABILITY

If the ship or cargo be insured for more than its contributory value, the underwriter pays what is assessed on the contributory value. But where insured for less than the contributory value, the underwriter pays on the insured value; and when there has been a particular average for damage which forms a deduction from the contributory value of the ship that must be deducted from the insured value to find upon what the underwriter contributes.

This rule does not apply to foreign adjustments, when the basis of contribution is something other than the net value of the thing insured.

That in practice, in applying the above rule for the purpose of ascertaining the liability of underwriters for contribution to general average and salvage charges, deduction shall be made from the insured value of all losses and charges for which underwriters are liable and which have been deducted in arriving at the contributory value.

In adjusting the liability of underwriters on freight for general average contribution and salvage charges, effect shall be given to Section 73 of the Marine Insurance Act, 1906, by comparing the gross and not the net amount of freight at risk with the insured value in the case of a valued policy or the insurable value in the case of an unvalued policy.

B34 THE DUTY OF ADJUSTERS IN CASES INVOLVING REFUNDS OF GENERAL AVERAGE DEPOSITS OR APPORTIONMENT OF SALVAGE, COLLISION RECOVERIES, OR OTHER FUNDS

That in cases of general average where deposits have been collected and it is likely that repayments will have to be made, measures be taken by the adjuster to ascertain the names of underwriters who have reimbursed their assured in respect of such deposits; that the names of any such underwriters be set forth in the adjustment as claimants of refund, if any, to which they are apparently entitled; and that on completion of the adjustment, notice be sent to all underwriters whose names are so set forth as to any refund of which they appear as claimants and as to the steps to be taken in order to obtain payment of the same.

That in cases where the names of any underwriters are not to be ascertained on completion of the adjustment, notice be sent to the Secretary of Lloyd's, to the Institute of London Underwriters, to the Liverpool Underwriters' Association, and to the Association of Underwriters of Glasgow, notifying such interests as have not been appropriated to underwriters.

And that in cases of apportionment of salvage or other funds for distribution, similar measures be taken by the adjuster to safeguard the interests of any underwriters who may be entitled to benefit under the apportionment.

B35 MEMORANDUM TO STATEMENTS SHOWING REFUNDS IN RESPECT OF GENERAL AVERAGE DEPOSITS

That the following memorandum shall appear at the end of statements which show refunds to be due in respect of General Average Deposits, viz:—

Memorandum — Refunds of general average deposits shown in this statement should only be paid on production of the original deposit receipts.

B36 INTEREST ON DEPOSITS

That, unless otherwise expressly provided, the interest accrued on deposits on account of salvage and/or general average and/or particular and/or other charges, or on the balance of such deposits after payments on account, if any, have been made, shall be credited to the depositor or those to whom his rights in respect of the deposits have been transferred.

B37   Apportionment of Interest on Amounts Made Good

That in practice (in the absence of express agreement between the parties concerned) interest allowed on amounts made good shall be apportioned between assured and underwriters, taking into account the sums paid by underwriters and the dates when such payments were made, notwithstanding that by the addition of interest the underwriter may receive a larger sum than he has paid.

SECTION C—YORK-ANTWERP RULES

C1   Salvage Services rendered under an Agreement

Expenses for salvage services rendered by or accepted under agreement shall in practice be treated as general average provided that such expenses were incurred for the common safety within the meaning of Rule " A " of the York–Antwerp Rules, 1924 or York–Antwerp Rules 1950.

An earlier Rule of Practice dealing with this subject was accepted in 1927, confirmed in 1928, and rescinded in 1942/43. The text of the earlier Rule is printed in the report for 1928, p. 32.

C2   Commission Allowed under York–Antwerp Rules

That the commission of 2 per cent allowed on general average disbursements under Rule XXI of York–Antwerp Rules 1924 and Rule XX of York–Antwerp Rules 1950 or 1974, shall be credited in full to the party who has authorised the expenditure and is liable for payment, except that where the funds for payment are provided in the first instance in whole or in part from the deposit funds, or by other parties to the adventure, or by underwriters, the commission on such advances shall be credited to the deposit funds or to the parties or underwriters providing the funds for payment.

C3   York–Antwerp Rules, 1924.   Rules X (a) and XX

That, in practice, where a vessel is at any port or place in circumstances in which the wages and maintenance of crew during detention there for the purpose of repairs necessary for the safe prosecution of the voyage would be admissible in general average under Rule XI of the York–Antwerp Rules, 1924, and the vessel is necessarily removed thence to another port or place because such repairs cannot be effected at the first port or place, the provisions of Rule X (a) shall be applied to the second port or place as if it were a port or place of refuge within that Rule and the provisions of Rule XX shall be applied to the prolongation of the voyage occasioned by such removal.

C4   York–Antwerp Rules 1950 and 1974   Rule X (a)

That in practice, in applying the second paragraph of Rule X (a), a vessel shall be deemed to be at a port or place of refuge when she is at any port or place in circumstances in which the wages and maintenance of the Master, Officers and crew incurred during any extra period of detention there would be admissible in General Average under the provisions of Rule XI.

SECTION D—DAMAGE AND REPAIRS TO SHIP

D1 EXPENSES OF REMOVING A VESSEL FOR REPAIR

Where a vessel is in need of repair at any port, and is removed thence to some other port for the purpose of repairs, either because the repairs cannot be effected, or cannot be effected prudently:

(a) The necessary expenses incurred in moving the vessel to the port of repair shall be allowed as part of the cost of repair, and where the vessel after repairing forthwith returns to the port from which she was removed, the necessary expenses incurred in so returning shall also be allowed.

(b) Where by moving the vessel to the port of repair any new freight is earned, or any expenses are saved in relation to the current voyage of the vessel, such net earnings or savings shall be deducted from the expenses of moving her, and where the vessel loads a new cargo at the port of repair no expenses subsequent to the completion of repair shall be allowed.

The expenses of removal include the cost of temporary repair, ballasting, wages and provisions of crew and/or runners, pilotage, towage, extra marine insurance, port charges, fuel and engine-room stores.

(c) This rule shall not admit any ordinary expenses incurred in fulfilment of a contract of affreightment, though such expenses are increased by the removal to a port of repair.

D2 FUEL AND STORES USED IN REPAIR OF DAMAGE TO THE VESSEL

That the cost of replacing fuel and stores consumed either in the repair of damage to a vessel, in working the engines or winches to assist in the repairs of damage, or in moving her to a place or repair within the limits of the port where she is lying, shall be treated as part of the cost of repairs.

D3 RIGGING CHAFED

Rigging injured by straining or chafing is not charged to underwriters, unless such injury is caused by blows of the sea, grounding, or contact; or by displacement, through sea peril, of the spars, channels, bulwarks, or rails.

D4 SAILS SPLIT OR BLOWN AWAY

Sails split by the wind, or blown away while set, unless occasioned by the ship's grounding or coming into collision, or in consequence of damage to the spars to which the sails are bent, are not charged to underwriters.

D5 DRY DOCK EXPENSES

1. That, in practice, where repairs, for the cost of which underwriters are liable, are necessarily effected in dry dock as an immediate consequence of the casualty, or the vessel is taken out of service especially to effect such repairs in dry dock,

the cost of entering and leaving the dry dock, in addition to so much of the dock dues as is necessary for the repair of the damage, shall be chargeable in full to the underwriters, notwithstanding that the shipowner may have taken advantage of the vessel being in dry dock to carry out survey for classification purposes or to effect repairs on his account which are not immediately necessary to make the vessel seaworthy.

2. (a) Where repairs on Owners' account which are immediately necessary to make the vessel seaworthy and which can only be effected in dry dock are executed concurrently with other repairs, for the cost of which underwriters are liable, and which also can only be effected in dry dock,

   (b) Where the repairs, for the cost of which underwriters are liable, are deferred until a routine dry-docking and are then executed concurrently with repairs on Owners' account which require the use of the dry dock, whether or not such Owners' repairs affect the seaworthiness of the vessel,

the cost of entering and leaving the dry dock, in addition to so much of the dock dues as is common to both repairs, shall be divided equally between the shipowner and the underwriters, irrespective of the fact that the repairs for which underwriters are liable may relate to more than one voyage or accident or may be payable by more than one set of underwriters.

3. Sub-division between underwriters of the proportion of dry-docking expenses chargeable to them shall be made on the basis of voyages, and/or such other franchise units as are specified in the policies.

4. In determining whether the franchise is reached the whole cost of dry-docking necessary for the repair of the damage, less the proportion (if any) chargeable to Owners when Section (a) of paragraph 2. applies, shall be taken into consideration, notwithstanding that there are other damages to which a portion of the cost of dry-docking has to be apportioned in ascertaining the amount actually recoverable.

An earlier Rule of Practice dealing with this subject was accepted in 1891, confirmed in 1892, and amended in 1903/4 after reference to a Special Committee. It was again referred to a Social Committee in November 1926, further amended in 1927/28, and rescinded in 1970/71. The texts are printed in the reports for 1892, p. 18; 1904, p. 42 and 1928, p. 31.

D6   TANKERS—TREATMENT OF THE COST OF TANK CLEANING AND/OR GAS-FREEING

1. That, in practice, where repairs, for the cost of which underwriters are liable, require the tanks to be rough cleaned and/or gas-freed as an immediate consequence of the casualty, or the vessel is taken out of service especially to effect such repairs, the cost of such rough cleaning and/or gas-freeing shall be chargeable in full to the underwriters, notwithstanding that the shipowner may have taken advantage of the vessel being rough cleaned and/or gas-freed to carry out survey for classification purposes or to effect repairs on his account which are not immediately necessary to make the vessel seaworthy.

2. (a) Where repairs on Owners' account which are immediately necessary to make the vessel seaworthy and which require the tanks being rough cleaned and/or gas-freed are executed concurrently with other repairs, for the cost of which underwriters are liable, and which also require the tanks being rough cleaned and/or gas-freed.

(*b*) Where the repairs, for the cost of which underwriters are liable, are deferred until a routine dry-docking or repair period, at which time repairs on Owners' account which also require the tanks being rough cleaned and/or gas-freed are effected, whether or not such Owners' repairs affect the seaworthiness of the vessel,

the cost of such rough-cleaning and/or gas-freeing as is common to both repairs shall be divided equally between the shipowners and the underwriters, irrespective of the fact that the repairs for which underwriters are liable may relate to more than one voyage or accident or may be payable by more than one set of underwriters.

3. The cost of fine cleaning specifically for a particular repair or particular repairs shall be divided in accordance with the principles set forth above.

4. Sub-division between underwriters of the proportion of rough tank cleaning and/or gas-freeing and/or fine cleaning chargeable to them shall be made on the basis of voyages, and/or such other franchise units as are specified in the policies.

5. In determining whether the franchise is reached the whole cost of rough cleaning and/or gas-freeing and/or fine cleaning necessary for the repair of the damage, less the proportion (if any) chargeable to Owners when Section (a) of paragraph 2. applies, shall be taken into consideration, notwithstanding that there are other damages to which a portion of the cost of rough tank cleaning and/or gas-freeing and/or fine cleaning has to be apportioned in ascertaining the amount actually recoverable.

D7   PARTICULAR AVERAGE ON SHIP: DEDUCTION OF ONE-THIRD

The deduction for new work in place of old is fixed by custom at one-third, with the following exceptions:

Anchors are allowed in full. Chain cables are subject to one-sixth only.

Metal sheathing is dealt with, by allowing in full the cost of a weight equal to the gross weight of metal sheathing stripped off minus the proceeds of the old metal. Nails, felt, and labour metalling are subject to one-third.

The rule applies to iron as well as to wooden ships, and to labour as well as material. It does not apply to the expense of straightening bent ironwork, and to the labour of taking out and replacing it.

It does not apply to graving dock expenses and removals, cartages, use of shears, stages, and graving dock materials.

It does not apply to a ship's first voyage.

D8   SCRAPING AND PAINTING

Where the Policy includes a Clause to the effect that:

"No claim shall in any case be allowed in respect of scraping or painting the vessel's bottom".

(*a*)   Gritblasting and/or other surface preparation of new bottom plates ashore and supplying and applying any " shop " primer thereto

(*b*)   Gritblasting and/or other surface preparation of:

(*i*)   the butts or area of plating immediately adjacent to any renewed or refitted plating damaged during the course of welding and/or repairs (*ii*) areas of plating damaged during the course of fairing, either in place or ashore

(*c*)   Supplying and applying the first coat of primer/anticorrosive to those particular areas mentioned in (*a*) and (*b*) above

shall be allowed as part of the reasonable cost of repairs in respect of bottom plating damaged by an insured peril and shall be deemed not to be excluded by the wording of this Clause. The gritblasting and⁵or other surface preparation and the painting of all other areas of the bottom is excluded by the Clause.

SECTION E—PARTICULAR AVERAGE ON GOODS

E1   ADJUSTMENT ON BONDED PRICES

In the following cases it is customary to adjust particular average on a comparison of bonded, instead of duty-paid prices:

In claims for damage to tea, tobacco, coffee, wine, and spirits imported into this country.

E2   ADJUSTMENT OF AVERAGE ON GOODS SOLD IN BOND

That in consequence of the facilities generally offered to bond goods at their destination, at which terms they are often sold, the term " Gross Proceeds " shall, for the purpose of adjustment, be taken to mean the price at which the goods are sold to the consumer, after payment of freight and landing charges, but exclusive of Customs duty, in cases where it is the custom of the port to sell or deal with the goods in bond.

E3   APPORTIONMENT OF INSURED VALUE OF GOODS

That where different qualities or descriptions of cargo are valued in the policy at a lump sum, such sum shall, for the purpose of adjusting claims, be apportioned on the invoice values where the invoice distinguishes the separate values of the said different qualities or descriptions; and over the net arrived sound values in all other cases.

E4   ALLOWANCE FOR WATER AND OR IMPURITIES IN PICKED COTTON

When bales of cotton are picked, and the pickings are sold wet, the allowance for water in the pickings (where there are no means of ascertaining it) is by custom fixed at one-third.

There is a similar custom to deduct one-sixth from the gross weight of pickings of country damaged cotton to take account of dirt, moisture and other impurities.

E5   ALLOWANCE FOR WATER IN CUT TOBACCO

When damaged tobacco is cut off, the allowance for water in the cuttings is one-fourth if the actual increase cannot be ascertained.

E6   ALLOWANCE FOR WATER IN WOOL

Damaged wool from Australia, New Zealand, and the Cape is subject to a
deduction of 3 per cent. for wet, if the actual increase cannot be ascertained.

E7   EXTRA CHARGES

Extra charges payable by underwriters, when incurred at the port of destination,
are recovered in full; but when charges of the same nature are incurred at an
intermediate port they are subjected to the same treatment in respect of insured
and contributory values, as general average charges.

SECTION F—GENERAL AVERAGE ADJUSTMENT UNDER ENGLISH LAW AND PRACTICE

F1   DECKLOAD JETTISON

The jettison of a deckload carried according to the usage of trade and not in
violation of the contracts of affreightment is general average.

   There is an excepton to this rule in the case of cargoes of cotton, tallow, acids
and some other goods.

F2   DAMAGE BY WATER USED TO EXTINGUISH FIRE

That damage done by water poured down a ship's hold to extinguish a fire be
treated as general average.

F3   EXTINGUISHING FIRE ON SHIPBOARD

Damage done to a ship and cargo, or either of them, by water or otherwise,
including damage by beaching or scuttling a burning ship, in extinguishing a
fire on board the ship, shall be made good as general average; except that no
compensation shall be made for damage by smoke or heat however caused.

*The earliest Rule of Practice dealing with this subject entitled " Damage caused by
water thrown upon burning goods " was accepted in 1874, confirmed in 1875, and
rescinded in 1968/69.*

*It was then replaced by a Rule under the present title which was in its turn rescinded
in 1974/75. The text of the original Rule is printed in the report for 1875, p. 22
and the subsequent Rule in the report for 1968, pp. 18/19.*

F4   VOLUNTARY STRANDING

When a ship is intentionally run on shore and the circumstances are such that if
that course were not adopted she would inevitably drive on shore or on rocks,
no loss or damage caused to the ship, cargo and freight or any of them by such
intentional running on shore shall be made good as general average, but loss or
damage incurred in refloating such a ship shall be allowed as general average.

In all other cases where a ship is intentionally run on shore for the common safety, the consequent loss or damage shall be allowed as general average.

The original Custom of Lloyd's under this headng, amended in 1876, was rescinded in 1968/69. The text of the Custom is printed, as confirmed as a Rule of Practice in the report for 1891, p. 69.

F5   EXPENSES LIGHTENING A SHIP WHEN ASHORE

When a ship is ashore in a position of peril and, in order to float her, cargo is put into lighters, and is then at once re-shipped, the whole cost of lightering, including lighter hire and re-shipping, is general average.

F6   SAILS SET TO FORCE A SHIP OFF THE GROUND

Sails damaged by being set, or kept set, to force a ship off the ground or to drive her higher up the ground for the common safety, are general average.

F7   STRANDED VESSELS: DAMAGE TO ENGINES IN GETTING OFF

That damage caused to machinery and boilers of a stranded vessel, in endeavouring to refloat for the common safety, when the interests are in peril, be allowed in general average.

F8   RESORT TO PORT OF REFUGE FOR GENERAL AVERAGE REPAIRS
                TREATMENT OF THE CHARGES INCURRED

That when a ship puts into a port of refuge in consequence of damage which is itself the subject of general average, and sails thence with her original cargo, or a part of it, the outward as well as the inward port charges shall be treated as general average; and when cargo is discharged for the purpose of repairing such damage, the warehouse rent and reloading of the same shall, as well as the discharge, be treated as general average. (See *Attwood* v. *Sellar*.)

F9   RESORT TO PORT OF REFUGE ON ACCOUNT OF PARTICULAR
                AVERAGE REPAIRS: TREATMENT OF THE CHARGES INCURRED

That when a ship puts into a port of refuge in consequence of damage which it itself the subject of particular average (or not of general average) and when the cargo has been discharged in consequence of such damage, the inward port charges and the cost of discharging the cargo shall be general average, the warehouse rent of cargo shall be a particular charge on cargo, and the cost of reloading and outward port charges shall be a particular charge on freight. (See *Svendsen* v. *Wallace*.)

F10   TREATMENT OF COSTS OF STORAGE AND RELOADING AT
                PORT OF REFUGE

That when the cargo is discharged for the purpose of repairing re-conditioning, or diminishing damage to ship or cargo which is itself the subject of general average, the cost of storage on it and of reloading it shall be treated as general average, equally with the cost of discharging it.

F11   INSURANCE ON CARGO DISCHARGED UNDER AVERAGE

That in practice, where the cost of insurance has been reasonably incurred by the shipowner, or his agents, on cargo discharged under average, such cost shall be treated as part of the cost of storage.

F12   EXPENSES AT A PORT OF REFUGE

When a ship puts into a port of refuge on account of accident and not in consequence of damage which is itself the subject of general average, then on the assumption that the ship was seaworthy at the commencement of the voyage, the Custom of Lloyd's is as follows:

(a) All cost of towage, pilotage, harbour dues, and other extraordinary expenses incurred in order to bring the ship and cargo into a place of safety, are general average. Under the term " extraordinary expenses " are not included wages or victuals of crew, coals, or engine stores, or demurrage.

(b) The cost of discharging the cargo, whether for the common safety, or to repair the ship, together with the cost of conveying it to the warehouse, is general average.

The cost of discharging the cargo on account of damage to it resulting from its own *vice propre*, is chargeable to the owners of the cargo.

(c) The warehouse rent, or other expenses which take the place of warehouse rent, of the cargo when so discharged, is, except as under, a special charge on the cargo.

(d) The cost of reloading the cargo, and the outward port charges incurred through leaving the port of refuge, are when the discharge of cargo falls in general average, a special charge on freight.

(e) The expenses referred to in clause (d) are charged to the party who runs the risk of freight—that is, wholly to the charterer —if the whole freight has been prepaid; and, if part only, then in the proportion which the part prepaid bears to the whole freight.

(f) When the cargo, instead of being sent ashore, is placed on board hulk or lighters during the ship's stay in port, the hulk-hire is divided between general average, cargo, and freight, in such proportions as may place the several contributing interests in nearly the same relative positions as if the cargo has been landed and stored.

F13   TREATMENT OF COSTS OF EXTRAORDINARY DISCHARGE

That no distinction be drawn in practice between discharging cargo for the common safety of ship and cargo, and discharging it for the purpose of effecting at an intermediate port or ports of refuge repairs necessary for the prosecution of the voyage.

F14   TOWAGE FROM A PORT OF REFUGE

That if a ship be in a port of refuge at which it is practicable to repair her, and if, in order to save expense, she be towed thence to some other port, then the extra cost of such towage shall be divided in proportion to the saving of expense thereby occasioned to the several parties to the adventure.

F15   CARGO FORWARDED FROM A PORT OF REFUGE

That if a ship be in a port of refuge at which it is practicable to repair her so as to enable her to carry on the whole cargo, but, in order to save expense, the cargo, or a portion of it, be transhipped by another vessel, or otherwise forwarded, then the cost of such transhipment (up to the amount of expense saved) shall be divided in proportion to the saving of expense thereby occasioned to the several parties to the adventure.

F16   CARGO SOLD AT A PORT OF REFUGE

That if a ship be in a port of refuge at which it is practicable to repair her so as to enable her to carry on the whole cargo, or such portion of it as is fit to be carried on, but, in order to save expense, the cargo, or a portion of it, be, with the consent of the owners of such cargo, sold at the port of refuge, then the loss by sale including loss of freight on cargo so sold (up to the amount of expense saved) shall be divided in proportion to the saving of expense thereby occasioned to the several parties to the adventure; provided always that the amount so divided shall in no case exceed the cost of transhipment and/or forwarding referred to in the preceding rule of the Association.

F17   INTERPRETATION OF THE RULE RESPECTING SUBSTITUTED EXPENSES

That for the purpose of avoiding any misinterpretation of the resolution relating to the apportionment of substituted expenses, it is declared that the saving of expense the reinmentioned is limited to a saving or reduction of the actual outlay, including the crew's wages and provisions, if any, which would have been incurred at the port of refuge, if the vessel has been repaired there, and does not include supposed losses or expenses, such as interest, loss of market, demurrage, or assumed damage by discharging.

F18   TREATMENT OF DAMAGE TO CARGO CAUSED BY DISCHARGE,
                          STORING, AND RELOADING

That damage necessarily done to cargo by discharging, storing, and reloading it, be treated as general average when, and only when the cost of those measures respectively is so treated.

A Custom of Lloyd's concerning cargo discharge at a port of refuge was rescinded in 1890/91, and an earlier Rule of Practice accepted in 1883 and confirmed in 1884 was rescinded in 1968/69. The text of the earlier Rule is printed in the report for 1884, p. 37.

F19   DEDUCTIONS FROM COST OF REPAIRS IN ADJUSTING
                                GENERAL AVERAGE

Repairs to be allowed in general average shall not be subject to deductions in respect of " new for old " where old materials or parts are replaced by new unless the ship is over fifteen years old in which case there shall be a deduction of one third. The deductions shall be regulated by the age of the ship from the 31st December of the year of completion of construction to the date of the general average act, except for insulation, life and similar boats, communications and navigational apparatus and equipment, machinery and boilers for which the deductions shall be regulated by the age of the particular parts to which they apply.

The deductions shall be made only from the cost of the new material or parts when finished and ready to be installed in the ship.

No deduction shall be made in respect of provisions, stores, anchors and chain cables.

Drydock and slipway dues and costs of shifting the ship shall be allowed in full.

The costs of cleaning, painting or coating of bottom shall not be allowed in general average unless the bottom has been painted or coated within the twelve months preceding the date of the general average act in which case one half of such costs shall be allowed.

F20   FREIGHT SACRIFICED: AMOUNT TO BE MADE
                                GOOD IN GENERAL AVERAGE

That the loss of freight to be made good in general average shall be ascertained by deducting from the amount of gross freight lost the charges which the owner thereof would have incurred to earn such freight, but has, in consequence of the sacrifice, not incurred.

F21   BASIS OF CONTRIBUTION TO GENERAL AVERAGE

When property saved by a general average act is injured or destroyed by subsequent accident, the contributing value of that property to a general average which is less than the total contributing value, shall, when it does not reach the port of destination, be its actual net proceeds; when it does it shall be its actual net value at the port of destination on its delivery there; and in all cases any values allowed in general average shall be added to and form part of the contributing value as above.

The above rule shall not apply to adjustments made before the adventure has terminated.

F22   CONTRIBUTORY VALUE OF FREIGHT

That freight at the risk of the shipowner shall contribute to general average upon its gross amount, deducting such charges and crew's wages as would not have been incurred in earning the freight had the ship and cargo been totally lost at the date of the general average act and have not been allowed as general average.

UNIFORMITY RESOLUTION

YORK-ANTWERP RULES 1924: APPLICATION OF RULE XIV

That, in practice, in applying Rule XIV of the York-Antwerp Rules, 1924, the cost of the temporary repair of the accidental damage there referred to shall be allowed in general average up to the saving to the general average by effecting such temporary repair, without regard to the saving (if any) to other interests.

Appendix 4

The York/Antwerp Rules, 1974

CONTRASTED WITH YORK/ANTWERP RULES, 1950

YORK/ANTWERP RULES, 1974	YORK/ANTWERP RULES, 1950
RULE OF INTERPRETATION. In the adjustment of general average the following lettered and numbered Rules shall apply to the exclusion of any Law and Practice inconsistent therewith.	RULE OF INTERPRETATION. In the adjustment of general average the following lettered and numbered Rules shall apply to the exclusion of any Law and Practice inconsistent therewith.
Except as provided by the numbered Rules, general average shall be adjusted according to the lettered Rules.	Except as provided by the numbered Rules, general average shall be adjusted according to the lettered Rules.
RULE A. There is a general average act when, and only when, any extraordinary sacrifice or expenditure is intentionally and reasonably made or incurred for the common safety for the purpose of preserving from peril the property involved in a common maritime adventure.	RULE A. There is a general average act when, and only when, any extraordinary sacrifice or expenditure is intentionally and reasonably made or incurred for the common safety for the purpose of preserving from peril the property involved in a common maritime adventure.
RULE B. General average sacrifices and expenses shall be borne by the different contributing interests on the basis hereinafter provided.	RULE B. General average sacrifices and expenses shall be borne by the different contributing interests on the basis hereinafter provided.
RULE C. Only such losses, damages or expenses which are the direct consequence of the general average act shall be allowed as general average.	RULE C. Only such losses, damages or expenses which are the direct consequence of the general average act shall be allowed as general average.
Loss or damage sustained by the ship or cargo through delay, whether on the voyage or subsequently, such as demurrage, and any indirect loss whatsoever, such as loss of market, shall not be admitted as general average.	Loss or damage sustained by the ship or cargo through delay, whether on the voyage or subsequently, such as demurrage, and any indirect loss whatsoever, such as loss of market, shall not be admitted as general average.

YORK/ANTWERP RULES, 1974

RULE D. Rights to contribution in general average shall not be affected, though the event which gave rise to the sacrifice or expenditure may have been due to the fault of one of the parties to the adventure, but this shall not prejudice any remedies *or defences* which may be open against *or to* that party *in respect* of such fault.

RULE E. The onus of proof is upon the party claiming in general average to show that the loss or expense claimed is properly allowable as general average.

RULE F. Any extra expense incurred in place of another expense which would have been allowable as general average shall be deemed to be general average and so allowed without regard to the saving, if any, to other interests, but only up to the amount of the general average expense avoided.

RULE G. General average shall be adjusted as regards both loss and contribution upon the basis of values at the time and place when and where the adventure ends.

This rule shall not affect the determination of the place at which the average statement is to be made up.

RULE I. JETTISON OF CARGO. No jettison of cargo shall be made good as general average, unless such cargo is carried in accordance with the recognized custom of the trade.

RULE II. DAMAGE BY JETTISON AND SACRIFICE FOR THE COMMON SAFETY. Damage done to a ship and cargo, or either of them, by or in consequence of a sacrifice made for the common safety, and by water which goes down a ship's hatches opened or other opening made for the purpose of making a jettison for the common safety, shall be made good as general average.

YORK/ANTWERP RULES, 1950

RULE D. Rights to contribution in general average shall not be affected, though the event which gave rise to the sacrifice or expenditure may have been due to the fault of one of the parties to the adventure; but this shall not prejudice any remedies which may be open against that party for such fault.

RULE E. The onus of proof is upon the party claiming in general average to show that the loss or expense claimed is properly allowable as general average.

RULE F. Any extra expense incurred in place of another expense which would have been allowable as general average shall be deemed to be general average and so allowed without regard to the saving, if any, to other interests, but only up to the amount of the general average expense avoided.

RULE G. General Average shall be adjusted as regards both loss and contribution upon the basis of values at the time and place when and where the adventure ends.

This rule shall not affect the determination of the place at which the average statement is to be made up.

RULE I. JETTISON OF CARGO. No jettison of cargo shall be made good as general average, unless such cargo is carried in accordance with the recognized custom of the trade.

RULE II. DAMAGE BY JETTISON AND SACRIFICE FOR THE COMMON SAFETY. Damage done to a ship and cargo, or either of them, by or in consequence of a sacrifice made for the common safety, and by water which goes down a ship's hatches opened or other opening made for the purpose of making a jettison for the common safety, shall be made good as general average.

YORK/ANTWERP RULES, 1974	YORK/ANTWERP RULES, 1950

RULE III. EXTINGUISHING FIRE ON SHIPBOARD. Damage done to a ship and cargo, or either of them, by water or otherwise, including damage by beaching or scuttling a burning ship, in extinguishing a fire on board the ship, shall be made good as general average; except that no compensation shall be made for damage *by smoke or heat however caused.*

RULE IV. CUTTING AWAY WRECK. Loss or damage sustained by cutting away wreck *or parts of the ship* which have been previously carried away *or are effectively lost by accident* shall not be made good as general average.

RULE V. VOLUNTARY STRANDING. When a ship is intentionally run on shore for the common safety, *whether or not she might have been driven on shore,* the consequent loss or damage shall be allowed in general average.

RULE VI. *SALVAGE REMUNERATION. Expenditure incurred by the parties to the adventure on account of salvage, whether under-contract or otherwise, shall be allowed in general average to the extent that the salvage operations were undertaken for the purpose of preserving from peril the property involved in the common maritime adventure.*

RULE III. EXTINGUISHING FIRE ON SHIPBOARD. Damage done to a ship and cargo, or either of them, by water or otherwise, including damage by beaching or scuttling a burning ship, in extinguishing a fire on board the ship, shall be made good as general average; except that no compensation shall be made for damage to such portions of the ship and bulk cargo, or to such separate packages of cargo, as have been on fire.

RULE IV. CUTTING AWAY WRECK. Loss or damage caused by cutting away the wreck or remains of spars or of other things which have previously been carried away by sea-peril, shall not be made good as general average.

RULE V. VOLUNTARY STRANDING. When a ship is intentionally run on shore, and the circumstances are such that if that course were not adopted she would inevitably drive on shore or on rocks, no loss or damage caused to the ship, cargo and freight or any of them by such intentional running on shore shall be made good as general average, but loss or damage incurred in refloating such a ship shall be allowed as general average.

In all other cases where a ship is intentionally run on shore for the common safety, the consequent loss or damage shall be allowed as general average.

RULE VI. CARRYING PRESS OF SAIL—DAMAGE TO OR LOSS OF SAILS. Damage to or loss of sails and spars, or either of them, caused by forcing a ship off the ground or by driving her higher up the ground, for the common safety, shall be made good as general average; but where a ship is afloat, no loss or damage caused to the ship, cargo and freight, or any of them, by carrying a press of sail, shall be made good as general average.

YORK/ANTWERP RULES, 1974

RULE VII. DAMAGE TO MACHINERY AND BOILERS. Damage caused to *any* machinery and boilers of a ship which is ashore and in a position of peril, in endeavouring to refloat, shall be allowed in general average when shown to have arisen from an actual intention to float the ship for the common safety at the risk of such damage; but where a ship is afloat no loss or damage caused by working the *propelling* machinery and boilers shall in any circumstances be made good as general average.

RULE VIII. EXPENSES LIGHTENING A SHIP WHEN ASHORE, AND CONSEQUENT DAMAGE. When a ship is ashore and cargo and ship's fuel and stores or any of them are discharged as a general average act, the extra cost of lightening, lighter hire and reshipping (if incurred), and the loss or damage sustained thereby, shall be admitted as general average.

RULE IX. SHIP'S MATERIALS AND STORES BURNT FOR FUEL. Ship's materials and stores, or any of them, necessarily burnt for fuel for the common safety at a time of peril, shall be admitted as general average, when and only when an ample supply of fuel had been provided; but the estimated quantity of fuel that would have been consumed, calculated at the price current at the ship's last port of departure at the date of her leaving, shall be credited to the general average.

RULE X. EXPENSES AT PORT OF REFUGE, ETC.

(a) When a ship shall have entered a port or place of refuge, or shall have returned to her port or place of loading in consequence of accident, sacrifice or other extraordinary circum-

YORK/ANTWERP RULES, 1950

RULE VII. DAMAGE TO MACHINERY AND BOILERS. Damage caused to machinery and boilers of a ship which is ashore and in a position of peril, in endeavouring to refloat, shall be allowed in general average when shown to have arisen from an actual intention to float the ship for the common safety at the risk of such damage; but where a ship is afloat no loss or damage caused by working the machinery and boilers, including loss or damage due to compounding of engines or such measures, shall in any circumstances be made good as general average.

RULE VIII. EXPENSES LIGHTENING A SHIP WHEN ASHORE, AND CONSEQUENT DAMAGE. When a ship is ashore and cargo and ship's fuel and stores or any of them are discharged as a general average act, the extra cost of lightening, lighter hire and reshipping (if incurred), and the loss or damage sustained thereby, shall be admitted as general average.

RULE IX. SHIPS'S MATERIALS AND STORES BURNT FOR FUEL. Ship's materials and stores, or any of them, necessarily burnt for fuel for the common safety at a time of peril, shall be admitted as general average, when and only when an amply supply of fuel had been provided; but the estimated quantity of fuel that would have been consumed, calculated at the price current at the ship's last port of departure at the date of her leaving, shall be credited to the general average.

RULE X. EXPENSES AT PORT OF REFUGE, ETC.

(a) When a ship shall have entered a port or place of refuge, or shall have returned to her port or place of loading in consequence of accident, sacrifice or other extraordinary circum-

YORK/ANTWERP RULES, 1974	YORK/ANTWERP RULES, 1950

stances, which render that necessary for the common safety, the expenses of entering such port or place shall be admitted as general average; and when she shall have sailed thence with her original cargo, or a part of it, the corresponding expenses of leaving such port or place consequent upon such entry or return shall likewise be admitted as general average.

When a ship is at any port or place of refuge and is necessarily removed to another port or place because repairs cannot be carried out in the first port or place, the provisions of this Rule shall be applied to the second port or place as if it were a port or place of refuge *and the cost of such removal including temporary repairs and towage shall be admitted as general average.* The provisions of Rule XI shall be applied to the prolongation of the voyage occasioned by such removal.

(b) The cost of handling on board or discharging cargo, fuel or stores whether at a port or place of loading, call or refuge shall be admitted as general average, when the handling or discharge was necessary for the common safety or to enable damage to the ship caused by sacrifice or accident to be repaired, if the repairs were necessary for the safe prosecution of the voyage, *except in cases where the damage to the ship is discovered at a port or place of loading or call without any accident or other extraordinary circumstances connected with such damage having taken place during the voyage.*

The cost of handling on board or discharging cargo, fuel or stores shall not be admissible as general average when incurred solely for the purpose of re-stowage due to shifting during the voyage unless such re-stowage is necessary for the common safety.

---

stances, which render that necessary for the common safety, the expenses of entering such port or place shall be admitted as general average; and when she shall have sailed thence with her original cargo, or a part of it, the corresponding expenses of leaving such port or place consequent upon such entry or return shall likewise be admitted as general average.

When a ship is at any port or place of refuge and is necessarily removed to another port or place because repairs cannot be carried out in the first port or place, the provisions of this Rule shall be applied to the second port or place as if it were a port or place of refuge. The provisions of Rule XI shall be applied to the prolongation of the voyage occasioned by such removal.

(b) The cost of handling on board or discharging cargo, fuel or stores whether at a port or place of loading, call or refuge, shall be admitted as general average when the handling or discharge was necessary for the common safety or to enable damage to the ship caused by sacrifice or accident to be repaired, if the repairs were necessary for the safe prosecution of the voyage.

YORK/ANTWERP RULES, 1974	YORK/ANTWERP RULES, 1950

(c) Whenever the cost of handling or discharging cargo, fuel or stores is admissible as general average, *the costs of storage, including insurance if reasonably incurred, reloading and stowing of such cargo, fuel or stores shall likewise be admitted as general average.*

But when the ship is condemned or does not proceed on her original voyage *storage expenses shall be admitted as general average only up to the date of the ship's condemnation or of the abandonment of the voyage or up to the date of completion of discharge of cargo if the condemnation or abandonment takes place before that date.*

(d) Deleted

(c) Whenever the cost of handling or discharging cargo, fuel or stores is admissible as general average, the cost of reloading and stowing such cargo, fuel or stores on board the ship, together with all storage charges (including insurance, if reasonably incurred) on such cargo, fuel or stores, shall likewise be so admitted. But when the ship is condemned or does not proceed on her original voyage, no storage expenses incurred after the date of the ship's condemnation or of the abandonment of the voyage shall be admitted as general average. In the event of the condemnation of the ship or the abandonment of the voyage before completion of discharge of cargo, storage expenses, as above, shall be admitted as general average up to the date of completion of discharge.

(d) If a ship under average be in a port or place at which it is practicable to repair her, so as to enable her to carry on the whole cargo, and if, in order to save expense, either she is towed thence to some other port or place of repair or to her destination, or the cargo or a portion of it is transshipped by another ship, or otherwise forwarded, then the extra cost of such towage, transshipment and forwarding, or any of them (up to the amount of the extra expense saved) shall be payable by the several parties to the adventure in proportion to the extraordinary expense saved.

RULE XI. WAGES AND MAINTENANCE OF CREW AND OTHER EXPENSES BEARING UP FOR AND IN A PORT OF REFUGE, ETC.

(a) Wages and maintenance of master, officers and crew reasonably incurred and fuel and stores consumed during the prolongation of the

RULE XI. WAGES AND MAINTENANCE OF CREW AND OTHER EXPENSES BEARING UP FOR AND IN A PORT OF REFUGE, ETC.

(a) Wages and maintenance of master, officers and crew reasonably incurred and fuel and stores consumed during the prolongation of the voyage occasioned by a ship entering a

voyage occasioned by a ship entering a port or place of refuge or returning to her port or place of loading shall be admitted as general average when the expenses of entering such port or place are allowable in general average in accordance with Rule X (a).

(b) When a ship shall have entered or been detained in any port or place in consequence of accident, sacrifice or other extraordinary circumstances which render that necessary for the common safety, or to enable damage to the ship caused by sacrifice or accident to be repaired, if the repairs were necessary for the safe prosecution of the voyage, the wages and maintenance of the master, officers and crew reasonably incurred during the extra period of detention in such port or place until the ship shall or should have been ready to proceed upon her voyage, shall be admitted in general average.

Provided that when damage to the ship is discovered at a port or place of loading or call without any accident or other extraordinary circumstance connected with such damage having taken place during the voyage, then the wages and maintenance of master, officers and crew and fuel and stores consumed during the extra detention for repairs to damages so discovered shall not be admissible as general average, even if the repairs are necessary for the safe prosecution of the voyage.

When the ship is condemned or does not proceed on her original voyage, *wages and maintenance of the master, officers and crew and fuel and stores consumed shall be admitted as general average only up to* the date of the ship's condemnation or of the abandonment of the voyage *or up to the date of completion of discharge of cargo if the condemnation or abandonment takes place before that date.*

port or place of refuge or returning to her port or place of loading shall be admitted as general average when the expenses of entering such port or place are allowable in general average in accordance with Rule X (a).

(b) When a ship shall have entered or been detained in any port or place in consequence of accident, sacrifice or other extraordinary circumstances which render that necessary for the common safety, or to enable damage to the ship caused by sacrifice or accident to be repaired, if the repairs were necessary for the safe prosecution of the voyage, the wages and maintenance of the master, officers and crew reasonably incurred during the extra period of detention in such port or place until the ship shall or should have been made ready to proceed upon her voyage, shall be admitted in general average. When the ship is condemned or does not proceed on her original voyage, the extra period of detention shall be deemed not to extend beyond the date of the ship's condemnation or of the abandonment of the voyage or, if discharge of cargo is not then completed, beyond the date of completion of discharge.

Fuel and stores consumed during the extra period of detention shall be admitted as general average, except such fuel and stores as are consumed in effecting repairs not allowable in general average.

Port charges incurred during the extra period of detention shall likewise be admitted as general average except such charges as are incurred solely by reason of repairs not allowable in general average.

YORK/ANTWERP RULES, 1974	YORK/ANTWERP RULES, 1950

Fuel and stores consumed during the extra period of detention shall be admitted as general average, except such fuel and stores as are consumed in effecting repairs not allowable in general average.

Port charges incurred during the extra period of detention shall likewise be admitted as general average except such charges as are incurred solely by reason of repairs not allowable in general average.

(c) For the purpose of this and the other Rules wages shall include all payments made to or for the benefit of the master, officers and crew, whether such payments be imposed by law upon the shipowners or be made under the terms or articles of employment.

(d) When overtime is paid to the master, officers or crew for maintenance of the ship or repairs, the cost of which is not allowable in general average, such overtime shall be allowed in general average only up to the saving in expense which would have been incurred and admitted as general average, had such overtime not been incurred.

RULE XII. DAMAGE TO CARGO IN DISCHARGING, ETC. Damage to or loss of cargo, fuel or stores caused in the act of handling, discharging, storing, reloading and stowing shall be made good as general average, when and only when the cost of those measures respectively is admitted as general average.

RULE XIII. DEDUCTIONS FROM COST OF REPAIRS. *Repairs to be allowed in general average shall not be subject to deductions in respect of "new for old" where old material or parts are replaced by new unless the ship is over fifteen years old in which case there shall be a deduction of one-third. The deductions shall be regu-*

(c) For the purpose of this and the other Rules wages shall include all payments made to or for the benefit of the master, officers and crew, whether such payments be imposed by law upon the shipowners or be made under the terms or articles of employment.

(d) When overtime is paid to the master, officers or crew for maintenance of the ship or repairs, the cost of which is not allowable in general average, such overtime shall be allowed in general average only up to the saving in expense which would have been incurred and admitted as general average, had such overtime not been incurred.

RULE XII. DAMAGE TO CARGO IN DISCHARGING, ETC. Damage to or loss of cargo, fuel or stores caused in the act of handling, discharging, storing, reloading and stowing shall be made good as general average, when and only when the cost of those measures respectively is admitted as general average.

RULE XIII. DEDUCTIONS FROM COST OF REPAIRS. In adjusting claims for general average, repairs to be allowed in general average shall be subject to deductions in respect of "new for old" according to the following rules, where old material or parts are replaced by new.

YORK/ANTWERP RULES, 1974

lated by the age of the ship from the 31st of December of the year of completion of construction to the date of the general average act, except for insulation, life- and similar boats, communications and navigational apparatus and equipment, machinery and boilers for which the deductions shall be regulated by the age of the particular parts to which they apply. The deductions shall be made only from the cost of the new material or parts when finished and ready to be installed in the ship.

No deduction shall be made in respect of provisions, stores, anchors and chain cables.

Drydock and slipway dues and costs of shifting the ship shall be allowed in full.

The costs of cleaning, painting or coating of bottom shall not be allowed in general average unless the bottom has been painted or coated within the twelve months preceding the date of the general average act in which case one-half of such costs shall be allowed.

YORK/ANTWERP RULES, 1950

The deductions to be regulated by the age of the ship from date of original register to the date of accident, except for provisions and stores, insulation, life- and similar boats, gyrocompass equipment, wireless, direction finding, echo sounding and similar apparatus, machinery and boilers for which the deductions shall be regulated by the age of the particular parts to which they apply.

No deduction to be made in respect of provisions, stores and gear which have not been in use.

The deduction shall be made from the cost of new material or parts, including labour and establishment charges, but excluding cost of opening up.

Drydock and slipway dues and costs of shifting the ship shall be allowed in full.

No cleaning and painting of bottom to be allowed, if the bottom has not been painted within six months previous to the date of the accident.

A. UP TO ONE YEAR OLD. All repairs to be allowed in full, except scaling and cleaning and painting or coating of bottom, from which one-third is to be deducted.

B. BETWEEN 1 AND 3 YEARS OLD. Deduction off scaling, cleaning and painting bottom as above under Clause A.

One-third to be deducted off sails, rigging, ropes, sheets and hawsers (other than wire and chain), awnings, covers, provisions, and stores and painting.

One-sixth to be deducted off woodwork of hull, including hold ceiling, wooden masts, spars and boats, furniture, upholstery, crockery, metal- and glass-ware, wire rigging, wire ropes and wire hawsers, gyrocompass equipment, wireless, direction finding, echo sounding and similar apparatus, chain cables and chains, insulation, auxiliary machinery, steering gear and connections, winches and cranes and connections and electrical machinery and connections other than electric propelling machinery; other repairs to be allowed in full.

Metal sheathing for wooden or composite ships shall be dealt with by allowing in full the cost of a weight equal to the gross weight of metal sheathing stripped off, minus the proceeds of the old metal. Nails, felt and labour metalling are subject to a deduction of one-third.

C. BETWEEN 3 AND 6 YEARS. Deductions as above under Clause B, except that one-third be deducted off woodwork of hull including hold ceiling, wooden masts, spars and boats, furniture, upholstery, and one-sixth be deducted off iron work of masts and spars and all machinery (inclusive of boilers and their mountings).

D. BETWEEN 6 AND 10 YEARS. Deductions as above under Clause C, except that one-third be deducted off all rigging, ropes, sheets, and hawsers, iron work of masts and spars, gyrocompass equipment, wireless, direction finding, echo sounding and similar apparatus, insulation, auxiliary machinery, steering gear, winches, cranes and connections and all other machinery, (inclusive of boilers and their mounting).

E. BETWEEN 10 AND 15 YEARS. One-third to be deducted off all renewals, except iron work of hull and cementing and chain cables, from which one-sixth to be deducted, and anchors, which are allowed in full.

F. OVER 15 YEARS. One-third to be deducted off all renewals, except chain cables, from which one-sixth to be deducted, and anchors, which are allowed in full.

RULE XIV. TEMPORARY RE-PAIRS. Where temporary repairs are effected to a ship at a port of loading, call or refuge, for the common safety, or of damage caused by general average sacrifice, the cost of such repairs shall be admitted as general average.

Where temporary repairs of accidental damage are effected *in order to* enable the adventure to be completed, the cost of such repairs shall be admitted as general average without regard to the saving, if any, to other interests, but only up to the saving in expense which would have been incurred and allowed in general average if such repairs had not been effected there.

No deductions "new for old" shall be made from the cost of temporary repairs allowable as general average.

RULE XV. LOSS OF FREIGHT. Loss of freight arising from damage to or loss of cargo shall be made good as general average, either when caused by a general average act, or when the damage to or loss of cargo is so made good.

Deduction shall be made from the amount of gross freight lost, of the charges which the owner thereof would have incurred to earn such freight, but has, in consequence of the sacrifice, not incurred.

RULE XVI. AMOUNT TO BE MADE GOOD FOR CARGO LOST OR DAMAGED BY SACRIFICE. The amount to be made good as general average for damage to or loss of *cargo* sacrificed shall be the loss which has *been* sustained thereby based on the *value at the time of discharge, ascertained from the commercial invoice rendered to the receiver or if there is no such invoice from the shipped value. The value at the time of discharge shall include the cost of insurance and freight except insofar as such freight is at the risk of interests other than the cargo.*

RULE XIV. TEMPORARY RE-PAIRS. Where temporary repairs are effected to a ship at a port of loading, call or refuge, for the common safety, or of damage caused by general average sacrifice, the cost of such repairs shall be admitted as general average.

Where temporary repairs of accidental damage are effected merely to enable the adventure to be completed, the cost of such repairs shall be admitted as general average without regard to the saving, if any, to other interests, but only up to the saving, in expense which would have been incurred and allowed in general average if such repairs had not been effected there.

No deductions "new for old" shall be made from the cost of temporary repairs allowable as general average.

RULE XV. LOSS OF FREIGHT. Loss of freight arising from damage to or loss of cargo shall be made good as general average, either when caused by a general average act, or when the damage to or loss of cargo is so made good.

Deduction shall be made from the amount of gross freight lost, of the charges which the owner thereof would have incurred to earn such freight, but has, in consequence of the sacrifice, not incurred.

RULE XVI. AMOUNT TO BE MADE GOOD FOR CARGO LOST OR DAMAGED BY SACRIFICE. The amount to be made good as general average for damage to or loss of goods sacrificed shall be the loss which the owner of the goods has sustained thereby, based on the market values at the last day of discharge of the vessel or at the termination of the adventure where this ends at a place other than the original destination.

Where goods so damaged are sold and the amount of the damage has not been otherwise agreed, the loss to be

YORK/ANTWERP RULES, 1974

When cargo so damaged *is* sold and the amount of the damage has not been otherwise agreed, the loss to be made good in general average shall be the difference between the net proceeds of sale and the net sound value *as computed in the first paragraph of this Rule.*

RULE XVII. CONTRIBUTORY VALUES. The contribution to a general average shall be made upon the actual net values of the property at the termination of the adventure *except that the value of cargo shall be the value at the time of discharge ascertained from the commercial invoice rendered to the receiver or if there is no such invoice from the shipped value. The value of the cargo shall include the cost of insurance and freight unless and insofar as such freight is at the risk of interests other than the cargo, deducting therefrom any loss or damage suffered by the cargo prior to or at the time of discharge. The value of the ship shall be assessed without taking into account the beneficial or detrimental effect of any demise or time charter party to which the ship may be committed.*

To *these* values shall be added the amount made good as general average for property sacrificed, if not already included, deduction being made from the freight and passage money at risk, of such charges and crew's wages as would not have been incurred in earning the freight had the ship and cargo been totally lost at the date of the general average act and have not been allowed as general average; deduction being also made from the value of the property of all *extra* charges incurred in respect thereof subsequently to the general average act, except such charges as are allowed in general average.

Where cargo is sold short of destination, however, it shall contribute upon the actual net proceeds of sale, with the addi-

YORK/ANTWERP RULES, 1950

made good in general average shall be the difference between the net proceeds of sale and the net sound value at the last day of discharge of the vessel or at the termination of the adventure where this ends at a place other than the original destination.

RULE XVII. CONTRIBUTORY VALUES. The contribution to a general average shall be made upon the actual net values of the property at the termination of the adventure, to which values shall be added the amount made good as general average for property sacrificed, if not already included, deduction being made from the shipowner's freight and passage money at risk, of such charges and crew's wages as would not have been incurred in earning the freight had the ship and cargo been totally lost at the date of the general average act and have not been allowed as general average; deduction being also made from the value of the property of all charges incurred in respect thereof subsequently to the general average act, except such charges as are allowed in general average.

Passengers' luggage and personal effects not shipped under bill of lading shall not contribute in general average.

*tion of any amount made good as general
average.*

Passengers' luggage and personal
effects not shipped under bill of lading shall not contribute in general
average.

RULE XVIII. DAMAGE TO SHIP.
The amount to be allowed as general
average for damage or loss to the ship,
her machinery and/or gear *caused by a
general average act shall be as follows:*

(*a*) *When repaired or replaced, the actual reasonable cost of repairing or replacing such damage or loss, subject to deductions in accordance with Rule XIII.*

(*b*) *When not repaired or replaced, the
reasonable depreciation arising from such
damage or loss, but not exceeding the estimated cost of repairs. But where the ship is
an actual total loss or when the cost of
repairs of the damage would exceed the
value of the ship when repaired, the
amount to be allowed as general average
shall be the difference between the estimated
sound value of the ship after deducting
therefrom the estimated cost of repairing
damage which is not general average and
the value of the ship in her damaged state
which may be measured by the net proceeds
of sale, if any.*

RULE XIX. UNDECLARED OR
WRONGFULLY DECLARED CAR-
GO. Damage or loss caused to goods
loaded without the knowledge of the
shipowner or his agent or to goods
wilfully misdescribed at time of shipment shall not be allowed as general
average, but such goods shall remain
liable to contribute, if saved.

Damage or loss caused to goods
which have been wrongfully declared
on shipment at a value which is lower
than their real value shall be contributed for at the declared value, but
such goods shall contribute upon
their actual value.

RULE XVIII. DAMAGE TO SHIP.
The amount to be allowed as general
average for damage or loss to the ship,
her machinery and/or gear when repaired or replaced shall be the actual
reasonable cost of repairing or replacing such damage or loss, subject to
deductions in accordance with Rule
XIII. When not repaired, the reasonable depreciation shall be allowed, not
exceeding the estimated cost of
repairs.

Where there is an actual or constructive total loss of the ship the
amount to be allowed as general average for damage or loss to the ship
caused by a general average act shall
be the estimated sound value of the
ship after deducting therefrom the estimated cost of repairing damage
which is not general average and the
proceeds of sale, if any.

RULE XIX. UNDECLARED OR
WRONGFULLY DECLARED CAR-
GO. Damage or loss caused to goods
loaded without the knowledge of the
shipowner or his agent or to goods
wilfully misdescribed at time of shipment shall not be allowed as general
average, but such goods shall remain
liable to contribute, if saved.

Damage or loss caused to goods
which have been wrongfully declared
on shipment at a value which is lower
than their real value shall be contributed for at the declared value, but
such goods shall contribute upon
their actual value.

YORK/ANTWERP RULES, 1974

RULE XX. PROVISION OF FUNDS. A commission of 2 per cent. on general average disbursements, other than the wages and maintenance of master, officers and crew and fuel and stores not replaced during the voyage, shall be allowed in general average, but when the funds are not provided by any of the contributing interests, the necessary cost of obtaining the funds required by means of a bottomry bond or otherwise, or the loss sustained by owners of goods sold for the purpose, shall be allowed in general average.

The cost of insuring money advanced to pay for general average disbursements shall also be allowed in general average.

RULE XXI. INTEREST ON LOSSES MADE GOOD IN GENERAL AVERAGE. Interest shall be allowed on expenditure, sacrifices and allowances charged to general average at the rate of 7 *per cent. per annum*, until the date of the general average statement, due allowance being made for any interim reimbursement from the contributory interests or from the general average deposit fund.

RULE XXII. TREATMENT OF CASH DEPOSITS. Where cash deposits have been collected in respect of cargo's liability for general average, salvage or special charges, such deposits shall be paid without any delay into a special account in the joint names of a representative nominated on behalf of the shipowner and a representative nominated on behalf of the depositors in a bank to be approved by both. The sum so deposited, together with accrued interest, if any, shall be held as security for payment to the parties entitled thereto of the general average, salvage or special

YORK/ANTWERP RULES, 1950

RULE XX. PROVISION OF FUNDS. A commission of 2 per cent. on general average disbursements, other than the wages and maintenance of master, officers and crew and fuel and stores not replaced during the voyage, shall be allowed in general average, but when the funds are not provided by any of the contributing interests, the necessary cost of obtaining the funds required by means of a bottomry bond or otherwise, or the loss sustained by owners of goods sold for the purpose, shall be allowed in general average.

The cost of insuring money advanced to pay for general average disbursements shall also be allowed in general average.

RULE XXI. INTEREST ON LOSSES MADE GOOD IN GENERAL AVERAGE. Interest shall be allowed on expenditure, sacrifices and allowances charged to general average at the rate of 5 per cent. per annum, until the date of the general average statement, due allowance being made for any interim reimbursement from the contributory interests or from the general average deposit fund.

RULE XXII. TREATMENT OF CASH DEPOSITS. Where cash deposits have been collected in respect of cargo's liability for general average, salvage or special charges, such deposits shall be paid without any delay into a special account in the joint names of a representative nominated on behalf of the shipowner and a representative nominated on behalf of the depositors in a bank to be approved by both. The sum so deposited, together with accrued interest, if any, shall be held as security for payment to the parties entitled thereto of the general average, salvage or special charges payable by cargo in respect to which the deposits have been collected. Payments on account or refunds of deposits may be made if certified to in writing by the average adjuster. Such deposits and payments or refunds shall be without prejudice to the ultimate liability of the parties.

charges payable by cargo in respect to which the deposits have been collected. Payments on account or refunds of deposits may be made if certified to in writing by the average adjuster. Such deposits and payments or refunds shall be without prejudice to the ultimate liability of the parties.

LOF 1980 # LLOYD'S

STANDARD FORM OF

SALVAGE AGREEMENT
(APPROVED AND PUBLISHED BY THE COMMITTEE OF LLOYD'S)

NO CURE—NO PAY

NOTES.

1. Insert name of person signing on behalf of Owners of property to be salved: The Master should sign wherever possible.

2. The Contractor's name should always be inserted in line 3 and whenever the Agreement is signed by the Master of the Salving vessel or other person on behalf of the Contractor the name of the Master or other person must also be inserted in line 3 before the words "for and on behalf of: The words "for and on behalf of" should be deleted where a Contractor signs personally.

3. Insert place if agreed in Clause 1(a) and currency if agreed in Clause 1(c).

On board the
Dated   19

IT IS HEREBY AGREED between Captain†   for and on
behalf of the Owners of the "   " her cargo freight bunkers and
stores and   for and on behalf of
(hereinafter called "the Contractor"*):—

1. (a) The Contractor agrees to use his best endeavours to salve the
and/or her cargo bunkers and stores and take them to ‡   or other
place to be hereafter agreed or if no place is named or agreed to a place of safety. The
Contractor further agrees to use his best endeavours to prevent the escape of oil from the
vessel while performing the services of salving the subject vessel and/or her cargo bunkers
and stores. The services shall be rendered and accepted as salvage services upon the
principle of "no cure—no pay" except that where the property being salved is a tanker
laden or partly laden with a cargo of oil and without negligence on the part of the
Contractor and/or his Servants and/or Agents (1) the services are not successful or (2) are
only partially successful or (3) the Contractor is prevented from completing the services
the Contractor shall nevertheless be awarded solely against the Owners of such tanker his
reasonably incurred expenses and an increment not exceeding 15 per cent of such
expenses but only if and to the extent that such expenses together with the increment are
greater than any amount otherwise recoverable under this Agreement. Within the
meaning of the said exception to the principle of "no cure—no pay" expenses shall in
addition to actual out of pocket expenses include a fair rate for all tugs craft personnel and

other equipment used by the Contractor in the services and oil shall mean crude oil fuel oil heavy diesel oil and lubricating oil.

(b) The Contractor's remuneration shall be fixed by arbitration in London in the manner herein prescribed and any other difference arising out of this Agreement or the operations thereunder shall be referred to arbitration in the same way. In the event of the services referred to in this Agreement or any part of such services having been already rendered at the date of this Agreement by the Contractor to the said vessel and/or her cargo bunkers and stores the provisions of this Agreement shall apply to such services.

(c) It is hereby further agreed that the security to be provided to the Committee of Lloyd's the Salved Values the Award and/or Interim Award and/or Award on Appeal of the Arbitrator and/or Arbitrator(s) on Appeal shall be in‡   currency. If this Clause is not completed then the security to be provided and the Salved Values the Award and/or Interim Award and/or Award on Appeal of the Arbitrator and/or Arbitrator(s) on Appeal shall be in Pounds Sterling.

(d) This Agreement shall be governed by and arbitration thereunder shall be in accordance with English law.

2.   The Owners their Servants and Agents shall co-operate fully with the Contractor in and about the salvage including obtaining entry to the place named in Clause 1 of this Agreement or such other place as may be agreed or if applicable the place of safety to which the salved property is taken. The Owners shall promptly accept redelivery of the salved property at such place. The Contractor may make reasonable use of the vessel's machinery gear equipment anchors chains stores and other appurtenances during and for the purpose of the operations free of expense but shall not unnecessarily damage abandon or sacrifice the same or any property the subject of this Agreement.

3.   The Master or other person signing this Agreement on behalf of the property to be salved is not authorised to make or give and the Contractor shall not demand or take any payment draft or order as inducement to or remuneration for entering into this Agreement.

PROVISIONS AS TO SECURITY

4.   The Contractor shall immediately after the termination of the services or sooner in appropriate cases notify the Committee of Lloyd's and where practicable the Owners of the amount for which he requires security (inclusive of costs expenses and interest). Unless otherwise agreed by the parties such security shall be given to the Committee of Lloyd's and security so given shall be in a form approved by the Committee and shall be given by persons firms or corporations resident in the United Kingdom either satisfactory to the Committee of Lloyd's or agreed by the Contractor. The Committee of Lloyd's shall not be responsible for the sufficiency (whether in amount or otherwise) of any security which shall be given nor for the default or insolvency of any person firm or corporation giving the same.

5.   Pending the completion of the security as aforesaid the Contractor shall have a maritime lien on the property salved for his remuneration. Where the aforementioned exception to the principle of "no cure—no pay" becomes likely to be applicable the Owners of the vessel shall on demand of the Contractor provide security for the Contractor's remuneration under the aforementioned exception in accordance with Clause 4 hereof. The salved property shall not without the consent in writing of the Contractor be removed from the place (within the terms of Clause 1) to which the property is taken by the Contractor on the completion of the salvage services until security has been given as aforesaid. The Owners of the vessel their Servants and Agents shall use their best endeavours to ensure that the Cargo Owners provide security in accordance with the provisions of Clause 4 of this Agreement before the cargo is released. The Contractor agrees not to arrest or detain the property salved unless (a) the security be not given within 14 days (exclusive of Saturdays and Sundays or other days observed as general holidays at Lloyd's) after the date of the termination of the services (the Committee of Lloyd's not being responsible for the failure of the parties concerned to provide the required security within the said 14 days) or (b) the Contractor has reason to believe that the removal of the property is contemplated contrary to the above agreement. In the event of security not being provided or in the event

of (1) any attempt being made to remove the property salved contrary to this agreement or (2) the Contractor having reasonable grounds to suppose that such an attempt will be made the Contractor may take steps to enforce his aforesaid lien. The Arbitrator appointed under Clause 6 or the person(s) appointed under Clause 13 hereof shall have power in their absolute discretion to include in the amount awarded to the Contractor the whole or such part of the expense incurred by the Contractor in enforcing or protecting by insurance or otherwise or in taking reasonable steps to enforce or protect his lien as they shall think fit.

PROVISIONS AS TO ARBITRATION

6. (a) Where security within the provisions of this Agreement is given to the Committee of Lloyd's in whole or in part the said Committee shall appoint an Arbitrator in respect of the interests covered by such security.
   (b) Whether security has been given or not the Committee of Lloyd's shall appoint an Arbitrator upon receipt of a written or telex or telegraphic notice of a claim for arbitration from any of the parties entitled or authorised to make such a claim.

7. Where an Arbitrator has been appointed by the Committee of Lloyd's and the parties do not wish to proceed to arbitration the parties shall jointly notify the said Committee in writing or by telex or by telegram and the said Committee may thereupon terminate the appointment of such Arbitrator as they may have appointed in accordance with Clause 6 of this Agreement.

.8. Any of the following parties may make a claim for arbitration viz.: — (1) The Owners of the ship. (2) The Owners of the cargo or any part thereof. (3) The Owners of any freight separately at risk or any part thereof. (4) The Contractor. (5) The Owners of the bunkers and/or stores. (6) Any other person who is a party to this Agreement.

9. If the parties to any such Arbitration or any of them desire to be heard or to adduce evidence at the Arbitration they shall give notice to that effect to the Committee of Lloyd's and shall respectively nominate a person in the United Kingdom to represent them for all the purposes of the Arbitration and failing such notice and nomination being given the Arbitrator or Arbitrator(s) on Appeal may proceed as if the parties failing to give the same had renounced their right to be heard or adduce evidence.

10. The remuneration for the services within the meaning of this Agreement shall be fixed by an Arbitrator to be appointed by the Committee of Lloyd's and he shall have power to make an Interim Award ordering such payment on account as may seem fair and just and on such terms as may be fair and just.

CONDUCT OF THE ARBITRATION

11. The Arbitrator shall have power to obtain call for receive and act upon any such oral or documentary evidence or information (whether the same be strictly admissible as evidence or not) as he may think fit and to conduct the Arbitration in such manner in all respects as he may think fit and shall if in his opinion the amount of the security demanded is excessive have power in his absolute discretion to condemn the Contractor in the whole or part of the expense of providing such security and to deduct the amount in which the Contractor is so condemned from the salvage remuneration. Unless the Arbitrator shall otherwise direct the parties shall be at liberty to adduce expert evidence at the Arbitration. Any Award of the Arbitrator shall (subject to appeal as provided in this Agreement) be final and binding on all the parties concerned. The Arbitrator and the Committee of Lloyd's may charge reasonable fees and expenses for their services in connection with the Arbitration whether it proceeds to a hearing or not and all such fees and expenses shall be treated as part of the costs of the Arbitration. Save as aforesaid the statutory provisions as to Arbitration for the time being in force in England shall apply.

12. Interest at a rate per annum to be fixed by the Arbitrator from the expiration of 21 days (exclusive of Saturdays and Sundays or other days observed as general holidays at Lloyd's) after the date of publication of the Award and/or Interim Award by the Committee of Lloyd's until the date payment

is received by the Committee of Lloyd's both dates inclusive shall (subject to appeal as provided in this Agreement) be payable upon any sum awarded after deduction of any sums paid on account.

PROVISIONS AS TO APPEAL

13. Any of the persons named under Clause 8 may appeal from the Award but not without leave of the Arbitrator(s) on Appeal from an Interim Award made pursuant to the provisions of Clause 10 hereof by giving written or telegraphic or telex Notice of Appeal to the Committee of Lloyd's within 14 days (exclusive of Saturdays and Sundays or other days observed as general holidays at Lloyd's) after the date of the publication by the Committee of Lloyd's of the Award and may (without prejudice to their right of appeal under the first part of this Clause) within 14 days (exclusive of Saturdays and Sundays or other days observed as general holidays at Lloyd's) after receipt by them from the Committee of Lloyd's of notice of such appeal (such notice if sent by post to be deemed to be received on the day following that on which the said notice was posted) give written or telegraphic or telex Notice of Cross-Appeal to the Committee of Lloyd's. As soon as practicable after receipt of such notice or notices the Committee of Lloyd's shall refer the Appeal to the hearing and determination of a person or persons selected by it. In the event of an Appellant or Cross-Appellant withdrawing his Notice of Appeal or Cross-Appeal the hearing shall nevertheless proceed in respect of such Notice of Appeal or Cross-Appeal as may remain. Any Award on Appeal shall be final and binding on all the parties concerned whether such parties were represented or not at either the Arbitration or at the Arbitration on Appeal.

CONDUCT OF THE APPEAL

14. No evidence other than the documents put in on the Arbitration and the Arbitrator's notes of the proceedings and oral evidence if any at the Arbitration and the Arbitrator's Reasons for his Award and Interim Award if any and the transcript if any of any evidence given at the Arbitration shall be used on the Appeal unless the Arbitrator(s) on the Appeal shall in his or their discretion call for or allow other evidence. The Arbitrator(s) on Appeal may conduct the Arbitration on Appeal in such manner in all respects as he or they may think fit and may act upon any such evidence or information (whether the same be strictly admissible as evidence or not) as he or they may think fit and may maintain increase or reduce the sum awarded by the Arbitrator with the like power as is conferred by Clause 11 on the Arbitrator to condemn the Contractor in the whole or part of the expense of providing security and to deduct the amount disallowed from the salvage remuneration. And he or they shall also make such order as he or they shall think fit as to the payment of interest on the sum awarded to the Contractor. The Arbitrator(s) on the Appeal may direct in what manner the costs of the Arbitration and of the Arbitration on Appeal shall be borne and paid and he or they and the Committee of Lloyd's may charge reasonable fees and expenses for their services in connection with the Arbitration on Appeal whether it proceeds to a hearing or not and all such fees and expenses shall be treated as part of the costs of the Arbitration on Appeal. Save as aforesaid the statutory provisions as to Arbitration for the time being in force in England shall apply.

PROVISIONS AS TO PAYMENT

15. (a) In case of Arbitration if no Notice of Appeal be received by the Committee of Lloyd's within 14 days (exclusive of Saturdays and Sundays or other days observed as general holidays at Lloyd's) after the date of the publication by the Committee of the Award and/or Interim Award the Committee shall call upon the party or parties concerned to pay the amount awarded and in the event of non-payment shall realize or enforce the security and pay therefrom to the Contractor (whose receipt shall be a good discharge to it) the amount awarded to him together with interest as hereinbefore provided but the Contractor shall reimburse the parties concerned to such extent as the final Award is less than the Interim Award.

(b) If Notice of Appeal be received by the Committee of Lloyd's in accordance with the provisions of Clause 13 hereof it shall as soon as but not until the Award on Appeal has been published by it call upon the party or parties concerned to pay the amount awarded and in the event of non-payment shall realize or enforce the security and pay therefrom to the Contractor (whose receipt shall be a good discharge to it) the amount awarded to him together with interest if any in such manner as shall comply with the provisions of the Award on Appeal.

(c) If the Award and/or Interim Award and/or Award on Appeal provides or provide that the costs of the Arbitration and/or of the Arbitration on Appeal or any part of such costs shall be borne by the Contractor such costs may be deducted from the amount awarded before payment is made to the Contractor by the Committee of Lloyd's unless satisfactory security is provided by the Contractor for the payment of such costs.

(d) If any sum shall become payable to the Contractor as remuneration for his services and/or interest and/or costs as the result of an agreement made between the Contractor and the parties interested in the property salved or any of them the Committee of Lloyd's in the event of non-payment shall realize or enforce the security and pay therefrom to the Contractor (whose receipt shall be a good discharge to it) the amount agreed upon between the parties.

(e) Without prejudice to the provisions of Clause 4 hereof the liability of the Committee of Lloyd's shall be limited in any event to the amount of security held by it.

GENERAL PROVISIONS

16.   Notwithstanding anything hereinbefore contained should the operations be only partially successful without any negligence or want of ordinary skill and care on the part of the Contractor his Servants or Agents and any portion of the vessel her appurtenances bunkers stores and cargo be salved by the Contractor he shall be entitled to reasonable remuneration and such reasonable remuneration shall be fixed in case of difference by Arbitration in the manner hereinbefore prescribed.

17.   The Master or other person signing this Agreement on behalf of the property to be salved enters into this Agreement as Agent for the vessel her cargo freight bunkers and stores and the respective owners thereof and binds each (but not the one for the other or himself personally) to the due performance thereof.

18.   In considering what sums of money have been expended by the Contractor in rendering the services and/or in fixing the amount of the Award and/or Interim Award and/or Award on Appeal the Arbitrator or Arbitrator(s) on Appeal shall to such an extent and in so far as it may be fair and just in all the circumstances give effect to the consequences of any change or changes in the value of money or rates of exchange which may have occurred between the completion of the services and the date on which the Award and/or Interim Award and/or Award on Appeal is made.

19.   Any Award notice authority order or other document signed by the Chairman of Lloyd's or any person authorised by the Committee of Lloyd's for the purpose shall be deemed to have been duly made or given by the Committee of Lloyd's and shall have the same force and effect in all respects as if it had been signed by every member of the Committee of Lloyd's.

20.   The Contractor may claim salvage and enforce any Award or agreement made between the Contractor and the parties interested in the property salved against security provided under this Agreement if any in the name and on behalf of any Sub-Contractors Servants or Agents including Masters and members of the Crews of vessels employed by him in the services rendered hereunder provided that he first indemnifies and holds harmless the Owners of the property salved against all claims by or liabilities incurred to the said persons. Any such indemnity shall be provided in a form satisfactory to such Owners.

21.   The Contractor shall be entitled to limit any liability to the Owners of the subject vessel and/or her cargo bunkers and stores which he and/or his Servants and/or Agents may incur in and about the services in the manner and to the extent provided by English law and as if the provisions of the Convention on Limitation of Liability for Maritime Claims 1976 were part of the law of England.

For and on behalf of the Contractor

For and on behalf of the Owners of property to be salved.

. . . .

. . . .

(To be signed either by the Contractor personally or by the Master of the salving vessel or other person whose name is inserted in line 3 of this Agreement.)

(To be signed by the Master or other person whose name is inserted in line 1 of this Agreement.)

Appendix 6

American Institute Hull Clauses

(June 2, 1977)

San Francisco

To be attached to and form a part of Policy No. .... of the ....

....

The terms and conditions of the following clauses are to be regarded as substituted for those of the policy form to which they are attached, the latter being hereby waived, except provisions required by law to be inserted in the Policy. All captions are inserted only for purposes of reference and shall not be used to interpret the clauses to which they apply.

ASSURED

This Policy insures 1

.... 2

.... hereinafter referred to as the Assured. 3

If claim is made under this Policy by anyone other than the Owner of the Vessel, such person shall not be entitled to recover to a greater extent 4
than would the Owner, had claim been made by the Owner as an Assured named in this Policy. 5

Underwriters waive any right of subrogation against affiliated, subsidiary or interrelated companies of the Assured, provided that such waiver shall 6
not apply in the event of a collision between the Vessel and any vessel owned, demise chartered or otherwise controlled by any of the aforesaid com- 7
panies, or with respect to any loss, damage or expense against which such companies are insured. 8

LOSS PAYEE

Loss, if any, payable to 9

.... 10

.... or order. 11

Provided, however, Underwriters shall pay claims to others as set forth in the Collision Liability clause and may make direct payment to persons 12
providing security for the release of the Vessel in Salvage cases. 13

VESSEL

The Subject Matter of this insurance is the Vessel called the 14
or by whatsoever name or names the said Vessel is or shall be called, which for purposes of this insurance shall consist of and be limited to her hull, 15
launches, lifeboats, rafts, furniture, bunkers, stores, supplies, tackle, fittings, equipment, apparatus, machinery, boilers, refrigerating machinery, insula- 16
tion, motor generators and other electrical machinery. 17

In the event any equipment or apparatus not owned by the Assured is installed for use on board the Vessel and the Assured has assumed respon- 18
sibility therefor, it shall also be considered part of the Subject Matter and the aggregate value thereof shall be included in the Agreed Value. 19

Notwithstanding the foregoing, cargo containers, barges and lighters shall not be considered a part of the Subject Matter of this insurance. 20

DURATION OF RISK

From the .... day of .... 19...., ... time 21
to the .... day of .... 19...., ... time. 22

Should the Vessel at the expiration of this Policy be at sea, or in distress, or at a port of refuge or of call, she shall, provided previous notice be 23
given to the Underwriters, be held covered at a pro rata monthly premium to her port of destination. 24

In the event of payment by the Underwriters for Total Loss of the Vessel this Policy shall thereupon automatically terminate. 25

AGREED VALUE

The Vessel, for so much as concerns the Assured, by agreement between the Assured and the Underwriters in this Policy, is and shall be valued at 26

.... Dollars. 27

AMOUNT INSURED HEREUNDER

.... Dollars. 28

DEDUCTIBLE

Notwithstanding anything in this Policy to the contrary, there shall be deducted from the aggregate of all claims (including claims under the Sue 29
and Labor clause and claims under the Collision Liability clause) arising out of each separate accident, the sum of $, unless the 30
accident results in a Total Loss of the Vessel in which case this clause shall not apply. A recovery from other interests, however, shall not operate to 31
exclude claims under this Policy provided the aggregate of such claims arising out of one separate accident if unreduced by such recovery exceeds that 32
sum. For the purpose of this clause each accident shall be treated separately, but it is agreed that (a) a sequence of damages arising from the same acci- 33
dent shall be treated as due to that accident and (b) all heavy weather damage, or damage caused by contact with floating ice, which occurs during a 34
single sea passage between two successive ports shall be treated as though due to one accident. 35

PREMIUM

The Underwriters to be paid in consideration of this insurance 36

.... Dollars being at the annual rate of .... per cent., which premium shall be due on attachment. If the Vessel 37
is insured under this Policy for a period of less than one year at pro rata of the annual rate, full annual premium shall be considered earned and immedi- 38
ately due and payable in the event of Total Loss of the Vessel. 39

RETURNS OF PREMIUM

Premium returnable as follows: 40
    Pro rata daily net in the event of termination under the Change of Ownership clause;   41
    Pro rata monthly net for each uncommenced month if it be mutually agreed to cancel this Policy;   42
    For each period of 30 consecutive days the Vessel may be laid up in port for account of the Assured,   43

            cents per cent. net not under repair, or   44

            cents per cent. net under repair;   45
provided always that: 46
    (a) a Total Loss of the Vessel has not occurred during the currency of this Policy;   47
    (b) in no case shall a return for lay-up be allowed when the Vessel is lying in exposed or unprotected waters or in any location not approved by   48
    the Underwriters;   49
    (c) in the event of any amendment of the annual rate, the above rates of return shall be adjusted accordingly;   50
    (d) in no case shall a return be allowed when the Vessel is used as a storage ship or for lightering purposes.   51
    If the Vessel is laid up for a period of 30 consecutive days, a part only of which attaches under this Policy, the Underwriters shall pay such pro-   52
portion of the return due in respect of a full period of 30 days as the number of days attaching hereto bears to 30. Should the lay-up period exceed 30   53
consecutive days, the Assured shall have the option to elect the period of 30 consecutive days for which a return is recoverable.   54

NON-PAYMENT OF PREMIUM

    In event of non-payment of premium 30 days after attachment, or of any additional premium when due, this Policy may be cancelled by the Under-   55
writers upon 10 days written or telegraphic notice sent to the Assured at his last known address or in care of the broker who negotiated this Policy.   56
Such proportion of the premium, however, as shall have been earned up to the time of cancellation shall be payable. In the event of Total Loss of the   57
Vessel occurring prior to any cancellation or termination of this Policy full annual premium shall be considered earned.   58

ADVENTURE

    Beginning the adventure upon the Vessel, as above, and so shall continue and endure during the period aforesaid, as employment may offer, in port or   59
at sea, in docks and graving docks, and on ways, gridirons and pontoons, at all times, in all places, and on all occasions, services and trades; with leave   60
to sail or navigate with or without pilots, to go on trial trips and to assist and tow vessels or craft in distress, but the Vessel may not be towed, except   61
as is customary or when in need of assistance, nor shall the Vessel render assistance or undertake towage or salvage services under contract previously   62
arranged by the Assured, the Owners, the Managers or the Charterers of the Vessel, nor shall the Vessel, in the course of trading operations, engage in   63
loading or discharging cargo at sea, from or into another vessel other than a barge, lighter or similar craft used principally in harbors or inland waters.   64
The phrase "engage in loading or discharging cargo at sea" shall include while approaching, leaving or alongside, or while another vessel is approaching,   65
leaving or alongside the Vessel.   66
    The Vessel is held covered in case of any breach of conditions as to cargo, trade, locality, towage or salvage activities, or date of sailing, or loading   67
or discharging cargo at sea, provided (a) notice is given to the Underwriters immediately following receipt of knowledge thereof by the Assured, and (b)   68
any amended terms of cover and any additional premium required by the Underwriters are agreed to by the Assured.   69

PERILS

    Touching the Adventures and Perils which the Underwriters are contented to bear and take upon themselves, they are of the Seas, Men-of-War, Fire,   70
Lightning, Earthquake, Enemies, Pirates, Rovers, Assailing Thieves, Jettisons, Letters of Mart and Counter-Mart, Surprisals, Takings at Sea, Arrests, Re-   71
straints and Detainments of all Kings, Princes and Peoples, of what nation, condition or quality soever, Barratry of the Master and Mariners and of all   72
other like Perils, Losses and Misfortunes that have or shall come to the Hurt, Detriment or Damage of the Vessel, or any part thereof, excepting, how-   73
ever, such of the foregoing perils as may be excluded by provisions elsewhere in the Policy or by endorsement thereon.   74

ADDITIONAL PERILS (INCHMAREE)

    Subject to the conditions of this Policy, this insurance also covers loss of or damage to the Vessel directly caused by the following: 75
    Accidents in loading, discharging or handling cargo, or in bunkering;   76
    Accidents in going on or off, or while on drydocks, graving docks, ways, gridirons or pontoons;   77
    Explosions on shipboard or elsewhere;   78
    Breakdown of motor generators or other electrical machinery and electrical connections thereto, bursting of boilers, breakage of shafts, or any   79
    latent defect in the machinery or hull, (excluding the cost and expense of replacing or repairing the defective part);   80
    Breakdown of or accidents to nuclear installations or reactors not on board the insured Vessel;   81
    Contact with aircraft, rockets or similar missiles, or with any land conveyance;   82
    Negligence of Charterers and/or Repairers, provided such Charterers and/or Repairers are not an Assured hereunder;   83
    Negligence of Masters, Officers, Crew or Pilots;   84
provided such loss or damage has not resulted from want of due diligence by the Assured, the Owners or Managers of the Vessel, or any of them.   85
Masters, Officers, Crew or Pilots are not to be considered Owners within the meaning of this clause should they hold shares in the Vessel.   86

DELIBERATE DAMAGE (POLLUTION HAZARD)

    Subject to the conditions of this Policy, this insurance also covers loss of or damage to the Vessel directly caused by governmental authorities   87
acting for the public welfare to prevent or mitigate a pollution hazard, or threat thereof, resulting directly from damage to the Vessel for which the   88
Underwriters are liable under this Policy, provided such act of governmental authorities has not resulted from want of due diligence by the Assured, the   89
Owners, or Managers of the Vessel or any of them to prevent or mitigate such hazard or threat. Masters, Officers, Crew or Pilots are not to be considered   90
Owners within the meaning of this clause should they hold shares in the Vessel.   91

CLAIMS (GENERAL PROVISIONS)

    In the event of any accident or occurrence which could give rise to a claim under this Policy, prompt notice thereof shall be given to the Under-   92
writers, and: 93
    (a) where practicable, the Underwriters shall be advised prior to survey, so that they may appoint their own surveyor, if they so desire;   94
    (b) the Underwriters shall be entitled to decide where the Vessel shall proceed for docking and/or repair (allowance to be made to the Assured for the   95
    actual additional expense of the voyage arising from compliance with the Underwriters' requirement);   96
    (c) the Underwriters shall have the right of veto in connection with any repair firm proposed;   97
    (d) the Underwriters may take tenders, or may require in writing that tenders be taken for the repair of the Vessel, in which event, upon acceptance   98
    of a tender with the approval of the Underwriters, an allowance shall be made at the rate of 30 per cent. per annum on the amount insured, for   99
    each day or pro rata for part of a day, for time lost between the issuance of invitations to tender and the acceptance of a tender, to the extent   100
    that such time is lost solely as the result of tenders having been taken and provided the tender is accepted without delay after receipt of the   101
    Underwriters' approval.   102
    Due credit shall be given against the allowances in (b) and (d) above for any amount recovered: 103
    (1) in respect of fuel, stores, and wages and maintenance of the Master, Officers or Crew allowed in General or Particular Average;   104
    (2) from third parties in respect of damages for detention and/or loss of profit and/or running expenses;   105
for the period covered by the allowances or any part thereof.   106
    No claim shall be allowed in Particular Average for wages and maintenance of the Master, Officers or Crew, except when incurred solely for the   107
necessary removal of the Vessel from one port to another for average repairs or for trial trips to test average repairs, in which cases wages and mainte-   108
nance will be allowed only while the Vessel is under way. This exclusion shall not apply to overtime or similar extraordinary payments to the Master,   109
Officers or Crew incurred in shifting the Vessel for tank cleaning or repairs or while specifically engaged in these activities, either in port or at sea.   110

· General and Particular Average shall be payable without deduction, new for old. 111
The expense of sighting the bottom after stranding shall be paid, if reasonably incurred especially for that purpose, even if no damage be found. 112
No claim shall in any case be allowed in respect of scraping or painting the Vessel's bottom. 113
In the event of loss or damage to equipment or apparatus not owned by the Assured but installed for use on board the Vessel and for which the 114
Assured has assumed responsibility, claim shall not exceed (1) the amount the Underwriters would pay if the Assured were owner of such equipment or 115
apparatus, or (2) the contractual responsibility assumed by the Assured to the owners or lessors thereof, whichever shall be less. 116
No claim for unrepaired damages shall be allowed, except to the extent that the aggregate damage caused by perils insured against during the period 117
of the Policy and left unrepaired at the expiration of the Policy shall be demonstrated by the Assured to have diminished the actual market value of the 118
Vessel on that date if undamaged by such perils. 119

GENERAL AVERAGE AND SALVAGE

General Average and Salvage shall be payable as provided in the contract of affreightment, or failing such provision or there be no contract of 120
affreightment, payable at the Assured's election either in accordance with York-Antwerp Rules 1950 or 1974 or with the Laws and Usages of the Port of 121
San Francisco. Provided always that when an adjustment according to the laws and usages of the port of destination is properly demanded by the owners 122
of the cargo, General Average shall be paid accordingly. 123
In the event of salvage, towage or other assistance being rendered to the Vessel by any vessel belonging in part or in whole to the same Owners or 124
Charterers, the value of such services (without regard to the common ownership or control of the vessels) shall be ascertained by arbitration in the man- 125
ner provided for under the Collision Liability clause in this Policy, and the amount so awarded so far as applicable to the interest hereby insured shall 126
constitute a charge under this Policy. 127
When the contributory value of the Vessel is greater than the Agreed Value herein, the liability of the Underwriters for General Average contribution 128
(except in respect to amounts made good to the Vessel), or Salvage, shall not exceed that proportion of the total contribution due from the Vessel which 129
the amount insured hereunder bears to the contributory value, and if, because of damage for which the Underwriters are liable as Particular Average, the 130
value of the Vessel has been reduced for the purpose of contribution, the amount of such Particular Average damage recoverable under this Policy shall 131
first be deducted from the amount insured hereunder, and the Underwriters shall then be liable only for the proportion which such net amount bears 132
to the contributory value. 133

TOTAL LOSS

In ascertaining whether the Vessel is a constructive Total Loss the Agreed Value shall be taken as the repaired value and nothing in respect of the 134
damaged or break-up value of the Vessel or wreck shall be taken into account. 135
There shall be no recovery for a constructive Total Loss hereunder unless the expense of recovering and repairing the Vessel would exceed the 136
Agreed Value. In making this determination, only expenses incurred or to be incurred by reason of a single accident or a sequence of damages arising 137
from the same accident shall be taken into account, but expenses incurred prior to tender of abandonment shall not be considered if such are to be 138
claimed separately under the Sue and Labor clause. 139
In the event of Total Loss (actual or constructive), no claim to be made by the Underwriters for freight, whether notice of abandonment has been 140
given or not. 141
In no case shall the Underwriters be liable for unrepaired damage in addition to a subsequent Total Loss sustained during the period covered by this 142
Policy. 143

SUE AND LABOR

And in case of any Loss or Misfortune, it shall be lawful and necessary for the Assured, their Factors, Servants and Assigns, to sue, labor and travel 144
for, in, and about the defense, safeguard and recovery of the Vessel, or any part thereof, without prejudice to this insurance, to the charges whereof 145
the Underwriters will contribute their proportion as provided below. And it is expressly declared and agreed that no acts of the Underwriters or Assured 146
in recovering, saving or preserving the Vessel shall be considered as a waiver or acceptance of abandonment. 147
In the event of expenditure under the Sue and Labor clause, the Underwriters shall pay the proportion of such expenses that the amount insured 148
hereunder bears to the Agreed Value, or that the amount insured hereunder (less loss and/or damage payable under this Policy) bears to the actual 149
value of the saved property, whichever proportion shall be less: provided always that their liability for such expenses shall not exceed their proportionate 150
part of the Agreed Value. 151
If claim for Total Loss is admitted under this Policy and sue and labor expenses have been reasonably incurred in excess of any proceeds realized 152
or value recovered, the amount payable under this Policy will be the proportion of such excess that the amount insured hereunder (without deduction 153
for loss or damage) bears to the Agreed Value or to the sound value of the Vessel at the time of the accident, whichever value was greater: provided 154
always that Underwriters' liability for such expenses shall not exceed their proportionate part of the Agreed Value. The foregoing shall also apply to 155
expenses reasonably incurred in salving or attempting to salve the Vessel and other property to the extent that such expenses shall be regarded as having 156
been incurred in respect of the Vessel. 157

COLLISION LIABILITY

And it is further agreed that: 158
(a) if the Vessel shall come into collision with any other ship or vessel, and the Assured or the Surety in consequence of the Vessel being at fault 159
shall become liable to pay and shall pay by way of damages to any other person or persons any sum or sums in respect of such collision, the 160
Underwriters will pay the Assured or the Surety, whichever shall have paid, such proportion of such sum or sums so paid as their respective sub- 161
scriptions hereto bear to the Agreed Value, provided always that their liability in respect to any one such collision shall not exceed their propor- 162
tionate part of the Agreed Value; 163
(b) in cases where, with the consent in writing of a majority (in amount) of Hull Underwriters, the liability of the Vessel has been contested, or pro- 164
ceedings have been taken to limit liability, the Underwriters will also pay a like proportion of the costs which the Assured shall thereby incur 165
or be compelled to pay. 166
When both vessels are to blame, then, unless the liability of the owners or charterers of one or both such vessels becomes limited by law, claims 167
under the Collision Liability clause shall be settled on the principle of Cross-Liabilities as if the owners or charterers of each vessel had been compelled 168
to pay to the owners or charterers of the other of such vessels such one-half or other proportion of the latter's damages as may have been properly allowed 169
in ascertaining the balance or sum payable by or to the Assured in consequence of such collision. 170
The principles involved in this clause shall apply to the case where both vessels are the property, in part or in whole, of the same owners or chart- 171
erers, all questions of responsibility and amount of liability as between the two vessels being left to the decision of a single Arbitrator, if the parties 172
can agree upon a single Arbitrator, or failing such agreement, to the decision of Arbitrators, one to be appointed by the Assured and one to be appointed 173
by the majority (in amount) of Hull Underwriters interested; the two Arbitrators chosen to choose a third Arbitrator before entering upon the reference, 174
and the decision of such single Arbitrator, or of any two of such three Arbitrators, appointed as above, to be final and binding. 175
Provided always that this clause shall in no case extend to any sum which the Assured or the Surety may become liable to pay or shall pay in conse- 176
quence of, or with respect to: 177
(a) removal or disposal of obstructions, wrecks or their cargoes under statutory powers or otherwise pursuant to law; 178
(b) injury to real or personal property of every description; 179
(c) the discharge, spillage, emission or leakage of oil, petroleum products, chemicals or other substances of any kind or description whatsoever; 180
(d) cargo or other property on or the engagements of the Vessel; 181
(e) loss of life, personal injury or illness. 182
Provided further that exclusions (b) and (c) above shall not apply to injury to other vessels or property thereon except to the extent that such injury 183
arises out of any action taken to avoid, minimize or remove any discharge, spillage, emission or leakage described in (c) above. 184

PILOTAGE AND TOWAGE

This insurance shall not be prejudiced by reason of any contract limiting in whole or in part the liability of pilots, tugs, towboats, or their owners 185
when the Assured or the agent of the Assured accepts such contract in accordance with established local practice. 186
Where in accordance with such practice, pilotage or towage services are provided under contracts requiring the Assured or the agent of the Assured: 187
(a) to assume liability for damage resulting from collision of the Vessel insured with any other ship or vessel, including the towing vessel, or 188
(b) to indemnify those providing the pilotage or towage services against loss or liability for any such damages, 189
it is agreed that amounts paid by the Assured or Surety pursuant to such assumed obligations shall be deemed payments "by way of damages to any other 190
person or persons" and to have been paid "in consequence of the Vessel being at fault" within the meaning of the Collision Liability clause in this Policy 191

to the extent that such payments would have been covered if the Vessel had been legally responsible in the absence of any agreement. Provided always 192
that in no event shall the aggregate amount of liability of the Underwriters under the Collision Liability clause, including this clause, be greater than 193
the amount of any statutory limitation of liability to which owners are entitled or would be entitled if liability under any contractual obligation referred to in 194
this clause were included among the liabilities subject to such statutory limitations. 195

CHANGE OF OWNERSHIP

In the event of any change, voluntary or otherwise, in the ownership or flag of the Vessel, or if the Vessel be placed under new management, or be 196
chartered on a bareboat basis or requisitioned on that basis, or if the Classification Society of the Vessel or her class therein be changed, cancelled or 197
withdrawn, then, unless the Underwriters agree thereto in writing, this Policy shall automatically terminate at the time of such change of ownership, flag, 198
management, charter, requisition or classification; provided, however, that: 199

(a) if the Vessel has cargo on board and has already sailed from her loading port, or is at sea in ballast, such automatic termination shall, if 200
required, be deferred until arrival at final port of discharge if with cargo, or at port of destination if in ballast; 201

(b) in the event of an involuntary temporary transfer by requisition or otherwise, without the prior execution of a written agreement by the 202
Assured, such automatic termination shall occur fifteen days after such transfer. 203

This insurance shall not inure to the benefit of any transferee or charterer of the Vessel and, if a loss payable hereunder should occur between 204
the time of change or transfer and any deferred automatic termination, the Underwriters shall be subrogated to all of the rights of the Assured against 205
the transferee or charterer in respect of all or part of such loss as is recoverable from the transferee or charterer, and in the proportion which the 206
amount insured hereunder bears to the Agreed Value. 207

The term "new management" as used above refers only to the transfer of the management of the Vessel from one firm or corporation to another, 208
and it shall not apply to any internal changes within the offices of the Assured. 209

ADDITIONAL INSURANCES

It is a condition of this Policy that no additional insurance against the risk of Total Loss of the Vessel shall be effected to operate during the cur- 210
rency of this Policy by or for account of the Assured, Owners, Managers, Operators or Mortgagees except on the interests and up to the amounts enum- 211
erated in the following Sections (a) to (g), inclusive, and no such insurance shall be subject to P.P.I., F.I.A. or other like term on any interests whatsoever 212
excepting those enumerated in Section (a); provided always and notwithstanding the limitation on recovery in the Assured clause a breach of this condition 213
shall not afford the Underwriters any defense to a claim by a Mortgagee who has accepted this Policy without knowledge of such breach: 214

(a) DISBURSEMENTS, MANAGERS' COMMISSIONS, PROFITS OR EXCESS OR INCREASED VALUE OF HULL AND MACHINERY, AND/OR SIMILAR INTER- 215
ESTS HOWEVER DESCRIBED, AND FREIGHT (INCLUDING CHARTERED FREIGHT OR ANTICIPATED FREIGHT) INSURED FOR TIME. An amount not exceeding 216
in the aggregate 25% of the Agreed Value. 217

(b) FREIGHT OR HIRE, UNDER CONTRACTS FOR VOYAGE. An amount not exceeding the gross freight or hire for the current cargo passage and next 218
succeeding cargo passage (such insurance to include, if required, a preliminary and an intermediate ballast passage) plus the charges of insur- 219
ance. In the case of a voyage charter where payment is made on a time basis, the amount shall be calculated on the estimated duration of the 220
voyage, subject to the limitation of two cargo passages as laid down herein. Any amount permitted under this Section shall be reduced, as the 221
freight or hire is earned, by the gross amount so earned. Any freight or hire to be earned under the form of Charters described in (d) below shall 222
not be permitted under this Section (b) if any part thereof is insured as permitted under said Section (d). 223

(c) ANTICIPATED FREIGHT IF THE VESSEL SAILS IN BALLAST AND NOT UNDER CHARTER. An amount not exceeding the anticipated gross freight 224
on next cargo passage, such amount to be reasonably estimated on the basis of the current rate of freight at time of insurance, plus the charges of 225
insurance. Provided, however, that no insurance shall be permitted by this Section if any insurance is effected as permitted under Section (b). 226

(d) TIME CHARTER HIRE OR CHARTER HIRE FOR SERIES OF VOYAGES. An amount not exceeding 50% of the gross hire which is to be earned under 227
the charter in a period not exceeding 18 months. Any amount permitted under this Section shall be reduced as the hire is earned under the charter 228
by 50% of the gross amount so earned but, where the charter is for a period exceeding 18 months, the amount insured need not be reduced while 229
it does not exceed 50% of the gross hire still to be earned under the charter. An insurance permitted by this Section may begin on the signing 230
of the charter. 231

(e) PREMIUMS. An amount not exceeding the actual premiums of all interest insured for a period not exceeding 12 months (excluding premiums 232
insured as permitted under the foregoing Sections but including, if required, the premium or estimated calls on any Protection and Indemnity or 233
War Risks and Strikes insurance) reducing pro rata monthly. 234

(f) RETURNS OF PREMIUM. An amount not exceeding the actual returns which are recoverable subject to "and arrival" or equivalent provision under 235
any policy of insurance. 236

(g) INSURANCE IRRESPECTIVE OF AMOUNT AGAINST:—Risks excluded by War, Strikes and Related Exclusions clause; risks enumerated in the American 237
Institute War Risks and Strikes Clauses; and General Average and Salvage Disbursements. 238

WAR STRIKES AND RELATED EXCLUSIONS

The following conditions shall be paramount and shall supersede and nullify any contrary provisions of the Policy. 239
This Policy does not cover any loss, damage or expense caused by, resulting from, or incurred as a consequence of: 240

(a) Capture, seizure, arrest, restraint or detainment, or any attempt thereat; or 241

(b) Any taking of the Vessel, by requisition or otherwise, whether in time of peace or war and whether lawful or otherwise; or 242
243

(c) Any mine, bomb or torpedo not carried as cargo on board the Vessel; or 243

(d) Any weapon of war employing atomic or nuclear fission and/or fusion or other like reaction or radioactive force or matter; or 244

(e) Civil war, revolution, rebellion, insurrection, or civil strife arising therefrom, or piracy; or 245

(f) Strikes, lockouts, political or labor disturbances, civil commotions, riots, martial law, military or usurped power; or 246

(g) Malicious acts or vandalism, unless committed by the Master or Mariners and not excluded elsewhere under this War Strikes and Related Exclu- 247
sions clause; or 248

(h) Hostilities or warlike operations (whether there be a declaration of war or not) but this subparagraph (h) not to exclude collision or contact with 249
aircraft, rockets or similar missiles, or with any fixed or floating object, or stranding, heavy weather, fire or explosion unless caused directly by 250
a hostile act by or against a belligerent power which act is independent of the nature of the voyage or service which the Vessel concerned or, in 251
the case of a collision, any other vessel involved therein, is performing. As used herein, "power" includes any authority maintaining, naval, mili- 252
tary or air forces in association with a power. 253

If war risks or other risks excluded by this clause are hereafter insured by endorsement on this Policy, such endorsement shall supersede the above 254
conditions only to the extent that the terms of such endorsement are inconsistent therewith and only while such endorsement remains in force. 255

Appendix 7

American Institute

EXCESS MARINE LIABILITIES CLAUSES
(November 3, 1977)

To be attached to and form a part of Policy No. .... of the ....

....

1. **Insures** 1

.... 2

.... 3

(hereinafter called the "Assured") against excess liabilities of the Assured as hereinafter described and subject to the terms and conditions hereinafter 4
set forth, in respect only of the liabilities or expenses checked and for which a premium is shown in the following schedule: 5

Section	Covered	Premium	6
(a) Excess Protection and Indemnity	☐	$_____	7
(b) Excess Collision Liability	☐	$_____	8
(c) Excess Collision, including Tower's Liability	☐	$_____	9
(d) Excess General Average and Salvage	☐	$_____	10
(e) Excess Sue and Labor Charges	☐	$_____	11
(f) Excess Ship Repairer's Legal Liability	☐	$_____	12
(g) Excess _____	☐	$_____	13
		TOTAL $_____	14

2. Period: At and from the .... day of .... 19...... . 15

   To the: .... day of .... 19...... . 16

Beginning and ending with .... Time. 17

EXCESS PROTECTION AND INDEMNITY 18
(a) These Underwriters agree to indemnify the Assured for all liability, loss, damage or expense insured against under the Protection and Indemnity 19
policies described in the Schedule of Underlying Insurances (hereinafter referred to in this Section and in the General Conditions as the "Primary 20
Policies"); but this insurance is warranted free from claim hereunder unless such liability in respect of the same accident (or occurrence, if the 21
Limits of Liability of the Primary Policies are written on an occurrence basis) exceeds the Limits of Liability of the Primary Policies in which 22
event these Underwriters shall be liable only for the amount by which such liability exceeds such underlying Limits of Liability, but in no 23
event for more than the Limit of Liability of this insurance. 24

EXCESS COLLISION 25
(b) These Underwriters agree to indemnify the Assured for sums not recoverable in full by the Assured under the Collision Clause of the policies 26
on Hull and Machinery (including Increased Value with excess liabilities, if any, or under any other policies insuring collision liability) described 27
in the Schedule of Underlying Insurance (hereinafter referred to in this Section and in the General Conditions as the "Primary Policies"), by 28
reason of the Assured's collision liability exceeding the amount insured against collision liability as stated in the Primary Policies, but in no 29
event for more than the Limit of Liability of this insurance. 30

EXCESS COLLISION INCLUDING TOWER'S LIABILITY 31
(c) These Underwriters agree to indemnify the Assured for sums not recoverable in full by the Assured under the Collision Clause incorporating 32
tower's liability, of the policies on Hull and Machinery (including Increased Values with excess liabilities, if any, or under any other policies 33
insuring collision and tower's liability) described in the Schedule of Underlying Insurances (hereinafter referred to in this Section and in 34

the General Conditions as the "Primary Policies"), by reason of the Assured's collision and or tower's liability exceeding the amounts insured   35
against collision and tower's liability as stated in the Primary Policies, but in no event for more than the Limit of Liability of this insurance.   36
These Underwriters shall not be required to indemnify the Assured under Section (b) of this Policy with respect to any vessel insured under   37
this Section (c).   38

EXCESS GENERAL AVERAGE AND SALVAGE   39
(d) These Underwriters agree to indemnify the Assured for General Average and Salvage not recoverable in full by the Assured under the policies on   40
Hull and Machinery (including Increased Value with excess liabilities, if any) described in the Schedule of Underlying Insurances (hereinafter   41
referred to in this Section and in the General Conditions as the "Primary Policies"), by reason of the difference between the insured value   42
of the Vessel as stated in the Primary Policies (or any reduced value arising from the deduction therefrom in the process of adjustment of any   43
claim which law or practice or the terms of the Primary Policies may have required) and the value of the Vessel adopted for the purpose of   44
contribution to General Average or Salvage charges, the liability under this Policy being for such proportion of the amount not recoverable as   45
the Limit of Liability of this insurance bears to the said difference or to the total sum insured against excess liabilities if it exceeds such   46
difference, but in no event for more than the Limit of Liability of this insurance.   47

EXCESS SUE AND LABOR CHARGES   48
(e) These Underwriters agree to indemnify the Assured for Sue and Labor Charges not recoverable in full by the Assured under the policies on   49
Hull and Machinery (including Increased Value with excess liabilities, if any) described in the Schedule of Underlying Insurances (hereinafter   50
referred to in this Section and in the General Conditions as the "Primary Policies"), by reason of the difference between the insured value   51
of the Vessel as stated therein (or any reduced value arising from the deduction therefrom of any claim which the terms of the policies cov-   52
ering Hull and Machinery may have required) and the value of the Vessel adopted for the purpose of ascertaining the amounts recoverable   53
under the policies on Hull and Machinery (including Increased Value with excess liabilities, if any), the liability under this Policy being for such pro-   54
portion of the amount not recoverable as the Limit of Liability of this insurance bears to the said difference or to the total sum insured   55
against excess liabilities if it exceeds such difference, but in no event for more than the Limit of Liability of this insurance.   56

EXCESS SHIP REPAIRER'S LEGAL LIABILITY   57
(f) These Underwriters agree to indemnify the Assured for all liability, loss, damage or expense insured against under the Ship Repairer's Legal   58
Liability policies described in the Schedule of Underlying Insurances (hereinafter referred to in this Section and in the General Conditions as   59
the "Primary Policies"), but this insurance is warranted free from claim hereunder unless such liability in respect of the same accident (or   60
occurrence if the Limits of Liability of the Primary Policies are written on an occurrence basis) exceeds the Limits of Liability of the Primary   61
Policies in which event these Underwriters shall be liable only for the amount by which such liability exceeds such underlying Limits of Liability,   62
but in no event for more than the Limit of Liability of this insurance.   63

EXCESS _____   64
(g) These Underwriters agree to indemnify the Assured for all liability, loss, damage or expense insured against under the   65

....   66

....   67
policies described in the Schedule of Underlying Insurances (hereinafter referred to in this Section and in the General Conditions as the   68
"Primary Policies"), but this insurance is warranted free from claim hereunder unless such liability in respect of the same accident (or occurrence   69
if the Limits of Liability of the Primary Policies are written on an occurrence basis) exceeds the Limits of Liability of the Primary Policies in   70
which event these Underwriters shall be liable only for the amount by which such liability exceeds such underlying limits of Liability, but in no   71
event for more than the Limit of Liability of this insurance.   72

GENERAL CONDITIONS

3. These Underwriters shall not be called upon to assume charge of the settlement or defense of any claim made or suit brought or proceeding   73
instituted against the Assured, but these Underwriters shall have the right and shall be given the opportunity (without incurring any liability for   74
costs or expenses thereof except as herein provided) to associate with the Assured or the underwriters on the Primary Policies, or both, in the   75
defense and control of any claim, suit or proceeding which involves or appears likely to involve these Underwriters, in which event the Assured,   76
the underwriters on the Primary Policies and these Underwriters shall cooperate in all matters in the defense of such claim, suit or proceeding.   77
4. In the event the Assured or the underwriters on the Primary Policies elect not to appeal a judgment in excess of the Limits of Liability as stated   78
in the Primary Policies, these Underwriters may, elect to make such an appeal at their sole cost and expense and shall be liable for the   79
taxable costs and disbursements and interest incidental thereto, but in no event shall the liability of these Underwriters exceed the Limit of Liability   80
of this insurance plus the cost and expense of any such appeal.   81
5. In the case of any payment made hereunder, these Underwriters may act together with all other interests (including the Assured) in the exercise   82
of any rights of recovery against third parties with respect to the loss paid by the Assured, underwriters on the Primary Policies and these Under-   83
writers. The apportionment of any amounts which may be recovered from third parties shall follow the principle that any interest (including that   84
of the Assured) that shall have paid an amount over and above any payment made hereunder by these Underwriters shall first be reimbursed up to   85
the amount paid thereby; these Underwriters will then be reimbursed out of any balance remaining up to the amount paid thereby and hereunder;   86
finally, the interests (including that of the Assured) of whom this Policy is in excess are entitled to claim the balance, if any. Expenses necessary   87
to the recovery of any such amounts shall be apportioned between the interests (including the Assured) concerned, in the proportion that their   88
respective recoveries are finally settled.   89
6. It is a condition of this Policy that all Primary Policies, in which the Assured has an interest, are scheduled and that the said Primary Policies   90
shall be maintained in full force and effect during the term of this Policy and that no changes shall be made in the Primary Policies which broaden   91
the insuring conditions thereof or reduce the amounts collectible thereunder. In the event of a breach of any of the aforesaid conditions this   92
Policy shall be null and void, unless otherwise agreed in writing by these Underwriters. These Underwriters shall be furnished with copies of the Primary   93
Policies and any amendments thereto at their request.   94
7. The term "Assured" is used severally and not collectively, but the inclusion herein of more than one Assured shall not operate to increase the   95
liability of these Underwriters.   96
8. The Assured, upon knowledge of any occurrence likely to give rise to a claim hereunder, shall give prompt written notice thereof to these Underwriters.   97
9. Either these Underwriters or the Assured may cancel this insurance by giving the other fifteen (15) days written notice, after which this Policy   98
shall be of no force or effect. Written or telegraphic notice sent to the Assured at its last known address shall constitute complete notice of   99
cancellation. Such notice sent to the Assured in care of the broker who negotiated this Policy shall have the same effect as if sent directly to the   100
Assured. If cancellation is at Assured's option, these Underwriters will retain earned premium hereunder as per customary short rate table; if   101
cancellation is at these Underwriters' option, pro rata unearned premium will be returned as soon as practicable. All returns shall be net.   102
10. Regardless of the number or types of liabilities insured against hereunder, or the number of vessels or risks involved, these Underwriters shall not   103
be liable under this Policy for more than $ .... any one accident or series of accidents arising out of the same event, but in no   104
event shall the liability of these Underwriters under any individual section of this Policy exceed the Limit of Liability scheduled for that section in   105
Column "A" below for any accident or series of accidents arising out of the same event.   106

11. This insurance shall cover only those excess liabilities specified in paragraph 1, but not exceeding the amounts specified under Limit of 107
Liability in Column "A" below, being excess of Primary Limits specified in column "B" below, but subject to the terms and conditions otherwise 108
specified herein. 109

The listing below of Underlying Insurances which include risks not otherwise insured against under this Policy, shall not be deemed to be 110
an acceptance by these Underwriters as protection against such risks, nor shall the Assured recover from these Underwriters any deductible or self- 111
insured retention under Primary Policies. 112

SCHEDULE OF UNDERLYING INSURANCES

Location or Vessel	Sections Applicable	Column "A" Limit of Liability	Column "B" Primary Limits

Appendix 8

American Institute

INCREASED VALUE AND EXCESS LIABILITIES CLAUSES
(November 3, 1977)

To be attached to and form a part of Policy No. .... of the ....

....

    The terms and conditions of the following clauses are to be regarded as substituted for those of the policy form to which they are attached, the latter being hereby waived, except provisions required by law to be inserted in the Policy. All captions are inserted only for purposes of reference and shall not be used to interpret the clauses to which they apply.

ASSURED

    This Policy insures   1

....   2

.... hereinafter referred to as the Assured.   3

    If claim is made under this Policy by anyone other than the Owner of the Vessel, such person shall not be entitled to recover to a greater   4
extent than would the Owner, had claim been made by the Owner as an Assured named in this Policy.   5

    Underwriters waive any right of subrogation against affiliated, subsidiary or interrelated companies of the Assured, provided that such waiver   6
shall not apply in the event of a collision between the Vessel and any vessel owned, demise chartered or otherwise controlled by any of the   7
aforesaid companies, or with respect to any loss, damage or expense against which such companies are insured.   8

    This insurance shall not be prejudiced by reason of any contract limiting in whole or in part the liability of pilots, tugs, towboats, or their   9
owners when the Assured or the Agent of the Assured accepts such contract in accordance with established local practice.   10

LOSS PAYEE

    Loss, if any, payable to   11

....   12

.... or order.   13

    Provided, however, Underwriters shall pay claims to others as set forth in the Collision Liability clause and may make direct payment to persons   14
providing security for the release of the Vessel in Salvage cases.   15

On INCREASED VALUE AND EXCESS LIABILITIES of the Vessel called the   16
(or by whatsoever name or names the said Vessel is or shall be called).   17

AMOUNT INSURED HEREUNDER

.... Dollars.   18

DURATION OF RISK

    From the .... day of .... 19 , ... time   19

    to the .... day of .... 19 , ... time.   20

    Should the Vessel at the expiration of this Policy be at sea, or in distress, or at a port of refuge or of call, she shall, provided previous notice   21
be given to the Underwriters, be held covered at a pro rata monthly premium to her port of destination.   22

    In the event of payment by the Underwriters for Total Loss of the Vessel this Policy shall thereupon automatically terminate.   23

PREMIUM

    The Underwriters to be paid in consideration of this insurance   24

.... Dollars being at the annual rate of .... per cent., which   25
premium shall be due on attachment. If the Vessel is insured under this Policy for a period of less than one year at pro rata of the annual rate,   26
full annual premium shall be considered earned and immediately due and payable in the event of Total Loss of the Vessel.   27

RETURNS OF PREMIUMS

Premium returnable as follows:

    Pro rata daily net in the event of termination under the Change of Ownership clause;   28 29

    Pro rata monthly net for each uncommenced month if it be mutually agreed to cancel this Policy;   30

    For each period of 30 consecutive days the Vessel may be laid up in port for account of the Assured,   31

    .... cents per cent. net not under repair, or   32

    .... cents per cent. net under repair;   33

provided always that: 34

    (a) A Total Loss of the Vessel has not occurred during the currency of this Policy;   35

    (b) In no case shall a return for lay-up be allowed when the Vessel is lying in exposed or unprotected waters or in any location not approved by   36
    the Underwriters;   37

    (c) In the event of any amendment of the annual rate, the above rates of return shall be adjusted accordingly;   38

    (d) In no case shall a return be allowed when the Vessel is used as a storage ship or for lightering purposes.   39

    If the Vessel is laid up for a period of 30 consecutive days, a part only of which attaches under this Policy, the Underwriters shall pay such   40
proportion of the return due in respect of a full period of 30 days as the number of days attaching hereto bears to 30. Should the lay-up period   41
exceed 30 consecutive days, the Assured shall have the option to elect the period of 30 consecutive days for which a return is recoverable.   42

NON-PAYMENT OF PREMIUM

In event of non-payment of premium 30 days after attachment, or of any additional premium when due, this Policy may be cancelled by the   43
Underwriters upon 10 days written or telegraphic notice sent to the Assured at his last known address or in care of the broker who negotiated this   44
Policy. Such proportion of the premium, however, as shall have been earned up to the time of cancellation shall be payable. In the event of Total Loss of   45
the Vessel occurring prior to any cancellation or termination of this Policy full annual premium shall be considered earned.   46

ADVENTURE

Beginning the adventure upon the Vessel, as above, and so shall continue and endure during the period aforesaid, as employment may offer, in   47
port or at sea, in docks and graving docks, and on ways, gridirons and pontoons, at all times, in all places, and on all occasions, services and trades;   48
with leave to sail or navigate with or without pilots, to go on trial trips and to assist and tow vessels or craft in distress, but the Vessel may not be   49
towed, except as is customary or when in need of assistance, nor shall the Vessel render assistance or undertake towage or salvage services under   50
contract previously arranged by the Assured, the Owners, the Managers or the Charterers of the Vessel, nor shall the Vessel, in the course of trading   51
operations, engage in loading or discharging cargo at sea, from or into another vessel other than a barge, lighter or similar craft used principally in   52
harbors or inland waters. The phrase "engage in loading or discharging cargo at sea" shall include while approaching, leaving or alongside, or while another   53
vessel is approaching, leaving or alongside the Vessel.   54

The Vessel is held covered in case of any breach of conditions as to cargo, trade, locality, towage or salvage activities, date of sailing, or loading   55
or discharging cargo at sea, provided (a) notice is given to the Underwriters immediately following receipt of knowledge thereof by the Assured, and   56
(b) any amended terms of cover and any additional premium required by the Underwriters are agreed to by the Assured.   57

COVERAGE

This insurance covers only: 58

(1) **TOTAL LOSS (ACTUAL OR CONSTRUCTIVE) OF THE VESSEL** directly caused by Perils of the Seas, Men-of-War, Fire, Lightning, Earthquake,   59
Enemies, Pirates, Rovers, Assailing Thieves, Jettisons, Letters of Mart and Counter-Mart, Surprisals, Takings at Sea, Arrests, Restraints and Detainments   60
of all Kings, Princes and Peoples, of what nation, condition or quality soever, Barratry of the Master and Mariners and of all other like Perils, Losses   61
and Misfortunes that have or shall come to the Hurt, Detriment or Damage of the Vessel, or any part thereof, excepting, however, such of the   62
foregoing perils as may be excluded by provisions elsewhere in the Policy or by endorsement thereon. It shall also cover Total Loss (actual or con-   63
structive) directly caused by the following:-   64
    Accidents in loading, discharging or handling cargo, or in bunkering;   65
    Accidents in going on or off, or while on drydocks, graving docks, ways, gridirons or pontoons;   66
    Explosions on shipboard or elsewhere;   67
    Breakdown of motor generators or other electrical machinery and electrical connections thereto, bursting of boilers, breakage of shafts, or   68
any latent defect in the machinery or hull, (excluding the cost and expense of replacing or repairing the defective part);   69
    Breakdown of or accidents to nuclear installations or reactors not on board the insured Vessel;   70
    Contact with aircraft, rockets or similar missiles, or with any land conveyance;   71
    Negligence of Charterers and/or Repairers, provided such Charterers and/or Repairers are not an Assured hereunder;   72
    Negligence of Masters, Officers, Crew or Pilots;   73
provided such loss or damage has not resulted from want of due diligence by the Assured, the Owners or Managers of the Vessel, or any of them.   74
Masters, Officers, Crew or Pilots are not to be considered Owners within the meaning of this clause should they hold shares in the Vessel.   75

Subject to the conditions of this Policy, this insurance also covers Total Loss (actual or constructive) of the Vessel directly caused by govern-   76
mental authorities acting for the public welfare to prevent or mitigate a pollution hazard, or threat thereof, resulting directly from damage to the   77
Vessel for which the Underwriters are liable under this Policy, provided such act of governmental authorities has not resulted from want of due   78
diligence by the Assured, the Owners, or Managers of the Vessel or any of them to prevent or mitigate such hazard or threat. Masters, Officers, Crew   79
or Pilots are not to be considered Owners within the meaning of this clause should they hold shares in the Vessel.   80
In ascertaining whether the Vessel is a constructive Total Loss the Agreed Value in the policies on Hull and Machinery shall be taken as the   81
repaired value and nothing in respect of the damaged or break-up value of the Vessel or wreck shall be taken into account.   82
There shall be no recovery for a constructive Total Loss hereunder unless the expense of recovering and repairing the Vessel would exceed the   83
Agreed Value in policies on Hull and Machinery. In making this determination, only expenses incurred or to be incurred by reason of a single   84
accident or a sequence of damages arising from the same accident shall be taken into account, but expenses incurred prior to tender of   85
abandonment shall not be considered if such are to be claimed separately under the Sue and Labor clause in said policies.   86
Provided that the policies on Hull and Machinery contain the above clauses with respect to the method of ascertaining whether the Vessel is a   87
constructive Total Loss (or clauses having a similar effect), the settlement of a claim for Total Loss under the policies on Hull and Machinery shall   88
be accepted as proof of the Total Loss of the Vessel under this Policy; and in the event of a claim for Total Loss being settled under the policies   89
on Hull and Machinery as a compromised total loss, the amount payable hereunder shall be the same percentage of the amount hereby insured as   90
the percentage paid on the amount insured under said policies.   91
Should the Vessel be a constructive Total Loss but the claim on the policies on Hull and Machinery be settled as a claim for partial loss, no   92
payment shall be due under this Section (1).   93
Full interest admitted; the Policy being deemed sufficient proof of interest.   94
In the event of Total Loss, the Underwriters waive interest in any proceeds from the sale or other disposition of the Vessel or wreck.   95

(2) **GENERAL AVERAGE AND SALVAGE** not recoverable in full under the policies on Hull and Machinery by reason of the difference between the   96
Agreed Value of the Vessel as stated therein (or any reduced value arising from the deduction therefrom in process of adjustment of any claim   97
which law or practice or the terms of the policies covering Hull and Machinery may have required) and the value of the Vessel adopted for the purpose   98
of contribution to General Average or Salvage, the liability under this Policy being for such proportion of the amount not recoverable as the amount   99
insured hereunder bears to the said difference or to the total amount insured against excess liabilities if it exceed such difference.   100

(3) **SUE AND LABOR CHARGES** not recoverable in full under the policies on Hull and Machinery by reason of the difference between the Agreed Value   101
of the Vessel as stated therein (or any reduced value arising from the deduction therefrom of any claim which the terms of the policies covering Hull   102
and Machinery may have required) and the value of the Vessel adopted for the purpose of ascertaining the amount recoverable under the policies on   103
Hull and Machinery, the liability under this Policy being for such proportion of the amount not recoverable as the amount insured hereunder bears to   104
the said difference or to the total amount insured against excess liabilities if it exceed such difference.   105

(4) **COLLISION LIABILITY** (Including Costs) not recoverable in full under the Collision Liability clause (including the Pilotage and Towage extension)   106
in the policies on Hull and Machinery by reason of such liability exceeding the Agreed Value of the Vessel as stated therein, in which case the   107
amount recoverable under this Policy shall be such proportion of the difference so arising as the amount hereby insured bears to the total amount   108
insured against excess liabilities.   109

Underwriters' liability under (1), (2), (3) and (4) is separate and shall not exceed the amount insured hereunder in any one section in respect of   110
any one claim.   111

NOTICE OF CLAIM

When it becomes evident that any accident or occurrence could give rise to a claim under this Policy, prompt notice thereof shall be given to the   112
Underwriters.   113

CHANGE OF OWNERSHIP

In the event of any change, voluntary or otherwise, in the ownership or flag of the Vessel, or if the Vessel be placed under new management,   114
or be chartered on a bareboat basis or requisitioned on that basis, or if the Classfiication Society of the Vessel or her class therein be changed, can-   115
celled or withdrawn, then, unless the Underwriters agree thereto in writing, this Policy shall automatically terminate at the time of such change of   116
ownership, flag, management, charter, requisition or classification; provided however, that: 117

(a) if the Vessel has cargo on board and has already sailed from her loading port, or is at sea in ballast, such automatic termination shall,   118
if required, be deferred until arrival at final port of discharge if with cargo, or at port of destination if in ballast;   119

(b) in the event of an involuntary temporary transfer by requisition or otherwise, without the prior execution of a written agreement by the   120
Assured, such automatic termination shall occur fifteen days after such transfer.   121

This insurance shall not inure to the benefit of any transferee or charterer of the Vessel and, if a loss payable hereunder should occur between   122
the time of change or transfer and any deferred automatic termination, the Underwriters shall be subrogated to all of the rights of the Assured against   123
the transferee or charterer in respect of all or part of such loss as is recoverable from the transferee or charterer, and in the proportion which the   124
amount insured hereunder bears to the Agreed Value.   125

The term "new management" as used above refers only to the transfer of the management of the Vessel from one firm or corporation to another,   126
and it shall not apply to any internal changes within the offices of the Assured.   127

WAR, STRIKES AND RELATED EXCLUSIONS

The following conditions shall be paramount and shall supersede and nullify any contrary provisions of the Policy.   128

This Policy does not cover any loss, damage or expense caused by, resulting from, or incurred as a consequence of: 129

(a) Capture, seizure, arrest, restraint or detainment, or any attempt thereat; or   130

(b) Any taking of the Vessel, by requisition or otherwise, whether in time of peace or war and whether lawful or otherwise; or   131

(c) Any mine, bomb or torpedo not carried as cargo on board the Vessel; or   132

(d) Any weapon of war employing atomic or nuclear fission and or fusion or other like reaction or radioactive force or matter; or   133

(e) Civil war, revolution, rebellion, insurrection, or civil strife arising therefrom, or piracy; or   134

(f) Strikes, lockouts, political or labor disturbances, civil commotions, riots, martial law, military or usurped power; or   135

(g) Malicious acts or vandalism, unless committed by the Master or Mariners and not excluded elsewhere under this War Strikes and Related Exclu-   136
sions clause; or   137

(h) Hostilities or warlike operations (whether there be a declaration of war or not) but this subparagraph (h) not to exclude collision or contact   138
with aircraft, rockets or similar missiles, or with any fixed or floating object, or stranding, heavy weather, fire or explosion unless caused   139
directly by a hostile act by or against a belligerent power which act is independent of the nature of the voyage or service which the Vessel   140
concerned or, in the case of a collision, any other vessel involved therein, is performing. As used herein "power" includes any authority   141
maintaining naval, military or air forces in association with a power.   142

If war risks or other risks excluded by this clause are hereafter insured by endorsement on this Policy, such endorsement shall supersede the   143
above conditions only to the extent that the terms of such endorsement are inconsistent therewith and only while such endorsement remains in force.   144

Appendix 9

American Institute
Hull War Risks and Strikes Clauses
(Including Automatic Termination and Cancellation Provisions)
For Attachment to American Institute Hull Clauses
December 1, 1977

To be attached to and form a part of Policy No. .... of the................ 1

.... 2

This insurance, subject to the exclusions set forth herein, covers only those risks which would be covered by the 3
attached Policy (including collision liability) in the absence of the WAR, STRIKES AND RELATED EXCLUSIONS clause 4
contained therein but which are excluded thereby and which risks shall be construed as also including: 5

   1. Any mine, bomb or torpedo not carried as cargo on board the Vessel; 6
   2. Any weapon of war employing atomic or nuclear fission and/or fusion or other like reaction or radioactive force 7
      or matter; 8
   3. Civil war, revolution, rebellion, insurrection, or civil strife arising therefrom; 9
   4. Strikes, lockouts, political or labor disturbances, civil commotions, riots, martial law, military or usurped power; 10
   5. Malicious acts or vandalism to the extent only that such risks are not covered by the attached Policy; 11
   6. Hostilities or warlike operations (whether there be a declaration of war or not) but this paragraph (6) shall not 12
      include collision or contact with aircraft, rockets or similar missiles, or with any fixed or floating object, or strand- 13
      ing, heavy weather, fire or explosion unless caused directly by a hostile act by or against a belligerent power 14
      which act is independent of the nature of the voyage or service which the Vessel concerned or, in the case of 15
      a collision, any other vessel involved therein, is performing. As used herein, "power" includes any authority 16
      maintaining naval, military or air forces in association with a power. 17

EXCLUSIONS

This insurance does not cover any loss, damage or expense caused by, resulting from, or incurred as a consequence 18
of: 19

   a. Any hostile detonation of any weapon of war described above in paragraph (2); 20
   b. Outbreak of war (whether there be a declaration of war or not) between any of the following countries: United 21
      States of America, United Kingdom, France, the Union of Soviet Socialist Republics or the People's Republic 22
      of China; 23
   c. Delay or demurrage; 24
   d. Requisition or preemption; 25
   e. Arrest, restraint or detainment under customs or quarantine regulations and similar arrests, restraints or detain- 26
      ments not arising from actual or impending hostilities; 27
   f. Capture, seizure, arrest, restraint, detainment, or confiscation by the Government of the United States or of the 28
      country in which the Vessel is owned or registered. 29

HELD COVERED AND OTHER PROVISIONS

The held covered clause appearing under the heading ADVENTURE in the attached Policy is deleted and the follow- 30
ing clause substituted therefore:— 31

        "Subject to the provisions of the Automatic Termination and Cancellation Clauses below, held covered in the 32
        event of any breach of conditions as to loading or discharging of cargo at sea, or towage or salvage activities 33
        provided (a) notice is given to the Underwriters immediately following receipt of knowledge thereof by the 34
        Assured, and (b) any amended terms of cover and any additional premium required by the Underwriters are 35
        agreed to by the Assured." 36

If at the natural expiry time of this insurance the Vessel is at sea, this insurance will be extended, provided previous 37
notice be given to the Underwriters, for an additional premium at a rate to be named by the Underwriters, until midnight 38

Local Time of the day on which the Vessel enters the next port to which she proceeds and for 24 hours thereafter, but | 39
in no event shall such extension affect or postpone the operation of the Automatic Termination and Cancellation Clauses | 40
below. | 41

Warranted not to abandon in case of capture, seizure or detention, until after condemnation of the property insured. | 42

The provisions of the attached Policy with respect to constructive Total Loss shall apply only to claims arising from | 43
physical damage to the Vessel. | 44

AUTOMATIC TERMINATION AND CANCELLATION CLAUSES

This insurance and any extension thereof, unless sooner terminated by the provisions of section B or C, shall terminate | 45
automatically upon and simultaneously with the occurrence of any hostile detonation of any nuclear weapon of war | 46
as defined above, wheresoever or whensoever such detonation may occur and whether or not the Vessel may be | 47
involved. | 48

B. This insurance and any extension thereof, unless sooner terminated by the provisions of section A or C, shall termi- | 49
nate automatically upon and simultaneously with the outbreak of war, whether there be a declaration of war or not, | 50
between any of the following countries: United States of America, United Kingdom, France, the Union of Soviet | 51
Socialist Republics or the People's Republic of China. | 52

C. This insurance and any extension thereof, unless sooner terminated by section A or B, shall terminate automatically | 53
if and when the Vessel is requisitioned, either for title or use. | 54

D. This insurance and any extension thereof may be cancelled at any time at the Assured's request, or by Underwriters | 55
upon 14 days' written notice being given to the Assured, but in no event shall such cancellation affect or postpone | 56
the operation of the provisions of sections A, B or C. Written or telegraphic notice sent to the Assured at his (its) | 57
last known address shall constitute a complete notice of cancellation and such notice mailed or telegraphed to | 58
the said Assured, care of the broker who negotiated this insurance, shall have the same effect as if sent to the | 59
said Assured direct. The mailing of notice as aforesaid shall be sufficient proof of notice and the effective date | 60
and hour of cancellation shall be 14 days from midnight Local Time of the day on which such notice was mailed or | 61
telegraphed as aforesaid. Underwriters agree, however, to reinstate this insurance subject to agreement between | 62
Underwriters and the Assured prior to the effective date and hour of such cancellation as to new rate of premium | 63
and/or conditions and/or warranties. | 64

RETURNS OF PREMIUM

The RETURNS OF PREMIUM clause of the attached Policy is deleted and the following substituted therefore:— | 65
"In the event of an automatic termination or cancellation of this insurance under the provisions of sections | 66
A, B, C or D above, or if the Vessel be sold, pro rata net return of premium will be payable to the Assured, | 67
provided always that a Total Loss of the Vessel has not occurred during the currency of this Policy. In no | 68
other event shall there be any return of premium." | 69

THIS INSURANCE SHALL NOT BECOME EFFECTIVE IF, PRIOR TO THE INTENDED TIME OF ITS ATTACHMENT, THERE | 70
HAS OCCURRED ANY EVENT WHICH WOULD HAVE AUTOMATICALLY TERMINATED THIS INSURANCE UNDER THE | 71
PROVISIONS OF SECTIONS A, B, OR C HEREOF HAD THIS INSURANCE ATTACHED PRIOR TO SUCH OCCURRENCE. | 72

Appendix 10

American Institute

BUILDER'S RISKS CLAUSES
(FEB. 8, 1979)

To be attached to and form a part of Policy No. ....of the ....

The terms and conditions of the following clauses are to be regarded as substituted for those of the policy form to which they are attached, the latter being hereby waived, except provisions required by law to be inserted in the Policy. All captions are inserted only for purposes of reference and shall not be used to interpret the clauses to which they apply.

ASSURED

This Policy insures	1
.... hereinafter referred to as the Assured.	2
If claim is made under this Policy by anyone other than the Owner of the Vessel, such person shall not be entitled to recover to a greater extent than would the Owner, had claim been made by the Owner as an Assured named in this Policy.	3 / 4
Underwriters waive any right of subrogation against affiliated, subsidiary or interrelated companies of the Assured, provided that such waiver shall not apply in the event of a collision between the Vessel and any vessel owned, demise chartered or otherwise controlled by any of the aforesaid companies, or with respect to any loss, damage or expense against which such companies are insured.	5 / 6 / 7

LOSS PAYEE

Loss, if any, payable to	8
.... or order.	9
Provided, however, Underwriters shall pay claims to others as set forth in the Collision Liability of the Protection and Indemnity clauses and may make direct payment to persons providing security for the release of the Vessel in Salvage cases.	10 / 11

SUBJECT MATTER

The Subject Matter of this insurance (herein referred to as the Vessel) is the hull, launches, lifeboats, rafts, furniture, bunkers, stores, tackle, fittings, equipment, apparatus, machinery, boilers, refrigeration machinery, insulation, motor generators and other electrical machinery, ordnance, munitions, and appurtenances, including materials, plans, patterns and moulds, staging, scaffolding and similar temporary construction to the extent only that the cost [12 / 13 / 14]

of any of the foregoing is included in the Agreed Value incorporated in or allocated to Hull No. .... Type .... [15]

building at the yard of the Builder at .... [16]

In the event of any material change in the specifications or design of the Vessel from that originally represented to the Underwriters, such change is held covered provided (a) notice is given to the Underwriters immediately following such change, and (b) any amended terms of cover and any additional premium required by the Underwriters are agreed to by the Assured. [17 / 18 / 19]

This Policy insures only while the Vessel (ashore or afloat) is at the building location named above; while in transit within the port of construction to and from such location; and while on trial trips (including proceeding to and returning from the trial course), as often as required, within a distance by water of 250 nautical miles of the port of construction, or held covered at an additional premium to be named by the Underwriters in the event of deviation of voyage, provided prompt notice thereof is given to the Underwriters. [20 / 21 / 22 / 23]

DURATION OF RISK

From the .... day of .... 19 .... time.	24
to the .... day of .... 19 .... time	25
or until delivery, if delivered at an earlier date.	26
In the event of delivery not being effected by the aforesaid expiration date, this Policy may be extended at .... per month,	27
provided prompt notice be given to the Underwriters but not for more than .... months from the date of original attachment, but held	28
covered for an additional period of time provided prompt notice is given the Underwriters and any amended terms of cover and any additional) premium	29
required by the Underwriters are agreed to by the Assured; provided, however, in no case shall this Policy extend beyond delivery of the Vessel.	30
In the event of payment by the Underwriters for Total Loss of the Vessel this Policy shall thereupon automatically terminate.	31

PREMIUM

The Underwriters to be paid in consideration of this insurance	32
.... Dollars being at the rate of	33
per cent., which premium shall be due on attachment.	34

RETURNS OF PREMIUM

In the event of delivery prior to the expiration date, or any extension thereof, to return pro rata daily of .... cents per cent.	35
net per month.	36

AGREED VALUE

The Vessel, for so much as concerns the Assured, by agreement between the Assured and the Underwriters in this Policy, is and shall be valued at the completed contract price plus the value of materials and equipment destined for the Vessel but not included in such price. If no amount is stated for such materials and equipment, Underwriters shall have no liability for any loss, damage or expense thereto or in connection therewith, and such materials and equipment shall not be deemed a part of the Vessel. [37 / 38 / 39 / 40]

The Agreed Value is provisionally declared as $ ...., being the contract price of $ .... and [41]

$ .... for materials and equipment destined for the Vessel but not included in the contract price. [42]

ESCALATION

In the event of any increase or decrease in the cost of labor or materials, or in the event of any change in the specifications or design of the Vessel (not constituting a material change for purposes of the held covered provisions of the Subject Matter clause), the Agreed Value shall be adjusted [43 / 44]

accordingly, but any increase shall be limited to .... per cent. of the Agreed Value as provisionally declared, and the Amount Insured shall be adjusted proportionately; provided that the Assured shall pay premium at the full Policy rate on the total construction cost of the Vessel of this insurance, but the Underwriters shall in no event be liable under this Policy for more than the Agreed Value provisionally declared plus said percentage thereof. [45 / 46 / 47 / 48]

AMOUNT INSURED HEREUNDER

Dollars. 49

In the event of a claim becoming payable under this Policy, the Underwriters shall not be liable for a greater proportion thereof than the Amount Insured Hereunder bears to the Agreed Value. 50 51

DEDUCTIBLE

Notwithstanding anything in this Policy to the contrary, there shall be deducted from the aggregate of all claims (including claims under the Sue and Labor, Collision Liability, and Protection and Indemnity clauses) arising out of each seperate accident, the sum of $ ⋅ unless the accident results in a Total Loss of the Vessel in which case this clause shall not apply. A recovery from other interests, however, shall not operate to exclude claims under this Policy provided the aggregate of such claims arising out of one separate accident if unreduced by such recovery exceeds that sum. For the purpose of this clause each accident shall be treated separately, but it is agreed that (a) a sequence of damages arising from the same accident shall be treated as due to that accident and (b) all heavy weather damage, or damage caused by contact with floating ice, which occurs during a single sea passage between two successive ports shall be treated as though due to one accident. 52 53 54 55 56 57 58

PART I — HULL SECTION

HULL RISKS

This Policy insures against all risks of physical loss of or damage to the Vessel occurring during the currency of this Policy, except as hereinafter provided. 59 60

In the event that faulty design of any part or parts should cause physical loss of or damage to the Vessel, this insurance shall not cover the cost or expense of repairing, replacing or renewing such part or parts, nor any expenditure incurred by reason of betterment or alteration in design. 61 62

DELIBERATE DAMAGE (Pollution Hazard)

Subject to the terms and conditions of this Policy, this insurance also covers loss of or damage to the Vessel directly caused by governmental authorities acting for the public welfare to prevent or mitigate a pollution hazard, or threat thereof, resulting directly from damage to the Vessel for which the Underwriters are liable under this Policy, provided such act of governmental authorities has not resulted from want of due diligence by the Assured, the Owners, or Managers of the Vessel or any of them to prevent or mitigate such hazard or threat. Masters, Officers, Crew or Pilots are not to be considered Owners within the meaning of this clause should they hold shares in the Vessel. 63 64 65 66 67

FAILURE TO LAUNCH

In case of failure to launch, the Underwriters shall bear, up to the Amount Insured Hereunder, their proportion of all necessary expenses incurred in completing launch. 68 69

GENERAL AVERAGE AND SALVAGE

General Average and Salvage shall be payable as provided in the contract of affreightment, or failing such provision or there be no contract of affreightment, payable at the Assured's election either in accordance with York-Antwerp Rules, 1950 or 1974 or with the Laws and Usages of the Port of New York. Provided always that when an adjustment according to the laws and usages of the port of destination is properly demanded by the owners of the cargo, General Average shall be paid accordingly. 70 71 72 73

In the event of salvage, towage or other assistance being rendered to the Vessel by any vessel belonging in part or in whole to the same Owners or Charterers, the value of such services (without regard to the common ownership or control of the vessels) shall be ascertained by arbitration in the manner provided for under the Collision Liability clause in this Policy, and the amount so awarded so far as applicable to the interest hereby insured shall constitute a charge under this Policy. 74 75 76 77

When the contributory value of the Vessel is greater than the Agreed Value herein, the liability of the Underwriters for General Average contribution (except in respect to amounts made good to the Vessel), or Salvage, shall not exceed that proportion of the total contribution due from the Vessel which the amount insured hereunder bears to the contributory value; and if, because of damage for which the Underwriters are liable as Particular Average, the value of the Vessel has been reduced for the purpose of contribution, the amount of such Particular Average damage recoverable under this Policy shall first be deducted from the Amount Insured Hereunder, and the Underwriters shall then be liable only for the proportion which such net amount bears to the contributory value. 78 79 80 81 82 83

TOTAL LOSS

There shall be no recovery for a constructive Total Loss under this Policy unless the expense of recovering and restoring the Vessel (as insured hereunder) to the stage of her construction at time of loss would exceed her value at such stage of construction (which value shall be taken to be the cost of labor actually expended by the Builder in the construction of the Vessel and material actually incorporated therein at the time of loss, including accrued overhead and profit on such labor and material, not exceeding the Agreed Value). In making this determination only expenses incurred or to be incurred by reason of a single accident or a sequence of damages arising from the same accident shall be taken into account, but expenses incurred prior to tender of abandonment shall not be considered if such are to be claimed separately under the Sue and Labor clause. 84 85 86 87 88 89

No claim for Total Loss (actual or constructive) shall exceed this Policy's proportion of the value of the Vessel at the stage of her construction at time of loss as computed in the manner set forth in the preceding paragraph. This Policy shall also pay its proportion of any physical loss or damage to material insured hereunder and not yet installed in the Vessel. 90 91 92

In no case shall the Underwriters be liable for unrepaired damage in addition to a subsequent Total Loss sustained during the period covered by this Policy, or any extension thereof. 93 94

SUE AND LABOR

And in case of any Loss or Misfortune, it shall be lawful and necessary for the Assured, their Factors, Servants and Assigns, to sue, labor and travel for, in and about the defense, safeguard and recovery of the Vessel, or any part thereof, without prejudice to this insurance, to the charges whereof the Underwriters will contribute their proportion as provided below. And it is expressly declared and agreed that no acts of the Underwriters or Assured in recovering, saving or preserving the Vessel shall be considered as a waiver or acceptance of abandonment. 95 96 97 98

In the event of expenditure under the Sue and Labor clause, the Underwriters shall pay the proportion of such expenses that the Amount Insured Hereunder bears to the Agreed Value, or that the Amount Insured Hereunder (less loss and/or damage payable under this Policy) bears to the actual value of the salved property; whichever proportion shall be less; provided always that their liability for such expenses shall not exceed their proportionate part of the Agreed Value. 99 100 101 102

If claim for Total Loss is admitted under this Policy and sue and labor expenses have been reasonably incurred in excess of any proceeds realized or value recovered, the amount payable under this Policy will be the proportion of such excess that the Amount Insured Hereunder (without deduction for loss or damage) bears to the Agreed Value or to the sound value of the Vessel at the time of the accident, whichever value was greater; provided always that Underwriters' liability for such expenses shall not exceed their proportionate part of the Agreed Value. The foregoing shall also apply to expenses reasonably incurred in salving or attempting to salve the Vessel and other property to the extent that such expenses shall be regarded as having been incurred in respect of the Vessel. 103 104 105 106 107 108

PART II — LIABILITY SECTION

COLLISION LIABILITY

And it is further agreed that: 109

(a) if the Vessel shall come into collision with any other ship or vessel, and the Assured or the Surety in consequence of the Vessel being at fault 110
shall become liable to pay and shall pay by way of damages to any other person or persons any sum or sums in respect of such collision, the 111
Underwriters will pay the Assured or the Surety, whichever shall have paid, ·such proportion of such sum or sums so paid as their respective 112
subscriptions hereto bear to the Agreed Value, provided always that 'their liability in respect to any one such collision shall not exceed their 113
proportionate part of the Agreed Value; 114

(b) in cases where, with the consent in writing of a majority (in amount) of Hull Underwriters, the liability of the Vessel has been contested, or pro- 115
ceedings have been taken to limit liability, the Underwriters will also pay a like proportion of the costs which the Assured shall thereby incur or 116
be compelled to pay. 117

When both vessels are to blame, then, unless the liability of the owners or charterers of one or both such vessels becomes limited by law, claims 118
under the Collision Liability clause shall be settled on the principle of Cross-Liabilities as if the owners or charterers of each vessel had been compelled 119
to pay to the owners or charterers of the other of such vessels such one-half or other proportion of the latter's damages as may have been properly allowed 120
in ascertaining the balance or sum payable by or to the Assured in consequence of such collision. 121

The principles involved in this clause shall apply to the case where both vessels are the property, in part or in whole, of the same owners or 122
charterers, all questions of responsibility and amount of liability as between the two vessels being left to the decision of a single Arbitrator, if the parties 123
can agree upon a single Arbitrator, or failing such agreement, to the decision of Arbitrators, one to be appointed by the Assured and one to be appointed 124
by the majority (in amount) of Hull Underwriters interested: the two Arbitrators chosen to choose a third Arbitrator before entering upon the reference, 125
and the decision of such single Arbitrator, or of any two of such three Arbitrators, appointed as above, to be final and binding. 126

Provided always that this clause shall in no case extend to any sum which the Assured or the Surety may become liable to pay or shall pay in 127
consequence of, or with respect to: 128

(a) removal or disposal of obstructions, wrecks or their cargoes under statutory powers or otherwise pursuant to law; 129

(b) injury to real or personal property of every description; 130

(c) the discharge, spillage, emission or leakage of oil, petroleum products, chemicals or other substances of any kind or description whatsoever; 131

(d) cargo or other property on or the engagements of the Vessel; 132

(e) loss of life, personal injury or illness. 133

Provided further that exclusions (b) and (c) above shall not apply to injury to other vessels or property thereon except to the extent that such injury 134
arises out of any action taken to avoid, minimize or remove any discharge, spillage, emission or leakage described in (c), above. 135

PROTECTION AND INDEMNITY

It is further agreed that if the Assured shall by reason of his interest in the Vessel, or the Surety in consequence of its undertaking, become 136
liable to pay and shall pay any sum or sums in respect of any responsibility, claim, demand, damages, and/or expenses arising from or occasioned by any 137
of the following matters or things during the currency of this Policy, that is to say: 138

(a) Loss of or damage to any other vessel or goods, merchandise, freight, or other things or interests whatsoever on board such other vessel, caused 139
proximately or otherwise by the Vessel, insofar as the same is not covered by the Collision Liability clause in this Policy; but the foregoing shall 140
not be construed to cover liability in excess of the amount recoverable under the Collision Liability clause; 141

(b) Loss of or damage to any goods, merchandise, freight or other things or interests whatsoever, other than as aforesaid, whether on board the 142
Vessel or not, which may arise from any cause whatsoever; provided that this subparagraph (b) shall not include Builder's gear, material or cargo 143
on the Vessel; 144

(c) Loss of or damage to any harbor, dock (graving or otherwise), slipway, way, gridiron, pontoon, pier, quay, jetty, stage, buoy, telegraphic cable 145
or other fixed or movable thing whatsoever, or to any goods or property in or on the same, howsoever caused; 146

(d) Loss of life of, or bodily injury to, or illness of any person (other than an employee of an Assured under this Policy); 147

(e) Payments made on account of life salvage; 148

(f) Any attempted or actual raising, removal or destruction of the wreck of the Vessel or the cargo thereof or any neglect or failure to raise, remove 149
or destroy the same; however, for the purpose of this paragraph only, the Assured shall be deemed liable for expenses, after deducting any 150
proceeds of the salvage, actually incurred by the Assured in removing the wreck of the Vessel from any place owned, leased or occupied by 151
the Assured; 152

(g) Any sum or sums for which the Assured may become liable or incur from causes not hereinbefore specified, but which are recoverable under 153
the Protection and Indemnity policy form known as Lazard No. SP 23; 154

the Underwriters will pay the Assured or the Surety such proportion of such sum or sums so paid, or which may be required to indemnify the Assured or 155
the Surety for such loss, as their respective subscriptions bear to the Agreed Value. Where the liability of the Assured has been contested with the consent 156
in writing of a majority (in amount) of the Underwriters, the Underwriters shall have the option of naming the attorneys who will defend the Vessel and 157
the Assured and will also pay a like proportion of the costs which the Assured shall thereby incur or be compelled to pay; provided that the total liability 158
of the Underwriters under all sections of these Protection and Indemnity clauses in respect of any one accident or series of accidents arising out of the 159
same event is limited to the Amount Insured Hereunder, plus costs as hereinabove provided. 160

Notwithstanding anything to the contrary contained in these Protection and Indemnity clauses, the Underwriters shall not be liable for nor indemnify 161
the Assured against any sum(s) paid with respect to any loss, damage, cost, liability, expense, fine, or penalty of any kind or nature whatsoever, and 162
whether statutory or otherwise, imposed on the Assured directly or indirectly in consequence of, or with respect to, the actual or potential discharge, 163
emission, spillage, or leakage upon or into the seas, waters, land or air, of oil, fuel, cargo, petroleum products, chemicals or other substances of any 164
kind or nature whatsoever. This exclusion, however, shall not apply to sums paid or payable, or liability of the Assured, for the physical loss of the 165
property discharged, emitted, spilled, or leaked, provided that such sums are covered elsewhere under the terms and conditions of this Policy. 166

In the event that Sections 182 to 189, both inclusive, of U.S. Code, Title 46, or any existing law or laws determining or limiting liability of 167
shipowners and carriers, or any of them, shall, while this Policy is in force, be modified, amended or repealed, or the liabilities of shipowners or 168
carriers be increased in any respect by legislative enactment, the Underwriters shall have the right to cancel the insurances afforded by these Pro- 169
tection and Indemnity clauses upon giving thirty (30) days' written notice in the manner prescribed in the Non-Payment of Premium clause; in the event 170
of such cancellation, Underwriters shall make an appropriate return of premium. 171

Underwriters' liability under these Protection and Indemnity clauses shall in no event exceed that which would be imposed on the Assured by law 172
in the absence of contract. 173

PART III — GENERAL PROVISIONS

CLAIMS

A. In the event of any accident or occurrence which could give rise to a claim under PART I of this Policy, prompt notice thereof shall be given to the 174
Underwriters, and: 175

(a) where practicable, the Underwriters shall be advised prior to survey, so that they may appoint their own surveyor, if they so desire;   176

(b) the Underwriters shall be entitled to decide where the Vessel shall proceed for docking and/or repair (allowance to be made to the Assured for   177
the actual additional expense of the voyage arising from compliance with the Underwriters' requirement);   178

(c) the Underwriters shall have the right of veto in connection with any repair firm proposed;   179

(d) the Underwriters may take tenders or may require in writing that tenders be taken for the repair of the Vessel, in which event, upon   180
acceptance of a tender with the approval of the Underwriters, an allowance shall be made at the rate of 30 per cent. per annum on the   181
amount insured, for each day or pro rata for part of a day, for time lost between the issuance of invitations to tender and the acceptance 182
of a tender, to the extent that such time is lost solely as the result of tenders having been taken and provided the tender is accepted without 183
delay after receipt of the Underwriters' approval;   184

(e) due credit shall be given against the allowances in (b) and (d) above for any amount recovered: 185
(1) in respect of fuel, stores, and wages and maintenance of the Master, Officers or Crew allowed in General or Particular Average;   186
(2) from third parties in respect of damages for detention and/or loss of profit and/or running expenses;   187
for the period covered by the allowances or any part thereof.   188

No claim shall be allowed in Particular Average for wages and maintenance of the Master, Officers or Crew, except when incurred solely for the   189

necessary removal of the Vessel from one port to another for average repairs or for trial trips made only to test average repairs, in which cases wages   190
and maintenance will be allowed only while the Vessel is under way. This exclusion shall not apply to overtime or similar extraordinary payments to Offi-   191
cers or Crew members incurred in shifting the Vessel for tank cleaning or repairs or while specifically engaged in these activities, either in port or   192
at sea.   193

General and Particular Average shall be payable without deduction, new for old.   194

The expense of sighting the bottom after stranding shall be paid, if reasonably incurred especially for that purpose, even if no damage be found.   195

No claim shall in any case be allowed in respect of scraping or painting the Vessel's bottom.   196

No claim for unrepaired damages shall be allowed, except to the extent that the aggregate damage insured against under the Policy and left unre-   197
paired at the expiration thereof shall be demonstrated by the Assured to have diminished the actual market value of the Vessel on that date if undamaged.   198

B. In the event of any occurrence which may result in a loss, damage or expense for which the Underwriters are or may become liable under PART   199
II of this Policy the Assured will give prompt notice thereof and forward to the Underwriters as soon as practicable after receipt thereof all com-   200
munications, processes, pleadings and other legal papers or documents relating to such occurrence.   201

No action shall lie against the Underwriters under PART II of this Policy for the recovery of any loss sustained by the Assured unless such action is   202
brought against the Underwriters within one year after the final judgment or decree is entered in the litigation against the Assured, or in case the claim   203
against the Underwriters accrues without the entry of such final judgment or decree, unless such action is brought within one year from the date of   204
the payment of such claim by the Assured.   205

NON-PAYMENT OF PREMIUM

In event of non-payment of premium 30 days after attachment, or of any additional premium when due, this Policy may be cancelled by the Under-   206
writers upon 10 days written or telegraphic notice sent to the Assured at his last known address or in care of the broker who negotiated this Policy.   207
Such proportion of the premium, however, as shall have been earned up to the time of cancellation shall be payable. In the event of Total Loss of the   208
Vessel occurring prior to any cancellation or termination of this Policy full premium shall be considered earned.   209

WAR, STRIKES AND OTHER EXCLUSIONS

The following conditions shall be paramount and shall supersede and nullify any contrary provisions of the Policy.   210

This Policy does not cover any loss, damage, liability or expense caused by, resulting from, or incurred as a consequence of: 211

(a) Capture, seizure, arrest, restraint or detainment, or any attempt thereat; or   212

(b) Any taking of the Vessel, by requisition or otherwise, whether in time of peace or war and whether lawful or otherwise; or   213

(c) Any mine, bomb or torpedo not carried as cargo on board the Vessel; or   214

(d) Any weapon of war employing atomic or nuclear fission and/or fusion or other like reaction or radioactive force or matter; or   215

(e) Civil war, revolution, rebellion, insurrection, or civil strife arising therefrom, or piracy; or   216

(f) Strikes, lockouts, political or labor disturbances, civil commotions, riots, martial law, military or usurped power; or   217

(g) Malicious acts or vandalism, unless committed by the Master or Mariners and not excluded elsewhere under this War Strikes and Related Exclu-   218
sions clause; or   219

(h) Hostilities or warlike operations (whether there be a declaration of war or not) but this subparagraph (h) not to exclude collision or contact with   220
aircraft, rockets or similar missiles, or with any fixed or floating object, or stranding, heavy weather, fire or explosion unless caused directly   221
by a hostile act by or against a belligerent power which act is independent of the nature of the voyage or service which the Vessel concerned   222
or, in the case of a collision, any other vessel involved therein, is performing. As used herein, "power" includes any authority maintaining naval,   223
military or air force in association with a power; or   224

(i) Delay or disruption of any type whatsoever, including, but not limited to, loss of earnings or use of the Vessel, howsoever caused, except to the   225
extent, if any, covered by the Collision Liability or the Protection and Indemnity clauses of this Policy; or   226

(j) The firing or testing of any weapon of war from, by or on the Vessel. This exclusion is in addition to and is not to be considered in whole or part   227
as a substitution for or modification of any other exclusion herein set forth; or   228

(k) Damage to docks, slipways, tools or any other property of the shipyard not intended to be incorporated in the Vessel, except as covered in Lines 12   229
through 16, and any damage to slipways occurring during a successful launch; or   230

(l) Any nuclear incident, reaction, radiation or any radioactive contamination, whether controlled or uncontrolled, and whether the loss, damage, liability   231
or expense be proximately or remotely caused thereby, or be in whole or in part caused by, contributed to, or aggravated by the risks and liabilities   232
insured under this Policy, and whether based on the Assured's negligence or otherwise; or   233

(m) Placing the Vessel in jeopardy as an act or measure of war taken in the actual process of a military engagement, including embarking or dis-   234
embarking troops or material of war in the immediate zone of such engagement; and any such loss, damage, liability or expense shall be excluded   235
from this Policy without regard to whether the Assured's liability in respect thereof is based on negligence or otherwise, and whether in time of   236
peace or war.   237

AMERICAN HULL INSURANCE SYNDICATE
ADDENDUM No. 2 TO THE
AMERICAN INSTITUTE BUILDER'S RISKS CLAUSES
(February 8, 1979)

HULL RISKS

Lines 61-62 of the attached policy are hereby deleted and the following
substituted therefor:

Subject to the provisions of exlusion (b) of the following paragraph,
in the event that faulty design of any part or parts should cause
physical loss of or damage to the Vessel this insurance shall not
cover the cost or expense of repairing, replacing or renewing such
part or parts, nor any expenditure incurred by reason of a betterment or alteration in the design. Faulty design shall include, but
not be limited to, errors, omissions or deficiencies in plans, draw-
ings, specifications or calculations.

Further, Underwriters shall not pay for any loss, damage or expense
caused by or arising in consequence of:

(a) faulty workmanship, or the installation or use of improper
or defective materials, unless resulting in destruction, deformation,
breaking, tearing, bursting, holing or cracking of the Vessel, or any
other like condition, and which loss, damage or expense is not otherwise excluded under the terms and conditions of the War, Strikes and
Other Exclusions Clause of the attached Policy; provided that Underwriters in no event shall respond for the cost or expense of repairing,
replacing or renewing any improper or defective materials;

(b) faulty production or assembly procedures even if constituting
faulty design.

SUBROGATION

The following provision is added after line 205 of the attached policy:

In case of any agreement or act, past or future, by the Assured whereby
any right of recovery of the Assured against any person or entity is released
or lost to which these Underwriters on payment of loss would be entitled to
subrogation but for such agreement or act, this insurance shall be vitiated
to the extent that the right of subrogation of these Underwriters has been
impaired thereby; and in such event the right of these Underwriters to retain
or collect any premium paid or due hereunder shall not be affected.

ALL OTHER TERMS AND CONDITIONS REMAIN UNCHANGED.

4/14/81

Appendix 11

American Institute
SHIP REPAIRERS LIABILITY CLAUSES
(November 3, 1977)

To be attached to and form a part of Policy No. .... of the 1

.... 2

The terms and conditions of the following clauses are to be regarded as substituted for those of the policy form to which they are attached, the 3
latter being hereby waived, except provisions required by law to be inserted in the policy. 4

1. This Policy insures 5

.... 6

.... (hereinafter referred to as the Assured). 7

2. Policy Period: From .... to .... 12:01 A.M. Standard Time at the Assured's 8
premises as stated in Clause 3. 9

3. In consideration of the payment of premium as hereinafter provided, and subject to the limits of liability, exclusions, conditions and other terms 10
of this Policy, this Company agrees to pay on behalf of the Assured all sums which the Assured, as Ship Repairer, shall become legally obligated 11
to pay: 12

    A. By reason of the liabilities imposed upon the Assured by law for physical loss of or damage to watercraft and their equipment, cargo, or 13
other interests on board, occurring only while such watercraft are in the care, custody or control of the Insured for the purpose of repair or 14
alteration at 15

                           16

    or while such watercraft are being moved via inland waters for a distance not in excess of .... miles in connection with repairs or 17
alteration; 18

    B. By reason of the liabilities imposed upon the Insured by law as damages because of property damage caused by a watercraft covered under "A" 19
above while in the care, custody, or control of the Assured and being navigated or operated away from premises described in "A" above 20
within permitted waters by an employee or employees of the Assured or in tow of a tug not owned by or demise chartered to the Assured. 21
It is a condition of this Clause 3B that any employee of the Assured engaged in the navigation of a watercraft described herein shall possess 22
such license as is required by the United States Coast Guard or any other applicable regulatory authority to perform the duties being carried 23
out by said employee; 24

    C. For the cost of defending any suit against the Assured on any claim based on a liability or an alleged liability of the Assured covered by this 25
insurance if the amount of the claim hereunder exceeds the amount deductible under this Policy, but this Company shall not be liable for the cost 26
or expense of prosecuting or defending any suit unless the same shall have been incurred with the written consent of this Company. This 27
Company, however, reserves the right to conduct the defense of any actions or suits at its own expense. The cost and expense of prosecuting 28
any claim in which the Assured shall have an interest by subrogation or otherwise, shall be divided between the Assured and this Company, 29
proportionately to the amounts which they would be entitled to receive, respectively, if the suit should be successful. 30

4. The maximum liability of this Company on account of any one occurrence shall be: 31
    A. $ .... with respect to each watercraft including its equipment, cargo, and other interests on board covered by Clause 3A; 32
    B. $ .... any one occurrence with respect to liability covered by Clause 3B; 33
    C. The legal costs, fees and expenses covered by Clause 3C. 34
The maximum aggregate liability of this Company on account of any one occurrence with respect to the coverage afforded under Sections 4 A, B 35
and C above shall be $ 36

5. The Assured, by acceptance of this Policy, agrees to keep an accurate record of all Gross Charges for operations covered under the terms and 37
conditions of this Policy, which record shall be open to examination by representatives of this Company at all times during business hours, dur- 38
ing the term of this Policy or thereafter, and further agrees to report to this Company on or before the last day of each month the total amount 39
thereof (collected and uncollected) for the preceding month or such period of time as is within the term of this Policy; the earned premium 40
hereunder to be computed thereon at the rate of $ .... per each $100.00 and applied against the Deposit Premium until same is 41
exhausted, following which all further earned premium shall be due and payable to this Company at time of filing the report on which the earned 42
premium is due: and any unearned premium, being the amount by which the Deposit Premium exceeds the earned premium, shall be refunded 43
upon expiration or cancellation of this Policy. This Company shall have the right of setoff against the claims payable under this Policy of any 44
premiums due hereunder. It is agreed that, except in the event of cancellation of this Policy by this Company, the Minimum Premium hereunder 45
shall be $ .... The Deposit Premium, payable upon attachment of this Policy, shall be $ 46

6. **NOTWITHSTANDING THE FOREGOING**, it is hereby expressly understood and agreed that this Policy does not cover against nor shall any liability 47
attach hereunder for: 48
    A. The first $ .... of any claim or claims, including legal fees and expenses, arising out of the same occurrence and insured against 49
hereunder; 50
    B. Death or personal injury: 51

C. Any liability assumed under contract or otherwise in extension of the liability which would have been imposed upon the Assured by law in the absence of contract; 52 53

D. Loss, damage or expense arising in connection with work on any vessel which has carried flammable or combustible liquid in bulk as fuel or cargo or any vessel which has carried flammable compressed gas in bulk, unless such work is done in accordance with the requirements of the rules and regulations of the National Fire Protection Association applicable to such work; 54 55 56

E. Demurrage, loss of time, loss of freight, loss of charter and/or similar and/or substituted expenses; 57

F. Loss, damage or expense which may be recoverable under any other insurance inuring to the benefit of the Assured except as to any excess over and above the amount recoverable thereunder; 58 59

G. Collision liability, tower's liability or liabilities insured against under the customary forms of hull or protection and indemnity policies arising out of the operation of any watercraft owned by, or demise chartered to, the Assured or any affiliated or subsidiary concern or party; 60 61

H. Loss of or damage to property owned, leased to, or in the possession of the Assured (other than watercraft which are in the custody of the Insured for the purpose of repair or alteration) or utilized by the Assured in its business as a ship repairer; 62 63

I. Loss of or damage to watercraft placed in the care, custody, or control of the Assured for the purpose of storage regardless of whether any work is also to be performed on the watercraft; provided that this exclusion shall not apply to any physical loss or damage to the watercraft (otherwise covered under this Policy) resulting directly from repairs or alterations to said watercraft carried out during such storage period; 64 65 66

J. The expense of redoing the work improperly performed by or on behalf of the Assured or the cost of replacement of materials, parts or equipment furnished in connection therewith; 67 68

K. The cost or expense of repairing, replacing or renewing any faultily designed part or parts which cause(s) loss of or damage to the watercraft, or for any expenditure incurred by reason of a betterment or alteration in design; 69 70

L. Any loss of or damage to watercraft occurring while in the care, custody or control of the Assured and otherwise covered under Section 3A hereof, but not discovered within sixty days of the delivery of the watercraft to the owner or demise charterer, or within sixty days after work is completed, whichever first occurs; 71 72 73

M. Loss, damage or expense caused by, resulting from or incurred by: 74

(a) Capture, seizure, arrest, taking, restraint, detainment, confiscation, preemption, requisition or nationalization, and the consequences thereof or any attempt thereat, whether in time of peace or war and whether or not the Assured's liability therefore is based on negligence or otherwise; 75 76

(b) Any weapon of war employing atomic or nuclear fission and/or fusion or other reaction or radioactive force or matter, or by any mine, bomb or torpedo; 77 78

(c) Hostilities or warlike operations (whether there be a declaration of war or not), but the phrase, "hostilities or warlike operations (whether there be a declaration of war or not)" shall not exclude collision or contact with aircraft, rockets or similar missiles or with any fixed or floating object, stranding, heavy weather, fire or explosion unless caused directly (independently of the nature of the voyage or service which the watercraft concerned or in the case of a collision, any other vessel involved therein, is performing) by a hostile act by or against a belligerent power: for the purposes of the foregoing, power includes any authority maintaining navy, military or air forces in association with a power. In addition to the foregoing exclusions this insurance shall not cover any loss, damage or expense to which a warlike act or the use of military or naval weapons is a contributing cause, whether or not the Assured's liability therefore is based on negligence or otherwise, and whether in time of peace or war. The embarkation, carriage and disembarkation of troops, combatants, or materiel of war, or the placement of the watercraft in jeopardy as an act or measure of war taken in the actual process of a military engagement, with or without the consent of the Assured, shall be considered a warlike act for the purposes of this Policy. 79 80 81 82 83 84 85 86 87 88

(d) The consequences of civil war, revolution, rebellion, insurrection, military or usurped power, the imposition of martial law, or civil strife arising therefrom, or piracy, or from any loss, damage or expense caused by or resulting directly or indirectly from the act or acts of one or more persons, whether or not agents of a sovereign power, carried out for political or terrorist purposes, and whether any loss, damage or expense resulting therefrom is accidental or intentional. 89 90 91 92

(e) Malicious acts or vandalism, strikes, lockouts, political or labor disturbances, civil commotions, riots, or the acts of any person or persons taking part in such occurrence or disorder; 93 94

N. The firing or testing of any weapon of war on the watercraft; 95

O. Any nuclear incident, reaction, radiation or any radioactive contamination, whether controlled or uncontrolled, and whether the loss, damage, liability or expense be proximately or remotely caused thereby, or be in whole or in part caused by, contributed to, or aggravated by the risks and liabilities insured under this Policy, and whether based on the Assured's negligence or otherwise; 96 97 98

P. Any sums paid with respect to any loss, damage, cost, liability, expense, fine or penalty of any kind or nature whatsoever and whether statutory or otherwise, incurred by or imposed on the Assured, directly or indirectly, in consequence of, or with respect to, the actual or potential discharge, emission, spillage, or leakage upon or into the seas, waters, land or air, of oil, petroleum products, chemicals or other substances of any kind or nature whatsoever. This exclusion, however, shall not apply to sums paid or payable, or liability of the Assured, for the physical loss of the property discharged, emitted, spilled or leaked, provided that such sums, or such liability, are (is) covered elsewhere under the terms and conditions of this Policy. 99 100 101 102 103 104

7. A. In the event of an occurrence with respect to which insurances are afforded under this Policy, written notice containing particulars sufficient to identify the Assured and also reasonably obtainable information with respect to the time, place and circumstances thereof, and the names and addresses of available witnesses, shall be given by or for the Assured to this Company as soon as practicable. 105 106 107

B. If claim is made or suit is brought against the Assured, the Assured shall immediately forward to this Company every demand, notice, summons or other process received by him or his representative. 108 109

C. The Assured shall cooperate with this Company and, upon this Company's request, assist in making settlements, in the conduct of suits and in enforcing any right of contribution or indemnity against any person or organization who may be liable to the Assured because of injury or damage with respect to which insurance is afforded under this Policy; and the Assured shall attend hearings and trials and assist in securing and giving evidence and obtaining the attendance of witnesses. This Policy shall be void and of no force or effect, in respect of any accident or occurrence, in the event the Assured shall make or shall have made any admission of liability either before or after such accident or occurrence in the event the Assured shall interfere in any negotiations of this Company for settlement or in any legal proceedings in respect of any claim for which this Company is or may be liable under this Policy. 110 111 112 113 114 115 116

8. It is expressly understood and agreed that no liability shall attach under this Policy until the liability of the Assured has been determined by final judgment against the Assured or by agreement between the Assured and the plaintiff with the written consent of this Company, in the event the Assured shall fail or refuse to settle any claim as authorized by this Company, the liability of this Company to the Assured shall be limited to the amount for which settlement could have been made. 117 118 119 120

9. No action shall lie against this Company for the recovery of any loss sustained by the Assured unless such action be brought against this Company within one year after the final judgment or decree is entered in the litigation against the Assured, or in case the claim against this Company accrues without the entry of such final judgment or decree, unless such action be brought within one year from the date of the payment of such claim, provided, however, that where such limitation of time is prohibited by the law of the State wherein this Policy is issued, then and in that event no action under this Policy shall be sustainable unless commenced within the shortest limitation permitted under the law of such State. 121 122 123 124 125

10. This Policy may be cancelled either by the Company or by the Assured giving 30 days' written or telegraphic notice to the other. Notice by the Company may be sent to the Assured's last known address, or in care of the broker who negotiated the placement of this Policy or the broker of record at the time the aforesaid notice is given. 126 127 128

Appendix 12

SHIP REPAIRERS LIABILITY

To be attached to and form a part of Policy No._____of the_____

_____ Dated_____

_____
(Hereinafter referred to as the Assured)
IS/ARE INSURED

In consideration of the Stipulations Herein Named and of_____

_____Dollars Deposit Premium and further premium as provided herein—

1. This insurance is to cover the legal liability of the Assured as ship repairers upon the terms and conditions and subject to the limitations hereinafter set forth.

   A. This insurance covers the legal liability of the Assured as ship repairers for loss or damage to vessels, craft, and equipment, cargoes, freights, and other interests on board, which are in their care, custody or control for the purpose of alteration or repair at locations within the United States or while such vessels or craft are being shifted and/or moved via inland waters for distances not in excess of fifteen miles in connection with their repair or alteration.

   B. This insurance also covers the legal liability of the Assured as ship repairers for loss or damage to property other than that referred to in paragraph A hereof within the port where such repairs or alterations are being carried out, caused by vessels or craft and their cargoes, which are in their care, custody or control for the purpose of alteration or repair, or by the Assured's employees while working on such vessel or craft.

2. During the period of time commencing at_____of the_____day of

   _____.19_____ and ending at_____of the_____day of

   _____.19_____ _____Time, unless this insurance be sooner terminated or made void as hereinafter provided.

3. The maximum liability of this Company on account of any one disaster or casualty shall not exceed:

   $_____with respect to each vessel including its equipment, cargo, freight, and other interests on board, in respect to which the Assured's legal liability is insured under Section 1A above.

   $_____with respect to the Assured's legal liability insured under Section 1B above.

4. No claim shall be payable under this policy unless the aggregate liability of the Assured arising out of the same accident or occurrence, and insured against hereunder, exceeds the sum of $_____ and this sum shall be deducted from the amount payable hereunder on account of liability arising from each such accident or occurrence.

5. Notwithstanding anything to the contrary contained in this policy, it is hereby expressly understood and agreed that this insurance does not cover any liability:

   A. For death or personal injury;

   B. Assumed under contract express or implied;

   C. Arising in connection with work on an oil burning or oil tank vessel or any craft or vessel previously engaged in carrying explosive or inflammable liquids unless such work is done in accordance with the requirements of the rules and regulations prepared by the National Fire Protective Association or American Bureau of Shipping, or any revision or amendment thereof;

   D. For demurrage, loss of time, loss of freight, loss of charter and/or similar and/or substituted expenses;

   E. For loss, damage or expense which may be recoverable under any other insurance inuring to the benefit of the Assured except as to any excess over and above the amount recoverable thereunder;

   F. For loss, damage or expense for collision liability, towers liability or protection and indemnity liability, arising out of the operation of any vessel or craft owned or operated by the Assured and/or any affiliated or subsidiary concern or individual or party;

   G. To property owned, leased to or in the possession of the Assured (other than vessels or craft and their cargo which are in the custody of the Assured for the purpose of alteration or repair), or utilized by the Assured in its business as ship repairer;

   H. To vessels or craft stored by the Assured;

   I. For loss, damage or expense caused by or resulting from strikes, lock-outs, labor disturbances, riots, civil commotions or the acts of any person or persons taking part in any such occurrence or disorder;

   J. In respect of loss or damage unless discovered prior to or within sixty days of the delivery to Owners or within sixty days after work is completed, whichever may first occur;

   K. For loss, damage or expense caused by or resulting from: (1) hostile or warlike action in time of peace or war, including action in hindering, combating or defending against an actual, impending or expected attack, (a) by any government or sovereign power (de jure or de facto), or by any authority maintaining or using military, naval or air forces; or (b) by military, naval or air forces; or (c) by an agent of any such government, power, authority or forces; (2) any weapon of war employing atomic fission or radioactive force whether in time of peace or war; (3) insurrection, rebellion, revolution, civil war, usurped power, or action taken by governmental authority in hindering, combating or defending against such an occurrence, seizure or destruction under quarantine or customs regulations, confiscation by order of any government or public authority.

6. The Assured, by the acceptance of this Policy, warrants and agrees to keep a complete and accurate record of all Gross Charges for operations covered by this Policy, which record shall be open to examination by representatives of the Assurers at all times during business hours, and further agrees to report to these Assurers, on or before the tenth (10th) day of each month, the total amount thereof (Collected and Uncollected) for the preceding month or such period of time as is within the term of this insurance; the earned premium hereunder to be computed thereon at the rate of

_____per each $100.00 and applied against the Deposit Premium until same is exhausted, following which all further earned premium shall be due and payable to the Assurers at time of filing the report on which the earned premium is due: and per contra, any unearned premium—being the amount by which the Deposit Premium exceeds the earned premium—shall be refunded upon expiration or termination of this Policy. It is, however, hereby agreed that, except in the event of cancellation of this Policy by the Assurers, the Minimum Premium hereunder shall be_____

_____Dollars.

(Over)

7. It is further stipulated and is a consideration for this insurance that in the event of any occurrence which may result in loss, damage and/or expense, for which these Assurers are or may become liable under this insurance, notice thereof shall be given to this Company as soon as practicable, and further, that any and every process, pleading and paper of any kind relating to such occurrence shall be forwarded promptly to this Company.

8. In respect of any accident or occurrence likely to give rise to a claim under this insurance, the Assured is obligated to and shall take such steps to protect its (and the Assurers') interests as would reasonably be taken in absence of this or similar insurance. This insurance, however, shall be void and of no force or effect, in respect of any accident or occurrence, in the event the Assured shall make or shall have made any admission of liability either before or after such accident or occurrence or in the event the Assured shall interfere in any negotiations of the Assurers for settlement or in any legal proceedings in respect of any claim for which the Assurers are or may be liable under this insurance.

9. It is expressly understood and agreed that no liability shall attach under this insurance until the liability of the Assured has been determined by final judgment against the Assured or by agreement between the Assured and the Plaintiff with the written consent of the Assurers; in the event the Assured shall fail or refuse to settle any claim, as authorized by the Assurers, the liability of the Assurers to the Assured shall be limited to the amount for which settlement could have been made.

10. Whenever required by the Assurers, the Assured shall aid in securing information, evidence, obtaining of witnesses, and cooperate with the Assurers (except in a pecuniary way) in all matters which the Assurers may deem necessary in the defense of any claim or suit or appeal from any judgment in respect of any occurrence as hereinbefore provided.

11. The cost of defending any suit against the Assured on any claim based on a liability or an alleged liability of the Assured covered by this insurance, shall be payable by the Assurers if the amount of the claim hereunder exceeds the amount deductible under this policy, but these Assurers shall not be liable for the cost or expense of prosecuting or defending any suit unless the same shall have been incurred with the written consent of these Assurers. This Company, however, reserves the right to conduct the defense of any actions or suits at their own expense. The cost and expense of prosecuting any claim in which these Assurers shall have an interest by subrogation or otherwise, shall be divided between the Assured and these Assurers, proportionately to the amounts which they would be entitled to receive respectively, if the suit should be successful.

12. The Assurers shall be subrogated to all the rights which the Assured may have against any other person or entity, in respect of any claim or payment made under this policy, to the extent of such payment, and the Assured shall, upon the request of the Assurers, execute all documents necessary to secure to the Assurers such rights.

13. No claim or demand against the Assurers under this policy shall be assigned or transferred, and no person, excepting a legally appointed Receiver of the property of the Assured, shall acquire any rights against the Assurers by virtue of this insurance without the expressed consent of the Assurers.

14. No action shall lie against the Assurers for the recovery of any loss sustained by the Assured unless such action be brought against the Assurers within one (1) year after the final judgment or decree is entered in the litigation against the Assured, or in case the claim against the Assurers accrues without the entry of such final judgment or decree, unless such action be brought within one (1) year from the date of the payment of such claim; provided, however, that where such limitation of time is prohibited by the laws of the State wherein this policy is issued, then and in that event no action under this policy shall be sustainable unless commenced within the shortest limitation permitted under the laws of such State.

15. This policy may be cancelled by either party on giving the other or its agent thirty (30) days notice in writing.

Appendix 13

TAYLOR
1953
(Rev. 70)

1   In consideration of the premium and the stipulations, terms and conditions hereinafter mentioned, this Company
2 does hereby insure:

3 Assured

4

5

6 Whose address is
7 Loss, if any, payable to

8

9

10 Upon the   called
11 Her hull, tackle, apparel, engines, boilers, machinery, appurtenances, equipment, stores, boats and furniture
12 From the   day of   19   Beginning and ending
13 Until the   day of   19   at noon Standard Time
                                                                                                at place of issuance.

	AMOUNT INSURED HEREUNDER	RATE	PREMIUM	AGREED VALUATION
14	$	%	$	$

15   Touching the adventures and perils which this Company is contented to bear and take upon itself, they are
16 of the waters named herein, fire, lightning, earthquake, assailing thieves, jettisons, barratry of the master and
17 mariners and all other like perils that shall come to the hurt, detriment or damage of the vessel named herein.

18   This insurance also covers loss of or damage to the vessel named herein caused by explosion on shipboard or
19 elsewhere.

20   This insurance also covers loss of or damage to the vessel named herein directly caused by:
21   Accidents in loading, discharging or handling cargo, or in bunkering;
22   Accidents in going on or off, or while on drydocks, graving docks, ways, marine railways, gridirons or
23   pontoons;
24   Breakdown of motor generators or other electrical machinery and electrical connections thereto, bursting
25   of boilers, breakage of shafts, or any latent defect in the machinery or hull, (excluding the cost and
26   expense of replacing or repairing the defective part);
27   Breakdown of or accidents to nuclear installations or reactors not on board the vessel named herein;
28   Contact with aircraft, rockets or similar missiles, or with any land conveyance;
29   Negligence of charterers and/or repairers, provided such charterers and/or repairers are not assured(s)
30   hereunder;
31   Negligence of master, mariners, engineers or pilots;
32 provided such loss or damage has not resulted from want of due diligence by the assured, the owners or managers
33 of the vessel, or any of them.

34   General average, salvage and special charges payable as provided in the contract of affreightment, or fail-
35 ing such provision, or there be no contract of affreightment, payable in accordance with the laws and usages
36 of the port of New York. Provided always that when an adjustment according to the laws and usages of the
37 port of destination is properly demanded by the owners of the cargo, general average shall be paid in accord-
38 ance with same.

39   And it is further agreed that if the vessel named herein and/or her tow, if any, shall come into collision with any
40 other ship or vessel other than her tow, if any, and the assured in consequence of the vessel named herein being at
41 fault shall become liable to pay and shall pay by way of damages to any other person or persons any sum or sums in
42 respect of such collision, this Company will pay its proportion of such sum or sums so paid as the amount insured
43 hereunder bears to the agreed valuation of the vessel named herein, provided always that this Company's liability in
44 respect of any one such collision shall not exceed the amount insured hereunder. And in cases where the liability of
45 the vessel named herein has been contested or proceedings have been taken to limit liability, with the consent in writ-
46 ing of this Company, this Company will also pay a like proportion of the costs which the assured shall thereby incur,
47 or be compelled to pay; but when both vessels are to blame, then, unless the liability of the owners of one or both such
48 vessels becomes limited by law, claims under this Collision Liability Clause shall be settled on the principle of cross-
49 liabilities as if the owners of each vessel had been compelled to pay to the owners of the other of such vessels such
50 one-half or other proportion of the latter's damages as may have been properly allowed in ascertaining the balance
51 or sum payable by or to the assured in consequence of such collision. Provided always that this clause shall in no
52 case extend to any sum which the assured may directly, indirectly, or otherwise incur or become liable to pay or
53 shall pay for: removal, destruction or abatement of, or any attempt or failure or neglect to remove, destroy or abate
54 obstructions or wrecks and/or their cargoes or any hazard resulting therefrom; loss of, or damage to, or expense,

55 including demurrage and/or loss of use thereof, in connection with any fixed or movable object, property or thing
56 of whatever nature (excepting other vessels, and property thereon); loss of or damage to her tow; cargo, baggage
57 or engagements of the vessel named herein or of her tow; or for loss of life of, or injury to, or illness of,
58 any person. And provided also that in the event of any claim under this clause being made by anyone other than the own-
59 ers of the vessel named herein, he shall not be entitled to recover in respect of any liability to which the owners of the
60 vessel as such would not be subject, nor to a greater extent than the owners would be entitled in such event to recover.

61 In case of any loss or misfortune it shall be lawful and necessary for the assured, their factors, servants and
62 assigns, to sue, labor and travel for, in and about the defense, safeguard and recovery of the vessel named herein,
63 or any part thereof, without prejudice to this insurance, to the charges whereof this Company will contribute as here-
64 inafter provided. It is agreed that the acts of the assured or this Company, or their agents, in recovering,
65 saving and preserving the property insured in case of disaster shall not be considered a waiver or an acceptance
66 of an abandonment, nor as affirming or denying any liability under this policy; but such acts shall be con-
67 sidered as done for the benefit of all concerned, and without prejudice to the rights of either party.

68 Warranted that in case of any casualty or loss which may result in a claim under this policy the assured shall
69 give this Company prompt notice thereof and reasonable opportunity to be represented on a survey of the damage,
70 each party to name a surveyor, which two surveyors shall proceed to draw specifications as to the extent of the
71 damage and the work required to make the damage good. If the two surveyors agree, such specifications shall be
72 binding on both this Company and the assured, subject nevertheless to policy terms and conditions and the question
73 of whether or not the disaster and resulting loss or damage are covered by this policy. In the event the two survey-
74 ors cannot agree, they must select an umpire, and in the event they cannot agree upon an umpire, either party
75 hereto may apply to the United States District Court for the district in which the home port of the vessel named
76 herein is located for the appointment of an umpire, pursuant to the United States Arbitration Act. The decision of
77 the umpire so appointed shall have the same force and effect as the specifications aforesaid. When specifications
78 have been drawn in either of the modes aforesaid, if the Company shall be dissatisfied with the terms which the
79 assured may obtain for the repair of the damage as specified by said survey, then this Company may require the
80 surveyors or the umpire to submit the specifications prepared as aforesaid to such shipyard, repair men, boat build-
81 ers and shipwrights, as may be selected by such surveyors or the umpire, with a request for bids for such repairs.
82 If after reception of such bids, the assured shall elect to accept some other bid than that of the lowest bidder, this
83 Company shall be liable only for its proportion of so much of the sum actually expended to effect repairs
84 specified by the surveyors for its account as does not exceed said lowest bid. In no event however shall this
85 Company respond for an amount in excess of its proportion of the amount actually expended by the assured in
86 effecting such repairs.

87 With respect to physical loss or damage to the vessel named herein this Company shall be liable only for
88 such proportion of such loss or damage as the amount insured hereunder bears to the agreed valuation.

89 In the event of expenditure under the sue and labor clause, this Company will pay the proportion of such
90 expenses that the amount insured hereunder bears to the agreed valuation of the vessel named herein, or that the
91 amount insured hereunder, less loss and/or damage payable under this policy, bears to the actual value of the
92 salved vessel, whichever proportion shall be less.

93 When the contributory value of the vessel named herein is greater than the agreed valuation stated herein
94 the liability of this Company for general average contribution (except in respect of amount made good to the
95 vessel) or salvage shall not exceed that proportion of the total contribution due from the vessel that the amount
96 insured hereunder bears to the contributory value; and if because of damage for which this Company is liable as
97 particular average the value of the vessel has been reduced for the purpose of contribution, the amount of the
98 particular average claim under this policy shall be deducted from the amount insured hereunder and this Com-
99 pany shall be liable only for the proportion which such net amount bears to the contributory value.

100 The sum of $ shall be deducted from the total amount of any or all claims (including claims
101 for sue and labor, collision liability, general average and salvage charges) resulting from any one accident. This
102 deduction does not apply to claims for total or constructive total loss. For the purpose of this clause each accident
103 shall be treated separately, but it is agreed that a sequence of damages arising from the same accident shall be
104 treated as due to that accident.

105 In case of loss, such loss to be paid in thirty days after satisfactory proof of loss and interest shall have
106 been made and presented to this Company, (the amount of any indebtedness due this Company from the assured
107 or any other party interested in this policy being first deducted).

108 Upon making payment under this policy the Company shall be vested with all of the assured's rights of re-
109 covery against any person, corporation, vessel or interest and the assured shall execute and deliver instruments
110 and papers and do whatever else is necessary to secure such rights.

111 Any agreement, contract or act, past or future, expressed or implied, by the assured whereby any right of re-
112 covery of the assured against any vessel, person or corporation is released, decreased, transferred or lost which
113 would, on payment of claim by this Company, belong to this Company but for such agreement, contract or act shall
114 render this policy null and void as to the amount of any such claim, but only to the extent and to the amount that
115 said agreement, contract or act releases, decreases, transfers, or causes the loss of any right of recovery of this
116 Company, but the Company's right to retain or recover the full premium shall not be affected.

117 This Company shall have the option of naming the attorneys who shall represent the assured in the prosecution
118 or defense of any litigation or negotiations between the assured and third parties concerning any claim, loss or inter-
119 est covered by this policy, and this Company shall have the direction of such litigation or negotiations. If the assured
120 shall fail or refuse to settle any claim as authorized by the Company, the liability of the Company to the assured
121 shall be limited to the amount for which settlement could have been made.

122 It is a condition of this policy that no suit, action or proceeding for the recovery of any claim for physical
123 loss of or damage to the vessel named herein shall be maintainable in any court of law or equity unless the same
124 be commenced within twelve (12) months next after the calendar date of the happening of the physical loss or
125 damage out of which the said claim arose. Provided, however, that if by the laws of the state within which this
126 policy is issued such limitation is invalid, then any such claim shall be void unless such action, suit or proceeding
127 be commenced within the shortest limit of time permitted, by the laws of such state, to be fixed herein.

128 In event of damage, cost of repairs to be paid without deduction of one-third, new for old.

129 If claim for total loss is admitted under this policy and sue and labor expenses have been reasonably incurred in
130 excess of any proceeds realized or value recovered, the amount payable under this policy will be the proportion of
131 such excess that the amount insured hereunder (without deduction for loss or damage) bears to the agreed valuation
132 or the sound value of the vessel named herein at the time of the accident, whichever value was greater.

133 It is a condition of this insurance that this Company shall not be liable for unrepaired damage in addition
134 to a total or constructive total loss.

135 No recovery for a constructive total loss shall be had hereunder unless the expense of recovering and re-
136 pairing the vessel named herein shall exceed the agreed valuation.

137 In ascertaining whether the vessel named herein is a constructive total loss the agreed valuation shall be
138 taken as the repaired value, and nothing in respect of the damaged or break-up value of the vessel or wreck shall
139 be taken into account.

140 In the event of total or constructive total loss, no claim to be made by this Company for freight, whether
notice of abandonment has been given or not.

141
142   Any deviation beyond the navigation limits provided herein shall void this policy; but on the return of the
143 vessel in a seaworthy condition, within the limits herein provided, this policy shall reattach and continue in full
144 force and effect, but in no case beyond the termination of this policy.
145   Warranted by the assured that there shall be no other insurance covering physical loss or damage to the
146 vessel named herein other than that which is provided in lines 15 through 33 hereof but permission is granted
147 to carry other insurance of whatever kind or nature not covered by this policy or additional amounts of insurance
148 of the kind or nature covered by this policy other than as provided in lines 15 through 33.
149   This insurance shall be void in case this policy or the vessel named herein, shall be sold, assigned, transferred
150 or pledged, or if there be any change of management or charter of the vessel, without the previous consent in
151 writing of this Company.
152   Notwithstanding anything to the contrary contained in this policy, this insurance is warranted free from
153 any claim for loss, damage or expense caused by or resulting from capture, seizure, arrest, restraint or detainment,
154 or the consequences thereof or of any attempt thereat, or any taking of the vessel, by requisition or otherwise,
155 whether in time of peace or war and whether lawful or otherwise; also from all consequences of hostilities or war-
156 like operations (whether there be a declaration of war or not), but the foregoing shall not exclude collision or
157 contact with aircraft, rockets or similar missiles, or with any fixed or floating object (other than a mine or
158 torpedo), stranding, heavy weather, fire or explosion unless caused directly (and independently of the nature of
159 the voyage or service which the vessel concerned or, in the case of a collision, any other vessel involved therein,
160 is performing) by a hostile act by or against a belligerent power, and for the purpose of this warranty "power"
161 includes any authority maintaining naval, military or air forces in association with a power; also warranted free,
162 whether in time of peace or war, from all loss, damage or expense caused by any weapon of war employing atomic
163 or nuclear fission and/or fusion or other reaction or radioactive force or matter.
164   Further warranted free from the consequences of civil war, revolution, rebellion, insurrection, or civil strife
165 arising therefrom, or piracy.
166   If war risks are hereafter insured by endorsement on the policy, such endorsement shall supersede the above
167 warranty only to the extent that their terms are inconsistent and only while such war risk endorsement remains
168 in force.
169   Warranted free of loss or damage in consequence of strikes, lockouts, political or labor disturbances, civil
170 commotions, riots, martial law, military or usurped power or malicious acts.
171   Either party may cancel this policy by giving ten days' notice in writing; if at the option of this Company
172 pro rata rates, if at the request of the assured short rates, will be charged—and arrival.

---

173   NAVIGATION LIMITS—SPECIAL CONDITIONS—ENDORSEMENTS, ETC.

Appendix 14

PACIFIC COAST TUG/BARGE FORM (1979)

To be attached to and form a part of Policy No. .... of the

....
   The terms and conditions of the following clauses are to be regarded as substituted for those of the policy form to which they are attached, the letter being hereby waived, except provisions required by law to be inserted in the Policy. All captions are inserted only for purposes of reference and shall not be used to interpret the clauses to which they apply.

ASSURED

This Policy insures 1

.... hereinafter referred to as the Assured. 2
   This Policy also covers the affiliated, subsidiary and interrelated companies of the Assured in whatever capacity, and Underwriters 3
waive any right of subrogation against such companies of the Assured, provided that such waiver shall not apply in the event of a 4
collision between the Vessel and any vessel owned, demise, chartered or otherwise controlled by any of the aforesaid companies, or with 5
respect to any loss, damage, expense or liability against which such companies are insured. 6
   If claim is made under this Policy by anyone other than the Owner of the Vessel, such person shall not be entitled to recover to a 7
greater extent than would the Owner, had claim been made by the Owner as an Assured named in this Policy. 8

LOSS PAYEE

Loss, if any, payable to 9

.... or order. 10
   Provided, however, Underwriters shall pay claims to others as set forth in the Collision and Tower's Liability clause and may make 11
direct payment to persons providing security for the release of the Vessel in Salvage cases. 12

VESSEL

The Subject Matter of this insurance is the Vessel called the 13
or by whatsoever name or names the said Vessel shall be called, which for purposes of this insurance shall consist of and be limited to 14
her hull, launches, lifeboats, rafts, furniture, bunkers, stores, supplies, tackle, fittings, equipment, apparatus, machinery, boilers, 15
refrigerating machinery, insulation, motor generators and other electrical machinery. 16
   In the event any equipment or apparatus not owned by the Assured is installed for use on board the Vessel and the Assured or any 17
of its affiliated, subsidiary or interrelated companies has assumed liability therefor, it shall also be considered part of the Subject 18
Matter and the aggregate value thereof shall be included in the Agreed Value. 19
   Notwithstanding the foregoing, cargo containers shall not be considered a part of the Subject Matter of this insurance. 20
   In the event that more than one Vessel is insured by this Policy, all of these clauses shall apply as though a separate policy had 21
been issued with respect to each Vessel. 22

DURATION OF RISK

From the .... day of .... 19......, ..., ... time 23

to the .... day of .... 19...... ...., ... time. 24
   Should the Vessel at the expiration of this Policy be at sea, or in distress, or at a port of refuge or of call, she shall, provided 25
previous notice be given the Underwriters, be held covered at a pro rata monthly premium to her port of destination. 26
   In the event of payment by the Underwriters for Total Loss of the Vessel this Policy shall thereupon automatically terminate. 27

TRADING WARRANTY

Held covered in case of any breach of the warranties in this clause, provided: 28
(a) such event occurs without the actual privity or prior knowledge of any owner or Assured, and 29
(b) the Assured give immediate notice of such event to Underwriters upon becoming aware thereof, and pay additional premium 30
     as required. 31

DEDUCTIBLE

Notwithstanding anything in this Policy to the contrary, there shall be deducted from the aggregate of all claims (including claims 32
under the Sue and Labor clause and claims under the Collision and Tower's Liability clause) arising out of each separate accident, the 33

sum of $ ...., unless the accident results in a Total Loss 34
of the Vessel in which case this clause shall not apply. A recovery from other interests, however, shall not operate to exclude claims under this Policy 35
provided the aggregate of such claims arising out of one separate accident if unreduced by such recovery exceed that sum. For the purpose of this clause 36
each accident shall be treated separately, but is it agreed that (a) a sequence of damages arising from the same accident shall be treated as due to that 37
accident and (b) all heavy weather damage, or damage caused by contact with floating ice (if otherwise covered hereunder), which occurs during a single 38
sea passage between two successive ports shall be treated as though due to one accident. 39

AGREED VALUE

The Vessel, for so much as concerns the Assured, by agreement between the Assured and the Underwriters in this Policy, is and 40

shall be valued at .... Dollars. 41

AMOUNT INSURED HEREUNDER

.... Dollars. 42

PREMIUM

The Underwriters to be paid in consideration of this insurance 43

Dollars being at the annual rate of .... per cent., which premium shall be due on attachment. If the Vessel is insured under this 44
Policy for less than one year at pro rata of the annual rate, full annual premium shall be considered earned and immediately due and 45
payable in the event of Total Loss of the Vessel. 46

RETURNS OF PREMIUM

Premium returnable as follows: 47
Pro rata daily in the event of termination under the Change of Ownership clause; 48
Pro rata daily if the Policy be cancelled by the Underwriters; Short rate will be charged if the Policy be cancelled by the Assured; 49
.... cents per cent. net for each period of 30 consecutive days the Vessel may be laid up in port without cargo on board, 50
out of commission and not under repair for Underwriters account; 51
provided always that: 52
  (a) from all cancellation or termination return premiums the same percentage of deduction (if any) shall be made as was allowed by the Underwriters 53
      on receipt of the original premium; 54
  (b) a Total Loss of the Vessel has not occurred during the currency of this Policy; 55
  (c) in the event of any amendment of the annual rate, the above rates of return shall be adjusted accordingly. 56
If the Vessel is laid up (as defined above) for a period of 30 consecutive days, a part only of which attaches under this Policy, the Underwriters shall pay 57
such proportion of the return due in respect of a full period of 30 days as the number of days attaching hereto bears to 30. Should the lay-up period exceed 30 58
consecutive days, the Assured shall have the option to elect the period of 30 consecutive days for which a return in recoverable. 59

CANCELLATION BY NOTICE

This Policy may be cancelled either by the Underwriters or by the Assured giving 15 days' written or telegraphic notice to the other. Underwriters' notice 60
may be sent to the Assured's last known address or in care of the broker who negotiated this Policy. In the event of Total Loss of the Vessel occurring prior 61
to any cancellation or termination of this Policy, full annual premium shall be considered earned. 62

ADVENTURE

Beginning the adventure upon the Vessel, as above, and so shall continue and endure during the period aforesaid, as employment may offer, in port or 63
at sea, in docks and graving docks, and on ways, gridirons and pontoons, at all times, in all places, and on all occasions, subject to all the terms, conditions 64
and warranties of this Policy. 65

PERILS

Touching the Adventures and Perils which the Underwriters are contented to bear and take upon themselves, they are of the Seas, 66
Men-of-War, Fire, Lightning, Earthquake, Enemies, Pirates, Rovers, Assailing Thieves, Jettisons, Letters of Mart and Counter-Mart, Surprisals, Takings at 67
Sea, Arrests, Restraints and Detainments of all Kings, Princes and Peoples, of what nation, condition or quality soever, Barratry of the Master and Mariners 68
and of all other like Perils, Losses and Misfortunes that have or shall come to the Hurt, Detriment or Damage of the Vessel, or any part thereof, excepting, 69
however, such of the foregoing perils as may be excluded by provisions elsewhere in the Policy or by endorsement thereon. 70

ADDITIONAL PERILS (INCHMAREE)

This Policy also covers loss of or damage to the Vessel directly caused by either: 71
  (a) breakdown of motor generators or other electrical machinery and electrical connections thereto, bursting of boilers, breakage of shafts, or any 72
      latent defect in the machinery or hull, (excluding the cost and expense of replacing or repairing the defective part); 73
                                  or 74
  (b) other causes of whatsoever nature arising either on shore or otherwise 75
      provided the loss or damage arising from those causes set forth in either (a) or (b) has not resulted from want of due diligence by the Assured, the 76
      Owners or Managers of the Vessel, or any of them. 77

COLLISION AND TOWER'S LIABILITY

And it is further agreed that if the Vessel and/or her tow shall come into collision with any other ship or vessel, and the Assured and/or any of its 78
affiliated and/or subsidiary and/or interrelated companies in consequence thereof or the Surety for any or all of them in consequence of its undertaking 79
shall become liable to pay and shall pay by way of damages to any other person or persons any sum or sums in respect of such collision, Underwriters will 80
pay the Assured and/or any of its affiliated and/or subsidiary and/or interrelated companies or the Surety, whichever shall have paid, such proportion of such 81
sum or sums so paid as their subscriptions hereto bear to the Agreed Value of the Vessel, provided always that their liability in respect of any one such 82
collision shall not exceed their proportionate part of the Agreed Value of the Vessel. 83
And it is further agreed that this Policy shall also cover the liability of the Vessel from any collision and/or grounding and/or stranding and/or loss or 84
damage which may occur to any vessel or vessels or craft or their cargo and/or freight while in tow of said Vessel, subject to all the terms and conditions of 85
the above clause. 86
And it is further agreed that if the Vessel and/or her tow shall come into collision or contact with any structure, floating or otherwise, or with any 87
substance or thing other than water, or shall cause any other ship, vessel or craft to strand, ground, collide or come into contact with any substance or thing 88
other than water, and the Assured and/or any of its affiliated and/or subsidiary and/or interrelated companies in consequence thereof or the Surety for any or 89
all of them in consequence of its undertaking shall become liable to pay and shall pay by way of damages to any other person or persons any sum or sums 90
in respect of any such accident, Underwriters will pay the Assured and/or any of its affiliated and/or subsidiary and/or interrelated companies or the Surety, 91
whichever shall have paid, such proportion of such sum or sums so paid as their subscriptions hereto bear to the Agreed Value of the Vessel, provided 92
always that their liability in respect of any one such accident shall not exceed their proportionate part of the Agreed Value of the Vessel. 93
In cases where the liability of the Vessel and/or her tow has been contested, or proceedings have been taken to limit liability, with the consent in writing 94
of a majority (in amount) of the Underwriters on the Hull, Underwriters will also pay a like proportion of the costs and expenses which the Assured and/or 95
any of its affiliated and/or subsidiary and/or interrelated companies shall thereby incur, or be compelled to pay; but in case of collision between two vessels 96
when both vessels are to blame, unless the liability of the Owners and/or Charterers and/or Operators and/or Lessees of one or both of such vessels 97
become limited by law, claims under this clause shall be settled on the principle of cross-liabilities as if the Owners and/or Charterers and/or Operators 98
and/or Lessees of each vessel had been compelled to pay to the Owners and/or Charterers and/or Operators and/or Lessees of the other such vessel such 99
proportion of the latter's damages as may have been properly allowed in ascertaining the balance or sum payable by or to the Assured and/or any of its 100
affiliated and/or subsidiary and/or interrelated companies in consequence of such collision. 101
It is hereby further agreed that the principles involved in the above clauses shall apply to the case where two or more the vessels or craft involved, or 102
structure, floating or otherwise, or any substance or thing damaged are the property in whole or in part of the same Owners and/or Charterers and/or 103
Operators and/or Lessees or are leased, controlled and/or in the custody of the same Owners and/or Charterers and/or Operators and/or Lessees, all 104
questions of responsibilty and amount of liability being left to the decision of a single Arbitrator, if the parties can agree on a single Arbitrator, or failing 105
such an agreement, to the decision of Arbitrators, one to be appointed by the Assured and one to be appointed by the majority (in amount) of Underwriters, 106
the two Arbitrators chosen to choose a third Arbitrator before entering upon the reference and the decision of such single or any two of such three 107
Arbitrators appointed as above, to be final and binding. 108
Provided always that this Collision and Tower's Liability clause shall in no case extend to any sum or sums which the Assured and/or any of its 109
affiliated and/or subsidiary and/or interrelated companies and/or the Surety may become liable to pay or shall pay: 110
  (a) for loss, damage or expense to vessel(s) in tow owned (other than vessel(s) bareboat chartered to others), bareboat chartered, managed or operated 111
      by the Assured and/or any of its affiliated and/or subsidiary and/or interrelated companies, or to cargo, owned by the Assured and/or any of its 112
      affiliated and/or subsidiary and/or interrelated companies, on board vessel(s) in tow of the Vessel; or 113
  (b) in consequence of, with respect to, or arising out of: 114
      (1) removal or disposal of obstructions, wrecks or their cargoes under statutory powers or otherwise pursuant to law; 115

(2) cargo, baggage or engagements of the Vessel;   116
(3) loss of life, personal injury or illness;   117
(4) the discharge, spillage, emission or leakage of oil, petroleum products, chemicals or other substances of any kind or description whatsoever.   118
   Provided, further that exclusion (b) (4) shall not apply to actual physical loss of or damage to such substances (if liability therefor is otherwise covered   119
under this Policy) except to the extent that such loss or damage arises out of any action taken to avoid, minimize or remove any discharge, spillage,   120
emission or leakage described in exclusion (b) (4).   121

GENERAL AVERAGE AND SALVAGE

   General Average and Salvage shall be payable as provided in the contract of affreightment, or failing such provision or there be no contract of   122
affreightment, payable at the Assured's election either in accordance with York-Antwerp Rules 1974 or with the Laws and Usages of the Port of San   123
Francisco. Provided always that when an adjustment according to the laws and usages of the port of destination is properly demanded by the owners of the   124
cargo, General Average shall be paid accordingly.   125
   In the event of salvage, towage or other assistance being rendered to the Vessel by any vessel belonging in part or in whole to the Assured and/or any of   126
its affiliated and/or subsidiary and/or interrelated companies, the value of such services (without regard to the common ownership or control of the vessels)   127
shall be ascertained by arbitration in the manner provided for under the Collision and Tower's Liability clause in this Policy, and the amount so awarded so   128
far as applicable to the interest hereby insured shall constitute a charge under this Policy.   129
   When the contributory value of the Vessel is greater than the Agreed Value herein, the liability of the Underwriters for General Average contribution   130
(except in respect to amounts made good to the Vessel), or Salvage, shall not exceed that proportion of the total contribution due from the Vessel which the   131
Amount Insured Hereunder bears to the contributory value; and if, because of damage for which the Underwriters are liable as Particular Average, the value   132
of the Vessel has been reduced for the purpose of contribution, the amount of such Particular Average damage recoverable under this Policy shall first be   133
deducted from the Amount Insured Hereunder, and the Underwriters shall then be liable only for the proportion which such net amount bears to the   134
contributory value.   135

SUE AND LABOR

   And in case of any Loss or Misfortune, it shall be lawful and necessary for the Assured, their Factors, Servants and Assigns, to sue, labor and travel for,   136
in, and about the defense, safeguard and recovery of the Vessel, or any part thereof, without prejudice to this insurance, to the charges whereof the   137
Underwriters will contribute their proportion as provided below. And it is expressly declared and agreed that no acts of the Underwriters or Assured in   138
recovering, saving or preserving the Vessel shall be considered as a waiver or acceptance of abandonment.   139
   In the event of expenditure under the Sue and Labor clause, the Underwriters shall pay the proportion of such expenses that the Amount Insured   140
Hereunder bears to the Agreed Value, or that the Amount Insured Hereunder (less loss and/or damage payable under this Policy) bears to the actual value of   141
the salved property, whichever proportion shall be less; provided always that their liability for such expenses shall not exceed their proportionate part of the   142
Agreed Value.   143
   If a claim for Total Loss is admitted under this Policy and sue and labor expenses have been reasonably incurred in excess of any proceeds realized or   144
value recovered, the amount payable under this Policy will be the proportion of such excess that the Amount Insured Hereunder (without deduction for loss   145
or damage) bears to the Agreed Value or to the sound value of the Vessel at the time of the accident, whichever value was greater: provided always that the   146
Underwriters' liability for such expenses shall not exceed their proportionate part of the Agreed Value. The foregoing shall also apply to expenses   147
reasonably incurred in salving or attempting to salve the Vessel and other property to the extent that such expenses shall be regarded as having been   148
incurred in respect of the Vessel.   149

CLAIMS (GENERAL PROVISIONS)

   In the event of any accident or occurrence which could give rise to a claim under this Policy, prompt notice thereof shall be given to the   150
Underwriters, and: 151
   (a) where practicable, the Underwriters shall be advised prior to survey, so that they may appoint their own surveyor, if they so desire;   152
   (b) the Underwriters shall be entitled to decide where the Vessel shall proceed for docking and/or repair (allowance to be made to the Assured for the   153
        actual additional expense of the voyage arising from compliance with the Underwriters' requirement);   154
   (c) the Underwriters shall have the right of veto in connection with any repair firm proposed;   155
   (d) in the event of failure to comply with the conditions of this clause 15 per cent. shall be deducted from the amount of the ascertained claim;   156
   (e) the Underwriters may take tenders, or may require in writing that tenders be taken for the repair of the Vessel, in which event, upon acceptance of a   157
        tender with the approval of the Underwriters, an allowance shall be made at the rate of 30 per cent. per annum on the Amount Insured Hereunder,   158
        for each day or pro rata part of a day, for time lost between the issuance of invitations to tender and the acceptance of a tender, to the extent that   159
        such time is lost solely as the result of tenders having been taken and provided the tender is accepted without delay after receipt of the   160
        Underwriters' approval.   161
Due credit shall be given against the allowances in (b) and (e) above for any amount recovered: 162
   (1) in respect of fuel, stores, and wages and maintenance of the Master, Officers or Crew allowed in General or Particular Average;   163
   (2) from third parties in respect of damages for detention and/or loss of profit and/or running expenses; for the period covered by the allowances or   164
        any part thereof.   165
   No claim shall be allowed in Particular Average for wages and maintenance of the Master, Officers or Crew, except when incurred solely for the   166
necessary removal of the Vessel from one port to another for average repairs or for trial trips to test average repairs, in which cases wages and maintenance   167
will be allowed only while the Vessel is under way. This exclusion shall not apply to overtime or similar extraordinary payments to the Master, Officers or   168
Crew incurred in shifting the Vessel for tank cleaning or repairs or while specifically engaged in these activities, either in port or at sea.   169
   General and Particular Average shall be payable without deduction, new for old.   170
   The expense of sighting the bottom after stranding shall be paid, if reasonably incurred especially for that purpose, even if no damage be found.   171
   From the cost of cleaning and painting the bottom of the Vessel (exclusive of dry dock charges) recoverable in average, there shall be deducted   172
one-twelfth for every month since the Vessel was last painted, but no allowance shall be made for cleaning and painting on account of exposure to air   173
unless the Vessel has been more than twenty-four hours on the dock.   174
   In the event of loss or damage to equipment or apparatus not owned by the Assured but installed for use on board the Vessel and for which the Assured   175
or any of its affiliated, subsidiary or interrelated companies has assumed responsibility, claim shall not exceed (a) the amount the Underwriters would pay if   176
the Assured were owner of such equipment or apparatus, or (b) the contractual responsibility assumed by the Assured or any of its affiliated, subsidiary or   177
interrelated companies to the owners or lessors thereof, whichever shall be less.   178
   No claim for unrepaired damage shall be allowed, except to the extent that the aggregate damage was caused by perils insured against during the   179
period of this Policy and left unrepaired at the expiration thereof shall be demonstrated by the Assured to have diminished the actual market value of the   180
Vessel on that date if undamaged by such perils.   181

TOTAL LOSS

   In ascertaining whether the Vessel is a constructive Total Loss the Agreed Value shall be taken as the repaired value and nothing in respect of   182
damaged or break-up value of the Vessel or wreck shall be taken into account.   183
   There shall be no recovery for a constructive Total Loss hereunder unless the expense of recovering and repairing the Vessel would exceed the Agreed   184
Value. In making this determination, only expenses incurred or to be incurred by reason of a single accident or a sequence of damages arising from the   185
same accident shall be taken into account, but expenses incurred prior to tender of abandonment shall not be considered if such are to be claimed   186
separately under the Sue and Labor clause.   187
   In the event of Total Loss (actual or constructive), no claim to be made by the Underwriters for freight, whether notice of abandonment has been given   188
or not.   189
   In no case shall the Underwriters be liable for unrepaired damage in addition to a subsequent Total Loss sustained during the period covered   190
by this Policy.   191

CHANGE OF OWNERSHIP

   In the event of any change, voluntary or otherwise, in the ownership of the Vessel, or if the Vessel be placed under new management, or be chartered on   192
a bareboat basis (other than a transfer or charter between the Assured and/or any of its affiliated and/or subsidiary and/or interrelated companies), or if the   193
Vessel be requisitioned on a bareboat basis, then, unless the Underwriters agree thereto in writing, this Policy shall automatically terminate at the time of   194

such change of ownership or management or requisition; provided, however, that if the Vessel has cargo on board and has already sailed from her loading   195
port, or is at sea in ballast, such automatic termination shall, if required, be deferred until arrival at final port of discharge if with cargo, or at port of   196
destination if in ballast.   197

This insurance shall not inure to the benefit of any transferee of the Vessel and, if a loss payable hereunder should occur between the time of change   198
or transfer and any deferred automatic termination, the Underwriters shall be subrogated to all the rights of the Assured against the transferee in respect of   199
all or part of such loss as is recoverable from the transferee, and in the proportion which the Amount Insured Hereunder bears to the Agreed Value.   200

ADDITIONAL INSURANCES

Privilege is hereby granted to insure Excess or Increased Value of the Vessel or other Policy Proof of Interest, Full Interest Admitted insurances to an   201
amount not exceeding 25% of the Agreed Value of the Vessel; and privilege is granted to insure, in addition, Voyage Freight and/or Charter Hire for an   202
estimated amount at risk, provided such Voyage Freight and/or Charter Hire is not insured Policy Proof of Interest or Full Interest Admitted.   203

WAR STRIKES AND RELATED EXCLUSIONS

The following conditions shall be paramount and shall supersede and nullify any contrary provisions of the Policy.   204
This Policy does not cover any loss, damage or expense caused by, resulting from, or incurred as a consequence of: 205
(a) Capture, seizure, arrest, restraint or detainment, or any attempt thereat; or   206
(b) Any taking of the Vessel, by requisition or otherwise, whether in time of peace or war and whether lawful or otherwise; or   207
(c) Any mine, bomb or torpedo not carried as cargo on board the Vessel; or   208
(d) Any weapon of war employing atomic or nuclear fission and/or fusion or other like reaction or radioactive force or matter; or   209
(e) Civil war, revolution, rebellion, insurrection, or civil strife arising therefrom, or piracy; or   210
(f) Strikes, lockouts, political or labor disturbances, civil commotions, riots, martial law, military or usurped power; or   211
(g) Malicious acts or vandalism, unless committed by the Master or Mariners and not excluded elsewhere under this War Strikes and Related   212
Exclusions clause; or   213
(h) Hostilities or warlike operations (whether there be a declaration of war or not) but this subparagraph (h) not to exclude collision or contact with   214
aircraft, rockets, or similar missiles, or with any fixed or floating object, or stranding, heavy weather, fire or explosion unless caused directly by a   215
hostile act by or against a belligerent power which act is independent of the nature of the voyage or service which the Vessel concerned or, in the   216
case of a collision, any other vessel involved therein, is performing. As used herein, "power" includes any authority maintaining naval, military or   217
air forces in association with a power.   218
If war risks or other risks excluded by this clause are hereafter insured by endorsement on this Policy, such endorsement shall supersede the above   219
condtions only to the extent that the terms of such endorsement are inconsistent therewith and only while such endorsement remains in force.   220

Appendix 15

BARGE HULL FORM
1955

FC & S Clause January 1970
Collision Liability Clause Revised June 1970

To be attached to Policy No.   of the.

1   INSURING

2   ITS SUCCESSORS OR ASSIGNS, FOR ACCOUNT OF WHOM IT MAY CONCERN.

3   LOSS, IF ANY, (Excepting Claims Required to be Paid to Others Under the Collision Clause) PAYABLE TO

OR ORDER.

4   DO MAKE INSURANCE AND CAUSE THEM TO BE INSURED, LOST OR NOT LOST, TO THE AMOUNT OF

DOLLARS ($

5   AT AND FROM THE   DAY OF   TO THE   DAY OF

beginning and ending with   time.

6   Should the Vessel at the expiration of this Policy be at sea, or in distress, or at a port of refuge or of call, she shall, provided previous notice be given to the Underwriters, be held covered at a pro rata monthly premium to her port of destination.

7   This Policy is agreed to cover the Vessel herein insured as employment may offer, in port and at sea, in docks and graving docks, and/or on ways, gridirons and pontoons, at all times, in all places and on all occasions, situations, services and trades whatsoever and wheresoever, under power or sail; with leave to sail or navigate with our without pilots, to tow and to be towed, and to assist vessels and/or craft in all situations and to any extent, to render salvage services and to go on trial trips; upon the Body, Tackle, Apparel, Machinery, Boilers, etc., equipment and everything connected there-with, Ordnance, Munitions, Stores, Artillery, Boats and other Furniture of and in the Vessel called the:—

or by whatsoever other name or names the said Vessel is or shall be named or called, beginning the adventure upon the said Vessel, etc., as above, and shall so continue and endure during the period as aforesaid. It shall be lawful for the said Vessel, &c., to proceed and sail to and touch and stay at any Ports or Places whatsoever and wheresoever without prejudice to this insurance. With liberty to discharge, exchange, and to take on board goods, specie, passengers and stores, wherever the Vessel may call at, or proceed to, without being deemed a deviation, and with liberty to carry goods, live stock, &c., on deck or otherwise, and underwriters' are liable for contribution towards the jettison of same. Including all risks of docking, undocking, changing docks or moving in harbour as often as may be required and going on or off slipway, gridiron and/or pontoon and/or in graving dock as often as may be done during the currency of this Policy and/or of adjusting compasses. The said Vessel, etc., for so much as concerns the Assured, by agreement be-tween the Assured and Assurers in this Policy, is and shall be valued at (as below) which value for purpose of franchise shall be divided as follows:—

8   Hull, Tackle, Apparel, Equipment, Stores, Boats and Furniture, etc., $

Machinery, Boilers, Equipment, Motor Generators and other Electrical
    Machinery and everything connected therewith $ $

    Winches, Cranes, Windlasses and Steering Gear shall be deemed to be part of the Hull and not of the Machinery.

9   The Insurers to be paid in consideration of this insurance

Dollars being at the rate of   per cent.

10   At the expiration of this Policy to return   per cent. net for every thirty consecutive days the Vessel may be laid up in port out of commission with no cargo on board and not under repair for Underwriters account; and to return   per cent. net for every thirty consecutive days of unexpired time if it be mutually agreed to cancel this Policy, but there shall be no cancellation or return of premium in event Vessel is lost from any cause whatsoever.

In the event of the Vessel being laid up in port for a period of 30 consecutive days, a part only of which attaches to this Policy, it is hereby agreed that the laying up period, in which either the commencing or ending date of this Policy falls, shall be deemed to run from the first day on which the Vessel is laid up and that on this basis Underwriter's shall pay such proportion of the return due in respect of a full period of 30 days as the number of days attaching thereto bears to thirty.

11   Held covered in the event of any breach of warranty, or deviation from the conditions of this Policy, at an equitable premium to be arranged, notice to be given on receipt of advices.

12   Particular Average payable if amounting to 3% or $ or the Vessel be stranded, sunk, burnt, on fire or in collision or in contact with any substance or thing other than water, and the expense of sighting the bottom after stranding or striking shall be paid if reasonably incurred, even if no damage be found.

13   Average payable on each valuation separately or on the whole, without deduction of thirds, new for old, whether the Average be Particular or General.

14   SPECIAL CONDITIONS AND WARRANTIES

15 In the event of accident whereby loss or damage may result in a claim under this Policy, notice shall be given in writing to the Underwriters, where practicable, prior to survey, so that they may appoint their own surveyor if they so desire. The Underwriters shall be entitled to decide the port to which a damaged Vessel shall proceed for docking or repairing (the actual additional expense of the voyage arising from compliance with Underwriters' requirements being refunded to the Assured) and Underwriters shall also have a right of veto in connection with the place of repair or repairing firm proposed and whenever the extent of the damage is ascertainable the majority (in amount) of the Underwriters may take or may require to be taken tenders for the repair of such damage. In the event of failure to comply with the conditions of this clause 15 per cent. shall be deducted from the amount of the ascertained claim.

In cases where a tender is accepted with the approval of Underwriters, an allowance shall be made at the rate of 30 per cent. per annum on the insured value for each day or pro rata for part of a day from the time of the completion of the survey until the acceptance of the tender provided that it be accepted without delay after receipt of Underwriters' approval.

No allowance shall be made for any time during which the Vessel is loading or discharging cargo or bunkering.

Due credit shall be given against the allowance as above for any amount recovered:—

(a) in respect of fuel and stores and wages and maintenance of the Master. Officers and Crew or any member thereof allowed in General or Particular Average;

(b) from third parties in respect of damages for detention and/or loss of profit and/or running expenses;

for the period covered by the tender allowance or any part thereof.

16 Radio apparatus and equipment and other apparatus or equipment whether used for the purpose of communication or as aids to navigation or safety devices, or otherwise, also equipment consisting of projection machines, sound apparatus and motion picture film shall be covered by this Policy and included within the agreed valuation of the hull, even when not owned by the Assured provided the Assured has assumed liability therefor; but the liability of Underwriters (either as to amount or as to the risks covered) shall not exceed the Assured's liability or liability to which Underwriters would be subject if the property were fully owned by the Assured, which ever shall be least.

17 TOUCHING the Adventures and Perils which we, the said Assurers, are contented to bear and take upon us, they are of the Seas, Men-of-War, Fire, Lightning, Earthquake, Enemies, Pirates, Rovers, Thieves, Jettisons, Letters of Mart and Countermart, Surprisals, Takings at Sea, Arrests, Restraints and Detainments of all Kings, Princes and Peoples, of what Nation, Condition or Quality soever, Barratry of the Master and Mariners, and all other Perils, Losses and Misfortunes that have or shall come to the Hurt, Detriment or Damage of the said Vessel, &c., or any part thereof. And in case of any Loss or Misfortune, it shall be lawful for the Assured and/or Charterers and/or Operators and/or Lessees their Factors, Servants and Assigns, to sue, labor and travel for, in and about the Defense, Safeguard and Recovery of the said Vessel, &c. or any part thereof, without prejudice to this Insurance; to the Charges whereof the said Insurance Company will contribute according to the Rate and Quantity of the sum herein insured. And it is expressly declared and agreed that no acts of the Assurers or Assured in recovering, saving or preserving the property insured shall be considered as a waiver or acceptance of abandonment.

18 This insurance also specially to cover (subject to the Average Warranty) cost of repairs or loss of or damage to the subject matter insured directly caused by accidents in loading, discharging or handling cargo or in bunkering or in taking in fuel or caused through negligence or error of judgment of Master, Mariners, Engineers, or other Servants or Employees of the Shipowners or Charterers or Operators or Lessees, Pilots, Servants or Employees of Port, Harbour or Dock Authorities, Stevedores, Labourers, Tradesmen or other Persons employed in near or about the Ship, or through contact with aircraft, explosions, bursting of boilers, breakage of shafts, or through any latent defect in the Machinery or Hull, or from other causes of whatsoever nature arising either on shore or otherwise, howsoever, causing loss of or injury to the property hereby insured, provided such loss or damage has not resulted from want or due diligence by the owners of the ship, or any of them, or by the Manager. Master, Mates, Engineers, Pilots or Crew not to be considered as part owners within the meaning of this clause should they hold shares in the Vessel.

19 And it is further agreed that in the event of salvage, towage or other assistance being rendered to the vessel hereby insured and/or her tow by any Vessel belonging in part or in whole to the same Owners or Charterers, and/or Operators, and/or Lessees, the value of such services (without regard to the common ownership or control of the Vessels) shall be ascertained by arbitration in the manner below provided for under the Collision Clause, and the amount so awarded so far as applicable to the interest hereby insured shall constitute a charge under this Policy.

20 General Average, Salvage and Special Charges payable as provided in the contract of affreightment, or failing such provision, or there be no contract of affreightment, payable in accordance with the Laws and Usages of the Port of San Francisco. Provided always that when an adjustment according to the laws and usages of the port of destination is properly demanded by the owners of the cargo, General Average shall be paid in accordance with same.

21 When the contributory value of the Vessel is greater than the valuation herein the liability of these Underwriters for General Average contribution (except in respect to amount made good to the Vessel) or salvage shall not exceed that proportion of the total contribution due from the Vessel that the amount insured hereunder bears to the contributory value; and if because of damage for which these Underwriters are liable as Particular Average the value of the Vessel has been reduced for the purpose of contribution, the amount of the Particular Average claim under this Policy shall be deducted from the amount insured hereunder and these Underwriters shall be liable only for the proportion which such net amount bears to the contributory value.

22 In the event of expenditure for Salvage, Salvage Charges, or under the Sue and Labour Clause, this Policy shall only be liable for its share of such proportion of the amount chargeable to the property hereby insured as the insured value, less loss and/or damage, if any, for which the Underwriters are liable bears to the value of the salved property. Provided that where there are no proceeds or there are expenses in excess of the proceeds, the expenses, or the excess of the expenses, as the case may be, shall be apportioned upon the basis of the sound value of the property at the time of the accident and this policy without any deduction for loss and/or damage shall bear its pro rata share of such expense or excess of expenses accordingly.

23 From the cost of cleaning and painting the bottom of the Vessel, (exclusive of dry-dock charges) recoverable in Average, there shall be deducted one-twelfth for every month since the Vessel was last painted, but no allowance shall be made for cleaning and painting on account of exposure to air unless the Vessel has been more than twenty-four hours on the dock.

24 No recovery for a Constructive Total Loss shall be had hereunder unless the expense of recovering and repairing the Vessel shall exceed the insured value.

25 In ascertaining whether the Vessel is a Constructive Total Loss the insured value shall be taken as the repaired value, and nothing in respect of the damaged or break-up value of the Vessel or wreck shall be taken into account.

26 In the event of Total Loss or Constructive Total Loss, no claim to be made by the Underwriters for freight, whether notice of abandonment has been given or not.

27 In no case shall Underwriters be liable for unrepaired damage in addition to a subsequent Total Loss sustained during the term covered by this Policy.

28 It is also agreed that any changes of interest in the Vessel hereby insured shall not affect the validity of this Policy.

This Policy also covers the affiliated companies of the Assured be they Owners, Subsidiaries, or Inter-related companies, and as Bareboat Charterers, or Charterers or Sub-charterers or Operators in whatever capacity and is without right of subrogation against them.

29 And it is further agreed that if any Vessel hereby insured shall come into collision with any other Ship or Vessel, and the Assured and/or Charterers and/or Operators and/or Lessees in consequence thereof or the Surety for any or all of them in consequence of their undertaking shall become liable to pay and shall pay by way of damages to any other person or persons any sum or sums in respect of such collision, this Company will pay the Assured and/or Charterers and/or Operators and/or Lessees or the Surety, whichever shall have paid, such proportion of such sum or sums so paid as its subcription hereto bears to the value of the Vessel hereby insured, provided always that its liability in respect of any one such collision shall not exceed its proportionate part of the value of the Vessel hereby insured, and in cases in which the liability of the Vessel and/or her tow has been contested, or proceedings have been taken to limit liability, with the consent in writing of a majority of the underwriters on the Hull and Machinery (in amount), this Company will also pay a like proportion of the costs and/or expenses which the Assured and/or Charterers and/or Operators and/or Lessees shall thereby incur, or be compelled to pay; but when both Vessels are to blame, then unless the the liability of the Owners and/or Charterers and/or Operators and/or Lessees of one or both of such Vessels becomes limited by law, claims under this clause shall be settled on the principle of cross-liabilities as if the Owners and/or Charterers and/or Operators and/or Lessees of each Vessel had been compelled to pay to the Owners and/or Charterers and/or Operators and/or Lessees of the other of such Vessels such one-half or other proportion of the latter's damages as may have been properly allowed in ascertaining the balance or sum payable by or to the Assured and/or Charterers and/or Operators and/or Lessees in consequence of such collision.

30 And it is further agreed that if the Vessel hereby insured shall come into collision or contact with any structure floating or otherwise or with any substance or things other than water or shall cause any other ship, vessel or craft to strand, ground, or collide or come into contact with any substance or thing other than water, and the Assured and/or Charterers and/or Operators and/or Lessees in consequence thereof or the Surety for any or all of them in consequence of their undertaking shall become liable to pay and shall pay by way of damages to any other person or persons any sum or sums in respect of any such accident, this Company will pay the Assured and/or Charterers and/or Operators and/or Lessees such proportion of such sum or sums so paid as its subcription hereto bears to the value of the Vessel hereby insured, provided always that its liability in respect of any one such accident shall not exceed its proportionate part of the value of the Vessel hereby insured.

It is hereby further agreed that the principles involved in the above clauses shall apply to the case where two or more of the vessels or craft involved, or structure, floating or otherwise, or any substance or thing damaged are the property in whole or in part of the same Owners and/or Charterers and/or Operators and/or Lessees or are leased, controlled and/or in the custody of the same Owners and/or Charterers and/or Operators and/or Lessees, all questions of responsibility and amount of liability being left to the decision of a single Arbitrator, if the parties can agree upon a single Arbitrator, or failing such an agreement to the decision of Arbitrators, one to be appointed by the managing Owners and/or Charterers and/or Operators and/or Lessees and one to be appointed by the majority (in amount) of underwriters interested, the two Arbitrators chosen to choose a third Arbitrator before entering upon the reference and the decision of such single or of any two of such three Arbitrators appointed as above, to be final and binding.

Provided always that this clause shall in no case extend to any sum which the Assured, or the Charterers, or the Surety may become liable to pay or shall pay in consequence of, or with respect to:

    (a)   removal or disposal of obstructions, wrecks or their cargoes under statutory powers or otherwise pursuant to law;
    (b)   cargo, baggage or engagements of the insured vessel;
    (c)   the discharge, spillage, emission or leakage of oil, petroleum products, chemicals or other substances of any kind or description whatsoever;
    (d)   loss of life, personal injury or illness.

Provided further that exclusion (c) above shall not apply to injury to other vessels or property thereon except to the extent that such injury arises out of any action taken to avoid, minimize or remove any discharge, spillage, emission or leakage described in (c).

PRIVILEGE TO INSURE INCREASED VALUE OF HULL & MACHINERY

31   Privilege is hereby granted to insure excess or increased value of Hull & Machinery or other P.P.I., F.I.A. insurances to an amount of not exceeding 25% of insured valuation of Vessel, all without prejudice to this Hull insurance; but permitted to insure in addition voyage freight and/or charter hire for estimated amount at risk provided such voyage freight and/or charter hire is not insured P.P.I. or F.I.A.

NON PAYMENT OF PREMIUM CLAUSE
(Applicable to Insurance placed in London)

32   The Assured shall be directly liable to the Assurer for all premiums under this Policy. If payment of premium is not made by the Assured within 10 days after attachment of the insurance, or, in the event the Assurers shall have agreed to accept deferred payments, if any payment of premium is not made on the day agreed, this Policy may be cancelled by the Assurers giving to the Assured named herein and third party payees named in the policy five days notice of such cancellation. A written and/or telegraphic notice by or through the brokers, or their American Correspondents, who negotiated the insurance, to said Assured and third party payees named in the policy at their last known address shall constitute a complete notice as required under this clause. Such cancellation shall be without prejudice to premiums earned and due for the period the policy is in force.

NON PAYMENT OF PREMIUM CLAUSE
(Applicable to Insurance placed in U.S.A.)

33   The Assured shall be directly liable to the Assurer for all premiums under this Policy. If payment of premium is not made by the Assured within thirty (30) days after attachment of the insurance, or, in the event the Assurer shall have agreed to accept deferred payments, if any payment of any premium is not made on the day agreed, this Policy may be cancelled at any time thereafter by the Assurer giving to the Assured named herein and to third party payee or payees (if any) named in the policy, five (5) days notice of such cancellation.

Such notice may be given either by the Assurer itself or in its behalf by the Board of Marine Underwriters of San Francisco, Incorporated.

Such cancellation shall be without prejudice to the premiums earned and due for the period the policy was in force.

34   Unless physically deleted by the Underwriters, the following warranty shall be paramount and shall supersede and nullify any contrary provisions of the Policy:

WAR, STRIKES AND RELATED EXCLUSIONS
(American Institute Hulls January 1970)

This Policy does not cover any loss, damage or expense caused by, resulting from, or incurred as a consequence of:

    (a)   Capture, seizure, arrest, restraint or detainment, or any attempt thereat; or
    (b)   Any taking of the Vessel, by requisition or otherwise, whether in time of peace or war and whether lawful or otherwise; or
    (c)   Any mine, bomb or torpedo not carried as cargo on board the Vessel; or
    (d)   Any weapon of war employing atomic or nuclear fission and/or fusion or other like reaction or radioactive force or matter; or
    (e)   Civil war, revolution, rebellion, insurrection, or civil strife arising therefrom, or piracy; or
    (f)   Strikes, lockouts, political or labor disturbances, civil commotions, riots, martial law, military or usurped power, malicious acts or vandalism; or
    (g)   Hostilities or warlike operations (whether there be a declaration of war or not) but this subparagraph (g) not to exclude collision or contact with aircraft, rockets or similar missiles, or with any fixed or floating object, or stranding, heavy weather, fire or explosion unless caused directly by a hostile act by or against a belligerent power which act is independent of the nature of the voyage or service which the Vessel concerned or, in the case of a collision, any other vessel involved therein, is performing. As used herein, "power" includes any authority maintaining naval, military or air forces in association with a power.

If war risks or other risks excluded by this clause are hereafter insured by endorsement on this Policy, such endorsement shall supersede the above conditions only to the extent that the terms of such endorsement are inconsistent therewith and only while such endorsement remains in force.

35   The terms and conditions of this form are to be regarded as substituted for those of the policy form to which it is attached, the latter being hereby waived, except provisions required by law to be inserted in the Policy.

Appendix 16

TUG HULL FORM
1965

FC & S Clause January 1970
Collision Liability Clause Revised June 1970

To be attached to Policy No._____ of the _____

1   INSURING:

2   ITS SUCCESSORS OR ASSIGNS, FOR ACCOUNT OF WHOM IT MAY CONCERN.

3   LOSS, IF ANY, (Excepting Claims Required to be Paid to Others Under the Collision Clause) PAYABLE TO

OR ORDER.

4   DO MAKE INSURANCE AND CAUSE THEM TO BE INSURED, LOST OR NOT LOST, TO THE AMOUNT OF

DOLLARS $

5   AT AND FROM THE   DAY OF   TO THE   DAY OF

beginning and ending with   time.

6   Should the Vessel at the expiration of this Policy be at sea, or in distress, or at a port of refuge or of call, she shall, provided previous notice be given to the Underwriters, be held covered at a pro rata monthly premium to her port of destination.

7   This Policy is agreed to cover the Vessel herein insured as employment may offer, in port and at sea, in docks and graving docks, and/or on ways, gridirons and pontoons, at all times, in all places and on all occasions, situations, services and trades whatsoever and wheresoever, under power or sail; with leave to sail or navigate with our without pilots, to tow and to be towed, and to assist vessels and/or craft in all situations and to any extent, to render salvage services and to go on trial trips; upon the Body, Tackle, Apparel, Machinery, Boilers, etc., equipment and everything connected therewith, Ordnance, Munitions, Stores, Artillery, Boats and other Furniture of and in the Vessel called the: –

or by whatsoever other name or names the said Vessel is or shall be named or called, beginning the adventure upon the said Vessel, etc., as above, and shall so continue and endure during the period as aforesaid. It shall be lawful for the said Vessel, &c., to proceed and sail to and touch and stay at any Ports or Places whatsoever and wheresoever without prejudice to this insurance. With liberty to discharge, exchange, and to take on board goods, specie, passengers and stores, wherever the Vessel may call at, or proceed to, without being deemed a deviation, and with liberty to carry goods, live stock, &c., on deck or otherwise, and underwriters are liable for contribution towards the jettison of same. Including all risks of docking, undocking, changing docks or moving in harbour as often as may be required and going on or off slipway, gridiron and/or pontoon and/or in graving dock as often as may be done during the currency of this Policy and/or of adjusting compasses. The said Vessel, etc., for so much as concerns the Assured, by agreement between the Assured and Assurers in this Policy, is and shall be valued at (as below) which value for purpose of franchise shall be divided as follows: –

8   Hull, Tackle, Apparel, Equipment, Stores, Boats and Furniture, etc., $

Machinery, Boilers, Equipment, Motor Generators and other Electrical
Machinery and everything connected therewith $ $

Winches, Cranes, Windlasses and Steering Gear shall be deemed to be part of the Hull and not of the Machinery.

9   The Insurers to be paid in consideration of this insurance.

Dollars being at the rate of   per cent.

10   At the expiration of this Policy to return   per cent. net for every thirty consecutive days the Vessel may be laid up in port out of commission with no cargo on board and not under repair for Underwriters account; and to return   per cent. net for every thirty consecutive days of unexpired time if it be mutually agreed to cancel this Policy, but there shall be no cancellation or return of premium in event Vessel is lost from any cause whatsoever.

In the event of the Vessel being laid up in port for a period of 30 consecutive days, a part only of which attaches to this Policy, it is hereby agreed that the laying up period, in which either the commencing or ending date of this Policy falls, shall be deemed to run from the first day on which the Vessel is laid up and that on this basis Underwriter's shall pay such proportion of the return due in respect of a full period of 30 days as the number of days attaching thereto bears to thirty.

11   Held covered in the event of any breach of warranty, or deviation from the conditions of this Policy, at an equitable premium to be arranged, notice to be given on receipt of advices.

12   Particular Average payable if amounting to 3% or $ _____ or the Vessel be stranded, sunk, burnt, on fire or in collision or in contact with any substance or thing other than water. and the expense of sighting the bottom after stranding or striking shall be paid if reasonably incurred, even if no damage be found.

13   Average payable on each valuation separately or on the whole, without deduction of thirds, new for old, whether the Average be Particular or General.

14   SPECIAL CONDITIONS AND WARRANTIES

15 **In the event of accident whereby loss or damage may result in a claim under this Policy, notice shall be given in writing to the Underwriters, where practicable, prior to survey, so that they may appoint their own surveyor if they so desire. The Underwriters shall be entitled to decide the port to which a damaged Vessel shall proceed for docking or repairing (the actual additional expense of the voyage arising from compliance with Underwriters' requirements being refunded to the Assured) and Underwriters shall also have a right of veto in connection with the place of repair or repairing firm proposed and whenever the extent of the damage is ascertainable the majority (in amount) of the Underwriters may take or may require to be taken tenders for the repair of such damage. In the event of failure to comply with the conditions of this clause 15 per cent. shall be deducted from the amount of the ascertained claim.**

In cases where a tender is accepted with the approval of Underwriters, an allowance shall be made at the rate of 30 per cent. per annum on the insured value for each day or pro rata for part of a day from the time of the completion of the survey until the acceptance of the tender provided that it be accepted without delay after receipt of Underwriters' approval.

No allowance shall be made for any time during which the Vessel is loading or discharging cargo or bunkering.

Due credit shall be given against the allowance as above for any amount recovered: -

(a) in respect of fuel and stores and wages and maintenance of the Master, Officers and Crew or any member thereof allowed in General or Particular Average;

(b) from third parties in respect of damages for detention and/or loss of profit and/or running expenses;

for the period covered by the tender allowance or any part thereof.

16 Radio apparatus and equipment and other apparatus or equipment whether used for the purpose of communication or as aids to navigation or safety devices, or otherwise, also equipment consisting of projection machines, sound apparatus and motion picture film shall be covered by this Policy and included within the agreed valuation of the hull, even when not owned by the Assured provided the Assured has assumed liability therefor; but the liability of Underwriters (either as to amount or as to the risks covered) shall not exceed the Assured's liability or liability to which Underwriters would be subject if the property were fully owned by the Assured, which ever shall be least.

17 TOUCHING the Adventures and Perils which we, the said Assurers, are contented to bear and take upon us, they are of the Seas, Men-of-War, Fire, Lightning, Earthquake, Enemies, Pirates, Rovers, Thieves, Jettisons, Letters of Mart and Countermart, Surprisals, Takings at Sea, Arrests, Restraints and Detainments of all Kings, Princes and Peoples, of what Nation, Condition or Quality soever, Barratry of the Master and Mariners, and all other Perils, Losses and Misfortunes that have or shall come to the Hurt, Detriment or Damage of the said Vessel, &c., or any part thereof. And in case of any Loss or Misfortune, it shall be lawful for the Assured and/or Charterers and/or Operators and/or Lessees their Factors, Servants and Assigns, to sue, labor and travel for, in and about the Defense, Safeguard and Recovery of the said Vessel, &c. or any part thereof, without prejudice to this Insurance; to the Charges whereof the said Insurance Company will contribute according to the Rate and Quantity of the sum herein insured. And it is expressly declared and agreed that no acts of the Assurers or Assured in recovering, saving or preserving the property insured shall be considered as a waiver or acceptance of abandonment.

18 This insurance also specially to cover (subject to the Average Warranty) cost of repairs or loss of or damage to the subject matter insured directly caused by accidents in loading, discharging or handling cargo or in bunkering or in taking in fuel or caused through negligence or error of judgment of Master, Mariners, Engineers, or other Servants or Employees of the Shipowners or Charterers or Operators or Lessees, Pilots, Servants or Employees of Port, Harbour or Dock Authorities, Stevedores, Labourers, Tradesmen or other Persons employed in near or about the Ship, or through contact with aircraft, explosions, bursting of boilers, breakage of shafts, or through any latent defect in the Machinery or Hull, or from other causes of whatsoever nature arising either on shore or otherwise, howsoever, causing loss of or injury to the property hereby insured, provided such loss or damage has not resulted from want or due diligence by the owners of the ship, or any of them, or by the Manager, Master, Mates, Engineers, Pilots or Crew not to be considered as part owners within the meaning of this clause should they hold shares in the Vessel.

19 And it is further agreed that in the event of salvage, towage or other assistance being rendered to the vessel hereby insured and/or her tow by any Vessel belonging in part or in whole to the same Owners or Charterers, and/or Operators, and/or Lessees, the value of such services (without regard to the common ownership or control of the Vessels) shall be ascertained by arbitration in the manner below provided for under the Collision Clause, and the amount so awarded so far as applicable to the interest hereby insured shall constitute a charge under this Policy.

20 General Average, Salvage and Special Charges payable as provided in the contract of affreightment, or failing such provision, or there be no contract of affreightment, payable in accordance with the Laws and Usages of the Port of San Francisco. Provided always that when an adjustment according to the laws and usages of the port of destination is properly demanded by the owners of the cargo, General Average shall be paid in accordance with same.

21 When the contributory value of the Vessel is greater than the valuation herein the liability of these Underwriters for General Average contribution (except in respect to amount made good to the Vessel) or salvage shall not exceed that proportion of the total contribution due from the Vessel that the amount insured hereunder bears to the contributory value; and if because of damage for which these Underwriters are liable as Particular Average the value of the Vessel has been reduced for the purpose of contribution, the amount of the Particular Average claim under this Policy shall be deducted from the amount insured hereunder and these Underwriters shall be liable only for the proportion which such net amount bears to the contributory value.

22 In the event of expenditure for Salvage, Salvage Charges, or under the Sue and Labour Clause, this Policy shall only be liable for its share of such proportion of the amount chargeable to the property hereby insured as the insured value, less loss and/or damage, if any, for which the Underwriters are liable bears to the value of the salved property. Provided that where there are no proceeds or there are expenses in excess of the proceeds, the expenses, or the excess of the expenses, as the case may be, shall be apportioned upon the basis of the sound value of the property at the time of the accident and this policy without any deduction for loss and/or damage shall bear its pro rata share of such expense or excess of expenses accordingly.

23 From the cost of cleaning and painting the bottom of the Vessel, (exclusive of dry-dock charges) recoverable in Average, there shall be deducted one-twelfth for every month since the Vessel was last painted, but no allowance shall be made for cleaning and painting on account of exposure to air unless the Vessel has been more than twenty-four hours on the dock.

24 No recovery for a Constructive Total Loss shall be had hereunder unless the expense of recovering and repairing the Vessel shall exceed the insured value.

25 In ascertaining whether the Vessel is a Constructive Total Loss the insured value shall be taken as the repaired value, and nothing in respect of the damaged or break-up value of the Vessel or wreck shall be taken into account.

26 In the event of Total Loss or Constructive Total Loss, no claim to be made by the Underwriters for freight, whether notice of abandonment has been given or not.

27 In no case shall Underwriters be liable for unrepaired damage in addition to a subsequent Total Loss sustained during the term covered by this Policy.

28 It is also agreed that any changes of interest in the Vessel hereby insured shall not affect the validity of this Policy.

This Policy also covers the affiliated companies of the Assured be they Owners, Subsidiaries, or Inter-related companies, and as Bareboat Charterers, or Charterers or Sub-charterers or Operators in whatever capacity and is without right of subrogation against them.

29 And it is further agreed that if any Vessel hereby insured and/or her tow shall come into collision with any other Ship or Vessel, and the Assured and/or Charterers and/or Operators and/or Lessees in consequence thereof or the Surety for any or all of them in consequence of their undertaking shall become liable to pay and shall pay by way of damages to any other person or persons any sum or sums in respect of such collision, this Company will pay the Assured and/or Charterers and/or Operators and/or Lessees or the Surety, whichever shall have paid, such proportion of such sum or sums so paid as its subscription hereto bears to the value of the Vessel hereby insured, provided always that its liability in respect of any one such collision shall not exceed its proportionate part of the value of the Vessel hereby insured, and in cases in which the liability of the Vessel and/or her tow has been contested, or proceedings have been taken to limit liability, with the consent in writing of a majority of the underwriters on the Hull and Machinery (in amount), this Company will also pay a like proportion of the costs and/or expenses which the Assured and/or Charterers and/or Operators and/or Lessees shall thereby incur, or be compelled to pay; but when both Vessels are to blame, then unless the liability of the Owners and/or Charterers and/or Operators and/or Lessees of one or both of such Vessels becomes limited by law, claims under this clause shall be settled on the principle of cross-liabilities as if the Owners and/or Charterers and/or Operators and/or Lessees of each Vessel had been compelled to pay to the Owners and/or Charterers and/or Operators and/or Lessees of the other of such Vessels such one-half or other proportion of the latter's damages as may have been properly allowed in ascertaining the balance or sum payable by or to the Assured and/or Charterers and/or Operators and/or Lessees in consequence of such collision.

30 And it is further agreed that this Policy shall also extend to and cover the liability of the vessel hereby insured from any collision and/or grounding and/or stranding and/or loss or damage which may occur to any vessel or vessels or craft or their cargo and/or freight while in tow of said vessel, subject to all the terms and conditions of the above clause.

And it is further agreed that if the Vessel hereby insured and/or her tow shall come into collision or contact with any structure floating or otherwise or with any substance or things other than water or shall cause any other ship, vessel or craft to strand, ground, or collide or come into contact with any substance or thing other than water, and the Assured and/or Charterers and/or Operators and/or Lessees in consequence thereof or the Surety for any or all of them in consequence of their undertaking shall become liable to pay and shall pay by way of damages to any other person or persons **any sum or sums in respect of any such accident, this Company will pay the Assured and/or Charterers and/or Operators and/or Lessees such proportion of such sum or sums so paid as its subscription hereto bears to the value of the Vessel hereby insured, ~~provided always that is liability in respect of any one such accident shall not exceed its proportionate part of the value of the Vessel hereby insured.~~**

It is hereby further agreed that the principles involved in the above clauses shall apply to the case where two or more of the vessels or craft involved, or structure, floating or otherwise, or any substance or thing damaged are the property in whole or in part of the same Owners and/or Charterers and/or Operators and/or Lessees or are leased, controlled and/or in the custody of the same Owners and/or Charterers and/or Operators and/or Lessees, all questions of responsibility and amount of liability being left to the decision of a single Arbitrator, if the parties can agree upon a single

Arbitrator, or failing such an agreement to the decision of Arbitrators, one to be appointed by the managing Owners and/or Charterers and/or Operators and/or Lessees and one to be appointed by the majority (in amount) of underwriters interested, the two Arbitrators chosen to choose a third Arbitrator before entering upon the reference and the decision of such single or of any two of such three Arbitrators appointed as above, to be final and binding.

Provided always that this clause shall in no case extend to any sum which the Assured, or the Charterers, or the Surety may become liable to pay or shall pay in consequence of, or with respect to:

(a)   removal or disposal of obstructions, wrecks or their cargoes under statutory powers or otherwise pursuant to law;
(b)   cargo, baggage or engagements of the insured vessel;
(c)   the discharge, spillage, emission or leakage of oil, petroleum products, chemicals or other substances of any kind or description whatsoever;
(d)   loss of life, personal injury or illness.

Provided further that exclusion (c) above shall not apply to injury to other vessels or property thereon except to the extent that such injury arises out of any action taken to avoid, minimize or remove any discharge, spillage, emission or leakage described in (c).

PRIVILEGE TO INSURE INCREASED VALUE OF HULL & MACHINERY

31   Privilege is hereby granted to insure excess or increased value of Hull & Machinery or other P.P.I., F.I.A. insurances to an amount of not exceeding 25% of insured valuation of Vessel, all without prejudice to this Hull insurance; but permitted to insure in addition voyage freight and/or charter hire for estimated amount at risk provided such voyage freight and/or charter hire is not insured P.P.I. or F.I.A.

NON PAYMENT OF PREMIUM CLAUSE
(Applicable to Insurance placed in London)

32   The Assured shall be directly liable to the Assurer for all premiums under this Policy. If payment of premium is not made by the Assured within 10 days after attachment of the insurance, or, in the event the Assurers shall have agreed to accept deferred payments, if any payment of premium is not made on the day agreed, this Policy may be cancelled by the Assurers giving to the Assured named herein and third party payees named in the policy five days notice of such cancellation. A written and/or telegraphic notice by or through the brokers, or their American Correspondents, who negotiated the insurance, to said Assured and third party payees named in the policy at their last known address shall constitute a complete notice as required under this clause. Such cancellation shall be without prejudice to premiums earned and due for the period the policy is in force.

NON PAYMENT OF PREMIUM CLAUSE
(Applicable to Insurance placed in U.S.A.)

33   The Assured shall be directly liable to the Assurer for all premiums under this Policy. If payment of premium is not made by the Assured within thirty (30) days after attachment of the insurance, or, in the event the Assurer shall have agreed to accept deferred payments, if any payment of any premium is not made on the day agreed, this Policy may be cancelled at any time thereafter by the Assurer giving to the Assured named herein and to third party payee or payees (if any) named in the policy, five (5) days notice of such cancellation.

Such notice may be given either by the Assurer itself or in its behalf by the Board of Marine Underwriters of San Francisco, Incorporated.

Such cancellation shall be without prejudice to the premiums earned and due for the period the policy was in force.

34   Unless physically deleted by the Underwriters, the following warranty shall be paramount and shall supersede and nullify any contrary provisions of the Policy:

WAR, STRIKES AND RELATED EXCLUSIONS
(American Institute Hulls January 1970)

This Policy does not cover any loss, damage or expense caused by, resulting from, or incurred as a consequence of:

(a)   Capture, seizure, arrest, restraint or detainment, or any attempt thereat; or
(b)   Any taking of the Vessel, by requisition or otherwise, whether in time of peace or war and whether lawful or otherwise; or
(c)   Any mine, bomb or torpedo not carried as cargo on board the Vessel; or
(d)   Any weapon of war employing atomic or nuclear fission and/or fusion or other like reaction or radioactive force or matter; or
(e)   Civil war, revolution, rebellion, insurrection, or civil strife arising therefrom, or piracy; or
(f)   Strikes, lockouts, political or labor disturbances, civil commotions, riots, martial law, military or usurped power, malicious acts or vandalism; or
(g)   Hostilities or warlike operations (whether there be a declaration of war or not) but this subparagraph (g) not to exclude collision or contact with aircraft, rockets or similar missiles, or with any fixed or floating object, or stranding, heavy weather, fire or explosion unless caused directly by a hostile act by or against a belligerent power which act is independent of the nature of the voyage or service which the Vessel concerned or, in the case of a collision, any other vessel involved therein, is performing. As used herein, "power" includes any authority maintaining naval, military or air forces in association with a power.

If war risks or other risks excluded by this clause are hereafter insured by endorsement on this Policy, such endorsement shall supersede the above conditions only to the extent that the terms of such endorsement are inconsistent therewith and only while such endorsement remains in force.

35   The terms and conditions of this form are to be regarded as substituted for those of the policy form to which it is attached, the latter being hereby waived, except provisions required by law to be inserted in the Policy.

Appendix 17

Revised June 1970

COLLISION CLAUSE, INCLUDING TOW   A

Endorsement to be attached to and made part of Policy No. ....

of ....

In consideration of an additional premium at the rate of .... it is understood and agreed that the following

clause is substituted for the Collision Clause in this policy, effective from ....

And it is further agreed that if the Vessel hereby insured and/or her tow shall come into collision with any other Ship or Vessel and the Assured or the Charterers in consequence thereof or the Surety for either or both of them in consequence of their undertaking shall become liable to pay and shall pay by way of damages to any other person or persons any sum or sums in respect of such collision, we, the Underwriters will pay the Assured or Charterers such proportion of such sum or sums so paid as our respective subscriptions hereto bear to the value of the Vessel hereby insured, provided always that our liability in respect of any one such collision shall not exceed our proportionate part of the value of the Vessel hereby insured. And in cases where the liability of the Vessel and/or her tow has been contested, or proceedings have been taken to limit liability, with the consent in writing of a majority (in amount) of the Underwriters on the hull and/or machinery, we will also pay a like proportion of the costs which the Assured or Charterers shall thereby incur, or be compelled to pay; but when both of the colliding Vessels are to blame, then, unless the liability of the Owners or Charterers of one or both of such Vessels becomes limited by law, claims under the Collision Clause shall be settled on the principle of Cross-Liabilities as if the Owners or Charterers of each Vessel has been compelled to pay to the Owners or Charterers of the other of such Vessels such one-half or other proportion of the latter's damages as may have been properly allowed in ascertaining the balance or sum payable by or to the Assured or Charterers in consequence of such collision; and it is further agreed that the principles involved in this clause shall apply to the case where both Vessels are the property, in part or in whole, of the same Owners or Charterers, all questions of responsibility and amount of liability as between the two Vessels being left to the decision of a single arbitrator, if the parties can agree upon a single arbitrator, or failing such agreement, to the decision of arbitrators, one to be appointed by the Managing Owners or Charterers of both Vessels, and one to be appointed by the majority (in amount) of Hull Underwriters interested; the two arbitrators chosen to choose a third arbitrator before entering upon the reference, and the decision of such single, or of any two of such three arbitrators, appointed as above, to be final and binding. Provided always that this clause shall in no case extend to any sum which the Assured, or the Charterers, or the Surety may become liable to pay or shall pay in consequence of, or with respect to:

a) removal or disposal of obstructions, wrecks or their cargoes under statutory powers or otherwise pursuant to law;
b) injury or potential injury to real or personal property of every description, excepting other vessels or property thereon;
c) the discharge, spillage, emission or leakage of oil, petroleum products, chemicals or other substances of any kind or description whatsoever;
d) cargo, baggage or engagements of either the insured vessel, or her tow, or a collision of the tow after breaking away, unless such break be the consequence of a collision as specified herein;
e) loss of life, personal injury or illness.

Provided further that exclusions (b) and (c) above shall not apply to injury to other vessels or property thereon except to the extent that such injury arises out of any action taken to avoid, minimize or remove any discharge, spillage, emission or leakage described in (c).

And provided also that in the event of any claim being made by Charterers under this clause they shall not be entitled to recover in respect of any liability to which the Owners of the Vessel, if interested in this Policy at the time of the collision in question, would not be subject, nor to a greater extent than the Shipowners would be entitled in such event to recover.

All other terms and conditions remaining unchanged.

Dated..19......•......

Revised June 1970

B

COLLISION CLAUSE, INCLUDING TOW AND LIMITED TOWER'S LIABILITY

Endorsement to be attached to and made part of Policy No...

of ....

In consideration of an additional premium at the rate of .... it is understood and agreed that the following

clause is substituted for the Collision Clause in this policy, effective from...

And it is further agreed that if the Vessel hereby insured and/or her tow shall come into collision with any other Ship, Vessel, Craft or Structure, floating or otherwise, or shall strand or ground such other Vessel or Craft, and the Assured or the Charterers in consequence thereof or the Surety for either or both of them in consequence of their undertaking shall become liable to pay and shall pay by way of damages to any other person or persons any sum or sums in respect of such casualty, we, the Underwriters, will pay the Assured or Charterers such proportion of such sum or sums so paid as our respective subscriptions hereto bear to the value of the Vessel hereby insured, provided always that our liability in respect of any one such casualty shall not exceed our proportionate part of the value of the Vessel hereby insured. And in cases where the liability of the Vessel and/or her tow has been contested, or proceedings have been taken to limit liability, with the consent in writing of a majority (in amount) of the Underwriters on the hull and/or machinery, we will also pay a like proportion of the costs which the Assured or Charterers shall thereby incur, or be compelled to pay; but when both Vessels are to blame, then, unless the liability of the Owners or Charterers of one or both of such Vessels becomes limited by law, claims under the Collision Clause shall be settled on the principle of Cross-Liabilities as if the Owners or Charterers of each Vessel had been compelled to pay to the Owners or Charterers of the other of such Vessels such one-half or other proportion of the latter's damages as may have been properly allowed in ascertaining the balance or sum payable by or to the Assured or Charterers in consequence of such collision; and it is further agreed that the principles involved in this clause shall apply to the case where both Vessels are the property, in part or in whole, of the same Owners or Charterers, all questions of responsibility and amount of liability as between the two Vessels being left to the decision of a single arbitrator, if the parties can agree upon a single arbitrator, or failing such agreement, to the decision of arbitrators, one to be appointed by the Managing Owners or Charterers of both Vessels, and one to be appointed by the majority (in amount) of Hull Underwriters interested: the two arbitrators chosen to choose a third arbitrator before entering upon the reference, and the decision of such single, or of any two of such three arbitrators, appointed as above, to be final and binding. Provided always that this clause shall in no case extend to any sum which the Assured, or the Charterers, or the Surety may become liable to pay or shall pay in consequence of, or with respect to:

a) removal or disposal of obstructions, wrecks or their cargoes under statutory or otherwise pursuant to law;
b) cargo, baggage or engagements of either the insured vessel, or her tow, or a collision of the tow after breaking away, unless such break be the consequence of a collision as specified herein;
c) the discharge, spillage, emission or leakage of oil, petroleum products, chemicals or other substances of any kind or description whatsoever;
d) loss of life, personal injury or illness.

Provided further that exclusion (c) above shall not apply to injury to other vessels or property thereon except to the extent that such injury arises out of any action taken to avoid, minimize or remove any discharge, spillage, emission or leakage described in (c).

And provided also that in the event of any claim being made by Charterers under this clause they shall not be entitled to recover in respect of any liability to which the Owners of the Vessel, if interested in this Policy at the time of the collision in question, would not be subject nor to a greater extent than the Shipowners would be entitled in such event to recover.

All other terms and conditions remaining unchanged.

Dated... 19.......

Revised June 1970

C

COLLISION CLAUSE, INCLUDING TOW
AND EXTENDED TOWER'S LIABILITY – EXCLUDING CARGO

Endorsement to be attached to and made part of Policy No..

of..it is understood and agreed that the following

In consideration of an additional premium at the rate of..., effective from...

clause is substituted for the Collision Clause in this policy.

And it is further agreed that if the Vessel hereby insured and/or her tow shall come into collision with any other Ship, Vessel, Craft, Structure or Object, other than water, floating or otherwise; or shall strand, ground or sink such other Vessel, Craft or Object and the Assured or the Charterers in consequence thereof or the Surety for either or both of them in consequence of their undertaking shall become liable to pay and shall pay by way of damages to any other person or persons any sum or sums in respect of such casualty, we, the Underwriters, will pay the Assured or Charterers such proportion of such sum or sums so paid as our respective subscription hereto bear to the value of the Vessel hereby insured, provided always that our liability, in respect of any one such casualty shall not exceed our proportionate part of the value of the Vessel hereby insured. And in cases where the liability of the Vessel and/or her tow has been contested, or proceedings have been taken to limit liability, with the consent in writing of a majority (in amount) of the Underwriters on the hull and/or machinery, we will also pay a like proportion of the costs which the Assured or Charterers shall thereby incur, or be compelled to pay; but when both Vessels are to blame, then, unless the liability of the Owners or Charterers of one or both of such Vessels becomes limited by law, claims under the Collision Clause shall be settled on the principle of Cross-Liabilities as if the Owners or Charterers of each Vessel had been compelled to pay to the Owners or Charterers of the other of such Vessels such one-half or other proportion of the latter's damages as may have been properly allowed in ascertaining the balance or sum payable by or to the Assured or Charterers in consequence of such collision; and it is further agreed that the principles involved in this clause shall apply to the case where both Vessels are the property, in part or in whole, of the same Owners or Charterers, all questions of responsibility and amount of liability as between the two Vessels being left to the decision of a single arbitrator, if the parties can agree upon a single arbitrator, or failing such agreement, to the decision of arbitrators, one to be appointed by the Managing Owners or Charterers of both Vessels, and one to be appointed by the majority (in amount) of Hull Underwriters interested: the two arbitrators chosen to choose a third arbitrator before entering upon the reference, and the decision of such single, or of any two of such three arbitrators, appointed as above, to be final and binding. And it is further agreed that this policy shall also extend to and cover the legal liability of the Vessel hereby insured arising from any collision, grounding, stranding or sinking which may occur to any Vessel(s) or Craft(s) while in tow of the said Vessel, subject to all other terms and conditions of this clause. Provided always that this clause shall in no way extend to any sum which the Assured, or the Charterers, or the Surety may become liable to pay or shall pay in consequence of, or with respect to:

a) removal or disposal of obstructions, wrecks or their cargoes under statutory powers or otherwise pursuant to law;
b) cargo, baggage or engagements of either the insured vessel, or her tow, or a collision of the tow after breaking away, unless such break be the consequence of a collision as specified herein;
c) the discharge, spillage, emission or leakage of oil, petroleum products, chemicals or other substances of any kind or description whatsoever; arises out of any action taken to avoid, minimize or remove any discharge, spillage, emission or leakage described in (c).
d) loss of life, personal injury or illness.

Provided further that exclusion (c) above shall not apply to injury to other vessels or property thereon except to the extent that such injury

And provided also that in the event of any claim being made by Charterers under this clause they shall not be entitled to recover in respect of any liability to which the Owners of the Vessel, if interested in this Policy at the time of the collision in question, would not be subject, nor to a greater extent than the Shipowners would be entitled to such event to recover.

All other terms and conditions remaining unchanged.

Dated..19.........

Revised June 1970   D

COLLISION CLAUSE, INCLUDING TOW
AND EXTENDED TOWER'S LIABILITY

Endorsement to be attached to and made part of Policy No...

of ....

In consideration of an additional premium at the rate of .... it is understood and agreed that the following

clause is substituted for the Collision Clause in this policy, effective from ....

And it is further agreed that if the Vessel hereby insured and/or her tow shall come into collision with any other Ship, Vessel, Craft, Structure or Object, other than water, floating or otherwise; or shall strand, ground or sink such other Vessel, Craft or Object and the Assured or the Charterers in consequence thereof or the Surety for either or both of them in consequence of their undertaking shall become liable to pay and shall pay by way of damages to any other person or persons any sum or sums in respect of such casualty, we, the Underwriters, will pay the Assured or Charterers such proportion of such sum or sums so paid as our respective subscription hereto bear to the value of the Vessel hereby insured, provided always that our liability, in respect of any one such casualty shall not exceed our proportionate part of the value of the Vessel hereby insured. And in cases where the liability of the Vessel and/or her tow has been contested, or proceedings have been taken to limit liability, with the consent in writing of a majority (in amount) of the Underwriters on the hull and/or machinery, we will also pay a like proportion of the costs which the Assured or Charterers shall thereby incur, or be compelled to pay; but when both Vessels are to blame, then, unless the liability of the Owners or Charterers of one or both of such Vessels becomes limited by law, claims under the Collision Clause shall be settled on the principle of Cross-Liabilities as if the Owners or Charterers of each Vessel had been compelled to pay to the Owners or Charterers of the other of such Vessels such one-half or other proportion of the latter's damages as may have been properly allowed in ascertaining the balance or sum payable by or to the Assured or Charterers in consequence of such collision; and it is further agreed that the principles involved in this clause shall apply to the case where both Vessels are the property, in part or in whole, of the same Owners or Charterers, all questions of responsibility and amount of liability as between the two Vessels being left to the decision of a single arbitrator, if the parties can agree upon a single arbitrator, or failing such agreement, to the decision of arbitrators, one to be appointed by the Managing Owners or Charterers of both Vessels, and one to be appointed by the majority (in amount) of Hull Underwriters interested; the two arbitrators chosen to choose a third arbitrator before entering upon the reference, and the decision of such single, or of any two of such three arbitrators, appointed as above, to be final and binding. And it is further agreed that this policy shall also extend to and cover the legal liability of the Vessel hereby insured arising from any, collision, grounding, stranding or sinking which may occur to any Vessel(s) or Craft(s) or their cargo and/or freight while in tow of the said Vessel, subject to all other terms and conditions of this clause. Provided always that this clause shall in no case extend to any sum which the Assured, or the Charterers, or the Surety may become liable to pay or shall pay in consequence of, or with respect to:

a) removal or disposal of obstructions, wrecks or their cargoes under statutory powers or otherwise pursuant to law;
b) cargo, baggage or engagements of the insured vessel, or a collision of the tow after breaking away, unless such break be the consequence of a collision as specified herein;
c) the discharge, spillage, emission or leakage of oil, petroleum products, chemicals or other substances of any kind or description whatsoever;
d) loss of life, personal injury or illness.

Provided further that exclusion (c) above shall not apply to injury to other vessels or property thereon except to the extent that such injury arises out of any action taken to avoid, minimize or remove any discharge, spillage, emission or leakage described in (c).

And provided also that in the event of any claim being made by Charterers under this clause they shall not be entitled to recover in respect of any liability to which the Owners of the Vessel, if interested in this Policy at the time of the collision in question, would not be subject, nor to a greater extent than the Shipowners would be entitled to such event to recover.

All other terms and conditions remaining unchanged.

Appendix 18

AMERICAN HULL INSURANCE SYNDICATE
LINER NEGLIGENCE CLAUSE
(MAY 1, 1964)

The so-called Inchmaree clause of the attached Policy is deleted and in place thereof the following inserted:

"This insurance also specially to cover, subject to the Average Warranty:

a. Breakdown of motor generators or other electrical machinery and electrical connections thereto; bursting of boilers; breakage of shafts; or any latent defect in the machinery or hull;

b. Loss of or damage to the subject matter insured directly caused by:

   1. Accidents on shipboard or elsewhere, other than breakdown of or accidents to nuclear installations or reactors on board the insured Vessel;

   2. Negligence, error of judgment or incompetence of any person;

excluding under both "a" and "b" above only the cost of repairing, replacing or renewing any part condemned solely as a result of a latent defect, wear and tear, gradual deterioration or fault or error in design or construction.

provided such loss or damage (either as described in said "a" or "b" or both) has not resulted from want of due diligence by the Assured(s), the Owner(s) or Manager(s) of the Vessel, or any of them. Masters, mates, engineers, pilots or crew not to be considered as part owners within the meaning of this clause should they hold shares in the Vessel."

Appendix 19

American Institute
(February 1949)
(F. C. & S. Warranty October, 1959)

32 B-9

AMERICAN INSTITUTE CARGO CLAUSES

1. This insurance attaches from the time the goods leave the Warehouse and/or Store at the place named in the policy for the commencement of the transit and continues during the ordinary course of transit, including customary transhipment if any, until the goods are discharged overside from the overseas vessel at the final port. Thereafter the insurance continues whilst the goods are in transit and/or awaiting transit until delivered to final warehouse at the destination named in the policy or until the expiry of 15 days (or 30 days if the destination to which the goods are insured is outside the limits of the port) whichever shall first occur. The time limits referred to above to be reckoned from midnight of the day on which the discharge overside of the goods hereby insured from the overseas vessel is completed. Held covered at a premium to be arranged in the event of transhipment, if any, other than as above and/or in the event of delay in excess of the above time limits arising from circumstances beyond the control of the Assured.

It is necessary for the Assured to give prompt notice to these Assurers when they become aware of an event for which they are "held covered" under this policy and the right to such cover is dependent on compliance with this obligation.

Warehouse to warehouse clause.

2. Including transit by craft and/or lighter to and from the vessel. Each craft and/or lighter to be deemed a separate insurance. The Assured are not to be prejudiced by any agreement exempting lightermen from liability.

Craft, &c., clause.

3. This insurance shall not be vitiated by any unintentional error in description of vessel, voyage or interest, or by deviation, over-carriage, change of voyage, transhipment or any other interruption of the ordinary course of transit, from causes beyond the control of the Assured. It is agreed, however, that any such error, deviation or other occurrence mentioned above shall be reported to this Company as soon as known to the Assured, and additional premium paid if required.

Deviation clause.

4. Warranted free from Particular Average unless the vessel or craft be stranded, sunk, or burnt, but notwithstanding this warranty these Assurers are to pay any loss of or damage to the interest insured which may reasonably be attributed to fire, collision or contact of the vessel and/or craft and/or conveyance with any external substance (ice included) other than water, or to discharge of cargo at port of distress. **The foregoing warranty, however, shall not apply where broader terms of Average are provided for hereon or in the certificate or policy to which these clauses are attached.**

F.P.A. clause.

5. Notwithstanding any average warranty contained herein, these Assurers agree to pay any landing, warehousing, forwarding and special charges for which this policy in the absence of such warranty would be liable. Also to pay the insured value of any package or packages which may be totally lost in loading, transhipment or discharge.

Warehousing & Forwarding Charges, Packages totally lost loading, etc.

6. In case of damage affecting labels, capsules or wrappers, these Assurers, if liable therefor under the terms of this policy, shall not be liable for more than an amount sufficient to pay the cost of new labels, capsules or wrappers, and the cost of reconditioning the goods, but in no event shall these Assurers be liable for more than the insured value of the damaged merchandise.

Labels clause.

7. When the property insured under this policy includes a machine consisting when complete for sale or use of several parts, then in case of loss or damage covered by this insurance to any part of such machine, these Assurers shall be liable only for the proportion of the insured value of the part lost or damaged, or at the Assured's option, for the cost and expense, including labor and forwarding charges, of replacing or repairing the lost or damaged part; but in no event shall these Assurers be liable for more than the insured value of the complete machine.

Machinery Clause

8. General Average and Salvage Charges payable according to United States laws and usage and/or as per Foreign Statement and/or as per York-Antwerp Rules (as prescribed in whole or in part) if in accordance with the Contract of Affreightment.

G/A clause.

9. Including the risk of explosion, howsoever or wheresoever occurring during the currency of this insurance, unless excluded by the F. C. & S. Warranty or the S. R. & C. C. Warranty set forth herein.

Explosion clause.

10. Where this insurance by its terms covers while on docks, wharves or elsewhere on shore, and/or during land transportation, it shall include the risks of collision, derailment, overturning or other accident to the conveyance, fire, lightning, sprinkler leakage, cyclones, hurricanes, earthquakes, floods (meaning the rising of navigable waters), and/or collapse or subsidence of docks or wharves, even though the insurance be otherwise F.P.A.

Shore Clause

11. The Assured are not to be prejudiced by the presence of the negligence clause and/or latent defect clause in the Bills of Lading and/or Charter Party. The seaworthiness of the vessel as between the Assured and these Assurers is hereby admitted and the wrongful act or misconduct of the shipowner or his servants causing a loss is not to defeat the recovery by an innocent Assured if the loss in the absence of such wrongful act or misconduct would have been a loss recoverable on the policy. With leave to sail with or without pilots, and to tow and assist vessels or craft in all situations, and to be towed.

Bill of Lading &c., clause.

12. This insurance is also specially to cover any loss of or damage to the interest insured hereunder, through the bursting of boilers, breakage of shafts or through any latent defect in the machinery, hull or appurtenances, or from faults or errors in the navigation and/or management of the vessel by the master, mariners, mates, engineers or pilots.
Inchmaree Clause

13. Warranted free of claim for loss of market or for loss, damage or deterioration arising from delay, whether caused by a peril insured against or otherwise, unless expressly assumed in writing hereon.
Delay clause.

14. Where goods are shipped under a Bill of Lading containing the so-called "Both to Blame Collision" Clause, these Assurers agree as to all losses covered by this insurance, to indemnify the Assured for this policy's proportion of any amount (not exceeding the amount insured) which the Assured may be legally bound to pay to the shipowners under such clause. In the event that such liability is asserted the Assured agree to notify these Assurers who shall have the right at their own cost and expense to defend the Assured against such claim.
Both to Blame clause.

15. No recovery for a Constructive Total Loss shall be had hereunder unless the property insured is reasonably abandoned on account of its actual total loss appearing to be unavoidable, or because it cannot be preserved from actual total loss without an expenditure which would exceed its value when the expenditure had been incurred.
Constructive Total Loss Clause

16. Warranted that this insurance shall not inure, directly or indirectly, to the benefit of any carrier or bailee.
Carrier clause.

17. The following Warranties shall be paramount and shall not be modified or superseded by any other provision included herein or stamped or endorsed hereon unless such other provision refers specifically to the risks excluded by these Warranties and expressly assumes the said risks:—

(A) Notwithstanding anything herein contained to the contrary, this insurance is warranted free from capture, seizure, arrest, restraint, detainment, confiscation, preemption, requisition or nationalization, and the consequences thereof or any attempt thereat, whether in time of peace or war and whether lawful or otherwise; also warranted free, whether in time of peace or war, from all loss, damage or expense caused by any weapon of war employing atomic or nuclear fission and/or fusion or other reaction or radioactive force or matter or by any mine or torpedo, also warranted free from all consequences of hostilities or warlike operations (whether there be a declaration of war or not), but this warranty shall not exclude collision or contact with aircraft, rockets or similar missiles or with any fixed or floating object (other than a mine or torpedo), stranding, heavy weather, fire or explosion unless caused directly (and independently of the nature of the voyage or service which the vessel concerned or, in the case of a collision, any other vessel involved therein, is performing) by a hostile act by or against a belligerent power; and for the purposes of this warranty "power" includes any authority maintaining naval, military or air forces in association with a power.
Further warranted free from the consequences of civil war, revolution, rebellion, insurrection, or civil strife arising therefrom, or piracy.
F. C. & S. Warranty.

(B) Warranted free of loss or damage caused by or resulting from strikes, lockouts, labor disturbances, riots, civil commotions or the acts of any person or persons taking part in any such occurrence or disorder.
S. R. & C. C. Warranty.

Special Terms and Conditions:—

Appendix 20

BULK OIL CLAUSES.

(Jan. 1962)

SP—13C

1. The Assured are not to be prejudiced by the presence of the negligence clause and/or latent defect clause in the bills of lading and/or charter party. The seaworthiness of the vessel and/or craft as between the Assured and Assurers is hereby admitted, and the Assurers agree that in the event unseaworthiness or a wrongful act or misconduct of shipowner, charterer, their agents or servants, shall directly or indirectly, cause loss or damage to the cargo insured by sinking, stranding, fire, explosion, contact with seawater, or by any other cause of the nature of any of the risks assumed in the policy, the Assurers will (subject to the terms of average and other conditions of the policy) pay to an innocent Assured the resulting loss. With leave to sail with or without pilots, and to tow and assist vessels or craft in all situations and to be towed.

2. Provided prompt notice be given the Assurers when such facts are known to the Assured and additional premium be paid if required, it is understood and agreed that if in case of short shipment in whole or in part by the vessel reported for insurance hereunder, or if the goods be transhipped by another vessel or vessels, or be carried beyond or discharged short of destination, or in the event of deviation, or change of voyage, or any interruption or other variation of the voyage or risk beyond the control of the Assured, this insurance shall nevertheless cover the goods until arrival at the final destination named in the policy or certificate of insurance or until the subject matter insured is no longer at the risk of the Assured, whichever may first occur. No additional risks (whether of delay or of any other description) are insured under this clause, which is intended merely to continue the insurance in force against the same risks named elsewhere in this policy or certificate and if the risks of War, Strikes, Riots or Civil Commotions, or any of these risks, are insured against, the insurance against such risks shall not be extended by this clause to cover contrary to any express provision of such insurance.

3. Including all risks of transhipment if required and of craft to and from the vessel, each lighter, craft or conveyance to be considered as if separately insured; also to cover any special or supplementary lighterage at additional premium if required. The Assured is not to be prejudiced by any agreement exempting lightermen from liability.

4. General Average, Salvage and Special Charges, as per foreign custom, payable according to foreign statement, and/or per York-Antwerp Rules and/or in accordance with the contract of affreightment, if and as required; or, failing any provision in or there be no contract of affreightment, payable in accordance with the Laws and Usages of the Port of New York; and it is agreed that in the event of salvage, towage or other assistance being rendered to the vessel and/or interest hereby insured by any vessel belonging in part or in whole to the same owner or under the same management, the value of

Claims are to be paid irrespective of percentage, but subject to deduction for normal shortage.

8. This insurance is also especially to cover any loss of and/or damage to the interest insured hereunder, including shortage and/or leakage and/or contamination, through the bursting of boilers, breakage of shafts or through any latent defect in the machinery, hull or appurtenances, or from faults or errors in the navigation, and/or management of the vessel by the Master, Mariners, Mates, Engineers or Pilots; provided, however, that this clause shall not be construed as covering loss arising out of delay, deterioration or loss of market, unless otherwise provided elsewhere in this policy.

9. These Assurers also agree that any action or proceeding against them for the recovery of any claim under or by virtue of this insurance shall not be barred if commenced within the time prescribed therefor in the Statutes of the State of New York.

10. The warranty that vessel be loaded under inspection of surveyors appointed by the underwriters is hereby waived.

11. In the event that this Policy is extended to cover property prior to the attachment or subsequent to the expiration of the cover provided by the attached Marine Extension Clauses, such extension shall always be subject to the following exclusion unless specifically otherwise stated in writing signed by this company in the extension endorsement or otherwise:

This Company shall not be liable for any claim for loss, damage or expense arising directly or indirectly from any nuclear incident, reaction, radiation or any radio-active contamination, all whether controlled, or uncontrolled, occurring while said property is within the United States or any territory of the United States, the Canal Zone or Puerto Rico, or arising from a source therein, and whether the loss, damage or expense be proximately or remotely caused thereby, or be in whole or in part caused by, contributed to, or aggravated by the peril(s) insured against in this Policy; however, subject to the foregoing and all provisions of this Policy, if this Policy insures against the peril of fire, then direct loss by fire resulting from nuclear incident, nuclear reaction, or nuclear radiation or radioactive contamination is insured against by this Policy.

12. Notwithstanding anything herein contained to the contrary, this insurance is warranted free from capture, seizure, arrest, restraint, detainment, confiscation, preemption, requisition or nationalization, and the consequences thereof or of any attempt thereat, whether in time

such services (without regard to the common ownership or management) shall be ascertained by arbitration and the amount so awarded, insofar as applicable to the interest hereby insured, shall constitute a charge under this policy.

5. In the event of accident, danger, damage or disaster before or after commencement of the voyage resulting from any cause whatsoever whether due to negligence or not, for which or for the consequences of which the Shipowner is not responsible by statute or contract or otherwise, these Assurers shall nevertheless pay Salvage and/or Special Charges incurred in respect of the interests hereby insured and shall contribute with the Shipowner in General Average to the payment of any sacrifices, losses or expenses of a General Average nature that may be made or incurred.

6. It is agreed that no right of subrogation except through General Average shall lie against any vessel or craft, or in respect to any pipe lines, on which cargo hereby insured is being carried or in respect of which freight insured hereunder is at risk, belonging in part or in whole to a subsidiary and/or affiliated company.

7. Against all risks whatsoever (excepting as hereinafter provided) excluding the risks excepted by the F. C. & S. and S. R. & C. C. warranties incorporated herein, from time of leaving tanks at port of shipment and whilst in transit and/or awaiting transit and until safely delivered in tanks at destination, but notwithstanding anything herein to the contrary, the Assurers are not liable for shortage and/or leakage and/or contamination (except as elsewhere in this policy provided) unless caused by or arising out of the vessel or craft being stranded, sunk, burnt, in collision or in contact with any substance or thing (ice included) other than water, fire, explosion (howsoever and wheresoever occurring) or there be a forced discharge of cargo; provided, however, that these Assurers are liable for contamination resulting from stress of weather.

It is agreed that notwithstanding anything herein to the contrary, this insurance is to pay the insured value of any oil lost from connecting pipe lines, flexible or otherwise, in loading, transhipment or discharge.

of peace or war and whether lawful or otherwise; also warranted free whether in time of peace or war, from all loss, damage or expense caused by any weapon of war employing atomic or nuclear fission and/or fusion or other reaction or radioactive force or matter or by any mine or torpedo, also warranted free from all consequences of hostilities or warlike operations (whether there be a declaration of war or not), but this warranty shall not exclude collision or contact with aircraft, rockets or similar missiles or with any fixed or floating object (other than a mine or torpedo), stranding, heavy weather, fire or explosion unless caused directly (and independently of the nature of the voyage or service which the vessel concerned or, in the case of a collision, any other vessel involved therein, is performing) by a hostile act by or against a belligerent power; and for the purposes of this warranty 'power' includes any authority maintaining naval, military or air forces in association with a power.

Further warranted free from the consequences of civil war, revolution, rebellion, insurrection, or civil strife arising therefrom, or piracy.

13. Warranted free of loss or damage caused by or resulting from strikes, lockouts, labor disturbances, riots, civil commotions or the acts of any person or persons taking part in any such occurrence or disorder.

14. If this policy is issued for a period of time, it is agreed that should the vessel at the expiration hereof be at sea, or in distress, or at a port of refuge or of call, the interest hereby insured shall, provided previous notice be given to the insurers, be held covered at a pro rata premium until arrival at port of destination.

15. Where goods are shipped under a bill of lading containing the so-called "Both to Blame Collision" Clause these Assurers agree, as to all losses covered by this insurance, to indemnify the Assured for any amount (up to the amount insured) which the Assured may be legally bound to pay to the shipowners under such clause. In the event that such liability is asserted the Assured agree to notify the Assurers who shall have the right at their own cost and expense, to defend the Assured against such claim.

Appendix 21

SPECIMEN

Policy No. **A**

AMERICAN STEAMSHIP OWNERS
MUTUAL PROTECTION AND INDEMNITY ASSOCIATION, INC.

NEW YORK, N. Y.

(Herein called the Association)

IN CONSIDERATION OF THE STIPULATIONS HEREIN NAMED

and of

Dollars being Premium at the rate of

per gross registered ton

DOES INSURE

Policyholder

and

Additional Assured

(Herein called collectively the Assured)

who in accepting this policy agree that the party described above as "Policyholder" shall exclusively be entitled to the rights of a policyholder and member as set forth in the charter and by-laws of the Association;

LOSS, IF ANY, PAYABLE TO

IN THE INSURED SUM OF   DOLLARS

at and from the   day of   19   , at   time

until the   day of   19   , at   time

against the risks and subject to the terms and conditions hereunder set forth in respect of the vessel called the
                                                                    of   gross registered tons or by
whatsoever other names the said vessel is or shall be named or called.

ASSESSABILITY. The Assured are subject to a contingent liability hereunder for assessment without limit of amount for their proportionate share of any deficiency or impairment as provided by law and fixed in accordance with the by-laws of the Association; provided, however, that any such assessment shall be for the exclusive benefit of holders of policies which provide for such a contingent liability, and the holders of policies subject to assessment shall not be liable to assessment in an amount greater in proportion to the total deficiency than the ratio that the deficiency attributable to the assessable business bears to the total deficiency.

THE ASSOCIATION AGREES TO INDEMNIFY THE ASSURED AGAINST ANY LOSS, DAMAGE OR EXPENSE WHICH THE ASSURED SHALL BECOME LIABLE TO PAY AND SHALL PAY BY REASON OF THE FACT THAT THE ASSURED IS THE OWNER (OR OPERATOR, MANAGER, CHARTERER, MORTGAGEE, TRUSTEE, RECEIVER OR AGENT, AS THE CASE MAY BE) OF THE INSURED VESSEL AND WHICH SHALL RESULT FROM THE FOLLOWING LIABILITIES, RISKS, EVENTS, OCCURRENCES AND EXPENDITURES:

(1) LIABILITY FOR LIFE SALVAGE, LOSS OF LIFE OF, OR PERSONAL INJURY TO, OR ILLNESS   **LOSS OF LIFE,**
OF ANY PERSON, NOT INCLUDING, HOWEVER, UNLESS OTHERWISE AGREED BY ENDORSE-   **INJURY AND**
MENT HEREON, LIABILITY TO AN EMPLOYEE (OTHER THAN HEREAFTER EXCEPTED) OF THE   **ILLNESS.**
ASSURED, OR IN CASE OF HIS DEATH TO HIS BENEFICIARIES, UNDER ANY COMPENSATION
ACT. LIABILITY HEREUNDER WITH RESPECT TO A MEMBER OF THE CREW SHALL INCLUDE
LIABILITY ARISING ASHORE OR AFLOAT. LIABILITY HEREUNDER SHALL ALSO INCLUDE
BURIAL EXPENSES NOT EXCEEDING $500., WHERE REASONABLY INCURRED BY THE ASSURED
FOR THE BURIAL OF ANY SEAMAN.

(a) Liability hereunder shall include the liability of the Assured for claims under any Compensation Act (other than hereafter excepted), in respect of an employee (i) who is a member of the crew of the insured vessel, or (ii) who is on board the insured vessel with the intention of becoming a member of her crew, or (iii) who, in the event of the vessel being laid up and out of commission, is engaged in the upkeep, maintenance or watching of the insured vessel, or (iv) who is engaged by the insured vessel or its Master to perform stevedoring work in connection with the vessel's cargo at ports in Alaska and ports outside the Continental United States where contract stevedores are not readily available. This insurance, however, shall not be considered as a qualification under any Compensation Act, but, without diminishing in any way the liability of the Association under this policy, the Assured may have in effect policies covering such liabilities. All claims under such Compensation Acts for which the Association is liable under the terms of this policy are to be paid without regard to such other policies.

(b) Liability hereunder shall not cover any liability under the provisions of the Act of Congress approved September 7th, 1916 and as amended, Public Act No. 267, Sixty-fourth Congress, known as the U. S. Employees Compensation Act.

(c) Liability hereunder in connection with the handling of cargo for the insured vessel shall commence from the time of receipt by the Assured of the cargo on dock or wharf, or on craft alongside for loading, and shall continue until due delivery thereof from dock or wharf of discharge or until discharge from the insured vessel on to a craft alongside.

(d) Liability hereunder may, by endorsement hereon, be made payable to an employee of the Assured or in the event of his death to his beneficiaries or estate.

(e) Claims hereunder, other than for burial expenses, are subject to a deduction of $ with respect to each accident or occurrence.

(2) LIABILITY FOR EXPENSES REASONABLY INCURRED IN NECESSARILY REPATRIATING ANY MEMBER OF THE CREW OR ANY OTHER PERSON EMPLOYED ON BOARD THE INSURED VESSEL; PROVIDED, HOWEVER, THAT THE ASSURED SHALL NOT BE ENTITLED TO RECOVER ANY SUCH EXPENSES INCURRED BY REASON OF THE EXPIRATION OF THE SHIPPING AGREEMENT, OTHER THAN BY SEA PERILS, OR BY THE VOLUNTARY TERMINATION OF THE AGREEMENT. WAGES SHALL BE RECOVERABLE HEREUNDER ONLY WHEN PAYABLE UNDER STATUTORY OBLIGATION DURING UNEMPLOYMENT DUE TO THE WRECK OR LOSS OF THE INSURED VESSEL.   REPATRIATION EXPENSES.

(a) Claims hereunder are subject to a deduction of $ with respect to each accident or occurrence.

(3) LIABILITY FOR LOSS OR DAMAGE ARISING FROM COLLISION OF THE INSURED VESSEL WITH ANOTHER SHIP OR VESSEL WHERE THE LIABILITY IS OF A TYPE, CHARACTER, OR KIND WHICH WOULD NOT BE COVERED IN ANY RESPECT BY THE FOLLOWING PORTIONS OF THE FOUR-FOURTHS COLLISION CLAUSE IN THE AMERICAN INSTITUTE HULL CLAUSES (JUNE 2, 1977) FORM.   COLLISION.

"And it is further agreed that:

(a) if the Vessel shall come into collision with any other ship or vessel, and the Assured or the Surety in consequence of the Vessel being at fault shall become liable to pay and shall pay by way of damages to any other person or persons any sum or sums in respect of such collision, the Underwriters will pay the Assured or the Surety, whichever shall have paid, such proportion of such sum or sums so paid as their respective subscriptions hereto bear to the Agreed Value, provided always that their liability in respect to any one such collision shall not exceed their proportionate part of the Agreed Value;

(b) in cases where, with the consent in writing of a majority (in amount) of Hull Underwriters, the liability of the Vessel has been contested, or proceedings have been taken to limit liability, the Underwriters will also pay a like proportion of the costs which the Assured shall thereby incur or be compelled to pay.

When both vessels are to blame, then, unless the liability of the owners or charterers of one or both such vessels becomes limited by law, claims under the Collision Liability clause shall be settled on the principle of Cross-Liabilities as if the owners or charterers of each vessel had been compelled to pay to the owners or charterers of the other of such vessels such one-half or other proportion of the latter's damages as may have been properly allowed in ascertaining the balance or sum payable by or to the Assured in consequence of such collision.

The principles involved in this clause shall apply to the case where both vessels are the property, in part or in whole, of the same owners or charterers, all questions of responsibility and amount of liability as between the two vessels being left to the decision of a single Arbitrator, if the parties can agree upon a single Arbitrator, or failing such agreement, to the decision of Arbitrators, one to be appointed by the Assured and one to be appointed by the majority (in amount) of Hull Underwriters interested; two Arbitrators chosen to choose a third Arbitrator before entering upon the reference, and the decision of such single Arbitrator, or of any two of such three Arbitrators, appointed as above, to be final and binding.

Provided that this clause shall in no case extend to any sum which the Assured or the Surety may become liable to pay or shall pay in consequence of, or with respect to:

(a) removal or disposal of obstructions, wrecks or their cargoes under statutory powers or otherwise pursuant to law;

(b) injury to real or personal property of every description;

(c) the discharge, spillage, emission or leakage of oil, petroleum products, chemicals or other substances of any kind or description whatsoever;

(d) cargo or other property on or the engagements of the Vessel;

(e) loss of life, personal injury or illness.

Provided further that exclusions (b) and (c) above shall not apply to injury to other vessels or property thereon except to the extent that such injury arises out of any action taken to avoid, minimize or remove any discharge, spillage, emission or leakage described in (c) above."

PROVIDED, HOWEVER, THAT INSURANCE HEREUNDER SHALL NOT EXTEND TO ANY LIABILITY, WHETHER DIRECT OR INDIRECT, IN RESPECT OF THE ENGAGEMENTS OF OR THE DETENTION OR LOSS OF TIME OF THE INSURED VESSEL.

(a) Claims hereunder shall be settled on the principles of Cross-Liabilities to the same extent only as provided in the four-fourths Collision Clause above mentioned.

(b) Where both vessels are the property, in part or in whole, of the same Owners or Charterers, claims hereunder shall be settled on the basis of the principles set forth in the four-fourths Collision Clause above mentioned.

(c) Claims hereunder shall be separated among and take the identity of the several classes of liability for loss, damage, and expense enumerated in this policy and each class shall be subject to the deductions, inclusions, exclusions and special conditions applicable in respect to such class.

(d) Notwithstanding the foregoing, the Association shall not be liable for any claims hereunder where the various liabilities resulting from such collision, or any of them, have been compromised, settled or adjusted without the written consent of the Association.

(4) LIABILITY FOR LOSS OF OR DAMAGE TO ANY OTHER VESSEL OR CRAFT, OR TO PROPERTY ON BOARD SUCH OTHER VESSEL OR CRAFT, CAUSED OTHERWISE THAN BY COLLISION OF THE INSURED VESSEL WITH ANOTHER VESSEL OR CRAFT. **DAMAGE CAUSED OTHERWISE THAN BY COLLISION.**

(a) Where such other vessel or craft or property on board such other vessel or craft belongs to the Assured, claims hereunder shall be adjusted as if it belonged to a third person; provided, however, that if such vessel, craft or property be insured, the Association shall be liable hereunder only in so far as the loss or damage, but for the insurance herein provided, is not or would not be recoverable by the Assured under such other insurance.

(b) Claims hereunder are subject to a deduction of $ with respect to each accident or occurrence.

(5) LIABILITY FOR DAMAGE TO ANY DOCK, PIER, JETTY, BRIDGE, HARBOR, BREAKWATER, STRUCTURE, BEACON, BUOY, LIGHTHOUSE, CABLE, OR TO ANY FIXED OR MOVABLE OBJECT OR PROPERTY WHATSOEVER, EXCEPT ANOTHER VESSEL OR CRAFT OR PROPERTY ON ANOTHER VESSEL OR CRAFT, OR TO PROPERTY ON THE INSURED VESSEL UNLESS PROPERTY ON THE INSURED VESSEL IS ELSEWHERE COVERED HEREIN. **DAMAGE TO DOCKS, BUOYS, ETC.**

(a) Where any such object or property belongs to the Assured, claims hereunder shall be adjusted as if it belonged to a third person; provided, however, that if such object or property be insured, the Association shall be liable hereunder only in so far as the damage, but for the insurance herein provided, is not or would not be recoverable by the Assured under such other insurance.

(b) Claims hereunder are subject to a deduction of $ with respect to each accident or occurrence.

(6) LIABILITY FOR COSTS OR EXPENSES OF OR INCIDENTAL TO THE REMOVAL OF THE WRECK OF THE INSURED VESSEL; PROVIDED, HOWEVER, THAT: **WRECK REMOVAL.**

(a) From such costs and expenses shall be deducted the value of any salvage from or which might have been recovered from the wreck inuring, or which might have inured, to the benefit of the Assured;

(b) The Association shall not be liable for any costs or expenses of a type, character or kind which would be payable under the terms of a policy written on the American Institute Hull Clauses (June 2, 1977) Form and a policy written on the American Institute Increased Value and Excess Liabilities Clauses (November 3, 1977) Form;

(c) In the event that the wreck of the insured vessel is upon property owned, leased, rented, or otherwise occupied by the Assured, the Association shall be liable for any liability for removal of the wreck which would be imposed upon the Assured by law in the absence of contract if the wreck had been upon the property belonging to another, but only for the excess over any amount recoverable under any other insurance applicable thereto;

(d) Each claim hereunder is subject to a deduction of $

(7) LIABILITY FOR LOSS OF OR DAMAGE TO OR IN CONNECTION WITH CARGO OR OTHER PROPERTY (EXCEPT MAIL OR PARCELS POST), INCLUDING BAGGAGE AND PERSONAL EFFECTS OF PASSENGERS, TO BE CARRIED, CARRIED OR WHICH HAS BEEN CARRIED ON BOARD THE INSURED VESSEL; PROVIDED, HOWEVER, THAT NO LIABILITY SHALL EXIST HEREUNDER FOR: **CARGO.**

(a) Loss, damage or expense incurred in connection with the custody, carriage or delivery of specie, bullion, precious metals, precious stones, jewelry, silks, furs, currency, bonds or other negotiable documents, or similar valuable property, unless specially agreed to and accepted for transportation under a form of contract approved, in writing, by the Association; **SPECIE, BULLION, JEWELRY, ETC.**

(b) Loss, damage or expense arising out of or in connection with the care, custody, carriage or delivery of cargo requiring refrigeration, unless the spaces, apparatus and means used for the care, custody and carriage thereof have been surveyed by a classification or other competent disinterested surveyor under working conditions before the commencement of each round voyage and found in all respects fit, and unless the Association has approved in writing the form of contract under which such cargo is accepted for transportation;

REFRIGERATION.

(c) Loss or damage to any passenger's baggage or personal effects, unless the form of ticket issued to the passenger shall have been approved, in writing, by the Association;

PASSENGERS' EFFECTS.

(d) Loss, damage or expense arising from any deviation in breach of the Assured's obligation to cargo, known to the Assured in time to enable him specifically to insure his liability therefor, unless notice thereof has been given the Association, and the Association has agreed, in writing, that such insurance was unnecessary;

DEVIATION.

(e) Loss, damage or expense arising from stowage of under deck cargo on deck, or stowage of cargo in spaces not suitable for its carriage, unless the Assured shall show that every reasonable precaution has been taken by him to prevent such improper stowage;

STOWAGE IN IMPROPER SPACES.

(f) Loss, damage or expense arising from issuance of clean bills of lading for goods known to be missing, unsound or damaged;

BILLS OF LADING.

(g) Loss, damage or expense arising from the intentional issuance of bills of lading prior to receipt of the goods described therein, or covering goods not received at all;

(h) Loss, damage or expense arising from delivery of cargo without surrender of bills of lading;

(i) Freight on cargo short-delivered, whether or not prepaid, or whether or not included in the claim and paid by the Assured;

FREIGHT.

AND PROVIDED FURTHER THAT:

(j) Liability hereunder shall in no event exceed that which would be imposed by law in the absence of contract;

(k) Liability hereunder shall be limited to such as would exist if the charter party, bill of lading or contract of affreightment contained (A) a negligence general average clause in the form hereinafter specified under Paragraph (12); (B) a clause providing that any provision of the charter party, bill of lading or contract of affreightment to the contrary notwithstanding, the Assured and the insured vessel shall have the benefit of all limitations of and exemptions from liability accorded to the owner or chartered owner of vessels by any statute or rule of law for the time being in force; (C) such clauses, if any, as are required by law to be stated therein; (D) and such other protective clauses as are commonly in use in the particular trade;

PROTECTIVE CLAUSES REQUIRED IN CONTRACT OF AFFREIGHTMENT.

(l) When cargo carried by the insured vessel is under a bill of lading or similar document of title subject or made subject to the Carriage of Goods by Sea Act of the United States or a law of any other country of similar import, liability hereunder shall be limited to such as is imposed by said Act or law, and if the Assured or the insured vessel assumes any greater liabiilty or obligation, either in respect of the valuation of the cargo or in any other respect, than the minimum liabilities and obligations imposed by said Act or law, such greater liability or obligation shall not be covered hereunder;

CARRIAGE OF GOODS BY SEA ACT.

(m) When cargo carried by the insured vessel is under a charter party, bill of lading or contract of affreightment not subject or made subject to the Carriage of Goods by Sea Act of the United States or a law of any other country of similar import, liability

LIMIT OF $500. PER PACKAGE.

hereunder shall be limited to such as would exist if said charter party, bill of lading or contract of affreightment contained a clause exempting the Assured and the insured vessel from liability for losses arising from unseaworthiness provided that due diligence shall have been exercised to make said vessel seaworthy and properly manned, equipped and supplied, and a clause effectively limiting the Assured's liability for total loss or damage to goods shipped to $500. per package, or in case of goods not shipped in packages, per customary freight unit, and providing for pro rata adjustment on such basis for partial loss or damage;

(n) In the event cargo is carried under an arrangement not reduced to writing, the Association's liability hereunder shall be no greater than if such cargo had been carried under a charter party, bill of lading or contract of affreightment containing the clauses referred to herein; **ORAL CONTRACT.**

(o) Where cargo on board the insured vessel is the property of the Assured, such cargo shall be deemed to be carried under a contract containing the protective clauses described in clauses (k), (l), and (m) herein; and such cargo shall be deemed to be fully insured under the usual form of cargo policy, and in case of loss of or damage to such cargo the Assured shall be insured hereunder in respect of such loss or damage only to the extent that he would have been if the cargo had belonged to another, but only in the event and to the extent that the loss or damage would not be recoverable from marine insurers under a cargo policy as above specified; **ASSURED'S OWN CARGO.**

(p) No liability shall exist hereunder for any loss, damage or expense in respect of cargo, or baggage and personal effects of passengers being transported on land or while on another vessel or craft unless such loss, damage or expense is caused directly by the insured vessel, her master, officers or crew; **TRANSPORTATION ON LAND OR OTHER CRAFT.**

(q) No liability shall exist hereunder for any loss, damage or expense in respect of cargo, or baggage and personal effects of passengers before loading on or after discharge from the insured vessel caused by flood, tide, windstorm, earthquake, fire, explosion, heat, cold, deterioration, collapse of wharf, leaky shed, theft or pilferage unless such loss, damage or expense is caused directly by the insured vessel, her master, officers or crew; **CARGO ON DOCK.**

(r) A deduction of $ shall be made from any claim or claims with respect to each cargo carried, including passengers' baggage and personal effects.

(8) LIABILITY FOR FINES AND PENALTIES FOR THE VIOLATION OF ANY LAWS OF THE UNITED STATES, OR OF ANY STATE THEREOF, OR OF ANY FOREIGN COUNTRY; PROVIDED, HOWEVER, THAT THE ASSOCIATION SHALL NOT BE LIABLE TO INDEMNIFY THE ASSURED AGAINST ANY SUCH FINES OR PENALTIES RESULTING DIRECTLY OR INDIRECTLY FROM THE FAILURE, NEGLECT OR FAULT OF THE ASSURED OR ITS MANAGING OFFICERS TO EXERCISE THE HIGHEST DEGREE OF DILIGENCE TO PREVENT A VIOLATION OF ANY SUCH LAWS. **FINES AND PENALTIES.**

(a) Claims hereunder are subject to a deduction of $ with respect to each fine or penalty.

(9) LIABILITY FOR EXPENSES INCURRED IN RESISTING ANY UNFOUNDED CLAIM BY A SEAMAN OR OTHER PERSON EMPLOYED ON BOARD THE INSURED VESSEL, OR IN PROSECUTING SUCH PERSON OR PERSONS IN CASE OF MUTINY OR OTHER MISCONDUCT; NOT INCLUDING, HOWEVER, COSTS OF SUCCESSFULLY DEFENDING CLAIMS ELSEWHERE PROTECTED IN THIS POLICY. **MUTINY, MISCONDUCT.**

(a) Claims hereunder are subject to a deduction of $ with respect to each occurrence.

(10) LIABILITY FOR EXTRAORDINARY EXPENSES, INCURRED IN CONSEQUENCE OF THE OUT- **QUARANTINE**
BREAK OF PLAGUE OR OTHER DISEASE ON THE INSURED VESSEL, FOR DISINFECTION OF THE **EXPENSES.**
VESSEL OR OF PERSONS ON BOARD, OR FOR QUARANTINE EXPENSES, NOT BEING THE
ORDINARY EXPENSES OF LOADING OR DISCHARGING, NOR THE ORDINARY WAGES OR
PROVISIONS OF CREW OR PASSENGERS; PROVIDED, HOWEVER, THAT NO LIABILITY SHALL
EXIST HEREUNDER IF THE VESSEL BE ORDERED TO PROCEED TO A PORT WHERE IT IS KNOWN
THAT SHE WILL BE SUBJECTED TO QUARANTINE.

(a) Each claim hereunder is subject to a deduction of $

(11) LIABILITY FOR PORT CHARGES INCURRED SOLELY FOR THE PURPOSE OF PUTTING IN TO **PUTTING IN**
LAND AN INJURED OR SICK SEAMAN OR PASSENGER, AND THE NET LOSS TO THE ASSURED **EXPENSES.**
IN RESPECT OF BUNKERS, INSURANCE, STORES AND PROVISIONS AS THE RESULT OF THE
DEVIATION.

(12) LIABILITY FOR CARGO'S PROPORTION OF GENERAL AVERAGE, INCLUDING SPECIAL **CARGO'S**
CHARGES, SO FAR AS THE ASSURED IS NOT ENTITLED TO RECOVER THE SAME FROM ANY **PROPN. G/A.**
OTHER SOURCE: PROVIDED, HOWEVER, THAT IF THE CHARTER PARTY, BILL OF LADING OR
CONTRACT OF AFFREIGHTMENT DOES NOT CONTAIN THE NEGLIGENCE GENERAL AVER-
AGE CLAUSE QUOTED BELOW, THE ASSOCIATION'S LIABILITY HEREUNDER SHALL BE
LIMITED TO SUCH AS WOULD EXIST IF SUCH CLAUSE WERE CONTAINED THEREIN: VIZ.,

"In the event of accident, danger, damage or disaster, before or after commence-   **NEGLIGENCE**
ment of the voyage resulting from any cause whatsoever, whether due to negligence   **G/A CLAUSE.**
or not, for which, or for the consequence of which, the Carrier is not responsible, by
statute, contract, or otherwise, the goods, the shipper and the consignee shall contribute with the Carrier in general average to the payment of any sacrifices, losses,
or expenses of a general average nature that may be made or incurred, and shall
pay salvage and special charges incurred in respect of the goods. If a salving ship
is owned or operated by the Carrier, salvage shall be paid for as fully and in the
same manner as if such salving ship or ships belonged to strangers."

(a) Claims hereunder are subject to a deduction of $ with
respect to each accident or occurrence.

(13) LIABILITY FOR EXPENSES ARISING OUT OF ACTION TAKEN IN COMPLIANCE WITH THE **DISCHARGE OF**
LAWS OF THE UNITED STATES OR ANY STATE OR SUBDIVISION THEREOF OR OF ANY **OIL OR OTHER**
COUNTRY TO AVOID DAMAGE FROM, OR TO MINIMIZE OR REMOVE, ANY DISCHARGE, **SUBSTANCE.**
SPILLAGE, EMISSION OR LEAKAGE OF OIL, PETROLEUM PRODUCTS, CHEMICALS OR OTHER
SUBSTANCES.

(a) Claims hereunder are subject to a deduction of $ with
respect to each accident or occurrence.

(14) LIABILITY FOR COSTS, CHARGES AND EXPENSES REASONABLY INCURRED AND PAID BY **EXPENSES OF**
THE ASSURED IN CONNECTION WITH ANY LIABILITY INSURED UNDER THIS POLICY, SUB- **INVESTIGATION**
JECT, HOWEVER, TO THE SAME DEDUCTION THAT WOULD BE APPLICABLE UNDER THIS POL- **AND DEFENSE.**
ICY TO THE LIABILITY DEFENDED; PROVIDED THAT IF ANY LIABILITY IS INCURRED AND PAID
BY THE ASSURED AS AFORESAID, THE DEDUCTION SHALL BE APPLIED TO THE AGGREGATE
OF THE CLAIM AND EXPENSES; AND PROVIDED FURTHER THAT THE ASSURED SHALL NOT
BE ENTITLED TO INDEMNITY FOR EXPENSES UNLESS THEY WERE INCURRED WITH THE
APPROVAL IN WRITING OF THE ASSOCIATION, OR THE ASSOCIATION SHALL BE SATISFIED
THAT SUCH APPROVAL COULD NOT HAVE BEEN OBTAINED UNDER THE CIRCUMSTANCES
WITHOUT UNREASONABLE DELAY, OR THAT THE EXPENSES WERE REASONABLY AND PROP-
ERLY INCURRED; AND PROVIDED FURTHER THAT ANY SUGGESTION OR APPROVAL OF
COUNSEL, OR INCURRING OF EXPENSES IN CONNECTION WITH LIABILITIES NOT INSURED
UNDER THIS POLICY, SHALL NOT BE DEEMED AN ADMISSION OF THE ASSOCIATION'S
LIABILITY.

(a) It is understood and agreed that the Association may undertake the investigation of any occurrence which might develop into a claim against the Assured, and may undertake the investigation and defense of any claim made against the Assured with respect to which the Assured shall be or may claim to be insured by the Association, and that during such investigation and/or defense the Association may incur expenses, which expenses shall be for the account of the Assured, and such investigation and/or defense shall not be considered as an admission of the Association's liability for such claim or expenses, and the liability of the Association to the Assured for any loss, damage or expense shall not be affected by any acts of the Association prior to formal presentation to the Association of the Assured's claim for reimbursement or indemnity.

(15) EXPENSES WHICH THE ASSURED MAY INCUR UNDER AUTHORIZATION OF THE ASSOCIATION IN THE INTEREST OF THE ASSOCIATION.

GENERAL CONDITIONS AND LIMITATIONS

(16) In the event of any happening which may result in loss, damage or expense for which the Association may become liable, prompt notice thereof, on being known to the Assured, shall be given by the Assured to the Association.

PROMPT NOTICE OF CLAIM.

(17) The Association shall not be liable for any claim not presented to the Association with proper proofs of loss within one year after payment by the Assured.

(18) In no event shall suit on any claim be maintainable against the Association unless commenced within two years after the loss, damage or expense resulting from liabilities, risks, events, occurrences and expenditures specified under this policy shall have been paid by the Assured.

TIME FOR SUIT.

(19) If the Assured shall fail or refuse to settle any claim as authorized or directed by the Association, the liability of the Association to the Assured shall be limited to the amount for which settlement could have been made, or, if the amount is unknown, to the amount which the Association authorized.

ASSURED'S FAILURE TO SETTLE CLAIMS.

(20) Whenever required by the Association, the Assured shall aid in securing information and evidence and in obtaining witnesses and shall cooperate with the Association in the defense of any claim or suit or in the appeal from any judgment, in respect of any occurrence as hereinbefore provided.

DEFENSE OF CLAIMS.

(21) Unless otherwise agreed by endorsement hereon, the Association's liability shall in no event exceed that which would be imposed on the Assured by law in the absence of contract; provided, however, that the Assured's right of indemnity from the Association shall include any loss, damage or expense covered under the provisions of this policy arising as a result of any contract for the employment of tugs where such contract is one which is substantially similar to those customarily in use or in force during the currency of this policy. The Assured's right of indemnity hereunder shall not include any liability for loss, damage or expense arising from collision between the insured vessel and another vessel or craft, other than liability consequent on such collision, (a) for removal of obstructions under statutory powers, (b) for damage to any dock,

ASSUMED CONTRACTUAL LIABILITY.

pier, jetty, bridge, harbor, breakwater, structure, beacon, buoy, lighthouse, cable or similar structures, (c) in respect of the cargo of the insured vessel and (d) for loss of life, personal injury and illness.

(22) No claim or demand against the Association shall be assigned or transferred without the written consent of the Association, and unless otherwise specifically agreed by endorsement hereon no person other than the Assured or Loss Payee named herein, or a receiver of the property or estate thereof, shall acquire any right against the Association hereunder. **ASSIGNMENT.**

(23) The Association shall be subrogated to all the rights which the Assured may have against any other person or entity, in respect of any payment made under this policy, to the extent of such payment, and the Assured shall, upon the request of the Association, execute all documents necessary to secure to the Association such rights. **SUBROGATION.**

(24) The Association shall not be liable for any loss, damage or expense against which, but for the insurance herein provided, the Assured is or would be insured under existing insurance. **OTHER INSURANCE.**

(25) If and when the Assured under this policy has any interest other than as an owner or bareboat charterer of the insured vessel, in no event shall the Association be liable hereunder to any greater extent than if such Assured were the owner or bareboat charterer and were entitled to all the rights of limitation to which a shipowner is entitled. **LIMITATION OF LIABILITY.**

(26) If an insured vessel shall be and remain in any safe port for a period of thirty (30) or more consecutive days after finally mooring there (such period being computed from the day of arrival to the day of departure, one only being included) the Association is to return   per cent of the initial annual premium, prorated daily, for the period the insured vessel shall be laid up without cargo and without crew (other than a skeleton crew) and to return   per cent of the initial annual premium, prorated daily, for the period the insured vessel shall be laid up with cargo or crew on board, provided the Assured give written notice to the Association as soon as practicable after the commencement and termination of such lay up period. The Association shall have absolute discretion to determine whether a port is safe and how many crew members constitute a skeleton crew within the meaning of this paragraph. **LAY-UP RETURNS.**

(27) Liability hereunder in respect of any one accident or occurrence is limited to the amount hereby insured. **LIMIT OF AMOUNT INSURED.**

CANCELLATION PROVISIONS:

(28) (a) If the insured vessel should be sold or requisitioned, the Association shall have the option to cancel insurance hereunder with respect to the insured vessel, the Association to return   per cent of the gross annual premium for each thirty (30) consecutive days of the unexpired term of the insurance with respect to said vessel. If the entire management, control and possession of the insured vessel be transferred whether by demise charter or by change in corporate ownership or control of the insured owner, the Association shall have the option to cancel insurance hereunder with respect to the insured vessel, the Association to return three (3) percent **CANCELLATION.**

of the gross annual premium for each thirty (30) consecutive days of the unexpired term of the insurance with respect to said vessel. Cancellation shall not relieve the Assured from liability for premiums under this policy and for assessments levied and to be levied for deficiencies and impairments in respect to the insurance year for which the policy was originally written.

(b) In the event of non-payment of the full premium within sixty (60) days after attachment, or, if installment payment of the premium has been arranged, in the event of non-payment of any installment thereof within twenty (20) days after it is due, this policy may be cancelled by the Association upon five (5) days' written notice being given the Assured. Should this policy be cancelled under the provisions of this clause or otherwise or should the Assured fail to pay any assessment within ten (10) days after it is due or should the Assured or any of them become insolvent or bankrupt or assign its property for the benefit of creditors or suffer the appointment of a receiver for its property or any part thereof or the institution of dissolution proceedings by or against it, the Association shall not be liable for any claims whatsoever under this policy unless within sixty (60) days from the date of such cancellation or the occurrence of such insolvency, bankruptcy, assignment, receivership or dissolution proceedings, there are paid to the Association by or on behalf of the Assured all premiums due, and the payment of any premiums to become due as well as all possible assessments is unconditionally guaranteed by a responsible surety.

(c) In the event that Sections 182 to 189, both inclusive, of U. S. Code, Title 46, or any other existing law or laws determining or limiting liability of shipowners and carriers, or any of them, shall, while this policy is in force, be modified, amended or repealed, or the liabilities of shipowners or carriers be increased in any respect by legislative enactment, the Association shall have the right to cancel said insurance upon giving thirty (30) days' written notice of their intention so to do, and in the event of such cancellation, make return of premium upon a pro rata daily basis.

(29) NOTWITHSTANDING ANYTHING TO THE CONTRARY CONTAINED IN THIS POLICY, THE **RISKS** ASSOCIATION SHALL NOT BE LIABLE FOR ANY LOSS, DAMAGE OR EXPENSE SUSTAINED, **EXCLUDED.** DIRECTLY OR INDIRECTLY, BY REASON OF:

(a) Loss, damage or expense to hull, machinery, equipment or fittings of the insured vessel, including refrigerating apparatus and wireless equipment, whether or not owned by the Assured;

(b) Cancelment or breach of any charter or contract, detention of the vessel, bad debts, insolvency, fraud of agents, loss of freight, passage money, hire, demurrage or any other loss of revenue;

(c) Any loss, damage, sacrifice or expense of a type, character or kind which would be payable under the terms of a policy written on the American Institute Hull Clauses (June 2, 1977) Form and a policy written on the American Institute Increased Value and Excess Liabilities Clauses (November 3, 1977) Form whether or not the insured vessel is fully covered under those policies by insurance and excess insurance sufficient in amount to pay in full and without limit all such loss, damage, sacrifice or expense;

(d) The insured vessel towing any other vessel or craft, unless such towage was to assist such other vessel or craft in distress to a port or place of safety; provided, however, that this exception shall not apply to claims covered under Paragraph (1) of this policy;

(e) For any claim for loss of life, personal injury or illness in relation to the handling of cargo where such claim arises under a contract of indemnity between the Assured and his sub-contractor.

(30) In every case where this policy insures tugs, Clause (b) of Paragraph (6) and Clause **TUGS.** (c) of Paragraph (29) shall be deemed to refer to the American Institute Tug Form, August 1, 1976 instead of the American Institute Hull Clauses (June 2, 1977) Form and Paragraph (3) shall be deemed to incorporate the Collision Clause contained in said policy (American Institute Tug Form, August 1, 1976) instead of the Collision Clause quoted in said Paragraph (3) and the following clause shall be substituted for and supersede Clause (d) of Paragraph (29) namely

"Loss of or damage to any vessel or vessels in tow and/or their cargoes, whether such loss or damage occurs before, during or after actual towage; provided, that this exception shall not apply to claims under Paragraph (1) of this policy."

(31) Notwithstanding anything to the contrary contained in this policy, the Association **WAR RISKS.** shall not be liable for or in respect of any loss, damage or expense sustained by reason of capture, seizure, arrest, restraint or detainment, or the consequences thereof or of any attempt thereat; or sustained in consequence of military, naval or air action by force of arms, including mines and torpedoes or other missiles or engines of war, whether of enemy or friendly origin; or sustained in consequence of placing the vessel in jeopardy as an act or measure of war taken in the actual process of a military engagement, including embarking or disembarking troops or material of war in the immediate zone of such engagement; and any such loss, damage and expense shall be excluded from this policy without regard to whether the Assured's liability therefor is based on negligence or otherwise, and whether before or after a declaration of war.

IN WITNESS WHEREOF the Association has caused this Policy to be signed in its behalf this..........................day of.., 19.............

AMERICAN STEAMSHIP OWNERS MUTUAL
PROTECTION AND INDEMNITY ASSOCIATION, INC.

By Shipowners Claims Bureau, Inc., Manager.

....
Authorized Signature

SPECIMEN

Appendix 22

AIMU
Protection and Indemnity (P and I) Clauses
June 2, 1983

To be attached to and form part of Policy No..............of.........................(hereinafter "the Underwriters"). 1

.... 2

THE FOLLOWING CLAUSES ARE SUBSTITUTED FOR THOSE OF THE POLICY FORM TO WHICH 3
THEY ARE ATTACHED, THE LATTER BEING VOID, EXCEPT FOR THOSE PROVISIONS REQUIRED 4
BY LAW. CAPTIONS, BELOW, ARE FOR EASE OF REFERENCE ONLY AND ARE NOT TO BE USED TO 5
INTERPRET THE CLAUSES. 6

ASSURED
This Policy insures 7

.... 8
(hereinafter, "the Assured"). The Underwriters waive all rights of subrogation against affiliated or subsidiary compa- 9
nies of the Assured but only to the extent that the liabilities of such companies are uninsured. 10

VESSEL
The Underwriters will indemnify the Assured in respect of the matters set forth at lines 46 through 76, below, subject 11
to all other terms hereof, in respect of the..........................of..............gross registered tons (hereinafter, the 12
"Vessel"). If more than one Vessel is named, all clauses shall apply as though a separate Policy had been issued for 13
each Vessel. 14

DURATION OF RISK
This Policy attaches on........................, 19......, at..............o'clock..........................time and expires on 15
..........................., 19...., at..........o'clock..........................time. Should the Vessel be at sea at the expiration of 16
this Policy, or in distress, or at a port of refuge or call, she shall be held covered until she reaches her port of destina- 17
tion, provided prior notice be given to the Underwriters and provided the Assured agrees to any amended terms of 18
cover and additional premium if required by the Underwriters. 19

LIMIT OF LIABILITY
Liability hereunder in respect of all consequences of any one casualty or occurrence, including defense costs, shall not 20
exceed the sum of $ less any applicable deductible, regardless of how many separate injuries or 21
claims arise out of such casualty or occurrence. 22

DEDUCTIBLES
There shall be deducted from the total amount payable by the Underwriters with respect to all claims, including costs 23
of defense and expenses, arising from any one casualty or occurrence: 24
    a) $.......................with respect to those claims for loss of life, bodily injury or illness, and 25
    b) $.......................with respect to all other claims; 26
PROVIDED, HOWEVER, that the maximum deductible for any one casualty or occurrence shall not exceed the 27
greater of the foregoing amounts. 28

PREMIUM
The Underwriters are to be paid premium of $ for this insurance, payable as follows: 29

.... 30

.... 31

RETURN PREMIUM
If the Vessel is sold, demise chartered or requisitioned this Policy shall terminate on the date and at the hour when 32
such disposition of the Vessel is effective and the Underwriters will return premium on a pro rata daily net basis for the 33
unexpired term. If the Policy is cancelled by the Assured, the Underwriters will return premium on the usual short rate 34
daily net basis for the unexpired term. If the Policy is cancelled by the Underwriters they will return premium on a pro 35
rata daily net basis for the unexpired term. 36

CANCELLATION

The Policy may be cancelled by the Underwriters or by the Assured upon fifteen days written or telegraphic notice. 37
The Underwriters may send notice to the Assured's last address known to them, or to the broker of record at the time 38
when notice is given. At noon local time at the place of the sending of the notice on the fifteenth day after such notice 39
shall have been mailed, telegraphed or telexed, the Policy shall cease to be in effect. The Policy may also be cancelled 40
at any time by mutual agreement of the Assured and the Underwriters. 41

TRADING WARRANTY

Warranted that the Vessel shall be confined to 42

.... 43

.... 44

.... 45

INDEMNITY

Subject to all exclusions and other terms of this Policy the Underwriters agree to indemnify the Assured for any sums 46
which the Assured, as owner of the Vessel, shall have become liable to pay, and shall have paid, in respect of any 47
casualty or occurrence during the currency of the Policy but only in consequence of any of the matters set forth here- 48
under PROVIDED, however, that if the interest of the Assured is or includes interests other than owner of the Vessel, 49
the Underwriters' liability shall not be greater than if the Assured was the owner entitled to all defenses and limita- 50
tions of liability to which a shipowner is entitled: 51

(1) Loss of life and bodily injury or illness; but excluding amounts paid under any compensation act. 52

(2) Hospital, medical or other expenses necessarily and reasonably incurred with respect to loss of life, bodily injury 53
to, or illness of, any person. 54

(3) Crew member burial expense not to exceed $1,000 per person. 55

(4) Repatriation expenses of crew member, excepting such as arise from the termination of any agreement in 56
accordance with its terms, or the sale of the Vessel or other voluntary act of the Assured. Wages may be included 57
in such expenses when a statute requires payment of wages while awaiting and during repatriation. 58

(5) Damage to any fixed or movable object or property, howsoever caused, excluding however, damage to another 59
vessel or any property aboard it caused by collision with the Vessel. 60

(6) Cost or expense of, or incidental to, any attempted or actual removal or disposal of obstructions, wrecks or their 61
cargoes under statutory power or otherwise pursuant to law, PROVIDED, however, that there shall be deducted from 62
such claim for cost or expenses, the value of any salvage from the wreck inuring to the benefit of the Assured or any 63
subrogee thereof. 64

(7) Fines and penalties, including expenses reasonably incurred in avoiding or mitigating same, for the violation of 65
any of the laws of the United States, or any State thereof, or of any foreign country; PROVIDED, however, that the 66
Underwriters shall not be liable to indemnify the Assured against any such fines or penalties resulting directly or 67
indirectly from the failure, neglect, or default of the Assured or his managing officers or managing agents to exercise 68
the highest degree of diligence to prevent a violation of any such laws. 69

(8) Extraordinary expense arising from an outbreak of contagious disease, PROVIDED that the Vessel was not 70
ordered by anyone acting on behalf of the Assured to proceed to a port where such disease was known or supposed 71
to exist. 72

(9) Costs incurred with the written consent of the Underwriters, or reasonably incurred prior to receipt of advices 73
from Underwriters, for investigation and defense of claims, valid or not, within the scope of the Policy. 74

(10) Port charges incurred solely for the purpose of putting in to land an injured or sick seaman or passenger, and the 75
net loss to the Assured in respect of bunkers, insurance, stores and provisions as the result of the deviation. 76

EXCLUSIONS

Notwithstanding anything to the contrary elsewhere herein the Underwriters will not indemnify the Assured in 77
respect of any of the following matters: 78

(A) Any liability assumed under contract or otherwise. 79

(B) Liability imposed on the Assured as punitive or exemplary damages, however described. 80

(C) Any liability for any loss of, damage to, or expense in respect of, cargo or other property (including baggage and 81
personal effects of passengers, mail and parcel post) carried, to be carried or which had been carried on board 82
the Vessel, EXCEPT, HOWEVER, such liability imposed under the doctrine of cross liabilities for cargo on 83
board the Vessel for which there is no coverage under any other policy held by the Assured. 84

(D) Any liability or claim for, or any loss of, damage to, or expense in respect of property owned, leased, chartered 85
or hired by the Assured. 86

(E) Engagement in unlawful trade or performance of an unlawful act with knowledge of the Assured. 87

(F) Cancellation or breach of any contract. 88

(G) Bad debts.   89

(H) Fraud, dishonesty or insolvency of the Assured, its agents or others.   90

(I) Salvage charges, special charges, general average, freight, detention, demurrage or loss of use, of the Vessel.   91

(J) Any liability for, or any loss, damage, or expense arising from or accruing by reason of the towage of any other   92
vessel or craft other than emergency towage of a vessel in distress at sea to a port or place of safety, EXCEPT,   93
HOWEVER, this exclusion shall not apply to claims for loss of life, or bodily injury to, or illness or any person.   94
Emergency towage is deemed to be towage undertaken as a salvage service while the Vessel is on a voyage wholly   95
unrelated to performance of such service.   96

(K) Any liability for, or any loss, damage or expense while engaged in, or resulting from, any commercial diving   97
operation or service from the Vessel, EXCEPT, HOWEVER, any liability incurred when the Vessel's crew is   98
engaged in inspection or repair of the Vessel which could not be deferred until commercial divers were available.   99

(L) Any liability for, or any loss, damage, injury or expense resulting from nuclear radiation, fission or fusion,   100
whether such loss, damage, injury or expense has been caused directly or indirectly or has arisen from any matter   101
for which the Assured has responsibility or otherwise, and whether the nuclear event be controlled or un-   102
controlled.   103

(M) Any liability for, or any loss, damage, injury or expense caused by, resulting from or incurred by reason of any   104
one or more of the following: 105

    1) Capture, seizure, arrest, taking, restraint, detainment, confiscation, preemption, requisition or national-   106
    ization, or the consequences thereof or any attempt thereat, whether in time of peace or war and whether   107
    lawful or otherwise;   108

    2) Any weapon of war employing atomic or nuclear fission and/or fusion or other reaction or radioactive   109
    force or matter, or by any mine, bomb or torpedo;   110

    3) Hostilities or warlike operations (whether there by a declaration of war or not), but the phrase, "hostilities   111
    or warlike operations (whether there be a declaration of war or not)", shall not exclude collision or contact   112
    with aircraft, rockets or similar missiles or with any fixed or floating object, stranding, heavy weather, fire   113
    or explosion unless caused directly (independently of the nature of the voyage or service which the watercraft   114
    concerned or in the case of a collision, any other vessel involved herein, is performing) by a hostile act by   115
    or against a belligerent power; for the purpose of the foregoing, power includes any authority maintaining   116
    naval, military or air forces in association with a power. In addition to the foregoing exclusions, this in-   117
    surance shall not cover any loss, damage or expense to which a warlike act or the use of military or naval   118
    weapons is a contributing cause, whether or not the Assured's liability therefor is based on negligence or   119
    otherwise, and whether in time of peace or war. The embarkation, carriage and disembarkation of troops,   120
    combatants, or material of war, or the placement of the watercraft in jeopardy as an act or measure of war   121
    taken in the actual process of a military engagement, with or without the consent of the Assured, shall be   122
    considered a warlike act for the purposes of this Policy.   123

    4) The consequences of civil war, revolution, rebellion, insurrection, military or usurped power, the imposition   124
    of martial law, or civil strife arising therefrom, or piracy; or from any loss, damage or expense caused by   125
    or resulting directly or indirectly from the act or acts of one or more persons, whether or not agents of a   126
    sovereign power, carried out for political, ideological or terrorist purposes, and whether any loss, damage   127
    or expense resulting therefrom is accidental or intentional.   128

    5) Malicious acts or vandalism, strikes, lockouts, political or labor disturbances, civil commotions, riots, or   129
    the acts of any person or persons taking part in such occurrence or disorder.   130

(N) Any liability for, or any loss, damage, cost, expense, fine or penalty of any kind or nature whatsoever, whether   131
statutory or otherwise, incurred by or imposed on the Assured, directly or indirectly, in consequence of, or with   132
respect to, the actual or potential discharge, emission, spillage or leakage upon or into the seas, waters, land or   133
air, of substances of any kind or nature whatsoever.   134

GENERAL CONDITIONS

NOTICE OF LOSS

It is a condition of this Policy that the Assured give prompt notice to the Underwriters of any casualty or occurrence   135
which may result in a claim under this Policy.   136

FORWARDING OF PROCESS

It is a condition of this Policy that the Assured forward to the Underwriters, promptly upon receipt, copies of all   137
communications, legal process and pleadings relating to any casualty or occurrence which may result in a claim under   138
this Policy.   139

SETTLEMENT OF CLAIMS

1) It is a condition of the Policy that the Assured shall not make any admission of nor agree to assume any liability   140
either before or after any casualty or occurrence which may result in a claim under this Policy.   141
2) It is a condition of this Policy that the Assured shall take such steps to minimize and avoid liability, before and after   142
any casualty or occurrence, as would be taken by a prudent uninsured person.   143
3) The Underwriters shall have the option of naming the attorneys who shall represent the Assured in the prose-   144
cution or defense of any litigation or negotiations between the Assured and third parties concerning any claim   145
covered by this Policy, and in any event, the Underwriters shall direct the progress of such litigation or nego-   146
tiations.   147

4) If the Assured shall fail, or refuse, to settle any claim as authorized by the Underwriters, the liability of the Under- 148
writers shall be limited to the amount for which settlement could have been made plus legal fees and disbursements 149
incurred to the date the Assured fails or refuses to settle any such claim, less the amount of any deductible provided 150
for in this Policy. If thereafter any amount is recovered against the Assured in excess of the amount of any settle- 151
ment authorized by the Underwriters (less the deductible), such excess amount, plus any additional legal fees and 152
disbursements, shall be solely for account of the Assured. 153

CLAIM COOPERATION

The Assured shall aid in securing information, evidence, obtaining witnesses, and shall cooperate with the Under- 154
writers in the defense of any claim or suit or in the appeal from any judgment, in respect of any casualty or occurence 155
as hereinbefore provided. 156

SUBROGATION

The Underwriters shall be subrogated to all the rights which the Assured may have against any other person or entity, 157
in respect of any payment made under this Policy, to the extent of such payment, and the Assured shall, upon the 158
request of the Underwriters, execute and shall deliver such instruments and papers as the Underwriters shall require 159
and do whatever else is necessary to secure such rights. In the event of any agreement or act, past or future, by the 160
Assured, whereby any right of recovery of the Assured against any person or entity is released or lost to which the 161
Underwriters on payment of loss would be entitled to subrogation, but for such agreement or act, the Underwriters 162
shall be relieved of liability under this Policy to the extent that their rights of subrogation have been impaired 163
thereby; in such event the right of the Underwriters to retain or collect any premium paid or due hereunder shall 164
not be affected. The Underwriters shall not be liable for the costs and expenses of prosecuting any claim or suit 165
unless the same shall have been incurred with the written consent of the Underwriters, or the Underwriters shall 166
be satisfied that such approval could not have been obtained under the circumstances without unreasonable delay 167
and that such costs and expenses were reasonably and properly incurred, such costs and expenses being subject to 168
the deductible. The Underwriters shall be entitled to take credit for any profit accruing to the Assured by reason 169
of any negligence or wrongful act of the Assured's servants or agents, up to the measure of their loss, or to recover 170
for their own account from third parties any damage that may be provable by reason of such negligence or 171
wrongful act. 172

OTHER INSURANCE

Provided that where the Assured is, irrespective of this insurance, covered or protected against any loss or claim 173
which would otherwise have been paid by the Underwriters under this Policy, there shall be no contribution or par- 174
ticipation by the Underwriters on the basis of excess, contributing, deficiency, concurrent, or double insurance 175
or otherwise. 176

ASSIGNMENTS

Neither this Policy nor any claim or demand against the Underwriters under this Policy shall be assigned or trans- 177
ferred, and no person, excepting a legally appointed Receiver of the property of the Assured, shall acquire any right 178
against the Underwriters by virtue of this insurance without the express consent of the Underwriters endorsed hereon. 179
This Policy shall cease to be in effect 10 days after appointment of a Receiver, Trustee or any other transferee of the 180
Assured's assets. 181

TIME FOR SUIT CLAUSE

No action shall lie against the Underwriters for the recovery of any loss sustained by the Assured unless such action 182
be brought against the Underwriters within one year after the final judgment or decree is entered in the litigation 183
against the Assured, OR in case the claim against the Underwriters accrues without the entry of such final judgment 184
or decree, unless such action be brought within one year from the date of the payment by the Assured of such claim, 185
PROVIDED, however, that where such limitation of time is prohibited by the law of the State wherein this Policy 186
is issued, then, and only in that event, no action under this Policy shall be sustainable unless commenced within the 187
shortest limitation permitted under the law of such State. 188

Appendix 23

PROTECTION AND INDEMNITY (P AND I CLAUSES)
Cargo Liability Endorsement
American Institute (*June 2, 1983*)

ENDORSEMENT to be attached to and made part of Policy No. . . . . of
. . . .

In consideration of the payment of an additional premium of $. . . . ,
and subject to the limit of liability, the deductible amount for claims other
than for loss of life, bodily injury or illness, the exclusions, the conditions
and the other terms of this Policy, this Policy is hereby extended to indemnify the Assured for any sum which the Assured, as owner of the Vessel
shall become liable to pay and shall have paid, in respect of any claim for
loss, damage or expense in respect of cargo, including baggage and personal
effects of passengers, on board the Vessel, carried, to be carried, or which
had been carried on board the Vessel SUBJECT ALSO to the Special Limits
of Liability hereinafter provided.

The Underwriters expressly agree to indemnify the Assured for any sums
which the Assured is unable to recover as cargo's proportion of general average, salvage charges and special charges from any other source PROVIDED
that cargo's proportion shall be determined as if the contract of carriage or
charter party contained the New Jason Clause.

EXCLUSIONS
Notwithstanding anything to the contrary contained in this Endorsement,
the Underwriters shall not be required to indemnify the Assured for any liability for, or any loss, damage or expense arising out of or in connection
with:

a) The custody, care, carriage or delivery of specie, bullion, precious
stones, precious metals, jewelry, furs, bank notes, bonds or other negotiable
documents or similar valuable property, unless specially agreed to by the
Underwriters and accepted for transportation under a form of contract approved in writing by the Underwriters.

b) The custody, care, carriage or delivery of mail and parcel post.

c) The custody, care, carriage or delivery of any cargo requiring refrigeration, unless the space, apparatus and means used for such care, custody, carriage and delivery thereof have been surveyed under working conditions by a
classification surveyor or other competent disinterested surveyor before the
commencement of each round voyage and found in all respects fit, and unless
the said cargo be accepted for transportation under a form of contract ap-
praoved in writing by the Underwriters.

d) The stowage of under deck cargo on deck or stowage of cargo in spaces not suitable for its carriage, unless the Assured shall show that he has taken every reasonable precaution to prevent such stowage.

e) Any deviation not authorized by the contract of affreightment, and known to the Assured in time to insure specifically the liability therefor, unless notice thereof is given to the Underwriters who agree in writing that such other insurance is unnecessary.

f) The refund of, or inability to collect, freight on cargo short delivered, whether or not prepaid or whether or not included in the claim and paid by the Assured.

g) The issuance of Bills of Lading or similar documents of title which, to the knowledge of the Assured, improperly describe the goods, their condition or quantity, their packing or their containers.

h) The delivery of cargo without surrender of Bills of Lading or similar documents of title.

i) Any unlawful act of the Assured or conversion of cargo or other property by the Assured.

SPECIAL LIMITS OF LIABILITY

It is specially further agreed and understood that under this Endorsement and subject always to the limit of liability of the Policy to which this Endorsement is attached,

A) with respect to cargo, not property of the Assured, carried by the Vessel, the liability of the Underwriters shall be limited:

(i) to the minimum liabilities and obligations imposed upon the Assured by the U.S. Carriage of Goods by Sea Act, April 16, 1936, regardless of whether the carriage is subject to the said Act, and

(ii) as may be reduced by any other lawful protective clauses commonly in use in the particular trade in which the Vessel is engaged,

regardless of whether the Assured or the Vessel assumes any greater liabilities or obligations;

B) with respect to cargo, property of the Assured, carried by the Vessel, the liability of the Underwriters shall be limited:

(i) as hereinbefore provided under the preceding clauses A(i) and A(ii),

(ii) subject however to reduction by the amount which would be recoverable for the loss under the usual form of All Risks Cargo Policy if fully insured,

(iii) regardless of whether such Policy had been obtained;

C) with respect to baggage and personal effects carried by the Vessel, the liability of the Underwriters shall in no event exceed the lesser of that which would be imposed upon the Assured in the absence of contract or that provided in the contract between the owner of the property and the Assured or Vessel.

All other terms and conditions remain unchanged.

. . . .

Dated . . . .

PROTECTION AND INDEMNITY

SP 23 (Revised

Amount Insured $......................

No. P.I. ....

Premium $......................

Rate ....

....

.... hereinafter called the Assured

Loss, if any, payable to ....

.... or order

In the sum of .... Dollars

at and from the.................day of........................, 19......, at.................................. time

until the ....day of........................, 19......, at.................................. time
against the liabilities of the Assured as hereinafter described, and subject to the terms and conditions hereinafter set forth,

in respect of the vessel called the ....(Tonnage................) or by whatsoever other names the
said vessel is or shall be named or called.

In consideration of the Stipulations Herein Named and of ....

.... Dollars, being Premium at the rate of ....

The Assurer hereby undertakes to make good to the Assured or the Assured's executors, administrators and/or successors, all
such loss and/or damage and/or expense as the Assured shall as owners of the vessel named herein have become liable to pay and
shall pay on account of the liabilities, risks, events and/or happenings herein set forth:

Loss of Life, injury and illness	(1) **Liability for loss of life of, or personal injury to, or illness of, any person, excluding, however, unless otherwise agreed by endorsement hereon,** liability under any Compensation Act to any employee of the Assured, (other than a seaman) or in case of death to his beneficiaries or others. Protection hereunder for loss of life or personal injury arising in connection with the handling of cargo of the vessel named herein shall commence from the time of receipt by the Assured of the cargo on dock or wharf or on craft alongside the said vessel for loading thereon and shall continue until delivery thereof from dock or wharf of discharge or until discharge from the said vessel on to another vessel or craft.
Hospital, medical, etc. expenses	(2) Liability for hospital, medical, or other expenses necessarily and reasonably incurred in respect of loss of life of, personal injury to, or illness of any member of the crew of the vessel named herein or any other person. Liability hereunder shall also include burial expenses not exceeding Two Hundred ($200) Dollars, when necessarily and reasonably incurred by the Assured for the burial of any seaman of said vessel.
Repatriation expenses	(3) Liability for repatriation expenses of any member of the crew of the vessel named herein, necessarily and reasonably incurred, under statutory obligation, excepting such expenses as arise out of or ensue from the termination of any agreement in accordance with the terms thereof, or by mutual consent, or by sale of the said vessel, or by other act of the Assured. Wages shall be included in such expenses when payable under statutory obligation, during unemployment due to the wreck or loss of the said vessel.
Damage to other vessel or property on board caused by collision	(4) **Liability for loss of, or damage to, any other vessel or craft, or to the freight thereof, or property on such other vessel or craft, caused by collision with the vessel named herein, insofar as such liability would not be covered by full insurance under the** ....(including the four-fourths running-down clause).
Principle of cross-liabilities to prevail	(a) Claims under this clause shall be settled on the principle of cross-liabilities to the same extent only as provided in the running-down clause above mentioned.
	(b) Claims under this clause shall be divided among the several classes of claims enumerated in this policy and each class shall be subject to the deduction and special conditions applicable in respect of such class.
	(c) Notwithstanding the foregoing, if any one or more of the various liabilities arising from such collision has been compromised, settled or adjusted without the written consent of the Assurer, the Assurer shall be relieved of liability for any and all claims under this clause.
Damage to other vessel or property on board not caused by collision	(5) **Liability for loss of or damage to any other vessel or craft, or to property on such other vessel or craft, not caused by collision, provided such liability does not arise by reason of a contract made by the assured.** Where there would be a valid claim hereunder but for the fact that the damaged property belongs to the Assured, the Assurer shall be liable as if such damaged property belonged to another, but only for the excess over any amount recoverable under any other insurance applicable on the property.
Damage to docks, piers, etc.	(6) **Liability for damage to any dock, pier, harbor, bridge, jetty, buoy, lighthouse, breakwater, structure, beacon, cable, or to any fixed or movable object or property whatsoever, except another vessel or craft, or property on another vessel or craft.**

Where there would be a valid claim hereunder but for the fact that the damaged property belongs to the Assured, the Assurer shall be liable as if such damaged property belonged to another, but only for the excess over any amount recoverable under any other insurance applicable on the property.

Removal of wreck

(7) **Liability for cost or expenses of, or incidental to, the removal of the wreck of the vessel named herein when such removal is compulsory by law, provided, however, that:**

   (a) There shall be deducted from such claim for cost or expenses, the value of any salvage from or which might have been recovered from the wreck, inuring, or which might have inured, to the benefit of the Assured.

   (b) The Assurer shall not be liable for such costs or expenses which would be covered by full insurance under the .... or claims arising out of hostilities or war-like operations, whether before or after declaration of war.

Cargo

(8) **Liability for loss of, or damage to, or in connection with cargo or other property, excluding mail and parcel post, including baggage and personal effects of passengers, to be carried, carried, or which has been carried on board the vessel named herein:**

Provided, however, that no liability shall exist under this provision for:

Specie, bullion, precious stones, etc.

   (a) Loss, damage or expense arising out of or in connection with the custody, care, carriage or delivery of specie, bullion, precious stones, precious metals, jewelry, silks, furs, bank notes, bonds or other negotiable documents or similar valuable property, unless specially agreed to and accepted for transportation under a form of contract approved, in writing, by the Assurer.

Refrigeration

   (b) Loss of, or damage to, or in connection with cargo requiring refrigeration unless the space, apparatus and means used for the care, custody, and carriage thereof have been surveyed by a classification surveyor or other competent disinterested surveyor under working conditions before the commencement of each voyage and found in all respects fit, and unless accepted for transportation under a form of contract approved, in writing, by the Assurer.

Passengers' effects

   (c) Loss, damage, or expense in connection with any passenger's baggage or personal effects, unless the form of ticket issued to the passenger shall have been approved, in writing, by the Assurer.

Stowage in improper places

   (d) Loss, damage, or expense arising from stowage of underdeck cargo on deck or stowage of cargo in spaces not suitable for its carriage, unless the Assured shall show that every reasonable precaution has been taken by him to prevent such improper stowage.

Deviation

   (e) Loss, damage, or expense arising from any deviation, or proposed deviation, not authorized by the contract of affreightment, known to the Assured in time to insure specifically the liability therefor, unless notice thereof is given to the Assurer and the Assurer agrees, in writing, that such insurance is unnecessary.

Freight on cargo short delivered

   (f) Freight on cargo short delivered, whether or not prepaid or whether or not included in the claim and paid by the Assured.

Misdescription of Goods

   (g) Loss, damage, or expense arising out of or as a result of the issuance of Bills of Lading which, to the knowledge of the Assured, improperly describe the goods or their containers as to condition or quantity.

Failure to surrender Bill of Lading

   (h) Loss, damage, or expense arising out of delivery of cargo without surrender of Bill of Lading.

And provided further that

   (aa) Liability hereunder shall in no event exceed that which would be imposed by law in the absence of contract.

Protective clauses required in contract of affreightment

   (bb) Liability hereunder shall be limited to such as would exist if the Charter Party, Bill of Lading or Contract of Affreightment contained the following clause (in substitution for the clause commonly known as the Jason Clause):

"In the event of accident, danger, damage or disaster before or after commencement of the voyage, resulting from any cause whatsoever, whether due to negligence or not, for which, or for the consequences of which, the shipowner is not responsible, by statute or contract or otherwise, the shippers, consignees or owners of the cargo shall contribute with the shipowner in general average to the payment of any sacrifices, losses or expenses of a general average nature that may be made or incurred, and shall pay salvage and special charges incurred in respect of the cargo."

When cargo is carried by the vessel named herein under a bill of lading or similar document of title subject or made subject to the Carriage of Goods by Sea Act, April 16, 1936, liability hereunder shall be limited to such as is imposed by said Act, and if the Assured or the vessel named herein assumes any greater liability or obligation than the minimum liabilities and obligations imposed by said Act, such greater liability or obligation shall not be covered hereunder.

Limit per package

When cargo is carried by the vessel named herein under a charter party, bill of lading or contract of affreightment not subject or made subject to the Carriage of Goods by Sea Act, April 16, 1936, liability hereunder shall be limited to such as would exist if said charter party, bill of lading, or contract of affreightment contained the following clauses: a clause limiting the Assured's liability for total loss or damage to goods shipped to Two Hundred and Fifty ($250) Dollars per package, or in case of goods not shipped in packages, per customary freight unit, and providing for pro rata adjustment on such basis for partial loss or damage; a clause exempting the Assured and the vessel named herein from liability for losses arising from unseaworthiness, even though existing at the beginning of the voyage, provided that due diligence shall have been exercised to make the vessel seaworthy and properly manned, equipped, and supplied; a clause providing that the carrier shall not be liable for claims in respect of cargo unless notice of claim is given within the time limited in such Bill of Lading and suit is brought thereon within the limited time prescribed therein; and such other protective clauses as are commonly in use in the particular trade; provided the incorporation of such clauses is not contrary to law.

The foregoing provisions as to the contents of the Bill of Lading and the limitation of the Assurer's liability may, however, be waived or altered by the Assurers on terms agreed, in writing.

Assured's own cargo

   (cc) Where cargo on board the vessel named herein is the property of the Assured, such cargo shall be deemed to be carried under a contract containing the protective clauses described in the preceding paragraph, and such cargo shall be deemed to be fully insured under the usual form of cargo policy, and in case of loss thereof or damage thereto the Assured shall be insured hereunder in respect of such loss or damage only to the extent that they would have been covered if said cargo had belonged to another, but only in the event and to the extent that the loss or damage would not be recoverable under a cargo policy as hereinbefore specified.

Cotton Bills of Lading

   (dd) The Assured's liability for claims under Custody Cotton Bills of Lading issued under the conditions laid down by the Liverpool Bill of Lading Conference Committee, is covered subject to previous notice of contract and payment of an extra premium of two (2¢) cents per bale per voyage, but such additional premium shall be waived provided every bale is re-marked at port of shipment on another portion of the bale.

Land transportation not included

   (ee) No liability shall exist hereunder for any loss, damage or expense in respect of cargo or other property being transported on land or on another vessel.

No liability shall exist hereunder for any loss, damage or expense in respect of cargo before loading on or after discharge from the vessel named herein caused by flood, tide, windstorm, earthquake, fire, explosion, heat, cold, deterioration, collapse of wharf, leaky steel, theft or pilferage unless such loss, damage or expense is caused directly by the vessel named herein, her master, officers or crew.

Customs, immigration or other fines or penalties

(9) **Liability for fines and penalties, including expenses necessarily and reasonably incurred in avoiding or mitigating same, for the violation of any of the laws of the United States, or of any State thereof, or of any foreign country; provided, however, that the Assurer shall not be liable to indemnify the Assured against any such fines or penalties resulting directly or indirectly from the failure, neglect, or default of the Assured or his managing officers or managing agents to exercise the highest degree of diligence to prevent a violation of any such laws.**

Mutiny or other misconduct

(10) Expenses incurred in resisting any unfounded claim by the master or crew or other persons employed on the vessel named herein, or in prosecuting such persons in case of mutiny or other misconduct.

Extraordinary expenses in case of quarantine, etc.

(11) Liability for extraordinary expenses resulting from outbreak of plague or other contagious disease, including such expenses incurred for disinfection of the vessel named herein or persons on board, or for quarantine, but excluding the ordinary expenses of loading and/or discharging, and the wages and provisions of crew and passengers; each claim under this provision is subject to a deduction of Two Hundred ($200) Dollars. It is provided further, however, that if the vessel named herein be ordered to proceed to a port when it is or should be known that calling there will subject the vessel to the extraordinary expenses above mentioned, or to quarantine or disinfection there or elsewhere, the Assurer shall be under no obligation to indemnify the Assured for any such expenses.

Deviation for purpose of landing injured or ill

(12) Net loss due to deviation incurred solely for the purpose of landing an injured or sick seaman in respect of port charges incurred, insurance, bunkers, stores, and provisions consumed as a result of the deviation.

Cargo's proportion of general average

(13) Liability for, or loss of, cargo's proportion of general average, including special charges, in so far as the Assured cannot recover same from any other source; subject however, to the exclusions of Section (8) and provided, that if the Charter Party, Bill of Lading, or Contract of Affreightment does not contain the quoted clause under Section 8 (bb) the Assurer's liability hereunder shall be limited to such as would exist if such clause were contained therein.

Costs and charges

(14) Costs, charges, and expenses, reasonably incurred and paid by the Assured in defense against any liabilities insured against hereunder in respect of the vessel named herein, subject to the agreed deductibles applicable, and subject further to the conditions and limitations hereinafter provided.

GENERAL CONDITIONS AND/OR LIMITATIONS

Prompt notice of claim

Warranted that in the event of any occurrence which may result in loss, damage and/or expense for which this Assurer is or may become liable, the Assured will use due diligence to give prompt notice thereof and forward to the Assurer as soon as practicable after receipt thereof, all communications, processes, pleadings and other legal papers or documents relating to such occurrences.

Settlement of claims

The Assured shall not make any admission of liability, either before or after any occurrence which may result in a claim for which the Assurer may be liable. The Assured shall not interfere in any negotiations of the Assurer, for settlement of any legal proceedings in respect of any occurrences for which the Assurer is liable under this policy; provided, however, that in respect of any occurrence likely to give rise to a claim under this policy, the Assured are obligated to and shall take steps to protect their (and/or the Assurer's) interests as would reasonably be taken in the absence of this or similar insurance. If the Assured shall fail or refuse to settle any claim as authorized by Assurer, the liability of the Assurer to the Assured shall be limited to the amount for which settlement could have been made.

Assured to assist with evidence in defense, etc.

Whenever required by the Assurer the Assured shall aid in securing information and evidence and in obtaining witnesses and shall cooperate with the Assurer in the defense of any claim or suit or in the appeal from any judgment, in respect of any occurrence as hereinbefore provided.

Law costs

The Assurer shall not be liable for the cost or expense of prosecuting or defending any claim or suit unless the same shall have been incurred with the written consent of the Assurer, or the Assurer shall be satisfied that such approval could not have been obtained under the circumstances without unreasonable delay, or that such costs and charges were reasonably and properly incurred, such cost or expense being subject to the deductible. The cost and expense of prosecuting any claim in which the Assurer shall have an interest by subrogation or otherwise, shall be divided between the Assured and the Assurer, proportionately to the amounts which they would be entitled to receive respectively, if the suit should be successful.

The Assurer shall be liable for the excess where the amount deductible under this policy is exceeded by (A) the cost of investigating and/or successfully defending any claim or suit against the Assured based on a liability or an alleged liability of the Assured covered by this insurance, or (B) the amount paid by the Assured either under a judgment or an agreed settlement based on the liability covered herein including all costs, expenses of defense and taxable disbursements.

Subrogation

The Assurer shall be subrogated to all the rights which the Assured may have against any other person or entity, in respect of any payment made under this policy, to the extent of such payment, and the Assured shall, upon the request of the Assurer, execute all documents necessary to secure to the Assurer such rights.

The Assurer shall be entitled to take credit for any profit accruing to the Assured by reason of any negligence or wrongful act of the Assured's servants or agents, up to the measure of their loss, or to recover for their own account from third parties any damage that may be provable by reason of such negligence or wrongful act.

Cover elsewhere

Provided that where the Assured is, irrespective of this insurance, covered or protected against any loss or claim which would otherwise have been paid by the Assurer, under this policy, there shall be no contribution by the Assurer on the basis of double insurance or otherwise.

Assignments

No claim or demand against the Assurer under this policy shall be assigned or transferred, and no person, excepting a legally appointed receiver of the property of the Assured, shall acquire any right against the Assurer by virtue of this insurance without the expressed consent of the Assurer.

Actions against Assurers

No action shall lie against the Assurer for the recovery of any loss sustained by the Assured unless such action is brought against the Assurer within one year after the final judgment or decree is entered in the litigation against the Assured, or in case the claim against the Assurer accrues without the entry of such final judgment or decree, unless such action is brought within one year from the date of the payment of such claim.

Time limitation

The Assurer shall not be liable for any claim not presented to the Assurer with proper proofs of loss within six (6) months after payment thereof by the Assured.

Lay-up returns

At the expiration of this policy, the Assurer is to return.................... for each thirty (30) consecutive days during the term of this insurance the vessel may be laid up in a safe port; or .... for each thirty (30) consecutive days during the term of this insurance the vessel may be laid up in a safe port without loading and/or discharging and without crew or cargo on board, provided the Assured give written notice to the Assurer as soon as practicable after the commencement and the termination of such lay-up period.

Cancellation provisions:

(a) If the vessel named herein should be sold or requisitioned and this policy be cancelled and surrendered, the Assurer to return................. for each thirty (30) consecutive days of the unexpired term of this insurance.

(b) In the event of non-payment of premium within sixty (60) days after attachment, this policy may be cancelled by the Assurer upon five (5) days' written notice being given the Assured.

(c) In the event that Sections 182 to 189, both inclusive, of U. S. Code, Title 46, or any other existing law or laws determining or limiting liability of shipowners and carriers, or any of them, shall, while this policy is in force, be modified, amended or repealed, or the liabilities of shipowners or carriers be increased in any respect by legislative enactment, the Assurer shall have the right to cancel said insurance upon giving thirty (30) days' written notice of their intention so to do, and in the event of such cancellation, make return of premium upon a pro rata daily basis.

Notwithstanding anything to the contrary contained in this policy, no liability attaches to the Assurer:

For any loss, damage, or expense which would be payable under the terms of the .... form of policy on hull and machinery, etc., if the vessel were fully covered by such insurance sufficient in amount to pay such loss, damage, or expense.

For any loss, damage or expense sustained by reason of capture, seizure, arrest, restraint or detainment, or the consequence thereof or of any attempt thereat; or sustained in consequence of military, naval or air action by force of arms, including mines and torpedoes or other missiles or engines of war, whether of enemy or friendly origin; or sustained in consequence of placing the vessel in jeopardy as an act or measure of war taken in the actual process of a military engagement, including embarking or disembarking troops or material of war in the immediate zone of such engagement; and any such loss, damage and expense shall be excluded from this policy without regard to whether The Assured's liability thereof is based on negligence or otherwise, and whether before or after a declaration of war.

For any loss, damage, or expense arising from the cancellation or breach of any charter, bad debts, fraud of agents, insolvency, loss of freight hire or demurrage, or as a result of the breach of any undertaking to load any cargo, or in respect of the vessel named herein engaging in any unlawful trade or performing any unlawful act, with the knowledge of the Assured.

For any loss, damage, expense, or claim arising out of or having relation to the towage of any other vessel or craft, whether under agreement or not, unless such towage was to assist such other vessel or craft in distress to a port or place of safety, provided, however, that this clause shall not apply to claims under this policy for loss of life or personal injury to passengers and/or members of the crew of the vessel named herein arising as a result of towing.

For any claim for loss of life or personal injury in relation to the handling of cargo where such claim arises under a contract of indemnity between the Assured and his sub-contractor.

It is expressly understood and agreed if and when the Assured under this policy has any interest other than as a shipowner in the vessel or vessels named herein, in no event shall the Assurer be liable hereunder to any greater extent than if such Assured were the owner and were entitled to all the rights of limitation to which a shipowner is entitled.

Unless otherwise agreed by endorsement to this policy, liability hereunder shall in no event exceed that which would be imposed on the Assured by law in the absence of contract.

Liability hereunder in respect of any one accident or occurrence is limited to the amount hereby insured.

Attached to and forming part of Policy No.   of

Appendix 25

PROTECTION AND INDEMNITY CLAUSES

1 Assured

2

3 Address

4

5 Loss, if any, payable to

6

7 From the _____ day of _____ 19___ Beginning and ending
8 Until the _____ day of _____ 19___ at noon Standard Time at place of issuance.

9 Amount hereby insured $_____ Rate_____ % Premium $_____

10 In consideration of the premium and subject to the warranties, terms and conditions herein mentioned, this Com-
11 pany hereby undertakes to pay up to the amount hereby insured and in conformity with lines 5 and 6 hereof,
12 such sums as the assured, as owner of the
13 shall have become legally liable to pay and shall have paid on account of:

14   Loss of life of, or injury to, or illness of, any person;

15   Hospital, medical, or other expenses necessarily and reasonably incurred in respect of loss of life of, in-
16 jury to, or illness of any member of the crew of the vessel named herein;

17   Loss of, or damage to, or expense in connection with any fixed or movable object or property of whatever
18 nature;

19   Costs or expenses of, or incidental to, the removal of the wreck of the vessel named herein when such
20 removal is compulsory by law; provided, however, that there shall be deducted from such claim the value
21 of any salvage recovered from the wreck by the assured;

22   Fines and penalties, including expenses reasonably incurred in attempting to obtain the remission or mitiga-
23 tion of same, for the violation of any of the laws of the United States, or of any state thereof, or of any
24 foreign country; provided, however, that this Company shall not be liable to indemnify the assured against
25 any such fines or penalties resulting directly or indirectly from the failure, neglect, or default of the as-
26 sured or his managing officers or managing agents to exercise the highest degree of diligence to prevent a
27 violation of any such laws;

28   Costs and expenses, incurred with this Company's approval, of investigating and/or defending any claim
29 or suit against the assured arising out of a liability or an alleged liability of the assured covered by this
30 policy.

31 Notwithstanding the foregoing this Company will not pay for:

32   The first $ of claims covered by lines 14, 15, 16, 28, 29 and 30 nor for the first $
33 of claims covered by any other parts of this policy, but, in no event shall the deductible exceed $
34 each occurrence. (For the purpose of this clause, each occurrence shall be treated separately, but a series
35 of claims hereunder arising from the same occurrence shall be treated as due to that occurrence.)

36   Loss of, or damage sustained by the vessel named herein or her tackle, apparel, furniture, boats, fittings,
37 equipment, stores, fuel, provisions or appurtenances;

38   Loss resulting from cancellation of charters, non-collectibility of freight, bad debts, insolvency of agents
39 or others, salvage, general average, detention, loss of use or demurrage of the vessel named herein;

40   Any loss, damage, expense or claim with respect to any vessel or craft in tow of the vessel named herein
41 and/or cargo thereon; provided this exclusion shall not apply to salvage services rendered in an emergency
42 to a ship or vessel in distress, nor to loss of life and/or injury to, or illness of any person;

43   Any claim for loss of, damage to, or expense in respect of cargo on board the vessel named herein;

44   Any claim arising directly or indirectly under the Longshoremen's and Harbor Workers' Compensation
45 Act or any workmen's compensation act of any state or nation;

46   Any liability assumed by the assured beyond that imposed by law; provided however that if by agree-
47 ment, or otherwise, the assured's legal liability is lessened, then this Company shall receive the benefit of
48 such lessened liability.

49   Any loss, damage or expense sustained by reason of any taking of the vessel by requisition or other-
50 wise, civil war, revolution, rebellion, or insurrection, or civil strife arising therefrom, capture, seizure,
51 arrest, restraint or detainment, or the consequences thereof or of any attempt thereat; or sustained in con-
52 sequence of military, naval or air action by force of arms; or sustained or caused by mines or torpedoes or
53 other missiles or engines of war, whether of enemy or friendly origin; or sustained or caused by any weapon

54 of war employing atomic fission or atomic fusion or radioactive material; or sustained in consequence of
55 placing the vessel in jeopardy as an act or measure of war taken in the actual process of a military engage-
56 ment, including embarking or disembarking troops or material of war in the immediate zone of such engage-
57 ment; and any such loss, damage and expense shall be excluded from this policy without regard to whether
58 the assured's liability in respect thereof is based on negligence or otherwise, and whether in time of peace
59 or war.

60 Any loss, damage, expense or claim collectible under the
61 form of policy, whether or not the vessel named herein is actually covered by such insurance and regardless
62 of the amount thereof.

63 Warranted that in the event of any occurrence which could result in a claim under this policy the assured
64 promptly will notify this Company upon receiving notice thereof and forward to this Company as soon
65 as practicable all communications, processes, pleadings or other legal papers or documents relating to such oc-
66 currence.

67 Whenever required by this Company, the assured shall aid in securing information and evidence and in obtaining
68 witnesses and shall cooperate with this Company in the defense of any claim or suit or in the appeal from any
69 judgment.

70 This Company shall have the option of naming the attorneys who shall represent the assured in the prosecution
71 or defense of any litigation or negotiations between the assured and third parties concerning any claim covered
72 by this policy, and shall have the direction of such litigation or negotiations. If the assured shall fail or refuse
73 to settle any claim as authorized by this Company, the liability of this Company shall be limited to the
74 amount for which settlement could have been made. The assured shall at the option of this Company
75 permit this Company to conduct, with an attorney of this Company's selection, at this Company's cost and expense
76 and under its exclusive control, a proceeding in the assured's name to limit the assured's liability to the extent,
77 and in the manner provided by the present and any future statutes relative to the limitation of a shipowner's
78 liability.

79 Liability hereunder in respect of loss, damage, costs, fees, expenses or claims arising out of or in consequence of
80 any one occurrence is limited to the amount hereby insured. (For the purpose of this clause each occurrence
81 shall be treated separately, but a series of claims hereunder arising from the same occurrence shall be treated
82 as due to that occurrence.)

83 The assured shall not make any admission of liability, either before or after any occurrence which could
84 result in a claim for which this Company may be liable. The assured shall not interfere in any negotia-
85 tions of this Company, for settlement of any legal proceedings in respect of any occurrence for which this
86 Company may be liable under this policy; provided, however, that in respect of any occurrence likely to give rise
87 to a claim under this policy, the assured is obligated to and shall take such steps to protect his and/or the
88 Company's interests as would reasonably be taken in the absence of this or similar insurance.

89 Upon making payment under this policy this Company shall be vested with all of the assured's rights of recovery
90 against any person, corporation, vessel or interest and the assured shall execute and deliver such instruments
91 and papers as this Company shall require and do whatever else is necessary to secure such rights.

92 No action shall lie against this Company for the recovery of any loss sustained by the assured unless such
93 action is brought within one year after the entry of any final judgment or decree in any litigation against the
94 assured, or in the event of a claim without the entry of such final judgment or decree, unless such action is
95 brought within one year from the date of the payment of such claim.

96 No claim or demand against this Company under this policy shall be assigned or transferred, and no person
97 shall acquire any right against this Company by virtue of this insurance without the express consent of this
98 Company.

99 It is expressly understood and agreed if and when the assured has any interest other than as a shipowner in
100 the vessel named herein, in no event shall this Company be liable hereunder to any greater extent than if the
101 assured were the sole owner and entitled to petition for limitation of liability in accordance with present and
102 future law.

103 Where the assured is, irrespective of this policy, covered or protected against any loss or claim which would
104 otherwise have been paid by this Company, under this policy, there shall be no contribution or participation by
105 this Company on the basis of excess, contributing, deficiency, concurrent, or double insurance or otherwise.

106 The navigation limits in the policy covering the hull, machinery, etc. of the vessel named herein are considered
107 incorporated herein.

108 This insurance shall be void in case the vessel named herein, or any part thereof, shall be sold, transferred or
109 mortgaged, or if there be any change of management or charter of the vessel, or if this policy be assigned or
110 pledged, without the previous consent in writing of this Company.

111 Either party may cancel this policy by giving ten days' notice in writing; if at the option of this Company
112 pro rata rates, if at the request of the assured short rates, will be charged—and arrival.

———————

113   SPECIAL CONDITIONS — WARRANTIES — ENDORSEMENTS, ETC.

114 Attached to and made part of Policy No.   of the

Appendix 26

AMERICAN HULL INSURANCE SYNDICATE
WAR RISK PROTECTION & INDEMNITY CLAUSES
JANUARY 18, 1970

To be attached to and form a part of Policy No. _____ of _____

_____

Insuring _____

_____

A. This insurance is also to cover the liability of the assured for Protection and Indemnity Risks excluded from Marine Protection and Indemnity Policies commonly issued by stock insurance companies in the United States by the following or a substantially similar F. C. & S. Clause:

   "Notwithstanding anything to the contrary contained in this policy, no liability attaches to the company, directly or indirectly, for or in respect of any loss, damage or expense sustained by reason of any taking of the vessel by requisition or otherwise, civil war, revolution, rebellion, or insurrection, or civil strife arising therefrom, capture, seizure, arrest, restraint or detainment, or the consequences thereof or of any attempt thereat; or sustained in consequence of military, naval or air action by force of arms, including mines and torpedoes or other missiles or engines of war, whether of enemy or friendly origin; or sustained in consequence of placing the vessel in jeopardy as an act or measure of war taken in the actual process of a military engagement, including embarking or disembarking troops or material of war in the immediate zone of such engagement; and any such loss, damage and expense shall be excluded from this policy without regard to whether the Assured's liability therefor is based on negligence or otherwise, and whether before or after a declaration of war."

B. This insurance includes liability of the assured arising out of strikes, riots and civil commotions and for contractual repatriation expenses of any member of the crew as a result of perils excluded by the aforesaid F.C.&S. Clause.

C. The Underwriters agree to accept the same percentage interest under these clauses as accepted under the Hull War Risks and Strikes Clauses.

D. The liability of the Underwriters under these clauses in respect of any one accident or series of accidents arising out of the same casualty shall be limited to the Amount Insured Hereunder.

E. Claims for which the Underwriters shall be liable under these clauses shall not be subject to any deduction.

F. This Protection and Indemnity Insurance shall terminate automatically at the same time as the insurance afforded by the Hull War Risks and Strikes Clauses and upon the terms and conditions contained in the Automatic Termination and Cancellation provisions of said Clauses.

G. Notwithstanding the provisions of Clause F, in the event of loss or shipwreck of the vessel from any cause prior to the natural expiry time or automatic termination of this policy, this insurance shall continue to cover the liability of the assured to the crew of the insured vessel, subject to its terms and conditions and at an additional premium if so required by Underwriters, until the crew shall be either discharged or landed at a port or place to which the owners or charterers are obliged to bring them.

H. Notwithstanding any of the foregoing provisions all liabilities covered by the Second Seamen's form of policy are excluded from this insurance.

All other terms and conditions remaining unchanged.

Dated _____   Signed _____

Appendix 27

1/10/83   (FOR USE ONLY WITH THE NEW MARINE POLICY FORM)

INSTITUTE TIME CLAUSES
HULLS

This insurance is subject to English law and practice

1 **NAVIGATION**   1

    1.1   The Vessel is covered subject to the provisions of this insurance at all times and has leave to sail or   2
navigate with or without pilots, to go on trial trips and to assist and tow vessels or craft in distress, but it   3
is warranted that the Vessel shall not be towed, except as is customary or to the first safe port or place   4
when in need of assistance, or undertake towage or salvage services under a contract previously arranged   5
by the Assured and/or Owners and/or Managers and/or Charterers. This Clause 1.1 shall not exclude   6
customary towage in connection with loading and discharging.   7

    1.2   In the event of the Vessel being employed in trading operations which entail cargo loading or discharging   8
at sea from or into another vessel (not being a harbour or inshore craft) no claim shall be recoverable   9
under this insurance for loss of or damage to the Vessel or liability to any other vessel arising from such   10
loading or discharging operations, including whilst approaching, lying alongside and leaving, unless   11
previous notice that the Vessel is to be employed in such operations has been given to the Underwriters   12
and any amended terms of cover and any additional premium required by them have been agreed.   13

    1.3   In the event of the Vessel sailing (with or without cargo) with an intention of being (a) broken up, or (b)   14
sold for breaking up, any claim for loss of or damage to the Vessel occurring subsequent to such sailing   15
shall be limited to the market value of the Vessel as scrap at the time when the loss or damage is sustained,   16
unless previous notice has been given to the Underwriters and any amendments to the terms of cover,   17
insured value and premium required by them have been agreed. Nothing in this Clause 1.3 shall affect   18
claims under Clauses 8 and/or 11.   19

2 **CONTINUATION**   20

Should the Vessel at the expiration of this insurance be at sea or in distress or at a port of refuge or of call, she   21
shall, provided previous notice be given to the Underwriters, be held covered at a pro rata monthly premium to her   22
port of destination.   23

3 **BREACH OF WARRANTY**   24

Held covered in case of any breach of warranty as to cargo, trade, locality, towage, salvage services or date of   25
sailing, provided notice be given to the Underwriters immediately after receipt of advices and any amended terms   26
of cover and any additional premium required by them be agreed.   27

4 **TERMINATION**   28

This Clause 4 shall prevail notwithstanding any provision whether written typed or printed in this insurance   29
inconsistent therewith.   30

Unless the Underwriters agree to the contrary in writing, this insurance shall terminate automatically at the time of   31

    4.1   change of the Classification Society of the Vessel, or change, suspension, discontinuance, withdrawal or   32
expiry of her Class therein, provided that if the Vessel is at sea such automatic termination shall be   33
deferred until arrival at her next port. However where such change, suspension, discontinuance or   34
withdrawal of her Class has resulted from loss or damage covered by Clause 6 of this insurance or which   35
would be covered by an insurance of the Vessel subject to current Institute War and Strikes Clauses Hulls-   36
Time such automatic termination shall only operate should the Vessel sail from her next port without the   37
prior approval of the Classification Society,   38

    4.2   any change, voluntary or otherwise, in the ownership or flag, transfer to new management, or charter on   39
a bareboat basis, or requisition for title or use of the Vessel, provided that, if the Vessel has cargo on   40
board and has already sailed from her loading port or is at sea in ballast, such automatic termination shall   41
if required be deferred, whilst the Vessel continues her planned voyage, until arrival at final port of   42
discharge if with cargo or at port of destination if in ballast. However, in the event of requisition for title   43

or use without the prior execution of a written agreement by the Assured, such automatic termination 44
shall occur fifteen days after such requisition whether the Vessel is at sea or in port. 45

A pro rata daily net return of premium shall be made. 46

5 ASSIGNMENT 47

No assignment of or interest in this insurance or in any moneys which may be or become payable thereunder is to 48
be binding on or recognised by the Underwriters unless a dated notice of such assignment or interest signed by the 49
Assured, and by the assignor in the case of subsequent assignment, is endorsed on the Policy and the Policy with 50
such endorsement is produced before payment of any claim or return of premium thereunder. 51

6 PERILS 52

6.1   This insurance covers loss of or damage to the subject-matter insured caused by 53

6.1.1   perils of the seas rivers lakes or other navigable waters 54

6.1.2   fire, explosion 55

6.1.3   violent theft by persons from outside the Vessel 56

6.1.4   jettison 57

6.1.5   piracy 58

6.1.6   breakdown of or accident to nuclear installations or reactors 59

6.1.7   contact with aircraft or similar objects, or objects falling therefrom, land conveyance, dock or 60
             harbour equipment or installation 61

6.1.8   earthquake volcanic eruption or lightning. 62

6.2   This insurance covers loss of or damage to the subject-matter insured caused by 63

6.2.1   accidents in loading discharging or shifting cargo or fuel 64

6.2.2   bursting of boilers breakage of shafts or any latent defect in the machinery or hull 65

6.2.3   negligence of Master Officers Crew or Pilots 66

6.2.4   negligence of repairers or charterers provided such repairers or charterers are not an Assured hereunder 67

6.2.5   barratry of Master Officers or Crew, 68

             provided such loss or damage has not resulted from want of due diligence by the Assured, Owners or 69
             Managers. 70

6.3   Master Officers Crew or Pilots not to be considered Owners within the meaning of this Clause 6 should 71
       they hold shares in the Vessel. 72

7 POLLUTION HAZARD 73

This insurance covers loss of or damage to the Vessel caused by any governmental authority acting under the 74
powers vested in it to prevent or mitigate a pollution hazard, or threat thereof, resulting directly from damage to 75
the Vessel for which the Underwriters are liable under this insurance, provided such act of governmental authority 76
has not resulted from want of due diligence by the Assured, the Owners, or Managers of the Vessel or any of them 77
to prevent or mitigate such hazard or threat. Master, Officers, Crew or Pilots not to be considered Owners within 78
the meaning of this Clause 7 should they hold shares in the Vessel. 79

8 3/4THS COLLISION LIABILITY 80

8.1   The Underwriters agree to indemnify the Assured for three-fourths of any sum or sums paid by the 81
       Assured to any other person or persons by reason of the Assured becoming legally liable by way of 82
       damages for 83

8.1.1   loss of or damage to any other vessel or property on any other vessel 84

8.1.2   delay to or loss of use of any such other vessel or property thereon 85

8.1.3   general average of, salvage of, or salvage under contract of, any such other vessel or property 86
             thereon, 87

             where such payment by the Assured is in consequence of the Vessel hereby insured coming into collision 88
             with any other vessel. 89

8.2   The indemnity provided by this Clause 8 shall be in addition to the indemnity provided by the other terms 90
       and conditions of this insurance and shall be subject to the following provisions: 91

8.2.1   Where the insured Vessel is in collision with another vessel and both vessels are to blame then, unless 92
             the liability of one or both vessels becomes limited by law, the indemnity under this Clause 8 shall be 93
             calculated on the principle of cross-liabilities as if the respective Owners had been compelled to pay 94
             to each other such proportion of each other's damages as may have been properly allowed in 95
             ascertaining the balance or sum payable by or to the Assured in consequence of the collision. 96

8.2.2   In no case shall the Underwriters' total liability under Clauses 8.1 and 8.2 exceed their proportionate 97
             part of three-fourths of the insured value of the Vessel hereby insured in respect of any one collision. 98

8.3   The Underwriters will also pay three-fourths of the legal costs incurred by the Assured or which the 99
       Assured may be compelled to pay in contesting liability or taking proceedings to limit liability, with the 100
       prior written consent of the Underwriters. 101

EXCLUSIONS   102
8.4 Provided always that this Clause 8 shall in no case extend to any sum which the Assured shall pay for or in 103
respect of 104

8.4.1 removal or disposal of obstructions, wrecks, cargoes or any other thing whatsoever 105

8.4.2 any real or personal property or thing whatsoever except other vessels or property on other vessels 106

8.4.3 the cargo or other property on, or the engagements of, the insured Vessel 107

8.4.4 loss of life, personal injury or illness 108

8.4.5 pollution or contamination of any real or personal property or thing whatsoever (except other 109
  vessels with which the insured Vessel is in collision or property on such other vessels). 110

9 SISTERSHIP 111

Should the Vessel hereby insured come into collision with or receive salvage services from another vessel belonging 112
wholly or in part to the same Owners or under the same management, the Assured shall have the same rights under 113
this insurance as they would have were the other vessel entirely the property of Owners not interested in the Vessel 114
hereby insured; but in such cases the liability for the collision or the amount payable for the services rendered shall 115
be referred to a sole arbitrator to be agreed upon between the Underwriters and the Assured. 116

10 NOTICE OF CLAIM AND TENDERS 117

10.1 In the event of accident whereby loss or damage may result in a claim under this insurance, notice shall be 118
given to the Underwriters prior to survey and also, if the Vessel is abroad, to the nearest Lloyd's Agent so 119
that a surveyor may be appointed to represent the Underwriters should they so desire. 120

10.2 The Underwriters shall be entitled to decide the port to which the Vessel shall proceed for docking or 121
repair (the actual additional expense of the voyage arising from compliance with the Underwriters' 122
requirements being refunded to the Assured) and shall have a right of veto concerning a place of repair or 123
a repairing firm. 124

10.3 The Underwriters may also take tenders or may require further tenders to be taken for the repair of the 125
Vessel. Where such a tender has been taken and a tender is accepted with the approval of the 126
Underwriters, an allowance shall be made at the rate of 30% per annum on the insured value for time lost 127
between the despatch of the invitations to tender required by Underwriters and the acceptance of a tender 128
to the extent that such time is lost solely as the result of tenders having been taken and provided that the 129
tender is accepted without delay after receipt of the Underwriters' approval. 130

Due credit shall be given against the allowance as above for any amounts recovered in respect of fuel and 131
stores and wages and maintenance of the Master Officers and Crew or any member thereof, including 132
amounts allowed in general average, and for any amounts recovered from third parties in respect of 133
damages for detention and/or loss of profit and/or running expenses, for the period covered by the 134
tender allowance or any part thereof. 135

Where a part of the cost of the repair of damage other than a fixed deductible is not recoverable from the 136
Underwriters the allowance shall be reduced by a similar proportion. 137

10.4 In the event of failure to comply with the conditions of this Clause 10 a deduction of 15% shall be made 138
from the amount of the ascertained claim. 139

11 GENERAL AVERAGE AND SALVAGE 140

11.1 This insurance covers the Vessel's proportion of salvage, salvage charges and/or general average, reduced 141
in respect of any under-insurance, but in case of general average sacrifice of the Vessel the Assured may 142
recover in respect of the whole loss without first enforcing their right of contribution from other parties. 143

11.2 Adjustment to be according to the law and practice obtaining at the place where the adventure ends, as if 144
the contract of affreightment contained no special terms upon the subject; but where the contract of 145
affreightment so provides the adjustment shall be according to the York-Antwerp Rules. 146

11.3 When the Vessel sails in ballast, not under charter, the provisions of the York-Antwerp Rules, 1974 147
(excluding Rules XX and XXI) shall be applicable, and the voyage for this purpose shall be deemed to 148
continue from the port or place of departure until the arrival of the Vessel at the first port or place 149
thereafter other than a port or place of refuge or a port or place of call for bunkering only. If at any such 150
intermediate port or place there is an abandonment of the adventure originally contemplated the voyage 151
shall thereupon be deemed to be terminated. 152

11.4 No claim under this Clause 11 shall in any case be allowed where the loss was not incurred to avoid or in 153
connection with the avoidance of a peril insured against. 154

12 DEDUCTIBLE 155

12.1 No claim arising from a peril insured against shall be payable under this insurance unless the aggregate of 156
all such claims arising out of each separate accident or occurrence (including claims under Clauses 8, 11 157

and 13) exceeds ....in which case this sum shall be 158
deducted. Nevertheless the expense of sighting the bottom after stranding, if reasonably incurred 159
specially for that purpose, shall be paid even if no damage be found. This Clause 12.1 shall not apply to a 160
claim for total or constructive total loss of the Vessel or, in the event of such a claim, to any associated 161
claim under Clause 13 arising from the same accident or occurrence. 162

12.2 Claims for damage by heavy weather occurring during a single sea passage between two successive ports 163
shall be treated as being due to one accident. In the case of such heavy weather extending over a period 164
not wholly covered by this insurance the deductible to be applied to the claim recoverable hereunder shall 165
be the proportion of the above deductible that the number of days of such heavy weather falling within 166
the period of this insurance bears to the number of days of heavy weather during the single sea passage. 167

1344 ENGLISH FORMS

The expression "heavy weather" in this Clause 12.2 shall be deemed to include contact with floating ice. 168

12.3 Excluding any interest comprised therein, recoveries against any claim which is subject to the above 169
deductible shall be credited to the Underwriters in full to the extent of the sum by which the aggregate of 170
the claim unreduced by any recoveries exceeds the above deductible. 171

12.4 Interest comprised in recoveries shall be apportioned between the Assured and the Underwriters, taking 172
into account the sums paid by the Underwriters and the dates when such payments were made, 173
notwithstanding that by the addition of interest the Underwriters may receive a larger sum than they have 174
paid. 175

13 DUTY OF ASSURED (SUE AND LABOUR)   176

13.1 In case of any loss or misfortune it is the duty of the Assured and their servants and agents to take such 177
measures as may be reasonable for the purpose of averting or minimising a loss which would be 178
recoverable under this insurance. 179

13.2 Subject to the provisions below and to Clause 12 the Underwriters will contribute to charges properly and 180
reasonably incurred by the Assured their servants or agents for such measures. General average, salvage 181
charges (except as provided for in Clause 13.5) and collision defence or attack costs are not recoverable 182
under this Clause 13. 183

13.3 Measures taken by the Assured or the Underwriters with the object of saving, protecting or recovering the 184
subject-matter insured shall not be considered as a waiver or acceptance of abandonment or otherwise 185
prejudice the rights of either party. 186

13.4 When expenses are incurred pursuant to this Clause 13 the liability under this insurance shall not exceed 187
the proportion of such expenses that the amount insured hereunder bears to the value of the Vessel as 188
stated herein, or to the sound value of the Vessel at the time of the occurrence giving rise to the expenditure 189
if the sound value exceeds that value. Where the Underwriters have admitted a claim for total loss and 190
property insured by this insurance is saved, the foregoing provisions shall not apply unless the expenses of 191
suing and labouring exceed the value of such property saved and then shall apply only to the amount of 192
the expenses which is in excess of such value. 193

13.5 When a claim for total loss of the Vessel is admitted under this insurance and expenses have been 194
reasonably incurred in saving or attempting to save the Vessel and other property and there are no 195
proceeds, or the expenses exceed the proceeds, then this insurance shall bear its pro rata share of such 196
proportion of the expenses, or of the expenses in excess of the proceeds, as the case may be, as may 197
reasonably be regarded as having been incurred in respect of the Vessel; but if the Vessel be insured for 198
less than its sound value at the time of the occurrence giving rise to the expenditure, the amount 199
recoverable under this clause shall be reduced in proportion to the under-insurance. 200

13.6 The sum recoverable under this Clause 13 shall be in addition to the loss otherwise recoverable under this 201
insurance but shall in no circumstances exceed the amount insured under this insurance in respect of the 202
Vessel. 203

14 NEW FOR OLD   204
Claims payable without deduction new for old. 205

15 BOTTOM TREATMENT   206
In no case shall a claim be allowed in respect of scraping gritblasting and/or other surface preparation or painting 207
of the Vessel's bottom except that 208

15.1 gritblasting and/or other surface preparation of new bottom plates ashore and supplying and applying 209
any "shop" primer thereto, 210

15.2 gritblasting and/or other surface preparation of: 211
the butts or area of plating immediately adjacent to any renewed or refitted plating damaged during the 212
course of welding and/or repairs, 213
areas of plating damaged during the course of fairing, either in place or ashore, 214

15.3 supplying and applying the first coat of primer/anti-corrosive to those particular areas mentioned in 15.1 215
and 15.2 above, 216

shall be allowed as part of the reasonable cost of repairs in respect of bottom plating damaged by an insured peril. 217

16 WAGES AND MAINTENANCE   218
No claim shall be allowed, other than in general average, for wages and maintenance of the Master, Officers and 219
Crew, or any member thereof, except when incurred solely for the necessary removal of the Vessel from one port 220
to another for the repair of damage covered by the Underwriters, or for trial trips for such repairs, and then only 221
for such wages and maintenance as are incurred whilst the Vessel is under way. 222

17 AGENCY COMMISSION   223
In no case shall any sum be allowed under this insurance either by way of remuneration of the Assured for time 224
and trouble taken to obtain and supply information or documents or in respect of the commission or charges of 225
any manager, agent, managing or agency company or the like, appointed by or on behalf of the Assured to 226
perform such services. 227

18 UNREPAIRED DAMAGE   228
18.1 The measure of indemnity in respect of claims for unrepaired damage shall be the reasonable depreciation 229
in the market value of the Vessel at the time this insurance terminates arising from such unrepaired 230
damage, but not exceeding the reasonable cost of repairs. 231

18.2	In no case shall the Underwriters be liable for unrepaired damage in the event of a subsequent total loss (whether or not covered under this insurance) sustained during the period covered by this insurance or any extension thereof.	232 233 234
18.3	The Underwriters shall not be liable in respect of unrepaired damage for more than the insured value at the time this insurance terminates.	235 236

19 CONSTRUCTIVE TOTAL LOSS   237

19.1   In ascertaining whether the Vessel is a constructive total loss, the insured value shall be taken as the repaired value and nothing in respect of the damaged or break-up value of the Vessel or wreck shall be taken into account.   238 239 240

19.2   No claim for constructive total loss based upon the cost of recovery and/or repair of the Vessel shall be recoverable hereunder unless such cost would exceed the insured value. In making this determination, only the cost relating to a single accident or sequence of damages arising from the same accident shall be taken into account.   241 242 243 244

20 FREIGHT WAIVER   245

In the event of total or constructive total loss no claim to be made by the Underwriters for freight whether notice of abandonment has been given or not.   246 247

21 DISBURSEMENTS WARRANTY   248

21.1   Additional insurances as follows are permitted: 249

21.1.1   *Disbursements, Managers' Commissions, Profits or Excess or Increased Value of Hull and Machinery.* A sum not exceeding 25% of the value stated herein.   250 251

21.1.2   *Freight, Chartered Freight or Anticipated Freight, insured for time.* A sum not exceeding 25% of the value as stated herein less any sum insured, however described, under 21.1.1.   252 253

21.1.3   *Freight or Hire, under contracts for voyage.* A sum not exceeding the gross freight or hire for the current cargo passage and next succeeding cargo passage (such insurance to include, if required, a preliminary and an intermediate ballast passage) plus the charges of insurance. In the case of a voyage charter where payment is made on a time basis, the sum permitted for insurance shall be calculated on the estimated duration of the voyage, subject to the limitation of two cargo passages as laid down herein. Any sum insured under 21.1.2 to be taken into account and only the excess thereof may be insured, which excess shall be reduced as the freight or hire is advanced or earned by the gross amount so advanced or earned.   254 255 256 257 258 259 260 261

21.1.4   *Anticipated Freight if the Vessel sails in ballast and not under Charter.* A sum not exceeding the anticipated gross freight on next cargo passage, such sum to be reasonably estimated on the basis of the current rate of freight at time of insurance plus the charges of insurance. Any sum insured under 21.1.2 to be taken into account and only the excess thereof may be insured.   262 263 264 265

21.1.5   *Time Charter Hire or Charter Hire for Series of Voyages.* A sum not exceeding 50% of the gross hire which is to be earned under the charter in a period not exceeding 18 months. Any sum insured under 21.1.2 to be taken into account and only the excess thereof may be insured, which excess shall be reduced as the hire is advanced or earned under the charter by 50% of the gross amount so advanced or earned but the sum insured need not be reduced while the total of the sums insured under 21.1.2 and 21.1.5 does not exceed 50% of the gross hire still to be earned under the charter. An insurance under this Section may begin on the signing of the charter.   266 267 268 269 270 271 272

21.1.6   *Premiums.* A sum not exceeding the actual premiums of all interests insured for a period not exceeding 12 months (excluding premiums insured under the foregoing sections but including, if required, the premium or estimated calls on any Club or War etc. Risk insurance) reducing pro rata monthly.   273 274 275 276

21.1.7   *Returns of Premium.* A sum not exceeding the actual returns which are allowable under any insurance but which would not be recoverable thereunder in the event of a total loss of the Vessel whether by insured perils or otherwise.   277 278 279

21.1.8   *Insurance irrespective of amount against:* Any risks excluded by Clauses 23, 24, 25 and 26 below.   280 281

21.2   Warranted that no insurance on any interests enumerated in the foregoing 21.1.1 to 21.1.7 in excess of the amounts permitted therein and no other insurance which includes total loss of the Vessel P.P.I., F.I.A., or subject to any other like term, is or shall be effected to operate during the currency of this insurance by or for account of the Assured, Owners, Managers or Mortgagees. Provided always that a breach of this warranty shall not afford the Underwriters any defence to a claim by a Mortgagee who has accepted this insurance without knowledge of such breach.   282 283 284 285 286 287

22 RETURNS FOR LAY-UP AND CANCELLATION   288

22.1   To return as follows: 289

22.1.1   Pro rata monthly net for each uncommenced month if this insurance be cancelled by agreement.   290

22.1.2   For each period of 30 consecutive days the Vessel may be laid up in a port or in a lay-up area provided such port or lay-up area is approved by the Underwriters (with special liberties as hereinafter allowed)   291 292 293

         (a)..................................per cent net not under repair   294

         (b)..................................per cent net under repair.   295

If the Vessel is under repair during part only of a period for which a return is claimable, the return shall be calculated pro rata to the number of days under (a) and (b) respectively. 296 297

22.2 PROVIDED ALWAYS THAT 298

22.2.1   a total loss of the Vessel, whether by insured perils or otherwise, has not occurred during the period covered by this insurance or any extension thereof 299 300

22.2.2   in no case shall a return be allowed when the Vessel is lying in exposed or unprotected waters, or in a port or lay-up area not approved by the Underwriters but, provided the Underwriters agree that such non-approved lay-up area is deemed to be within the vicinity of the approved port or lay-up area, days during which the Vessel is laid up in such non-approved lay-up area may be added to days in the approved port or lay-up area to calculate a period of 30 consecutive days and a return shall be allowed for the proportion of such period during which the Vessel is actually laid up in the approved port or lay-up area 301 302 303 304 305 306 307

22.2.3   loading or discharging operations or the presence of cargo on board shall not debar returns but no return shall be allowed for any period during which the Vessel is being used for the storage of cargo or for lightering purposes 308 309 310

22.2.4   in the event of any amendment of the annual rate, the above rates of return shall be adjusted accordingly 311 312

22.2.5   in the event of any return recoverable under this Clause 22 being based on 30 consecutive days which fall on successive insurances effected for the same Assured, this insurance shall only be liable for an amount calculated at pro rata of the period rates 22.1.2(a) and/or (b) above for the number of days which come within the period of this insurance and to which a return is actually applicable. Such overlapping period shall run, at the option of the Assured, either from the first day on which the Vessel is laid up or the first day of a period of 30 consecutive days as provided under 22.1.2(a) or (b), or 22.2.2 above. 313 314 315 316 317 318 319

The following clauses shall be paramount and shall override anything contained in this insurance inconsistent therewith. 320 321

23 WAR EXCLUSION 322

In no case shall this insurance cover loss damage liability or expense caused by 323

23.1   war civil war revolution rebellion insurrection, or civil strife arising therefrom, or any hostile act by or against a belligerent power 324 325

23.2   capture seizure arrest restraint or detainment (barratry and piracy excepted), and the consequences thereof or any attempt threat 326 327

23.3   derelict mines torpedoes bombs or other derelict weapons of war. 328

24 STRIKES EXCLUSION 329

In no case shall this insurance cover loss damage liability or expense caused by 330

24.1   strikers, locked-out workmen, or persons taking part in labour disturbances, riots or civil commotions 331 332

24.2   any terrorist or any person acting from a political motive. 333

25 MALICIOUS ACTS EXCLUSION 334

In no case shall this insurance cover loss damage liability or expense arising from 335

25.1   the detonation of an explosive 336

25.2   any weapon of war 337

and caused by any person acting maliciously or from a political motive. 338

26 NUCLEAR EXCLUSION 339

In no case shall this insurance cover loss damage liability or expense arising from any weapon of war employing atomic or nuclear fission and/or fusion or other like reaction or radioactive force or matter. 340 341

Appendix 28

1/10/83   (FOR USE ONLY WITH THE NEW MARINE POLICY FORM)

INSTITUTE TIME CLAUSES — HULLS
DISBURSEMENTS AND INCREASED VALUE
(Total Loss only, including Excess Liabilities)

This insurance is subject to English law and practice

NAVIGATION   1

1.1   The subject-matter insured is covered subject to the provisions of this insurance at all times and the Vessel   2
has leave to sail or navigate with or without pilots, to go on trial trips and to assist and tow vessels or craft   3
in distress, but it is warranted that the Vessel shall not be towed, except as is customary or to the first safe   4
port or place when in need of assistance, or undertake towage or salvage services under a contract   5
previously arranged by the Assured and/or Owners and/or Managers and/or Charterers. This Clause 1.1   6
shall not exclude customary towage in connection with loading and discharging.   7

1.2   In the event of the Vessel being employed in trading operations which entail cargo loading or discharging   8
at sea from or into another vessel (not being a harbour or inshore craft) no claim shall be recoverable   9
under this insurance in respect of loss of or damage to the subject-matter insured or for liability to any   10
other vessel arising from such loading or discharging operations, including whilst approaching, lying   11
alongside and leaving, unless previous notice that the Vessel is to be employed in such operations has been   12
given to the Underwriters and any amended terms of cover and any additional premium required by them   13
have been agreed.   14

1.3   In the event of the Vessel sailing (with or without cargo) with an intention of being (a) broken up, or (b)   15
sold for breaking up, no claim shall be recoverable under this insurance in respect of loss or damage to the   16
Vessel occurring subsequent to such sailing unless previous notice has been given to the Underwriters and   17
any amendments to the terms of cover, amount insured and premium required by them have been agreed.   18

CONTINUATION   19

Should the Vessel at the expiration of this insurance be at sea or in distress or at a port of refuge or of call, the   20
subject-matter insured shall, provided previous notice be given to the Underwriters, be held covered at a pro rata   21
monthly premium to her port of destination.   22

BREACH OF WARRANTY   23

Held covered in case of any breach of warranty as to cargo, locality, trade, towage, salvage services   24
or date of sailing, provided notice be given to the Underwriters immediately after receipt of advices   25
and any amended terms of cover and any additional premium required by them be agreed.   26

TERMINATION   27

This Clause 4 shall prevail notwithstanding any provision whether written typed or printed in this insurance   28
inconsistent therewith.   29

Unless the Underwriters agree to the contrary in writing, this insurance shall terminate automatically at the time of   30

4.1   change of the Classification Society of the Vessel, or change, suspension, discontinuance, withdrawal or   31
expiry of her Class therein, provided that if the Vessel is at sea such automatic termination shall be   32
deferred until arrival at her next port. However where such change, suspension, discontinuance or   33
withdrawal of her Class has resulted from loss or damage which would be covered by an insurance of the   34
Vessel subject to current Institute Time Clauses Hulls or Institute War and Strikes Clauses Hulls-Time   35
such automatic termination shall only operate should the Vessel sail from her next port without the prior   36
approval of the Classification Society,   37

4.2   any change, voluntary or otherwise, in the ownership or flag, transfer to new management, or charter on   38
a bareboat basis, or requisition for title or use of the Vessel, provided that, if the Vessel has cargo on   39

board and has already sailed from her loading port or is at sea in ballast, such automatic termination shall 40
if required be deferred, whilst the Vessel continues her planned voyage, until arrival at final port of 41
discharge if with cargo or at port of destination if in ballast. However, in the event of requisition for title 42
or use without the prior execution of a written agreement by the Assured, such automatic termination 43
shall occur fifteen days after such requisition whether the Vessel is at sea or in port. 44

A pro rata daily net return of premium shall be made. 45

5   **ASSIGNMENT** 46
No assignment of or interest in this insurance or in any moneys which may be or become payable thereunder is to 47
be binding on or recognised by the Underwriters unless a dated notice of such assignment or interest signed by the 48
Assured, and by the assignor in the case of subsequent assignment, is endorsed on the Policy and the Policy with 49
such endorsement is produced before payment of any claim or return of premium thereunder. 50

6   **PERILS** 51
6.1   This insurance covers total loss (actual or constructive) of the subject-matter insured caused by 52
6.1.1   perils of the seas rivers lakes or other navigable waters 53
6.1.2   fire, explosion 54
6.1.3   violent theft by persons from outside the Vessel 55
6.1.4   jettison 56
6.1.5   piracy 57
6.1.6   breakdown of or accident to nuclear installations or reactors 58
6.1.7   contact with aircraft or similar objects, or objects falling therefrom, land conveyance, dock or 59
harbour equipment or installation 60
6.1.8   earthquake volcanic eruption or lightning. 61
6.2   This insurance covers total loss (actual or constructive) of the subject-matter insured caused by 62
6.2.1   accidents in loading discharging or shifting cargo or fuel 63
6.2.2   bursting of boilers breakage of shafts or any latent defect in the machinery or hull 64
6.2.3   negligence of Master Officers Crew or Pilots 65
6.2.4   negligence of repairers or charterers provided such repairers or charterers are not an Assured 66
hereunder 67
6.2.5   barratry of Master Officers or Crew, 68
provided such loss or damage has not resulted from want of due diligence by the Assured, Owners or 69
Managers. 70
6.3   Master Officers Crew or Pilots not to be considered Owners within the meaning of this Clause 6 should 71
they hold shares in the Vessel. 72
6.4   This insurance covers: 73
6.4.1   **General Average, Salvage and Salvage Charges** not recoverable in full under the insurances on hull 74
and machinery by reason of the difference between the insured value of the Vessel as stated therein 75
(or any reduced value arising from the deduction therefrom in process of adjustment of any claim 76
which law or practice or the terms of the insurances covering hull and machinery may have required) 77
and the value of the Vessel adopted for the purpose of contribution to general average, salvage or 78
salvage charges, the liability under this insurance being for such proportion of the amount not 79
recoverable as the amount insured hereunder bears to the said difference or to the total sum insured 80
against excess liabilities if it exceed such difference. 81
6.4.2   **Sue and Labour Charges** not recoverable in full under the insurances on hull and machinery by 82
reason of the difference between the insured value of the Vessel as stated therein and the value of the 83
Vessel adopted for the purpose of ascertaining the amount recoverable under the insurances on hull 84
and machinery, the liability under this insurance being for such proportion of the amount not 85
recoverable as the amount insured hereunder bears to the said difference or to the total sum insured 86
against excess liabilities if it exceed such difference. 87
6.4.3   **Collision Liability (three-fourths)** not recoverable in full under the Institute 3/4ths Collision 88
Liability and Sistership Clauses in the insurances on hull and machinery by reason of such three- 89
fourths liability exceeding three-fourths of the insured value of the Vessel as stated therein, in which 90
case the amount recoverable under this insurance shall be such proportion of the difference so 91
arising as the amount insured hereunder bears to the total sum insured against excess liabilities. 92
6.5   The Underwriters' liability under 6.4.1, 6.4.2 and 6.4.3 separately, in respect of any one claim, shall not 93
exceed the amount insured hereunder. 94

7   **POLLUTION HAZARD** 95
This insurance covers total loss (actual or constructive) of the Vessel caused by any governmental authority acting 96
under the powers vested in it to prevent or mitigate a pollution hazard, or threat thereof, resulting directly from 97
damage to the Vessel caused by a peril covered by this insurance, provided such act of governmental authority has 98
not resulted from want of due diligence by the Assured, the Owners, or Managers of the Vessel or any of them to 99
prevent or mitigate such hazard or threat. Master, Officers, Crew or Pilots not to be considered Owners within the 100
meaning of this Clause 7 should they hold shares in the Vessel. 101

8   **NOTICE OF CLAIM** 102
In the event of accident whereby loss or damage may result in a claim under this insurance, notice shall be given to 103
the Underwriters prior to survey and also, if the Vessel is abroad, to the nearest Lloyd's Agent so that a surveyor 104
may be appointed to represent the Underwriters should they so desire. 105

9   CONSTRUCTIVE TOTAL LOSS   106

   9.1   In ascertaining whether the Vessel is a constructive total loss, the insured value in the insurances on hull   107
and machinery shall be taken as the repaired value and nothing in respect of the damaged or break-up   108
value of the Vessel or wreck shall be taken into account.   109

   9.2   No claim for constructive total loss based upon the cost of recovery and/or repair of the Vessel shall be   110
recoverable hereunder unless such cost would exceed the insured value in the insurances on hull and   111
machinery. In making this determination, only the cost relating to a single accident or sequence of   112
damages arising from the same accident shall be taken into account.   113

   9.3   Provided that the Constructive Total Loss Clause in the current Institute Time Clauses Hulls or a clause   114
having a similar effect is contained in the insurances on hull and machinery, the settlement of a claim for   115
constructive total loss thereunder shall be accepted as proof of the constructive total loss of the Vessel.   116

   9.4   Should the Vessel be a constructive total loss but the claim on the insurances on hull and machinery be   117
settled as a claim for partial loss, no payment shall be due under this Clause 9.   118

10   COMPROMISED TOTAL LOSS   119

In the event of a claim for total loss or constructive total loss being settled on the insurances on hull and machinery   120
as a compromised total loss the amount payable hereunder shall be the same percentage of the amount insured as   121
is paid on the said insurances.   122

11   RETURNS FOR LAY-UP AND CANCELLATION   123

   11.1   To return as follows: 124

   11.1.1   Pro rata monthly net for each uncommenced month if this insurance be cancelled by agreement.   125

   11.1.2   For each period of 30 consecutive days the Vessel may be laid up in a port or in a lay-up area   126
provided such port or lay-up area is approved by the Underwriters (with special liberties as   127
hereinafter allowed)   128

         (a).....................................per cent net not under repair   129

         (b).....................................per cent net under repair: 130

         If the Vessel is under repair during part only of a period for which a return is claimable, the return shall   131
be calculated pro rata to the number of days under (a) and (b) respectively.   132

   11.2   PROVIDED ALWAYS THAT   133

   11.2.1   a total loss of the Vessel, whether by insured perils or otherwise, has not occurred during the period   134
covered by this insurance or any extension thereof   135

   11.2.2   in no case shall a return be allowed when the Vessel is lying in exposed or unprotected waters, or in a   136
port or lay-up area not approved by the Underwriters but, provided the Underwriters agree that   137
such non-approved lay-up area is deemed to be within the vicinity of the approved port or lay-up   138
area, days during which the Vessel is laid up in such non-approved lay-up area may be added to days   139
in the approved port or lay-up area to calculate a period of 30 consecutive days and a return shall be   140
allowed for the proportion of such period during which the Vessel is actually laid up in the approved   141
port or lay-up area   142

   11.2.3   loading or discharging operations or the presence of cargo on board shall not debar returns but no   143
return shall be allowed for any period during which the Vessel is being used for the storage of cargo   144
or for lightering purposes   145

   11.2.4   in the event of any amendment of the annual rate, the above rates of return shall be adjusted   146
accordingly   147

   11.2.5   in the event of any return recoverable under this Clause 11 being based on 30 consecutive days which   148
fall on successive insurances effected for the same Assured, this insurance shall only be liable for an   149
amount calculated at pro rata of the period rates 11.1.2 (a) and/or (b) above for the number of days   150
which come within the period of this insurance and to which a return is actually applicable. Such   151
overlapping period shall run, at the option of the Assured, either from the first day on which the   152
Vessel is laid up or the first day of a period of 30 consecutive days as provided under 11.1.2 (a) or   153
(b), or 11.2.2 above.   154

The following clauses shall be paramount and shall override anything contained in this insurance inconsistent   155
therewith.   156

12   WAR EXCLUSION   157

In no case shall this insurance cover loss damage liability or expense caused by   158

   12.1   war civil war revolution rebellion insurrection, or civil strife arising therefrom, or any hostile act by or   159
against a belligerent power   160

   12.2   capture seizure arrest restraint or detainment (barratry and piracy excepted), and the consequences   161
thereof or any attempt thereat   162

   12.3   derelict mines torpedoes bombs or other derelict weapons of war.   163

13   STRIKES EXCLUSION   164

In no case shall this insurance cover loss damage liability or expense caused by   165

   13.1   strikers, locked-out workmen, or persons taking part in labour disturbances, riots or civil commotions   166

   13.2   any terrorist or any person acting from a political motive.   167

14   MALICIOUS ACTS EXCLUSION   168

In no case shall this insurance cover loss damage liability or expense arising from   169

15 NUCLEAR EXCLUSION   173

In no case shall this insurance cover loss damage liability or expense arising from any weapon of war employing   174
atomic or nuclear fission and/or fusion or other like reaction or radioactive force or matter.   175

Appendix 29

1/10/83   (FOR USE ONLY WITH THE NEW MARINE POLICY FORM)

INSTITUTE TIME CLAUSES — HULLS
TOTAL LOSS, GENERAL AVERAGE AND 3/4THS COLLISION LIABILITY
(Including Salvage, Salvage Charges and Sue and Labour)

This insurance is subject to English law and practice

1	**NAVIGATION**	1
1.1	The Vessel is covered subject to the provisions of this insurance at all times and has leave to sail or	2
	navigate with or without pilots, to go on trial trips and to assist and tow vessels or craft in distress, but it	3
	is warranted that the Vessel shall not be towed, except as is customary or to the first safe port or place	4
	when in need of assistance, or undertake towage or salvage services under a contract previously arranged	5
	by the Assured and/or Owners and/or Managers and/or Charterers. This Clause 1.1 shall not exclude	6
	customary towage in connection with loading and discharging.	7
1.2	In the event of the Vessel being employed in trading operations which entail cargo loading or discharging	8
	at sea from or into another vessel (not being a harbour or inshore craft) no claim shall be recoverable	9
	under this insurance for loss of or damage to the Vessel or liability to any other vessel arising from such	10
	loading or discharging operations, including whilst approaching, lying alongside and leaving, unless	11
	previous notice that the Vessel is to be employed in such operations has been given to the Underwriters	12
	and any amended terms of cover and any additional premium required by them have been agreed.	13
1.3	In the event of the Vessel sailing (with or without cargo) with an intention of being (a) broken up, or (b)	14
	sold for breaking up, any claim for loss of or damage to the Vessel occurring subsequent to such sailing	15
	shall be limited to the market value of the Vessel as scrap at the time when the loss or damage is sustained,	16
	unless previous notice has been given to the Underwriters and any amendments to the terms of cover,	17
	insured value and premium required by them have been agreed. Nothing in this Clause 1.3 shall affect	18
	claims under Clauses 8 and/or 11.	19
2	**CONTINUATION**	20
	Should the Vessel at the expiration of this insurance be at sea or in distress or at a port of refuge or of call, she	21
	shall, provided previous notice be given to the Underwriters, be held covered at a pro rata monthly premium to her	22
	port of destination.	23
3	**BREACH OF WARRANTY**	24
	Held covered in case of any breach of warranty as to cargo, trade, locality, towage, salvage services or date of	25
	sailing, provided notice be given to the Underwriters immediately after receipt of advices and any amended terms	26
	of cover and any additional premium required by them be agreed.	27
4	**TERMINATION**	28
	This Clause 4 shall prevail notwithstanding any provision whether written typed or printed in this insurance	29
	inconsistent therewith.	30
	Unless the Underwriters agree to the contrary in writing, this insurance shall terminate automatically at the time of	31
4.1	change of the Classification Society of the Vessel, or change, suspension, discontinuance, withdrawal or	32
	expiry of her Class therein, provided that if the Vessel is at sea such automatic termination shall be	33
	deferred until arrival at her next port. However where such change, suspension, discontinuance or	34
	withdrawal of her Class has resulted from loss or damage which would be covered by an insurance of the	35
	Vessel subject to current Institute Time Clauses Hulls or Institute War and Strikes Clauses Hulls-Time	36
	such automatic termination shall only operate should the Vessel sail from her next port without the prior	37
	approval of the Classification Society,	38
4.2	any change, voluntary or otherwise, in the ownership or flag, transfer to new management, or charter on	39
	a bareboat basis, or requisition for title or use of the Vessel, provided that, if the Vessel has cargo on	40
	board and has already sailed from her loading port or is at sea in ballast, such automatic termination shall	41
	if required be deferred, whilst the Vessel continues her planned voyage, until arrival at final port of	42
	discharge if with cargo or at port of destination if in ballast. However, in the event of requisition for title	43
	or use without the prior execution of a written agreement by the Assured, such automatic termination	44
	shall occur fifteen days after such requisition whether the Vessel is at sea or in port.	45
	A pro rata daily net return of premium shall be made.	46

5   ASSIGNMENT   47

No assignment of or interest in this insurance or in any moneys which may be or become payable thereunder is to   48
be binding on or recognised by the Underwriters unless a dated notice of such assignment or interest signed by the   49
Assured, and by the assignor in the case of subsequent assignment, is endorsed on the Policy and the Policy with   50
such endorsement is produced before payment of any claim or return of premium thereunder.   51

6   PERILS   52

6.1   This insurance covers total loss (actual or constructive) of the subject-matter insured caused by   53
6.1.1   perils of the seas rivers lakes or other navigable waters   54
6.1.2   fire, explosion   55
6.1.3   violent theft by persons from outside the Vessel   56
6.1.4   jettison   57
6.1.5   piracy   58
6.1.6   breakdown of or accident to nuclear installations or reactors   59
6.1.7   contact with aircraft or similar objects, or objects falling therefrom, land conveyance, dock or   60
             harbour equipment or installation   61
6.1.8   earthquake volcanic eruption or lightning.   62
6.2   This insurance covers total loss (actual or constructive) of the subject-matter insured caused by   63
6.2.1   accidents in loading discharging or shifting cargo or fuel   64
6.2.2   bursting of boilers breakage of shafts or any latent defect in the machinery or hull   65
6.2.3   negligence of Master Officers Crew or Pilots   66
6.2.4   negligence of repairers or charterers provided such repairers or charterers are not an Assured   67
             hereunder   68
6.2.5   barratry of Master Officers or Crew,   69
             provided such loss or damage has not resulted from want of due diligence by the Assured, Owners or   70
             Managers.   71
6.3   Master Officers Crew or Pilots not to be considered Owners within the meaning of this Clause 6 should   72
        they hold shares in the Vessel.   73

7   POLLUTION HAZARD   74

This insurance covers total loss (actual or constructive) of the Vessel caused by any governmental authority acting   75
under the powers vested in it to prevent or mitigate a pollution hazard, or threat thereof, resulting directly from   76
damage to the Vessel caused by a peril covered by this insurance, provided such act of governmental authority has   77
not resulted from want of due diligence by the Assured, the Owners, or Managers of the Vessel or any of them to   78
prevent or mitigate such hazard or threat. Master, Officers, Crew or Pilots not to be considered Owners within the   79
meaning of this Clause 7 should they hold shares in the Vessel.   80

8   3/4THS COLLISION LIABILITY   81

8.1   The Underwriters agree to indemnify the Assured for three-fourths of any sum or sums paid by the   82
        Assured to any other person or persons by reason of the Assured becoming legally liable by way of   83
        damages for   84
8.1.1   loss of or damage to any other vessel or property on any other vessel   85
8.1.2   delay to or loss of use of any such other vessel or property thereon   86
8.1.3   general average of, salvage of, or salvage under contract of, any such other vessel or property   87
             thereon,   88
             where such payment by the Assured is in consequence of the Vessel hereby insured coming into collision   89
             with any other vessel;   90
8.2   The indemnity provided by this Clause 8 shall be in addition to the indemnity provided by the other terms   91
        and conditions of this insurance and shall be subject to the following provisions: 92
8.2.1   Where the insured Vessel is in collision with another vessel and both vessels are to blame then, unless   93
             the liability of one or both vessels becomes limited by law, the indemnity under this Clause 8 shall be   94
             calculated on the principle of cross-liabilities as if the respective Owners had been compelled to pay   95
             to each other such proportion of each other's damages as may have been properly allowed in   96
             ascertaining the balance or sum payable by or to the Assured in consequence of the collision.   97
8.2.2   In no case shall the Underwriters' total liability under Clauses 8.1 and 8.2 exceed their proportionate   98
             part of three-fourths of the insured value of the Vessel hereby insured in respect of any one collision.   99
8.3   The Underwriters will also pay three-fourths of the legal costs incurred by the Assured or which the   100
        Assured may be compelled to pay in contesting liability or taking proceedings to limit liability, with the   101
        prior written consent of the Underwriters.   102

EXCLUSIONS   103

8.4   Provided always that this Clause 8 shall in no case extend to any sum which the Assured shall pay for or in   104
        respect of   105
8.4.1   removal or disposal of obstructions, wrecks, cargoes or any other thing whatsoever   106
8.4.2   any real or personal property or thing whatsoever except other vessels or property on other vessels   107
8.4.3   the cargo or other property on, or the engagements of, the insured Vessel   108
8.4.4   loss of life, personal injury or illness   109

8.4.5　　　　　pollution or contamination of any real or personal property or thing whatsoever (except other　110
　　　　　　　vessels with which the insured Vessel is in collision or property on such other vessels).　　　111

9　SISTERSHIP　112

Should the Vessel hereby insured come into collision with or receive salvage services from another vessel belonging　113
wholly or in part to the same Owners or under the same management, the Assured shall have the same rights under　114
this insurance as they would have were the other vessel entirely the property of Owners not interested in the Vessel　115
hereby insured; but in such cases the liability for the collision or the amount payable for the services rendered shall　116
be referred to a sole arbitrator to be agreed upon between the Underwriters and the Assured.　117

10　NOTICE OF CLAIM　118

In the event of accident whereby loss or damage may result in a claim under this insurance, notice shall be given to　119
the Underwriters prior to survey and also, if the Vessel is abroad, to the nearest Lloyd's Agent so that a surveyor　120
may be appointed to represent the Underwriters should they so desire.　121

11　GENERAL AVERAGE AND SALVAGE　122

11.1　　This insurance covers the Vessel's proportion of salvage, salvage charges and/or general average, reduced　123
　　　　in respect of any under-insurance.　124

11.2　　**This insurance does not cover partial loss of and/or damage to the Vessel except for any proportion of**　125
　　　　general average loss or damage which may be recoverable under Clause 11.1 above.　126

11.3　　Adjustment to be according to the law and practice obtaining at the place where the adventure ends, as if　127
　　　　the contract of affreightment contained no special terms upon the subject; but where the contract of　128
　　　　affreightment so provides the adjustment shall be according to the York-Antwerp Rules.　129

11.4　　When the Vessel sails in ballast, not under charter the provisions of the York-Antwerp Rules, 1974　130
　　　　(excluding Rules XX and XXI) shall be applicable, and the voyage for this purpose shall be deemed to　131
　　　　continue from the port or place of departure until the arrival of the Vessel at the first port or place　132
　　　　thereafter other than a port or place of refuge or a port or place of call for bunkering only. If at any such　133
　　　　intermediate port or place there is an abandonment of the adventure originally contemplated the voyage　134
　　　　shall thereupon be deemed to be terminated.　135

11.5　　No claim under this Clause 11 shall in any case be allowed where the loss was not incurred to avoid or in　136
　　　　connection with the avoidance of a peril insured against.　137

12　DEDUCTIBLE　138

12.1　　No claim arising from a peril insured against shall be payable under this insurance unless the aggregate of　139
　　　　all such claims arising out of each separate accident or occurrence (including claims under Clauses 8 and　140

　　　　13) exceeds...in which case this sum shall be deducted.　141
　　　　This Clause 12.1 shall not apply to a claim for total or constructive total loss of the Vessel or, in the event　142
　　　　of such a claim, to any associated claim under Clause 13 arising from the same accident or occurrence.　143

12.2　　Excluding any interest comprised therein, recoveries against any claim which is subject to the above　144
　　　　deductible shall be credited to the Underwriters in full to the extent of the sum by which the aggregate of　145
　　　　the claim unreduced by any recoveries exceeds the above deductible.　146

12.3　　Interest comprised in recoveries shall be apportioned between the Assured and the Underwriters, taking　147
　　　　into account the sums paid by the Underwriters and the dates when such payments were made,　148
　　　　notwithstanding that by the addition of interest the Underwriters may receive a larger sum than they have　149
　　　　paid.　150

13　DUTY OF ASSURED (SUE AND LABOUR)　151

13.1　　In case of any loss or misfortune it is the duty of the Assured and their servants and agents to take such　152
　　　　measures as may be reasonable for the purpose of averting or minimising a loss which would be　153
　　　　recoverable under this insurance.　154

13.2　　Subject to the provisions below and to Clause 12 the Underwriters will contribute to charges properly and　155
　　　　reasonably incurred by the Assured their servants or agents for such measures. General average, salvage　156
　　　　charges (except as provided for in Clause 13.5) and collision defence or attack costs are not recoverable　157
　　　　under this Clause 13.　158

13.3　　Measures taken by the Assured or the Underwriters with the object of saving, protecting or recovering the　159
　　　　subject-matter insured shall not be considered as a waiver or acceptance of abandonment or otherwise　160
　　　　prejudice the rights of either party.　161

13.4　　When expenses are incurred pursuant to this Clause 13 the liability under this insurance shall not exceed　162
　　　　the proportion of such expenses that the amount insured hereunder bears to the value of the Vessel as　163
　　　　stated herein, or to the sound value of the Vessel at the time of the occurrence giving rise to the　164
　　　　expenditure if the sound value exceeds that value. Where the Underwriters have admitted a claim for total　165
　　　　loss and property insured by this insurance is saved, the foregoing provisions shall not apply unless the　166
　　　　expenses of suing and labouring exceed the value of such property saved and then shall apply only to the　167
　　　　amount of the expenses which is in excess of such value.　168

13.5　　When a claim for total loss of the Vessel is admitted under this insurance and expenses have been　169
　　　　reasonably incurred in saving or attempting to save the Vessel and other property and there are no　170
　　　　proceeds, or the expenses exceed the proceeds, then this insurance shall bear its pro rata share of such　171
　　　　proportion of the expenses, or of the expenses in excess of the proceeds, as the case may be, as may　172
　　　　reasonably be regarded as having been incurred in respect of the Vessel; but if the Vessel be insured for　173
　　　　less than its sound value at the time of the occurrence giving rise to the expenditure, the amount　174
　　　　recoverable under this clause shall be reduced in proportion to the under-insurance.　175

13.6　　The sum recoverable under this Clause 13 shall be in addition to the loss otherwise recoverable under this　176
　　　　insurance but shall in no circumstances exceed the amount insured under this insurance in respect of the　177
　　　　Vessel.　178

1354

14 NEW FOR OLD 179

General average payable without deduction new for old. 180

15 AGENCY COMMISSION 181

In no case shall any sum be allowed under this insurance either by way of remuneration of the Assured for time 182
and trouble taken to obtain and supply information or documents or in respect of the commission or charges of 183
any manager, agent, managing or agency company or the like, appointed by or on behalf of the Assured to 184
perform such services. 185

16 CONSTRUCTIVE TOTAL LOSS 186

16.1 In ascertaining whether the Vessel is a constructive total loss, the insured value shall be taken as the 187
repaired value and nothing in respect of the damaged or break-up value of the Vessel or wreck shall be 188
taken into account. 189

16.2 No claim for constructive total loss based upon the cost of recovery and/or repair of the Vessel shall be 190
recoverable hereunder unless such cost would exceed the insured value. In making this determination, 191
only the cost relating to a single accident or sequence of damages arising from the same accident shall be 192
taken into account. 193

17 FREIGHT WAIVER 194

In the event of total or constructive total loss no claim to be made by the Underwriters for freight whether notice 195
of abandonment has been given or not. 196

18 DISBURSEMENTS WARRANTY 197

18.1 Additional insurances as follows are permitted: 198

18.1.1 *Disbursements, Managers' Commissions, Profits or Excess or Increased Value of Hull and* 199
Machinery. A sum not exceeding 25% of the value stated herein. 200

18.1.2 *Freight, Chartered Freight or Anticipated Freight, insured for time.* A sum not exceeding 25% of 201
the value as stated herein less any sum insured, however described, under 18.1.1. 202

18.1.3 *Freight or Hire, under contracts for voyage.* A sum not exceeding the gross freight or hire for the 203
current cargo passage and next succeeding cargo passage (such insurance to include, if required, a 204
preliminary and an intermediate ballast passage) plus the charges of insurance. In the case of a 205
voyage charter where payment is made on a time basis, the sum permitted for insurance shall be 206
calculated on the estimated duration of the voyage, subject to the limitation of two cargo passages 207
as laid down herein. Any sum insured under 18.1.2 to be taken into account and only the excess 208
thereof may be insured, which excess shall be reduced as the freight or hire is advanced or earned by 209
the gross amount so advanced or earned. 210

18.1.4 *Anticipated Freight if the Vessel sails in ballast and not under Charter.* A sum not exceeding the 211
anticipated gross freight on next cargo passage, such sum to be reasonably estimated on the basis of 212
the current rate of freight at time of insurance plus the charges of insurance. Any sum insured under 213
18.1.2 to be taken into account and only the excess thereof may be insured. 214

18.1.5 *Time Charter Hire or Charter Hire for Series of Voyages.* A sum not exceeding 50% of the gross 215
hire which is to be earned under the charter in a period not exceeding 18 months. Any sum insured 216
under 18.1.2 to be taken into account and only the excess thereof may be insured, which excess shall 217
be reduced as the hire is advanced or earned under the charter by 50% of the gross amount so 218
advanced or earned but the sum insured need not be reduced while the total of the sums insured 219
under 18.1.2 and 18.1.5 does not exceed 50% of the gross hire still to be earned under the charter. 220
An insurance under this Section may begin on the signing of the charter. 221

18.1.6 *Premiums.* A sum not exceeding the actual premiums of all interests insured for a period not 222
exceeding 12 months (excluding premiums insured under the foregoing sections but including, if 223
required, the premium or estimated calls on any Club or War etc. Risk insurance) reducing pro rata 224
monthly. 225

18.1.7 *Returns of Premium.* A sum not exceeding the actual returns which are allowable under any 226
insurance but which would not be recoverable thereunder in the event of a total loss of the Vessel 227
whether by insured perils or otherwise. 228

18.1.8 *Insurance irrespective of amount against:* 229
Any risks excluded by Clauses 20, 21, 22 and 23 below. 230

18.2 Warranted that no insurance on any interests enumerated in the foregoing 18.1.1 to 18.1.7 in excess of the 231
amounts permitted therein and no other insurance which includes total loss of the Vessel P.P.I., F.I.A., 232
or subject to any other like term, is or shall be effected to operate during the currency of this insurance by 233
or for account of the Assured, Owners, Managers or Mortgagees. Provided always that a breach of this 234
warranty shall not afford the Underwriters any defence to a claim by a Mortgagee who has accepted this 235
insurance without knowledge of such breach. 236

RETURNS FOR LAY-UP AND CANCELLATION 237

19.1 To return as follows: 238

19.1.1 Pro rata monthly net for each uncommenced month if this insurance be cancelled by agreement. 239

19.1.2 For each period of 30 consecutive days the Vessel may be laid up in a port or in a lay-up area 240
provided such port or lay-up area is approved by the Underwriters (with special liberties as 241
hereinafter allowed) 242

(a).....................................per cent net not under repair 243

(b).....................................per cent net under repair. 244

If the Vessel is under repair during part only of a period for which a return is claimable, the return 245
shall be calculated pro rata to the number of days under (a) and (b) respectively 246

19.2   PROVIDED ALWAYS THAT   247
19.2.1   a total loss of the Vessel, whether by insured perils or otherwise, has not occurred during the period   248
         covered by this insurance or any extension thereof   249
19.2.2   in no case shall a return be allowed when the Vessel is lying in exposed or unprotected waters, or in a   250
         port or lay-up area not approved by the Underwriters but, provided the Underwriters agree that   251
         such non-approved lay-up area is deemed to be within the vicinity of the approved port or lay-up   252
         area, days during which the Vessel is laid up in such non-approved lay-up area may be added to days   253
         in the approved port or lay-up area to calculate a period of 30 consecutive days and a return shall be   254
         allowed for the proportion of such period during which the Vessel is actually laid up in the approved   255
         port or lay-up area   256
19.2.3   loading or discharging operations or the presence of cargo on board shall not debar returns but no   257
         return shall be allowed for any period during which the Vessel is being used for the storage of cargo   258
         or for lightering purposes   259
19.2.4   in the event of any amendment of the annual rate, the above rates of return shall be adjusted   260
         accordingly   261
19.2.5   in the event of any return recoverable under this Clause 19 being based on 30 consecutive days which   262
         fall on successive insurances effected for the same Assured, this insurance shall only be liable for an   263
         amount calculated at pro rata of the period rates 19.1.2 (a) and/or (b) above for the number of days   264
         which come within the period of this insurance and to which a return is actually applicable. Such   265
         overlapping period shall run, at the option of the Assured, either from the first day on which the   266
         Vessel is laid up or the first day of a period of 30 consecutive days as provided under 19.1.2 (a) or (b)   267
         or 19.2.2 above.   268

The following clauses shall be paramount and shall override anything contained in this insurance inconsistent   269
therewith.   270

20   WAR EXCLUSION   271
In no case shall this insurance cover loss damage liability or expense caused by   272
20.1   war civil war revolution rebellion insurrection, or civil strife arising therefrom, or any hostile act by or   273
       against a belligerent power   274
20.2   capture seizure arrest restraint or detainment (barratry and piracy excepted), and the consequences   275
       thereof or any attempt thereat   276
20.3   derelict mines torpedoes bombs or other derelict weapons of war.   277

21   STRIKES EXCLUSION   278
In no case shall this insurance cover loss damage liability or expense caused by   279
21.1   strikers, locked-out workmen, or persons taking part in labour disturbances, riots or civil commotions   280
21.2   any terrorist or any person acting from a political motive.   281

22   MALICIOUS ACTS EXCLUSION   282
In no case shall this insurance cover loss damage liability or expense arising from   283
22.1   the detonation of an explosive   284
22.2   any weapon of war   285
and caused by any person acting maliciously or from a political motive.   286

23   NUCLEAR EXCLUSION   287
In no case shall this insurance cover loss damage liability or expense arising from any weapon of war employing   288
atomic or nuclear fission and/or fusion or other like reaction or radioactive force or matter.   289

Appendix 30

1/10/83 (FOR USE ONLY WITH THE NEW MARINE POLICY FORM)

INSTITUTE TIME CLAUSES — HULLS
TOTAL LOSS ONLY
(Including Salvage, Salvage Charges and Sue and Labour)

This insurance is subject to English law and practice

1 NAVIGATION   1

1.1 The Vessel is covered subject to the provisions of this insurance at all times and has leave to sail or   2
navigate with or without pilots, to go on trial trips and to assist and tow vessels or craft in distress, but it   3
is warranted that the Vessel shall not be towed, except as is customary or to the first safe port or place   4
when in need of assitance, or undertake towage or salvage services under a contract previously arranged   5
by the Assured and/or Owners and/or Managers and/or Charterers. This Clause 1.1 shall not exclude   6
customary towage in connection with loading and discharging.   7

1.2 In the event of the Vessel being employed in trading operations which entail cargo loading or discharging   8
at sea from or into another vessel (not being a harbour or inshore craft) no claim shall be recoverable   9
under this insurance for loss of or damage to the Vessel from such loading or discharging operations,   10
including whilst approaching, lying alongside and leaving, unless previous notice that the Vessel is to be   11
employed in such operations has been given to the Underwriters and any amended terms of cover and any   12
additional premium required by them have been agreed.   13

1.3 In the event of the Vessel sailing (with or without cargo) with an intention of being (a) broken up, or (b)   14
sold for breaking up, any claim for loss of or damage to the Vessel occurring subsequent to such sailing   15
shall be limited to the market value of the Vessel as scrap at the time when the loss or damage is sustained,   16
unless previous notice has been given to the Underwriters and any amendments to the terms of cover,   17
insured value and premium required by them have been agreed. Nothing in this Clause 1.3 shall affect   18
claims under Clause 9.   19

2 CONTINUATION   20

Should the Vessel at the expiration of this insurance be at sea or in distress or at a port of refuge or of call, she   21
shall, provided previous notice be given to the Underwriters, be held covered at a pro rata monthly premium to her   22
port of destination.   23

3 BREACH OF WARRANTY   24

Held covered in case of any breach of warranty as to cargo, trade, locality, towage, salvage services or date of   25
sailing, provided notice be given to the Underwriters immediately after receipt of advices and any amended terms   26
of cover and any additional premium required by them be agreed.   27

4 TERMINATION   28

This Clause 4 shall prevail notwithstanding any provision whether written typed or printed in this insurance   29
inconsistent therewith.   30

Unless the Underwriters agree to the contrary in writing, this insurance shall terminate automatically at the time of   31

4.1 change of the Classification Society of the Vessel, or change, suspension, discontinuance, withdrawal or   32
expiry of her Class therein, provided that if the Vessel is at sea such automatic termination shall be   33
deferred until arrival at her next port. However where such change, suspension, discontinuance or   34
withdrawal of her Class has resulted from loss or damage which would be covered by an insurance of the   35
Vessel subject to current Institute Time Clauses Hulls or Institute War and Strikes Clauses Hulls-Time   36
such automatic termination shall only operate should the Vessel sail from her next port without the prior   37
approval of the Classification Society,   38

4.2 any change, voluntary or otherwise, in the ownership or flag, transfer to new management, or charter on   39
a bareboat basis, or requisition for title or use of the Vessel, provided that, if the Vessel has cargo on   40
board and has already sailed from her loading port or is at sea in ballast, such automatic termination shall   41
if required be deferred, whilst the Vessel continues her planned voyage, until arrival at final port of   42

discharge if with cargo or at port of destination if in ballast. However, in the event of requisition for title   43
or use without the prior execution of a written agreement by the Assured, such automatic termination   44
shall occur fifteen days after such requisition whether the Vessel is at sea or in port.   45

A pro rata daily net return of premium shall be made.   46

5   **ASSIGNMENT**   47

No assignment of or interest in this insurance or in any moneys which may be or become payable thereunder is to   48
be binding on or recognised by the Underwriters unless a dated notice of such assignment or interest signed by the 49
Assured, and by the assignor in the case of subsequent assignment, is endorsed on the Policy and the Policy with   50
such endorsement is produced before payment of any claim or return of premium thereunder.   51

6   **PERILS**   52

6.1   This insurance covers total loss (actual or constructive) of the subject-matter insured caused by   53

6.1.1   perils of the seas rivers lakes or other navigable waters   54

6.1.2   fire, explosion   55

6.1.3   violent theft by persons from outside the Vessel   56

6.1.4   jettison   57

6.1.5   piracy   58

6.1.6   breakdown of or accident to nuclear installations or reactors   59

6.1.7   contact with aircraft or similar objects, or objects falling therefrom, land conveyance, dock or   60
              harbour equipment or installation   61

6.1.8   earthquake volcanic eruption or lightning.   62

6.2   This insurance covers total loss (actual or constructive) of the subject-matter insured caused by   63

6.2.1   accidents in loading discharging or shifting cargo or fuel   64

6.2.2   bursting of boilers breakage of shafts or any latent defect in the machinery or hull   65

6.2.3   negligence of Master Officers Crew or Pilots   66

6.2.4   negligence of repairers or charterers provided such repairers or charterers are not an Assured   67
              hereunder   68

6.2.5   barratry of Master Officers or Crew,   69

              provided such loss or damage has not resulted from want of due diligence by the Assured, Owners or   70
              Managers.   71

6.3   Master Officers Crew or Pilots not to be considered Owners within the meaning of this Clause 6 should   72
        they hold shares in the Vessel.   73

7   **POLLUTION HAZARD**   74

This insurance covers total loss (actual or constructive) of the Vessel caused by any governmental authority acting 75
under the powers vested in it to prevent or mitigate a pollution hazard, or threat thereof, resulting directly from 76
damage to the Vessel caused by a peril covered by this insurance, provided such act of governmental authority has   77
not resulted from want of due diligence by the Assured, the Owners, or Managers of the Vessel or any of them to   78
prevent or mitigate such hazard or threat. Master, Officers, Crew or Pilots not to be considered Owners within the   79
meaning of this Clause 7 should they hold shares in the Vessel.   80

8   **NOTICE OF CLAIM**   81

8.1   In the event of accident whereby loss or damage may result in a claim under this insurance, notice shall be 82
        given to the Underwriters prior to survey and also, if the Vessel is abroad, to the nearest Lloyd's Agent so 83
        that a surveyor may be appointed to represent the Underwriters should they so desire.   84

9   **SALVAGE**   85

9.1   This insurance covers the Vessel's proportion of salvage and salvage charges, reduced in respect of any   86
        under-insurance.   87

9.2   No claim under this Clause 9 shall in any case be allowed where the loss was not incurred to avoid or in   88
        connection with the avoidance of a peril insured against.   89

10 **SISTERSHIP**   90

Should the Vessel hereby insured receive salvage services from another vessel belonging wholly or in part to the   91
same Owners or under the same management, the Assured shall have the same rights under this insurance as they   92
would have were the other vessel entirely the property of Owners not interested in the Vessel hereby insured; but in 93
such cases the amount payable for the services rendered shall be referred to a sole arbitrator to be agreed upon   94
between the Underwriters and the Assured.   95

11 **DUTY OF ASSURED (SUE AND LABOUR)**   96

11.1   In case of any loss or misfortune it is the duty of the Assured and their servants and agents to take such   97
        measures as may be reasonable for the purpose of averting or minimising a loss which would be   98
        recoverable under this insurance.   99

11.2   Subject to the provisions below the Underwriters will contribute to charges properly and reasonably   100
        incurred by the Assured their servants or agents for such measures. General average, salvage charges and   101
        collision defence or attack costs are not recoverable under this Clause 11.   102

11.3   Measures taken by the Assured or the Underwriters with the object of saving, protecting or recovering the   103
        subject-matter insured shall not be considered as a waiver or acceptance of abandonment or otherwise   104
        prejudice the rights of either party.   105

11.4   When expenses are incurred pursuant to this Clause 11 the liability under this insurance shall not exceed the proportion of such expenses that the amount insured hereunder bears to the value of the Vessel as stated herein, or to the sound value of the Vessel at the time of the occurrence giving rise to the expenditure if the sound value exceeds that value. Where the Underwriters have admitted a claim for total loss and property insured by this insurance is saved, the foregoing provisions shall not apply unless the expenses of suing and labouring exceed the value of such property saved and then shall apply only to the amount of the expenses which is in excess of such value.

11.5   When a claim for total loss of the Vessel is admitted under this insurance and expenses have been reasonably incurred in saving or attempting to save the Vessel and other property and there are no proceeds, or the expenses exceed the proceeds, then this insurance shall bear its pro rata share of such proportion of the expenses, or of the expenses in excess of the proceeds, as the case may be, as may reasonably be regarded as having been incurred in respect of the Vessel; but if the Vessel be insured for less than its sound value at the time of the occurrence giving rise to the expenditure, the amount recoverable under this clause shall be reduced in proportion to the under-insurance.

11.6   The sum recoverable under this Clause 11 shall be in addition to the loss otherwise recoverable under this insurance but shall in no circumstances exceed the amount insured under this insurance in respect of the Vessel.

CONSTRUCTIVE TOTAL LOSS

12.1   In ascertaining whether the Vessel is a constructive total loss, the insured value shall be taken as the repaired value and nothing in respect of the damaged or break-up value of the Vessel or wreck shall be taken into account.

12.2   No claim for constructive total loss based upon the cost of recovery and/or repair of the Vessel shall be recoverable hereunder unless such cost would exceed the insured value. In making this determination, only the cost relating to a single accident or sequence of damages arising from the same accident shall be taken into account.

FREIGHT WAIVER

In the event of total or constructive total loss no claim to be made by the Underwriters for freight whether notice of abandonment has been given or not.

DISBURSEMENTS WARRANTY

14.1   Additional insurances as follows are permitted:

14.1.1   *Disbursements, Managers' Commissions, Profits or Excess or Increased Value of Hull and Machinery.* A sum not exceeding 25% of the value stated herein.

14.1.2   *Freight, Chartered Freight or Anticipated Freight, insured for time.* A sum not exceeding 25% of the value as stated herein less any sum insured, however described, under 14.1.1.

14.1.3   *Freight or Hire, under contracts for voyage.* A sum not exceeding the gross freight or hire for the current cargo passage and next succeeding cargo passage (such insurance to include, if required, a preliminary and an intermediate ballast passage) plus the charges of insurance. In the case of a voyage charter where payment is made on a time basis, the sum permitted for insurance shall be calculated on the estimated duration of the voyage, subject to the limitation of two cargo passages as laid down herein. Any sum insured under 14.1.2 to be taken into account and only the excess thereof may be insured, which excess shall be reduced as the freight or hire is advanced or earned by the gross amount so advanced or earned.

14.1.4   *Anticipated Freight if the Vessel sails in ballast and not under Charter.* A sum not exceeding the anticipated gross freight on next cargo passage, such sum to be reasonably estimated on the basis of the current rate of freight at time of insurance plus the charges of insurance. Any sum insured under 14.1.2 to be taken into account and only the excess thereof may be insured.

14.1.5   *Time Charter Hire or Charter Hire for Series of Voyages.* A sum not exceeding 50% of the gross hire which is to be earned under the charter in a period not exceeding 18 months. Any sum insured under 14.1.2 to be taken into account and only the excess thereof may be insured, which excess shall be reduced as the hire is advanced or earned under the charter by 50% of the gross amount so advanced or earned but the sum insured need not be reduced while the total of the sums insured under 14.1.2 and 14.1.5 does not exceed 50% of the gross hire still to be earned under the charter. An insurance under this Section may begin on the signing of the charter.

14.1.6   *Premiums.* A sum not exceeding the actual premiums of all interests insured for a period not exceeding 12 months (excluding premiums insured under the foregoing sections but including, if required, the premium or estimated calls on any Club or War etc. Risk insurance) reducing pro rata monthly.

14.1.7   *Returns of Premium.* A sum not exceeding the actual returns which are allowable under any insurance but which would not be recoverable thereunder in the event of a total loss of the Vessel whether by insured perils or otherwise.

14.1.8   *Insurance irrespective of amount against:*
Any risks excluded by Clauses 16, 17, 18 and 19 below.

14.2   Warranted that no insurance on any interests enumerated in the foregoing 14.1.1 to 14.1.7 in excess of the amounts permitted therein and no other insurance which includes total loss of the Vessel P.P.I., F.I.A., or subject to any other like term, is or shall be effected to operate during the currency of this insurance by or for account of the Assured, Owners, Managers or Mortgagees. Provided always that a breach of this warranty shall not afford the Underwriters any defence to a claim by a Mortgagee who has accepted this insurance without knowledge of such breach.

15   RETURNS FOR LAY-UP AND CANCELLATION

15.1   To return as follows:

| 15.1.1 | Pro rata monthly net for each uncommenced month if this insurance be cancelled by agreement. | 176 |

15.1.2   For each period of 30 consecutive days the Vessel may be laid up in a port or in a lay-up area | 177
provided such port or lay-up area is approved by the Underwriters (with special liberties as | 178
hereinafter allowed) | 179

         (a)....................................per cent net not under repair | 180

         (b)....................................per cent net under repair. | 181

If the Vessel is under repair during part only of a period for which a return is claimable, the return | 182
shall be calculated pro rata to the number of days under (a) and (b) respectively. | 183

15.2   PROVIDED ALWAYS THAT | 184

15.2.1   a total loss of the Vessel, whether by insured perils or otherwise, has not occurred during the period | 185
covered by this insurance or any extension thereof | 186

15.2.2   in no case shall a return be allowed when the Vessel is lying in exposed or unprotected waters, or in a | 187
port or lay-up area not approved by the Underwriters but, provided the Underwriters agree that | 188
such non-approved lay-up area is deemed to be within the vicinity of the approved port or lay-up | 189
area, days during which the Vessel is laid up in such non-approved lay-up area may be added to days | 190
in the approved port or lay-up area to calculate a period of 30 consecutive days and a return shall be | 191
allowed for the proportion of such period during which the Vessel is actually laid up in the approved | 192
port or lay-up area | 193

15.2.3   loading or discharging operations or the presence of cargo on board shall not debar returns but no | 194
return shall be allowed for any period during which the Vessel is being used for the storage of cargo | 195
or for lightering purposes | 196

15.2.4   in the event of any amendment of the annual rate, the above rates of return shall be adjusted | 197
accordingly | 198

15.2.5   in the event of any return recoverable under this Clause 15 being based on 30 consecutive days which | 199
fall on successive insurances effected for the same Assured, this insurance shall only be liable for an | 200
amount calculated at pro rata of the period rates 15.1.2 (a) and/or (b) above for the number of days | 201
which come within the period of this insurance and to which a return is actually applicable. Such | 202
overlapping period shall run, at the option of the Assured, either from the first day on which the | 203
Vessel is laid up or the first day of a period of 30 consecutive days as provided under 15.1.2 (a) | 204
or (b), or 15.2.2 above. | 205

The following clauses shall be paramount and shall override anything contained in this insurance inconsistent | 206
therewith. | 207

16   WAR EXCLUSION | 208

In no case shall this insurance cover loss damage liability or expense caused by | 209

16.1   war civil war revolution rebellion insurrection, or civil strife arising therefrom, or any hostile act by or | 210
against a belligerent power | 211

16.2   capture seizure arrest restraint or detainment (barratry and piracy excepted), and the consequences | 212
thereof or any attempt thereat | 213

16.3   derelict mines torpedoes bombs or other derelict weapons of war. | 214

17   STRIKES EXCLUSION | 215

In no case shall this insurance cover loss damage liability or expense caused by | 216

17.1   strikers, locked-out workmen, or persons taking part in labour disturbances, riots or civil commotions | 217

17.2   any terrorist or any person acting from a political motive. | 218

18   MALICIOUS ACTS EXCLUSION | 219

In no case shall this insurance cover loss damage liability or expense arising from | 220

18.1   the detonation of an explosive | 221

18.2   any weapon of war | 222

and caused by any person acting maliciously or from a political motive. | 223

19   NUCLEAR EXCLUSION | 224

In no case shall this insurance cover loss damage liability or expense arising from any weapon of war employing | 225
atomic or nuclear fission and/or fusion or other like reaction or radioactive force or matter. | 226

Appendix 31

1/10/83

(FOR USE ONLY WITH THE NEW MARINE POLICY FORM)
INSTITUTE WAR AND STRIKES CLAUSES.
Hulls—Time
This insurance is subject to English law and practice

1 PERILS 1

Subject always to the exclusions hereinafter referred to, this insurance covers loss of or damage to the Vessel 2
caused by 3

1.1 war civil war revolution rebellion insurrection, or civil strife arising therefrom, or any hostile act by or 4
against a belligerent power 5

1.2 capture seizure arrest restraint or detainment, and the consequences thereof or any attempt thereat 6

1.3 derelict mines torpedoes bombs or other derelict weapons of war 7

1.4 strikers, locked-out workmen, or persons taking part in labour disturbances, riots or civil commotions 8

1.5 any terrorist or any person acting maliciously or from a political motive 9

1.6 confiscation or expropriation. 10

2 INCORPORATION 11

The Institute Time Clauses—Hulls 1/10/83 (including 4/4ths Collision Clause) except Clauses 1.2, 2, 3, 4, 6, 12, 12
21.1.8, 22, 23, 24, 25 and 26 are deemed to be incorporated in this insurance in so far as they do not conflict with 13
the provisions of these clauses. 14

Held covered in case of breach of warranty as to towage or salvage services provided notice be given to the Under- 15
writers immediately after receipt of advices and any additional premium required by them be agreed. 16

3 DETAINMENT 17

In the event that the Vessel shall have been the subject of capture seizure arrest restraint detainment confiscation 18
or expropriation, and the Assured shall thereby have lost the free use and disposal of the Vessel for a continuous 19
period of 12 months then for the purpose of ascertaining whether the Vessel is a constructive total loss the Assured 20
shall be deemed to have been deprived of the possession of the Vessel without any likelihood of recovery. 21

4 EXCLUSIONS 22

This insurance excludes 23

4.1 loss damage liability or expense arising from 24

4.1.1 any detonation of any weapon of war employing atomic or nuclear fission and/or fusion or other 25
like reaction or radioactive force or matter, hereinafter called a nuclear weapon of war 26

4.1.2 the outbreak of war (whether there be a declaration of war or not) between any of the following 27
countries: 28

United Kingdom, United States of America, France, 29
the Union of Soviet Socialist Republics, 30
the People's Republic of China 31

4.1.3 requisition or pre-emption 32

4.1.4 capture seizure arrest restraint detainment confiscation or expropriation by or under the order of the 33
government or any public or local authority of the country in which the Vessel is owned or registered 34

4.1.5 arrest restraint detainment confiscation or expropriation under quarantine regulations or by reason 35
of infringement of any customs or trading regulations 36

4.1.6 the operation of ordinary judicial process, failure to provide security or to pay any fine or penalty or 37
any financial cause 38

4.1.7 piracy (but this exclusion shall not affect cover under Clause 1.4), 39

4.2 loss damage liability or expense covered by the Institute Time Clauses—Hulls 1/10/83 (including 4/4ths 40
Collision Clause) or which would be recoverable thereunder but for Clause 12 thereof, 41

4.3 any claim for any sum recoverable under any other insurance on the Vessel or which would be recoverable 42
under such insurance but for the existence of this insurance, 43

4.4 any claim for expenses arising from delay except such expenses as would be recoverable in principle in 44
English law and practice under the York-Antwerp Rules 1974. 45

5   TERMINATION   46

5.1   This insurance may be cancelled by either the Underwriters or the Assured giving 7 days notice (such   47
cancellation becoming effective on the expiry of 7 days from midnight of the day on which notice of   48
cancellation is issued by or to the Underwriters). The Underwriters agree however to reinstate this   49
insurance subject to agreement between the Underwriters and the Assured prior to the expiry of such   50
notice of cancellation as to new rate of premium and/or conditions and/or warranties.   51

5.2   Whether or not such notice of cancellation has been given this insurance shall TERMINATE   52
AUTOMATICALLY   53

5.2.1   upon the occurrence of any hostile detonation of any nuclear weapon of war as defined in Clause   54
4.1.1 wheresoever or whensoever such detonation may occur and whether or not the Vessel may be   55
involved   56

5.2.2   upon the outbreak of war (whether there be a declaration of war or not) between any of the   57
following countries: 58

United Kingdom, United States of America, France,   59
the Union of Soviet Socialist Republics,   60
the People's Republic of China   61

5.2.3   in the event of the Vessel being requisitioned, either for title or use.   62

5.3   In the event either of cancellation by notice or of automatic termination of this insurance by reason of the   63
operation of this Clause 5, or of the sale of the Vessel, pro rata net return of premium shall be payable to   64
the Assured.   65

**This insurance shall not become effective if, subsequent to its acceptance by the Underwriters and prior to the intended
time of its attachment, there has occurred any event which would have automatically terminated this insurance under
the provisions of Clause 5 above.**

Appendix 32

1/10/83   (FOR USE ONLY WITH THE NEW MARINE POLICY FORM)

INSTITUTE ADDITIONAL PERILS CLAUSES — HULLS

(For use only with the Institute Time Clauses — Hulls 1/10/83)

1   In consideration of an additional premium this insurance is extended to cover   1

1.1   the cost of repairing or replacing   2

1.1.1   any boiler which bursts or shaft which breaks   3

1.1.2   any defective part which has caused loss or damage to the Vessel covered by Clause 6.2.2 of the   4
Institute Time Clauses — Hulls 1/10/83,   5

1.2   loss of or damage to the Vessel caused by any accident or by negligence, incompetence or error of   6
judgement of any person whatsoever.   7

2   Except as provided in 1.1.1 and 1.1.2, nothing in these Additional Perils Clauses shall allow any claim for the cost   8
of repairing or replacing any part found to be defective as a result of a fault or error in design or construction and   9
which has not caused loss of or damage to the Vessel.   10

3   The cover provided in Clause 1 is subject to all other terms, conditions and exclusions contained in this insurance   11
and subject to the proviso that the loss or damage has not resulted from want of due diligence by the Assured,   12
Owners or Managers. Master Officers Crew or Pilots not to be considered Owners within the meaning of this   13
Clause should they hold shares in the Vessel.   14

Appendix 33

1/10/83

(FOR USE ONLY WITH THE NEW MARINE POLICY FORM)

INSTITUTE MACHINERY DAMAGE ADDITIONAL DEDUCTIBLE CLAUSE

(For use only with the Institute Time Clauses — Hulls 1/10/83)

Notwithstanding any provision to the contrary in this insurance a claim for loss of or damage to any machinery, shaft, 1
electrical equipment or wiring, boiler condenser heating coil or associated pipework, arising from any of the perils 2
enumerated in Clauses 6.2.2 to 6.2.5 inclusive of the Institute Time Clauses — Hulls 1/10/83 or from fire or 3

explosion when either has originated in a machinery space, shall be subject to a deductible of 4
Any balance remaining, after application of this deductible, with any other claim arising from the same accident or 5
occurrence, shall then be subject to the deductible in Clause 12.1 of the Institute Time Clauses — Hulls 1/10/83. 6

The provisions of Clauses 12.3 and 12.4 of the Institute Time Clauses — Hulls 1/10/83 shall apply to recoveries and 7
interest comprised in recoveries against any claim which is subject to this Clause. 8

This Clause shall not apply to a claim for total or constructive total loss of the Vessel. 9

Appendix 34

1/3/85   (FOR USE ONLY WITH THE NEW MARINE POLICY FORM)

INSTITUTE TIME CLAUSES HULLS
PORT RISKS including LIMITED NAVIGATION
This insurance is subject to English law and practice

1   NAVIGATION   1

1.1   The Vessel has leave to proceed to and from any wet or dry docks harbours ways cradles and pontoons,   2
within the limits specified in this insurance.   3

1.2   The Vessel is held covered in case of deviation or change of voyage, provided notice be given immediately   4
after receipt of advices and any amended terms of cover and any additional premium required be agreed.   5

2   CONTINUATION   6

Should the Vessel at the expiration of this insurance be at sea or in distress or at a port of refuge or of call, she   7
shall, provided previous notice be given to the Underwriters, be held covered at a pro rata monthly premium to her   8
port of destination.   9

3   TERMINATION   10

This Clause 3 shall prevail notwithstanding any provision whether written typed or printed in this insurance   11
inconsistent therewith.   12

Unless the Underwriters agree to the contrary in writing, this insurance shall terminate automatically at the time of   13

3.1   change of the Classification Society of the Vessel, or change, suspension, discontinuance, withdrawal or   14
expiry of her Class therein, provided that if the Vessel is at sea such automatic termination shall be   15
deferred until arrival at her next port. However where such change, suspension, discontinuance or   16
withdrawal of her Class has resulted from loss or damage covered by Clause 5 of this insurance or which   17
would be covered by an insurance of the Vessel subject to current Institute War and Strikes Clauses Hulls-   18
Time such automatic termination shall only operate should the Vessel sail from her next port without the   19
prior approval of the Classification Society,   20

3.2   any change, voluntary or otherwise, in the ownership or flag, transfer to new management, or charter on   21
a bareboat basis, or requisition for title or use of the Vessel. However, in the event of requisition for title   22
or use without the prior execution of a written agreement by the Assured, such automatic termination   23
shall occur fifteen days after such requisition whether the Vessel is in port or at sea.   24

4   ASSIGNMENT   25

No assignment of or interest in this insurance or in any moneys which may be or become payable thereunder is to   26
be binding on or recognised by the Underwriters unless a dated notice of such assignment or interest signed by the   27
Assured, and by the assignor in the case of subsequent assignment, is endorsed on the Policy and the Policy with   28
such endorsement is produced before payment of any claim or return of premium thereunder.   29

5   PERILS   30

5.1   This insurance covers loss of or damage to the subject-matter insured caused by   31

5.1.1   perils of the seas rivers lakes or other navigable waters   32

5.1.2   fire lightning explosion   33

5.1.3   violent theft by persons from outside the Vessel   34

5.1.4   jettison   35

5.1.5   piracy   36

5.1.6   breakdown of or accident to nuclear installations or reactors   37

5.1.7   contact with aircraft or similar objects, or objects falling therefrom, land conveyance, dock or   38
harbour equipment or installation.   39

5.2   This insurance covers loss of or damage to the subject-matter insured caused by   40

5.2.1   accidents in loading discharging or shifting cargo or fuel   41

5.2.2   bursting of boilers breakage of shafts or any latent defect in the machinery or hull   42

5.2.3   negligence of Master Officers Crew or Pilots   43

5.2.4   negligence of repairers or charterers provided such repairers or charterers are not an Assured   44
hereunder   45

5.2.5	barratry of Master Officers or Crew,	46
	provided such loss or damage has not resulted from want of due diligence by the Assured, Owners or Managers.	47 48
5.3	Master Officers Crew or Pilots not to be considered Owners within the meaning of this Clause 5 should they hold shares in the Vessel.	49 50

6   EARTHQUAKE AND VOLCANIC ERUPTION EXCLUSION   51

In no case shall this insurance cover loss damage liability or expense caused by earthquake or volcanic eruption. This exclusion applies to all claims including claims under Clauses 8, 10, 12 and 14.   52 53

7   POLLUTION HAZARD   54

This insurance covers loss of or damage to the Vessel caused by any governmental authority acting under the powers vested in it to prevent or mitigate a pollution hazard, or threat thereof, resulting directly from damage to the Vessel for which the Underwriters are liable under this insurance, provided such act of governmental authority has not resulted from want of due diligence by the Assured, the Owners, or Managers of the Vessel or any of them to prevent or mitigate such hazard or threat. Master, Officers, Crew or Pilots not to be considered Owners within the meaning of this Clause 7 should they hold shares in the Vessel.   55 56 57 58 59 60

8   COLLISION LIABILITY   61

8.1	The Underwriters agree to indemnify the Assured for any sum or sums paid by the Assured to any other person or persons by reason of the Assured becoming legally liable by way of damages for	62 63
8.1.1	loss of or damage to any other vessel or property on any other vessel	64
8.1.2	delay to or loss of use of any such other vessel or property thereon	65
8.1.3	general average of, salvage of, or salvage under contract of, any such other vessel or property thereon,	66 67
	where such payment by the Assured is in consequence of the Vessel hereby insured coming into collision with any other vessel.	68 69
8.2	The indemnity provided by this Clause 8 shall be in addition to the indemnity provided by the other terms and conditions of this insurance and shall be subject to the following provisions:	70 71
8.2.1	Where the insured Vessel is in collision with another vessel and both vessels are to blame then, unless the liability of one or both vessels becomes limited by law, the indemnity under this Clause 8 shall be calculated on the principle of cross-liabilities as if the respective Owners had been compelled to pay to each other such proportion of each other's damages as may have been properly allowed in ascertaining the balance or sum payable by or to the Assured in consequence of the collision.	72 73 74 75 76
8.2.2	In no case shall the Underwriters' total liability under Clauses 8.1 and 8.2 exceed their proportionate part of the insured value of the Vessel hereby insured in respect of any one such collision.	77 78
8.3	The Underwriters will also pay the legal costs incurred by the Assured or which the Assured may be compelled to pay in contesting liability or taking proceedings to limit liability, with the prior written consent of the Underwriters.	79 80 81

EXCLUSIONS   82

8.4	Provided always that this Clause 8 shall in no case extend to any sum which the Assured shall pay for or in respect of	83 84
8.4.1	removal or disposal of obstructions, wrecks, cargoes or any other thing whatsoever	85
8.4.2	any real or personal property or thing whatsoever except other vessels or property on other vessels	86
8.4.3	the cargo or other property on, or the engagements of, the insured Vessel	87
8.4.4	loss of life, personal injury or illness	88
8.4.5	pollution or contamination of any real or personal property or thing whatsoever (except other vessels with which the insured Vessel is in collision or property on such other vessels).	89 90

9   SISTERSHIP   91

Should the Vessel hereby insured come into collision with or receive salvage services from another vessel belonging wholly or in part to the same Owners or under the same management, the Assured shall have the same rights under this insurance as they would have were the other vessel entirely the property of Owners not interested in the Vessel hereby insured; but in such cases the liability for the collision or the amount payable for the services rendered shall be referred to a sole arbitrator to be agreed upon between the Underwriters and the Assured.   92 93 94 95 96

10   PROTECTION AND INDEMNITY   97

10.1	The Underwriters agree to indemnify the Assured for any sum or sums paid by the Assured to any other person or persons by reason of the Assured becoming legally liable, as owner of the Vessel, for any claim, demand, damages and/or expenses, where such liability is in consequence of any of the following matters or things and arises from an accident or occurrence during the period of this insurance:	98 99 100 101
10.1.1	loss of or damage to any fixed or movable object or property or other thing or interest whatsoever, other than the Vessel, arising from any cause whatsoever in so far as such loss or damage is not covered by Clause 8	102 103 104
10.1.2	any attempted or actual raising, removal or destruction of any fixed or movable object or property or other thing, including the wreck of the Vessel, or any neglect or failure to raise, remove, or destroy the same	105 106 107
10.1.3	liability assumed by the Assured under contracts of customary towage for the purpose of entering or leaving port or manoeuvring within the port during the ordinary course of trading	108 109

| 10.1.4 | loss of life, personal injury, illness or payments made for life salvage | 110 |

10.1.4 loss of life, personal injury, illness or payments made for life salvage 110

10.1.5 liability under Clause 1(a) of the current Lloyd's Standard Form of Salvage Agreement in respect of unsuccessful, partially successful, or uncompleted services if and to the extent that the salvor's expenses plus the increment exceed any amount otherwise recoverable under the Agreement. 111 112 113

10.2 The Underwriters agree to indemnify the Assured for any of the following arising from an accident or occurrence during the period of this insurance: 114 115

10.2.1 the additional cost of fuel, insurance, wages, stores, provisions and port charges reasonably incurred solely for the purpose of landing from the Vessel sick or injured persons or stowaways, refugees, or persons saved at sea 116 117 118

10.2.2 additional expenses brought about by the outbreak of infectious disease on board the Vessel or ashore 119 120

10.2.3 fines imposed on the Vessel, on the Assured, or on any Master Officer crew member or agent of the Vessel who is reimbursed by the Assured, for any act or neglect or breach of any statute or regulation relating to the operation of the Vessel, provided that the Underwriters shall not be liable to indemnify the Assured for any fines which result from any act neglect failure or default of the Assured their agents or servants other than Master Officer or crew member 121 122 123 124 125

10.2.4 the expenses of the removal of the wreck of the Vessel from any place owned, leased or occupied by the Assured 126 127

10.2.5 legal costs incurred by the Assured, or which the Assured may be compelled to pay, in avoiding, minimising or contesting liability with the prior written consent of the Underwriters. 128 129

EXCLUSIONS 130

10.3 Notwithstanding the provisions of Clauses 10.1 and 10.2 this Clause 10 does not cover any liability cost or expense arising in respect of: 131 132

10.3.1 any direct or indirect payment by the Assured under workmen's compensation or employers' liability acts and any other statutory or common law liability in respect of accidents to or illness of workmen or any other persons employed in any capacity whatsoever by the Assured or others in on or about or in connection with the Vessel or her cargo materials or repairs 133 134 135 136

10.3.2 liability assumed by the Assured under agreement expressed or implied in respect of death or illness of or injury to any person employed under a contract of service or apprenticeship by the other party to such agreement 137 138 139

10.3.3 punitive or exemplary damages, however described 140

10.3.4 cargo or other property carried, to be carried or which has been carried on board the Vessel but this Clause 10.3.4 shall not exclude any claim in respect of the extra cost of removing cargo from the wreck of the Vessel 141 142 143

10.3.5 property, owned by builders or repairers or for which they are responsible, which is on board the Vessel 144 145

10.3.6 liability arising under a contract or indemnity in respect of containers, equipment, fuel or other property on board the Vessel and which is owned or leased by the Assured 146 147

10.3.7 cash, negotiable instruments, precious metals or stones, valuables or objects of a rare or precious nature, belonging to persons on board the Vessel, or non-essential personal effects of any Master, Officer or crew member 148 149 150

10.3.8 fuel, insurance, wages, stores, provisions and port charges arising from delay to the Vessel while awaiting a substitute for any Master, Officer or crew member 151 152

10.3.9 fines or penalties arising from overloading or illegal fishing 153

10.3.10 pollution or contamination of any real or personal property or thing whatsoever (This Clause 10.3.10 shall not exclude any amount recoverable under Clause 10.1.5) 154 155

10.3.11 general average, sue and labour and salvage charges, salvage, and/or collision liability to any extent that they are not recoverable under Clauses 8, 12 and 14 by reason of the agreed value and/or the amount insured in respect of the Vessel being inadequate. 156 157 158

10.4 The indemnity provided by this Clause 10 shall be in addition to the indemnity provided by the other terms and conditions of this insurance but in no case shall the Underwriters' liability under this Clause 10 exceed their proportionate part of the insured value of the Vessel in respect of each separate accident or occurrence or series of accidents arising out of the same event. 159 160 161 162

10.5 PROVIDED ALWAYS THAT 163

10.5.1 prompt notice must be given to the Underwriters of every casualty event or claim upon the Assured which may give rise to a claim under this Clause 10 and of every event or matter which may cause the Assured to incur liability costs or expense for which he may be insured under this Clause 10. 164 165 166

10.5.2 the Assured shall not admit liability for or settle any claim for which he may be insured under this Clause 10 without the prior written consent of the Underwriters. 167 168

11 NOTICE OF CLAIM AND TENDERS 169

11.1 In the event of accident whereby loss or damage may result in a claim under this insurance, notice shall be given to the Underwriters prior to survey and also, if the Vessel is abroad, to the nearest Lloyd's Agent so that a surveyor may be appointed to represent the Underwriters should they so desire. 170 171 172

11.2 The Underwriters shall be entitled to decide the port to which the Vessel shall proceed for docking or repair (the actual additional expense of the voyage arising from compliance with the Underwriters' requirements being refunded to the Assured) and shall have a right of veto concerning a place of repair or a repairing firm. 173 174 175 176

11.3 The Underwriters may also take tenders or may require further tenders to be taken for the repair of the Vessel. Where such a tender has been taken and a tender is accepted with the approval of the 177 178

Underwriters, an allowance shall be made at the rate of 30% per annum on the insured value for time lost 179
between the despatch of the invitations to tender required by Underwriters and the acceptance of a tender 180
to the extent that such time is lost solely as the result of tenders having been taken and provided that the 181
tender is accepted without delay after receipt of the Underwriters' approval. 182

Due credit shall be given against the allowance as above for any amounts recovered in respect of fuel and 183
stores and wages and maintenance of the Master Officers and Crew or any member thereof, including 184
amounts allowed in general average, and for any amounts recovered from third parties in respect of 185
damages for detention and/or loss of profit and/or running expenses, for the period covered by the 186
tender allowance or any part thereof. 187

Where a part of the cost of the repair of damage other than a fixed deductible is not recoverable from the 188
Underwriters the allowance shall be reduced by a similar proportion. 189

11.4   In the event of failure to comply with the conditions of this Clause 11, a deduction of 15% shall be made 190
from the amount of the ascertained claim. 191

12   GENERAL AVERAGE AND SALVAGE   192

12.1   This insurance covers the Vessel's proportion of salvage, salvage charges and/or general average, reduced 193
in respect of any under-insurance, but in case of general average sacrifice of the Vessel the Assured may 194
recover in respect of the whole loss without first enforcing their right of contribution from other parties. 195

12.2   Adjustment to be according to the law and practice obtaining at the place where the adventure ends, as if 196
the contract of affreightment contained no special terms upon the subject; but where the contract of 197
affreightment so provides the adjustment shall be according to the York-Antwerp Rules. 198

12.3   When the Vessel sails in ballast, not under charter, the provisions of the York-Antwerp Rules, 1974 199
(excluding Rules XX and XXI) shall be applicable, and the voyage for this purpose shall be deemed to 200
continue from the port or place of departure until the arrival of the Vessel at the first port or place 201
thereafter other than a port or place of refuge or a port or place of call for bunkering only. If at any such 202
intermediate port or place there is an abandonment of the adventure originally contemplated the voyage 203
shall thereupon be deemed to be terminated. 204

12.4   No claim under this Clause 12 shall in any case be allowed where the loss was not incurred to avoid or in 205
connection with the avoidance of a peril insured against. 206

13   DEDUCTIBLE   207

13.1   No claim arising from a peril insured against shall be payable under this insurance unless the aggregate of 208
all such claims arising out of each separate accident or occurrence (including claims under Clauses 8, 10, 209

12 and 14) exceeds . . . . in which case this sum shall be 210
deducted. Nevertheless the expense of sighting the bottom after stranding, if reasonably incurred 211
specially for that purpose, shall be paid even if no damage be found. This Clause 13.1 shall not apply to a 212
claim for total or constructive total loss of the Vessel or, in the event of such a claim, to any associated 213
claim under Clause 14 arising from the same accident or occurrence. 214

13.2   Excluding any interest comprised therein, recoveries against any claim which is subject to the above 215
deductible shall be credited to the Underwriters in full to the extent of the sum by which the aggregate of 216
the claim unreduced by any recoveries exceeds the above deductible. 217

13.3   Interest comprised in recoveries shall be apportioned between the Assured and the Underwriters, taking 218
into account the sums paid by the Underwriters and the dates when such payments were made, 219
notwithstanding that by the addition of interest the Underwriters may receive a larger sum than they have 220
paid. 221

14   DUTY OF ASSURED (SUE AND LABOUR)   222

14.1   In case of any loss or misfortune it is the duty of the Assured and their servants and agents to take such 223
measures as may be reasonable for the purpose of averting or minimising a loss which would be 224
recoverable under this insurance. 225

14.2   Subject to the provisions below and to Clause 13 the Underwriters will contribute to charges properly and 226
reasonably incurred by the Assured their servants or agents for such measures. General average, salvage 227
charges (except as provided for in Clause 14.5) collision defence or attack costs and costs incurred by the 228
Assured in avoiding, minimising or contesting liability covered by Clause 10 are not recoverable under 229
this Clause 14. 230

14.3   Measures taken by the Assured or the Underwriters with the object of saving, protecting or recovering the 231
subject-matter insured shall not be considered as a waiver or acceptance of abandonment or otherwise 232
prejudice the rights of either party. 233

14.4   When expenses are incurred pursuant to this Clause 14 the liability under this insurance shall not exceed 234
the proportion of such expenses that the amount insured hereunder bears to the value of the Vessel as 235
stated herein, or to the sound value of the Vessel at the time of the occurrence giving rise to the 236
expenditure if the sound value exceeds that value. Where the Underwriters have admitted a claim for total 237
loss and property insured by this insurance is saved, the foregoing provisions shall not apply unless the 238
expenses of suing and labouring exceed the value of such property saved and then shall apply only to the 239
amount of the expenses which is in excess of such value. 240

14.5   When a claim for total loss of the Vessel is admitted under this insurance and expenses have been 241
reasonably incurred in saving or attempting to save the Vessel and other property and there are no 242
proceeds, or the expenses exceed the proceeds, then this insurance shall bear its pro rata share of such 243
proportion of the expenses, or of the expenses in excess of the proceeds, as the case may be, as may 244
reasonably be regarded as having been incurred in respect of the Vessel; but if the Vessel be insured for 245
less than its sound value at the time of the occurrence giving rise to the expenditure, the amount 246
recoverable under this clause shall be reduced in proportion to the under-insurance. 247

14.6   The sum recoverable under this Clause 14 shall be in addition to the loss otherwise recoverable under this 248
insurance but shall in no circumstances exceed the amount insured under this insurance in respect of the 249
Vessel. 250

15 NEW FOR OLD   251

Claims payable without deduction new for old.   252

16 BOTTOM TREATMENT   253

In no case shall a claim be allowed in respect of scraping gritblasting and/or other surface preparation or painting   254
of the Vessel's bottom except that   255

   16.1   gritblasting and/or other surface preparation of new bottom plates ashore and supplying and applying   256
         any "shop" primer thereto,   257

   16.2   gritblasting and/or other surface preparation of: 258

         the butts or area of plating immediately adjacent to any renewed or refitted plating damaged during the   259
         course of welding and/or repairs,   260

         areas of plating damaged during the course of fairing, either in place or ashore,   261

   16.3   supplying and applying the first coat of primer/anti-corrosive to those particular areas mentioned in 16.1   262
         and 16.2 above.   263

shall be allowed as part of the reasonable cost of repairs in respect of bottom plating damaged by an insured peril.   264

17 WAGES AND MAINTENANCE   265

No claim shall be allowed, other than in general average, for wages and maintenance of the Master, Officers and   266
Crew, or any member thereof, except when incurred solely for the necessary removal of the Vessel, with the   267
agreement of the Underwriters, from one port to another for the repair of damage covered by the Underwriters, or   268
for trial trips for such repairs, and then only for such wages and maintenance as are incurred whilst the Vessel is   269
under way.   270

18 AGENCY COMMISSION   271

In no case shall any sum be allowed under this insurance either by way of remuneration of the Assured for time   272
and trouble taken to obtain and supply information or documents or in respect of the commission or charges of   273
any manager, agent, managing or agency company or the like, appointed by or on behalf of the Assured to   274
perform such services.   275

19 UNREPAIRED DAMAGE   276

   19.1   The measure of indemnity in respect of claims for unrepaired damage shall be the reasonable depreciation   277
         in the market value of the Vessel at the time this insurance terminates arising from such unrepaired   278
         damage, but not exceeding the reasonable cost of repairs.   279

   19.2   In no case shall the Underwriters be liable for unrepaired damage in the event of a subsequent total loss   280
         (whether or not covered under this insurance) sustained during the period covered by this insurance or   281
         any extension thereof.   282

   19.3   The Underwriters shall not be liable in respect of unrepaired damage for more than the insured value at   283
         the time this insurance terminates.   284

20 CONSTRUCTIVE TOTAL LOSS   285

   20.1   In ascertaining whether the Vessel is a constructive total loss, the insured value shall be taken as the   286
         repaired value and nothing in respect of the damaged or break-up value of the Vessel or wreck shall be   287
         taken into account.   288

   20.2   No claim for constructive total loss based upon the cost of recovery and/or repair of the Vessel shall be   289
         recoverable hereunder unless such cost would exceed the insured value. In making this determination only   290
         the cost relating to a single accident or sequence of damages arising from the same accident shall be taken   291
         into account.   292

21 FREIGHT WAIVER   293

In the event of total or constructive total loss no claim to be made by the Underwriters for freight whether notice   294
of abandonment has been given or not.   295

22. DISBURSEMENTS WARRANTY   296

   22.1   Additional insurances as follows are permitted   297

   22.1.1   *Disbursements, Managers' Commissions, Profits or Excess or Increased Value of Hull and*   298
          Machinery. A sum not exceeding 25% of the value stated herein.   299

   22.1.2   *Freight, Chartered Freight or Anticipated Freight, insured for time.* A sum not exceeding 25% of   300
          the value as stated herein less any sum insured, however described, under 22.1.1.   301

   22.1.3   *Freight or Hire, under contracts for voyage.* A sum not exceeding the gross freight or hire for the   302
          current cargo passage and next succeeding cargo passage (such insurance to include, if required, a   303
          preliminary and an intermediate ballast passage) plus the charges of insurance. In the case of a   304
          voyage charter where payment is made on a time basis, the sum permitted for insurance shall be   305
          calculated on the estimated duration of the voyage, subject to the limitation of two cargo passages   306
          as laid down herein. Any sum insured under 22.1.2 to be taken into account and only the excess   307
          thereof may be insured, which excess shall be reduced as the freight or hire is advanced or earned by   308
          the gross amount so advanced or earned.   309

   22.1.4   *Anticipated Freight if the Vessel sails in ballast and not under Charter.* A sum not exceeding the   310
          anticipated gross freight on next cargo passage, such sum to be reasonably estimated on the basis of   311
          the current rate of freight at time of insurance plus the charges of insurance. Any sum insured under   312
          22.1.2 to be taken into account and only the excess thereof may be insured.   313

   22.1.5   *Time Charter Hire or Charter Hire for Series of Voyages.* A sum not exceeding 50% of the gross   314
          hire which is to be earned under the charter in a period not exceeding 18 months. Any sum insured   315

under 22.1.2 to be taken into account and only the excess thereof may be insured, which excess shall 316
be reduced as the hire is advanced or earned under the charter by 50% of the gross amount so 317
advanced or earned but the sum insured need not be reduced while the total of the sums insured 318
under 22.1.2 and 22.1.5 does not exceed 50% of the gross hire still to be earned under the charter. 319
An insurance under this Section may begin on the signing of the charter. 320

22.1.6 *Premiums.* A sum not exceeding the actual premiums of all interests insured for a period not 321
exceeding 12 months (excluding premiums insured under the foregoing sections but including, if 322
required, the premium or estimated calls on any Club or War etc. Risk insurance) reducing pro rata 323
monthly. 324

22.1.7 *Returns of Premium.* A sum not exceeding the actual returns which are allowable under any 325
insurance but which would not be recoverable thereunder in the event of a total loss of the Vessel 326
whether by insured perils or otherwise. 327

22.1.8 *Insurance irrespective of amount against:* 328
Any risks excluded by Clauses 6, 24, 25, 26 and 27. 329

22.2 Warranted that no insurance on any interests enumerated in the foregoing 22.1.1 to 22.1.7 in excess of the 330
amounts permitted therein and no other insurance which includes total loss of the Vessel P.P.I., F.I.A., 331
or subject to any other like term, is or shall be effected to operate during the currency of this insurance by 332
or for account of the Assured, Owners, Managers or Mortgagees. Provided always that a breach of this 333
warranty shall not afford the Underwriters any defence to a claim by a Mortgagee who has accepted this 334
insurance without knowledge of such breach. 335

23 RETURNS FOR CANCELLATION 336

To return pro rata monthly net for each uncommenced month if this insurance be cancelled either by agreement or 337
by the operation of Clause 3 provided that a total loss of the Vessel, whether by insured perils or otherwise, has 338
not occurred during the period of this insurance or any extension thereof. 339

The following clauses shall be paramount and shall override anything contained in this insurance inconsistent 340
therewith. 341

24 WAR EXCLUSION 342

In no case shall this insurance cover loss damage liability or expense caused by 343

24.1 war civil war revolution rebellion insurrection, or civil strife arising therefrom, or any hostile act by or 344
against a belligerent power 345

24.2 capture seizure arrest restraint or detainment (barratry and piracy excepted), and the consequences 346
thereof or any attempt thereat 347

24.3 derelict mines torpedoes bombs or other derelict weapons of war. 348

25 STRIKES EXCLUSION 349

In no case shall this insurance cover loss damage liability or expense caused by 350

25.1 strikers, locked-out workmen, or persons taking part in labour disturbances, riots or civil commotions 351

25.2 any terrorist or any person acting from a political motive. 352

26 MALICIOUS ACTS EXCLUSION 353

In no case shall this insurance cover loss damage liability or expense arising from 354

26.1 the detonation of an explosive 355

26.2 any weapon of war 356

and caused by any person acting maliciously or from a political motive. 357

27 NUCLEAR EXCLUSION 358

In no case shall this insurance cover loss damage liability or expense arising from any weapon of war employing 359
atomic or nuclear fission and/or fusion or other like reaction or radioactive force or matter. 360

Appendix 35

1/3/85 (FOR USE ONLY WITH THE NEW MARINE POLICY FORM)

INSTITUTE TIME CLAUSES HULLS
PORT RISKS

This insurance is subject to English law and practice

1 NAVIGATION 1

The Vessel has leave to proceed to and from any wet or dry docks harbours ways cradles and pontoons, within the 2
limits specified in this insurance. 3

2 TERMINATION 4

This Clause 2 shall prevail notwithstanding any provision whether written typed or printed in this insurance 5
inconsistent therewith. 6

Unless Underwriters agree to the contrary in writing, this insurance shall terminate automatically at the time of 7

2.1 change of the Classification Society of the Vessel, or change, suspension, discontinuance, withdrawal or 8
expiry of her Class therein. However where such change, suspension, discontinuance or withdrawal of her 9
Class has resulted from loss or damage covered by Clause 4 of this insurance or which would be covered 10
by an insurance of the Vessel subject to current Institute War and Strikes Clauses Hulls-Time such 11
automatic termination shall not operate. 12

2.2 any change, voluntary or otherwise, in the ownership or flag, transfer to new management, or charter on 13
a bareboat basis, or requisition for title or use of the Vessel. However, in the event of requisition for title 14
or use without the prior execution of a written agreement by the Assured, such automatic termination 15
shall occur fifteen days after such requisition whether the Vessel is in port or at sea. 16

3 ASSIGNMENT 17

No assignment of or interest in this insurance or in any moneys which may be or become payable thereunder is to 18
be binding on or recognised by the Underwriters unless a dated notice of such assignment or interest signed by the 19
Assured, and by the assignor in the case of subsequent assignment, is endorsed on the Policy and the Policy with 20
such endorsement is produced before payment of any claim or return of premium thereunder. 21

4 PERILS 22

4.1 This insurance covers loss of or damage to the subject-matter insured caused by 23
4.1.1 perils of the seas rivers lakes or other navigable waters 24
4.1.2 fire lightning explosion 25
4.1.3 violent theft by persons from outside the Vessel 26
4.1.4 jettison 27
4.1.5 piracy 28
4.1.6 breakdown of or accident to nuclear installations or reactors 29
4.1.7 contact with aircraft or similar objects, or objects falling therefrom, land conveyance, dock or 30
harbour equipment or installation. 31

4.2 This insurance covers loss of or damage to the subject-matter insured caused by 32
4.2.1 accidents in loading discharging or shifting cargo or fuel 33
4.2.2 bursting of boilers breakage of shafts or any latent defect in the machinery or hull 34
4.2.3 negligence of Master Officers Crew or Pilots 35
4.2.4 negligence of repairers or charterers provided such repairers or charterers are not an Assured 36
hereunder 37
4.2.5 barratry of Master Officers or Crew, 38

provided such loss or damage has not resulted from want of due diligence by the Assured, Owners or 39
Managers. 40

4.3 Master Officers Crew or Pilots not to be considered Owners within the meaning of this Clause 4 should 41
they hold shares in the Vessel. 42

5 EARTHQUAKE AND VOLCANIC ERUPTION EXCLUSION 43

In no case shall this insurance cover loss damage liability or expense caused by earthquake or volcanic eruption. 44
This exclusion applies to all claims including claims under Clauses 7, 9, 11 and 13. 45

6	**POLLUTION HAZARD**		46

This insurance covers loss of or damage to the Vessel caused by any governmental authority acting under the 47
powers vested in it to prevent or mitigate a pollution hazard, or threat thereof, resulting directly from damage to 48
the Vessel for which the Underwriters are liable under this insurance, provided such act of governmental authority 49
has not resulted from want of due diligence by the Assured, the Owners, or Managers of the Vessel or any of them 50
to prevent or mitigate such hazard or threat. Master, Officers, Crew or Pilots not to be considered Owners within 51
the meaning of this Clause 6 should they hold shares in the Vessel. 52

7   COLLISION LIABILITY   53

7.1   The Underwriters agree to indemnify the Assured for any sum or sums paid by the Assured to any other   54
person or persons by reason of the Assured becoming legally liable by way of damages for   55

7.1.1   loss of or damage to any other vessel or property on any other vessel   56

7.1.2   delay to or loss of use of any such other vessel or property thereon   57

7.1.3   general average of, salvage of, or salvage under contract of, any such other vessel or property   58
thereon,   59

where such payment by the Assured is in consequence of the Vessel hereby insured coming into collision   60
with any other vessel.   61

7.2   The indemnity provided by this Clause 7 shall be in addition to the indemnity provided by the other terms   62
and conditions of this insurance and shall be subject to the following provisions: 63

7.2.1   Where the insured Vessel is in collision with another vessel and both vessels are to blame then, unless   64
the liability of one or both vessels becomes limited by law, the indemnity under this Clause 7 shall be   65
calculated on the principle of cross-liabilities as if the respective Owners had been compelled to pay   66
to each other such proportion of each other's damages as may have been properly allowed in   67
ascertaining the balance or sum payable by or to the Assured in consequence of the collision.   68

7.2.2   In no case shall the Underwriters' total liability under Clauses 7.1 and 7.2 exceed their proportionate   69
part of the insured value of the Vessel hereby insured in respect of any one such collision.   70

7.3   The Underwriters will also pay the legal costs incurred by the Assured or which the Assured may be   71
compelled to pay in contesting liability or taking proceedings to limit liability, with the prior written   72
consent of the Underwriters.   73

EXCLUSIONS   74

7.4   Provided always that this Clause 7 shall in no case extend to any sum which the Assured shall pay for or in   75
respect of   76

7.4.1   removal or disposal of obstructions, wrecks, cargoes or any other thing whatsoever   77

7.4.2   any real or personal property or thing whatsoever except other vessels or property on other vessels   78

7.4.3   the cargo or other property on, or the engagements of, the insured Vessel   79

7.4.4   loss of life, personal injury or illness   80

7.4.5   pollution or contamination of any real or personal property or thing whatsoever (except other   81
vessels with which the insured Vessel is in collision or property on such other vessels).   82

8   SISTERSHIP   83

Should the Vessel hereby insured come into collision with or receive salvage services from another vessel belonging   84
wholly or in part to the same Owners or under the same management, the Assured shall have the same rights under   85
this insurance as they would have were the other vessel entirely the property of Owners not interested in the Vessel   86
hereby insured; but in such cases the liability for the collision or the amount payable for the services rendered shall   87
be referred to a sole arbitrator to be agreed upon between the Underwriters and the Assured.   88

9   PROTECTION AND INDEMNITY   89

9.1   The Underwriters agree to indemnify the Assured for any sum or sums paid by the Assured to any other   90
person or persons by reason of the Assured becoming legally liable, as owner of the Vessel, for any claim,   91
demand, damages and/or expenses, where such liability is in consequence of any of the following matters   92
or things and arises from an accident or occurrence during the period of this insurance: 93

9.1.1   loss of or damage to any fixed or movable object or property or other thing or interest whatsoever,   94
other than the Vessel, arising from any cause whatsoever in so far as such loss or damage is not   95
covered by Clause 7   96

9.1.2   any attempted or actual raising, removal or destruction of any fixed or movable object or property   97
or other thing, including the wreck of the Vessel, or any neglect or failure to raise, remove, or   98
destroy the same   99

9.1.3   liability assumed by the Assured under contracts of customary towage for the purpose of entering or   100
leaving port or manoeuvring within the port during the ordinary course of trading   101

9.1.4   loss of life, personal injury, illness or payments made for life salvage   102

9.1.5   liability under Clause 1(a) of the current Lloyd's Standard Form of Salvage Agreement in respect of   103
unsuccessful, partially successful, or uncompleted services if and to the extent that the salvor's   104
expenses plus the increment exceed any amount otherwise recoverable under the Agreement.   105

9.2   The Underwriters agree to indemnify the Assured for any of the following arising from an accident or   106
occurrence during the period of this insurance: 107

9.2.1   the additional cost of fuel, insurance, wages, stores, provisions and port charges reasonably   108
incurred solely for the purpose of landing from the Vessel sick or injured persons or stowaways,   109
refugees, or persons saved at sea   110

9.2.2   additional expenses brought about by the outbreak of infectious disease on board the Vessel or   111
ashore   112

9.2.3	fines imposed on the Vessel, on the Assured, or on any Master Officer crew member or agent of the	113
	Vessel who is reimbursed by the Assured, for any act or neglect or breach of any statute or	114
	regulation relating to the operation of the Vessel, provided that the Underwriters shall not be liable	115
	to indemnify the Assured for any fines which result from any act neglect failure or default of the	116
	Assured their agents or servants other than Master Officer or crew member	117
9.2.4	the expenses of the removal of the wreck of the Vessel from any place owned, leased or occupied by	118
	the Assured	119
9.2.5	legal costs incurred by the Assured, or which the Assured may be compelled to pay, in avoiding,	120
	minimising or contesting liability with the prior written consent of the Underwriters.	121

EXCLUSIONS   122

9.3	Notwithstanding the provisions of Clauses 9.1 and 9.2 this Clause 9 does not cover any liability cost or	123
	expense arising in respect of:	124
9.3.1	any direct or indirect payment by the Assured under workmen's compensation or employers'	125
	liability acts and any other statutory or common law liability in respect of accidents to or illness of	126
	workmen or any other persons employed in any capacity whatsoever by the Assured or others in on	127
	or about or in connection with the Vessel or her cargo materials or repairs	128
9.3.2	liability assumed by the Assured under agreement expressed or implied in respect of death or illness	129
	of or injury to any person employed under a contract of service or apprenticeship by the other party	130
	to such agreement	131
9.3.3	punitive or exemplary damages, however described	132
9.3.4	cargo or other property carried, to be carried or which has been carried on board the Vessel but this	133
	Clause 9.3.4 shall not exclude any claim in respect of the extra cost of removing cargo from the	134
	wreck of the Vessel	135
9.3.5	property, owned by builders or repairers or for which they are responsible, which is on board the	136
	Vessel	137
9.3.6	liability arising under a contract or indemnity in respect of containers, equipment, fuel or other	138
	property on board the Vessel and which is owned or leased by the Assured	139
9.3.7	cash, negotiable instruments, precious metals or stones, valuables or objects of a rare or precious	140
	nature, belonging to persons on board the Vessel, or non-essential personal effects of any Master,	141
	Officer or crew member	142
9.3.8	fuel, insurance, wages, stores, provisions and port charges arising from delay to the Vessel while	143
	awaiting a substitute for any Master, Officer or crew member	144
9.3.9	fines or penalties arising from overloading or illegal fishing	145
9.3.10	pollution or contamination of any real or personal property or thing whatsoever (This Clause 9.3.10	146
	shall not exclude any amount recoverable under Clause 9.1.5)	147
9.3.11	general average, sue and labour and salvage charges, salvage, and/or collision liability to any extent	148
	that they are not recoverable under Clauses 7, 11 and 13 by reason of the agreed value and/or the	149
	amount insured in respect of the Vessel being inadequate.	150

9.4	The indemnity provided by this Clause 9 shall be in addition to the indemnity provided by the other terms	151
	and conditions of this insurance but in no case shall the Underwriters' liability under this Clause 9 exceed	152
	their proportionate part of the insured value of the Vessel in respect of each separate accident or	153
	occurrence or series of accidents arising out of the same event.	154
9.5	PROVIDED ALWAYS THAT	155
9.5.1	prompt notice must be given to the Underwriters of every casualty event or claim upon the Assured	156
	which may give rise to a claim under this Clause 9 and of every event or matter which may cause the	157
	Assured to incur liability costs or expense for which he may be insured under this Clause 9.	158
9.5.2	the Assured shall not admit liability for or settle any claim for which he may be insured under this	159
	Clause 9 without the prior written consent of the Underwriters.	160

10 NOTICE OF CLAIM AND TENDERS   161

10.1	In the event of accident whereby loss or damage may result in a claim under this insurance, notice shall be	162
	given to the Underwriters prior to survey and also, if the Vessel is abroad, to the nearest Lloyd's Agent so	163
	that a surveyor may be appointed to represent the Underwriters should they so desire.	164
10.2	The Underwriters shall be entitled to decide the port to which the Vessel shall proceed for docking or	165
	repair (the actual additional expense of the voyage arising from compliance with the Underwriters'	166
	requirements being refunded to the Assured) and shall have a right of veto concerning a place of repair or	167
	a repairing firm.	168
10.3	The Underwriters may also take tenders or may require further tenders to be taken for the repair of the	169
	Vessel. Where such a tender has been taken and a tender is accepted with the approval of the	170
	Underwriters, an allowance shall be made at the rate of 30% per annum on the insured value for time lost	171
	between the despatch of the invitations to tender required by Underwriters and the acceptance of a tender	172
	to the extent that such time is lost solely as the result of tenders having been taken and provided that the	173
	tender is accepted without delay after receipt of the Underwriters' approval.	174
	Due credit shall be given against the allowance as above for any amounts recovered in respect of fuel and	175
	stores and wages and maintenance of the Master Officers and Crew or any member thereof, including	176
	amounts allowed in general average, and for any amounts recovered from third parties in respect of	177
	damages for detention and/or loss of profit and/or running expenses, for the period covered by the	178
	tender allowance or any part thereof.	179
	Where a part of the cost of the repair of damage other than a fixed deductible is not recoverable from the	180
	Underwriters the allowance shall be reduced by a similar proportion.	181

10.4	In the event of failure to comply with the conditions of this Clause 10, a deduction of 15% shall be made from the amount of the ascertained claim.	182 183

11 GENERAL AVERAGE AND SALVAGE   184

11.1	This insurance covers the Vessel's proportion of salvage, salvage charges and/or general average, reduced in respect of any under-insurance, but in case of general average sacrifice of the Vessel the Assured may recover in respect of the whole loss without first enforcing their right of contribution from other parties.	185 186 187
11.2	Adjustment to be according to the law and practice obtaining at the place where the adventure ends, as if the contract of affreightment contained no special terms upon the subject; but where the contract of affreightment so provides the adjustment shall be according to the York-Antwerp Rules.	188 189 190
11.3	No claim under this Clause 11 shall in any case be allowed where the loss was not incurred to avoid or in connection with the avoidance of a peril insured against.	191 192

12 DEDUCTIBLE   193

12.1	No claim arising from a peril insured against shall be payable under this insurance unless the aggregate of all such claims arising out of each separate accident or occurrence (including claims under Clauses 7, 9, 11 and 13) exceeds . . . . in which case this sum shall be deducted. Nevertheless the expense of sighting the bottom after stranding, if reasonably incurred specially for that purpose, shall be paid even if no damage be found. This Clause 12.1 shall not apply to a claim for total or constructive total loss of the Vessel or, in the event of such a claim, to any associated claim under Clause 13 arising from the same accident or occurrence.	194 195 196 197 198 199 200
12.2	Excluding any interest comprised therein, recoveries against any claim which is subject to the above deductible shall be credited to the Underwriters in full to the extent of the sum by which the aggregate of the claim unreduced by any recoveries exceeds the above deductible.	201 202 203
12.3	Interest comprised in recoveries shall be apportioned between the Assured and the Underwriters, taking into account the sums paid by the Underwriters and the dates when such payments were made, notwithstanding that by the addition of interest the Underwriters may receive a larger sum than they have paid.	204 205 206 207

13 - DUTY OF ASSURED (SUE AND LABOUR)   208

13.1	In case of any loss or misfortune it is the duty of the Assured and their servants and agents to take such measures as may be reasonable for the purpose of averting or minimising a loss which would be recoverable under this insurance.	209 210 211
13.2	Subject to the provisions below and to Clause 12 the Underwriters will contribute to charges properly and reasonably incurred by the Assured their servants or agents for such measures. General average, salvage charges (except as provided for in Clause 13.5) collision defence or attack costs and costs incurred by the Assured in avoiding, minimising or contesting liability covered by Clause 9 are not recoverable under this Clause 13.	212 213 214 215 216
13.3	Measures taken by the Assured or the Underwriters with the object of saving, protecting or recovering the subject-matter insured shall not be considered as a waiver or acceptance of abandonment or otherwise prejudice the rights of either party.	217 218 219
13.4	When expenses are incurred pursuant to this Clause 13 the liability under this insurance shall not exceed the proportion of such expenses that the amount insured hereunder bears to the value of the Vessel as stated herein, or to the sound value of the Vessel at the time of the occurrence giving rise to the expenditure if the sound value exceeds that value. Where the Underwriters have admitted a claim for total loss and property insured by this insurance is saved, the foregoing provisions shall not apply unless the expenses of suing and labouring exceed the value of such property saved and then shall apply only to the amount of the expenses which is in excess of such value.	220 221 222 223 224 225 226
13.5	When a claim for total loss of the Vessel is admitted under this insurance and expenses have been reasonably incurred in saving or attempting to save the Vessel and other property and there are no proceeds, or the expenses exceed the proceeds, then this insurance shall bear its pro rata share of such proportion of the expenses, or of the expenses in excess of the proceeds, as the case may be, as may reasonably be regarded as having been incurred in respect of the Vessel; but if the Vessel be insured for less than its sound value at the time of the occurrence giving rise to the expenditure, the amount recoverable under this clause shall be reduced in proportion to the under-insurance.	227 228 229 230 231 232 233
13.6	The sum recoverable under this Clause 13 shall be in addition to the loss otherwise recoverable under this insurance but shall in no circumstances exceed the amount insured under this insurance in respect of the Vessel.	234 235 236

14 NEW FOR OLD   237

Claims payable without deduction new for old.   238

15 BOTTOM TREATMENT   239

In no case shall a claim be allowed in respect of scraping gritblasting and/or other surface preparation or painting of the Vessel's bottom except that   240 241

15.1	gritblasting and/or other surface preparation of new bottom plates ashore and supplying and applying any "shop" primer thereto,	242 243
15.2	gritblasting and/or other surface preparation of:	244
	the butts or area of plating immediately adjacent to any renewed or refitted plating damaged during the course of welding and/or repairs,	245 246
	areas of plating damaged during the course of fairing, either in place or ashore,	247
15.3	supplying and applying the first coat of primer/anti-corrosive to those particular areas mentioned in 15.1 and 15.2 above,	248 249

shall be allowed as part of the reasonable cost of repairs in respect of bottom plating damaged by an insured peril.   250

16 WAGES AND MAINTENANCE   251

No claim shall be allowed, other than in general average, for wages and maintenance of the Master, Officers and   252
Crew, or any member thereof, except when incurred solely for the necessary removal of the Vessel, with the   253
agreement of the Underwriters, from one port to another for the repair of damage covered by the Underwriters, or   254
for trial trips for such repairs, and then only for such wages and maintenance as are incurred whilst the Vessel is   255
under way.   256

17 AGENCY COMMISSION   257

In no case shall any sum be allowed under this insurance either by way of remuneration of the Assured for time   258
and trouble taken to obtain and supply information or documents or in respect of the commission or charges of   259
any manager, agent, managing or agency company or the like, appointed by or on behalf of the Assured to   260
perform such services.   261

18 UNREPAIRED DAMAGE   262

18.1   The measure of indemnity in respect of claims for unrepaired damage shall be the reasonable depreciation   263
in the market value of the Vessel at the time this insurance terminates arising from such unrepaired   264
damage, but not exceeding the reasonable cost of repairs.   265

18.2   In no case shall the Underwriters be liable for unrepaired damage in the event of a subsequent total loss   266
(whether or not covered under this insurance) sustained during the period covered by this insurance or   267
any extension thereof.   268

18.3   The Underwriters shall not be liable in respect of unrepaired damage for more than the insured value at   269
the time this insurance terminates.   270

19 CONSTRUCTIVE TOTAL LOSS   271

19.1   In ascertaining whether the Vessel is a constructive total loss, the insured value shall be taken as the   272
repaired value and nothing in respect of the damaged or break-up value of the Vessel or wreck shall be   273
taken into account.   274

19.2   No claim for constructive total loss based upon the cost of recovery and/or repair of the Vessel shall be   275
recoverable hereunder unless such cost would exceed the insured value. In making this determination only   276
the cost relating to a single accident or sequence of damages arising from the same accident shall be taken   277
into account.   278

20. DISBURSEMENTS WARRANTY   279

20.1.   Additional insurances as follows are permitted: 280

20.1.1   *Disbursements, Managers' Commissions, Profits or Excess or Increased Value of Hull and*   281
Machinery. A sum not exceeding 25% of the value stated herein.   282

20.1.2   *Earnings or Anticipated Freight, insured for time.* A sum not exceeding 25% of the value as stated   283
herein less any sum insured, however described, under 20.1.1.   284

20.1.3   *Freight or Hire, under contracts for voyage.* A sum not exceeding the gross freight or hire for the   285
first passage and next succeeding cargo passage plus the charges of insurance. In the case of a   286
voyage charter where payment is made on a time basis, the sum permitted for insurance shall be   287
calculated on the estimated duration of the voyage, subject to the limitation of two cargo passages   288
as laid down herein. Any sum insured under 20.1.2 to be taken into account and only the excess   289
thereof may be insured.   290

20.1.4   *Time Charter Hire or Charter Hire for Series of Voyages.* A sum not exceeding 50% of the gross   291
hire which is to be earned under the charter in a period not exceeding 18 months. Any sum insured   292
under 20.1.2 to be taken into account and only the excess thereof may be insured. An insurance   293
under this Section may begin on the signing of the charter.   294

20.1.5   *Premiums.* A sum not exceeding the actual premiums of all interests insured for a period not   295
exceeding 12 months (excluding premiums insured under the foregoing sections but including, if   296
required, the premium or estimated calls on any Club or War etc. Risk insurance) reducing pro rata   297
monthly.   298

20.1.6   *Returns of Premium.* A sum not exceeding the actual returns which are allowable under any   299
insurance but which would not be recoverable thereunder in the event of a total loss of the Vessel   300
whether by insured perils or otherwise.   301

20.1.7   *Insurance irrespective of amount against:*   302
Any risks excluded by Clauses 5, 22, 23, 24 and 25.   303

20.2   Warranted that no insurance on any interests enumerated in the foregoing 20.1.1 to 20.1.6 in excess of the   304
amounts permitted therein and no other insurance which includes total loss of the Vessel P.P.I., F.I.A.,   305
or subject to any other like term, is or shall be effected to operate during the currency of this insurance by   306
or for account of the Assured, Owners, Managers or Mortgagees. Provided always that a breach of this   307
warranty shall not afford the Underwriters any defence to a claim by a Mortgagee who has accepted this   308
insurance without knowledge of such breach.   309

21 RETURNS FOR CANCELLATION   310

To return pro rata monthly net for each uncommenced month if this insurance be cancelled either by agreement or   311
by the operation of Clause 2 provided that a total loss of the Vessel, whether by insured perils or otherwise, has   312
not occurred during the period of this insurance or any extension thereof.   313

The following clauses shall be paramount and shall override anything contained in this insurance inconsistent   314
therewith.   315

APPENDIX 35

1375

Appendix 36

1/5/71

INSTITUTE FISHING VESSEL CLAUSES

Navigation.

1. (*a*) The Vessel is covered subject to the provisions of this Policy at all times and has leave to sail or navigate with or without pilots, to go on trial trips and to assist and tow vessels or craft in distress, but it is warranted that the Vessel shall not be towed, except as is customary or when in need of assistance, or undertake towage or salvage services under a contract previously arranged by the Assured and/or Owners and/or Managers and/or Charterers. This clause shall not exclude customary towage in connection with loading and discharging.

Removals Ashore.

(*b*) Any part or parts of the subject matter insured are covered subject to the provisions of this Policy whilst ashore for the purpose of repair, overhaul or refitting, including transit from and to the Vessel.

Continuation.

2. Should the Vessel at the expiration of this Policy be at sea or in distress or at a port of refuge or of call, she shall, provided previous notice be given to the Underwriters, be held covered at a pro rata monthly premium to her port of destination.

Breach of Warranty.

3. Held covered in case of any breach of warranty as to cargo, trade, locality, towage, salvage services or date of sailing, provided notice be given to the Underwriters immediately after receipt of advices and any amended terms of cover and any additional premium required by them be agreed.

Additional Damage.

4. This insurance includes loss of or damage to the subject matter insured directly caused by:—

- Accidents in loading discharging or shifting catch cargo fuel or stores
- Explosions on shipboard or elsewhere
- Breakdown of or accident to nuclear installations or reactors on shipboard or elsewhere
- Bursting of boilers breakage of shafts or any latent defect in the machinery or hull
- Negligence of Master Officers Crew or Pilots
- Negligence of repairers
- Contact with aircraft
- Contact with any land conveyance, dock or harbour equipment or installation
- Earthquake, volcanic eruption or lightning

provided such loss or damage has not resulted from want of due diligence by the Assured, Owners or Managers.

Masters Officers Crew or Pilots not to be considered as part Owners within the meaning of this clause should they hold shares in the Vessel.

Machinery Co-insurance.

5. In the event of a claim for loss of or damage to any boiler, shaft, machinery or associated equipment, arising from any of the causes enumerated in Clause 4, attributable in part or in whole to negligence of Master Officers or Crew and recoverable under this insurance only by reason of Clause 4, then the Assured shall, in addition to the deductible, also bear in respect of each accident or occurrence an amount equal to 10% of the balance of such claim. This clause shall not apply to a claim for total or constructive total loss of the Vessel.

General Average and Salvage.

6. Any claim for general average and salvage to be on the basis of an adjustment according to York-Antwerp Rules if so required by the Underwriters but the insured value of Hull and Machinery to be taken as the contributory value without deduction.

Wages and Maintenance.

7. The Underwriters to pay the cost of wages and maintenance of members of crew necessarily retained whilst the Vessel is undergoing repairs for which the Underwriters are liable under this Policy.

Salvage Expenses.

8. Where a claim for total loss of the Vessel is admitted under this Policy and expenses have been reasonably incurred in salving or attempting to salve the Vessel and other property and there are no proceeds, or the expenses exceed the proceeds, then the Underwriters shall pay the expenses, or the expenses in excess of the proceeds, as the case may be.

Average No Thirds.

9. Average payable without deduction new for old, whether the average be particular or general.

Deductible.

10. No claim arising from a peril insured against shall be payable under this insurance unless the aggregate of all such claims arising out of each separate accident or occurrence (including claims under the Suing and Labouring Clause and under Clauses 16, 17, 18 and 19 of these clauses) exceeds .... in which case this sum shall be deducted. Nevertheless the expense of sighting the bottom after stranding, if reasonably incurred specially for that purpose, shall be paid even if no damage be found. This paragraph shall not apply to a claim for total or constructive total loss of the Vessel.

Excluding any interest comprised therein, recoveries against any claim which is subject to the above deductible shall be credited to the Underwriters in full to the extent of the sum by which the aggregate of the claim unreduced by any recoveries exceeds the above deductible.

Interest comprised in recoveries shall be apportioned between the Assured and the Underwriters, taking into account the sums paid by Underwriters and the dates when such payments were made, notwithstanding that by the addition of interest the Underwriters may receive a larger sum than they have paid.

Painting Bottom.

11. No claim shall in any case be allowed in respect of scraping or painting the Vessel's bottom.

Fishing Gear.

12. No claim to attach hereto for loss of or damage to fishing gear during and as a result of fishing operations.

Unrepaired Damage.

13. In no case shall the Underwriters be liable for unrepaired damage in addition to a subsequent total loss sustained during the period covered by this Policy or any extension thereof under Clause 2.

Constructive Total Loss.

14. In ascertaining whether the Vessel is a constructive total loss the insured value shall be taken as the repaired value and nothing in respect of the damaged or break-up value of the Vessel or wreck shall be taken into account.

No claim for constructive total loss based upon the cost of recovery and/or repair of the Vessel shall be recoverable hereunder unless such cost would exceed the insured value.

No Claim for Freight.

15. In the event of total or constructive total loss no claim to be made by the Underwriters for freight whether notice of abandonment has been given or not.

4/4ths Collision Liability.

16. It is further agreed that if the Vessel hereby insured shall come into collision with any other vessel and the Assured shall in consequence thereof become liable to pay and shall pay by way of damages to any other person or persons any sum or sums in respect of such collision for

(i) loss of or damage to any other vessel or property on any other vessel,
(ii) delay to or loss of use of any such other vessel or property thereon, or
(iii) general average of, salvage of, or salvage under contract of, any such other vessel or property thereon,

the Underwriters will pay the Assured such proportion of such sum or sums so paid as their respective subscriptions hereto bear to the value of the Vessel hereby insured, provided always that their liability in respect of any one such collision shall not exceed their proportionate part of the value of the Vessel hereby insured, and in cases in which, with the prior consent in writing of the Underwriters, the liability of the Vessel has been contested or proceedings have been taken to limit liability, they will also pay a like proportion of the costs which the Assured shall thereby incur or be compelled to pay; but when both vessels are to blame, then unless the liability of the Owners of one or both of such vessels becomes limited by law, claims under this clause shall be settled on the principle of cross-liabilities as if the Owners of each vessel had been compelled to pay to the Owners of the other of such vessels such one-half or other proportion of the latter's damages as may have been properly allowed in ascertaining the balance or sum payable by or to the Assured in consequence of such collision.

Provided always that this clause shall in no case extend or be deemed to extend to any sum which the Assured may become liable to pay or shall pay for or in respect of:—

(*a*) *removal or disposal, under statutory powers or otherwise, of obstructions, wrecks, cargoes or any other thing whatsoever,*
(*b*) *any real or personal property or thing whatsoever except other vessels or property on other vessels,*
(*c*) *the cargo or other property on or the engagements of the insured Vessel,*
(*d*) *loss of life, personal injury or illness.*

Sister Ship.

17. Should the Vessel hereby insured come into collision with or receive salvage services from another vessel belonging wholly or in part to the same Owners or under the same management, the Assured shall have the same rights under this Policy as they would have were the other vessel entirely the property of Owners not interested in the Vessel hereby insured; but in such cases the liability for the collision or the amount payable for the services rendered shall be referred to a sole arbitrator to be agreed upon between the Underwriters and the Assured.

Protection and Indemnity.

18. It is further agreed that if by reason of interest in the Vessel during the period covered by this Policy, the Assured:—

(i) shall become liable to pay and shall pay any sum or sums in respect of any liability, claim, demand, damages or expenses arising from or occasioned by any of the following events or happenings which occur during the period covered by this Policy:—

(*a*) Loss of or damage to any other vessel or goods, merchandise, freight, or other things or interests whatsoever, on board such other vessel, caused proximately or otherwise by the Vessel hereby insured,
(*b*) Loss of or damage to any goods, merchandise, freight, or other things or interests whatsoever, other than as aforesaid (not being the Vessel hereby insured),
(*c*) Loss of or damage to any harbour, dock (graving or otherwise), slipway, way, gridiron, pontoon, pier, quay, jetty, stage, buoy, telegraph cable or other fixed or moveable thing whatsoever (not being the Vessel hereby insured),
(*d*) Any attempted or actual raising, removal, or destruction of the wreck of the Vessel hereby insured, or the cargo, catch or fishing gear thereof, or any neglect or failure to raise, remove or destroy the same,
(*e*) Loss of life, personal injury, illness or life salvage,

(ii) shall pay any sum or sums consequent upon any event or happening during the period covered by this Policy but not specified in (i) above, and which would be recoverable absolutely or conditionally under that part, described as "Protection Clause", of the standard terms of entry of the United Kingdom Trawlers Mutual Insurance Company Limited in force at the inception of this Policy,

the Underwriters will pay the Assured such proportion of such sum or sums so paid, or which may be required to indemnify the Assured for such loss, as their respective subscriptions hereto bear to the insured value of the Vessel hereby insured, provided always that their liability under this clause, together with any liability there may be under Clause 19, in respect of any one accident or series of accidents arising out of the same event or happening, shall not exceed their proportionate part of the insured value of the Vessel hereby insured, and in cases in which, with the prior consent in writing of the Underwriters, the liability of the Assured has been contested or proceedings have been taken to limit liability, they will also pay a like proportion of the costs which the Assured shall thereby incur or be compelled to pay.

Removal of Wreck from own Premises.

19. This insurance also to pay the expenses, after deduction of the proceeds of the salvage, not recoverable under Clause 18, of the removal of the wreck of the Vessel hereby insured, or the cargo, catch or fishing gear thereof, from any place owned, leased or occupied by the Assured. Underwriters' liability under this clause is subject to the limitations in amount provided in Clause 18. The provisions of that clause regarding the payment of legal costs shall also apply hereto.

Protection and Indemnity Exclusions.

20. (i) The cover provided by this insurance under Clauses 18 and 19 shall in no case extend or be deemed to extend to include any claim arising:—

(*a*) directly or indirectly under Workmen's Compensation or Employers' Liability Acts and any other Statutory or Common Law Liability in respect of loss of life of or personal injury to or

...ness of any person employed in any capacity whatsoever by the 177
Assured in on or about or in connection with the Vessel hereby 178
insured or her cargo catch materials or repairs. 179
   This sub-clause shall not exclude a claim for which the Assured 180
shall become liable under Sections 34, 35, 40, 41 and 42 of the 181
Merchant Shipping Act, 1906, or any statutory modification 182
thereof, except so far as such claim is for wages or remuneration 183
in the nature of wages. 184
  (b) from strikes, lock-outs, labour disturbances, riots or civil 185
commotions, 186
  (c) from liability assumed by the Assured under agreement expressed 187
or implied in respect of death or illness of or injury to any person 188
employed under a contract of service or apprenticeship by the other 189
party to such agreement except to the extent that the Assured is or 190
would be liable independently of such agreement. 191
 (ii) The cover provided by Clause 18 shall not extend to collision liability 192
covered by Clause 16 nor to any sum or sums paid by the Assured 193
which are not recoverable by the Assured from the Underwriters in the 194
terms of Clause 16 because the total of the sum or sums paid by the 195
Assured exceeds the insured value of the Vessel hereby insured. 196

Catch etc., Exclusion.
21.   Notwithstanding the provisions of Clauses 16 and 18 no liability shall 197
attach thereunder for any claim in respect of goods, catch, fishing gear, merchan- 198
dise, freight, or other things or interests whatsoever on board the Vessel hereby 199
insured or in respect of the engagements of the Vessel hereby insured. 200

Notice of Claim and Tender Clause.
22.   In the event of accident whereby loss or damage may result in a claim 201
under this Policy, notice shall be given to the Underwriters prior to survey and 202
also, if the Vessel is abroad, to the nearest Lloyd's Agent so that a surveyor may 203
be appointed to represent the Underwriters should they so desire. The Under- 204
writers shall be entitled to decide the port to which the Vessel shall proceed for 205
docking or repair (the actual additional expense of the voyage arising from 206
compliance with the Underwriters' requirements being refunded to the Assured) 207
and shall have a right of veto concerning a place of repair or a repairing firm. The 208
Underwriters may also take tenders or may require further tenders to be taken 209
for the repair of the Vessel. Where a tender so taken is accepted with the approval 210
of the Underwriters an allowance shall be made at the rate of 30% per annum on the 211
insured value for time lost between the despatch of the invitations to tender and 212
the acceptance of a tender to the extent that such time is lost solely as the result 213
of tenders having been taken and provided that the tender is accepted without delay 214
after receipt of the Underwriters' approval. 215
  Due credit shall be given against the allowance as above for any amount 216
recovered:— 217
  (a) in respect of fuel and stores and wages and maintenance of the 218
master officers and crew or any member thereof allowed in general 219
or particular average, 220
  (b) from third parties in respect of damages for detention and/or loss 221
of profit and/or running expenses, 222
for the period covered by the tender allowance or any part thereof. 223
  Where a part of the cost of average repairs other than a fixed deductible is not 224
recoverable from the Underwriters the allowance shall be reduced by a similar 225
proportion. 226
  In the event of failure to comply with the conditions of this clause, 15% shall be 227
deducted from the amount of the ascertained claim. 228

Returns for Lying up and Cancelling.
23.   To return as follows:— 229
           per cent. net for each uncommenced month if⌉ 230
this Policy be cancelled by agreement. 231
and for each period of 30 consecutive days the Vessel may be laid up in a 232
port or in a lay-up area provided such port or lay-up area is approved by 233
the Underwriters (with special liberties as hereinafter allowed):— 234

  (a)   per cent. net not under repair ⌉ 235
  (b)   per cent. net under repair. 236
  If the Vessel is under repair during part only of a period for which a 237
return is claimable, the return payable shall be calculated pro rata to the 238
number of days under (a) and (b) respectively. 239
  Provided always that: 240
 (i) in no case shall a return be allowed when the Vessel is lying in 241
exposed or unprotected waters, or in a port or lay-up area not 242
approved by the Underwriters but, provided the Underwriters 243
agree that such non-approved lay-up area is deemed to be within 244
the vicinity of the approved port or lay-up area, days during which 245
the Vessel is laid up in such non-approved lay-up area may be 246
added to days in the approved port or lay-up area to calculate a 247
period of 30 consecutive days and a return shall be allowed for 248
the proportion of such period during which the Vessel is actually 249
laid up in the approved port or lay-up area 250
 (ii) loading or discharging operations or the presence of catch or 251
cargo on board shall not debar returns but no return shall be 252
allowed for any period during which the Vessel is being used for 253
the storage of catch or cargo 254
(iii) in the event of a return for special trade or any other reason 255
being recoverable, the above rates of return of premium shall be 256
reduced accordingly. 257
  In the event of any return recoverable under this clause being based on 30 258
consecutive days which fall on successive policies, effected for the same Assured, 259
this Policy shall only be liable for an amount calculated at pro rata of the period 260
rates (a) and/or (b) above for the number of days which come within the period 261
of this Policy and to which a return is actually applicable. Such overlapping period 262
shall run, at the option of the Assured, either from the first day on which the 263
Vessel is laid up or the first day of a period of 30 consecutive days as provided 264
under (a) or (b) or (i) above. 265

Disbursements Warranty.
24.   Warranted that no insurance is or shall be effected to operate during 266
the currency of this Policy by or for accounts of the Assured, Owners, Mana- 267
gers or Mortgagees on:— 268
  (a) disbursements, commissions or similar interests, P.P.I., F.I.A. or sub- 269
ject to any other like term, 270
  (b) excess or increased value of hull and machinery however described. 271
  Provided always that a breach of this warranty shall not afford the Under- 272
writers any defence to a claim by a Mortgagee who has accepted this Policy with- 273
out knowledge of such breach. 274

Sale or Transfer of Vessel.
25.   If the Vessel is sold or transferred to new management then unless the 275
Underwriters agree in writing to continue the insurance this Policy shall become 276
cancelled from the time of sale or transfer, unless the Vessel is at sea, in which case 277
such cancellation shall, if required, be suspended until arrival at final port of 278
discharge or at port of destination. A pro rata daily return of premium shall be 279
made. 280
  This clause shall prevail notwithstanding any provision whether written, typed 281
or printed in the Policy inconsistent therewith. 282

Assignment.
26.   No assignment of or interest in this Policy or in any moneys which may 283
be or become payable thereunder is to be binding on or recognised by the Under- 284
writers unless a dated notice of such assignment or interest signed by the Assured, 285
and by the assignor in the case of subsequent assignment, is endorsed on this 286
Policy and the Policy with such endorsement is produced before payment of any 287
claim or return of premium thereunder; but nothing in this clause is to have 288
effect as an agreement by the Underwriters to a sale or transfer to new manage- 289
ment. 290

Strikes and Riots Exclusion.
27.   Warranted free of loss or damage caused by strikers, locked-out workmen, 291
or persons taking part in labour disturbances, riots or civil commotions. 292

Unless deleted by the Underwriters the following clauses shall be paramount and shall override anything contained in this insurance inconsistent therewith. 293

War Exclusion.
28.   Warranted free of capture, seizure, arrest, restraint or detainment, and the consequences thereof or of any attempt thereat; also from the consequences of 294
hostilities or warlike operations, whether there be a declaration of war or not; but this warranty shall not exclude collision, contact with any fixed or floating object 295
(other than a mine or torpedo), stranding, heavy weather or fire unless caused directly (and independently of the nature of the voyage or service which the Vessel 296
concerned or, in the case of a collision, any other vessel involved therein, is performing) by a hostile act by or against a belligerent power: and for the purpose of this 297
warranty "power" includes any authority maintaining naval, military or air forces in association with a power. 298
  Further warranted free from the consequences of civil war, revolution, rebellion, insurrection, or civil strife arising therefrom, or piracy. 299

Malicious Acts.
29.   Warranted free of claim arising from:— 300
  (a) the detonation of an explosive 301
  (b) any weapon of war 302
and caused by any person acting maliciously or from a political motive. 303

Nuclear Exclusion.
30.   Warranted free of claim arising from any weapon of war employing atomic or nuclear fission and/or fusion or other like reaction or radioactive force or matter. 304

Appendix 37

1/5/70   **INSTITUTE FISHING VESSEL CLAUSES**

—ADDITIONAL PERILS CLAUSE—

Clause 4 of this Policy is deemed to be renumbered 4(a) and the following clause is deemed to be inserted thereunder:—

(b) This insurance includes:—

Loss of or damage to any boiler, shaft or machinery howsoever caused, but excluding wear and tear and the cost of repairing, replacing or renewing any defective part condemned solely in consequence of latent defect, faulty design or faulty construction

Loss of or damage to the subject matter insured caused by persons acting maliciously

provided such loss or damage has not resulted from want of due diligence by the Assured, Owners or Managers.

Masters, Officers, Crew or Pilots not to be considered as part Owners within the meaning of this clause should they hold shares in the Vessel.

Any reference to Clause 4 in this Policy shall apply to Clauses 4(a) and 4(b).

Appendix 38

26/3/80 INSTITUTE LOCATION CLAUSE

Notwithstanding anything to the contrary contained in this contract Underwriters' liability in respect of any one accident or series of accidents arising from the same event in any one location shall not exceed the sum of ....

....

Appendix 39

1/10/71   **INSTITUTE FISHING VESSEL CLAUSES (1/5/71)**

1/10/71 AMENDMENT

Clauses 16 and 20 are hereby deleted and the following clauses included in this insurance.

4/4ths Collision Liability.

(A) It is further agreed that if the Vessel hereby insured shall come into collision with any other vessel and the Assured shall in consequence thereof become liable to pay and shall pay by way of damages to any other person or persons any sum or sums in respect of such collision for

- (i) loss of or damage to any other vessel or property on any other vessel,
- (ii) delay to or loss of use of any such other vessel or property thereon, or
- (iii) general average of, salvage of, or salvage under contract of, any such other vessel or property thereon,

the Underwriters will pay the Assured such proportion of such sum or sums so paid as their respective subscriptions hereto bear to the value of the Vessel hereby insured, provided always that their liability in respect of any one such collision shall not exceed their proportionate part of the value of the Vessel hereby insured, and in cases in which, with the prior consent in writing of the Underwriters, the liability of the Vessel has been contested or proceedings have been taken to limit liability, they will also pay a like proportion of the costs which the Assured shall thereby incur or be compelled to pay; but when both vessels are to blame, then unless the liability of the Owners of one or both of such vessels becomes limited by law, claims under this clause shall be settled on the principle of cross-liabilities as if the Owners of each vessel had been compelled to pay to the Owners of the other of such vessels such one-half or other proportion of the latter's damages as may have been properly allowed in ascertaining the balance or sum payable by or to the Assured in consequence of such collision.

Provided always that this clause shall in no case extend or be deemed to extend to any sum which the Assured may become liable to pay or shall pay for or in respect of:—

- (a) *removal or disposal, under statutory powers or otherwise, of obstructions, wrecks, cargoes or any other thing whatsoever,*
- (b) *any real or personal property or thing whatsoever except other vessels or property on other vessels,*
- (c) *pollution or contamination of any real or personal property or thing whatsoever (except other vessels with which the insured Vessel is in collision or property on such other vessels),*
- (d) *the cargo or other property on or the engagements of the insured Vessel,*
- (e) *loss of life, personal injury or illness.*

Protection and Indemnity Exclusions.

(B) (i) The cover provided by this insurance under Clauses 18 and 19 shall in no case extend or be deemed to extend to include any claim arising:—

- (a) directly or indirectly under Workmen's Compensation or Employers' Liability Acts and any other Statutory or Common Law Liability in respect of loss of life of or personal injury to or illness of any person employed in any capacity whatsoever by the Assured in on or about or in connection with the Vessel hereby insured or her cargo catch materials or repairs.

This sub-clause shall not exclude a claim for which the Assured shall become liable under Sections 34, 35, 40, 41 and 42 of the Merchant Shipping Act, 1906, or any statutory modification thereof, except so far as such claim is for wages or remuneration in the nature of wages.

(b) from strikes, lock-outs, labour disturbances, riots or civil commotions.

(c) from liability assumed by the Assured under agreement expressed or implied in respect of death or illness of or injury to any person employed under a contract of service or apprenticeship by the other party to such agreement except to the extent that the Assured is or would be liable independently of such agreement.

(ii) The cover provided by Clause 18 shall not extend to collision liability covered by Clause (A) nor to any sum or sums paid by the Assured which are not recoverable by the Assured from the Underwriters in the terms of Clause (A) because the total of the sum or sums paid by the Assured exceeds the insured value of the Vessel hereby insured.

(iii) The cover provided by this insurance under Clauses 18 and 19 shall in no case extend or be deemed to extend to include any claim in respect of or arising directly or indirectly from

(a) pollution or contamination of any real or personal property or any person or thing whatsoever (other than property on the Insured Vessel),

(b) any measures taken by any person (including measures taken by, on behalf of, or on the direction of any government or authority) to avert or minimise such pollution or contamination arising from any discharge or escape (whether actual or apprehended).

Appendix 40

1/11/85   (FOR USE ONLY WITH THE NEW MARINE POLICY FORM)

INSTITUTE YACHT CLAUSES

This insurance is subject to English law and practice

1   VESSEL

Vessel means the hull, machinery, boat(s), gear and equipment, such as would normally be sold with her if she changed hands.

2   IN COMMISSION AND LAID UP

2.1   The Vessel is covered subject to the provisions of this insurance

2.1.1   while in commission at sea or on inland waters or in port, docks, marinas, on ways, gridirons, pontoons, or on the hard or mud or at place of storage ashore, including lifting or hauling out and launching, with leave to sail or navigate with or without pilots, to go on trial trips and to assist and to tow vessels or craft in distress, or as is customary, but it is warranted that the Vessel shall not be towed, except as is customary or when in need of assistance, or undertake towage or salvage services under a contract previously arranged by Owners, Masters, Managers or Charterers

2.1.2   while laid up out of commission as provided for in Clause 4 below, including lifting or hauling out and launching, while being moved in shipyard or marina, dismantling, fitting out, overhauling, normal maintenance or while under survey, (also to include docking and undocking and periods laid up afloat incidental to laying up or fitting out and with leave to shift in tow or otherwise to or from her lay-up berth but not outside the limits of the port or place in which the Vessel is laid up) but excluding, unless notice be given to the Underwriters and any additional premium required by them agreed, any period for which the Vessel is used as a houseboat or is under major repair or undergoing alteration.

2.2   Notwithstanding Clause 2.1 above the gear and equipment, including outboard motors, are covered subject to the provisions of this insurance while in place of storage or repair ashore.

3   NAVIGATING AND CHARTER HIRE WARRANTIES

3.1   Warranted not navigating outside the limits stated in the Schedule to the policy or, provided previous notice be given to the Underwriters, held covered on terms to be agreed.

3.2   Warranted to be used solely for private pleasure purposes and not for hire charter or reward, unless specially agreed by the Underwriters.

4   LAID UP WARRANTY

Warranted laid up out of commission as stated in the Schedule to the policy, or held covered on terms to be agreed provided previous notice be given to the Underwriters.

5   SPEED WARRANTY

5.1   Warranted that the maximum designed speed of the Vessel, or the parent Vessel in the case of a Vessel with boat(s), does not exceed 17 knots.

5.2   Where the Underwriters have agreed to delete this warranty, the conditions of the Speedboat Clause 19 below shall also apply.

6   CONTINUATION

Should the Vessel at the expiration of this insurance be at sea or in distress or at a port or place of refuge or of call, she shall, provided prompt notice be given to the Underwriters, be held covered at a premium to be agreed until anchored or moored at her next port of call in good safety.

7   ASSIGNMENT

No assignment of or interest in this insurance or in any moneys which may be or become payable thereunder is to be binding on or recognised by the Underwriters unless a dated notice of such assignment or interest signed by the

Assured, and by the assignor in the case of subsequent assignment, is endorsed on the policy and the policy with such endorsement is produced before payment of any claim or return of premium thereunder.

8   CHANGE OF OWNERSHIP

This Clause 8 shall prevail notwithstanding any provision whether written typed or printed in this insurance inconsistent herewith.

8.1   Should the Vessel be sold or transferred to new ownership, or, where the Vessel is owned by a company, should there be a change in the controlling interest(s) of the company, then, unless the Underwriters agree in writing to continue the insurance, this insurance shall become cancelled from the time of such sale transfer or change and a pro rata daily net return of premium be made calculated on the premium charged for the in commission and/or laid up period.

8.2   If however the Vessel shall have left her moorings or be at sea at the time of sale or transfer such cancellation shall if required by the Assured be suspended until arrival at port or place of destination.

9   PERILS

Subject always to the exclusions in this insurance

9.1   this insurance covers loss of or damage to the subject-matter insured caused by

9.1.1   perils of the seas rivers lakes or other navigable waters

9.1.2   fire

9.1.3   jettison

9.1.4   piracy

9.1.5   contact with dock or harbour equipment or installation, land conveyance, aircraft or similar objects or objects falling therefrom

9.1.6   earthquake volcanic eruption or lightning

9.2   and, provided such loss or damage has not resulted from want of due diligence by the Assured Owners or Managers, this insurance covers

9.2.1   loss of or damage to the subject-matter insured caused by

9.2.1.1   accidents in loading, discharging or moving stores, gear, equipment, machinery or fuel

9.2.1.2   explosions

9.2.1.3   malicious acts

9.2.1.4   theft of the entire Vessel or her boat(s), or outboard motor(s) provided it is securely locked to the Vessel or her boat(s) by an anti-theft device in addition to its normal method of attachment, or, following upon forcible entry into the Vessel or place of storage or repair, theft of machinery including outboard motor(s), gear or equipment

9.2.2   loss of or damage to the subject-matter insured, *excepting motor and connections (but not strut shaft or propeller) electrical equipment and batteries and connections,* caused by

9.2.2.1   latent defects in hull or machinery, breakage of shafts or bursting of boilers (excluding the cost and expense of replacing or repairing the defective part broken shaft or burst boiler)

9.2.2.2   the negligence of any person whatsoever, but excluding the cost of making good any defect resulting from either negligence or breach of contract in respect of any repair or alteration work carried out for the account of the Assured and/or the Owners or in respect of the maintenance of the Vessel.

9.3   this insurance covers the expense of sighting the bottom after a stranding, if reasonably incurred specially for that purpose, even if no damage be found.

10   EXCLUSIONS

No claim shall be allowed in respect of any

10.1   outboard motor dropping off or falling overboard

10.2   ship's boat having a maximum designed speed exceeding 17 knots, unless such boat is specially covered herein and subject also to the conditions of the Speedboat Clause 19 below, or is on the parent Vessel or laid up ashore

10.3   ship's boat not permanently marked with the name of the parent Vessel

10.4   sails and protective covers split by the wind or blown away while set, unless in consequence of damage to the spars to which sails are bent, or occasioned by the Vessel being stranded or in collision or contact with any external substance (ice included) other than water

10.5   sails, masts, spars or standing and running rigging while the Vessel is racing, unless the loss or damage is caused by the Vessel being stranded, sunk, burnt, on fire or in collision or contact with any external substance (ice included) other than water

10.6   personal effects

10.7   consumable stores, fishing gear or moorings

10.8   sheathing, or repairs thereto, unless the loss or damage has been caused by the Vessel being stranded, sunk, burnt, on fire or in collision or contact with any external substance (ice included) other than water

10.9   loss or expenditure incurred in remedying a fault in design or construction or any cost or expense incurred by reason of betterment or alteration in design or construction

10.10   motor and connections (but not strut shaft or propeller) electrical equipment and batteries and connections, where the loss or damage has been caused by heavy weather, unless the loss or damage has been caused by the Vessel being immersed, but this clause 10.10 shall not exclude loss or damage caused by the Vessel, being stranded or in collision or contact with another vessel, pier or jetty.

11 LIABILITIES TO THIRD PARTIES

This Clause only to apply when a sum is stated for this purpose in the Schedule to the policy.

11.1   The Underwriters agree to indemnify the Assured for any sum or sums which the Assured shall become legally liable to pay and shall pay, by reason of interest in the insured Vessel and arising out of accidents occurring during the currency of this insurance, in respect of

11.1.1   loss of or damage to any other vessel or property whatsoever

11.1.2   loss of life, personal injury or illness, including payments made for life salvage, caused on or near the Vessel or any other vessel

11.1.3   any attempted or actual raising, removal or destruction of the wreck of the insured Vessel or the cargo thereof or any neglect or failure to raise, remove or destroy the same.

11.2   LEGAL COSTS

The underwriters will also pay, provided their prior written consent has been obtained,

11.2.1   the legal costs incurred by the Assured or which the Assured may be compelled to pay in contesting liability or taking proceedings to limit liability

11.2.2   the costs for representation at any coroner's inquest or fatal accident enquiry.

11.3   SISTERSHIP

Should the Vessel hereby insured come into collision with or receive salvage services from another vessel belonging wholly or in part to the same Owners or under the same management, the Assured shall have the same rights under this insurance as they would have were the other vessel entirely the property of Owners not interested in the Vessel hereby insured; but in such cases the liability for the collision or the amount payable for the services rendered shall be referred to a sole arbitrator to be agreed upon between the Underwriters and the Assured.

11.4   NAVIGATION BY OTHER PERSONS

The provisions of this Clause 11 shall extend to any person navigating or in charge of the insured Vessel with the permission of the Assured named in this insurance (other than a person operating, or employed by the operator of, a shipyard, marina, repair yard, slipway, yacht club, sales agency or similar organisation) and who while so navigating or in charge of the Vessel shall in consequence of any occurrence covered by this Clause 11 become liable to pay and shall pay any sum or sums to any person or persons, other than to the Assured named in this insurance, but indemnity under this Clause shall inure to the benefit of the Assured and only to a person navigating or in charge of the Vessel as described above, at the written request of and through the agency of the Assured. Nothing in this extension shall increase the Underwriters' liability beyond the limitation of liability imposed by Clause 11.8 below and this extension shall be subject to all other terms conditions and warranties of this insurance.

Nothing in this Clause 11.4 shall be deemed to override the provisions of Clause 3.2 above.

11.5   REMOVAL OF WRECK EXTENSION

This insurance also to pay the expenses, after deduction of the proceeds of the salvage, of the removal of the wreck of the insured Vessel from any place owned, leased or occupied by the Assured.

11.6   LIABILITIES SECTION EXCLUSIONS

Notwithstanding the provisions of this Clause 11 this insurance does not cover any liability cost or expense arising in respect of

11.6.1   any direct or indirect payment by the Assured under workmen's compensation or employers' liability acts and any other statutory or common law liability in respect of accidents to or illness of workmen or any other persons employed in any capacity whatsoever by the Assured or by any person to whom the protection of this insurance is afforded by reason of the provisions of Clause 11.4 above, in on or about or in connection with the Vessel hereby insured or her cargo, materials or repairs

11.6.2   any boat belonging to the Vessel and having a maximum designed speed exceeding 17 knots, unless such boat is specially covered herein and subject also to the conditions of the Speedboat Clause 19 below, or is on the parent Vessel or laid up ashore

11.6.3   any liability to or incurred by any person engaged in water skiing or aquaplaning, while being towed by the Vessel or preparing to be towed until safely on board or ashore

11.6.4   any liability to or incurred by any person engaged in a sport or activity, other than water skiing or aquaplaning, while being towed by the Vessel or preparing to be towed or after being towed until safely on board or ashore

11.6.5   punitive or exemplary damages, however described.

11.7   WATER-SKIERS LIABILITIES

Should Clause 11.6.3 and/or Clause 11.6.4 above be deleted, the liabilities mentioned in such clause(s) shall be covered hereunder, subject always to the warranties, conditions and limits of this insurance.

11.8   LIMIT OF LIABILITY
        The liability of the Underwriters under this Clause 11, in respect of any one accident or series of accidents arising out of the same event, shall in no case exceed the sum stated for this purpose in the Schedule to the policy, but when the liability of the Assured has been contested with the consent in writing of the Underwriters, the Underwriters will also pay a like proportion of the costs which the Assured shall thereby incur or be compelled to pay.

12   EXCESS AND DEDUCTIBLE
12.1   No claim arising from a peril insured against shall be payable under this insurance unless the aggregate of all such claims arising out of each separate accident or occurrence (including claims under Clauses 11, 14 and 15) exceeds the amount stated for this purpose in the Schedule to the policy, in which case this sum shall be deducted. This Clause 12.1 shall not apply to a claim for total or constructive total loss of the Vessel or, in the event of such a claim, to any associated claim under Clause 15 arising from the same accident or occurrence.

12.2   Prior to the application of Clause 12.1 above and in addition thereto, deductions new for old not exceeding one-third may be made at the Underwriters' discretion in respect of loss of or damage to

12.2.1   protective covers, sails and running rigging

12.2.2   outboard motors whether or not insured by separate valuation under this insurance.

13   NOTICE OF CLAIM AND TENDERS
13.1   Prompt notice shall be given to the Underwriters in the event of any occurrence which may give rise to a claim under this insurance, and any theft or malicious damage shall also be reported promptly to the Police.

13.2   Where loss or damage has occurred, notice shall be given to the Underwriters prior to survey and, if the Vessel is abroad, also to the nearest Lloyd's Agent so that a surveyor may be appointed to represent the Underwriters should they so desire.

13.3   The Underwriters shall be entitled to decide the port to which the Vessel shall proceed for docking or repair (the actual additional expense of the voyage arising from compliance with Underwriters' requirements being refunded to the Assured) and shall have a right of veto concerning a place of repair or a repairing firm.

13.4   The Underwriters may also take tenders or may require tenders to be taken for the repair of the Vessel.

14   SALVAGE CHARGES
        Subject to any express provision in this insurance, salvage charges incurred in preventing a loss by perils insured against may be recovered as a loss by those perils.

15   DUTY OF ASSURED
15.1   In case of any loss or misfortune it is the duty of the Assured and their servants and agents to take such measures as may be reasonable for the purpose of averting or minimising a loss which would be recoverable under this insurance.

15.2   Subject to the provisions below and to Clause 12 the Underwriters will contribute to charges properly and reasonably incurred by the Assured their servants or agents for such measures. General average, salvage charges, collision defence or attack costs and costs incurred by the Assured in contesting liability covered by Clause 11.2 are not recoverable under this Clause 15.

15.3   The Assured shall render to the Underwriters all possible aid in obtaining information and evidence should the Underwriters desire to take proceedings at their own expense and for their own benefit in the name of the Assured to recover compensation or to secure an indemnity from any third party in respect of anything covered by this insurance.

15.4   Measures taken by the Assured or the Underwriters with the object of saving, protecting or recovering the subject-matter insured shall not be considered as a waiver or acceptance of abandonment or otherwise prejudice the rights of either party.

15.5   The sum recoverable under this Clause 15 shall be in addition to the loss otherwise recoverable under this insurance but in no circumstances shall amounts recoverable under Clause 15.2 exceed the sum insured under this insurance in respect of the Vessel.

16   UNREPAIRED DAMAGE
16.1   The measure of indemnity in respect of claims for unrepaired damage shall be the reasonable depreciation in the market value of the Vessel at the time this insurance terminates arising from such unrepaired damage, but not exceeding the reasonable cost of repairs.

16.2   In no case shall the Underwriters be liable for unrepaired damage in the event of a subsequent total loss (whether or not covered under this insurance) sustained during the period covered by this insurance or any extension thereof.

16.3   The Underwriters shall not be liable in respect of unrepaired damage for more than the insured value at the time this insurance terminates.

17   CONSTRUCTIVE TOTAL LOSS
17.1   In ascertaining whether the Vessel is a constructive total loss, the insured value shall be taken as the repaired value and nothing in respect of the damaged or break-up value of the Vessel or wreck shall be taken into account.

17.2   No claim for constructive total loss based upon the cost of recovery and/or repair of the Vessel shall be recoverable hereunder unless such cost would exceed the insured value. In making this determination, only the cost relating to a single accident or sequence of damages arising from the same accident shall be taken into account.

18   DISBURSEMENTS WARRANTY

Warranted that no amount shall be insured policy proof of interest or full interest admitted for account of the Assured, Mortgagees or Owners on disbursements, commission, profits or other interests or excess or increased value of hull or machinery however described unless the insured value of the Vessel is over £50,000 and then not to exceed 10 per cent of the total amount insured in respect of the Vessel as stated in the Schedule to the policy.

Provided always that a breach of this warranty shall not afford the Underwriters any defence to a claim by a Mortgagee who has accepted this insurance without knowledge of such breach.

19   SPEEDBOAT CLAUSE

WHERE THIS CLAUSE 19 APPLIES IT SHALL OVERRIDE ANY CONFLICTING PROVISIONS IN THE CLAUSES ABOVE.

19.1   **It is a condition of this insurance that when the Vessel concerned is under way the Assured named in the Schedule to the policy or other competent person(s) shall be on board and in control of the Vessel.**

19.2   No claim shall be allowed in respect of loss of or damage to the Vessel or liability to any third party or any salvage services

19.2.1   caused by or arising from the Vessel being stranded sunk swamped immersed or breaking adrift, while left moored or anchored unattended off an exposed beach or shore

19.2.2   arising while the Vessel is participating in racing or speed tests, or any trials in connection therewith.

19.3   No claim shall be allowed in respect of rudder strut shaft or propeller

19.3.1   under Clauses 9.2.2.1 and 9.2.2.2

19.3.2   for any loss or damage caused by heavy weather, water or contact other than with another vessel, pier or jetty, but this Clause 19.3.2 shall not exclude damage caused by the Vessel being immersed as a result of heavy weather.

19.4   If the Vessel is fitted with inboard machinery no liability shall attach to this insurance in respect of any claim caused by or arising through fire or explosion unless the Vessel is equipped in the engine room (or engine space) tank space and galley, with a fire extinguishing system automatically operated or having controls at the steering position and properly installed and maintained in efficient working order.

20   CANCELLATION AND RETURN OF PREMIUM

This insurance may be cancelled by the Underwriters at any time subject to 30 days notice to the Assured or by mutual agreement, when a pro rata daily net return of premium shall be made calculated on the premium charged for the in commission and/or laid up period.

THE FOLLOWING CLAUSES SHALL BE PARAMOUNT AND SHALL OVERRIDE ANYTHING CONTAINED IN THIS INSURANCE INCONSISTENT THEREWITH.

21   WAR EXCLUSION

In no case shall this insurance cover loss damage liability or expense caused by

21.1   war civil war revolution rebellion insurrection, or civil strife arising therefrom, or any hostile act by or against a belligerent power

21.2   capture seizure arrest restraint or detainment (barratry and piracy excepted), and the consequences thereof or any attempt thereat

21.3   derelict mines torpedoes bombs or other derelict weapons of war.

22   STRIKES AND POLITICAL ACTS EXCLUSION

In no case shall this insurance cover loss damage liability or expense caused by

22.1   strikers, locked-out workmen, or persons taking part in labour disturbances, riots or civil commotions

22.2   any terrorist or any person acting from a political motive.

23   NUCLEAR EXCLUSION

In no case shall this insurance cover loss damage liability or expense arising from

23.1   any weapon of war employing atomic or nuclear fission and/or fusion or other like reaction or radioactive force or matter

23.2   ionising radiations from or contamination by radioactivity from any nuclear fuel or from any nuclear waste from the combustion of nuclear fuel

23.3   the radioactive, toxic, explosive or other hazardous properties of any explosive nuclear assembly or nuclear component thereof.

Appendix 41

1/11/85   (FOR USE ONLY WITH THE NEW MARINE POLICY FORM)

INSTITUTE WAR AND STRIKES CLAUSES
YACHTS
This insurance is subject to English law and practice

1 **PERILS**

Subject always to the exclusions hereinafter referred to, this insurance covers loss of or damage to the Vessel caused by

1.1   war civil war revolution rebellion insurrection, or civil strife arising therefrom, or any hostile act by or against a belligerent power

1.2   capture seizure arrest restraint or detainment, and the consequences thereof or any attempt thereat

1.3   derelict mines torpedoes bombs or other derelict weapons of war

1.4   strikers, locked-out workmen, or persons taking part in labour disturbances, riots or civil commotions

1.5   any terrorist or any person acting from a political motive

1.6   confiscation or expropriation.

Provided that the insurance against the perils under Clause 1 above (with the exception of Clause 1.4) shall not apply before the Vessel has been launched or whilst she is hauled out ashore.

2 **INCORPORATION**

The Institute Yacht Clauses 1/11/85 except Clauses 2, 3, 4, 5, 6, 8, 9, 10, 12.1, 19, 20, 21, 22 and 23 are deemed to be incorporated in this insurance in so far as they do not conflict with the provisions of these clauses and providing that any indemnity in respect of any sum or sums for which the Assured may become legally liable in respect of any one accident or series of accidents arising out of the same event shall be limited to the sum stated for this purpose in this insurance or, if no such amount is stated, to the sum insured in respect of the Vessel.

3 **DETAINMENT**

In the event that the Vessel shall have been the subject of capture seizure arrest restraint detainment confiscation or expropriation, and the Assured shall thereby have lost the free use and disposal of the Vessel for a continuous period of 12 months then for the purpose of ascertaining whether the Vessel is a constructive total loss the Assured shall be deemed to have been deprived of the possession of the Vessel without any likelihood of recovery.

4 **EXCLUSIONS**

This insurance excludes

4.1   loss damage liability or expense arising from

4.1.1   any detonation of any weapon of war employing atomic or nuclear fission and/or fusion or other like reaction or radioactive force or matter, hereinafter called a nuclear weapon of war

4.1.2   the outbreak of war (whether there be a declaration of war or not) between any of the following countries:

United Kingdom, United States of America, France, the Union of Soviet Socialist Republics, the People's Republic of China

4.1.3   requisition or pre-emption

4.1.4   capture seizure arrest restraint detainment confiscation or expropriation by or under the order of the government or any public or local authority of the country in which the Vessel is owned or registered

4.1.5   arrest restraint detainment confiscation or expropriation under quarantine regulations or by reason of infringement of any customs or trading regulations

4.1.6   the operation of ordinary judicial process, failure to provide security or to pay any fine or penalty or any financial cause

4.1.7   piracy (but this exclusion shall not affect cover under Clause 1.4)

4.2   loss damage liability or expense covered by the Institute Yacht Clauses 1/11/85 or which would be recoverable thereunder but for Clause 12 thereof

4.3   any claim for any sum recoverable under any other insurance on the Vessel or which would be recoverable under such insurance but for the existence of this insurance

4.4   any claim for expenses arising from delay except such expenses as would be recoverable in principle in English law and practice under the York-Antwerp Rules 1974.

5   TERMINATION

5.1   This insurance may be cancelled by either the Underwriters or the Assured giving 7 days notice (such cancellation becoming effective on the expiry of 7 days from midnight of the day on which notice of cancellation is issued by or to the Underwriters). The Underwriters agree however to reinstate this insurance subject to agreement between the Underwriters and the Assured prior to the expiry of such notice of cancellation as to new rate of premium and/or conditions and/or warranties.

5.2   Whether or not such notice of cancellation has been given this insurance shall TERMINATE AUTOMATICALLY

5.2.1   upon the occurrence of any hostile detonation of any nuclear weapon of war as defined in Clause 4.1.1 wheresoever or whensoever such detonation may occur and whether or not the Vessel may be involved

5.2.2   upon the outbreak of war (whether there be a declaration of war or not) between any of the following countries:

United Kingdom, United States of America, France, the Union of Soviet Socialist Republics, the People's Republic of China

5.2.3   in the event of the Vessel being requisitioned, either for title or use.

5.3   In the event either of cancellation by notice or of automatic termination of this insurance by reason of the operation of this Clause 5, or of the sale of the Vessel, pro rata net return of premium shall be payable to the Assured.

This insurance shall not become effective if, subsequent to its acceptance by the Underwriters and prior to the intended time of its attachment, there has occurred any event which would have automatically terminated this insurance under the provisions of Clause 5 above.

Appendix 42

1/11/85

(FOR USE ONLY WITH THE NEW MARINE POLICY FORM)

INSTITUTE YACHT CLAUSES
MACHINERY DAMAGE EXTENSION CLAUSE

Notwithstanding the provisions of Clauses 9.2.2.1, 9.2.2.2 and 10.10 of the Institute Yacht Clauses 1/11/85, but subject always to the other terms and conditions of this insurance, cover is extended to include loss of or damage to motor and connections electrical equipment and batteries and connections caused by:—

(1) latent defects in hull or machinery, breakage of shafts or bursting of boilers (excluding the cost and expense of replacing or repairing the defective part, broken shaft or burst boiler)

(2) the negligence of any person whatsoever, but excluding the cost of making good any defect resulting from either negligence or breach of contract in respect of any repair or alteration work carried out for the account of the Assured and/or the Owners or in respect of the maintenance of the Vessel

(3) heavy weather.

Appendix 43

1/11/85   (FOR USE ONLY WITH THE NEW MARINE POLICY FORM)

INSTITUTE YACHT CLAUSES
PERSONAL EFFECTS CLAUSES
(For use only with the Institute Yacht Clauses 1/11/85 in
insurances covering Vessels with lockable cabin accommodation)

The following extension shall apply provided that a separate amount insured in respect of Personal Effects is stated in the Schedule to the policy.

1   Subject always to its terms and conditions, this insurance is extended to cover (without reference to any excess and deductible in Clause 12.1 of the Institute Yacht Clauses 1/11/85, all risks of loss of or damage to Personal Effects, being the personal property of the Assured and/or of the Assured's family, and crew's clothes provided by the Owners, while on board or in use in connection with the insured Vessel, including while in transit from the Assured's place of residence to the insured Vessel, and until return to such place of residence, but EXCLUDING CLAIMS ARISING FROM:

  1.1   wear and tear, gradual deterioriation, damp, mould, mildew, vermin, moth and mechanical derangement

  1.2   breakage of articles of a brittle nature, unless caused by the vessel being stranded, sunk, burnt, on fire or in collision, or by stress of weather, burglars or thieves

  1.3   loss of cash, currency, banknotes or travellers cheques

  1.4   loss of water-skis or diving equipment, unless as a result of fire or theft following forcible entry or of total loss of the Vessel

  1.5   perils excluded by Clauses 21, 22 and 23 of the Institute Yacht Clauses 1/11/85.

2   **AVERAGE**

This insurance is subject to the condition of average, that is to say, if the property covered by this extension shall at the time of any loss be of greater value than the amount insured hereunder in respect thereof, the Assured shall only be entitled to recover such proportion of the said loss as such amount insured bears to the total value of the said property.

3   **NON-CONTRIBUTION**

This insurance does not cover any loss or damage which at the time of the happening of such loss or damage is or would, but for the existence of this insurance, be insured under any other insurance, except in respect of any excess beyond the amount which would have been payable under such other insurance had this insurance not been effected.

4   **LIMIT OF INDEMNITY**

The amount recoverable under this Personal Effects extension shall be limited to the amount insured in respect thereof, as stated in the Schedule to the policy, (any single article valued at £100 or more to be specially declared).

Appendix 44

1/11/85 (FOR USE ONLY WITH THE NEW MARINE POLICY FORM)

INSTITUTE YACHT CLAUSES
RACING RISK EXTENSION CLAUSE
(for use only with the Institute Yacht Clauses 1/11/85)

1   In consideration of the payment of an additional premium as stated in the Schedule to the policy it is agreed that, notwithstanding the provisions of Clauses 10.4 and 10.5 of the Institute Yacht Clauses 1/11/85:

 1.1   The cost of replacing or repairing sails, masts, spars, standing and running rigging lost or damaged by an insured peril whilst the Vessel hereby insured is racing shall be recoverable hereunder, to the extent only of 2/3rds of such cost (without application of Clause 12 Excess and Deductible of the Institute Yacht Clauses 1/11/85 in this insurance), unless the loss or damage be caused by the Vessel being stranded, sunk, burnt, on fire, in collision or in contact with any external substance (ice included) other than water, when the cost of replacement or repair shall be recoverable in full, subject only to the deduction new for old and to the excess or deductible in the said Clause 12 in this insurance.

 Warranted that no additional insurance is or shall be placed covering any part of the cost of replacement or repair not recoverable under the foregoing Clause 1.1.

 1.2   The Underwriters' liability under Clause 1.1 above arising out of any one occurrence whilst racing shall be calculated upon the basis that the full replacement cost of all sails carried whether set or not, masts, spars, standing and running rigging shall not exceed the sum stated for this purpose in the Schedule to the policy.

Appendix 45

INSTITUTE CLAUSES FOR BUILDERS' RISKS

1/12/72

VESSEL..

BUILDERS..
....

BUILDERS' YARDS... Contract or Yard No.......................

SUBJECT OF INSURANCE

(Where more than one part of the subject matter insured is described in Section I(A), Section I(B) or Section II below, then the respective wording of Section I(A), Section I(B) or Section II shall be applied to each part separately.)

SECTION I. Provisional Period .... from........................
but this insurance to terminate upon delivery to Owners if prior to expiry of Provisional Period.

(A) HULL and MACHINERY etc. under construction at the yard or other premises of the Builders.

Description	Contract or Yard No.	Provisionally valued at	To be built at/by

The subject matter of this sub-section (A) is covered whilst at Builders' Yard and at Builders' premises elsewhere within the port or place of construction at which the Builders' Yard is situated and whilst in transit between such locations.   Underwriters' liability in respect of each item of this sub-section (A) which is at such locations shall attach from the time:—

   (i) of inception of this Section I if such item has already been allocated to the Vessel;
   (ii) of delivery to Builders of such item (if allocated) when delivered after inception of this Section I;
   (iii) of allocation by Builders if allocated after inception of this Section I.

(B) MACHINERY etc. insured hereon whilst under construction by Sub-Contractors.

Description	Contract or Yard No.	Provisionally valued at	To be built at/by

The subject matter of this sub-section (B) is covered whilst at Sub-Contractors' works and at Sub-Contractors' premises elsewhere within the port or place of construction at which the Sub-Contractors' works are situated and whilst in transit between such locations. Underwriters' liability in respect of each item of this sub-section (B) which is at such locations shall attach from the time:—

(i) of inception of this Section I if such item has already been allocated to the Vessel;

(ii) of delivery to the Sub-Contractors of such item (if allocated) when delivered after inception of this Section I;

(iii) of allocation by the Sub-Contractors if allocated after inception of this Section I.

The subject matter of this sub-section (B) is also covered whilst:—

(a) in transit to Builders if the transit is within the port or place of construction at which the Builders' Yard is situated;

(b) at Builders' Yard and at Builders' premises elsewhere within the port or place of construction at which the Builders' Yard is situated and whilst in transit between such locations.

SECTION II. Provisional Period.................from................
   but this insurance to terminate upon delivery to.......ners if prior to expiry of Provisional Period.

MACHINERY etc. insured hereon from delivery to Builders.

Description	Contract or Yard No.	Provisionally valued at	To be built at/by

The subject-matter of this Section II is covered whilst at Builders' Yard and at Builders' premises elsewhere within the port or place of construction at which the Builders' Yard is situated and whilst in transit between such locations. Underwriters' liability in respect of each item of this Section II shall attach from the time of delivery to Builders.

1. Whereas the value stated herein is provisional, it is agreed that the final contract price, or the total building cost plus............% whichever is the greater, of the subject matter of this insurance shall be the Insured Value.

Should the Insured Value, determined as above,

(i) exceed the provisional value stated herein, the Assured agree to declare to the Underwriters hereon, the amount of such excess and to pay premium thereon at the full policy rates, and the Underwriters agree to accept their proportionate shares of the increase,

or (ii) be less than the provisional value stated herein, the sum insured by this policy shall be reduced proportionately and Underwriters agree to return premium at the full policy rates, on the amounts by which their respective lines are reduced.

Nevertheless, should the Insured Value exceed 125% of the provisional value, then the limits of indemnity under this insurance shall be 125% of the provisional value, any one accident or series of accidents arising out of the same event.

Notwithstanding the above it is understood and agreed that any variation of the value for insurance on account of a material alteration in the plans or fittings of the vessel or a change in type from that originally contemplated does not come within the scope of this clause and such a variation requires the specific agreement of the Underwriters.

2. Held covered at a premium to be arranged for transit not provided for in section I or II above.

3. Held covered at a premium to be arranged in the event of delivery to owners being delayed beyond the provisional period(s) mentioned above, but in no case shall any additional period of cover extend beyond 30 days from completion of Builders' Trials.

4. Held covered in case of deviation or change of voyage, provided notice be given to the Underwriters immediately after receipt of advices and any amended terms of cover and any additional premium required by them be agreed.

5. SUBJECT ALWAYS TO ITS TERMS, CONDITIONS AND EXCLUSIONS this insurance is against all risks of loss of or damage to the subject matter insured including the cost of repairing replacing or renewing any defective part condemned solely in consequence of the discovery therein during the period of this insurance of a latent defect.

In case of failure of launch, Underwriters to bear all subsequent expense necessarily incurred in completing launch.

Average payable without deduction new for old, whether the average be particular or general.

6. Notwithstanding anything to the contrary which may be contained in the Policy or the clauses attached thereto, this insurance includes loss of or damage to the subject matter insured arising from faulty design of any part or parts thereof but in no case shall this insurance extend to cover the cost or expense of repairing, modifying, replacing or renewing such part or parts, nor any cost or expense incurred by reason of betterment or alteration in design.

Provided always that this clause shall in no case extend or be deemed to extend to any sum which the Assured may become liable to pay or shall pay for or in respect of:—

(a) removal or disposal, under statutory powers or otherwise, of obstructions, wrecks, cargoes or any other thing whatsoever,

(b) any real or personal property or thing whatsoever except other vessels or property on other vessels.

(c) pollution or contamination of any real or personal property or thing whatsoever (except other vessels with which the insured Vessel is in collision or property on such other vessels),

(d) the cargo or other property on or the engagements of the insured Vessel,

(e) loss of life, personal injury or illness.

16. Should the Vessel hereby insured come into collision with or receive salvage services from another vessel belonging wholly or in part to the same Owners or under the same management, the Assured shall have the same rights under this Policy as they would have were the other vessel entirely the property of Owners not interested in the Vessel hereby insured; but in such cases the liability for the collision or the amount payable for the services rendered shall be referred to a sole arbitrator to be agreed upon between the Underwriters and the Assured.

17. It is further agreed that if by reason of interest in the Vessel hereby insured during the period covered by this Policy, the Assured

(i) shall become liable to pay and shall pay any sum or sums in respect of any liability, claim, demand, damages or expenses arising from or occasioned by any of the following events or happenings which occur during the period covered by this Policy:

(a) loss of or damage to any other vessel or goods, merchandise, freight, or other things or interests whatsoever, on board such other vessel, caused proximately or otherwise by the Vessel hereby insured,

(b) loss of or damage to any goods, merchandise, freight, or other things or interests whatsoever, other than as aforesaid (not being property on board the Vessel hereby insured and owned by builders or repairers or for which they may be responsible), whether or not on board the Vessel hereby insured, which may arise from any cause whatsoever,

(c) loss of or damage to any harbour, dock (graving or otherwise), slipway, way, gridiron, pontoon, pier, quay, jetty, stage, buoy, telegraph cable or other fixed or moveable thing whatsoever (not being the Vessel hereby insured),

(d) any attempted or actual raising, removal, or destruction of the wreck of the Vessel hereby insured, or the cargo thereof, or any neglect or failure to raise, remove, or destroy the same,

(e) loss of life, personal injury, illness or life salvage,

(ii) shall pay any sum or sums consequent upon any event or happening during the period covered by this Policy but not specified in (i) above, and which would be recoverable absolutely or conditionally under the Protecting and Indemnity Club rules of the standard terms of entry of the United Kingdom Mutual Steam Ship Assurance Association (Bermuda) Limited in force at the inception of this Policy,

the Underwriters will pay the Assured such proportion of such sum or sums so paid, or which may be required to indemnify the Assured for such loss, as their respective subscriptions hereto bear to the insured value of the Vessel hereby insured, provided always that their liability under this clause, together with any liability there may be under Clause 18, in respect

---

7. With leave to proceed to and from any wet or dry docks, harbours, ways, cradles and pontoons within the port or place of construction and to proceed under own power, loaded or in ballast, as often as required, for fitting out, docking, trials or delivery, within a distance by water of 250 nautical miles of the Port or place of construction, or held covered at a premium to be arranged in the event of such distance being exceeded.

Any movement of the Vessel in tow outside the port or place of construction held covered at a premium to be arranged, provided previous notice be given to the Underwriters.

8. No claim arising from a peril insured against shall be payable under this insurance unless the aggregate of all such claims arising out of each separate accident or occurrence (including claims under the Suing and Labouring Clause and Clauses 15, 16, 17 and 18 of these Clauses) exceeds

.... in which case this sum shall be deducted.

Nevertheless the expense of sighting the bottom after stranding, if reasonably incurred specially for that purpose, shall be paid even if no damage be found. This paragraph shall not apply to a claim for total or constructive total loss of the subject matter insured.

Claims for damage by heavy weather occurring during a single sea passage between two successive ports shall be treated as being due to one accident. In the case of such heavy weather extending over a period not wholly covered by this insurance the proportion of the above deductible that the number of days of such heavy weather falling within the period of this insurance bears to the number of days of heavy weather during the single sea passage.

The expression "heavy weather" in the preceding paragraph shall be deemed to include contact with floating ice.

Excluding any interest comprised therein, recoveries against any claim which is subject to the above deductible shall be credited to the Underwriters in full to the extent of the sum by which the aggregate of the claim unreduced by any recoveries exceeds the above deductible.

Interest comprised in recoveries shall be apportioned between the Assured and the Underwriters, taking into account the sums paid by Underwriters and the dates when such payments were made, notwithstanding that by the addition of interest the Underwriters may receive a larger sum than they have paid.

9. In no case shall the Underwriters be liable for unrepaired damage in addition to a subsequent total loss sustained during the period covered by this Policy or any extension thereof.

10. In ascertaining whether the subject matter insured is a constructive total loss the Insured Value shall be taken as the repaired value and nothing in respect of the damaged or break-up value shall be taken into account.

No claim for constructive total loss based upon the cost of recovery and/or repair shall be recoverable hereunder unless such cost would exceed the Insured Value.

11. General average and salvage to be adjusted according to the law and practice obtaining at the place where the adventure ends, as if the contract of affreightment if any contained no special terms upon the subject; but where the contract of affreightment so provides the adjustment shall be according to York-Antwerp Rules.

When the Vessel sails in ballast, not under charter the provisions of the York-Antwerp Rules, 1950 (excluding Rules XX and XXI) shall be applicable, and the voyage for this purpose shall be deemed to continue from the port or place of departure until the arrival of the Vessel at the first port or place thereafter other than a port or place of refuge or a port or place of call for bunkering only. If at any such intermediate port or place there is an abandonment of the adventure originally contemplated the voyage shall thereupon be deemed to be terminated.

12. In the event of loss, damage liability or expense which may result in a claim under this Policy, prompt notice shall be given to the Underwriters prior to repair and, if the subject matter is under construction abroad, to the nearest Lloyd's Agent so that a surveyor may be appointed to represent the Underwriters should they so desire.

13. Any change of interest in the subject matter insured shall not affect the validity of this Policy.

14. No assignment of or interest in this Policy or in any moneys which may be or become payable thereunder is to be binding on or recognised by the Underwriters unless a dated notice of such assignment or interest signed by the Assured, and by the assignor in the case of subsequent assignment, is endorsed on this Policy and the Policy with such endorsement is produced before payment of any claim or return of premium thereunder.

15. It is further agreed that if the Vessel hereby insured shall come into collision with any other vessel and the Assured shall in consequence thereof become liable to pay and shall pay by way of damages to any other person or persons any sum or sums in respect of such collision for

(i) loss of or damage to any other vessel or property on any other vessel,
(ii) delay to or loss of use of any such other vessel or property thereon or
(iii) general average of, salvage of, or salvage under contract of, any such other vessel or property thereon,

the Underwriters will pay the Assured such proportion of such sum or sums so paid as their respective subscriptions hereto bear to the value of the Vessel hereby insured, provided always that their liability in respect of any one such collision shall not exceed their proportionate part of the value of the Vessel hereby insured, and in cases in which, with the prior consent in writing of the Underwriters, the liability of the Vessel has been contested or proceedings have been taken to limit liability, they will also pay a like proportion of the costs which the Assured shall thereby incur or be compelled to pay; but when both vessels are to blame, then unless the liability of the Owners of one or both of such vessels becomes limited by law, claims under this clause shall be settled on the principle of cross-liabilities as if the Owners of each vessel had been compelled to pay to the Owners of the other of such vessels such one-half or other proportion of the latter's damages as may have been properly allowed in ascertaining the balance or sum payable by or to the Assured in consequence of such collision.

of any one accident or series of accidents arising out of the same event or happening, shall not exceed their proportionate part of the insured value of the Vessel hereby insured, and in cases in which, with the prior consent in writing of the Underwriters, the liability of the Assured has been contested or proceedings have been taken to limit liability, they will also pay a like proportion of the costs which the Assured shall thereby incur or be compelled to pay.

18. This insurance also to pay the expenses, after deduction of the proceeds of the salvage, not recoverable under Clause 17, of the removal of the wreck of the Vessel hereby insured, or the cargo thereof, from any place owned, leased or occupied by the Assured. Underwriters' liability under this clause is subject to the limitations in amount provided in Clause 17. The provisions of that clause regarding the payment of legal costs shall also apply hereto.

19. The cover under Clauses 17 and 18 shall in no case extend or be deemed to extend to include any claim arising

(a) directly or indirectly under Workmen's Compensation or Employers' Liability Acts and any other Statutory or Common Law Liability in respect of loss of life or of personal injury to or illness of any person employed in any capacity whatsoever by the Assured or sub-contractors in on or about or in connection with the Vessel hereby insured or her cargo materials or repairs,

(b) from strikes, lock-outs, labour disturbances, riots or civil commotions.

(c) from liability assumed by the Assured under agreement expressed or implied in respect of death or illness of or injury to any person employed under a contract of service or of apprenticeship by the other party to such agreement except to the extent that the Assured is or would be liable independently of such agreement.

20. Warranted free of loss or damage caused by strikers, locked-out workmen, or persons taking part in labour disturbances, riots or civil commotions.

Unless deleted by the Underwriters the following clauses shall be paramount and shall override anything contained in this insurance inconsistent therewith.

21. Warranted free of capture, seizure, arrest, restraint or detainment, and the consequences thereof or of any attempt thereat; also from the consequences of hostilities or warlike operations, whether there be a declaration of war or not; but this warranty shall not exclude collision, contact with any fixed or floating object (other than a mine or torpedo), stranding, heavy weather or fire unless caused directly (and independently of the nature of the voyage or service which the Vessel concerned or, in the case of a collision, any other vessel involved therein, is performing) by a hostile act by or against a belligerent power; and for the purpose of this warranty "power" includes any authority maintaining naval, military, or air forces in association with a power.
Further warranted free from the consequences of civil war, revolution, rebellion, insurrection, or civil strife arising therefrom, or piracy.

22. Warranted free of any claim based upon loss of, or frustration of, the insured voyage or adventure caused by arrests restraints or detainments of Kings Princes Peoples Usurpers or persons attempting to usurp power.

23. Warranted free from loss damage liability or expense arising from:—
(a) the detonation of an explosive
(b) any weapon of war
and caused by any person acting maliciously or from a political motive.

24. Warranted free from loss damage liability or expense directly or indirectly caused by or contributed to by or arising from
(a) ionising radiations from or contamination by radio activity from any nuclear fuel or from any nuclear waste from the combustion of nuclear fuel;
(b) the radioactive, toxic, explosive or other hazardous properties of any explosive nuclear assembly or nuclear component thereof;
(c) any weapon of war employing atomic or nuclear fission and/or fusion or other like reaction or radioactive force or matter.

25. Warranted free of claim arising from earthquake or volcanic eruption, or tidal wave arising therefrom.

Appendix 46

1/12/72

INSTITUTE STRIKES CLAUSES

BUILDERS' RISKS

1.   This insurance covers   1

        loss of or damage to the subject matter insured caused by strikers 2
locked-out workmen or persons taking part in labour disturbances 3
riots or civil commotions,   4

but excludes any loss of or damage to the subject matter insured covered by 5
the Institute War Clauses for Builders' Risks.   6

2.   Warranted free of any claim for expenses arising from delay except such 7
expenses as would be recoverable in principle in English law and practice under 8
York-Antwerp Rules 1950.   9

3.   Claims payable irrespective of percentage.   10

4.   This insurance also covers, subject to the limitation of liability provided 11
for in Clause 17 of the Institute Clauses for Builders' Risks, the liability under 12
Clauses 17 and 18 of the Institute Clauses for Builders' Risks which is excluded 13
by Clause 19 (b).   14

5.   The Institute Clauses for Builders' Risks are deemed to be incorporated in 15
this insurance, in so far as they do not conflict with the provisions of these 16
clauses, but this insurance excludes any claim which would be recoverable under 17
the Standard Form of English Marine Policy with the said clauses attached.   18

6.   No return of premium hereunder unless specially agreed.   19

Appendix 47

1/12/72

INSTITUTE DEDUCTIBLE CLAUSE

BUILDERS' RISKS

Notwithstanding anything to the contrary which may be contained in the 1
Policy or the clauses attached thereto, no claim arising from a peril insured against 2
shall be payable under this insurance unless the aggregate of all such claims arising 3
out of each separate accident or occurrence (including claims under the Collision, 4
Protection and Indemnity, Removal of Wreck, and Suing and Labouring Clauses) 5

exceeds..in which case this sum shall be deducted. 6

Nevertheless the expense of sighting the bottom after stranding, if reasonably 7
incurred specially for that purpose, shall be paid even if no damage be found. This 8
paragraph shall not apply to a claim for total or constructive total loss of the 9
subject matter insured. 10

Claims for damage by heavy weather occurring during a single sea passage 11
between two successive ports shall be treated as being due to one accident. In the 12
case of such heavy weather extending over a period not wholly covered by this 13
insurance the deductible to be applied to the claim recoverable hereunder shall be 14
the proportion of the above deductible that the number of days of such heavy 15
weather falling within the period of this insurance bears to the number of days of 16
heavy weather during the single sea passage. 17

The expression "heavy weather" in the preceding paragraph shall be deemed 18
to include contact with floating ice. 19

Excluding any interest comprised therein, recoveries against any claim which 20
is subject to the above deductible shall be credited to the Underwriters in full to 21
the extent of the sum by which the aggregate of the claim unreduced by any 22
recoveries exceeds the above deductible. 23

Interest comprised in recoveries shall be apportioned between the Assured and 24
the Underwriters, taking into account the sums paid by Underwriters and the dates 25
when such payments were made, notwithstanding that by the addition of interest 26
the Underwriters may receive a larger sum than they have paid. 27

Appendix 48

BUILDERS' RISKS

INSTITUTE CLAUSE FOR LIMITATION OF LIABILITY IN RESPECT OF FAULTY DESIGN & P. & I. RISKS
(INST. F.D. & P. & I. CLAUSE).

Notwithstanding anything to the contrary which may be contained in the Policy or the clauses attached thereto:—

(1) This insurance includes loss of or damage to the subject matter insured arising from faulty design of any part or parts thereof but in no case shall this insurance extend to cover the cost or expense of repairing, modifying, replacing or renewing such part or parts, nor any cost or expense incurred by reason of betterment or alteration in design.

(2) The amount recoverable under the Protection and Indemnity Clause in respect of any one accident or series of accidents arising out of the same event shall in no case exceed the sum hereby insured. Costs are payable in addition as provided in the Protection and Indemnity Clauses of the current Institute Clauses for Builders' Risks.

Appendix 49

1/12/72

	INSTITUTE WAR CLAUSES	
	BUILDERS' RISKS	

1. **Subject always to the exclusions hereinafter referred to, this insurance covers only** 1

(1)(a) the risks excluded from the Standard Form of English Marine Policy by the clause:— 2
"Warranted free of capture, seizure, arrest, restraint or detainment, and the consequences 3
thereof or of any attempt thereat; also from the consequences of hostilities or warlike 4
operations, whether there be a declaration of war or not; but this warranty shall not exclude 5
collision, contact with any fixed or floating object (other than a mine or torpedo), stranding, 6
heavy weather or fire unless caused directly (and independently of the nature of the voyage 7
or service which the vessel concerned or, in the case of a collision, any other vessel involved 8
therein, is performing) by a hostile act by or against a belligerent power; and for the purpose 9
of this warranty 'power' includes any authority maintaining naval, military or air forces 10
in association with a power. 11

Further warranted free from the consequences of civil war, revolution, rebellion, 12
insurrection, or civil strife arising therefrom, or piracy."; 13

(b) the cover excluded from the Standard Form of English Marine Policy with the Institute 14
Clauses for Builders' Risks attached, by the clause:— 15

"Warranted free from loss damage liability or expense arising from:— 16

(a) the detonation of an explosive 17
(b) any weapon of war 18

and caused by any person acting maliciously or from a political motive."; 19

(2) loss of or damage to the property hereby insured caused by:— 20

(a) hostilities, warlike operations, civil war, revolution, rebellion, insurrection, or civil strife 21
arising therefrom; 22
(b) mines, torpedoes, bombs or other engines of war. 23

Nevertheless this insurance is warranted free of any claim based upon loss of, or frustration 24
of, the insured voyage or adventure caused by arrests restraints or detainments of Kings 25
Princes Peoples Usurpers or persons attempting to usurp power. 26

Provided that the insurance against the risks under (1) and (2) above shall not attach to 27
the subject matter insured until the Vessel is launched and then shall attach only to 28
such part of the subject matter as is built into or is in or on the Vessel at the time of the 29
launch. The insurance against the said risks shall attach to the remainder of the subject 30
matter insured only as it is placed in or on the Vessel subsequent to the launch. 31

2. Claims payable irrespective of percentage. 32

3. This insurance also covers, subject to the limitation of liability provided for in Clause 17 of 33
the Institute Clauses for Builders' Risks, the liability under Clauses 17 and 18 of the 34
Institute Clauses for Builders' Risks which is excluded by Clauses 21 and 23. 35

Provided however that such cover shall not attach until the vessel is launched. 36

4. The Institute Clauses for Builders' Risks except Clauses 4, 21, 23 and 24 are deemed to be 37
incorporated in this insurance, in so far as they do not conflict with the provisions of these clauses. 38

5. **This insurance excludes** 39

(1) loss, damage, liability or expense arising from 40

(a) any hostile detonation of any weapon of war employing atomic or nuclear fission 41
and/or fusion or other like reaction or radioactive force or matter, hereinafter called 42
a nuclear weapon of war; 43

(b) the outbreak of war (whether there be a declaration of war or not) between any of the 44
following countries:— 45

United Kingdom, United States of America, France, 46
the Union of Soviet Socialist Republics, 47
the People's Republic of China; 48

(c) requisition or pre-emption; 49

(d) capture, seizure, arrest, restraint, detainment or confiscation by the Government of the 50
country in which the Vessel is owned or registered; 51

(e) arrest, restraint or detainment under quarantine regulations or by reason of infringement   52
of any customs regulations;   53

(2) (a) loss, damage or expense covered by the Standard Form of English Marine Policy, with the   54
Free of Capture etc. Clause (as quoted in Clause 1(1) (a) above) inserted therein and with   55
the Institute Clauses for Builders' Risks attached or which would be recoverable under   56
such insurance but for Clause 8 thereof;   57

(b) any claim for any sum recoverable under any other insurance on the property hereby   58
insured or which would be recoverable under such insurance but for the existence of this   59
insurance;   60

(3) any claim for expenses arising from delay except such expenses as would be recoverable in   61
principle in English law and practice under the York Antwerp Rules 1950.   62

6.   NOTICE OF CANCELLATION AND   63
      AUTOMATIC TERMINATION OF COVER CLAUSE   64

(a) This insurance may be cancelled by either the Underwriters or the Assured giving 14 days   65
notice (such cancellation becoming effective on the expiry of 14 days from midnight of the   66
day on which notice of cancellation is issued by or to the Underwriters). The Underwriters   67
agree however to reinstate this insurance subject to agreement between the Underwriters   68
and the Assured prior to the expiry of such notice of cancellation as to new rate of premium   69
and/or conditions and/or warranties.   70

Whether or not such notice of cancellation has been given this insurance shall TERMINATE   71
AUTOMATICALLY   72

(i)   upon the occurrence of any hostile detonation of any nuclear weapon of war as defined   73
in Clause 5(1) (a) wheresoever or whensoever such detonation may occur and whether   74
or not the Vessel may be involved;   75

(ii) upon the outbreak of war (whether there be a declaration of war or not) between any   76
of the following countries:—   77

United Kingdom, United States of America, France,   78
the Union of Soviet Socialist Republics,   79
the People's Republic of China;   80

(iii) in the event of the Vessel being requisitioned, either for title or use.   81

(b) In the event either of cancellation by notice or of automatic termination of this insurance   82
by reason of the operation of section (a) of this clause, or of the sale of the Vessel, pro rata   83
net return of premium shall be payable to the Assured.   84

This insurance shall not become effective if, prior to the intended time of its attachment, there has occurred any event which would have automatically terminated this insurance under the provisions of Clause 6 above had this insurance attached prior to such occurrence.

Appendix 50

1/8/73   INSTITUTE POLLUTION HAZARD CLAUSE

Subject to the terms and conditions of this Policy, this insurance covers loss of or damage to the Vessel directly caused by any governmental authority acting under the powers vested in them to prevent or mitigate a pollution hazard or threat thereof, result ng directly from damage to the Vessel for which the Underwriters are liable under this Policy, provided such act of governmental authority has not resulted from want of due diligence by the Assured, the Owners, or Managers of the Vessel or any of them to prevent or mitigate such hazard or threat. Masters, Officers. Crew or Pilots not to be considered Owners within the meaning of this clause should they hold shares in the Vessel.

All other terms and conditions remain unchanged.

For use with:

Institute Time Clauses-Hulls.
Institute Voyage Clauses-Hulls.
Standard Dutch Hull Form.
Institute T.me Clauses, Hulls-Port Risks.
Institute Clauses for Builders' Risks.
Institute Yacht Clauses.
Institute Fishing Vessel Clauses.
Institute War and Strikes Clauses Hulls-Time.
Institute War and Strikes Clauses Hulls-Voyage.

Appendix 51

1/1/82.   (FOR USE ONLY WITH THE NEW MARINE POLICY FORM)

INSTITUTE CARGO CLAUSES (A)

RISKS COVERED

1   This insurance covers all risks of loss of or damage to the subject-matter insured except as provided in   Risks
    Clauses 4, 5, 6 and 7 below.   Clause

2   This insurance covers general average and salvage charges, adjusted or determined according to the contract of   General
    affreightment and/or the governing law and practice, incurred to avoid or in connection with the avoidance of   Average
    loss from any cause except those excluded in Clauses 4, 5, 6 and 7 or elsewhere in this insurance.   Clause

3   This insurance is extended to indemnify the Assured against such proportion of liability under the   "Both to
    contract of affreightment "Both-to-Blame Collision" Clause as is in respect of a loss recoverable hereunder.   Blame
    In the event of any claim by shipowners under the said Clause the Assured agree to notify the Under-   Collision'
    writers who shall have the right, at their own cost and expense, to defend the Assured against such claim.   Clause

EXCLUSIONS

4   In no case shall this insurance cover   General
                                                                                Exclusions

    4.1   loss damage or expense attributable to wilful misconduct of the Assured   Clause

    4.2   ordinary leakage, ordinary loss in weight or volume, or ordinary wear and tear of the subject-matter
            insured

    4.3   loss damage or expense caused by insufficiency or unsuitability of packing or preparation of the subject-
            matter insured (for the purpose of this Clause 4.3 "packing" shall be deemed to include stowage in a
            container or liftvan but only when such stowage is carried out prior to attachment of this insurance or by
            the Assured or their servants)

    4.4   loss damage or expense caused by inherent vice or nature of the subject-matter insured

    4.5   loss damage or expense proximately caused by delay, even though the delay be caused by a risk insured
            against (except expenses payable under Clause 2 above)

    4.6   loss damage or expense arising from insolvency or financial default of the owners managers charterers
            or operators of the vessel

    4.7   loss damage or expense arising from the use of any weapon of war employing atomic or nuclear fission
            and/or fusion or other like reaction or radioactive force or matter.

5   5.1   In no case shall this insurance cover loss damage or expense arising from   Unseaworthiness
                                                                                        and Unfitness
            unseaworthiness of vessel or craft,   Exclusion
                                                                                          Clause
            unfitness of vessel craft conveyance container or liftvan for the safe carriage of the subject-matter
            insured,

            where the Assured or their servants are privy to such unseaworthiness or unfitness, at the time the
            subject-matter insured is loaded therein.

    5.2   The Underwriters waive any breach of the implied warranties of seaworthiness of the ship and fitness
            of the ship to carry the subject-matter insured to destination, unless the Assured or their servants are
            privy to such unseaworthiness or unfitness.

6   In no case shall this insurance cover loss damage or expense caused by   War
                                                                                    Exclusion

    6.1   war civil war revolution rebellion insurrection, or civil strife arising therefrom, or any hostile act by or   Clause
            against a belligerent power

    6.2   capture seizure arrest restraint or detainment (piracy excepted), and the consequences thereof or any
            attempt thereat

    6.3   derelict mines torpedoes bombs or other derelict weapons of war

7   In no case shall this insurance cover loss damage or expense   Strikes
                                                                                       Exclusion

    7.1   caused by strikers, locked-out workmen, or persons taking part in labour disturbances, riots or civil   Clause
            commotions

    7.2   resulting from strikes, lock-outs, labour disturbances, riots or civil commotions

    7.3   caused by any terrorist or any person acting from a political motive.

DURATION

8   8.1   This insurance attaches from the time the goods leave the warehouse or place of storage at the   Transit
            place named herein for the commencement of the transit, continues during the ordinary course of   Clause
            transit and terminates either

        8.1.1   on delivery to the Consignees' or other final warehouse or place of storage at the destination
                    named herein,

8.1.2   on delivery to any other warehouse or place of storage, whether prior to or at the destination named herein, which the Assured elect to use either

8.1.2.1   for storage other than in the ordinary course of transit or

8.1.2.2   for allocation or distribution,

           or

8.1.3   on the expiry of 60 days after completion of discharge overside of the goods hereby insured from the oversea vessel at the final port of discharge,

           whichever shall first occur.

8.2   If, after discharge overside from the oversea vessel at the final port of discharge, but prior to termination of this insurance, the goods are to be forwarded to a destination other than that to which they are insured hereunder, this insurance, whilst remaining subject to termination as provided for above, shall not extend beyond the commencement of transit to such other destination.

8.3   This insurance shall remain in force (subject to termination as provided for above and to the provisions of Clause 9 below) during delay beyond the control of the Assured, any deviation, forced discharge, reshipment or transhipment and during any variation of the adventure arising from the exercise of a liberty granted to shipowners or charterers under the contract of affreightment.

9   If owing to circumstances beyond the control of the Assured either the contract of carriage is terminated at a port or place other than the destination named therein or the transit is otherwise terminated before delivery of the goods as provided for in Clause 8 above, then this insurance shall also terminate *unless prompt notice is given to the Underwriters and continuation of cover is requested when the insurance shall remain in force, subject to an additional premium if required by the Underwriters*, either   Termination of Contract of Carriage Clause

     9.1   until the goods are sold and delivered at such port or place, or, unless otherwise specially agreed, until the expiry of 60 days after arrival of the goods hereby insured at such port or place, whichever shall first occur,

            or

     9.2   if the goods are forwarded within the said period of 60 days (or any agreed extension thereof) to the destination named herein or to any other destination, until terminated in accordance with the provisions of Clause 8 above.

10   Where, after attachment of this insurance, the destination is changed by the Assured, *held covered at a premium and on conditions to be arranged subject to prompt notice being given to the Underwriters.*   Change of Voyage Clause

CLAIMS

11   11.1   In order to recover under this insurance the Assured must have an insurable interest in the subject-matter insured at the time of the loss.   Insurable Interest Clause

     11.2   Subject to 11.1 above, the Assured shall be entitled to recover for insured loss occurring during the period covered by this insurance, notwithstanding that the loss occurred before the contract of insurance was concluded, unless the Assured were aware of the loss and the Underwriters were not.

12   Where, as a result of the operation of a risk covered by this insurance, the insured transit is terminated at a port or place other than that to which the subject-matter is covered under this insurance, the Underwriters will reimburse the Assured for any extra charges properly and reasonably incurred in unloading storing and forwarding the subject-matter to the destination to which it is insured hereunder.   Forwarding Charges Clause

     This Clause 12, which does not apply to general average or salvage charges, shall be subject to the exclusions contained in Clauses 4, 5, 6 and 7 above, and shall not include charges arising from the fault negligence insolvency or financial default of the Assured or their servants.

13   No claim for Constructive Total Loss shall be recoverable hereunder unless the subject-matter insured is reasonably abandoned either on account of its actual total loss appearing to be unavoidable or because the cost of recovering, reconditioning and forwarding the subject-matter to the destination to which it is insured would exceed its value on arrival.   Constructive Total Loss Clause

14   14.1   If any Increased Value insurance is effected by the Assured on the cargo insured herein the agreed value of the cargo shall be deemed to be increased to the total amount insured under this insurance and all Increased Value insurances covering the loss, and liability under this insurance shall be in such proportion as the sum insured herein bears to such total amount insured.   Increased Value Clause

            In the event of claim the Assured shall provide the Underwriters with evidence of the amounts insured under all other insurances.

     14.2   **Where this insurance is on Increased Value the following clause shall apply:**
            The agreed value of the cargo shall be deemed to be equal to the total amount insured under the primary insurance and all Increased Value insurances covering the loss and effected on the cargo by the Assured, and liability under this insurance shall be in such proportion as the sum insured herein bears to such total amount insured.

            In the event of claim the Assured shall provide the Underwriters with evidence of the amounts insured under all other insurances.

BENEFIT OF INSURANCE

15   This insurance shall not inure to the benefit of the carrier or other bailee.   Not to Inure Clause

MINIMISING LOSSES

16   It is the duty of the Assured and their servants and agents in respect of loss recoverable hereunder   Duty of Assured Clause

     16.1   to take such measures as may be reasonable for the purpose of averting or minimising such loss,

            and

     16.2   to ensure that all rights against carriers, bailees or other third parties are properly preserved and exercised

            and the Underwriters will, in addition to any loss recoverable hereunder, reimburse the Assured for any charges properly and reasonably incurred in pursuance of these duties.

17 Measures taken by the Assured or the Underwriters with the object of saving, protecting or recovering   Waiver
    the subject-matter insured shall not be considered as a waiver or acceptance of abandonment or   Clause
    otherwise prejudice the rights of either party.

AVOIDANCE OF DELAY

18 It is a condition of this insurance that the Assured shall act with reasonable despatch in all circumstances   Reasonable
    within their control.   Despatch
                                                                                                                    Clause

LAW AND PRACTICE

19 This insurance is subject to English law and practice.   English Law
                                                                                                             and Practice
                                                                                                             Clause

---

NOTE:— It is necessary for the Assured when they become aware of an event which is "held covered" under this insurance to give prompt notice to the Underwriters and the right to such cover is dependent upon compliance with this obligation.

Appendix 52

1/1/82   (FOR USE ONLY WITH THE NEW MARINE POLICY FORM)

INSTITUTE CARGO CLAUSES (B)

RISKS COVERED

1   This insurance covers, except as provided in Clauses 4, 5, 6 and 7 below   Risks
                                                                                                 Clause

   1.1   loss of or damage to the subject-matter insured reasonably attributable to

   1.1.1   fire or explosion

   1.1.2   vessel or craft being stranded grounded sunk or capsized

   1.1.3   overturning or derailment of land conveyance

   1.1.4   collision or contact of vessel craft or conveyance with any external object other than water

   1.1.5   discharge of cargo at a port of distress

   1.1.6   earthquake volcanic eruption or lightning,

   1.2   loss of or damage to the subject-matter insured caused by

   1.2.1   general average sacrifice

   1.2.2   jettison or washing overboard

   1.2.3   entry of sea lake or river water into vessel craft hold conveyance container liftvan or place of storage,

   1.3   total loss of any package lost overboard or dropped whilst loading on to, or unloading from, vessel or craft.

2   This insurance covers general average and salvage charges, adjusted or determined according to the contract of   General
affreightment and/or the governing law and practice, incurred to avoid or in connection with the avoidance of   Average
loss from any cause except those excluded in Clauses 4, 5, 6 and 7 or elsewhere in this insurance.   Clause

3   This insurance is extended to indemnify the Assured against such proportion of liability under the   "Both to
contract of affreightment "Both to Blame Collision" Clause as is in respect of a loss recoverable hereunder.   Blame
In the event of any claim by shipowners under the said Clause the Assured agree to notify the Under-   Collision"
writers who shall have the right, at their own cost and expense, to defend the Assured against such claim.   Clause

EXCLUSIONS

4   In no case shall this insurance cover   General
                                                                                                 Exclusions
   4.1   loss damage or expense attributable to wilful misconduct of the Assured   Clause

   4.2   ordinary leakage, ordinary loss in weight or volume, or ordinary wear and tear of the subject-matter insured

   4.3   loss damage or expense caused by insufficiency or unsuitability of packing or preparation of the subject-matter insured (for the purpose of this Clause 4.3 "packing" shall be deemed to include stowage in a container or liftvan but only when such stowage is carried out prior to attachment of this insurance or by the Assured or their servants)

   4.4   loss damage or expense caused by inherent vice or nature of the subject-matter insured

   4.5   loss damage or expense proximately caused by delay, even though the delay be caused by a risk insured against (except expenses payable under Clause 2 above)

   4.6   loss damage or expense arising from insolvency or financial default of the owners managers charterers or operators of the vessel

   4.7   deliberate damage to or deliberate destruction of the subject-matter insured or any part thereof by the wrongful act of any person or persons

   4.8   loss damage or expense arising from the use of any weapon of war employing atomic or nuclear fission and/or fusion or other like reaction or radioactive force or matter.

5   5.1   In no case shall this insurance cover loss damage or expense arising from   Unseaworthiness
                                                                                                 and Unfitness
      unseaworthiness of vessel or craft,   Exclusion
                                                                                                 Clause
      unfitness of vessel craft conveyance container or liftvan for the safe carriage of the subject-matter insured,

      where the Assured or their servants are privy to such unseaworthiness or unfitness, at the time the subject-matter insured is loaded therein.

   5.2   The Underwriters waive any breach of the implied warranties of seaworthiness of the ship and fitness of the ship to carry the subject-matter insured to destination, unless the Assured or their servants are privy to such unseaworthiness or unfitness.

6   In no case shall this insurance cover loss damage or expense caused by   War
                                                                                                 Exclusion
   6.1   war civil war revolution rebellion insurrection, or civil strife arising therefrom, or any hostile act by or   Clause
against a belligerent power

6.2   capture seizure arrest restraint or detainment, and the consequences thereof or any attempt thereat

6.3   derelict mines torpedoes bombs or other derelict weapons of war.

7   In no case shall this insurance cover loss damage or expense   *Strikes*
                                                                                              Exclusion
7.1   caused by strikers, locked-out workmen, or persons taking part in labour disturbances, riots or civil   *Clause*
        commotions

7.2   resulting from strikes, lock-outs, labour disturbances, riots or civil commotions

7.3   caused by any terrorist or any person acting from a political motive.

DURATION

8   8.1   This insurance attaches from the time the goods leave the warehouse or place of storage at the   *Transit*
              place named herein for the commencement of the transit, continues during the ordinary course of   *Clause*
              transit and terminates either

      8.1.1   on delivery to the Consignees' or other final warehouse or place of storage at the destination
                named herein,

      8.1.2   on delivery to any other warehouse or place of storage, whether prior to or at the destination
                named herein, which the Assured elect to use either

      8.1.2.1   for storage other than in the ordinary course of transit or

      8.1.2.2   for allocation or distribution,

                  or

      8.1.3   on the expiry of 60 days after completion of discharge overside of the goods hereby insured
                from the oversea vessel at the final port of discharge,

              whichever shall first occur.

      8.2   If, after discharge overside from the oversea vessel at the final port of discharge, but prior to
              termination of this insurance, the goods are to be forwarded to a destination other than that to
              which they are insured hereunder, this insurance, whilst remaining subject to termination as
              provided for above, shall not extend beyond the commencement of transit to such other
              destination.

      8.3   This insurance shall remain in force (subject to termination as provided for above and to the
              provisions of Clause 9 below) during delay beyond the control of the Assured, any deviation,
              forced discharge, reshipment or transhipment and during any variation of the adventure arising
              from the exercise of a liberty granted to shipowners or charterers under the contract of
              affreightment.

9   If owing to circumstances beyond the control of the Assured either the contract of carriage is terminated at a port   *Termination*
      or place other than the destination named therein or the transit is otherwise terminated before delivery of the   *of Contract*
      goods as provided for in Clause 8 above, then this insurance shall also terminate *unless prompt notice is given to*   *of Carriage*
      the Underwriters and continuation of cover is requested when the insurance shall remain in force, subject to an   *Clause*
      additional premium if required by the Underwriters, either

      9.1   until the goods are sold and delivered at such port or place, or, unless otherwise specially agreed, until the
              expiry of 60 days after arrival of the goods hereby insured at such port or place, whichever shall first
              occur,

              or

      9.2   if the goods are forwarded within the said period of 60 days (or any agreed extension thereof) to the
              destination named herein or to any other destination, until terminated in accordance with the provisions
              of Clause 8 above.

10   Where, after attachment of this insurance, the destination is changed by the Assured, *held covered at a*   *Change of*
      premium and on conditions to be arranged subject to prompt notice being given to the Underwriters.   *Voyage*
                                                                                                                  Clause

CLAIMS

11   11.1   In order to recover under this insurance the Assured must have an insurable interest in the   *Insurable*
               subject-matter insured at the time of the loss.   *Interest*
                                                                                                                  Clause
      11.2   Subject to 11.1 above, the Assured shall be entitled to recover for insured loss occurring during the
               period covered by this insurance, notwithstanding that the loss occurred before the contract of insurance
               was concluded, unless the Assured were aware of the loss and the Underwriters were not.

12   Where, as a result of the operation of a risk covered by this insurance, the insured transit is terminated at a port   *Forwarding*
      or place other than that to which the subject-matter is covered under this insurance, the Underwriters will   *Charges*
      reimburse the Assured for any extra charges properly and reasonably incurred in unloading storing and   *Clause*
      forwarding the subject-matter to the destination to which it is insured hereunder.

      This Clause 12, which does not apply to general average or salvage charges, shall be subject to the exclusions
      contained in Clauses 4, 5, 6 and 7 above, and shall not include charges arising from the fault negligence insolvency
      or financial default of the Assured or their servants.

13   No claim for Constructive Total Loss shall be recoverable hereunder unless the subject-matter insured   *Constructive*
      is reasonably abandoned either on account of its actual total loss appearing to be unavoidable or because   *Total Loss*
      the cost of recovering, reconditioning and forwarding the subject-matter to the destination to which it is   *Clause*
      insured would exceed its value on arrival.

14   14.1   If any Increased Value insurance is effected by the Assured on the cargo insured herein the   *Increased*
               agreed value of the cargo shall be deemed to be increased to the total amount insured under this   *Value*
               insurance and all Increased Value insurances covering the loss, and liability under this insurance   *Clause*
               shall be in such proportion as the sum insured herein bears to such total amount insured.

               In the event of claim the Assured shall provide the Underwriters with evidence of the amounts
               insured under all other insurances.

      14.2   Where this insurance is on Increased Value the following clause shall apply:
               The agreed value of the cargo shall be deemed to be equal to the total amount insured under the

primary insurance and all Increased Value insurances covering the loss and effected on the cargo by the Assured, and liability under this insurance shall be in such proportion as the sum insured herein bears to such total amount insured.

In the event of claim the Assured shall provide the Underwriters with evidence of the amounts insured under all other insurances.

BENEFIT OF INSURANCE

15   This insurance shall not inure to the benefit of the carrier or other bailee.   Not to
                                                                                                        Inure Clause

MINIMISING LOSSES

16   It is the duty of the Assured and their servants and agents in respect of loss recoverable hereunder   Duty of
                                                                                                        Assured Clause
    16.1   to take such measures as may be reasonable for the purpose of averting or minimising such loss, and

    16.2   to ensure that all rights against carriers, bailees or other third parties are properly preserved and exercised

and the Underwriters will, in addition to any loss recoverable hereunder, reimburse the Assured for any charges properly and reasonably incurred in pursuance of these duties.

17   Measures taken by the Assured or the Underwriters with the object of saving, protecting or recovering   Waiver
     the subject-matter insured shall not be considered as a waiver or acceptance of abandonment or   Clause
     otherwise prejudice the rights of either party.

AVOIDANCE OF DELAY

18   It is a condition of this insurance that the Assured shall act with reasonable despatch in all circumstances   Reasonable
     within their control.   Despatch
                                                                                                        Clause

LAW AND PRACTICE

19   This insurance is subject to English law and practice.   English Law
                                                                                                        and Practice
                                                                                                        Clause

---

NOTE:— It is necessary for the Assured when they become aware of an event which is "held covered" under this insurance to give prompt notice to the Underwriters and the right to such cover is dependent upon compliance with this obligation.

Appendix 53

INSTITUTE CARGO CLAUSES (C)

RISKS COVERED

1   This insurance covers, except as provided in Clauses 4, 5, 6 and 7 below:

   1.1   loss of or damage to the subject-matter insured reasonably attributable to

   1.1.1   fire or explosion

   1.1.2   vessel or craft being stranded grounded sunk or capsized

   1.1.3   overturning or derailment of land conveyance

   1.1.4   collision or contact of vessel craft or conveyance with any external object other than water

   1.1.5   discharge of cargo at a port of distress,

   1.2   loss of or damage to the subject-matter insured caused by

   1.2.1   general average sacrifice

   1.2.2   jettison.

2   This insurance covers general average and salvage charges, adjusted or determined according to the contract of affreightment and/or the governing law and practice, incurred to avoid or in connection with the avoidance of loss from any cause except those excluded in Clauses 4, 5, 6 and 7 or elsewhere in this insurance.   *General Average Clause*

3   This insurance is extended to indemnify the Assured against such proportion of liability under the contract of affreightment "Both to Blame Collision" Clause as is in respect of a loss recoverable hereunder. In the event of any claim by shipowners under the said Clause the Assured agree to notify the Underwriters who shall have the right, at their own cost and expense, to defend the Assured against such claim.   *"Both to Blame Collision" Clause*

EXCLUSIONS

4   In no case shall this insurance cover   *General Exclusions Clause*

   4.1   loss damage or expense attributable to wilful misconduct of the Assured

   4.2   ordinary leakage, ordinary loss in weight or volume, or ordinary wear and tear of the subject-matter insured

   4.3   loss damage or expense caused by insufficiency or unsuitability of packing or preparation of the subject-matter insured (for the purpose of this Clause 4.3 "packing" shall be deemed to include stowage in a container or liftvan but only when such stowage is carried out prior to attachment of this insurance or by the Assured or their servants)

   4.4   loss damage or expense caused by inherent vice or nature of the subject-matter insured

   4.5   loss damage or expense proximately caused by delay, even though the delay be caused by a risk insured against (except expenses payable under Clause 2 above)

   4.6   loss damage or expense arising from insolvency or financial default of the owners managers charterers or operators of the vessel

   4.7   deliberate damage to or deliberate destruction of the subject-matter insured or any part thereof by the wrongful act of any person or persons

   4.8   loss damage or expense arising from the use of any weapon of war employing atomic or nuclear fission and/or fusion or other like reaction or radioactive force or matter.

5   5.1   In no case shall this insurance cover loss damage or expense arising from   *Unseaworthiness and Unfitness Exclusion Clause*

       unseaworthiness of vessel or craft,

       unfitness of vessel craft conveyance container or liftvan for the safe carriage of the subject-matter insured,

       where the Assured or their servants are privy to such unseaworthiness or unfitness, at the time the subject-matter insured is loaded therein.

   5.2   The Underwriters waive any breach of the implied warranties of seaworthiness of the ship and fitness of the ship to carry the subject-matter insured to destination, unless the Assured or their servants are privy to such unseaworthiness or unfitness.

6   In no case shall this insurance cover loss damage or expense caused by   *War Exclusion Clause*

   6.1   war civil war revolution rebellion insurrection, or civil strife arising therefrom, or any hostile act by or against a belligerent power

   6.2   capture seizure arrest restraint or detainment, and the consequences thereof or any attempt thereat

6.3   derelict mines torpedoes bombs or other derelict weapons of war.

7   In no case shall this insurance cover loss damage or expense   Strikes
                                                                                                Exclusion
7.1   caused by strikers, locked-out workmen, or persons taking part in labour disturbances, riots or civil   Clause
       commotions

7.2   resulting from strikes, lock-outs, labour disturbances, riots or civil commotions

7.3   caused by any terrorist or any person acting from a political motive.

DURATION

8   8.1   This insurance attaches from the time the goods leave the warehouse or place of storage at the   Transit
              place named herein for the commencement of the transit, continues during the ordinary course of   Clause
              transit and terminates either

       8.1.1   on delivery to the Consignees' or other final warehouse or place of storage at the destination
                named herein,

       8.1.2   on delivery to any other warehouse or place of storage, whether prior to or at the destination
                named herein, which the Assured elect to use either

       8.1.2.1   for storage other than in the ordinary course of transit or

       8.1.2.2   for allocation or distribution,

              or

       8.1.3   on the expiry of 60 days after completion of discharge overside of the goods hereby insured
                from the oversea vessel at the final port of discharge,

              whichever shall first occur.

       8.2   If, after discharge overside from the oversea vessel at the final port of discharge, but prior to
              termination of this insurance, the goods are to be forwarded to a destination other than that to
              which they are insured hereunder, this insurance, whilst remaining subject to termination as
              provided for above, shall not extend beyond the commencement of transit to such other
              destination.

       8.3   This insurance shall remain in force (subject to termination as provided for above and to the
              provisions of Clause 9 below) during delay beyond the control of the Assured, any deviation,
              forced discharge, reshipment or transhipment and during any variation of the adventure arising
              from the exercise of a liberty granted to shipowners or charterers under the contract of
              affreightment.

9   If owing to circumstances beyond the control of the Assured either the contract of carriage is terminated at a port   Termination
       or place other than the destination named therein or the transit is otherwise terminated before delivery of the   of Contract
       goods as provided for in Clause 8 above, then this insurance shall also terminate unless prompt notice is given   of Carriage
       to the Underwriters and continuation of cover is requested when the insurance shall remain in force, subject to   Clause
       an additional premium if required by the Underwriters, either

       9.1   until the goods are sold and delivered at such port or place, or, unless otherwise specially agreed, until
              the expiry of 60 days after arrival of the goods hereby insured at such port or place, whichever shall first
              occur,

              or

       9.2   if the goods are forwarded within the said period of 60 days (or any agreed extension thereof) to the
              destination named herein or to any other destination, until terminated in accordance with the provisions
              of Clause 8 above.

10   Where, after attachment of this insurance, the destination is changed by the Assured, held covered at a   Change of
       premium and on conditions to be arranged subject to prompt notice being given to the Underwriters.   Voyage
                                                                                                                            Clause

CLAIMS

11   11.1   In order to recover under this insurance the Assured must have an insurable interest in the   Insurable
               subject-matter insured at the time of the loss.   Interest
                                                                                                                            Clause

       11.2   Subject to 11.1 above, the Assured shall be entitled to recover for insured loss occurring during the period
               covered by this insurance, notwithstanding that the loss occurred before the contract of insurance was
               concluded, unless the Assured were aware of the loss and the Underwriters were not.

12   Where, as a result of the operation of a risk covered by this insurance, the insured transit is terminated at a port   Forwarding
       or place other than that to which the subject-matter is covered under this insurance, the Underwriters will   Charges
       reimburse the Assured for any extra charges properly and reasonably incurred in unloading storing and   Clause
       forwarding the subject-matter to the destination to which it is insured hereunder.

       This Clause 12, which does not apply to general average or salvage charges, shall be subject to the exclusions
       contained in Clauses 4, 5, 6 and 7 above, and shall not include charges arising from the fault negligence
       insolvency or financial default of the Assured or their servants.

13   No claim for Constructive Total Loss shall be recoverable hereunder unless the subject-matter insured   Constructive
       is reasonably abandoned either on account of its actual total loss appearing to be unavoidable or because   Total Loss
       the cost of recovering, reconditioning and forwarding the subject-matter to the destination to which it is   Clause
       insured would exceed its value on arrival.

14   14.1   If any Increased Value insurance is effected by the Assured on the cargo insured herein the   Increased
               agreed value of the cargo shall be deemed to be increased to the total amount insured under this   Value
               insurance and all Increased Value insurances covering the loss, and liability under this insurance   Clause
               shall be in such proportion as the sum insured herein bears to such total amount insured.

               In the event of claim the Assured shall provide the Underwriters with evidence of the amounts
               insured under all other insurances.

       14.2   Where this insurance is on Increased Value the following clause shall apply:
               The agreed value of the cargo shall be deemed to be equal to the total amount insured under the
               primary insurance and all Increased Value insurances covering the loss and effected on the cargo

by the Assured, and liability under this insurance shall be in such proportion as the sum insured herein bears to such total amount insured.

In the event of claim the Assured shall provide the Underwriters with evidence of the amounts insured under all other insurances.

BENEFIT OF INSURANCE

15   This insurance shall not inure to the benefit of the carrier or other bailee.   Not to Inure Clause

MINIMISING LOSSES

16   It is the duty of the Assured and their servants and agents in respect of loss recoverable hereunder   Duty of Assured Clause

    16.1   to take such measures as may be reasonable for the purpose of averting or minimising such loss, and

    16.2   to ensure that all rights against carriers, bailees or other third parties are properly preserved and exercised

    and the Underwriters will, in addition to any loss recoverable hereunder, reimburse the Assured for any charges properly and reasonably incurred in pursuance of these duties.

17   Measures taken by the Assured or the Underwriters with the object of saving, protecting or recovering the subject-matter insured shall not be considered as a waiver or acceptance of abandonment or otherwise prejudice the rights of either party.   Waiver Clause

AVOIDANCE OF DELAY

18   It is a condition of this insurance that the Assured shall act with reasonable despatch in all circumstances within their control.   Reasonable Despatch Clause

LAW AND PRACTICE

19   This insurance is subject to English law and practice.   English Law and Practice Clause

NOTE:— It is necessary for the Assured when they become aware of an event which is "held covered" under this insurance to give prompt notice to the Underwriters and the right to such cover is dependent upon compliance with this obligation.

Appendix 54

1/1/82 (FOR USE ONLY WITH THE NEW MARINE POLICY FORM)

MALICIOUS DAMAGE CLAUSE
(For use with Institute Cargo Clauses (B) and (C))

In consideration of an additional premium, it is hereby agreed that Clause 4.7 of the Institute Cargo Clauses is deemed to be deleted and further that this insurance covers loss of or damage to the subject-matter insured caused by malicious acts vandalism or sabotage, subject always to the other exclusions contained in this insurance.

Appendix 55

(FOR USE ONLY WITH THE NEW MARINE POLICY FORM)

INSTITUTE STRIKES CLAUSES (CARGO)

RISKS COVERED

1   This insurance covers, except as provided in Clauses 3 and 4 below, loss of or damage to the subject-matter insured caused by   *Risks Clause*

     1.1   strikers, locked-out workmen, or persons taking part in labour disturbances, riots or civil commotions,

     1.2   any terrorist or any person acting from a political motive

2   This insurance covers general average and salvage charges, adjusted or determined according to the contract of affreightment and/or the governing law and practice, incurred to avoid or in connection with the avoidance of loss from a risk covered under these clauses.   *General Average Clause*

EXCLUSIONS

3   In no case shall this insurance cover   *General Exclusions Clause*

     3.1   loss damage or expense attributable to wilful misconduct of the Assured

     3.2   ordinary leakage, ordinary loss in weight or volume, or ordinary wear and tear of the subject-matter insured

     3.3   loss damage or expense caused by insufficiency or unsuitability of packing or preparation of the subject-matter insured (for the purpose of this Clause 3.3 "packing" shall be deemed to include stowage in a container or liftvan but only when such stowage is carried out prior to attachment of this insurance or by the Assured or their servants)

     3.4   loss damage or expense caused by inherent vice or nature of the subject-matter insured

     3.5   loss damage or expense proximately caused by delay, even though the delay be caused by a risk insured against (except expenses payable under Clause 2 above)

     3.6   loss damage or expense arising from insolvency or financial default of the owners managers charterers or operators of the vessel

     3.7   loss damage or expense arising from the absence shortage or withholding of labour of any description whatsoever resulting from any strike, lockout, labour disturbance, riot or civil commotion

     3.8   any claim based upon loss of or frustration of the voyage or adventure

     3.9   loss damage or expense arising from the use of any weapon of war employing atomic or nuclear fission and/or fusion or other like reaction or radioactive force or matter

     3.10   loss damage or expense caused by war civil war revolution rebellion insurrection, or civil strife arising therefrom, or any hostile act by or against a belligerent power.

4   4.1.   In no case shall this insurance cover loss damage or expense arising from   *Unseaworthiness and Unfitness Exclusion Clause*

       unseaworthiness of vessel or craft,

       unfitness of vessel craft conveyance container or liftvan for the safe carriage of the subject-matter insured,

       where the Assured or their servants are privy to such unseaworthiness or unfitness, at the time the subject-matter insured is loaded therein.

     4.2   The Underwriters waive any breach of the implied warranties of seaworthiness of the ship and fitness of the ship to carry the subject-matter insured to destination, unless the Assured or their servants are privy to such unseaworthiness or unfitness.

DURATION

5   5.1   This insurance attaches from the time the goods leave the warehouse or place of storage at the place named herein for the commencement of the transit, continues during the ordinary course of transit and terminates either   *Transit Clause*

     5.1.1   on delivery to the Consignees' or other final warehouse or place of storage at the destination named herein,

     5.1.2   on delivery to any other warehouse or place of storage, whether prior to or at the destination named herein, which the Assured elect to use either

     5.1.2.1   for storage other than in the ordinary course of transit or

     5.1.2.2   for allocation or distribution,

       or

5.1.3   on the expiry of 60 days after completion of discharge overside of the goods hereby insured from the oversea vessel at the final port of discharge,

whichever shall first occur.

5.2   If, after discharge overside from the oversea vessel at the final port of discharge, but prior to termination of this insurance, the goods are to be forwarded to a destination other than that to which they are insured hereunder, this insurance, whilst remaining subject to termination as provided for above, shall not extend beyond the commencement of transit to such other destination.

5.3   This insurance shall remain in force (subject to termination as provided for above and to the provisions of Clause 6 below) during delay beyond the control of the Assured, any deviation, forced discharge, reshipment or transhipment and during any variation of the adventure arising from the exercise of a liberty granted to shipowners or charterers under the contract of affreightment.

6   If owing to circumstances beyond the control of the Assured either the contract of carriage is terminated at a port or place other than the destination named therein or the transit is otherwise terminated before delivery of the goods as provided for in Clause 5 above, then this insurance shall also terminate *unless prompt notice is given to the Underwriters and continuation of cover is requested when the insurance shall remain in force, subject to an additional premium if required by the Underwriters, either*   Termination of Contract of Carriage Clause

28\1\1

6.1   until the goods are sold and delivered at such port or place, or, unless otherwise specially agreed, until the expiry of 60 days after arrival of the goods hereby insured at such port or place, whichever shall first occur,

or

6.2   if the goods are forwarded within the said period of 60 days (or any agreed extension thereof) to the destination named herein or to any other destination, until terminated in accordance with the provisions of Clause 5 above.

7   Where, after attachment of this insurance, the destination is changed by the Assured, *held covered at a premium and on conditions to be arranged subject to prompt notice being given to the Underwriters.*   Change of Voyage Clause

CLAIMS

8   8.1   In order to recover under this insurance the Assured must have an insurable interest in the subject-matter insured at the time of the loss.   Insurable Interest Clause

8.2   Subject to 8.1 above, the Assured shall be entitled to recover for insured loss occurring during the period covered by this insurance, notwithstanding that the loss occurred before the contract of insurance was concluded, unless the Assured were aware of the loss and the Underwriters were not.

9   9.1   If any Increased Value insurance is effected by the Assured on the cargo insured herein the agreed value of the cargo shall be deemed to be increased to the total amount insured under this insurance and all Increased Value insurances covering the loss, and liability under this insurance shall be in such proportion as the sum insured herein bears to such total amount insured.   Increased Value Clause

In the event of claim the Assured shall provide the Underwriters with evidence of the amounts insured under all other insurances.

9.2   **Where this insurance is on Increased Value the following clause shall apply:**
The agreed value of the cargo shall be deemed to be equal to the total amount insured under the primary insurance and all Increased Value insurances covering the loss and effected on the cargo by the Assured, and liability under this insurance shall be in such proportion as the sum insured herein bears to such total amount insured.

In the event of claim the Assured shall provide the Underwriters with evidence of the amounts insured under all other insurances.

BENEFIT OF INSURANCE

10   This insurance shall not inure to the benefit of the carrier or other bailee.   Not to Inure Clause

MINIMISING LOSSES

11   It is the duty of the Assured and their servants and agents in respect of loss recoverable hereunder   Duty of Assured Clause

11.1   to take such measures as may be reasonable for the purpose of averting or minimising such loss, and

11.2   to ensure that all rights against carriers, bailees or other third parties are properly preserved and exercised

and the Underwriters will, in addition to any loss recoverable hereunder, reimburse the Assured for any charges properly and reasonably incurred in pursuance of these duties.

12   Measures taken by the Assured or the Underwriters with the object of saving, protecting or recovering the subject-matter insured shall not be considered as a waiver or acceptance of abandonment or otherwise prejudice the rights of either party.   Waiver Clause

AVOIDANCE OF DELAY

13   It is a condition of this insurance that the Assured shall act with reasonable despatch in all circumstances within their control.   Reasonable Despatch Clause

LAW AND PRACTICE

14   This insurance is subject to English law and practice.   English Law and Practice Clause

---

NOTE:— *It is necessary for the Assured when they become aware of an event which is "held covered" under this insurance to give prompt notice to the Underwriters and the right to such cover is dependent upon compliance with this obligation.*

Appendix 56

(FOR USE ONLY WITH THE NEW MARINE POLICY FORM)

INSTITUTE WAR CLAUSES (CARGO)

RISKS COVERED

This insurance covers except as provided in Clauses 3 and 4 below, loss of or damage to the subject-matter insured caused by   Risks Clause

1.1   war civil war revolution rebellion insurrection, or civil strife arising therefrom, or any hostile act by or against a belligerent power

1.2   capture seizure arrest restraint or detainment, arising, from risks covered under 1.1 above, and the consequences thereof or any attempt thereat

1.3   derelict mines torpedoes bombs or other derelict weapons of war.

2   This insurance covers general average and salvage charges, adjusted or determined according to the contract of affreightment and/or the governing law and practice, incurred to avoid or in connection with the avoidance of loss from a risk covered under these clauses.   General Average Clause

EXCLUSIONS

3   In no case shall this insurance cover   General Exclusions Clause

3.1   loss damage or expense attributable to wilful misconduct of the Assured

3.2   ordinary leakage, ordinary loss in weight or volume, or ordinary wear and tear of the subject-matter insured

3.3   loss damage or expense caused by insufficiency or unsuitability of packing or preparation of the subject-matter insured (for the purpose of this Clause 3.3 "packing" shall be deemed to include stowage in a container or liftvan but only when such stowage is carried out prior to attachment of this insurance or by the Assured or their servants)

3.4   loss damage or expense caused by inherent vice or nature of the subject-matter insured

3.5   loss damage or expense proximately caused by delay, even though the delay be caused by a risk insured against (except expenses payable under Clause 2 above)

3.6   loss damage or expense arising from insolvency or financial default of the owners managers charterers or operators of the vessel

3.7   any claim based upon loss of or frustration of the voyage or adventure

3.8   loss damage or expense arising from any hostile use of any weapon of war employing atomic or nuclear fission and/or fusion or other like reaction or radioactive force or matter.

4   4.1   In no case shall this insurance cover loss damage or expense arising from   Unseaworthiness and Unfitness Exclusion Clause

unseaworthiness of vessel or craft,

unfitness of vessel craft conveyance container or liftvan for the safe carriage of the subject-matter insured,

where the Assured or their servants are privy to such unseaworthiness or unfitness, at the time the subject-matter insured is loaded therein.

4.2   The Underwriters waive any breach of the implied warranties of seaworthiness of the ship and fitness of the ship to carry the subject-matter insured to destination, unless the Assured or their servants are privy to such unseaworthiness or unfitness.

DURATION

5   5.1   This insurance   Transit Clause

5.1.1   attaches only as the subject-matter insured and as to any part as that part is loaded on an oversea vessel

and

5.1.2   terminates, subject to 5.2 and 5.3 below, either as the subject-matter insured and as to any part as that part is discharged from an oversea vessel at the final port or place of discharge,

or

on expiry of 15 days counting from midnight of the day of arrival of the vessel at the final port or place of discharge,

whichever shall first occur;

nevertheless,

subject to prompt notice to the Underwriters and to an additional premium, such insurance

5.1.3   reattaches when, without having discharged the subject-matter insured at the final port or place of discharge, the vessel sails therefrom,

and

5.1.4   terminates, subject to 5.2 and 5.3 below, either as the subject-matter insured and as to any part as that part is thereafter discharged from the vessel at the final (or substituted) port or place of discharge,

or

on expiry of 15 days counting from midnight of the day of re-arrival of the vessel at the final port or place of discharge or arrival of the vessel at a substituted port or place of discharge,

whichever shall first occur.

5.2   If during the insured voyage the oversea vessel arrives at an intermediate port or place to discharge the subject-matter insured for on-carriage by oversea vessel or by aircraft, or the goods are discharged from the vessel at a port or place of refuge, then, subject to 5.3 below and to an additional premium if required, this insurance continues until the expiry of 15 days counting from midnight of the day of arrival of the vessel at such port or place, but thereafter reattaches as the subject-matter insured and as to any part as that part is loaded on an on-carrying oversea vessel or aircraft. During the period of 15 days the insurance remains in force after discharge only whilst the subject-matter insured and as to any part as that part is at such port or place. If the goods are on-carried within the said period of 15 days or if the insurance reattaches as provided in this Clause 5.2

5.2.1   where the on-carriage is by oversea vessel this insurance continues subject to the terms of these clauses,

or

5.2.2   where the on-carriage is by aircraft, the current Institute War Clauses (Air Cargo) (excluding sendings by Post) shall be deemed to form part of this insurance and shall apply to the on-carriage by air.

5.3   If the voyage in the contract of carriage is terminated at a port or place other than the destination agreed therein, such port or place shall be deemed the final port of discharge and such insurance terminates in accordance with 5.1.2. If the subject-matter insured is subsequently reshipped to the original or any other destination, then *provided notice is given to the Underwriters before the commencement of such further transit and subject to an additional premium*, such insurance reattaches

5.3.1   in the case of the subject-matter insured having been discharged, as the subject-matter insured, and as to any part as that part is loaded on the on-carrying vessel for the voyage;

5.3.2   in the case of the subject-matter not having been discharged, when the vessel sails from such deemed final port of discharge;

thereafter such insurance terminates in accordance with 5.1.4.

5.4   The insurance against the risks of mines and derelict torpedoes, floating or submerged, is extended whilst the subject-matter insured or any part thereof is on craft whilst in transit to or from the oversea vessel, but in no case beyond the expiry of 60 days after discharge from the oversea vessel unless otherwise specially agreed by the Underwriters.

5.5   *Subject to prompt notice to Underwriters, and to an additional premium if required, this insurance shall remain in force within the provisions of these Clauses during any deviation, or any variation of the adventure arising from the exercise of a liberty granted to shipowners or charterers under the contract of affreightment.*

(For the purpose of Clause 5

"arrival" shall be deemed to mean that the vessel is anchored, moored or otherwise secured at a berth or place within the Harbour Authority area. If such a berth or place is not available, arrival is deemed to have occurred when the vessel first anchors, moors or otherwise secures either at or off the intended port or place of discharge

"oversea vessel" shall be deemed to mean a vessel carrying the subject-matter from one port or place to another where such voyage involves a sea passage by that vessel)

6   Where, after attachment of this insurance, the destination is changed by the Assured, *held covered at a premium and on conditions to be arranged subject to prompt notice being given to the Underwriters.*   Change of Voyage Clause

7   Anything contained in this contract which is inconsistent with Clauses 3.7, 3.8 or 5 shall, to the extent of such inconsistency, be null and void.

CLAIMS

8   8.1   In order to recover under this insurance the Assured must have an insurable interest in the subject-matter insured at the time of the loss.   Insurable Interest Clause

8.2   Subject to 8.1 above, the Assured shall be entitled to recover for insured loss occurring during the period covered by this insurance, notwithstanding that the loss occurred before the contract of insurance was concluded, unless the Assured were aware of the loss and the Underwriters were not.

9   9.1   If any Increased Value insurance is effected by the Assured on the cargo insured herein the agreed value of the cargo shall be deemed to be increased to the total amount insured under this insurance and all Increased Value insurances covering the loss, and liability under this insurance shall be in such proportion as the sum insured herein bears to such total amount insured.   Increased Value Clause

In the event of claim the Assured shall provide the Underwriters with evidence of the amounts insured under all other insurances.

9.2   **Where this insurance is on Increased Value the following clause shall apply:**
The agreed value of the cargo shall be deemed to be equal to the total amount insured under the primary insurance and all Increased Value insurances covering the loss and effected on the cargo by the Assured, and liability under this insurance shall be in such proportion as the sum insured herein bears to such total amount insured.

In the event of claim the Assured shall provide the Underwriters with evidence of the amounts insured under all other insurances.

BENEFIT OF INSURANCE

10   This insurance shall not inure to the benefit of the carrier or other bailee.   Not to Inure Clause

MINIMISING LOSSES

11 It is the duty of the Assured and their servants and agents in respect of loss recoverable hereunder   Duty of Assured Clause

  11.1 to take such measures as may be reasonable for the purpose of averting or minimising such loss,

    and

  11.2 to ensure that all rights against carriers, bailees or other third parties are properly preserved and exercised

and the Underwriters will, in addition to any loss recoverable hereunder, reimburse the Assured for any charges properly and reasonably incurred in pursuance of these duties.

12 Measures taken by the Assured or the Underwriters with the object of saving, protecting or recovering the subject-matter insured shall not be considered as a waiver or acceptance of abandonment or otherwise prejudice the rights of either party.   Waiver Clause

AVOIDANCE OF DELAY

13 It is a condition of this insurance that the Assured shall act with reasonable despatch in all circumstances within their control.   Reasonable Despatch Clause

LAW AND PRACTICE

14 This insurance is subject to English law and practice.   English Law and Practice Clause

---

NOTE:— It is necessary for the Assured when they become aware of an event which is "held covered" under this insurance to give prompt notice to the Underwriters, and the right to such cover is dependent upon compliance with this obligation.

Appendix 57

(1/2/83)   (FOR USE ONLY WITH THE NEW MARINE POLICY FORM)

INSTITUTE BULK OIL CLAUSES

RISKS COVERED

1   This insurance covers, except as provided in Clauses 4,5,6 and 7 below,   Risks Clause

    1.1   loss of or contamination of the subject-matter insured reasonably attributable to

        1.1.1   fire or explosion

        1.1.2   vessel or craft being stranded grounded sunk or capsized

        1.1.3   collision or contact of vessel or craft with any external object other than water

        1.1.4   discharge of cargo at a port or place of distress

        1.1.5   earthquake volcanic eruption or lightning,

    1.2   loss of or contamination of the subject-matter insured caused by

        1.2.1   general average sacrifice

        1.2.2   jettison

        1.2.3   leakage from connecting pipelines in loading transhipment or discharge

        1.2.4   negligence of Master Officers or Crew in pumping cargo ballast or fuel,

    1.3   contamination of the subject-matter insured resulting from stress of weather

2   This insurance covers general average and salvage charges, adjusted or determined according to the contract of affreightment and/or the governing law and practice, incurred to avoid or in connection with the avoidance of loss from any cause except those excluded in Clauses 4, 5, 6 and 7 or elsewhere in this insurance.   General Average Clause

3   This insurance is extended to indemnify the Assured against such proportion of liability under the contract of affreightment "Both to Blame Collision" Clause as is in respect of a loss recoverable hereunder. In the event of any claim by shipowners under the said Clause the Assured agree to notify the Underwriters who shall have the right, at their own cost and expense, to defend the Assured against such claim.   "Both to Blame Collision" Clause

EXCLUSIONS

4   In no case shall this insurance cover   General Exclusions Clause

    4.1   loss damage or expense attributable to wilful misconduct of the Assured

    4.2   ordinary leakage, ordinary loss in weight or volume, or ordinary wear and tear of the subject-matter insured

    4.3   loss damage or expense caused by inherent vice or nature of the subject-matter insured

    4.4   loss damage or expense proximately caused by delay, even though the delay be caused by a risk insured against (except expenses payable under Clause 2 above)

    4.5   loss damage or expense arising from insolvency or financial default of the owners managers charterers or operators of the vessel

    4.6   loss damage or expense arising from the use of any weapon of war employing atomic or nuclear fission and/or fusion or other like reaction or radioactive force or matter.

5   5.1   In no case shall this insurance cover loss damage or expense arising from   Unseaworthiness and Unfitness Exclusion Clause

        unseaworthiness of vessel or craft,

        unfitness of vessel craft or conveyance for the safe carriage of the subject-matter insured,

        where the Assured or their servants are privy to such unseaworthiness or unfitness, at the time the subject-matter insured is loaded therein.

    5.2   The Underwriters waive any breach of the implied warranties of seaworthiness of the ship and fitness of the ship to carry the subject-matter insured to destination, unless the Assured or their servants are privy to such unseaworthiness or unfitness.

6   In no case shall this insurance cover loss damage or expense caused by   War Exclusion Clause

    6.1   war civil war revolution rebellion insurrection, or civil strife arising therefrom, or any hostile act by or against a belligerent power

6.2   capture seizure arrest restraint or detainment (piracy excepted), and the consequences thereof or any attempt thereat

6.3   derelict mines torpedoes bombs or other derelict weapons of war.

7   In no case shall this insurance cover loss damage or expense   *Strikes Exclusion Clause*

7.1   caused by strikers, locked-out workmen, or persons taking part in labour disturbances, riots or civil commotions

7.2   resulting from strikes, lock-outs, labour disturbances, riots or civil commotions

7.3   caused by any terrorist or any person acting from a political motive.

DURATION

8   8.1   This insurance attaches as the subject-matter insured leaves tanks for the purpose of loading at the place named herein for the commencement of the transit, continues during the ordinary course of transit and terminates either   *Transit Clause*

8.1.1   as the subject-matter insured enters tanks on discharge to place of storage or to storage vessel at the destination named herein,

or

8.1.2   on the expiry of 30 days after the date of arrival of the vessel at the destination named herein, whichever shall first occur.

8.2   If, after discharge from the oversea vessel into craft at the final port or place of discharge, but prior to the termination of this insurance under 8.1 above, the subject-matter insured or any part thereof is to be forwarded to a destination other than that to which it is insured hereunder, the insurance on the subject-matter insured or such part thereof shall not extend beyond the commencement of transit to such other destination, *unless otherwise agreed by the Underwriters upon receipt of prompt notice from the Assured.*

8.3   *Subject to prompt notice being given to the Underwriters and to an additional premium if required by them,* this insurance shall remain in force (until terminated under 8.1 or 8.2 above, and subject to the provisions of Clause 9 below) during delay beyond the control of the Assured, any deviation, forced discharge, reshipment or transhipment and during any other variation of the adventure provided such other variation is beyond the control of the Assured.

9   If owing to circumstances beyond the control of the Assured either the contract of carriage is terminated at a port or place other than the destination named therein or the transit is terminated otherwise than as provided in Clause 8 above, then this insurance shall also terminate *unless prompt notice is given to the Underwriters and continuation of cover is requested when the insurance shall remain in force, subject to an additional premium if required by the Underwriters,* either   *Termination of Contract of Carriage Clause*

9.1   until the goods are sold and delivered at such port or place, or, unless otherwise specially agreed, until the expiry of 30 days after arrival of the goods hereby insured at such port or place, whichever shall first occur,

or

9.2   if the goods are forwarded within the said period of 30 days (or any agreed extension thereof) to the destination named herein or to any other destination, until terminated in accordance with the provisions of Clause 8 above.

10   Where, after attachment of this insurance, the destination is changed by the Assured, held covered at a premium and on conditions to be arranged subject to prompt notice being given to the Underwriters.   *Change of Voyage Clause*

CLAIMS

11   11.1   In order to recover under this insurance the Assured must have an insurable interest in the subject-matter insured at the time of the loss.   *Insurable Interest Clause*

11.2   Subject to 11.1 above, the Assured shall be entitled to recover for insured loss occuring during the period covered by this insurance, notwithstanding that the loss occured before the contract of insurance was concluded, unless the Assured were aware of the loss and the Underwriters were not.

12   Where, as a result of the operation of a risk covered by this insurance, the insured transit is terminated at a port or place other than that to which the subject-matter is covered under this insurance, the Underwriters will reimburse the Assured for any extra charges properly and reasonably incurred in unloading storing and forwarding the subject-matter to the destination to which it is insured hereunder.   *Forwarding Charges Clause*

This Clause 12, which does not apply to general average or salvage charges, shall be subject to the exclusions contained in Clauses 4, 5, 6 and 7 above, and shall not include charges arising from the fault negligence insolvency or financial default of the Assured or their servants

13   No claim for Constructive Total Loss shall be recoverable hereunder unless the subject-matter insured is reasonably abandoned either on account of its actual total loss appearing to be unavoidable or because the cost of recovering, reconditioning and forwarding the subject-matter to the destination to which it is insured would exceed its value on arrival.   *Constructive Total Loss Clause*

14.1   If any Increased Value Insurance is effected by the Assured on the cargo insured herein the agreed value of the cargo shall be deemed to be increased to the total amount insured under this insurance and all Increased Value insurances covering the loss, the liability under this insurance shall be in such proportion as the sum insured herein bears to such total amount insured.   *Increased Value Clause*

In the event of claim the Assured shall provide the Underwriters with evidence of the amounts insured under all other insurances.

14.2   **Where this insurance is on Increased Value the following clause shall apply:**

The agreed value of the cargo shall be deemed to be equal to the total amount insured under the primary insurance and all Increased Value insurances covering the loss and effected on the cargo by the Assured, and liability under this insurance shall be in such proportion as the sum insured herein bears to such total amount insured.

In the event of claim the Assured shall provide the Underwriters with evidence of the amounts insured under all other insurances.

15 Claims for leakage and shortage recoverable under this insurance are to be adjusted as follows:- Adjustment Clause

15.1   The amount recoverable shall be the proportionate insured value of the volume of oil lost, to be ascertained by a comparison of the gross volume certified as having left tanks for loading on to the vessel with the gross volume certified as having been delivered to tanks at the termination of the transit, except that where the contract of sale is based on weight and not on volume the amount recoverable may be calculated on a weight basis from such certified quantities.

The term "gross volume" in this Clause 15.1 means total volume without deduction of sediment and water content and free water, except to the extent that the amount of water can be shown by the Assured to have increased abnormally during the insured transit as a result of the operation of a risk covered by this insurance.

15.2   Adjustment shall be made to the calculation under 15.1 above to eliminate any change in volume caused by variation in temperature and any apparent change in quantity arising from the use of inconsistent procedures in determining the certified quantities.

15.3   Where this insurance provides for an excess to be applied to claims for leakage or shortage, such excess shall be deemed to include ordinary loss in weight or volume except when caused by variation in temperature or settling out of water. Where there is no such provision, the amount recoverable in accordance with Clauses 15.1 and 15.2 shall be subject to reduction for any ordinary loss excluded by Clause 4.2 above.

BENEFIT OF INSURANCE

16 This insurance shall not inure to the benefit of the carrier or other bailee. Not to Inure Clause

MINIMISING LOSSES

17 It is the duty of the Assured and their servants and agents in respect of loss recoverable hereunder Duty of Assured Clause

17.1   to take such measures as may be reasonable for the purpose of averting or miniming such loss,

and

17.2   to ensure that all rights against carriers, bailees or other third parties are properly preserved and exercised

and the Underwriters will, in addition to any loss recoverable hereunder, reimburse the Assured for any charges properly and reasonably incurred in pursuance of these duties.

18 Measures taken by the Assured or the Underwriters with the object of saving, protecting or recovering the subject-matter insured shall not be considered as a waiver or acceptance of abandonment or otherwise prejudice the rights of either party. Waiver Clause

AVOIDANCE OF DELAY

19 It is a condition of this insurance that the Assured shall act with reasonable despatch in all circumstances within their control. Reasonable Despatch Clause

LAW AND PRACTICE

20 This insurance is subject to English law and practice. English Law and Practice Clause

---

NOTE:— *It is necessary for the Assured when they become aware of an event which is "held covered" under this insurance to give prompt notice to the Underwriters and the right to such cover is dependent upon compliance with this obligation.*

Appendix 58

1/2/83   (FOR USE ONLY WITH THE NEW MARINE POLICY FORM)

INSTITUTE STRIKES CLAUSES (BULK OIL)

RISKS COVERED

1   This insurance covers, except as provided in Clauses 3 and 4 below, loss of or damage to the subject-matter insured caused by   Risks Clause

    1.1   strikers, locked-out workmen, or persons taking part in labour disturbances, riots or civil commotions

    1.2   any terrorist or any person acting from a political motive.

2   This insurance covers general average and salvage charges, adjusted or determined according to the contract of affreightment and/or the governing law and practice, incurred to avoid or in connection with the avoidance of loss from a risk covered under these clauses.   General Average Clause

EXCLUSIONS

3   In no case shall this insurance cover   General Exclusions Clause

    3.1   loss damage or expense attributable to wilful misconduct of the Assured

    3.2   ordinary leakage, ordinary loss in weight or volume, or ordinary wear and tear of the subject-matter insured

    3.3   loss damage or expense caused by inherent vice or nature of the subject-matter insured

    3.4   loss damage or expense proximately caused by delay, even though the delay be caused by a risk insured against (except expenses payable under Clause 2 above)

    3.5   loss damage or expense arising from insolvency or financial default of the owners managers charterers or operators of the vessel

    3.6   loss damage or expense arising from the absence shortage or withholding of labour of any description whatsoever resulting from any strike, lockout, labour disturbance, riot or civil commotion

    3.7   any claim based upon loss of or frustration of the voyage or adventure

    3.8   loss damage or expense arising from the use of any weapon of war employing atomic or nuclear fission and/or fusion or other like reaction or radioactive force or matter

    3.9   loss damage or expense caused by war civil war revolution rebellion insurrection, or civil strife arising therefrom, or any hostile act by or against a belligerent power.

4   4.1   In no case shall this insurance cover loss damage or expense arising from   Unseaworthiness and Unfitness Exclusion Clause

        unseaworthiness of vessel or craft,

        unfitness of vessel craft or conveyance for the safe carriage of the subject-matter insured,

    where the Assured or their servants are privy to such unseaworthiness or unfitness, at the time the subject-matter insured is loaded therein.

    4.2   The Underwriters waive any breach of the implied warranties of seaworthiness of the ship and fitness of the ship to carry the subject-matter insured to destination, unless the Assured or their servants are privy to such unseaworthiness or unfitness.

DURATION

5   5.1   This insurance attaches as the subject-matter insured leaves tanks for the purpose of loading at the place named herein for the commencement of the transit, continues during the ordinary course of transit and terminates either   Transit Clause

    5.1.1   as the subject-matter insured enters tanks on discharge to place of storage or to storage vessel at the destination named herein,

        or

    5.1.2   on the expiry of 30 days after the date of arrival of the vessel at the destination named herein,

    whichever shall first occur.

    If, after discharge from the oversea vessel into craft at the final port or place of discharge, but prior to the termination of this insurance under 5.1 above, the subject-matter insured or any part thereof is to be forwarded to a destination other than that to which it is insured hereunder, the insurance on the subject-matter insured or such part thereof shall not extend beyond the commencement of transit to such other destination, *unless otherwise agreed by the Underwriters upon receipt of prompt notice from the Assured.*

5.3   *Subject to prompt notice being given to the Underwriters and to an additional premium if required by them*, this insurance shall remain in force (until terminated under 5.1 or 5.2 above and subject to the provisions of Clause 6 below) during delay beyond the control of the Assured, any deviation, forced discharge, reshipment or transhipment and during any other variation of the adventure provided such other variation is beyond the control of the Assured.

6   If owing to circumstances beyond the control of the Assured either the contract of carriage is terminated at a port or place other than the destination named therein or the transit is terminated otherwise than as provided in Clause 5 above, then this insurance shall also terminate *unless prompt notice is given to the Underwriters and continuation of cover is requested when the insurance shall remain in force, subject to an additional premium if required by the Underwriters,* either   *Termination of Contract of Carriage Clause*

6.1   until the goods are sold and delivered at such port or place, or, unless otherwise specially agreed, until the expiry of 30 days after arrival of the goods hereby insured at such port or place, whichever shall first occur,

or

6.2   if the goods are forwarded within the said period of 30 days (or any agreed extension thereof) to the destination named herein or to any other destination, until terminated in accordance with the provisions of Clause 5 above.

7   Where, after attachment of this insurance, the destination is changed by the Assured, *held covered at a premium and on conditions to be arranged subject to prompt notice being given to the Underwriters.*   *Change of Voyage Clause*

CLAIMS

8   8.1   In order to recover under this insurance the Assured must have an insurable interest in the subject-matter insured at the time of the loss.   *Insurable Interest Clause*

8.2   Subject to 8.1 above, the Assured shall be entitled to recover for insured loss occurring during the period covered by this insurance, notwithstanding that the loss occurred before the contract of insurance was concluded, unless the Assured were aware of the loss and the Underwriters were not.

9   9.1   If any Increased Value insurance is effected by the Assured on the cargo insured herein the agreed value of the cargo shall be deemed to be increased to the total amount insured under this insurance and all Increased Value insurances covering the loss, and liability under this insurance shall be in such proportion as the sum insured herein bears to such total amount insured.   *Increased Value Clause*

In the event of claim the Assured shall provide the Underwriters with evidence of the amounts insured under all other insurances.

9.2   **Where this insurance is on Increased Value the following clause shall apply;**
The agreed value of the cargo shall be deemed to be equal to the total amount insured under the primary insurance and all Increased Value insurances covering the loss and effected on the cargo by the Assured and liability under this insurance shall be in such proportion as the sum insured herein bears to such total amount insured.

In the event of claim the Assured shall provide the Underwriters with evidence of the amounts insured under all other insurances.

10   Claims for leakage and shortage recoverable under this insurance are to be adjusted as follows: *Adjustment Clause*

10.1   The amount recoverable shall be the proportionate insured value of the volume of oil lost, to be ascertained by a comparison of the gross volume certified as having left tanks for loading on to the vessel with the gross volume certified as having been delivered to tanks at the termination of the transit, except that where the contract of sale is based on weight and not on volume the amount recoverable may be calculated on a weight basis from such certified quantities:
The term "gross volume" in this Clause 10.1 means total volume without deduction of sediment and water content and free water, except to the extent that the amount of water can be shown by the Assured to have increased abnormally during the insured transit as a result of the operation of a risk covered by this insurance.

10.2   Adjustment shall be made to the calculation under 10.1 above to eliminate any change in volume caused by variation in temperature and any apparent change in quantity arising from the use of inconsistent procedures in determining the certified quantities.

10.3   Where this insurance provides for an excess to be applied to claims for leakage or shortage, such excess shall be deemed to include ordinary loss in weight or volume except when caused by variation in temperature or settling out of water. Where there is no such provision, the amount recoverable in accordance with Clauses 10.1 and 10.2 shall be subject to reduction for any ordinary loss excluded by Clause 3.2 above.

BENEFIT OF INSURANCE

11   This insurance shall not inure to the benefit of the carrier or other bailee.   *Not to Inure Clause*

MINIMISING LOSSES

12   It is the duty of the Assured and their servants and agents in respect of loss recoverable hereunder   *Duty of Assured Clause*

12.1   to take such measures as may be reasonable for the purpose of averting or minimising such loss, and

12.2   to ensure that all rights against carriers, bailees or other third parties are properly preserved and exercised

and the Underwriters will, in addition to any loss recoverable hereunder, reimburse the Assured for any charges properly and reasonably incurred in pursuance of these duties.

13   Measures taken by the Assured or the Underwriters with the object of saving, protecting or recovering the subject-matter insured shall not be considered as a waiver or acceptance of abandonment or otherwise prejudice the rights of either party.   *Waiver Clause*

AVOIDANCE OF DELAY

14   It is a condition of this insurance that the Assured shall act with reasonable despatch in all circumstances within their control.   *Reasonable Despatch Clause*

LAW AND PRACTICE

15 This insurance is subject to English law and practice

English Law
and Practice
Clause

NOTE:— It is necessary for the Assured when they become aware of an event which is "held covered" under this insurance to give prompt notice to the Underwriters and the right to such cover is dependent upon compliance with this obligation.

Appendix 59

1/4/82 **(FOR USE ONLY WITH THE NEW MARINE POLICY FORM)**

INSTITUTE STANDARD CONDITIONS FOR CARGO CONTRACTS

1   This contract is to insure the subject-matter specified for the transits and on the conditions named shipped by or for account of

....

....
or the insurance of which is under their control as selling or purchasing agent unless insured elsewhere prior to inception of this contract or to insurable interest being acquired.

This contract does not cover the interest of any other person, but this shall not prevent a transfer of the insurance by the Assured or Assignee.

2   It is a condition of this contract that the Assured are bound to declare hereunder every consignment without exception, Underwriters being bound to accept up to but not exceeding the amount specified in clause 3 below.

3   3.1   This contract is for an open amount but the amount declarable may not exceed the sum of .... in respect of any one vessel, aircraft or conveyance.

    3.2   Should this contract be expressed in the form of a floating policy the total amount declarable hereunder may not exceed

      .... subject always to the provisions of clause 3.1 above.

4   Notwithstanding anything to the contrary contained in this contract Underwriters' liability in respect of any one accident

or series of accidents arising from the same event in any one location shall not exceed the sum of ....

....

5   In the event of loss accident or arrival before declaration of value it is agreed that the basis of valuation shall be the prime cost of the goods or merchandise plus the expenses of and incidental to shipping, the freight for which the Assured are liable, the

charges of insurance and .... %.

6   This contract is subject to the Institute Classification Clause.

7   Should the risks of war, strikes, riots and civil commotions be included in the cover granted by this contract the relevant Institute War Clauses and Institute Strikes Clauses shall apply.

8   The Institute Clauses referred to herein are those current at the inception of this contract but should such clauses be revised during the period of this contract, and provided that Underwriters shall have given at least 30 days notice thereof, then the revised Institute Clauses shall apply to risks attaching subsequent to the date of expiry of the said notice.

9   This contract may be cancelled by either Underwriters or the Assured giving .... days notice in writing to take

effect from... but risks covered by Institute War Clauses may be cancelled at seven days notice and risks covered by the Institute Strikes Clauses may be cancelled at seven days notice, or at forty-eight hours notice in respect of shipments to or from the United States of America. Notice shall commence from midnight of the day when it is issued but cancellation shall not apply to any risks which have attached in accordance with the cover granted hereunder before the cancellation becomes effective.

NOTE   The Assured are required to give the earliest provisional notice of intended shipments advising in each case the name of the vessel and approximate value of the shipments.

Appendix 60

5/9/83 (FOR USE ONLY WITH THE NEW MARINE POLICY FORM)

INSTITUTE COMMODITY TRADES CLAUSES (A)
Agreed with The Federation of Commodity Associations
for the insurance of shipments of
Cocoa, Coffee, Cotton, Fats and Oils not in bulk,
Hides and Skins, Metals, Oil Seeds, Refined Sugar, and Tea

RISKS COVERED

1 This insurance covers all risks of loss of or damage to the subject-matter insured except as provided in Clauses 4, 5, 6 and 7 below. — *Risks Clause*

2 This insurance covers general average and salvage charges, adjusted or determined according to the contract of affreightment and/or the governing law and practice, incurred to avoid or in connection with the avoidance of loss from any cause except those excluded in Clauses 4, 5, 6 and 7 or elsewhere in this insurance. — *General Average Clause*

3 This insurance is extended to indemnify the Assured against such proportion of liability under the contract of affreightment "Both to Blame Collision" Clause as is in respect of a loss recoverable hereunder. In the event of any claim by shipowners under the said Clause the Assured agree to notify the Underwriters who shall have the right, at their own cost and expense, to defend the Assured against such claim. — *"Both to Blame Collision" Clause*

EXCLUSIONS

4 In no case shall this insurance cover — *General Exclusions Clause*

4.1 loss damage or expense attributable to wilful misconduct of the Assured

4.2 ordinary leakage, ordinary loss in weight or volume, or ordinary wear and tear of the subject-matter insured

4.3 loss damage or expense caused by insufficiency or unsuitability of packing or preparation of the subject-matter insured (for the purpose of this Clause 4.3 "packing" shall be deemed to include stowage in a container or liftvan but only when such stowage is carried out prior to attachment of this insurance or by the Assured or their servants)

4.4 loss damage or expense caused by inherent vice or nature of the subject-matter insured

4.5 loss damage or expense proximately caused by delay, even though the delay be caused by a risk insured against (except expenses payable under Clause 2 above)

4.6 loss damage or expense caused by insolvency or financial default of the owners managers charterers or operators of the vessel where, at the time of loading of the subject-matter insured on board the vessel, the Assured are aware, or in the ordinary course of business should be aware, that such insolvency or financial default could prevent the normal prosecution of the voyage
This exclusion shall not apply where this insurance has been assigned to the party claiming hereunder who has bought or agreed to buy the subject-matter insured in good faith under a binding contract

4.7 loss damage or expense arising from the use of any weapon of war employing atomic or nuclear fission and/or fusion or other like reaction or radioactive force or matter.

5 5.1 In no case shall this insurance cover loss damage or expense arising from — *Unseaworthiness and Unfitness Exclusion Clause*

5.1.1 unseaworthiness of vessel or craft or unfitness of vessel or craft for the safe carriage of the subject-matter insured, where the Assured are privy to such unseaworthiness or unfitness, at the time the subject-matter insured is loaded therein

5.1.2 unfitness of container liftvan or land conveyance for the safe carriage of the subject-matter insured, where loading therein is carried out prior to attachment of this insurance or by the Assured or their servants.

5.2 Where this insurance has been assigned to the party claiming hereunder who has bought or agreed to buy the subject-matter insured in good faith under a binding contract, exclusion 5.1.1 above shall not apply.

5.3 The Underwriters waive any breach of the implied warranties of seaworthiness of the ship and fitness of the ship to carry the subject-matter insured to destination.

6 In no case shall this insurance cover loss damage or expense caused by — *War Exclusion Clause*

6.1 war civil war revolution rebellion insurrection, or civil strife arising therefrom, or any hostile act by or against a belligerent power

6.2 capture seizure arrest restraint or detainment (piracy excepted), and the consequences thereof or any attempt thereat

6.3 derelict mines torpedoes bombs or other derelict weapons of war.

7 In no case shall this insurance cover loss damage or expense — *Strikes Exclusion Clause*

7.1 caused by strikers, locked-out workmen, or persons taking part in labour disturbances, riots or civil commotions

	7.2	resulting from strikes, lock-outs, labour disturbances, riots or civil commotions	
	7.3	caused by any terrorist or any person acting from a political motive.	

DURATION

8	8.1	This insurance attaches from the time the goods leave the warehouse or place of storage at the place named herein for the commencement of the transit, continues during the ordinary course of transit and terminates either	Transit Clause
	8.1.1	on delivery to the Consignees' or other final warehouse or place of storage at the destination named herein,	
	8.1.2	on delivery to any other warehouse or place of storage, whether prior to or at the destination named herein, which the Assured elect to use either	
	8.1.2.1	for storage other than in the ordinary course of transit or	
	8.1.2.2	for allocation or distribution,	
		or	
	8.1.3	on the expiry of 60 days after completion of discharge overside of the goods hereby insured from the oversea vessel at the final port of discharge,	
		whichever shall first occur.	
	8.2	If, after discharge overside from the oversea vessel at the final port of discharge, but prior to termination of this insurance, the goods are to be forwarded to a destination other than that to which they are insured hereunder, this insurance, whilst remaining subject to termination as provided for above, shall not extend beyond the commencement of transit to such other destination.	
	8.3	This insurance shall remain in force (subject to termination as provided for above and to the provisions of Clause 9 below) during delay beyond the control of the Assured, any deviation, forced discharge, reshipment or transhipment and during any variation of the adventure arising from the exercise of a liberty granted to shipowners or charterers under the contract of affreightment.	
9		If owing to circumstances beyond the control of the Assured either the contract of carriage is terminated at a port or place other than the destination named therein or the transit is otherwise terminated before delivery of the goods as provided for in Clause 8 above, then this insurance shall also terminate *unless prompt notice is given to the Underwriters and continuation of cover is requested when the insurance shall remain in force, subject to an additional premium if required by the Underwriters*, either	Termination of Contract of Carriage Clause
	9.1	until the goods are sold and delivered at such port or place, or, unless otherwise specially agreed, until the expiry of 60 days after arrival of the goods hereby insured at such port or place, whichever shall first occur,	
		or	
	9.2	if the goods are forwarded within the said period of 60 days (or any agreed extension thereof) to the destination named herein or to any other destination, until terminated in accordance with the provisions of Clause 8 above.	
10		Where, after attachment of this insurance, the destination is changed by the Assured, *held covered at a premium and on conditions to be arranged subject to prompt notice being given to the Underwriters.*	Change of Voyage Clause

CLAIMS

11	11.1	In order to recover under this insurance the Assured must have an insurable interest in the subject-matter insured at the time of the loss.	Insurable Interest Clause
	11.2	Subject to 11.1 above, the Assured shall be entitled to recover for insured loss occurring during the period covered by this insurance, notwithstanding that the loss occurred before the contract of insurance was concluded, unless the Assured were aware of the loss and the Underwriters were not.	
12		Where, as a result of the operation of a risk covered by this insurance, the insured transit is terminated at a port or place other than that to which the subject-matter is covered under this insurance, the Underwriters will reimburse the Assured for any extra charges properly and reasonably incurred in unloading storing and forwarding the subject-matter to the destination to which it is insured hereunder.	Forwarding Charges Clause
		This Clause 12, which does not apply to general average or salvage charges, shall be subject to the exclusions contained in Clauses 4, 5, 6 and 7 above, and shall not include charges arising from the fault negligence insolvency or financial default of the Assured or their servants.	
13		No claim for Constructive Total Loss shall be recoverable hereunder unless the subject-matter insured is reasonably abandoned either on account of its actual total loss appearing to be unavoidable or because the cost of recovering, reconditioning and forwarding the subject-matter to the destination to which it is insured would exceed its value on arrival.	Constructive Total Loss Clause
14	14.1	If any Increased Value insurance is effected by the Assured on the cargo insured herein the agreed value of the cargo shall be deemed to be increased to the total amount insured under this insurance and all Increased Value insurances covering the loss, and liability under this insurance shall be in such proportion as the sum insured herein bears to such total amount insured	Increased Value Clause
		In the event of claim the Assured shall provide the Underwriters with evidence of the amounts insured under all other insurances.	
	14.2	**Where this insurance is on Increased Value the following clause shall apply:** The agreed value of the cargo shall be deemed to be equal to the total amount insured under the primary insurance and all Increased Value insurances covering the loss and effected on the cargo by the Assured, and liability under this insurance shall be in such proportion as the sum insured herein bears to such total amount insured.	
		In the event of claim the Assured shall provide the Underwriters with evidence of the amounts insured under all other insurances.	

BENEFIT OF INSURANCE

| 15 | | This insurance shall not inure to the benefit of the carrier or other bailee. | Not to Inure Clause |

MINIMISING LOSSES

16 It is the duty of the Assured and their servants and agents in respect of loss recoverable hereunder   *Duty of Assured Clause*

   16.1 to take such measures as may be reasonable for the purpose of averting or minimising such loss; and

   16.2 to ensure that all rights against carriers, bailees or other third parties are properly preserved and exercised

and the Underwriters will, in addition to any loss recoverable hereunder, reimburse the Assured for any charges properly and reasonably incurred in pursuance of these duties.

17 Measures taken by the Assured or the Underwriters with the object of saving, protecting or recovering the subject-matter insured shall not be considered as a waiver or acceptance of abandonment or otherwise prejudice the rights of either party.   *Waiver Clause*

AVOIDANCE OF DELAY

18 It is a condition of this insurance that the Assured shall act with reasonable despatch in all circumstances within their control.   *Reasonable Despatch Clause*

LAW AND PRACTICE

19 This insurance is subject to English law and practice.   *English Law and Practice Clause*

NOTE:— It is necessary for the Assured when they become aware of an event which is "held covered" under this insurance to give prompt notice to the Underwriters and the right to such cover is dependent upon compliance with this obligation.

Appendix 61

(FOR USE ONLY WITH THE NEW MARINE POLICY FORM)

INSTITUTE FROZEN FOOD CLAUSES (A)

(Excluding Frozen Meat)

RISKS COVERED

1   This insurance covers, except as provided in Clauses 4, 5, 6 and 7 below,

    1.1   all risks of loss of or damage to the subject-matter insured, other than loss or damage resulting from any variation in temperature howsoever caused,   *Risks Clause*

    1.2   loss of or damage to the subject-matter insured resulting from any variation in temperature attributable to

        1.2.1   breakdown of refrigerating machinery resulting in its stoppage for a period of not less than 24 consecutive hours

        1.2.2   fire or explosion

        1.2.3   vessel or craft being stranded grounded sunk or capsized

        1.2.4   overturning or derailment of land conveyance

        1.2.5   collision or contact of vessel craft or conveyance with any external object other than water

        1.2.6   discharge of cargo at a port of distress.

2   This insurance covers general average and salvage charges, adjusted or determined according to the contract of affreightment and/or the governing law and practice, incurred to avoid or in connection with the avoidance of loss from any cause except those excluded in Clauses 4, 5, 6 and 7 or elsewhere in this insurance.   *General Average Clause*

3   This insurance is extended to indemnify the Assured against such proportion of liability under the contract of affreightment "Both to Blame Collision" Clause as is in respect of a loss recoverable hereunder. In the event of any claim by shipowners under the said Clause the Assured agree to notify the Underwriters who shall have the right, at their own cost and expense, to defend the Assured against such claim.   *"Both to Blame Collision" Clause*

EXCLUSIONS

4   In no case shall this insurance cover   *General Exclusions Clause*

    4.1   loss damage or expense attributable to wilful misconduct of the Assured

    4.2   ordinary leakage, ordinary loss in weight or volume, or ordinary wear and tear of the subject-matter insured

    4.3   loss damage or expense caused by insufficiency or unsuitability of packing or preparation of the subject-matter insured (for the purpose of this Clause 4.3 "packing" shall be deemed to include stowage in a container or liftvan but only when such stowage is carried out prior to attachment of this insurance or by the Assured or their servants)

    4.4   loss damage or expense caused by inherent vice or nature of the subject-matter insured (except loss damage or expense resulting from variation in temperature specifically covered under Clause 1.2 above)

    4.5   loss damage or expense proximately caused by delay, even though the delay be caused by a risk insured against (except expenses payable under Clause 2 above)

    4.6   loss damage or expense arising from insolvency or financial default of the owners managers charterers or operators of the vessel

    4.7   loss damage or expense arising from the use of any weapon of war employing atomic or nuclear fission and/or fusion or other like reaction or radioactive force or matter

    4.8   loss damage or expense arising from any failure of the Assured or their servants to take all reasonable precautions to ensure that the subject-matter insured is kept in refrigerated or, where appropriate, properly insulated and cooled space

    4.9   any loss damage or expense otherwise recoverable hereunder unless prompt notice thereof is given to the Underwriters and, in any event, not later than 30 days after the termination of this insurance.

5   5.1   In no case shall this insurance cover loss damage or expense arising from   *Unseaworthiness and Unfitness Exclusion Clause*

        unseaworthiness of vessel or craft,

        unfitness of vessel craft conveyance container or liftvan for the safe carriage of the subject-matter insured, where the Assured or their servants are privy to such unseaworthiness or unfitness, at the time the subject-matter insured is loaded therein.

5.2   The Underwriters waive any breach of the implied warranties of seaworthiness of the ship and fitness of the ship to carry the subject-matter insured to destination, unless the Assured or their servants are privy to such unseaworthiness or unfitness.

6   In no case shall this insurance cover loss damage or expense caused by   *War Exclusion Clause*

6.1   war civil war revolution rebellion insurrection, or civil strife arising therefrom, or any hostile act by or against a belligerent power

6.2   capture seizure arrest restraint or detainment (piracy excepted), and the consequences thereof or any attempt thereat

6.3   derelict mines torpedoes bombs or other derelict weapons of war.

7   In no case shall this insurance cover loss damage or expense   *Strikes Exclusion Clause*

7.1   caused by strikers, locked-out workmen, or persons taking part in labour disturbances, riots or civil commotions

7.2   resulting from strikes, lock-outs, labour disturbances, riots or civil commotions

7.3   caused by any terrorist or any person acting from a political motive.

DURATION

8   8.1   This insurance attaches from the time the goods are loaded into the conveyance at freezing works or cold store at the place named herein for the commencement of the transit, continues during the ordinary course of transit and terminates either   *Transit Clause*

8.1.1   on delivery to the cold store or place of storage at the destination named herein,

8.1.2   on delivery to any other cold store or place or storage, whether prior to or at the destination named herein, which the Assured elect to use either

8.1.2.1   for storage other than in the ordinary course of transit or

8.1.2.2   for allocation or distribution,

     or

8.1.3   on the expiry of 5 days after discharge overside of the goods hereby insured from the oversea vessel at the final port of discharge,

     whichever shall first occur.

8.2   If, after discharge overside from the oversea vessel at the final port of discharge, but prior to termination of this insurance, the goods are to be forwarded to a destination other than that to which they are insured hereunder, this insurance, whilst remaining subject to termination as provided for above, shall not extend beyond the commencement of transit to such other destination.

8.3   This insurance shall remain in force (subject to termination as provided for above and to the provisions of Clause 9 below) during delay beyond the control of the Assured, any deviation, forced discharge, reshipment or transhipment and during any variation of the adventure arising from the exercise of a liberty granted to shipowners or charterers under the contract of affreightment.

9   If owing to circumstances beyond the control of the Assured either the contract of carriage is terminated at a port or place other than the destination named therein or the transit is otherwise terminated before delivery of the goods as provided for in Clause 8 above, then this insurance shall also terminate *unless prompt notice is given to the Underwriters and continuation of cover is requested when the insurance shall remain in force, subject to an additional premium if required by the Underwriters*, either   *Termination of Contract of Carriage Clause*

9.1   until the goods are sold and delivered at such port or place, or, unless otherwise specially agreed, until the expiry of 30 days after arrival of the goods hereby insured at such port or place, whichever shall first occur,

     or

9.2   if the goods are forwarded within the said period of 30 days (or any agreed extension thereof) to the destination named herein or to any other destination, until terminated in accordance with the provisions of Clause 8 above.

10   Where, after attachment of this insurance, the destination is changed by the Assured, *held covered at a premium and on conditions to be arranged subject to prompt notice being given to the Underwriters:*   *Change of Voyage Clause*

CLAIMS

11   11.1   In order to recover under this insurance the Assured must have an insurable interest in the subject-matter insured at the time of the loss.   *Insurable Interest Clause*

11.2   Subject to 11.1 above, the Assured shall be entitled to recover for insured loss occurring during the period covered by this insurance, notwithstanding that the loss occurred before the contract of insurance was concluded, unless the Assured were aware of the loss and the Underwriters were not.

12   Where, as a result of the operation of a risk covered by this insurance, the insured transit is terminated at a port or place other than that to which the subject-matter is covered under this insurance, the Underwriters will reimburse the Assured for any extra charges properly and reasonably incurred in unloading storing and forwarding the subject-matter to the destination to which it is insured hereunder.   *Forwarding Charges Clause*

     This Clause 12, which does not apply to general average or salvage charges, shall be subject to the exclusions contained in Clauses 4, 5, 6 and 7 above; and shall not include charges arising from the fault negligence insolvency or financial default of the Assured or their servants.

13   No claim for Constructive Total Loss shall be recoverable hereunder unless the subject-matter insured is reasonably abandoned either on account of its actual total loss appearing to be unavoidable or because the cost of recovering,   *Constructive Total Loss Clause*

reconditioning and forwarding the subject-matter to the destination to which it is insured would exceed its value on arrival.

14 **14.1** If any Increased Value insurance is effected by the Assured on the cargo insured herein the agreed value of the cargo shall be deemed to be increased to the total amount insured under this insurance and all Increased Value insurances covering the loss, and liability under this insurance shall be in such proportion as the sum insured herein bears to such total amount insured. Increased
Value
Clause

In the event of claim the Assured shall provide the Underwriters with evidence of the amounts insured under all other insurances.

14.2 Where this insurance is on Increased Value the following clause shall apply:
The agreed value of the cargo shall be deemed to be equal to the total amount insured under the primary insurance and all Increased Value insurances covering the loss and effected on the cargo by the Assured, and liability under this insurance shall be in such proportion as the sum insured herein bears to such total amount insured.

In the event of claim the Assured shall provide the Underwriters with evidence of the amounts insured under all other insurances.

BENEFIT OF INSURANCE

15 This insurance shall not inure to the benefit of the carrier or other bailee. Not to
Inure Clause

MINIMISING LOSSES

16 It is the duty of the Assured and their servants and agents in respect of loss recoverable hereunder Duty of
Assured Clause

    16.1 to take such measures as may be reasonable for the purpose of averting or minimising such loss, and

    16.2 to ensure that all rights against carriers, bailees or other third parties are properly preserved and exercised

and the Underwriters will, in addition to any loss recoverable hereunder, reimburse the Assured for any charges properly and reasonably incurred in pursuance of these duties.

17 Measures taken by the Assured or the Underwriters with the object of saving, protecting or recovering the subject-matter insured shall not be considered as a waiver or acceptance of abandonment or otherwise prejudice the rights of either party. Waiver
Clause

AVOIDANCE OF DELAY

18 It is a condition of this insurance that the Assured shall act with reasonable despatch in all circumstances within their control. Reasonable
Despatch
Clause

LAW AND PRACTICE

19 This insurance is subject to English law and practice. English Law
and Practice
Clause

NOTE:— It is necessary for the Assured when they become aware of an event which is "held covered" under this insurance to give prompt notice to the Underwriters and the right to such cover is dependent upon compliance with this obligation.

SPECIAL NOTE:— This insurance does not cover loss damage or expense caused by embargo, or by rejection prohibition or detention by the government of the country of import or their agencies or departments, but does not exclude loss of or damage to the subject-matter insured caused by risks insured hereunder and sustained prior to any such embargo rejection prohibition or detention.

Appendix 62

1/4/86

(FOR USE ONLY WITH THE NEW MARINE POLICY FORM)

INSTITUTE TIMBER TRADE FEDERATION CLAUSES
Agreed with the Timber Trade Federation

RISKS COVERED

1 **Cargo whilst stowed on deck**

1.1 This insurance covers, except as provided in Clauses 4, 5, 6 and 7 below,   *Risks Clause*

1.1.1 loss of or damage to the subject-matter insured whilst stowed on deck of the oversea vessel, or any part or item thereof whilst so stowed, reasonably attributable to

1.1.1.1 fire or explosion

1.1.1.2 vessel being stranded grounded sunk or capsized

1.1.1.3 collision or contact of vessel with any external object other than water

1.1.1.4 discharge of cargo at a port of distress,

1.1.2 loss of or damage to the subject-matter insured whilst stowed on deck of the oversea vessel, or any part or item thereof whilst so stowed, caused by

1.1.2.1 general average sacrifice

1.1.2.2 jettison or washing overboard

1.1.2.3 theft or non-delivery

1.1.2.4 malicious act.

Cargo whilst not stowed on deck

1.2 This insurance covers all risks of loss of or damage to the subject-matter insured excluding any part or item thereof whilst stowed on deck on the oversea vessel, as provided in Clauses 4, 5, 6 and 7 below. Subject-matter insured or any part or item thereof stowed in poop, forecastle, deck house, shelter deck, other enclosed space, or in a container, shall be deemed to be subject-matter insured not stowed on deck.

2 This insurance covers general average and salvage charges, adjusted or determined according to the contract of affreightment and/or the governing law and practice, incurred to avoid or in connection with the avoidance of loss from any cause except those excluded in Clauses 4, 5, 6 and 7 or elsewhere in this insurance.   *General Average Clause*

3 This insurance is extended to indemnify the Assured against such proportion of liability under the contract of affreightment "Both to Blame Collision" Clause as is in respect of a loss recoverable hereunder. In the event of any claim by shipowners under the said Clause the Assured agree to notify the Underwriters who shall have the right, at their own cost and expense, to defend the Assured against such claim.   *"Both to Blame Collision" Clause*

EXCLUSIONS

4 In no case shall this insurance cover   *General Exclusions Clause*

4.1 loss damage or expense attributable to wilful misconduct of the Assured

4.2 ordinary leakage, ordinary loss in weight or volume, or ordinary wear and tear of the subject-matter insured

4.3 loss damage or expense caused by insufficiency or unsuitability of packing or preparation of the subject-matter insured (for the purpose of this Clause 4.3 "packing" shall be deemed to include stowage in a container or liftvan but only when such stowage is carried out prior to attachment of this insurance or by the Assured or their servants)

4.4 loss damage or expense caused by inherent vice or nature of the subject-matter insured

4.5 loss damage or expense proximately caused by delay, even though the delay be caused by a risk insured against (except expenses payable under Clause 2 above)

4.6 loss damage or expense caused by insolvency or financial default of the owners managers charterers or operators of the vessel where, at the time of loading of the subject-matter insured on board the vessel, the Assured are aware, or in the ordinary course of business should be aware, that such insolvency or financial default could prevent the normal prosecution of the voyage
This exclusion shall not apply where this insurance has been assigned to the party claiming hereunder who has bought or agreed to buy the subject-matter insured in good faith under a binding contract

4.7 loss damage or expense arising from the use of any weapon of war employing atomic or nuclear fission and/or fusion or other like reaction or radioactive force or matter.

5 5.1 In no case shall this insurance cover loss damage or expense arising from   *Unseaworthiness and Unfitness Exclusion Clause*

5.1.1 unseaworthiness of vessel or craft or unfitness of vessel or craft for the safe carriage of the subject-matter insured, where the Assured are privy to such unseaworthiness or unfitness at the time the subject-matter insured is loaded therein

5.1.2　　unfitness of container liftvan or land conveyance for the safe carriage of the subject-matter insured, where loading therein is carried out prior to attachment of this insurance or by the Assured or their servants.

5.2　　Where this insurance has been assigned to the party claiming hereunder who has bought or agreed to buy the subject-matter insured in good faith under a binding contract, exclusion 5.1.1 above shall not apply.

5.3　　The Underwriters waive any breach of the implied warranties of seaworthiness of the ship and fitness of the ship to carry the subject-matter insured to destination.

6　In no case shall this insurance cover loss damage or expense caused by

6.1　　war civil war revolution rebellion insurrection, or civil strife arising therefrom, or any hostile act by or against a belligerent power

6.2　　capture seizure arrest restraint or detainment (piracy excepted), and the consequences thereof or any attempt thereat

6.3　　derelict mines torpedoes bombs or other derelict weapons of war.

War Exclusion Clause

7　In no case shall this insurance cover loss damage or expense

7.1　　caused by strikers, locked-out workmen, or persons taking part in labour disturbances, riots or civil commotions

7.2　　resulting from strikes, lock-outs, labour disturbances, riots or civil commotions

7.3　　caused by any terrorist or any person acting from a political motive.

Strikes Exclusion Clause

8　8.1　　This insurance attaches on or after the loading of the goods insured hereunder on land and/or water conveyances or their floating at the mill, warehouse, factory, yard or premises wheresoever, from which the despatch to the oversea vessel is made, continues during the ordinary course of transit and terminates either

Transit Clause

8.1.1　　on delivery of the goods by land or water into the mill, warehouse, factory, yard or premises at their final destination, whether at the port of discharge of the oversea vessel or (further sea voyage excepted) elsewhere, and are there made available to the Assured or Receivers

8.1.2　　on delivery to any other warehouse or place of storage which the Assured elect to use for storage other than in the ordinary course of transit

or

8.1.3　　on the expiry of 60 days after completion of discharge overside of the goods hereby insured from the oversea vessel at the final port of discharge,

whichever shall first occur.

8.2　　This insurance shall remain in force (subject to termination as provided for above and to the provisions of Clause 9 below) during delay beyond the control of the Assured, any deviation, forced discharge, reshipment or transhipment and during any variation of the adventure arising from the exercise of a liberty granted to shipowners or charterers under the contract of affreightment.

8.3　　Each bill of lading to be deemed a separate insurance if required by the Assured at any time.

8.4　　The provisions of Clause 8 shall apply notwithstanding that the description of the voyage in the body of the policy may state only the ports and places of shipment and discharge.

9　If owing to circumstances beyond the control of the Assured either the contract of carriage is terminated at a port or place other than the destination named therein or the transit is otherwise terminated before delivery of the goods as provided for in Clause 8 above, then this insurance shall also terminate *unless prompt notice is given to the Underwriters and continuation of cover is requested when the insurance shall remain in force, subject to an additional premium if required by the Underwriters* either

Termination of Contract of Carriage Clause

9.1　　until the goods are sold and delivered at such port or place, or, unless otherwise specially agreed, until the expiry of 60 days after arrival of the goods hereby insured at such port or place, whichever shall first occur,

or

9.2　　if the goods are forwarded within the said period of 60 days (or any agreed extension thereof) to the destination named herein or to any other destination until terminated in accordance with the provisions of Clause 8 above.

10　Where, after attachment of this insurance, the destination is changed by the Assured, *held covered at a premium and on conditions to be arranged subject to prompt notice being given to the Underwriters.*

Change of Voyage Clause

CLAIMS

11　11.1　　In order to recover under this insurance the Assured must have an insurable interest in the subject-matter insured at the time of the loss.

Insurable Interest Clause

11.2　　Subject to 11.1 above, the Assured shall be entitled to recover for insured loss occurring during the period covered by this insurance, notwithstanding that the loss occurred before the contract of insurance was concluded, unless the Assured were aware of the loss and the Underwriters were not.

12　Where, as a result of the operation of a risk covered by this insurance, the insured transit is terminated at a port or place other than that to which the subject-matter is covered under this insurance, the Underwriters will reimburse the Assured for any extra charges properly and reasonably incurred in unloading storing and forwarding the subject-matter to the destination to which it is insured hereunder.

Forwarding Charges Clause

This Clause 12, which does not apply to general average or salvage charges, shall be subject to the exclusions contained in Clauses 4, 5, 6 and 7 above, and shall not include charges arising from the fault negligence insolvency or financial default of the Assured or their servants.

13　No claim for Constructive Total Loss shall be recoverable hereunder unless the subject-matter insured is reasonably abandoned either on account of its actual total loss appearing to be unavoidable or because the cost of recovering, reconditioning and forwarding the subject-matter to the destination to which it is insured would exceed its value on arrival.

Constructive Total Loss Clause

14　14.1　If any Increased Value insurance is effected by the Assured on the cargo insured herein the agreed value of the cargo shall be deemed to be increased to the total amount insured under this insurance and all Increased Value insurances covering the loss, and liability under this insurance shall be in such proportion as the sum insured herein bears to such total amount insured.　　　　　*Increased Value Clause*

　　　　　In the event of claim the Assured shall provide the Underwriters with evidence of the amounts insured under all other insurances.

　　14.2　**Where this insurance is on Increased Value the following clause shall apply:**

　　　　　The agreed value of the cargo shall be deemed to be equal to the total amount insured under the primary insurance and all Increased Value insurances covering the loss and effected on the cargo by the Assured, and liability under this insurance shall be in such proportion as the sum insured herein bears to such total amount insured.

　　　　　In the event of claim the Assured shall provide the Underwriters with evidence of the amounts insured under all other insurances.

BENEFIT OF INSURANCE

15　This insurance shall not inure to the benefit of the carrier or other bailee.　　　　　*Not to Inure Clause*

MINIMISING LOSSES

16　It is the duty of the Assured and their servants and agents in respect of loss recoverable hereunder　　　　　*Duty of Assured Clause*

　　16.1　to take such measures as may be reasonable for the purpose of averting or minimising such loss

　　　　　and

　　16.2　to ensure that all rights against carriers, bailees or other third parties are properly preserved and exercised

　　and the Underwriters will, in addition to any loss recoverable hereunder, reimburse the Assured for any charges properly and reasonably incurred in pursuance of these duties.

17　Measures taken by the Assured or the Underwriters with the object of saving, protecting or recovering the subject-matter insured shall not be considered as a waiver or acceptance of abandonment or otherwise prejudice the rights of either party.　　　　　*Waiver Clause*

AVOIDANCE OF DELAY

18　It is a condition of this insurance that the Assured shall act with reasonable despatch in all circumstances within their control.　　　　　*Reasonable Despatch Clause*

LAW AND PRACTICE

19　This insurance is subject to English law and practice.　　　　　*English Law and Practice Clause*

Note:— It is necessary for the Assured when they become aware of an event which is "held covered" under this insurance to give prompt notice to the Underwriters and the right to such cover is dependent upon compliance with this obligation.

Appendix 63

1/4/86

(FOR USE ONLY WITH THE NEW MARINE POLICY FORM)

INSTITUTE STRIKES CLAUSES (TIMBER TRADE FEDERATION)
Agreed with the Timber Trade Federation

RISKS COVERED

1   This insurance covers, except as provided in Clauses 3 and 4 below, loss of or damage to the subject-matter insured caused by — *Risks Clause*

   1.1   strikers, locked-out workmen, or persons taking part in labour disturbances, riots or civil commotions

   1.2   any terrorist or any person acting from a political motive.

2   This insurance covers general average and salvage charges, adjusted or determined according to the contract of affreightment and/or the governing law and practice, incurred to avoid or in connection with the avoidance of loss from a risk covered under these clauses. — *General Average Clause*

EXCLUSIONS

3   In no case shall this insurance cover — *General Exclusions Clause*

   3.1   loss damage or expense attributable to wilful misconduct of the Assured

   3.2   ordinary leakage, ordinary loss in weight or volume, or ordinary wear and tear of the subject-matter insured

   3.3   loss damage or expense caused by insufficiency or unsuitability of packing or preparation of the subject-matter insured (for the purpose of this Clause 3.3 "packing" shall be deemed to include stowage in a container or liftvan but only when such stowage is carried out prior to attachment of this insurance or by the Assured or their servants)

   3.4   loss damage or expense caused by inherent vice or nature of the subject-matter insured

   3.5   loss damage or expense proximately caused by delay, even though the delay be caused by a risk insured against (except expenses payable under Clause 2 above)

   3.6   loss damage or expense caused by insolvency or financial default of the owners managers charterers or operators of the vessel where, at the time of loading of the subject-matter insured on board the vessel, the Assured are aware, or in the ordinary course of business should be aware, that such insolvency or financial default could prevent the normal prosecution of the voyage
This exclusion shall not apply where this insurance has been assigned to the party claiming hereunder who has bought or agreed to buy the subject-matter insured in good faith under a binding contract

   3.7   loss damage or expense arising from the absence shortage or withholding of labour of any description whatsoever resulting from any strike, lockout, labour disturbance, riot or civil commotion

   3.8   any claim based upon loss of or frustration of the voyage or adventure

   3.9   loss damage or expense arising from the use of any weapon of war employing atomic or nuclear fission and/or fusion or other like reaction or radioactive force or matter

   3.10   loss damage or expense caused by war civil war revolution rebellion insurrection, or civil strife arising therefrom, or any hostile act by or against a belligerent power.

4   4.1   In no case shall this insurance cover loss damage or expense arising from — *Unseaworthiness and Unfitness Exclusion Clause*

   4.1.1   unseaworthiness of vessel or craft or unfitness of vessel or craft for the safe carriage of the subject-matter insured, where the Assured are privy to such unseaworthiness or unfitness, at the time the subject-matter insured is loaded therein

   4.1.2   unfitness of container liftvan or land conveyance for the safe carriage of the subject-matter insured, where loading therein is carried out prior to attachment of this insurance or by the Assured or their servants.

   4.2   Where this insurance has been assigned to the party claiming hereunder who has bought or agreed to buy the subject-matter insured in good faith under a binding contract, exclusion 4.1.1 above shall not apply.

   4.3   The Underwriters waive any breach of the implied warranties of seaworthiness of the ship and fitness of the ship to carry the subject-matter insured to destination.

DURATION

5   5.1   This insurance attaches on or after the loading of the goods insured hereunder on land and/or water conveyances or their floating at the mill, warehouse, factory, yard or premises wheresoever, from which the despatch to the oversea vessel is made, continues during the ordinary course of transit and terminates either — *Transit Clause*

   5.1.1   on delivery of the goods by land or water into the mill, warehouse, factory, yard or premises at their final destination, whether at the port of discharge of the oversea vessel or (further sea voyage excepted) elsewhere, and are there made available to the Assured or Receivers

   5.1.2   on delivery to any other warehouse or place of storage which the Assured elect to use for storage other than in the ordinary course of transit or

5.1.3   on the expiry of 60 days after completion of discharge overside of the goods hereby insured from the oversea vessel at the final port of discharge,

    whichever shall first occur.

5.2   This insurance shall remain in force (subject to termination as provided for above and to the provisions of Clause 6 below) during delay beyond the control of the Assured, any deviation, forced discharge, reshipment or transhipment and during any variation of the adventure arising from the exercise of a liberty granted to shipowners or charterers under the contract of affreightment.

5.3   Each bill of lading to be deemed a separate insurance if required by the Assured at any time.

5.4   The provisions of Clause 5 shall apply notwithstanding that the description of the voyage contained in the body of the policy may state only the ports and places of shipment and discharge.

6   If owing to circumstances beyond the control of the Assured either the contract of carriage is terminated at a port or place other than the destination named therein or the transit is otherwise terminated before delivery of the goods as provided for in Clause 5 above, then this insurance shall also terminate *unless prompt notice is given to the Underwriters and continuation of cover is requested when the insurance shall remain in force, subject to an additional premium if required by the Underwriters,* either   *Termination of Contract of Carriage Clause*

6.1   until the goods are sold and delivered at such port or place, or, unless otherwise specially agreed, until the expiry of 60 days after arrival of the goods hereby insured at such port or place, whichever shall first occur,

    or

6.2   if the goods are forwarded within the said period of 60 days (or any agreed extension thereof) to the destination named herein or to any other destination, until terminated in accordance with the provisions of Clause 5 above.

7   Where, after attachment of this insurance, the destination is changed by the Assured, *held covered at a premium and on conditions to be arranged subject to prompt notice being given to the Underwriters.*   *Change of Voyage Clause*

CLAIMS

8 8.1   In order to recover under this insurance the Assured must have an insurable interest in the subject-matter insured at the time of the loss.   *Insurable Interest Clause*

8.2   Subject to 8.1 above, the Assured shall be entitled to recover for insured loss occurring during the period covered by this insurance, notwithstanding that the loss occurred before the contract of insurance was concluded, unless the Assured were aware of the loss and the Underwriters were not.

9 9.1   If any Increased Value insurance is effected by the Assured on the cargo insured herein the agreed value of the cargo shall be deemed to be increased to the total amount insured under this insurance and all Increased Value insurances covering the loss, and liability under this insurance shall be in such proportion as the sum insured herein bears to such total amount insured.   *Increased Value Clause*

    In the event of claim the Assured shall provide the Underwriters with evidence of the amounts insured under all other insurances.

9.2   **Where this insurance is on Increased Value the following clause shall apply:**

    The agreed value of the cargo shall be deemed to be equal to the total amount insured under the primary insurance and all Increased Value insurances covering the loss and effected on the cargo by the Assured, and liability under this insurance shall be in such proportion as the sum insured herein bears to such total amount insured.

    In the event of claim the Assured shall provide the Underwriters with evidence of the amounts insured under all other insurances.

BENEFIT OF INSURANCE

10   This insurance shall not inure to the benefit of the carrier or other bailee.   *Not to Inure Clause*

MINIMISING LOSSES

11   It is the duty of the Assured and their servants and agents in respect of loss recoverable hereunder   *Duty of Assured Clause*

11.1   to take such measures as may be reasonable for the purpose of averting or minimising such loss,

    and

11.2   to ensure that all rights against carriers, bailees or other third parties are properly preserved and exercised

    and the Underwriters will, in addition to any loss recoverable hereunder, reimburse the Assured for any charges properly and reasonably incurred in pursuance of these duties.

12   Measures taken by the Assured or the Underwriters with the object of saving, protecting or recovering the subject-matter insured shall not be considered as a waiver or acceptance of abandonment or otherwise prejudice the rights of either party.   *Waiver Clause*

AVOIDANCE OF DELAY

13   It is a condition of this insurance that the Assured shall act with reasonable despatch in all circumstances within their control.   *Reasonable Despatch Clause*

LAW AND PRACTICE

14   This insurance is subject to English law and practice.   *English Law and Practice Clause*

NOTE:— *It is necessary for the Assured when they become aware of an event which is "held covered" under this insurance to give prompt notice to the Underwriters and the right to such cover is dependent upon compliance with this obligation.*

Appendix 64

1/10/69.

INSTITUTE CONTAINER CLAUSES
TIME (ALL RISKS)

SCHEDULE

| Type & Size | Subject Matter Insured | | Sea and Territorial Limits |
	Identification Mark	Value	(which are deemed to include normal flying routes between points within these Sea and Territorial Limits)
			Oversea Vessels
Deductible			

or as per schedule attached

THE CONTAINER MUST BEAR CLEAR MARKS OF IDENTIFICATION.

1. This insurance is against all risks of loss of or damage to the subject matter insured, including whilst on deck, occurring within the Sea and Territorial Limits specified in the Schedule above during the period covered by this insurance but shall in no case be deemed to cover loss damage or expense arising on Oversea Vessels other than those to which the entry in the said Schedule applies.

Breach of these Sea and Territorial Limits held covered, at an additional premium to be agreed, subject to prompt notice.

2. This insurance shall in no case be deemed to extend to cover:—
   (a) ordinary wear and tear or gradual deterioration;
   (b) loss damage or expense proximately caused by delay or inherent vice or nature of the subject matter insured.

3. In relation to any claim for loss of or damage to the machinery of the container Underwriters shall only be liable:—
   (a) when the container is a total loss;
   or (b) for damage proximately caused by:—
      (i) stranding or sinking of the vessel or craft;
      (ii) collision, overturning or other accident to the land conveyance or aircraft;
      (iii) general average sacrifice;
   or (c) for damage reasonably attributable to:—
      (i) fire or explosion originating externally to the machinery;
      (ii) collision or contact of the vessel or craft with any external substance (ice included) other than water.

4. Each container shall be deemed to be a separate insurance.

5. (a) Where a claim is payable under this insurance for a container which is damaged but is not a total loss, the measure of indemnity shall not exceed the reasonable cost of repairing such damage.
   (b) Underwriters only to be liable for the excess of the amount specified in the Schedule above as the deductible in respect of each container any one accident or series of accidents arising out of the same occurrence but this deductible shall not apply to
      (i) total loss;
      (ii) general average, salvage charges and sue and labour.

6. In respect of any one container Underwriters shall not be liable for unrepaired damage in addition to a subsequent total loss sustained during the period covered by this insurance.

7. In ascertaining whether a container is a constructive total loss the insured value shall be taken as the repaired value and nothing in respect of the damaged or scrap value of the container shall be taken into account.
   No claim for constructive total loss based upon the cost of recovery and/or repair of a container shall be recoverable hereunder unless such cost would exceed the insured value.

8. In the event of accident whereby loss or damage may result in a claim under this insurance, notice shall be given to Underwriters or, if the container is abroad, to the nearest Lloyd's Agent so that a surveyor may be appointed to represent Underwriters should they so desire.

9. It is the duty of the Assured and their Agents, in all cases, to take such measures as may be reasonable for the purpose of averting or minimising a loss and to ensure that all rights against carriers, bailees or other third parties are properly preserved and exercised.

10. General average and salvage charges payable according to Foreign Statement or to York-Antwerp Rules if in accordance with the contract of affreightment. Should the contributory value exceed the insured value, then the contribution shall be paid in full by Underwriters.

11. This insurance is extended to indemnify the Assured against such proportion of liability under the contract of affreightment "Both to Blame Collision" Clause as is in respect of a loss recoverable hereunder.
   In the event of any claim by shipowners under the said Clause the Assured agrees to notify Underwriters who shall have the right, at their own cost and expense, to defend the Assured against such claim.

12. In the event of loss the Assured's right of recovery hereunder shall not be prejudiced by the fact that the loss may have been attributable to the wrongful act or misconduct of the carriers or their servants, committed without the privity of the Assured.

13. This insurance shall not inure to the benefit of the carrier or other bailee.

14. No assignment of or interest in this Policy or in any moneys which may be or become payable thereunder is to be binding on or recognised by Underwriters unless a dated notice of such assignment or interest signed by the Assured, and by the assignor in the case of subsequent assignment, is endorsed on this Policy and the Policy with such endorsement is produced before payment of any claim or return of premium thereunder; but nothing in this clause is to have effect as an agreement by Underwriters to a sale.

15. If a container is sold, the insurance by this Policy of that container shall become cancelled from the time of sale, unless Underwriters agree in writing to continue the cover.
   This clause shall prevail notwithstanding any provision whether written, typed or printed in this Policy inconsistent therewith.

16. This insurance may be cancelled by either Underwriters or the Assured giving 30 days' notice (such cancellation becoming effective on the expiry of 30 days from midnight of the day on which notice of cancellation is issued by or to Underwriters). In the event of cancellation by Underwriters, they shall allow pro rata net return of premium to the Assured. In the event of cancellation by the Assured, Underwriters shall allow such return of premium as may be agreed.

17. Warranted free of capture, seizure, arrest, restraint or detainment, and the consequences thereof or of any attempt thereat; also from the consequences of hostilities or warlike operations, whether there be a declaration of war or not; but this warranty shall not exclude collision, contact with any fixed, floating or airborne object (other than a mine, torpedo or other warlike missile), stranding, heavy weather or fire unless caused directly (and independently of the nature of the venture or service which the vessel or aircraft concerned or, in the case of a collision, any other vessel or aircraft involved therein, is performing) by a hostile act by or against a belligerent power; and for the purpose of this warranty "power" includes

any authority maintaining naval, military or air forces in association with   97
a power.   98
    Further warranted free from the consequences of civil war, revolu-   99
tion, rebellion, insurrection, or civil strife arising therefrom, or piracy.   100

18. Warranted free of loss or damage or expense directly or indirectly   101
caused by or contributed to by or arising from   102
   (a) ionising radiations from or contamination by radio activity   103
      from any nuclear fuel or from any nuclear waste from   104
      the combustion of nuclear fuel;   105

   (b) the radioactive, toxic, explosive or other hazardous proper-   106
      ties of any explosive nuclear assembly or nuclear component   107
      thereof.   108

19. Warranted free of loss or damage or expense arising from confisca-   109
tion or nationalisation or requisition or pre-emption.   110

20. Warranted free of loss or damage or expense caused by strikers,   111
locked-out workmen, or persons taking part in labour disturbances, riots   112
or civil commotions.   113

Appendix 65

INSTITUTE CONTAINER CLAUSES
TIME (Total Loss, General Average, Salvage, Salvage Charges, Sue and Labour)

SCHEDULE

	Subject Matter Insured		Sea and Territorial Limits
Type & Size	Identification Mark	Value	(which are deemed to include normal flying routes between points within these Sea and Territorial Limits)
			Oversea Vessels

or as per schedule attached

THE CONTAINER MUST BEAR CLEAR MARKS OF IDENTIFICATION.

1 1. This insurance only covers
2   (a) all risks of total loss of the subject matter insured
3   (b) general average, salvage and salvage charges
4   (c) sue and labour charges incurred for the purpose of averting or
5   diminishing any loss covered by this insurance
6 including whilst on deck, within the Sea and Territorial Limits specified
7 in the Schedule above during the period covered by this insurance but
8 shall in no case be deemed to cover loss damage or expense arising on Over-
9 sea Vessels other than those to which the entry in the said Schedule applies.

10   Breach of these Sea and Territorial Limits held covered, at an
11 additional premium to be agreed, subject to prompt notice.

12 2. This insurance shall in no case be deemed to cover:—
13   (a) ordinary wear and tear or gradual deterioration;
14   (b) loss damage or expense proximately caused by delay or inherent
15   vice or nature of the subject matter insured.

16 3. Each container shall be deemed to be a separate insurance.

17 4. In ascertaining whether a container is a constructive total loss the
18 insured value shall be taken as the repaired value and nothing in respect
19 of the damaged or scrap value of the container shall be taken into account.

20   No claim for constructive total loss based upon the cost of recovery
21 and/or repair of a container shall be recoverable hereunder unless such cost
22 would exceed the insured value.

23 5. In the event of accident whereby loss or damage may result in a
24 claim under this insurance, notice shall be given to Underwriters, or, if
25 the container is abroad, to the nearest Lloyd's Agent so that a surveyor
26 may be appointed to represent Underwriters should they so desire.

27 6. It is the duty of the Assured and their Agents, in all cases, to take
28 such measures as may be reasonable for the purpose of averting or mini-
29 mising a loss and to ensure that all rights against carriers, bailees or other
30 third parties are properly preserved and exercised.

31 7. General average and salvage charges payable according to Foreign
32 Statement or to York-Antwerp Rules if in accordance with the contract
33 of affreightment. Should the contributory value exceed the insured value,
34 then the contribution shall be paid in full by Underwriters.

35 8. This insurance is extended to indemnify the Assured against such
36 proportion of liability under the contract of affreightment "Both to Blame
37 Collision" Clause as is in respect of a loss recoverable hereunder.

38   In the event of any claim by shipowners under the said Clause the
39 Assured agrees to notify Underwriters who shall have the right, at their
40 own cost and expense, to defend the Assured against such claim.

41 9. In the event of loss the Assured's right of recovery hereunder shall
42 not be prejudiced by the fact that the loss may have been attributable
43 to the wrongful act or misconduct of the carriers or their servants, com-
44 mitted without the privity of the Assured.

45 10. This insurance shall not inure to the benefit of the carrier or other
46 bailee.

47 11. No assignment of or interest in this Policy or in any moneys which
48 may be or become payable thereunder is to be binding on or recognised by
49 Underwriters unless a dated notice of such assignment or interest signed
49 by the Assured, and by the assignor in the case of subsequent assignment,
50 is endorsed on this Policy and the Policy with such endorsement is produced.
51 before payment of any claim or return of premium thereunder; but nothing
52 in this clause is to have effect as an agreement by Underwriters to a sale.
53

54 12. If a container is sold, the insurance by this Policy of that container
55 shall become cancelled from the time of sale, unless Underwriters agree in
56 writing to continue the cover.

57   This clause shall prevail notwithstanding any provision whether
58 written, typed or printed in this Policy inconsistent therewith.

59 13. This insurance may be cancelled by either Underwriters or the
60 Assured giving 30 days' notice (such cancellation becoming effective on the
61 expiry of 30 days from midnight of the day on which notice of cancellation
62 is issued by or to Underwriters). In the event of cancellation by Under-
63 writers, they shall allow pro rata net return of premium to the Assured.
64 In the event of cancellation by the Assured, Underwriters shall allow such
65 return of premium as may be agreed.

66 14. Warranted free of capture, seizure, arrest, restraint or detainment,
67 and the consequences thereof or of any attempt thereat; also from the
68 consequences of hostilities or warlike operations, whether there be a
69 declaration of war or not; but this warranty shall not exclude collision,
70 contact with any fixed, floating or airborne object (other than a mine,
71 torpedo or other warlike missile), stranding, heavy weather or fire unless
72 caused directly (and independently of the nature of the venture or service
73 which the vessel or aircraft concerned or, in the case of a collision, any other
74 vessel or aircraft involved therein, is performing) by a hostile act by or
75 against a belligerent power; and for the purpose of this warranty "power"
76 includes any authority maintaining naval, military or air forces in
77 association with a power.

78   Further warranted free from the consequences of civil war, revolution,
79 rebellion, insurrection, or civil strife arising therefrom, or piracy.

80 15. Warranted free of loss or damage or expense directly or indirectly
81 caused by or contributed to by or arising from

82   (a) ionising radiations from or contamination by radioactivity
83   from any nuclear fuel or from any nuclear waste from the
84   combustion of nuclear fuel;

Appendix 66

1/10/69.

INSTITUTE WAR AND STRIKES CLAUSES
CONTAINERS—TIME

SCHEDULE

Type & Size	Subject Matter Insured Identification Mark	Value	Sea and Territorial Limits (which are deemed to include normal flying routes between points within these Sea and Territorial Limits)
			Oversea Vessels
Deductible			

or as per schedule attached

THE CONTAINER MUST BEAR CLEAR MARKS OF IDENTIFICATION.

1. Subject always to the exclusions hereinafter referred to, this insurance covers only the risks of loss of or damage to the subject matter insured which would be recoverable under the Standard Form of English Marine Policy, with the Institute Container Clauses Time -(All Risks) (1/10/69) attached, but for the following clauses:

(a) Warranted free of capture, seizure, arrest, restraint or detainment, and the consequences thereof or of any attempt thereat; also from the consequences of hostilities or warlike operations, whether there be a declaration of war or not; but this warranty shall not exclude collision, contact with any fixed, floating or airborne object (other than a mine, torpedo or other warlike missile), stranding, heavy weather or fire unless caused directly (and independently of the nature of the venture or service which the the vessel or aircraft concerned or, in the case of a collision, any other vessel or aircraft involved therein, is performing) by a hostile act by or against a belligerent power; and for the purpose of this warranty "power" includes any authority maintaining naval, military or air forces in association with a power.

Further warranted free from the consequences of civil war, revolution, rebellion, insurrection, or civil strife arising therefrom, or piracy.

(b) Warranted free of loss or damage or expense caused by strikers, locked-out workmen, or persons taking part in labour disturbances, riots or civil commotions.

The Institute Container Clauses Time (All Risks) (1/10/69), except lines 7 and 8 in Clause 1, Clause 16 and the words "confiscation or" in Clause 19, are deemed to be incorporated in this insurance in so far as they do not conflict with the provisions of these clauses.

2. This insurance excludes

(a) any claim for expenses arising from delay except such expenses as would be recoverable in principle in English law and practice under the York-Antwerp Rules 1950.

(b) loss damage or expense covered by the Standard Form of English Marine Policy with the Institute Container Clauses Time (All Risks) attached.

(c) loss damage or expense arising

(i) from the outbreak of war (whether there be a declaration of war or not) between any of the following countries:— United Kingdom, United States of America, France, the Union of Soviet Socialist Republics, the People's Republic of China;

(ii) from capture, seizure, arrest, restraint, detainment or confiscation by the Government of the country in which the container is owned;

(iii) from arrest, restraint or detainment under quarantine regulations or by reason of infringement of any customs regulations;

(iv) whilst the container is not on board an aircraft or oversea vessel except as provided in Clause 3 below (for the purpose of this clause an oversea vessel shall be deemed to mean a vessel carrying the container from one port or place to another where such voyage involves a sea passage by that vessel).

Anything contained in this insurance which is inconsistent with this Clause 2 (c) (iv) shall to the extent of such inconsistency be null and void.

3. Notwithstanding Clause 2(c)(iv) but subject in all other respects to the terms, exclusions and conditions of this insurance, whilst the container is

(a) on board any vessel or craft, this insurance covers loss of or damage to such container caused by piracy, mines or derelict engines of war;

(b) on board any vessel or craft, or is ashore, this insurance covers loss of or damage to such container caused by strikers, locked-out workmen, or persons taking part in labour disturbances, riots or civil commotions, not being loss or damage arising from hostilities, warlike operations, civil war, revolution, rebellion, insurrection or civil strife arising therefrom.

NOTICE OF CANCELLATION AND AUTOMATIC TERMINATION OF COVER CLAUSE

4. (a) This insurance may be cancelled by either Underwriters or the Assured giving 14 days notice (such cancellation becoming effective on the expiry of 14 days from midnight of the day on which notice of cancellation is issued by or to Underwriters). Underwriters agree however to reinstate this insurance subject to agreement between Underwriters and the Assured prior to the expiry of such notice of cancellation as to new rate of premium and/or conditions and/or warranties.

Whether or not such notice of cancellation has been given this insurance shall TERMINATE AUTOMATICALLY

(i) upon the occurrence of any hostile detonation of any weapon of war employing atomic or nuclear fission and/or fusion or other like reaction or radioactive force or matter, wheresoever or whensoever such detonation may occur and whether or not the subject matter insured may be involved;

(ii) upon the outbreak of war (whether there be a declaration of war or not) between any of the following countries:— United Kingdom, United States of America, France, the Union of Soviet Socialist Republics, the People's Republic of China;

(iii) in the event of the container being requisitioned either for title or use.

(b) In the event either of cancellation by notice or of automatic termination of this insurance by reason of the operation of section (a) of this clause, or of the sale of the subject matter insured, pro rata net return of premium shall be payable to the Assured.

This insurance shall not become effective if, prior to the intended time of its attachment, there has occurred any event which would have automatically terminated this insurance under the provisions of Clause 4 above had this insurance attached prior to such occurrence.

Appendix 67

ORIGINAL

ASSOCIATION OF MARINE UNDERWRITERS OF BRITISH COLUMBIA

For signature only by Companies or firms whose officials or partners are Underwriting Members of the Association of Marine Underwriters of British Columbia.

Be it known that

HULL POLICY NO.

as well in *their* own Name, as for and in the Name and Names of all and every other Person or Persons to whom the same doth, may, or shall appertain, in part or in all, doth make Assurance, and cause *themselves* and them and every of them, to be assured, lost or not lost, at and from

upon the Body, Tackle, Apparel, Ordnance, Munition, Artillery, Boat and other Furniture, of and in the good Ship or Vessel called the

whereof is Master, under God, for this present Voyage,
or whosoever else shall go for Master in the said Ship, or by whatsoever other Name or Names the said Ship, or the Master thereof, is or shall be named or called, beginning the Adventure upon the said Ship, &c., *as above*, and shall so continue and endure during her Abode there; and further, until the said ship, with all her Ordnance, Tackle, Apparel, &c., shall be arrived at *as above*, and until she hath moored at Anchor in good Safety; and it shall be lawful for the said Ship, &c., in this Voyage to proceed and sail to and touch and stay at any Ports or Places whatsoever without Prejudice to this Assurance. The said Ship &c., for so much as concerns the Assured by Agreement between the Assured and Assurers in this Policy, are and shall be valued at

TOUCHING the Adventures and Perils which the Assurers are contented to bear and do take upon themselves in this Voyage, they are of the Seas, Men-of-War, Fire, Enemies, Pirates, Rovers, Assailing Thieves, Jettisons, Letters of Mart and Countermart, Surprisals, Takings at Sea, Arrests, Restraints and Detainments of all Kings, Princes and People, of what Nation, Condition, or Quality soever, Barratry of the Master and Mariners, and of all other Perils, Losses and Misfortunes, that have or shall come to the Hurt, Detriment or Damage of the subject matter of this Assurance: and in case of any Loss or Misfortune, it shall be lawful to the Assured, their Factors, Servants and Assigns, to sue, labour, and travel for, in and about the Defence, Safeguard and Recovery of the said subject matter of Assurance without Prejudice to this Assurance; to the Charges whereof the Assurers will contribute, each company rateably according to the amount of their respective subscriptions hereto. And it is especially declared and agreed that no acts of the Assurer or Assured in recovering, saving, or preserving the property Assured, shall be considered as a waiver or acceptance of abandonment. And it is agreed by us, the Assurers, that this Writing or Policy of Assurance shall be of as much Force and Effect as the surest Writing or Policy of Assurance heretofore made in Lombard Street, or in the Royal Exchange, or elsewhere in London.

Warranted free of capture, seizure, arrest, restraint or detainment, and the consequences thereof or of any attempt thereat; also from the consequences of hostilities or warlike operations, whether there be a declaration of war or not; but this warranty shall not exclude collision, contact with any fixed or floating object (other than a mine or torpedo), stranding, heavy weather or fire unless caused directly (and independently of the nature of the voyage or service which the vessel concerned or, in the case of a collision, any other vessel involved therein, is performing) by a hostile act by or against a belligerent power; and for the purpose of this warranty "power" includes any authority maintaining naval, military or air forces in association with a power.

Further warranted free from the consequences of civil war, revolution, rebellion, insurrection, or civil strife arising therefrom, or piracy.

NOW THIS POLICY WITNESSETH that we, the Assurers, the Companies whose names are set out herein, take upon ourselves the burden of this Assurance each of us to the extent of the amount underwritten by us respectively, and promise and bind ourselves, each Company for itself only and not the one for the other and in respect only of the due proportion of each Company to the Assured, their Executors, Administrators and Assigns for the true performance and fulfilment of the contract contained in this Policy in consideration of the person or persons effecting this Policy promising to pay a premium at and after the Rate of

IN WITNESS whereof we, the Assurers, have subscribed our names and sums assured in Vancouver, B.C.

as hereinafter appears, this .... day of .... 19 ....

N.B. — The Ship and Freight are warranted free from Average under Three per cent., unless general, or the Ship be stranded, sunk or burnt.

AMOUNT	PROP'N.	ASSURERS	AUTHORIZED SIGNATURE

1/10/74
1974

Appendix 68

CANADIAN HULLS (PACIFIC) CLAUSES

1974

1. Touching the Adventures and Perils which we, the assurers, are contented to bear and take upon us, they are of the Seas, Men-of-War, Fire, Enemies, Pirates, Rovers, Thieves, Jettisons, Letters of Mart and Counter-Mart, Surprisals, Takings at Sea, Arrests, Restraints and Detainments of all Kings, Princes and Peoples, of what nation, condition or quality soever, Barratry of the Master and Mariners and of all other like Perils, Losses and Misfortunes that have or shall come to the Hurt, Detriment or Damage of the said Vessel, &c., or any part thereof; excepting, however, such of the foregoing Perils as may be excluded by provisions elsewhere in these clauses or by endorsement.

And in case of any Loss or Misfortune, it shall be lawful for the Assured, their Factors, Servants and Assigns, to sue, labour and travel for, in, and about the Defence, Safeguard and Recovery of the said Vessel, &c., or any part thereof, without prejudice to this Insurance, to the Charges whereof the Underwriters will contribute their proportion as provided below. And it is expressly declared and agreed that no acts of the Underwriters or Assured in recovering, saving or preserving the property insured shall be considered as a waiver or acceptance of abandonment.

2. This insurance includes loss of or damage to the subject matter insured directly caused by: –

  (a) Accidents in loading, discharging or shifting cargo or fuel

Explosions on shipboard or elsewhere

Breakdown of or accident to nuclear installations or reactors on shipboard or elsewhere

Bursting of boilers, breakage of shafts or any latent defect in the machinery or hull

Negligence of Master, Charterers other than an Assured,

When the contributory value of the Vessel is greater than the valuation herein the liability of these Underwriters for General Average contribution (except in respect to amount made good to the Vessel) or Salvage shall not exceed that proportion of the total contribution due from the Vessel that the amount insured hereunder bears to the contributory value; and if because of damage for which these Underwriters are liable as Particular Average the value of the Vessel has been reduced for the purpose of contribution, the amount of the Particular Average loss under this Policy shall be deducted from the amount insured hereunder and these Underwriters shall be liable only for the proportion which such net amount bears to the contributory value.

9. In the event of expenses being incurred pursuant to the Suing and Labouring Clause, the liability under this Policy shall not exceed the proportion of such expenses that the amount insured hereunder bears to the value of the Vessel as stated herein, or to the sound value of the Vessel at the time of the occurrence giving rise to the expenditure if the sound value exceeds that value. Where Underwriters have admitted a claim for total loss and property insured by this Policy is saved, the foregoing provisions shall not apply unless the expenses of suing and labouring exceed the value of such property saved and then shall apply only to the amount of the expenses which is in excess of such value.

Where a claim for total loss of the Vessel is admitted under this Policy and expenses have been reasonably incurred in salving or attempting to salve the Vessel and other property and there are no proceeds, or the expenses exceed the proceeds, then this Policy shall bear its pro rata share of such proportion of the expenses, or of the expenses in excess of the proceeds, as the case

Officers, Crew or Pilots
Negligence of repairers provided such repairers are not
Assured(s) hereunder
(b) Contact with aircraft
Contact with any land conveyance, dock or harbour
equipment or installation
Earthquake, volcanic eruption or lightning
Provided such loss or damage has not resulted from want of
due diligence by the Assured, Owners or Managers.
Masters, Officers, Crew or Pilots not to be considered as part
Owners within the meaning of this Clause should they hold shares
in the vessel.
3. Warranted free from claims due to or resulting from ice
and/or freezing howsoever caused on inland waters above ocean
tidal influence.
4. The Vessel is covered subject to the provisions of this Policy
at all times and has leave to sail or navigate with or without pilots,
to go on trial trips and to assist and tow vessels or craft in distress,
but it is warranted that the Vessel shall not otherwise tow or be
towed, except as is customary or to the first safe port or place
when in need of assistance.
5. The sum of $ shall be deducted from the
total of all claims arising out of one accident or occurrence
(including claims under the Running Down Clause). Nevertheless,
the expense of sighting the bottom after stranding, if reasonably
incurred specially for that purpose, shall be paid in full even if no
damage be found. This paragraph shall not apply to Sue and
Labour, Salvage Expenses, General Average nor to a claim for
Total or Constructive Total Loss.
Claims for damage by heavy weather (which includes contact
with floating ice) occurring during a single sea passage between
two successive ports shall be treated as being due to one accident.
In the case of such heavy weather extending over a period not
wholly covered by this insurance the deductible to be applied to
the claim recoverable hereunder shall be the proportion of the
above deductible that the number of days of such heavy weather
falling within the period of this insurance bears to the number of
days of heavy weather during the single sea passage.
Unless the Assured and Underwriters shall have agreed in
writing prior to commencement of suit to participate jointly in
recoveries and concomitant legal costs, then recoveries (excluding

may be, as may reasonably be regarded as having been incurred in
respect of the Vessel; but if the Vessel be insured for less than its
sound value at the time of the occurrence giving rise to the
expenditure, the amount recoverable under this clause shall be
reduced in proportion to the under-insurance.
10. In ascertaining whethere the Vessel is a constructive total
loss the insured value shall be taken as the repaired value and
nothing in respect of the damaged or break-up value of the Vessel
or wreck shall be taken into account.
No claim for constructive total loss based upon the cost of
recovery and/or repair of the Vessel shall be recoverable hereunder unless such cost would exceed the insured value.
11. In the event of total or constructive total loss no claim to be
made by the Underwriters for freight whether notice of abandonment has been given or not.
12. In no case shall Underwriters be liable for unrepaired damage
in addition to a subsequent total loss sustained during the term
covered by this Policy or extension thereof.
13. It is further agreed that if the Vessel hereby insured shall
come into collision with any other vessel and the Assured shall in
consequence thereof become liable to pay and shall pay by way
of damages to any other person or persons any sum or sums in
respect of such collision for
(i) loss of or damage to any other vessel or property on
any other vessel,
(ii) delay to or loss of use of any such other vessel or
property thereon, or
(iii) general average of, salvage of, or salvage under contract
of, any such other vessel or property thereon,
the Underwriters will pay the Assured such proportion of such
sum or sums so paid as their respective subscriptions hereto bear
to the value of the Vessel hereby insured, provided always that
their liability in respect of any one such collision shall not exceed
their proportionate part of the value of the Vessel hereby
insured, and in cases in which, with the prior consent in
writing of the Underwriters, the liability of the Vessel has
been contested or proceedings have been taken to limit the
liability, they will also pay a like proportion of the costs which
the Assured shall thereby incur or be compelled to pay; but when
both vessels are to blame, then unless the liability of the Owners
of one or both of such vessels becomes limited by law, claims

72 interest comprised therein) made against any claim subject to the
73 above deductible, or any other deductions by reason of the
74 difference between the insured and sound values, shall first be
75 credited to Underwriters up to the amount of the claim paid by
76 them and then to the Assured.
77   Interest comprised in recoveries shall be apportioned be-
78 tween the Assured and the Underwriters, taking into account the
79 sums paid by Underwriters and the dates when such payments
80 were made.
81 6. Average payable without deduction of thirds, new for old,
82 whether the average be particular or general.
83 7. From the cost of cleaning and painting the bottom of a
84 Vessel, (exclusive of dry-dock charges) recoverable in average,
85 there shall be deducted one-twelfth for every month since the
86 Vessel was last painted, but no allowance shall be made for
87 cleaning and painting on account of exposure to air unless the
88 Vessel has been more than twenty-four hours on the dock.
89   Notwithstanding the foregoing no claim in respect to bottom
90 painting shall be recoverable hereunder unless evidence is pro-
91 vided to show date of the last bottom painting prior to the loss.
92 8. General Average, Salvage and Special Charges payable as
93 provided in the contract of affreightment, or failing such
94 provision, or there be no contract of affreightment, payable in
95 accordance with the York-Antwerp Rules. Provided always that
96 when an adjustment according to the laws and usages of the port
97 of destination is properly demanded by the owners of the cargo,
98 General Average shall be paid in accordance with same.
99   When the Vessel sails in ballast, not under charter, the
100 provisions of the York-Antwerp Rules, 1974 (excluding Rules XX
101 and XXI) shall be applicable, and the voyage for this purpose shall
102 be deemed to continue from the port or place of departure until
103 the arrival of the Vessel at the first port or place thereafter other
104 than a port or place of refuge or a port or place of call for
105 bunkering only. If at any such intermediate port or place there is
106 an abandonment of the adventure originally contemplated the
107 voyage shall thereupon be deemed to be terminated.

179 under this clause shall be settled on the principle of cross-liabili-
180 ties as if the Owners of each vessel had been compelled to pay to
181 the Owners of the other of such vessels such one-half or other
182 proportion of the latter's damages as may have been properly
183 allowed in ascertaining the balance or sum payable by or to the
184 Assured in consequence of such collision.
185   Provided always that this clause shall in no case extend or be
186 deemed to extend to any sum which the Assured may become
187 liable to pay or shall pay for or in respect of: —
188 (a) removal or disposal, under statutory powers or other-
189 wise, of obstructions, wrecks, cargoes or any other thing
190 whatsoever,
191 (b) any real or personal property or thing whatsoever except
192 other vessels or property on other vessels,
193 (c) pollution or contamination of any real or personal
194 property or thing whatsoever (except other vessels with
195 which the insured Vessel is in collision or property on
196 such other vessels),
197 (d) the cargo or other property on or the engagements of
198 the insured Vessel,
199 (e) loss of life, personal injury or illness.
200 14. Should the Vessel hereby insured come into collision with or
201 receive salvage services from another vessel belonging wholly or in
202 part to the same Owners or under the same management, the
203 Assured shall have the same rights under this Policy as they would
204 have were the other vessel entirely the property of Owners not
205 interested in the Vessel hereby insured; but in such cases the
206 liability for the collision or the amount payable for the services
207 rendered shall be referred to a sole arbitrator to be agreed upon
208 between the Underwriters and the Assured.
209 15. This insurance covers loss of or damage to the Vessel directly
210 caused by any governmental authority acting under the powers
211 vested in them to prevent or mitigate a pollution hazard, or threat
212 thereof, resulting directly from damage to the Vessel for which
213 the Underwriters are liable under this Policy, provided such act of
214 governmental authority has not resulted from want of due

diligence by the Assured, the Owners, or Managers of the Vessel or any of them to prevent or mitigate such hazard or threat. Masters, Officers, Crew or Pilots not to be considered Owners within the meaning of this clause should they hold shares in the Vessel.

16. This insurance also covers loss of or damage to the property hereby insured caused by strikers, locked-out workmen or persons taking part in labour disturbances, riots or civil commotions; destruction of or damage to the property hereby insured caused by persons acting maliciously.

17. In the event of accident whereby loss or damage may result in a claim under this Policy, notice shall be given in writing to the Underwriters, where practicable, prior to survey, so that they may appoint their own surveyor if they so desire. The Underwriters shall be entitled to decide the port to which a damaged Vessel shall proceed for docking or repairing (the actual additional expense of the voyage arising from compliance with Underwriters' requirements being refunded to the Assured) and Underwriters shall also have a right of veto in connection with the place of repair or repairing firm proposed and whenever the extent of the damage is ascertainable the majority (in amount) of the Underwriters may take, or may require to be taken, tenders for the repair of such damage.

In the event of failure to comply with the conditions of this clause, 15 per cent shall be deducted from the amount of the ascertained claim.

18. If the Vessel is sold or transferred to new management or chartered on a bare boat basis, then unless the Underwriters agree in writing to continue the insurance, this Policy shall become cancelled from the time of sale or transfer, unless the Vessel has cargo on board and has already sailed from her loading port or is at sea in ballast, in either of which cases such cancellation shall, if required, be suspended until arrival at final port of discharge if with cargo, or at port of destination if in ballast. A *pro rata* daily return of net premium shall be made.

This clause shall prevail notwithstanding any provision whether written, typed or printed in the Policy inconsistent therewith.

19. If payment of premium is not made by the Assured within thirty (30) days after attachment of the insurance, or, in the event the Underwriters shall have agreed to accept deferred payments, if any payment of any premium is not made on the

for the current cargo passage and next succeeding cargo passage (such insurance to include, if required, a preliminary and an intermediate ballast passage) plus the charges of insurance. In the case of a voyage charter where payment is made on a time basis, the sum permitted for insurance shall be calculated on the estimated duration of the voyage, subject to the limitation of two cargo passages as laid down herein. Any sum insured under this Section shall be reduced as the freight or hire is earned by the gross amount so earned.

(c) ANTICIPATED FREIGHT IF THE VESSEL SAILS IN BALLAST AND NOT UNDER CHARTER. A sum not exceeding the anticipated gross freight on next cargo passage, such sum to be reasonably estimated on the basis of the current rate of freight at time of insurance, plus the charges of insurance. Provided, however, that no insurance shall be permitted under this Section if any insurance is effected under Section (b).

(d) TIME CHARTER HIRE OR CHARTER HIRE FOR SERIES OF VOYAGES. A sum not exceeding 50% of the gross hire which is to be earned under the charter in a period not exceeding 18 months. Any sum insured under this Section shall be reduced as the hire is earned under the charter by 50% of the gross amount so earned but where the charter is for a period exceeding 18 months the sum insured need not be reduced while it does not exceed 50% of the gross hire still to be earned under the charter. An insurance under this Section may begin on the signing of the charter.

(e) PREMIUMS. A sum not exceeding the actual premiums of all interests insured for a period not exceeding 12 months (excluding premiums insured under the fore-going Sections but including if required, the premium or estimated calls on any Protection and Indemnity or War &c. Risk insurance) reducing pro rata monthly.

(f) RETURNS OF PREMIUM. A sum not exceeding the actual returns which are recoverable subject to "and arrival" under any policy of insurance.

(g) INSURANCE IRRESPECTIVE OF AMOUNT AGAINST: – Risks excluded by the F.C. & S. Clause, and risks enumerated in the Institute War and Strikes Clauses and General Average and Salvage Disbursements.

Warranted that no insurance on any interests enumerated in the foregoing Sections (a) to (f), inclusive, in excess of the amounts permitted therein and no insurance subject to P.P.I., F.I.A. or other like term, on any interests whatever excepting those enumerated in Section (a), is or shall be effected to operate during the currency of this Policy by or for account of the Assured, Owners, Managers or Mortgagees. Provided always that a breach of this warranty shall not afford Underwriters any defense to a claim by a Mortgagee who has accepted this Policy without knowledge of such breach.

23. Should the Vessel at the expiration of this Policy be at sea, or in distress, or at a port of refuge or of call, she shall, provided previous notice be given to the Underwriters, be held covered at a pro rata monthly premium, to her port of destination.

24. Notwithstanding anything to the contrary contained in these clauses, warranted free of capture, seizure, arrest, restraint or detainment, and the consequences thereof or of any attempt thereat; also from the consequences of hostilities or warlike operations, whether there be a declaration of war or not; but this warranty shall not exclude collision, contact with any fixed or floating object (other than a mine or torpedo), stranding, heavy weather or fire unless caused directly (and independently of the nature of the voyage or service which the Vessel concerned or, in the case of a collision, any other vessel involved therein, is performing) by a hostile act by or against a belligerent power; and for the purpose of this warranty "power" includes any authority maintaining naval, military or air forces in association with a power.

Further warranted free from the consequences of civil war, revolution, rebellion, insurrection, or civil strife arising therefrom, or piracy.

25. Warranted free from loss, damage, liability or expense arising from any weapon of war employing atomic or nuclear fission and/or fusion or other like reaction or radioactive force or matter.

26. This insurance is:
(1) Warranted free from loss, damage, liability or expense arising from:—
(a) The detonation of an explosive
(b) Any weapon of war
and caused by any person acting from a political motive.

27. Warranted to be subject to Canadian law and usage as to liability for and settlement of any and all claims.

day agreed, this policy may be cancelled at any time thereafter by the Underwriter giving to the Assured named herein, and to third party payee or payees (if any) named in the policy, five (5) days' notice of such cancellation.

Such notice may be given by the Underwriter or on his behalf by an authorized Agent or by the Agent or Broker effecting this insurance.

Such cancellation shall be without prejudice to the premiums earned and due for the period the policy was in force.

In event of Total or Constructive Total Loss occurring prior to cancellation full annual premium shall be deemed earned.

20. At the expiration of this Policy to return per cent, net for every thirty consecutive days the Vessel may be laid up in port out of commission with no cargo on board and not under repair for Underwriters' account; and to return per cent, net for every thirty days of unexpired time if it be mutually agreed to cancel this Policy, but there shall be no cancellation or return of premium in event Vessel is lost from any cause whatsoever.

In the event of the Vessel being laid up in port for a period of thirty consecutive days, a part only of which attaches to this Policy, it is hereby agreed that the laying up period, in which either the commencing or ending date of this Policy falls, shall be deemed to run from the first day on which the Vessel is laid up and that on this basis Underwriters shall pay such proportion of the return due in respect of a full period of thirty days as the number of days attaching thereto bear to thirty.

21. Held covered in case of any breach of warranty as to cargo, employment, towage, salvage services or date of sailing, provided notice be given to the Underwriters immediately after receipt of advices and any amended terms of cover and any additional premium required by them be agreed.

22. Additional insurances as follows are permitted:
(a) DISBURSEMENTS, MANAGERS' COMMISSIONS, PROFITS OR EXCESS OR INCREASED VALUE OF HULL AND MACHINERY AND/OR SIMILAR INTERESTS HOWEVER DESCRIBED, AND FREIGHT (INCLUDING CHARTERED FREIGHT OR ANTICIPATED FREIGHT) INSURED FOR TIME. A sum not exceeding in the aggregate 25% of the insured value of the vessel.
(b) FREIGHT OR HIRE, UNDER CONTRACTS FOR VOYAGE. A sum not exceeding the gross freight or hire

Appendix 69

CANADIAN (Pacific) TOTAL LOSS AND EXCESS LIABILITIES CLAUSES

1. Touching the Adventures and Perils which we, the assurers, are
contented to bear and take upon us, they are of the Seas, Men-of-War,
Fire, Enemies, Pirates, Rovers, Thieves, Jettisons, Letters of Mart and
Counter-Mart, Surprisals, Takings at Sea, Arrests, Restraints and Detainments of all Kings, Princes and Peoples, of what nation, condition or
quality soever, Barratry of the Master and Mariners and of all other
like Perils, Losses and Misfortunes that have or shall come to the Hurt,
Detriment or Damage of the said Vessel, &c., or any part thereof;
excepting, however, such of the foregoing Perils as may be excluded
by provisions elsewhere in these clauses or by endorsement.
 And in case of any Loss or Misfortune, it shall be lawful for the
Assured, their Factors, Servants and Assigns, to sue, labour and travel
for, in, and about the Defence, Safeguard and Recovery of the said
Vessel, &c., or any part thereof, without prejudice to this Insurance, to
the Charges whereof the Underwriters will contribute their proportion
as provided below. And it is expressly declared and agreed that no acts
of the Underwriters or Assured in recovering, saving or preserving the
property insured shall be considered as a waiver or acceptance of
abandonment.

2. This insurance covers only:

(a) **Total Loss (Actual or Constructive) of the Vessel**
 (including total loss, actual or constructive, directly caused by:
 (i) Accidents in loading discharging or shifting cargo or fuel
  Explosions on shipboard or elsewhere
  Breakdown of or accident to nuclear installations or reac-
   tors on shipboard or elsewhere
  Bursting of boilers, breakage of shafts or any latent defect
   in the machinery or hull
  Negligence of Master, Charterers other than an Assured,
   Officers, Crew or Pilots
  Negligence of repairers provided such repairers are not
   Assured(s) hereunder
 (ii) Contact with aircraft
  Contact with any land conveyance, dock or harbour equip-
   ment or installation
  Earthquake, volcanic eruption or lightning
  Provided such loss or damage has not resulted from want of
   due diligence by the Assured, Owners or Managers.
  Masters, Officers, Crew or Pilots not to be considered as
   part Owners within the meaning of this Clause should they
   hold shares in the vessel.)

(c) the discharge, spillage, emission or leakage of oil, petroleum
 products, chemicals or other substances of any kind or description whatsoever;

(d) cargo or other property on or the engagements of the Vessel;

(e) loss of life, personal injury or illness.
 Provided further that exclusions (b) and (c) above shall not apply
to injury to any other vessel with which the Vessel is in collision or to
property on such other vessel except to the extent that such injury
arises out of any action taken to avoid, minimize or remove any discharge, spillage, emission or leakage described in (c).

3. This insurance is:—

(1) Warranted free from loss, damage, liability or expense arising
 from:—
  (a) The detonation of an explosive
  (b) Any weapon of war
   and caused by any person acting maliciously or from a political
   motive.

(2) Warranted free from claims due to or resulting from ice and/
 or freezing howsoever caused on inland waters above ocean
 tidal influence.

4. The Vessel is covered subject to the provisions of this Policy at
all times and has leave to sail or navigate with or without pilots, to go
on trial trips and to assist and tow vessels or craft in distress, but it is
warranted that the Vessel shall not otherwise tow or be towed, except
as is customary or to the first safe port or place when in need of
assistance.

5. Held covered in case of any breach of warranty as to cargo, employment, towage, salvage services or date of sailing, provided notice
be given to the Underwriters immediately after receipt of advices and
any amended terms of cover and any additional premium required by
them be agreed.

6. Should the Vessel at the expiration of this Policy be at sea, or in
distress, or at a port of refuge or of call, she shall, provided previous
notice be given to the Underwriters, be held covered at a pro rata
monthly premium, to her port of destination.

7. If the Vessel is sold or transferred to new management or chartered
on a bare boat basis, then unless the Underwriters agree in writing to
continue the insurance, this Policy shall become cancelled from the time

In ascertaining whether the Vessel is a constructive total loss the insured value in the policies on hull and machinery shall be taken as the repaired value and nothing in respect of the damaged or breakup value of the Vessel or wreck shall be taken into account.

No claim for constructive total loss based upon the cost of recovery and/or repair of the Vessel shall be recoverable hereunder unless such cost would exceed the insured value in the policies on hull and machinery.

Should the Vessel be a constructive total loss but the claim on the policies on hull and machinery be settled as a claim for partial loss, no payment shall be due under this clause 2(a).

Provided that the Valuation Clause, lines 42/50 above, or a clause having a similar effect, is contained in the policies on hull and machinery, the settlement of a claim for constructive total loss thereunder shall be accepted as proof of the constructive total loss of the Vessel and in the event of a claim for total loss or constructive total loss being settled on the policies on hull and machinery as a compromised total loss the amount payable hereunder shall be the same percentage of the sum Insured as is paid on the said policies.

(b) General Average, Salvage and Salvage Charges not recoverable in full under the policies on hull and machinery by reason of the difference between the insured value of the Vessel as stated therein (or any reduced value arising from the deduction therefrom in process of adjustment of any claim which law or practice or the terms of the policies covering hull and machinery may have required) and the value of the Vessel adopted for the purpose of contribution to general average, salvage or salvage charges, the liability under this Policy being for such proportion of the amount not recoverable as the amount insured hereunder bears to the said difference or to the total sum insured against excess liabilities if it exceeds such difference.

(c) Sue and Labour Charges not recoverable in full under the policies on hull and machinery by reason of the difference between the insured value of the Vessel as stated therein and the value of the Vessel adopted for the purpose of ascertaining the amount recoverable under the policies on hull and machinery, the liability under this policy being for such proportion of the amount not recoverable as the amount insured hereunder bears to the said difference or to the total sum insured against excess liabilities if it exceeds such difference.

(d) Collision Liability not recoverable in full under the Running Down and Sister Ship Clauses in the policies on hull and machinery by reason of such liability exceeding the insured value of the Vessel as stated herein, in which case the amount recoverable under this Policy shall be such proportion of the difference so arising as the amount insured hereunder bears to the total sum insured against excess liabilities.

of sale or transfer, unless the Vessel has cargo on board and has already sailed from her loading port or is at sea in ballast, in either of which cases such cancellation shall, if required, be suspended until arrival at final port of discharge if with cargo, or at port of destination if in ballast. A pro rata daily return of net premium shall be made.

The foregoing provisions with respect to cancellation in the event of change in ownership, management or charter shall apply even in the case of insurance "for whom it may concern".

This clause shall prevail notwithstanding any provision whether written, typed or printed in the Policy inconsistent therewith.

8. Notwithstanding anything to the contrary contained in these clauses, warranted free of capture, seizure, arrest, restraint or detainment, and the consequences thereof or of any attempt thereat; also from the consequences of hostilities or warlike operations, whether there be a declaration of war or not; but this warranty shall not exclude collision, contact with any fixed or floating object (other than a mine or torpedo), stranding, heavy weather or fire unless caused directly (and independently of the nature of the voyage or service which the Vessel concerned or, in the case of a collision, any other vessel involved therein, is performing) by a hostile act by or against a belligerent power; and for the purpose of this warranty "power" includes any authority maintaining naval, military or air forces in association with a power.

Further warranted free from the consequences of civil war, revolution, rebellion, insurrection, or civil strife arising therefrom, or piracy.

9. Warranted free from loss, damage, liability or expense arising from any weapon of war employing atomic or nuclear fission and/or fusion or other like reaction or radioactive force or matter.

10. If payment of premium is not made by the Assured within thirty (30) days after attachment of the insurance, or, in the event the Underwriters shall have agreed to accept deferred payments, if any payment of any premium is not made on the day agreed, this policy may be cancelled at any time thereafter by the Underwriter giving to the Assured named herein, and to third party payee or payees (if any) named in the policy, five (5) days notice of such cancellation.

Such notice may be given by the Underwriter or on his behalf by an authorized Agent or by the Agent or Broker effecting this insurance.

Such cancellation shall be without prejudice to the premiums earned and due for the period the policy was in force.

In event of Total or Constructive Total Loss occurring prior to cancellation full annual premium shall be deemed earned.

11. At the expiration of this policy to return per cent. net for every thirty consecutive days the Vessel may be laid up in port out of commission with no cargo on board and not under repair for underwriters' account; and to return per cent. net for every thirty days of unexpired time if it be mutually agreed to cancel this Policy, but there shall be no cancellation or return of premium in event Vessel is lost from any cause whatsoever.

In the event of the Vessel being laid up in port for a period of thirty consecutive days, a part only of which attaches to this Policy, it

92 Underwriters' liability under (a), (b), (c), and (d), separately, in
93 respect of any one claim, shall not exceed the amount insured hereunder.
94 Provided always that this clause shall in no case extend or be
95 deemed to extend to any sum which the Assured may become liable
96 to pay or shall pay for or in respect of:—
97 (a) removal or disposal of obstructions, wrecks or their cargoes
98 under statutory powers or otherwise pursuant to law:
99 (b) injury to real or personal property of every description;

(Association of Marine Underwriters of British Columbia)

187 is hereby agreed that the laying up period, in which either the com-
188 mencing or ending date of this Policy falls, shall be deemed to run
189 from the first day on which the Vessel is laid up and that on this basis
190 Underwriters shall pay such proportion of the return due in respect of
191 a full period of thirty days as the number of days attaching thereto
192 bears to thirty.

193 12. Warranted to be subject to Canadian law and usage as to liability
194 for and settlement of any and all claims.

Appendix 70

BRITISH COLUMBIA HULL (FIRE AND TOTAL LOSS FROM MARINE PERILS) FORM – 1962

1 (1) This insurance covers:—
2   (a) loss and/or damage caused by or arising from fire
3   and/or explosion and/or lightning
4   (b) total and/or constructive total loss from marine perils,
5   as enumerated in Clause No. 2.

6   (2) Touching the Adventures and Perils which we, the assurers,
7 are contented to bear and take upon us, they are of the Seas,
8 Men-of-War, Fire, Enemies, Pirates, Rovers, Thieves, Jettisons,
9 Letters of Mart and Counter-Mart, Surprisals, Takings at Sea,
10 Arrests, Restraints and Detainments of all Kings, Princes and
11 Peoples, of what nation, condition or quality soever, Barratry of
12 the Master and Mariners and of all other like Perils, Losses and
13 Misfortunes that have or shall come to the Hurt, Detriment or
14 Damage of the said Vessel, &c., or any part thereof; excepting,
15 however, such of the foregoing Perils as may be excluded by pro-
16 visions elsewhere in these clauses or by endorsement.

17   (3) In case of any Loss or Misfortune arising from a peril in-
18 sured against hereunder it shall be lawful for the Assured, their
19 Factors, Servants and Assigns, to sue, labour and travel for, in, and
20 about the Defence, Safeguard and Recovery of the said Vessel, &c.,
21 or any part thereof, without prejudice to this insurance, to the
22 Charges whereof the Underwriters will contribute their proportion as
23 provided below. And it is expressly declared and agreed that no acts
24 of the Underwriters or Assured in recovering, saving or preserving
25 the property insured shall be considered as a waiver or acceptance
26 of abandonment.

27   (4) The vessel is covered subject to the provisions of this policy
28 as employment may offer, in port and at sea, in docks and graving
29 docks, and on ways, gridirons and pontoons, at all times, in all
30 places, and on all occasions, services and trades whatsoever and
31 wheresoever, under steam, motor power or sail: with leave to sail
32 or navigate with or without pilots, to go on trial trips and to
33 assist and tow vessels or craft in distress, but if without the ap-
34 proval of Underwriters the Vessel be towed, except as is customary
35 or when in need of assistance, or undertakes towage or salvage
36 services under a pre-arranged contract made by Owners and/or
37 Charterers, the Assured shall notify Underwriters immediately and
38 pay an additional premium if required but no such premium shall
39 be required for customary towage by the Vessel in connection with
40 loading and discharging. With liberty to discharge, exchange and
41 take on board goods, specie, passengers and stores, wherever the
42 Vessel may call at or proceed to, and with liberty to carry goods,
43 live cattle, &c., on deck or otherwise.

94   (9) In no case shall Underwriters be liable for unrepaired
95 damage in addition to a subsequent total loss sustained during the
96 terms covered by this Policy or extension thereof.

97   (10) In ascertaining whether the Vessel is a constructive total
98 loss the insured value shall be taken as the repaired value, and
99 nothing in respect of the damage or break-up value of the Vessel
100 or wreck shall be taken into account.

101   (11) In the event of total or constructive total loss, no claim
102 to be made by the Underwriters for freight, whether notice of
103 abandonment has been given or not.

104   (12) In the event of accident whereby loss or damage may
105 result in a claim under this Policy, notice shall be given in writing
106 to the Underwriters, where practicable, prior to survey, so that they
107 may appoint their own surveyor if they so desire. The Underwriters
108 shall be entitled to decide the port to which a damaged Vessel shall
109 proceed for docking or repairing (the actual additional expense of
110 the voyage arising from compliance with Underwriters' requirements
111 being refunded to the Assured) and Underwriters shall also have a
112 right of veto in connection with the place of repair or repairing
113 firm proposed and whenever the extent of the damage is ascertain-
114 able the majority (in amount) of the Underwriters may take or may
115 require the lowest tenders for the repair of such damage.

116   In the event of failure to comply with the conditions of this
117 clause, 15 per cent. shall be deducted from the amount of the
118 ascertained claim.

119   (13) In the event of any change, voluntary or otherwise, in the
120 ownership of the Vessel or if the Vessel be placed under new man-
121 agement or be chartered on a bareboat basis or requisitioned on
122 that basis, then, unless the Underwriters agree thereto in writing,
123 this Policy shall thereupon become cancelled from time of such
124 change in ownership or management, charter or requisition: pro-
125 vided, however, that in the case of an involuntary temporary trans-
126 fer by requisition or otherwise, without the prior execution of any
127 written agreement by the Assured, such cancellation shall take
128 place fifteen days after such transfer; and provided further that
129 if the Vessel has cargo on board and has already sailed from her
130 loading port, or is at sea in ballast, such cancellation shall be
131 suspended until arrival at final port of discharge if with cargo or
132 at port of destination if in ballast. This insurance shall not insure
133 to the benefit of any such charterer or transferee of the Vessel,
134 and if a loss payable hereunder should occur between such trans-
135 fer and such cancellation the Underwriters shall be subrogated to
136 all the rights of the Assured against the transferee, by reason of

(5) Held covered in case of any breach of warranty as to cargo, trade, locality, towage, salvage services or date of sailing, provided notice be given immediately after receipt of advices and any additional premium required be agreed.

(6) General Average, Salvage and Special Charges (arising from fire and/or explosion and/or lightning) payable as provided in the contract of affreightment, or failing such provision, or there be no contract of affreightment, payable in accordance with the York Antwerp Rules. Provided always that when an adjustment according to the laws and usages of the port of destination is properly demanded by the owners of the cargo, General Average shall be paid in accordance with same.

When the contributory value of the Vessel is greater than the valuation herein the liability of these Underwriters for General Average contribution (except in respect to amount made good to the Vessel) or Salvage shall not exceed that proportion of the total contribution due from the Vessel that the amount insured hereunder bears to the contributory value; and if because of damage for which these Underwriters are liable as Particular Average the value of the Vessel has been reduced for the purpose of contribution, the amount of the Particular Average loss under this Policy shall be deducted from the amount insured hereunder and these Underwriters shall be liable only for the proportion which such net amount bears to the contributory value.

(7) In the event of expenses being incurred pursuant to the Suing and Labouring Clause arising from a peril insured against hereunder the liability under this Policy shall not exceed the proportion of such expenses that the amount insured hereunder bears to the value of the Vessel as stated herein, or to the sound value of the Vessel at the time of the occurrence giving rise to the expenditure if the sound value exceeds that value. Where Underwriters have admitted a claim for total loss and property insured by this Policy is saved, the foregoing provisions shall not apply unless the expenses of suing and labouring exceed the value of such property saved and then shall apply only to the amount of the expenses which is in excess of such value.

Where a claim for total loss of the Vessel is admitted under this Policy and expenses have been reasonably incurred in salving or attempting to salve the Vessel and other property and there are no proceeds, or the expenses exceed the proceeds, then this Policy shall bear its pro rata share of such proportion of the expenses, or of the expenses in excess of the proceeds, as the case may be, as may reasonably be regarded as having been incurred in respect of the Vessel; but if the Vessel be insured for less than its sound value at the time of the occurrence giving rise to the expenditure, the amount recoverable under this clause shall be reduced in proportion to the under-insurance.

(8) Average payable irrespective of percentage without deduction of thirds new for old whether the Average be Particular or General.

such transfer, in respect of all or part of such loss as is recoverable from the transferee and in the proportion which the respective amounts insured bear to the insured value. A pro rata daily return of net premium shall be made. The foregoing provisions with respect to cancellation in the event of change in ownership or management, charter or requisition shall apply even in the case of insurance "for account of whom it may concern."

(14) If payment of premium is not made by the Assured within thirty (30) days after attachment of the insurance, or, in the event the Underwriters shall have agreed to accept deferred payments, if any payment of any premium is not made on the day agreed, this Policy may be cancelled at any time thereafter by the Underwriter giving to the Assured named herein, and to third party payee or payees (if any) named in the policy, five (5) days' notice of such cancellation.

Such notice may be given by the Underwriter or on his behalf by an authorized Agent or by the Agent or Broker effecting this insurance.

Such cancellation shall be without prejudice to the premiums earned and due for the period the policy was in force.

In event of Total or Constructive Total Loss occurring prior to cancellation full annual premium shall be deemed earned.

(15) To return.........per cent. net for every thirty days of unexpired time if it be mutually agreed to cancel this Policy, but no returns whatsoever to be paid in case of loss of the Vessel.

(16) Should the Vessel at the expiration of this Policy be at sea, or in distress, or at a port of refuge or of call, she shall, provided previous notice be given to the Underwriters, be held covered at a pro rata monthly premium to her port of destination.

(17) Notwithstanding anything to the contrary contained in these clauses, warranted free of capture, seizure, arrest, restraint or detainment, and the consequences thereof or of any attempt thereat; also from the consequences of hostilities or warlike operations, whether there be a declaration of war or not; but this warranty shall not exclude collision, contact with any fixed or floating object (other than a mine or torpedo), stranding, heavy weather or fire unless caused directly (and independently of the nature of the voyage or service which the Vessel concerned or, in the case of a collision, any other vessel involved therein, is performing) by a hostile act by or against a belligerent power; and for the purpose of this warranty "power" includes any authority maintaining naval, military or air forces in association with a power.

Further warranted free from the consequences of civil war, revolution, rebellion, insurrection, or civil strife arising therefrom, or piracy.

(18) Warranted to be subject to English law and usage as to liability for and settlement of any and all claims.

Appendix 71

BRITISH COLUMBIA HULL (FIRE ONLY) FORM - 1954

1   (1) Covering only loss and/or damage caused by or arising from
2 fire and/or explosion and/or lightning, including General Average
3 and/or Salvage Charges arising from fire and/or explosion and/or
4 lightning.

5   (2) In case of any Loss or Misfortune arising from a peril insured
6 against hereunder it shall be lawful for the Assured, their Factors,
7 Servants and Assigns, to sue, labour and travel for, in, and about
8 the Defence, Safeguard and Recovery of the said Vessel, &c., or any
9 part thereof, without prejudice to this Insurance, to the Charges
10 whereof the Underwriters will contribute their proportion as provided
11 below. And it is expressly declared and agreed that no acts of the
12 Underwriters or Assured in recovering, saving or preserving the
13 property insured shall be considered as a waiver or acceptance of
14 abandonment.

15   (3) The vessel is covered subject to the provisions of this policy
16 as employment may offer, in port and at sea, in docks and graving
17 docks, and on ways, gridirons and pontoons, at all times, in all
18 places, and on all occasions, services and trades whatsoever and
19 wheresoever, under steam, motor power or sail; with leave to sail
20 or navigate with or without pilots, to go on trial trips and to
21 assist and tow vessels or craft in distress, but if without the ap-
22 proval of Underwriters the Vessel be towed, except as is customary
23 or when in need of assistance, or undertakes towage or salvage
24 services under a pre-arranged contract made by Owners and/or
25 Charterers, the Assured shall notify Underwriters immediately and
26 pay an additional premium if required but no such premium shall
27 be required for customary towage by the Vessel in connection with
28 loading and discharging. With liberty to discharge, exchange and
29 take on board goods, specie, passengers and stores, wherever the
30 Vessel may call at or proceed to, and with liberty to carry goods,
31 live cattle, &c., on deck or otherwise.

32   (4) Held covered in case of any breach of warranty as to cargo,
33 trade, locality, towage, salvage services or date of sailing, provided
34 notice be given immediately after receipt of advices and any ad-
35 ditional premium required be agreed.

36   (5) General Average, Salvage and Special Charges (arising from
37 a peril insured against hereunder) payable as provided in the contract

88 or wreck shall be taken into account.

89   (10) In the event of total or constructive total loss, no claim
90 to be made by the Underwriters for freight, whether notice of
91 abandonment has been given or not.

92   (11) In the event of accident whereby loss or damage may
93 result in a claim under this Policy, notice shall be given in writing
94 to the Underwriters, where practicable, prior to survey, so that they
95 may appoint their own surveyor if they so desire. The Underwriters
96 shall be entitled to decide the port to which a damaged Vessel shall
97 proceed for docking or repairing (the actual additional expense of
98 the voyage arising from compliance with Underwriters' requirements
99 being refunded to the Assured) and Underwriters shall also have a
100 right of veto in connection with the place of repair or repairing firm
101 proposed and whenever the extent of the damage is ascertainable
102 the majority (in amount) of the Underwriters may take or may re-
103 quire to be taken tenders for the repair of such damage.

104   In the event of failure to comply with the conditions of this
105 clause, 15 per cent. shall be deducted from the amount of the
106 ascertained claim.

107   (12) In the event of any change, voluntary or otherwise, in the
108 ownership of the Vessel or if the Vessel be placed under new man-
109 agement or be chartered on a bareboat basis or requisitioned on
110 that basis, then, unless the Underwriters agree thereto in writing,
111 this Policy shall thereupon become cancelled from time to time of such
112 change in ownership or management, charter or requisition; pro-
113 vided, however, that in the case of an involuntary temporary trans-
114 fer by requisition or otherwise, without the prior execution of any
115 written agreement by the Assured, such cancellation shall take
116 place fifteen days after such transfer; and provided further that
117 if the Vessel has cargo on board and has already sailed from her
118 loading port, or is at sea in ballast, such cancellation shall be
119 suspended until arrival at final port of discharge if with cargo or
120 at port of destination if in ballast. This insurance shall not inure
121 to the benefit of any such charterer or transferee of the Vessel,
122 and if a loss payable hereunder should occur between such trans-
123 fer and such cancellation the Underwriters shall be subrogated to
124 all the rights of the Assured against the transferee, by reason of

38 or affreightment, or failing such provision, or there be no contract of
39 affreightment, payable in accordance with the York Antwerp Rules.
40 Provided always that when an adjustment according to the laws and
41 usages of the port of destination is properly demanded by the
42 owners of the cargo, General Average shall be paid in accordance
43 with same.

44 When the contributory value of the Vessel is greater than the
45 valuation herein the liability of these Underwriters for General
46 Average contribution (except in respect to amount made good to the
47 Vessel) or Salvage shall not exceed that proportion of the total
48 contribution due from the Vessel that the amount insured hereunder
49 bears to the contributory value; and if because of damage for which
50 these Underwriters are liable as Particular Average the value of the
51 Vessel has been reduced for the purpose of contribution, the amount
52 of the Particular Average loss under this Policy shall be deducted
53 from the amount insured hereunder and these Underwriters shall be
54 liable only for the proportion which such net amount bears to the
55 contributory value.

56 (6) In the event of expenses being incurred pursuant to the
57 Suing and Labouring Clause arising from a peril insured against
58 hereunder the liability under this Policy shall not exceed the pro-
59 portion of such expenses that the amount insured hereunder bears
60 to the value of the Vessel as stated herein, or to the sound value
61 of the Vessel at the time of the occurrence giving rise to the
62 expenditure if the sound value exceeds that value. Where Under-
63 writers have admitted a claim for total loss and property insured by
64 this Policy is saved, the foregoing provisions shall not apply unless
65 the expenses of suing and labouring exceed the value of such
66 property saved and then shall apply only to the amount of the
67 expenses which is in excess of such value.

68 Where a claim for total loss of the Vessel is admitted under
69 this Policy and expenses have been reasonably incurred in salving
70 or attempting to salve the Vessel and other property and there
71 are no proceeds, or the expenses exceed the proceeds, then this
72 Policy shall bear its pro rata share of such proportion of the ex-
73 penses, or of the expenses in excess of the proceeds, as the case
74 may be, as may reasonably be regarded as having been incurred
75 in respect of the Vessel; but if the Vessel be insured for less than
76 its sound value at the time of the occurrence giving rise to such
77 expenditure, the amount recoverable under this clause shall be
78 reduced in proportion to the under-insurance.

79 (7) In no case shall Underwriters be liable for unrepaired
80 damage in addition to a subsequent total loss sustained during the
81 term covered by this Policy or extension thereof.

82 (8) Average payable irrespective of percentage without deduc-
83 tion of thirds new for old whether the Average be Particular or
84 General.

85 (9) In ascertaining whether the Vessel is a constructive total
86 loss the insured value shall be taken as the repaired value, and
87 nothing in respect of the damage or break-up value of the Vessel

125 such transfer, in respect of all or part of such loss as is recover-
126 able from the transferee and in the proportion which the respective
127 amounts insured bear to the insured value. A pro rata daily return
128 of net premium shall be made. The foregoing provisions with re-
129 spect to cancellation in the event of change in ownership or man-
130 agement, charter or requisition shall apply even in the case of
131 insurance "for account of whom it may concern."

132 (13) If payment of premium is not made by the Assured within
133 thirty (30) days after attachment of the insurance, or, in the event
134 the Underwriters shall have agreed to accept deferred payments, if
135 any payment of any premium is not made on the day agreed, this
136 policy may be cancelled at any time thereafter by the Underwriter
137 giving to the Assured named herein, and to third party payee or
138 payees (if any) named in the policy, five (5) days' notice of such
139 cancellation.

140 Such notice may be given by the Underwriter or on his behalf
141 by an authorized Agent or by the Agent or Broker effecting this
142 insurance.

143 Such cancellation shall be without prejudice to the premiums
144 earned and due for the period the policy was in force.

145 In event of Total or Constructive Total Loss occurring prior to
146 cancellation full annual premium shall be deemed earned.

147 (14) To return _____ per cent. net for every thirty
148 days of unexpired time if it be mutually agreed to cancel this
149 Policy, but no returns whatsoever to be paid in case of loss of the
150 Vessel.

151 (15) Should the Vessel at the expiration of this Policy be at sea,
152 or in distress, or at a port of refuge or of call, she shall, provided
153 previous notice be given to the Underwriters, be held covered at a
154 pro rata monthly premium to her port of destination.

155 (16) Notwithstanding anything to the contrary contained in these
156 clauses, warranted free of capture, seizure, arrest, restraint or de-
157 tainment, and the consequences thereof or of any attempt thereat;
158 also from the consequences of hostilities or warlike operations,
159 whether there be a declaration of war or not; but this warranty
160 shall not exclude collision, contact with any fixed or floating object
161 (other than a mine or torpedo), stranding, heavy weather or fire
162 unless caused directly (and independently of the nature of the
163 voyage or service which the Vessel concerned or, in the case of a
164 collision, any other vessel involved therein, is performing) by a
165 hostile act by or against a belligerent power; and for the purpose
166 of this warranty "power" includes any authority maintaining naval,
167 military or air forces in association with a power.

168 Further warranted free from the consequences of civil war, revo-
169 lution, rebellion, insurrection, or civil strife arising therefrom, or
170 piracy.

171 (17) Warranted to be subject to English law and usage as to
172 liability for and settlement of any and all claims.

Appendix 72

CANADIAN (Pacific) SCOW CARGO CLAUSES — 1966

1. It is understood and agreed that this risk attaches from the time of commencement of loading the cargo on board the vessel for shipment and continues during the ordinary course of transit until discharge at destination.

This insurance shall remain in force (subject to termination as provided for above) during delay beyond the control of the Assured, any deviation, forced discharge, reshipment or transhipment and during any variation of the adventure arising from the exercise of a liberty granted to shipowners or charterers under the contract of affreightment, but shall in no case be deemed to extend to cover loss damage or expense proximately caused by delay or inherent vice or nature of the subject matter insured.

2. Warranted Free from Particular Average unless directly caused by the vessel being stranded, sunk, or burnt, but notwithstanding this warranty, Underwriters to pay for:

(a) any loss of or damage to the interest insured which may reasonably be attributed to fire, explosion, collision or contact of the vessel with any external substance (ice included) other than water,

(b) loss or damage directly caused by jettison, fortuitous washing and/or failing overboard or by capsizing of the carrying vessel,

(c) accidental physical loss or damage to the interest insured occurring whilst being loaded on or unloaded from the carrying vessel or caused by other interests being moved during the process of loading or unloading from the carrying vessel.

(d) special charges for landing warehousing and forwarding if incurred at an intermediate port of call or refuge, for which Underwriters would be liable under the standard form of English Marine Policy with Institute Cargo Clauses (W.A.) attached.

3. Held covered at a premium to be arranged in case of change of voyage or of any omission or error in the description of the interest vessel or voyage.

4. No claim for Constructive Total Loss shall be recoverable hereunder unless the goods are reasonably abandoned either on account of their actual total loss appearing to be unavoidable or because the cost of recovering, reconditioning, and forwarding the goods to the destination to which they are insured would exceed their value on arrival.

5. General Average and Salvage Charges payable according to Foreign Statement or to York-Antwerp Rules if in accordance with the contract of affreightment.

6. The seaworthiness of the vessel as between the Assured and Underwriters is hereby admitted.

In the event of loss the Assured's right of recovery hereunder shall not be prejudiced by the fact that the loss may have been attributable to the wrongful act or misconduct of the shipowners or their servants, committed without the privity of the Assured.

7. It is the duty of the Assured and their Agents, in all cases, to take such measures as may be reasonable for the purpose of averting or minimising a loss and to ensure that all rights against carriers, bailees or other third parties are properly preserved and exercised.

8. This insurance shall not inure to the benefit of the carrier or other bailee.

9. This insurance is extended to indemnify the Assured against such proportion of liability under the contract of affreightment "Both to Blame Collision" Clause as is in respect of a loss recoverable hereunder.

In the event of any claim by shipowners under the said Clause the Assured agree to notify the Underwriters who shall have the right, at their own cost and expense, to defend the Assured against such claim.

10. Warranted free of capture, seizure, arrest, restraint or detainment, and the consequences thereof or of any attempt thereat; also from the consequences of hostilities or warlike operations, whether there be a declaration of war or not: but this warranty shall not exclude collision, contact with any fixed or floating object (other than a mine or torpedo), stranding, heavy weather or fire unless caused directly (and independently of the nature of the voyage or service which the vessel concerned or, in the case of a collision, any other vessel involved therein, is performing) by a hostile act by or against a belligerent power; and for the purpose of this warranty "power" includes any authority maintaining naval, military or air forces in association with a power.

Further warranted free from the consequences of civil war, revolution, rebellion, insurrection, or civil strife arising therefrom, or piracy.

SHOULD CLAUSE NO. 10 BE DELETED, THE RELEVANT CURRENT INSTITUTE WAR CLAUSES SHALL BE DEEMED TO FORM PART OF THIS INSURANCE.

11. Warranted free of loss or damage

(a) caused by strikers, locked-out workmen, or persons taking part in labour disturbances, riots or civil commotions;

(b) resulting from strikes, lock-outs, labour disturbances, riots or civil commotions.

SHOULD CLAUSE NO. 11 BE DELETED, THE RELEVANT CURRENT INSTITUTE STRIKES, RIOTS AND CIVIL COMMOTIONS CLAUSES SHALL BE DEEMED TO FORM PART OF THIS INSURANCE.

12. IT IS A CONDITION OF THIS INSURANCE THAT THE ASSURED SHALL ACT WITH REASONABLE DESPATCH IN ALL CIRCUMSTANCES WITHIN THEIR CONTROL.

NOTE—It is necessary for the Assured when they become aware of an event which is "held covered" under this insurance to give prompt notice to Underwriters and the right to such cover is dependent upon compliance with this obligation.

Appendix 73

BRITISH COLUMBIA BUILDERS RISK FORM (1946)

....for account of themselves and/or any owner or owners of the vessel as interest may appear at the time of the happening of the loss. Loss, if any, payable in funds current in the Dominion of Canada to

....or order

do make insurance and cause to be insured to the amount of...

....Dollars

for the period of time commencing..(which is

warranted by the assured to be the date of laying of the keel) and ending...

or until delivery at...if delivered at an earlier date.

In the event of such delivery not being effected by...

this policy may be extended at................................monthly additional premium provided notice of the

extension be given to this Underwriter prior to..

In no case shall this insurance extend beyond delivery of the vessel.

In the event of cancellation to return...............per cent. net for each uncommenced month cancelled, but such return shall not exceed in all...

On Hull, Tackle, Apparel, Ordnance, Munitions, Artillery, Engines, Boilers, Machinery, Appurtenances, etc. (including plans, patterns, moulds, etc.) Boats and other Furniture and Fixtures and all material belonging to and/or destined for.............

....................building at

....

....
as per clauses hereinbelow specified.

This policy does not cover any materials, apparel, furniture and equipment for this vessel furnished by the owner, the cost of which is not included in the construction contract price, but permission is granted to effect additional insurance covering the value of such material, etc.

In the event of loss the underwriters shall not be liable for a greater proportion thereof than the amount of this insurance bears to the completed contract price.

This Underwriter to be paid in consideration of this insurance ....Dollars

being at the rate of...............per cent.

TOUCHING the Adventures and Perils which we, ...id Underwriters, are contented to bear and take upon us, they are of the Seas, Men-of-War, Fire, Enemies, Pirates, Rovers, T....ves, Jettisons, Letters of Mart and Counter-Mart, Surprisals, Takings at Sea, Arrests, Restraints and Detainments of all Kings, Princes and Peoples, of what nation, condition or quality soever, Barratry of the Master and Mariners, and of all other like Perils, Losses and Misfortunes that have or shall come to the Hurt, Detriment or Damage of the said Vessel, etc., or any part thereof; excepting, however, such of the foregoing Perils as may be excluded by provisions elsewhere in the Policy or by endorsement. And in case of any loss or misfortune it shall be lawful for the Assured, their factors, servants and assigns, to sue, labor and travel for, in, and about the defence, safeguard and recovery of the said ship, etc., or any part thereof, without prejudice to this insurance; to the charges whereof the said Underwriter will contribute according to the Rate and Quantity of the sum herein assured. And it is expressly declared and agreed that no acts of the Underwriter or insured in recovering, saving or preserving the property insured shall be considered as a waiver or acceptance of abandonment. With leave to sail with or without pilots, to tow and be towed, and to assist vessels and/or craft in all situations and to any extent, and to go on trial trips. With liberty to discharge, exchange, and take on board goods, specie, passengers, and stores, wherever the vessel may call at or proceed to. Including all risks of docking, undocking, changing docks, or moving in harbour and going on or off gridiron, slipways, graving docks, and/or pontoons or dry docks as often as may be done during the currency of this policy.

CLAUSES FOR BUILDERS RISKS

1. This Insurance is also to cover all risks, including fire, while under construction and/or fitting out, including materials in Buildings, wo: ps, yards and docks of the Assured, or on quays, pontoons, craft, etc., and all risks while in transit to and from the works and/or the vessel wherever she may be lying, also all risks of loss or damage through collapse of supports or ways from any cause whatever, and all risks of launching and breakage of the ways.

2. This Insurance is also to cover all risks of trial trips, loaded or otherwise, as often as required, and all risks whilst proceeding to and returning from the trial course but warranted that all trials shall be

one or both of such Vessels becomes limited by law, claims under this clause shall be settled on the principle of cross-liabilities as if the Owners of each Vessel had been compelled to pay to the Owners of the other of such Vessels such one-half or other proportion of the latter's damage as may have been properly allowed in ascertaining the balance or sum payable by or to the Assured in consequence of such collision.

And it is further agreed that the principles involved in this clause shall apply to the case where both Vessels are the property, in part or in whole, of the same owners, all questions of responsibility and amount of liability as between the two Ships being left to the decision of a single Arbitrator, if the parties can agree upon a single Arbitrator, or failing such agreement, to the decision of Arbitrators, one to be appointed by the managing owners of both Vessels, and one to be appointed by the majority in amount of Underwriters interested in each Vessel; the two Arbitrators chosen to choose a third Arbitrator before entering upon the reference, and the decision of such single, or of any two of such three Arbitrators, appointed as above, to be final and binding.

This clause shall also extend to any sum which the Assured may become liable to pay, or shall pay for removal of obstructions under statutory powers, for injury to harbours, wharves, piers, stages, and similar structures, or for loss of life or personal injury consequent on such collision.

PROTECTION AND INDEMNITY CLAUSE

14. It is further agreed that if the Assured by reason of its interest in the insured ship or the Surety for the Assured in consequence of its undertaking shall become liable to pay and shall pay any sum or sums in respect of any responsibility, claim, demand, damages, and/or expenses arising from or occasioned by any of the following matters or things during the currency of this policy, that is to say:—

Loss of or damage to any other ship or goods, merchandise, freight, or other things or interests, whatsoever, on board such other ship, caused proximately or otherwise by the ship insured in so far as the same is not covered by the running down clause set out above:

Loss or damage to any goods, merchandise, freight, or other things or interest whatsoever, other than as aforesaid (not being builders' gear or material or cargo on the insured ship), whether on board the insured ship or not, which may arise from any cause whatsoever:

Loss of or damage to any harbour, dock (graving or otherwise), slipway, way, gridiron, pontoon, pier, quay, jetty, stage, buoy, telegraph cable or other fixed or movable thing whatsoever, or to any goods or property in or on the same, howsoever caused:

Any attempted or actual raising, removal, or destruction of the wreck of the insured ship or the cargo thereof, or any neglect or failure to raise, remove, or destroy the same:

Any sum or sums for which the Assured may become liable or incur from causes not hereinbefore specified, but which are absolutely or conditionally recoverable from or undertaken by the Liverpool and London Steamship Protection and Indemnity Association Limited, and/or North of England Protecting and Indemnity Association, but excluding loss of life and personal injury and matters expressly excluded from any of the above clauses:

the Underwriters will pay the Assured such proportion of such sum or sums so paid, or which may be required to indemnify the Assured for such loss, as their respective subscriptions bear to the insured value of the ship hereby insured, provided always that the amount recoverable hereunder in respect of any one accident or series of accidents arising out of the same event shall not exceed the sum hereby insured, and where the liability of the Assured has been contested with the consent in writing of a majority (in amount) of the Underwriters on the ship hereby insured, the Underwriters will also pay a like proportion of the

carried out within a distance by water of 100 nautical miles of the place of construction or held covered at a rate to be arranged.

3. With leave to proceed to and from any wet or dry docks, harbours, ways, cradles, and pontoons during the currency of this policy.

4. With leave to fire guns and torpedoes but no claim to attach hereto for loss of or damage to same or to ship or machinery unless the accident results in the total loss of the Vessel.

5. In case of failure to launch, underwriters to bear all subsequent expenses incurred in completing launch.

6. Average payable irrespective of percentage, and without deduction of one-third, whether the Average be particular or general.

7. General Average and Salvage to be adjusted according to the law and practice obtaining at the place where the adventure ends, as if the contract of affreightment contained no special terms upon the subject; but where the contract of affreightment so provides the adjustment shall be according to York-Antwerp Rules 1890 (omitting in the case of wool cargoes the first word, "No," of Rule 1) or York-Antwerp Rules 1924; and in the event of Salvage, towage, or other assistance being rendered to the Vessel hereby insured by any Vessel belonging in part or in whole to the same owners, it is hereby agreed that the value of such services (without regard to the common ownership of the Vessels) shall be ascertained by Arbitration in the manner hereinafter provided for under "Collision Clause," and the amount so awarded, so far as applicable to the interest hereby insured, shall constitute a charge under this policy.

8. In event of deviation to be held covered at an additional premium to be hereafter arranged.

9. ... to cover while building all damage to hull, machinery, apparel, materials, or furniture, caused by settling of the stocks, or failure or breakage of shores, blocking or staging, or of hoisting or other gear, either before or after launching and while fitting out.

10. It is agreed that any changes of interest in the vessel hereby insured shall not affect the validity of this policy.

11. And it is expressly declared and agreed that no acts of the Underwriter or Insured, in recovering, saving, or preserving the property insured shall be considered as a waiver or acceptance of abandonment.

12. This Insurance also specially to cover loss of or damage to the hull or machinery, through negligence of Master, Mariners, Engineers or Pilots, or through explosions, bursting of boilers, breakage of shafts, or through any latent defect in the Machinery, or Hull, or from other causes, Arising either on shore or otherwise, causing loss of or injury to the property hereby insured, provided such loss or damage has not resulted from want of due diligence by the Owners of the Ship or any of them, or by the Manager, and to cover all risks incidental to navigation, or in graving docks.

COLLISION CLAUSE

13. And it is further agreed that if the Ship hereby insured shall come into collision with any other Ship or Vessel, and the Assured in consequence thereof or the Surety for them in consequence of their undertaking shall become liable to pay, and shall pay by way of damages to any other person or persons any sum or sums in respect of such

collision the Underwriters will pay the Assured such proportion of such sum or sums so paid as their respective subscriptions hereto bear to the insured value of the Ship hereby insured, provided always, that their liability in respect of any one such collision shall not exceed their proportionate part of the value of the Ship hereby insured, and in cases in which the liability of the ship has been contested, or proceedings have been taken to limit liability, with the consent in writing of a majority (in amount) of the Underwriters on the Hull and/or Machinery, we, the Underwriters, will also pay a like proportion of the costs which the Assured shall thereby incur, or be compelled to pay; but when both Vessels are to blame, then, unless the liability of the Owners of

costs which the Assured shall thereby incur or be compelled to pay.

15. It is agreed that no assignment of or interest in this policy or in any moneys which may be or become payable thereunder is to be binding on or recognized by the Underwriters unless a dated notice of such assignment or interest signed by the Assured and (in the case of subsequent assignment) by the assignor be endorsed on this policy and the policy with such endorsement be produced before payment of any claim or return of premium thereunder. But nothing in this clause is to have effect as an agreement by the Underwriters to a sale or transfer to new management.

Unless physically deleted by the Underwriters, the following warranty shall be paramount and shall supersede and nullify any contrary provision of the Policy including any endorsements or attachments thereto:

Warranted free of capture, seizure, arrest, restraint, or detainment, and the consequences thereof or of any attempt thereat; also from the consequences of hostilities or warlike operations, whether there be a declaration of war or not; but this warranty shall not exclude collision, contact with any fixed or floating object (other than a mine or torpedo), stranding, heavy weather or fire unless caused directly (and independently of the nature of the voyage or service which the vessel concerned or, in the case of a collision, any other vessel involved therein, is performing) by a hostile act by or against a belligerent power; and for the purpose of this warranty "power" includes any authority maintaining naval, military or air forces in association with a power.

Further warranted free from the consequences of civil war, revolution, rebellion, insurrection, or civil strife arising therefrom, or piracy.

If war risks are hereafter insured by endorsement on the Policy, such endorsement shall supersede the above warranty only to the extent that their terms are inconsistent and only while such war risk endorsement remains in force.

NOTWITHSTANDING THE FOREGOING, this Policy is:—

(A) Warranted free from any claim arising directly or indirectly under Workmen's Compensation or Employers Liability Acts and any other Statutory or Common Law liability in respect of accidents to any person or persons whomsoever, excepting claims payable under the Collision Clause above set forth.

(B) Warranted free of loss or damage caused by strikers, locked-out workmen or persons taking part in labour disturbances or riots or civil commotions.

(C) Warranted free of loss or damage caused by earthquake.

(D) Warranted free of any consequential damages or claims for loss through delay however caused.

(E) Warranted free from claim for loss or damage to engines, boilers and all other materials while in transport, except in the port at which the vessel is being built.

This policy shall not be vitiated by any unintentional error in description of interest or voyage, provided the same be communicated to Underwriters as soon as known to the Assured, and an additional premium paid if required.

The words "Owner" and "Assured" as used in this policy shall be interpreted to mean "Builder," "Owner" or both.

There shall be no recovery for a Constructive Total Loss under this policy unless the expense of recovering the vessel and restoring her to the condition she was in prior to the loss would exceed her value in that condition, which value shall be determined by applying to the completed contract price the percentage of the vessel which was completed on the ways, while being launched or after launching as the case may be at the time of the loss; and no claim for a Constructive Total Loss hereunder shall exceed this policy's proportion of the value so computed, plus this policy's proportion of any damage to material insured hereunder and not yet installed in the vessel, plus any salvage and special charges, and sue and labor expenses.

Nothing in this policy shall be construed to insure against or cover any loss, damage or expense in connection with docks, ship-ways, tools or any other property of the shipyard not intended to be incorporated in the vessel, excepting staging, scaffolding and similar temporary construction the value of which is included in the contract price of the vessel and excepting any loss, damage or expense for which Underwriters may be liable under the Protection and Indemnity clauses; provided, nevertheless, that in case of failure of launch, Underwriters shall bear all subsequent expenses incurred in completing launch.

Warranted to be subject to English Law and Usage as to liability for and settlement of any and all claims.

The terms and conditions of this form are to be regarded as substituted for those of the policy to which it is attached, the latter being hereby waived, except provisions required by law to be inserted in the policy.

Attached to Policy No._____ of the _____

Dated_____
_____
Association of Marine Underwriters of British Columbia

Appendix 74

1/7/73

MARINE INSURANCE- LOGS

Approved by the Association of Marine Underwriters of British Columbia

CONTRACTUAL CONDITIONS

Assurers:

In consideration of premium at rates to be agreed, does insure:

Assured:
  (1)

  (2) For account of whom it may concern.

Loss Payable:
  (3) Loss, if any, payable to:

Subject Matter Insured:
  (4) Upon logs (including piling, boomsticks and swifters), but excluding Alder, Maple and Cottonwood logs, unless otherwise specifically agreed upon prior to attachment of risk.

  The Assured has the privilege of insuring Chains and other Equipment, provided they specify their intention to do so prior to attachment of risk.

Wire Swiftered Rafts:
  (5) Unless otherwise agreed prior to attachment of risk, all wire swiftered flat booms are excluded from this Contract.

F.B.M. (or C.M.) Per Section:
  (6) It is understood and agreed that all booms averaging less than 20,000 F.B.M. (or equivalent C.M.) per section excepting such booms moving on the Fraser River and its tributaries, are subject to an additional premium to be agreed.
  NOTE: For the purpose of these clauses 1 CM = 6 FBM

Attachment Date:
  (7) This contract to be deemed continuous and to cover and attach on all shipments made on and after
          19

Valuation:
  (8) Valued at invoice value if logs are purchased or sold, or market value at destination if logs are unsold, exclusive of unearned towing charges, unless otherwise specially agreed upon prior to attachment of risk.

Geographical Limits:
  (9) To be insured, lost or not lost, at, from and between ports and/or places in British Columbia and/or the inside waters of Northwest Washington, but warranted flat and/or bundled booms are not covered while in transit to, from or between ports and/or places on the Queen Charlotte Islands or on the west coast of Vancouver Island between Owen Point and Cape Sutil.

Reporting Clause:
  (10) It is agreed that every shipment shall be reported to:
  at the end of each month with the following particulars of all booms or logs at the risk of these Underwriters during the preceding month.
    (a) Transit
        (i)   Number of logs
        (ii) Species
        (iii) Estimated measurement
        (iv) Date and location of attachment
        (v)   Destination
        (vi) Name of towing Vessel or Company or carrying vessel
    (b) Storage
        The assured agrees to keep an accurate record of all logs in storage and report the maximum total FBM (or equivalent CM) and value thereof during the previous 30 days.

  It is understood and agreed, however, that shipments insured hereunder are held covered in the event of inadvertent omission to declare such shipments; the Assured agreeing on their part to report any such omissions as soon as they are aware of same and to pay premium thereon.

It is understood and agreed that these Underwriters or their duly appointed representative shall be permitted at all reasonable times during the term of this policy, or within a year after its expiration, to inspect the property covered hereunder and to examine the Assured's books, records and such policies as are relevant to any property covered hereunder. This inspection and/or examination shall not waive nor in any manner affect any of the terms and conditions of this policy.

Construction:

(11) It is understood and agreed that so far as is possible all booms shall be constructed in accordance with the current log boom specifications published by the Marine Surveyors of Western Canada.

Limit of Liability:

(12) These Assurers are not to be liable under this contract for more than (a) $ any one tow
(b) $ any one barge
(c) $ any one location,
unless otherwise agreed upon in writing prior to the attachment of the risk.

Premiums:

(13) Premiums payable on all shipments coming under the terms of this Contract at rates shown hereafter, or as arranged.

Change of Ownership:

(14) Should the interest insured hereunder be sold at an intermediate storage ground, cover ceases immediately, unless permission to assign the cover is granted by the Underwriters or their Agent at an additional premium to be agreed.

Sue and Labour:

(15) In case of any loss or misfortune, it shall be lawful for the Assured, their Factors, Servants and Assigns, to sue, labour and travel for, in and about the Defence, Safeguard and Recovery of the subject matter of this insurance or any part thereof, without prejudice to this insurance; to the charges whereof, we, the Assurers, will contribute, each one rateably according to the amount of his subscription hereto. And it is specially declared and agreed that no acts of the Assurer or Assured in recovering, saving or preserving the property insured shall be considered as a waiver or acceptance of abandonment.

Cancellation:

(16) This Contract may be cancelled at any time by either party having given the other party Thirty (30) days' notice in writing, but such cancellation shall not prejudice any risk or risks which shall have already attached.

Canadian Law & Practice

(17) This insurance is understood and agreed to be subject to Canadian Law & Practice as to Liability for settlement of all claims. Should the Assurers own form of policy be attached hereto, these clauses shall supercede and annul any clauses of same or similar effect printed in such attached policy.

WARRANTIES

Boomsticks, Swifters and Other Equipment:

(1) Warranted that all boomsticks, swifters, chains, wire and other equipment used in making up any boom are fit and seaworthy for the intended voyage.

Reporting of Loss:

(2) Warranted that no loss shall be recoverable hereunder unless discovered and reported to Underwriters within ninety (90) days of the date of loss.

INSURING CONDITIONS

(1) Subject to the Assured having an insurable interest, this insurance shall attach on
  (a) Logs in Transit per:
    (i) Flat or Bundled Booms - at any time after the logs are made up into a flat or bundled boom and shall continue during the course of the voyage until the boom is sold or until commencement of the intentional breaking up of the boom at destination, whichever shall first occur, but for a period not to exceed forty-five (45) days in all. Provided notice in writing is given to these Underwriters prior to the expiry of the forty-five (45) days mentioned above and in consideration of an additional premium to be agreed for each consecutive 30 day period, or part thereof, it is understood and agreed that the insurance under this policy is extended to cover booms of logs in storage after the expiry of the original forty-five (45) day period.   *Commencement and Termination Clause*
    (ii) Log Barges - from the time of loading on board the barge and shall continue until all logs have been dumped at destination.
  (b) Logs in Approved Storage Grounds:
From the time of arrival or dumping and shall continue to time of removal or until commencement of the intentional breaking up of a boom whichever shall first occur.

(2) Subject to the provisions of the foregoing Clause and Clause 3 hereunder, this insurance shall remain in force during any deviation or delay in transit beyond the control of the Assured.   *Extended Cover Clause*

(3) If, owing to circumstances beyond the control of the Assured, either the Contract of Towage is terminated at a port or place other than the destination named therein or the adventure is otherwise terminated before delivery of the logs as provided in Clause 1(a) above then subject to prompt notice being given to Underwriters and to an additional premium if required, this insurance shall remain in force until either:
  (a) The logs are sold and delivered at such port or place, or
  (b) if the logs are forwarded within the said period of forty-five (45) days (or any agreed extension thereof) to the destination named in the policy or any other destination, until terminated in accordance with the provisions of clause 1(a) above.

(4) Each boom and/or barge load to be deemed a separate insurance.

Separate
Insurance
Clause

(5) Held covered at a premium to be arranged in case of change of voyage or of any omission or error in the description of the interest, towing vessel or voyage.

Change Of
Voyage
Clause

(6) This insurance is against all risks of:
    (a) Total loss of an entire boom or log barge shipment
    (b) Total loss of part of a boom or barge shipment or of logs in storage. Each claim for Total loss of part shall be subject to a deductible of

Perils
Clause

        $ each Boom
        $ each Barge
        $ any one Storage Location
and in addition thereto Hemlock and Balsam logs are subject to a deduction of six percent (6%) of the insured value of such logs, excluding Boomsticks and Swifters, contained in a boom or storage ground.

In no case shall this insurance extend to cover loss, damage or expense proximately caused by sinking of the insured interest, delay, inherent vice, or nature of the subject matter insured or arising through depreciation.

(7) To pay General Average, Salvage and/or Special Charges if properly incurred. All such charges incurred are limited to the actual cost to the Assured or their agents.

G.A. Clause

(8) Warranted no claim for services rendered by towing vessel for first twenty-four (24) hours after occurence of accident.

Salvage
Clause

(9) The seaworthiness of the towing vessel as between the Assured and Underwriters is hereby admitted.

In the event of loss the Assured's right of recovery hereunder shall not be prejudiced by the fact that the loss may have been attributable to the wrongful act or misconduct of the operators of the towing vessel or their servants, committed without the privity of the Assured.

Seaworthiness
Admitted
Clause

(10) It is the duty of the Assured and their Agents, in all cases, to take such measures as may be reasonable for the purpose of averting or minimizing a loss and to ensure that all rights against the operators of the towing vessel, bailees or other third parties are properly preserved and exercised.

Bailee
Clause

(11) This insurance shall not inure to the benefit of the operator of the towing vessel or other bailee.

Not To Inure
Clause

(12) Warranted free of capture, seizure, arrest, restraint or detainment, and the consequences thereof or of any attempt thereat, also from the consequences of hostilities or warlike operations, whether there be a declaration of war or not; but this warranty shall not exclude collision, contact with any fixed or floating object (other than a mine or torpedo), stranding, heavy weather or fire unless caused directly (and independently of the nature of the voyage or service which the vessel concerned, or in the case of a collision, any other vessel involved therein, is performing) by a hostile act by or against a belligerent power; and for the purpose of this warranty "power" includes any authority maintaining naval, military or air forces in association with a power. Further warranted free from the consequences of civil war, revolution, rebellion, insurrection, or civil strife arising therefrom, or piracy.
        Should Clause No. 12 be deleted, the relevant current Institute War Clauses shall be deemed to form part of this insurance.

F.C. & S.
Clause

(13) Warranted free of loss
    (a) Caused by strikers, locked-out workmen, or persons taking part in labor disturbances, riots, or civil commotions;
    (b) Resulting from strikes, lock-outs, labor disturbances, riots, or civil commotions;
        Should Clause No. 13 be deleted, the relevant current Institute Strikes, Riots and Civil Commotions Clause shall be deemed to form part of this insurance.

F.S.R. &
C.C. Clause

(14) It is a condition of this insurance that the Assured shall act with reasonable despatch in all circumstances within their control.

Reasonable
Despatch
Clause

Appendix 75

B.C. YACHT FORM (FULL COVER) 1964

In consideration of the premium hereinafter mentioned, these Assurers do hereby insure:

Upon the   Built

from Noon   to Noon

                                                         Pacific Standard Time

This Insurance is limited to those coverages named in the schedule below which are indicated by a premium set opposite thereto

COVERAGES	AMOUNT OF INSURANCE	AGREED VALUATION AS PER VALUATION CLAUSE IN SEC. A PAGE 2	RATE	PREMIUM
1 (a) Hull Insurance, as per Section A			%	$
1 (b) As per Endorsement attached			%	$
2 Land Transportation as included under Section A of these clauses within............miles of vessel's home port			%	$

	LOSS OF LIFE AND BODILY INJURY		PROPERTY DAMAGE
	LIMIT, ANY ONE PERSON	LIMIT, ANY ONE ACCIDENT	LIMIT, ANY ONE ACCIDENT
3 (a) Protection and Indemnity Insurance as per Section B of these clauses	$	$	$
3 (b) Medical Payments Insurance, as per Section C of these clauses	LIMIT, ANY ONE ACCIDENT $		
TOTAL PREMIUM			$

WARRANTED that the said vessel shall be laid up and out of commission from .... at noon P.S.T., until .... at noon P.S.T.

RETURN PREMIUMS FOR LAYUP

Return premium will be paid at the rate of ....% net for each period of 15 consecutive days during which the vessel, while at the risk of these Assurers, shall be laid up and out of commission during the navigating period, and arrival.

RETURN PREMIUMS FOR CANCELLATION

If this policy be cancelled, return premiums will be paid as follows:

(1) With respect to Coverage 1 (a) above, for each 15 consecutive days of unexpired time, of the navigating period, at the rate of ....% net; of the layup period at the rate of ....% net.

(2) With respect to Land Transportation Insurance, Coverage 2 above, no return of premium.

(3) With respect to Coverage 3 above:

Should this policy be cancelled in accordance with its terms by the Assured or by this Assurer after the premium has been paid return premium payable under this section shall be computed as follows:

Where this policy provides for six (6) months navigation or less, these Assurers shall return under this section of the policy 6% net of the annual premium for every fifteen (15) consecutive days of the unexpired time of the navigating period and 1% net of the annual premium for every fifteen (15) consecutive days of the unexpired time of the layup period. Minimum premium to be retained $10.00.

Where this policy provides for more than six (6) months navigation, these Assurers shall return 8% net of the annual premium for every fifteen (15) consecutive days of the unexpired time. Minimum premium to be retained $10.00.

SPECIAL CONDITIONS

GENERAL CONDITIONS

PRIVATE PLEASURE WARRANTY

Warranted to be used solely for private pleasure purposes and not to be chartered unless approval and permission is endorsed hereon.

TRANSFER OF INTEREST

Warranted this Insurance shall be void in case this policy or the interest insured thereby shall be sold or transferred without the previous consent in writing of these Assurers.

PRIVILEGES

To cover in port and at sea, at all times, in all places on shore or afloat, and on all occasions not conflicting with warranties and clauses contained herein and with leave to sail with or without pilots, to be towed by vessels, and to assist vessels in all situations.

CONTINUATION CLAUSE

If the vessel insured hereunder is at sea at the expiration of this policy this insurance may be continued until the vessel has been anchored or moored at her port of destination for twenty-four (24) hours in good safety, provided notice be given to these Assurers and additional premium paid as required.

NOTICE OF PAYMENT OF LOSS

In the event of any accident, loss, damage or injury for which claim may be made under this policy, the Assured must give immediate notice thereof to these Assurers or their authorized agent, as soon as such loss or accident becomes known to the Assured.

In case of loss covered by this policy, such loss to be paid within thirty (30) days after proof of loss and proof of interest in the said vessel, all indebtedness between the Assured and these Assurers being first deducted.

NOTICE OF CANCELLATION

This policy may be cancelled at any time at the Assured's request, or by these Assurers giving ten (10) days written notice of such cancellation, calculated from the time of receipt of the letter of cancellation at the Post Office, at the point of mailing.

TIME FOR SUIT

It is a condition of this policy that no suit, action or proceeding for the recovery of any claim under this policy shall be sustainable in any court of law or equity unless the same be commenced within twelve months next after the time a cause of action for the loss accrues. Provided, however, that if by the laws of the province within which this policy is issued such limitation is invalid, then any such claim shall be void unless such action, suit or proceeding be commenced within the shortest limit of time permitted, by the laws of such province, to be fixed therein.

NEGLIGENCE AND PRIVITY

Personal negligence or fault of the Assured in the navigation of the vessel or privity or knowledge in respect thereto (excepting loss, damage or liability wilfully or intentionally caused by the Assured) shall not relieve these Assurers of liability under this policy.

LEGAL REPRESENTATION AND COOPERATION CLAUSE

The Assured shall not assume any obligation or admit any liability for which the Assurers may be liable, without the written approval of the Assurers. In case the liability of the Assured shall be contested with the written approval of the Assurers first obtained, the Assurers will pay the cost and expense of such defense, in which event the Assurers shall have the option of naming the attorneys who shall represent the Assured in the said defense, and, if such option is exercised, shall have the exclusive direction and control thereof. The Assured shall, whenever required, attend hearings and trials and shall assist in effecting settlements, securing and giving evidence, obtaining the attendance of witnesses, and in the conduct of suits and limitation proceedings.

OMNIBUS CLAUSE

It is understood and agreed that the word Assured whenever used in the Collision Clause, Section A of these clauses, and in the Protection and Indemnity Insurance, Section B of these clauses, includes in addition to the named Assured any person, firm, corporation or other legal entity who may be operating the insured vessel with the prior permission of the named Assured, but does not include a paid master or a paid member of the crew of the insured vessel or a person, firm, corporation or other legal entity, or any agent or employee thereof, operating a shipyard, boat repair yard, marina, yacht club, sales agency, boat service station, or similar organization. Notwithstanding anything contained herein this insurance provided by this clause does not cover liability of such additional Assureds to the Assured and/or Assureds named in this policy. The insurance provided by this clause is conditional upon compliance by an Assured with all the terms, conditions and warranties applicable to the named Assured. Nothing contained in this clause shall be construed to increase the limits of the Assurers' liability as stated in the policy.

PROPORTION OF LOSSES COVERED

Where the amount of insurance as set forth in Coverage 1(a) is less than the Agreed Valuation stated therein, these Assurers shall be liable only for such proportion of any loss recoverable under this policy as the said amount of insurance bears to the said Agreed Valuation.

STRIKES AND RIOTS

Warranted free of loss or damage caused by strikers, locked out workmen or persons taking part in labor disturbances, riots or civil commotions.

F.C. AND S. CLAUSE

Unless physically deleted by these Assurers, the following warranty shall be paramount and shall supersede and nullify any contrary provision of these clauses:

Warranted free of capture, seizure, arrest, restraint or detainment, and the consequences thereof or of any attempt thereat; also from the consequences of hostilities or warlike operation, whether there be a declaration of war or not; but this warranty shall not exclude collision, contact with any fixed or floating object (other than a mine or torpedo), stranding heavy weather or fire unless caused directly (and independently of the nature of the voyage or service which the vessel concerned or, in the case of a collision, any other vessel involved therein, is performing) by a hostile act by or against a belligerent power; and for the purpose of this warranty "power" includes any authority maintaining naval, military or air forces in association with a power.

Further warranted free from the consequences of civil war, revolution, rebellion, insurrection, or civil strife arising therefrom, or piracy.

ENGLISH LAW AND USAGE

Warranted to be subject to English Law and Usage as to liability for and settlement of any and all claims.

SECTION A — HULL AND MACHINERY INSURANCE

COVERAGES

The insurance provided by this Section shall cover, subject to the exclusions, stipulations, conditions and warranties contained herein, afloat and ashore, against ALL RISKS of direct physical loss or damage including physical loss or damage directly caused by the following:

Explosions, bursting of boilers, breakage of shafts, or any latent defect in the Hull or Machinery (excluding the cost of repairing or replacing the defective part);

Negligence of Master, Mariners, Engineers or Pilots; providing such loss or damage has not resulted from want of due diligence by the Assured, or any of them, or by the Manager.

COLLISION CLAUSE

It is further agreed that if the vessel hereby insured shall come into collision while water borne, with any other vessel or craft, and the Assured shall, in consequence thereof, become legally liable to pay and shall pay by way of damages to any other person or persons any sum or sums in respect of such collision, the Assurers will pay the Assured such sum or sums so paid not exceeding in respect of any one such collision the total limit of liability specified in Coverage No. 1, "Agreed Valuation". And in cases where the liability of the Assured has been contested, with the consent, in writing, of the Assurers, the Assurers will also bear a like proportion of the costs and expenses that may be incurred in contesting the liability resulting from said collision.

PROVIDED always that the foregoing clause shall in no case extend to any sum which the Assured may become liable to pay, or shall pay for removal of obstructions under statutory powers, or for loss of life or personal injury.

PROPERTY COVERED

Upon the vessel including her sails, tackle, apparel, machinery, dinghies, tenders, outboard motors, furniture and such other equipment as is generally required aboard for the operation and maintenance of the vessel.

HULL VALUATION

The vessel, including all the property insured under this Section, for so much, as concerns the Assured by agreement between the Assured and these Assurers, is and shall be valued at the amount stated in "Agreed Valuation" on Page 1, but no recovery for a Total or Constructive Total Loss shall be had hereunder unless all said property is lost absolutely or unless the expenses of recovering and repairing the vessel shall exceed such amount.

DEDUCTIBLE

The sum of $ shall be deducted from each and every claim under this policy except for total and/or Constructive Total Loss.

Notwithstanding the foregoing, where the vessel is being loaded to or from, or conveyed in or on, any land conveyance a deductible of 5% of the insured value or a maximum of $250 whichever shall be the less, shall apply to each and every claim. For purposes of this clause, a marine railway, dockside crane or elevator are not to be regarded as land conveyances.

DEPRECIATION

Losses payable without deduction for depreciation, except in respect to sails, protective covers and running rigging. No deductions to be made for depreciation in the event of Total or Constructive Total Loss of the vessel due to perils insured against.

EQUIPMENT SEPARATED AND ON SHORE

It is also agreed that should any part of the furniture, tackle, boats, or other property of the said vessel be separated and laid up on shore during the period of this policy then this shall cover the same to an amount not exceeding   % of the sum stated under the heading "Amount of Insurance" in Coverage 1 on Page 1. The amount attaching on the said vessel shall be decreased by the amount so covered.

SUE AND LABOUR

In case of any loss or misfortune, it shall be lawful and necessary for the Assured, their factors, servants and assigns, to sue, labour and travel for, in and about the defense, safeguard and recovery of the said property or any part thereof, without prejudice to this insurance, to the charges whereof these Assurers will contribute their proportion, not exceeding the "Agreed Valuation" as specified in Coverage 1 on Page 1. And it is especially declared and agreed that no acts of these Assurers or the Assured in recovering, saving or preserving the property insured shall be considered as a waiver or acceptance of abandonment.

UNREPAIRED DAMAGE

In no case shall these Assurers be liable for unrepaired damage in addition to a subsequent total loss sustained during the period covered by this policy.

FIBERGLASS AND PATCH CLAUSE

If the hull of the insured vessel is made in whole or in part of Flywood, Plastic, Fiberglass or other material of similar nature, it is understood and agreed that in the event of damage caused by a peril insured against, these Assurers shall only be liable for repairs made by applying suitable patches to the damaged hull area, in accordance with good repair practice.

It is also agreed that these Assurers will not be liable for the cost or expense of painting or impregnating colour beyond the immediate damaged area or areas. These principles shall also govern in determining whether or not the insured vessel is a Constructive Total Loss.

GENERAL AVERAGE AND SALVAGE CHARGES

Also to pay General Average and Salvage Charges, where properly and reasonably incurred, not exceeding however, the amount in Coverage 1 on Page 1, of this policy under "Agreed Valuation".

OTHER INSURANCE

Warranted that the Assured shall not insure excess or increased value of Hull and Machinery or other total loss Policy Proof of Interest or Full Interest Admitted Insurances, without the written consent of these Assurers.

EXCLUSIONS

THIS POLICY DOES NOT COVER:

Loss, damage or expense, caused directly or indirectly by wear and tear, gradual deterioration (including Marine life), marring, denting, scratching, electrolysis, corrosion, rust, dampness of atmosphere, ice or in consequence of ice freezing other than collision with floating ice, extremes of temperature, weathering or wilful misconduct of the Assured;

Loss or damage to electrical apparatus, including wiring, caused by electricity other than lightning, unless fire ensues and then only for loss or damage by such ensuing fire;

Wrongful conversion or infidelity of persons to whom the insured property may be entrusted.

Loss or damage to spars and/or sails while racing unless added hereon by endorsement at an additional premium to be agreed upon;

Appendix 76

CANADIAN BOARD OF MARINE UNDERWRITERS
GREAT LAKES HULL CLAUSES
September 1, 1971

To be attached to and form a part of Policy No.   of the

The terms and conditions of the following clauses are to be regarded as substituted for those of the policy form to which they are attached, the latter being hereby waived, except provisions required by law to be inserted in the Policy. All captions are inserted only for purposes of reference and shall not be used to interpret the clauses to which they apply.

ASSURED

This Policy insures

hereinafter referred to as the Assured.

If claim is made under this Policy by anyone other than the Owner of the Vessel, such person shall not be entitled to recover to a greater extent than would the Owner, had claim been made by the Owner as an Assured named in this Policy.

Underwriters waive any right of subrogation against affiliated, subsidiary or interrelated companies of the Assured, provided that such waiver shall not apply in the event of a collision between the Vessel and any vessel owned, demise chartered or otherwise controlled by any of the aforesaid companies, or with respect to any loss, damage or expense against which such companies are insured.

LOSS PAYEE

Loss, if any, (excepting claims required to be paid to others under the Collision Liability clause), payable to or order.

VESSEL

The Subject Matter of this insurance is the Vessel called the or by whatsoever name or names the said Vessel is or shall be called, which for purposes of this insurance shall consist of and be

1
2
3
4
5
6
7
8
9
10
11
12
13
14

limited to her hull, launches, lifeboats, rafts, furniture, bunkers, stores, supplies, tackle, fittings, equipment, apparatus, machinery, boilers, refrigerating machinery, insulation, motor generators and other electrical machinery.

In the event any such equipment or apparatus not owned by the Assured is installed for use on board the Vessel and the Assured has assumed responsibility therefor, it shall also be considered part of the Subject Matter and the aggregate value thereof shall be included in the Agreed Value.

Notwithstanding the foregoing, cargo containers, barges and lighters shall not be considered a part of the Subject Matter of this insurance.

DURATION OF RISK

From the   day of   19 ,   C.S.T.

to the   day of   19 ,   C.S.T.

In the event of payment by the Underwriters for Total Loss of the Vessel this Policy shall thereupon automatically terminate.

AGREED VALUE

The Vessel, for so much as concerns the Assured, by agreement between the Assured and the Underwriters in this Policy, is and shall be valued at   Dollars.

EASTERN LIMIT OF NAVIGATION (line 76)

AMOUNT INSURED HEREUNDER

    Dollars.

DEDUCTIBLE

Notwithstanding anything in this Policy to the contrary, there shall be deducted from the aggregate of all claims (including claims under the Collision Liability clause) arising out of each separate accident, the sum of $, unless the accident results in a Total Loss or Constructive Total Loss of the Vessel in which case this clause shall not apply. A recovery from other interests, however, shall not operate to exclude claims under this Policy provided the aggregate of such claims arising out of one separate accident if unreduced by such recovery exceeds that sum. For the purpose of this clause each accident shall be treated separately, but it is agreed that (a) a sequence of damages arising from the same accident shall be treated as due to that accident and (b) all heavy weather damage which occurs during a single sea passage between two successive ports shall be treated as though due to one accident. Also there shall be no deductible average applied to claims arising under the Sue and Labor Clause, nor claims for salvage expenses, or general average.

PROVIDED, however, that claims arising from damage by ice, (excepting claim for Total or Constructive Total Loss), shall be subject to a deductible of $50,000. or 10% of the insured value of the entire Vessel as stated herein, whichever is less, in respect of

15
16
17
18
19
20
21

22
23
24

25
26
27

28

29
30
31
32
33
34
35
36
37
38
39

each accident as defined herein, but in no case less than the deductible stated in line 30 above. Also there shall be no deductible 40
average applied to claims arising under the Sue and Labor Clause, nor claims for salvage expenses, or general average. 41
    In the event of a claim for loss of or damage to any boiler, shaft, machinery or associated equipment, arising from any of the 42
causes enumerated in the ADDITIONAL PERILS (INCHMAREE) clause, lines 106 to 115 hereunder, attributable in part or in whole 43
to negligence of Master Officers or Crew and recoverable under this insurance only by reason of the said Clause, then the Assured 44
shall, in addition to the deductible, also bear in respect of each accident or occurrence an amount equal to 10% of the balance 45
of such claim, but not to exceed a further $50,000. This clause shall not apply to a claim for total or constructive total loss of the 46
Vessel. 47

PREMIUM

    The Underwriters to be paid in consideration of this insurance 48
                              Dollars 49

being at the rate of   per cent.   payable in cash, and in case the said premium shall not be paid to these 50
Underwriters within sixty days after the date of attachment of navigating insurance in force under this Policy, or before November 51
first next succeeding the date of attachment if there be less than sixty days between the date of attachment and such November 52
first, this Policy shall automatically terminate upon such sixtieth day, at noon, or upon November first at noon, as the case may be. 53
Such proportional part of the premium, however, as shall have been earned up to the time of such termination shall thereupon 54
remain and become immediately due and payable. 55
    Additional premiums, if any, shall be due at commencement of the risk for which such additional premiums have been 56
assessed. 57
    Full premium (Port Risk, Navigating for the entire Season of Navigation and any additional premium due) shall be considered 58
earned in the event the Vessel becomes a Total Loss during the term of this Policy. 59

UNDERWRITER'S SURVEYOR

60

RETURNS OF PREMIUM

    Port Risk and/or Navigating premium returnable as follows: 61
    Pro rata daily net in the event of termination under the Change of Ownership clause; 62
    Pro rata monthly net for each uncommenced month if it be mutually agreed to cancel this Policy; 63
    Pro rata daily net of the Navigating rate for each period of 15 consecutive days between March 31st — December 15th, 64
Midnight C.S.T. that the Vessel may be laid up in port not under repair and for which Navigating premium has been paid; 65
provided always that: 66

(a) a Total Loss of the Vessel has not occurred during the currency of this Policy;

(b) in no case shall a return for lay-up be allowed when the Vessel is lying in exposed or unprotected waters or in any location not approved by the Underwriters;

(c) in no case shall a return be allowed when the Vessel is used for lightering purposes.

If, for account of the Assured, the Vessel is laid up for a period of 15 consecutive days, a part only of which attaches under this Policy, the Underwriters shall pay such proportion of the return due in respect of a full period of 15 days as the number of days attaching hereto bears to 15. Should the lay up period exceed 15 consecutive days, the Assured shall have the option to elect the period of 15 consecutive days for which a return is recoverable.

TRADING WARRANTY AND SEASON OF NAVIGATION

Warranted that the vessel shall be confined to the waters, bays, harbors, rivers, canals and other tributaries of the Great Lakes, not east of the point specified in line 27 above and shall engage in navigation only between March 31st, Midnight and December 15th, Midnight, C.S.T. (referred to in this Policy as the Season of Navigation).

Navigation prior to March 31st, Midnight, C.S.T. and subsequent to December 15th, Midnight, C.S.T. is held covered provided (a) prompt notice is given to the Underwriters (b) any amended terms of cover and any additional premium required by the Underwriters are agreed to by the Assured and (c) prior approval of each sailing is obtained from Underwriter's Surveyor.

The Vessel may discharge inward cargo, take in outward cargo, retain cargo on board, and move in port during the period she is in Winter lay-up. For purposes of this provision such of the following places as are designated by a single numeral shall be deemed one port: (1) Duluth   Superior (2) Detroit   Dearborn   River Rouge   Ecorse   Wyandotte   Windsor (3) Kingston Portsmouth.

Permission is hereby granted for the Vessel to carry grain without shifting boards on the Great Lakes. This privilege also applies to navigation on the St. Lawrence River as far as permitted hereunder, but not East of 65° West Longitude.

WINTER MOORINGS

Warranted that the Vessel be properly moored in a safe place and under conditions satisfactory to the Underwriter's Surveyor during the period the Vessel is in Winter lay-up.

ADVENTURE

Beginning the adventure upon the Vessel, as above, and so shall continue and endure, subject to the terms and conditions of this Policy, as employment may offer, in port or at sea, in docks and graving docks, and on ways, gridirons and pontoons, at all times, in all places, and on all occasions, services and trades; with leave to sail or navigate with or without pilots, to go on trial trips and to assist and tow vessels or craft in distress, but the Vessel may not be towed, except as is customary or when in need of assistance, nor shall the Vessel render assistance or undertake towage or salvage services under contract previously arranged by the Assured, the Owners, the Managers or the Charterers of the Vessel.

The Vessel is held covered in case of any breach of conditions as to towage or salvage activities, provided (a) notice is given to the Underwriters immediately following receipt of knowledge thereof by the Assured, and (b) any amended terms of cover and any additional premium required by the Underwriters are agreed to by the Assured.

PERILS

Touching the Adventures and Perils which the Underwriters are contented to bear and take upon themselves, they are of the Seas, Men-of-War, Fire, Lightning, Earthquake, Enemies, Pirates, Rovers, Assailing Thieves, Jettisons, Letters of Mart and Counter-Mart, Surprisals, Takings at Sea, Arrests, Restraints and Detainments of all Kings, Princes and Peoples, of what nation, condition or quality soever, Barratry of the Master and Mariners and of all other like Perils, Losses and Misfortunes that have or shall come to the Hurt, Detriment or Damage of the Vessel, or any part thereof, excepting, however, such of the foregoing perils as may be excluded by provisions elsewhere in the Policy or by endorsement thereon.

ADDITIONAL PERILS (INCHMAREE)

Subject to the conditions of this Policy, this insurance also covers loss of or damage to the Vessel directly caused by the following:

Accidents in loading, discharging or handling cargo, or in bunkering;

Accidents in going on or off, or while on drydocks, graving docks, ways, gridirons or pontoons;

Explosions on shipboard or elsewhere;

Breakdown of motor generators or other electrical machinery and electrical connections thereto, bursting of boilers, breakage of shafts, or any latent defect in the machinery or hull, (excluding the cost and expense of replacing or repairing the defective part);

Breakdown of or accidents to nuclear installations or reactors not on board the insured Vessel;

Contact with aircraft, rockets or similar missiles, or with any land conveyence;

Negligence of Charterers and/or Repairers, provided such Charterers and/or Repairers are not an Assured hereunder;

Negligence of Master, Officers, Crew or Pilots;

provided such loss or damage has not resulted from want of due diligence by the Assured, the Owners or Managers of the Vessel, or any of them. Masters, Officers, Crew or Pilots are not to be considered Owners within the meaning of this clause should they hold shares in the Vessel.

CLAIMS (GENERAL PROVISIONS)

In the event of any accident or occurrence which could give rise to a claim under this Policy, prompt notice thereof shall be given to the Underwriters, and:

93
94
95
96
97

98
99
100
101
102
103

104
105
106
107
108
109
110
111
112
113
114
115
116
117
118

119
120

(a) where practicable, the Underwriters shall be advised prior to survey, so that they may appoint their own surveyor, if they so desire;

(b) the Underwriters shall be entitled to decide where the Vessel shall proceed for docking and/or repair (allowance to be made to the Assured for the actual additional expense of the voyage arising from compliance with the Underwriters' requirement);

(c) the Underwriters shall have the right of veto in connection with any repair firm proposed;

(d) the Underwriters may take tenders or may require tenders to be taken for the repair of the Vessel, in which event, upon acceptance of a tender with the approval of the Underwriters, an allowance shall be made at the rate of 30 per cent. per annum on the amount insured, for each day or pro rata for part of a day, for time lost between the issuance of invitations to tender and the acceptance of a tender, to the extent that such time is lost solely as the result of tenders having been taken and provided the tender is accepted without delay after receipt of the Underwriters' approval.

Due credit shall be given against the allowances in (b) and (d) above for any amount recovered:

(1) in respect of fuel, stores, and wages and maintenance of the Master, Officers and Crew members allowed in General or Particular Average;

(2) from third parties in respect of damages for detention and/or loss of profit and/or running expenses;

for the period covered by the allowances or any part thereof.

No claim shall be allowed in Particular Average for wages and maintenance of the Master, Officers and Crew, except when the Crew are employed in lieu of shore or other labour with the view to minimizing expense or when incurred solely for the necessary removal of the vessel from one port to another for average repairs or for trial trips to test average repairs, in which cases wages and maintenance will be allowed only while the vessel is under way.

General and Particular Average shall be payable without deduction, new for old.

Claims hereunder to be adjusted in accordance with the Rules of Practice for the Great Lakes of the Association of Average Adjusters of Canada so far as they may be applicable.

The expense of sighting the bottom after stranding shall be paid, if reasonably incurred especially for that purpose, even if no damage be found.

If repairs have not been executed within 15 months from the date of the accident, Underwriters are not to be liable for any increased cost of repairs which may be incurred by reason of such repairs being executed after 15 months from the date of the accident.

No claim shall in any case be allowed in respect of scraping or painting the Vessel's bottom.

In the event of failure to comply with the conditions of this clause 15 per cent. shall be deducted from the amount of the ascertained claim.

In the event of loss or damage to equipment or apparatus as covered hereunder not owned by the Assured but installed for use on board the Vessel and for which the Assured has assumed responsibility, claim shall not exceed (1) the amount the Underwriters would pay if the Assured were owner of such equipment or apparatus, or (2) the contractual responsibility assumed by the Assured to the owners or lessors thereof, whichever shall be less.

It is understood and agreed that the fees of the Assured, his Superintendent, and the Assured's Officers, Manager and/or other servants are not collectible under this Policy, except that in the event of loss or damage, where the Assured chooses not to employ an Owner's surveyor and uses his own Marine Superintendent, a reasonable fee will be allowed.

GENERAL AVERAGE AND SALVAGE

General Average and Salvage shall be payable as provided in the contract of affreightment, or failing such provision or there be no contract of affreightment payable in accordance with the Rules of Practice for the Great Lakes of the Association of Average Adjusters of Canada. Provided always that when an adjustment according to the laws and usages of the port of destination is properly demanded by the owners of the cargo, General Average shall be paid accordingly.

In the event of salvage, towage or other assistance being rendered to the Vessel by any vessel belonging in part or in whole to the same Owners or Charterers, the value of such services (without regard to the common ownership or control of the vessels) shall be ascertained by arbitration in the manner provided for under the Collision Liability clause in this Policy, and the amount so awarded so far as applicable to the interest hereby insured shall constitute a charge under this Policy.

When the contributory value of the Vessel is greater than the Agreed Value herein, the liability of the Underwriters for General Average contribution (except in respect to amounts made good to the Vessel), or Salvage, shall not exceed that proportion of the total contribution due from the Vessel which the amount insured hereunder bears to the contributory value; and if, because of damage for which the Underwriters are liable as Particular Average, the value of the Vessel has been reduced for the purpose of contribution, the amount of such Particular Average damage recoverable under this Policy shall first be deducted from the amount insured hereunder, and the Underwriters shall then be liable only for the proportion which such net amount bears to the contributory value.

TOTAL LOSS

There shall be no recovery for a constructive Total Loss hereunder unless the expense of recovering and repairing the Vessel shall exceed the Agreed Value. In making this determination, only expenses incurred by reason of a single accident or a sequence of damages arising from the same accident shall be taken into account.

In ascertaining whether the Vessel is a constructive Total Loss the Agreed Value shall be taken as the repaired value and nothing in respect of the damaged or break-up value of the Vessel or wreck shall be taken into account.

In the event of Total Loss (actual or constructive), no claim to be made by the Underwriters for freight, whether notice of abandonment has been given or not.

In no case shall the Underwriters be liable for unrepaired damage in addition to a subsequent Total Loss sustained during the period covered by this Policy.

SUE AND LABOR

And in case of any Loss or Misfortune, it shall be lawful and necessary for the Assured, their Factors, Servants and Assigns, to sue, labor and travel for, in, and about the defense, safeguard and recovery of the Vessel, or any part thereof, without prejudice to this insurance, to the charges whereof the Underwriters will contribute their proportion as provided below. And it is expressly declared and agreed that no acts of the Underwriters or Assured in recovering, saving or preserving the Vessel shall be considered as a waiver or acceptance of abandonment.

In the event of expenditure under the Sue and Labor clause, the Underwriters shall pay the proportion of such expenses that the amount insured hereunder bears to the Agreed Value, or that the amount insured hereunder, less loss and/or damage payable under this Policy, bears to the actual value of the salved property; whichever proportion shall be less.

If claim for Total Loss is admitted under this Policy and sue and labor expenses have been reasonably incurred in excess of any proceeds realized or value recovered, the amount insured hereunder (without deduction for loss or damage) bears to the Agreed Value or to the sound value of the Vessel at the time of the accident, whichever value was greater. The foregoing shall also apply to expenses reasonably incurred in salving or attempting to salve the Vessel and other property to the extent that such expenses shall be regarded as having been incurred in respect of the Vessel.

COLLISION LIABILITY

And it is further agreed that:

(a) if the Vessel shall come into collision with any other ship or vessel, and **the Assured or the Surety** in consequence of the Vessel being at fault shall become liable to pay and shall pay by way of **damages** to any other person or persons any sum or sums in respect of such collision, the Underwriters will pay the Assured or the Surety, whichever shall have paid, such proportion of such sum or sums so paid as their respective subscriptions hereto bear to the Agreed Value, provided always that their liability in respect to any one such collision shall not exceed their proportionate part of the Agreed Value;

(b) in cases where, with the consent in writing of a majority (in amount) of Hull Underwriters, the liability of the Vessel has been contested, or proceedings have been taken to limit liability, the Underwriters will also pay a like proportion of the costs which the Assured shall thereby incur or be compelled to pay.

When both vessels are to blame, then, unless the liability of the owners or charterers of one or both such vessels becomes limited by law, claims under the Collision Liability clause shall be settled on the principle of Cross-Liabilities as if the owners or charterers of each vessel had been compelled to pay to the owners or charterers of the other of such vessels such one-half or other proportion of the latter's damages as may have been properly allowed in ascertaining the balance or sum payable by or to the Assured in consequence of such collision.

The principles involved in this clause shall apply to the case where both vessels are the property, in part or in whole, of the same owners or charterers, all questions of responsibility and amount of liability as between the two vessels being left to the decision of a single Arbitrator, if the parties can agree upon a single Arbitrator, or failing such agreement, to the decision of

183
184
185
186
187
188
189
190
191
192
193
194
195
196
197
198
199
200
201
202
203
204
205
206
207
208
209
210
211
212
213

Arbitrators, one to be appointed by the Assured and one to be appointed by the majority (in amount) of Hull Underwriters interested; the two Arbitrators chosen to choose a third Arbitrator before entering upon the reference, and the decision of such single Arbitrator, or of any two of such three Arbitrators, appointed as above, to be final and binding.

Provided always that this clause or any other provision of this policy shall in no case extend to any sum which the Assured or the Surety may become liable to pay or shall pay in consequence of, or with respect to:

(a) removal or disposal of obstructions, wrecks, cargoes, or any other thing whatsoever under statutory powers or otherwise pursuant to law;

(b) injury to real or personal property of every description;

(c) the discharge, spillage, emission or leakage of oil, petroleum products, chemicals or other substances of any kind or description whatsoever;

(d) cargo or other property on or the engagements of the Vessel;

(e) loss of life, personal injury or illness.

Provided further that exclusions (b) and (c) above shall not apply to injury to other vessels or property thereon except to the extent that such injury arises out of any action taken to avoid, minimize or remove any discharge, spillage, emission or leakage described in (c).

CHANGE OF OWNERSHIP

In the event of any change, voluntary or otherwise, in the ownership or flag of the Vessel, or if the Vessel be placed under new management, or be chartered on a bareboat basis or requisitioned on that basis, or if the Classification Society of the Vessel or her class therein be changed, cancelled or withdrawn, then, unless the Underwriters agree thereto in writing, this Policy shall automatically terminate at the time of such change of ownership, flag, management, charter, requisition or classification; provided, however, that:

(a) if the Vessel has cargo on board and has already sailed from her loading port, or is at sea in ballast, such automatic termination shall, if required, be deferred until arrival at final port of discharge if with cargo, or at port of destination if in ballast;

(b) in the event of an involuntary temporary transfer by requisition or otherwise, without the prior execution of a written agreement by the Assured, such automatic termination shall occur fifteen days after such transfer.

This insurance shall not inure to the benefit of any transferee or charterer of the Vessel and, if a loss payable hereunder should occur between the time of change or transfer and any deferred automatic termination, the Underwriters shall be subrogated to all of the rights of the Assured against the transferee or charterer in respect of all or part of such loss as is recoverable from the transferee or charterer, and in the proportion which the amount insured hereunder bears to the Agreed Value.

The term "new management" as used above refers only to the transfer of the management of the Vessel from one firm or corporation to another, and it shall not apply to any internal changes within the offices of the Assured.

ADDITIONAL INSURANCES

It is a condition of this Policy that no additional insurance against the risk of Total Loss of the Vessel shall be effected to operate during the currency of this Policy by or for account of the Assured, Owners, Managers, Operators or Mortgagees except on the interests and up to the amounts enumerated in the following Sections (a) to (g), inclusive, and no such insurance shall be subject to P.P.I., F.I.A. or other like term on any interests whatever excepting those enumerated in Section (a): provided always and notwithstanding the limitation on recovery in the Assured clause a breach of this condition shall not afford the Underwriters any defense to a claim by a Mortgagee who has accepted this Policy without knowledge of such breach:

(a) DISBURSEMENTS, MANAGERS' COMMISSIONS, PROFITS OR EXCESS OR INCREASED VALUE OF HULL AND MACHINERY AND/OR SIMILAR INTERESTS HOWEVER DESCRIBED, AND FREIGHT (INCLUDING CHARTERED FREIGHT OR ANTICIPATED FREIGHT) INSURED FOR TIME. An amount not exceeding in the aggregate 25% of the Agreed Value.

(b) FREIGHT OR HIRE, UNDER CONTRACTS FOR VOYAGE. An amount not exceeding the gross freight or hire for the current cargo passage and next succeeding cargo passage (such insurance to include, if required, a preliminary and an intermediate ballast passage) plus the charges of insurance. In the case of a voyage charter where payment is made on a time basis, the amount shall be calculated on the estimated duration of the voyage, subject to the limitation of two cargo passages as laid down herein. Any amount permitted under this Section shall be reduced, as the freight or hire is earned, by the gross amount so earned. Any freight or hire to be earned under the form of Charters described in (d) below shall not be permitted under this Section (b) if any part thereof is insured as permitted under said Section (d).

(c) ANTICIPATED FREIGHT IF THE VESSEL SAILS IN BALLAST AND NOT UNDER CHARTER. An amount not exceeding; the anticipated gross freight on next cargo passage, such amount to be reasonably estimated on the basis of the current rate of freight at time of insurance, plus the charges of insurance. Provided, however, that no insurance shall be permitted by this Section if any insurance is effected as permitted under Section (b).

(d) TIME CHARTER HIRE OR CHARTER HIRE FOR SERIES OF VOYAGES. An amount not exceeding 50% of the gross hire which is to be earned under the charter in a period not exceeding 18 months. Any amount permitted under this Section shall be reduced as the hire is earned under the charter by 50% of the gross amount so earned but, where the charter is for a period exceeding 18 months, the amount insured need not be reduced while it does not exceed 50% of the gross hire still to be earned under the charter. An insurance permitted by this Section may begin on the signing of the charter.

(e) PREMIUMS. An amount not exceeding the actual premiums of all interests insured for a period not exceeding 12 months (excluding premiums insured as permitted under the foregoing Sections but including, if required, the estimated calls or premium on any Protection and Indemnity or War Risks and Strikes Insurance) reducing pro rata monthly.

(f) RETURNS OF PREMIUM. An amount not exceeding the actual returns which are recoverable subject to "and arrival" or equivalent provision under any policy of insurance.

(g) INSURANCE IRRESPECTIVE OF AMOUNT AGAINST: — Risks excluded by the War, Strikes and Related Exclusions clause; risks enumerated in the American Institute War Risks and Strikes Clauses; and General Average and Salvage Disbursements.

WAR STRIKES AND RELATED EXCLUSIONS

The following conditions shall be paramount and shall supersede and nullify any contrary provisions of the Policy.

This Policy does not cover any loss, damage or expense caused by, resulting from, or incurred as a consequence of:

(a) Capture, seizure, arrest, restraint or detainment, or any attempt thereat; or

(b) Any taking of the Vessel, by requisition or otherwise, whether in time of peace or war and whether lawful or otherwise; or

(c) Any mine, bomb or torpedo not carried as cargo on board the Vessel; or

(d) Any weapon of war employing atomic or nuclear fission and/or fusion or other like reaction or radioactive force or matter; or

(e) Civil war, revolution, rebellion, insurrection, or civil strife arising therefrom, or piracy; or

(f) Strikes, lockouts, political or labor disturbances, civil commotions, riots, martial law, military or usurped power, malicious acts or vandalism; or

(g) Hostilities or warlike operations (whether there be a declaration of war or not) but this subparagraph (g) not to exclude collision or contact with aircraft, rockets or similar missiles, or with any fixed or floating object, or stranding, heavy weather, fire or explosion unless caused directly by a hostile act by or against a belligerent power which act is independent of the nature of the voyage or service which the Vessel concerned or, in the case of a collision, any other vessel involved therein, is performing. As used herein, "power" includes any authority maintaining naval, military or air forces in association with a power.

If war risks or other risks excluded by this clause are hereafter insured by endorsement on this Policy, such endorsement shall supersede the above conditions only to the extent that the terms of such endorsement are inconsistent therewith and only while such endorsement remains in force.

Appendix 77

Canadian (Pacific) Protection and Indemnity Policy

Policy No.

ORIGINAL

For signature only by Companies or firms whose officials or partners are Underwriting Members of the Association of Marine Underwriters of British Columbia.

ASSURED

Loss, if any, payable to

Vessel(s)

LIMIT OF LIABILITY
(Any One Accident or Occurrence)

(Inclusive of Legal Fees and Costs)

From　　　　　　　　　　　Noon, Pacific Standard Time

To　　　　　　　　　　　　Noon, Pacific Standard Time

PREMIUM:

Deductibles

The following deductibles will be borne by the Assured:

(i) $ in respect of damage done any one accident or occurrence.

(ii) $ in respect of bodily injury and all other claims any one accident or occurrence.

(iii) $ in respect of any one accident or occurrence directly resulting from pollution.

But in no event shall the combined deductibles exceed the largest applicable deductible in (i), (ii) or (iii) as shown above any one accident or occurrence.

NOW THIS POLICY WITNESSETH that we, the Assurers, the Companies whose names are set out herein, take upon ourselves the burden of this Assurance each of us to the extent of the amount underwritten by us respectively, and promise and bind ourselves, each Company for itself only and not the one for the other and in respect only of the due proportion of each Company to the Assured, their Executors, Administrators and Assigns for the true performance and fulfillment of the contract contained in this Policy in consideration of the person or persons effecting this Policy promising to pay a premium as above.

IN WITNESS whereof we, the Assurers, have subscribed our names and limits of liability in Vancouver, B.C.

as hereinafter appears, this .... day of .... 19 ....

Subject to CANADIAN (PACIFIC) PROTECTION AND INDEMNITY CLAUSES as attached.

AMOUNT	PROP'N.	ASSURERS	AUTHORIZED SIGNATURE:

Appendix 78

1/1/83
1983

1983

CANADIAN (PACIFIC) PROTECTION AND INDEMNITY CLAUSES

1 The Assurer(s) hereby undertakes to make good to the Assured or the
2 Assured's executors, administrators and/or successors all such Liabilities
3 and/or Expenses as the Assured or the Assured's executors, administrators
4 and/or successors shall have become liable to pay and shall have in fact
5 paid on account of the liabilities, risks, events and/or happenings arising
6 out of ownership, use or operation of the vessel(s) hereby insured (herei-
7 nafter referred to as "The Vessel"), as follows:

8 **1. LIABILITY FOR LOSS OF LIFE, BODILY INJURY**

9 Liability for loss of life of, or bodily injury to, or illness of any
10 person, excluding however, unless otherwise agreed by endorsement
11 hereon, liability to any employee of the Assured or in the case of
12 death, to his beneficiaries or others, under any Compensation Acts
13 or similar legislation, order or regulations, where the Assured is
14 required to insure under such compensation provisions.

15 Protection hereunder for loss of life or injury arising in connection
16 with the handling of cargo shall commence from the time of receipt
17 by the Assured of the cargo on dock or wharf or on craft alongside
18 the vessel for loading thereon, and shall continue until delivery
19 thereof from dock or wharf of discharge or until discharge from the
20 vessel on to another vessel or craft.

21 **2. HOSPITAL, MEDICAL OR OTHER EXPENSES**

22 (a) Liability for hospital, medical or other expenses necessarily
23 and reasonably incurred in respect of loss of life of or bodily

89 **5. LIABILITY FOR DAMAGE TO FIXED OR MOVABLE**
90 **OBJECTS**

91 (i) Loss of or damage to any fixed or movable object or property
92 thereon, except another vessel or craft or property on board
93 another vessel or craft.

94 (ii) Where there would be a valid claim hereunder but for the fact
95 that the damaged property belongs to the Assured, the Assur-
96 er(s) shall be liable in the same way and shall have the same
97 rights as if the damaged property belongs to different owners.

98 **6. LIABILITY FOR POLLUTION**

99 Loss, damage, cost, liability or expense that the Assured, as owner
100 of the vessel(s), shall have become liable to pay and shall pay in
101 consequence of the accidental, actual or potential discharge, spillage
102 or leakage of oil, fuel, cargo, petroleum products, chemicals or
103 other substances of any kind or description; Provided, However,
104 that this policy shall not insure any liability resulting directly or
105 indirectly, or arising out of or having relation to:

106 (a) Any loss, damage, cost, liability or expense paid or incurred in
107 consequence of any such actual or potential discharge, spillage
108 or leakage unless proximately caused by fault on the part of
109 the Assured.

110 (b) Punitive or exemplary damages.

injury to, or illness of any member of the crew of the vessel or any other person. Protection hereunder shall also include burial expenses not exceeding $500.00 when necessarily and reasonably incurred by the Assured for the burial of any seaman of the vessel and such burial expenses shall not be subject to any deductible provision in the policy.

This insurance EXCLUDES any claim recoverable under any Provincial or other applicable Hospital or Medical Insurance Plan where the claimant is required to be insured under such a plan.

(b) Port Charges and Owner's Expenses

Port Charges incurred solely for the purpose of landing an injured or sick person shall be allowed as well as the net loss of the Assured in respect of bunkers, insurance, stores and provisions solely caused by the landing of such person.

3. REPATRIATION EXPENSES

Liability for repatriation expenses of any members of the crew of the vessel necessarily and reasonably incurred in case of wreck or abandonment of the vessel or under statutory obligation, excepting such liability and expenses as arise out of or ensue from the termination of any agreement in accordance with the terms thereof, or by mutual consent, or by the sale of the vessel, or by any other act of the Assured. Wages shall only be included in such expenses where payable under statutory obligations during unemployment due to wreck or loss of the vessel.

4. LIABILITY FOR DAMAGE TO OTHER VESSELS

(a) By Collision

(i) Loss of or damage to any other vessel or craft or to the freight thereof or property thereon, caused by collision with the vessel to the extent that the same would not be recoverable if the vessel where at all times fully insured under hull and machinery and, where applicable, excess liabilities policies on terms at least equivalent to those of the current Canadian Hulls (Pacific) Clauses and current

7. REMOVAL OF WRECK

Liability for costs or expenses of, or incidental to the removal of the wreck of the vessel, when such removal is compulsory by law, PROVIDED HOWEVER, that the value of all stores and materials saved as well as the value of the wreck itself, shall first be deducted from such costs or expenses and only the balance thereof, if any, shall be recoverable from the Assurers, ALWAYS PROVIDED THAT the Assurers are not liable for such costs, or expenses as would be covered by insurance under the current Canadian Hulls (Pacific) Clauses, and where applicable, current Canadian (Pacific) Total Loss and Excess Liabilities Clauses.

8. FINES IMPOSED BY GOVERNMENT OR CUSTOMS' AUTHORITIES

Liability for fines and penalties, including expenses necessarily and reasonably incurred in avoiding or mitigating same, for the violation of any laws of Canada or of any Province thereof, or of any foreign country including fines imposed by Government or Customs' Authorities in respect of short or over delivery of cargo, smuggling, breach of Immigration Regulations or in respect of other neglect or default of captains or crew for which the vessel or Assured may be held responsible; PROVIDED HOWEVER that the Assurer(s) shall not be liable to indemnify the Assured against any such fines or penalties resulting directly or indirectly from the failure, neglect or default of the Assured or his managing officers or managing agents to exercise the highest degree of diligence to prevent a violation of any such laws.

With respect to claims for pollution, this policy shall not indemnify the Assured against any fine or penalty arising out of the actual or potential discharge, spillage or leakage of oil, fuel, cargo, petroleum products, chemicals or other substances of any kind or description.

9. EXTRAORDINARY EXPENSES IN CASES OF QUARANTINE ETC.

Extraordinary expenses incurred in cases of outbreak of plague or

Canadian (Pacific) Total Loss and Excess Liabilities Clauses.

(ii) Where there would be a valid claim hereunder but for the fact that the damaged property belongs to the same Assured, the Assurer(s) shall be liable in the same way and shall have the same rights as if the damaged property belonged to different owners.

(iii) When both vessels are to blame, then unless the liability of the Owners of one or both of such vessels becomes limited by law, claims under this clause shall be settled on the principle of cross liabilities as if the Owner of each vessel had been compelled to pay to the Owner of the other vessel one-half or other proportion of the latter's damages as may have been properly allowed in ascertaining the balance or sum payable by or to the Assured in consequence of such collision.

Notwithstanding the foregoing, if any one or more of the various liabilities arising from such collision has been compromised, settled or adjusted without the written consent of the Assurer(s), the Assurer(s) shall be relieved of liability for any and all claims under this clause.

(b) Other Than By Collision

(i) Loss of or damage to any other vessel or craft or to the freight thereof or property thereon not caused by collision with the vessel provided such liability does not arise solely by reasons of a contract made by the Assured.

(ii) Where there would be a valid claim hereunder but for the fact that the damaged property belongs to the Assured, the Assurer(s) shall be liable in the same way and shall have the same rights as if the damaged property belongs to different owners.

other contagious disease, for disinfection of the vessel or persons on board, or for quarantine but not including the ordinary expenses of loading or discharge, nor the wages and/or provisions of crew or passengers. Where the vessel is chartered or, not being under contract is ordered to proceed to a port where it is or ought to be known that she will be subjected to quarantine, the Assured shall receive no benefit from the Assurer(s) under this clause.

10. MUTINY OR OTHER MISCONDUCT

Expenses incurred in resisting any unfounded claim by the master or crew or other persons employed on the vessel, or in prosecuting such persons in case of mutiny or other misconduct.

11. COSTS

(a) Legal Costs

Where the Assured is successful in defending a claim or suit, the Legal Costs incurred with the Assurer(s) or their agent's approval shall be payable by Assurers without application of any deductible. Where however, payment has to be made to dispose of a claim and the amount so paid by the Assured, including Legal Costs, exceeds the amount of the deductible stipulated in this policy, the Assurer(s) shall be liable only for the amount in excess of such deductible.

(b) Costs and Charges

Other costs, charges and expenses, reasonably incurred and paid by the Assured in defence against any liabilities herein insured against in respect of the vessel shall be subject to the agreed deductibles applicable, and subject further to the conditions and limitations herein provided.

GENERAL CONDITIONS AND/OR LIMITATIONS

171 PROMPT NOTICE OF CLAIM — WARRANTED that in the event
172 of any occurrence which may result in loss, damage and/or expense for
173 which the Assurer(s) is/are or may become liable, the Assured will give
173 prompt notice thereof and forward to the Assurer(s) as soon as practicable
175 after receipt thereof, all communications, processes, pleadings and other
176 legal papers or documents relating to such occurrences.

177 SETTLEMENT OF CLAIM — The Assured shall not make any
178 admission of liability, either before or after any occurrence which may
179 result in a claim for which the Assurer(s) may be liable without the
180 Assurer(s) prior written consent.

181 The Assured shall not interfere in any negotiations of the Assurer(s) for
182 settlement of any legal proceedings in respect of any occurrences for
183 which the Assurer(s) are liable under this policy; PROVIDED, HOW-
184 EVER, that in respect of any occurrence likely to give rise to a claim
185 under this insurance, the Assured is obligated to and shall take steps to
186 protect its (and/or the Assurer(s)) interests as would reasonably be taken
187 in the absence of this or similar insurance. If the Assured shall fail or
188 refuse to settle any claim as authorized by the Assurer(s) the liability of
189 the Assurer(s) to the Assured shall be limited to the amount for which
190 settlement could have been made.

191 ASSURED TO ASSIST WITH EVIDENCE IN DEFENCE ETC.
192 — Whenever required by the Assurer(s), the Assured shall aid in securing
193 information and evidence and in obtaining witnesses and shall co-operate
194 with the Assurer(s) in the defence of any claim or suit or appeal from any
195 judgement, in respect of any occurrence as herein before provided.

196 SUBROGATION — The Assurer(s) shall be subrogated to all the rights
197 which the Assured may have against any other person or entity in respect
198 of any payment made under this insurance, to the extent of such payment,
199 and the Assured shall, upon the request of the Assurer(s), execute all
200 documents necessary to secure to the Assurer(s) such rights. The Assur-
201 er(s) shall be entitled to take credit for any profit accruing to the Assured

245 ASSIGNMENTS — This insurance shall be void in case the vessel or
246 any part thereof, shall be sold, transferred or mortgaged, or if there be any
247 change of management or charter of the vessel, or if this policy be
248 assigned or pledged, without the previous consent in writing of the
249 Assurer(s).

250 TITLES OF PARAGRAPH — The titles of paragraphs of this Policy
251 including endorsement and supplementary contracts, if any, now or
252 hereafter attached to this Policy are included solely for the convenience of
253 reference and should not be deemed in any way to limit, alter or affect the
254 provisions to which they relate.

255 ACTIONS AGAINST THE ASSURER — No Action shall lie against
256 the Assurer(s) for the recovery of any loss sustained by the Assured unless
257 such action is brought against the Assurer(s) within one year of the final
258 judgement or decree is entered in the litigation against the Assurer(s) or, in
259 case the claim against the Assurer(s) accrues without the entry of such
260 final judgment or decree, unless such action is brought within one year of the
261 date of the payment of such claim.

262 CONTINUATION CLAUSE — Should the vessel at the expiration of
263 this insurance be at sea, or in distress, or at a port of refuge or of call, she
264 shall, provided previous written notice be given to the Assurer(s), be held
265 covered to her port of destination and until completion of discharge upon
266 payment of a pro-rata monthly premium each 30 days (or part thereof)
267 during which this insurance is held covered.

268 CANCELLATION CLAUSE — A pro rata net premium for every
269 thirty consecutive days of unexpired time shall be returned if it be mutu-
270 ally agreed to cancel this policy, but there shall be no cancellation or
271 return of premium in event vessel is lost from any cause whatsoever.

272 It is understood and agreed that in the event of non payment of premiums
273 by the Assured to the Agent or to the Assurer(s), the Agent or the
274 Assurer(s) may cancel this insurance by giving to the Assured five days
275 notice in writing by registered letter.

276 If the vessel named herein should be sold or requisitioned and this policy

277 be cancelled and surrendered, a pro rata net premium for each thirty
278 consecutive days of the unexpired term of this insurance shall be
279 returned.

280 EACH VESSEL SEPARATELY INSURED CLAUSE — As a
281 matter of convenience one policy is issued covering the vessels scheduled
282 herein, but as a matter of construction the limit of liability applicable to
283 each vessel is to be deemed a separate interest, separately insured, in all
284 respects as if a separate policy for the limit of liability set against each
285 vessel were issued, and the policy is to be read and applied accordingly.
286 The limit of liability on one vessel is not applicable to any other.

287 (iii) For any loss, damage, or expense arising from the cancellation or
288 breach of any charter, bad debts, fraud of agents, insolvency,
289 loss of freight, hire or demurrage, or as a result of the breach of
290 any undertaking to load any cargo, or in respect of the vessel
291 engaging in any unlawful trade or performing any unlawful act,
292 with the knowledge of the Assured.

293 (iv) For any loss, damage, expense or claim arising out of or having
294 relation to the towage by the vessel (not being a tug) of any
295 other vessel or craft, whether under agreement or not, unless
296 such towage was to assist such other vessel or craft in distress to
297 a port or place of safety, PROVIDED, HOWEVER, that this
298 clause shall not apply to claims under this policy for loss of life
299 or bodily injury to passengers and/or members of the crew of
300 the vessel arising as a result of towing.

301 (v) When the insured vessel is a tug this insurance shall remain in
302 force during the towage of any other vessel, craft or log raft but
303 shall in no way extend to cover loss, damage or expense to (or
304 caused by) her tow or the property thereon, whether liability
305 arises under contract or otherwise.

202 by reason of any negligence or wrongful act of the Assured's servants or
203 agents, up to the measure of their loss, or to recover for their own
204 account from third parties any damage that may be provable by reason of
205 such negligence or wrongful act.

206 COVER ELSEWHERE — Where the Assured is, irrespective of this
207 insurance covered or protected against any loss or claim which would
208 otherwise have been paid by the Assurer(s) under this insurance, there
209 shall be no contribution by the Assurer(s) on the basis of double insurance
210 or otherwise.

EXCLUSIONS AND WARRANTIES

211 Notwithstanding anything to the contrary contained in this policy, no
212 liability attaches to the Assurer(s);

213 (i) For any loss, damage, or expense which would be payable if the
214 vessel were fully insured under the Hull & Machinery and Excess
215 Liability policies on terms at least equivalent to those of the
216 current Canadian Hulls (Pacific) Clauses and where applicable
217 current Canadian (Pacific) Total Loss and Excess Liabilities
218 Clauses.

219 (ii) For any loss, damage or expense sustained by reason of capture,
220 seizure, arrest, restraint or detainment, and the consequences
221 thereof or of any attempt thereof; also from the consequences of
222 hostilities or warlike operations, whether there be a declaration
223 of war or not; but this shall not exclude collision, contact with
224 any fixed or floating object (other than a mine or torpedo),
225 stranding, heavy weather or fire unless caused directly (and
226 independently of the nature of the voyage or service which the
227 vessel or, in the case of a collision, any other vessel involved

228 therein, is performing) by a hostile act by or against a belligerent
229 power; and for the purpose of this exclusion "power" includes
230 any authority maintaining naval, military or air forces in associa-
231 tion with a power.

232 Warranted free from the consequences of civil war, revolution,
234 rebellion, insurrection, or civil strife arising therefrom, or
235 piracy.

236 Warranted free from loss, damage, liability or expense arising
237 from any weapon of war employing atomic or nuclear fission
238 and/or fusion or other like reaction or radioactive force or
239 matter.

240 Warranted free from loss, damage, liability or expense arising
241 from: —

242 (a) The detonation of an explosive
243 (b) Any weapon of war
244 and caused by any person acting from a political motive.

(vi)   306 For any claim involving loss of life or bodily injury resulting
307 from or in relation to the handling of cargo where such claim
308 arises from a contract of indemnity between the Assured and a
309 third party.

(vii)   310 For any claim in respect of cargo carried on board the vessel.

(viii)   311 Oil pollution resulting from or during services provided under a
312 contract of salvage.

(ix)   313 The U.S. Water Quality Improvement Act and/or any similar
314 acts enacted by any State or duly constituted legal authority, or
315 any statutory amendment or modification thereof.

316 It is expressly understood and agreed if and when the Assured under this
317 policy has any interest other than as a shipowner in the vessel, in no event
318 shall the Assurer(s) be liable hereunder to any greater extent that if such
319 Assured where the owner and were entitled to all the rights of limitation
320 to which a shipowner is entitled.

321 Unless otherwise agreed by endorsement to this insurance, liability
322 hereunder shall in no event exceed that which would be imposed on the
323 Assured by law in the absence of contract.

Appendix 79

UNITED STATES DISTRICT COURT

DISTRICT OF OREGON

SAFETY SHIPPING CO., INC.   )
)   No._____
                    Plaintiff   )
)   COMPLAINT FOR BREACH
          v.   )   OF INSURANCE CONTRACT
)
ST. PAUL FIRE & MARINE INS. CO.,)   JURY DEMAND
INC., a corporation,   )
)
                    Defendant   )
_____   )

     The plaintiff Safety Shipping Co., Inc. alleges the
following in its complaint for breach of contract against St.
Paul Fire & Marine Ins. Co., Inc.

     1. Jurisdiction is founded on diversity of citizenship and
amount. The matter in controversy exceeds, exclusive of interest
and costs, the sum of ten thousand dollars. Alternatively,
jurisdiction is based on the fact that this is a suit on a marine
insurance policy and an admiralty and maritime claim within the
meaning of Rule 9(h), F.R.C.P.

     2. The plaintiff is a corporation incorporated under the
laws of the State of Delaware and has its principal place of
business in the State of Delaware. The defendant is a
corporation incorporated under the laws of the State of Michigan
and has its principal place of business in a state other than
the State of Oregon. Defendant is an insurance company licensed
to do business in the State of Oregon.

     3. On January 1, 1987, in consideration of a premium paid
by plaintiff, the defendant by its agent duly authorized thereto,
issued and delivered its "all risk" policy of insurance, Marine
Open Cargo Policy No. 123456, with endorsements (hereinafter the
"Policy") and thereby agreed to pay plaintiff, after proof of
loss and interest, for all loss of and damage to goods, including
heavy machinery, shipped on or after January 1, 1987, and duly
declared by plaintiff under said Marine Open Cargo Policy.

     4. Thereafter, on or about February 1, 1987, plaintiff
purchased a shipment of heavy machinery, which on or about
said date was shipped in good order and condition from Hamburg,
Germany to Portland, Oregon on board the vessel GOOD HOPE

consigned to plaintiff. At all times relevant, plaintiff was the
lawful owner of said shipment and had an insurable interest in
said shipment.

5. Plaintiff duly declared said shipment under Marine Open
Cargo Policy No. 123456, and has paid to defendant all premiums
required.

6. During the transit described above, and while coverage
under said policy was in full force and effect, said shipment
became bent, warped and twisted, and otherwise damaged and
depreciated in value in the amount of $350,000.

7. Said bending, warping and twisting and other damage to
said shipment was due to a peril insured against under the
policy, and occurred while coverage afforded by the said policy
was in full force and effect.

8. Plaintiff has heretofore made claim against defendant
under said policy for said loss and damage, and fulfilled all
conditions required of it under said policy.

9. Defendant has, in breach of said contract of insurance,
wrongfully refused to pay said claim or any portion thereof.

10. By reason of the premises, there is now due and owing
from defendant to plaintiff the sum of $350,000, together with
interest thereon from February 1, 1987 until paid.

WHEREFORE, plaintiff prays for judgment against defendant as
follows:

(1) For $350,000 for breach of said contract of insurance;

(2) For prejudgment interest; and

(3) For such other and further relief as may be just and
proper.

Dated: April 1, 1987.

_____
Of Attorneys for Plaintiff

Appendix 80

IN THE SUPREME COURT
OF QUEENSLAND

NO. 123 OF 1987

WRIT ISSUED THE 1ST DAY OF MARCH, 1987
BETWEEN

JOALDEK PTY LTD.,

Plaintiff

AND:

STATEMENT
OF CLAIM

AUGUSTUS A. SMITH, who is being
sued as the representative of
various insurance underwriters who
entered into a policy of insurance
with the plaintiff on or about March,
1986

Defendant

DELIVERED the 2nd day of March, 1987.

1. The plaintiff was at all material times,
and still is, duly incorporated according
to law.

2. The plaintiff is the registered owner of
the sailing and motor vessel "Ayesha."

3. The defendant is sued as the representative of members of insurance companies and
or underwriters connected with, or in respect
of, the policy of insurance referred to in
paragraph 4 hereof and is authorized by the
said companies and or underwriters to act as
such representative.

WHITE & BLACK
SOLICITORS
1 EAGLE ST.
BRISBANE, QLD 400

4. By a policy of marine insurance dated 1
March, 1986 made by the defendant and other
underwriters in consideration of premiums
paid and to be paid to them by the plaintiff,
the defendant insured the said vessel against
loss or damage for the sum of $310,000.

5. Pursuant to the said policy the premiums
were payable annually and for the year ending
the 1st day of March, 1987, the plaintiff

paid to the defendant, or to its servants or
agents, a premium of $3,100 plus stamp duty
levied in respect thereof.

6. At all material times the plaintiff was
interested in the said vessel to the extent
of the amount so insured pursuant to the
policy.

7. On or about the 24th day of December,
1986, while the said policy was in force,
the said vessel sank and as a result thereof
the plaintiff has suffered loss and damage.

Particulars

The total loss of the said vessel $310,000

8. In the premises therefore, the plaintiff
became and is entitled to the payment of the
said sum of $310,000 arising from the loss of
or damage to the said vessel.

9. The plaintiff has duly notified the defendant of the said loss and damage but the
defendant has not nor have any of the other
underwriters paid to the plaintiff the said
sum of $310,000 or any part thereof.

10. AND the plaintiff claims against the
defendant, as the said representative, the
sum of $310,000 pursuant to the said policy
of insurance together with interest thereon
pursuant to the Common Law Practice Act 1867,
as amended.

Place of trial: Brisbane

                        Solicitors for the Plaintiff

This pleading was settled by Mr. G.H. Black-
stone of Counsel

The defendant is required to plead to the
within Statement of Claim within 28 days from
the time limited for appearance or from the
delivery of the Statement of Claim whichever
is the later, otherwise the plaintiff may
obtain judgment against him.

Appendix 81

IN THE SUPREME COURT OF BRITISH COLUMBIA

BETWEEN:

SEATECH CHARTERS LTD.
Plaintiff

AND: FIREMAN'S FUND INSURANCE COMPANY, THE CONTINENTAL
INSURANCE CO., TALBOT BIRD COMPANY LTD., AND BLACK
SEA & BALTIC GENERAL INSURANCE CO. LTD.
Defendants

STATEMENT OF CLAIM

1. The Plaintiff is a company duly incorporated under the laws
of the Province of British Columbia having an office and place of
business at 9999 West Vancouver Road, Sidney, British Collumbia.

2. The Plaintiff was interested to the amount of $312,000 under
a policy of marine insurance numbered FAW81/569 dated June 10,
1986 for that amount on the hull and machinery of the Plaintiff's
diesel vessel "SEA KING" subscribed by the Defendants in the
following percentages:

(a) Fireman's Fund Insurance Company   -   30%
(b) The Continental Insurance Co.   -   25%
(c) Talbot Bird Company Ltd.   -   25%
(d) Black Sea & Baltic General Ins. Co. -   20%

3. The terms of the said policy was from June 1, 1986 to June 1,
1987.

4. On or about tdhe 3rd day of January, 1987, the insured vessel
while at dock in the inner harbour of Victoria, British Columbia,
sustained damage and loss arising from the flooding of the vessel
by salt water.

5. The aforesaid damage and losses to the insured vessel arose
from a cause or causes insured against by the said policy, in
particular, loss and misfortunes that came to the hurt, detriment
or damage of the insured vessel from a peril of the sea, namely,
a fortuitous incursion of sea water when the ship was weighted
down and immersed below here normal water line by a heavy
snowfall.

6. In the alternative, the damage and losses to the insured vessel were caused by a latent defect in the hull which allowed an incursion of sea water when the vessel was weighted down and immersed as aforesaid.

7. The Plaintiff has suffered damage, losses and expenses as a result of the physical damage to the vessel and for costs and expenses incurred by way of sue and labour.

8. The Plaintiff has provided to the Defendants particulars of its damage, losses and expenses and has demanded payment from the Defendants of its losses incurred, but the Defendants have denied that the damage, losses and expenses incurred as a result of the said incursion of sea water is covered by the terms of the said policy.

9. The Defendants have continued to deny liability under the said policy, despite the provision of full particulars as to the circumstances of the incursion of the sea water and full access to the vessel provided to the Defendants' representatives.

WHEREFORE THE PLAINTIFF CLAIMS:

(a) Judgment upon the contract of marine insurance in the amount of the Plaintiff's claim, losses and expenses;

(b) A reference, if necessary, to the learned Registrar to determine the amount of the said damage, losses and expenses;

(c) Prejudgment interest at such rate per annum as may be determined by this Honourable Court from the date or dates as may be decided by this Honourable Court to the date of payment;

(d) An Order that the Defendants indemnify the Plaintiff for all expenses and costs incurred by the Plaintiff by way of sue and labour expense;

(e) Costs;

(f) Such other and further relief as this Honourable Court may deem meet.

PLACE OF TRIAL: Vancouver, British Columbia

DATED at Vancouver, British Columbia this 19th day of May, 1987.

_____
Solicitor for Plaintiff

This STATEMENT OF CLAIM is filed by John Doe, Q.C. of the law firm of Smith, Doe & Black, whose place of business and address for service is 15th Floor, 000 Burrard Street, Vancouver, British Columbia, V7X 1K9, Telephone No. 688-0000.

Appendix 82

IN THE SUPREME COURT OF BRITISH COLUMBIA

BETWEEN:

SEATECH CHARTERS LTD.

Plaintiff

AND:

FIREMAN'S FUND INSURANCE COMPANY
and Others

Defendants

STATEMENT OF DEFENCE

1.   The Defendants admit each and every allegation of fact
contained in paragraphs 1 to 3 of the Statement of Claim.

2.   The Defendants deny each and every allegation of fact
contained in paragraphs 4 to 7 of the Statement of Claim.

3.   The Defendants deny each and every allegation of fact
contained in paragraphs 8 and 9 of the Statement and Claim save
and except that Defendants have denied liability under the said
policy for the alleged losses claimed by the Plaintiff.

4.   In answer to the entire Statement of Claim the Defendants
say that if the vessel "SEA KING" sustained damage and losses
arising from the flooding of the vessel by sea water, which is
not admitted but specifically denied, that alleged damage was not
caused by a peril insured against under the policy, but resulted
from wear and tear and deterioration of the vessel, and the
Defendants rely on Section 56(1)(c) of the Insurance (Marine) Act
R.S.B.C. 1979 Chapter 203.

5.   In answer to paragraph 6 of the Statement of Claim the
Defendants say that the deteriorated condition of the caulking
and fittings of the hull of the vessel was not a latent defect,
as the vessel had leaked for some years prior to January, 1987,
and the cause of that leakage could have been ascertained if any
reasonable inspection of the vessel had been undertaken.

WHEREFORE, the Defendants pray that the Plaintiff's claim be
dismissed with costs to the Defendants.

DATED at the City of Vancouver, in the Province of British
Columbia, this 21st day of June, 1987.

_____
Solicitor for Defendants

INDEX

G

Gaming contract, policy must not be, 23

Garbling. *See* Particular average

General average

affreightment contracts: Cogsa, obligations of carrier, 521-24; contrast, Harter vs. Cogsa, 516, 517; deviation, 549-53; deviation, effect of, 524, 525; deviation, whether reasonable, 550-52; deviation—fundamental breach, 552, 553; due diligence, obligation as to, 516-21; effect of fault, 513-15; Fire Statute, 544, 555; Harter Act, evolution of, 515, 516; Jason Clause, 525-31; negligence, care, custody, and control of cargo, 545-48; negligence, navigation, and management, 548; unseaworthiness, 518-19; unseaworthiness, discussion of, 532-36; vessel found seaworthy, 536-44; vessel found unseaworthy, 533-36

American development, 483-87

amount to be made good: allowances, 589; cargo, 587, 588; contributory values, 589-91; freight, 588-89; in general, 584, 585; vessel, 585-87

common safety versus mutual benefit, 485-87

contribution, rules as to: cargo, 627; freight, 627; general average sacrifices, 628; generally, 624, 625; vessels, 625-27

definition of, 21

differences in English and American practice, 485-87

English development, 481-83

extraordinary sacrifice or expenditure: damage to cargo in discharging, 563, 564; definition, 553; extinguishing fire, 558-61; fuel supply short, 562, 563; jettison, 554-58; port of refuge expenses, 570-77; Rule F, and Rules X and XI, port of refuge, 570-77; salvage, 582-84; stranding, 565-69; substituted expenses,

577-80; vessel sacrifices, 564, 565

extraordinary sacrifices or expenditures, temporary repairs, 581

general average act: common safety, 499-503; consequences of, 504; direct consequences, examples of, 504-9; engines, abnormal use of, 494-96; extraordinary sacrifice or expenditure, 493-504; intentionally and reasonably made, 496-99; loss by delay not admitted, 504; peril, imminence of, 500-3; property involved, 503; Rule A, 493-504; Rule B—borne by contributing interests, 509; Rule C—direct consequences, 504-9; Rule E—burden of proof, 509; Rule F—substituted expenses, 513; Rule G—values at end of adventure, 511, 512

history of, 480, 481

Institute Time Hulls Clauses, provisions relating to, 105

introduction, 480

marine insurance, independent of, 3

marine policies, relation to, 620-24

practice of: average disbursements, insuring, 608-10; funds, provisions for, 607, 608; general average adjustments, examples, 615-20; insurance of average disbursements, 608-10; interest, 606, 607; introduction, 601-3; limitation of liability, 610-12; rates of exchange, 612-14; security, 603-6

tug and tow: in general, 591-99; towage versus salvage, 599-601

York-Antwerp Rules, contracts of affreightment, applicable to, 491-93

York-Antwerp Rules, effect of, 487-93

York-Antwerp Rules, lettered versus numbered rules, 488-91

Good safety. *See* Voyage policy

Grounding. *See* Perils clause

H

Hanseatic League, 4-5

Heat, sweat, and spontaneous combustion, 350, 351